Using WordPerfect for Windows, Special Edition

QUE® DEVELOPMENT GROUP

Using WordPerfect for Windows, Special Edition

Copyright© 1991 by Que® Corporation

Library of Congress Catalog: 91-62307

ISBN: 0-88022-556-4

94   93   92   4   3

Interpretation of the printing code: the rightmost double-digit number is the year of the book's printing; the rightmost single-digit number, the number of the book's printing. For example, a printing code of 91-1 shows that the first printing of the book occurred in 1991.

Screen reproductions in this book were created with Collage Plus from Inner Media, Inc., Hollis, NH.

This book is based on WordPerfect Corporation's WordPerfect 5.1 for Windows.

Publisher: Lloyd J. Short

Associate Publisher: Karen A. Bluestein

Acquisitions Manager: Rick Ranucci

Product Development Manager: Thomas H. Bennett

Managing Editor: Paul Boger

Book Designer: Scott Cook

Production Team: Jeff Baker, Claudia Bell, Brad Chinn, Michelle Cleary, Mark Enochs, Sandy Grieshop, Denny Hager, Audra Hershman, Phil Kitchel, Bob LaRoche, Laurie Lee, Anne Owen, Juli Pavey, Louise Shinault, Allan Wimmer, Phil Worthington, Lisa Wilson, Christine Young

CREDITS

Product Director
Charles O. Stewart III

Senior Editor
Jeannine Freudenberger

Production Editors
Robin Drake
Frances R. Huber
Gregory R. Robertson
Diane L. Steele

Editors
Sara Allaei
Tracy L. Barr
Kelly D. Dobbs
Barbara K. Koenig
Susan M. Shaw

Acquisitions Editors
Chris Katsaropoulos
Tim Ryan

Technical Editors
Margaret Hobbic
Gary Karasik
Judy Petersen
Tom Simondi

Composed in *Cheltenham* and *MCP Digital* by Que Corporation

Charles O. Stewart III is a senior product development specialist and staff writer at Que Corporation. He was instrumental in determining the emphases for this book, assembled the team of contributors, and worked closely with the authors through manuscript development, editing, and final review. Stewart cowrote *WordPerfect Tips, Tricks, and Traps* and contributed to *Using WordPerfect 5*; *Using WordPerfect 5.1*, Special Edition; *Upgrading to 1-2-3 Release 3*; and *Introduction to Business Software*.

Eric Baatz has held a variety of managerial and programming jobs in the New England computer industry during the last 15 years. Currently, he is developing applications in a UNIX environment, and he has been an enthusiastic user of many word processors and desktop publishing systems.

Robert M. Beck is a computer consultant for small-to-medium-sized law offices. Beck was a technical editor and contributing author for *Using WordPerfect 5.1*, Special Edition; a contributing author for *WordPerfect 5.1 Tips, Tricks, and Traps*, 3rd Edition; and author of *Using LetterPerfect*. He is a regular participant on the WordPerfect Support Group's A and B forums under CIS identification number 72707,1765.

Read Gilgen, Ph.D., is Director of Learning Support Services at the University of Wisconsin, Madison, and editor of *The IALL Journal of Language Learning Technologies*. He started using computers in 1981 and WordPerfect shortly thereafter. He also is a WordPerfect Certified Resource and independent trainer/consultant.

Steve Konicki is a Miami, Florida, computer consultant who specializes in Microsoft Windows and Windows applications, as well as computer systems design for businesses. Konicki also teaches beginning, intermediate, and advanced classes in Windows and Windows applications.

Gordon Nelder-Adams is the WordPerfect expert for the Sacramento PC Users Group. He writes a monthly WordPerfect column for the Group's magazine, *Sacra Blue*, which then is reprinted in other user groups' newsletters nation-wide, and he is Chair of the WordPerfect Special Interest Group. He is also a Computing Assistant at the University of California, Davis, where his duties include word processing, desktop publishing, and other computer-related tasks.

Judy Petersen is a WordPerfect instructor/resource staffperson for the Leon County (Florida) School Board Vocational Program. In her own business, Judy is a lawyer and computer software consultant/trainer for businesses and individuals in the Tallahassee area.

Gary Pickavet is an assistant superintendent for the Santa Barbara County Education Office, where he is responsible for business and data processing services. He is a member of the California Department of Education Statewide Microcomputer Advisory Committee. Pickavet has used WordPerfect extensively since Version 3.0.

Anthony W. Rairden is the principal in Rairden Associates, a strategic marketing consulting firm based in Nashville, Tennessee. A microcomputer user since 1980, he is a long-time WordPerfect user; he also has provided computer systems consulting for many of his marketing consulting clients.

Eric Rintell is a New York-based author, reviewer, and independent computer consultant who specializes in WordPerfect training. He has been a WordPerfect user since Version 3.0.

Joseph E. Rosenman is the principal consultant of PCC Resources, a New York City consulting concern that specializes in PC installations, word processing, and desktop publishing. He moderates several conferences on the ILink BBS network.

ACKNOWLEDGMENTS

Using WordPerfect for Windows, Special Edition, is the result of the immense efforts of many dedicated and talented people. Que Corporation thanks the following people for their contributions to the development of this book:

The many WordPerfect and Windows experts who contributed to this book, for their expertise, enthusiasm, professionalism, and dogged determination to ensure a timely and authoritative book. Their excellent work reinforces our belief that collaborative computer book efforts represent a tremendous value for readers. Although group efforts are fraught with their own set of problems, this book is *much* stronger for having been a collaboration. Special thanks go to Eric Mark Rintell for critical assistance early on in determining the scope of the book and developing an outline.

Senior editor Jeannine Freudenberger, for her exceptional efforts in coordinating the editing of the book and keeping it on schedule. Many thanks to production editors Robin Drake, Fran Huber, Greg Robertson, and Diane Steele for their outstanding work and the innumerable hours they put in to help ensure the accuracy, quality, and readability of the text. Thanks also to copy editors Sara Allaei, Tracy Barr, Barbara Koenig, and Susan Shaw for their fine work. And to G.P., for encouragement as well as those "strange and beautiful fish."

Technical editors Margaret Hobbie, Gary Karasik, Judy Petersen, and Tom Simondi, for their attentive technical review of the manuscript. Publisher Lloyd Short, for making this project possible and for providing direction, support, and guidance. Acquisitions editors Chris Katsaropoulos and Tim Ryan, for managing the crucial tasks of arranging schedules and contracts, and communicating with the many contributors during the book's genesis. Stacey Beheler and Dorothy Aylward, for their support to the product development and editing staff working on this book. Scott Cook, for his design of the book, and Karen Bluestein, for her suggested refinements to the design. Graphic imaging specialist Dennis Sheehan for his patient work in adjusting figures.

WordPerfect Corporation, for the incredible effort that went into the development of an impressive Windows word processing program.

TRADEMARK ACKNOWLEDGMENTS

Que Corporation has made every effort to supply trademark information about company names, products, and services mentioned in this book. Trademarks indicated below were derived from various sources. Que Corporation cannot attest to the accuracy of this information.

1-2-3, Lotus, Ami Pro, and DIF are registered trademarks of Lotus Development Corporation. Agfa Compugraphic is a registered trademark of Agfa Corporation. Aldus, Persuasion, and PageMaker are registered trademarks of Aldus Corporation. ANSI is a registered trademark of the American National Standards Institute. ARTS & LETTERS is a trademark of Computer Support Corporation. Ashton-Tate, MultiMate, and dBASE are registered trademarks of Ashton-Tate Corporation. Bitstream is a registered trademark and FaceLift is a trademark of Bitstream Inc. CompuServe is a registered trademark of CompuServe Incorporated and H&R Block, Inc. CorelDRAW! is a registered trademark of Corel Systems Corporation. EPSON is a registered trademark and Epson FX-80 is a trademark of EPSON America, Inc. Harvard Graphics is a trademark of Software Publishing Corporation. IBM and IBM PC are registered trademarks and DisplayWrite is a trademark of International Business Machines Corporation. LaserJet, HP, and Hewlett-Packard Graphics Language are registered trademarks of Hewlett-Packard Co. Microsoft, Microsoft Windows 3.0, Microsoft Excel, Microsoft Word for Windows, PowerPoint, and MS-DOS are registered trademarks of Microsoft Corporation. NEC and SilentWriter are registered trademarks of NEC Information Systems Inc. Norton Utilities is a registered trademark of Symantec Corporation. PC Paintbrush is a registered trademark of ZSoft Corp. PC Tools is a trademark of Central Point Software. PostScript and ATM are registered trademarks and Adobe Type Manager is a trademark of Adobe Systems, Inc. Quattro Pro and Quattro are registered trademarks of Borland International, Inc. Ventura Publisher is a trademark of Xerox Corporation and a registered trademark of Ventura Software, Inc. WordPerfect, PlanPerfect, DataPerfect, WordPerfect Office, and DrawPerfect are registered trademarks and Button Bar is a trademark of WordPerfect Corporation. WordStar is a registered trademark of WordStar International Inc. XyWrite III and XyWrite II Plus are registered trademarks of XyQuest, Inc.

Trademarks of other products mentioned in this book are held by the companies producing them.

CONTENTS AT A GLANCE

Part I   Getting Started 7

Part II   Mastering Basic Word Processing Tasks 45

Part III   Mastering More Advanced Procedures 277

Part IV   Producing Professional Output 457

Part V   Automating Your Work 621

Part VI   Managing Large Projects 773

Part VII Becoming an Expert User 903

Appendix A Installing and Setting Up WordPerfect for
           Windows 1093

Appendix B WordPerfect: Windows vs. DOS 1113

TABLE OF CONTENTS

Introduction 1

    Who Should Use This Book? 2
    How To Use This Book 2
    How This Book Is Organized 3
    Where To Find More Help 4
    Conventions Used in This Book 5

I Getting Started

1 Preparing To Use WordPerfect for Windows 9

    An Overview of WordPerfect for Windows 10
    Understanding WordPerfect's File Manager 18
    Starting Windows 20
    Starting WordPerfect 20
        Understanding the Editing Screen 21
        Troubleshooting Problems Starting
            WordPerfect 24
    Understanding Document Windows 25
    Maneuvering in a WordPerfect Document 27
        Using the Mouse 29
        Using the Keyboard 31
    Choosing Commands 33
        Choosing Menu Options 34
        Making Choices in Dialog Boxes 36
        Using the Button Bar To Streamline Your Work ... 37
        Using the Ruler To Make Choices in Your
            Documents 39
    Understanding Hidden Codes 39
    Using Help 40
        What Is 41

How Do I 41
Standard Help Features 41
Exiting WordPerfect for Windows 42
Looking Ahead 43
Chapter Summary 43

II Mastering Basic Word Processing Tasks

2 Creating, Printing, and Saving a Document 47

Writing with a Word Processor 48
Understanding WordPerfect's Built-In Settings 50
Entering Text 50
Inserting Blank Lines 52
Moving the Insertion Point and Scrolling the
     Document 53
     Moving with the Mouse 54
     Moving with the Directional Keys 55
     Moving around the Sample Letter 55
     Completing the Sample Letter 57
     Moving the Insertion Point with Go To ... 58
Inserting Text 60
Using Typeover 60
Printing a Document 61
Saving a Document to Disk 64
Clearing the Screen and Exiting WordPerfect 67
Using WordPerfect To Develop Ideas 68
     Handling Writer's Block 69
     Planning Documents 72
Chapter Summary 77

3 Managing Files 79

Understanding File Management Terms 80
Planning File Storage Requirements 81
Using the File Manager 83
     Understanding the File Manager Screen ... 84
     Finding Existing Directories 84
     Creating New Directories 84
Setting the Default Document Directory 86
Using the Open File Dialog Box 86
     Opening a File 87
     Using the Files List 88
     Locking Files 89

Using the View Window 90
Changing the Current Directory 91
Using the Open File Options 92
Using a Quick List 100
Creating a Quick List 101
Editing or Deleting Quick List Entries 104
Chapter Summary 105

4 Editing a Document 107

Opening and Retrieving Files 108
Opening a File 109
Locating a "Lost" File 110
Using Retrieve To Combine Files 111
Revising Text 112
Inserting Text 113
Overwriting Text 113
Deleting Text 113
Restoring Deleted Text 115
Understanding Hidden Codes 117
Working with Reveal Codes 124
Changing the Size of the Reveal Codes
   Window 124
Using Boldface and Underline 125
Removing Boldface and Underline Codes 127
Searching and Replacing 128
Searching 128
Searching and Replacing Text 131
Using Search or Replace in Other Ways 133
Using Document Comments 133
Creating a Comment 135
Editing and Deleting Comments 135
Hiding Comments 136
Converting Text to Comments and Comments
   to Text 137
Chapter Summary 137

5 Selecting and Editing Text 139

Understanding the Select Process 141
Highlighting a Selection 141
Using the Mouse To Highlight a Selection 142
Using the Keyboard To Highlight a Selection 145
Using Select Mode To Highlight a Selection 146
Canceling a Highlighted Selection 147

Performing Functions on Selections 148
Transferring Selected Text to Another Location 148
   Moving or Copying a Selection 149
   Appending a Selection 150
   Transferring Selections to Other Windows
      Applications 150
Deleting and Undeleting a Selection 151
Saving a Selection in a File 151
Printing a Selection 152
Changing the Appearance of a Selection 153
   Enhancing the Appearance of Text 154
   Changing the Font or Font Size 154
   Changing the Layout of a Selection 155
   Changing Selections to Uppercase or
      Lowercase 157
Working with Rectangular Selections 158
Using Styles with Selections 159
Chapter Summary 159

6 Formatting Text **161**

Understanding Formatting in WordPerfect 162
   Default Format Settings 162
   The Ruler 163
   Auto Code Placement 164
Formatting Lines and Paragraphs 165
   Controlling Line Spacing and Line Height 166
   Setting Margins 169
   Setting Header and Footer Margins 170
   Using Indent and Margin Release 170
   Setting and Using Tabs 172
   Locating Text on the Line 180
Using Justification 182
Using Hyphenation 184
   Splitting Words with Codes 184
   Preventing Hyphenation 185
   Using Automatic Hyphenation 185
   Setting the Hyphenation Zone 186
   Choosing a Hyphenation Point 186
   Removing Hyphenation from a Document 188
   Modifying the Hyphenation Decision
      Resources 190
Chapter Summary 190

7 Introduction to Graphics 193

WordPerfect's Graphics Categories 194
Understanding Line Art, or Vector Graphics 194
Understanding Bit-Map, or Raster Graphics 195
WordPerfect's Graphics Formats 196
WordPerfect's Five Graphics Box Types 199
WordPerfect's Figure Graphics 200
Creating a Figure Graphic 201
Using a Figure Graphic as an Ornament 205
Working with More Than One Graphic on the
Page 207
Combining Graphics and Text 210
Going beyond Simple Graphics 213
Chapter Summary 213

8 Using the Speller and the Thesaurus 215

Using the Speller 216
Setting Up the Speller 217
Starting the Speller 218
Specifying Speller Options 219
Spell Checking the Document 223
Looking Up a Word 229
Spell Checking Other Languages 230
Using a Supplementary Dictionary 230
Using the Speller Utility 232
Adding and Deleting Dictionary Words 234
Compressing and Expanding a Dictionary 235
Using the Thesaurus 236
Starting the Thesaurus 236
Looking Up Words 237
Understanding the Thesaurus Window 238
Replacing a Word 239
Looking Up References 239
Chapter Summary 240

9 Basic Printing 241

Choosing a Printer Driver 242
WordPerfect Printer Drivers 243
Windows Printer Drivers 244
Using a WordPerfect Printer Driver 245
Installing a WordPerfect Printer Driver 246

Adding a WordPerfect Printer Driver 248
Selecting a WordPerfect Printer 251
Setting Up a WordPerfect Printer 252
Copying a WordPerfect Printer Driver 256
Deleting a WordPerfect Printer Driver 256
Using the Info Option 257
Updating a WordPerfect Printer Driver 257
Using a Windows Printer Driver.....................................257
Selecting a Windows Printer Driver 258
Configuring and Updating a Windows Printer
Driver 259
Printing a Document 260
Understanding the Current Print Job Dialog
Box 261
Printing from the Screen 262
Printing Documents from Disk 263
Printing Multiple Pages 266
Canceling a Print Job 267
Using Document Print Settings 267
Using the Windows Print Manager 270
Using Print Preview 271
Using the View Menu Options 273
Using the Pages Menu Options 275
Understanding Print Preview's Limitations 276
Chapter Summary 276

III Mastering More Advanced Procedures

10 Working with Fonts 279

Understanding the Vocabulary of Typography 280
Using Different Fonts 282
Soft Fonts 283
Cartridges 283
Windows Typeface Packages 285
Installing Fonts in a WordPerfect Printer Driver 288
Adding a Cartridge in a WordPerfect Printer
Driver 288
Adding Soft Fonts in a WordPerfect Printer
Driver 291
Adding Print Wheels in a WordPerfect Printer
Driver 294
Installing Fonts in a Windows Printer Driver 295

Selecting Fonts in WordPerfect for Windows 296
    Specifying Initial Fonts 297
    Using Several Fonts in a Document 300
Changing Font Attributes 301
    Changing the Size Attributes 302
    Changing the Appearance Attributes 304
    Applying Font Attributes to Existing Text 307
Chapter Summary 307

11 Formatting Pages and Designing Documents 309

Formatting Pages 310
    Placing Format Codes 311
    Deleting Format Codes 312
    Setting Margins 312
    Keeping Text Together 314
    Centering a Page 318
    Using the Advance Command 319
    Using Headers and Footers 320
    Numbering Pages 328
    Choosing Paper Size and Type 333
    Setting the Initial Font 339
    Setting Initial Codes 340
    Using the Redline Method 341
    Changing the Display Pitch 342
Creating a Document Summary 342
    Creating a Document Summary on Save or Exit . 346
    Choosing Document Summary Options 346
Chapter Summary 348

12 Using Styles 349

When To Use Styles 350
How To Create Styles 351
    Creating an Open Style 352
    Creating a Paired Style 356
    Placing Graphics in Styles 359
    Creating a Style from Existing Text 359
Using Styles in Documents 361
    Checking Styles with Reveal Codes 362
    Applying Paired Styles to Existing Text in a
        Document 363
    Editing Style Codes 363
    Editing Style Names 364

Editing the Information in the Style Properties
    Dialog Box 366
Saving Styles in a Document 367
Replacing a Style with Another Style....................367
Deleting Style Codes from a Document 369
Deleting Styles from the Style List 369
Style Libraries 371
Using Multiple Style Libraries 371
Using Default Style Libraries 372
Saving Styles in a Style Library 373
Retrieving a Style Library 374
Sample Style Library 375
LIBRARY.STY 375
Styles and Style Libraries 376
Chapter Summary 380

13 Working with Text Columns 381

Newspaper Columns 382
Defining Newspaper Columns by Using the
    Ruler 383
Defining Newspaper Columns by Using the
    Dialog Box 385
Working with Columnar Text 388
Previewing Newspaper Columns 392
Parallel Columns 394
Defining Parallel Columns 394
Typing Text in Parallel Columns 397
Changing Columns by Using the Ruler 398
Editing Parallel Columns 400
Inserting Parallel Columns 401
Moving Parallel Columns 402
Limitations of Using Columns 402
Automating Columns with Macros and the Button
    Bar 403
Chapter Summary 404

14 Working with Tables...405

Planning Your Tables 407
Creating and Using Tables: The Basics 408
Creating a Table 408
Moving within a Table 410
Entering Text 411
Cutting, Pasting, and Deleting Text 412

Selecting and Deleting a Cell 413
Deleting or Moving a Table 415
Saving and Printing a Table 415
Editing the Table Structure 416
Changing Column Widths 417
Changing the Table Size 419
Inserting Rows and Columns 420
Deleting Rows and Columns 421
Restoring Deleted Rows and Columns 422
Joining Cells 422
Splitting Cells 423
Changing Table Lines 424
Changing Row Height 427
Creating Header Rows 428
Locking Cells 429
Positioning Tables 430
Understanding Table Codes 430
Formatting Table Text 431
Understanding Formatting Precedence 431
Formatting Columns 432
Formatting Cells 434
Setting Global Table Options 436
Using Table Math 437
Creating Formulas 437
Copying Formulas 439
Using Totaling Functions 439
Creating Tax and Total Formulas 440
Calculating and Changing Values 441
Deleting and Modifying Formulas 442
Creating and Using Tables: The Next Step 442
Converting Tabular Columns to Tables 443
Sorting Tables 445
Converting Parallel Columns to Tables 445
Importing a Spreadsheet to a Table 447
Adding Graphics to a Table 448
Creating Forms with Irregular Columns 449
Placing Tables Side-by-Side 450
Placing Tables in Newspaper Columns 451
Cross-Referencing Tables 452
Using Merge Codes with Tables 453
Exploring Other Uses for Tables 453
Calendars 453
Phone Message Forms 455
Chapter Summary 455

IV Producing Professional Output

15 Working with Advanced Printing Techniques 459

Using the Paper Size Feature 460
    Creating and Editing Paper Definitions 460
    Selecting a Paper Definition 465
    Using the [ALL OTHERS] Definition 466
    Editing the [ALL OTHERS] Definition 467
    Copying Paper Definitions 468
    Deleting Paper Definitions 469
    Using Paper Definitions with Windows Printer
        Drivers 469
Printing on Envelopes 470
Printing on Labels 473
    Creating and Editing Label Definitions 474
    Using Label Definitions in a Document 481
    Using Labels with Windows Printer Drivers 483
Adjusting Textual Appearance 484
    Using Advance 485
    Kerning 486
    Using Letterspacing and Word Spacing 489
    Setting Word Spacing Justification Limits 490
    Adjusting Line Height (Leading) 490
    Using the First Baseline at Top Margin Option ...492
    Using the Underline Options 493
    Using the Printer Command Option 493
Chapter Summary 495

16 Using Lines To Add Effects 497

Creating Horizontal Lines 498
    Creating a Full Horizontal Line 499
    Specifying Vertical Position 500
    Specifying Horizontal Position and Length 501
    Specifying Line Characteristics 502
    Editing a Horizontal Line 503
Creating Vertical Lines 506
    Creating a Full Vertical Line 507
    Specifying Position, Length, and
        Characteristics 510
    Using Vertical Lines with Columns 510
    Editing a Vertical Line 514
Combining Vertical and Horizontal Lines 515

Using Line Draw 516
   Moving the Insertion Point in Line Draw 518
   Drawing Lines 518
   Erasing Lines 520
   Printing Line Draw Lines 520
Chapter Summary 521

17 Understanding Advanced Graphics 523

WordPerfect's Five Graphics Boxes 524
Figure Graphics 525
Options for the Graphics Boxes 527
   Graphics Box and Text 528
   Border Lines for Boxes 529
   Gray Shading 529
   Creating Captions 530
Graphics Defaults 531
Figure Editor 536
   Figure Editor File Commands 538
   Box Position and Size Dialog Box 541
   Figure Editor Menu Commands 544
Text Boxes and the Text Editor 553
Caption Editor 555
Some Examples of Graphics 555
The GRAPHCNV Program 572
Graphics Resources 573
   DrawPerfect 574
   Other Graphics Packages 574
   Scanners 575
   Autotracing 576
   Clip-Art Vendors 576
Chapter Summary 577

18 Desktop Publishing with WordPerfect 579

Integrating Text and Graphics 580
Designing Successful Publications 581
Understanding Typefaces 583
   Typeface Essentials 584
   Type Styles 585
   Typography 586
Presenting a Page 589
   Creating a Page 590
   Fitting Type on the Page 592
   Enhancing a Page 592

Creating a Flier 593
   Using Graphics in the Flier 595
   Using Fonts in the Flier 596
   Laying Out the Flier 597
   Settings for the Flier 597
Creating a Trifold Mailer 599
   Designing the Outside 600
   Designing the Inside 602
   Creating Columns 603
   Settings for the Trifold Mailer 604
Creating a Newsletter 606
   Designing the First Page 606
   Designing the Second Page 609
   Designing the Third Page 613
   Settings for the Newsletter 615
   Finishing the Newsletter 618
Chapter Summary 619

V Automating Your Work

19 Using the Button Bar 623

Why Use the Button Bar? 624
Selecting a Button Bar 625
Examining the Button Bar 627
Creating Personal Button Bars 628
   Saving a Button Bar 629
   Editing Button Bars 630
Changing the Button Bar's Position and Style 632
Creating Specialized Button Bars 636
Using Macros with the Button Bar 638
   Creating Macros To Control Button Bars 638
   Assigning Macros to a Button Bar 639
   Creating a Macros Button Bar 640
Editing Built-in Button Bars 641
Chapter Summary 642

20 Creating Macros 643

Recording Macros 645
Playing Macros 648
Using Control-Key Macros 649
Stopping Macros 650
Replacing Macros 650

Changing Format with Macros 651
   A Macro That Changes Tab Settings 652
   A Macro That Changes Margins 653
Making Macros Pause 654
Creating Some Useful Macros 656
   A Macro That Inserts a Special Character 656
   A Macro That Transposes Two Characters 657
   A Macro That Prints an Envelope 658
Using Macros with Styles and Merges 660
   A Macro That Selects a Style 661
   A Macro That Starts a Merge 662
   A Combination of Macros, Merges, and Styles 663
Playing Macros in Other Ways 665
   Assigning Macros to the Menu 666
   Assigning Macros to the Button Bar 669
   Assigning Macros to the Keyboard 670
Managing Macro Files 673
   Using Different Extensions 673
   Using Different Directories 674
   Manipulating and Viewing Macro Files 675
Editing Macros 678
   Understanding the Differences from
      WordPerfect 5.1 for DOS Macros 679
   Understanding Macro Syntax 680
   Making a Simple Text Change 682
   Editing WordPerfect Commands 684
Compiling Macros 686
Using Advanced Macros 687
Chapter Summary 688

21 Assembling Documents with Merge **689**

Planning a Merge Operation 690
Setting Up Merge Files 691
   Creating the Secondary Merge File 693
   Creating the Primary Merge File 700
Merging Files 704
Merging with Labels and Envelopes 706
   Merging with Envelopes 706
   Merging with Labels 709
Dealing with Special Situations 710
   Changing Fields in a Secondary File 711
   Using Other Secondary Files 712
   Using Keyboard Input 713
   Inserting Dates 714

Using Empty Fields 715
Removing Hard Page Breaks 719
Merging Directly to the Printer 719
Chapter Summary 719

22 Sorting and Selecting Data 721

Understanding Data Files 721
Designing a Data File 723
Understanding Basic Terms 726
Understanding Formatting Codes 728
Organizing and Formatting Your Data 728
Choosing a Record Format 731
Creating a Data File 737
Creating a Line Record 737
Creating a Paragraph Record 742
Creating a Merge Record 744
Creating a Table-Row Record 747
Sorting Data File Records 750
Understanding Size Limitations 751
Specifying the Records To Sort 751
Accessing the Sort Dialog Box 752
Defining the Sort Parameters 753
Starting the Sort Operation 759
Sorting Paragraph Records 760
Extracting Records 762
Defining Selection Parameters 762
Sorting and Selecting Table-Row Records 769
Chapter Summary 771

VI Managing Large Projects

23 Using Footnotes and Endnotes 775

Choosing between Footnotes and Endnotes 776
Using Footnotes 776
Creating Footnotes 777
Viewing Footnotes 779
Editing Footnotes 780
Numbering Footnotes Automatically 781
Adding Footnotes 782
Moving Footnotes 783
Deleting Footnotes 785

Changing Footnote Options 785
Formatting Footnotes 788
Continuing Footnotes across Documents 790
Using Endnotes 791
Creating Endnotes 791
Changing Endnotes' Location 793
Changing Footnotes to Endnotes 794
Chapter Summary 795

24 Line Numbering, Paragraph Numbering, and Outlining 797

The Line Numbering Feature 798
Understanding Line Numbering Options 798
Specifying Line Numbering Settings 800
Turning Off Line Numbering 801
Viewing Line Numbers 802
The Paragraph Numbering Feature 803
Defining Number Style 804
Creating Numbered Paragraphs with
    Automatic Levels 806
Overriding Automatic Levels with Manual
    Levels 807
Editing Paragraph Numbers 808
The Outline Feature 809
Turning On Outline 811
Understanding the Outline Keys 811
Turning Off Outline 812
Creating a Sample Outline 813
Editing an Outline 814
The Define Paragraph Numbering Dialog Box 821
Using the Define Options 821
Using the Starting Outline Number Option 825
Using the Current Outline Style Option 825
Using the Options Features 826
Outline Styles 827
Using Predefined Outline Styles 827
Using an Outline Style 828
Creating and Editing Outline Styles 829
Chapter Summary 831

25 Assembling Other Document References 833

Creating Lists 834
Marking Text for Lists 835

Defining a List and Choosing Numbering
Formats 837
Generating Document References 839
Creating a Table of Contents 840
Marking Text for a Table of Contents 840
Defining a Table of Contents 842
Generating a Table of Contents 844
Using Multiple Tables of Contents 844
Creating a Table of Authorities 844
Adjusting Setup for the Table of Authorities 846
Choosing Sections and Marking Text for a
Table of Authorities 846
Defining and Generating a Table of Authorities .. 851
Creating an Index 854
Specifying Text for an Index 855
Defining and Generating an Index 860
Preparing Indexes for Multiple Related
Documents 862
Using Automatic Cross-References 863
Marking Text for Automatic Cross-Referencing .. 864
Generating Cross-References 870
Using Document Compare 870
Comparing a New Version to an Old Version 871
Purging Marked Changes from a Saved
Document 873
Chapter Summary 874

26 Working with Master Documents 875

Creating Master and Subdocuments 876
Working with Subdocuments 877
Building the Master Document 878
Adding and Deleting a Subdocument 882
Expanding the Master Document 883
Creating a Table of Contents, List, Index, or Table
of Authorities 885
Marking Text for the Table of Contents 887
Defining the Table of Contents 888
Generating the Table of Contents 890
Printing the Master Document 893
Condensing the Master Document 894
Saving the Master Document 895
Using Other Features in a Master Document 896
Inserting a New Page Number 897
Using Search, Replace, and Speller 898

Adding Footnotes and Endnotes 899
Using Cross-References 901
Creating Subdocuments within Subdocuments 901
Finding Other Uses for Master Documents 902
Chapter Summary 902

VII Becoming an Expert User

27 Using the Equation Editor 905

Starting the Equation Editor 906
Examining the Equation Editor Screen 908
Creating an Equation in the Editing Pane 910
Creating a Simple Fraction 912
Creating Superscripts and Subscripts 913
Reviewing Key Concepts 914
Defining Terms 914
Understanding Syntax 917
Using the Equation Editor 918
Using the Editing Pane 918
Using an Equation Keyboard 919
Using the Equation Palette 919
Using WordPerfect Characters 921
Altering the Equation Display 921
Using Functions and Commands to Create
      Equations 923
Using Functions in the Equation Editor 923
Using FUNC, BOLD and ITAL to Format
      Equations 925
Using \ To Format Literals 926
Forming Fractions with the OVER, LEFT, and
      RIGHT Commands 927
Creating Sums and Integrals 929
Creating Roots 930
Using the Matrix Commands 930
Creating Multiline Expressions with STACK
      and STACKALIGN...932
Using Other Commands and Symbols 934
Positioning and Sizing Equations 935
Numbering Equations 936
Embedding Equations in Text 938
Saving and Retrieving Equation Files 940
Printing Equations 941
Chapter Summary 943

28 Creating and Displaying Special Characters 945

Using WordPerfect Characters 946
   Creating Shortcuts for Special Characters 950
   Displaying Special Characters 950
   Printing Special Characters 952
Creating and Editing Overstrike Characters 956
Working with Multiple Languages 958
   Entering WordPerfect Language Codes 958
   Using Dictionary, Thesaurus, and Hyphenation
      Files 961
   Using the Language Resource File 962
Chapter Summary 962

29 Customizing WordPerfect with Preferences 963

Introducing the Preferences Menu 965
Customizing Location of Files 967
Backing Up Your Work 968
   Creating Timed Backups 969
   Creating Original Document Backups 970
Customizing the Environment 971
   Auto Code Placement 972
   Confirm on Code Deletion 974
   Fast Save 975
   Allow Undo 975
   Allow Graphics Boxes To Bump to Next Page 975
   Format Retrieved Documents for Default
      Printer 976
   Customize the Beep 977
   Customize Menu Display 977
   Customize the Ruler 979
   Customize Hyphenation 980
Customizing the Display 982
   Customizing the Display in Draft Mode 983
   Customizing the Display in WYSIWYG Mode 985
Customizing Your Print Jobs 990
   Multiple Copies 992
   Binding Offset 993
   Graphics Quality 993
   Text Quality 995
   Redline Method 995
   Size Attribute Ratio 996
   Windows Print Drivers Fast Graphics Printing ...996
Customizing Keyboards 997

Selecting a Keyboard 998
Creating a Keyboard 999
Adding Your Keystrokes to the WordPerfect
    Menus 1004
Retaining Home Key Options 1005
Editing a Keyboard 1005
Editing Text Assigned to a Keyboard 1006
Removing Text or Macros Added to a
    Keyboard 1006
Using Initial Codes 1007
Customizing the Document Summary 1009
Using Subject Search Text 1009
Using Default Descriptive Type 1010
Creating a Summary on Save/Exit 1011
Dating Your Documents 1011
Inserting the Date or Time into Your
    Document 1012
Changing the Date Format 1013
Changing the Date Format in Preferences 1016
Customizing Merge Preferences 1016
Customizing the Table of Authorities 1018
Customizing the Equation Editor 1019
Standardizing Equation Settings 1019
Using an Equation Keyboard 1021
Chapter Summary 1022

30 Advanced File Management Techniques 1023

Understanding and Using File Manager Windows ...1025
Using the Navigator 1026
Using the Viewer 1026
Using the File List 1027
Using the Quick List 1029
Determining and Changing Active Windows 1029
Closing File Manager Windows 1029
Using File Manager Commands 1030
Changing Directories 1030
Opening a File 1031
Copying a File 1031
Copying Files by "Dragging and Dropping" 1033
Copying Multiple Files 1033
Deleting Files 1035
Deleting Multiple Files 1036
Deleting (Removing) a Directory 1036

Renaming and Moving Files 1037
Printing Files from the File Manager 1039
Finding Files 1039
    Searching the File List and Viewer Windows 1040
    Using Search Patterns in Find File and Find
        Word Searches 1041
    Using Advanced Find 1042
    Narrowing a Search 1043
Using the File Manager Button Bar 1044
Changing File Manager Layouts 1044
    Selecting a Defined Layout................................1044
    Sizing the Windows 1045
    Customizing the File List Column Headings 1046
    Changing Fonts 1046
    Saving Layouts 1047
    Changing the Start-Up Layout 1048
Getting System Information 1048
Changing File Attributes 1049
Printing and Saving Information from the File
    Lists 1051
    Using the Clipboard 1051
    Printing File Lists 1052
Launching Applications 1052
    Adding Applications to the File Manager 1053
    Associating Applications with Files 1054
    Using the WordPerfect File Manager as a
        Program Manager 1055
Chapter Summary 1056

31 Importing Data and Working with Other Programs 1057

Understanding Conversion Strategies 1060
Converting Word Processing Files............................1062
    Using WordPerfect's Convert 1063
    Using the Windows Clipboard 1070
    Using Dynamic Data Exchange (DDE) 1075
    Using an Intermediate Format 1077
Using Spreadsheet Information 1079
    Using the Import Spreadsheet Function 1080
    Creating a WordPerfect Spreadsheet Link.........1081
    Creating a DDE Spreadsheet Link 1082
    Using the Clipboard 1083
    Handling Wide Spreadsheets 1084
    Dealing with Problem Spreadsheets....................1085
Using WordPerfect with Graphics Programs 1085

CorelDRAW! 1086
Arts & Letters 1087
Using Database Conversions 1087
Chapter Summary 1089

A Installing and Setting Up WordPerfect for Windows 1093

Installing WordPerfect for Windows 1095
Initial Installations 1097
Interim Releases 1103
Reinstallations 1108
Setting Up and Starting WordPerfect 1109
Defining a Documents Subdirectory 1110
Activating the Ruler 1111
Using WordPerfect Start-Up Switches 1111

B WordPerfect: Windows vs. DOS 1113

Why Use WordPerfect 5.1 for Windows? 1114
Advantages 1114
Costs 1115
New Features 1117
Button Bar 1117
Convert 1117
DDE Links 1118
Macro Features 1119
Multiple Documents 1119
Quick List 1119
Ruler 1120
Undo 1120
WordPerfect Characters 1120
WPG Images 1120
Comparing Terminology 1121
Comparing Procedures 1122
Auto Code Placement 1122
Clipboard 1123
File Manager 1123
Graphics 1123
Macros 1124
Menu versus Command Key Access 1124
Reveal Codes 1125
Save and Save As 1125
Search 1125
Special Codes 1125

Speller and Thesaurus 1126
WordPerfect Characters 1126
WYSIWYG versus Draft Mode 1126
Windows-Specific Considerations 1127
Comparing Keyboard Layouts 1127
Common User Access (CUA) Keystrokes 1128
WordPerfect for Windows CUA Keyboard
Layout 1129
WordPerfect for Windows DOS-Compatible
Keyboard Layout 1129
Keyboard Layout Comparisons 1130
Chapter Summary 1142

Index 1143

Introduction

*U*sing *WordPerfect for Windows*, Special Edition, pools the talents of a diverse collection of Windows and WordPerfect experts, providing extensive coverage of all WordPerfect's features and combining tutorial steps and reference information. The authors have made this book unique among books about WordPerfect for Windows because this book is a collaboration in the best sense of that word.

Why a collaboration? When you need to accomplish a complex, tough job on a tight schedule, an excellent strategy is to pull together a team of experts, each one specializing in a particular aspect of the overall discipline. The resulting product in a collaborative effort can be superior to even the best efforts of any individual contributors. This book on WordPerfect 5.1 for Windows, a collaboration, pools the knowledge of a range of WordPerfect experts, all experts in particular areas or applications.

As software companies adapt their programs to work with graphical user interfaces (GUIs) and as word processors become more complex, powerful, feature-laden, and useful to a diversity of users, the need for in-depth expertise across a range of experience becomes clear. This kind of coverage is unavailable in a single-author book. Only a team of experts can adequately cover a program as advanced, complex, and versatile as WordPerfect 5.1 for Windows.

Who Should Use This Book?

WordPerfect 5.1 for Windows is based closely on the best-selling WordPerfect 5.1 for DOS. If you have never used any version of WordPerfect, this book's complete coverage of program features, mix of step-by-step procedures with reference information, real-world examples, and clear instructions can help you master WordPerfect quickly.

If you're switching from WordPerfect 5.1 for DOS, this book can help you make a smooth, painless transition to the Windows version of WordPerfect 5.1. Appendix B, "WordPerfect: Windows vs. DOS," addresses compatibility issues, describes in detail the similarities and differences between the DOS and Windows versions of WordPerfect 5.1, and orients you to what you need to know about WordPerfect 5.1 for Windows to begin using it effectively. Experienced WordPerfect users will appreciate the tips, cues, warnings, shortcuts, and Button Bar ideas in each chapter.

Note: To ensure your success with WordPerfect 5.1 for Windows, you should have a basic understanding of Windows 3. This book assumes that you are familiar with Windows. As you learn about WordPerfect in Chapter 1, you also learn about Windows. If you are new to Windows, however, you may want to consult any of the following books published by Que Corporation for information on Windows' basic operation: *Easy Windows*, by Shelley O'Hara; *Windows 3 QuickStart*, by Ron Person and Karen Rose; or *Using Microsoft Windows 3*, 2nd Edition, by Ron Person and Karen Rose.

How To Use This Book

Using WordPerfect for Windows, Special Edition, is designed to complement the reference manual and workbook that come with WordPerfect. Beginners will find the step-by-step information in this book helpful; experienced users will appreciate the comprehensive coverage and expert advice. After you become proficient with WordPerfect 5.1 for Windows, you can use this book as a desktop reference.

Each chapter in this book focuses on a particular WordPerfect operation or set of operations. Overall, the movement of the book is from the steps typical of any document's creation (such as entering text, checking spelling, and printing) to more specialized topics (such as macros, styles, equations, and desktop publishing). *Using WordPerfect for Windows*, Special Edition, distills the real-world experience of many WordPerfect experts, making the book workplace-based and applications-oriented.

The tips included in the body of the text either point out information often overlooked in the documentation or help you use WordPerfect more efficiently. You will find many of these tips useful or pertinent as you become more comfortable with the software. Cues, located in the margins, are abbreviated versions of tip information and also point out how to use the program more efficiently. Cautions and warnings alert you to potential loss of data or harm to your computer system.

How This Book Is Organized

This book is organized to follow the natural flow of learning and using WordPerfect 5.1 for Windows. *Using WordPerfect for Windows*, Special Edition, is divided into seven parts:

- Part I: Getting Started
- Part II: Mastering Basic Word Processing Tasks
- Part III: Mastering More Advanced Procedures
- Part IV: Producing Professional Output
- Part V: Automating Your Work
- Part VI: Managing Large Projects
- Part VII: Becoming an Expert User

Part I introduces you to WordPerfect 5.1 for Windows and prepares you to begin working with the program.

Part II shows you how to use WordPerfect to accomplish a range of basic word processing tasks as you complete the cycle of document preparation: planning, creating, editing, formatting, managing, printing, and checking the spelling of documents. In Part II, you also learn how easily you can import graphics images into WordPerfect.

Part III covers more advanced word processing techniques, such as working with fonts and font packages, formatting pages, using styles to automate document formatting, using parallel and newspaper-style columns, and creating tables.

Part IV focuses on high-quality printed output and WordPerfect's capabilities as a desktop publishing system. This part of the book begins with a look at advanced printing techniques; moves to the use of graphic lines for embellishing documents; covers the complexities and fine points of including graphics in your documents and working with WordPerfect's Figure Editor; includes a brief primer on page layout, typography, design, and graphics; and takes you through the mechanics of integrating text and graphics. The last chapter in this section showcases several attractive documents produced with WordPerfect.

Part V shows you how to take advantage of a number of WordPerfect features to streamline your work. You see how to use the innovative Button Bar to place frequently used commands and macros on buttons for instant access, use macros to accomplish simple and complex tasks, use merge to create mass mailings, and use sort and select to rearrange information in data files.

Part VI is especially useful to persons who must work with large documents. You see how to structure documents with footnotes and endnotes; use paragraph numbering, line numbering, and outlining; and use other document reference tools, such as tables of contents, lists, indexes, tables of authority, and cross-references. In the final chapter, you see how to use the Master Document feature for large projects that need to be broken into smaller, connected elements.

Part VII is addressed to those users who want to become more expert with WordPerfect. This section begins with use of the Equation Editor, moves to creating and displaying special characters, explores changing default program settings, covers more advanced use of the File Manager, and concludes with a look at how to import text, graphics, or spreadsheet data from other programs into WordPerfect.

The first appendix covers installation, program setup, and WordPerfect's start-up options. The second appendix orients WordPerfect 5.1 for DOS users to WordPerfect 5.1 for Windows.

Where To Find More Help

If you find yourself stymied on a particular point, WordPerfect's built-in Help feature may answer your questions. Help is explained in Chapter 1. In addition, you can turn to this book or to WordPerfect's manual and workbook for help.

Should all else fail, WordPerfect Corporation provides toll-free telephone support. Call the appropriate number to receive assistance:

1-800-228-6076	Installation
1-800-228-1029	Features
1-800-228-6013	Graphics/Tables/Equations
1-800-228-1032	Macro/Merge/Labels
1-800-228-1023	Laser/PostScript Printers
1-800-228-1017	Dot-Matrix/All Other Printers
1-800-228-6066	Networks

You can also reach WordPerfect Customer Support by dialing the following number, which is not toll-free: (801) 228-9907.

WordPerfect Corporation operates an electronic bulletin board that you can call at 1-801-225-4414.

One of the best sources of help is the WordPerfect Support Group (WPSG), an independent group not affiliated with WordPerfect Corporation. The group publishes an excellent monthly newsletter, *The WordPerfectionist*. You can subscribe to *The WordPerfectionist* for $36 a year by writing to the following address:

The WordPerfectionist
Newsletter of the WordPerfect Support Group
P.O. Box 130
McHenry, MD 21541

The WordPerfectionist is intended for all levels of users and is filled with helpful hints, clever techniques, solid guidance, and objective reviews of books and software.

Conventions Used in This Book

The conventions used in this book have been established to help you learn to use the program quickly and easily. Instructions in this book emphasize use of the *mouse* to access commands, make choices in dialog boxes, and so forth. WordPerfect enables you to use both keyboard and mouse to select menu and dialog box items: you can press a letter or you can select an item by clicking it with the mouse. The letter you press appears in boldface: Select **P**rint. If you use a mouse with WordPerfect, you place the mouse pointer on the relevant menu or dialog box item and click the left mouse button to make your selection. Instructions for getting around in WordPerfect for Windows appear in Chapters 1 and 2.

For commands used with the Common User Access (CUA) compliant keyboard, the name of the command is presented first, followed by the keystrokes used to invoke the command. Common User Access keystrokes are keystrokes that perform the same function in many Windows applications. For example, Help (F1) means that you press F1 to invoke Help. A special icon identifies all CUA keystrokes:

 Press Help (F1).

Uppercase letters are used to distinguish file names, macro names, and merge commands, such as {END FIELD}. In most cases, the keys on the keyboard are represented as they appear on your keyboard (for example, G, Enter, Tab, Ctrl, Ins, and Backspace). For keystrokes separated by hyphens, such as Speller (Ctrl-F1), hold down the first key (Ctrl in this example) and press the second key (F1 in this example) to invoke the command. When a series of keys is separated by commas, press and release each key in sequence. To move to the beginning of the line before any hidden codes, for example, press and release Home twice (Home, Home).

A special Button Bar icon in the margin identifies Button Bar ideas mentioned in the text:

 Create a Print Preview button to take you quickly to the Print Preview mode.

Text you are asked to type is shown in **boldface**. On-screen messages and WordPerfect hidden codes are shown in a monospaced font: `[Tab]`. Special words or phrases defined for the first time appear in *italic* type.

Charles O. Stewart III
Carmel, Indiana

Getting Started

PART

I

OUTLINE

Preparing To Use WordPerfect for Windows

Preparing To Use WordPerfect for Windows

WordPerfect 5.1 for Windows is one of the most powerful word processors available for Windows or for DOS. WordPerfect for Windows builds on the popular and powerful DOS versions, WordPerfect 5.0 and 5.1, and makes excellent use of Windows' simple, intuitive, icon- and menu-based graphical user interface (GUI). In addition, WordPerfect for Windows has beautifully simple graphics handling.

This chapter begins with an overview of the important and powerful features of WordPerfect for Windows and then provides a hands-on introduction to the program's basic components. In this chapter, you learn how to do the following:

■ Launch and exit WordPerfect

■ Understand components of the editing window

■ **Steve Konicki** is a computer consultant and teacher who specializes in Microsoft Windows and Windows applications and in computer systems design for business.

■ Understand document windows

■ Edit up to nine documents at a time

■ Use the mouse and keyboard, as well as special keyboard shortcuts

■ Understand WordPerfect's menus and dialog boxes

■ Make selections and execute commands

■ Understand the function of the Button Bar and the Ruler

■ Understand hidden codes

■ Use WordPerfect's special Help function

Despite all the changes and new features in WordPerfect for Windows, WordPerfect for DOS veterans will be delighted to know that the Windows version includes the same features that made WordPerfect 4.0 through WordPerfect 5.1 among the largest selling computer programs in history. In fact, documents written in WordPerfect for Windows use the same format as documents written in WordPerfect 5.1, so your work is interchangeable between the two versions. For a detailed comparison of WordPerfect for Windows and WordPerfect 5.1 for DOS, see Appendix B, "WordPerfect: Windows vs. DOS."

If you need help installing WordPerfect for Windows, turn to Appendix A, "Installing and Setting Up WordPerfect for Windows." If you have not yet installed Windows, refer to the Microsoft Windows User's Guide, which comes with the Windows software.

An Overview of WordPerfect for Windows

WordPerfect for Windows makes full use of Windows' WYSIWYG (what you see is what you get) capabilities: WordPerfect for Windows accurately portrays graphics, fonts, and other elements of the page to enable you to see on-screen what the printed document will look like (see fig. 1.1). The simplicity of the Windows interface makes choosing and sizing fonts and importing graphics as easy as a few mouse clicks. Even using multiple graphics on the same page is not difficult. If you have ever thought that a graphic designer may live in your soul, waiting to get out, WordPerfect for Windows could be the program to help release that talent.

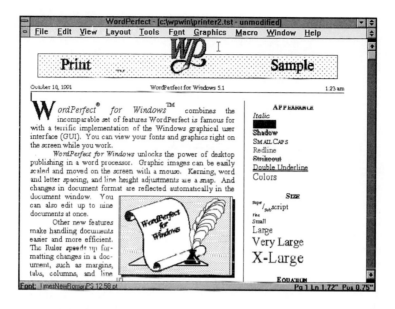

FIG. 1.1

A WordPerfect
for Windows
WYSIWYG
display.

In fact, because WordPerfect makes such good use of WYSIWYG, the program is ideal for almost any kind of business publishing task. Placing a small chart or graph in a letter to the field sales staff or designing company newsletters, brochures, and fliers is made easy by WordPerfect. WordPerfect for Windows is also sophisticated enough to meet the word processing needs of people who are responsible for more complex desktop publishing chores, such as preparing the company's annual reports.

Another new WordPerfect feature, the Button Bar, puts you in control of your word processor. With the Button Bar, shown in figure 1.2, you can launch a frequently accessed function, such as the Speller, with a single click of the left mouse button. The Button Bar gives you more freedom to work the way you want—with power and simplicity—than almost any other word processor.

Cue: The Button Bar puts you in control of your word processor.

FIG. 1.2

The default
WordPerfect
Button Bar.

The Button Bar also can cut dramatically the amount of time a new user needs to learn WordPerfect for Windows. Using the Button Bar saves time because frequently used functions can be found easily on the Button Bar; new users do not have to stumble through menus looking for them.

Cue: Using the Button Bar saves time because frequently used functions can be found easily on the Button Bar.

As illustrated in figure 1.3, placing the Thesaurus button beside the Speller button can speed final document preparation. Placing the Print Preview and Print buttons side-by-side on the Button Bar enables you to view document formatting at full-screen size and, when you are satisfied, print without opening a menu.

FIG. 1.3

The Thesaurus and Print Preview buttons added to the default Button Bar.

Another example of the power and versatility of WordPerfect for Windows is its capability of converting documents from more than 40 popular word processing formats to WordPerfect format or converting WordPerfect documents to all those other document formats. This capability may make WordPerfect for Windows the optimal word processor for businesses that use several different word processors. Instead of forcing die-hard computer users to abandon their favorite word processors, you can use WordPerfect to translate documents back and forth between formats. Figure 1.4 shows the Save As dialog box, which is used for converting a file from one word processor format to another, and some of the many document format choices WordPerfect offers.

FIG. 1.4

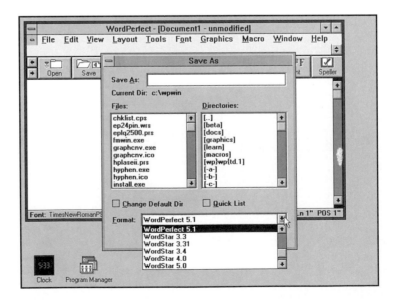

The Save As dialog box for converting a file to a different format.

WordPerfect for Windows comes with a File Manager, which you can use to keep track of documents and do housekeeping chores on your hard drive. The program also includes a thesaurus and spelling checker, which can be used for final document preparation before printing.

Although these utilities are designed to be used with WordPerfect, each also works as a stand-alone application when run from Windows. For example, you can launch the spelling checker to find the spelling of a word without having first to start WordPerfect. You can use the File Manager to delete, move, and rename any file, not just WordPerfect documents. WordPerfect's Setup program installs these utilities in Windows in the WordPerfect Group.

WordPerfect for Windows' powerful new features include the following:

- *Icon- and menu-based Windows interface.* Most commands are available from pull-down and cascading menus and 3-D buttons by using the mouse instead of the complex command structure that can make other word processors hard to learn (see fig. 1.5).

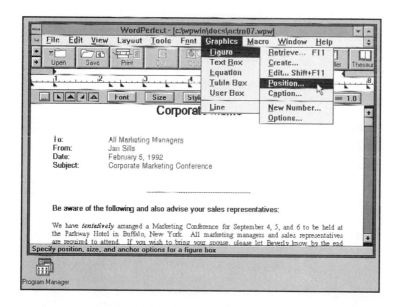

FIG. 1.5

The WordPerfect Graphics Figure menu.

- *WYSIWYG.* WYSIWYG is an on-screen display of document fonts, margins, graphics, indents, tables, and other document details. WordPerfect's WYSIWYG capabilities are detailed in the chapters on fonts, text formatting, and graphics.

■ *Simplified graphics handling.* Importing graphics into WordPerfect involves a few simple choices from the Graphics menu instead of obscure commands like those that make using graphics difficult in some word processors. As shown in figure 1.6, text automatically wraps around the graphic. You can reposition the graphic by dragging it with the mouse to virtually anywhere in the document. A Graphics Editor launched from WordPerfect for Windows enables you to size and shape a graphic to suit your project.

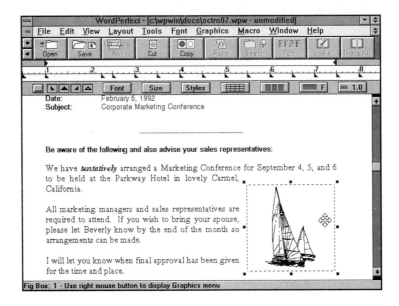

FIG. 1.6

Text wrapped around a graphic.

■ *Button Bar.* This feature enables you to place your choice of important WordPerfect commands where they are always available with a single mouse click, thus circumventing the menus and other commands.

■ *On-screen Ruler.* This feature enables you to set margins and tabs by dragging, or moving, graphics symbols. The Ruler also includes 3-D buttons that enable you to select typefaces and font sizes; instantly set up a table; set type in columns; select left, right, or full justification of type; and choose line spacing. Figure 1.7 shows the Ruler's pull-down menu that appears when you click the 3-D line spacing button. The ease with which you can format a WordPerfect document is greatly increased by the on-screen Ruler.

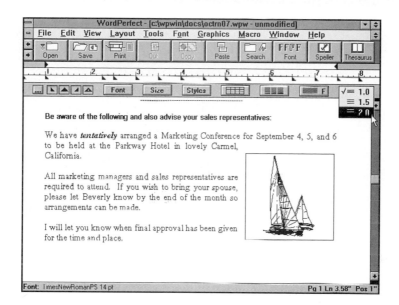

■ *Context-sensitive help.* This feature includes an extremely helpful "How Do I" feature, which explains basic program operation, and a "What Is" feature that enables you to click a mouse button nearly anywhere on the WordPerfect screen to learn the area's name and see a short description of its function. After you know the area's name, you can quickly find more information in WordPerfect's extensive help files.

■ *Capability to convert documents.* You can convert documents from and to more than 40 popular word processor formats

■ *New editing capabilities.* You can edit up to nine documents at once, with the capability of copying text from one document into any or all the other documents or copying a graphic, such as your company logo, into all nine. This capability also enables you to compare documents side-by-side and switch instantly from one to another by using the mouse. Figure 1.8 shows WordPerfect with two documents on-screen at the same time, side-by-side.

■ *Undo command.* This command reverses the most recent change made to your document. This feature, combined with Word-Perfect's Undelete command, enables you to reverse nearly any action you have taken. The Undo and Undelete commands are located on the Edit menu.

■ **Cue:** The Undo command reverses only the most recent change made to your document.

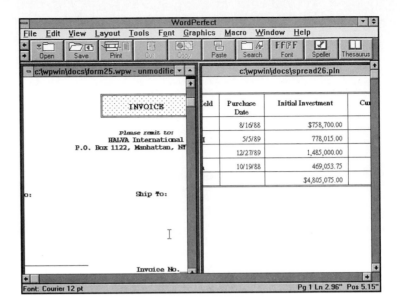

FIG. 1.8

Side-by-side
document
windows.

- *Mouse and keyboard capabilities.* You can activate commands by using the mouse or the keyboard, including special shortcut key combinations. The shortcut combinations can be faster than using the mouse because the keyboard shortcut bypasses the menu system (not all commands have keyboard shortcuts). Mouse and keyboard methods for choosing commands in WordPerfect for Windows are discussed later in this chapter.

- *Quick printer configuration.* Nearly all printer commands are located in one place, and you can make choices by using Windows' pull-down menu structure and the mouse.

- *Print Preview.* This feature enables you to see how your document looks at full-page size. Print Preview includes a view of headers and footers, footnotes, or formats that aren't shown in WordPerfect's editing window. An example of Print Preview is shown in figure 1.9.

- *Draft mode.* This feature speeds writing and editing when several graphics, font changes, columns, or tables are present in a document. In effect, this feature disables WYSIWYG by replacing proportional on-screen fonts with monospaced characters like the screen characters in the DOS version of WordPerfect. Chapter 10 details the use of fonts.

■ *Dynamic Data Exchange (DDE).* Dynamic Data Exchange enables you to link data imported from a Windows program into
WordPerfect. By using DDE, WordPerfect automatically updates
the data in WordPerfect when you change data in the Windows
program that created the data. Chapter 31 details the use of
Dynamic Data Exchange.

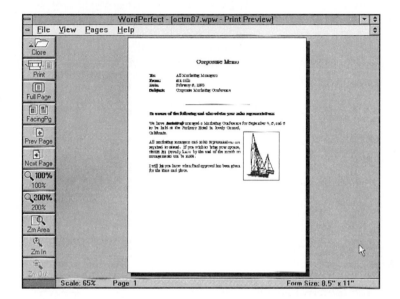

FIG. 1.9

A Print Preview
of a document.

■ *New macro features.* These new features include the capability of
pausing a macro, performing a task, and then resuming the macro.
You can assign macros to your Macro menu for easier access.
This feature also enables you to create a menu item for nearly any
WordPerfect function. A macro also may be retrieved, edited, and
saved like a document. The macro language itself has been rewritten to make creating and using macros even easier.

■ *Special characters.* Besides standard keyboard characters,
WordPerfect provides many special characters, including languages, such as Greek, and typesetting characters and symbols to
help dress up your document. These symbol sets are accessed
through the Font menu. Chapter 28 discusses special characters.

Understanding WordPerfect's File Manager

WordPerfect includes a File Manager designed for managing documents and graphics when they are spread throughout several directories, more than one hard drive, or even a network. The File Manager's functions include routine file management chores: deleting, moving, and renaming files. Like WordPerfect itself, the File Manager enables you to add a Button Bar containing the functions you are most likely to use.

The File Manager includes the following features:

- A Navigator that enables you to move quickly from a view of subdirectories to a listing of individual files

- A Viewer that quickly shows you the contents of a document without your having to take the time to open the file in WordPerfect

- A Find command that can search for a certain file on all directories of a drive

- A sophisticated Advanced Find command that can search inside all documents in a directory or on an entire drive for a specific word or phrase

- An Applications menu that enables you to add programs to run from the File Manager

  The programs installed from the Applications menu by the WordPerfect Install program include the Speller, Thesaurus, and WordPerfect itself. You can install any Windows program you choose, including any of the utilities that come with Windows, such as Clock, Calendar, Terminal, Cardfile, Write, Paintbrush, and Calculator.

- An Info menu that provides detailed information on your DOS version, system hardware, Windows and its current operating mode, as well as the currently selected printer and your floppy and hard disk drives.

Cue: You can activate the File Manager from within WordPerfect by choosing the File menu and then the File Manager option.

You can activate the File Manager from within WordPerfect by choosing the File menu and then the File Manager option. You also can run the File Manager as a stand-alone application from Windows. If you launch File Manager before WordPerfect, you can use File Manager to launch WordPerfect by selecting the Applications menu and then choosing WordPerfect.

T I P

File Manager also can be used to load a specific file into WordPerfect, bypassing WordPerfect's own File, Open menu selection. If WordPerfect is running, you can use the mouse or keyboard to select the file you want to load, and File Manager loads it into a WordPerfect document window, ready to edit. If WordPerfect is not already running, selecting a file in the File Manager launches WordPerfect with that file loaded in a document window.

A particularly useful feature of the File Manager is its Quick List capability. Quick List enables you to create both a list of the directories you use most often and descriptions that refer to each of the directories. When you need to access a directory, you select the desired directory from the descriptive names (see fig. 1.10).

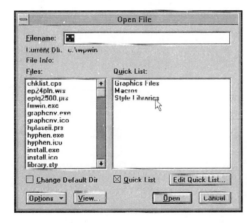

FIG 1.10

The Open File dialog box with a Quick List.

The Navigator enables you to move from directory to directory by double-clicking the name of a directory you want to enter. The files in the directory appear in the File List window. When you are in the root directory, the File List window displays all the root directory's subdirectories.

T I P

Choosing the Layouts option from the File Manager's View menu enables you to determine exactly what is displayed in the File Manager. Using the Layouts option, you can display a list of files in a window on the left side of the screen and on the right open a window to view the contents of an individual file.

Chapters 3 and 30 explain the File Manager and tell you how to configure it for maximum usefulness.

Starting Windows

You launch Windows from the C> prompt by typing **win** and pressing Enter. The Windows Program Manager appears.

The WordPerfect Program Group may be open when Windows loads, enabling you to see the icons for WordPerfect for Windows, the Speller, the Thesaurus, and the File Manager. If the WordPerfect group is an icon when Windows loads, double-click the icon to open the group (see fig. 1.11).

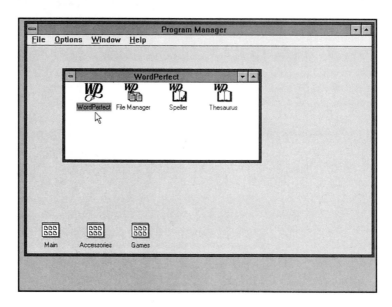

FIG. 1.11

The WordPerfect group in the Windows Program Manager.

Starting WordPerfect

To launch WordPerfect for Windows, double-click its icon. WordPerfect appears on-screen with the default configuration (see fig. 1.12). The Button Bar and the Ruler have not been turned on yet, so they are absent. You will activate them shortly, but for now concentrate on what you need to know about the basic WordPerfect setup.

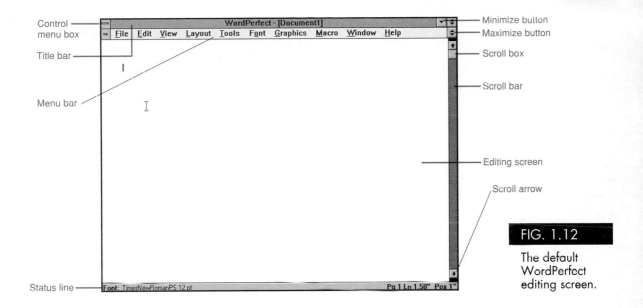

FIG. 1.12

The default WordPerfect editing screen.

Understanding the Editing Screen

The basic WordPerfect for Windows editing screen, where you do your work, appears immediately after you launch the program. Before you try to open your first document, take a moment to examine the WordPerfect screen. Acquaint yourself with the way that the WordPerfect screen uses many of the same basic elements as Windows.

Note the open editing space, the title bar, the Minimize and Maximize buttons, the scroll bars, the status line, and the menu bar. Refer to figure 1.12, which identifies the elements of the WordPerfect screen.

The Title Bar

When you launch WordPerfect, it creates a document called DOCUMENT1. The document's name is displayed on WordPerfect's title bar. You can begin typing immediately, and WordPerfect prompts you to name and save the document before you exit.

The best way to protect your work is to give the new document a name immediately by clicking the File menu and selecting Save. A dialog box prompts you for the file name (see Chapter 2 for information about naming files).

T I P   You should always name new documents immediately and save them frequently so that your work is not lost if a power outage or other problem with your computer occurs.

The Menu Bar

Cue: WordPerfect menus control nearly every operation.

Beneath the title bar is WordPerfect's menu bar. The menu bar is a key focus of the editing screen, as important in WordPerfect for Windows as the function keys are in WordPerfect for DOS, because the menus control nearly every operation. The 10 pull-down menus in Word-Perfect contain virtually all the commands with which you work. As with other Windows programs, when a menu choice requires additional information, you are presented with an additional menu or dialog box so that you can make the required choices or enter the necessary information.

The Scroll Bars

Along the right side of the WordPerfect editing screen, and optionally across the bottom, are the scroll bars you use to move quickly through a document too long to fit on one screen. To use a scroll bar, place the mouse pointer on the scroll arrow that points in the direction you want to move and press the left mouse button. Holding down the left mouse button continues the scroll through the document. To move quickly from one part of the document to another—to move from the top to the bottom, for example—place the mouse pointer on the scroll box and drag.

The Status Line

The status line, which is the bar across the bottom of the screen, displays a great deal of helpful information regarding your location in the current document. Refer again to figure 1.12 to see the status line as it looks when you launch WordPerfect.

The right side of the status line displays the number of the page you are typing, the line number within the page, and the number of inches your insertion point is from the left edge of the paper. If you are using default one-inch margins, the status line will read 1" (for one inch) when the insertion point is at the beginning of a line.

The left side of the status line offers *Long Prompts*, which change, depending on the operation you are performing. While you are typing in a document, for example, the left side of the status line displays the name and point size of the font being used at that point in the document. When you are using the menus, the status line changes to provide quick help on nearly any WordPerfect function.

To see the way WordPerfect's Long Prompts provide quick help, activate a menu by placing the mouse pointer on the menu name and clicking the left button. Then place the mouse pointer over the menu choice you want help with. While the pointer is on the proper menu choice, press and hold down the left mouse button without moving the pointer. The status line displays a short explanation of the function you have chosen. For example, click the File menu and hold down the mouse button while the pointer is on Open. The status line now reads Open an existing file and retrieve it into a new window.

 CAUTION: Although you can use the mouse pointer to get help at any time, this feature can be tricky. If you release the mouse button while the pointer is on a command you wanted help with, WordPerfect executes that command. Be sure that you don't release the mouse button while the pointer is on the menu option. Instead, move the mouse until the pointer is on the title bar. Then you can release the mouse button safely.

The quick help WordPerfect provides on the status line works in the following ways:

■ To get help on the way commands are grouped in a menu, put the mouse pointer on the menu name; press and hold the left mouse button. The status line displays a short description of the kinds of commands grouped in the menu. For example, selecting the View menu prompts the status line to read Change what you see in the WordPerfect window.

■ If you hold the mouse button with the pointer on a menu choice, the status line displays quick help about that operation. For example, when you hold the mouse pointer on the Layout menu's Justification option, the status line says Align text in document.

- If you press the Ins (Insert) key while typing in the editing screen, the text on the left side of the status line changes to indicate that you are in Typeover mode.

- When you save a document, the status line confirms the operation and displays the file's drive, path, and name on the left side of the status line. For example, the status line may display the following while you are saving a document: `Saving Document: C:\WPWIN\DOCS\CABANA.WPW.`

Troubleshooting Problems Starting WordPerfect

Cue: If you have trouble launching WordPerfect for Windows, try reinstalling the program.

If you have problems launching WordPerfect for Windows, retracing the steps for installation detailed in Appendix A may help. As much as possible, try to determine whether you followed the installation instructions exactly. If you skipped a step, or if you are not sure that you followed the directions closely, you may need to reinstall WordPerfect. Make sure that you provide setup with the proper information for the floppy drive from which you are installing WordPerfect, the drive and directory to which you are installing WordPerfect, and the correct information about your printer.

Cue: If reinstalling WordPerfect does not solve the problem, you need to determine whether the problem is in Windows.

If reinstalling WordPerfect does not solve the problem, you need to determine whether the problem is in Windows, because Windows serves as the basic system software under which WordPerfect runs. One way to ensure that Windows is working properly is to launch a few Windows utilities, such as the Clock, Calendar, Terminal, Cardfile, Write, Paintbrush, and Calculator. If these utilities work as they should, chances are the problem is not in Windows. If Windows is not working properly, you may need to reinstall it or call Microsoft technical support for assistance.

If Windows is working properly, and you are sure that you have installed WordPerfect properly, the next step is to call WordPerfect technical support for assistance. Be sure that you are in front of your computer when you call so that you can answer questions about your system and take the steps suggested by technical support. The telephone numbers for WordPerfect technical support are listed in the Introduction.

When you call technical support, you need to have your program serial number at hand, as well as basic inforamtion about your computer: its CPU (80286, 80386, or 80486), amount of installed RAM, the brand name of your video card and monitor, and the amount of hard drive space available (the DOS CHKDSK command gives you the total space available).

WARNING: Do not run CHKDSK inside Windows, because doing so can destroy data on your hard disk drive.

Understanding Document Windows

WordPerfect for Windows enables you to open as many as nine documents at a time. This capability gives you an exceptional amount of freedom to exchange information between documents. With several documents open, for example, you can move quickly from one document to the next, copying parts of each to create a new document. Or you can import a single graphic into several different documents.

WordPerfect loads each document into what is termed a *document window*. Document windows can be displayed in the same basic ways that Windows displays programs—as a full screen, in a window, or as an icon. Each document window can be moved around the screen, and each can be opened or closed without affecting the others. By displaying documents in these ways, WordPerfect enables you to accomplish the following:

■ **Cue:** You can have as many as nine document windows open at once and work with each without affecting the others.

■ Remove a document almost completely from the screen by minimizing it, that is, reducing it to an icon so that you have room for other documents on-screen

■ Move a document window from one location to another

■ Make one document window overlap another, enabling you to switch between them by clicking the mouse on one or the other

■ Position two or more document windows side-by-side so that you can compare files or cut and paste data from one to the other

The most common way to work in a WordPerfect document is to maximize its window, or give it the entire editing area. Maximizing the window provides the best view of the entire document. A double-headed arrow on the menu bar, shown in figure 1.13, is one indication that a document window is maximized. Clicking the double-headed arrow reduces the document window so that it uses only part of the main WordPerfect screen.

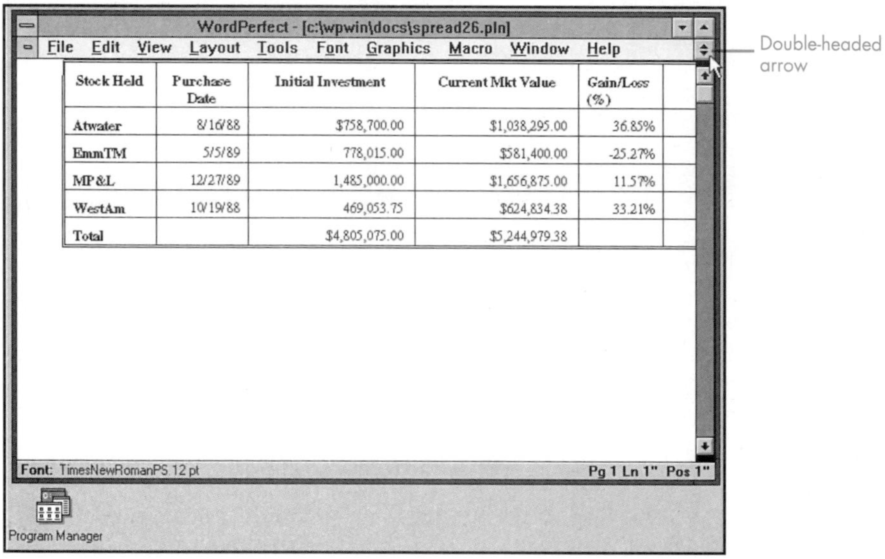

Double-headed arrow

FIG. 1.13

A double-headed arrow indicating a maximized window.

When several documents are open at once, you can make changes only to the *foreground document*, the document in front on the editing screen. To work on a background document, you first need to bring it to the foreground. Additionally, a document must be in the foreground before you can close it or save it. In figure 1.14, which shows several open documents, the foreground document's title bar says c:\wpwin\docs\octrn12.wpw.

To switch from one document to another, click anywhere on the window to which you want to switch. You also can open the Window menu and click the name of the document you want to edit. This method is the most simple for moving between documents when your document windows are maximized.

To help you arrange multiple documents so that you can switch more easily from one to another, WordPerfect enables you to tile or cascade your documents. You make your choice in the Window menu.

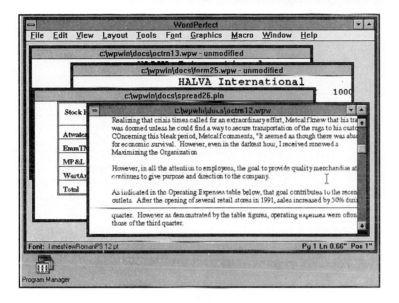

FIG. 1.14

Several open
document
windows.

Tiling windows gives each window the same amount of screen space without overlapping. *Cascading* overlaps windows but leaves each title bar showing. Figure 1.15 shows nine WordPerfect document windows that have been tiled; figure 1.16 shows the same nine windows cascaded.

Maneuvering in a WordPerfect Document

This section explains how to get around in a WordPerfect document by using the keyboard and the mouse. Even if you have not launched WordPerfect yet, the Windows navigation techniques you learned in running other Windows programs translate to valuable experience for WordPerfect.

All basic elements of the Windows GUI are present in WordPerfect for Windows; therefore, you maneuver in WordPerfect in the same ways that you maneuver in Windows.

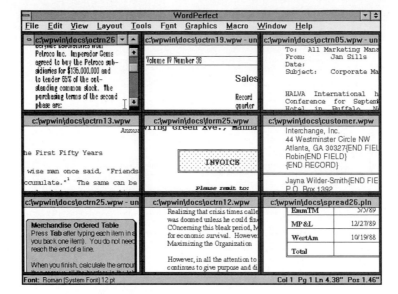

FIG .15

Tiled
WordPerfect
document
windows.

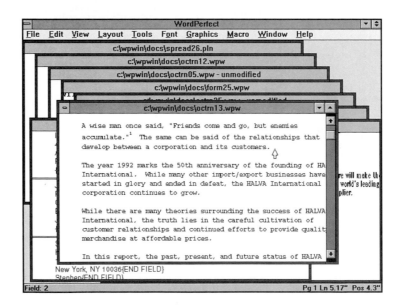

FIG .16

Cascaded
WordPerfect
document
windows.

Using the Mouse

You have probably noticed how many of WordPerfect's features are activated and controlled through the mouse. Use of the mouse is almost a requirement in WordPerfect for Windows. Although many mouse functions have keyboard equivalents, using the keyboard is usually slower and more difficult. In addition, some WordPerfect functions cannot be used without a mouse.

If you are new to using a mouse, chances are that, after learning to use it effectively, you will find the mouse quick and convenient. You may even wonder why you didn't begin to use one sooner. With a mouse, actions that take numerous keystrokes or complex keystroke combinations can be done by moving the mouse pointer to a menu choice and pressing a mouse button. The use of the mouse is a skill that can help you with many programs. All Windows programs, as well as many DOS programs, depend heavily on the mouse.

Cue: Using the mouse is a skill that can help you work with all Windows programs and many DOS programs.

The first step in using a mouse is moving the mouse across an empty area next to your keyboard while keeping the mouse in contact with the desk or, preferably, a mouse pad. Moving the mouse this way rotates a ball on the underside of the mouse. That ball, in turn, generates an electronic signal that moves the mouse pointer on your computer screen.

Depending on the manufacturer, a mouse can have two or three buttons. Figure 1.17 shows a standard two-button mouse. By default, the left button is the primary mouse button. If you prefer another button as your primary mouse button, you can make this change in the Windows Control Panel.

FIG. 1.17

A standard two-button mouse.

The three basic mouse operations are clicking, double-clicking, and dragging. A short description of these common mouse functions follows:

■ *Clicking.* To click, quickly press and release the primary mouse button once while the pointer is on a menu option, an icon, or some other graphic symbol. Clicking the name of a menu causes that menu to appear on-screen. Clicking the Button Bar's Speller button launches WordPerfect's spelling checker feature.

■ *Double-clicking.* To double-click, quickly press and release the primary mouse button twice. Double-clicking often functions like the Enter key. You launch WordPerfect for Windows, or any other program in Windows, by double-clicking the program's icon.

■ *Dragging.* To drag, hold down the primary mouse button while you move the mouse on your desk or mouse pad. You drag to move document windows from place to place in WordPerfect. Within a document, dragging is used to select blocks of text for cutting, copying, or performing other changes.

The arrow pointer is the most common mouse pointer in Windows. The mouse pointer is used primarily in operations that involve selecting from menus, clicking icons, and performing other simple tasks. WordPerfect displays this pointer when the mouse is in the title bar, menu bar, Button Bar, Ruler, or scroll bars, which are places where most tasks are simple selection operations.

When you move the mouse pointer into WordPerfect's text editing area, the mouse pointer changes into what is called the *I-beam.* The I-beam is particularly important to maneuvering with the mouse in a WordPerfect document. The place where you enter words, or where you make changes to a document, is marked by the *insertion point,* a thin flashing bar. Figure 1.18 shows both the I-beam and the insertion point.

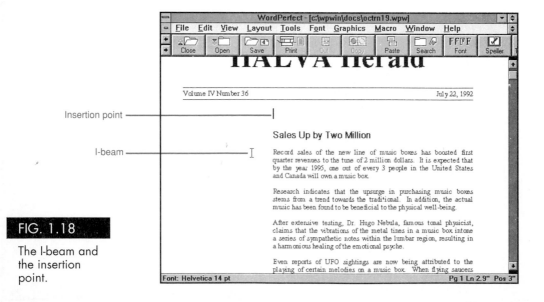

FIG. 1.18

The I-beam and the insertion point.

With the mouse, you use the I-beam to move the insertion point. By moving the mouse on your desktop or mouse pad, you can move the I-beam to any part of your WordPerfect document.

To use the I-beam to move the insertion point, place the I-beam at the beginning of any word in the document and click the left mouse button. The insertion point moves immediately to where the I-beam is located. Using this mouse technique to move from one part of a document to another is much quicker than using the directional keys.

> The I-beam is particularly handy used in combination with keyboard keys when you move through a long document. Use the scroll bars or the PgDn and PgUp keys, to move from page to page, and when you reach the page you want to edit, move the I-beam to the word you want to change and click. The insertion point moves instantly to where you need it.

T I P

Using the Keyboard

You can move the insertion point in a document by using the keyboard's up-, down-, left-, and right-arrow keys. You probably will use the directional keys almost exclusively to move around in the current WordPerfect editing screen, where moving the insertion point from one line to another by using the keyboard is the quick way.

Chapter 2 shows you how to use many of the basic keys in combination with the Ctrl or Alt key to accelerate movement through a document.

Because WordPerfect is designed to run on modern computers, such as 286, 386, and 486 machines, most people using the program will work on Enhanced keyboards, which generally have 12 function keys. See figure 1.19 for a diagram showing the layout of an Enhanced keyboard. If you are working on an older keyboard, however, your keyboard may have fewer function keys, and your cursor-movement keys or numeric keypad may be slightly different from the diagram.

The basic keys used most often to move around in a WordPerfect document are the arrow keys, Home, End, Del, Backspace, PgUp, and PgDn. These keys move you through a WordPerfect document in the following ways:

Key	Action
Up arrow	Insertion point moves up one line
Down arrow	Insertion point moves down one line
Left arrow	Insertion point moves left one character
Right arrow	Insertion point moves right one character
Home	Insertion point moves to beginning of current line
End	Insertion point moves to end of current line
Del	Deletes character at insertion point
Backspace	Deletes character to left of insertion point
PgUp	Insertion point moves to previous screen
PgDn	Insertion point moves to next screen
Ctrl-Home	Moves to the beginning of the document
Ctrl-End	Moves to the end of the document

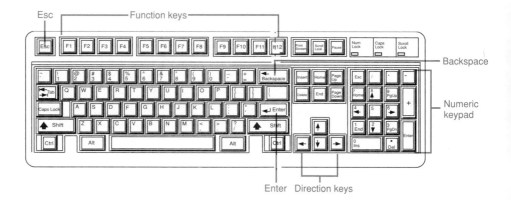

FIG. 1.19

The Enhanced keyboard.

As explained in the next section, WordPerfect offers special shortcut key combinations that are much faster than using regular keyboard or mouse techniques because the shortcut keys enable you to bypass the menus when executing certain commands. You should become familiar with the location of the Shift, Alt, Ctrl, Backspace, and function keys on your keyboard if you plan to use shortcut key combinations.

If you select the File menu's Preferences option, you can choose whether to use Windows' shortcut key combinations, known as *Common User Access (CUA)*, or a keyboard setup comparable to that of

WordPerfect 5.1 for DOS. WordPerfect enables you to customize your keyboard by *remapping* (changing the function of) certain keys. Appendix B provides an extensive listing of the shortcut key combinations and other keystrokes available in WordPerfect for Windows.

 Cue: You can choose to use Common User Access keys or a setup compatible with WordPerfect 5.1 for DOS.

CAUTION: When you use the WordPerfect 5.1 compatible keyboard in WordPerfect for Windows, in dialog boxes the CUA keyboard overrides the current keyboard.

If you are new to word processing but have used a typewriter, you must keep in mind an important difference between your keyboard and a typewriter's keyboard. When typing in WordPerfect, you do not need to end each line by pressing Enter, which is the key that corresponds to the carriage return on a typewriter. When you reach the end of a line in WordPerfect, the program automatically *wraps text*, or ends the line and moves to the next. When you edit your document, WordPerfect automatically adjusts the length of each line to fit the margins after you add or delete text.

Choosing Commands

Nearly every function of WordPerfect for Windows is done more easily and quickly with the mouse. Whether creating and editing documents, setting margins and tabs, adding graphics to a document, choosing the document typeface and point size, dividing text into columns similar to those in newspapers or magazines, setting single- or double-spaced lines, or creating tables and using styles, you can accomplish the task more quickly with the mouse.

Still, WordPerfect goes to great lengths to make itself accessible to those who prefer the keyboard. In fact, WordPerfect enables you to use certain special keystroke combinations as shortcuts to powerful functions. Pressing F1, for example, is quicker than using the mouse to launch Help.

This section can help you learn those commands you can use with the keyboard or keyboard shortcuts that are quicker than a mouse. You cannot do without the mouse completely, however, because several important WordPerfect functions require the mouse. Even if you are uncomfortable with the mouse right now, you will find that you learn WordPerfect more quickly and make greater use of its power if you take the time to become familiar with the mouse.

Choosing Menu Options

Take a moment now to open WordPerfect's menus one at a time and note the commands contained in each. Although you cannot expect to memorize the location of every command, note that each menu is a logical group of commands.

T I P   After you understand the logic behind the grouping of commands in the WordPerfect menus, you will find yourself speeding through writing, editing, and document-formatting tasks.

The Graphics menu, for example, controls the importing of graphics and the creation of text boxes, tables, and equations. In the File menu, as in most Windows programs, you find the Open, Close, Save, and Print commands, which enable you to manipulate documents. Also in the File menu is WordPerfect's Preferences option, which enables you to change many WordPerfect defaults and make the program run the way you want.

WordPerfect's menus are shown on the tear-out command card in the back of this book; the following list tells you some of the commands available on each menu:

- *The File menu* contains basic document commands: Open, Save, Print, and New (for creating a document). The File menu also contains the Save As command. From the File menu, you can password protect a file or launch the File Manager. This menu also contains the Preferences option, which you use to customize WordPerfect for Windows.

- *The Edit menu* contains the Cut, Copy, Paste, Undo, and Undelete commands, as well as commands to search a document for a certain text string and, if you want, replace it with different text. Using the Select command, you can select a sentence or a paragraph. The Convert Case command makes selected text all uppercase or lowercase letters. The Go To command takes you immediately to the page number you enter in the dialog box.

- *The View menu* contains options that determine the configuration of the WordPerfect screen. You activate the Button Bar and Ruler and choose between short or long menus from the View menu. You also can decide to display graphics on-screen or show just a frame where graphics are to be located. This menu also contains the Draft Mode option, which improves typing and editing speed by turning off the WYSIWYG display, as explained earlier in this chapter.

- *The Layout menu* contains numerous options that enable you to decide the appearance of your document, including Margins, Justification, Typesetting, Footnote, Columns, Tables, and Styles.

- *The Tools menu* contains the Speller and Thesaurus, as well as the Word Count, Outline, Sort, and Merge commands. The Tools menu also includes Master Document and Spreadsheet options. In addition, you can choose from the 28 languages supported by WordPerfect for Windows.

- *The Font menu* contains the Font and Size options. Using this menu enables you to set type styles like Bold, Italic, Underline, Double Underline, Strikeout, Subscript, and Superscript. In addition, you can choose from the 13 special WordPerfect character sets, including Greek, Hebrew, Japanese, Math/Scientific, Typographic Symbols, and ASCII.

- *The Graphics menu* contains the commands for importing and editing WordPerfect (WPG) format graphics and creating text boxes, equations, table boxes, and performing other functions.

- *The Macro menu* contains the commands to record and play a *macro*, a series of keystrokes you can save and use later to automate a task. This menu enables you to assign completed macros to the menu so that they can be executed when you want.

- *The Window menu* contains a list of all documents currently loaded. You can choose to tile or cascade document windows when more than one document is loaded.

- *The Help menu* offers context-sensitive help, which is help that pertains to the task you are currently doing. Anytime in WordPerfect that you forget what to do next or how to do it, press F1 or click the Help menu. The use of the Help utility is explained later in this chapter.

Making Menu Choices with the Mouse

WordPerfect's menus, like those of any Windows program, are designed to make executing commands easy by using the mouse. To open a menu, click its name. Then click the required option or command. The simplicity of making selections with the mouse is one of the major reasons many people find Windows programs so easy to learn and use.

Making Menu Choices with the Keyboard

WordPerfect offers two basic techniques for executing menu commands with the keyboard.

■ **Cue:** You can execute
WordPerfect menu com-
mands by using the mouse or
the keyboard.

Although not the fastest, the simplest method for accessing the menus
from the keyboard begins by pressing the Alt key. The menu bar's Control Menu box is highlighted. Using the directional keys, move the highlight to the menu you want to open and press Enter. Use the directional
keys to scroll through the menu until the option you want is highlighted. Press Enter to execute the command.

The second method involves *mnemonic* menu options, commands that
give you clues to jog your memory about which keystrokes to use. In
WordPerfect, for instance, you can activate any menu by pressing the
Alt key at the same time as the underlined letter in each menu's name.
To open the File menu, for example, press Alt-F. Then press a
command's underlined letter to execute the command.

WordPerfect also offers shortcut key combinations for bypassing the
menu system when executing certain commands. For example, pressing
Alt-F4 exits WordPerfect. Shortcut key combinations are displayed next
to the menu options to which they correspond. These combinations
are shown in the menus only as a reminder. You do not need to open a
menu to use a shortcut key combination; you simply enter the combination at any time. Menu commands that do not list shortcut keys, such
as the Edit menu's Link and Select options, do not have shortcut keys.

Making Choices in Dialog Boxes

When you make a choice in one of WordPerfect's menus that requires
additional information before the command can be executed, you are
presented with a dialog box. Some dialog boxes require you to click an
option box or button or require you to type the needed information.
Other dialog boxes present choices in a scrolling list of options.

■ **Cue:** In dialog boxes,
you use the mouse or the Tab
and cursor-movement keys to
choose options.

In dialog boxes that present you with several options, you use the Tab
key to move from area to area. In a scrolling list box, make your selection with the cursor-movement keys. When you must choose from several check boxes, move from one to the other by pressing Tab and
make your selection by pressing the space bar. In dialog boxes where
buttons indicate your choices, make your selection with the cursor-
movement keys.

For example, a dialog box that will become quite familiar to you as you
use WordPerfect is the Open File dialog box, shown in figure 1.20. To
display this dialog box, you select Files, Open. Suppose that you want
to examine the list of files shown in the Files list at the left side of this

dialog box. This list shows in alphabetical order all the files in the current directory. To use the Files list, you place the mouse pointer anywhere in the Files list box and click the left mouse button. From the keyboard, you press Alt-I, or you press Tab to move the cursor to the Files list box. The Files list then becomes the active window. You can browse through the files with the up- or down-arrow key or by using the mouse with the scroll bar at the right side of the box. To exit the Open File dialog box, you use the mouse to click the Cancel button, or you press Tab to move the cursor to the Cancel button before pressing Enter or the space bar.

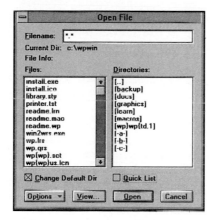

FIG. 1.20

A typical
dialog box.

Using the Button Bar To Streamline Your Work

The Button Bar is easily WordPerfect's fastest way to make choices, because the Button Bar enables you to place the most important WordPerfect commands where they are always available with a single mouse click, thus circumventing the menus and other commands. Each button's graphic depiction of its function helps remind you what that button does.

The power of the Button Bar is simple to illustrate. WordPerfect has 10 pull-down menus, and each menu has numerous options or functions. Using a frequently accessed option like the Speller, for example, involves clicking the mouse button on the Tools menu and then on the Speller option. But with the Button Bar that comes with WordPerfect, you can launch the Speller with a single mouse click anytime you want.

This speed and ease of use make the Button Bar one of the most power-ful, and yet simplest, features of WordPerfect for Windows.

T I P With the Button Bar, someone new to WordPerfect for Windows can create, edit, save, and print a document within the first few minutes of working in the program. The Button Bar is that powerful and simple.

If you have not activated the Button Bar, do so now by opening the View menu and clicking the Button Bar option. Figure 1.21 illustrates the default Button Bar.

FIG. 1.21

The default Button Bar.

The following is a quick overview of the commands on the default Button Bar:

Button	Function
Open	Retrieve a document
Save	Save a document
Print	Send the current document to the printer
Close	Exit the current document but remain in WordPerfect
Cut	Delete highlighted text in the current document
Copy	Copy highlighted text to the Windows Clipboard, where the text is stored until you need it
Paste	Retrieve Clipboard text and insert it into the current document at the location of the insertion point
Search	Find a specific word, phrase, or other text string in the current document
Font	Choose the typeface and point size of text
Speller	Check the spelling of the current document

The simplicity of the Button Bar extends to enabling you to customize it easily. Chapter 19 contains detailed information on creating, customizing, and using the Button Bar.

Using the Ruler To Make Choices in Your Documents

The on-screen Ruler is another example of the ease with which WordPerfect enables you to make choices regarding your documents. The Ruler includes 3-D buttons that enable you to select typefaces and font sizes with the mouse, as well as set type in columns, select the document's justification, create tables, set up and change columns, choose line spacing, and select from WordPerfect's styles. Figure 1.22 shows the Ruler.

■ **Cue:** Use the Ruler to select typefaces, set up a table, and choose line spacing.

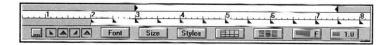

FIG. 1.22

WordPerfect's Ruler.

Understanding Hidden Codes

Hidden codes may seem complex at first, but you cannot afford to ignore them. When you press a key in WordPerfect, many times a hidden code is inserted into your document. These codes indicate margin settings, tabs, carriage returns, indents, and a great deal of other information about the way your document looks in the editing window. In addition, hidden codes contain information about headers, footnotes or endnotes, font changes, document comments, and nonprinting notes.

Other hidden codes turn a feature on and off. Such codes are found in pairs, like the [Bold on] [Bold off] codes shown in figure 1.23, which also shows other examples of hidden codes. To see the hidden codes in a document, choose the View menu's Reveal Codes option.

WordPerfect novices quickly learn that if they are having trouble formatting documents, the trouble lies in the way the hidden codes have been entered in the document. You do not need to understand hidden codes fully at this time; they are covered in greater detail in Chapter 4. For now, be aware that hidden codes do control the appearance of your document.

■ **Cue:** WordPerfect's hidden codes control the appearance of a document.

40

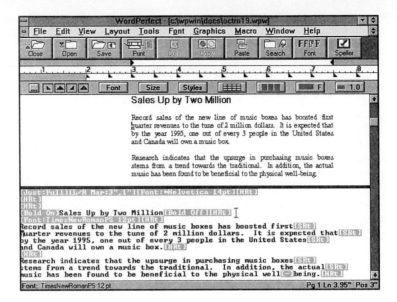

FIG. 1.23

FIG. 1.23

WordPerfect's
hidden codes.

Using Help

WordPerfect's context-sensitive help is another excellent example of taking the simplicity of a basic Windows feature a step further. WordPerfect's help contains Windows' standard features, including the alphabetical index and glossary of terms you use to find most help subjects quickly.

WordPerfect's Help goes beyond just listing topics. Help anticipates your questions about the program and its workings, and understands that you might not know enough about the program's terminology to look for answers in an index. Two Help options in particular assist you in finding the information you need:

What Is

How Do I

Cue: WordPerfect Help is a great tool for finding your way around Windows.

Both of these imaginative features help someone new to WordPerfect find out about a puzzling feature. In fact, because WordPerfect's Help feature often explains the way WordPerfect uses the standard Windows interface, WordPerfect Help is a great tool for finding your way around Windows in general. If you cannot find out what something is called when using Windows Help, the solution most likely will be found and fully explained in WordPerfect Help.

What Is

What Is enables you to place the special mouse pointer on almost any part of the WordPerfect screen and click to learn the area's correct name and to get quick help about how to use that part of the screen. For example, placing the mouse pointer on the status bar and clicking gets this short explanation:

> Displayed in the status bar at the bottom of the WordPerfect window, these information lines provide a brief synopsis of the menu item or option you are currently highlighting.

The information provided by What Is is especially useful because in giving you the name of the area you click (in this case, the status bar), What Is enables you to use the standard Help index to read its longer and more detailed explanation.

How Do I

How Do I can save you the several minutes of frustration that occur when you know what you want to do but have no idea how to do it. Clicking the How Do I help selection gives you a plain-English list of common tasks you need to know.

How Do I starts with the basics—retrieving, opening, saving, and printing a document—and then offers help on a great number of subjects that includes common editing commands, as well as what you need to know about graphics, printing, password protecting, creating a macro, and searching for a lost document.

■ **Cue:** Clicking the How Do I help selection gives you a plain-English list of common tasks you need to know.

> Chances are that if a task is possible, How Do I can tell you how to do it without the frustration of your having to look through the program documentation for a feature you cannot name.

T I P

Standard Help Features

WordPerfect's standard help features are also helpful. Anytime you are unable to recall how to perform a WordPerfect function, press F1 or click the Help menu for immediate context-sensitive help.

Help is broken down by topics in both an index and a glossary. The index provides a list of tasks, arranged alphabetically, that you can do in WordPerfect. The glossary provides an alphabetical list of all the terms used in Help. If you cannot find exactly what you want by looking in the index, you probably will find it when you look in the glossary.

As in Windows Help, when you move the mouse pointer to a topic or task listing with more information available, the pointer becomes a hand. Click to view the additional information. Figure 1.24 shows WordPerfect's Help index.

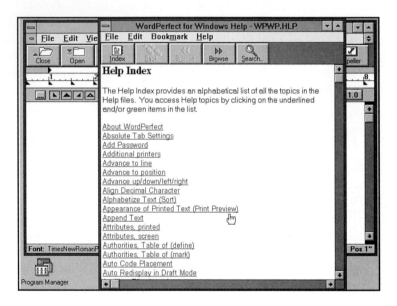

FIG. 1.24

The WordPerfect Help index.

Clicking the command buttons at the top of the help screen move you forward to the next topic or back to the preceding one. The command buttons also enable you to browse or see an index of help topics. WordPerfect also provides special help on using either the Windows Common User Access (CUA) keyboard or the WordPerfect 5.1 for DOS keyboard.

Exiting WordPerfect for Windows

When you are finished with a session of using WordPerfect for Windows, you need to exit from the program. Follow these steps to exit WordPerfect:

1. Save your document by choosing the File menu and then selecting Save.

2. Choose the File menu and then select Exit. If you have not saved your document, WordPerfect asks whether you want to save the file before exiting.

3. Click Yes or press Enter to save and exit; click No (or Tab to No and press Enter) to exit without saving; or click Cancel (or Tab to Cancel and press Enter) to abort the exit and return to editing the current document.

If you are using the keyboard, use the shortcut key combination Alt-F4.

Looking Ahead

Chapter 2, "Creating, Printing, and Saving a Document," provides the basic information you need to begin using WordPerfect for Windows immediately. The subsequent chapters build on the basics covered in these first three chapters, as well as cover the use of WordPerfect's more sophisticated features.

After you have finished Chapter 2, you may want to look through the tutorial workbook included with the documentation for WordPerfect for Windows. Even if you are an experienced WordPerfect for DOS user, you may want to browse these lessons so that you can learn quickly the new ways WordPerfect for Windows does things and become better acquainted with its many new features.

Chapter Summary

In this chapter, you got a brief introduction to WordPerfect for Windows and learned how its use of the Windows GUI makes WordPerfect more useful and easy for you.

This chapter provides you with important information on using WordPerfect for Windows effectively by discussing the basics of starting and exiting the program; the components of the editing screen, such as the status line, Ruler, menus, and hidden codes; and the special capabilities of WordPerfect that enable you to edit as many as nine documents simultaneously, use the Button Bar to save time, and use the special Help command to access immediate context-sensitive help. In addition, this chapter covers how to use both the mouse and keyboard, as well as keyboard shortcuts, to access and run the various menus and commands. The chapters that follow build on the information you have gathered here.

PART II

Mastering Basic Word Processing Tasks

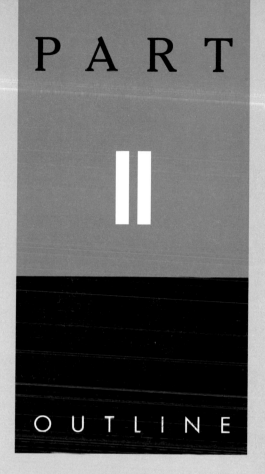

OUTLINE

Creating, Printing, and Saving
    a Document
Managing Files
Editing a Document
Selecting and Editing Text
Formatting Text
Introduction to Graphics
Using the Speller
    and the Thesaurus
Basic Printing

Creating, Printing, and Saving a Document

C hapter 1 covers WordPerfect fundamentals, such as how to start the program, how to understand the information the editing screen gives you, how to use the mouse and the keyboard, how to access menus and dialog boxes, how to manipulate windows, how to make menu choices and execute commands, how to get on-line help, and how to exit WordPerfect. With that introduction to WordPerfect, you're now ready to learn more about how to create memos, short notes, letters—any kind of basic document—with WordPerfect.

In this chapter, you learn in much more detail how to use your computer and WordPerfect to compose the documents you need. After an introduction to writing with a word processor, you look at procedures for the following:

■ **Charles O. Stewart III** served as product director for *Using WordPerfect for Windows*, Special Edition, determining content, assembling the team of contributors, and working closely with them throughout the project.

- Entering text, inserting blank lines, using Typeover, and inserting new text
- Moving the insertion point through a document with the keyboard or the mouse
- Scrolling a document with the mouse
- Printing a single page or an entire document
- Saving a document to disk
- Exiting WordPerfect
- Using multiple document windows when writing a rough draft
- Using WordPerfect to develop ideas for writing

As a bonus, this chapter provides some advice on how you can use WordPerfect to plan and draft your documents. If you have trouble getting started or suffer from writer's block, you will see how word processing can be of tremendous assistance. This advice is based on research about the ways writing habits change with word processors. If you are new to word processing, you will find that many of these tips help you realize the benefits of word processing immediately. Even old hands at word processing can come away from this chapter with new ideas for getting started.

Writing with a Word Processor

Writing is never easy, even for experienced writers. Paul Heckel, author of the classic *The Elements of Software Design: The New Edition*, attributes the following sentiment to Ptahhotep, Vizier to Isesi, Fifth Egyptian Dynasty, 2300 B.C.: "Writing is harder than all other work."[1] The good fortune for writers in the late twentieth century is that a word processor can make writing easier. Researchers looking at what happens when people learn to write with word processors have discovered a heartening fact: people who once dreaded writing become much more positive about it after they learn to write with a word processor.

Word processing in the graphical environment of Windows 3 offers additional attractions to writers. WordPerfect's WYSIWYG (what you see is what you get) display shows you on-screen how your document will appear when printed: you see italic, boldface, underlining, different size fonts, graphics, columns, and so on.

A graphical user interface is sometimes referred to as a "direct manipulation interface." You no longer have to type a line of obscure command syntax and then press Enter to start a program. Instead, you manipulate an on-screen object—in this case, an *icon* (a visual symbol) representing a particular application program—by placing the mouse pointer on the icon and clicking the left mouse button. WordPerfect provides many examples of this kind of direct involvement: sizing and resizing document windows, using pull-down and cascading menus, selecting buttons, using scroll bars to move through documents, to name just a few.

Examples of direct manipulation of screen objects in WordPerfect include working with graphics and using the Button Bar. You use the mouse to resize a graphic image in a document or drag the image across the screen. WordPerfect's Button Bar is helpful to writers because they can create and manipulate graphical buttons to automate the processes of opening files, retrieving text into documents, saving, printing, searching, formatting, revising, and many other word-processing tasks. Adding, moving, and deleting buttons from the Button Bar are examples of direct manipulation of objects on the screen.

As suggested in Chapter 1, the Windows interface is almost endlessly adaptable. The fluid nature of a GUI provides an especially rich environment for the early exploratory phase of writing. For example, with WordPerfect's multiple editing windows you can work on up to nine documents at the same time. You can switch between documents and use the Windows Clipboard to cut and paste text effortlessly among them.

Composing with a word processor is different from composing in longhand or at the typewriter. Ann Berthoff writes that "composing—putting things together—is a continuum, a process that continues without any sharp breaks."[2] WordPerfect is matched perfectly to this process, enabling you to put things together as well as to take them apart with ease at any stage of the writing process. Some WordPerfect features, such as document summaries or comments, prove helpful when you are creating documents in collaboration with colleagues and need to see comments, suggestions, and alterations from others. Rearranging, deleting, or embellishing your words—or the words of a colleague—on-screen is far easier than doing so at the typewriter or in longhand.

With a word processor, you can get words on-screen as fast as you can type them, so you are freed from the frustration of not being able to record thoughts almost as fast as they occur. Researchers tell us that short-term memory lasts about five seconds—all the more reason to have a tool that enables you to record your ideas quickly. You can use a word processor across the full range of writing tasks—to create, format, revise, edit, save, open, and print documents.

Unlike a typewriter, a word processor gives you freedom to alter what you write. With a word processor, you can easily insert new words, delete words you don't want, or move up and down through a document to see what you have written. Because altering what you have written can be accomplished so effortlessly, you can focus on getting words on-screen.

With WordPerfect's many formatting features, you can change the look of the text on the page. You can change margins, indent text, vary line spacing, put text in columns or tables, create headers and footers, center text, and so on. In this chapter, though, you focus on the built-in settings, which WordPerfect assumes that most people use (at least initially). Later you learn how to modify these defaults to meet your needs.

Understanding WordPerfect's Built-In Settings

Even before you begin typing, WordPerfect has been at work for you. With a typewriter, you must set margins, line spacing, and tabs, for example, before you begin composing. With WordPerfect, you don't have to make any formatting decisions before you begin unless the present values don't suit you.

You should be familiar with the basic default settings before you begin writing. Subsequent chapters, especially the chapters devoted to formatting, printing, and desktop publishing, explore the many ways you can alter the look of a document. For now, assume that the default settings are acceptable.

Table 2.1 lists just a few of WordPerfect's many built-in settings. To change any of these settings, see Chapter 29, "Customizing WordPerfect with Preferences."

Entering Text

■ **Cue:** To keep the Button Bar on-screen but reduce it in size, choose the Text Only or Graphics Only option. See Chapter 19 for details.

In this section, you begin a short letter and get a feel for entering text in a WordPerfect window. Over the course of the chapter, you type the body of the letter, followed by the closing; then you insert the date, recipient's address, and salutation before printing the letter. If you haven't started WordPerfect and you want to follow along in this chapter, see the steps in Chapter 1 for launching WordPerfect.

Table 2.1. Some of WordPerfect's Built-In Settings

Setting	Preset Value
Margins	1-inch top, bottom, left, and right
Tabs	Left-aligned, every 1/2-inch
Initial font	Depends on printer; typically Courier 10 cpi
Line spacing	Single-spaced
Page number	None
Justification	Full
Hyphenation	Off
Paper size	Letter-size paper (8 1/2-by-11 inches)*
Date format	Month, day, year: July 4, 1992
Automatic backup of files	None

For U.S. versions only

With WordPerfect's "clean" editing screen you can see as much of the text as possible. If you choose not to display the Button Bar and the Ruler, you free up even more screen space for your text.

T I P

To display as much of your text on-screen as possible during the initial drafting of a document, leave the Button Bar and Ruler turned off. Later, when you need to format the text, you can display the Button Bar and Ruler again.

The purpose of this exercise is to give you a feel for the ease of composing with a word processor. Don't worry about errors. If you do make an error, use the Backspace key to erase your error and start over. (Keys for deleting text are discussed in detail in Chapter 4, "Editing a Document.") If you have WordPerfect running and want to get started right away, type the following paragraph:

> Thank you for inquiring about "The Seed and the Soil: A Biodynamic Perspective," the Midwest Regional Conference of the Biodynamic Farming and Gardening Association. The conference will be held from April 3-5, 1992, in the Barn Abbey at New Harmony, Indiana. The registration packet you requested is enclosed.

After you type a few words, look at the Pos indicator on the status line. This value increases as you type and as the insertion point moves across the line to the right.

WordPerfect doesn't require that you press Enter to end a line. Instead, if WordPerfect cannot fit a word on a line, the program inserts a hidden formatting code called a *soft return*. This code ends the line and wraps the word to the next line. This feature is often referred to as *wordwrap*.

Inserting Blank Lines

■ **Cue:** Consider working in Draft mode, which makes entering and editing text easier and faster. Select **V**iew, **D**raft Mode. See Chapter 29 for details.

To end a paragraph or insert blank lines into the text, you press the Enter key, which inserts what WordPerfect calls a *hard return*. If you're following the example, when you come to the end of the last sentence, press Enter twice and type the next paragraph:

> This conference marks the first of its kind in the Midwest. If you're new to biodynamic gardening, you'll have a rare opportunity to learn from the experts. If you're an experienced biodynamic gardener, you'll be able to mingle and swap secrets with like-minded enthusiasts. New Harmony's chief biodynamic gardener, Mark Trela, will present the keynote speech on "planetary stewardship." He will show slides from the workshop on eco-theology he attended last summer in Assisi, Italy, hosted by Father Thomas Berry, author of *The Dream of the Earth*.

Your screen should look like the one shown in figure 2.1. When you press Enter the first time, WordPerfect inserts a hard-return code. When you press Enter the second time, WordPerfect inserts another hard-return code, creating a blank line between paragraphs.

Type the third and fourth paragraphs of the letter:

> New Harmony, once the site of two utopian and agrarian communities in the early nineteenth century, is an ideal setting for our conference. Driving time from Chicago is approximately 5 1/2 hours.

> Thank you for your interest in the Midwest Regional Conference of the Biodynamic Farming and Gardening Association. We look forward to meeting and working with you in April.

Press Enter twice to end the last paragraph and insert a blank line between the last paragraph and the closing.

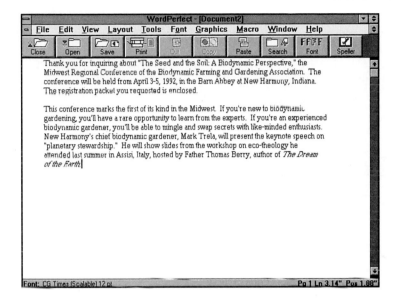

Thank you for inquiring about "The Seed and the Soil: A Biodynamic Perspective," the Midwest Regional Conference of the Biodynamic Farming and Gardening Association. The conference will be held from April 3-5, 1992, in the Barn Abbey at New Harmony, Indiana. The registration packet you requested is enclosed.

This conference marks the first of its kind in the Midwest. If you're new to biodynamic gardening, you'll have a rare opportunity to learn from the experts. If you're an experienced biodynamic gardener, you'll be able to mingle and swap secrets with like-minded enthusiasts. New Harmony's chief biodynamic gardener, Mark Trela, will present the keynote speech on "planetary stewardship." He will show slides from the workshop on eco-theology he attended last summer in Assisi, Italy, hosted by Father Thomas Berry, author of *The Dream of the Earth.*

FIG. 2.1

A blank line inserted with the Enter key.

Complete the letter with the following steps:

1. Type **Sincerely yours,** (be sure to type the comma) and press Enter five times to insert four blank lines for the signature.

2. Type **Gertrude Jekyll**.

Moving the Insertion Point and Scrolling the Document

Because you need easy access to any part of your document regardless of where in the document you are working, WordPerfect provides various ways to move the insertion point to a different position in the text or to scroll the document. You can use both mouse and keyboard methods to move around in a document.

Your movement can be as little as one character at a time, or you can *scroll* the document. When you think of scrolling a document, imagine a continuous sheet of paper that you can roll up or down. (You can, however, view only a certain number of text lines at a time.) Depending on the method you choose, you may or may not move the insertion point as you scroll.

If you are not familiar with the basic parts of the WordPerfect screen or Windows screens in general, see Chapter 1 for details. This chapter assumes that you can use a mouse and understand the basic parts of the screen and the keyboard. The sections that follow explain the various ways to scroll and move the insertion point around a document.

Moving with the Mouse

In Chapter 1, you learned that when you move the arrow-shaped mouse pointer into the text editing area of the screen, the pointer changes into the I-beam pointer.

If you prefer to use the mouse to scroll through a document and reposition the insertion point, you need to keep one important point in mind: when you use a mouse to scroll through a document, the insertion point does not move until you stop scrolling, place the I-beam pointer in the editing screen, and press the left mouse button.

You can position the insertion point anywhere on the editing screen with the mouse by following these general steps:

1. Use the mouse to position the I-beam pointer at a specific spot in your document.

2. Click the left mouse button to reposition the insertion point.

■ **Cue:** You can use the mouse to scroll through a document without moving the insertion point.

To scroll line-by-line through a document, do the following:

1. Place the mouse pointer on an up or down scroll bar arrow.

2. Press and hold down the left mouse button. Text on the screen scrolls.

Scrolling stops when you reach the top or bottom of the document.

Another way to scroll vertically in a document is the following:

1. Position the mouse pointer on a scroll bar box.

2. Drag the scroll bar box up or down the scroll bar.

T I P If you choose to have WordPerfect display a horizontal scroll bar at the bottom of the screen, you can click and drag the scroll bar box to scroll left or right in the text. You may want to enable this feature if your line length extends beyond the visible borders of the editing screen or if you are working with a very large table. See Chapter 29 for details on customizing the display.

Moving with the Directional Keys

The Enhanced Keyboard has a separate set of directional keys beside those on the numeric keypad, which you use with the Num Lock key off. (You use these same keys with the Num Lock key on to type numbers.) When you use the directional keys to move through a document, you don't have to be concerned with a pointer—you are always moving the insertion point. Whether you move one character at a time or scroll through the document, the location of the insertion point is always where you stop.

The eight directional keys are Home, End, PgUp, PgDn, up arrow, down arrow, left arrow, and right arrow. As table 2.2 illustrates, you can use these keys alone or in combinations (including combinations with the Alt and Ctrl keys) to move easily throughout your document.

Note: Table 2.2 is based on the assumption that you are using the default CUA-compatible keyboard.

Keep in mind that WordPerfect's hidden codes are treated like characters. If you have hidden codes in the document, and you press the left or right arrow, the insertion point may not appear to move; actually, the insertion point is moving through the hidden code.

Moving around the Sample Letter

In this section, you return to the sample letter to practice some of the insertion-point movement commands shown in table 2.2. Follow these steps:

1. Move the insertion point several characters into the last word, *Earth*, of the paragraph you just typed. Press and release the left arrow several times and notice the insertion point's movement.

   If you hold down the arrow key, the insertion point continues to move across the line. Notice that if you press the left arrow and reach the beginning of the line, the insertion point moves to the end of the preceding line. Similarly, if you press the right arrow and reach the end of the line, the insertion point moves to the beginning of the next line.

2. Use the mouse or Ctrl-right arrow and Ctrl-left arrow to move from word to word in the second paragraph of your sample letter.

3. Use the mouse or the up- and down-arrow keys to scroll up and down, line-by-line, in your sample letter.

■ **Cue:** Here's a handy way to check page breaks: Press Alt-PgUp or Alt-PgDn, followed by the up arrow.

■ **Cue:** You can't move the insertion point through "dead space" (space with no text or codes) beyond where you stop typing.

■ **Cue:** Use Ctrl-up arrow and Ctrl-down arrow to examine the comparative length of each paragraph, assess the flow of thought from paragraph to paragraph, or check for topic sentences in each paragraph.

Table 2.2. Moving the Insertion Point with the Keyboard

Movement	Key
One character left	Left arrow
One character right	Right arrow
One word left	Ctrl-left arrow
One word right	Ctrl-right arrow
One line up	Up arrow
One line down	Down arrow
Beginning of the preceding paragraph	Ctrl-up arrow
Beginning of the following paragraph	Ctrl-down arrow
Beginning of the current line (after codes)	Home
Beginning of the current line (before codes)	Home, Home
End of the current line	End
Top of the editing screen	PgUp
Bottom of the editing screen	PgDn
First line of preceding page	Alt-PgUp
First line of following page	Alt-PgDn
Top of the document	Ctrl-Home
Bottom of the document	Ctrl-End

4. With the insertion point anywhere in the second paragraph of your letter, press Ctrl-up arrow. Note that the position of the insertion point is now just before *This conference* in the first line.

5. Use the arrow keys to place the insertion point in the middle of the first sentence of the second paragraph of your letter.

   Press Home and watch the insertion point move to just before *This* at the start of the line.

Press End and watch the insertion point move to the end of the line, just after *biodynamic*.

6. Unless you have chosen to display the Button Bar, your entire sample letter should be visible on-screen. Press PgUp to move to the top line of your letter. When you press PgDn, the insertion point moves to the last line of the letter.

Completing the Sample Letter

In this section, you complete the sample letter. You move the insertion point to the top of the document; then you enter the date, type the recipient's address, and complete the salutation. Follow these steps:

1. Press Ctrl-Home to move the insertion point to the beginning of the first paragraph of the letter.

2. Press Enter twice to insert two blank lines.

3. Press Ctrl-Home to move the insertion point to the top of the document.

4. To enter today's date, select **Tools**, **Date**, **Text**.

    Press Date (Ctrl-F5).

   WordPerfect inserts the current date, based on your computer's internal clock. If the clock is working properly but the date and time are incorrect, use the Date/Time option in the Windows Control Panel to make the appropriate adjustments.

5. Press Enter twice.

6. Type the following name and address, remembering to press Enter after each line:

   Mr. Rudolf Steiner
   23 Goethe Street
   Chicago, Illinois 60610

7. Press Enter and type the following salutation:

   Dear Mr. Steiner:

Your screen should now resemble figure 2.2.

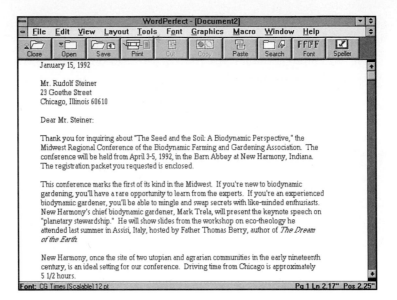

FIG. 2.2

The beginning of
the sample letter.

Moving the Insertion Point with Go To

With WordPerfect's Go To command (**E**dit, **G**o To), you can move the insertion point in great "leaps" through a document. For example, with Go To, you can move the insertion point in the following ways:

- To a particular page number

- To the top of the current page

- To the bottom of the current page

- To the previous location of the insertion point after you have moved the insertion point with commands such as Go To, Search and Replace, PgDn, and PgUp

Perhaps the most common use of Go To is to move the insertion point to a specific page when you work with documents longer than one page.

Return to the sample letter, insert a page break, and use Go To to move between pages:

1. Press Alt-PgDn or use the mouse to move the insertion point to the end of the letter.

2. Select **L**ayout, **P**age, **P**age Break to insert a hard page break, thereby creating a two-page document.

Notice that a double line stretches across the screen just below *Gertrude Jekyll* (see fig. 2.3). The insertion point is now on the first line of page 2.

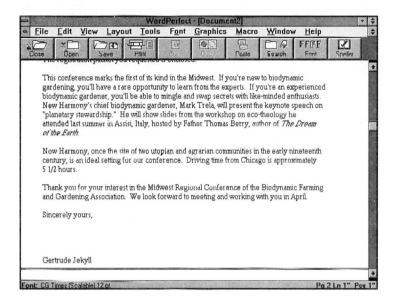

This conference marks the first of its kind in the Midwest. If you're new to biodynamic gardening, you'll have a rare opportunity to learn from the experts. If you're an experienced biodynamic gardener, you'll be able to mingle and swap secrets with like-minded enthusiasts. New Harmony's chief biodynamic gardener, Mark Trela, will present the keynote speech on "planetary stewardship." He will show slides from the workshop on eco-theology he attended last summer in Assisi, Italy, hosted by Father Thomas Berry, author of *The Dream of the Earth.*

New Harmony, once the site of two utopian and agrarian communities in the early nineteenth century, is an ideal setting for our conference. Driving time from Chicago is approximately 5 1/2 hours.

Thank you for your interest in the Midwest Regional Conference of the Biodynamic Farming and Gardening Association. We look forward to meeting and working with you in April.

Sincerely yours,

Gertrude Jekyll

FIG. 2.3

A hard page break inserted to create a two-page document.

3. To move the insertion point to the top of page 1, press Alt-PgUp or use the mouse.

4. To move the insertion point to the top of page 2, select **Edit, Go To.**

    Press Go To (Ctrl-G).

5. In the Go To dialog box, type **2** in the text field, and press Enter or click OK.

   WordPerfect moves the insertion point to the top of page 2.

6. To restore the letter to its original one-page status, press Backspace to delete the hard page break.

Go To also functions as a kind of place marker in the text. Suppose that the insertion point is in the middle of a sentence on the last page of a 29-page document. You want to check a reference that you know is on page 2, so you use Go To to move quickly to that page. To return to the sentence you were completing on page 29, do the following:

1. Select **E**dit, **G**o To.

      Press Go To (Ctrl-G).

2. In the Go To dialog box, select **L**ast Position or press Alt-L.

   The insertion point returns to the position it occupied on the last page, before the preceding Go To command.

   For easy access to this feature, assign the Go To command to a button on the Button Bar. See Chapter 19 for full instructions.

Inserting Text

One advantage of word processing is the freedom to add text to what is already written. To add a word, phrase, or sentence, place the insertion point where you want to insert the text. You can insert text by typing it directly at the insertion point or by cutting and pasting. With WordPerfect's Select feature, you can cut and paste text anywhere in a document or between documents. If you store *boilerplate* text (frequently used text), you can easily retrieve this text into a document. Whether you type or cut and paste, what you insert appears to the left of the insertion point.

Suppose that you want to add a sentence to the third paragraph of your sample letter. Use the mouse or the arrow keys to place the insertion point at the beginning of the last sentence, right before *Driving*.

1. Type the following:

   You'll find a map in the registration packet to help you find your way here.

2. Press the space bar twice.

Notice that as you enter new text, existing text pushes ahead and wraps to the next line, reformatting automatically to accommodate the insertion. Your screen should now look like figure 2.4.

Using Typeover

The Ins key on your keyboard works like a toggle switch, enabling you to switch between Insert mode ("push ahead") and Typeover mode. When you press the Ins key, the program switches to Typeover mode, and new text replaces old text. Using Typeover mode is most useful when making one-for-one replacements, such as changing *adn* to *and*. Chapter 4 discusses Typeover in greater detail.

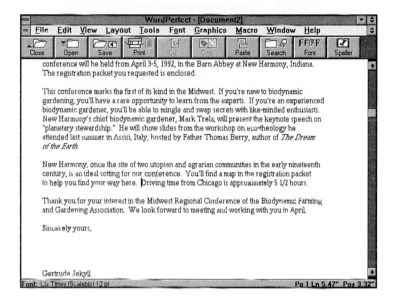

FIG. 2.4

Sample letter after insertion of additional sentence in the middle of the third paragraph.

Printing a Document

With WordPerfect, you can be flexible about printing. If you do not want to save a document, WordPerfect enables you to print the document without first having to save it to disk. Printing in this manner is called *making a screen print*, because you print what has been created and stored in temporary memory.

Note: The steps that follow assume that you have installed your printer properly. For information on running the Install program, see Appendix A. WordPerfect will not print unless you have installed the proper printer driver. If you have trouble printing or questions about printer drivers, see Chapter 9, "Basic Printing." For now all you need to know how to do is to give the print command to print the current page.

Your first act is to select a printer; follow these steps:

1. Choose **File**, **Select Printer**.

   The Select Printer dialog box appears (see fig. 2.5).

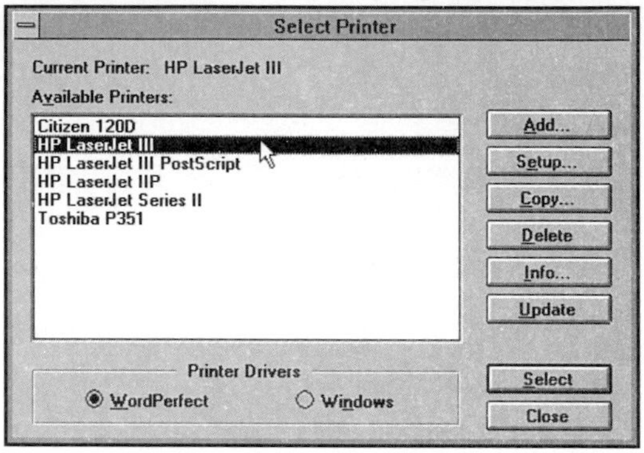

FIG. 2.5

The Select Printer
dialog box.

2. Double-click the appropriate printer name, or highlight the
   appropriate printer name and choose **S**elect.

To print your sample letter, follow these steps:

1. Select **F**ile, **P**rint.

   CUA   Press Print (F5).

   The Print dialog box appears. The Full Document option is the
   default (see fig. 2.6).

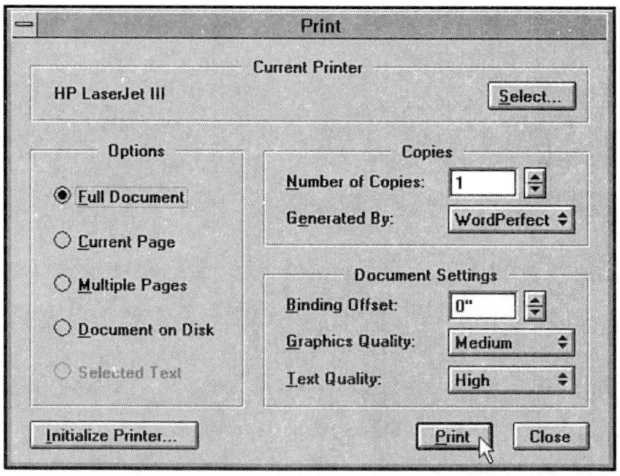

FIG. 2.6

The Print dialog
box.

Because the letter you want to print is less than a page, leave the
default setting at Full Document. When you want to print just the
current page in a multiple page document, you select the **C**urrent
Page option.

2. Choose **P**rint to send your document to the current printer.

The Current Print Job dialog box appears. This dialog box indicates that WordPerfect is preparing your document for the printer. With very short documents, such as the sample letter, the Current Print Job dialog box is on-screen for only a few moments. On longer documents, the box displays the print status until every page of the document has been prepared for the printer. To cancel printing, choose Cancel Print Job. When the Current Print Job dialog box is no longer on-screen, printing should begin.

Figure 2.7 shows the printed letter.

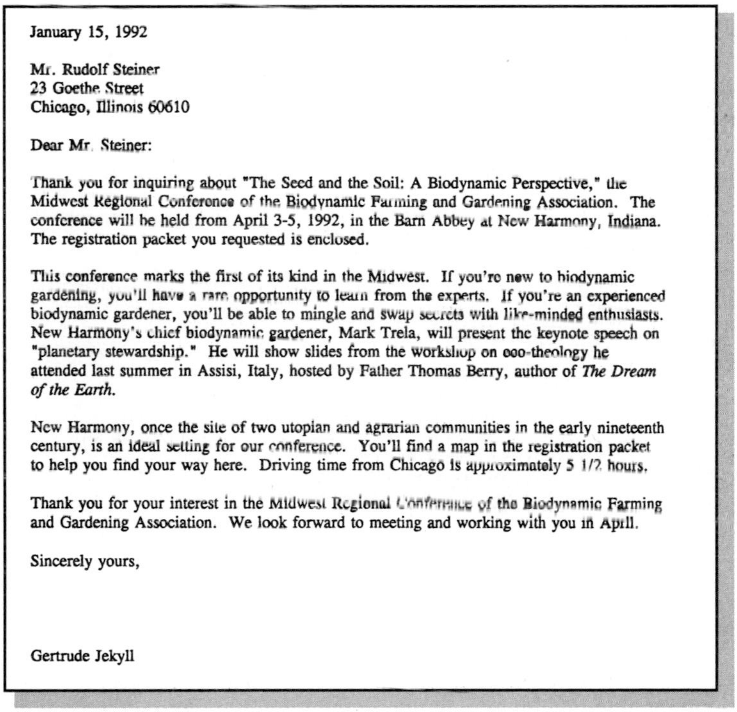

January 15, 1992

Mr. Rudolf Steiner
23 Goethe Street
Chicago, Illinois 60610

Dear Mr. Steiner:

Thank you for inquiring about "The Seed and the Soil: A Biodynamic Perspective," the Midwest Regional Conference of the Biodynamic Farming and Gardening Association. The conference will be held from April 3-5, 1992, in the Barn Abbey at New Harmony, Indiana. The registration packet you requested is enclosed.

This conference marks the first of its kind in the Midwest. If you're new to biodynamic gardening, you'll have a rare opportunity to learn from the experts. If you're an experienced biodynamic gardener, you'll be able to mingle and swap secrets with like-minded enthusiasts. New Harmony's chief biodynamic gardener, Mark Trela, will present the keynote speech on "planetary stewardship." He will show slides from the workshop on eco-theology he attended last summer in Assisi, Italy, hosted by Father Thomas Berry, author of *The Dream of the Earth*.

New Harmony, once the site of two utopian and agrarian communities in the early nineteenth century, is an ideal setting for our conference. You'll find a map in the registration packet to help you find your way here. Driving time from Chicago is approximately 5 1/2 hours.

Thank you for your interest in the Midwest Regional Conference of the Biodynamic Farming and Gardening Association. We look forward to meeting and working with you in April.

Sincerely yours,

Gertrude Jekyll

FIG. 2.7

The printed letter.

Your document doesn't have to be on-screen for you to print it. With WordPerfect, you can print any number of documents stored on disk (floppy or hard). You can even have documents in various windows and print a document stored on disk. Chapter 9 explores the various ways of printing. But you know enough now to make a quick print of on-screen text.

T I P   To review your writing, print frequent copies of your on-screen work. One limitation of composing on-screen is that for most documents, you cannot see the entire text at once. With such a small window for text, you can easily lose a sense of the whole, repeat yourself, or lose a feel for the sequence of your ideas.

Saving a Document to Disk

Usually you keep copies on disk of the documents you create. WordPerfect gives you two methods of saving a file:

- With the Save or Save As command, you save a copy of the on-screen document to disk. When you use Save or Save As, the document remains on-screen for additional work.

- With the Close command, you save a copy of the document to disk, and the document window closes. Close asks you whether you want to save the latest editing changes to the document.

The first time you save a document, the Save As dialog box appears and prompts you for a file name.

A file name consists of two parts: a root *name* (or *primary file name*) and an optional *extension* (or *suffix*). The root name can have one to eight characters. You can use the root name to describe the file's contents. The extension can have one to three characters. If you use an extension, separate it from the root name by a period. When you name a file, you need to observe the operating system (MS-DOS) guidelines for naming files.

To save the sample letter, follow these steps:

1. With the sample letter on-screen, select **F**ile, **S**ave.

     Press Save (Shift-F3).

    The Save As dialog box appears. The insertion point is in the Save As text box, where you give the document a name.

2. If you want to save the file to a drive and directory other than the current drive and directory—indicated next to Current Dir in the Save As dialog box—enter a full path name. You can type a new path name in the Save As text box, or you can use the mouse or

the Tab and arrow keys to highlight a drive and directory in the Directories list. When you highlight an alternative drive and directory in the Directories list, the path information in the Save As text box changes accordingly. Unless you actually select another drive and directory, the default drive and directory does not change, but the file is saved to the alternative drive and directory you have specified in the Save As text box.

3. Type **confer.let** as a file name for your sample letter.

Recall that for every new window you open, WordPerfect assigns a default name of Document1, Document2, Document3 up through Document9 in the title bar (see Chapter 3 for details). When you name and save a file for the first time, WordPerfect replaces the default document name in the title bar with the name you specify for the document.

Note in figure 2.8 that confer.let has been entered in the Save As text box to name the file.

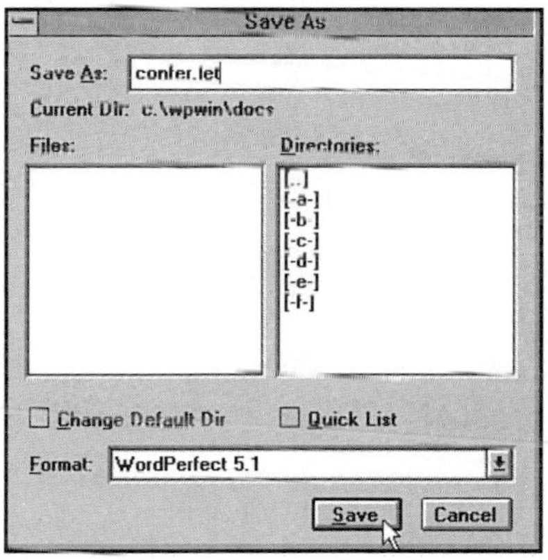

FIG. 2.8

The sample letter file name in the Save As dialog box.

4. Select **S**ave or press Enter to save your sample letter.

WordPerfect responds with a * Please Wait * prompt on the status line, followed by a prompt indicating that WordPerfect is saving the file to the current drive and directory—or to the drive and directory specified in the Save As text box. In this instance, WordPerfect saves the file to the default directory, C:\WPWIN\DOCS. If you followed the directions in Appendix A for installing and setting up WordPerfect, you created a documents directory under the main \WPWIN directory. Chapter 3, "Managing Files," contains a complete primer on file management, including steps on how to create subdirectories to store your working documents.

WordPerfect responds differently when you are saving a file you have already named and saved before. When you select **File**, **S**ave, WordPerfect saves the file without stopping to display the Save As dialog box.

Unless you specify otherwise, WordPerfect assumes that you want to save files in WordPerfect 5.1 format. The Format list box in the Save As dialog box lists 42 file formats that WordPerfect supports. For a complete listing of these formats, see Chapter 31, "Importing Data and Working with Other Programs." To select a different format in the Save As dialog box, choose **F**ormat or press Alt-F to display the pop-up list, as shown in figure 2.9. Use the mouse or the arrow keys to scroll this list, or press the first letter of the format you want. For example, pressing A brings up Ami Pro 1.2. If you keep pressing A, the list cycles through the other formats beginning with A.

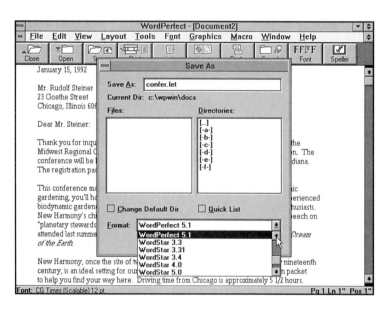

FIG. 2.9

The Format pop-up list of file format options for saving text.

When you want to save an existing file under a different name or in a different format, follow these steps:

1. Select **F**ile, Save **A**s.

   CUA Press Save As (F3).

2. Choose **F**ormat; from the pop-up list, select the desired file format.

3. Specify the drive and directory where you want the file to be saved.

4. Type a file name in the Save As text box.

5. Choose **S**ave to save the file.

   If you enter a file name that duplicates an existing file name, WordPerfect indicates that the file already exists and queries whether you want to replace it. Choose **Y**es to replace the file, or **N**o to return to the Save As dialog box and type a new file name. If you choose to replace the file on disk, the new file will overwrite the old file that has the same file name.

6. Select **S**ave or press Enter.

WordPerfect 5.1 for DOS and WordPerfect 5.1 for Windows use the same file format, enabling you to transfer files between these programs without the need for conversion. The WordPerfect 5.1 format option in the Save As dialog box applies to both programs.

T I P

Clearing the Screen and Exiting WordPerfect

You can close a document but continue editing another document in WordPerfect, or you can exit WordPerfect and return to the Windows Program Manager. This section describes both methods.

To stay in WordPerfect but close the document you're working on, do the following:

1. Select **F**ile, **C**lose.

    Press Close (Ctrl-F4).

   If you have modified the document during the current editing session, WordPerfect asks whether you want to save the changes.

2. Select **Y**es if you want to save the file again, or select **N**o if you want to close the document without saving it again.

You can continue editing in a new document window.

To save the document on-screen and exit WordPerfect, follow these steps:

1. Select **F**ile, E**x**it.

    Press Exit (Alt-F4).

   WordPerfect prompts you to indicate whether you want to save your open document.

2. Respond **Y**es to the prompt if you want WordPerfect to save the file and then exit to Windows. If you respond **N**o, WordPerfect exits immediately to Windows. If you have more than one document window open, WordPerfect displays this prompt for each document in sequence, and then exits to Windows.

   If you have made no changes to your document since you last opened it, WordPerfect exits immediately to Windows.

If you have just exited WordPerfect but want to continue in this chapter, restart WordPerfect now by double-clicking the WordPerfect icon in Windows.

Using WordPerfect To Develop Ideas

This section is an "extra" for readers who want tips on writing with a word processor. If you're new to word processing, the information in this section may help you adapt your old writing habits to the "electronic scribe." Even if you have been using a word processor—any word processor—for a while, you will find some fresh ideas in this section.

Most writing done on the job does not require that you determine a subject or an idea for a document. You usually write letters, memos, and reports, for example, in response to a request or a predetermined need: you respond to a customer's complaint; you write a memo recommending a certain course of action; you draw up a progress report explaining your work to date on a project.

Whether you are writing an essay at school or a memo on the job, you must plan before you write. You need to determine the scope of your message and its purpose, analyze your audience, and consider how you want to present yourself. No matter what the writing task, you may find yourself stymied, or blocked, at certain points. If you have trouble getting started, or if you're not sure what you want to say, you can use WordPerfect to generate ideas.

Writing is a recursive process, one in which many activities overlap. Writing does not proceed neatly in lockstep fashion by stages from planning to drafting to revising to final editing and polishing. For example, while editing a draft, writers may find themselves looping back to rethink the basic ideas of a document and explore additional possibilities. WordPerfect is a marvelous tool for assisting writers through each loop of the writing process. In *Word Processing in a Community of Writers*, authors Elder, Schwartz, Bowen, and Goswami point out that a word processor is perfectly adapted to the centrifugal, exploratory aspect of the writing process, which is characterized by "a broadening of the circle of thought, in order to discover and connect new elements."[3] WordPerfect is particularly helpful with the exploratory aspect of the writing process.

As you adapt your writing habits to the computer, keep in mind that you don't have to abandon all your old ways of doing things. If you have a penchant for jotting notes on restaurant napkins, the backs of envelopes, or in a pocket notebook, fine. You don't have to use WordPerfect for the entire composing process. But remember that WordPerfect is an ideal electronic notepad for jotting down ideas as they occur to you.

■**Cue:** If you're having trouble getting started with your writing or if you're not sure what you want to say, use WordPerfect to generate ideas.

The following sections present tips on warming up to the writing task, discovering what you want to say, and dealing with those moments when you cannot get started or are blocked. You also find tips on planning and drafting documents.

Handling Writer's Block

In *When a Writer Can't Write: Studies in Writer's Block and Other Composing Process Problems*, Mike Rose comments: "No one writes effortlessly. Our composing is marked by pauses, false starts, gnawing feelings of inadequacy, crumpled paper."[4]

WordPerfect can save you a mountain of crumpled paper, but WordPerfect cannot prevent those sometimes agonizing moments when the words just don't come. By removing much of the drudgery of writing, however, WordPerfect helps you record your thoughts and even stimulate your own creativity.

If you're a halfway decent typist, you will be amazed at how quickly you can transfer your thoughts to the screen. Researchers have found that writers talk to themselves as they compose. Many talk out loud, rehearsing and changing phrases, clauses, sentences, and whole passages. With WordPerfect, you can keep up with your running commentary and make changes and additions nearly as fast as you can speak. As an electronic scribe, WordPerfect ensures that you don't lose fleeting thoughts.

Two strategies that writers find useful for combatting writer's block are brainstorming and freewriting.

Brainstorming

When you have trouble determining a sharp focus for a document—when you're not sure what you want to say—consider trying a semistructured writing exercise known as *brainstorming.*

When you brainstorm a writing assignment on-screen, you record your ideas in list form—words, phrases, even entire sentences—as they occur to you. When you brainstorm, you don't worry about typos, spelling errors, or style; you can handle those matters later. Your goal is to generate as many ideas as possible about the topic, the purpose, or the audience. You can create and save a file for each brainstorming session.

Brainstorming can be useful before you reach the point where a prewriting template (described later in this chapter) may help.

If your computer system has enough memory available, you can open up to nine document windows in WordPerfect. Take advantage of this capability to jot notes to yourself in multiple windows. You can keep several *idea files* of notes that relate to a particular project.

Suppose that you are drafting a proposal for new guidelines to be used for collaborative writing. You might keep separate idea files of notes from interviews with authors, editors, product managers, marketing staff, and articles dealing specifically with the considerations surrounding projects with multiple authors. While working in your main document file, you can open the idea files in overlapping windows "cascaded" on screen for easy access (see fig. 2.10).

You can save these idea files and open them when you want to add more ideas to them. You can use the Windows Clipboard to cut and paste notes between document windows; or you can use the Select feature to mark selected text, save it to disk, and then retrieve this text into another idea file at a later date. (See Chapter 5, "Selecting and Editing Text," for the use of Select to save highlighted text to disk and the use of Select with the Clipboard to cut and paste text; retrieving text is addressed in Chapter 4.)

When you have multiple windows open and you have maximized the active window, quick keyboard methods for cycling through the windows are

■ To move to the next document, press Next Document (Ctrl-F6).

■ To move to a previous document, press Previous Document (Ctrl-Shift-F6).

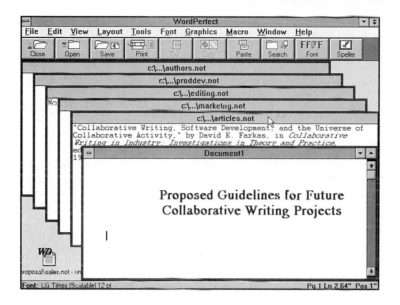

FIG. 2.10

Multiple idea files in open windows for easy access while drafting a document.

The capability to open multiple document windows is a real advantage to writers. In a typical situation, you may be working on a letter to a business contact and suddenly need to fire off a quick memo. No problem. You open a second document window, type the memo, print it, close the window, and resume working on the letter.

> **T I P**
>
> Use WordPerfect's multiple document windows capability to enable you to see two parts of the same document at once. Open two windows, each containing the same document you want to edit. Choose **W**indow, **T**ile to split the screen in half in order to display both windows at once. If you are working on a long report, you may want to keep the Introduction visible in the top window as you continue to edit the body of the report in the bottom window. But be careful to make changes in only one window and save the correct version of the file—the one that reflects your latest changes—at the end of your editing session. Instead of viewing two parts of the same document, you can put a document in one window and use the second tiled window to make notes or comments about parts of the primary document.

Freewriting

Freewriting is less structured than brainstorming, but the two techniques are similar. Writing teacher Peter Elbow has been credited with popularizing the practice of freewriting. He defines a freewriting session as follows: "To do a freewriting exercise, simply force yourself to write without stopping for ten minutes."[5] Elbow justifies freewriting because it "separates the producing process from the revising process."

Begin a freewriting session with an idea or topic, and without planning or deliberation, write anything that comes into your mind about that topic. Write nonstop for at least 10 minutes. Obviously, this exercise is easier and less tiring with WordPerfect than with a typewriter or a pen or pencil. The most important point is to keep going, even if you find yourself writing what appears to be nonsense. Don't make any changes or corrections. Don't worry about typos, spelling, or other errors. The most important goal in freewriting—as in brainstorming—is to stimulate your thinking and get you writing.

One variation on the freewriting technique is to examine your text after each session, extract key ideas, and use these ideas as the basis for subsequent sessions of on-screen freewriting. You can save these key ideas to one idea file or have several document windows open while you are freewriting and copy and paste your key ideas to these other document windows. Within each window, you can develop that "kernel" idea. This strategy, called *looping*, forces you to find the natural coherence in the text you have produced. You can create as many loops as you want or need. As your writing becomes more focused through this process of discovery, you can use the results of these looping sessions in a prewriting template or outline.

Planning Documents

Brainstorming and freewriting at the keyboard are excellent strategies for warming up, generating ideas, and pushing your material toward a productive, critical mass. Both methods exemplify the unique role WordPerfect can play during the exploratory aspect of writing. Out of chaos can come order; out of an undeveloped sprawl of text on the screen—or the printout—can come the key points and direction of your message. Brainstorming and freewriting can move you toward a first draft, but many writers need still more preparation before formal drafting. They need interim planning.

Research into cognitive processes and the writing process suggests that experienced writers tend to have certain established mental frameworks to help them in their writing tasks. That is, they know the requirements of a particular piece of writing—whether it is a letter conveying bad news, a progress report, or a research paper—before they put fingers to keyboard. In a sense, these writers have already accomplished some planning.

Experienced writers also tend to plan *more*: they make outlines, take notes, or make lists of ideas before they create a first draft. Experienced writers try to anticipate how a reader will respond to the text— what meaning may arise out of the coming together of reader, text, and author. Inexperienced writers, on the other hand, often lack these internalized guidelines and have trouble meeting the demands of particular writing tasks.

Interestingly, current research suggests that writers who use computers may indeed do *less* planning than they did before writing with a computer. You may use paper to do some prewriting, or you may consider some of the strategies presented in this chapter. Find the best match between your writing habits and the word processor for composing.

Just as experienced writers have in mind good examples for particular documents, readers have built-in expectations for the documents. Readers expect documents to follow logical patterns. When these expectations are met or surpassed, readers are usually appreciative and receptive.

Readers have expectations even about the sequence of elements in a paragraph or sentence. They expect the first sentence of a paragraph to orient them to the rest of the paragraph. If you begin a sentence with new information but follow with something the reader already knows, you may force the reader to reread the sentence. The movement from new to old is unnatural and makes sentences less readable. If you don't plan your documents carefully—from sentence structure to overall design—you run the risk of violating the expectations of your readers. Frustrated readers lose confidence in the writer and may stop reading.

As part of the planning process, consider two effective tools: prewriting templates and outlines.

Cue: Resist the temptation to begin immediately composing that first draft at the keyboard. Don't let the ease with which you can put words on-screen deceive you into assuming that planning isn't necessary.

Using a Prewriting Template

Prewriting is everything you do up to the actual step of writing the first draft. Prewriting is very much a part of the planning stage.

A prewriting template is a set of prompts that forces you to answer some basic questions before you begin drafting your document. As you plan the document, you may find using a prewriting template helpful in refining your thinking about a particular writing task. You can ask the basic reporter's questions of Who? What? Where? Why? and When? Alternatively, you can simplify your planning to consider these questions:

- Who are you? What is your role in the organization? How do you want to present yourself, to be perceived?

- What is your subject? What do you need to say? What do you want to say?

- What is your purpose in writing? Why are you writing this document? What do you hope to achieve?

- Who is your audience? What do they already know? What do they need to know? What is your relationship to the audience? What will your readers do with your message? How will your readers react to your message? Can you anticipate this reaction and shape your message accordingly? Can you consider your message from your reader's point of view?

To create a prewriting template, begin with a fresh screen and enter the text you see in figure 2.11. Put each prompt in a large boldface font and leave several blank lines between items. Save this document to disk as PREWRITE.TEM or just TEMPLATE. When you need this prewriting template, you can open it and use it again.

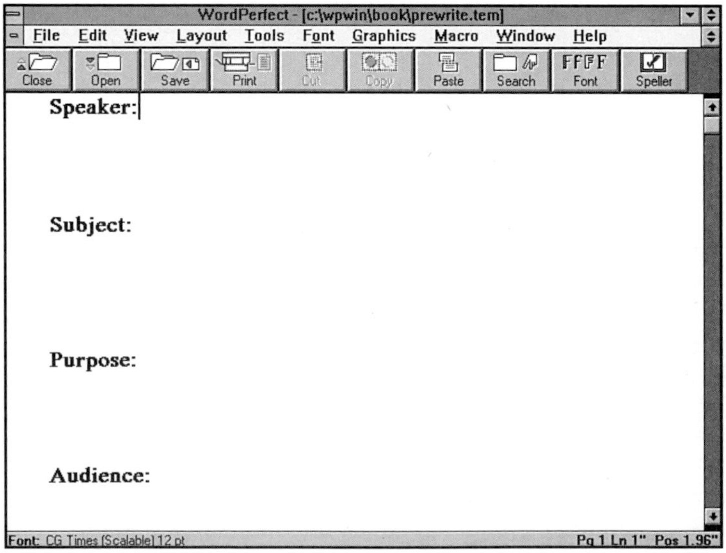

FIG. 2.11

A prewriting template.

If you prefer to prewrite or plan on hard copy, you can add more lines between prompts, print the template, and enter your responses by hand.

> Create a macro that opens your prewriting template file. Assign this macro to a button on your Button Bar so that you can call up a new prewriting template at any time. For details on creating macros, see Chapter 20; for details on working with the Button Bar, see Chapter 19.
>
> **T I P**

To use the on-screen template, move the insertion point to the right of each prompt and type notes. When you have a clear sense of how you want to present yourself, what you need to say, why you need to say it, and who your audience is—you are considerably closer to creating that first draft. You then save the prewriting template to disk; be sure to use the Save As option to save the file under a different file name so that you won't overwrite the original blank template.

Open a second document window and begin the first draft of the letter, memo, or report. Consider using the Window, Tile option to split the screen in half and display parts of both documents at once, as shown in figure 2.12. (Turn off the Button Bar to display more of both document windows.) You can refer to your prewriting template while composing your draft in the other window. If you're writing a report that entails research, you may want to create an outline next, based in part on your template responses.

Using an Outline

An *outline* can also function as a kind of template. The structure of an outline isn't easy to conceive, however, especially if the writing task promises to be lengthy. Besides, you may have been force-fed outlines in elementary school and high school and balk at the idea of working from one.

Whether you use an outline depends, in part, on what type of writer you are. Some writers make elaborate plans and don't diverge much from those plans when they compose. Other writers do less planning or structuring and heavily revise their text. When you are in the middle of a writing task, however, even an informal or loose outline can give you some scaffolding on which to place your ideas.

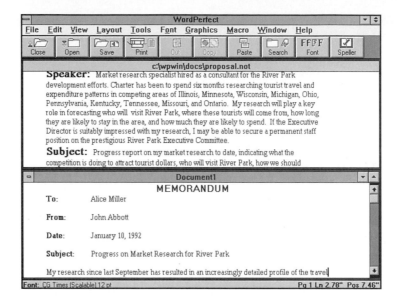

FIG. 2.12

Tiled windows
that display a
prewriting
template and a
memo document.

In fact, you might even consider using a *transitional* outline after you have written the first rough draft. A transitional outline functions as a description of what you have already written and is therefore useful in revealing the coherence (or lack of coherence) of your first draft. You can use outlines in general to help you understand the logical flow of your topics. If you work up an outline before beginning to write, don't feel that you have to follow it slavishly while you are composing; you can slot ideas here and there as they occur to you. You don't have to supply all the headings and subheadings, either; you can begin with a few major categories and flesh out sections here and there. You can even use brainstorming and freewriting to generate additional ideas for sections. Later, you can go back and supply transitions and add, cut, or relocate material. With WordPerfect's Outline feature, covered in detail in Chapter 24, you can move entire outline "families" when revising your outline.

If you have trouble getting started, try the timeworn method of creating an outline first. Successful writers have learned the importance of beginning a writing task with a road map that supplies some sense of the structure and outcome. A transitional outline, which you extract later from a rough draft of your document, enables you to test the coherence of your writing-in-progress.

Chapter Summary

In this chapter, you have learned a great deal about using a word processor to help you write. You have learned about the ways in which WordPerfect's graphical user interface offers some unique benefits to writers. You have read about how you can type, print, and save a document with WordPerfect; brainstorm and freewrite using WordPerfect as a composing tool; use multiple windows and move text between them during drafting; and create templates to help you plan your writing tasks.

Now that you have created, printed, and saved your first document file, you are ready to learn about basic file management in the next chapter.

---

[1] Paul Heckel, *The Elements of Friendly Software Design: The New Edition* (Alameda, CA: Sybex, 1991), p. 50.

[2] Ann Berthoff, *Forming, Thinking, Writing: The Composing Imagination* (Montclair, NJ: Boynton/Cook Publishers, Inc., 1982), p. 11.

[3] John Elder, Betsy Bowen, Jeffrey Schwartz, Dixie Goswami, *Word Processing in a Community of Writers: An Introduction to Composition* (New York: Garland Publishing, 1989), p. 14.

[4] Mike Rose, *When a Writer Can't Write: Studies in Writer's Block and Other Composing Process Problems* (New York:Guilford Press, 1985), p. 9.

[5] Peter Elbow, *Writing with Power: Techniques for Mastering the Writing Process* (New York: Oxford University Press, 1981), p. 13-14.

Managing Files

I n Chapter 2, you learned how to save and print your documents.
This process is important because you will keep nearly all your
WordPerfect documents in printed or electronic form (or both). Sooner
or later, you probably will need to copy your files to backup disks,
move them from one location to another on the hard disk, delete them,
or find old versions. Even if you are relatively new to computing, you
must learn more than just how to create files; you also must know how
to manage them.

One problem with using the DOS environment for file management is
that you must remember commands to type at the DOS prompt. Also,
you cannot easily see which files are where on the disk, or deal with
selected groups of files.

Over the years, several software producers have marketed file management programs, including WordPerfect's own Office File Manager.
(WordPerfect 5.1 for DOS also includes a capable List Files feature for
file management.) In the Windows environment, a few companies have
attempted to improve on the relatively simple File Manager that comes
with Windows. With WordPerfect for Windows, however, in addition to
some built-in, basic file management capabilities, you get a powerful file
management program that replaces other Windows file management
programs and works with WordPerfect.

■ **Read Gilgen** is
Director of Learning Support
Services at the University of
Wisconsin, Madison.
Known as Dr. DOS in his
local user's group, since
1982 he has taught
workshops on and authored
a series of articles about
DOS and file management.

Suppose that you hand-wrote a memo. If you had to place the memo in a file folder, place the file folder in a filing cabinet, and shut and lock the file drawer before being allowed to edit another memo, you would think the process absurd. Likewise, when you use a word processor, you want to be able to find, open, edit, and save many different files without first having to exit the program. WordPerfect's File Manager program enables you to find, use, copy, and delete files, and makes these processes easy.

The emphasis in this chapter is on the basic procedures for file management you need on a regular basis, primarily using the Open File dialog box. This chapter also introduces the WordPerfect File Manager program, discussed in depth in Chapter 30, "Advanced File Management Techniques."

Understanding File Management Terms

The following paragraphs discuss some important terms and concepts related to file management.

- *File*. Each document you create is saved as a file on the hard disk or a floppy disk.

- *File name*. The names of your files must adhere to certain limitations imposed by the operating system (DOS) in which Windows runs. The root of the file name uses a maximum of eight characters, followed by a period and an optional extension of up to three characters (for example, *FILENAME.EXT*).

  File names can use any combination of letters and numerals, but the use of symbols and punctuation marks is limited. See your DOS manual for complete details.

- *Directory*. A directory is part of the disk (floppy or hard) where you store a subset of files. You can think of a directory as the file folder in which you store files.

  Directories are arranged in a *tree* structure. The main directory is the *root directory*. *Subdirectories* are "related" much like listings in a genealogical tree, and the directory directly above a subdirectory is called the *parent directory*.

- *Drive*. The device that stores files on floppy or hard disks is called a drive. Local drives (physically installed in your computer) are designated drive A, drive B, drive C, and so on. Network drives (located on a network) are called drive F, drive G, and so on.

■ *Path name.* A path name consists of the complete name of a stored file and its location. The file MYDOC.TXT, for example, if stored in the DOCS subdirectory of the WPWIN directory on drive C, has the following path name:

C:\WPWIN\DOCS\MYDOC.TXT

Note the backslashes that separate the different parts of the path name: *drive:\directory\filename.*

■ *Default.* When you change directory locations, the new location becomes the *current* or *default* directory. To use a file in the current directory, you use only the file name (although you can use the entire path name if you prefer). To use a file in a different directory, you must specify the full path name of the file.

■ *Wild-card characters.* To speed up or simplify file management, you often can substitute wild-card characters for parts of file names. You use a question mark to replace a single character; MYDO?.TXT, for example, can refer to MYDOC.TXT, MYDOG.TXT, and so on. An asterisk (*) stands for a range of characters. MYDO*.TXT, for example, refers to MYDOC.TXT, MYDOCTOR.TXT, MYDOG.TXT, and so on. The wild-card designation *.* refers to all files.

Planning File Storage Requirements

When you begin working with WordPerfect, the number of files you use is relatively small. That number changes, however, as you generate many documents of different kinds. The ability to find these documents quickly depends on good file management practices.

The first step in organizing your files is to try to determine work patterns. If you use many different types of computer programs (word processing, spreadsheets, database management, and communications programs, for example), you may want to create subdirectories for each activity. If you use only word processing, on the other hand, the directories you create may relate instead to types of documents (memos, letters, reports), or to the types of activities for which you create the documents (reports, sales, publicity, forms, and so on).

Sketching your proposed organization in the form of a tree can be helpful, as shown in the following illustration (where the tree appears to be lying on its side). The trunk corresponds to your root (or main) directory, and the major categories you use become first level directories, with other subdirectories branching from them.

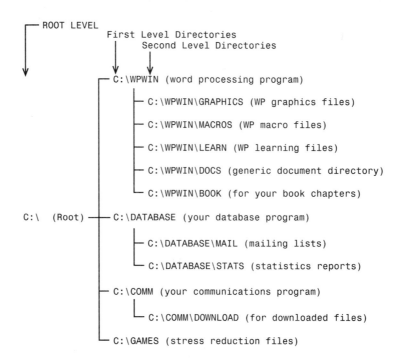

Sample Hard Disk Tree Structure

```
         ┌─ ROOT LEVEL
         │            First Level Directories
         │               Second Level Directories
         │                 │        │
         ▼                 ▼        ▼
                  ┌─ C:\WPWIN (word processing program)
                  │
                  │   ┌─ C:\WPWIN\GRAPHICS (WP graphics files)
                  │   │
                  │   ├─ C:\WPWIN\MACROS (WP macro files)
                  │   │
                  │   ├─ C:\WPWIN\LEARN (WP learning files)
                  │   │
                  │   ├─ C:\WPWIN\DOCS (generic document directory)
                  │   │
                  │   └─ C:\WPWIN\BOOK (for your book chapters)
                  │
  C:\  (Root) ────┼─ C:\DATABASE (your database program)
                  │
                  │   ┌─ C:\DATABASE\MAIL (mailing lists)
                  │   │
                  │   └─ C:\DATABASE\STATS (statistics reports)
                  │
                  ├─ C:\COMM (your communications program)
                  │
                  │   └─ C:\COMM\DOWNLOAD (for downloaded files)
                  │
                  └─ C:\GAMES (stress reduction files)
```

T I P   Although this example uses a "tall tree" structure with several sublevels, you often can save time by using a "flat bush" approach to your tree structure. With this method, you attach more directories to your root directory, thus avoiding long path names with several subdirectory levels (for example, C:\DOCS rather than C:\WPWIN\DOCS).

The second step in organizing your files is to determine the directories currently on your hard disk. The "Finding Existing Directories" section of this chapter describes how to find directories on your disk. As you discover existing directories, add them to your sketch of the proposed tree structure.

The third step in organizing your files is to create the directories you need. You use the File Manager for this task (described later in this chapter).

T I P

Depending on the installation process you chose (Basic or Custom), WordPerfect for Windows automatically created certain directories, including C:\WPWIN for WordPerfect program files, and C:\WPC for WordPerfect shared resource files. You also may find other directories, such as C:\WPWIN\GRAPHICS or C:\WPWIN\LEARN.

Finally, you create files, save them in appropriate directories, and copy or move files from one directory to another as needed to establish an orderly system. The remaining sections of this chapter describe the procedures you use to accomplish these file management objectives.

Using the File Manager

The WordPerfect File Manager is a comprehensive program that can run as part of WordPerfect for Windows or separately in Windows. To start the File Manager outside WordPerfect, you choose the WP File Manager icon from the Windows Program Manager menu or window.

For this section, however, use the File Manager with WordPerfect. To start the program from WordPerfect for Windows, choose File, File Manager. The File Manager window appears on-screen. Figure 3.1 shows one version of the File Manager window; you can change the arrangement of the layout.

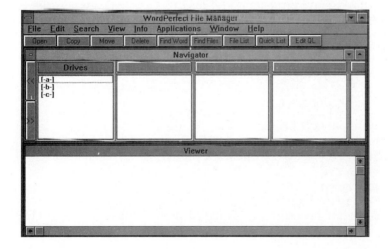

FIG. 3.1

WordPerfect's File Manager with the Navigator and Viewer windows.

T I P   To switch quickly between WordPerfect for Windows and the File Manager, press Alt-Tab to leave both programs active and enable you to move more quickly between them.

Understanding the File Manager Screen

When you start the File Manager, you should see two windows. The Navigator window shows the tree structure of the disk drive you specify. This window is the "active" window; commands you use apply to the file(s) selected in this window. The Viewer window enables you to look at the contents of any file you select in the Navigator window.

Finding Existing Directories

When you need to determine which directories exist on your disk, the Navigator is the perfect tool. The box at the left of the Navigator window shows a list of disk drives. The drive names appear in brackets (for example, [-a-], [-b-], or [-c-]). Because you want to look at the structure of your hard disk (drive C), highlight [-c-] and press Enter or double-click the mouse.

The directories and files that appear in the second box of the Navigator are in the root directory of drive C. Directories are listed in brackets without hyphens (for example, [dos] or [wpwin]). Directories appear alphabetically before file names. File names appear without brackets.

To see additional subdirectories, select a directory and press Enter (or double-click the directory name with the mouse). Repeat this process with each directory, and add the directory names to your paper diagram of the tree structure until all the directories on your hard disk are listed on the diagram.

Creating New Directories

You may need to add directories to your disk. For example, you may want to create a special directory to store chapters of a book. The only way to create new directories in WordPerfect is by using the File Manager. To create a new directory, follow these steps:

1. From the File Manager menu, choose **File, Create Directory** (or press Ctrl-T).

   The Create Directory dialog box appears, as shown in figure 3.2. The New Directory text box shows the name of the current directory.

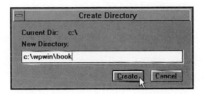

FIG. 3.2

The Create Directory dialog box with the current directory name displayed.

2. To create a new directory, type the directory path name in the New Directory text box. Be sure to type the entire path name, including the drive specifier (C:), backslashes (the first backslash marks the beginning of the root directory), and any directories found between the root directory and the directory you are creating.

   For this example, type **C:\WPWIN\BOOK**.

3. Choose **Create** or press Enter.

   If a directory exists with the specified name, the File Manager displays an error message. Press Enter or click OK to return to the Create Directory dialog box.

   If no other message appears, you have created the new directory.

4. Repeat steps 2 and 3 to add the next directory.

5. When you finish adding directories, choose **File, Exit** to return to WordPerfect.

    Press Exit (Alt-F4).

   If you prefer to leave File Manager active in the background, press Alt-Tab to return to WordPerfect.

Create other directories as necessary to complete your tree structure. Don't worry if you don't know all the directories you may need. You can return to the File Manager later to create additional directories.

Setting the Default Document Directory

WordPerfect uses the C:\WPWIN directory as the default start-up directory unless you change the default. Because you should avoid storing your documents in the same directory as the WordPerfect program files, this section describes how to change the default directory.

To change the default document directory, follow these steps:

1. Choose **F**ile, **P**references, **L**ocation of Files.

   WordPerfect displays a dialog box that you can use to specify the default directories for several types of files.

2. Move to the **D**ocuments text box.

3. Type the complete path name for the directory you want to use for storing documents. (If the directory listed in the **D**ocuments text box is the one you want, choose Cancel or press Esc.)

   For this example, type **C:\WPWIN\DOCS**.

4. Press Enter or choose OK to set the specified directory as the default document directory.

Using the Open File Dialog Box

In this section, you learn the basic WordPerfect file management procedures: opening, retrieving, deleting, copying, and renaming files.

When WordPerfect opens a document, the software copies the contents of the file stored on disk into the computer's memory. The original file remains on your disk, but you or the computer can change and use the data in the open file. WordPerfect actually opens documents in the following four ways:

■ *Opening* a file brings a copy of the file into a new editing screen.

■ *Retrieving* a file places a copy of the file in an editing screen that contains data. For example, you can retrieve a graphic image into a newsletter document.

■ You *select* a file when WordPerfect needs the file for a task, such as a Button Bar display. WordPerfect must open the file to use the information found in that file.

■ When you *play* a macro that is recorded on disk, WordPerfect opens the macro file before playing the macro.

Because these four processes are similar, their dialog boxes are nearly identical. Figure 3.3 shows the Open File dialog box. The function used to access files (in this case, Open File) appears at the top of the dialog box. The top portion of the dialog box displays information about the current directory and any selected files.

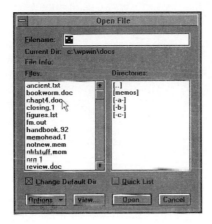

FIG. 3.3

The Open File
dialog box.

If you retrieve, select, or play a file, the specified function replaces the Open File name at the top of the dialog box. In all other ways, each dialog box is identical to the Open File dialog box, but only the Open File and Retrieve File dialog boxes enable you to view the contents of the files.

Opening a File

To open a file, select File, Open or press Open (F4). WordPerfect displays the Open File dialog box. When this dialog box first appears in an editing session, the listing for Current Dir is the default directory you specified at installation or with the File, Preferences, Location of Files command discussed earlier. If you didn't change the default, the specified directory is the location of your WordPerfect program files (for example, C:\WPWIN).

The Filename text box shows *.*, indicating that all files in the current directory are displayed, but no files have been selected. If you know the path and file name for the file you want to open, you can type that information in the Filename text box and press Enter or choose Open to open the file. The dialog box disappears, and WordPerfect opens the document in a new screen.

If you decide that you don't want to open a file, press Esc or choose Cancel to close the Open File dialog box.

Using the Files List

In most cases, you probably don't know the name or location of the file you want to open. WordPerfect helps you by listing the files in the current directory in the Files list at the left side of the Open File dialog box. The Files list shows all files in the current directory in alphabetical order.

To use the Files list, choose Files. The Files list becomes the active window. You can browse through the files by pressing the down- or up-arrow key or by using the mouse with the scroll bar at the right side of the box. If the directory contains too many files to fit in the window, you can continue scrolling until you have seen all the files.

You can move quickly to a file in the list by typing the first few characters of the file name. To find the file called CHAPT4.DOC, for example, you can type **ch** to move to the part of the Files list beginning with those letters (see fig. 3.4).

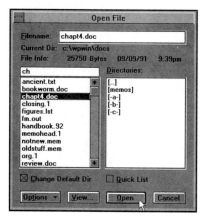

FIG. 3.4

Searching for a file with the Files list.

When you highlight a file name, the file name reverses colors (for example, changing from black letters on a white background to white letters on a black background). This change indicates that you have *selected* the file. Simultaneously, the name of the selected file appears in the **Filename** text box, and basic information about the file appears next to File Info. The file information includes the following data:

- The size of the file in bytes (roughly equivalent to the number of characters in the document)

- The date on which the file was last modified

- The time at which the file was last modified

If you want to open the selected file, press Enter or choose **Open**. This action closes the dialog box and opens the selected document in a new screen. To cancel the Open File dialog box, press Esc or select Cancel.

You can select and open a file in one step by double-clicking the mouse on the file name.

T I P

Locking Files

You can assign a password to files so that no one but you can use them. If you decide to guard your files with password protection, keep one important caution in mind: if you forget the password, the file will be inaccessible to you. After you lock a file, every time you attempt to open, retrieve, view, print, or merge the file, WordPerfect prompts you to enter your password.

■ **Cue:** After locking a file, don't forget your password!

To save and "lock" an open file with a password, follow these steps:

1. Choose **File**, **Password**. The Password dialog box appears (see fig. 3.5).

FIG. 3.5

The Password dialog box.

2. Type a password of up to 24 characters in the Type Password for Document text box. Note that WordPerfect displays asterisks in the text box instead of the actual characters you type.

3. Choose Set and retype the password when prompted by WordPerfect. If you make a mistake when retyping your password, you must start over at step 2.

4. Save the document to lock the document.

To unprotect a file, first make certain that the document from which you want to remove the password is open. Then follow these steps:

1. Choose **File**, **Password**. The Password dialog box is displayed.

2. Choose **Remove**.

3. Save the document.

■ **Cue:** You are prompted to specify a file password for locked documents searched during a Find Files or Word Search operation in File Manager.

To verify that your document is unlocked, open a second copy of the document in another window. WordPerfect no longer prompts you for a password.

Using the View Window

Sometimes you may not remember what is in a file, or you may be uncertain whether a file name that sounds correct is the file you want. WordPerfect provides a handy View function to let you peek into the file before opening it.

To use the View function, select a file in the Files list, and then choose **View**. WordPerfect displays the View window in the upper right corner of the screen (see fig. 3.6). This window remains visible until you close the Open File dialog box.

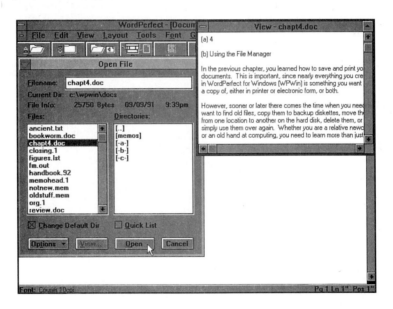

The View window displays ASCII text, text created in WordPerfect Versions 4.2 and later, WordPerfect graphics, and Windows 3.0 bit-mapped graphics. With other documents, the View window may display part of the document, "garbage" characters, or nothing. (***Note:*** The View window cannot display text and graphics at the same time. When a file includes both, the View window displays the text.)

Changing the Current Directory

After browsing and viewing files in the Files List, you may discover that the current directory doesn't contain the file you want. If you saved a file in the C:\WPWIN\BOOK directory, for example, it will not appear in the Files list for the default C:\WPWIN\DOCS directory.

Before changing directories, note the full path name of the current directory, listed next to Current Dir. Knowing the path can help you determine where you are relative to other directories in your tree. (Refer to the tree structure diagram you created earlier.)

If you know the full path name of the directory you want to change to, you can type that information in the **Filename** text box and press Enter or choose **O**pen to open that directory. To change from the C:\WPWIN\DOCS directory to the C:\WPWIN\BOOK directory, for example, move to the **Filename** text box, type **C:\WPWIN\BOOK**, and press Enter or choose **O**pen.

If you decide not to change directories after all, press Esc or choose Cancel to close the Open File dialog box.

When you change the default directory in this manner, the change is temporary. The next time you start WordPerfect, the original default directory is restored. Note the check mark in the **Change Default Dir** box. By default, changing to a new directory makes that directory the new default directory until you change directories again or until you exit WordPerfect.

If you change directories, and you later want to save a file to the original directory, (for example, to the C:\WPWIN\DOCS documents directory), you must specify the full path name or change directories again, or you may save the file to a different directory than you expected.

The next time you start WordPerfect, the initial current directory is the same one you specified when you set the default document directory (see "Setting the Default Document Directory," earlier in this chapter).

If you don't remember the name of the directory where you stored a file, WordPerfect enables you to browse through your directories to find the one you want.

The **Directories** list at the right side of the Open File dialog box shows a list of drives and directories. Drives appear in brackets with a hyphen on each side (for example, [-a-], [-b-], or [-c-]). Other directories related to the current directory also appear in brackets, but without hyphens (for example, [drafts]). If you are working in a subdirectory, the parent directory of that subdirectory is indicated by two periods in brackets ([..]).

T I P

Choosing [-c-] doesn't give you the root directory of drive C, but the current or default directory of drive C (listed next to Current Dir at the top of the dialog box).

To change from C:\WPWIN\DOCS to C:\WPWIN\BOOK, you change to the parent directory first (in this case, to C:\WPWIN). To change to the parent directory, highlight the [..] entry and choose **O**pen or press Enter, or just double-click the [..] entry. A new list of subdirectories appears, from which you can choose the desired directory.

■**Cue:** To move to the parent directory for a new list of directories, select [..].

To change from the C:\WPWIN directory to the C:\WPWIN\BOOK directory, you highlight the [book] entry and press Enter or choose **O**pen, or double-click the [book] entry.

Using the Open File Options

The Options button in the lower left corner of the Open File dialog box performs some basic file management procedures. To view or select these options, choose Options and then press the space bar or press and hold the left mouse button. A pull-down menu appears, as shown in figure 3.7.

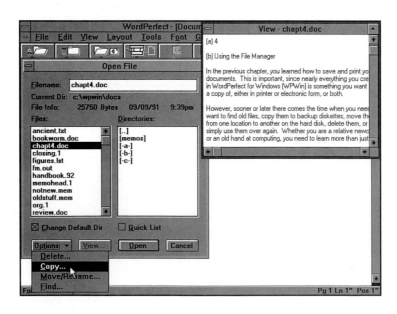

FIG. 3.7

The Options pull-down menu in the Open File dialog box.

Copying Files

You copy files for a number of reasons. You may need to consolidate files from several different locations in the same directory to simplify using the files. You may want to transfer files from one computer to another. Often you need to make backup copies of files on a floppy disk or a network storage disk for protection.

■ **Cue:** Before choosing one of the options on the Options pull-down menu, select the desired file from the Files list.

You can use the Copy command on the Open File Options menu to copy your files. This command copies files from one hard disk location to another, from the hard disk to a floppy disk, and from a floppy disk to the hard disk.

Before choosing the Copy option, select a file in the Files list. Then choose Options, press the space bar or left mouse button to pull down the Options menu, and choose Copy. The Copy File dialog box appears, as shown in figure 3.8.

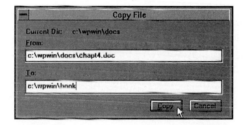

FIG. 3.8

The Copy File dialog box.

The dialog box shows the current directory and the full path name of the selected file. To tell WordPerfect where you want to copy the file, you type the full path name of the target directory in the **To** text box.

If the target directory is in the same drive as the current directory, you can omit the drive designation (C:) from the path name. You must include the rest of the path name, however (for example, \WPWIN\BOOK).

■ **Cue:** You need not type the name of the file unless you want to change the name of the file while copying.

In this example, you copy the file CHAPT4.DOC from the C:\WPWIN\DOCS directory to the C:\WPWIN\BOOK directory. To copy a single file, follow these steps:

1. Select the desired file in the Files list. For this example, highlight CHAPT4.DOC.

2. Choose Options.

3. Press the space bar or the left mouse button to pull down the Options menu.

4. Choose **C**opy from the pull-down menu.

   The selected file name appears in the **F**rom text box. For this example, the file should be C:\WPWIN\DOCS\CHAPT4.DOC.

   If the file name is not correct, return to step 1 and select the correct file, or type the correct path and file name.

5. Type the path and file name for the target file in the **T**o text box. For this example, type **\WPWIN\BOOK**.

6. Choose **C**opy or press Enter to copy the file.

If the target directory doesn't exist (for example, if you type the path name incorrectly), the following error message appears:

```
Invalid directory specified in path
```

CAUTION: If only the final directory of your path name is incorrect, WordPerfect copies the file to a different file name. If you specify C:\WPWIN\BOOC as the target directory, for example, WordPerfect copies the file to C:\WPWIN and changes the name of the file to BOOC.

If a file with the specified name exists in the target directory, WordPerfect displays a warning message to ask whether you want to replace the file with the source file (see fig. 3.9).

FIG. 3.9

The warning prompt that appears if you try to copy a file to an existing file name.

WordPerfect

c:\wpwin\book\chapt4.doc already exists. Do you want to replace it?

[Yes] [No]

If you want to replace the existing file, choose **Y**es. If you choose **N**o, WordPerfect returns to the Copy File dialog box, where you can change the target name or cancel the copy procedure.

WARNING: If you copy a file to an existing file name, WordPerfect replaces the old file with the new one. If you aren't sure you want to replace the existing file, use the **V**iew option to look at the target file before continuing.

The process for copying a file from the hard disk to a floppy disk is the same except that you designate a drive (for example, drive A) rather than a directory in the **To** text box. If you're copying a file to a subdirectory on a floppy disk, designate the drive and appropriate subdirectory in the **To** text box.

This copy procedure is useful for occasions when you need to copy one or two files. If you need to copy several files, use the File Manager. See Chapter 30, "Advanced File Management Techniques," for more information.

Deleting Files

If you decide that you no longer need a file, you can use the **Delete** command from the Open File Options menu.

To delete a file, follow these steps:

1. Select the file in the Files list.

2. Choose Options and press the space bar or left mouse button to pull down the Options menu.

3. Select **Delete** from the pull-down menu. The Delete File dialog box appears, as shown in figure 3.10.

   The **File** to Delete text box displays the target file to be deleted. If the file name is not correct, type the correct path and file name in the **File** to Delete text box or return to step 1 and select the correct file.

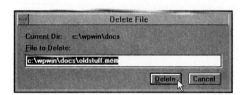

FIG. 3.10

The Delete File dialog box.

4. Choose **Delete** to delete the file. If you don't want to delete the file, press Esc or choose Cancel.

WARNING: The Delete File dialog box is the only warning that you are about to delete a file. If you choose **Delete**, WordPerfect deletes the file and you cannot retrieve it without a special utility program.

If you accidentally delete an important file, get help immediately. The longer you wait, the less likely the possibility that you can recover deleted files. If you have the Norton Utilities or PC Tools, you can use the file recovery capabilities of these utilities to recover your file.

The delete procedure is useful for occasions when you need to delete just one or two files. If you need to delete many files at a time, use the File Manager.

CAUTION: Before deleting a large number of files, make a backup copy of the files. Accidentally deleting the wrong files is easy when you work with many different files at once.

Renaming and Moving Files

An important part of good file management is being able to identify the files on your disk. Sometimes you must change the name of a file to make identification easier or to free a name you want to use for another file.

■ **Cue:** You need not provide the drive designation and path name in a Rename operation.

The Move/Rename File dialog box is nearly identical to the Copy File dialog box. To rename the file, you supply the new file name in the **To** text box. If you want to move the file, enter a new directory name but don't add the file name (unless you also want to change the name). When you are ready to rename or move the file, select **M**ove or press Enter.

■ **Cue:** When you move files, you copy and delete in one operation.

When you rename a file, WordPerfect replaces the old file name with the new file name. When you move a file, WordPerfect copies the file to the new location, and deletes the original file.

In this example, you change a file named END (the conclusion to Chapter 4) to CHAPT4.END. To rename or move a file, follow these steps:

1. Select the file from the Files list. For this example, you select the END file.

2. Choose Op**t**ions and press the space bar or left mouse button to pull down the Options menu.

3. Select **M**ove/Rename from the pull-down menu. The Move/Rename File dialog box appears, as shown in figure 3.11. The original path and file name appear in the **F**rom text box.

   If the source file name is not correct, type the correct path and file name, or return to step 1 and select the correct file. For this example, the source file name is C:\WPWIN\BOOK\END.

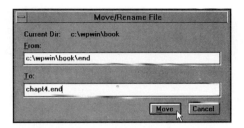

FIG. 3.11

The Move/
Rename File
dialog box.

4. Type the target path and file name in the To text box. For this example, type **CHAPT4.END**.

5. Choose **Move** or press Enter to move or rename the file. If you don't want to move or rename the file, choose Cancel or press Esc.

Searching for Files

Suppose that you need a list of product codes that you created several weeks ago. Creating the list again can take hours, so you use the Open File dialog box to browse through your directories, looking for a file that contains the list. Unfortunately, the file names don't offer much help.

Fortunately, the powerful Find command in the Open File Options menu can help you find misplaced files by searching your entire disk for file name patterns, or by searching files for words that you may remember from the desired document.

Finding Words

Suppose that you remember one of the parts listed in the missing file is a widget. The chance that the word *widget* appears in many files is unlikely, so you can use the Find command to search for files containing the word *widget*.

To find files that contain a specific word, follow these steps from the Open File dialog box:

1. Choose Options and press the space bar or left mouse button to pull down the Options menu.

2. Choose Find from the pull-down menu. The Find dialog box appears, as shown in figure 3.12.

   At this point, you can use only two options in the Find dialog box: Find **F**iles and Find **W**ords. After you have found some files, you can use the other options.

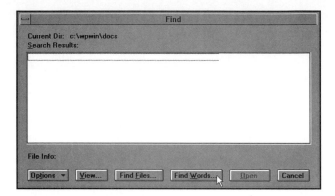

FIG. 3.12

The Find dialog
box.

3. Select Find **W**ords. The Find Words dialog box appears, as shown
   in figure 3.13.

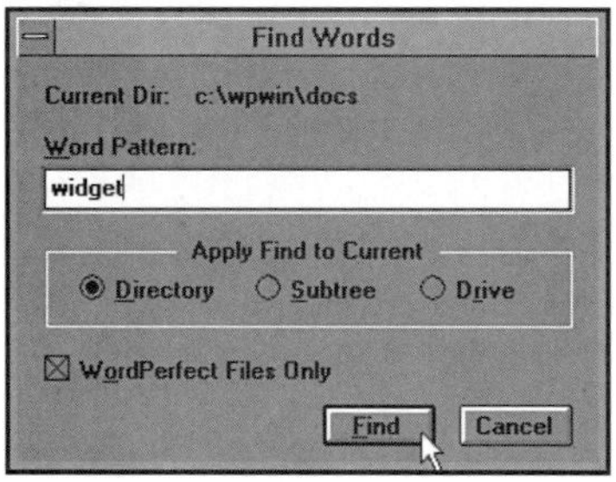

FIG. 3.13

The Find Words
dialog box.

4. In the **W**ord Pattern text box, type the word you want to find. For
   this example, type **widget**.

5. Choose the D**r**ive, **D**irectory, or **S**ubtree option to tell WordPerfect
   where to search for the word (**D**irectory is the default). For this
   example, choose **D**irectory.

6. If you want to search all files, not just WordPerfect files, deselect
   the W**o**rdPerfect Files Only option (press Alt-O or click the check
   box with the mouse).

7. Choose **F**ind to begin searching (choose Cancel or press Esc if you
   don't want to conduct the search).

WordPerfect looks at every file specified by the search criteria. The
options that you chose in the Find Words dialog box direct the search
process as follows:

- Choosing **D**irectory causes WordPerfect to search the files in the current directory only. In the example shown in figure 3.13, WordPerfect searches the C:\WPWIN\DOCS directory.

- If you choose **S**ubtree, WordPerfect searches all files in the current directory and in any subdirectories of the current directory. In the C:\WPWIN\DOCS directory, for example, WordPerfect searches the C:\WPWIN\DOCS\PERSONAL and C:\WPWIN\DOCS\MEMOS directories.

- Choosing the **D**rive option causes WordPerfect to search all files in all directories on the current drive (for example, on drive C).

WordPerfect lists all files that match your search criteria in the **S**earch Results window of the Find dialog box. The Find dialog box then works like the Open File dialog box, offering the following functions:

- Selecting a file

- Opening a selected file

- Viewing a selected file

- Deleting a selected file (on the Options menu)

- Copying a selected file (on the Options menu)

- Moving/renaming a selected file (on the Options menu)

You can conduct another search if the first search didn't yield the results you expected.

Finding Files

Suppose that you find three files containing the word *widget*. After viewing each, you determine that none of them is the file you want. Perhaps the report doesn't contain the word *widget* after all. You decide to look for file names that end in the extension RPT.

To find file names that match a specific pattern, follow these steps from the Open File dialog box:

1. Choose Options and pull down the Options menu.

2. Choose **F**ind. The Find dialog box appears.

3. Choose Find Files. The Find Files dialog box appears, as shown in figure 3.14.

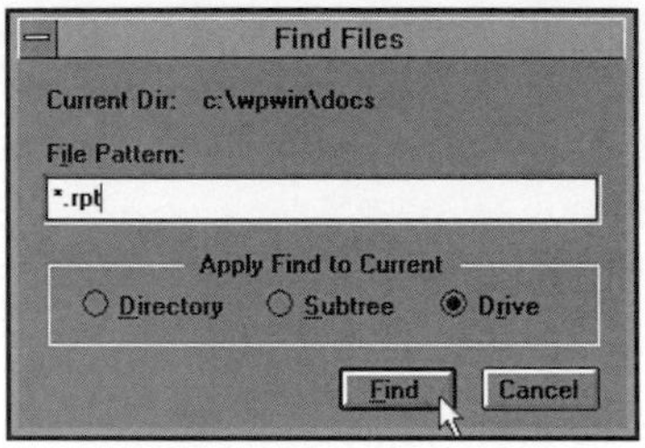

FIG. 3.14

The Find Files
dialog box.

4. In the File Pattern text box, type the file name or file name pattern you want to find (for example, type ***.RPT**).

5. Choose the **D**irectory, **S**ubtree, or **D**rive option to tell WordPerfect where to search for the word. D**r**ive is the default.

6. Choose **F**ind to begin the search (choose Cancel or press Esc if you don't want to conduct the search).

WordPerfect looks at every file specified by your search criteria and lists the results in the **S**earch Results window of the Find dialog box. At this point, the other buttons and options in the dialog box can be used for files listed in the window.

For more information on searching for words and file names, see Chapter 30, "Advanced File Management Techniques."

Using a Quick List

While reading this chapter, you may have wondered whether an easier method exists for changing directories, especially those you use often. Typing **C:\WPWIN\BOOK\CHAPT1.DOC** isn't very efficient; it takes too long and is too error-prone. Again, WordPerfect provides some powerful functions to simplify this process.

As you have seen, when you ask WordPerfect to open, retrieve, or save a file, a dialog box appears, displaying the files in the current directory at the left side of the box. The right side of the dialog box displays all directories or drives directly accessible from the current directory (parent directories, subdirectories, and other drives). By choosing the **Q**uick List option, you can display a custom list of directories and drives, thus easing the task of changing directories.

Creating a Quick List

If you have changed directories with the File, Preferences, Location of Files command, *and* allowed WordPerfect to merge those locations into your Quick List (the default setting), you already have a short Quick List that includes those directories. The Location of Files dialog box contains an Update Quick List with Changes check box. The default is to have WordPerfect update the Quick List automatically when you make any changes in the Location of Files dialog box.

When you choose the Quick List option in the Open File dialog box, WordPerfect displays a list that may resemble the one shown in figure 3.15.

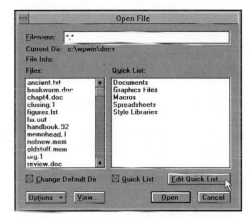

FIG. 3.15

The Open File dialog box with a typical Quick List.

You can add descriptive names to your Quick List to ease the task of choosing directories and drives. The following list shows some directory designations and descriptive names:

Drive and directory	Descriptive name
C:\WPWIN\GRAPHICS	Pretty WordPerfect Pictures
C:\WPWIN\BOOK	My Book Stuff
C:\WPWIN\DOCS	WPWin Documents
A:\	Drive A

To add descriptive names to your Quick List, follow these steps:

1. Choose **File, O**pen.

    Press Open (F4).

   The Open File dialog box appears.

2. Choose the **Q**uick List option. The Edit Quick List button appears in the dialog box (again see fig. 3.15).

3. Choose **E**dit Quick List. The Edit Quick List dialog box appears, as shown in figure 3.16.

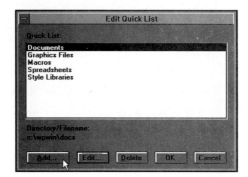

FIG. 3.16

Editing a Quick List.

If you have never used the **Q**uick List option, you may not see any entries in this dialog box. If you specified directories for the Quick List when you installed WordPerfect or set the location of your files, those entries appear in the dialog box.

To add directories to the Quick List, choose **A**dd. WordPerfect displays the Add Quick List Item dialog box, as shown in figure 3.17.

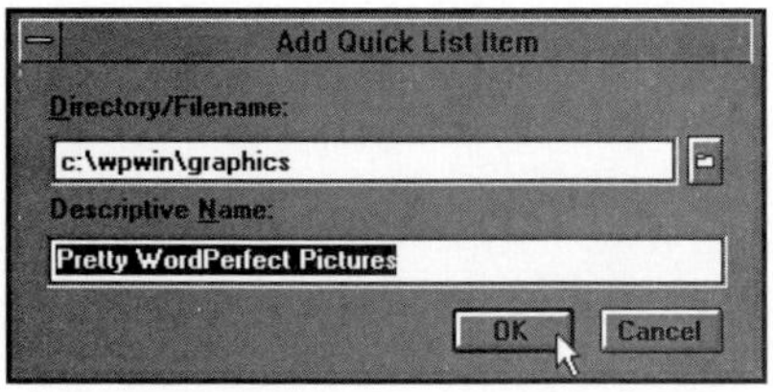

FIG. 3.17

The Add Quick List Item dialog box.

For each item that you add, you must provide the path name for the directory you want to include. In the **Directory**/Filename text box, type the full path name for your entry (for example, type **C:\WPWIN\GRAPHICS**).

If you cannot remember the name of the directory you want, click the folder icon at the right of the Directory/Filename text box (or press Alt and the up-arrow or down-arrow key). WordPerfect displays the Select Directory dialog box (shown in figure 3.18), which lists the parent directory and any subdirectories of the current directory.

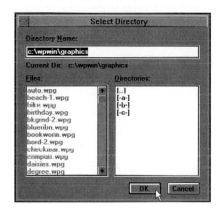

The Select Directory dialog box.

The Files and Directories lists in the Select Directory dialog box are similar to those in the Open File dialog box (without the Quick List), but the files in the Files list are always dimmed. This action reminds you that you are selecting a directory, not a file. Use the same methods you learned earlier to change directories. Then select OK or press Enter to copy the directory name into the **Directory**/Filename text box.

Now move to the Descriptive **Name** text box and type a descriptive name for the directory (for example, type **Pretty WordPerfect Pictures**). If you don't specify a descriptive name, WordPerfect uses the path name as the descriptive name.

■ **Cue:** Add any directories that you use frequently to your Quick List.

Choose OK or press Enter to add the new item to your Quick List. Repeat this process for other directories you want to add.

You can add a specific file name to your Quick List by including the full path name and file name.

T I P

Editing or Deleting Quick List Entries

The procedure for editing or deleting Quick List entries parallels the procedure for adding items. Follow these steps to edit or delete an entry:

1. Choose **File**, **O**pen.

    Press Open (F4).

   The Open File dialog box appears.

2. If the Quick List check box isn't enabled, choose **Q**uick List.

3. Choose **E**dit Quick List.

4. Select the entry you want to edit or delete.

5. Choose **D**elete or **E**dit.

6. If you chose **D**elete, confirm that you want to delete the entry.

   If you chose **E**dit, follow the procedures you learned earlier to change the path name or the descriptive name for the directory.

Deleting a Quick List entry doesn't delete the directory or the files in that directory.

T I P   You can set up partial directories in your Quick List by using wild-card characters (see the "Understanding File Management Terms" section of this chapter). If you want a list of memos, for example, even though other documents may be in the same directory, you can specify C:\WPWIN\DOCS*.MEM to list all files with the extension MEM.

Your Quick List is available for any situation where you must open, save, retrieve, play, or select a file or directory. If you enable the **Q**uick List option in one dialog box (for example, in the Open File dialog box), the Quick List is activated in all dialog boxes with a Quick List option. In the same manner, disabling the **Q**uick List option in one dialog box turns it off in all others.

Chapter Summary

In this chapter, you learned procedures for managing files in WordPerfect with the Open File dialog box and the WordPerfect File Manager. You learned how to list and view files; create and change directories; copy, delete, move, and rename files; find files by looking for word and file name patterns; and create and use a Quick List for easier access to your directories.

The procedures you learned in this chapter are basic file management tools that you will use every day. The File Manager program has many other features not discussed in this chapter; these functions are discussed in Chapter 30, "Advanced File Management Techniques."

Editing a Document

I f you are new to word processing, this chapter gives you a taste of what electronic editing is all about. Using WordPerfect to create, save, and print text is like the appetizer to your word processing feast. Editing is more like the main course. After you become accustomed to the power of WordPerfect's editing features, you may wonder how you got along without them.

Preparing a document from beginning to end involves at least three basic, essential steps:

- Creating
- Editing
- Formatting

Word processing has dramatically changed the method of document preparation in the work place. Before the advent of word processing, often one person created original material, perhaps by dictation, and another person transcribed, edited, and formatted the material. That pattern still holds in some cases today, but more often those persons who create material now also edit for content before turning over the document to another person for final formatting. Some writers find formatting so easy and fun that they no longer pass on that job to someone else; instead, they oversee the preparation of the document from start to finish.

■ **Read Gilgen** is Director of Learning Support Services at the University of Wisconsin, Madison. He started using computers in 1981 and WordPerfect shortly thereafter. His only regret is that WordPerfect wasn't around when he had to type and edit his own dissertation.

WordPerfect's power lies in its capacity to accommodate your needs in working with a document at any stage of its development. Even more, WordPerfect becomes a valuable tool that extends your editing power and also saves you time.

In this chapter you learn how to do the following:

- Open an existing document

- Retrieve an existing document into a document you have open

- Edit the content of a document by inserting, deleting, and emphasizing text

- Use hidden codes for better control of your document

- Search for and replace text and codes

- Add document comments to assist group editing efforts

T I P   The key to efficient word processing is learning to minimize the number of keystrokes (or mouse clicks) required to accomplish a task. When alternative procedures are offered, try to learn and use the alternatives that save time.

Opening and Retrieving Files

Chapter 2, "Creating, Printing, and Saving a Document," shows you how to save a document. In this section, you learn to bring that document (or any other document) to your editing screen by using WordPerfect's Open and Retrieve features.

The command terms *open* and *retrieve* may appear to have essentially the same meaning, but in WordPerfect the commands serve two different purposes.

Open means to bring a previously saved file to a blank editing screen. The document retains all its initial settings, such as margins, font, file name, and so on. If you already are working in a document, Word-Perfect opens another blank screen for the next file you open. When you save an open file, WordPerfect replaces the original file of the same name on your disk with the open version of the file.

Retrieve means to bring a previously saved file into another document that you already have on-screen. WordPerfect ignores the file's initial settings in favor of the settings in the on screen document. When you save your current (open) document, WordPerfect saves the retrieved file along with it. The original document from which you retrieved the file isn't changed. If you are working on ANNUAL.RPT, for example, and decide you must incorporate a list of company sites found in the file SITES.LST, you retrieve SITES.LST to become part of ANNUAL.RPT. Saving the information from SITES.LST along with ANNUAL.RPT doesn't change the original SITES.LST.

Opening a File

In Chapter 3, "Managing Files," you learned several ways to open a file. Perhaps the easiest method is to follow these steps:

1. Choose **File**, **O**pen.

    Press Open File (F4).

   WordPerfect displays the Open File dialog box with the current (or default) directory and a list of the files in that directory (see fig. 4.1). Most likely you specified this directory when you installed WordPerfect.

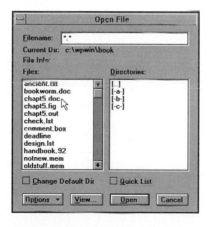

FIG. 4.1

The Open File dialog box.

2. Press Alt-I or place the mouse pointer in the Files window and click. Then highlight the file you want in the Files list.

   If your file list is long, some files may not appear in the Files list window. Use the direction keys or the scroll bar to move through the Files list to highlight the file you want.

■ **Cue:** Double-clicking a file name in the Files list selects *and* opens that file.

3. To open the selected file, choose **O**pen, press Enter, or double-click the file name.

T I P When searching for a file in the Files list, begin typing the file name. WordPerfect moves to the first file name that matches what you type. Type **ch**, for example, to move to the section of file names beginning with *ch* (see fig. 4.2).

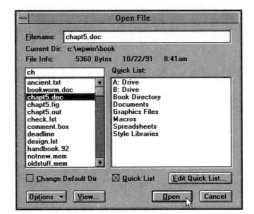

FIG. 4.2

The name search option for locating a file name in the Files list window.

Locating a "Lost" File

If you cannot find a file that you want to open, usually the problem isn't that the file is gone but that you just don't know where the file is. Several methods can help you find your "lost" file:

■ Carefully scan the Files list to see whether you can find the file. You easily can forget what you named a file, especially the exact spelling of the file name. Because computers are picky about precise names, use the Files list to jog your memory.

■ A second method is to use the **V**iew option in the Open File dialog box. Choose **V**iew; as you highlight a file in the Files list, WordPerfect displays the contents in the View window, next to the Open File dialog box (see fig. 4.3).

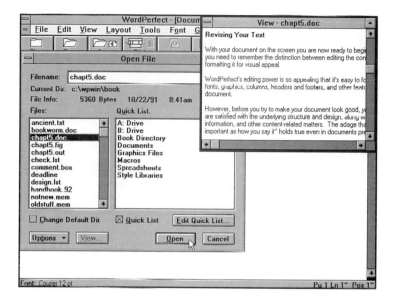

FIG. 4.3

Using the View window to find a file.

- Finally, you can select another directory in the Quick List and repeat the process for opening a file. (See Chapter 3, "Managing Files," for information on creating a Quick List.) In most cases, you can find your "lost" file in one of the directories you use most often.

- If none of the other approaches works, you must search through the directories on your disk. For a more detailed discussion of directories, paths, and how to find files, see Chapter 3, "Managing Files."

Perhaps the most important key to finding files is making sure that you save them where you intend to save them. When you save a file, double-check the Current Directory information in the Save or Save As dialog box.

T I P

Using Retrieve To Combine Files

The procedure for retrieving a file is like that for opening a file, except that WordPerfect inserts a retrieved file directly into your current file, at the insertion point. To retrieve a file, follow these steps:

1. Position the insertion point where you want to insert the retrieved file.

2. Choose **File**, **Retrieve**.

   The Retrieve File dialog box that appears is nearly identical to the Open File dialog box.

3. Type the file name you want in the **Filename** text box or highlight the file in the **Files** list window; then press Enter or choose **Retrieve**.

   WordPerfect prompts you to confirm that you want to insert the document into your current document (see fig. 4.4). Choose **Yes** or press Enter to retrieve the file.

You can use this procedure effectively for assembling a longer document from prepared smaller documents. You may have several standard paragraphs, for example, that you use in various documents. Rather than retyping the paragraphs repeatedly, you can create them once, save them as separate files, and then build the document by retrieving the paragraphs you need.

T I P Save your current document before you retrieve or open another document. If you retrieve rather than open, for example, or retrieve to the wrong location in your current file, you can close the current document without saving it and then open the version you saved just before the mistake.

Revising Text

With the document displayed, you can begin editing. WordPerfect's editing power is so appealing that you easily can focus on layout, fonts, graphics, columns, headers and footers, and other features that polish your document. Before you try to make your document look good, however, determine that the underlying structure and design, along with grammar, accuracy of information, and other content-related matters, are satisfactory.

The remainder of this chapter focuses on the tools you can use for editing the content of your document. Other chapters—Chapter 6, "Formatting Text," and Chapter 11, "Formatting Pages and Designing Documents"—deal with formatting your document to make it visually attractive.

Inserting Text

With a standard typewriter, you cannot insert new words into a sentence without retyping the entire sentence—or page. Like all word processors, WordPerfect enables you to insert new text at the insertion point without having to retype anything. Text following the insertion point moves to the right and down to make room for what you type. Lines, paragraphs, and pages are automatically reformatted to account for the added text.

Overwriting Text

By default, WordPerfect *inserts* new text at the insertion point. To *type over* existing text, press the Ins (or Insert) key to turn on Typeover mode.

When Typeover is active, anything you type writes over existing text—in effect, deleting the original text. To return to normal Insert mode, press the Ins key again.

Deleting a few characters and typing new ones is more efficient than changing to Typeover, typing the characters, and then changing back to Insert. The main reason is that the new word rarely is the same length as the old one, forcing you to delete the extra characters. Switching back and forth between Insert and Typeover modes actually requires more keystrokes and causes more confusion.

■**Cue:** After you press the Ins key, the word Typeover appears at the left side of the status bar; press Ins again and Typeover disappears, indicating that you have returned to Insert mode.

Deleting Text

Deleting or replacing unwanted text is basic to the editing process. WordPerfect quickly and easily helps you to delete characters, lines, sentences, paragraphs, and full pages. You even can restore deleted text if you make a mistake.

Two different keys enable you to delete one character at a time. Learning which key to use in which situation can help you to edit more efficiently. The Backspace key is the one you use more often when entering new text. Pressing Backspace moves the insertion point to the left, erasing character-by-character as it goes. When you make a typing mistake, press Backspace to erase the wrong character and then type the correct one.

T I P   If you are a relatively fast touch typist, backspacing through five or six characters to erase an incorrect character and then retyping often is faster than moving the insertion point to the left, deleting and retyping the character, and then moving the insertion point back to the right to continue.

The Del (or Delete) key, used more often while editing text, leaves the insertion point in its current location and deletes characters to the right.

Use the key that gets the job done more quickly. When you must delete the character immediately to the left of the insertion point, for example, pressing Backspace is more efficient than pressing the left arrow and then Del.

Holding down the Backspace or Del key repeats the action, enabling you to delete several characters at once. Generally, any codes in the affected text remain intact (see "Understanding Hidden Codes," later in this chapter).

Deleting Words and Lines

With faster computers, you can be tempted to hold down the Backspace or Del key to delete all characters in a word. This technique can be inaccurate, however, and can force you to retype accidentally deleted characters.

■ **Cue:** Press Ctrl-Backspace to delete a word at a time.

Instead, to delete an entire word, position the insertion point anywhere in the word and press Ctrl-Backspace. This method also deletes any spaces or punctuation that follow the word (up to the next word).

To delete text from the insertion point to the end of the line, press Ctrl-Del. This key combination deletes everything except text that precedes the insertion point and any hard return ([HRt], placed in your text when you press the Enter key) at the end of the line. If the line ends with a soft return ([SRt], placed in the text by WordPerfect when wrapping text to the next line), press Ctrl-Del to continue deleting lines of text.

WordPerfect has no special method for deleting an entire line of text, but you can accomplish the same result by pressing Home and then Ctrl-Del. This key combination places the insertion point at the beginning of the line and then deletes the entire line.

Deleting Large Amounts of Text

A quick and easy method for deleting a large amount of text involves using the mouse to specify an area of text to delete. Follow these steps:

1. Move the mouse pointer to the beginning of the text you want to delete.

2. Press and hold the left mouse button while you drag the pointer to the other end of the text you want to delete. The text you select appears in reverse video (for example, white letters on a black background).

3. Release the mouse button.

4. Press Del or Backspace to delete the selected text.

■ **Cue:** Deleting lines or blocks of text also deletes any format codes found within that text. Deleting text with Backspace or Del, one character at a time, leaves most codes intact.

See Chapter 5, "Selecting and Editing Text," for details on how to select and delete predefined blocks of text, such as sentences, paragraphs, and pages, and how to select blocks of text by using the keyboard.

Restoring Deleted Text

If you accidentally delete a character or word, retyping the deleted text is relatively simple. Accidentally deleting larger portions of text, however, can be quite frustrating. Fortunately, WordPerfect offers two useful features to recover and restore deleted text: Undo and Undelete.

Of these two methods, Undelete is designed to be more forgiving. Each time you delete something, WordPerfect remembers the deletion in a *buffer*, a special storage area of your computer's memory. In fact, WordPerfect keeps track of the last three deletions made during your current editing session.

■ **Cue:** You can restore text deleted with Typeover by using the Undelete feature.

To restore deleted text, follow these steps:

1. Position the insertion point where you want to restore your deleted text (not necessarily at the same place where the text was deleted).

2. Choose **E**dit, **U**ndelete.

 Press Undelete (Alt-Shift-Backspace).

WordPerfect opens the Undelete dialog box and displays the most recently deleted text in reverse video at the insertion point in your text (see fig. 4.5). To restore or view a previous deletion, choose **P**revious. Each time you use this option, WordPerfect cycles among your three most recent deletions.

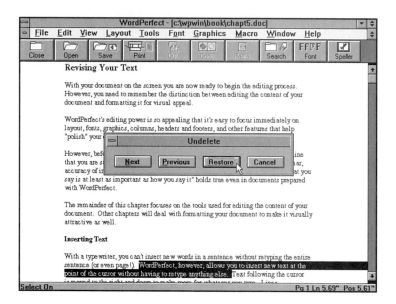

FIG. 4.5

The Undelete dialog box and deleted text to be restored.

3. When you are ready to restore one of the three deletions, choose **R**estore.

CAUTION: You can use the Undelete feature to restore accidentally deleted text, but be sure to restore as soon as possible. You probably don't realize how often you delete when you edit; the deletion you think WordPerfect safely remembers may have been replaced in quick succession by three more recent deletions.

Another, less reliable method for restoring deleted text is the Undo feature. Undo enables you to reverse the effect of nearly any procedure you mistakenly use. When you Undo a deletion, the result is similar to what happens when you Undelete a deletion. Unlike Undelete, however, Undo also reverses the effect of a deletion followed by any cursor movement. If you delete a word and then move the insertion point to the beginning of the document, for example, Undo returns to the place of the deletion and restores the word.

CAUTION: Don't depend on Undo to restore deleted text. After you begin a new procedure in WordPerfect, the act of deleting is forgotten and Undo forgets the deleted text.

Undo and Undelete aren't good substitutes for cutting, copying, and pasting. For more information on cutting, copying, and pasting, see Chapter 5, "Selecting and Editing Text."

Understanding Hidden Codes

What you see on-screen is almost exactly what you get when you print your document, because WordPerfect uses various hidden codes to control the display of your text. WordPerfect places a code at the end of every line, for example, to make the text return to the left side and move down one line. In fact, the code even reflects whether you pressed Enter ([HRt]) or WordPerfect wrapped the text because the line reached the margin ([SRt]).

To see the text with its hidden codes, choose View, Reveal Codes or press Reveal Codes (Alt-F3). WordPerfect splits the screen, showing the text as you normally see it in the upper half and the same text with the codes revealed in the lower half (see fig. 4.6).

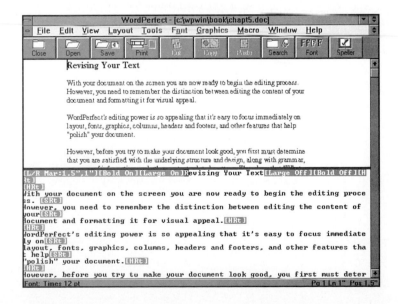

FIG. 4.6

A typical Reveal Codes display.

Codes always appear in brackets. Among the codes shown in figure 4.6 are ones that turn the boldface attribute on ([Bold On]) and off ([Bold Off]), several soft returns ([SRt]), and a margin setting ([L/R Mar:1.5",1"]).

Knowing more about codes, how they work, and where they are placed can help you to understand how WordPerfect controls the display of text. At times your display just doesn't look right; a quick peek into the Reveal Codes window may provide an answer as to why and what to do. (See the section "Using Boldface and Underline" for more examples of working with Reveal Codes.)

You don't need to memorize all the WordPerfect control codes. If you encounter a code you want to know more about, refer to table 4.1, which lists WordPerfect codes that may appear in Reveal Codes. Attribute codes always appear in pairs; the first includes On and the second includes Off.

Table 4.1. WordPerfect's Hidden Codes

Code	Definition
[-]	Hyphen Character
-	Soft Hyphen
[Adv]	Advance
[Bline:On]	Baseline Placement On
[Bline:Off]	Baseline Placement Off
[Block Pro]	Block Protection
[Bold On]	Boldface On
[Bold Off]	Boldface Off
[Box Num]	Caption in Graphics Box
[Cell]	Table Cell
[Center]	Center
[Center Pg]	Center Page Top to Bottom
[Cndl EOP]	Conditional End of Page
[Cntr Tab]	Centered Tab
[Col Def]	Column Definition
[Col On]	Beginning of Text Columns
[Col Off]	End of Text Columns
[Color]	Print Color

Code	Definition
[Comment]	Document Comment
[Date]	Date/Time Function
[Dbl Indent]	Double Indent
[Dbl Und On]	Double Underline On
[Dbl Und Off]	Double Underline Off
[DDE Link Begin]	DDE Link Begin
[DDE Link End]	DDE Link End
[Dec Tab]	Decimal-Aligned Tab
[Decml/Algn Char]	Decimal Character/Thousands Separator
[Def Mark:Index]	Index Definition
[Def Mark:List]	List Definition
[Def Mark:ToA]	Table of Authorities Definition
[Def Mark:ToC]	Table of Contents Definition
[Dorm HRt]	Dormant Hard Return
[DSRt]	Deletable Soft Return
[Embedded]	Embedded Code for Macro
[End C/A]	End Centering/Alignment
[End Def]	End of Index, List, or Table of Contents
[End Mark]	End of Marked Text
[End Opt]	Endnote Options
[Endnote]	Endnote
[Endnote Placement]	Endnote Placement
[Equ Box]	Equation Box
[Equ Opt]	Equation Box Options
[Ext Large On]	Extra Large Print On
[Ext Large Off]	Extra Large Print Off
[Fig Box]	Figure Box
[Fig Opt]	Figure Box Options
[Fine On]	Fine Print On
[Fine Off]	Fine Print Off

continues

Table 4.1. *(continued)*

Code	Definition
[Flsh Rgt]	Flush Right
[Font]	Base Font
[Footer A]	Footer A
[Footer B]	Footer B
[Footnote]	Footnote
[Force]	Force Odd/Even Page
[Ftn Opt]	Footnote Options
[HdCntrTab]	Hard Centered Tab
[HdDecTab]	Hard Decimal-Aligned Tab
[HdRgtTab]	Hard Right-Aligned Tab
[HdSpc]	Hard Space
[HdTab]	Hard Left-Aligned Tab
[Header A]	Header A
[Header B]	Header B
[HLine]	Horizontal Line
[HPg]	Hard Page Break
[Hrd Row]	Hard Row
[HRt]	Hard Return
[HRt-SPg]	Hard Return-Soft Page
[Hyph Ign Wrd]	Hyphenation Ignore Word
[Hyph On]	Hyphenation On
[Hyph Off]	Hyphenation Off
[HyphSRt]	Hyphenation Soft Return
[HZone]	Hyphenation Zone
[Indent]	Indent
[Index]	Index Entry
[Insert Pg Num]	Insert Page Number
[Italc On]	Italic on
[Italc Off]	Italic off
[Just Lim]	Word Spacing Justification Limits

Code	Definition
[Just:Center]	Center Justification
[Just:Full]	Full Justification
[Just:Left]	Left Justification
[Just:Right]	Right Justification
[Kern]	Kerning
[L/R Mar]	Left and Right Margins
[Lang]	Language
[Large On]	Large Print On
[Large Off]	Large Print Off
[Line Height Adj]	Line Height Adjustment
[Link]	Spreadsheet Link
[Link End]	Spreadsheet Link End
[Ln Height]	Line Height
[Ln Num On]	Line Numbering On
[Ln Num Off]	Line Numbering Off
[Ln Spacing]	Line Spacing
[Mar Rel]	Left Margin Release
[Mark:List]	List Entry
[Mark:ToC]	Table of Contents Entry
[New End Num]	New Endnote Number
[New Equ Num]	New Equation Box Number
[New Fig Num]	New Figure Box Number
[New Ftn Num]	New Footnote Number
[New Tbl Num]	New Table Number
[New Txt Num]	New Text Box Number
[New Usr Num]	New User Box Number
[Note Num]	Footnote/Endnote Number
[Open Style]	Open Style
[Outline Lvl Open Style]	Open Outline Style
[Outline Lvl Style On]	Paired Outline Style On
[Outline Lvl Style Off]	Paired Outline Style Off

continues

Table 4.1. *(continued)*

Code	Definition
[Outline On]	Outline On
[Outline Off]	Outline Off
[Outln On]	Outline On (Attribute)
[Outln Off]	Outline Off (Attribute)
[Ovrstk]	Overstrike
[Paper Sz/Typ]	Paper Size and Type
[Par Num]	Paragraph Number
[Par Num Def]	Paragraph Numbering Definition
[Pg Num]	New Page Number
[Pg Num Style]	Page Number Style
[Pg Numbering]	Page Numbering
[Ptr Cmnd]	Printer Command
[Redln On]	Redline On
[Redln Off]	Redline Off
[Ref]	Reference (Cross-reference)
[Rgt Tab]	Right-Aligned Tab
[Row]	Table Row
[Select]	Beginning of a Selection (Block)
[Shadw On]	Shadow on
[Shadw Off]	Shadow Off
[Sm Cap On]	Small Caps On
[Sm Cap Off]	Small Caps Off
[Small On]	Small Print On
[Small Off]	Small Print Off
[SPg]	Soft Page Break
[SRt]	Soft Return
[Stkout On]	Strikeout On
[Stkout Off]	Strikeout Off
[Style On]	Style On
[Style Off]	Style Off

Code	Definition
[Subdoc]	Subdocument (Master Documents)
[Subdoc Start]	Beginning of Subdocument
[Subdoc End]	End of Subdocument
[Subscpt On]	Subscript On
[Subscpt Off]	Subscript Off
[Suppress]	Suppress Page Format
[Suprscpt On]	Superscript On
[Suprscpt Off]	Superscript Off
[T/B Mar]	Top and Bottom Margins
[Tab]	Left-Aligned Tab
[Tab Set]	Tab Set
[Target]	Target (Cross-reference)
[Tbl Box]	Table Box
[Tbl Def]	Table Definition
[Tbl Off]	Table Off
[Tbl Opt]	Table Box Options
[Text Box]	Text Box
[ToA]	Table of Authorities Entry
[Txt Opt]	Text Box Options
[Und On]	Underlining On
[Und Off]	Underlining Off
[Undrln]	Underline Spaces/Tabs
[Unknown]	Code not recognized by WordPerfect for Windows
[Usr Box]	User-defined Box
[Usr Opt]	User-defined Box Options
[VLine]	Vertical Line
[Vry Large On]	Very Large Print On
[Vry Large Off]	Very Large Print Off
[W/O On]	Widow/Orphan On
[W/O Off]	Widow/Orphan Off
[Wrd/Ltr Spacing]	Word and Letter Spacing

Working with Reveal Codes

To become comfortable with hidden codes and their locations, try working for a while with Reveal Codes on to display the Reveal Codes window. With Reveal Codes on you can enter text and codes normally—but you see both screens change as you type.

In the Reveal Codes window, the insertion point and characters don't appear the same as in the document window. The characters are always boldfaced and monospaced; the insertion point's position displays in reverse video the character or code it rests on; for example, white letters on a black background.

If you must delete a specific code (such as a margin setting or a [Bold On] code), or if you want to make sure that a format code is placed in the proper location, you often can position the insertion point more accurately by using the Reveal Codes window as a guide. Move the insertion point with the direction keys, observing its location in the Reveal Codes window. Alternatively, you can use the mouse to position the insertion point by pointing at the location in the document window (or by pointing directly at the code in the Reveal Codes window) and clicking.

Changing the Size of the Reveal Codes Window

Some WordPerfect users prefer to work with Reveal Codes on. Others find the window distracting. One way to reduce the distraction is to reduce the size of the Reveal Codes window, using the mouse (no equivalent keyboard method exists). Follow these steps:

1. Position the mouse pointer on the sizing bar separating the upper and lower screens. The pointer turns into a double arrow.

2. Hold down the mouse button and drag the sizing bar down (see fig. 4.7) until the screens are split the way you want; then release the mouse button.

Until you change this setting again or exit WordPerfect, the size of your Reveal Codes window remains as you just set it.

After you turn off Reveal Codes, notice the small black bars at the top and bottom of the vertical scroll bar (see fig. 4.8). You can turn on Reveal Codes and set the window size at the same time by positioning the mouse pointer on a black bar (the pointer turns into a double arrow), holding the mouse button down, and dragging the sizing bar up or down until you get the window size you want. To turn off Reveal Codes, drag the sizing bar to the top or bottom of your screen.

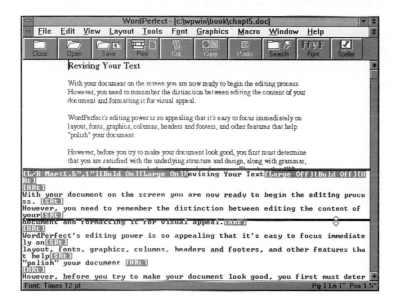

FIG. 4.7

Double-arrow pointer on the sizing bar resizing the Reveal Codes window.

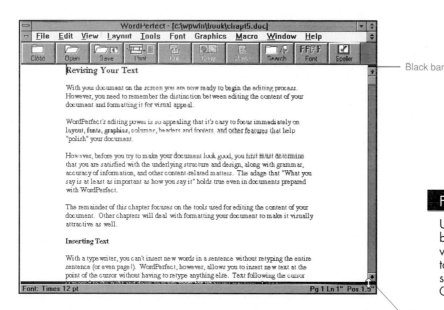

Black bar

FIG. 4.8

Using the black bars on the vertical scroll bar to turn on and size the Reveal Codes window.

Black bar

Using Boldface and Underline

Enhancing text generally is part of the formatting process that *follows* a thorough edit of the document's contents. Nevertheless, adding certain enhancements as you create your document often makes sense. You usually think of emphasizing a word or phrase at the time you create the text; if you wait until later, you may forget what you wanted to emphasize.

You can use boldfaced text to emphasize words, phrases, titles, and so on. Because at times boldfaced text can come across like shouting, use it sparingly. Underlined text has a somewhat gentler effect on the reader. Because underlining often crosses the descenders of certain letters, however (*y*, *p*, and *q* have descenders, *b*, *c*, and *t* don't), underlined text often is more difficult to read.

To boldface or underline characters as you create text, move the insertion point to where you want the enhanced text to begin. Then follow these steps:

1. To use boldfacing, press Ctrl-B or choose Font, **Bold**. To use underlining, press Ctrl-U or choose Font, **Underline**.

   Notice that the name of the font displayed on the left side of the status bar is boldfaced or underlined to indicate the enhancement for the text you are about to type.

2. Type the text. (Fig. 4.9 shows text that has been enhanced with boldface.)

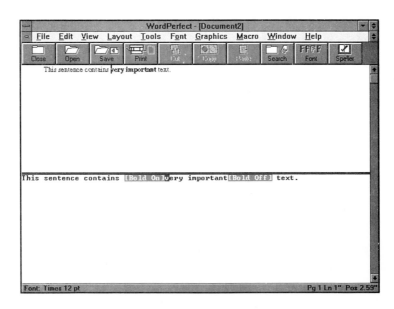

Split screen with bold attribute codes shown in Reveal Codes window and boldfaced text shown in document window.

3. To return to normal text, press Ctrl-B or Ctrl-U again (or choose **Font** and then **Bold**/**Underline** or **Normal**).

   Notice that the name of the font on the status bar is no longer boldfaced or underlined.

To see the effect of your creation, open the Reveal Codes window. In figure 4.9, a [Bold On] code precedes the boldfaced text and a [Bold Off] code follows the text. If you typed underlined text, you see [Und On] and [Und Off] codes instead.

Position the insertion point to the left of the [Bold On] or [Und On] code and note that the font displayed on the status bar is normal. Move the insertion point to the right until it highlights the [Bold On] or [Und On] code or is to the right of the code. Note that the font displayed on the status bar now is boldfaced or underlined. Continue moving the insertion point to the right until you pass the [Bold Off] or [Und Off] code. Again, the status bar font returns to normal.

Cue: Attribute codes such as [Bold On] and [Bold Off] always appear in pairs.

> **T I P**
>
> The more you work with WordPerfect, the more you rely on the status bar to tell where your insertion point is positioned in relationship to your attribute codes. The status bar saves you the time and trouble of turning Reveal Codes on and off.

For more information on font attributes, see Chapter 10, "Working with Fonts."

Removing Boldface and Underline Codes

In Reveal Codes, position the insertion point to the right of the [Bold On] or [Und On] code. Then turn off Reveal Codes. When you press Backspace, you may expect to delete the [Bold On] or [Und On] code, but instead you delete the space preceding the boldfaced or underlined word.

By default, WordPerfect prevents you from accidentally deleting attribute codes when using Backspace or Del. You must turn on Reveal Codes before WordPerfect enables you to delete the attribute codes.

Turn on Reveal Codes again and move the insertion point until it highlights one of the codes. Press Del. Notice that both the [Bold On] and [Bold Off] (or [Und On] and [Und Off]) codes disappear; because they always appear in pairs, deleting one code also deletes the other.

You can change the default so that WordPerfect prompts you to delete attribute codes when Reveal Codes is off. Choose File, Preferences, Environment; in the Environment Settings dialog box, choose Confirm on Code Deletion and then press Enter.

When both attribute codes are included in a block of selected text, deleting the selected text also deletes the attribute codes.

Attribute codes thus cannot be deleted with Backspace or Del except under one of the following conditions:

- Reveal Codes is turned on.

- The Confirm on Code Deletion option is selected in Preferences.

- Both attribute codes (on and off) are included in selected text that is deleted.

Searching and Replacing

One of WordPerfect's more powerful editing tools is its capacity to find words, phrases, and codes—and replace them with other words, phrases, and codes. Suppose that you are working with a long document, such as an annual report. You remember mentioning the Baxter Company but don't remember where. The Search feature can help you quickly find the name. You also may discover that the vice president's name has been spelled *Johnson* when it should have been *Jonson*. Using Search and Replace, you can fix that problem within seconds.

Searching

You can search for text from any point in your document, forward to the end or backward to the beginning. Suppose that you want to search for the word *Baxter* from your current location at the beginning of the document. Follow these steps:

1. Choose **Edit, Search**.

    Press Search (F2).

   The Search dialog box appears (see fig. 4.10).

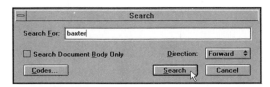

The Search
dialog box.

2. In the Search **For** text box, type **baxter**.

3. If you want to ignore headers, footers, footnotes, graphics, captions, and the like, choose Search Document **B**ody Only.

4. The default search **D**irection is Forward. If you want to search backward, choose Backward from the **D**irection pop-up list.

5. To search for codes, choose **C**odes (see "Searching for Codes," later in this chapter).

6. To begin the search, choose **S**earch or press Enter.

WordPerfect looks for an exact match for the *search string* you specify. In this example, the search string is the letters *baxter*. A search string also can include codes.

When WordPerfect finds the first occurrence of the search string, the program positions the insertion point immediately following the string and closes the dialog box. If the word or phrase doesn't exist in the text, WordPerfect briefly displays the message String Not Found on the left side of the status bar and returns to the last insertion point position.

Choosing Search Criteria

WordPerfect looks for an exact match to the search string. The exception is that lowercase letters find both lower- and uppercase equivalents, and uppercase letters find only uppercase equivalents. The string *baxter* finds *baxter*, *Baxter*, or *BAXTER*, but *JONES* finds only *JONES*.

WordPerfect may find an exact match in part of a word. If you search for *he*, for example, WordPerfect stops for *them*, *rather*, or *she*. Sometimes you can add spaces or punctuation to make your search more accurate. Searching for " *her* " (with spaces preceding and following the word) avoids finding *there* but also misses finding " *her*," which is followed by a comma rather than a space.

Repeating a Search

If the first match isn't the one you want, you can repeat the search in the same direction by choosing **E**dit, **S**earch or pressing Search (F2). Because WordPerfect remembers your last search request, you just press Enter.

A quicker way to repeat a search is to choose **E**dit, Search Next or press Search Next (Shift-F2) to find the next occurrence; or choose **E**dit, Search Previous or press Search Previous (Alt-F2) to find the preceding occurrence.

Searching for Codes

You cannot type even simple codes such as [Tab] or [HRt] in the Search **F**or text box of the Search dialog box. Instead, you must select codes from a list in the Codes dialog box that WordPerfect displays when you choose **C**odes. To enter codes in the text box, follow these steps:

1. Choose C**o**des in the Search dialog box. WordPerfect displays the Codes dialog box with codes that can appear in the search string listed (see fig. 4.11).

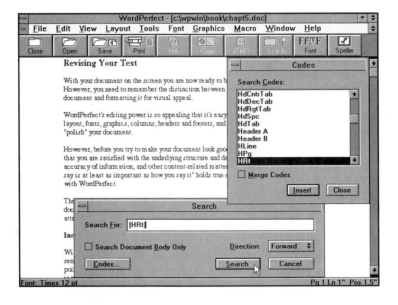

FIG. 4.11

Searching for a code.

2. Scroll through the list to select the code you want to find. If you know the spelling of the hidden code (refer to table 4.1), you can type the first characters; WordPerfect scrolls to that name. Typing **hrt**, for example, takes you directly to [HRt].

3. Choose **Insert**. WordPerfect enters the code in the Search For text box of the Search dialog box.

   The Codes dialog box closes when you begin the search or close the Search dialog box.

■ **Cue:** Only those codes that can appear in a search string are displayed in the Codes list box.

With the Search feature, you can search for font changes, margin settings, boldfacing codes, and more. If you are having problems with your format, for example, Search can help you quickly find the offending codes.

> If you don't remember how a word is spelled, you can substitute the code [Any Char] for any letter in your search string. The string sm[Any Char]th[Any Char], for example, finds *Smith*, *Smythe*, or *smother*.

T I P

Searching and Replacing Text

At times you must replace the search string with something else. Suppose that you must replace *Johnson* with *Jonson* throughout your document. Follow these steps:

1. Position the insertion point at the beginning of the document.

2. Choose **Edit**, **Replace**.

    Press Replace (Ctrl-F2).

   The Search and Replace dialog box appears (see fig. 4.12).

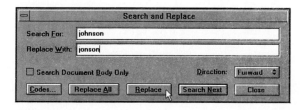

FIG. 4.12

The Search and Replace dialog box.

3. In the Search **For** text box, type **johnson**, the string you want to find and replace.

You can use lowercase strings to find upper- and lowercase occurrences. If a capitalized word is found, WordPerfect changes only the first letter of the replace string to a capital letter. When you replace *Johnson*, for example, *jonson* becomes *Jonson*. When you replace a completely uppercase word, only the first character of the replacement string is capitalized. The string *TITLE*, for example, when replaced by *chapter*, becomes *Chapter*.

4. Choose Replace **W**ith. Type **jonson**, the string you want to insert in place of the existing text.

5. Choose Search Document **B**ody Only if you don't want to search headers, footers, footnotes, captions, and so on.

6. Specify the search **D**irection by selecting Forward or Backward from the pop-up list. (Forward is the default.)

7. Choose **C**odes to insert codes into the search or replace string (refer to fig. 4.11). You cannot include certain searchable codes in the replace string. If you try to select such a code, WordPerfect displays the message Selected Code NOT allowed in replace string.

After you type the search and the replace strings and are ready to begin replacing, you have two more options:

- ■ Cue: The Search and Replace dialog box remains on-screen throughout a search and replace operation.

- ■ You can decide which occurrences WordPerfect replaces. Choose Search **N**ext to move to the first occurrence of your search string. Then choose **R**eplace to replace that occurrence with your replace string or Search **N**ext to skip that occurrence and move to the next. If you choose **R**eplace, WordPerfect makes the replacement and moves to the next occurrence.

- ■ Choose Replace **A**ll to have WordPerfect replace all specified occurrences.

With either method, WordPerfect searches and replaces until it no longer finds a match, and then reports String Not Found and returns to the last location where the program found the string.

CAUTION: Search and Replace can become "search and destroy" if not used carefully. When you specify the search and replace strings, consider the effect the replacement will have. Replacing all cases of *he* with *she*, for example, can result in words like *tsheir* or *cshecking account*. When in doubt, use **R**eplace and Search **N**ext to verify each replacement.

Save yourself headaches by saving your document before replacing. If necessary, you can close the current document without saving and open the original "unreplaced" document.

T I P

Using Search or Replace in Other Ways

Besides the examples mentioned earlier, Search/Replace is a powerful tool for editing the content of your document. Consider the following ideas:

■ **Cue:** You can use Search and Replace for more than changing misspelled words.

■ You have a habit of using certain cliches or jargon. Search can help you find whether you have used such words in your document. You can replace each occurrence by deleting the old word and typing something different, or just use Search and Replace.

■ You must use an unusually long phrase that appears repeatedly in your document. Suppose that in a report you often refer to a client's company, Allied Manufacturing and Skateboard Rentals Inc. Rather than typing the entire name each time, you can type **amsr** and then replace it later with the full name.

■ You created your document using two hard returns between each single-spaced paragraph. Now you want to use double-spaced text but don't want four lines of space between each paragraph. You can search for [HRt][HRt] and replace with [HRt].

■ Your editor tells you to get rid of the underlined text throughout your document. You can search for and replace all occurrences of [Und On] with nothing (that is, don't type anything in the Replace With text box).

Using Document Comments

You are familiar, no doubt, with the sticky little note papers that offices use to attach comments to documents. WordPerfect's electronic equivalent is the Comment box (see fig. 4.13).

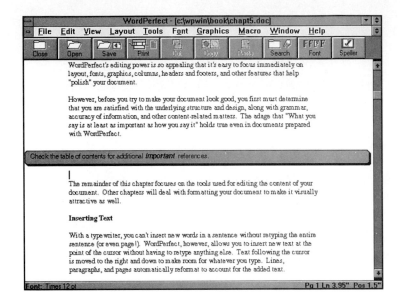

FIG. 4.13

A sample
comment box.

Cue: Text in a comment box doesn't print.

You can create an on-screen comment box anywhere in your document. You can hide comment boxes, convert existing text to a comment box, or convert comment boxes to regular text.

As a writing tool, comments can be quite useful. You probably can imagine many uses for the Comment feature. Consider the following:

- As you create text, you get an idea you want to develop, but you aren't sure where the idea should go. Create a comment box with the basics of the idea. Later, the comment reminds you to find a place for the idea and to develop it fully.

- As you edit text, you come across a statement you think is incorrect. Create a comment to remind yourself or someone else to check the statement and to make corrections if necessary.

- You create a new form for the clerical staff to use. You want to prompt them to follow certain procedures without having to look for printed instructions. Place the instructions in a comment box.

- You want to keep a certain paragraph in a document but don't always want the paragraph printed. Place the paragraph in a comment box; when you need it, convert the comment to text.

Creating a Comment

To create a comment box, follow these steps:

1. Position the insertion point where you want the comment box to appear.

2. Choose **Tools, Comment, Create.** The Create Comment dialog box appears (see fig. 4.14).

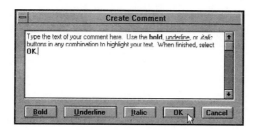

FIG. 4.14

The Create Comment dialog box.

3. In the text box, type the text you want to include in your comment.

4. Choose the **Bold, Underline,** or **Italic** buttons in any combination to enhance your text. **Note:** Pressing Ctrl-B, Ctrl-U, or Ctrl-I doesn't work in this text box.

5. Choose OK to place the comment box in your text.

If you use comments often, you can add a button to your Button Bar that enables you to create comments just by clicking the Comment button. See Chapter 19 for instructions.

Editing and Deleting Comments

As the Reveal Codes window in figure 4.15 shows, comment boxes are codes that you can delete, move, or edit. If you insert a comment in the middle of a line of text, the text is split on-screen.

To change the contents of an existing comment box, position the insertion point anywhere past the comment box and choose **Tools, Comment, Edit.** An easier method is to position the mouse pointer on the comment box and double-click.

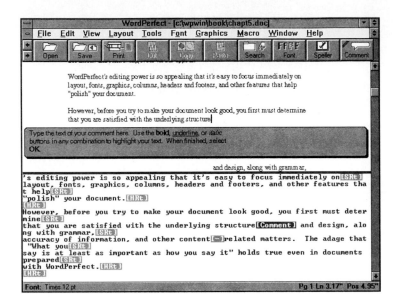

FIG. 4.15

A Comment code
shown in the
Reveal Codes
window.

In either case, WordPerfect displays the Edit Comment dialog box, which looks and functions like the Create Comment dialog box (refer to fig. 4.14). After making your changes, choose OK.

To delete a comment, you must first turn on Reveal Codes (Alt-F3) and then delete the [Comment] code. This procedure removes the comment code and the text of the comment.

T I P   To remove all comments from your document, use Search and Replace to find the [Comment] codes; then replace them with nothing (that is, don't type anything in the Replace With text box).

Hiding Comments

If you or other users find comment boxes distracting, hide the comments by choosing View, Comments.

Hiding comment boxes doesn't remove them. You can view them again at any time by choosing View, Comments again. Choosing to hide comments affects the display of comments in all your documents until you choose View, Comments to display them again.

Converting Text to Comments and Comments to Text

Sometimes you may have text that you don't want to print, or text that you may not want to use all the time. Suppose that you are an attorney, for example, and you have a paragraph used only in severe cases. You can convert this text to comment boxes and later convert the comments to text if you want to print the text.

To convert text to a comment, follow these steps:

1. Position the insertion point at the beginning of the text you want to convert.

2. Hold down the mouse button, drag the pointer to the end of the text you want to convert, and release the mouse button.

3. Choose **Tools**, **Comment**, **Create** to convert the selected text to a comment.

When you want to include or print the comment in the document text, follow these steps:

1. Position the insertion point after the comment box you want to convert.

2. Choose **Tools**, Comment, Convert to **Text** to insert the text of the comment box into your document.

Chapter Summary

In this chapter you learned how easily you can change the contents of your document. In fact, you now can use the tools that comprise the heart and soul of word processing.

Practice and learn the procedures found in this chapter, because what you learn from this point builds on these fundamentals: opening and retrieving documents; inserting, overwriting, and deleting text; restoring deleted text; working with hidden codes; using basic enhancements; searching for and replacing text and codes; and using document comments as an editing aid.

Selecting and Editing Text

After you have written a document in WordPerfect, you may need to edit and revise your work. Through the Select Text function, WordPerfect for Windows enables you to use many powerful word processing features on a selected portion of your document.

Before word processors, text that needed revision required the writer to retype the page. Moving a portion of a document to another location wasn't possible. Even minor corrections were noticeable, making the document look less professional.

With computerized word processing came the capability to modify text without retyping the entire page. Revising text required deleting and retyping only the affected portion of the document.

WordPerfect's Select Text feature takes this capability one step further. With the Select Text feature, you no longer need to delete text and retype to make revisions. To move a paragraph, for example, you *select* the paragraph you want to move, *cut* the selection to remove it from the current location, and *paste* the text to the desired location.

■ Gary Pickavet is the Assistant Superintendent for business and Data Processing Services for the Santa Barbara County Education Office. He uses WordPerfect regularly for research projects and for preparing supporting materials for presentations.

The capability to select text and execute WordPerfect commands on the selected text makes many editing procedures easy. To use italic for a word or paragraph, for example, you select the text and choose the WordPerfect Italic command (Ctrl-I). To change the margins for a portion of the document, you select the text where you want to apply the command, choose **Layout**, **M**argins (or press Ctrl-F8) and specify the desired settings for the selected text.

In short, with the advanced editing capabilities of the Select Text feature in WordPerfect for Windows, you can focus on your writing as you compose a document, instead of concentrating on how the text looks. After you finish typing the text, you then can focus energy on editing the text and improving the look of the document.

When you use the Select Text feature, the selected portion of your document is highlighted on your computer screen (in reverse video). The highlighting shows graphically that the selected text is ready for a command and shows to which portion of the document the command will apply.

A selection can be as small as one character or as large as the entire document. Despite the name of the feature (Select Text), you can include graphics in the selection and apply *some* WordPerfect features (such as Cut and Paste) to the selected text and graphics. When you use the Select Text feature, WordPerfect displays a `Select On` or `Select Mode` message on the left side of the status bar at the bottom of the WordPerfect window.

This chapter shows you how to do the following:

- Select text with the mouse and keyboard
- Move or copy selected text and graphics to another location within your document
- Append selected text and graphics
- Move or copy selected text and graphics to another Windows application
- Delete selected text and graphics
- Save a portion of a document as a file
- Print a portion of a document
- Enhance selected text with attributes such as underlining, boldface, and italic
- Change the typeface and size of selected text
- Change the layout (margins, alignment, line spacing, and so forth) of selected text

■ Change selected text to upper- or lowercase characters

■ Work with a rectangular selection

■ Apply styles to selected text

Besides applying common features described in this chapter to a selection, the text selection process can be used with other specialized WordPerfect features, such as working with tables, using the speller, and creating an index. The individual chapters on those features describe how to use these specialized functions with selections.

Understanding the Select Process

The Select Text feature enables you to perform various editing functions on a selected portion of your document. Why work with selections? Often, after you create a document, you want to change the document's appearance or the arrangement of your words. The capacity to work with selected text enables you to make those changes—quickly. You don't need to delete and retype text to edit it.

The steps used to apply a WordPerfect command to a selected portion of your document are always the same:

1. Position the insertion point at the beginning of the information you want to select.

2. Highlight the text with the mouse or keyboard.

3. Choose a WordPerfect operation to be performed on the selection.

4. Cancel the selection, if necessary, using the mouse or keyboard.

Highlighting a Selection

You must highlight a selection before performing any operation on that selection. WordPerfect highlights your selection on-screen (see fig. 5.1). The highlighted text shows the portion of your document that will change when you choose the function to perform. (***Note:*** Graphics and captions don't appear highlighted but are included in the selection. Only text is highlighted.)

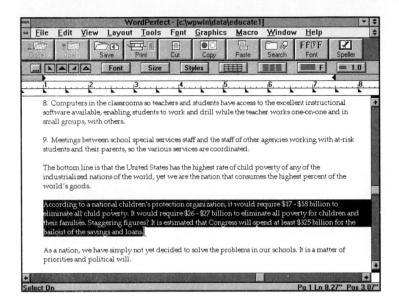

FIG. 5.1

An example of
selected text.

You can make selections by using the mouse, the keyboard, or a combination of both. Experiment with the different methods and use the method you find most comfortable.

Using the Mouse To Highlight a Selection

If you have used a mouse with other programs, you should feel right at home with WordPerfect for Windows. The mouse techniques are similar to techniques in other Windows applications and even the Macintosh computer.

In WordPerfect, selecting a portion of your document with the mouse is quick and easy. Follow these steps:

1. Move the mouse pointer to the left side of the first character you want to select. (While in the document, the mouse pointer looks like a tall, thin capital letter *I* and is called the *I-beam* pointer.)

2. Press the left mouse button to move the insertion point to the location of the mouse pointer. This *click* anchors your selection at that location. The insertion point blinks on the left side of the first character to be included in the selection.

(*Note:* If the Reveal Codes window is open at the bottom of the screen, the first character in the selection is highlighted.)

3. Press and hold down the left mouse button while you move the mouse pointer to the end of the area you want to select—a process called *dragging*. As you select text, WordPerfect highlights the characters on-screen. Release the mouse button when you have highlighted all the information you want to include in the selection.

■ **Cue:** Keep the left mouse button pressed while you drag the mouse pointer to highlight a selection.

If you release the mouse button while dragging, you can continue selecting text by pressing and holding down the Shift key before you press the mouse button again. (Pressing the mouse button without Shift cancels the current selection and moves the anchor point to the location of the mouse pointer.) After you resume dragging, you can release the Shift key.

T I P

When you want to include formatting codes with your selection, remember that these codes don't appear on-screen, but you can view them with Reveal Codes by choosing View, Reveal Codes (or press Alt-F3). When you select part of the document, the [Select] code appears in Reveal Codes to show where the selection starts. The formatting codes you want to include in the selection must appear between [Select] and the end of the selection (shown by a box representing the current location of the insertion point). For more information about using Reveal Codes, see Chapter 4, "Editing a Document."

T I P

While dragging the mouse, if you want to highlight a selection that extends beyond the portion of the document displayed on-screen, continue to hold down the mouse button while you move the mouse pointer beyond the edge of the document window in the direction you want to move. WordPerfect scrolls the document and highlights text until you bring the mouse pointer back into the document window. When you see the place where you want to stop the selection, move the mouse pointer to the desired ending point and release the mouse button.

T I P Besides dragging to highlight a selection, you can click the mouse to anchor the insertion point and then move the mouse pointer to the desired ending point of the selection. Then press and hold the Shift key and click the left mouse button. This action highlights the selection from the anchored location at the insertion point to the location of the mouse pointer. This method is especially useful when highlighting the entire document or large sections.

After you highlight a selection, if you change your mind about the amount of text selected, press and hold Shift while you click the mouse pointer at a new location. The highlighted text area is enlarged if you click farther from the anchor point or reduced if you click closer to the anchor point.

CAUTION: Pressing a character while a selection is highlighted deletes and replaces the selected text with the character you type. This shortcut can save you the trouble of pressing Del first, but a problem can occur if you unintentionally press a letter. To remove the unwanted text and restore the deleted material, immediately choose **U**ndo from the **E**dit menu.

WordPerfect provides several mouse shortcuts you can use when highlighting selections. These methods are shown in table 5.1. Using these shortcuts saves time when you want to highlight words, sentences, and paragraphs quickly.

Table 5.1. Other Mouse Selection Methods

Selection Action	Result
Double-click	Selects a word
Triple-click	Selects a sentence
Quadruple-click	Selects a paragraph
Shift-click	Selects from insertion point to location of mouse pointer

Using the Keyboard To Highlight a Selection

You can highlight text from the keyboard without using a mouse. Follow these steps:

1. Move the insertion point to the first character you want to include in the selection.

2. Press Shift-right arrow or Shift-left arrow, depending on the area you want to select.

3. While holding down the Shift key, use the direction keys (left arrow, up arrow, PgDn, and so on) to move to the end of the text you want to select.

To deselect highlighted text, press a direction key without pressing Shift.

WordPerfect provides several shortcuts you can use when highlighting text with the keyboard. These methods are shown in Table 5.2. Using these shortcuts saves time when you highlight words, sentences, and paragraphs.

Cue: To include hidden formatting codes in your selection, choose **V**iew Reveal **C**odes (or press Alt-F3) and be sure that the codes appear within the selected section of the document.

The keyboard shortcuts in table 5.2 work properly only if you have specified the CUA Compliant keyboard as your preference. (CUA stands for Common User Access, a standard used in Windows applications to ensure that keystrokes for standard commands are the same in each program.) To determine the keyboard preference in use, choose **P**references from the **F**ile menu and **K**eyboard from the Preferences menu. If you are using the CUA Compliant keyboard, you see the following in the WordPerfect Keyboard dialog box:

```
Name: [CUA Keyboard]
```

You can find more information about specifying keyboard preferences in Chapter 29, "Customizing WordPerfect with Preferences."

T I P

Table 5.2. Other CUA Keyboard Selection Methods	
Selection Action	**Result**
Shift-right arrow or Shift-left arrow	Selects one character to the right or left, respectively
Shift-up arrow or Shift-down arrow	Selects up or down one line, respectively
Shift-End	Selects to end of line (before codes)
Shift-End, Shift-End	Selects to end of line (after codes)
Shift-Home	Selects to beginning of line (after codes)
Shift-Home, Shift-Home	Selects to beginning of line (before codes)
Shift-PgUp	Selects to top of screen and then up one more screen each time you press Shift-PgUp
Shift-PgDn	Selects to bottom of screen and then down one more screen each time you press Shift-PgDn
Shift-Alt-PgUp	Selects to first line on preceding page
Shift-Alt-PgDn	Selects to first line on next page
Shift-Ctrl-right arrow or Shift-Ctrl-left arrow	Selects one word to the right or left, respectively
Shift-Ctrl-up arrow or Shift-Ctrl-down arrow	Selects up or down one paragraph, respectively
Shift-Ctrl-Home	Selects to beginning of document (after codes)
Shift-Ctrl-Home, Shift-Ctrl-Home	Selects to beginning of document (before codes)
Shift-Ctrl-End	Selects to end of document (after codes)

Using Select Mode To Highlight a Selection

Select mode works much like the WordPerfect 5.1 for DOS Block feature. When you type a character in Select mode, instead of deleting and replacing the highlighted selection with the typed text, the selected area extends to the next occurrence of the letter pressed. Pressing Enter, for example, extends the selection to the end of the paragraph.

You can activate Select mode only with a CUA Compliant keyboard.

After you activate Select mode with the Select command (F8), you can change the size of the selection by using the standard WordPerfect direction keys, without holding down the Shift key. You also can use Select mode with the keyboard selection methods shown in table 5.2.

■ **Cue:** Pressing Shift and clicking the left mouse button switches from Select mode to WordPerfect for Windows normal Select On function.

To use Select mode, follow these steps:

1. Move the insertion point to the first character you want to include in the selection.

2. Press Select (F8). Select Mode appears in the status line at the bottom of the screen. (*Note:* If the Reveal Codes screen is open, the first character in the selection is highlighted.)

3. Use the direction keys to move to the end of the text you want to select. The text is highlighted on-screen as you select.

Canceling a Highlighted Selection

After highlighting text, you may decide to cancel the selection. If you started the selection by using the mouse or holding the Shift key and moving the insertion point, Select On appears at the bottom of the screen. You can cancel this type of selection with any of the following methods:

■ Click the mouse anywhere in the document (without holding down the Shift key)

■ Move the insertion point with one of the direction keys (for example, the right-arrow key)

■ Press Select (F8)

If you selected the text by pressing Select (F8) and entering Select mode, cancel the selection with any of the following methods:

■ Click the mouse anywhere in the document (without holding down the Shift key)

■ Press Select (F8) again

Performing Functions on Selections

After you highlight a selection, you can perform the desired WordPerfect operation on the selected portion of your document. Note that while information is selected, the message Select On or Select Mode appears on the status line at the bottom of the screen and the text is highlighted on-screen. This message indicates that WordPerfect is ready to perform a function on just the highlighted portion of text.

After you perform a WordPerfect command, the selection remains highlighted so that you can apply more changes to the selection without having to reselect the text. When you finish applying commands, cancel the selection.

After you highlight a selection, you can perform the following functions with the highlighted text (these functions are discussed throughout this book):

- Append
- Block Protect
- Bold
- Center
- Columns
- Copy
- Cut
- Delete
- Flush Right
- Font Size and Appearance
- Move (Cut & Paste)
- Print
- Paste
- Save
- Search
- Sort
- Speller
- Style
- Underline

Transferring Selected Text to Another Location

Good information belongs in the right places. As you work with a document, you probably find information you want to move or copy to another location. A graphical user interface (GUI) product like WordPerfect for Windows makes the transfer of information easy.

WordPerfect uses the commands Cut, Copy, and Append to transfer text to the Windows Clipboard. Then you can use the Paste command to place the text elsewhere in the current document, in other WordPerfect documents, or in other Windows applications. The current Clipboard information remains unchanged until the next Cut, Copy, or Append operation is performed. To view the Clipboard's contents, use the Windows Clipboard program. See your Windows manual for more information about the Clipboard and the Clipboard program. When you exit Windows, any information on the Clipboard is erased.

T I P

If you include the codes in the selected text, information that you cut, copy, or append to the Clipboard retains its size and text enhancement attributes (such as Large or Italic). Unless the typeface (such as Helvetica) is defined within the selected area, however, the selection assumes the typeface in effect at the location where you paste the information.

Moving or Copying a Selection

When you finish typing a document, you often find text that you want to place elsewhere in the document. You can move or copy this text easily with WordPerfect's Cut and Paste functions.

To move or copy a selection, follow these steps:

1. Select the text, graphics, or combination of text and graphics that you want to move or copy.

2. To move a selection, choose Cut from the Edit menu.

   CUA Press Cut (Shift-Delete).

   To copy a selection, choose Copy from the Edit menu.

   CUA Press Copy (Ctrl-Ins).

3. Move the insertion point to where you want to place the selection.

4. Choose Paste from the Edit menu.

   CUA Press Paste (Shift-Insert).

■ **Cue:** The Cut, Copy, and Paste commands are on the Button Bar provided with WordPerfect; selecting these commands from the Button Bar saves time.

Appending a Selection

Cue: The selection remains on the Clipboard until you issue another Cut, Copy, or Append command or leave Windows—a capability that enables you to paste the same information repeatedly.

When you choose the Cut or Copy commands in WordPerfect, the information transferred to the Windows Clipboard replaces any previous selection. The Append command doesn't replace Clipboard information; instead Append adds the new information to any existing selection on the Clipboard.

Because WordPerfect offers no Append command shortcut keys, consider adding the Append command to the Button Bar. Figure 5.2 shows an example of the Button Bar with an Append button. (See Chapter 19 for information on adding a command to the Button Bar.)

FIG. 5.2

The Button Bar with an Append command button.

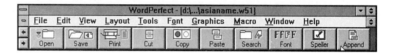

To append a selection to the Clipboard, follow these steps:

1. Select the text, graphics, or text and graphics combination you want to append.
2. Choose **A**ppend from the **E**dit menu, or if you have added the Append command to the Button Bar, click the Append button.

You can now paste the original information and the new information to the location of your choice with the Paste command, described previously.

Transferring Selections to Other Windows Applications

In WordPerfect for Windows, information saved on the Windows Clipboard is available by choosing the **P**aste command on the **E**dit menu of other Windows applications. In the same way, you can paste into WordPerfect documents information that was cut or copied to the Clipboard from other Windows applications.

Information on the Clipboard stays there until you cut or copy more information to the Clipboard, clear the Clipboard with the Windows Clipboard commands, or exit Windows. Refer to your Windows manual for more details about the Windows Clipboard.

Deleting and Undeleting a Selection

Deleting a selection is as simple as highlighting the selection and pressing the Backspace or Del key. If you type text while a selection is highlighted, you delete the selection and replace it with the new text (except in Select mode, described in the section "Using Select Mode To Highlight a Selection" in this chapter).

A deleted selection is not placed on the Clipboard and cannot be retrieved using the Paste command. You can restore (undelete) the deleted selection, however, if you act quickly. WordPerfect stores your last three deletions so that you can restore them if you change your mind.

To undelete a selection, follow these steps:

■ **Cue:** You can undelete only the last three deletions.

1. Move the insertion point to the location where you want to retrieve the deleted selection.

2. Choose Undelete from the Edit menu.

   CUA Press Undelete (Alt-Shift-Backspace).

3. The latest deletion appears at the insertion point.

4. The Undelete dialog box appears, enabling you to see other deletions (by choosing Next or Previous), Restore the deletion shown on-screen, or Cancel the Undelete command. Figure 5.3 shows the Undelete dialog box.

FIG. 5.3

The Undelete dialog box.

5. Choose Next or Previous until the deleted selection you want to restore is displayed. Then choose Restore.

Saving a Selection in a File

You can save a selected part of your document to a file to be retrieved later in another document or in an application that doesn't have access to the Windows Clipboard.

■ **Cue:** You can move selections between WordPerfect documents or Windows applications immediately by using the Cut or Copy and Paste commands.

To save a selection to a file, follow these steps:

1. Highlight the selection you want to save as a separate file.

2. Choose **S**ave or Save **A**s from the **F**ile menu.

    Press Save (Shift-F3) or Save As (F3).

3. If you want to save the file in a format other than the WordPerfect format, choose the desired file format from the **F**ormat list. (See Chapter 3, "Managing Files," for more information about other file formats.)

4. If you want to save the file in a directory different from the current directory, specify the desired drive and directory.

5. Type a file name in the Save **A**s text box.

6. Choose Sa**v**e to save the selection as a file and return to your document.

Printing a Selection

Sometimes you need to print only part of a document, or even part of one page—maybe one or two paragraphs. Just as you can save a selection from the document as a file, you can print a selection.

Follow these steps to print a selection:

1. Highlight the selection you want to print.

2. Choose **P**rint from the **F**ile menu.

    Press Print (F5).

   The Print dialog box appears.

3. Specify the desired print options. (See Chapter 9, "Basic Printing," for a description of print options.)

4. Choose **P**rint to print the selection and return to your document.

Changing the Appearance of a Selection

When you are using your creative talents to type a WordPerfect document, you probably don't want to give much thought to the document's appearance until you finish typing. By using selections, you can go through the finished document and quickly modify the appearance of selected portions. Figure 5.4 shows an example of many of the enhancement attributes that you can use with text in WordPerfect. The next section describes these attributes and methods for applying the attributes to selected text.

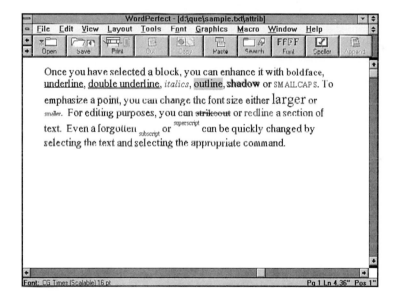

CAUTION: Some printers—daisywheel and certain dot-matrix printers, for example—don't support the font or size choices shown on the WordPerfect menus. Also, not all text attributes are available for all typefaces—even for laser printers. Consult your printer manual for more information about the fonts and attributes available for your printer.

Enhancing the Appearance of Text

On the Font menu, WordPerfect provides various enhancements to change your text's appearance. The list of enhancements includes Normal, Bold, Italic, Underline, Double Underline, Redline, and Strikeout. If you have a color printer, you also can change the color of a selection of text.

Selecting the Font option from the Font menu provides the additional enhancements Outline, Shadow, and Small Caps. These text enhancements are described in detail in Chapter 10, "Working with Fonts."

 WordPerfect Corporation provides the bold attribute on the Button Bar. If you regularly use certain enhancements (such as italic or outlining), consider adding them to the Button Bar.

To change the appearance of a selection of text, select the text that you want to change. Choose Font and choose the desired enhancement(s). The selection remains highlighted so that you can apply additional enhancements to the block.

If you change your mind about an enhancement you applied to selected text, reselect the text and choose the enhancement again. WordPerfect removes the enhancement from the text.

Changing the Font or Font Size

As you enter text, WordPerfect displays the currently used font on the status line at the bottom of the screen, as shown here:

```
Font: CG Times (Scalable) 12pt
```

After you compose a document in WordPerfect, you may want to change selected portions of the text to different typefaces or sizes. If you typed the document with a Times Roman font in a 12-point type size, for example, you can change the title line to a larger point size with a boldfaced attribute and change a quotation to a smaller font size (for example, 10-point). Figure 5.5 shows an example of an extra-large boldfaced headline and its impact on a document. These seemingly complex changes are simplified by applying the appropriate WordPerfect commands to the highlighted selection.

You can change the font in various ways. Using the Size option on the Font menu, you can change the font size of a text block to any of these font sizes: Fine, Small, Large, Very Large, Extra Large.

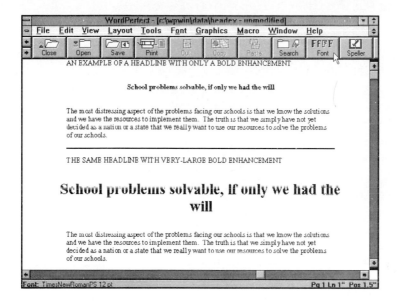

FIG. 5.5

Using a large font size for a headline.

By choosing the Font option from the Font menu, or pressing Font (F9), you can specify a point size or scroll through a list of predefined font sizes to apply to the selection. Only point sizes supported by the selected font and printer are shown.

You can choose superscript and subscript sizes directly from the Font menu.

To change the font or font size, follow these steps:

1. Highlight a selection whose font or font size you want to change.

2. From the Font menu, choose the desired font attribute.

The selection remains highlighted to enable you to apply additional enhancements, or more font or size changes.

Changing the Layout of a Selection

Besides the choices you make for fonts and text enhancement in your document, the layout of the document can greatly enhance readability and impact. WordPerfect provides a wide range of layout options, such as text justification, line spacing, and margin settings.

The various layout commands appear on the Layout menu and subsequent menus and dialog boxes. From the **L**ayout menu, for example, you can choose the **M**argins command to access the Margins dialog box, where you can change the left and right margins for the selection.

Many (but not all) Layout commands can be applied to selections. Layout commands that cannot be applied to selections are dimmed on-screen, indicating that the commands are not available.

From the **L**ayout, **L**ine menu, you can choose the following commands to apply to the selection:

Command	Purpose
Tab Set	Changes tab settings
Spacing	Changes spacing between lines
Height	Changes line height
Numbering	Applies line numbering to lines
Center	Centers between left and right margins
Flush Right	Aligns selection with right margin

When you choose **T**ab Set, **S**pacing, **H**eight, or **N**umbering, WordPerfect displays a dialog box requesting setting information appropriate to the option. For more information about **L**ayout, **L**ine commands, see Chapter 6, "Formatting Text."

By selecting **J**ustification from the **L**ayout menu, you can apply one of the following text alignment formats to your selection:

Left

Right

Center

Full

T I P Normally, you use the **C**enter and **F**lush Right commands on the **L**ayout, **L**ine menu to change the alignment of the current line only. When you press Enter, the next line returns to the left margin. The **R**ight and **C**enter options on the **L**ayout, **J**ustification menu change the center or right alignment of text until you choose another justification command. When applied to selected text, these commands justify all the highlighted text.

From the **L**ayout, **P**age menu, you can choose **B**lock Protect to prevent the selected text from being split between two pages. When a selection of text is protected, WordPerfect moves the entire block to a subsequent page if the block doesn't fit on the page where the protected block begins.

From the **L**ayout, Typesetting menu, you can specify whether WordPerfect underlines spaces between words and the space between tabs when you are using the underline feature. The Typesetting menu also has several advanced features—such as Word Spacing, Letter Spacing, and Kerning—that can be applied to a selection. These advanced features are described in detail in Chapter 15, "Working with Advanced Printing Techniques."

To change the layout of a selection, highlight the selection whose layout you want to change. Choose **L**ayout and then choose the desired layout command(s). The selection remains highlighted so that you can apply additional WordPerfect commands.

Changing Selections to Uppercase or Lowercase

You can use case to emphasize a point in your document. If you use a printer that doesn't support other enhancements, you may want to use uppercase letters for emphasis.

You don't need to delete and retype text to change the case. WordPerfect's Convert Case command changes a block of lowercase text to uppercase, or vice versa. Note that when you switch from upper- to lowercase, certain letters remain capitalized, such as the letter *I* (when occurring by itself) or any character that begins a sentence.

■ **Cue:** If you change from upper- to lowercase, be sure to check your converted block for accuracy because WordPerfect leaves some letters capitalized in certain circumstances.

To change the case of a selection, follow these steps:

1. Highlight a selection whose case you want to change.

2. Choose **C**onvert Case from the **E**dit menu.

3. Choose **U**ppercase to convert the block to uppercase or **L**owercase to convert the block to lowercase.

   The selection remains highlighted so that you can apply additional WordPerfect commands.

If you often convert the case of selected text, consider adding Upper and Lower buttons to the Button Bar.

`BUTTON`

Working with Rectangular Selections

In WordPerfect, you can select text within a defined rectangle. Figure 5.6 shows an example of a rectangular selection.

WordPerfect - [d:\que\sample.txt\refeinfo]

| File | Edit | View | Layout | Tools | Font | Graphics | Macro | Window | Help |

Open Save Print Cut Copy Paste Search Font Speller Append

Scheduling Preferences:

- I can't referee at all this year, contact me next year: _____
- Please remove me from the referee list permanently: _____
- I prefer to referee in the following divisions (please check all that apply):

Division 6 (ages 6 & 7) _____ Boys Girls Either
Division 5 (ages 8 & 9) _____ Boys Girls Either
Division 4 (ages 10 & 11) _____ Boys Girls Either
Division 3 (ages 12 & 13) _____ Boys Girls Either
Division 2 (ages 14 & 15) _____ Boys Girls Either

- Please indicate any other scheduling preferences: (such as early/late games; geographic preference; dates unavailable to referee; number of games per Saturday; etc.)

_____
_____
_____
_____

- Comments/Feedback/Questions:

_____

Select On   Pg 1 Ln 6.71" Pos 2"

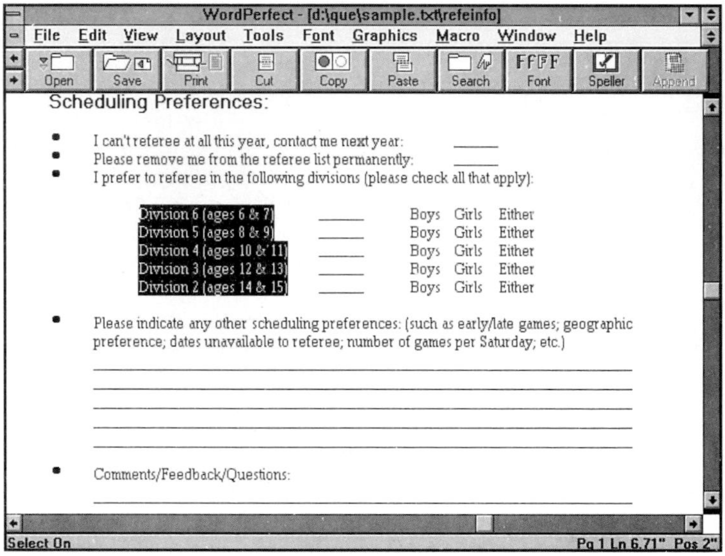

FIG. 5.6

A highlighted rectangular selection.

To highlight a rectangular selection of text, follow these steps:

1. Move the insertion point to the beginning or ending corner of the rectangle you want to select.

2. Move the mouse pointer to the diagonally opposite corner and Shift-click, or hold down the left mouse button and drag the mouse pointer to the opposite corner.

   At first you may think that more text is being selected than you actually want to select. After you perform the next step, the highlighted area shrinks to the intended *rectangle* size (as shown in fig. 5.6.)

3. Choose Select from the Edit menu; then choose Rectangle.

You now can cut, copy, or delete the rectangular selection. To place the selected rectangle in a different location, choose Cut or Copy, move the insertion point to the desired location, and choose Paste from the Edit menu.

If you plan to delete or cut the rectangle, each line of text from which you are removing a section must end with a hard return, to ensure that the selection is removed without disturbing other text on the page. If the lines end without hard returns, text will wrap unpredictably from line to line when you Cut the rectangle.

T I P

Using Styles with Selections

With the Style command, you can apply multiple formatting commands to selected text many times throughout a document without retyping the commands each time. You may want to apply the Underline and Large attributes, for example, to each headline in your document. Rather than selecting each headline and applying the two attributes each time, you can create and name a style that applies this formatting to any text where the style is applied, thus saving time.

When you edit a style, the modified codes also are applied to the text at every location where you applied the style throughout the document. If you highlight each headline and individually apply the codes instead of using a style, later modification of text formatting requires finding each headline and changing the attributes individually. For a complete description of styles, see Chapter 12, "Using Styles."

To apply a style to a selection, follow these steps:

1. Highlight the selection where you want to apply the style.

2. Select **S**tyles from the **L**ayout menu.

 Press Styles (Alt-F8).

3. Choose the style you want to use and then choose **On.**

Chapter Summary

This chapter has shown you how to use the selection process to specify a portion of your document where you want to perform WordPerfect functions. Rather than deleting and retyping sections of text, you can apply WordPerfect commands to the selected text.

In this chapter, you learned how to highlight a selection with the mouse and keyboard; move or copy a selection to another location, document, or Windows application; append selected text; delete, undelete, and print a selection; and save a selection as a file. You also learned how to enhance selected text with attributes such as underlining, boldface, and italic; change the typeface, size, or layout; change selected text to uppercase or lowercase characters; work with a rectangular selection; and apply styles to selections.

When you are ready to edit a document, the Select Text feature enables you to change the look of the document quickly and easily.

Formatting Text

When you set words, numbers, and pictures to paper, regardless of the tools you use, your objective is to communicate ideas. When you use a word processing package like WordPerfect on a computer and print your output on a sophisticated printer, you can greatly increase the effectiveness with which your ideas are communicated through the way you format your text, pages, and documents.

■ **Tony Rairden** is a strategic-marketing consultant with extensive experience using WordPerfect Corporation's products.

Formatting is the visual organization and placement, or laying out, of text and graphics in a document. Formatting includes selecting the base font in which you compose the document, setting margins and line and paragraph spacing, selecting paragraph style (block or indented) and justification, and choosing many other details of the document's layout on the page.

In this chapter, you learn to format lines and paragraphs on the page, both as you enter text and after the fact. You explore WordPerfect's default formats and broad range of text formatting capabilities and learn the following:

- How to change or override default formatting settings
- How to use the Ruler to expedite formatting tasks
- How to use WordPerfect's "smart" Auto Code Placement to affect formatting commands

■ How to set and use margins and different kinds of tabs, and how to use indents and margin releases

■ How to use and control justification and hyphenation

Chapter 11, "Formatting Pages and Designing Documents," extends what you do here into page layouts and ways of working with page layouts to produce coherent document designs. To learn how to apply WordPerfect's many text appearance and size attributes to enhance text, see Chapter 10, "Working with Fonts."

Understanding Formatting in WordPerfect

WordPerfect Corporation makes some assumptions and generalizations about what constitutes an acceptable, reasonably professional-looking document and about which tools and features are most useful in producing such a document. Those assumptions and generalizations are reflected in WordPerfect's default settings and in the tools and features made available in the Ruler and the default Button Bar.

Default Format Settings

■ **Cue:** WordPerfect sets your document margins at one inch all around by default.

If you don't change the default settings, WordPerfect sets your document margins at one inch all around (top, bottom, left, and right) and sets left-aligned tab stops every half inch beginning at the left margin. The program sets as your default font one of the more basic, monospaced fonts available on your printer; the default font often is Courier in 10 pitch (10 characters per inch) or 12 point (which is approximately the same size as 10 pitch). (Monospaced font is also called *fixed pitch;* every character occupies the same horizontal space. In *proportional* fonts, the characters occupy only the horizontal space required by their particular shapes.)

When you load WordPerfect into Windows, WordPerfect opens an empty document screen with your default font shown at the lower left in the status bar. WordPerfect also defaults to single-spacing and full justification for lines.

You can change these defaults and many other formatting parameters temporarily at specific locations within a document or for the entire document. If you change defaults and parameters for the entire document, you can make still other local changes to any parameter.

You can see and edit the codes causing the changes. Use View, Reveal Codes (Alt-F3), go to the beginning of the document, and follow any of the procedures discussed throughout this chapter.

Many changes to the defaults also can be "hidden" by selecting Layout, Document, Initial Font, or Initial Codes, following the procedures discussed in this chapter, and then clicking the Close button or pressing Alt-C. (See Chapter 11 for a more extensive discussion of Document Initial Codes and Chapter 10 for more on Document Initial Font.) You cannot see or edit Document Initial Codes and Fonts through Reveal Codes; you must use the Document Initial menus to edit these codes, or you must override them by entering new codes at the top of the document. Editing the codes is preferable to overriding them.

This chapter discusses temporarily varying from the default values for a document and making local changes within a document. To change the formatting and font choices permanently, see Chapter 29, "Customizing WordPerfect with Preferences."

The Ruler

In WordPerfect, you can change margins, tab settings, fonts, justification, and line spacing. You can create columns and tables. You then can apply styles from the appropriate menus. You also can take advantage of one of WordPerfect's most powerful and versatile tools: the Ruler (see fig. 6.1). The Ruler lets you handle all these formatting functions with click-and-drag efficiency and provides you with ready visual references to their effects.

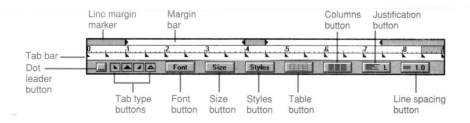

The ruler not only gives you access to many of the most important formatting functions, it also serves as an indicator, providing detailed information about the current format.

The status bar at the bottom of the screen tells you what font and size are active and where you are on the page and in the document. The Ruler graphically adds information about the margins, tab settings, line spacing, and justification in effect at the insertion point. If the insertion point is in a column or a table, the Ruler also shows you where the column margins or cell divider positions are.

With the mouse, you can modify any formatting parameter on the Ruler. Clicking most of the buttons displays drop-down menus on which you change the current setting. (The Dot Leader button is a toggle.) You can drag tab settings onto or off the tab bar. You can drag margins left or right. If you're in columns or a table, you can adjust the column widths and gutters and the table cell widths by dragging.

To see the Ruler on your screen, select **V**iew, **R**uler or press View Ruler (Alt-Shift-F3). When you display the Ruler from within a document, the Ruler's display and contents are document-specific. If you save the document, when you retrieve it, the Ruler comes up again; but if you open a new document or exit and reenter WordPerfect, the Ruler will not be visible until you display it.

To have the Ruler display whenever you load WordPerfect and be visible for every document unless you turn off the Ruler, you must change the default (see Chapter 29, "Customizing WordPerfect with Preferences," for more information).

BUTTON

The Button Bar is a versatile and powerful tool designed to increase your productivity by giving you one-click implementation of any menu selections or macros you use frequently. You can set up as many different Button Bars as you need; users typically set up Button Bars for special functions, such as editing and formatting text, creating and editing tables, and outlining and marking for tables of contents and indexes. Chapter 19, "Using the Button Bar," covers creating, editing, and using Button Bars.

The only text-formatting button on the basic Button Bar is Font, which brings up the Fonts menu. You probably will want to add any formatting commands you use frequently, such as Indent, to the Basic Button Bar or to one you create as described in Chapter 19. (The Button Bars shown in this chapter are not the default version. The author has chosen to show his working Button Bars, positioned as he feels makes them easiest to use.)

Auto Code Placement

WordPerfect formats by placing hidden codes in the document. You can see the codes at any time by selecting **V**iew, Reveal **C**odes or by pressing Alt-F3. Because Reveal Codes is a toggle, giving the command again hides the codes and returns the screen to its normal configuration.

WordPerfect features "smart" placement of these codes, called Auto Code Placement, as its default mode of operation. WordPerfect places codes that normally affect entire paragraphs, such as codes for left and right margins and justification, at the beginning of the paragraph, regardless of where the insertion point is located in the paragraph when you activate the formatting command. Similarly, WordPerfect places page formatting codes at the top of the page in which you invoke them.

If you deactivate Auto Code Placement, through File, Preferences, Environment, line and paragraph formatting commands take effect from the insertion point onward in the document; page formatting commands take effect beginning with the *next* page. Most users normally operate with Auto Code Placement on and deactivate it only under specific circumstances.

■ **Cue:** WordPerfect features "smart" placement of codes, called Auto Code Placement, as its default mode.

Formatting Lines and Paragraphs

You access WordPerfect's line and paragraph formatting commands through the Layout menu (see figs. 6.2 and 6.3). The Ruler makes many of these same commands readily available so that you can bypass the menus and dialog boxes and set parameters on-screen, or bypass the menus and go directly to the commands' dialog boxes.

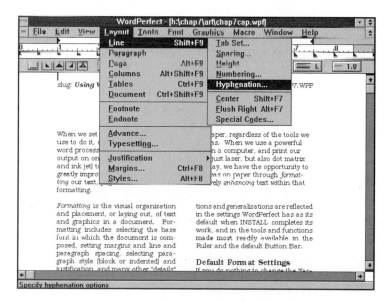

FIG. 6.2

The Layout and Line menus.

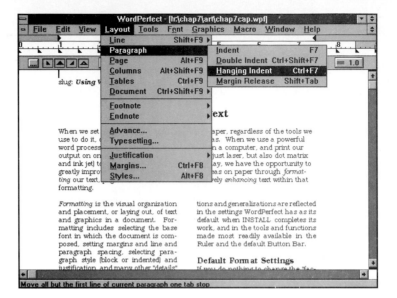

Controlling Line Spacing and Line Height

WordPerfect defaults to single-spaced lines and automatically sets the line height (measured from baseline to baseline of single-spaced type) according to the type font and size selected. You can adjust line spacing and line height for part of a document or for the entire document, or you can adjust these values permanently (by changing WordPerfect's default values).

As with most formatting values discussed in this chapter, you make permanent changes to WordPerfect's defaults for line spacing or line height through the File, Preferences, Initial Codes command (see Chapter 29, "Customizing WordPerfect with Preferences"). You can override the program's defaults temporarily by changing base values for a document through the Layout, Document, Initial Codes menu.

Cue: You can apply
changes in the value for line
spacing or line height to
selected text or simply insert
the changes into the
document.

You can apply changes in the value for line spacing or line height to selected text or simply insert the changes into the document. If you apply them to selected text, WordPerfect inserts a code to restore the preceding value at the end of the selected block of text. If you insert the changes into the document with no text selected and Auto Code Placement on, WordPerfect places either code (Line Height or Line Spacing) at the beginning of the current paragraph. If Auto Code Placement is off, WordPerfect inserts the codes at the insertion point. Either code affects all text following the code unless another code of the same type is encountered later in the document.

Line Spacing

A change in line spacing doesn't change the line height measurement but changes the multiple of that height by which the lines are spaced.

Using the Line Spacing button on the Ruler (refer to fig. 6.1) is the quickest and easiest way to make routine line spacing changes among single-spacing, double-spacing, and space-and-a-half. Simply click the Line Spacing button on the Ruler and drag to the desired value on the pull-down menu. WordPerfect places the appropriate code [Ln Spacing: x] in your text in accordance with the status of Auto Code Placement.

To access the full line-spacing feature for spacing other than single, double, and space-and-a-half, follow these steps:

1. Select **Layout, Line**.

    Press Layout Line (Shift-F9).

2. Select **S**pacing to open the Line Spacing dialog box (see fig. 6.4).

3. Type your desired spacing in the text box or scroll to select your spacing.

4. Click OK or press Enter.

WordPerfect places the appropriate line spacing code in the document, and the dialog box closes, returning you to your editing screen.

You can enter any value between .5 and 160. The predefined values fall in increments of .5. You can type any value that falls within the range, specifying up to three decimal places; WordPerfect rounds your number to two decimal places for the dialog box and code displays.

Line Height

WordPerfect's automatic line height feature works well under normal circumstances, because the automatic height for a line is based on the largest point size on that line. Line height varies, however, if you use multiple point sizes of type; you will get some interesting-looking results if you change type sizes within a paragraph or use different type sizes for different entries in a list, as shown in figure 6.5.

> WordPerfect's default automatic line height works very well under normal circumstances. Since the automatic height is based on the **largest** point size on a line, however, it will vary if you use multiple sizes of type; you will get some interesting-looking results if you change type sizes within a paragraph for em-
>
> phasis, or use different type sizes for different entries in a list

FIG. 6.5

The effects of automatic line height.

If your layout needs multiple type sizes, WordPerfect enables you to change the line height setting from automatic to fixed and specify the height for the lines directly. You specify fixed line heights by placing the code in the text. You can have the code affect all subsequent text or apply the code only to selected text by placing a code specifying automatic line height at the end of the selected block.

To change line height settings, follow these steps:

1. Select **Layout, Line**.

   CUA Press Layout Line (Shift-F9).

2. Select **Height** to display the Line Height dialog box (see fig. 6.6).

FIG. 6.6

The Line Height dialog box.

3. Select **Auto** or **Fixed**. If you are in Auto (WordPerfect's default) and select Fixed, the window in the box initially shows you the current line height. You can accept that entry or type another height in the text box.

4. Click OK or press Enter to accept your change and return to your document.

You can fine-tune line height further through the Typesetting dialog box, discussed in Chapter 15, "Working with Advanced Printing Techniques."

Setting Margins

Because WordPerfect sets margins from each edge of the specified page, they are independent of the paper size and the font in use. Margins are expressed as distance from the edge of the page in inches (or other units if you have altered the setting in Preferences).

You can set the margins in several ways. For any individual margin (top, bottom, left, or right); both side margins; top and bottom margins; or all margins; follow these steps:

1. Select Layout, Margins to display the Margins dialog box.

   DUA Press Margins (Ctrl-F8).

2. Enter the new setting(s) in the dialog box, as shown in figure 6.7.

3. Click OK or press Enter.

The new margin codes are inserted into your document, and you are returned to your editing screen.

> Although you may change all the margins in a single dialog box, WordPerfect still generates separate codes for the Left/Right and the Top/Bottom margins.   **T I P**

■ **Cue:** You can double-click in the margin areas or on the margin indicators in the Margin bar on the Ruler to display the Margins dialog box.

You can change just the side margins even more easily from the Ruler. Just drag the Line Margin markers in the Margin bar of the Ruler. As soon as you release the mouse button, you see the effect of your change on the screen.

With Auto Code Placement on (the default), a left/right margin setting entered in text is placed at the beginning of the paragraph and a top/bottom setting is placed at the beginning of the page. With Auto Code Placement off, WordPerfect immediately generates a hard return followed by the new margin setting, which will affect the text following the new setting.

You can change margins for selected text, too. WordPerfect uses the new margins only in the selected block of text and places a code reverting to the original margin settings at the end of the selected text. If you go through the Margins dialog box, you will see that the Top and Bottom options are gray, indicating that you cannot change those margins within selected text.

Setting Header and Footer Margins

Left and right margins for headers and footers are determined by the margin settings (default, document initial, or code-specified) at the point in your document where you insert the header or footer code. You can make your header or footer margins independent of the document's text margins, however, by setting margins in the header or footer itself.

Using Indent and Margin Release

■ **Cue:** After you establish the basic margins for a document or a section of a document, you can vary those margins.

After you establish the basic margins for a document or a section of a document, you can vary those margins in order to emphasize areas of your text or to indicate hierarchical relationships among elements of your text. Although you could reset the left and right margins repeatedly to vary the margins, WordPerfect has built-in tools to simplify the process and to give you consistent results. Those tools—Indent, Double Indent, Margin Release, and Hanging Indent—are accessible through the Layout, Paragraph menu.

Indent and Double Indent

To indent a paragraph from your normal left margin, select **L**ayout, **P**aragraph, **I**ndent, or press Indent (F7) at the beginning of the paragraph. WordPerfect indents all text from the left margin to the first tab stop, until the program encounters a hard return. (Use the Ruler to see where any Paragraph Layout commands will be affected.) After the hard return, WordPerfect again places text at the normal left margin. You can use multiple indents to indent the margin to the corresponding tab stops.

To indent both the left and the right margins, select **Layout**, **Paragraph**, **D**ouble Indent or press Double Indent (Ctrl-Shift-F7) at the beginning of the paragraph.

If you haven't changed the default tab settings (see "Setting and Using Tabs" in this chapter), each indent temporarily shifts the margin(s) one-half inch toward the center of the page. In figure 6.8, the second paragraph illustrates a single indent from the left margin, and the third paragraph shows a double indent from both margins.

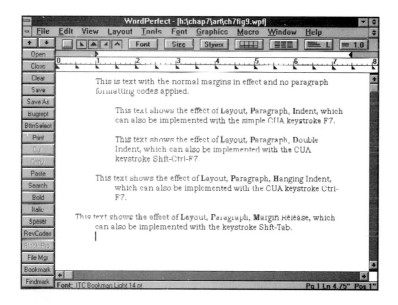

FIG. 6.8

Indenting from the left and right margins.

CAUTION: Don't try to create indents or tabs by inserting spaces with the space bar at the beginning of each line and hard returns at the end of each line. If you're using a nonproportional typeface, you may get satisfactory results on-screen or even in a printout, but you cannot edit the text without reworking the layout. The text probably will not print satisfactorily in a proportional font and probably will pose printing and editing problems to anyone working with the file on another computer.

Margin Release

To begin the first line of a paragraph outside the current left margin (refer to fig. 6.8, last paragraph), select **L**ayout, **P**aragraph, **M**argin Release or press Margin Release (Shift-Tab).

You can use the Margin Release command to call attention to specific sections of text, usually instructional or annotational. You can release the margin only as far to the left as your printer can print. For most printers, this limit is to the right of the edge of the page. The margin release command is probably most useful as part of the Hanging Indent command.

Hanging Indent

Hanging Indent, although a single command, is, in effect, a combination of an indent and a margin release. To insert a hanging indent into a document, select **L**ayout, **P**aragraph, **H**anging Indent or press Hanging Indent (Ctrl-F7).

This single command inserts separate Indent and Margin Release codes into the text. Hanging indents are useful for composing simple numbered or bulleted lists. A hanging indent clearly separates a number or bullet from a list item and aligns the number or bullet on the original document margin.

T I P   Because hanging indents use separate indent and margin release codes, be sure that you delete *both* codes if you delete a hanging indent. Use Reveal Codes when you edit or delete codes in your text.

Setting and Using Tabs

Unlike indents, which affect all text until a hard return is encountered, tabs position text only in the current line (unless Outlining is turned on; see Chapter 24, "Line Numbering, Paragraph Numbering, and Outlining," for a discussion of outlining).

Tabs are used primarily for the following three purposes:

■ To indent the first line of a paragraph when you use an indented-paragraph style of writing

- To provide an orderly arrangement of tabular data
- To determine the points to which the Indent codes (and Hard Tab codes with Outlining turned on) temporarily shift margins

Types of Tabs

WordPerfect has four types of tabs and a dot leader attribute that you can apply to any one or to all four. The four types of tabs are listed in the Tab Set dialog box and shown on the Ruler. The tab types follow:

- *Left Align.* Text flows from the tab setting to the right; this alignment is the most commonly used type of tab.

- *Center.* Text centers at the tab setting; text extends alternately to the right and left. This tab works similarly to the Layout, Line, Center (Shift-F7) command, except that you can place the tab setting at any point on the line rather than only at the center point.

- *Right Align.* Text flows from the tab setting to the left. This tab works similarly to the Layout, Line, Flush Right (Alt-F7) command, except that you can place the tab anywhere on the line rather than only at the right margin.

- *Decimal Align.* Text flows from the tab setting to the left until you enter the alignment character. WordPerfect places the alignment character on the tab setting, and subsequent text flows to the right. The default alignment character is a period, or decimal point.

You can embellish all four types of tabs with dot leaders so that a line of dots bridges the space from the position where you pressed the Tab key to the beginning of the tabbed text. Dot leaders are useful when the space between tabular columns is wide, and the reader's eye has difficulty associating elements across the gap.

The default tab settings in WordPerfect are relative, left-aligned, every 1/2 inch for 14 inches, from –1 inch to 13 inches.

Setting Tabs on the Ruler

You can see and modify directly on the Ruler all tabs that fall within your paper size. The Ruler has a button for each type of tab and a Dot Leader button for toggling the dot leaders on and off. (Click the Dot Leader button, and a line of dots appears below the markers in each of

- **Cue:** You can see and modify directly on the Ruler all tabs that fall within your paper size.

the tab buttons.) Figure 6.1 shows the Ruler without active dot leaders; figure 6.9 shows the tab type buttons and several tab position markers in the Ruler with dot leaders active.

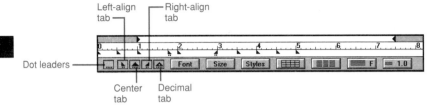

FIG. 6.9

The tab alignment buttons.

To add or replace a tab anywhere on the Ruler, click the appropriate tab type button and drag to the left or right. A marker for the tab appears on the Ruler, and a vertical dotted line runs below the marker through your text, showing you where the tab will be placed. Word-Perfect places the new tab wherever the marker and dotted line are located when you release the mouse button. To replace a tab, be sure that the new marker is superimposed over the old one. If you want a dot leader tab, toggle the dot leaders on with the Dot Leader button before dragging your tab to its location.

Deleting and moving tabs is easy when you use the Ruler. To delete a tab, click and drag it off the Ruler; to move a tab, just click and drag it to its new position. If you change your mind about moving or deleting a tab, continue to hold down the mouse button and drag the tab above the top of the Ruler into the title bar. The tab marker snaps back to its original position.

Notice that the tab markers move and that the tab position indication at the right end of the status bar changes in 1/16-inch increments. These increments in the Ruler make the tabs easier to place consistently. To bypass these increments temporarily, you can move or place tabs in one-pixel increments by holding down the Shift key while dragging. You can eliminate the 1/16-inch increments permanently by turning off the Tabs Snap to Ruler Grid option with the Preferences command (see Chapter 29, "Customizing WordPerfect with Preferences").

You can delete, move, and copy multiple tabs on the Ruler. First, select the desired tabs by clicking on (or toward the nearest margin from) the first tab and dragging across the other tabs to highlight your target group.

To delete the group, hold down the mouse button with the pointer in the band, drag the band down off the Ruler, and release the button. When you release the button, the band and the markers in the Ruler disappear.

To move the group, hold down the mouse button with the pointer in the band and drag the group to its new location. When you release the button, the tabs remain in their new locations and the band and markers in the old locations disappear.

To copy the group, hold down the Ctrl key when you initially click in the band; then drag the copy of the group to its new location and release the button. The band disappears, and the duplicate group of tabs remains in the new location.

Setting Tabs from the Tab Set Dialog Box

As versatile as the Ruler is for working with tabs, it doesn't do everything. You must use the Tab Set dialog box for the following tasks:

- Specify whether tabs are absolute or relative
- Clear all tabs and easily create a new set at different intervals
- Position tabs with 1/1000-inch precision
- Restore WordPerfect's default tabs
- See or edit tabs that aren't accessible on the Ruler (that are beyond the width of your current paper size)

Follow these steps to display the Tab Set dialog box:

1. Select **Layout**, **Line**.

   CUA Press Layout Line (Shift-F9).

2. Choose **Tab** Set from the Line menu.

   The Tab Set dialog box appears (see fig. 6.10).

FIG. 6.10

The Tab Set dialog box.

T I P If you're using the Ruler, the fastest and easiest way to display the Tab Set dialog box is to double-click any tab or tab type button in the Ruler.

Cue: The Tab Set dialog box shows you the tab settings in effect at the current location.

The Tab Set dialog box shows you the tab settings in effect at the current location. The top box under **P**osition tells you the point on the line from which any action selected in the dialog box will take effect. Any number you type there defines where a tab will be set or cleared if you select the **S**et Tab or Clear T**a**b button. You can position tabs anywhere from 0 inches to 54 1/2 inches. You also can select existing tabs for replacement or clearing by scrolling in the Position box and clicking a position. WordPerfect then highlights that position, and it also appears in the top text box. To replace the tab with a different type of tab, choose the appropriate tab type button, select **S**et Tab, and click OK or press Enter. To clear (delete) the tab, simply choose the Clear T**a**b button and then click OK or press Enter.

To revert to WordPerfect Corporation's default tab settings from tabs you have set, select the De**f**ault button, and then click OK or press Enter.

CAUTION: Choosing the Default button in the Tab Set dialog box always restores WordPerfect's original *every 1/2 inch*, *left-aligned*, *relative* tab settings, even if you have changed the program's default tab settings in Preferences, Initial Codes, or the document's default tab settings.

To eliminate all tabs, select Clear Ta**b**s and then click OK or press Enter.

To set repetitive tabs at intervals other than WordPerfect's default half inch, select **E**venly Spaced.

T I P To replace the current tabs with new Evenly Spaced tabs rather than just add to them, select Clear Ta**b**s before selecting **E**venly Spaced.

The Position box indicates the left edge of the paper or a position you selected or typed before toggling on Evenly Spaced. The position shown in the box is the starting point for your repetitive tabs; to change it, simply type the new position. WordPerfect accepts values in this box from –1 inch to 40 inches but doesn't generate tabs on or beyond the left edge of your currently defined paper size. Next, select Repea**t** Every and type your desired interval for the tabs. Acceptable values are 0.100 inch to 10 inches.

Now select **S**et Tab; the new tabs are listed in the Position list box. Click OK or press Enter, and you return to your document, where the new tabs now appear on the Ruler.

CAUTION: In WordPerfect, you can set a maximum of 40 tabs, regardless of their interval or position. When you generate evenly spaced tabs from the Tab Set dialog box, they use all remaining available tabs. If, therefore, you are creating additional tabs and haven't cleared any of WordPerfect's 29 default tabs, you can create only 11 additional tabs. This limitation applies to tabs inserted manually as well as to automatically generated evenly spaced tabs. To create more than 11 tabs, you first must clear those you don't want to use.

Whether you have set your tabs through the Ruler or the Tab Set dialog box, WordPerfect places a tab set code in the text according to whether Auto Code Placement is on or off.

Relative and Absolute Tabs

In WordPerfect, you can specify whether to position your tabs (and your indents) from the left margin or from the left edge of the page. You make your choice through the Tab Set dialog box, shown in figure 6.10.

Follow these steps:

1. Select **L**ayout, **L**ine.

   CUA Press Layout Line (Shift-F9).

2. Choose **T**ab Set from the Line menu to open the Tab Set dialog box.

3. Choose Left **E**dge or Left **M**argin under Position From or click the corresponding button.

4. Press Enter or click on OK.

WordPerfect places a TabSet code in your text (placed in compliance with your AutoCode setting), and you are returned to your editing screen.

◼Cue: In WordPerfect, you can specify whether to position your tabs relative to the left margin or the left edge of the page.

Tabs positioned from the left margin are called *relative* because their positions shift if the left margin is shifted. Tabs positioned from the left edge of the page are called *absolute* because the margin settings do not affect their position on the page. Figure 6.11 shows the codes for the same set of tabs in both relative and absolute forms. The 0-inch point is the left margin for relative tabs, so you can have negative numbers indicating relative tab settings, as shown in the top set. The 0-inch point for absolute tabs is the left edge of the page, with the result that all absolute tab settings are expressed as positive numbers.

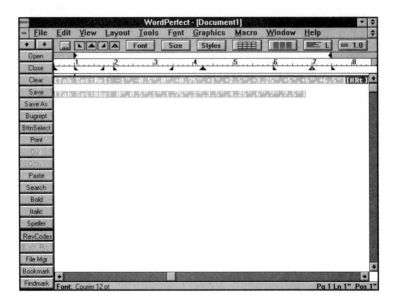

FIG. 6.11

Relative and absolute tab settings designating the same points on a line with a 1-inch left margin.

Hard Tabs

When you press the Tab key, WordPerfect inserts into your text a tab code based on the type of the next defined tab, the insertion point jumps to that tab, and text flows into the document in accordance with the tab type. To change a tab in one specific location from, for example, a left-aligned tab (typical for text) to a decimal-aligned tab (for a column of financial figures), you could change the tab type through the Tab Set dialog box or the Ruler. Either way, however, creates a new tab set code that remains in effect throughout your document until you reverse the change.

■ **Cue:** Use Hard Tab codes to make temporary tab changes.

WordPerfect offers a less disruptive alternative for making temporary changes: Hard Tab codes. When you insert a Hard Tab code into the text, the Hard Tab code takes the place of the tab codes generated when you press the Tab key. You therefore can specify that a new type of tab be used without generating a new tab set code. Hard Tab codes for all four tab types (left, center, right, and decimal) are available with and without dot leaders.

To insert a Hard Tab code, first make sure that your insertion point is where you want the hard tab; then follow these steps:

1. Select Layout, Line.

    CUA Press Layout Line (Shift-F9).

2. Select Special Codes from the Line menu. The Insert Special Codes dialog box opens (see fig. 6.12).

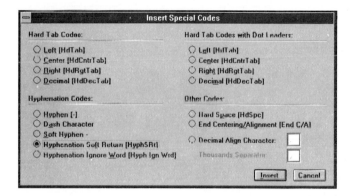

FIG. 6.12

The Insert Special Codes dialog box.

3. Select the specific code you want and select Insert.

The dialog box closes, and you are returned to your editing screen with the Hard Tab code in place and the insertion point at the tab stop, waiting to flow text into the document in the manner specified by the Hard Tab type.

Changing the Decimal Align Character

You change the decimal align character through the Insert Special Codes dialog box (again see fig. 6.12). WordPerfect's default decimal align character is the decimal point, typically used for numbers and financial data. To change the default, select Decimal Align Character under Other Codes in the Insert Special Codes dialog box. Type the new alignment character in the text box, and select Insert to return to your document. Colons are used frequently in descriptive lists. Compare the readability of a list composed with left-aligned tabs in the upper part of figure 6.13 with the same list composed with decimal-aligned tabs (with the colon as the align character) in the lower part of the screen.

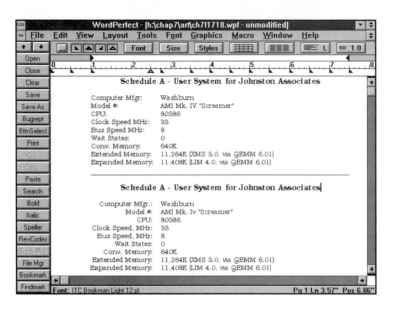

FIG. 6.13

A list with left-aligned tabs and decimal-aligned tabs.

Unlike indents, which affect all text until a hard return is encountered, tabs position text only in the current line. This limitation means that tabs to position data in tabular columns must be entered between all data items on every line. For simple two- or three-column tables, such as the example shown in figure 6.13, tabs offer a reasonably effective approach.

For more complex tables, however, WordPerfect's Table feature automates the placement of text elements and adds built-in math commands and various line and shading options. Chapter 14, "Working with Tables," discusses the Table feature.

Locating Text on the Line

Selecting **L**ayout, **L**ine, **C**enter (Shift-F7) centers text on a line. The text you enter begins at the center of the line and flows left and right from the center point, rather than from the left margin. Centered text is used typically for titles or headings and often is combined with boldface or a larger type size or both.

You also can enter text at the right margin of a line rather than the left, so that it flows "backward" to the left. Select **Layout**, **Line**, **Flush Right** (Alt-F7).

Center and Flush Right both apply only to a single line of text; a hard return cancels their effect and returns text entry to the left margin. You can use either code at the beginning of a line of text or apply the code after you have entered text on the line. You can use the codes on left-justified or full-justified text, but not on centered or right-justified text (see "Using Justification" in this chapter). Both often are used in headers and footers, discussed in Chapter 11, "Formatting Pages and Designing Documents."

The End Centering/Alignment code [End C/A] enables you to end centered text without entering a hard return; the code causes subsequent text on the same line to continue from the end of the centered text or causes the insertion of a Flush Right code to shift remaining text on the line to the right margin. Figure 6.14 shows the use of this code with the Center and Flush Right codes.

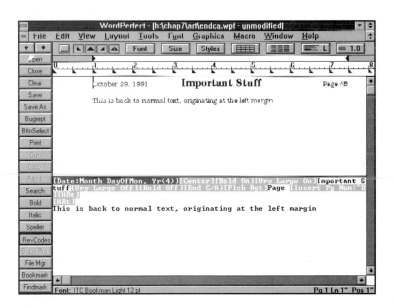

FIG. 6.14

The use of Center and End Center/Align codes.

Place End Centering/Alignment in a line by placing the insertion point where you want the code and following these steps:

1. Select **Layout**, **Line**.

    Press Layout Line (Shift-F9).

2. Select Special Codes. The Insert Special Codes dialog box opens.

3. Choose End Centering/Alignment under Other Codes.

4. Press Enter or click Insert.

An End Centering/Alignment code is placed in your text, and you are returned to your editing screen.

If you apply Center or Flush Right when text is selected, WordPerfect inserts a Justify Center or Justify Right code at the beginning of the selected block and inserts the appropriate "restore justification" code at the selection's end.

Using Justification

Justification aligns text to or between margins. WordPerfect has four different forms of justification: full, left, right, and center, as shown in figure 6.15.

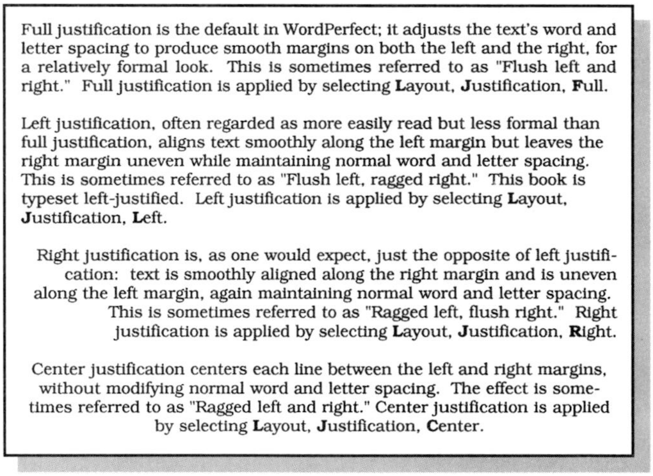

Full justification is the default in WordPerfect; it adjusts the text's word and letter spacing to produce smooth margins on both the left and the right, for a relatively formal look. This is sometimes referred to as "Flush left and right." Full justification is applied by selecting **Layout, Justification, Full.**

Left justification, often regarded as more easily read but less formal than full justification, aligns text smoothly along the left margin but leaves the right margin uneven while maintaining normal word and letter spacing. This is sometimes referred to as "Flush left, ragged right." This book is typeset left-justified. Left justification is applied by selecting **Layout, Justification, Left.**

Right justification is, as one would expect, just the opposite of left justification: text is smoothly aligned along the right margin and is uneven along the left margin, again maintaining normal word and letter spacing. This is sometimes referred to as "Ragged left, flush right." Right justification is applied by selecting **Layout, Justification, Right.**

Center justification centers each line between the left and right margins, without modifying normal word and letter spacing. The effect is sometimes referred to as "Ragged left and right." Center justification is applied by selecting **Layout, Justification, Center.**

FIG. 6.15

WordPerfect's four forms of justification.

■ *Full justification*, the default in WordPerfect, adjusts the text's word and letter spacing to produce even margins on the left and the right, resulting in a relatively formal look. Apply full justification by selecting **Layout, Justification, Full** or by pressing Ctrl-F.

■ *Left justification*, sometimes referred to as *flush left, ragged right*, retains normal word and letter spacing, aligns text evenly along the left margin, and leaves the right margin uneven. Left justification, used in most of this book, often is considered to be easier to read but less formal than full justification. Apply left justification by selecting **L**ayout, **J**ustification, **L**eft or by pressing Ctrl-L.

- *Right justification*, sometimes called *ragged left, flush right,* is the opposite of left justification. Right justification retains normal word and letter spacing, aligns text evenly along the right margin, and leaves the left margin uneven. Apply right justification by selecting **L**ayout, **J**ustification, **R**ight or by pressing Ctrl-R.

- *Center justification* centers each line between the left and right margins without modifying normal word and letter spacing. The effect is sometimes called *ragged left and right.* Apply center justification by selecting **L**ayout, **J**ustification, **C**enter or by pressing Ctrl-J.

Using hyphenation (see "Using Hyphenation" in this chapter) makes the right, unjustified margin in left-justified text more even; hyphenation also improves the word and letter spacing in fully justified text. Automatic hyphenation does not function in right-justified and centered text.

T I P

Justification codes placed in a document remain in effect until another justification code is encountered. If you select text when a justification code is applied, WordPerfect places the new justification code at the beginning of the block. At the end of the block, WordPerfect inserts a code for the justification in effect before you selected the block.

The CUA keyboard commands and the Justification button on the Ruler are quicker for most users than the menu sequences. The Ruler's Justification button gives you quick and easy ways to see what justification is in effect at the insertion point and to change that justification. To change the justification, just click the button and drag the cursor bar (reverse video highlight) to the desired justification and release the mouse button.

With Auto Code Placement off, WordPerfect places the justification code at the insertion point; if the insertion point is not at the beginning or end of a line, a deletable soft return precedes the justification code to create a new line.

Using Hyphenation

Cue: The WordPerfect Hyphenation feature splits long words that extend beyond the right margin instead of wrapping them to the next line.

Use WordPerfect's Hyphenation feature to reduce gaps at the ends of lines in left-justified text or between words in fully justified text. The Hyphenation feature splits long words that extend beyond the right margin instead of wrapping them completely to the next line. Some people prefer not to use hyphenation, and some document formats specify that it not be used. When hyphenation is acceptable, however, WordPerfect can automate the process substantially or completely for you.

The codes WordPerfect uses to hyphenate words or to prevent their hyphenation are placed in the document in several different ways. You can enter most hyphenation codes directly from the Insert Special Codes dialog box (again see fig. 6.12). WordPerfect inserts some codes without any user involvement if Hyphenation is on; and you can enter many codes from the Position Hyphen dialog box during prompted automatic hyphenation (see "Choosing a Hyphenation Point").

Splitting Words with Codes

You can split words in WordPerfect by inserting one of four different hyphenation codes, each of which serves a different purpose. These codes are as follows:

- *Hard hyphen*. Produces a visible hyphen and hyphenates even with hyphenation off. You enter the hard hyphen by pressing the hyphen key on the top row of your keyboard or the minus key on the numeric keypad. The hidden code is [-].

- *Soft hyphen*. Produces an invisible hyphen that becomes visible if the word is split. You enter a soft hyphen by pressing Ctrl-Shift-hyphen or choosing it through the Special Codes dialog box. The hidden code is a highlighted hyphen (-).

- *Hyphenation soft return*. Accessible only through the Special Codes dialog box, this code splits a word without a hyphen if a split is required. The hidden code is [HyphSRt].

- *Deletable soft return*. Splits a word at the right margin if the word extends from the left margin to beyond the right (usually found only in very narrow margins). Inserted only automatically, the hidden code is [DSRt].

Preventing Hyphenation

Sometimes you don't want WordPerfect to split certain words or phrases, such as corporate or product names (Du Pont) or long or hyphenated proper names (Santos-Dumas). WordPerfect has three different codes to meet these needs, as follows:

- *Hyphenation ignore word.* Causes entire word to wrap to next line. Codes accessible only through Special Codes dialog box. The hidden code is [Hyph Ign Wrd].

- *Hyphen.* Prints as a hyphen, doesn't split word. You enter it by pressing Ctrl-hyphen (on the top row of your keyboard). The hidden code is a hyphen (-).

- *Hard space.* Prints as a space but keeps two words together on the same line. You enter it by pressing Home, space bar. The hidden code is simply a space—[ ].

Using Automatic Hyphenation

WordPerfect's default mode is Hyphenation Off; words wrap to the next line intact rather than hyphenated. Of course, you can hyphenate words manually as you enter them.

To turn on hyphenation in a document, follow these steps:

1. Select Layout, Line.

    Press Layout Line (Shift-F9).

2. Choose Hyphenation. The Line Hyphenation dialog box opens, as shown in figure 6.16.

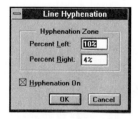

FIG. 6.16

The Line Hyphenation dialog box.

3. Select Hyphenation On and then select OK or press Enter.

WordPerfect places the Hyphenation On code in the text at the insertion point, where the code affects all text that follows it. (Auto Code Placement has no effect on Hyphenation On.)

To turn on Hyphenation for the entire document, go to the top of the document (Ctrl-Home, Ctrl-Home) and follow the preceding steps. WordPerfect places a Hyphenation On code [Hyph On], which you can see with Reveal Codes, in front of all text in the document. Alternatively, select **L**ayout, **D**ocument, Initial **C**odes and then follow the procedure in the preceding numbered steps, which places the [Hyph On] code in the Initial Codes window. Then select **C**lose. Hyphenation will be on throughout the document (except where specifically turned off through the Line Hyphenation dialog box), and the top of the document will not be cluttered with the code.

Auto Code Placement does not control the placement of hyphenation on and off codes; WordPerfect always places them at the insertion point.

To open every new document with Hyphenation On, change the settings through the File, Preferences command (see Chapter 29, "Customizing WordPerfect with Preferences").

Setting the Hyphenation Zone

The Hyphenation Zone setting determines whether WordPerfect wraps a word to the next line or hyphenates it. The hyphenation zone is composed of two areas, one on either side of the right margin, each a percentage of the total line length (the distance between left and right margins). You can set the percentages in the Line Hyphenation dialog box (again see fig. 6.16). A word must span the entire hyphenation zone, crossing both the left and right boundaries, for WordPerfect to hyphenate it. The larger the hyphenation zone, the fewer words WordPerfect hyphenates; the smaller the hyphenation zone, the more words WordPerfect hyphenates. If Auto Code Placement is on, WordPerfect places Hyphenation Zone definition codes at the beginning of the current paragraph, affecting that paragraph and all following text. WordPerfect also places Hyphenation Zone definition codes at the insertion point if Auto Code Placement is off.

Choosing a Hyphenation Point

Before WordPerfect hyphenates a word, it consults the dictionary file, WP{WP}US.LEX (or the equivalent for another language), which contains correct hyphenation points and correct spellings for approximately 115,000 words. If the word is in the dictionary, WordPerfect inserts a soft hyphen at the break point nearest the margin and splits the word at that point.

If WordPerfect doesn't find the word in the dictionary and therefore cannot find a hyphenation point for the word, the program displays the Position Hyphen dialog box and asks you where to put the hyphen (see fig. 6.17).

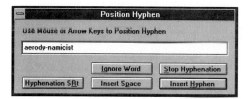

The word to be split is displayed with a hyphen initially positioned at the right margin. You can use the mouse or the arrow keys to place the hyphen where you want to break the word (you can position the word break only within the hyphenation zone). After you have selected your break point, you can split the word in the following ways:

- To split the word with a hyphen, select Insert **Hyphen**. WordPerfect inserts a soft hyphen code at your chosen point and splits the word with a visible hyphen.

- To split the word or phrase without a hyphen, select Hyphenation **SRt**. WordPerfect inserts a hyphenation soft return code [HyphSRt] at your chosen point and splits the word without a hyphen.

  If you later edit the text and move a word hyphenated by a soft hyphen or a hyphenation soft return away from the hyphenation zone, WordPerfect rejoins the word with no action on your part.

- To break the word or phrase into two distinct elements separated by an ordinary space, select Insert **Space**. No hidden code is involved in this option. The elements subsequently function as if you originally entered them as two distinct words.

  The Insert **Space** option is probably most useful when you insert text that abuts another word, and the combination pushes across the hyphenation zone. With hyphenation on, WordPerfect treats the inserted text and adjoining word as a single word requiring hyphenation. You cannot continue until you choose one of the options in the Position Hyphen dialog box. By choosing Insert

Space, you put a space between elements that probably will end up separated by a space anyhow. (If the natural break point isn't visible in the window, select **S**top Hyphenation.

■ To keep the word intact, with no break, select **I**gnore Word. WordPerfect inserts a Hyphenation Ignore Word code [Hyph Ign Wrd] before the word and wraps the word to the next line.

When you are in the middle of an editing sequence that is scrolling through the entire document (for example, running a looping formatting macro or checking spelling), you probably don't want to deal with hyphenation. WordPerfect has an option to Stop Hyphenation, which temporarily turns off hyphenation until the command sequence is completed.

Removing Hyphenation from a Document

■ **Cue:** WordPerfect hyphenation codes remain embedded in words even after you turn off hyphenation.

The hyphenation codes WordPerfect inserts, whether automatically or as a result of your selections from the Position Hyphen dialog box or the Special Codes dialog box, remain embedded in the words even after you turn off hyphenation. (The deletable soft return is the exception; WordPerfect eliminates this code automatically if the conditions forcing its insertion are resolved.) If a word containing an embedded hyphenation code spans the hyphenation zone, the code takes effect whether hyphenation is on or off.

If you decide after using hyphenation that you would rather have a completely unhyphenated document, you must remove the hyphenation codes. You can remove them manually by selecting Reveal Codes and editing them out individually, or you can remove them all at once by replacing them all with nothing. To remove all hyphenation from your document at once, follow these steps:

1. Press Ctrl-Home, Ctrl-Home to go to the beginning of the document.

2. Select **E**dit, **R**eplace.

   [CUA] Press Replace (Ctrl-F2).

   The Search and Replace dialog box opens.

3. Select **C**odes to open the Codes dialog box (see fig. 6.18).

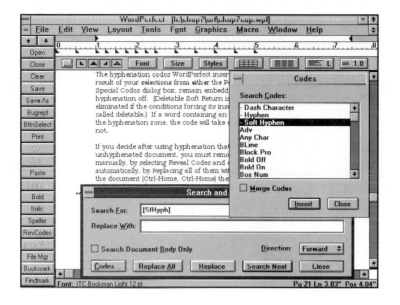

FIG. 6.18

The Search and
Replace dialog
box with the
Codes dialog
box.

4. In the Codes dialog box, select -Soft Hyphen, and then **Insert**, followed by **Close**.

   WordPerfect inserts a [SfHyph] code (not the same highlighted
   hyphen that you see in Reveal Codes) in the Search **For** box of the
   Search and Replace dialog box.

5. Select Replace **All** in the Search and Replace dialog box, without
   entering anything in the Replace **With** box. This procedure is
   essentially "search and delete."

WordPerfect executes its search and replace throughout the document,
stopping at the last place the searched-for code was deleted. Select
Close to return to the editing screen.

You also can delete any Hyphenation Soft Return codes that you have
used in the document. Repeat the preceding steps, but select HyphSRt
rather than -Soft Hyphen in the Codes dialog box.

To scroll quickly to the desired item in the Codes dialog box, simply **T I P**
begin typing the item with the dialog box active. WordPerfect jumps
to the entry corresponding to what you're typing. This "speed scroll"
capability is built into all WordPerfect's scrollable list boxes.

Cue: WordPerfect gives the user full control over hyphenation.

WordPerfect Corporation's philosophy is to give the user full control over the program's functions—in hyphenation as in almost all parts of the program. You can control several aspects of hyphenation from the Environment Settings dialog box. See Chapter 29, "Customizing WordPerfect with Preferences," for a full discussion of the aspects of hyphenation you can control.

Modifying the Hyphenation Decision Resources

If you use automatic hyphenation, you probably use words that WordPerfect cannot hyphenate (the words always display the Position Hyphen dialog box) or hyphenates in a way you think is wrong. You can add your own words and hyphenation point preferences to the resources WordPerfect consults, whether you use the External or the Internal Hyphenation option (see Chapter 29).

If you use external hyphenation, WordPerfect's SPELL.EXE utility provides several ways to add words and their hyphenation points to the dictionaries. To override WordPerfect's hyphenation of a word that is already in the dictionary, delete the word and reenter it with your preferred hyphenation. See Chapter 8, "Using the Speller and the Thesaurus," for more information.

If you use internal hyphenation, you can use WordPerfect's HYPHEN.EXE maintenance utility to create and edit a hyphenation exception dictionary, WP{WP}US.HYD (or another language equivalent). The first time you use the utility, WordPerfect asks whether you want to create the file. Choose **Y**es. WordPerfect creates the file and presents you with HYPHEN.EXE's self-explanatory main menu. The procedures for using HYPHEN.EXE are similar to those detailed in Chapter 8 for using SPELL.EXE on the main dictionary file.

Chapter Summary

In this chapter, you have explored WordPerfect's broad range of text formatting capabilities. You became acquainted with many of WordPerfect's default format settings and learned how to change or override them. You learned to use the Ruler to expedite formatting tasks. You also learned how to set and use margins and the various forms of tabs, how to use indents and margin releases, and how to use and control justification and hyphenation. You saw how WordPerfect's Auto Code Placement affects various formatting commands.

WordPerfect offers several additional tools for formatting and enhancing text. For a discussion of WordPerfect's text appearance and size attributes, see Chapter 10, "Working with Fonts." Chapter 12, "Using Styles," shows you how to set up styles for formatting and text enhancement conventions that you use frequently. Chapter 13, "Working with Text Columns," covers WordPerfect's capability to format text into columns. Finally, if you are presenting data that is too complex to put into simple tabular columns, see Chapter 14, "Working with Tables."

Introduction to Graphics

M odern word processing provides a rich and complex selection of features, ranging from simple text editing to desktop publishing and page composition. With a *graphical user interface (GUI)*, you easily can manage text, graphics, typefaces, page layout, and all the other complicated elements that make up modern word processing.

In particular, a GUI like Microsoft Windows is a natural environment for graphics-mode programs. WordPerfect for Windows uses the Windows facilities to display text in a WYSIWYG (what you see is what you get) format, and to manipulate graphical elements easily. Previous versions of WordPerfect for the DOS environment supported graphics, but didn't give you the kind of control you needed to *see* what you were doing. By showing you nearly everything just as it will be printed, WordPerfect for Windows changes this historic limitation.

This chapter introduces graphics terms and ideas so that you can work more comfortably with different programs and formats. This chapter also introduces the most important type of WordPerfect graphics—the figure graphic—and shows you how to use it in a document. Chapter 17, "Understanding Advanced Graphics," continues with a more

■ **Joseph E. Rosenman** is the principal consultant of PCC Resources, an NYC consulting concern that specializes in PC installations, word processing, and desktop publishing.

complete look at WordPerfect's graphics facilities. In this chapter, you do the following:

- Learn what graphics are
- Review the different graphics formats
- Become acquainted with WordPerfect's graphics formats
- Create WordPerfect figure graphics
- Resize the figure graphics
- Move the graphics

WordPerfect's Graphics Categories

As the saying goes, "a picture is worth a thousand words." Graphics can make complicated text easy to understand. For example, look at this book. Imagine trying to follow the examples without figures. The screen examples, which are actually graphic "pictures" of the WordPerfect screen in action, make following along much easier to do. Can you imagine a biography without a photograph or portrait of the subject? Or an advertisement for a car without a picture of the car?

In the past, to illustrate a document, you had to leave a blank space to "paste up" a photograph. Although that process is still followed for the best quality reproduction, many applications work well with graphics incorporated into the document itself.

At first, you may be confused by the many graphics formats and types that are available. In fact, all graphics fall into one of two categories: *vector* or *raster graphics*.

Understanding Line Art, or Vector Graphics

Vector graphics are images made up of lines. The lines can be straight lines, curved lines, circles, squares, or triangles. If the lines form a solid object like a circle or a rectangle, the object might be "filled" with a color or pattern. In all cases, though, the graphics are made up of line segments (see fig. 7.1).

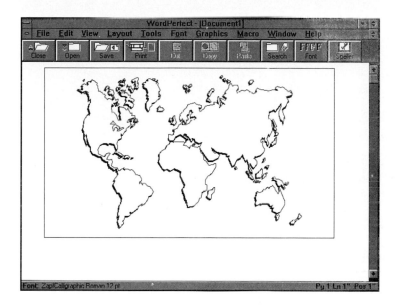

Line art is called vector graphics because each line segment starts at one specific point and ends at another specific point. Because everything is so *definite*, this format lends itself to rescaling. Because you easily can make line art larger or smaller without losing detail and clarity, line art is useful in situations where you may have to resize the graphic.

Although WordPerfect supports both types of graphics format, all the clip art available through WordPerfect Corporation is in vector format, so you can change it easily to suit your particular needs.

Understanding Bit-Map, or Raster Graphics

Raster graphics are images made up of dots. Each dot can be a different color or a different shade of gray, if the image is black-and-white. Bit maps are described as raster graphics because they are similar to television and computer screens, which are considered "raster" devices. Televisions create their images by activating dots (picture elements) on the screen. The dots are arranged in a matrix (columns and rows). Bit-mapped graphics work in the same way; they consist of a matrix of dots that are present or absent (see fig. 7.2).

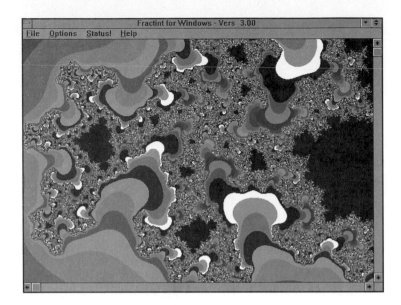

FIG. 7.2

A bit-map
graphic of a
mathematically
derived image
called a fractal.

Bit maps are good for presenting images that look "realistic." Because of their capability to have many colors (or shades of gray) in a small area, bit maps can produce detailed textures. Photographs and pictures are almost always converted into bit maps.

Bit maps have two major disadvantages: they cannot be resized without distortion, and the files containing bit maps are large.

WordPerfect can accept bit-map files, but many WordPerfect editing features that are available for vector files do not work for bit-map files. The best practice is to use bit maps only in their original size. You can crop them (leave parts out), but you *cannot* enlarge them or manipulate them as you can vector graphics.

WordPerfect's Graphics Formats

Cue: Vector graphics can be sized and modified with excellent results. Raster graphics can have images like photographs but cannot be modified without loss of quality.

A perfect world might have only two formats: one for vector and another for raster. However, many different graphics formats are in use. In the world of personal computers, eight formats are of special concern to WordPerfect users.

WordPerfect automatically converts seven of the eight formats (see table 7.1) to WPG format when you retrieve them; the exception is the GIF format. You can convert GIF files for use in WordPerfect with another conversion product.

Table 7.1. WordPerfect's Eight Graphics Formats

Graphics Name	Format	Description
WP Graphics (WPG)	Both	The format native to WordPerfect is unusual because it can be either a vector or raster format—but not at the same time. The source of the graphic usually determines what type of WPG graphic it becomes. Photographs generally become raster graphics, and graphics created in drawing programs (like DrawPerfect) become vector graphics. Most WPG files are vector graphics, because that format can be scaled and modified effectively. WPG vector format graphics are similar to the CGM format. The WPG raster format is similar to the PCX format.
Computer Graphics Metafile (CGM)	Vector	Probably the most common vector format for line art, this format converts nicely into WPG format. Many clip art collections of CGM graphics are available.
Hewlett-Packard Graphics Language (HPGL)	Vector	The format recognized by most HP plotters, HPGL is a standard in the plotter industry and is often the only "compatible" format in CAD (Computer Aided Design) programs. HPGL converts well into WPG format.
PC Graphics (PCX)	Raster	The graphics format used by PC PaintBrush, this format is one of the most popular "paint" programs. PCX has become a de facto standard for bit-map graphics. The format often features "blends" from one color to another, or shading from light to dark if the picture is black and white. Resizing distorts the graphic.

continues

Table 7.1. (continued)

Graphics Name	Format	Description
Tagged-Image	Raster	This format is the graphics format that File Format (TIFF) scanners usually create. Scanners are often used to "capture" photographs. TIFF files can be as large as 24 megabytes. Although the current generation of PCs are limited to 256 simultaneous colors, TIFF files can store 16 million colors at once. TIFF images are subject to the same limitations as PCX files.
Bit Map (BMP)	Raster	This format, popularized in Microsoft Windows, is essentially a "raw" bit map. Windows "wallpaper" uses BMP files.
Encapsulated PostScript (EPS)	Vector	PostScript printing language created the EPS format. It includes PostScript printing commands, plus an optional TIFF graphical display header. If the optional header is present, WordPerfect can print EPS graphics on any graphics-capable printer. EPS graphics print at full resolution *only* on PostScript printers.
Graphical Interchange Format (GIF)	Raster	CompuServe, Inc. created this format as a way to transfer graphics across different types of computers. GIF is a raster format that supports a maximum of 256 colors and comes in a variety of resolutions. GIF (pronounced "Jiff") is primarily a display format. Although GIF files can be printed, they are not the best format for printing. Most GIFs are created from TIFF files. If you know that the graphic will be used in a WordPerfect document, you should work with the original TIFF file if at all possible.

WordPerfect can convert many other formats into its native graphics format, performing most conversions when the graphic is loaded. You must use the GRAPHCNV program (included with WordPerfect) to convert other formats—Autocad's DFX format, in particular. For more information on graphics conversions, see the section on conversion in Chapter 17, "Understanding Advanced Graphics."

WordPerfect's Five Graphics Box Types

WordPerfect always places graphical information into special graphics boxes. Whenever you want to use a graphic, you must first create a graphics box. WordPerfect provides five types of graphics boxes:

- Figure box
- Text box
- Equation box
- Table box
- User box

WordPerfect's graphics boxes are all treated the same after you create them and place them in the document. WordPerfect associates each box with a specific type of editor (or choice of editors). For example, the figure box automatically uses the Figure Editor, and the text box automatically uses the Text Editor. You can use all three editors—Figure, Text, Equation—with the table box.

WordPerfect uses separate settings for each graphics box—for example, the types of lines that surround the graphics and whether the box has a gray background or a clear background. Each variety of graphics box has options which can be set for that type of box. These options enable you to determine the type of border around the box, whether the background is gray or clear, the spacing inside and outside of the box, and so on (see fig. 7.3).

Because WordPerfect for Windows has five types of graphics boxes, each box can have its own options settings. The option setting is a code that you can place in the document; therefore, the options also can change within the document. You can use the names *Table* or *Text* to help differentiate options selections, even though they may contain the same kind of graphics.

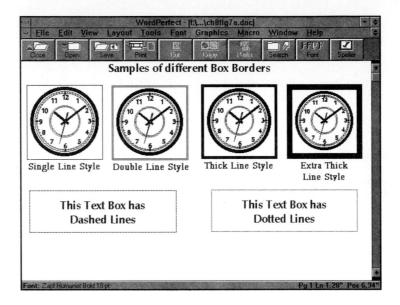

FIG. 7.3

Box Border
samples.

Although equations work just like other WordPerfect graphics, they are different because you actually *create* them in WordPerfect's Equation Editor. You learn more about the Equation Editor in Chapter 27, "Using the Equation Editor."

Chapter 17, "Understanding Advanced Graphics," explores the Options command in more detail. The following sections in this chapter focus on the most frequently used type of graphics, figure graphics.

WordPerfect's Figure Graphics

When you work with graphics in WordPerfect, you really work with boxes that contain graphical images (often called *clip art*) created elsewhere. WordPerfect for Windows comes with a collection of sample clip art created in DrawPerfect, WordPerfect Corporation's DOS-based graphics editor.

When you work with WordPerfect graphics, you can manipulate the graphics box itself, or you can change what's *in* the graphics box. Chapter 17 discusses editing the contents of the graphics box. The following section explores figure graphics using the clip art Word-Perfect has included with WordPerfect for Windows.

Creating a Figure Graphic

If you haven't already done so, start WordPerfect. You should be in a blank document screen. The following steps assume that you installed all the Graphics files when you installed WordPerfect for Windows:

1. Select **G**raphics, **F**igure, **R**etrieve to open the Retrieve Figure dialog box.

    Press Figure Retrieve (F11).

   The Retrieve Figure dialog box displays the default Graphics Files directory, which should contain the sample clip art included with WordPerfect for Windows.

2. Choose DUCKLING.WPG from the file list on the left, then click the Retrieve button (or press Alt-R). Figure 7.4 shows the Retrieve Figure dialog box with the file selected and ready to be retrieved. The file automatically loads into the figure box using WordPerfect's default settings, and your screen looks like the example in figure 7.5.

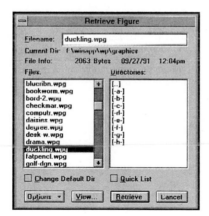

FIG. 7.4

The Retrieve Figure dialog box with a graphics file selected and ready to be retrieved.

If you frequently work with a specific graphics box type, you can add a Button Bar selection for that choice.

BUTTON

The figure box that WordPerfect creates is a square one-half the width of the page. WordPerfect adjusts the box to a different size if you retrieve a rectangular graphic. Sizing a graphic to fit exactly can be a tricky operation. WordPerfect for Windows helps make the task easier, because you can see exactly what you are doing.

■ **Cue:** If the graphics box is located on a document margin, the sizing handles along that margin are suppressed.

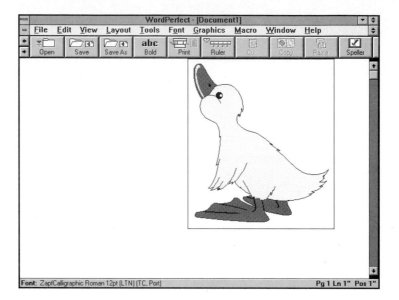

FIG. 7.5

A graphic inserted in a WordPerfect figure box.

If you click the graphics box, the box becomes highlighted, and WordPerfect switches into Graphic Edit mode. The box is surrounded by dashed lines, with eight sizing handles around the box (see fig. 7.6). Although each box has eight sizing handles associated with it, some of them may not be visible. If a box edge is on a margin, the three handles along the margin are suppressed. WordPerfect's default location is along the top margin. As a result, only five sizing handles are visible in figure 7.6.

In Graphic Edit mode, the pointer changes shape, appearing as a four-headed arrow inside the box or a two-headed arrow if positioned on one of the sizing handles. When the pointer changes to a two-headed arrow, you can drag (or push) the box into a different size. A two-headed arrow pointer *resizes* the box, and a four-headed arrow pointer *moves* the box within the document page.

■ Cue: Double-click the Figure Graphic to invoke the Figure Editor.

You can initiate the Figure Editor by double-clicking the mouse button when either the two- or four-headed arrow pointer is present. Chapter 17 discusses editing graphics in more detail.

Now, enlarge the graphics box to fill the upper half of the page. Move the figure box to the upper right-hand corner of the screen, using the following steps:

1. Move the mouse pointer onto the box, and click the mouse button. The mouse pointer switches to a four-headed arrow.

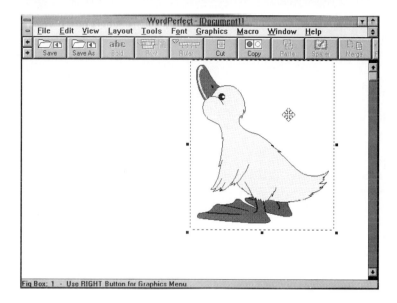

FIG. 7.6

Dashed lines and
sizing handles
indicate Graphic
Edit mode.

2. Click and hold the mouse button. Drag the mouse to move the figure into the upper right-hand corner of the screen. Don't worry about placing the figure exactly; if you push it past the document margins, WordPerfect makes sure that the figure is "placed" within the current margins. Note that after you start moving the box, the sizing handles disappear, but reappear when you stop moving the box.

3. Release the mouse button.

The next task is to stretch the box to fill the entire top of the page. Perform the following three steps:

1. Position the mouse pointer on the middle left sizing handle. The pointer switches to a two-headed arrow (facing left and right).

2. Click and hold the mouse button, and move the pointer to the extreme left side of the screen.

3. Release the mouse button.

   The image itself remains exactly the same size, but is centered within the box (see fig. 7.7). Unless you are using a very fast PC, some time passes before WordPerfect displays the graphics image.

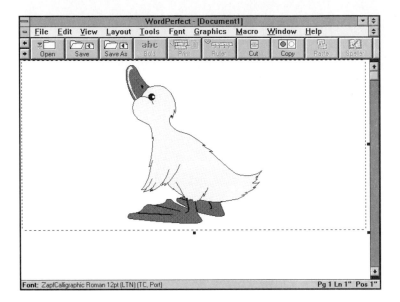

FIG. 7.7

Horizontally
expanding the
graphics box
centers the
graphics image.

The final step involves stretching the box downward. The process is the same as for centering the box—you simply work with a different sizing handle.

1. Position the mouse pointer on the center bottom sizing handle. The pointer switches to a two-headed arrow (facing up and down).

2. Click and hold the mouse button, and drag the pointer down as far as you can toward the bottom of the screen.

3. Release the mouse button.

Because you now have changed both the height and width of the box, WordPerfect resizes the graphic inside the box to fit the enlarged box's new measurements (see fig. 7.8). This method of sizing works well for boxes that fit on the viewing screen. For anything larger, such as a full-page graphic, you must use the Position option (choose **G**raphics, **F**igure, **P**osition). The Box Position and Size dialog box is discussed in Chapter 17.

The dashed lines surrounding the graphics box tell you that the box is still selected. After you position the box, deselect it by simply clicking somewhere else on the page. The insertion point appears, and the mouse pointer returns to a vertical bar (or arrow, if you move it onto the graphics box).

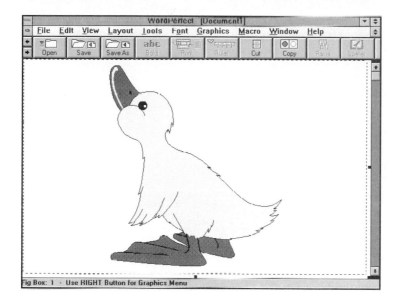

FIG. 7.8

Vertically expanding the graphics box resizes the graphics image.

Using a Figure Graphic as an Ornament

Graphics that are normally large can be effective as "ornaments" accompanying text. For example, a graphical check mark placed next to a list can reinforce the message you want to convey. In this section, you retrieve the check mark graphic (assuming that you installed the Graphics files) and reduce it to a small size.

For purposes of this example, you need to work from a fresh document. If you haven't issued a File Close for the duckling document you just created, do so now. A fresh WordPerfect document should say Document#-unmodified at the top (the # can be any number from 1 through 9).

The first task is to retrieve the figure graphic.

1. Select **G**raphics, **F**igure, **R**etrieve.

 Press Figure Retrieve (F11).

2. When the Retrieve Figure dialog box appears, select checkmar.wpg, then click the Retrieve button. Alternatively, you can double-click the file name.

WordPerfect retrieves the figure box and positions it near the upper right corner (see fig. 7.9). WordPerfect places a newly created graphic near the current position of the insertion point. In a new document,

WordPerfect places the graphic in the upper right corner. You easily can select and move the graphics after they have been retrieved.

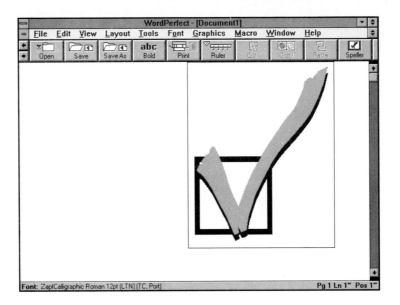

FIG. 7.9

The check mark graphic inserted in the editing window.

To move the check mark box to the left side of the screen, do the following:

1. Position the mouse pointer roughly in the middle of the figure box, and click the mouse button. A four-headed arrow appears.

T I P Make sure that you don't go too quickly to step 2. If you do, WordPerfect interprets the movement as a double-click and opens the Figure Edit window. If this mistake happens, select **Close** on the Figure Editor Button Bar.

2. Click and hold the mouse button, and move the mouse pointer to the left of the screen. An outline of the box moves with the mouse pointer.

3. When the box is properly positioned, release the mouse pointer (see fig. 7.10).

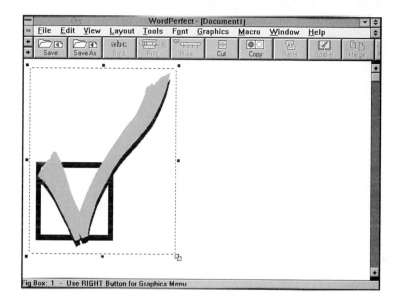

FIG. 7.10

The check mark graphic at the left edge of the page.

The next task is to shrink the figure box, using the following steps:

1. Position the pointer on the sizing handle in the lower right-hand corner. When properly positioned, the pointer changes into a two-headed arrow facing upper left and lower right (on the diagonal).

2. Click and hold the mouse button, and move the pointer toward the upper left corner. The box shrinks (to enlarge the box, move the pointer to the lower right corner).

3. When the box is the right size, release the pointer.

Figure 7.11 shows the figure after resizing, with a sentence added so that you can see how the graphic looks next to text. To deselect the graphics box, click the mouse pointer somewhere outside the box.

Working with More Than One Graphic on the Page

In WordPerfect, you can use as many graphics boxes in the document as you like. In the next example, you combine two graphics boxes. The first box contains desert scenery, and the second shows a flying airplane.

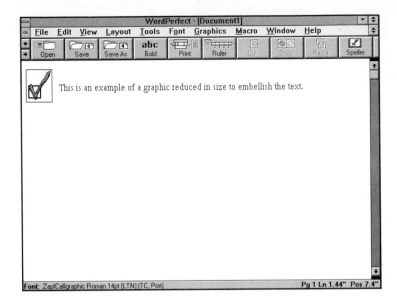

FIG. 7.11

The resized
check mark
graphic with
added text.

First, retrieve, size, and position the desert scenery. Use the same procedure you used for the preceding two graphics.

1. To retrieve the file BKGRND-2.WPG, select **G**raphics, **F**igure,
   Retrieve.

   CUA Press Figure Retrieve (F11).

2. Select the file, and click the Retrieve button (or press Alt-R).
   Alternatively, double-click the file name.

3. Click the box to select it.

4. Move the box to the left side of the screen and down a bit (see
   fig. 7.12 for the correct position).

5. Position the pointer on the upper right-hand sizing handle (the
   pointer switches into a two-headed arrow pointing from the lower
   left to the upper right), and stretch the box to the right and up.
   Don't stretch it all the way to the top; you want to leave some
   room for the airplane. Figure 7.13 shows the graphic after resizing.

6. Retrieve the file JET-2.WPG into a figure box by selecting
   Graphics, **F**igure, **R**etrieve.

   CUA Press Figure Retrieve (F11).

   Figure 7.14 shows the screen with the second graphic on top of
   the first.

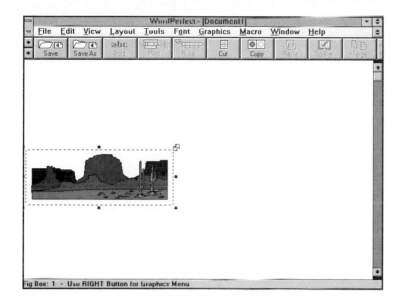

FIG. 7.12

The desert
graphic moved
to the left and
down.

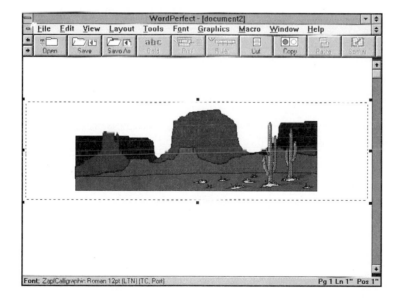

FIG. 7.13

Desert graphic
after resizing.

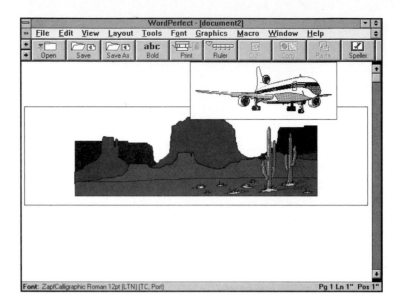

FIG. 7.14

A second graphic on top of the first.

7. Click the second box to select it. Only one box can be selected at a time.

8. Move the airplane box to a position about one-third the distance from the left side of the screen.

9. Position the pointer on the upper right-hand sizing handle, and shrink the box. The final result should look like figure 7.15. You may need to adjust the position and the size a couple times before you can match the location in figure 7.15. You can alter the position and size as often as necessary.

10. Click somewhere in the document screen to deselect the box.

Combining Graphics and Text

Cue: The Box Position and Size dialog box enables you to choose whether text wraps around a graphics box or is superimposed over the graphics box.

Now that you have worked with graphics, you can incorporate them into a document with text. WordPerfect can wrap text around the graphics box or ignore the box completely. If you choose to wrap the text, WordPerfect handles everything automatically. A text-free zone is created around the graphics box, and the text flows around it. If you turn off word wrap, however, the graphic figure lands right on top of the text. Sometimes, this image is exactly what you want. Other times, it is exactly what you *don't* want.

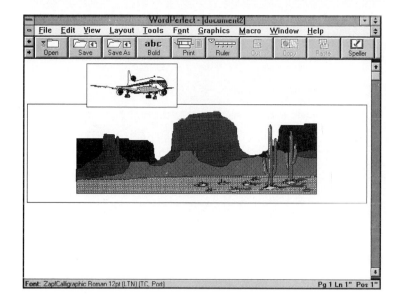

FIG. 7.15

Second graphic
resized and
repositioned.

If you add a graphics box (with wrap on) to a document that already
contains text, WordPerfect reformats the document so that the text
flows around the box. If you start with a graphics box and then add
text, WordPerfect places text only in the areas unoccupied by the
graphics box. Either way, WordPerfect keeps your text where it belongs. Figures 7.16, 7.17, and 7.18 demonstrate text with a graphics box
inserted with wrap on and wrap off.

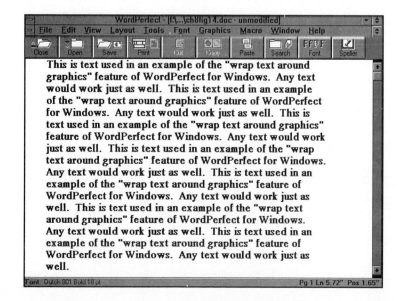

FIG. 7.16

A screen with
text.

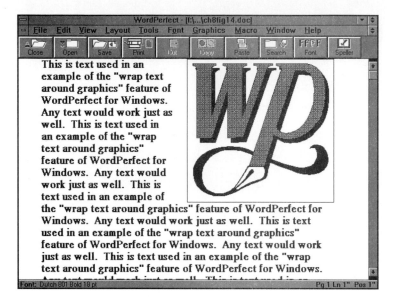

FIG. 7.17

A graphics box added to text with wrap on.

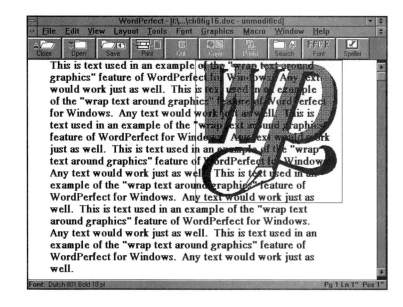

FIG. 7.18

A graphics box added to text with wrap off.

Chapter 17 explores in detail all the options for graphics. Chapter 18, "Desktop Publishing with WordPerfect," covers effective and easy ways to use text and graphics together.

Going beyond Simple Graphics

WordPerfect includes a Figure Editor you can use to enlarge specific portions of the graphics image, mirror and rotate the image, move the image around within the box, and so on. Chapter 17 explores the different features of the Figure Editor and describes the different defaults for the various boxes. For example, each box in the graphics you created had a thin line around it. You can remove that line, make it thicker, and so on. You can add a gray background (at various intensities) to the box. Chapter 16, "Using Lines To Add Effects," explores these subjects, and more.

WordPerfect, however, *cannot* create or modify the graphic itself. WordPerfect includes a small collection of clip art. Additional clip art collections are available from a variety of vendors. To modify the clip art itself, you need to purchase a graphics editor. WordPerfect sells a graphics editor called DrawPerfect that works well with WordPerfect graphics. DrawPerfect is currently available as a DOS application. All the clip art used in this chapter, and included with WordPerfect, was created in DrawPerfect.

Chapter Summary

Adding and manipulating graphics in WordPerfect is easy to do. The primary graphics box used in WordPerfect, the figure graphic, can be placed anywhere in the document and can be moved or resized with just a click of the mouse. In this chapter, you learned about types of graphics and about WordPerfect's graphics boxes. You created figure boxes and retrieved graphics into figure boxes. You then learned to move, enlarge, and reduce figure boxes, and to position two figure boxes together.

Chapter 17, "Understanding Advanced Graphics," expands on this chapter—introducing the other box types, discussing the box options, exploring in detail the various graphics editors. In addition, Chapter 17 explores several examples of complex graphics in documents.

Using the Speller and the Thesaurus

Whether you write memos, reports, or novels, you occasionally need to find the correct spelling or meaning of a word or a synonym for a word you have used too frequently. You no longer have to juggle a dictionary and thesaurus while you type at the keyboard. WordPerfect includes two powerful tools that can do the work for you—the Speller and the Thesaurus—available at the press of a key.

The Speller contains more than 100,000 words. You can use the Speller to check the spelling of your documents, to find certain types of irregular capitalization, and to look for duplicate words (the same word occurring twice consecutively). A variety of options also enables you to fine-tune the Speller's operation.

■ **Gary Pickavet** is the Assistant Superintendent for Business and Data Processing Services for the Santa Barbara County Education Office. He uses WordPerfect regularly for research projects and preparing supporting materials for presentations.

With the Speller Utility, you can maintain your dictionary files. You use the Speller Utility to add words to and delete words from a dictionary and to compress and optimize dictionaries for more efficient performance.

Using the Thesaurus, you can make a document more interesting or present thoughts more precisely. You can look for the word that is *just right* for your document. The Thesaurus looks up and displays synonyms (words with the same or similar meanings) and antonyms (words with the opposite meaning).

In this chapter, you learn how to use the Speller, the Speller Utility, and the Thesaurus to do the following:

- Check the spelling of a document
- Look up words that sound alike or that match a pattern
- Correct misspellings
- Add and delete words in the dictionaries
- Create your own supplementary dictionary
- Compress and expand supplementary dictionaries
- Check for duplicate words (for example, *the the*)
- Check for irregular capitalization (such as *THe* or *tHe*)
- Use the Thesaurus to look up and display synonyms and antonyms

Using the Speller

The Speller is a powerful editing tool. Even if you are a proficient speller and typist, you probably find misspelled or duplicate words or irregular capitalization in documents you compose. The longer the document, the greater the chance of these problems occurring and the more likely you are to miss problem words.

Cue: To increase the Speller's usefulness, you can purchase foreign language dictionaries (contact Word-Perfect Corporation for more information).

You also can look up words with the Speller, searching phonetically (to display words that sound similar) or displaying all words that match a pattern of known and unknown characters. The Speller doesn't contain the definitions of words—you need to use a regular dictionary for that purpose. The Speller does contain hyphenation information for the words in its dictionary, however, to enable WordPerfect to break words properly as necessary.

The Speller doesn't catch every mistake. Words found in the dictionaries are considered to be spelled correctly. A word may be spelled properly but not be the word you mean to use. The phrase *Thank you for you support!* passes the spelling check, for example, although the second *you* should have been *your*. The Speller is not a substitute for proofreading your document. The Speller is a tool to use to ensure that your final document is of the highest possible quality.

Setting Up the Speller

The Speller must be copied to your computer by using the INSTALL program. See Appendix A, "Installing and Setting Up WordPerfect for Windows," for information on the installation procedure.

The Speller uses two dictionaries—a main dictionary and a supplementary dictionary. The two letters of the file name immediately preceding the extension LEX indicate the dictionary's language. The file WP{WP}US.LEX, for example, is the United States *main* dictionary file; WP{WP}FR.LEX is the French National main dictionary file. The United States *supplementary* dictionary file name is WP{WP}US.SUP.

The supplementary dictionary is where the Speller places words you tell it to add during a spelling check. Although the Speller checks the supplementary dictionary for exact word matches, only words in the main dictionary or a *compressed* supplementary dictionary are offered as suggested replacements for misspelled words. Normally, you will work with a supplementary dictionary that has not been compressed.

The Speller must find the main dictionary file, and first checks to see whether you have indicated a path to the location of dictionary files. The path was specified when you installed WordPerfect and can be changed by using the Location of Files feature.

To change the path for the dictionary files or to see where WordPerfect currently looks for them, follow these steps:

1. Choose Preferences from the File menu.

2. Choose Location of Files. The Location of Files dialog box appears, as shown in figure 8.1. The paths to the Main and Supplementary dictionary files are shown in the Thesaurus/Speller/Hyphenation section of the dialog box.

If the dictionary files are not found in the location specified or if no path is specified, the Speller checks for the dictionary files in the directory where the Speller program files are located. If the main dictionary file is not found in any of the directories checked, you see a dialog box indicating that the dictionary was not found. You also can choose the Select Dictionary option to specify where the main dictionary file is located. If the supplementary dictionary isn't found, WordPerfect creates a new one when you have the Speller add words. Figure 8.2 shows the Speller dialog box that appears when the main dictionary is not found.

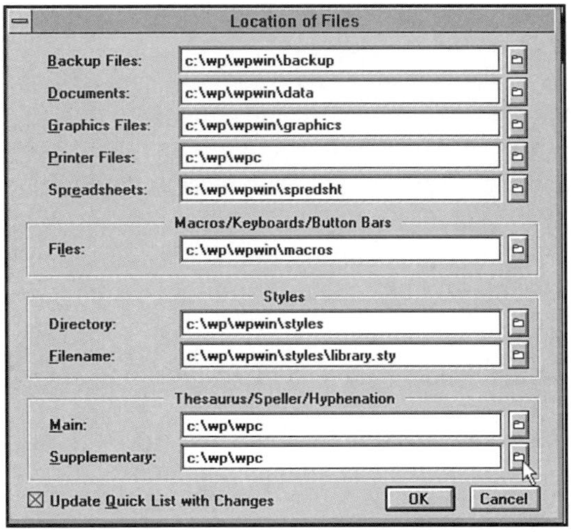

Location of Files

Backup Files:	c:\wp\wpwin\backup
Documents:	c:\wp\wpwin\data
Graphics Files:	c:\wp\wpwin\graphics
Printer Files:	c:\wp\wpc
Spreadsheets:	c:\wp\wpwin\spredsht

Macros/Keyboards/Button Bars

Files:	c:\wp\wpwin\macros

Styles

Directory:	c:\wp\wpwin\styles
Filename:	c:\wp\wpwin\styles\library.sty

Thesaurus/Speller/Hyphenation

Main:	c:\wp\wpc
Supplementary:	c:\wp\wpc

☒ Update Quick List with Changes   OK   Cancel

FIG. 8.1

Locating the dictionary files.

FIG. 8.2

The dialog box that appears when you use the wrong path.

Speller

Dictionary not found or bad format:
WP{WP}US.LEX

Select Dictionary...   Skip Language   Exit

Starting the Speller

The first step to checking the spelling of a document is to start the Speller. When you start the Speller, you are starting it as another Windows application.

CAUTION: Expect the unexpected! When you start any computer program, your computer may lock up. To be safe, *always* save your document before starting the Speller or any other application. Saving your file ensures that your document is safe on disk if you need to restart the computer.

You can start the Speller in the following ways:

- Click the Speller button on the Button Bar. To run the Speller from the Button Bar, move the mouse pointer to the Speller button and click the left mouse button (see fig. 8.3).

- Choose **S**peller from the **T**ools menu.

 Press Speller (Ctrl-F1).

When you start the Speller, the Speller window appears on-screen (see fig. 8.4).

FIG. 8.3

The Speller button on the Button Bar.

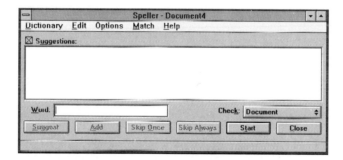

FIG. 8.4

Starting the Speller.

Like WordPerfect, the Speller is a Windows application, which means that you can run the Speller from Windows without running WordPerfect. You can use the word look-up features of the Speller outside of WordPerfect, but you cannot check the spelling of documents in other Windows applications.

■ **Cue:** To move the Speller screen out of the way without closing it, click the Speller's Minimize icon to reduce the screen to an icon.

Specifying Speller Options

When you start the Speller, you may want to change some of the Speller's default settings. You can change the dictionary that the Speller uses to check words, for example, or specify which types of errors you want the Speller to find. This section describes how to set the Speller options to meet your needs.

T I P   The Speller checks document text, endnotes, captions, text boxes, headers, footers, footnotes, and so on. The Speller *doesn't* check graphics, equations, or the text included in a style. To check the spelling of text in a header, footer, and so on (without checking the document), start the spelling check while you are in the window or dialog box for that feature. Text defined in a style can be checked by starting the spelling check while you are using the Style Editor.

Specifying a Different Dictionary

You may want to use different dictionaries for different documents. Supplementary dictionaries with specialized medical or legal terminology, for example, are available, and you may find them useful when checking the spelling of a document in one of those disciplines.

After you start the Speller—but before you start the spell-check operation—you can specify which main and supplementary dictionaries you want the Speller to use. To use a different main or supplementary dictionary, follow these steps:

1. Start the Speller.

2. Choose **M**ain or **S**upplementary, as appropriate, from the **D**ictionary menu. A directory dialog box is displayed.

3. Specify the appropriate drive, directory, and file in the dialog box. The Speller will use that dictionary.

T I P   The supplementary dictionaries are regular WordPerfect files and can be protected with passwords. If you choose a dictionary that has a password, WordPerfect prompts you for the password.

The Speller dictionaries are identical to the WordPerfect 5.1 dictionaries. If you are switching from WordPerfect 5.1 to WordPerfect for Windows and have added a substantial number of words to the main dictionary in WordPerfect 5.1, you can use the WordPerfect 5.1 dictionary. Just indicate where to find the dictionary by using the Location of Files command.

If possible, use the WordPerfect for Windows or WordPerfect 5.1 dictionary. Older WordPerfect dictionaries aren't hyphenated and don't work as well with the WordPerfect for Windows automatic hyphenation feature. If you must use an older dictionary, keep in mind the following:

- WordPerfect 5.0 dictionaries work with the Speller, but the words don't include hyphenation information.

- WordPerfect 4.2 users must convert the dictionary to WordPerfect 5.1 format by using the Speller Utility. The converted dictionary doesn't contain hyphenation information.

Setting the Speller Options

You can change several options to affect the operation of the Speller. These options enable you to specify what the Speller looks for as it checks spelling and also to change the position of the Speller window. You use the Options menu to make these changes (see fig. 8.5).

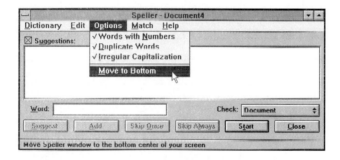

FIG. 8.5

Setting the Speller's options.

The Words with Numbers, Duplicate Words, and Irregular Capitalization options are switched on and off by choosing the option. A check mark to the left of the option indicates that the Speller will perform that function as it checks spelling.

The Words with Numbers option determines whether the Speller checks the spelling of words containing a number (for example, FILE1234).

The Speller alerts you to the occurrence of duplicate words, such as *the the*, if you check the Duplicate Words option.

The Speller also can check for certain unusual mixtures of upper- and lowercase letters in words if the Irregular Capitalization option is checked.

The Move to Bottom option moves the Speller window to the bottom of the screen, and the text with problems is displayed above the Speller window.

These options are covered in detail later in the chapter.

Specifying What You Want To Check

After starting the Speller, you can specify what you want the Speller to check. If you have highlighted a selection of text, the Speller initially indicates that it will check selected text. Otherwise, the Speller will check the entire document; the Check section shows Document.

Choose Check to check a different portion of your document. A pop-up list is displayed with several choices (see fig. 8.6).

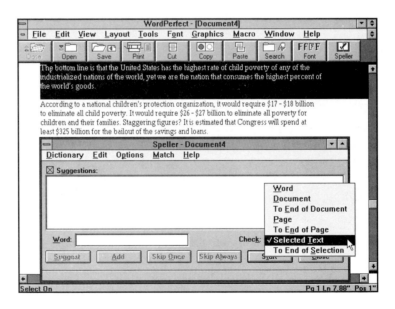

FIG. 8.6

Specifying the portion of the document to check.

■ **Cue:** Save time by limiting the spelling check to the portion of the document you have revised.

The pop-up list gives you a great deal of flexibility in determining which part of your document the Speller checks. The options named To End of begin checking at the location of the insertion point. The available options work as follows:

■ Choosing **W**ord checks the word where the insertion point is located. After looking up the word, the Speller moves the insertion point to the next word.

- Choosing **D**ocument checks the entire document regardless of the location of the insertion point.

- Choosing To **E**nd of Document checks from the insertion point to the end of the document.

- Choosing **P**age checks the current page regardless of the location of the insertion point.

- Choosing To E**n**d of Page checks from the insertion point to the end of the current page.

- Choosing Selected **T**ext checks a highlighted selection. (See Chapter 5 for more information on highlighting selections.)

- Choosing To End of **S**election checks from the location of the insertion point to the end of a highlighted selection.

Spell Checking the Document

To begin the spelling check, choose Start. The Speller informs you of its progress by displaying the message Spell Checking Page ## in the status line at the bottom of the Speller window as it checks each page.

> If you minimize the Speller rather than close it, you receive three benefits: the Speller is available very quickly; you don't need to reset any options you specified; and if you told the Speller to make certain replacements (for example, to replace the misspelled word *teh* with *the*), the Speller remembers and performs those replacements for subsequent spelling checks.
>
> **T I P**

Using Suggested Replacement Words

The primary function of the Speller is to check your document for misspelled words. The dictionary provided with WordPerfect doesn't have every word in the English language, but the dictionary *is* extensive. You also can add words to make the Speller even more useful.

To check your document as quickly as possible, the Speller first compares each word in your document to a list of common words in the main dictionary. If the word is found, the Speller continues to the next word.

- **Cue:** The Speller checks each word before moving to the next; a spelling check is always performed in the forward direction.

If the word isn't found, the Speller checks the word against the other words in the main dictionary. If the word still doesn't match, the Speller checks the supplementary dictionary. If the word isn't in the main or supplementary dictionaries, the Speller highlights the word and displays the message Not Found: followed by the word not found in the status line at the bottom of the Speller window. Figure 8.7 shows an example of a word not found in the dictionaries.

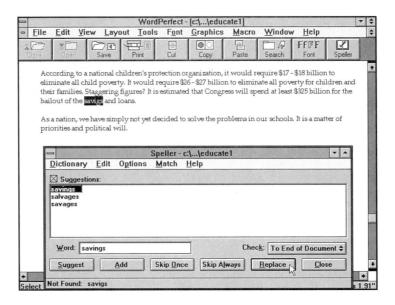

FIG. 8.7

Finding a word unknown to the Speller.

■ **Cue:** Turn off Suggestions to speed the spelling check.

In addition to informing you that a word wasn't found, the Speller suggests replacement words (if you checked the Suggestions check box). The suggestions include words differing by one letter, words with transposed letters, and words that sound similar to the word being checked.

■ **Cue:** If you requested suggestions and the correct word is displayed in the Word text box, choose **R**eplace.

If you are a proficient speller, you may not want the Speller to spend time finding alternate words. You may feel comfortable correcting misspelled words or skipping correctly spelled words without being offered suggestions. If you didn't check Suggestions, the word not found is displayed in the Word text box. Even if you turned off Suggestions, you can select **S**uggest after the Speller indicates that a word was not found, and the Speller displays a list of suggested replacement words.

If you checked the Suggestions box, the first word in the list of suggestions is displayed in the Word text box. To replace the misspelled word with one from the list of suggestions, scroll through the list of alternate words until the desired word is displayed in the list. Move the mouse pointer to the desired word. You can select this alternate word with either of the following methods:

- Click the mouse to move the desired word to the Word text box in the Speller window. Then choose **R**eplace.

- Double-click the mouse to select the replacement word and simultaneously replace the misspelled word with the selected word.

If none of the suggestions is appropriate, you can type the desired word in the Word text box and choose **R**eplace. You also can edit the misspelled word by clicking the mouse in the document. Move the mouse pointer to the misspelled word and click the mouse to move the insertion point to that location. Make the desired change and then choose **R**esume. See the "Editing a Word" section for more information.

The Speller offers only alternative word choices contained in the main dictionary and a compressed supplementary dictionary. As you add words to the supplementary dictionary, you may decide to move the added words to the main dictionary or compress the supplementary dictionary so that the new words can be offered as suggestions by the Speller. These processes are described in the "Using the Speller Utility" section of this chapter.

Handling Correctly Spelled Words

Because the Speller's main dictionary is extensive but not exhaustive, some words will not be found. Surnames, street names, technical jargon, and so on are especially likely not to be found. Many common proper names or common terms from various professions are included in the WordPerfect dictionary. Names like *Gary* and *Debbie* are in the dictionary, for example, but *Wendy* isn't.

If the Speller indicates that a word is not found, and you know the word is spelled correctly, you may want to add the word to build the Speller's vocabulary. Selecting **A**dd adds the word to the supplementary dictionary. The word will not be shown as Not Found during the rest of the current spelling check or in future spelling checks.

If you accidentally add a misspelled word, you can delete that word from the supplementary dictionary. See the section "Viewing and Modifying a Supplementary Dictionary" later in this chapter.

T I P

You can use the Speller Utility to add words from the supplementary dictionary to the main dictionary or to delete words from the main dictionary. See the "Adding and Deleting Dictionary Words" section of this chapter for more information.

Added words aren't placed in the supplementary dictionary until the Speller is closed. Added and skipped words are stored in a temporary area in your computer's memory. If you skip and add many words while the Speller is open, the Speller may run out of room in this storage area. The Speller then removes skipped words to make room for added words. This situation can cause the Speller to indicate that a word is Not Found, even though you had told the Speller earlier always to skip the word.

If the temporary storage area becomes full of *added* words, the message Dictionary Full appears on-screen. To write the added words to the supplementary dictionary and free the temporary storage area for more words, close the Speller. Then restart the Speller and use the Check pop-up menu to have the Speller continue the spelling check from the insertion point to the end of the document or selection, as appropriate.

Another option when a word is not found is to skip the word. You may want to skip the word if it's spelled correctly but you don't want to add the word to the supplementary dictionary. You also may want to skip the word if you aren't sure of the spelling but want to be alerted during the next spelling check that the word isn't in the dictionary. Words that you aren't likely to use on a regular basis are candidates for skipping. A good example of this situation is the last name of a person whose name you are unlikely to use in the future.

The Speller enables you to skip a word once or always. If you choose Skip **O**nce, the Speller continues past the word but shows the word as Not Found if the word occurs again later in the spelling check. Choosing Skip A**l**ways causes the Speller to continue past the word and to ignore the word if it occurs again later in the spelling check.

Editing a Word

If a word isn't found because it's misspelled, you can edit the word to correct the spelling in one of the following ways:

- Correct the word by typing it correctly in the Word text box and selecting **R**eplace.

- Correct the word by clicking the mouse pointer on the highlighted misspelled word in your document. The insertion point moves to the location of the mouse pointer, and you can use standard text editing techniques to edit the word. After correcting the word, click the Speller window (if the Speller window is not visible, reselect the Speller) and then choose **R**esume. The Speller

continues to check the document from the insertion point to the
end of the specified section (page, document, or selection).
The word you just edited will be spell-checked again. If it still isn't
found, it will be highlighted again. If the word is spelled correctly,
choose **A**dd, Skip **O**nce, or Skip A**l**ways, as desired.

When you replace a word with a suggested alternative, WordPerfect
will correct subsequent occurrences of the misspelled word with the
same replacement. If you edit the word using one of these two methods, however, WordPerfect continues to stop at subsequent occurrences of the misspelled word and request action.

Correcting Irregular Capitalization

In addition to checking the spelling of a document, the Speller checks
for five types of irregular capitalization. Irregular capitalization occurs
when upper- and lowercase letters are mixed in a way that doesn't
"make sense" to the Speller. The Irregular Capitalization Found dialog
box appears when the Speller finds such a mixture (see fig. 8.8).

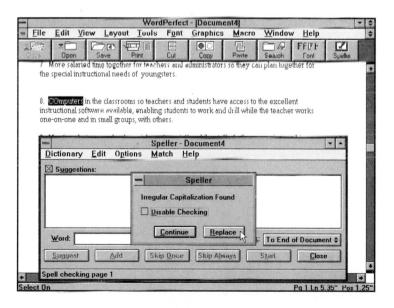

FIG. 8.8

Finding irregular
capitalization
with the Speller.

The Speller finds and replaces (upon your request) the irregularities as
shown in table 8.1 (where X indicates an uppercase letter, x indicates a
lowercase letter).

Table 8.1. Irregular Capitalization Error/Conversion

Irregular Capitalization	Changed Capitalization	Example
XXx	Xxx	THis becomes This
xXx	Xxx	tHis becomes This
xXX	XXX	tHIS becomes THIS
xxX	xxx	thIs becomes this
xX	Xx	as becomes As

If the Speller corrects irregular capitalization, the capitalization of the entire word is determined by the first three letters. Capitalization of letters after the first three has no effect on the way the capitalization of the word is changed. If a word is changed to all lowercase or all upper-case based on the first three characters, all letters in the word are changed. The word *fRAgile*, for example, is replaced by *FRAGILE* because the first three letters (*fRA*) match the *xXX* criterion as shown in table 8.1.

Eliminating Duplicate Words

Another important task the Speller can perform is checking your document for the occurrence of duplicate words. A duplicate word that often is missed in proofreading is the word *the*, as in *the the*. Sometimes the reader sees the first *the* but not the second.

When the Speller finds a duplicate word, you see the Duplicate Words Found dialog box (see fig. 8.9). The dialog box gives you the option to Continue (with no action by the Speller) or to delete the second word (by choosing Delete 2nd). If you don't want the Speller to check for duplicate words, choose Disable Checking (an X is placed in the box) and then choose Continue. The Speller stops checking for duplicate words.

Finishing the Spelling Check

When the Speller finishes checking the specified text, you see the message Spell check completed in a dialog box. To cancel the spelling check before it is completed, press Esc. The message Spell check cancelled appears on-screen.

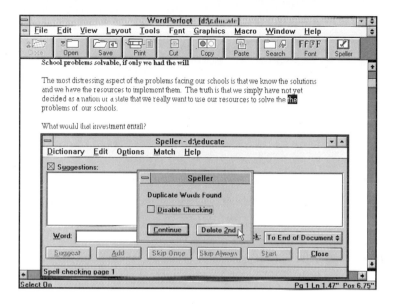

FIG. 8.9

Locating
duplicate words
with the Speller.

If you replaced or changed any words or made other revisions during
the spelling check, choose **Save** or **Save As** from the File menu to save
the modified document.

Looking Up a Word

You can type in the Word text box any word you want to find. Typing a
word in the Word text box and choosing **Suggest** causes the Speller to
do a phonetic word search. The Speller lists suggested replacement
words that sound similar to the word you typed in the Word text box.

In addition to looking up phonetically similar words, you can type wild-
card characters in the Word text box and have the Speller look up a
word that matches a pattern. Wild-card characters represent unknown
letters; a question mark (?) represents one character and an asterisk
(*) represents any number of characters. Choosing **Suggest** to match
c?p, for example, lists *cop*, *cup*, and *cap*. Matching *water** results in a
long list that includes *waterfall*, *waterproof*, and *watermark*. You can mix
wild-card characters and text. Matching the pattern *water*l* lists *waterfall*, *waterfowl*, and *waterwheel*.

The status line of the Speller window indicates the number of replacement words listed and shows `Pattern Matches` or `Phonetic Matches`,
as appropriate.

■ **Cue:** You can enter a
word in the Word text box
by cutting the word to the
Windows Clipboard in
WordPerfect or another
Windows application and
then pasting the word into
the Word text box (choose
Paste from the **E**dit menu).

During a spelling check, words with numbers can be excluded from the check. If you are checking a document with items containing a mix of letters and numbers (for example, *x1234* or *FILE123*), you may want to have the Speller skip them automatically. To skip words with numbers, be sure that the Words with **N**umbers item on the **O**ptions menu of the Speller window *doesn't* have a check mark.

Spell Checking Other Languages

If your documents contain mixed languages, during the spelling check the Speller can change to a dictionary for that language. Contact WordPerfect Corporation to learn which language dictionaries are available.

■ **Cue:** Choose **V**iew, Reveal **C**odes (Alt-F3) to see the hidden codes.

To spell check other languages, select the text you want to check with the alternative language dictionaries. Then choose **L**anguage from the **T**ools menu. A dialog box opens to enable you to choose the dictionary's language; specify the appropriate language. WordPerfect inserts a hidden code (such as [Lang:NL] for the Dutch language) at the beginning of the selected text. At the end of the selected text, another code (such as [Lang:US] for the English-U.S. language) alerts the Speller to return to the default language.

When the Speller reaches the code, the Speller uses dictionaries for the specified foreign language. If the Speller cannot find the language's main dictionary, a dialog box appears, enabling you either to indicate where the dictionary is located or to skip the language. If you choose **S**kip Language, the text identified for that language isn't spell checked. At the end of the selected text, the Speller switches back to the default language dictionaries.

Using a Supplementary Dictionary

After the Speller has looked for a word in the main dictionary, it looks for the word in the supplementary dictionary. You can use supplementary dictionaries to keep special words that are unique to your profession or situation. You also can buy supplementary dictionaries containing collections of words from the medical, legal, data processing, and other professions.

■ **Cue:** A supplementary dictionary is a regular WordPerfect file if it hasn't been compressed with the Speller Utility.

You can create a custom supplementary dictionary by typing the words in WordPerfect, saving the file, and specifying the file as the supplementary dictionary you want the Speller to use. You then can add words to your custom dictionary one at a time by choosing the **A**dd option as you check the spelling of a document.

You can open and edit a supplementary dictionary file in the same way as any other WordPerfect document. Additional words can be made available to the Speller by adding them to the document, and words can be eliminated by deleting them from the document. Save the file to make the changes permanent.

> If a word is in the main dictionary, don't add it to the supplementary dictionary. To determine whether a word is in the main dictionary, choose a supplementary dictionary that you know *doesn't* include the word and spell check the list of words you want to place in the supplementary dictionary. Words that *aren't* flagged as Not Found are in the main dictionary and don't need to be added to the supplementary dictionary you are creating.

T I P

To create a custom supplementary dictionary, choose **New** from the **File** menu to create the file. Then type the words you want in your supplementary dictionary, pressing Enter after each word. When you finish entering the words, save the file.

■ **Cue:** If you sort the words in the supplementary dictionary alphabetically, spell checking is faster.

For convenience, you can use the file extension SUP when you create a new supplementary dictionary. (When you choose the Dictionary Supplementary command to use a custom dictionary, the Speller uses *.SUP as the default entry in the Filename text box.)

You need not alphabetize the words or use capitalization. The Speller checks spelling without regard to capitalization of words and offers suggested replacement words with capitalization based on the word being replaced.

Include hyphens when entering a word only if you intend to add the word to the main dictionary or you plan to compress the supplementary dictionary. Adding hyphens in these cases tells WordPerfect where the word can be broken if hyphenation is necessary.

If you will not be adding the word to the main dictionary or compressing the supplementary dictionary, don't use hyphens in the words; hyphens cause the Speller to treat the word as two or more separate words. Use a supplementary dictionary with hyphenated words only after the dictionary has been compressed.

Combining Supplementary Dictionaries

The Speller can use only one supplementary dictionary at a time. To use words from more than one supplementary dictionary in spelling

■ Cue: The size of a supplementary dictionary has no practical limit; however, if the dictionary is enormous, the spelling check takes more time.

checks, you can combine the dictionaries. (Supplementary dictionaries must be expanded to be combined. For details, see the section "Compressing and Expanding a Dictionary" later in this chapter.)

To combine supplementary dictionaries, follow these steps:

1. Open one of the dictionaries by choosing **O**pen from the **F**ile menu.

2. Move the insertion point to the end of the file and choose **R**etrieve from the **F**ile menu. The Retrieve File dialog box appears on-screen.

3. Specify the directory and file name for the second supplementary dictionary and then choose **R**etrieve. Another dialog box appears, containing the message Insert file into current document? Choose **Y**es.

   To combine additional supplementary dictionaries, repeat steps 2 and 3 until all dictionaries are combined.

4. To save the combined dictionary, choose Save **A**s from the **F**ile menu. Specify a directory and file name for the combined dictionary.

You now can select the new combined supplementary dictionary from the Speller's **D**ictionary menu.

Viewing and Modifying a Supplementary Dictionary

As you add words by choosing **A**dd during the spelling check, the words are placed into the supplementary dictionary being used by the Speller. Unless you compress it, a supplementary dictionary is a regular WordPerfect file that you can view or open in the same way as any other file. After you compress a supplementary dictionary, however, you must expand it before you can view or open it. (For information on compressing and expanding supplementary dictionaries, see the section "Compressing and Expanding a Dictionary" in this chapter.)

After opening a supplementary dictionary, you can delete or add words as you want and then save the file with the changes.

Using the Speller Utility

The Speller Utility is provided with WordPerfect to enable you to perform various editing operations on a main dictionary or a compressed supplementary dictionary. You can use the Speller Utility to add words to or delete words from a dictionary, to display the common word list, or to see whether a word is in the common word list. You also can use the Speller Utility to look up words by matching patterns or by phonetic similarity, or to compress a supplementary dictionary.

The Speller Utility is a DOS character-based program rather than a Windows application. In fact, the Speller Utility is identical to the WordPerfect 5.1 Speller Utility. Like other character-based, non-Windows applications, the Speller Utility can be run from Windows. To run the Speller Utility, follow these steps:

1. Choose **R**un from the Windows Program Manager **F**ile menu.

2. Type the full path name, followed by the file name SPELL.EXE. If the file SPELL.EXE is in the WPC directory, for example, type **C:\WPC\SPELL.EXE**.

After you start the Speller Utility program, you can choose from many options. Figure 8.10 shows the main menu of the Speller Utility.

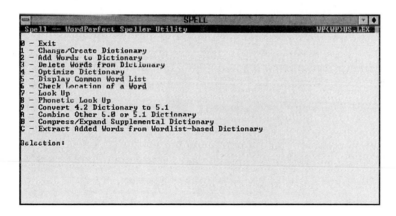

FIG. 8.10

Choosing options from the Speller Utility main menu.

Most of the options on the main menu are performed on the dictionary file listed in the upper right corner of the screen. As figure 8.10 shows, the Speller Utility is using the main United States dictionary WP{WP}US.LEX. If you decide to create or change a main or supplemental dictionary, choose **1**, Change/Create Dictionary. The Speller Utility offers the default main dictionary file name, WP{WP}US.LEX, or the default supplementary dictionary file name, WP{WP}US.SUP. Generally, you will use these default file names because they are the dictionaries normally used by the Speller. To choose a custom main or supplementary dictionary, type the appropriate file name.

A supplementary dictionary doesn't have both a common and main word list as does a main dictionary. If a supplementary dictionary is selected and you choose options that add or delete words from the common word list, you see the message Not functional with supplemental dictionary.

Adding and Deleting Dictionary Words

Cue: To speed the spelling check, add words you use often to the common word list of the main dictionary.

As described earlier, when the Speller performs a spelling check, it first looks for words in the common word list of the main dictionary. This list contains the most commonly used words in the language. By looking in the common word list first, the program performs the spelling check faster than if the Speller looked only in the main dictionary. If the word is not found in the common word list, the Speller looks for the word in the main word list of the main dictionary.

When you add a word to the main dictionary, you can choose whether to place the word in the common word list. If the word you are adding is one you use on a regular basis, place the word in the common word list. Don't place infrequently used words in the common word list, because making the list too large slows down the spelling check.

Cue: When adding words to the dictionary, add as many words as possible at once.

You can add words from the keyboard or from a file; for example, you may want to add words from a supplementary dictionary. (A compressed supplementary dictionary must be expanded before its words can be added to a main dictionary.)

To add words to a dictionary, choose option **2** (Add Words to Dictionary) from the Speller Utility main menu. From the resulting Spell—Add Words menu, choose option **1** or **2** (Add to Common Word List) to add words to the common word list of a main dictionary, or option **3** or **4** (Add to Main Word List) to add words to a supplementary dictionary or to the main word list of the main dictionary.

CAUTION: When you receive upgrades to the WordPerfect program, the main dictionary may have changes you want to install. WordPerfect Corporation may have added words, for example, or deleted misspelled words found during testing. If you install the main dictionary from a WordPerfect upgrade, any words you added and changes you made to the old dictionary are replaced. You may want to keep track of words you add to the main dictionary. For words added from a file, consider printing the file containing the words to be added. For words added from the keyboard, keep a manual list for future reference.

Just as you can add words to the dictionaries, you can delete words singly from the keyboard or as a group of words contained in a file.

To delete words from a dictionary, choose option **3** (Delete Words from Dictionary) from the Speller Utility main menu. From the resulting Spell—Delete Words menu, choose option **1** or **2** (Delete from Common Word List) to delete words from the common word list of a main dictionary, or option **3** or **4** (Delete from Main Word List) to delete words from a supplementary dictionary or from the main word list of a main dictionary.

 Cue: Deleting a word from the main word list also deletes it from the common word list if the word was in both places.

Compressing and Expanding a Dictionary

Compressing a supplementary dictionary is a matter of personal preference. The differences are listed here to help you decide what will work best for you.

An expanded supplementary dictionary is a normal WordPerfect file. You can view, add, delete, or change words by opening the file with WordPerfect. You make the changes permanent by saving the file.

The expanded supplementary dictionary has some disadvantages. The Speller can compare a word listed as Not Found to the words in an expanded supplementary dictionary but cannot offer any of the dictionary words as suggested alternatives. Words in an expanded supplementary dictionary also aren't hyphenated by WordPerfect.

Compressing the supplementary dictionary makes the file smaller (a side benefit) and speeds the spelling check process. The words are offered as suggested replacements when appropriate. If hyphenation is selected in WordPerfect, and you placed hyphens in words you entered in the supplementary dictionary, hyphenation occurs (when needed) at the point where you placed a hyphen.

CAUTION: *Don't* use dashes (Home-hyphen) to indicate hyphenation points. Use a hyphen instead of a dash. (Hyphens are displayed in the Reveal Codes screen as [-].) If you use a dash, the Speller treats it as a space and each part of a word is treated by the Speller Utility as a separate word.

To compress or expand a supplementary dictionary, follow these steps:

1. Start the Speller Utility and choose Change/Create Dictionary (**1**) from the main menu. Then choose Change/Create Supplemental Dictionary (**2**) from the resulting menu.

2. The message Name of supplemental dictionary to use appears on-screen. The default supplementary file name is displayed (for the United States, WP{WP}US.SUP). Press Enter to use the displayed file name, or type an alternative path and file name.

3. To *compress* the supplementary dictionary, choose Compress Supplemental Dictionary (**1**).

   To *expand* the supplementary dictionary, choose Expand Supplemental Dictionary (**2**).

Using the Thesaurus

Cue: Use the Thesaurus to find words that express what you want to say.

Using a thesaurus, you can make your document more interesting to read. A thesaurus helps you find the *right* words to express your thoughts. Some words are stronger or softer than others, and the right word conveys exactly the message you want to get across to the reader.

The WordPerfect Thesaurus searches for and displays synonyms (words with the same or very similar meanings) and antonyms (words with opposite meanings) for a word found in your document or entered in the Thesaurus. You may find that not all synonyms or antonyms fit correctly in your sentence. The Thesaurus offers you a list of words— you must select the best word from the list.

Starting the Thesaurus

Before starting the Thesaurus, you must copy the Thesaurus files to your computer by using the INSTALL program. See Appendix A for information on the installation procedure.

To look up a word with the Thesaurus, follow these steps:

1. Place the insertion point anywhere within the word you want to look up.

2. Choose **T**hesaurus from the **T**ools menu.

    Press Thesaurus (Alt-F1).

The Thesaurus window appears on-screen (see fig. 8.11).

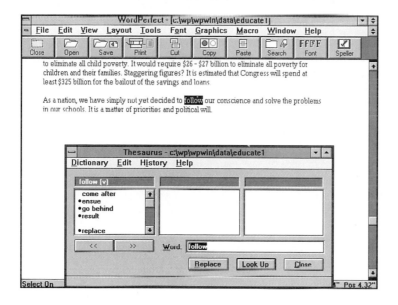

FIG. 8.11

Using the
Thesaurus.

If you use the Thesaurus regularly, consider adding a Thesaurus button to the Button Bar.

BUTTON

If the program cannot find the Thesaurus file (for example, WP{WP}US.THS for the United States thesaurus), the Select a WordPerfect Thesaurus dialog box appears with directory and file name windows to enable you to select a Thesaurus file.

Looking Up Words

When the Thesaurus window appears, in addition to looking up the word where the insertion point is located, you can look up words by typing them in the **W**ord text box and then choosing **L**ook Up. Synonyms and antonyms are displayed.

Because the Thesaurus is a separate Windows application, you can start the Thesaurus without running WordPerfect. You cannot select a word in another Windows application and automatically look it up with the Thesaurus, but you can *copy* a word in a Windows application to the Windows Clipboard and then choose **P**aste from the **E**dit menu of the Thesaurus to place the word in the Word text box. Then choose **L**ook Up to list the synonyms and antonyms of the word you copied to the Clipboard.

Cue: Start the Thesaurus from the Windows Program Manager to look up words without running WordPerfect.

You can minimize the Thesaurus window when you aren't using it by clicking the window's Minimize icon. This action reduces the Thesaurus window to an icon but doesn't close the window. When you maximize the Thesaurus again, you see the window with almost no delay.

Understanding the Thesaurus Window

The word you look up is called a *headword*. (If the message Word not found is displayed in the status line at the bottom of the Thesaurus window, the word you're looking up is not a headword in the Thesaurus dictionary.) The headword is listed at the top of the column and a list of *references* is displayed below it. If all the references don't fit in the list box, use the scroll bar to see more of the list.

References shown with a bullet (•) also are headwords that, if selected, display additional references. Looking up additional headword references can help you to refine your search for the right word. As many as three headwords with reference lists can be displayed at one time. You can use the << and >> buttons under the first column to move between the lists.

The references are identified as nouns [(n)], verbs [(v)], adjectives [(a)], or antonyms [(ant)]. If the headword is used in more than one way, the headword appears again in the list of references with the appropriate identification. Figure 8.12 shows an example of a headword, *minute*, shown as a noun [(n)] and as an adjective [(a)].

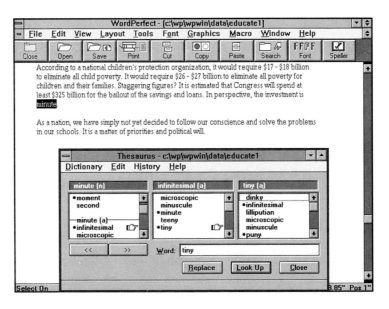

FIG. 8.12

The headword *minute* shown as a noun and an adjective.

If the headword has more than one meaning, the references are divided into subgroups and separated by their meanings.

Replacing a Word

Changing your document by using a word from the Thesaurus list is easy. If the word is an exact replacement, move the mouse pointer to the desired word and press the left mouse button to place the word in the Word text box. Then choose **R**eplace.

The replacement word may need some minor editing. Suppose that you looked up the word *assigning* (see fig. 8.13). The headword is shown as *assign* (a verb) and one of the reference words is *distribute*. If you want to use the reference word *distribute*, you need to edit it. Move the mouse pointer to the word *distribute* and press the left mouse button to move the word to the Word text box. Delete the *e*, add *ing*, and choose **R**eplace. The word *assigning* is replaced in your document by the word *distributing*.

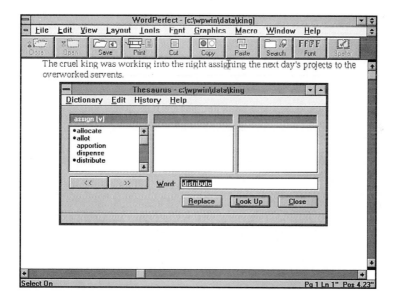

FIG. 8.13

Editing a replacement word.

Looking Up References

If the reference word list doesn't contain the word you want, you can select any of the reference words that also are headwords and look up additional references. Follow these steps:

1. Move the mouse pointer to the reference word marked as a headword (the word is preceded by a bullet).

2. Press the left mouse button to select the word and move it to the Word text box.

3. Choose **Look** Up. The headword at the top of the column is replaced by the new headword and a new reference list appears in the column.

■ **Cue:** To look up a word again quickly, use the History option.

As you look up different words, you may want to review the words you have looked up, or you may want to go back to one of the previous words and look at the reference words again. To see which words you have looked up since you started the Thesaurus, choose History. To look up one of the words on the history list again, highlight the word and then press the left mouse button.

You also can display the headwords in separate columns. When you double-click a reference word marked with a bullet, the Thesaurus places a hand symbol next to the word and that word becomes the headword in the next column (refer to fig. 8.12). This system enables you to see the synonyms and antonyms for several headwords as you look for the right word. Only three columns can be displayed at a time. If you have more than three lists of words, use the << and >> buttons below the first column to scroll the columns left and right.

Chapter Summary

WordPerfect for Windows' Speller and Thesaurus enable you to polish your documents and present thoughts in an accurate and interesting way. These tools cannot do your work for you, but they help ensure that your document is of the highest quality.

The Speller can help you to use the words in your document accurately. Use the Speller to check spelling, look for duplicate words, and check for certain kinds of irregular capitalization.

The Thesaurus cannot choose the right word for you but can provide lists of synonyms and antonyms, enabling you to select the word that best expresses what you want to say. Using appropriate words can make your document hard-hitting or soft, colorful or straightforward.

Basic Printing

With WordPerfect for Windows, you can do much more than just basic printing on standard paper; you can express your *ideas* in print. One of WordPerfect's strengths is the variety, depth, and power of its printer functions. This book discusses printing in three separate chapters: "Basic Printing" (this chapter), "Working with Fonts" (Chapter 10), and "Working with Advanced Printing Techniques" (Chapter 15). This chapter provides the basic information you need to print your documents from WordPerfect for Windows.

In this chapter, you learn how to set up and configure a printer for WordPerfect, how to view your document before printing, and how to print all or part of your document. Specifically, this chapter includes the following topics:

- Understanding WordPerfect and Windows printer drivers
- Installing and configuring a WordPerfect printer driver
- Using a Windows printer driver

■ **Eric Mark Rintell** is a computer consultant who advises clients about WordPerfect. He enjoys print-related topics so much that he wrote much of the print-related material in this book.

■ Printing documents

■ Managing your printing with Print Manager

■ Previewing documents before printing

If you already have installed a printer driver or want to begin printing documents immediately, you can skip to the section "Printing a Document."

Choosing a Printer Driver

Each printer has its own set of commands, and WordPerfect must "speak" the printer's language to operate the printer properly. A command to print text in boldface on one printer, for example, may command another printer to underline text. WordPerfect would be difficult to use if you had to remember all the printer commands. Fortunately, printer drivers remember them for you. A *printer driver* is a file that translates WordPerfect's printer commands into the commands your printer uses.

In WordPerfect for Windows, you can use the printer drivers of both WordPerfect and Windows; however, you can have only one printer driver at a time active in a document. In theory, your output should look the same on your printer regardless of which printer driver you select. In reality, you may have problems switching between drivers if the printers are configured differently. Because the WordPerfect printer driver may support a package that isn't available for the Windows printer driver, you may lose some functionality in switching between printer drivers. The printer driver options are discussed in the following sections.

CAUTION: If you didn't install and select a printer driver during installation, WordPerfect defaults to its "standard printer." This setting may be adequate for simple text, but not for graphics. To get the most out of printing in WordPerfect for Windows, you must install a printer driver for your printer.

WordPerfect Printer Drivers

The WordPerfect for Windows printer drivers are the printer drivers from WordPerfect for DOS, a character-based program. The advantages of using WordPerfect printer drivers are as follows:

- You can access all printers supported by WordPerfect, including many printers that Windows doesn't support.

- You can use existing WordPerfect 5.1 for DOS drivers. If you also use WordPerfect 5.1 for DOS, you don't have to install a printer driver during installation—just tell WordPerfect where to find your existing WordPerfect 5.1 for DOS printer driver. After you select your existing driver in WordPerfect 5.1 for Windows, you can begin printing.

- Documents print identically in the Windows and DOS versions of WordPerfect.

- Printing speed is fast.

- Several WordPerfect printing features work only with the WordPerfect printer drivers. You can set the graphics and text print quality independently, for example.

- You can select more than one paper size in a document.

- WordPerfect printer drivers contain more information than Windows printer drivers, giving you better printer control.

- You can customize WordPerfect printer drivers with the Printer (PTR) program.

The disadvantages of selecting WordPerfect printer drivers include the following:

- You can use a WordPerfect printer driver only in WordPerfect. If no printer driver for your printer is available in Windows, you cannot use the WordPerfect printer driver with other Windows applications.

- Windows font packages may not print properly with the WordPerfect driver.

- You may lose some WYSIWYG capabilities if you have a printer font in your printer file and Windows doesn't have a matching screen font. Windows approximates the appearance of the font.

- A third-party font package for WordPerfect for DOS (for example, FaceLift for WordPerfect) may not work in the Windows environment.

■ Information contained in WordPerfect printer drivers cannot be shared with other Windows applications. Fonts installed in the WordPerfect printer drivers may not be accessible to other Windows applications. If you modify a WordPerfect printer driver with the Printer (PTR) program, you can use the modifications only in WordPerfect for Windows.

■ You cannot install WordPerfect printer drivers from Windows or WordPerfect for Windows. You must install them from DOS.

Use WordPerfect printer drivers if you use WordPerfect 5.1 for DOS *and* WordPerfect 5.1 for Windows, especially if you have modified your WordPerfect printer drivers. WordPerfect printer drivers are faster than their Windows counterparts, and more sophisticated users often prefer the extra printer control and customization offered by these drivers. If you don't intend to share data with another Windows application or if WordPerfect for Windows is your primary Windows application, use the WordPerfect printer drivers.

Windows Printer Drivers

WordPerfect printer drivers may seem to be the better choice, but Windows printer drivers have the following advantages:

■ Windows printer drivers are written specifically for the Windows environment and conform to Windows' standards of device independence.

■ You can install Windows printer drivers from Windows without exiting WordPerfect for Windows.

■ You can use Windows printer drivers with Windows applications. All fonts, cartridges, and so on installed in a Windows printer driver are available to other Windows applications.

■ Windows system fonts are available in every Windows printer driver. If you choose a Windows system font as your initial font, the font appears the same in your document, regardless of which Windows printer driver you select.

■ Windows printer drivers work with Windows font packages such as Adobe Type Manager, FaceLift for Windows, and so on. These font packages include matching screen fonts to ensure WYSIWYG capability.

■ Windows printer drivers extend uniformity (with respect to printing) across Windows applications.

- You can fax your document from WordPerfect with a fax card If you select a Windows fax printer driver.

The disadvantages of using the Windows printer drivers include the following:

- Not all WordPerfect printing features work with the Windows printer drivers. You cannot use some font attributes, for example, with Windows printer drivers (see Chapter 10, "Working with Fonts").

- You cannot modify (customize) Windows printer drivers with WordPerfect's Printer (PTR) program.

- You can select only one paper size in a document.

- Documents may print differently in WordPerfect 5.1 for Windows than in WordPerfect 5.1 for DOS. A document that prints on 2 pages with a WordPerfect printer driver may require 2 1/4 pages with a Windows printer driver.

- The printing speed is slower than with WordPerfect printer drivers.

- If you own WordPerfect 5.1 for DOS, you need to store two sets of printer drivers.

Choose Windows printer drivers if you own a Windows typeface package. You also should choose Windows printer drivers to send a fax while running WordPerfect for Windows. If you use other Windows packages, such as Microsoft Excel for Windows, Aldus PageMaker, and so on, use the Windows rather than the WordPerfect drivers.

- **Cue:** Remember that you can switch printer drivers as needed.

Using a WordPerfect Printer Driver

Before you can access a printer in WordPerfect for Windows, you must install the printer driver file on the hard disk. You can install more than one printer driver to use with WordPerfect. After you install the printer driver, you select the printer (see "Selecting a WordPerfect Printer," later in this chapter).

Note: If you already have installed and selected a printer for WordPerfect for Windows, you can skip ahead to "Setting Up a WordPerfect Printer."

Installing a WordPerfect Printer Driver

You must install your printer driver from the DOS command level. First, save any documents in the WordPerfect editing window to protect them, and then exit WordPerfect and Windows. You can install more than one printer at a time.

T   I   P   If you also use WordPerfect 5.1 for DOS, you don't need to install a printer driver. Instead, tell WordPerfect for Windows where to find your existing WordPerfect 5.1 for DOS printer driver. Choose File, Preferences, Location of Files to display the Location of Files dialog box (see fig. 9.1). Choose Printer Files and type the path and name of the directory where your WordPerfect 5.1 for DOS printer files are located.

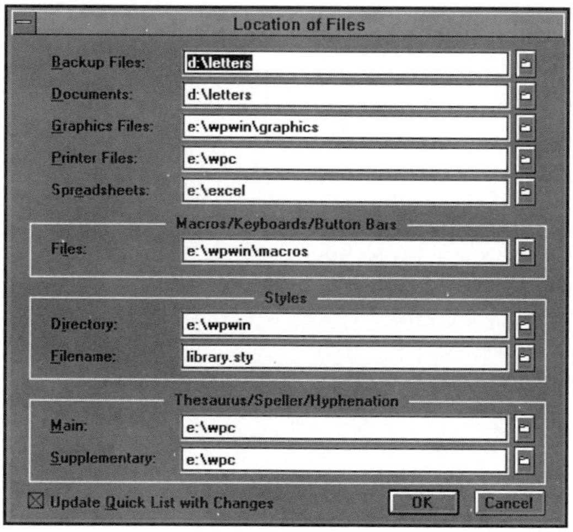

FIG. 9.1

The Location of Files dialog box.

To install a printer driver, follow these steps:

1. Place the WordPerfect Install disk in your floppy disk drive. If the floppy disk drive is A, type **A:INSTALL** at the DOS command prompt. If your floppy drive is B, type **B:INSTALL**.

2. Press Enter. The WordPerfect for Windows Installation screen appears.

3. To continue the installation, choose **Yes**.

CAUTION: If you used the Custom Installation option (#2) when you installed WordPerfect for Windows and you installed the shared WordPerfect files in a different directory, ignore step 4. Instead, choose Custom Installation (#2) again and check the file locations in the Install To screen option (#2). Change the file locations to match your setup and then exit (#9) to return to the Custom Installation screen. Choose option #4, Select Printer(s), and then continue with step 5.

4. Select option #4, Printer.

5. Make sure that Install has the correct floppy disk drive from which to install; if not, type the correct drive letter and press Enter.

6. When prompted, remove the Install disk from your floppy drive and insert the disk labeled Printer 1. If you have a supplemental disk from WordPerfect Corporation that contains the printer driver you want, insert that disk instead of Printer 1. Be sure to place the printer disk in the floppy disk drive listed in step 5. The Install program displays an alphabetized list of printers, as shown in figure 9.2.

```
  1 - NEC Pinwriter P3300          Printers marked with a '*' are
  2 - NEC Pinwriter P5             not included with the diskettes
  3 - NEC Pinwriter P5200          in your WordPerfect package.
  4 - NEC Pinwriter P5300          Selecting one of these printers
  5 - NEC Pinwriter P6             will provide you with
  6 - NEC Pinwriter P6 Plus        information on how to order
  7 - NEC Pinwriter P60            that printer definition.
  8 - NEC Pinwriter P6200
  9 - NEC Pinwriter P6300          The printers you select are
 10 - NEC Pinwriter P7             marked with a '♦.'
 11 - NEC Pinwriter P7 Plus
 12 - NEC Pinwriter P70
 13 - NEC Pinwriter P90
 14 - NEC Pinwriter P9300
 15 - NEC Pinwriter P9XL
 16 - NEC Silentwriter 2 260
 17 - NEC Silentwriter 2 290
 18 - NEC Silentwriter 2 Model S60P
▶19 - NEC Silentwriter 2 Model 90
 20 - NEC Silentwriter 2 S60
 21 - NEC Silentwriter LC-815
 22 - NEC Silentwriter LC-850

N Name Search; PgDn More Printers; PgUp Previous Screen; Esc Cancel; F7 Install;
Selection: 19
```

FIG. 9.2

The list of printers in Install.

7. Use the up-arrow and down-arrow keys to move the cursor (triangle) to your printer's name.

   Because so many printers are listed, you may need a few minutes to find the printer driver you want. To speed up the process, press **N** for Name Search. Type the first few letters of your printer manufacturer's name; Install moves immediately to that vendor's printers. Press Enter to exit Name Search mode.

8. Press Enter or the space bar to select the printer. The Install program displays a diamond in front of the selected printer's name. To install additional printers, repeat steps 7 and 8 until you have selected all the printers you want to install.

   If your printer isn't on the printer disks included with WordPerfect for Windows, you need to order a supplemental printer disk from WordPerfect Corporation.

   ■ **Cue:** Emulations may not take advantage of all the printer's features.

   If your printer isn't on the list but emulates one that is listed (see your printer manual for emulation information), install the driver of the emulated printer for temporary use. Many dot-matrix printers emulate the Epson FX-80, for example, and many laser printers emulate the HP LaserJet II.

9. Press F7 to install the selected printer driver. The Install program may instruct you to insert a different disk to install the specified printer driver.

10. Choose the Exit Install option to exit the Install program.

T I P   To speed up the installation, you can make a \TEMP directory on the drive where you want to install the program and copy all the WordPerfect disks to that directory. Then type **INSTALL** and press Enter from the \TEMP directory. This method is the fastest if you have sufficient space available on the drive. Erase the \TEMP directory and its contents when you complete the installation.

Adding a WordPerfect Printer Driver

In the preceding section, you learned how to copy your printer driver files to your hard disk. But WordPerfect doesn't yet know that these printer drivers are available. In this section, you learn how to add a printer driver to WordPerfect's available printer list.

Before you begin, you must specify where the printer driver is located. Choose File, Preferences, Location of Files to display the Location of Files dialog box. Choose Printer Files and type the path and name of the directory where your WordPerfect 5.1 for DOS printer driver files are located.

To add a printer driver to WordPerfect's list of available printers, follow these steps:

1. Choose File, Select Printer.

   If you prefer, you can choose File, Print to access the Print dialog box, and then choose Select (Current Printer).

   WordPerfect displays the Select Printer dialog box, as shown in figure 9.3.

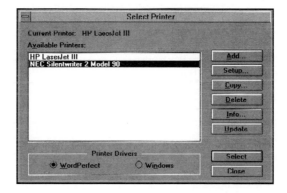

The Select Printer dialog box.

2. Choose WordPerfect in the Printer Drivers section to ensure that you are working with WordPerfect printer drivers.

   Note: If you choose WordPerfect in the Select Printer dialog box, WordPerfect displays options different from the options displayed when you choose Windows. (See the "Configuring and Updating a Windows Printer Driver" section of this chapter for the options available when you choose Windows.)

3. Choose Add to display the Add Printer dialog box (shown in fig. 9.4), which you use to add individual printers.

4. Choose Additional Printers (*.ALL) from the Printers section.

   WordPerfect printer files are of two forms: ALL files and PRS files. The ALL files contain printer drivers for several printers, and the PRS (Printer Resource) files are printer drivers for specific

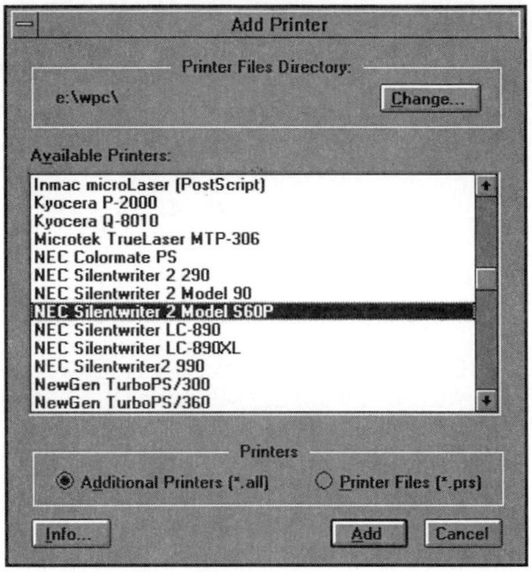

FIG. 9.4

The Add Printer
dialog box.

printers. Choose the Additional Printers (*.all) option when you
want to use printers that may not have individual PRS files on
disk. The Printer Files (*.prs) option is useful for reviewing individual printer files.

If no printers are listed under Available Printers, verify that the
printer files directory is correct. If not, choose Change and type
the path of the directory containing the printer files.

5. Choose Available Printers and select your printer. Alternatively,
you can type the first letter of your printer's name.

If you want helpful hints and information about using the selected
printer, you can choose Info to open the Printer Information dialog box. This dialog box indicates the printer driver release date
at the top. After you read the information in the dialog box,
choose Close.

6. Choose Add to add the specified printer to the Available Printers
list in the Select Printer dialog box. WordPerfect displays the
Copy Printer dialog box, which contains a file name ending in PRS
(see fig. 9.5). This file is the individual printer driver for the
printer you selected in step 4.

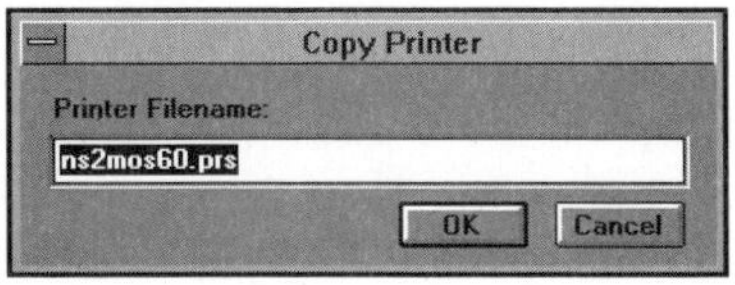

FIG. 9.5

The Copy Printer
dialog box.

7. Choose OK to confirm the file name.

   If the printer file exists on disk, WordPerfect asks whether you want to replace the existing file. If you choose **Yes**, WordPerfect overwrites the existing PRS file, which you may not be able to recover. To be safe, answer **No** and change the file name. Don't worry about having more than one printer driver for a printer on disk; you can change the name of one printer driver so that you can tell them apart (see "Copying a WordPerfect Printer Driver," later in this chapter).

8. Verify that the printer you added is listed in the Select Printer dialog box. Choose Close to exit the dialog box.

Selecting a WordPerfect Printer

You can use several printers with WordPerfect for Windows, but only one printer at a time can be active. The active (or current) printer is the printer to which WordPerfect sends your output. To select a printer, follow these steps:

■ **Cue:** You need to select a printer only if you are changing printers or printer drivers (WordPerfect or Windows).

1. Choose File, Select Printer.

   Alternatively, choose File, Print to access the Print dialog box, and then choose Select (Current Printer).

   WordPerfect displays the Select Printer dialog box.

2. Choose **WordPerfect** in the Printer Drivers section (if this option isn't selected already).

   WordPerfect shows the current printer at the top of the Select Printer dialog box. This printer is where the program sends output. If no printer is selected, the Current Printer line displays none.

3. Choose Available Printers and select the printer you want to use.

4. Choose **Select** to confirm your choice of the current printer. WordPerfect closes the dialog box.

   The next time you access the Select Printer dialog box, WordPerfect displays the name of the printer you just selected on the Current Printer line.

After you select a printer, you are ready to print, assuming that you don't need to edit the printer settings. If you are ready to print, see "Printing a Document," later in this chapter.

Setting Up a WordPerfect Printer

■ **Cue:** You don't need to select a printer to edit the Printer Resource file.

After you add your printer to the list of available WordPerfect printers in the Select Printer dialog box, you can edit the Printer Resource file to fit your specific printer configuration. For most users, WordPerfect's standard printer driver suffices. You can change the printer driver settings, however, when you add memory to your printer, add a sheet feeder, cartridges, or fonts, or change the initial base font.

To alter a printer setting, follow these steps:

1. Choose **F**ile, Se**l**ect Printer.

    Alternatively, choose **F**ile, **P**rint to access the Print dialog box, and then choose Se**l**ect (Current Printer).

    WordPerfect displays the Select Printer dialog box.

2. Choose **W**ordPerfect in the Printer Drivers section (if this option isn't selected already).

3. Choose A**v**ailable Printers and select the printer you want to modify.

4. Choose S**e**tup to display the Printer Setup dialog box (see fig. 9.6).

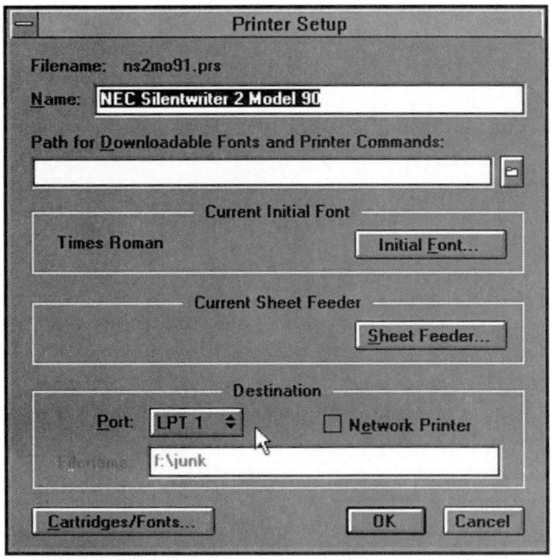

FIG. 9.6

The Printer Setup dialog box.

From the Printer Setup dialog box, you can view or change any of the features described in the following sections. When you finish making changes, choose OK to close the Printer Setup dialog box and return to your document. Keep in mind that any changes you make remain in effect until you make more changes. Exiting WordPerfect doesn't cause the program to revert to its previous settings.

Printer Names

The Name text box in the Printer Setup dialog box shows the name WordPerfect for Windows uses for the selected printer. You can use this text box to change the printer name if you need to distinguish between printers. If you have two cartridges for a printer that uses only one cartridge at a time, for example, you can name one printer HP LaserJet IIP (IQ cartridge) and the other HP LaserJet IIP (TypeCity cartridge).

■ **Cue:** Unless you have multiple copies of a printer definition, you probably don't need to change the printer name.

Sheet Feeders

If your printer is equipped with a sheet feeder, you use the Current Sheet Feeder section of the dialog box to specify your sheet feeder so that WordPerfect can use it. (For most printers, this area is empty.) To add a sheet feeder to your printer definition, follow these steps:

1. From the Printer Setup dialog box, choose **S**heet Feeder to display the Select Sheet Feeder dialog box (see fig. 9.7).

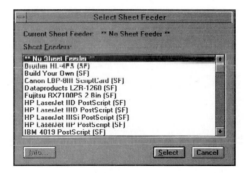

FIG. 9.7

The Select Sheet Feeder dialog box.

2. Select the desired sheet feeder in the Sheet **F**eeders list box.

   Before selecting a sheet feeder, you can determine whether the selected sheet feeder matches your printer by choosing **I**nfo. WordPerfect displays the same Printer Information dialog box you viewed when you added a printer, except that the dialog box provides details on the sheet feeder. Choose **C**lose to exit the Printer Information box and continue.

CAUTION: If your ALL file includes printers that support sheet feeders, WordPerfect may list sheet feeders even though no sheet feeders are compatible with your printer. Use this option only if you have a sheet feeder.

3. Choose **S**elect to confirm your sheet feeder selection and close the Select Sheet Feeder dialog box.

   WordPerfect lists the sheet feeder in the Current Sheet Feeder section of the Printer Setup dialog box.

To remove the sheet feeder, choose **S**heet Feeder from the Printer Setup dialog box, and then select **No Sheet Feeder**.

Destinations

In the Destination section of the Printer Setup dialog box, you specify whether you want WordPerfect to send output to a *port* or to a network printer. A port is analogous to a wall outlet into which you plug your telephone; the port is the "outlet" that connects your printer to your computer. Choose **P**ort to display the Port pop-up list, as shown in figure 9.8.

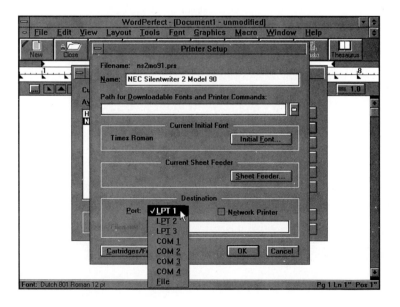

FIG. 9.8

The Printer Setup Port options.

Two types of ports exist: parallel and serial. If your printer has both types of ports, use the parallel port for faster printing. A printer with a parallel port is connected to a parallel port in the computer; parallel port names begin with LPT. The first parallel port on the computer is called LPT1, the second LPT2, and the third LPT3. Specify the parallel computer port to which your printer is connected.

If you use a serial connection, the first serial port in the computer is called COM1, the second COM2, and so on. Windows supports up to four serial ports; specify the COM port to which your printer is connected.

If you aren't sure what type of printer you have, refer to your printer manual.

Choose the **File** port option if you want WordPerfect to print to disk rather than to the printer. Then choose Filename and type the name of the file to which you want to print. You cannot choose Filename unless you choose **File** as the port. In the Filename text box, you can include a drive and path name.

> **CAUTION:** Be careful when you write to a file; WordPerfect continues to write to the specified file until you specify a new destination by changing the port setting.

Cartridges and Fonts

Additional typefaces for your printer are available in two forms: plug-in cartridges and font files (soft fonts) stored on your hard disk. Not all printers can accommodate these optional fonts, but some accommodate both cartridges and soft fonts. To view or change these additional printer typefaces, choose **C**artridges/Fonts from the Printer Setup dialog box. If your printer is equipped with built-in fonts, you don't need to use the Cartridges/Fonts option to access them.

You also can change the default font that WordPerfect uses to print by changing the initial font setting in the Current Initial Font section of the Printer Setup dialog box. Choose Initial **F**ont to change the default font.

In the Path for Downloadable Fonts and Printer Commands text box, WordPerfect displays the current path that the program uses to locate the files for your downloadable fonts and printer commands.

WordPerfect for Windows automatically sends commands to your printer; however, a printer vendor may provide disk files to access special features in your printer (called *printer command files*). To specify the location of these special files, choose Path for

■ **Cue:** Keep your downloadable font files and your printer command files in the same location; in the Printer Setup dialog box, you can specify only one path for both types of files.

Downloadable Fonts and Printer Commands, and then type the path and directory where the printer command files reside on disk. If you leave this text box blank, WordPerfect assumes that the files are stored in your printer files directory.

For more information on using fonts with WordPerfect, see Chapter 10, "Working with Fonts."

Copying a WordPerfect Printer Driver

You can copy a printer file that is listed under Available Printers in the Select Printer dialog box. You can use this feature, for example, to make a backup copy of your printer file before updating it with a newer version.

To copy a printer file, choose File, Select Printer and specify Word-Perfect (if it isn't selected already). Then choose Copy to display the Copy Printer dialog box (again see fig. 9.5). WordPerfect automatically assigns and displays a new PRS file name. To differentiate the new file from the original, the program changes a letter in the original file name or adds a number. You can change the file name, but you shouldn't change the PRS extension, which WordPerfect uses to identify the file as a Printer Resource file. When you are satisfied with the file name, choose OK.

You may now have two printers with the same name listed in the Available Printers section of the Select Printer dialog box. To change one or both of the printer name(s) so that you can tell them apart, refer to the "Setting Up a WordPerfect Printer" section, earlier in this chapter.

Deleting a WordPerfect Printer Driver

From the Select Printer dialog box, you can choose Delete to remove a printer from the list of available printers. Choose Yes from the resulting dialog box to remove the printer; choose No to cancel the Delete command.

The Delete command removes the printer's name from the Available Printers list, but the Printer Resource file remains on your hard disk in your printer files directory. If you need the printer file again, choose Add to restore it to the Available Printers list (see "Adding a Word-Perfect Printer Driver," earlier in this chapter).

If you are certain that you will not need the printer file again, you can erase the PRS file from your printer files directory (see Chapter 3, "Managing Files," for information on erasing files).

Using the Info Option

Choosing the **I**nfo button in the Select Printer or Add Printer dialog boxes displays the release date of your WordPerfect printer driver. You also can access helpful hints about using your printer with WordPerfect for Windows. The Select Sheet Feeder dialog box also contains an Info button, which enables you to access information about sheet feeders. When you choose Info, WordPerfect displays the Printer Information dialog box. To close the Printer Information dialog box after you review the information, choose **C**lose.

■ **Cue:** Knowing the printer driver release date may assist WordPerfect Corporation in determining whether the driver is current and whether you have a "bug" in the driver.

Updating a WordPerfect Printer Driver

WordPerfect Corporation frequently revises and enhances its printer drivers. The corporation doesn't ship updated printer files as individual Printer Resource files, however, because the files would require too many disks. Instead, several printer files with similar characteristics are shipped in an ALL file. As a general rule, you shouldn't install an updated printer driver if your printer is operating without any difficulty; use updates to correct a problem or to add support for a new feature.

■ **Cue:** Before installing a new printer file, choose **C**opy from the Select Printer dialog box to make a backup copy of your old printer resource file.

Copy the ALL file into your printer files directory. Then return to the Select Printer dialog box, select the printer you want to update, and choose **U**pdate. WordPerfect overwrites your original PRS file with the newer version.

Using a Windows Printer Driver

In contrast to WordPerfect printer drivers, Windows printer drivers are accessed only in the Windows environment. You must install your Windows printer driver before you can select and use the driver in WordPerfect. For information on installing a Windows printer, consult your Windows documentation or Que's *Using Microsoft Windows 3*, Second Edition.

This section describes how to select, configure, and update a Windows printer driver.

To use a Windows printer driver, you must turn on the Fast Graphics Printing option. This option speeds graphics printing through the Windows driver without affecting the speed of text printing. Leave this option enabled unless you experience problems printing graphics through your Windows printer driver.

To turn on Fast Graphics Printing, follow these steps:

1. Choose **F**ile, **P**references.

     Press Preferences (Ctrl-Shift-F1).

2. Choose **P**rint to display the Print Settings dialog box, as shown in figure 9.9.

Print Settings

Multiple Copies

Number of Copies: `1`

Generated By: `Printer`

Document Settings

Binding Offset: `0"`

Graphics Quality: `Medium`

Text Quality: `High`

Redline Method
- ⦿ Printer Dependent
- ○ Mark Left Margin
- ○ Mark Alternating Margins
- Redline Character: `|`

Size Attribute Ratio

Fine: `60%`

Small: `80%`

Large: `120%`

Very Large: `150%`

Extra Large: `200%`

Super/Subscript: `60%`

Windows Print Drivers
- ☒ Fast Graphics Printing

`OK` `Cancel`

3. Choose Fa**s**t Graphics Printing in the Windows Print Drivers section of the dialog box to display an X in the check box.

4. Choose OK.

The Fast Graphics Printing option remains selected until you deselect it, even if you exit and restart WordPerfect.

Selecting a Windows Printer Driver

◼ Cue: WordPerfect for Windows defaults to WordPerfect printer files unless you indicated otherwise when installing the software.

When you want to use a Windows printer driver in WordPerfect, you don't need to add the driver to the list of available printers in the Select Printer dialog box (as you must do with WordPerfect printer drivers), but you must select the Windows driver to use it. (***Note:*** You must install a Windows printer driver before you can use the driver in WordPerfect.) To select a Windows printer driver in WordPerfect, follow these steps:

1. Choose **F**ile, Select Printer.

Alternatively, choose File, Print to access the Print dialog box, and then choose Select (Current Printer).

WordPerfect displays the Select Printer dialog box.

2. Choose Windows in the Printer Drivers section of the dialog box.

WordPerfect displays the Select Printer dialog box shown in figure 9.10. Notice that this version of the dialog box contains fewer options than the dialog box displayed when you choose Word-Perfect.

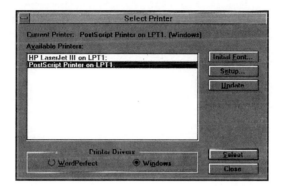

FIG. 9.10

The Select Printer dialog box when the Windows option is selected.

3. Choose Available Printers.

4. Highlight the Windows printer you want to use.

5. Choose Select to confirm your choice and to close the dialog box. The next time you access the dialog box, WordPerfect displays the name of your Windows printer, followed by (Windows), on the Current Printer line.

WordPerfect copies information from the Windows printer driver to your disk as a Windows printer resource file, with the extension WRS. You then can use the Windows printer driver to print. Note that because Windows printer drivers don't contain as much information as WordPerfect printer drivers, fewer options are available.

Configuring and Updating a Windows Printer Driver

You can change print options from within WordPerfect, but you also may need to make some changes within the Windows printer driver. You may need to customize the driver, for example, if WordPerfect cannot access all the printer's features (such as printer resolution or page orientation) with its Windows Printer Resource file. You also occasionally may need to install an updated version of the printer driver.

For these functions, you use the Setup and Update options in the Select Printer dialog box. To use these options, make sure that the Windows option is selected in the Select Printer dialog box and then select the printer you want to reconfigure.

■**Cue:** Using the Printers-Configure dialog box saves time because you don't have to access the Windows Control Panel.

To reconfigure a Windows printer driver, choose Setup in the Select Printer dialog box. The Printers-Configure dialog box appears. Options in this dialog box vary according to the printer selected in the Select Printer dialog box. Make any desired changes in the options shown and then choose OK to confirm your changes and close the dialog box. Finally, choose Close to exit the Select Printer dialog box.

For information on Windows printer configuration options, consult your Windows documentation and your printer manual.

CAUTION: Changes you make in your Windows printer drivers also affect your other Windows programs.

If you receive an updated version of a Windows printer driver, install it in Windows before using the Update option in the Select Printer dialog box. To update the WordPerfect PRS file, select the printer you want to update in the Available Printers list box of the Select Printer dialog box. Then choose Update. WordPerfect reads the Windows printer file and copies the updated information into the PRS file.

Printing a Document

With WordPerfect for Windows, you have several alternatives for printing documents, regardless of which type of printer driver (WordPerfect or Windows) you use. Printing from the screen is the most widely used printing method. The second printing method, printing from a disk, enables you to print a document without retrieving it in WordPerfect. With this method you also can specify which pages to print.

Understanding the Current Print Job Dialog Box

Regardless of which printing method you use, WordPerfect displays the Current Print Job dialog box (shown in figure 9.11) after you select a print option. This dialog box shows the status of your print requests.

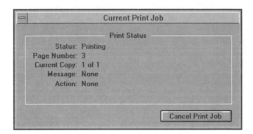

FIG. 9.11

The Current Print Job dialog box.

The Current Print Job dialog box contains the following information:

- The Status line indicates what WordPerfect is doing. If the program encounters no problems, it displays the message Printing.

- The Page Number line shows the number of the page WordPerfect currently is sending to the printer. (If you have activated the Windows Print Manager, WordPerfect sends pages to the Print Manager instead of the printer. For more information on the Print Manager, see "Using the Windows Print Manager," later in this chapter.)

- The Current Copy line shows which copy is printing and the number of copies requested.

- The Message line displays a message if WordPerfect encounters a problem when printing. If no printing problems occur, WordPerfect displays the message None. (If you have activated the Windows Print Manager, error messages are displayed in the Print Manager.)

- The Action line displays WordPerfect's suggestion about how to solve the problem shown in the Message line. When no problems are present, the Action line displays the message None.

- The Cancel Print Job button terminates the print job.

Printing from the Screen

You have several alternatives when printing from the screen: you can print the entire document, a specific page, several pages, or selected sections. To print selected text, you first must select the desired section (see Chapter 5, "Selecting and Editing Text," for more information on selecting sections of text).

To print from the screen, you access the Print dialog box by choosing **File**, **Print** (see fig. 9.12).

 Press Print (F5).

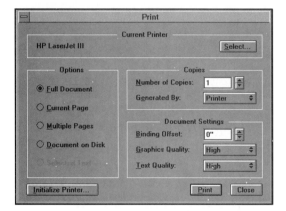

FIG. 9.12

The Print dialog box.

Cue: Press Ctrl-P to print a full document quickly.

In the Options section of the dialog box, you specify the amount of text you want to print. To print the entire document, choose **Full Document** (the default option). To print only the current page, choose **Current Page**. To print a selected section, choose Selected Text. (This option isn't available unless a section is selected before you access the Print dialog box.)

When you finish specifying options, choose **Print**. WordPerfect displays the Current Print Job dialog box. If you are printing only the current page, the Page Number line counts your document pages from the beginning page to the current page, and WordPerfect ensures that the format codes (margins, line spacing, and so on) are correct.

If you haven't requested other print jobs before this job, the document begins printing after WordPerfect closes the Current Print Job dialog box.

You also can print specified pages, rather than the current page. See the "Printing Multiple Pages" section, later in this chapter.

Printing Documents from Disk

You don't need to retrieve a WordPerfect document to print it. The Document on Disk option in the Print dialog box enables you to print documents from your disk drive.

■ **Cue:** Documents saved with the Fast Save feature may take longer to print.

To print a document from disk, follow these steps:

1. Choose **F**ile, **P**rint to display the Print dialog box.

   [CUA] Press Print (F5).

2. Choose **D**ocument on Disk.

3. Choose **P**rint.

   The Document on Disk dialog box appears, as shown in figure 9.13.

The Document on Disk dialog box.

4. In the **F**ilename text box, type the name of the file you want to print.

   Alternatively, click the Folder icon to open the Select File dialog box, highlight the desired file, and choose **S**elect to close the Select File dialog box and return to the Document on Disk dialog box.

5. Specify any desired print options (described later in this section).

6. Choose **P**rint to close the Document on Disk dialog box and start the printing process.

If the document you are printing was formatted for a printer other than the one currently selected, WordPerfect displays the message Document has not been formatted for current printer. Continue?

Choose **No** to cancel the print job or **Yes** to continue printing. If you choose **Yes**, the output may look different from what you expected because the formatting codes in the document on disk were intended for a different printer. *Note:* WordPerfect doesn't change the codes stored in the document on disk.

The following sections explain the Range, Document Summary, and Odd/Even Pages options in the Multiple Pages and Document on Disk dialog boxes.

Range

The Range option specifies which pages WordPerfect prints. By default, WordPerfect prints the entire document (All). To print specific pages, specify in the **R**ange text box the pages you want to print.

WordPerfect doesn't require that the pages be consecutive; however, you must type the numbers of the pages you want to print in numeric order. If you specify page 5 before page 2, WordPerfect prints only page 5. Table 9.1 shows several ways to specify page ranges.

Table 9.1. Specifying a Page Range

To Print	Type
Pages 4, 8–11, 23, 30–33	**4,8-11,23,30-33**
Page 36 to the end	**36-**
Page 36	**36**
From beginning to page 7	**-7**
Pages 4, 8, 11, 23, 30, 33	**4,8,11,23,30,33**
Pages 1–8, and 38 to the end	**1-8,38-**

If you use the New Page Number feature to divide your document into sections (see Chapter 11, "Formatting Pages and Designing Documents"), type the section number in the **R**ange text box, followed by a colon and the pages you want to print from that section. To specify pages 4 through 6 in Chapter 3, for example, type **3:4-6** in the Range text box.

Sections numbered with Roman numerals are counted separately from sections using Arabic numerals. If you use Roman numerals for your document's preface and appendix, for example, and you type **2:iii** in the **R**ange text box, WordPerfect prints page iii of the appendix (the second section using Roman numerals). If you type **2:3**, however, WordPerfect prints page 3 of Chapter 2.

Table 9.2 shows examples of how to specify a range of pages from a document containing sections. For this example, assume that the document contains pages numbered as follows:

Section	Page Numbers
Preface	i–iv
Chapter 1	1–8
Chapter 2	1–12
Chapter 3	1–7
Appendix	i–ix

If you don't specify a section number, WordPerfect prints the specified page of the first section matching the numbering style—Roman or Arabic—used for the page number.

Table 9.2. Specifying Pages with Sections

To Print	Type
Preface, page ii	**1:ii**
Appendix, page ii	**2:ii**
Chapter 1, page 2	**1:2**
Chapter 3, page 2	**3:2**
All of the Preface and Appendix	**i-v, i-ix**
Ch. 1, page 2 through Ch. 2, page 4	**1:2-2:4**
Preface, page ii to the end	**ii-**

Odd/Even Pages

The Odd/Even Pages option saves time if you want to print only odd or even pages. This option is especially useful if you want to print on both sides of your paper but don't have a duplex printer—you can print the odd pages, flip the paper, and then print the even pages on the other side.

You can choose from five options in the Odd/Even Pages pop-up list: None (the default), Odd, Even, Logical Odd, and Logical Even. If you choose **O**dd or **E**ven, WordPerfect uses the actual page numbers to print pages, ignoring any page numbers you may have changed with formatting codes. If you choose **L**ogical Odd or Lo**g**ical Even, the program doesn't use the actual page numbers; instead, it uses the page numbers in formatting codes.

Suppose that you use the code [Pg Num:4] to change page number 3 to page number 4 in a five-page document. If you choose **O**dd and specify the range **1-5** in the **R**ange text box, WordPerfect uses the actual page numbers and prints pages 1, 3, and 5. If you choose **L**ogical Odd with the same page range, however, WordPerfect uses the formatting codes and prints only pages 1 and 5.

Document Summary

The Document Summary feature (see Chapter 11, "Formatting Pages and Designing Documents") stores information about your WordPerfect document. You enter any information you want to store; for example, the date of last revision, comments, or the author's name.

To print the document summary with the document, choose the **D**ocument Summary option. To print the document summary alone, don't specify a range in the **R**ange text box, and choose None in the Odd/Even Pages section of the dialog box. To print specified pages of the document summary, specify odd or even pages, or type the desired page range.

Printing Multiple Pages

You can print multiple pages from the screen or from disk. To print multiple pages from the screen, follow these steps:

1. Choose **F**ile, **P**rint.

    Press Print (F5).

2. Choose **M**ultiple Pages. The Multiple Pages dialog box appears.

3. Specify the desired options. Options in the Multiple Pages dialog box are the same as the options in the Document on Disk dialog box, except that you cannot enter a file name in the Multiple Pages dialog box.

4. Choose **P**rint to close the Multiple Pages dialog box and begin printing.

Canceling a Print Job

Occasionally, you may need to cancel a print job while it's printing—if the job prints incorrectly, the wrong paper is in the printer, the wrong typeface is printing, and so on. You can terminate a print job by choosing **C**ancel Print Job in the Current Print Job dialog box. After WordPerfect removes the Current Print Job dialog box from your editing window, however, you cannot cancel printing from within WordPerfect for Windows.

You can cancel the print job if the Windows Print Manager is active, but if the Print Manager isn't active, and WordPerfect is printing directly to your printer, the job continues to print. When your printer has finished printing, you may need to reset it to clear its buffers to prevent ruining future output.

Using Document Print Settings

You can modify print settings (for example, print quality and binding offset) in one of two ways. To make permanent changes, modify the default settings in the Print Settings dialog box (shown in fig. 9.14). These changes remain in effect until you change the default settings again. To make temporary changes on a document-by-document basis, you can change the print settings in the Print dialog box (shown in fig. 9.15).

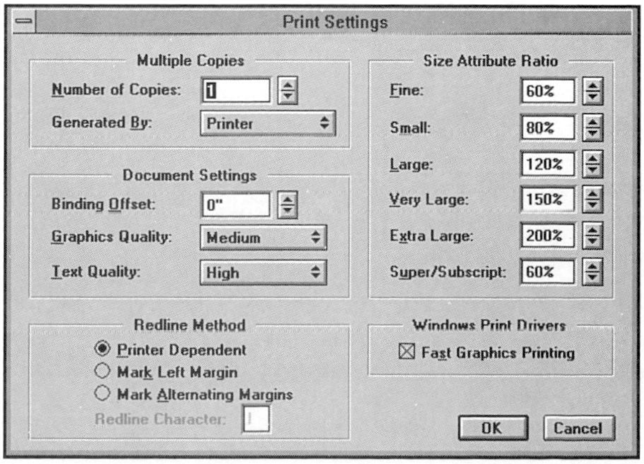

The Print Settings dialog box.

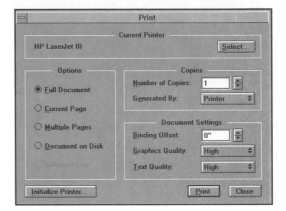

FIG. 9.15

The Print dialog
box.

To access the Print Settings dialog box, choose **File**, **Preferences**, **Print**. The options in the Multiple Copies and Document Settings sections of the Print Settings dialog box are the same as the options in the Copies and Document Settings sections of the Print dialog box. The following sections describe these options. (Other sections of the Print Settings dialog box are discussed in Chapter 10, "Working with Fonts.")

Note: Changes you make in the Print dialog box for the current document override the default settings in the Print Settings dialog box. When you save the document, the print settings also are saved with the document.

Multiple Copies

You can print more than one copy of a print job by specifying the number of copies needed in the Number of Copies text box. Then specify (with the Generated By option) whether the additional copies are generated by WordPerfect or the **P**rinter.

If your printer can print multiple copies of a page, choose **P**rinter for the Generated By option. With this method, WordPerfect tells the printer to print the specified number of copies of each page. If you type **5** in the Number of Copies text box, for example, the printer prints five copies of page 1, five copies of page 2, and so on. (Note that the documents aren't collated and must be separated.)

If your printer cannot print multiple copies, choosing **W**ordPerfect prints multiple copies by sending the document to the printer as many times as needed. This method may take longer to generate multiple copies than generating the copies from the printer.

Binding Offset

Use the Binding Offset option when you plan to bind the printed pages. This option shifts the printed text to the right on odd-numbered pages and to the left on even-numbered pages to provide extra white space along the inside edges of the pages of a bound document.

Be careful about using the Binding Offset option in the Print Settings dialog box; every document you print will be affected unless you override the offset in the Print dialog box.

Graphics Quality

The Graphics Quality setting determines the resolution (sharpness) of the graphics you print. The four settings available are High, Medium, Draft, and Do Not Print. The higher the resolution, the longer the graphics take to print.

If you are printing with a Windows printer driver, the available settings are Set in Driver, Draft, and Do Not Print. Choosing Set in Driver instructs WordPerfect to use the current resolution set in the Windows printer driver.

If your printer has trouble printing graphics or has difficulty printing text and graphics simultaneously, choose Do Not Print and print only the text of the document. Then return the printed pages to the printer, choose a Graphics Quality setting, and choose Do Not Print for the Text Quality option (described in the next section). WordPerfect then prints only the graphics on the pages.

Text Quality

Like the Graphics Quality setting, the Text Quality setting affects the printing resolution; however, the Text Quality option determines the resolution of the text instead of the graphics.

When you print a character from a character set that isn't supported by your printer, WordPerfect creates the character from its DRS (driver resource) file. DRS characters print at the Graphics Quality setting unless you choose High for the Text Quality. With this setting, DRS characters print at high resolution, regardless of the Graphics Quality setting. If you choose Do Not Print for *either* quality setting, DRS characters don't print.

If you use a Windows printer driver, the available Text Quality settings are Set in Driver, Draft, and Do Not Print. Choosing Set in Driver instructs WordPerfect to use the current resolution set in the Windows printer driver.

Using the Windows Print Manager

If you want to continue working in your document editing window while you print, you must use the Windows Print Manager (see fig. 9.16). The Print Manager's *background printing* feature (not available in Word-Perfect) can handle your print job while you continue working in Word-Perfect. Using background printing can save time, especially when you need to print high-resolution graphics or use fonts that must be down-loaded.

In addition to background printing, you can use the Print Manager to pause printing temporarily, cancel printing, or change printing speed.

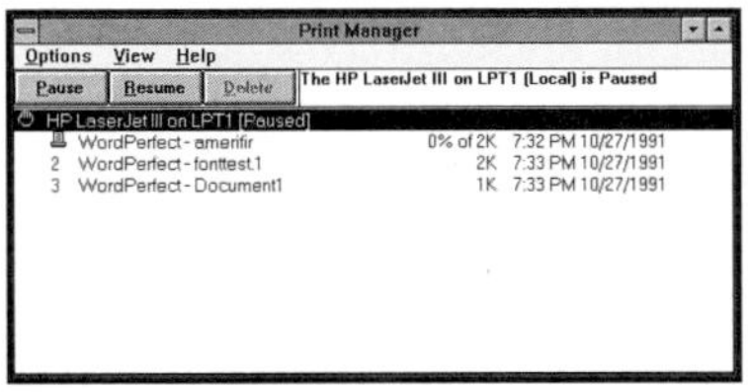

FIG. 9.16

The Windows
Print Manager.

If the Windows Print Manager is active, WordPerfect sends output di-rectly to the Print Manager rather than to the printer. You can resume working when WordPerfect closes the Current Print Job dialog box (described earlier in the section "Understanding the Current Print Job Dialog Box"), indicating that the program has finished sending your output to the Print Manager.

The Print Manager window shows the document being printed and the documents in the *print queue* (the list of documents waiting to be printed). If you are using more than one printer, each printer has its own print queue. The document currently printing is indicated with a printer icon to the left of the document name, and other jobs in the queue are sequentially numbered in the order in which they will print.

You can interrupt printing temporarily to change a ribbon, load paper, and so on, by pausing the printer. Select the printer for which you want to interrupt printing, and then choose **P**ause. The printer stops printing (if the printer's buffer contains pages, however, printing may not stop immediately). To continue printing from a paused printer, select the paused printer and then choose **R**esume.

To remove a print job from the print queue, select the document name and choose **D**elete. If the document already is printing when you cancel it, you may need to turn the printer off and on again to clear its buffer. If you don't clear the buffer, future print jobs may not print correctly.

> The Delete option enables you to cancel a print job that you didn't have time to cancel in WordPerfect's Current Print Job dialog box.
>
> **T I P**

To reposition a print job, select the document you want to move in the queue. Then press Ctrl and the up- or down-arrow key to move the document to its new position in the queue. (*Note:* You cannot move a print job after the printer has begun printing it.) After you reposition the document, Print Manager adjusts the print queue numbers to reflect the new printing order.

If your documents take too long to print, you can speed the printing process by choosing **O**ptions and specifying a priority. You have three choices: Low Priority, Medium Priority, and High Priority. The higher the priority, the faster your document prints. If you specify High Priority, however, your computer allocates more resources to Print Manager. Depending on the speed and installed memory of your computer, choosing High Priority may slow your work in WordPerfect. In general, a high priority slows all your other Windows applications.

For more information on using the Windows Print Manager, consult your Windows documentation or Que's *Using Microsoft Windows 3*, Second Edition.

Using Print Preview

Unless you are working in Draft mode, WordPerfect's editing window displays text and graphics in WYSIWYG. The editing window doesn't show your document as it will look when printed, though; for example, you cannot see WordPerfect graphic characters, footnotes, headers, footers, or vertical bars.

To see how your printed document will look, use WordPerfect's Print Preview feature. This feature also is useful for viewing changes that occur in your document after you select a different printer.

■ **Cue:** Print Preview enables you to see output before you print it, but you cannot edit your document in Print Preview.

To view your document in the Print Preview window, choose **F**ile, Print Pre**v**iew. WordPerfect displays the Print Preview window (see fig. 9.17), which shows the current page from your document.

 Press Print Preview (Shift-F5).

FIG. 9.17

A page shown in the Print Preview window.

BUTTON   Print Preview has its own Button Bar that you can customize. Instead of selecting an option from the menu, you can click the appropriate button. From the Edit menu, you can turn on, turn off, or edit the Button Bar. To learn more about the Button Bar, see Chapter 19, "Using the Button Bar."

Except when you are using Print Preview to view a full page, you can use the cursor keys and the scroll bars to view different parts of the page. Press PgUp to move up by one full screen or PgDn to move down by one full screen. You also can move the page left or right by pressing Ctrl-PgUp or Ctrl-PgDn, respectively.

To exit Print Preview, choose **F**ile, **C**lose. WordPerfect returns to the document editing window.

In this section, you learn about the Print Preview options and the limitations of this feature. Before you continue, you should know the following facts about Print Preview:

- Print Preview uses many computing resources to display your page, which can slow the display process.

- To interrupt Print Preview for any reason, press Esc. Print Preview stops what it is displaying, enabling you to choose a different action.

- You must select a printer before you can use Print Preview. Documents are displayed in the format contained in the current printer driver.

- Print Preview displays graphics even if you have selected a nongraphics printer.

- Print Preview remembers the settings specified the last time you used the Print Preview feature. The next time you use Print Preview, the same settings are in effect.

■ Cue: To see how your document would look from a printer you don't have, select that printer and view the document in Print Preview.

Using the View Menu Options

When you use Print Preview, many viewing options are available. These options enable you to select different page views and size ratios for the pages you display from your document. *Note:* The status bar at the bottom of the Print Preview window shows the page number and the size ratio (*scale*) at which the page is displayed.

The Zoom In option enlarges the size of the displayed text and graphics by a factor ranging from 25 to 400 percent. Zoom Out reduces the viewing size by 25 percent and can shrink the area until the entire page is shown on-screen. The Zoom to Full Width option shows the full width of the current page (text and graphics).

■ Cue: Because you can use more than one form size per document with WordPerfect printer drivers but not with Windows printer drivers, the form size shown in Print Preview may vary.

The 100 percent option displays the current page at actual size, as shown in figure 9.18. WordPerfect approximates the size of the text and graphics. Unless you have a monitor large enough to show an entire page at actual size, WordPerfect displays only a portion of the page, but you should be able to read the text. To view different areas of the page, use the cursor keys or scroll bars to move around the page.

The 200 percent option displays the current page at twice its actual printed size.

To display the entire page in the Print Preview window, use the Full Page option. WordPerfect *greeks* the text (displays lines or bars instead of text) to shrink the page so that it fits on-screen, making the text illegible.

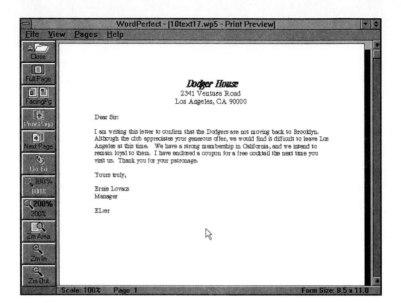

FIG. 9.18

A page shown
at 100 percent
in Print Preview.

The Zoom Area option enlarges the displayed size of a particular area
of a page. (You must use a mouse with this feature.) To enlarge a specific area of text and graphics, follow these steps:

1. Choose **View**, **Z**oom Area. WordPerfect displays *cross hairs* (inter-
   secting vertical and horizontal lines) in the document area. When
   you move the mouse, the cross hairs move.

2. Position the cross hairs at the top left corner of the area you want
   to enlarge.

3. Press and hold the left mouse button. WordPerfect replaces the
   cross hairs with a rectangle. Holding the left mouse button, drag
   the mouse until the rectangle covers the area you want to enlarge.

4. Release the mouse button to fill the Print Preview window with
   the area you selected.

■ **Cue:** If you are satisfied
with the appearance of your
document in Print Preview,
choose **F**ile, **P**rint to close
the Print Preview screen and
open the Print dialog box;
then print the document.

If you interrupt Print Preview while WordPerfect is displaying a page
view or if your view doesn't look right, you can use the Reset option to
refresh the Print Preview window. This option is useful for cleaning up
the Print Preview display or for restoring a view.

Using the Pages Menu Options

You can use the Pages menu in Print Preview to move from page to page in a displayed document, to display multiple pages, and to specify which pages you want Print Preview to display.

To jump to a specific page in the displayed document, use the Go To Page option. WordPerfect displays the Go To dialog box; type the number of the page you want to view and choose OK. The page you specified becomes the current page.

You can view two pages on-screen with the Facing Pages option. WordPerfect displays two consecutive pages from the document as they would appear in a book (see fig. 9.19)—even-numbered pages on the left side of the screen and odd-numbered pages on the right. Keep in mind that because the first page in a book is on the right, WordPerfect doesn't display a left-facing page when page 1 is the current page—unless you have a page 0.

■**Cue:** You cannot use the Facing Pages option if your current page is an odd-numbered page.

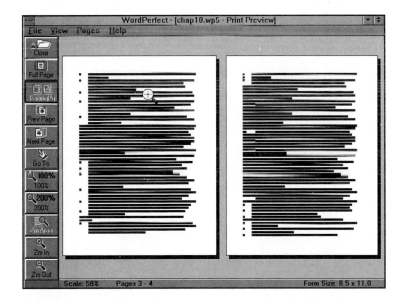

FIG. 9.19

Facing pages displayed in Print Preview.

Use the Next Page option to display the page following the current page (which then becomes the current page). If you are viewing page 3, for example, and you choose Next Page, WordPerfect makes page 4 the current page and displays it in the Print Preview screen. If you are using the Facing Pages option to view pages 2 and 3, choosing Next Page displays pages 4 and 5 as facing pages.

The effect of the Previous Page option is the opposite of the Next Page option. When you choose Previous Page, the preceding page becomes the current page displayed on-screen. If the current page is page 4, for example, choosing Previous Page displays page 3 and makes it the current page. If you are using the Facing Pages option to view pages 4 and 5, choosing Previous Page displays pages 2 and 3 as facing pages.

Understanding Print Preview's Limitations

The Print Preview feature is useful, but it has the following limitations:

- Print Preview approximates what your document will look like when printed. The document you preview on-screen may not exactly match the printed document.

- The document editing window in WordPerfect uses Windows fonts to display text. Print Preview doesn't have access to Windows fonts; instead, it accesses your printer driver and the WordPerfect Driver Resource file (WP.DRS), so Print Preview text may look different from a printed copy or the same text shown in the document editing window.

- Because Print Preview isn't WYSIWYG, use this feature only to view document pages in their entirety, to see the page layout before printing, or to view the output of another printer.

Chapter Summary

This chapter has explained how to print all or part of a document from the screen and from disk. You learned the purpose of a printer driver and the features of WordPerfect and Windows printer drivers. You also learned how to set up printer drivers in WordPerfect for Windows. You learned how to adjust the print quality of your text and graphics and how to use the Windows Print Manager to control your print jobs. Finally, you learned the many ways to use WordPerfect's Print Preview feature to display the pages of your documents.

PART

III

Mastering More Advanced Procedures

OUTLINE

Working with Fonts

Formatting Pages and
    Designing Documents

Using Styles

Working with Text Columns

Working with Tables

Working with Fonts

In Chapter 9, "Basic Printing," you learned how to print using WordPerfect 5.1 for Windows. This chapter shows you how to use fonts to make your printed documents look more professional and have a greater impact.

This chapter first defines the terminology used in discussing typefaces. The chapter next provides an overview of cartridges, soft fonts, and other typeface packages and explains how they interact with WordPerfect 5.1 for Windows. You learn how to do the following:

- Add typefaces to your printer
- Install additional typefaces in a WordPerfect printer driver and in a Windows printer driver
- Select an initial font to use in all your documents
- Select other fonts for use within a document
- Change the typeface appearance by using attributes, such as bold-face or italic

■ **Eric Mark Rintell** is a New York-based reviewer and author who has been using WordPerfect since Version 3.0. He teaches WordPerfect and has a computer consulting practice.

■ **Tony Rairden**, who contributed to the sections on attributes, is a strategic marketing consultant with extensive experience using WordPerfect Corporation products.

The information contained in this chapter is not dependent on your using any particular type of printer (laser, dot-matrix, or inkjet). Not all the features discussed are available on every printer, however. Check your printer manual to see what features your printer supports.

Understanding the Vocabulary of Typography

At the most basic level, *type* is the printed characters that appear on paper. But type is much more than that; type can be an extension of your personality (compare, for example, the second and third paragraphs in figure 10.1). A change in type can make your message easier or more difficult to read. To understand how to use type, you first need to understand the vocabulary of typography.

A *typeface* is a specific design for a set of characters (including letters, numbers and symbols). Figure 10.1 shows three typefaces that represent three categories of typefaces[1]. Palatino is a *serif* typeface: it has small finishing cross strokes on the ends of the main strokes of the characters. ITC Avant Garde is a *sans serif* typeface: the main strokes are the beginning and ending of the characters (notice the absence of cross strokes). Finally, Park Avenue is a *decorative* typeface that has a customized look.

This is Palatino, a serif typeface; the font is 14-point Palatino. Notice the cross strokes on each letter (in contrast to the following font). Serif typefaces are usually good for smaller point sizes and are used in the body of text in magazines and newspapers.

This is ITC Avant Garde, a sans serif typeface.
The font is 14-point ITC Avant Garde.
Sans serif typefaces look good in larger point sizes.

Park Avenue is a decorative typeface; it is not as easy to read as the other two categories of typefaces. The font is 18-point Park Avenue. Decorative typefaces should be used sparingly for impact.

FIG. 10.1

Examples of three typefaces.

---

[1] *All the print samples in this chapter were printed on an NEC SilentWriter 2 Model 90 PostScript laser printer.*

A *font* is a set of characters with specific typeface, point size, weight (Roman or bold), and posture (upright or italic). In figure 10.1, 14-point ITC Avant Garde is a font from the ITC Avant Garde typeface family.

WordPerfect uses *point size* to determine basic character height; 72 points equal 1 inch. For example, 72-point Times Roman characters are approximately 1 inch high. As a better measure of the height of a font, however, use as a guideline the lowercase letter *x* as it appears in that font. Although two fonts with identical point sizes are the same height overall, the font with the larger *x-height* looks larger.

An *ascender* is the part of a letter that rises above the x-height. The lowercase letters *b*, *d*, *f*, *h*, *k*, *l*, and *t* have ascenders. Ascenders don't always align at the top. *Descenders*, seen on the lowercase letters *g*, *j*, *p*, *q*, and *y*, are the opposite of ascenders. A descender is the part of a lowercase character that falls below the baseline, and descenders do align at the bottom.

Posture refers to the slant of the characters. Upright type is known as *Roman*, and slanted type is called *italic*.

Weight refers to the thickness of the characters. Most typefaces come in a thin (*light*), medium (*normal*), or thick (*bold*) weight.

Width refers to the width of the characters. A typeface can have a normal, condensed, or expanded width. A *condensed* typeface is a narrow version of the typeface; an *expanded* typeface is a wide version.

Typefaces are spaced according to one of two methods, depending on character width. *Fixed-spaced* fonts (usually called *monospaced*) are typewriter-like fonts in which every character is the same width. *Proportionally spaced* fonts vary the width of each letter according to its size; an uppercase *W* requires more space than a lowercase *i*, for example. Figure 10.2 shows examples of character spacing.

```
Courier is a fixed-space typeface. Each letter uses
the same amount of space.
```

Times Roman is a proportionally spaced typeface. Letters use whatever space they actually require.

FIG. 10.2

Monospaced and proportionally spaced fonts.

Pitch refers to the number of characters that can fit into a horizontal inch. The term applies only to fixed-spaced fonts, because in proportional fonts, the number of characters per inch varies. In a LaserJet printer, Courier 10 is a 10-pitch font with 10 characters per inch (cpi).

Computer fonts can be broken down into two groups: bit-mapped and outline (or scalable) fonts. This classification is determined by the way the program forms the characters. In a *bit-mapped* font, the characters consist of patterns of dots. The typeface designer has filled in all the dots that make up each character, much like filling in the shape of the character on graph paper. Because each character is formed by a group of dots, bit-mapped fonts are usually of high quality, but they are fixed to a particular size. To your printer, 11-point Times Roman and 11.5-point Times Roman, for example, are separate bit-mapped fonts. Each bit-mapped font takes up disk space and printer memory.

An *outline*, or *scalable*, font is a collection of character outlines. Each outline contains a description of that character shape in that typeface. A mathematical formula is applied to the outline typeface to generate the font at a given point size. A single Times Roman outline typeface, therefore, can generate Times Roman in 6, 11, 16, and many other point sizes. Outline fonts require less disk space than bit-mapped fonts and save printer memory because the printer can use the Times Roman outline (for example) for any size font. Some outlines may contain *hints* to ensure the quality of the characters at different sizes; others may not. The hints ensure that the characters are correctly shaped; for example, that the descender on the letter *y* curves correctly.

Using Different Fonts

Printer fonts are available in several different forms. Fonts can be supplied with the printer as *internal*, or *built-in*, fonts. Built-in fonts are useful for personal correspondence and draft copies of documents. You may want to purchase additional fonts for business correspondence, presentations, and letterhead. You can purchase an additional font on a plug-in cartridge. Fonts can be installed on your hard disk as *soft* fonts. Before you use printer fonts in WordPerfect, however, you must inform your printer driver (the "translator" between WordPerfect and your printer) that the fonts are available (usually when you install them).

Printers include at least one built-in font (or print wheel in the case of print-wheel printers), usually a fixed-space Courier 10- or 12-pitch font. The benefit of built-in internal fonts is that they are always ready when you turn on the printer. WordPerfect and Windows printer drivers are set up to work with the built-in fonts supplied with your printer, so you don't need to install these fonts. To begin printing with built-in fonts, skip to the section "Selecting Fonts in WordPerfect for Windows."

As you become more experienced with fonts, you probably will want to add more fonts to your printer. You may want to add memory to your printer so that it can hold additional fonts. This section discusses different cartridges and outline typeface packages for Windows. You may opt for cartridges, typeface packages, or both.

Soft Fonts

Soft fonts are fonts stored on disk rather than in the printer or on a cartridge. You can add and delete soft fonts as often as you want. Before you can print with soft fonts, however, you must transfer, or *download*, the fonts into the printer's internal memory. Downloading soft fonts takes time; the larger the file size, the more time needed to download to your printer. Moreover, the font size as well as the number of fonts available for printing might be limited by your printer's internal memory. You lose soft fonts as soon as you turn off the printer; to use them again, you must download them again. If you have many fonts and little printer memory, you may have to download the same font several times during a print job.

Soft fonts vary in price: some are available for free on electronic bulletin board systems, while other packages sell for over a hundred dollars. Soft fonts are available from Adobe, Bitstream, Agfa Compugraphic, Linotype, Monotype, and other vendors.

Cartridges

Cartridges are plug-in modules that contain several fonts. Cartridges are fast because the fonts are readily available and do not use the printer's internal memory. Even if the printer is turned off, the cartridge fonts are available as long as the cartridge is plugged into the printer. With the exception of erasable and modular cartridges, you cannot change the fonts included with the cartridge. Cartridges are typically more expensive than soft fonts.

Before you purchase a cartridge, make sure that the cartridge can be used with Windows or WordPerfect. Because cartridges are more expensive than soft fonts, do not purchase a cartridge for a single font; the soft font version of the font you want is probably cheaper. Three types of cartridges are available: fixed, modular, and erasable.

Fixed Cartridges

Fixed cartridges are so named because the fonts they contain cannot be changed. The cartridge vendor chooses the limited number of fonts (usually fewer than 50) that go into the cartridge. Recent improvements in technology have produced high-capacity fixed cartridges that can hold more than 100 fonts in a single cartridge.

The first cartridges released contained bit-mapped fonts from only three or four font families. The bit-mapped fonts were high quality because they were hand-tuned by a typographer. As printer vendors have begun incorporating scalable typeface technology into their printers, cartridge vendors have made fixed scalable cartridges available. Scalable cartridges enable you to select the type size, but the quality of scalable cartridges is uneven.

A popular type of fixed cartridge is the PostScript cartridge, which turns a LaserJet series printer into a PostScript printer. *PostScript* is an industry-standard page description language (a programming language that describes printer output in device-independent commands); all PostScript printers accept the same typefaces and graphics. PostScript supports a standard scalable typeface known as PostScript Type 1. Professional printers and service bureaus use PostScript. If you have a PostScript cartridge, you can supply a service bureau with your type-set-ready WordPerfect file and have it printed directly on the bureau's PostScript printer.

Another advantage of using a PostScript cartridge is that your documents will print identically on another PostScript printer. Consider a PostScript cartridge if you want printer-independence, 35 built-in scalable fonts, and high quality graphics. You can use a PostScript cartridge to print any of the thousands of PostScript Type 1 fonts available. PostScript, however, is slow, and the typefaces are expensive.

Modular Cartridges

Modular cartridges are an extension of fixed cartridges. With a modular cartridge, however, you select the fonts that the cartridge will contain. When you purchase a modular cartridge, the package usually consists of a cartridge with at least one expansion module containing fonts. You can purchase additional expansion modules if you need more typefaces. Modular cartridges have another advantage: you may be able to purchase a custom expansion module that contains your company logo, a specific font, a signature, a graphic, and so on. Modular cartridges, however, cost slightly more than fixed cartridges, and the cartridge vendor dictates the price of custom expansion modules.

Erasable Cartridges

A recent development is the erasable cartridge, in which you can erase the fonts. Erasable cartridges come with no fonts. You can transfer soft fonts from a floppy disk or your hard disk to this kind of cartridge, which is faster than downloading soft fonts. The erasable cartridge enables you to use soft fonts with all the advantages of a cartridge. Consider purchasing this type of cartridge If downloading soft fonts to your printer takes too long, or if you always use the same set of fonts that are not available in a fixed or modular cartridge. The disadvantage to using an erasable cartridge is that you have to purchase both the soft fonts and the erasable cartridge.

Windows Typeface Packages

The packages surveyed in this section work with your printer and also help your computer screen more accurately display what your printer output will look like. Windows contains several system fonts that it uses to display your text in WordPerfect for Windows. Windows may not have an exact match for the font you are using, however, and letters appear irregular at large point sizes. The packages described in this section solve both of these problems.

The packages discussed here feature scalable typeface technology. One of the benefits of the packages is that you can use scalable typefaces with your printer even if your printer does not support scalable typefaces. Unlike cartridges, the Windows typeface packages typically require one to two megabytes of hard disk space for the program and additional disk space for each typeface; they also are slower than cartridge-based fonts. You can combine any of these packages with cartridges; you even can combine the different Windows packages.

CAUTION: The Windows typeface packages described in this section do *not* install into printer drivers. They install themselves into the Windows environment. You must select a Windows printer driver to print with them. The fonts may not appear WYSIWYG in Print Preview (because WordPerfect uses its own driver resource file, WP.DRS, to display text in Print Preview). The fonts should appear closer to WYSIWYG in your editing screen. For more information on selecting printer drivers and Print Preview, refer to Chapter 9, "Basic Printing."

Micrologic's MoreFonts

Micrologic Software's MoreFonts includes support for the DOS-based WordPerfect and Windows. MoreFonts supports LaserJet-compatible laser printers, inkjet printers, and most dot-matrix printers. To use MoreFonts with WordPerfect 5.1 for Windows, you must select a Windows printer driver. The package includes 14 typefaces, and Micrologic will send you an additional 14 typefaces for registering the package. The package includes several decorative typefaces (Showtime, Burlesque, Pageant, Opera, and Poster) in addition to serif and sans serif typefaces.

Like other Windows typeface packages, MoreFonts features scalable typefaces. MoreFonts, however, includes special effects that aren't included with the other packages. You can fill your letters with different patterns, add backgrounds, and use outlines and shadows. MoreFonts prints faster than its competition because it sends the printer only the characters needed for printing, whereas the other packages always send the entire character set to the printer. Although MoreFonts uses a proprietary type format, you can use any PostScript Type 1 typeface with a utility supplied by Micrologic when you register Morefonts.

Intellifont for Windows

If you own a Hewlett-Packard LaserJet III printer, Hewlett-Packard will send you a free copy of Intellifont for Windows (IFW). IFW is used only for displaying type. IFW comes with the screen fonts for the built-in scalable typefaces included in every LaserJet III: CG Times (Hewlett-Packard's equivalent of Times Roman) and Univers (its equivalent of Helvetica). If you purchase Hewlett-Packard printer fonts or a Hewlett-Packard scalable cartridge, IFW displays these fonts as well. You can use IFW regardless of the printer driver (WordPerfect or Windows) you have selected.

Bitstream's FaceLift for Windows

FaceLift for Windows is a display and type package for Windows. The scalable typefaces are in Bitstream's Speedo format. FaceLift works with dot-matrix, inkjet, and laser printers. Bitstream also sells a version of FaceLift for the character-based WordPerfect 5.1; this version uses the same Speedo font technology. FaceLift for WordPerfect, however, does not work in the Windows environment (unless you run it with WordPerfect 5.1 for DOS at the DOS prompt), so you cannot use FaceLift for WordPerfect 5.1 for DOS with WordPerfect 5.1 for Windows.

T I P   If you own both versions of FaceLift, install new fonts in the Windows version first because it can read only from floppy disks. FaceLift for WordPerfect can read the typefaces from the hard disk.

Unless you use FaceLift for Windows as a display font for PostScript printers or WordPerfect printer drivers, you must use the Windows printer driver with this program. FaceLift for Windows comes with 13 typefaces, including a fixed-space typeface (Monospace 821), a thick typeface called Bitstream Cooper Black, and Bitstream's versions of Times (Dutch 801) and Helvetica (Swiss 721).

Because FaceLift for WordPerfect uses the same Speedo typefaces, you need only one directory on your hard disk to store the fonts for both versions of FaceLift. Speedo typefaces are moderately priced, and Bitstream sells groups of typefaces in Headlines packages for use in desktop publishing and artwork, and for other purposes. The disadvantage of FaceLift is that the Speedo fonts are available only from Bitstream, so the font selection is not as great as the selection of PostScript Type 1 fonts.

Adobe Type Manager for Windows

Adobe Type Manager (ATM) for Windows is a display and typeface package from Adobe, the creators of the PostScript page description language. ATM is an inexpensive way to get PostScript Type 1 fonts without having to purchase a PostScript printer. Although ATM does not provide a page description language, ATM does enable most laser printers and EPSON and IBM dot-matrix printers to use Type 1 fonts.

For PostScript printer owners, ATM provides a better font display at larger sizes. The basic ATM package comes with 13 typefaces, Symbol, and 4 weights (normal, boldface, italic, and boldface italic) of Times, Helvetica, and Courier. Adobe sells additional typefaces at premium prices and has one of the largest digital typeface collections available. Because Type 1 is an open published format, you also can purchase these fonts from other vendors. ATM also works with a companion product called Adobe Type Align, which you can use to add type effects (such as rotation and curves) to your Type 1 fonts. ATM is a good choice for PostScript printer owners and for users who want access to the vast Adobe type library.

If you own a PostScript printer, use one of the WordPerfect PostScript printer drivers and ATM for screen display. With this combination, you have WYSIWYG in Windows while taking advantage of the flexibility offered by the WordPerfect printer driver.

T I P

Installing Fonts in a WordPerfect Printer Driver

WordPerfect stores printer information in ALL files (see Chapter 9, "Basic Printing," for more information about ALL files and for a discussion of when to use WordPerfect printer drivers rather than Windows printer drivers). Before you can use your fonts in WordPerfect, you must install them into an ALL file. Because fonts from different companies are installed in different ways, this chapter doesn't discuss adding typefaces to ALL printer files. Follow the instructions included with your cartridges and soft fonts to install your fonts, if you haven't done so already. Note that if you do not install the fonts (including cartridges) into the ALL file, you will not be able to select and use them with a WordPerfect printer driver.

CAUTION: One benefit of using WordPerfect 5.1 for Windows is its capability to use WordPerfect 5.1 for DOS flexible printer drivers. When you use WordPerfect printer drivers, however, you may not have matching Windows screen fonts for the typefaces in the 5.1 printer driver. If you do not have the same screen fonts, what is displayed in your editing window may be different from your printer output.

To work around this problem, verify that your Windows and WordPerfect printer drivers contain the same typefaces. Be careful: the same font may have different names in WordPerfect and in Windows; the names must match exactly for screen fonts to work in your Windows environment. Windows uses the corresponding screen font when its WordPerfect counterpart is selected (as long as the corresponding Windows printer driver is the active printer in the Printers dialog box of the Windows Control Panel).

Adding a Cartridge in a WordPerfect Printer Driver

Although you have installed your cartridge fonts in your ALL file, you cannot use them yet. You must tell WordPerfect what cartridge you are using. To select a cartridge installed in your WordPerfect ALL file, follow these steps:

1. Choose Select Printer from the File menu.

    Press Print (F5).

2. Choose Select to open the Select Printer dialog box.

3. Verify that you have selected WordPerfect in the Printer Drivers area.

4. Highlight the name of the printer with which you want to use the cartridge.

5. Choose Setup. The Printer Setup dialog box opens (see fig. 10.3).

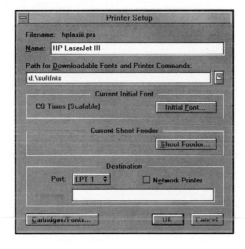

The Printer Setup dialog box.

6. Select Cartridges/Fonts. The Cartridges and Fonts dialog box opens (see fig. 10.4).

7. Highlight the Cartridges line. (If your printer does not support cartridges, WordPerfect does not show a Cartridges line in this dialog box.)

8. Choose Select. The Select Fonts dialog box opens (see fig. 10.5).

9. The Quantity area in the upper right corner shows the total number of cartridge slots in your printer and the number of slots currently available. The Cartridges list displays all the cartridges WordPerfect is configured to use. Highlight the name of the cartridge you have just added to your printer.

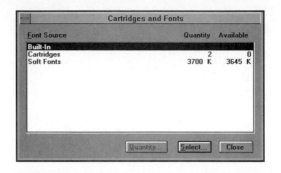

FIG. 10.4

The Cartridges and Fonts dialog box.

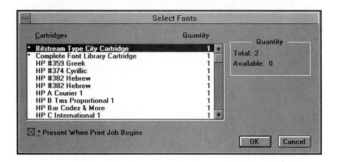

FIG. 10.5

The Select Fonts dialog box for cartridges.

10. Press the asterisk (*) key to indicate to WordPerfect that the cartridge is present. Notice that the number of available cartridge slots decreases by one. If you need to add any more cartridges, highlight each cartridge name and press *.

   To indicate to WordPerfect that you no longer have a cartridge, highlight the cartridge name and press *. The cartridge no longer is selected, and the number of available cartridge slots increases by one.

11. Choose OK. The Select Fonts dialog box closes.

12. Close the Cartridges and Fonts dialog box, which now reflects any changes you have made. If you have made changes in the printer setup, WordPerfect displays on the status line an Updating Font message followed by a font number as WordPerfect counts down the number of fonts available.

13. Choose OK to close the Printer Setup dialog box.

14. Close the Select Printer dialog box.

> When you install your fonts into a WordPerfect printer driver, remember to mark your most frequently used fonts with *. Write a macro to download the fonts marked with * to your printer when you start WordPerfect.
>
> **T I P**

If you have no soft fonts to add, you can skip to "Selecting Fonts in WordPerfect for Windows" to begin using your printer cartridge fonts.

> Place your most frequently used fonts on the Font button on the Ruler (using the **A**ssign to Ruler option in the Font dialog box). When you need to select a font, click the Font button and select the font.
>
> **T I P**

Adding Soft Fonts in a WordPerfect Printer Driver

Just as you must inform WordPerfect about cartridge fonts, you must tell WordPerfect about your soft fonts before you can use them. You also must tell the program where they are located and the path to this location. Before you continue, be sure to read "Installing Fonts in a WordPerfect Printer Driver," if you haven't done so already.

Selecting Soft Fonts

To select soft fonts with a WordPerfect printer driver, follow these steps:

1. Choose Se**l**ect Printer from the **F**ile menu.

   `CUA` Press Print (F5).

2. Choose **S**elect to open the Select Printer dialog box.

3. Verify that you have selected **W**ordPerfect in the Printer Drivers area.

4. Highlight the appropriate printer.

5. Choose S**e**tup. The Printer Setup dialog box opens (again see fig. 10.3).

6. Select **C**artridges/Fonts. The Cartridges and Fonts dialog box opens (again see fig. 10.4).

7. Highlight the Soft Fonts line. WordPerfect indicates how much memory is available in your printer for soft fonts. If you have added memory to your printer's internal memory, select **Q**uantity and enter the new amount. Any soft fonts marked with an asterisk reduce the amount of available printer memory.

8. Choose **S**elect.

   The Font Groups dialog box opens (see fig. 10.6). Instead of listing all available soft fonts in a cluttered screen, WordPerfect separates the fonts into font groups. If you have just installed a new soft font package, look for its name in this dialog box.

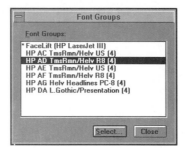

FIG. 10.6

The Font Groups dialog box.

9. Highlight the font group from which you want to select your fonts.

   The Select Fonts dialog box opens, listing the fonts in the font group you have highlighted (see fig. 10.7).

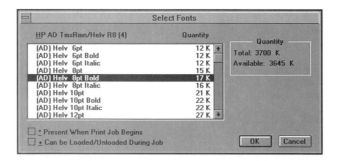

FIG. 10.7

The Select Fonts dialog box for soft fonts.

10. Highlight, one at a time, the fonts you want to use, choosing one of the two options listed at the bottom of the dialog box.

If you use a soft font frequently, mark it as Present When a Print Job Begins by pressing *.

For soft fonts you use less often, select Can Be Loaded/Unloaded during Job, by pressing the plus sign (+).

11. Choose OK to close the Select Fonts dialog box.

12. Close the Font Groups dialog box.

13. Close the Cartridges and Fonts dialog box. WordPerfect updates the font list for your printer.

14. Choose OK to close the Printer Setup dialog box.

15. Close the Select Printer dialog box.

When you select Present When Print Job Begins, you are telling WordPerfect that this soft font will be in your printer's internal memory before you begin printing. The upper right corner of the dialog box lists the total printer memory and the amount of printer memory available. Every time you mark a soft font with *, WordPerfect subtracts from the available printer memory the memory required for that soft font.

Soft fonts selected with the second option, Can be Loaded/Unloaded During Job, do not reduce the available printer memory because they are temporary fonts that can be overwritten by other fonts in the printer's internal memory. You cannot select a font that is larger than the remaining available printer memory. During a print job, WordPerfect automatically downloads soft fonts marked with +.

 **Cue:** If you need to use attributes or fonts temporarily, consider placing them in a style. To learn about styles, see Chapter 12, "Using Styles."

You can mark fonts as *swappable* by using both * and +. If a soft font is marked with both settings, WordPerfect writes over the font in the printer's internal memory if the program needs space for another soft font. At the end of the print job, WordPerfect reloads the font marked with both settings into the printer's internal memory.

Some printers can hold only a limited number of fonts (usually 32) in memory, regardless of the amount of printer memory available. If your printer's font capacity is limited, WordPerfect displays a Fonts Available counter; you cannot mark soft fonts when this number reaches zero. You may be able to mark a few more fonts by labeling some fonts as swappable.

WARNING: Before you can use soft fonts marked with *, you must select Download Fonts in the Print dialog box at the beginning of your work session or if you turned off or reset your printer. WordPerfect initializes the printer by downloading the fonts to make them available for print jobs. You also need to indicate where the fonts are located before they are downloaded (see the following section).

Specifying the Path for Downloadable Fonts

Before you can begin using soft fonts, you must tell WordPerfect where the fonts are stored. WordPerfect accepts only one directory for printer command files and soft fonts, so make sure that you keep them all in the same place.

To tell WordPerfect where to find your soft fonts when you are using a WordPerfect printer driver, follow these steps:

1. Choose Select Printer from the File menu.

    Press Print (F5).

2. Choose Select to open the Select Printer dialog box.

3. Verify that you have selected WordPerfect in the Printer Drivers area.

4. Highlight the appropriate printer.

5. Choose Setup. The Printer Setup dialog box opens.

6. Choose Path for Downloadable Fonts and Printer Commands.

7. Type the full path name for the soft fonts. If the fonts are stored in the SOFTFNTS directory on drive D, for example, type **d:\softfnts** (again see fig. 10.3).

8. Choose OK to close the Printer Setup dialog box.

9. Close the Select Printer dialog box.

You now can select soft fonts in the same manner you select any built-in or cartridge-based font, as explained in "Selecting Fonts in WordPerfect for Windows," in this chapter.

Adding Print Wheels in a WordPerfect Printer Driver

If your printer supports print wheels, you select them in the same manner as soft fonts. Highlight the Print Wheels line in the Cartridges and Fonts dialog box and refer to the preceding section for instructions. If you have marked a print wheel with + (Can Be Loaded/Unloaded during Job), a dialog box prompts you to change the print wheel during a print job. After you change the print wheel, select Go to continue printing.

Installing Fonts in a Windows Printer Driver

Many vendors provide additional typefaces for the Windows environment. To install the fonts, follow the directions provided by the font vendor. Be sure to install the screen fonts that accompany your Windows typefaces so that your display matches your printer output. If you have added any fonts in your Windows printer driver, you may have to reselect the printer driver in order for WordPerfect to recognize the additional fonts (see Chapter 9, "Basic Printing").

■ **Cue:** Consider purchasing a Windows typeface package so that Windows can display your text more accurately.

CAUTION: Your fonts may appear different in Print Preview because WordPerfect uses its own Driver Resource file, WP.DRS, in Print Preview. In some cases, the editing screen will be closer to WYSIWYG than Print Preview. Please see Chapter 9, "Basic Printing" for more information about Print Preview.

Like their WordPerfect counterparts, Windows printer drivers are set up to recognize whether your printer supports plug-in cartridges, additional memory, and soft fonts. To inform Windows what printer you are using, follow these steps:

1. Choose Select Printer from the File menu.

    Press Print (F5).

2. Choose Select (Current Printer)

3. Choose Windows in the Printer Drivers area if it has not been selected. The WordPerfect Select Printers dialog box changes slightly to the Windows Select Printers dialog box, with fewer options available. Highlight your printer.

4. Choose Setup.

5. The Printer Driver dialog box opens. Figure 10.8 shows the dialog box for a Hewlett-Packard LaserJet III printer.

   An option appears in a Windows Printer Driver dialog box only if the printer supports that option. If you are using a printer that does not accept cartridges, for example, the Cartridge option does not appear.

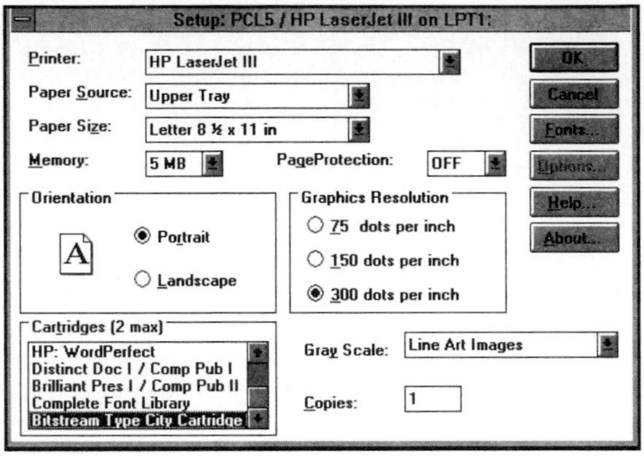

FIG. 10.8

The Windows
LaserJet III Printer
Driver dialog
box.

The following table summarizes how to modify the Windows
printer driver.

To change	Select	Then
Cartridges	Cartridges	Highlight the cartridge you are using with your printer.
Printer Memory	Memory	Select the amount with which your printer is configured.
Fonts	Fonts	Follow directions in the Font dialog box, which varies by printer.

6. Choose OK to close the dialog box for your printer driver.

7. Close the Select Printer dialog box.

Selecting Fonts in WordPerfect for Windows

After you have informed your printer driver about your printer fonts,
you can begin to use these fonts in your document. In this section, you
learn how to specify an initial font and how to select different fonts in a
document.

T I P

You can select and print special characters in WordPerfect 5.1 for Windows; however, WordPerfect may not be capable of displaying those characters in your editing window. Special characters are mapped into WordPerfect character sets and cannot be accessed with Windows printer drivers.

To select special characters, load the CHARMAP.TST file (usually placed in the \WPC directory) and go to the end of the document (Ctrl-End). Before Character Map 12, select a character set as you select any other font and print the current page on your printer so that you can tell what characters your printer is capable of printing and what their character numbers are. For example, select Zapf Dingbats before Character Map 12 and print the current page. You can use the page you have just printed as a map to the Zapf Dingbat character set in WordPerfect. To use any of the characters in a document, select the font and use WordPerfect Characters (Ctrl-W) to select the character you want to print. For more information on character sets, see Chapter 28, "Creating and Displaying Special Characters."

Specifying Initial Fonts

When you select a printer, WordPerfect assigns an *initial font* to print standard text for all documents. Any text enhancements (such as boldface or italic) you make are variations of and deviations from the initial font. The initial font, therefore, sets the tone for the document as much as any other design element. The initial font is also called the *base font*, because it is the basis for all variations used for enhancement.

Cue: If you are using a symbol set such as Zapf Dingbats in a Windows printer driver, remember to select the font explicitly, or it will not print.

In WordPerfect, you can select fonts through three dialog boxes: the Printer Initial Font dialog box, the Document Initial Font dialog box, and the Font dialog box. Fonts selected through the Font dialog box have first precedence, followed by fonts selected through the Document Initial Font dialog box.

Keep in mind the following things about font selection precedence:

- If you specify a different font in each of these three dialog boxes, your text is formatted in the font selected in the Font dialog box.

- In a document with different fonts selected in the Printer Initial Font and Document Initial Font dialog boxes (but not the Font dialog box), the text is formatted in the font specified in the Document Initial Font dialog box.

■ In a document with no other fonts selected, WordPerfect uses the Printer Initial font.

Selecting a Printer Initial Font

The default initial font is usually a fixed-space font such as Courier 10. Regardless of which printer driver (WordPerfect or Windows) you have selected, you can change the initial font to any font you want. You can use any internal font, cartridge, or soft font for the initial font. When you assign an initial font in a printer driver, all documents printed with that printer driver have the same base font. To select an initial font for a printer, follow these steps:

1. Choose Select Printer from the File menu.

    Press Print (F5) and choose Select.

   The Select Printer dialog box opens.

2. Highlight the printer for which you want to establish an initial font.

3. If you are using a Windows printer driver, choose Initial Font.

   If you are using a WordPerfect printer driver, choose Setup; then select Initial Font from the Printer Setup dialog box.

   The Printer Initial Font dialog box opens (see fig. 10.9). This box displays all the fonts WordPerfect is configured to use, including built-in, cartridge, and soft fonts. The font and size you currently are using are highlighted. A text box displays The Quick Brown Fox Jumps... in the current font. As you change fonts and sizes, WordPerfect previews the selection for you by displaying the font in the preview text box. Experiment by changing the font and point size.

4. Highlight the font and point size you want to use as your initial font. Verify that the font is the one you want by looking at the preview text.

5. Select OK to close the Printer Initial Font dialog box.

6. If you are using a WordPerfect printer driver, close the Printer Setup dialog box by choosing OK.

7. Close the Select Printer dialog box.

The left side of the status bar shows the font you have selected as your initial font.

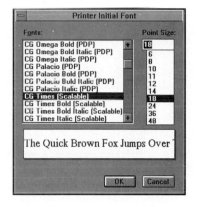

FIG. 10.9

The Printer Initial
Font dialog box.

Selecting a Document Initial Font

If you have a document in which you want to use a different initial font,
you can override the Printer Initial Font selection by selecting a *document initial font*. The document initial font becomes the default font for
text, headers, footnotes, and so on, in the document with which you are
working. This choice does not affect other documents.

> The initial font you select in a document affects the body of the
> document. If you select a font in a header, footer, footnote, or
> endnote, that font selection affects only the text in the element
> selected.
>
> **T I P**

To change the initial font in your document, follow these steps:

1. Choose **D**ocument from the Layout menu.

   CUA Press Layout Document (Ctrl-Shift-F9).

2. Select Initial **F**ont from the Document submenu.

   The Document Initial Font dialog box opens; it looks (and works)
   like the Printer Initial Font dialog box shown in figure 10.9. The
   current font and size are highlighted, and sample text appears in
   the preview text box.

3. Highlight the font and point size you want to use for your document initial font. Look at the preview text to verify that the font is
   what you want.

4. Choose OK to close the Document Initial Font dialog box.

The font listed in the left corner of the status line changes to the font and size you have selected in the Document Initial Font dialog box. The font you have chosen is the initial font for your active document only; this selection does not affect other documents. When you save the document, your font selection is saved with it.

CAUTION: If you open a document formatted for a different printer, WordPerfect formats the document for your currently selected printer. You may not have some of the fonts originally used in the document. WordPerfect uses the font closest to the original font and prefixes the font name with *. If you switch printers after using 12-point Palatino, for example, WordPerfect selects 12-point Times Roman because it is the nearest match. (The font code shows as Font:*Times Roman 12pt.)

Using Several Fonts in a Document

You can override initial fonts and use multiple fonts in a document by selecting fonts from the Font dialog box or by using the Font button on the Ruler. The font you select remains the current font until you change fonts again.

To choose a new font, follow these steps:

1. Select Font from the Font menu, or double-click the Font button on the Ruler.

    Press Font (F9).

   The Font dialog box opens (see fig. 10.10).

2. Choose the font and point size you want to use in your document.

   Remember that 72 points equal 1 inch; 18 points is a 1/4-inch font. WordPerfect previews your font selection in the text box. Whenever you change the font or point size, look at this box to see how the change affects your text.

3. Choose OK to close the Font dialog box and begin using the new font in your text. By selecting Reveal Codes from the View menu (Alt-F3), you can see a font code with the name of the font you selected.

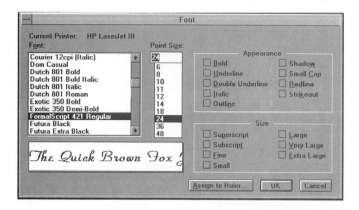

FIG. 10.10

The Font dialog
box.

Move frequently used fonts to the Ruler by selecting **Assign to Ruler** before you close the Font dialog box. With the Ruler on, you can select fonts without opening the Font dialog box by clicking the Font button on the Ruler. Holding down the mouse button, drag the mouse until the font you want is highlighted; then release the mouse button. You can adjust the font size by clicking the Size button on the Ruler, holding down the mouse button, and dragging the mouse until the size you want is highlighted, and then releasing the mouse button.

T I P

Your printer may be able to rotate fonts from portrait to landscape. If your printer does not have this capability, you need different fonts for portrait and landscape orientation. If you do not have a landscape font for each portrait font, you may find that you have fewer font selections for landscape printing than you have for portrait printing.

T I P

Changing Font Attributes

WordPerfect has two categories of font attributes: size and appearance. *Size attributes* enable you to change the size of text, and *appearance attributes* enable you to create a different look by using features such as underlining and italic.

Size variations often are combined with appearance attributes. For example, you can use a contrasting font in a larger size and in boldface for headings and subheads; headings in Helvetica Boldface 14-point type might be paired with Times Roman 11-point body text.

You can insert any attribute into your document, and it will affect all subsequent text until you enter an ending attribute code (by reselecting the attribute or by reentering the keystroke). Alternatively, you can apply any attribute to selected text, in which case WordPerfect automatically places the ending code at the end of the block.

Changing the Size Attributes

In WordPerfect, you can set relative type sizes as a percentage of the base font point size. Type size variations can be used for emphasis, to indicate headings, annotations, and other structural elements, and to help separate quoted material from original text.

Changing font size is dependent on using WordPerfect's printer driver; you cannot use this method reliably if you are using a Windows printer driver. The advantage of using WordPerfect printer drivers is that WordPerfect can substitute a similar font if you print your document on another printer that does not have the same typefaces.

You can choose from the following size attributes: Fine, Small, Large, Very Large, Extra Large, Superscript, Subscript (see fig. 10.11). (For more information on using superscript and subscript, see Chapter 27, "Using the Equation Editor.") Relative size attributes are defined in terms of a percentage of the base font size and can be accessed from the Font menu or through shortcut keystrokes. Table 10.1 shows the sizes, the keystrokes, and WordPerfect's default percentages for the font attribute ratios. To see what sizes you can use with your printer, retrieve PRINTER.TST (located in the directory where WPWIN.EXE is stored) and print this text document on your printer.

When you adjust the size of a font, WordPerfect automatically adjusts the spacing between lines. The font listed at the left end of the status line is affected by the change in size. You can use more than one size font on a single line.

To change a font size, follow these steps:

1. Select **S**ize from the Font menu or press Font Size Menu (Ctrl-S).

2. Choose **F**ine, **S**mall, **L**arge, **V**ery Large, or **E**xtra Large.

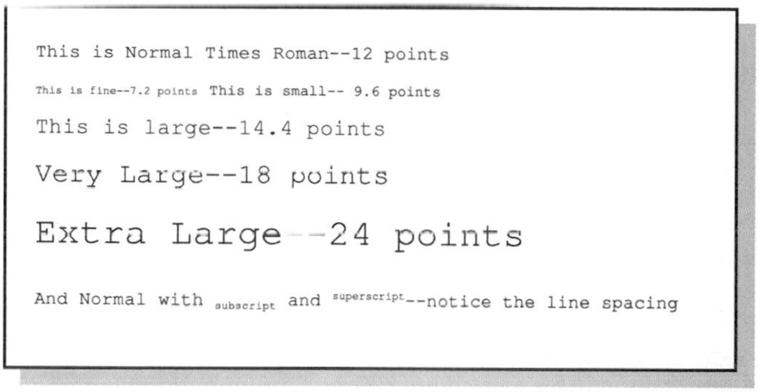

```
This is Normal Times Roman--12 points
This is fine--7.2 points This is small-- 9.6 points
This is large--14.4 points
Very Large--18 points
Extra Large--24 points
And Normal with subscript and superscript--notice the line spacing
```

FIG. 10.11

Text printed using different size attributes. (note: not shown to scale)

Table 10.1. Size Attributes

Font Size Attribute	Keystrokes	Default Font Attribute Ratio
Fine	(Ctrl-S, F)	60%
Small	(Ctrl-S, S)	80%
Normal	(Ctrl-S, N)	100%
Large	(Ctrl-S, L)	120%
Very Large	(Ctrl-S, V)	150%
Extra Large	(Ctrl-S, E)	200%
Superscript/Subscript	(No Shortcut)	60%

T I P

To select size more quickly, press Font (F9) or double-click the Font button on the Ruler. The Font dialog box opens, and you can click the size you want.

When you enter new text, it appears in the size you have chosen. Changing the size attribute of text does not change the initial font. A pair of hidden codes changes the size of the font. If you turn on Reveal Codes (Alt-F3), a format code appears in front of the text you have just entered. If you have selected Small, for example, you see a pair of [Small On] and [Small Off] codes before and after your text, respectively.

To find out what font size is in effect, select **S**ize from the Font menu or press Font Size Menu (Ctrl-S). The size in effect has a check mark (✔) in front of the name. To turn off a size selection, press Normal (Ctrl-N), or press the right-arrow key to move the insertion point past the font size code.

If you have a printer that supports outline fonts (such as a PostScript or Hewlett-Packard LaserJet III printer), you can set the size for Fine, Small, Large, Very Large, Extra Large, Superscript, and Subscript by changing the default size attribute ratios in Preferences (see Chapter 29, "Customizing WordPerfect with Preferences").

Changing the Appearance Attributes

The appearance attributes include typographic and typing conventions such as boldface, italic, and underlining. You can use the attributes alone on the base font or in combination with size attributes, depending on what you want to communicate with the variations from the base font.

You can use any appearance attribute on-screen, but your printer may not be capable of printing all appearance attributes. To determine what your printer can do, retrieve the PRINTER.TST file (stored in the directory where WPWIN.EXE is located) and print this file.

The following appearance attributes are available in WordPerfect (see fig. 10.12). Notice that you can combine appearance attributes to obtain the desired effect.

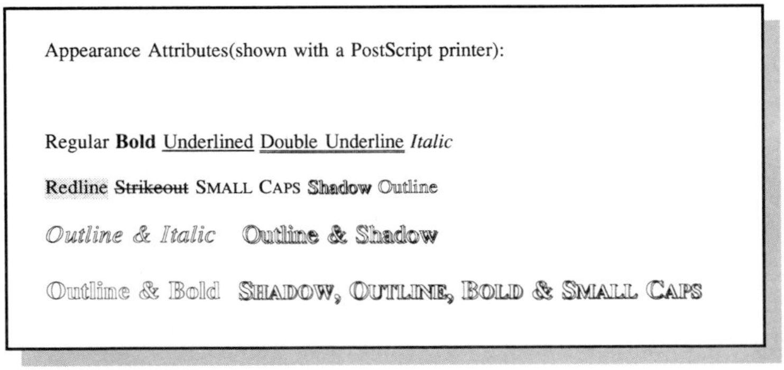

Appearance Attributes(shown with a PostScript printer):

Regular **Bold** Underlined Double Underline *Italic*

Redline Strikeout SMALL CAPS Shadow Outline

Outline & Italic Outline & Shadow

Outline & Bold SHADOW, OUTLINE, BOLD & SMALL CAPS

FIG. 10.12

Text illustrating the appearance attributes.

- *Boldface* (Ctrl-B). Boldface typically is used for headings and for strong emphasis in body text.

- *Italic* (Ctrl-I). Italic typically is used for moderate emphasis in text and to indicate quoted text.

■ *Underlining* (Ctrl-U) and *Double Underlining*. WordPerfect, as its default, underlines blank spaces as well as regular letter and number characters. You can make WordPerfect underline tabs or skip underlining spaces and tabs (see Chapter 15, "Working with Advanced Printing Techniques").

Underlining on the typewriter is a substitute for typographic italic. You should restrict underlining in word processing, which has access to italic and boldface, to numeric data, underlined blank spaces for signatures and other fill-ins, and specified format requirements. You should not use underlining for simple emphasis unless your printer cannot produce boldface or italic.

■ *Redline* and *Strikeout*. Redline marks text with characters (typically nonalphanumeric, such as WordPerfect's default |) in the margins or with shading, depending on your printers' capabilities and the selections you make in the Preferences, Print Settings dialog box (see Chapter 29, "Customizing WordPerfect with Preferences"). Redline usually is used to indicate new or added text in a document. Strikeout marks text with a line through it, indicating text that has been deleted or needs to be deleted. Although these attributes are used primarily by the legal profession, WordPerfect also uses these attributes to compare documents. See the discussion of Document Compare in Chapter 25, "Assembling Other Document References," for more information about Redline and Strikeout.

■ *Special Effects*. WordPerfect comes with three built-in special effects, *Shadow*, *Outline*, and *Small Caps*, which you can use if your printer supports them. These effects are used typically for decorative or design purposes in documents (such as presentations) and on the cover pages of proposals. Small Caps often are used to set company or product names apart from body text. These special effects are available from the Fonts dialog box (F9), but not from the Fonts menu.

The Outline attribute does not display on-screen as shown in figure 10.12. When you turn on the Outline attribute, the text is displayed in a different color. This difference is not a WordPerfect for Windows limitation; Windows displays outlined characters in this manner. If you are using a monochrome monitor, you have to use Print Preview to view outlined characters on-screen (see Chapter 9, "Basic Printing").

You can choose the appearance attributes from the Font dialog box. Except for Shadow, Small Caps, and Outline, the appearance attributes also are listed on the Font menu.

Appearance attributes, like size attributes, are paired codes. If you select the Underline attribute, for example, the On code [Und On] and the Off code [Und Off] are inserted into your document at the insertion point, and any text between the two codes takes on the Underline attribute. You can select your appearance attribute before you type the text. You also can apply attributes to existing text in your document; see "Applying Font Attributes to Existing Text" in this chapter. You can verify the appearance attributes you have selected by using Reveal Codes from the View menu.

To turn on an appearance attribute before you type your text, follow these steps:

1. Choose the appearance attribute you want from the Font menu if that attribute is listed, or choose Font from the Font menu to open the Font dialog box.

    Press Font (F9).

   The following table shows keyboard shortcuts available for several appearance attributes.

Attribute	Keyboard Shortcut
Boldface	Ctrl-B
Italic	Ctrl-I
Underline	Ctrl-U
Normal	Ctrl-N

2. If you have opened the Font dialog box, choose the appearance attribute(s) you want to use in your document.

3. Type your text.

4. Again choose the attribute in the Font menu or the Font dialog box to turn off the attribute.

T I P   To turn off all attributes, choose Normal from the Font menu (or press Normal (Ctrl-N)). If you have Reveal Codes on, you also can press the right-arrow key to move the insertion point past the attribute Off code.

Applying Font Attributes to Existing Text

You can apply font attributes to existing text by selecting the text and applying the attributes. Follow these steps:

1. Place the insertion point before the text to which you want to apply the attribute.

2. Press Select (F8). Move the insertion point to the last character to which you want to apply the attribute. (You also can use the mouse to select text; see Chapter 5, "Selecting and Editing Text.")

3. Choose the attribute from the Font menu or the Font dialog box (press F9). The text remains selected so that you can apply other attributes if you want.

4. Press Select (F8) to deselect the text.

> Hold down the Shift key and use the directional keys to highlight the text. For example, for a quick select to end of line, press Shift-End.   **T I P**

When text is selected, you can determine the attributes applied to the text in the Font menu or the Font dialog box. If all the text selected is affected by an attribute, a check mark (✔) appears before the attribute in the Font menu and an X in the box before the attribute in the Font dialog box. If only a portion of the text selected is affected by an attribute, a bullet (•) appears before the attribute in the Font menu, and gray shading appears in the box before the attribute in the Font dialog box.

You can delete an attribute by deleting its On code (for example, [Und On] for Underline). Select Reveal Codes from the View menu and delete the code.

Chapter Summary

This chapter covers the basics of using fonts, including the vocabulary of typography and the differences between internal, cartridge, and soft fonts. You have learned how to select additional typefaces in WordPerfect and Windows printer drivers. The chapter also explains how to select fonts in documents and how to change the size and appearance of fonts in WordPerfect.

This chapter is only a basic introduction to fonts. You can do much more with fonts. You can use the Overstrike feature to create new characters by combining characters (see Chapter 28, "Creating and Displaying Special Characters"). You can use kerning to remove unwanted white space by moving letters closer together. Chapter 15, "Working with Advanced Printing Techniques," covers kerning and other typesetting variables and Automatic Font Control. Refer to this chapter for more ideas on improving your output without changing your text.

Formatting Pages and Designing Documents

The amount of reading people must do today is a persuasive reason for making your documents as easy to read as possible. The longer the document, the more important readability and manageability become. Are the page numbers well located? If several documents are shuffled together does each page have a header or footer indicating where it belongs?

A variety of WordPerfect features control the layout of pages; you can use them to change the appearance of your document in ways previously available only with more complex and specialized desktop publishing software. These effects often encourage the reader to delve into a document. Many of the features are road maps that guide the eyes of the reader through the document. This chapter focuses on the following:

Judith Petersen is a WordPerfect instructor/ resource staffperson for the Leon County (Florida) School Board Vocational Program. In her own business, Judy is a lawyer and computer software consultant/trainer for businesses and individuals in the Tallahassee area.

- Keeping text together on a page in a variety of ways and determining when each method is most suitable

- Setting margins for your document

- Centering text on a page and advancing text to specific page locations

- Designing, creating, and editing headers and footers

- Numbering pages in simple and complex multipart documents

- Selecting paper sizes and paper types that determine printed appearance

- Modifying font, redline, and other initial code settings for your document

- Creating a database of document summaries

Formatting Pages

You need to make decisions about the layout of a document at many levels, including the layout of individual lines of text, paragraphs, entire pages, and the document as a whole. WordPerfect for Windows groups these formatting commands in the Layout pull-down menu, shown in figure 11.1.

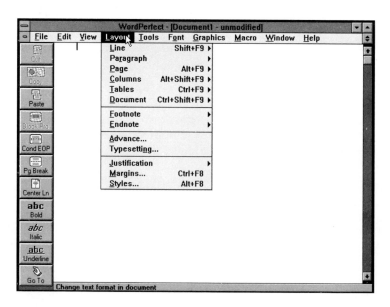

FIG. 11.1

The WordPerfect for Windows document screen displaying the Layout menu and a customized editing Button Bar.

Placing Format Codes

All the features discussed in this chapter place hidden codes in your text. Refer to Chapter 4, "Editing a Document," for a full discussion of codes. You must place WordPerfect document codes and page codes that format the entire document at the beginning of the document before any text and before any hard returns or spaces. Similarly, when you use a page code to change the appearance of a page, you must insert the page code before any text on that page. If you tab or center or type text before the page format code, the format change does not take effect until the following page.

The Auto Code Placement feature automates this code placement process for you. You can turn on Auto Code Placement to insert all page codes at the top of the current page, regardless of the location of the insertion point at the time you choose a page layout command. The Auto Code Placement feature places paragraph and line layout codes at the beginning of the paragraph. Refer to Chapter 6, "Formatting Text," for more about Auto Code Placement, and to Chapter 29, "Customizing WordPerfect with Preferences," for a table of codes that Auto Code Placement controls. The instructions in this chapter are based on the assumption that the Auto Code Placement feature is on.

■ **Cue:** Use the Auto Code Placement feature to make sure that page and document codes are inserted properly.

You may choose to leave Auto Code Placement off, or you may want to insert a code that is not controlled by Auto Code Placement. In either case, before you choose page layout commands, move the insertion point to the beginning of the document or page in one of the following ways:

■ To the beginning of the document: press Ctrl-Home to place the insertion point *after* any codes at the beginning of the document, or press Ctrl-Home, Ctrl-Home to move *in front of* any codes at the beginning of the document.

  Alternatively, use the mouse to move to the top of your document, open the Reveal Codes window, place the mouse pointer before or after any codes, and then click the left button.

■ To the top of a page: choose **E**dit, **G**o To; then type the page number and choose OK. On the keyboard, press Ctrl-G to activate the Go To box.

  If you want to move to the top or bottom of the *current* page, choose **P**osition while in the Go To box; then choose **T**op of Current Page or **B**ottom of Current Page.

CAUTION: In spite of your efforts at proper code placement as you create your document, codes located at the top of pages subsequent to the first page *will be moved to new locations* when you add or delete text, change margins, and make other formatting changes. Give careful attention to the effects of editing with the goal of developing a work pattern that addresses this issue; for example, you can add page and document formatting after you finish editing the text.

Deleting Format Codes

WordPerfect protects many of the codes you insert into your document so that you don't accidentally delete them. However, in the Reveal Codes window, you can delete any code in one of the following two ways:

- Highlight the code using the direction keys or by placing the mouse pointer on the code and clicking the left mouse button; then press Del.

- Highlight the character after the code in the same manner; then press Backspace.

The format codes that you can delete without opening the Reveal Codes window include Page Break, Indent, Double-Indent, Flush Right, and Center. All other codes used to format lines, pages, and documents can be deleted only with the Reveal Codes window open.

You can modify this code protection by turning on Confirm on Code Deletion in the Preferences, Environment menu. You find information and instructions for this feature in Chapter 29, "Customizing WordPerfect with Preferences." All the instructions in this chapter assume that Confirm on Code Deletion remains off.

Setting Margins

Margins are the areas of white space that surround the text on a page. Margins are measured from the edge of the page to the edge of the text. The default margins in WordPerfect are one inch on all four sides; they are measured in decimal inches that you can specify to two decimal places. WordPerfect inserts a [T/B Mar:#,##] for the top and bottom margins, and a [L/R Mar:#,##] for the left and right margins. Figure 11.2 shows the Margins dialog box, which you access through the Layout menu.

FIG. 11.2

The Margins
dialog box with
the default 1-inch
margins.

To set margins, follow these steps:

1. Choose **Layout**, **Margins**.

   CUA Press Margins (Ctrl-F8).

2. Enter new margins in each text box as required. Move from box to
   box by pressing Tab, by pressing Alt plus the underlined letter, or
   by clicking with the mouse.

3. Choose OK to save the changes and return to your document.

   Alternatively, with the Ruler on, click the triangle at the end of
   either margin bar and drag the triangle to the new location, as in
   figure 11.3. (For more information on the Ruler, see Chapter 6,
   "Formatting Text.")

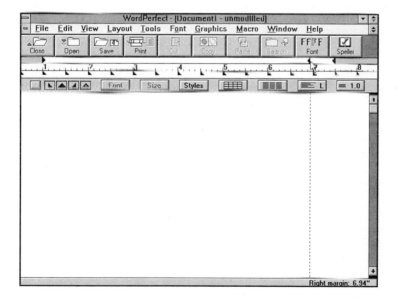

FIG. 11.3

Click the marker
on the Ruler to
set margins.

You can change margins in a document at any time. The change remains in effect until WordPerfect encounters another margin code. To change a margin, follow the steps described in this section for creating the new margin setting.

The Auto Code Placement feature handles each margin code differently. When Auto Code Placement is on, it inserts the Top/Bottom margin code at the top of the current page and places the Left/Right margin code at the beginning of the paragraph where the insertion point is located. If the feature is off, the program inserts the codes at the insertion point location. The Top/Bottom margin takes effect on the next page if the code does not appear at the top of the current page. The Left/Right margin change inserts a hard return code ([HRt]) and takes effect immediately.

Some printers have a minimum margin requirement. If you enter a margin setting smaller than the minimum setting your printer accepts, WordPerfect notifies you of the required minimum margin, and automatically resets the margin to that minimum.

T I P If your most frequent jobs, such as printing on letterhead or in a standard report format, require margin settings that differ from the default settings, choose Preferences, Initial Codes to change the default margin settings to your specifications. The new default settings remain in effect for all documents you create in the future.

If you want your document to print on facing pages, the appropriate adjustment to the margins is made with Binding Offset in the Print dialog box (see Chapter 9, "Basic Printing"). You also can start text in the bottom line of the top margin.

Other than binding offset, typesetting adjustments, numbering lines, or marking redlined text in the margin area, *all* text appears within the margin settings, including headers, footers, page numbers, and footnotes. These features, including a blank line that separates the feature from the main text, appear in the space subtracted from the main body of the document.

Keeping Text Together

The capability of word processing software to automate the layout of typed text may be the most common reason for personal computer purchases. To enhance the capabilities of automated layout,

WordPerfect uses standard formatting rules for document layout, controlling the way that automated layout divides pages. You can use the Page Break, Conditional End of Page, Block Protect, and Widow/Orphan Protection commands to prevent problems such as section names that dangle at the bottom of a page or page breaks that occur in the middle of a list or table.

This section addresses keeping text together on the larger scale; refer to Chapter 6, "Formatting Text," for information on keeping words together.

Soft Page Breaks

WordPerfect automatically divides your document into pages based on the margins and paper size you establish. These automatic page breaks are called *soft page breaks* and appear on-screen as a thin solid line. When you access Reveal Codes, you see that each page of text ends with a [SPg] code. If the soft page break falls on the location of a hard return, WordPerfect saves the hard return and the new code appears as [HRt-SPg].

A soft page break often occurs at a blank line, such as when a break falls on the hard return. To prevent this blank line from being carried to the top of the next page, but to retain it should later editing move the page break location elsewhere, WordPerfect inserts a dormant hard return [DORM HRt] to save the blank line.

Hard Page Breaks

As you edit a document, adding and deleting text and changing formats, WordPerfect recalculates the soft page break locations. To ensure that a page always breaks at a specific location that cannot be affected by the changing soft page breaks, use the Page Break feature.

To ensure that a page always breaks at a specific location, use a hard page break. Place the insertion point at the exact location where you want the page to break, and follow these steps:

1. Choose **L**ayout, **P**age.

   CUA Press Layout Page (Alt-F9).

2. Choose **P**age Break from the Page menu (see fig. 11.4).

   A hard page break code appears on-screen as a double solid line; in the Reveal Codes window, a hard page break appears as [HPg].

Cue: Use the Page Break feature to end specific sections of a document so that a new section starts on the next page. Hard Page Breaks are appropriate to end a cover page, a preface, a chapter, an appendix, or a table of contents.

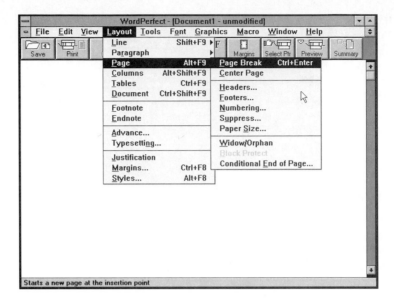

FIG. 11.4

The Layout and
Page menus.

The only way to override the hard page break is to delete it, while in
the document window, in one of the following two ways:

- Place the insertion point in the space immediately above the
  double line and press Del.

- Place the insertion point immediately after the double line and
  press Backspace.

Block Protect

Cue: Use Block Protect
to keep all the text in a list, a
table, a figure and its
accompanying text, or a
series of numbered para-
graphs on the same page.

The Block Protect feature places codes at the beginning and end of a
section of text you want to keep together on the same page. As you edit
the protected text, the block expands or shrinks to accommodate your
changes.

When WordPerfect encounters a Block Protect code, the program determines whether there is sufficient room to place the entire block of
text in the space remaining on the present page. If sufficient space is
not available, WordPerfect inserts a soft page break above the block,
and the block of text begins the next page.

To protect a block of text, move the insertion point to the beginning of
the text you want to protect and follow these steps:

1. Highlight the block of text by pressing the left mouse button and
   dragging the highlight with the mouse to the end of the text.

Press Select (F8) and use the direction keys to move the insertion point to highlight the desired text.

2. Choose **Layout**, **P**age. The Block Protect feature, which is usually dimmed to indicate that it is unavailable, is now a choice on the menu, along with Conditional End of Page. All other Page features are dimmed when text is selected.

3. Choose **B**lock Protect.

   The codes that appear in the Reveal Codes window at the beginning and end of the selected text are [Block Pro:On] and [Block Pro:Off]. You can end the protection by deleting either code.

CAUTION: Block Protect is designed to protect a page or less of text. If you add text to a protected block so that the amount of protected text exceeds one page, the Block Off code moves to the end of the amount of text that will fit on one page. This change is permanent; the original location of the Block Off code will not be restored by later format changes or deletions of text. If you need to include more than a page of text, try using a smaller font size.

Conditional End of Page

The Conditional End of Page feature acts to protect a specific number of lines rather than specific text. Use this feature to ensure that titles, headings and subheadings are not left alone at the bottom of a page. You can continue to add text in the protected area, but the text that follows is pushed out of the protected area.

Use Conditional End of Page at the beginning of sections or subsections to ensure that three to six lines of text follow on the page. Remember also to count the lines needed for double- or triple-spacing between headings and text.

To insert a Conditional End of Page, move the insertion point to the beginning of the text you want to protect and follow these steps:

1. Choose **Layout**, **P**age

    Press Layout Page (Alt-F9).

■ **Cue:** Use Conditional End of Page to keep a section heading and a few of the following lines of text together on a page.

2. Choose Conditional **E**nd of Page.

3. In the Conditional End of Page dialog box, enter the number of lines you want to keep together.

4. Choose OK to save the changes and return to your document.

The single code [Cndl EOP:#] appears at the beginning of the protected text in the Reveal Codes window, where # is the number of lines you choose to include. You can override a Conditional End of Page by inserting a page break within the lines that the command protects.

Widows and Orphans

A heading or subheading dangling at the bottom of a page is not the only time a line appears to be lost. A single line of a paragraph appearing by itself on the bottom of a page is called an *orphan*. A single line from the end of a paragraph that is pushed to the top of the next page is referred to as a *widow*.

■ **Cue:** Widow/Orphan protection is most often used to protect an entire document. If you use this feature regularly, consider including it in the Initial Codes you specify in Preferences from the File menu.

Widow/Orphan Protection is usually, but not necessarily, placed at the beginning of the document to protect the entire document. Unlike other page codes, WordPerfect places the Widow/Orphan code at the insertion point location, even when the Auto Code Protection feature is on.

To place Widow/Orphan protection in a document, place the insertion point where you want protection to begin, or press Ctrl-Home to move to the beginning of the document, and follow these steps:

1. Choose **L**ayout, **P**age.

    CUA Press Layout Page (Alt-F9).

2. Choose **W**idow/Orphan.

    The [W/O On] code appears in the Reveal Codes window.

The protected lines always move to the top of the next page, leaving blank lines at the bottom of the preceding page. WordPerfect moves two-line and three-line paragraphs in their entirety.

Centering a Page

■ **Cue:** Use Center Page to place a short note on letterhead stationery, for title and cover pages, acknowledgments, and a preface.

Centering a page between the top and bottom margins is an easy way to format a page that stands alone. Centering a page repositions the material in relation to the top and bottom margins only. To center from top to bottom, the text should not start or end with extra hard returns unless you want the blank lines to place the text slightly below center.

The Center Page command centers text only on the page where the code appears. To center a page, follow these steps:

1. Choose **L**ayout, **P**age.

   [CUA] Press Layout Page (Alt-F9).

2. Choose **C**enter Page.

   The single code, [Center Pg], appears in the Reveal Codes window.

3. Insert a page break at the end of the centered text.

The centered material does not appear differently on-screen. To see the centered page as it will print, you must view it in Print Preview.

Whether or not the Auto Code Placement feature is on, to delete the code, you can choose Center Page again while the insertion point is anywhere on the centered page. You also can open the Reveal Codes window and delete the code manually.

Using the Advance Command

The Advance command enables you to place text at a precise location on the page. Advance is useful in starting multipage letters with a first-page-only allowance for letterhead, helps you fill in preprinted forms, and enables you to ignore line height changes that occur when larger or smaller font sizes are chosen.

Advance has two positioning schemes. You can use it to place text a measured distance up, down, left, or right of the Advance code. If you edit the preceding text, the code relocates accordingly. The measurements are always relative to the final location of the Advance code.

■ **Cue**: Use Advance to place text or graphics at a specific location on the page.

With the second method, you specify a particular line and column position just as they appear in the status line in the lower right corner of the screen. This method results in absolute placement of the text, regardless of the final location of the Advance code.

You can include only one direction of movement in an Advance code. You need separate Advance codes to specify vertical distance and horizontal distance.

To advance text to a specific location, place the insertion point immediately before the text you want to advance and follow these steps:

1. Choose **L**ayout, **A**dvance to display the Advance dialog box (see fig. 11.5).

FIG. 11.5

The Advance
dialog box.

2. To choose one of the directions, click it with the mouse or press the underlined letter so that a dot appears in the circle next to your choice.

   If the text you want to advance cannot be moved in a certain direction, that direction is dimmed in the dialog box.

3. Choose **A**dvance; in the text box, type either the amount to move the text, or the line and column position.

4. Choose OK to save the changes and return to your document.

If you want to add text at your original location, return to it by using Advance to specify that point.

CAUTION: Subsequent editing of text preceding or between Advance codes can negate or distort the result of the measurement specified in the codes. Think through the result of any additions or deletions of text, checking the document in Print Preview regularly to ensure that you are getting the results you want.

Advance is a powerful tool for integrating text and graphics. You can find a discussion of this feature in greater detail in Chapter 15, "Working with Advanced Printing Techniques," and Chapter 18, "Desktop Publishing with WordPerfect."

Using Headers and Footers

Headers and footers are blocks of text that appear at the top or bottom of a page. They can include graphics, page numbers, the section title, or any other information about the document. Headers and footers can improve the appearance of your work and serve as a road map of its features.

WordPerfect enables you to use two headers and two footers on each page, and they can be different on every page. They can appear on only even or odd pages. They can be suppressed where one would conflict with letterhead or figure placement.

If you are using two headers or two footers on the same page, design each so that they do not overlap. You can use flush-right, centering, or alternating lines, for example. Headers and footers start at the edge of the margin and print into the main text area with a blank line added to separate them from the main text. They can be as long as one page, although that is unlikely to happen!

Headers and footers do not appear on-screen. You can view them by using **File**, Print Preview (or by pressing Shift-F5).

Creating a Header or Footer

You can create different headers and footers on any page in your document, although they are typically created at the beginning of the document. You may want to create new headers and footers at the beginning of each new chapter.

Headers and footers appear on the page the way they are designed. Creating one as A or B does not determine the order in which they appear on the printed page.

The Headers or Footers dialog box shown in figure 11.6 opens the editing screen shown in figure 11.7. The editing screen contains a button to close the screen when you are finished, one to insert a page number, and one that opens a Placement dialog box.

When you are in the header or footer editing window, the WordPerfect formatting commands and menus are available. The settings in effect at the location of the header or footer code control what appears in the document. Headers or footers created in a succeeding portion of the document, where new margin settings or fonts are in effect, conform to the new settings.

All the instructions that follow refer to Header A because the steps for Header A or B are the same as the steps for Footer A or B. To create a new header, follow these steps:

1. Choose **Layout**, **P**age.

    Press Layout Page (Alt-F9).

2. Choose **H**eaders to open the Headers dialog box shown in figure 11.6.

FIG. 11.6

The Headers dialog box.

3. Choose Header **A**.

4. In the editing window, as shown in figure 11.7, type the text of the header. Insert any formatting codes you want in the header. Features not available for creating a header are dimmed on the menus. Make sure that you change current document settings in the header where appropriate. Do not end with a hard return unless you want an extra blank line.

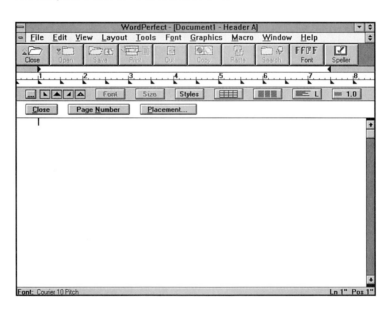

FIG. 11.7

The Header editing window.

In addition to the Layout and Font menus, several particularly useful commands are available while you work in the editing window. You can automate your layout with styles and with macros, or enhance the text with graphics and graphics lines.

5. By default, the header will appear on every page. To change this selection, choose **P**lacement to open the Placement dialog box shown in figure 11.8. Then choose **O**dd Pages if the header is to appear only on odd pages, and E**v**en Pages if you want the header or footer only on even pages.

FIG. 11.8

The Placement dialog box.

6. If you want to include page numbering in the header, refer to the discussion in "Using Page Numbers in Headers and Footers" in this chapter.

7. Choose **C**lose to return to the document.

As an example, a code that appears in the Reveal Codes window is `[Header A:Every page;`*`text[code]text`*`..]`. Up to three lines of text, including all codes, are displayed.

The Retrieve command is available when you create a header or footer. After you design a header or footer you want to use in the future, select the form text (using F8 or highlighting with the mouse), and then choose Edit, Copy, Close the header or footer, open a new window and paste in the text; then save the file. When you create the same header or footer in your next report, choose File, **R**etrieve at the time you open the blank header or footer window to retrieve your form text.

T I P

Editing Headers and Footers

You can edit headers and footers as easily as you edit the main body of a document. You can begin the editing process at any point in the document where the header or footer you want to edit is in effect.

324

■ **Cue:** Remember that you can display the Reveal Codes window while in the header/footer window. Use Reveal Codes to locate, insert, and delete codes.

To edit the header created in the preceding section, follow these steps:

1. Choose **Layout**, **Page**.

    Press Layout Page (Alt-F9).

2. Choose **H**eaders to access the header you want to edit.

3. Choose Header **A**; then choose **E**dit. WordPerfect displays the Header editing window with the text you entered.

4. Type the changes and choose **C**lose to save your changes and return to your document.

Using Page Numbers in Headers and Footers

When you are working in a header or footer editing window, as shown in figure 11.7, you can include a page number code by placing the insertion point where you want the page number to appear and selecting Page Numbering to insert the ^B character. When the document is formatted for printing, WordPerfect replaces the ^B with the actual page number. Page numbers are often enhanced with text so that they read *Page 24* or *- 24 -*, for example. To include text with the page number, type it before or after you insert the ^B.

Alternatively, you can use the instructions in the section "Numbering Pages," to set up header or footer page numbers using the Page Numbering dialog box.

You can use one of four ways to remove or override a header or footer as follows:

■ You can delete the header or footer in the Reveal Codes window as discussed in "Deleting Format Codes," a previous section in this chapter.

■ You can replace the header or footer by creating another one with the same letter later in the document.

■ You can suppress a header or footer on any one document page by using the procedure explained in the following section.

■ You can discontinue a header or footer that you do not want to appear again in the document by using the procedure in the section, "Discontinuing Headers and Footers."

Suppressing Headers and Footers

You usually create headers and footers on the first page of a document. However, because headers usually do not appear on the first page of a document (especially when you use letterhead) and page number footers often start on the second page of a document, you can suppress the printing of headers and footers on a page. You also can suppress headers and footers at the beginnings of chapters or elsewhere in a document when you don't want them to appear.

■ **Cue:** You can suppress the printing of a header or footer on one page, and it will continue to print on the succeeding pages of the document.

To suppress the header you created in the first section, place the insertion point at the top of the page where you want to suppress the header and follow these steps:

1. Choose Layout, Page.

   CUA Press Layout Page (Alt-F9).

2. Choose Suppress. From the Suppress dialog box, choose Header A (see fig. 11.9).

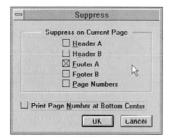

FIG. 11.9

The Suppress dialog box.

3. Choose OK to return to your document.

You can delete the suppress code ([Suppress:HA]) in the Reveal Codes window. The reference in header and footer codes is HA, HB, FA, FB for Header or Footer A or B, respectively.

Discontinuing Headers and Footers

To *replace* a header or footer, you simply create a new header or footer and assign it the same letter. The header or footer that appears when you edit is the one in effect on the page that contains the insertion point at the time you choose Edit.

To *discontinue* a header or footer if you do not want it to print again and you do not replace it immediately with another header or footer of the same letter (for example, the header you created previously in the index of a report), follow these steps:

1. Choose **L**ayout, **P**age.

    Press Layout Page (Alt-F9).

2. Choose **H**eaders to access the header that you want to discontinue.

3. Choose Header **A**; then choose **D**iscontinue.

4. Choose OK to return to your document.

T I P   If you want to record extensive editing and printing information about a document, create and then discontinue a header or footer that you can use for a specialized document summary which will not appear in your printed document. You might include the following information:

Created date:
Printed date:
Revisions from ABC: Second revision:
Revisions from XYZ: Second revision:
Revisions from LMN: Second revision:
Revision printed: Second revised printing:
Mailed date:

After creating this header or footer, immediately discontinue it, making sure that no intervening codes or text exist. The header or footer remains in your document and can be edited to update the information as long as you do not create another one of the same name. If you use this format regularly, save the text as a file and retrieve it into the header or footer window when you want to use it in another document.

Using Other WordPerfect Features with Headers and Footers

Headers and footers have an interesting hybrid status in a document. They may include all the structured layout found in the main body of the document but otherwise seem to have the status of Post-it Notes: they are only nominally part of the document. This characteristic becomes more obvious as you explore other WordPerfect features.

Incorporating Graphics in Headers and Footers

The full range of graphics commands is available in the header or footer window. Choose from one to all of the following to enhance your header or footer:

- *Line Draw.* Press Ctrl-D to access Line Draw when in the header or footer window. Ten different line styles are available for drawing boxes, shading areas, and so on. For a complete discussion of this feature, see Chapter 16, "Using Lines To Add Effects."

- *Graphics lines.* The Line feature in the Graphics menu places horizontal or vertical lines of any length, thickness, and shading into your header or footer. You easily can center a short horizontal line above a page number in a footer or use a full-width horizontal line to set off a header from the main text. Insert these lines using the instructions set out in Chapter 16, "Using Lines to Add Effects."

- *Graphics figures.* You can use any of the box styles available in the Graphics menu in a header or footer. You can import and link part of a spreadsheet into a table box in the header or footer, use any of the WPG figures that come with WordPerfect, or import other graphics. The size of a figure requires careful consideration when used in what will probably be a small area. Nevertheless, many of the WPG figures can be used effectively in a two-line footer that appears on second sheets of personal letterhead stationery. Specific instructions for using graphics are in given in Chapter 17.

Using the Speller

The Speller checks headers and footers only if you choose to check the entire document or if you choose to check a page on which there is a header or footer code.

Chapter 8, "Using the Speller and the Thesaurus," provides instructions on how to use the Speller.

Using Search and Replace

Both the Search feature and the Replace feature have a check box titled Search Document Body Only. Leave this box empty if you want to include headers and footers in searches. To include headers and footers, you still need to press Ctrl-Home twice to make sure that you start a forward search or replace before any header or footer codes.

If you do not return to the beginning of your document, you can search or replace backwards to find any headers and footers you may have missed. Refer to Chapter 4, "Editing a Document," for instructions on how to use Search and Replace.

Cutting, Copying, and Pasting

You can use the Cut, Copy, and Paste editing features when creating headers and footers. You can cut or copy text or a graphic from a document window or from another header or footer, and then paste the text or graphic into the current header or footer editing window. The reverse is as simple. You also can cut or copy the contents of a header or footer in one document and paste into the header or footer window in another document.

Instructions for selecting text and using Cut, Copy, and Paste are in Chapter 5, "Selecting and Editing Text."

Numbering Pages

WordPerfect has the capability to number pages automatically, even for complex documents with multiple chapters and introductions and appendixes. You can number chapters individually and assign different numbering styles to opening and closing sections.

Page numbers do not appear on-screen, but you can preview them by choosing **F**ile, **P**rint Preview. To be able to read the numbers in Print Preview, however, you need to magnify the size of the page and use the vertical and horizontal scroll bars.

The page number prints in the top or bottom line of the text area. WordPerfect inserts a blank line to separate the number from the rest of the text. If you use the default 1-inch top and bottom margins for 8 1/2-by-11-inch paper and a Courier 10 cpi font, the text area contains 54 lines. Adding page numbers decreases the number of lines to 52.

You find all page numbering options in the Page Numbering dialog box. Although the options are discussed here in separate sections, you can choose all the options you want to select before finally closing the dialog box.

Choosing Page Number Position

WordPerfect provides eight preset page number positions, including two that place numbers on alternating pages. You choose the position you want from the Page Numbering dialog box, as shown in figure 11.10.

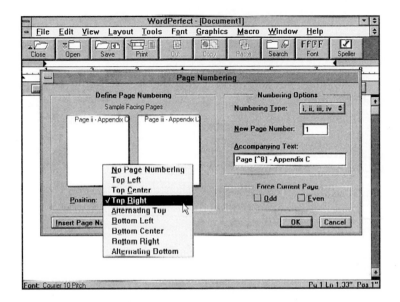

FIG. 11.10

The Page Numbering dialog box with the Position pop up list.

You can place numbers in the left, center, or right of the top or bottom of the page and on alternating outside top or bottom of facing pages, as in a book. The code inserted at the beginning of the page is [Pg Numbering:location], which you can see in the Reveal Codes window.

To choose a position for your page numbers, follow these steps:

1. Choose **L**ayout, **P**age.

    CUA Press Layout Page (Alt-F9).

2. Choose **N**umbering to display the Page Numbering dialog box.

3. Choose **P**osition in the Define Page Numbering section of the dialog box; highlight your choice in the positions list.

4. Check the Sample Facing Pages area in the dialog box to see a rough preview of your position selection.

5. When you finish configuring your page numbers, choose OK to save your changes and return to the document.

T I P   Use alternating numbering when you plan to print text and staple the document in the upper corner. If you number pages in the upper right corner, the number on the back of the page is covered by the staple.

Choosing a Numbering Type

You easily can number introductory pages, the body of a document, and closing sections differently with the three page-numbering styles available in WordPerfect. In addition to Arabic numerals (1, 2, 3, 4), you can use upper- and lowercase Roman numerals (I, II, III, IV or i, ii, iii, i).

To set the page numbering type, move to the page where the new style should begin and follow these steps:

1. Choose **L**ayout, **P**age.

   [CUA]   Press Layout Page (Alt-F9).

2. Choose **N**umbering to display the Page Numbering dialog box.

3. From the Numbering Options, choose Numbering **T**ype and scroll to highlight your selection.

4. When you finish configuring your page number, choose OK to save the changes and return to the document.

In the Reveal Codes window, the code appears as `[Pg Num:1]` (or `i` or `I`), reflecting the numbering type you have chosen. To start a new numbering type in a succeeding place in the document, follow the preceding steps, placing the insertion point where you want the numbering type to change.

T I P   When you include page numbers in a header or footer, Numbering Type is dimmed when you open the Page Numbering dialog box, limiting you to using only Arabic numbers.

New Page Number

Occasionally you may want to begin page numbering with a number other than 1. Saving chapters as separate files, for example, may require that you start each chapter with a specific page number.

To start numbering with a new page number, follow these steps:

1. Choose **L**ayout, **P**age.

    Press Layout Page (Alt-F9).

2. Choose **N**umbering to display the Page Numbering dialog box.

3. Choose New Page Number. Regardless of the numbering type you are using, type the new number as an Arabic numeral. It appears in the code in the format you are using.

4. Choose OK to save your changes and return to the document.

Text with Page Number

You do not have to use a header or footer in order to include text with a page number. Appendixes, for example, often are numbered A-1, A-2, B-1, B-2, B-3, and so forth. Reference manuals often give the section name before the page number. You can place up to 28 characters around a page number, including ASCII or WordPerfect characters. Extended characters may require more space than standard characters.

To include text with a page number, follow these steps:

1. Choose **L**ayout, **P**age.

    Press Layout Page (Alt-F9).

2. Choose **N**umbering to display the Page Numbering dialog box.

3. Choose **A**ccompanying Text from the Numbering Options area. In the text box, type the text as you want it to appear on either or both sides of the page number.

   Text can precede and follow the page number ([^B]), as shown in fig. 11.10. Do not delete the [^B] code, if you want text before and after the number. If you delete the code, WordPerfect places it at the end of the text for you. If you accidentally delete the code, close the box and start over.

4. Choose OK to save your changes and return to the document.

The code appears as [Pg Num Style:Page iii - Appendix B], for example, in the Reveal Codes window. To change the text in another section of the document, repeat the steps listed in this section.

Inserting a Page Number

In addition to the eight page-number placement options available, you can place a page number anywhere else on the page. You can include page numbers in headers or footers, in a specific location to avoid a header or footer, or in text where you want to refer to the current page number.

When you insert a page number, WordPerfect ignores the Auto Code Placement feature and places the code at the exact location of the insertion point.

The code appears as [Insert Pg Num:text ^B] in the Reveal Codes window. The actual appearance of the page number on-screen and when printed incorporates all the changes previously made in the dialog box, including accompanying text. Therefore, place the insertion point where you want the page number to appear and follow these steps carefully to insert a page number:

1. Choose **L**ayout, **P**age.

    Press Layout Page (Alt-F9).

2. Choose **N**umbering to display the Page Numbering dialog box.

3. Review the selections already recorded in the dialog box to make sure that accompanying text, if any, numbering type, and other information are all appropriate for the new location. Accompanying text, for example, is probably inappropriate if the number is to appear in the middle of a sentence.

4. Choose **I**nsert Page Number.

5. Choose OK to save your changes and return to the document.

Suppressing Page Numbering

The first page of most documents is not numbered. On some pages, the page number may interfere with the position of a graphic or table. You can suppress the page number on that page so that the number does not appear in the printed version and still maintain the numbering of subsequent pages in proper order.

To suppress page numbering on one page, follow these steps:

1. Choose **L**ayout, **P**age.

    Press Layout Page (Alt-F9).

2. Choose **S**uppress to open the Suppress dialog box.

3. From the Suppress box, choose **P**age Numbering (an X appears in the adjacent check box).

   If you want to relocate the page number to the bottom center position for this page, choose Print Page Number at Bottom Center.

4. Choose OK to save your changes and return to the document.

The Suppress code appears as [Suppress:PgNum] in the Reveal Codes window. You can suppress page numbering on any page and as often as necessary.

Forcing Odd or Even Page Numbers

A simple way to make sure that chapters or sections begin on the right side of facing pages is to force that page to be an odd page number. Forcing an odd page number ensures this right-side placement regardless of text inserts or deletions.

To force an odd or even page number, follow these steps:

1. Choose **L**ayout, **P**age.

   Press Layout Page (Alt-F9).

2. Choose **N**umbering to display the Page Numbering dialog box.

3. In the Force Current Page area, choose **O**dd or **E**ven. An X appears in the adjacent check box.

4. Choose OK to save your changes and return to the document.

Choosing Paper Size and Type

The paper size and type options available by default in WordPerfect depend on the printer you have chosen. You can choose other sizes and types, such as continuous-fold labels or 5 1/2-by-8 1/2-inch invoices. A specific paper size or type is called a *paper definition*. The paper definitions you can create are limited only by the demands of your task and the capabilities of your printer.

The default paper definition in the U.S. version of WordPerfect for Windows is Standard, 8 1/2-by-11-inch continuous paper. This setting is the default even if a printer has not been chosen or no printer has been installed. You can choose any other paper definition. The paper definition you choose also manages the print job.

Choosing a Different Paper Size

In addition to the 8 1/2-by-11-inch standard paper definition, most printers have several additional paper definitions available, including legal size (8 1/2-by-14-inch) and label size.

The steps you follow to choose a different paper definition depend on whether you have chosen a printer and whether it is a WordPerfect or a Windows printer driver. You choose a printer in the Select Printer dialog box (accessed through the File menu), which includes options for choosing WordPerfect or Windows printer drivers.

After you choose a different paper definition, WordPerfect inserts a code, for example [Paper Sz/Typ:8.5" x 14",Legal]. Unless you are using a Windows printer driver, you can change the definition at any point in your document by choosing another definition. You can delete the paper size code in the Reveal Codes window.

Using a WordPerfect Printer Driver

If you have chosen a WordPerfect printer driver, change the default paper definition as follows:

1. Choose **L**ayout, **P**age.

    Press Layout Page (Alt-F9).

2. Choose **P**aper Size to display the Paper Size dialog box (see fig. 11.11).

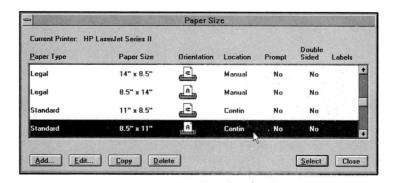

Paper Type	Paper Size	Orientation	Location	Prompt	Double Sided	Labels
Legal	14" x 8.5"		Manual	No	No	
Legal	8.5" x 14"		Manual	No	No	
Standard	11" x 8.5"		Contin	No	No	
Standard	8.5" x 11"		Contin	No	No	

Current Printer: HP LaserJet Series II

[Add...] [Edit...] [Copy] [Delete]   [Select] [Close]

FIG: 11.11

The Paper Size dialog box.

3. Move the highlight bar in the Paper Size dialog box to the paper definition you want to use; then choose Select, or double-click the appropriate paper size with the mouse to return to your document.

Using a Windows Printer Driver

If you are using a Windows printer driver, the procedure and the dialog box are different from those of a WordPerfect printer driver. If you use the usual Layout, Page, Paper Size process, the dialog box displays only one paper definition. To choose a different paper size, follow these steps to use the Windows Printer dialog box:

1. Choose File, Select Printer, Windows Printer.

2. Move the highlight bar to the name of the printer you want in the list of Windows printer drivers; then choose Setup.

   The Microsoft Windows printer setup box for the printer you highlighted appears.

3. At this point, almost every printer dialog box is unique. In the two most common paper size layouts for this setup box, one displays paper widths and paper heights in separate boxes (see fig. 11.12), and the other lists both width and height paper sizes in one bar or box (see fig. 11.13). Choose the paper size you want to use.

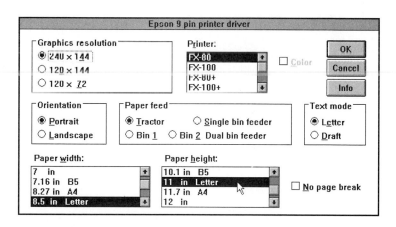

FIG. 11.12

A Windows printer driver dialog box with separate width and height lists.

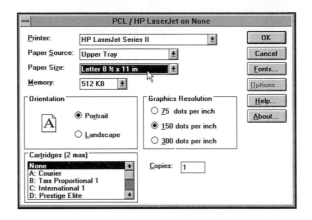

FIG. 11.13

A Windows
printer driver
dialog box with
one Paper Size
box for width
and height.

4. Choose OK to close the Windows printer driver dialog box; then choose **S**elect in the WordPerfect Select Printer dialog box to return to the document.

Note that Portrait and Landscape options, if available, change automatically as you choose the height and width or paper size you want to use.

You can choose only one paper size per document when using a Windows printer driver. Choosing another paper size later in the document changes the original paper size choice.

T I P   If you require different paper definitions in your print job, and you are using a Windows driver, select the first paper size or type needed, print those pages, and then select the next paper size or type and print the remaining pages. Refer to Chapter 9, "Basic Printing," for instructions on how to print selected pages.

Choosing Paper Size When No Printer Is Selected or Installed

If you have not yet chosen a printer, you may still change the default paper definition, but the dialog box is again different. To display the Edit Paper Size box, follow these steps:

1. Choose **L**ayout, **P**age.

  Press Layout Page (Alt-F9).

2. Choose Paper Size to display the Edit Paper Size (No Printer Selected) dialog box (see fig. 11.14).

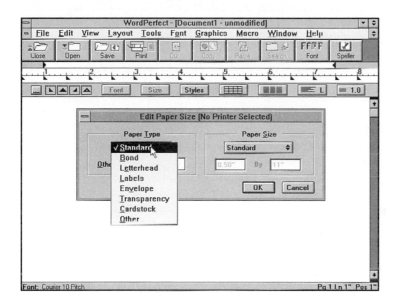

FIG. 11.14

The Edit Paper Size (No Printer Selected) dialog box with Paper Type pop-up list.

3. Choose a paper type. Choosing one of the first seven options changes the name in the Paper Type button. If you choose Other, the pointer appears in the Other text box, enabling you to type a different name for your definition.

4. Choose a paper size from the pop-up list shown in figure 11.15. If you choose one of the first nine sizes, the name for the size appears in the Paper Size button. Choosing Other places default sizes of 8.5" and 11" in the two size text boxes, enabling you to edit each dimension.

Note that this dialog box provides no option for printing landscape (sideways, along the long edge of the paper). If you have landscape fonts, you can force landscape printing by specifying a paper size that is wider than it is long. The [Paper Sz/Typ] code then includes the dimensions in a landscape format. If you choose a width that exceeds the width available to your printer and is less than the length of the paper, the [Paper Sz/Typ] code appears with an asterisk (*) in front of the width, and the maximum width is the number displayed.

5. Choose OK to confirm your choices and return to the document.

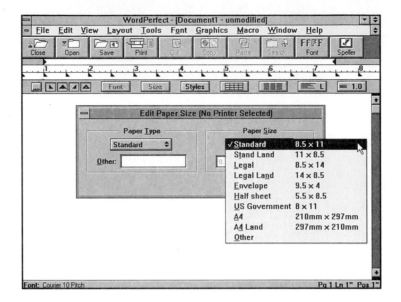

FIG. 11.15

Paper sizes available in the Edit Paper Size (No Printer Selected) dialog box.

Using Additional Paper Size and Type Considerations

Because WordPerfect saves the paper size and type code with your document, selecting a different printer may modify the code so that it is unacceptable for your job. For example, if you specify 11-by-8 1/2-inch (wide) paper and later select a printer that cannot print this width, the code changes to the maximum width available (with an asterisk in front of it) by 8 1/2 inches, as long as that printer selection is in effect. If you change printer selections, check the paper size and type code in the Reveal Codes window before printing documents created for another printer.

If you routinely use a paper size other than 8 1/2 by 11 inches, you can replace the default definition for all new documents by choosing another definition in Preferences, Initial Codes, as explained in Chapter 29, "Customizing WordPerfect with Preferences."

When you attempt to change paper definitions while using the columns feature, the paper size and type feature is dimmed. When you try to change paper definitions in the middle of a table while the Auto Code Placement feature is off, a warning box appears, and your new selection is ignored.

T I P

If you have a printer with multiple paper trays, or bins, a frequent print job layout is to specify the bin containing letterhead for the first page of a document and a second bin containing second sheets for the rest of the document.

When the paper size and type code for the second sheets is placed at the top of the second page, the code can be moved around easily when you edit the document. To avoid this problem, choose the second-page paper definition as soon as you have typed some text—such as the date—on the first page. This intervening text forces the second paper size and type code to take effect on the next page, exactly where you want it to be. Subsequent editing is not likely to move the code when you place it this early in the document.

When you change paper definitions, the positions of soft page breaks automatically change in your document. In addition, changes occur in some menus, such as fonts, where the paper definition may restrict selections to only landscape or only portrait fonts.

For information about actual printing of your document, refer to Chapter 9, "Basic Printing." Information on the relationship between fonts and paper orientation is available in Chapter 10, "Working with Fonts." You can create new paper definitions to accommodate almost any print job, as discussed in Chapter 15, "Working with Advanced Printing Techniques."

Setting the Initial Font

You can change the initial font used in your document at any time from any location in your document. When you use Initial Font to perform this task, the change extends to text in headers, footers, footnotes, and endnotes. To change the initial font in the document you are currently editing, follow these steps:

1. Choose **Layout, Document.**

   [CUA] Press Layout Document (Ctrl-Shift-F9).

2. Choose Initial **Font.**

3. In the Fonts area, choose the name of the font you want; then in the Point Size area, choose the size you want. *Note:* Unless you have a printer with built-in scalable fonts or have installed a font package such as Bitstream fonts, Point Size is gray and unavailable.

4. Choose OK to save the changes and return to your document.

This command is particularly useful if you have not yet changed fonts in your document. If you have already changed fonts, the Initial Font change takes effect at the beginning of your document and continues until it encounters a code for a different font name or size.

Refer to Chapter 10, "Working with Fonts," for a full discussion of fonts and how they affect the appearance of your document.

Setting Initial Codes

You can specify a document's initial codes without those codes appearing in the Reveal Codes window by choosing Preferences, Initial Codes; or Document, Initial Codes. If you choose to use Preferences, Initial Codes, the codes you set up are thereafter used initially in every document you create. If you choose Document, Initial Codes, the codes you set up are used initially in the current document only and take precedence over those codes chosen in Preference, Initial Codes.

Regardless of how you set initial codes, you are presented with an Initial Codes window with the Reveal Codes window already displayed and a button to close the Initial Codes window. If you have set up codes with Preferences, Initial Codes, these codes appear, and you can edit, rearrange, or delete them as appropriate.

The procedure for either method is the same and is discussed fully in Chapter 29, "Customizing WordPerfect with Preferences," which includes a list of the codes that can serve as initial codes.

To set up initial codes in your document, follow these steps:

1. Choose **L**ayout, **D**ocument.

    Press Layout Document (Ctrl-Shift-F9).

2. Choose Initial **C**odes.

3. Use the menu, Button Bar, or keyboard commands to create codes for the features you want initially in your document. The codes you create appear in the Reveal Codes window.

4. Choose **C**lose to save your changes and return to the document.

If you want to change the codes you have chosen, follow the same steps to open the Document Initial Codes window and make the changes you want. Any codes you insert later in your document take precedence over the initial codes. This preference is important if you create new headers or footers, because the codes in effect at the point you insert the header or footer prevail.

Using the Redline Method

Redline and Strikeout are special features that enable you to edit documents in WordPerfect by noting suggested additions (Redline) and deletions (Strikeout).

If you have a color monitor, the redlined text is red on-screen. On a monochrome monitor, the appearance is controlled by the setting you choose for the Redline attribute in Display (from the Preferences menu). Strikeout shows as a horizontal line drawn through the stricken text on either monitor.

You choose Redline and Strikeout from the Font menu. These editing tools are discussed further in Chapter 10, "Working with Fonts," but the printed appearance of these fonts is an important consideration for formatting documents.

To choose the Redline method, follow these steps:

1. Choose Layout, Document.

   CUA Press Layout Document (Ctrl-Shift-F9).

2. Choose Redline Method.

   You can access the same Redline selections by choosing File, Preferences, Print, or by pressing Alt-F, E, P.

3. Choose one of the following three methods for marking Redlined text:

   - *Printer Dependent.* Prints a shaded background for most laser printers or dots for most dot-matrix printers.

   - *Mark Left Margin.* Places a vertical bar (|) in the margin area along your text.

   - *Mark Alternating Margins.* Places the vertical bar on either margin, alternating left and right.

4. If you choose to mark text in the margins, the Redline Character dialog box appears. If you want to use a character other than the vertical bar, delete the bar and type another character. To use a WordPerfect character, press Ctrl-W to access the WordPerfect Characters box. Choose the appropriate character **S**et and the

Character you want to use; then choose **I**nsert and **C**lose. Chapter 28, "Creating and Displaying Special Characters," provides information on the WordPerfect characters.

5. Choose OK to return to the document.

Choosing a different Redline method does not change the on-screen appearance. Because this choice affects only the way the text appears when you print, you may change the method as often as you want. Your final selection takes precedence over previous selections.

Changing the Display Pitch

Changing the on-screen display pitch enables you to display several columns or a wide table of text by reducing the amount of space contained in tabs, indents, and margins. The display pitch adjusts the width of characters on-screen without changing the way the actual characters appear. You can see more easily how this feature works by changing settings with the Ruler displayed.

To change the display pitch, follow these steps:

1. Choose **L**ayout, **D**ocument.

   CUA Press Layout Document (Ctrl-Shift-F9).

2. Choose **D**isplay Pitch.

3. Choose **M**anual to activate the text box.

4. Type the new display pitch value in the text box.

5. Choose OK to save the changes and return to your document.

   The space used for tabs, margins, spacing between columns, and so on, decreases as the percentage of normal decreases; in Draft mode, the space used decreases as the inch increment increases.

Creating a Document Summary

Creating a document summary enables you to maintain a database about your documents from which you can obtain information without retrieving the individual documents. You can store a substantial amount of information in the document summary. In addition to the document creation date and revision date, which WordPerfect automatically fills in, you can include eight separate pieces of information about your document (see fig. 11.16).

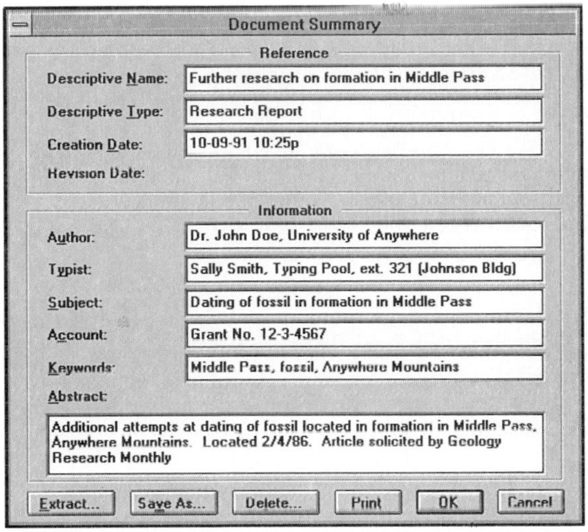

FIG. 11.16

A completed
Document
Summary dialog
box.

The following list describes the text boxes in the Document Summary
dialog box:

- *Descriptive Name.* This option enables you to enter for your document a name longer than the 8 characters (plus 3-character extension) you can use in DOS file-naming conventions. In WordPerfect
  you can use up to 68 characters to describe the document.

- *Descriptive Type.* This option enables you to enter up to 20 characters to classify your documents into categories such as Letter,
  Proposal, or Payroll Report. The WordPerfect File Manager uses
  the information in this text box to sort your documents by type.
  Read about the File Manager feature in Chapter 3, "Managing
  Files," before you design a list of descriptive types for your
  documents.

- *Creation Date.* WordPerfect fills in the Creation Date box when you
  create your document. You can change this information in the
  following format, using slashes or hyphens in the date and *a* or *p*
  following the time:

  08/07/1991 10:25a

  8-7-99 04:13p

If you do not use the correct format, you receive an error message
when you choose OK to return to your document. Any other information you have already filled in is retained, however.

- *Revision Date.* WordPerfect updates the revision date every time you save your document. You cannot enter information in this field.

CAUTION: The Creation Date and Revision Date are obtained from the current date and time available in your computer. Check the system date and time frequently to make sure that they are correct.

- *Author.* This option enables you to type up to 60 characters that describe the document author's name, job title, address, or other information.

- *Typist.* This option enables you to type up to 60 characters that describe the typist's name, job title, extension number, or other information. (If you choose to extract information, WordPerfect inserts the contents of this text box from your last document summary here; see the section on Extract in this chapter.)

- *Subject.* You can enter up to 160 characters about the subject matter of your document in the Subject text box. (If you choose to extract information, WordPerfect inserts the 160 characters following the default subject text here; see the section on Extract in this chapter.)

- *Account.* You can enter up to 160 characters of any information you want in the Account text box. This box provides an additional area for descriptive information.

  Use the Account text box to identify a client, customer, or job that may not be apparent in the document summary. You can record an account number, court case number, or case style. This box can be particularly useful if you regularly prepare routine correspondence to the same individuals about the same subject on behalf of a different client or job.

- *Keywords.* Through the Advanced Find feature in File Manager, WordPerfect can search document summaries for keywords. Use the Keywords text box to enter descriptive information about the document that can be useful for a speedy file search. Refer to Chapter 30, "Advanced File Management," for detailed information about the File Manager's Advanced Find feature.

- *Abstract.* The Abstract text box accepts up to 400 characters of text to describe your document. (If you choose to extract information, WordPerfect inserts the first 400 characters of your document here. If the document is a letter, the text inserted includes the recipient's name, address, salutation, and opening paragraph without hard returns. You can edit freely in the Abstract box, but the Copy, Cut, Paste, and Undelete commands are not available. See the section on Extract in this chapter.)

You access the Document Summary dialog box through the Layout menu. Figure 11.17 shows the commands in the Layout, Document section of the menu bar. These commands affect the entire document.

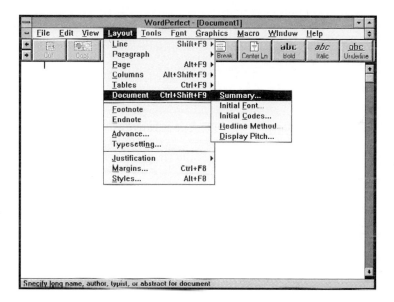

FIG. 11.17

The Document menu.

Using the text boxes in the Document Summary dialog box, create a document summary by following these steps:

1. Choose **Layout**, **Document**.

   CUA Press Layout Document (Ctrl-Shift-F9).

2. Choose **S**ummary to display the Document Summary dialog box (again see fig. 11.16).

3. Type the information you want to include in the text boxes, moving from box to box with the Tab key or Alt plus the underlined letter, or by clicking the mouse.

4. Choose OK to save the summary and return to your document.

Creating a Document Summary on Save or Exit

You can choose to have WordPerfect prompt you to fill in the document summary each time you save or exit your document. When you are prompted, you can choose Cancel to exit the dialog box. The dialog box continues to appear each time you save or exit until you enter text in it.

To instruct WordPerfect to prompt you to complete the summary, follow these steps:

1. Choose File, Preferences, Document Summary.

2. Choose Create Summary on Save/Exit to place an X in the check box.

3. Choose OK to return to your document.

If you decide you no longer want to be prompted for document summaries, follow the same steps, choosing Create Summary on Save/Exit to turn off the feature.

If you do not want to create a document summary for *every* document, yet you create one fairly often, consider installing Document Summary on the Button Bar. With Document Summary on the Button Bar, you have the option handy but are not confronted with the dialog box every time you save or exit.

Choosing Document Summary Options

Several options are available that delete, save, or extract information from the document summary. These options are available as buttons along the bottom of the Document Summary dialog box (again see fig. 11.16).

Extract

When you choose Extract, Yes, WordPerfect performs the following tasks:

■ Retrieves into their respective text boxes in the new document the Author and Typist entries from the last document summary you saved.

- Retrieves the first 160 characters of text following the Subject text. WordPerfect searches your document for text that identifies the subject of the document and places the text in the Subject box. The default text for the search is *RE:*. You can change this text if you use other words in your documents to introduce the subject. (Refer to Chapter 29, "Customizing WordPerfect with Preferences," for instructions to complete this task.)

- Retrieves the first 400 characters of text into the Abstract box. You may want to edit the text that appears in the Subject box because, in a letter, this feature includes a string of the name, address, salutation and repeat of the subject with the first words of the body of the letter.

Save As

You can save document summaries as separate files by choosing Save As. The regular Save As box prompts you to type a file name. The saved file lists each entry, the system file name (the complete DOS path name), and the system file type (the version of WordPerfect used to create the document).

If you enter a file name that already exists, an Overwrite/Append dialog box warns that a file of that name already exists. Choose **Overwrite** if you want to replace the existing file; choose **Append** if you want to add the text to the end of the existing file. If you choose to append, WordPerfect adds a hard return to the end of the existing file before appending the new text.

Delete

The only way to remove a document summary after you create it is to delete it by choosing the Delete button and then choosing OK. You cannot restore a summary after you have deleted it; you must create a new summary for that document. If you have chosen to be prompted to complete a summary, the prompt resumes the next time you save or exit the document.

Print

To print the document summary you created, choose the **P**rint button. Note that you also can print the document summary from the Print menu by choosing **M**ultiple Pages, which enables you to print only the document summary.

System File Name and System File Type

The system file name and system file type print automatically when you print a document summary. The *system file name* is the complete DOS path name of your document, as in the following example:

C:\WPWIN\FILES\FILENAME.EXT

The *system file type* is the version of WordPerfect used to create your document.

Chapter Summary

This chapter focuses on a number of WordPerfect features that provide the kind of layout details usually available only from professional type-setters. You learned how to keep text together on a page in a variety of ways and learned when each method is most suitable. Setting margins, centering text on a page, and selecting paper sizes and types are explained as ways to control the spacing of text on the page.

You also learned how to enhance your document by designing, creating, and editing headers and footers and by numbering pages in simple and complex multipart documents. You learned to modify font, redline, and other initial code settings for your document.

Finally, this chapter covers the benefits of creating a database of document summaries, and you learned about the kinds of information that you can include in those summaries.

Using Styles

This chapter describes the WordPerfect for Windows Styles feature. A *style* is a set of formatting instructions that you can use in a single document or reuse in a group of related documents. The program supports three types of styles, which can contain format codes, text, and graphics. These types are open styles, paired styles, and outline styles. This chapter covers open and paired styles. For a discussion of outline styles, see Chapter 24, "Line Numbering, Paragraph Numbering, and Outlining."

In this chapter, you learn how to do the following:

- Create open and paired styles
- Create styles from existing text
- Activate and view styles in a document
- Edit and save styles with a document
- Delete style codes and style definitions in a document

■ **Eric Mark Rintell** is a reviewer and author who uses Styles to format his work for different publishers. He teaches WordPerfect and has a computer consulting practice.

■ Create, edit, retrieve, and maintain a style library

■ Use and enhance the style library included with WordPerfect for Windows

When To Use Styles

You can use styles to make your documents adaptable to convenient changes in format. Suppose that you write a report for your boss at Lucky Widgets, Inc. You format the report with double-spacing, a one-inch right margin, and italicized headings. An hour before you turn in the report, you discover that it must be single-spaced, have the page number and date on the bottom of each page, with headings in boldface and a two-inch right margin for space to write comments.

If your report is only 2 pages long, you probably can make the format changes, item by item, in an hour. If your report is 65 pages long, however, going through it page-by-page to change the headings and the individual codes will take you some time—even if you search for codes.

In this situation, the use of styles provides a quick and simple solution to your problem. Documents formatted with styles are indistinguishable from documents formatted with individual formatting codes, so you can make formatting changes through styles instead of searching the document to make one change at a time. If, for example, you have defined a style for headings, which you might call Headings, you can change the headings in your report from italic to boldface simply by editing the style. You do not have to alter each heading individually. The new style definition for Headings takes effect for every similarly coded heading in the document.

You also can create new styles for single-spaced text, for a footer containing the page number and date, and for two-inch right margins. By saving the styles in a style library, you can use them in all your company reports. If you get a new boss who likes reports in a different format, you don't have to edit your report formats one at a time, you simply edit the style library.

Using styles rather than individual formatting provides the following advantages:

■ Styles can contain text, format codes, and graphics.

■ Styles save time and keystrokes.

■ Styles create a consistent look within a single document and, when you use a style library, among groups of documents.

■ Styles make document revisions easier and less time-consuming.

■ Styles enable different users to share a uniform look among their documents.

■ Styles have fewer hidden codes in Reveal Codes; named styles replace several individual format codes.

CAUTION: You cannot use features that WordPerfect generates (such as Cross-Reference and Subdocuments) in styles.

You can save time on repetitive formatting tasks by using styles and macros; however, you need to be aware of the differences between the two features. Macros leave formatting codes in your document. If you edit a macro after using it in a document and want the document to reflect the formatting changes of the edited macro, you have to search for and edit every individual formatting code that the macro left in the document.

Styles, on the other hand, leave only [Style] codes in the document. Because the [Style] code contains all the formatting codes, you simply edit the style definition if you need to change the codes. WordPerfect then updates the document with the changes.

To use the Lucky Widgets, Inc. report as an example, remember that you had italicized the original headings, but you now have to change the formatting to boldface. If you used a macro to format the headings, you would have to search for each heading and reformat to boldface, one heading at a time. If, however, you create a style called *Headings*, you can redefine the Headings style from italic to boldface and, with one edit, reformat every heading in the report.

How To Create Styles

In WordPerfect for Windows, you create most of the styles you use in a document. Suppose that you need a style that affects the entire document, such as the style that establishes a two-inch right margin. Perhaps you want a style to format only a specific part of a document, like the Headings style definition. You may need a style to help you build an outline with Roman numerals. In WordPerfect for Windows, you can create the following kinds of styles to fit these requirements:

■ An *open style* is a style that you cannot turn off; an open style affects the entire document after the [Style on] code. For example, from the point in your document where you place an open style code that sets the right margin at two inches, the rest of the document has a two-inch right margin (unless you place a new right margin code later in the document). Often you place open

styles at the beginning of a document to format permanent settings, such as margin settings, binding offsets, headers, footers,
and so on.

■ A *paired style* is a style that you can turn on and off. In contrast to
an open style, a paired style does not affect an entire document,
but only the text between the [Style On] and [Style Off]
codes. Using the Headings style discussed previously, the text
between the [Style On:Headings] code and the [Style
Off:Headings] code in the report appears in boldface. If you
need to change the look of your section headings from boldface to
underline, you edit the style, not the text. If you need to change
the text of a section heading, you can edit the text between
the on and off style codes. Paired styles are useful for indented
paragraphs, quotations, temporary margin changes, and titles.

■ The *outline style* feature is a hybrid of the Outline and Styles features and is useful for producing formatted hierarchical outlines
with formats for up to eight levels. In terms of formatting, the Outline feature is helpful for numbering and indenting paragraphs.
Outline style adds the capability to format automatically the text
for different levels in the outline. For more information on Outline
styles, see Chapter 24, "Line Numbering, Paragraph Numbering,
and Outlining."

Creating an Open Style

Your boss at Lucky Widgets wants each page of your report single-
spaced with a two-inch right margin and a footer containing the page
number and date. An Open style, which affects the entire document, is
appropriate for this task. Beginning at the top of an empty document,
create the Widget style as follows:

1. Select **S**tyles from the **L**ayout menu.

     Press Styles (Alt-F8).

    Alternatively, with the Ruler on, double-click the Styles button.

    WordPerfect displays the Styles dialog box, as shown in
    figure 12.1.

2. Choose **C**reate to display the Style Properties dialog box (see
    fig. 12.2).

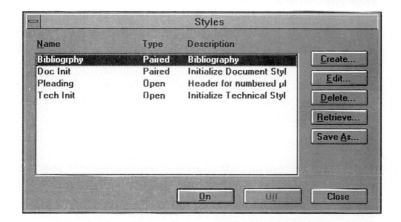

FIG. 12.1

The Styles
dialog box.

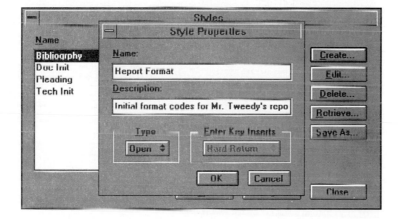

FIG. 12.2

The Style
Properties
dialog box for
an open style.

3. In the Name text box, type a name that describes the style. You can use up to 20 characters, including characters from the WordPerfect character set (see Chapter 28, "Creating and Displaying Special Characters"). For the Lucky Widgets report, type **Report Format**. Do not press Enter.

Be careful when you choose a name for any style you create. Pick a name that conveys what the style does; Report Format is more meaningful than Style1. When you click the Styles button on the Ruler, the name you give your style appears in the list that drops down.

If you enter a style name that you have used previously, a message box informs you that the style name already exists. Press Enter to return to the Name text box and enter a new name.

4. Press Tab or choose **D**escription. In the Description text box, enter up to 54 characters (fewer characters if you use WordPerfect character sets to describe what the style does. Type **Initial format codes for Mr. Tweedy's report** and press Tab.

   Be careful how you describe the style—do not waste the description by repeating the name of the style. The description should augment the style name to give you a more detailed information about the style. The style's description appears to the right of the style name in the Styles dialog box.

5. Select **T**ype and choose **O**pen from the pop-up list. (*Note:* Style Type defaults to Paired styles.) Your screen should look like the screen in figure 12.2.

6. Click OK or press Enter to open the Style Editor screen.

The next step in the process of creating an open style is to enter in the Style Editor screen the codes and text that you want in the style, using the same method you use to enter codes in the document window (see Chapter 4, "Editing a Document").

When you create an open style, be careful not to use a paired style code unless you really want the code to affect the entire document. For example, if you choose Bold for an open style, a [Bold On] code displays in the Style Editor screen without a matching [Bold Off] code. Your entire document could end up in boldface type!

To insert the open style codes for the Lucky Widget report document format, follow these steps:

1. Set the format for single-spacing. Select **L**ine from the **L**ayout menu.

    Press Layout Line (Shift-F9).

   Select **S**pacing from the Line menu. Type **1** in the Line Spacing dialog box. Click OK or press Enter.

2. To enter the format code for a two-inch right margin, choose **M**argins from the **L**ayout menu.

    Press Margins (Ctrl-F8).

   In the Margins dialog box, press Alt-R and type **2** to set the right margin. Click OK or press Enter to close the Margins dialog box.

3. Use the Footer feature to insert a page number and the current date on the bottom of each page.

   Choose **P**age from the **L**ayout menu.

    Press Page (Alt-F9).

   Select **F**ooters to open the Footers dialog box. Choose **C**reate in the Footers dialog box to open the Footers A screen. Type **Page** and press the space bar once. Choose Page **N**umber and ^B appears in the Footer A window. The date will appear on the right side of the footer, so press Flush Right (Alt-F7). To make sure that the document prints with today's date, press Ctrl-Shift-F5 for the Date code.

   Your screen should look like the screen shown in figure 12.3.

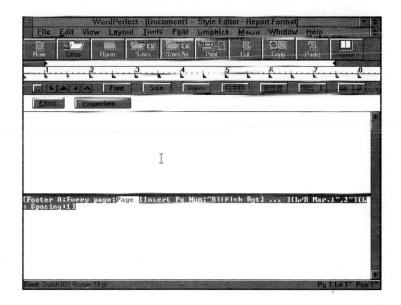

FIG. 12.3

The Style Editor screen shown with codes for Report Format.

4. To return to the Styles dialog box, press Alt-C twice. Verify that Report Format is an open style in the style list. Close the Style dialog box; congratulations, you have created your first style!

Creating a Paired Style

You create paired styles in the same way that you create open styles, but the process is more involved, because paired styles have a beginning and an end. Because they affect only text between the [Style On] and [Style Off] codes, a paired style is the best choice for text formatted differently from the rest of a document (like the headings in the Lucky Widgets report). To create the Heading style for the Lucky Widgets report, follow these steps:

1. Select **S**tyles from the **L**ayout menu.

    Press Styles (Alt-F8).

   Alternatively, with the Ruler on, double-click the Styles button.

   WordPerfect displays the Styles dialog box.

2. Choose **C**reate to display the Style Properties dialog box.

3. In the Name text box, type **Headings** for the style name and press Tab or choose **D**escription.

   (If you enter a style name that you have used previously, a message box informs you that the style name already exists. Press Enter to return to the Name text box and enter a new name.)

4. In the Description text box, type **Section head in bold type**. Because the default Style Type is paired, you can bypass the Type button. Click OK or press Enter to open the Style Editor screen.

> **Cue:** When you choose a style name, be sure to choose a name that conveys what the style does.

T I P The description you enter into the Description text box should augment the style name to give you more information about the style. Your description can be up to 54 characters long (fewer characters if you use WordPerfect character sets).

Because paired styles have a beginning and an end, a paired Style Editor screen is different from an Open Style Editor screen. WordPerfect inserts a *comment* to separate the On section of the screen from the Off section (refer to fig. 12.4).

You place codes and text *before* the comment to affect the text that follows the [Style On] code. With a few exceptions, when you turn off the style, codes in the [Style On] section no longer affect text. For example, if you place a [Bold On] code in the section before the comment, you do not have to place a matching [Bold Off] code in the

[Style Off] section *after* the comment. You place the codes in the [Style Off] section that you want to have take effect after the style is turned off.

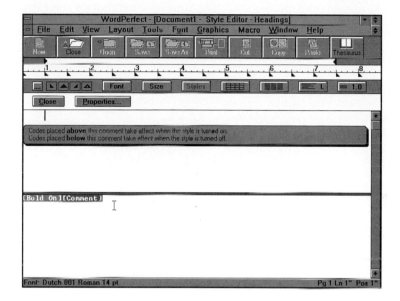

FIG. 12.4

Paired Styles "headings" in the Style Editor screen.

CAUTION: Codes that you insert into a document take precedence over codes that you place in a style. When you turn on a paired style that sets line spacing at 2 and you insert a [Ln spacing:1] code into your document, the single-spacing command affects the text that follows up to the point that you turn off the paired style. The text that follows the [Style Off] code reverts back to the original line-spacing setting of the document.

To insert the paired style codes for the Lucky Widget report document format, follow these steps:

1. Because you want the Lucky Widgets report headings formatted in boldface, press Ctrl-B to insert the [Bold On] code before the comment. Notice that no matching [Bold Off] code appears in the Reveal Codes screen after the comment (see fig. 12.4).

2. Choose **Close** to exit the Style Editor screen.

   WordPerfect displays the entry Headings in the style list as a paired style.

CAUTION: You can nest paired styles in a document, but you cannot turn on a paired style that is already on. You can turn on paired style B when paired style A is on, for example, but you cannot turn on paired style A when paired style A is already on.

When you create the paired style, you may notice the Enter Key Inserts area of the Style Properties dialog box. Select Enter Key Inserts and choose from the pop-up list one of the following three options for activating the Enter key in a paired style (see fig. 12.5):

FIG. 12.5

The Enter Key Inserts pop-up lists.

- *Hard Return.* If you choose this option, the Enter key inserts a [HRt] code into the document. The Enter key functions as usual, and the paired style remains turned on; you can turn off the paired style in the Styles dialog box. Use the Hard Return option for a paired style to change the margin settings for unindented paragraphs.

- *Style Off.* If you choose this option, the Enter key turns off the paired style. With one keystroke (Enter), you turn off the style and move the insertion point past the [Style Off] code. The Headings style you created in the preceding section is a good candidate for the Style Off Enter Key Inserts option because it saves you the trouble of turning off the style each time you use the style in the document. (You can edit the Headings style to use this feature.) This option is suited for one-line or one-paragraph styles, like a title or an indented paragraph.

- *Style Off/On.* Suppose that you need to indent a bulleted list. With the Style Off option, you have to turn on the bullet style after each time you press Enter. The Style Off/On option rectifies this situation. By placing a [Style Off] code in the document, followed by a [Style On] code, the Enter key turns off a paired style, and then turns it on again. When you use this option, however, pressing Enter does not place a [HRt] between the [Style On] and [Style Off] codes. (You can insert a [HRt] in the Style Editor screen in the Off section, after the comment.) For the Enter key to function normally again, you have to turn off the Style from the Style dialog box or from the Ruler.

Placing Graphics in Styles

By using the WordPerfect for Windows Graphics feature, you can place figures, equations, and charts into a style. Be sure that you set any graphics options—border, shading, and so on—before the graphics box. For graphics to work in a style, the graphics must be present on disk. Use the Graphics on Disk option when creating or editing the graphics box (see Chapter 7, "Introduction to Graphics").

Creating a Style from Existing Text

In the previous examples, you created your styles before you inserted them into your document. Suppose, however, that you want to put format codes and text from your document into a style. You can take codes from your editing screen (document window) and put them into a style definition.

For this example, you create a paired style to make numbers at the bottom of columns (as in a spreadsheet) more noticeable. The column totals will be in boldface and double underlined. First, place the formatting codes in a document. Press Ctrl-B to turn on boldface. For double underline, choose **D**ouble Underline from the **F**ont menu. To verify that your codes are correct, type **$1,000,000.00**. Follow these steps to copy the formatting for the column totals into a paired style:

1. Copy the formatting codes (not the text, because not all columns will total $1,000,000.00) into the paired style. Position the insertion point so that the first hidden code, [Bold On], is highlighted in the Reveal Codes window. To move the insertion point to the beginning of the line, press Home, Home.

Cue: When creating a style from existing text, turn on Reveal Codes (Alt+3) to make it easier to select hidden codes in the document.

■ **Cue:** In WordPerfect for Windows you cannot use the mouse to block hidden codes by themselves (without text).

2. To select the hidden codes that you want to copy from the document into the style definition, press Select (F8), right arrow, right arrow.

   The hidden code [Select] appears in front of the [Bold On] code in the Reveal Codes window (see fig. 12.6).

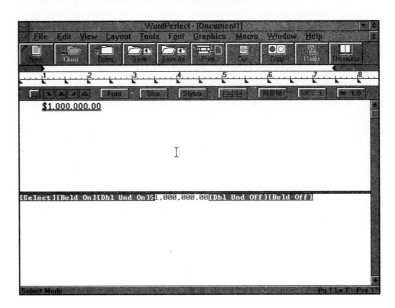

FIG. 12.6

Selected hidden codes.

3. Copy the selected codes into the Clipboard by pressing Copy (Ctrl-Ins).

4. Press Styles (Alt-F8) to open the Styles dialog box.

5. Choose **Create** to open the Style Properties dialog box.

6. Type **Total Numbers** in the Name text box. Press Tab or choose **Description**.

7. Type **double underlined column totals** in the Description text box.

8. Remember that when you create a style, paired is the default type of style. Select Enter Key Inserts and choose Style Off from the pop-up list; when you use the Total Numbers style in a document, you can turn off the style automatically by pressing the Enter key.

9. Click OK or press Enter. Notice that the codes you selected appear in the Style Editor window.

10. Choose **Close** to exit the Style Editor screen.

11. Choose **Close** to exit the Styles dialog box.

Using Styles in Documents

After you create your styles, you can use them in documents. Selecting a style is easy. As an example, create a sample report, in which you will use the Report Format style that you created in the section "Creating an Open Style." For this example, begin with an empty document. Choose **New** from the **File** menu for a blank document.

To place a style in a document, follow these steps:

1. Select **Styles** from the **Layout** Menu.

     Press Styles (Alt-F8).

    WordPerfect displays the Styles dialog box.

> If the Ruler is on, you can activate styles by moving the pointer to the Styles button. Click and hold the left mouse button to display the pop-up list of style names. Drag the mouse to the style you want to insert into your document and release the button.
>
> **T I P**

2. Highlight the Report Format style (which you created in the section "Creating an Open Style") to insert into your document.

3. Choose **On** to turn on the style in the document.

4. Highlight the Headings style and choose **On**.

5. Choose **Close** to exit the Styles dialog box and return to the document window.

6. Type **Double Duck Disasters**. Notice that every character you type appears in boldface.

7. To turn off the paired style, select **Styles** from the **Layout** Menu.

     Press Styles (Alt-F8).

8. Highlight Headings in the Style list.

9. Because the Headings style is on, or active, the Off option is now available. Choose **Off** to deactivate the Headings style.

10. Press Enter, Enter to return to the document window.

■ **Cue:** To turn off a paired style, use the right-arrow key to move the insertion point past the [Styles Off] code.

11. Type the first line of text under the heading, **Ducks, deer, doves and widgets don't mix.** Notice that the characters are not in boldface because the paired style is not active.

Checking Styles with Reveal Codes

Although the effects of styles are visible in your documents, styles are hidden codes and are not visible on the document screen. If you accidentally turned on a paired style, you will have difficulty in figuring out the problem by looking at the document screen. You can view styles' hidden codes, however, in the Reveal Codes screen. To check the codes for the styles you have just created, choose Reveal **C**odes (Alt-F3) from the **L**ayout menu (see fig. 12.7).

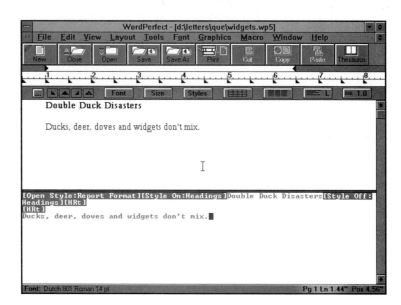

FIG 12.7

Hidden style codes displayed in Reveal Codes.

Notice the [Open Style:Report Format] code in the upper left corner of the Reveal Codes window. The [Open Style] code indicates that you inserted the open style, Report Format, at the top of the document. If you move the insertion point to the [Open Style:Report Format] code, it expands to show you the codes contained in the Report Format style.

To move the insertion point to the code, press Ctrl-Home, Home, Home. The highlighted code changes to include the style name and the format codes.

WordPerfect displays paired style codes in a similar manner, except that two codes display: one to turn on the style and the other to turn it off. The [Style On:Headings] code turns on the Headings style, and the [Style Off:Headings] code turns off the Headings style. If you move the insertion point to the right (press the right arrow), the [Style On:Headings] code reveals the underlying codes (as with open styles). Press End, left arrow to move to the [Style Off:Headings] code; WordPerfect reveals the underlying [Bold Off] code. (Remember that you did not press **B**old a second time to turn it off when you created the Headings style!)

Applying Paired Styles to Existing Text in a Document

Just as you can create a style from your document, you can apply a paired style to existing text in a document. This practice is useful if you have forgotten to apply a paired style when you entered the text. To apply a style to existing text, select the text and turn on the paired style.

In the Lucky Widgets window, press Enter, Enter. Without using a style code, type the heading **The 5-Hour Plan**. To apply the Headings style to the heading after you typed it, follow these steps:

1. Make sure that the insertion point is past the *n* in *Plan*. Press Select (F8). Press Shift-Home to highlight *The 5 Hour Plan*.

2. Select **S**tyles from the Layout menu.

    Press Styles (Alt-F8).

3. Highlight Headings in the style list.

4. Choose **O**n to turn on the style in the document.

   In the document window, you can see that the text is in boldface. If you look in Reveal Codes (Alt-F3), the [Style On:Headings] precedes *The 5 Hour Plan* with a matching [Style Off:Headings] after the text of the heading.

Editing Style Codes

Suppose that, after creating the Headings style for headings in boldface, you get a new boss who prefers section heads underlined and in italic typeface. In this scenario, using styles is more advantageous than using individually applied format codes because the style codes update with the changes as you scroll through a document. You do not have to search and modify *each* section heading because the editing affects *all* style codes with the edited style name. To edit a style, follow these steps:

1. Select **S**tyles from the **L**ayout menu.

     Press Styles (Alt-F8).

   Alternatively, with the Ruler on, double-click the Styles button.

   WordPerfect displays the Styles dialog box.

2. Highlight the style you want to edit. Highlight Headings.

3. Choose **E**dit to display the Style Editor screen.

   You can insert or delete codes and text in the Style Editor window, the same as you can in the document window. The insertion point rests in the On section before the comment separating the On and Off sections.

4. To delete the [Bold On] code, press Delete; to insert the [Italics On] code, press Ctrl-I; to insert the [Underline On] code, press Ctrl-U.

5. Choose **C**lose to exit the Style Editor window.

6. Choose **C**lose to exit the Styles dialog box.

When you edit a style, you may have to change its description, too (see the section "Editing the Information in the Style Properties Dialog Box" in this chapter).

T   I   P   You can bypass the WordPerfect for Windows menus and edit styles. With the Ruler on, double-click the Styles button. Using the mouse, highlight the styles you want to edit and double-click.

Editing Style Names

You also can edit the name of a style. The Editing Style Names feature is a powerful tool for copying between styles without using Cut and

Paste. When you change the name of a style, WordPerfect asks whether you want to rename all the styles in the document. Choose **Yes** to re-place the old style name with the new style name in the styles list and in the document. If you choose **No**, WordPerfect places the old style name back in the style list when you scroll across it in a document.

Suppose that you need to add a paired style called Titles to your docu-ment. The Titles style definition is identical to the Headings style defini-tion, with the additional instruction to center the text. To add a style based on an existing style, follow these steps:

1. Select **S**tyles from the **L**ayout menu.

    Press Styles (Alt-F8).

   Alternatively, with the Ruler on, double-click the Styles button.

   WordPerfect displays the Styles dialog box.

2. Highlight Headings.

3. Choose **E**dit to open the Style Editor screen.

4. To add centering to the style, press Center Line (Shift-F7).

5. Choose **P**roperties to open the Style Properties dialog box (the same dialog box you use to create a style).

6. Choose **N**ame and type **Titles** in the Name text box.

7. Change the description to reflect what the Titles style does: choose **D**escription and type **Centered underlined titles** in the Description text box.

8. Click OK or press Enter to return to the Style Editor screen.

9. Choose **C**lose to exit the Style Editor screen.

10. A dialog box prompts Rename Styles in Document? Choose **No**. WordPerfect does not alter the Headings style in the document.

    In the Styles dialog box, WordPerfect adds Titles to the style list and removes Headings.

11. Choose **C**lose to exit the Styles dialog box.

12. Scroll through your report for Lucky Widgets. When you en-counter a Headings style, WordPerfect adds the Headings style back to the style list (without the description). To confirm that WordPerfect has a Headings style, press Styles (Alt-F8).

Editing the Information in the Style Properties Dialog Box

WordPerfect enables you to edit the contents of any text box in the Style Properties dialog box. When you rename a style, you do not change the name or update the description in this dialog box. Even if you don't change the name of a style, you may want to edit the description if you think of an explanation that better describes the style.

To change the description after you edit the style, follow these steps:

1. Choose **P**roperties in the Style Editor screen.

2. Choose **D**escription in the Style Properties dialog box.

3. Type the new description in the Description text box, and then click OK or press Enter.

4. Choose **C**lose to exit the Style Properties dialog box.

In the Style Properties dialog box, you also can change the style type. If you change a paired style to an open style, the program deletes in the [Style Off] section of the paired style the codes that are no longer necessary. (Because open styles don't have a beginning and end, they do not need an Off section.)

When you change an open style to a paired style, WordPerfect places all the codes from the open style into the [Style On] section of the paired style. Because this change does not affect open styles with the same name in the document, you may end up with open and paired styles with the same name. The better practice is to copy the open style into a paired style by renaming it (see the "Editing Style Names" section in this chapter) and answering **N**o to the Rename Styles in a Document? prompt.

For paired styles, you also can edit the effect of the Enter key in the Style Properties dialog box. The Headings style is a one-line style; you may find it useful to turn off the style by pressing Enter. To add the Enter key function to the style, edit the Headings style as follows:

1. Select **S**tyles from the **L**ayout menu.

     Press Styles (Alt-F8).

    Alternatively, with the Ruler on, double-click the Styles button.

    WordPerfect displays the Styles dialog box.

2. Highlight Headings in the style list.

3. Choose **E**dit to open the Style Editor screen.

4. Choose **P**roperties to open the Style Properties dialog box.

5. Choose **E**nter Key Inserts to display the pop-up list of options that alter the behavior of the Enter key in paired styles.

6. Choose Style Off, so that the Enter key turns off the Headings style.

7. Click OK or press Enter to close the Style Properties dialog box.

8. Choose **C**lose to exit the Style Editor screen.

9. Choose **C**lose to exit the Styles dialog box.

10. To verify that you can turn off the Headings style with the Enter key, go to the end of the document (Ctrl-End). Turn on the Headings style and type some text. Press Enter and type more text. The Headings style does not affect the later text.

Saving Styles in a Document

When you save your document, you also save all the styles listed in the Styles dialog box. Even if you don't modify a document, remember to save the document if you edited any style definitions. If you do not save the document, you lose the edited style (unless you previously saved it in a style library). If you add a style to a document but not to a style library, the style is available only to that particular document. To learn how to make styles available to more than one document, see the "Style Libraries" section in this chapter.

Replacing a Style with Another Style

Suppose that you need to replace only some occurrences of a style with another style. In WordPerfect, you cannot search and replace a [Style On:Headings] with [Style On:Titles]. You can search, however, for generic style codes without the style name.

WordPerfect enables you to search for [Open Style], [Style On], and [Style Off]. The disadvantage to this method is that you have to change each style code in the document that requires an alteration. Before you change the style, choose Reveal **C**odes (Alt-F3) from the **V**iew menu. Go to the beginning of the document by pressing Ctrl-Home, Home, Home. To change *Double Duck Disasters* from the Headings style to the Titles style, follow these steps:

1. Press Search (F2) to open the Search dialog box.

2. Choose **C**odes to open the Codes dialog box.

3. Press **S** to move directly to the *s*'s in the Search Codes list; then highlight [Style On].

4. Choose **I**nsert to place [Style On] in the Search For text box in the Search dialog box (see fig. 12.8).

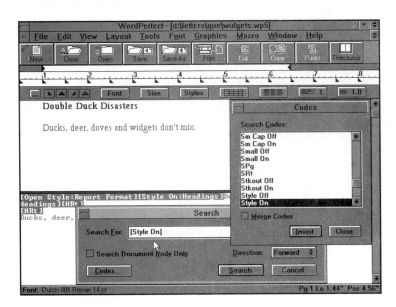

A search by generic style code.

5. Choose **C**lose to exit the Codes dialog box.

6. Choose **S**earch in the Search dialog box. The insertion point should be the *D* in *Double* that follows the [Style On:Headings] code.

7. Press the Backspace key to delete the [Style On:Headings] code; the operation deletes the matching [Style Off:Headings] at the same time. To verify the deletion, check the Reveal Codes window.

8. Select *Double Duck Disasters* by pressing Shift-End.

    WordPerfect highlights *Double Duck Disasters*.

9. Select **S**tyles from the **L**ayout menu.

    CUA Press Styles (Alt-F8).

10. Highlight the Titles style in the style list.

    Alternatively, click and drag the mouse on the Styles button on the Ruler. WordPerfect displays the pop-up styles list; highlight Titles and release the mouse.

11. Choose **On** to turn on the Titles style.

    With the Titles style, WordPerfect centers *Double Duck Disasters* at the top of the page.

Deleting Style Codes from a Document

When you need to delete some, but not all, occurrences of a style from a document, use the Search function to find the style code. Used with Reveal Codes, you can delete styles from portions of a document. When you delete the style, it no longer affects the text that follows the style code. When you want to delete all occurrences of a style from a document, you can save time by using the method described in the following section.

Deleting Styles from the Style List

If you need to remove a style from an entire document, use WordPerfect's style deletion function as follows:

1. Select Styles from the Layout menu.

     Press Styles (Alt-F8).

    Alternatively, with the Ruler on, double-click the Styles button.

    WordPerfect displays the Styles dialog box.

2. Highlight Titles in the style list.

3. Choose **D**elete to open the Delete Style dialog box (see fig. 12.9).

    The Delete Style dialog box contains the following three options (see fig. 12.9):

FIG. 12.9

The Delete Style dialog box.

Leave Format Codes. In this example, WordPerfect erases all oc-currences of the Titles style from the document, replacing them with matched pairs of [Und On], [Italc On], [Und Off], and [Italc Off]. This option enables you to delete the style code and replace it with the codes contained in the style. In other words, you can use this option to remove the style code but leave the document unaffected.

Delete Format Codes. This option erases not only the style code from the document, but also erases the codes contained within the style from the document. Using the Titles style as an example, with this option you erase all Titles style codes from the docu-ment as well as the formatting codes [Center] and the code pairs [Und] and [Italc].

Delete Definition Only. The least destructive choice, this option removes the style name from the style list, but does not affect any style codes in the document. This option is useful for erasing un-used style codes; WordPerfect adds back the style name to the style list when the program encounters a style code with that name in the document.

4. All three options remove the highlighted style name from the styles list. Choose Delete Definition **O**nly.

5. Choose **C**lose to exit the Styles dialog box.

T I P   You cannot delete all the styles in a style list with a single command. You must delete each style individually through the Styles dialog box.

Style Libraries

To this point, the discussion of styles has been limited to their application to one document. The power of the Styles feature lies in its capability to apply uniform formatting in more than one document. As an employee of Lucky Widgets, Inc., you must write all your papers to the company specifications. Styles would be difficult to use if you had to cut and paste your style definitions from one document to another. By using style libraries, you can use styles in several documents.

WordPerfect saves styles in a special file called a *style library*. A style library is a file that contains only style names and definitions. You can store all your styles in a default style library and tell WordPerfect to use that style library for all your documents.

WordPerfect for Windows does not restrict you to one style library; you can have multiple style libraries stored on disk. With multiple style libraries, you can retrieve the suitable style library for each document. WordPerfect enables you to reuse style names in different libraries; the only restriction is that the style name must be a unique name within each style library.

Using Multiple Style Libraries

Using style libraries, you can reformat material differently from the original format. Suppose that you write a screenplay you want to send to movie companies. Each movie company wants the script in a different format: Big Budget Movies wants scripts formatted with double-spacing, boldface character names, and italicized stage directions. Warped Movies prefers the character names in small capital letters, 1 1/2 line spacing, and boldface stage directions. Another movie company may want scripts submitted with a different appearance.

You can create a different style library for the script for each movie company. The names in each style sheet are the same, but the style definitions are different in each library. By retrieving the appropriate style library, WordPerfect automatically reformats the script for each movie company. The style for Char Name, for example, is boldface for Big Budget Movies and small capital letters for Warped Movies. With style libraries, you do not have to change the names of the styles in the screenplay or change any codes individually.

Using Default Style Libraries

To help you manage your style libraries, you can set a style library directory and a default style library. If you use only one set of files, the better choice is a default style library. Then, whenever you use styles, WordPerfect loads the default style library.

■ **Cue:** If you use more than two style libraries, create a separate subdirectory only for style library files and keep all style libraries in that directory.

On the other hand, if you use multiple style libraries, do not set a default style library. You should designate a separate directory to store your style libraries.

The default directory is where WordPerfect saves and looks for style library files. The default directory for the storage of style library files is the \WPWIN subdirectory. For directions for changing the default styles directory, see Chapter 29, "Customizing WordPerfect with Preferences."

T   I   P   To ensure a consistent design in documents among users, place style libraries in a common, shared network directory. If your company does not have a network, provide each user with a read-only copy of your default style library.

T   I   P   In an environment where you share styles (through style libraries), include in the file the initials or employee number of the person who created the style. Anyone who modifies the style should add appropriate identification. Using this procedure, anyone sharing the styles can identify the original author and the last person to modify a style.

The *default style library* is the style library that WordPerfect normally uses (unless you specifically retrieve a different style library). WordPerfect's default style library is called LIBRARY.STY. To change the default style library, see Chapter 29, "Customizing WordPerfect with Preferences."

CAUTION: WordPerfect does not check the file name that you type, so the program doesn't prevent you from entering a nonexistent file name. When attempting to access your default style library, WordPerfect tells you at that time that It cannot find the style library file. The Styles button on the Ruler will display the message, No Styles Available, and the Styles dialog box will not list any style names in the Names text field.

Saving Styles in a Style Library

If you plan to use the styles from your current document in other documents, you have to save the styles in a style library. Remember that WordPerfect saves styles with documents; if you create or edit a style without saving it in a style library, the style is available only in the document with which you saved it. When you save the styles in a style library, all edited and new styles are available for use in other documents. To save a style library, follow these steps:

1. Select **Styles** from the **Layout** menu.

     Press Styles (Alt F8).

    Alternatively, with the Ruler on, double-click the Styles button.

2. Choose Save **As** from the Styles dialog box.

3. When the Save Styles dialog box appears, type the name you want to give to the style library. To distinguish style libraries from other files (a useful practice when you do not have a separate directory for style libraries), type a file name with a STY extension. Note that existing STY files will show up for reference.

4. Choose Save to save the style library. The Save Styles dialog box closes.

5. Choose **C**lose to exit the Styles dialog box.

Remember the following points when you save style libraries:

■ The style library includes Outline styles when you write the style to disk.

■ If you do not need to share styles among documents, you do not need to save a style library (because you save styles used in a document automatically when you save the document).

T   I   P   If you have only one set of styles, save them in a default style library. You do not need a separate subdirectory for style library files, nor does the default style library need to contain a copy of every style you use. Keep only the styles you use most in your default library.

■ When you delete a style name from a style library, remember to save the style library after the deletion, so that you save the edited style library.

■ If you receive a warning message that the file already exists, and WordPerfect asks, Do You Want to Replace It?, think carefully before you answer. If you answer **Yes**, you will lose any style definitions in the style library that are not on the current style list. To protect those styles, you first can retrieve the older style library, as described in the following section.

T   I   P   Be careful when replacing style libraries on disk. If you overwrite unused style definitions, you may not be able to recover them. Before saving a style library file, retrieve the disk version. Answer **No** to the replace existing style definitions prompt. Your style list then includes all styles from that library, whether you use them in the document or not. After this safety check, save the style on disk.

Retrieving a Style Library

To use a style library in your current document, use the Retrieve option on the Styles dialog box. You also can use this option to update styles in more than one document or to retrieve different style libraries for use in a single document. To retrieve a style library into a document, follow these steps:

1. Select **S**tyles from the **L**ayout menu.

    Press Styles (Alt-F8).

   Alternatively, with the Ruler on, double-click the Styles button to open the Styles dialog box.

2. Choose **Retrieve** to open the Retrieve Styles dialog box.

3. In the Name text box, type the name of the style you want to use in this document.

4. Choose **Retrieve** to retrieve the style library.

   WordPerfect compares the style names from your current style list against the style names from the style library you are retrieving. Finding a match, WordPerfect prompts Style(s) Already Exist. Replace? If you answer **Yes**, WordPerfect replaces the styles in your current style list with the styles of the same names that are in the style library you are retrieving.

   If you press **No** at the prompt, WordPerfect retrieves only those styles with names that do not appear on your current style list. You can use this tool for preventing accidental deletion of unused styles. Before you save a style library, retrieve the previous version from disk and answer **No** to the replace existing style definitions prompt. Your style list then contains both styles used in the document and unused styles that were stored on disk. At this point, you safely can save the style library.

5. Choose **Close** to exit the Styles dialog box.

Before retrieving a style library, save the document (not the style library). If you don't like what you see after you retrieve the style library, you can exit the document without saving it and, therefore, without saving the style library in the document. Retrieve the document to verify that the style library is not attached.

T I P

Sample Style Library

WordPerfect ships with a sample style library, LIBRARY.STY. You can use this file with the styles you create in this chapter to explore ideas for creating your own styles and style library.

LIBRARY.STY

WordPerfect for Windows includes the LIBRARY.STY style library file, which is copied to your computer's hard disk during installation if you answer **Yes** to the prompt. The installation program normally copies

LIBRARY.STY to your WordPerfect for Windows program directory. If you run a customized installation and supply a separate directory for style files, LIBRARY.STY resides in that directory.

The following styles are included in LIBRARY.STY:

- *Bibliography.* Use this paired style with the Enter key set to Style Off/On for creating bibliographies. When the Bibliography style is turned on, WordPerfect formats paragraphs with the first line at the left margin and indents subsequent lines in the paragraph. Pressing Enter turns the style off and on so that you can format several paragraphs more easily.

- *Doc Init.* A paired style used in a outline document to help define the Table of Contents. This style also turns on the Outline feature in the [Style Off] section.

- *Pleading.* An open style useful in law offices to format the text with line numbers and a vertical line (redline) in the left margin.

- *Tech Init.* An open style that sets the Outline style and turns on the Outline feature. When you place this style at the beginning of a document, first-level outlines appear in a large typeface. The style indents second-level paragraphs and formats the text in a smaller typeface than first-level text.

Styles and Style Libraries

The following sections contain examples of practical applications of styles and style libraries in WordPerfect. Use them as the foundations for your own style libraries.

You can customize styles to suit your individual tastes. You can change any aspect in the following examples to suit your own needs. Like LIBRARY.STY, these sample library styles represent only a starting point for you to explore the power of styles. Although this section does not include step-by-step instructions for creating each style, after studying this chapter, you can create these styles (or variations) on your own. Note that the figures in the following sections show the codes for the styles and not the styles themselves.

Letterhead Style

A letterhead is a useful application for an open style. Although the example illustrated here is for personal letterhead, you can modify the operation for a company letterhead. The open style for the letterhead should be activated by a macro that inserts the current date after the style is turned on. Due to the nature of styles, you should not insert WordPerfect's Date code or Date Text in a style definition. Use a paired style for the name and a different paired style for the address.

When you modified the Lucky Widgets Report Format style, you included a footer that contained the Date code. When you retrieve a document that contains a Date code in the style, the date automatically changes to the current date. Date Text inserts the date you wrote the style; this date never changes. When you put the Date code in a macro, the macro stamps the document with the date the macro runs. When you retrieve the document a month later, the document retains the date you wrote it. Figure 12.10 shows codes you can place in letterhead style(s).

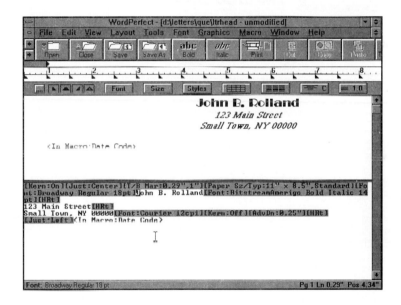

FIG. 12.10

Letterhead Style.

Envelope Style

You should have matching envelopes to go with your letterhead. Envelope style is an open style, because the codes placed at the top of document set the paper size and type, margins, and so on. By using the paired styles for name and address, you can be sure that the envelopes and letterhead retain the same look. You can use another macro to copy and paste the addressee's name into an envelope file for printing. Figure 12.11 shows the codes for the Envelope style. Figure 12.12 shows how the envelope will look when it prints.

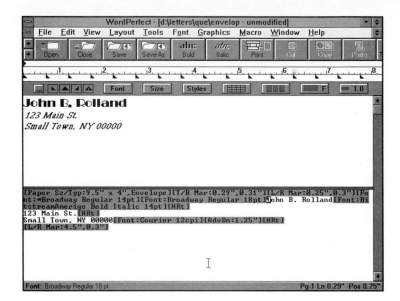

FIG. 12.11

Envelope Style.

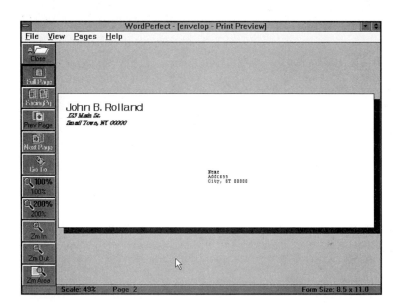

FIG. 12.12

Envelope in
Print Preview.

Paragraph Styles

Paragraph style is a simple time-saving paired style that enables you to reformat the body of a document by editing the style. Press Enter to turn the style off and on. (Turn off the Paragraph style by pressing right arrow to move the insertion point past the [Style Off:Paragraph].)

In its unedited form, the Paragraph style formats paragraphs with line spacing set to 1 1/2 lines and unindented paragraphs separated by 2 [HRt] codes in the Off section of the style (see fig. 12.13). You can modify the Paragraph style for indented double-spaced paragraphs by placing the following codes in the On section before the Comment: indented paragraph [Indent] and double-spacing [Ln Spacing:2]. Delete the second hard return [HRt] following the comment in the Off section.

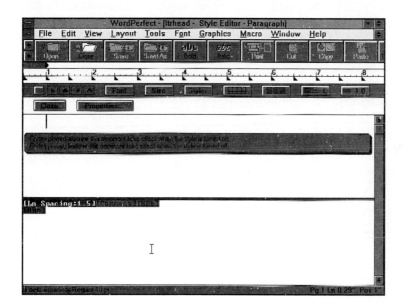

FIG. 12.13

Unindented 1 1/2 line Paragraph style in the Style Editor screen.

Quotation Style

When you need to quote more than a line of text, use this paired style, Quote. You can use the Quote style to offset quoted material in research papers. The Quote paired style, shown in figure 12.14, is composed of the following codes in the On section: indented paragraph [Indent], italic typeface [Italc], and an opening quotation mark (", which can be found in the typographic symbol set). The Off code section after the comment contains a closing quotation mark (") and a hard return [HRt] (the [HRt] advances the insertion point beyond the closing quotation mark). Press Enter to turn off the style.

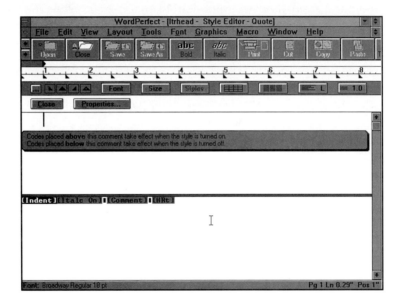

FIG. 12.14

The Quote style in the Style Editor screen.

Chapter Summary

The Styles feature offers you control of your document formatting. In this chapter, you learned to create an open style to format an entire document, create paired styles to format sections of a document, edit styles to reformat documents, use styles for easier document revision, and create style libraries to store styles for use in multiple documents.

Working with Text Columns

Many specialized documents, including newsletters and three-fold brochures, have text laid out in more than one column. Columns can add visual drama to your document and make it easier to read. With WordPerfect's powerful Columns feature, you can format all or part of a document into columns, maintaining complete control over the number and width of columns, gutter space (the white space between columns), and even the manner in which text flows from column to column.

You can make two types of columns in WordPerfect: newspaper columns and parallel columns. *Newspaper columns* typically contain moderate to large amounts of continuous text, which flows down the complete length of each column on a page, then wraps to the top of the next column or to the top of the first column on the next page. *Parallel columns* consist of short blocks of text placed side-by-side in columns. Each side-by-side group effectively forms a row, which is read from left to right.

■ **Gordon Nolder-Adams**
is the WordPerfect expert for the Sacramento PC Users Group and a Computing Assistant at the University of California, Davis. He frequently uses columns for newsletters and other documents.

In this chapter, you learn how to do the following:

- Define newspaper columns
- Define parallel columns
- Type and edit in columns
- Adjust column margins with the Ruler
- Preview your document in final form

Newspaper Columns

With WordPerfect's newspaper columns feature, you can lay out an entire document (or shorter sections within a document) in multiple columns (see fig. 13.1). A columnar format adds visual appeal and is easier to read than a full page of text, especially at smaller point sizes. When you read text printed at full page width, your eye often has trouble finding the correct line when scanning from one line to the next. For this reason, most large-format magazines are printed in two or three columns.

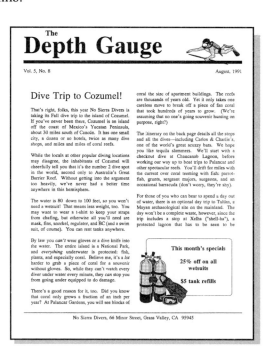

FIG. 13.1

A document formatted with newspaper columns.

Defining Newspaper Columns by Using the Ruler

WordPerfect enables you to control every aspect of your column formatting, including number of columns, the width of the gutter (the space between columns), and equal or unequal widths. If you find WordPerfect's default values acceptable, with a single mouse action you can select two to five evenly spaced parallel columns by using the Columns icon contained in the Ruler (see fig. 13.2).

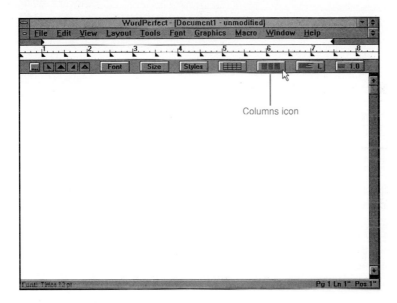

FIG. 13.2

The Ruler's Columns icon.

To select two parallel columns, follow these steps:

1. If the Ruler is not displayed, select View, Ruler.

   CUA   Press View Ruler (Alt-Shift-F3).

2. Start with a new document, or select an insertion point in an existing document where you want columns to begin.

3. Using the mouse, press and hold the Columns icon. A drop-down menu appears (see fig. 13.3).

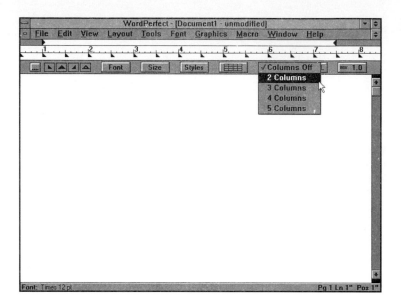

FIG. 13.3

The Ruler's drop-
down Columns
menu.

4. Drag down to select the number of columns you desire; in this case, select 2 Columns and release the mouse button.

WordPerfect inserts into your document two codes: a column definition code and a column on code. If you are editing an existing document, all text below your insertion point now appears in two parallel columns with a half-inch gutter between them. If you are creating a new document, all subsequent text you type is formatted into two columns with a half-inch gutter.

If your insertion point is in the middle of a paragraph, Auto Code Placement affects precisely where WordPerfect inserts these codes. If Auto Code Placement is on, WordPerfect places the codes at the beginning of the current paragraph. If Auto Code Placement is off, WordPerfect places the codes at the insertion point and inserts a hard return ([HRt]) immediately before them, effectively breaking the paragraph in two. (See Chapter 6, "Formatting Text," for more information on Auto Code Placement.)

WordPerfect requires a column definition code ([Col Def:]) and a Column on code ([Col On]) to format a document in columns. In Reveal Codes, these codes appear as follows:

```
[Col Def:Newspaper;2;1",4";4.5",7.5"][Col On]
```

The column definition code specifies the type of columns, number of columns, and the left and right margins of each column. The column on code tells WordPerfect to turn on columns at that point. You cannot turn on columns without a column definition code, but after columns have been defined you can turn them on and off repeatedly by inserting additional column on and column off ([Col Off]) codes.

To turn columns off, use your mouse to select Columns Off from the drop-down Columns menu in the Ruler, or use WordPerfect's main menu to select **Layout**, **Columns**, Columns Off. WordPerfect inserts a [Col Off] code into your document. To turn columns *back* on, you use a similar procedure. After columns have been defined, you can use your mouse to select the Columns On option that appears in the Ruler's drop-down Columns menu. Alternatively, you can select **Layout**, **Columns**, Columns **O**n from WordPerfect's main menu. WordPerfect inserts a [Col On] code into your document.

Defining Newspaper Columns by Using the Dialog Box

You can use the drop-down menu in the Ruler to select 3, 4, or 5 evenly spaced parallel columns. In each case, however, the gutter width remains fixed at 0.5 inch. If the default settings are not acceptable, you can specify the settings you prefer by using the Define Columns dialog box (see fig. 13.4).

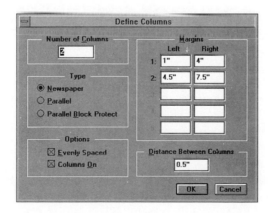

FIG. 13.4

The Define Columns dialog box.

Before calling up the Define Columns dialog box, you should decide how many columns you need, how much space you want between columns, and whether all your columns should be the same width. You are not locked into these choices; you can edit your column layout at any time (see the section "Changing Columns by Using the Ruler" in this chapter).

To create a custom column definition, follow these steps:

1. Select an insertion point where you want the columns to begin.

■ **Cue:** Display the Define Columns dialog box by double-clicking the Columns icon in the Ruler.

2. Select **L**ayout, **C**olumns, **D**efine. The Define Columns dialog box appears. If you already have defined columns in your document, the box displays your current settings. If you have not defined columns yet, the settings displayed are WordPerfect's defaults, which are for two newspaper columns with a 0.5-inch gutter between them.

   WordPerfect automatically suggests column margins based on the current document's left and right margins, the number of columns selected, and the specified distance between columns. Whenever you change the Number of **C**olumns or the **D**istance Between Columns, WordPerfect recalculates the column margins.

3. Enter the desired number of columns in the Number of **C**olumns text box. The default is two columns.

   This Number of **C**olumns value is highlighted when the dialog box appears, so you can change the number immediately by typing a new number. You can define up to 24 columns.

4. If necessary, select **N**ewspaper in the Type section. Newspaper columns are the default, so in most circumstances this option will be selected already.

5. Select **D**istance Between Columns to change the default 0.5-inch gutter between your columns. Type a new value, which generally will be smaller than the default (0.5 inch is usually too much). You can insert any decimal value up to the width of the document, or you can enter fractions, such as 1/3 or 1/5.

   In general, the more columns you have, the smaller the space you want between them. Remember that the gutter between columns is not available for text, and that the total amount of space lost from a page is the distance between columns multiplied by the number of gutters (which is one fewer than the number of columns). If you have six columns on a page 8.5 inches wide (with left and right margins 1 inch wide), for example, and the distance between columns is set to 0.5 inch, you lose 2.5 inches of usable space, and have only 4.0 inches left on a standard page. With the distance between set to 0.25 inch, you lose only 1.25 inches, and have 5.25 inches of usable space. *Some* gutter space is necessary, so avoid settings that approach 0. Note that if you select a value that, multiplied by the number of gutters, is greater than the document's width, the values for column margins drop to 0.

6. If you *don't* want all your columns to be the same width, deselect the Evenly Spaced check box under Options. If you want evenly spaced columns, skip to step 8. (For newspaper style columns, you usually want all columns to be the same width.)

   Other changes you make in the Define Columns dialog box can affect the Evenly Spaced setting. Changing the Number of Columns or the Distance Between Columns automatically *selects* Evenly Spaced, and changing any individual column margin *deselects* Evenly Spaced.

7. Select **Margins** to edit individual columns (only if you do not need evenly spaced columns). The left margin setting of column 1 is highlighted. Enter a new value (or leave it unchanged); then press Tab to highlight the right margin setting. Successive tabbing highlights the left and then right margin settings of each subsequent column. You also can use your mouse to select any column margin setting. The dialog box displays the margins for only five columns at a time; if you have specified six or more columns, a scroll bar appears so that you can move through the settings for all the columns.

   Do not press Enter until you are finished, or you will insert the column definition as is. After you have set custom column margins, be aware that if you check the Evenly Spaced check box or change the setting in the Distance Between Columns or Number of Columns text box, WordPerfect replaces your custom margins with evenly spaced margins.

8. If you want to insert a column definition code but *not* a column on code at this point, deselect the Columns **On** check box.

   By default, WordPerfect inserts the [Col On] and [Col Off] codes at the same time when you close the Define Columns dialog box. If, however, you want to insert a column definition into Initial Codes (or some other place early in your document) but actually do not want to turn on columns yet, deselect the Columns **On** box before selecting OK. (You also can delete the [Col On] code after it is inserted.)

9. Select OK or press Enter when you are satisfied with all your settings.

WordPerfect inserts a [Col Def:] code and, unless you deselected the option, a [Col On] code. If you deselect the Columns **On** check box, your document is not formatted in columns until you insert a [Col On] code. Otherwise, any new or existing text below the [Col On] code is formatted in columns according to your specifications.

■ **Cue:** You can make changes directly from the editing screen by dragging column markers on the Ruler.

If you are not satisfied with your column margins when you see the formatted text, you can return to the Define Columns dialog box and change the settings. Before activating the Define Columns dialog box, select an insertion point in the first paragraph that is formatted in columns, or you will insert a *second* column definition at the beginning of the current paragraph. (If Auto Code Placement is off, move the insertion point to *immediately* after the original column definition code.) Then repeat any steps necessary to make your desired changes.

Working with Columnar Text

Typing in columns is the same as typing in a normal document. Text automatically wraps at the end of each line within the column and from the bottom of one column to the top of the next. Because of the narrower line width, however, your printed text may look less pleasing. The right side of left-justified text may be too ragged, and with justification set to Full, some lines may be spread out or compressed to achieve even margins. WordPerfect gives you several ways to combat these problems.

Consider changing your type size; large type and small columns don't mix. A different type face at the same point size also may take up less space. Proportionally spaced fonts adjust better than fixed-width fonts. Consider decreasing the number of columns to make each remaining column wider. In general, although you should make such overall layout decisions in advance, appearance should always be your final guide.

You will want to hyphenate some words manually, but avoid placing hyphens on several successive lines. If WordPerfect is hyphenating for you, you may need to adjust the hyphenation zone settings in extreme cases for tighter hyphenation (covered in Chapter 6, "Formatting Text"). Again, this problem is far less severe with proportionally spaced fonts than with fixed-width fonts.

Moving the Insertion Point

Insertion point movement *within* a column is the same as in a normal document, but movement *between* columns is not. The easiest way to move from one column to another is to select a new insertion point with your mouse. If you do not have a mouse, however, or if you prefer to use the keyboard, WordPerfect offers several commands for moving the insertion point in columns. You *must* use these commands when creating a macro that moves between columns, because macros don't record the movement of a mouse.

Alt-right arrow and Alt-left arrow are the easiest ways to move between columns. Alt-right arrow moves the insertion point one column to the right, until you reach the last column; Alt-left arrow moves the insertion point one column to the left, until you reach the first column. More complex, but more powerful, is movement through the Go To dialog box (select **Edit**, **G**o To, or press Ctrl-G). Typically, you use the Go To dialog box's **P**osition option to go to a specific page number or to the top or the bottom of the current page (see fig. 13.5). Chapter 2, "Creating, Printing, and Saving a Document," explains the use of the Go To command.

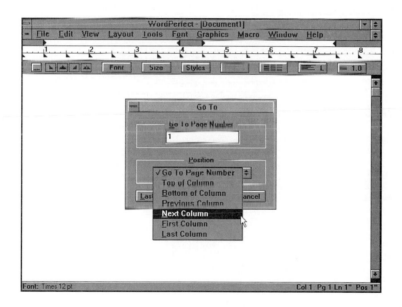

When the insertion point is within a column, however, the following options become available:

Go to Page Number

Top of Column

Bottom of Column

> **P**revious Column
>
> **N**ext Column
>
> **F**irst Column
>
> **L**ast Column

To select one of these options from the keyboard, follow these steps:

1. Select Go To (select **E**dit, **G**o To, or press Ctrl-G). The Go To dialog box appears.

2. Press Alt-P or Tab to select **P**osition.

3. Press the space bar to access the drop-down menu.

4. Type Alt-*letter* for the desired option.

5. Press Enter.

   The insertion point moves to the desired location.

Displaying One Column at a Time

■ **Cue:** For ease and speed of editing, turn off side-by-side column display (at least temporarily).

WordPerfect can display columns side-by-side, exactly as they will print, or WordPerfect can display only one column at a time. By default, WordPerfect displays columns side-by-side, which is ideal for clarity. WordPerfect has to work harder, however, to display two or more columns simultaneously, which slows down program performance. Furthermore, you can scroll from column to column more easily with a single column displayed.

In regular text, you simply scroll downward through a page break on-screen. In columns, however, the text that follows the bottom of the first column is the text at the top of the second column on the same page. If you scroll *down* through a column with side-by-side display enabled, the insertion point scrolls directly to the following page, skipping any text in adjacent columns. You must scroll *right* from the bottom row to reach the top of the next column.

With side-by-side column display disabled, the insertion point automatically jogs over to the next column when it reaches the end of a column. You can change the side-by-side column display option by following these steps:

1. Select **F**ile, **P**references.

    Press Preferences (Ctrl-Shift-F1).

2. Choose **D**isplay.

3. Press Alt-C to select or deselect Display **C**olumns Side by Side.

Editing in Newspaper Columns

Editing within newspaper columns is not much different from editing standard text. WordPerfect has no special keys for selecting text within columns. For instance, Alt-Shift-PgDn still selects all text to the end of the page, *not* to the end of the column. You must be aware, however, of the codes that create the columns themselves. Deleting a [Col On] code reformats your document as normal text to the end of the document or to the next [Col On] code, whichever comes first. Deleting a [Col Off] code formats any following text into columns. Deleting a [Col Def:] code removes *all* columns in the document, unless a subsequent [Col Def:] code appears. Note that deleting any of these codes can alter drastically the pagination of your document.

If you want to change the format of part of your document to match that of the preceding section, delete the intervening [Col Off] or [Col On] code, just as you would remove a double-spacing code to revert the following text to single-spacing. If, however, you delete a [Col On] code by accident, select Undo (press Alt-Backspace or select **E**dit, **U**ndo) *immediately*, or you will lose the following [Col Off] code (if any). If you delete a [Col Def:] code by accident, you may have to reenter all subsequent column codes.

When columns have been turned on, WordPerfect uses normal page break codes to indicate column breaks. At the bottom of each column you see a [SPg] code or the equivalent. To force a column break at some point, insert a [HPg] code, which leaves the rest of that column empty and forces the following text to the top of the next column.

After you have defined columns, you can turn columns on and off within a document simply by inserting additional [Col Off] and [Col On] codes in the appropriate locations. Both options are available under the Columns icon in the Ruler or by selecting **L**ayout, **C**olumns. Turning on columns part of the way through a document presents no problems, but turning them off before the end inserts a [HPg] code for each remaining column, leaving the remainder of the column and any subsequent columns empty. Unfortunately, WordPerfect provides no method by which adjacent columns automatically can be adjusted to the same length. You can insert [HPg] codes to force a column break at the end of a particular line, but this technique destroys the justification of that line and does not adjust if you later edit the text.

T I P

To justify the last line in a column, insert one space, then enough hard spaces to cause the line of hard spaces to wrap. Insert a few more hard spaces; then insert a [HPg] code to start the next column. You need to accommodate the extra "blank" line in your formatting, but the last text line will be justified. Editing, of course, requires extra work, because the group of hard spaces becomes a "word."

Still, under certain circumstances, such as chapter breaks and other major divisions, changing between columns and normal text can be effective. For instance, you can start each chapter with a title and other prefatory material at full width, and then switch to columns for the body text. Extra white space at chapter or section breaks usually is acceptable, so a [Col Off] code can be inserted without detracting from the appearance of your document.

Note that the appearance of centered headings in a document with columns depends on the location of the headings. WordPerfect centers text between the current margins, whether those margins are the full page width or a single column. A centered heading within a column, therefore, is centered between the column margins, while a centered heading in normal text is centered between the overall page margins. If additional [Col Off] or [Col On] codes are added to the document, subsequent Center commands adjust accordingly.

Previewing Newspaper Columns

The side-by-side columns display gives an accurate view of the way your document will print, but cannot display a full page at a time or items such as headers, footers, and endnotes. (**Note:** you *cannot* use footnotes within a column.) To see all these items as they will print, use Print Preview. With Print Preview, you can view one or two pages at a time (the more pages, the smaller the image), view part of a single page at 100 percent or 200 percent resolution, or zoom in on a selected area (see figs. 13.6 and 13.7).

BUTTON

To select Print Preview, select **F**ile, Print Pre**v**iew, or press Shift-F5. You can enlarge the view that appears through options in the **V**iew and **P**ages menus, or by adding a Print Preview button to the Button Bar (see Chapter 19 for instructions). If you are satisfied with the appearance of your document, you can print immediately by selecting **F**ile, **P**rint (or press F5), or by selecting the Print button on the Button Bar. If you are not satisfied, you must close the Print Preview window and edit your document accordingly.

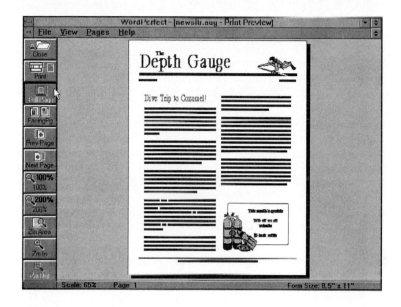

FIG. 13.6

Print Preview at Full Page.

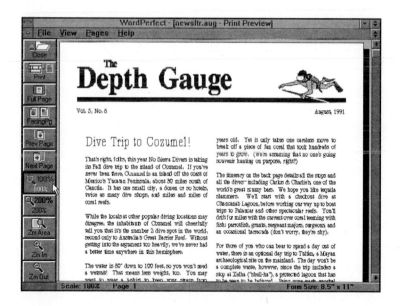

FIG. 13.7

Print Preview at 100 percent.

Parallel Columns

Parallel columns, although more closely related to newspaper columns, also have much in common with WordPerfect's Tables feature. Where newspaper columns typically feature large amounts of text flowing continuously from column to column, parallel columns contain shorter blocks of text that you read across the page from left to right (see fig. 13.8). These blocks of text can be any length, from individual words and short phrases to long paragraphs. As a result, you can use parallel columns for a wide variety of documents, from itineraries to screenplays.

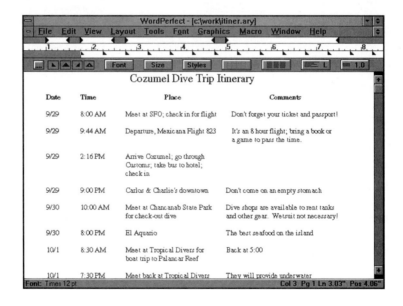

FIG. 13.8

An example of parallel columns.

Defining Parallel Columns

The steps for defining parallel columns are similar to those for creating newspaper columns. You can define parallel columns, however, only through the Define Columns dialog box. You cannot use the Columns icon on the Ruler as a shortcut, as you can for simple newspaper columns. Also, whereas newspaper columns are usually evenly spaced and need little, if any, adjustment after definition, parallel columns are usually of greatly differing widths. The appearance of parallel columns depends on the actual contents of the various columns. For the best appearance, you usually need to edit your parallel columns definition after you have entered some text. Although you should plan in advance the number of columns you need and their approximate relative widths, don't spend a great deal of time making complex calculations that you will change anyway.

To create your initial parallel columns definition, follow these steps:

1. Select an insertion point where you want the columns to begin.

2. Select **L**ayout, **C**olumns, **D**efine. Alternatively, double-click the Columns icon in the Ruler.

   The Define Columns dialog box appears (see fig. 13.9).

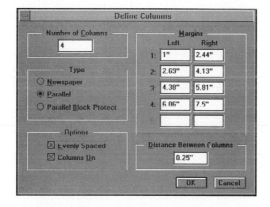

FIG. 13.9

Defining parallel columns.

3. Enter the number of columns you want. The default is 2 columns.

   This value is highlighted when the dialog box appears, so you can change the number immediately simply by typing a new number. You can define up to 24 columns. If you have made other changes, you can return to the Number of **C**olumns text box by pressing Alt-C, by pressing Tab until the box is highlighted, or by selecting the text box with your mouse.

4. In the Type section, select **P**arallel or Parallel **B**lock Protect. The two types are similar, but in the latter type WordPerfect places Block Protect codes around each group of parallel columns so that individual text blocks cannot be split by page breaks.

5. Select **D**istance Between Columns to change the default 0.5-inch gutter space between your columns. Type a new value, which usually will be smaller than the default (0.5 inch is usually too much space). You can insert any decimal value up to the width of the document, and you can enter fractions, such as 1/3 or 1/5.

The more columns you have, the smaller you should make the distance between them. Because individual text blocks within parallel columns are often different lengths, the extra white space below short columns helps compensate for the narrow distance between them and prevents your columns from appearing crowded.

6. If you don't want all your columns to be the same width, deselect the **E**venly Spaced box under Options. If you want evenly spaced columns, skip to step 7. Changing one column margin also automatically deselects the **E**venly Spaced check box.

7. Press Alt-M to edit individual column margins (only if you do not need evenly spaced columns). The left margin setting of column 1 is highlighted. (You can use your mouse to select any column margin setting.) Enter a new value or leave it unchanged, and tab to the next setting. The dialog box can display the margins for only five columns at a time; if you have specified six or more columns, a scroll bar appears so that you can move through the settings for all the columns.

Do not press Enter until you are finished, or you will insert the column definition as is. After you have set custom column margins, be aware that if you select the **E**venly Spaced option, or change the **D**istance Between Columns or the Number of **C**olumns, WordPerfect replaces your custom margins with evenly spaced ones. (You can use this technique to reset column margins if you are not satisfied with your initial settings.)

8. To insert a column definition *without* turning on columns at this point, deselect the Columns **O**n option box.

The Columns **O**n option is the default, and WordPerfect inserts a [Col On] code with the column definition. If, however, you want to insert a column definition in Initial Codes, for example, but don't want to turn on columns immediately, deselect the box before selecting OK. (You also can delete the [Col On] code after it is inserted.)

9. Select OK or press Enter when you are satisfied with all your settings.

WordPerfect inserts a [Col Def:Parallel] code or a [Col Def:Parallel/Block Pro] code, depending on which type of parallel columns you selected. The Ruler, if selected, now displays your column margins between your page margins. You can change the widths of your columns by dragging the column guides in the Ruler, but before doing so, you should type several rows of text.

Typing Text in Parallel Columns

In newspaper columns, WordPerfect automatically wraps text from column to column, although you can insert a [HPg] code to force a column break at a given location. In parallel columns, however, you *must* insert a [HPg] code (press Ctrl-Enter) at the end of each block of text to tell WordPerfect where to break text between columns. If you do not press Ctrl-Enter, WordPerfect treats everything that follows as part of the same column.

After you type text in the last column, press Ctrl-Enter. The insertion point returns to the beginning of the first column, below any text in the first row. In Reveal Codes, you see the codes [Col Off][HRt][Col On] in immediate succession. WordPerfect assumes that you want to continue adding text in parallel columns, and after the program turns columns off and adds a carriage return, WordPerfect turns columns on again.

This pattern repeats as you type successive rows of information. WordPerfect starts each group of parallel columns with a [Col On], requires a [HPg] between columns, and ends each group with a [Col Off]. WordPerfect also adds [HRt][Col On] after each group to start the next group automatically.

Parallel columns with Block Protect work in exactly the same way, with the addition of block protect codes around each group of columns. When you specify Parallel Block Protect in the Define Columns dialog box, the column definition code appears as [Col Def:Parallel/Block Pro;...]. Each group of columns then begins with [Block Pro:On] [Col On], has a [HPg] code between columns, and ends with [Block Pro:Off][Col Off]. Without block protection, a block of text can extend over a page break. This situation is acceptable in screenplays and other documents in which a single text block may be several paragraphs or even several pages long, but when text blocks are relatively short, such page breaks become intrusive.

CAUTION: If you have selected in Preferences not to display columns side-by-side in order to work with newspaper columns, you will have difficulty working with parallel columns. Change your setting as described in the section "Displaying One Column at a Time."

To create the itinerary shown in figure 13.8, do the following:

1. Define parallel columns as described in the preceding section. Select 4 columns with 0.25 inch space between them. You need not adjust column margins. Leave Columns **O**n checked.

2. Select Bold (select **F**ont, **B**old, or press Ctrl-B), and type **Date**.

3. Press Ctrl-Enter to go to the next column. In Reveal Codes, you can see a [HPg] code.

4. Type **Time**, and press Ctrl-Enter to go to the third column.

5. Select Center (**L**ayout, **L**ine, **C**enter or press Shift-F7), type **Place**, and press Ctrl-Enter to go to the final column.

6. Select Center (**L**ayout, **L**ine, **C**enter or press Shift-F7), type **Comments**, and turn off Bold (**F**ont, **B**old or Ctrl-B).

7. Press Ctrl-Enter to return to the first column.

8. Continue to type text in column format, pressing Ctrl-Enter at the end of each column. You can use any text attributes, choose justification or alignment options, change line spacing, and so on.

9. If you finish typing columns and want to resume typing normal text, turn off columns.

   Select **L**ayout, **C**olumns, Columns O**ff**.

■ **Cue:** You can use the Columns icon on the Ruler to turn off columns.

If you forget to turn off columns, and press Ctrl-Enter instead, simply delete the final [Col On] code. The following text does not appear in columns.

Changing Columns by Using the Ruler

After you have entered some text into your columns, you can see which columns are too wide and too narrow. Figure 13.10 shows an itinerary without adjustments. Compare this result with figure 13.8, which shows the finished version of the same document. In the rough version, the Date and Time columns clearly are too wide and are nearly empty, whereas the Place and Comments columns are far too narrow.

The Ruler displays page margins and the gutters as blocks of gray and displays margin markers representing page and column margins as triangles pointing away from those gray areas (see fig 13.10). Whenever you move a margin or tab setting in the Ruler, a vertical line appears down the screen to aid in placing the setting with respect to the existing text.

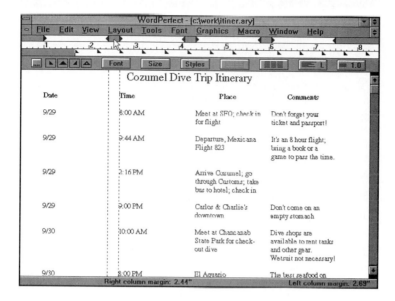

FIG. 13.10

Dragging
column margins
in the Ruler.

Dragging a margin marker to the left or right changes that margin *and* the adjacent gutter. For example, if you drag the triangle representing the left margin of the second column to the right, you decrease the width of that column and increase the width of the space between the first and second columns. The widths of the other columns are not affected.

Dragging the gray area between two columns to the left or right changes the respective widths of those columns but *not* the space between them. If you drag the gray area between the first and second columns to the left, you decrease the width of the first column and increase the width of the second column. The width of the space *between* the columns remains unchanged, as do the widths of all other columns.

To adjust the columns of the itinerary, do the following:

1. Select an insertion point in the first block of text. If your insertion point is not in the first "row" of text blocks, you will add a *new* column definition at your currently selected row instead of editing the original column definition at the beginning of the columns.

2. Select **View**, **R**uler to display the Ruler if it is hidden.

    CUA Press View Ruler (Alt-Shift-F3).

3. Using the mouse, drag the gutter space between the first two columns. Because you are moving the right margin of the first column and the left margin of the second column simultaneously, two vertical lines appear.

4. Drag to the left until the left vertical line approaches the text in the first column.

5. Release the gutter, being careful not to drag it down off the Ruler (which would delete it). The text in column 2 moves to the left; columns 3 and 4 remain unchanged.

6. Drag the gutter between columns 2 and 3 to the left in the same way that you dragged the first gutter.

   When you release the gutter, the text in column 3 adjusts to the new column width, and blocks of text that were 4 and 5 lines long are now 1 or 2 lines long.

7. Finally, drag the gutter between columns 3 and 4 so that the two columns are about the same width.

   The text in column 4 now spreads out as well. With most blocks of text now 1 or 2 lines, and none longer than 3 lines, the entire document takes up far less space, and the text is reasonably well balanced between columns. You can make further adjustments at any time to fine-tune column widths, remembering first to select an insertion point in the first block of text.

Editing Parallel Columns

Editing in newspaper columns is essentially the same as editing normal text. When you edit in parallel columns, however, you must remain aware of the codes that give the columns their structure and work within that structure. At times, you will want to cut and paste text between columns, insert new groups of columns between existing ones, and move groups of columns to different locations.

You can cut and paste text from one location to another with few restrictions. You must pay attention, however, to your location within the columns. Remember that each group of columns begins with a [Col On] code, ends with [Col Off], and that columns are separated by [HPg] codes (and Block Protect codes are optional). In WordPerfect, you *cannot* delete an individual [HPg] or [Col Off] necessary to the structure of a group of parallel columns, although you *can* delete a [Col On] code. If you do, the [HPg] codes between that group of columns now act as true hard page breaks, and you must restore the [Col On] code or delete the [HPg] codes to reformat your document.

Avoid cutting and pasting text that spans two or more adjacent columns. WordPerfect always prevents you from adding or deleting the [HPg] codes between columns that are necessary to maintain the column structure. When you paste a selection that contains [HPg] codes, then, the results are unpredictable. WordPerfect maintains the column structure, but several of your columns may be squeezed into one column as a result. If you cut text from the last column of one group into the first column of the next group, the selection will contain a [Col On] code, whose removal will destroy the column formatting of both groups of columns.

The safest way, therefore, to move small amounts of text around within parallel columns is to copy rather than cut the desired information, then selectively delete the original. Alternatively, make your selections with Reveal Codes on, and make sure that your selections do not include essential column formatting codes.

Inserting Parallel Columns

What if you need to add a new event to the middle of your itinerary? You must insert a new group of parallel columns within existing text. Select an insertion point at the *end* of the *preceding* group of columns, immediately before the [Col Off] code (or in front of the [Block Pro:Off] code, if present), and press Ctrl-Enter. WordPerfect immediately inserts a complete, empty set of [Col On], [HPg], and [Col Off] codes between the two existing groups of columns, and places the insertion point in the first column for you to enter text. You may need to add or delete some [HRt] codes to preserve spacing. WordPerfect still recognizes Ctrl-Enter as the command to go to the next column, but does not insert [HPg] codes, because they are already there. In this case, however, you also can press the right arrow once to scroll past the [HPg] code to the next column. If you need to insert additional groups of columns at the same location, press Ctrl-Enter again in the last column, and WordPerfect will insert another set of codes.

 **CAUTION:** When inserting a new group of parallel columns within your text, you may be tempted simply to select an insertion point at the beginning of the following event and begin typing. When you press Ctrl-Enter to move to the second column, however, WordPerfect pushes the next group's first-column text ahead of you and combines it with the following second-column text. If you continue in this manner, you will squash the entire following group of columns into a single column.

Moving Parallel Columns

Moving existing groups of parallel columns can be difficult. To move one or more groups of columns, you *must* include both the [Col On] and the [Col Off] codes, or you will destroy the column structure for the selected text. Reveal Codes is essential for properly selecting and inserting columns. Note that you cannot move a group of columns *above* the column definition without losing the column format.

To move a group of parallel columns, do the following:

1. Select Reveal Codes (**V**iew, Reveal **C**odes) if it is not already active.

    Press Reveal Codes (Alt-F3).

2. Select an insertion point in the desired group of columns before the [Col On] code (or [Block Pro:On][Col On] codes, if present).

3. If necessary, press Home twice to move the insertion point before the code.

4. Press Select (F8) and press the down arrow twice. The selection should now include the [HRt] between groups of columns but *not* the [Col On] code for the following group.

   Alternatively, press Shift-down arrow twice.

5. Select Cut (choose **E**dit, Cu**t** or press Shift-Del or Ctrl-X).

6. Move the insertion point to where you want to move the block, and position it before the [Col On] code.

7. Select Paste (choose **E**dit, **P**aste or press Shift-Ins or Ctrl-V).

Limitations of Using Columns

WordPerfect's Columns feature is powerful but has some limitations you should keep in mind.

First, you cannot place a WordPerfect table directly into a column. This restriction is absolute; however, you *can* place a graphics box into columns, and then place the table inside the graphics box.

Working with Tables

O f all WordPerfect's special features, the Tables feature offers you more practical uses and enables you to do more to enhance the attractiveness of your documents than any other feature. That statement is a bold one, but it is substantiated, as you learn in this chapter.

"What is a table?" is a good question, because people use the term in different contexts. In WordPerfect, a *table* is rows and columns of data arranged and formatted to make that data easy to read or understand. For example, consider the following list:

Item	Part #	Bin #
Widget	34-222	24-A
Gadget	33-245	26-B
Do-Dad	33-249	13-F

■ **Read Gilgen** is Director of Learning Support Services at the University of Wisconsin, Madison. He teaches workshops on WordPerfect's Tables feature.

In the past, most word processing programs could format this list only by separating the columns with tabs and by using underlining and different fonts to make the information easy to follow. Not only are such lists boring, but as you read them, you easily can lose your place, especially if the lists are wide and contain many details.

On the other hand, consider the same list in a printed WordPerfect for Windows table (see fig. 14.1). Already you can see a difference—the program separates the items clearly, and the entire table is neat and attractive.

Item	Part#	Bin#
Widget	34-222	24-A
Gadget	33-245	26-B
Do-Dad	33-249	13-F

The structure of a table is much like the structure of a spreadsheet: WordPerfect labels the rows with numbers (1, 2, 3...) and the columns with letters (A, B, C...). The intersection of a column and a row is a *cell*. You can identify each cell according to the row and column in which it resides (A1, B3, C14, and so on). In figure 14.1, for example, the word *Widget* is in the first column (A) and the second row (2); therefore, *Widget* is in cell A2.

The other table features are optional. For example, you can change the lines that WordPerfect inserts, or you can omit them altogether. You can change the text justification, and you can add text attributes, such as boldface or italic. You can adjust the width and height of any column or row. You even can create formulas to calculate numeric information.

Using WordPerfect's table formatting options, you can create any kind of table—from simple lists to complex invoices, from schedules to calendars, from programs to scripts, and more.

In this chapter, you first learn how to create a simple table by using a sample invoice as a model (see fig. 14.2). You learn how to enter text into table cells, how to change the table structure, how to format table text, and how to use the table for calculating numeric information.

■ **Cue:** Don't be afraid to
experiment and add your
own ideas to tables.

Designing, creating, and modifying a table is a visual and artistic venture. Although this chapter describes how to obtain certain results when creating a table, you have your own needs and sense of what looks good. Don't be afraid to experiment, and don't be upset if the results are not quite what you expected. Simply try again.

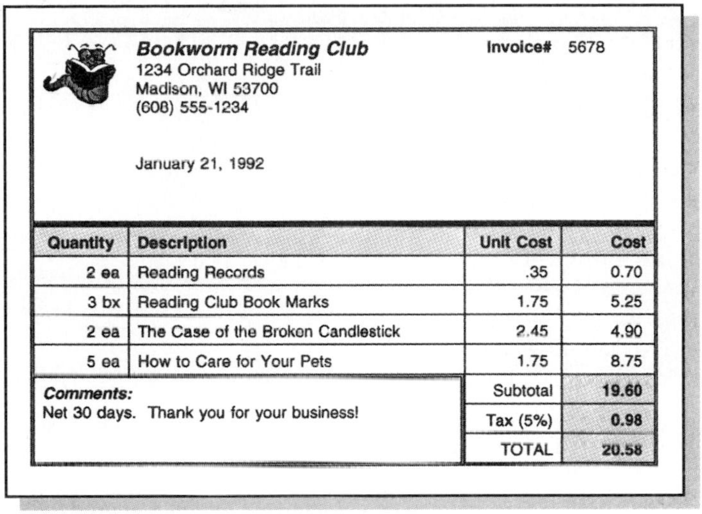

Bookworm Reading Club
1234 Orchard Ridge Trail
Madison, WI 53700
(608) 555-1234

Invoice# 5678

January 21, 1992

Quantity	Description	Unit Cost	Cost
2 ea	Reading Records	.35	0.70
3 bx	Reading Club Book Marks	1.75	5.25
2 ea	The Case of the Broken Candlestick	2.45	4.90
5 ea	How to Care for Your Pets	1.75	8.75
Comments: Net 30 days. Thank you for your business!		Subtotal	19.60
		Tax (5%)	0.98
		TOTAL	20.58

FIG. 14.2

An invoice
created with the
Tables feature.

Planning Your Tables

Before actually creating a table, you can save yourself a great deal of time by doing some preliminary planning. First, ask yourself what you want to accomplish with your table. Do you merely want to present straightforward information more clearly, or do you want to design a more complex, heavily formatted form?

Next, determine the approximate number of rows and columns you want. You can have up to 32 columns and 32,765 rows (or 1,048,480 cells), although you are most unlikely to use that many. You do not need to know the *exact* number of rows or columns because you can add or delete them while you work with your table. Knowing this information in advance, however—especially the number of columns— can make creating, modifying, and using your table easier.

You also can benefit from determining and selecting the font style and size you want to use. Again, this planning is not critical because you can change fonts as you work with your table.

Finally, you must consider where in your document you plan to locate the table. You cannot place tables in newspaper columns, nor can you create side-by-side tables. You must use graphics boxes to create these kinds of tables (see Chapter 17, "Understanding Advanced Graphics," for a detailed discussion of graphics boxes).

Creating and Using Tables: The Basics

Even in their simplest form, tables are easy to create and yet can be quite effective. Learning the basic procedures described in this section is important because the more complex procedures explained later in this chapter build on these fundamentals.

Creating a Table

■ **Cue:** You can create WordPerfect tables by using the menus or the Ruler.

At least two different methods of creating a table are available. The first method is to use WordPerfect's menu system to specify the number of columns and rows you want; the second method is to determine the shape of the table by using the mouse to choose rows and columns from the Ruler.

To use the menus to create a table, follow these steps:

1. In your document, position the insertion point where you want to insert your table.

2. Select **L**ayout, **T**ables.

    Press Layout Tables (Ctrl-F9).

3. Select **C**reate to display the Create Table dialog box, which prompts you to specify the number of columns and rows you want in your table (see fig. 14.3).

FIG. 14.3

The Create Table dialog box.

4. In the **C**olumns text box, type the number of columns you want and press Tab to advance to the **R**ows text box.

5. Type the number of rows you want, and press Enter to display the table you have defined.

If you specify four columns and five rows, WordPerfect displays on-screen the table shown in figure 14.4.

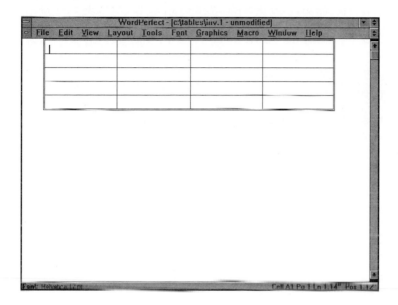

FIG. 14.4

A table with four columns and five rows.

By default, the outside border of a table is a double line, and the lines separating the cells are single lines. Also by default, WordPerfect left-justifies the table. When you first create a table, however, the program extends the table to the right margin. (See "Positioning Tables" in this chapter, for more details about changing the position of a table.)

The other, perhaps easier, method for creating tables involves using the Ruler. To use the Ruler to create a table, follow these steps:

1. If the Ruler isn't already displayed, select View, Ruler.

 Press View Ruler (Alt-Shift-F3).

WordPerfect displays several buttons at the bottom of the Ruler, including the Tables button, which displays a grid icon and is located to the immediate right of the Styles button (see fig. 14.5.)

FIG. 14.5

WordPerfect's Ruler.

2. Place the insertion point at the place in your document where you want to locate the table.

3. Click the Tables button, and press the mouse button to display a large grid.

4. Drag the mouse pointer down and to the right until the pop-up grid highlights the number of columns and rows you want (see fig. 14.6).

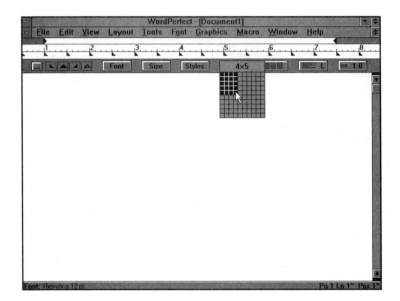

FIG. 14.6

The Tables button pop-up grid.

If you need more columns and rows than are displayed on the grid, keep dragging the mouse; WordPerfect expands the grid up to 32 columns by 45 rows. At the top of the grid, WordPerfect specifies the number of columns and rows, in that order, that you have selected (4x5 in this example).

5. After you have displayed the number of columns and rows you want, release the mouse button. WordPerfect creates the table according to the size you indicated.

Moving within a Table

After you create a table, WordPerfect positions the cursor at the upper left corner of the table, in cell A1. On the status bar, at the lower right corner of the screen, WordPerfect displays not only the usual information—Pg, Ln, and Pos—but also displays the current cell location, Cell A1. When you move the cursor to a new cell, WordPerfect indicates on the status bar the new cell location.

To move the cursor one cell to the right, press the Tab key. The status bar now indicates that the cursor is in Cell B1. If you want to move the cursor one cell to the left, press Shift-Tab.

■ **Cue:** To move the cursor to the right or left in a table, press Tab or Shift-Tab, respectively.

If the cursor is in the rightmost column, pressing Tab moves the cursor to column A and down one row. Pressing Shift-Tab while the cursor is in column A moves the cursor to the rightmost column and up one row.

Using the mouse to position the cursor in the cell you want is sometimes a quicker and easier way to move from one cell to another. If you are typing, however, using the Tab key usually is easier than interrupting your typing to use the mouse.

You also can use the arrow keys to move from one cell to the next, but using the Tab key or the mouse generally is easier, especially when cells are filled with text or numbers.

Although all three methods provide the same results, you will find that you use a specific method for certain tasks. For example, when browsing and editing a table, you probably will use the mouse. On the other hand, you probably will use the Tab key and arrow keys when entering text into a table.

Entering Text

When you enter text into your table, consider each cell a miniature document with its own margins and formatting. As you enter text, WordPerfect wraps the words within the cell, vertically expanding the row to accommodate what you type (see fig. 14.7). You can enter and edit the text in a cell just as you work in a document.

Suppose that you want to create an invoice table in which you list in four columns the quantity, description, unit cost, and extended price of various products. You simply move the cursor from cell to cell and type the information that you want in each cell. (You learn later about adjusting the structure of your table. For now, focus on the mechanics of using a simple table structure.)

As you follow the development of the sample invoice table, you may not see explicit instructions to enter text. Nevertheless, when you see new text in the sample figures, enter that text into your own invoice table.

FIG. 14.7

The table with
two lines of text
in cell A1.

Cutting, Pasting, and Deleting Text

You delete text from table cells the same way you delete text from
documents; however, you must take certain precautions to avoid
deleting more than text.

To delete text from a cell, first position the cursor in the cell from
which you want to delete text. Then use the Del or Backspace key; or
select the text you want to delete (press F8 and use the arrow keys)
and press Del or Backspace. To restore deleted text to any cell, position the cursor in that cell, and press Alt-Shift-Backspace or select **E**dit,
U**n**delete.

Cue: To restore deleted
text to any cell, position the
cursor in that cell, and press
Alt-Shift-Backspace or select
Edit, U**n**delete.

CAUTION: If you want to select text from more than one cell, you
must use the Select key (F8) and the arrow keys. If you
use the mouse, and remain within the table, you select
cells rather than text.

You can copy or cut and paste text from one cell to another, from a
document to a cell, or from a cell to a document; however, you cannot
copy data from a document to more than one cell at a time.

If you position the cursor at the beginning of cell A1, press Select (F8),
and move the cursor or click and drag the mouse pointer beyond the
bottom of the table, you can delete, cut, or copy all the contents of the
table.

If you cut or delete text from several table cells, you cannot use normal procedures to paste it into its original location. You first must paste or restore the text to your document, outside of the table; then you can cut each part of the restored text and paste it into its original cell—a tedious process at best.

Remember, however, that you can undo the action you last initiated. If you accidentally delete more than you intended, select **E**dit, **U**ndo (or press Alt-Backspace) to return the table to the stage it was in before you made the deletion (assuming, of course, that you haven't made any other changes before trying to undo the deletion).

T I P

When working with tables, save your document frequently. Sometimes remembering the changes you have made to your table is difficult—especially the steps you took to make those changes. Frequently saving your work means that you have a backup copy of your table to which you can return if you try a procedure or design that doesn't work.

Selecting and Deleting a Cell

Another method for deleting cell text, and a method you use with table formatting, is to select an entire cell rather than just its text or parts of its text. To select an entire cell, position the mouse pointer within the cell you want to select and move the pointer slowly toward the left or the top line of the cell until WordPerfect displays an arrow. This arrow indicates that your next command will affect the entire cell, not just its contents.

Click once to select the cell. WordPerfect reverses the colors of the cell, such as from black text in a white cell to white text in a black cell (see fig. 14.8). If you press Backspace or Del, the program deletes the contents of that cell. Of course, you can undo this action, but you cannot use Undelete to recover text deleted in this manner.

To select an entire row of cells, click twice with the arrow pointing to the left side of the cell. Again, the program reverses the colors of the cells in that row. When you press Backspace or Del, however, WordPerfect displays the Delete Row dialog box so that you can choose whether you want to delete the row (text and structure) or just the text in that row (see fig. 14.9).

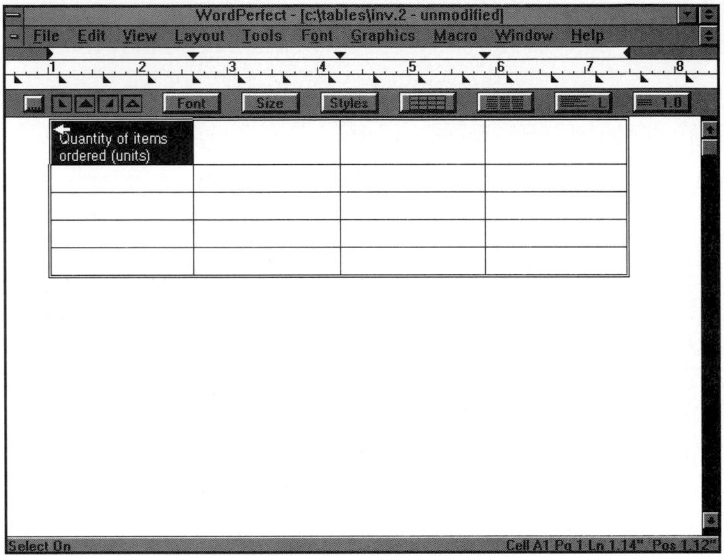

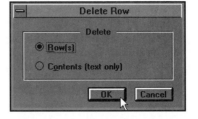

FIG. 14.8

A selected cell.

FIG. 14.9

The Delete Row dialog box.

■ **Cue:** To select an entire column of cells, click twice with the arrow pointing to the top of the cell.

To select an entire column of cells, click twice with the arrow pointing to the top of the cell. When you press Backspace or Del, the Delete Column dialog box asks you whether you want to delete the column (text and structure) or just the text in that column.

To select all the cells in a table (all rows and columns), click three times with the arrow pointing either to the side or to the top of the cell. Again, the reversed colors indicate that you have selected those cells. Pressing Backspace or Del opens the Delete Table dialog box, which enables you to delete the whole table, only the text from the cells, or only the table structure, leaving the text with each column of information separated by tabs (see fig. 14.10).

To select a group of cells, click the upper left cell of the group and drag down and to the right until you have selected the block you want.

FIG. 14.10

The Delete Table dialog box.

You also can use the keyboard to accomplish the same task. Position the cursor in the first cell, press and hold the Shift key, and use the directional keys to select the group of cells. As soon as you move the cursor from the first cell to the next cell, WordPerfect "assumes" that you want to select cells rather than text and selects one cell at a time as you move the cursor.

If the group of cells you select does not extend to both sides of the table and you press Backspace or Del, WordPerfect deletes the contents of the selected cells without prompting you.

■ **Cue:** The Undo feature (select **E**dit, **U**ndo or press Alt-Backspace) is extremely useful when working with tables; you quickly can reverse mistakes you make when deleting text and changing the structure of a table.

Deleting or Moving a Table

To delete, cut, or copy an entire table, including its structure, position the cursor before the table, press Select (F8), and use the directional keys (or click and drag the mouse) to extend the selection beyond the end of the table. Then delete, cut, or copy the table.

This method enables you to undelete or to paste the entire table in another location. Of course, you also can restore the table to its original location, or you can undo the action.

■ **Cue:** A quick way to delete a table is to place the insertion point on the [Tbl Def] code in Reveal Codes and press **D**el to open the Delete Table dialog box.

Saving and Printing a Table

A table always is part of a document, even when the table is the only element in the document. The procedure for saving tables, therefore, is exactly the same as the method for saving documents (see Chapter 2).

You print tables the same way you print other kinds of text; however, keep in mind the following points:

■ WordPerfect never splits table rows with page breaks. The entire last row on a page always prints with a line at the bottom of the row of cells, and the next entire row prints at the top of the next page with a line at the top of the row of cells.

- Table lines print properly regardless of the font you use or the format of the text and graphics in the cells.

- WordPerfect prints table lines graphically, so you can print them on any dot-matrix or laser printer.

- Graphic printing always takes longer than regular text printing without graphics. Depending on the printer you use, printing tables can dramatically increase the printing time of your document.

- You can decrease printing time by turning off table lines (see "Editing the Table Structure" in this chapter).

Editing the Table Structure

You now know the basics of creating, working with, printing, and saving tables. Up to this point, you have learned only the default WordPerfect table settings, which include the following:

- Evenly spaced columns and rows that fit neatly between the margins of your document

- Double lines around the outer edge of the table

- Single lines between the cells of the table

- Left-justified tables

The real beauty of the Tables feature, however, is that you can make all kinds of adjustments and modifications to these default settings. When you make changes to the shape and size of table cells, columns, and rows, you are editing the layout of the table, or the *table structure*.

■ **Cue:** You can change a table layout by using the menus, the Ruler, or the Button Bar.

WordPerfect enables you to use several methods of changing the layout of your table: the menu system, the Ruler, and the Button Bar.

The first and most obvious editing tool is WordPerfect's menu system. Before you access the menus, you must position the cursor inside the table you want to edit. Then, to display the table editing options, select **L**ayout, **T**ables. WordPerfect displays the Tables menu (see fig. 14.11). If the cursor is outside the table when you access the Tables menu, the menu's options are gray.

Another important table editing tool is the Ruler. If you don't have the Ruler turned on, select **V**iew, **R**uler. Although you can make many table adjustments from the menus, adjusting the table structure with the Ruler often is much easier.

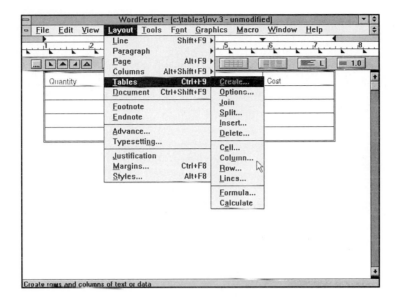

FIG. 14.11

The Tables menu.

The adjustments you make to a table sometimes cause WordPerfect to extend the table horizontally beyond the edges of the screen. If this extension happens, you need to turn on the horizontal scroll bar to assist you in scrolling from one side of the table to the other. Select File, Preferences, Display, and select Display Horizontal Scroll Bar from the dialog box.

The final editing tool you can use to change the table structure is a Button Bar for working with tables. Because you often use the Tables menu while editing a table, using a Button Bar can save you time. (Refer to Chapter 19, "Using the Button Bar," for more information on creating and modifying Button Bars.) WordPerfect comes with a special Button Bar for working with tables. To turn on the Tables Button Bar, select View, Button Bar Setup, Select and from the dialog box select TABLES.WWB.

BUTTON

Changing Column Widths

Often you need a table with columns of unequal widths rather than evenly spaced columns. To change the widths of columns quickly, position the mouse pointer on the inverted triangle (on the Ruler) that indicates the column margin you want to change, and drag the triangle to the desired position on the Ruler.

When you click the triangle and hold down the mouse button, WordPerfect displays a dotted ruler line to help you position the new column margin (see fig. 14.12). You can use the measurements on the status bar or Ruler to set your new column margin, or you can just notice how the column margin looks in the document before you release the mouse button. Note that the status bar displays `Table Split: x.x` while you hold down the mouse button.

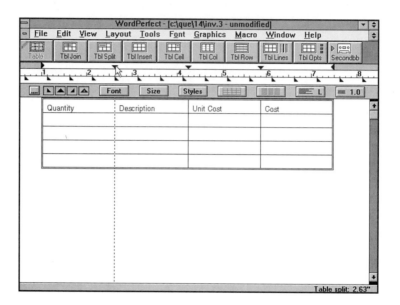

FIG. 14.12

Using the Ruler to change a table column margin.

As you increase the width of a column, all columns to the right of that column move to the right until they reach the document margin, at which point the columns begin to decrease in width (the largest column decreases first) to make room for the expanded column.

Because the table is left-justified, by default, decreasing the width of a column causes all columns to the right of it simply to move left, without changing size.

If you want precise column widths, position the cursor in any cell in the column you want to change. Then select **L**ayout, **T**ables, Col**u**mn, or you can select the Tbl Col button from the Tables Button Bar. WordPerfect displays the Format Column dialog box (see fig. 14.13).

Type the exact width measurement you want in the **C**olumn Width text box. For this example, make columns A, C, and D 1 inch wide, and column B 3 1/2 inches wide. Select OK to confirm your adjustments.

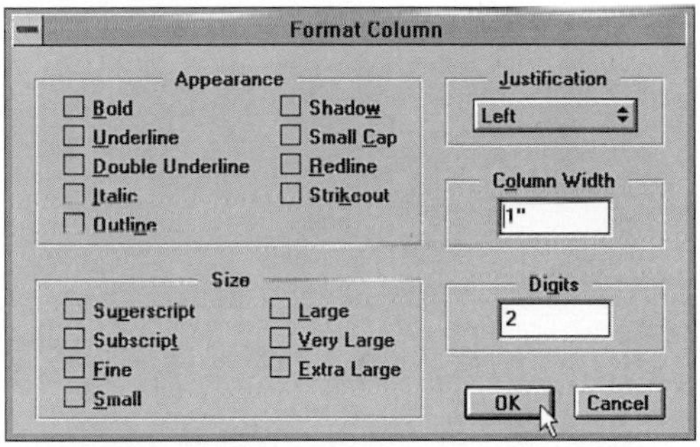

FIG. 14.13

The Format
Column dialog
box.

You can specify the column width measurement in decimals (the
default unit of measurement) or in fractions of an inch, such as
1 5/16. Other units of measurement you can use include centimeters, points, and WordPerfect Units (such as 1w, which is equal to
1/1200 inch). WordPerfect for Windows converts inches, centimeters, points, and WordPerfect Units to decimal amounts.

T I P

Changing the Table Size

After you create a table, you often discover that it has too many or too
few columns or rows. To add columns or rows, select **Layout, Tables,
Options.** You see the Table Options dialog box (see fig. 14.14). In the
Table Size text boxes, enter the number of columns or rows you want,
and then select OK to confirm the change. For example, you may create
a table that contains five rows, but later you determine that it requires
a minimum of eight rows. To change the table size, type **8** in the Rows
text box and select OK.

■ **Cue:** After you create a
table, you can change the
number of rows or columns.

WordPerfect adds rows at the bottom of the table and columns to the
right of the table. The columns and rows you add assume the special
formatting attributes—such as lines and text formats—of the columns
and rows to which they are attached.

Similarly, when you decrease the size of a table, WordPerfect removes
rows (including any text) from the bottom of the table and columns
(including any text) from the right. WordPerfect does not warn you that
you are about to lose text. If you accidentally remove important data,
you can use the Undo feature to return to your original table.

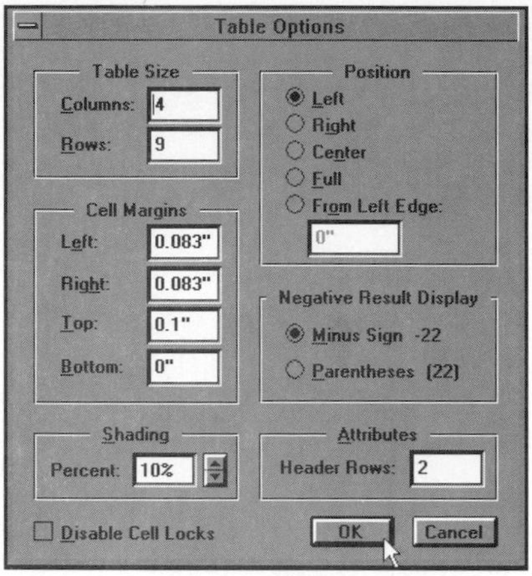

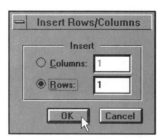

FIG. 14.14

The Table Options dialog box.

Inserting Rows and Columns

Sometimes you want to insert rows or columns somewhere in the middle of the table. For this example, suppose that you want to insert a row at the top of your invoice for your company logo and address.

To insert a new row, follow these steps:

1. Position the cursor at the location where you want to insert the new row. For this example, place the cursor in row 1.

2. Select **L**ayout, **T**ables, **I**nsert to display the Insert Rows/Columns dialog box (see fig. 14.15).

FIG. 14.15

The Insert Rows/Columns dialog box.

3. Choose **R**ows and type the number of rows you want to insert. For this example, type **1**.

4. Select OK.

To insert a column, you follow the same procedures, but select **C**olumns instead of **R**ows. Remember that when you insert a column or columns, WordPerfect may decrease the width of the existing columns so that all the columns fit within the margins of your document. As a result, you may need to readjust the width of your columns (see "Changing Column Widths" in this chapter).

Deleting Rows and Columns

When you want to remove a row or column of information, you may want to remove it entirely, or you may want to remove only its text without altering the table's structure. WordPerfect for Windows enables you to choose between two different approaches for deleting a row or a column.

The first approach to deleting rows or columns enables you to remove both text and structure. To use this method of deleting rows and columns, follow these steps:

1. Position the cursor in the row or column you want to delete.

2. Select **L**ayout, **T**ables, **D**elete.

3. From the Delete Columns/Rows dialog box, select either **R**ows or **C**olumns.

4. Enter the number of columns or rows you want to delete (including the column or row in which the cursor is positioned and counting columns to the right or counting rows down).

5. Select OK.

Although WordPerfect doesn't warn you that you are about to delete the rows or columns, if you make a mistake, you can undo the deletion by pressing Alt-Backspace.

 WARNING: You use Undo, not Undelete, to recover a deleted row or column. Make sure that you undo the deletion before doing anything else.

The second approach to deleting rows and columns enables you to choose whether you want to delete both the text and the structure or only the text. To use this method of deleting a row or column, follow these steps:

1. Use the mouse to select the row or column of cells you want to delete (see "Selecting and Deleting a Cell" in this chapter).

2. After you select the cells in a row or column, press Del or Backspace. WordPerfect displays the Delete Row or Delete Column dialog box, depending on your selection of cells.

3. In the dialog box, indicate whether you want to delete the entire structure or only the content (text or graphics).

4. Select OK.

Restoring Deleted Rows and Columns

WordPerfect has no special provision for keeping track of deleted rows or columns so that you can restore them later. The only way for you to restore them is to use the Undo feature.

 **Cue:** You cannot delete a column or row structure from one location in the table and restore it to another location.

If you accidentally delete a row or column—both its structure and its content—you can use the Undo feature to restore the lost structure and text to its original location. Note, however, that you cannot delete the structure from one location in the table and restore it to another location.

If you delete only the text from a row or column, you also can use the Undo feature to restore the text to its original location. You cannot use the Undelete feature to restore text you delete in this manner, either to a table or to anywhere else in your document.

WARNING: If you delete a row or column and then proceed to do something else (edit, add text, make deletions, choose another procedure), you won't be able to undo the row or column deletion.

Joining Cells

Suppose that you want the row at the top of your invoice to consist of one cell that extends all the way across the top of the table. You want one cell, rather than the four currently displayed, so that you can include your company name. WordPerfect for Windows enables you to join two or more cells into one.

To join the four cells in the top row of your table, follow these steps:

1. Position the cursor in the top row of the table.

2. Use the mouse to select the four cells in the top row (move the cursor toward the left edge of a cell in that row until you see the arrow pointer, and click twice to select the row).

3. Select **Layout**, **Tables**, **Join** to join the four cells into a single cell (A1) across the top of your table (see fig. 14.16). Note that B1, C1, and D1 no longer exist.

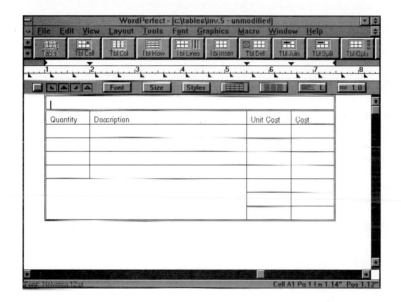

FIG. 14.16

The table with joined cells.

You can use this method to join any number of cells in rows, columns, or blocks. Joined cells become one cell occupying the space formerly taken by the individual cells.

Suppose that in the lower left corner of your invoice, you want a box for comments. Select cells A7, A8, A9, B7, B8, and B9, and follow the preceding steps to join the cells. WordPerfect replaces the six cells you selected with one, large cell (again see fig. 14.16). Any text you enter has to fill the entire cell before the cell expands.

Splitting Cells

WordPerfect also enables you to split a cell into two or more cells. Suppose that you now want to split the top cell into two cells, a small

■ Cue: WordPerfect enables you to split a cell into two or more cells.

cell on the left for a graphic of your company's logo and a longer cell on the right for your company's name and address. Position the cursor anywhere in the top cell, and select **L**ayout, **T**ables, **S**plit. WordPerfect displays the Split Column/Row dialog box (see fig. 14.16), prompting you to specify the number of columns you want. Because you want two columns, type **2** and select OK.

The Split Column/Row dialog box.

WordPerfect divides the top cell into two cells, but the left cell is as wide as the two leftmost columns in the table, and the right cell is as wide as the two rightmost columns. Although WordPerfect splits the cell evenly (two columns worth on each side), the margin between the two new cells matches the margins of adjoining cells (for example, the margin between columns B and C). If the cells have no corresponding margin, the cells are split evenly.

To get the results you want—a small cell on the left and a longer cell on the right—follow these steps:

1. Split the left cell (A1) into two cells. WordPerfect displays three cells in the top row.

2. Join the two right cells (B1 and C1). WordPerfect displays one small cell on the left and one large cell on the right (see fig. 14.18).

You also can split a cell into two or more rows. Simply position the cursor in the cell you want to split, select **L**ayout, **T**ables, **S**plit, and in the Split Column/Row dialog box, select **R**ow and indicate the number of rows you want.

Joining and splitting cells may take some getting used to, but the procedure is easy and the effect can be quite attractive.

Changing Table Lines

Part of the effectiveness of a table is that its lines help the reader better understand the information you present. For tables in which a user needs to fill in information, lines also help the user know where to enter appropriate data.

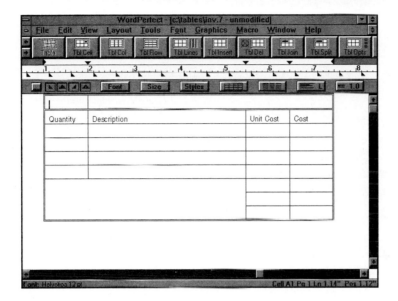

FIG. 14.18

Row 1, split into
a small and a
large cell.

WordPerfect for Windows offers you several options for table lines, other than the default double-line border and single-line cell separators.

Understanding the types of lines in each cell of your table is helpful. By default, each cell has a line on the left and on the top. The cells in the rightmost column also have lines on the right side, and the cells in the bottom row have lines on the bottom side. If you were to "explode" a typical table of three rows and three columns, the cells would look like the cells shown in figure 14.19.

To change the double line at the bottom of the first row in your invoice, therefore, you actually change the top line of the second row. You even can create special effects by using two double lines or by combining a double line and a single line. Using figure 14.19 as a guide, you should be able to change the appropriate cell lines.

Continuing with the invoice example, you change the lines in the table to separate the company logo and address from the rest of the invoice by a thick line. Follow these steps:

1. Position the cursor in the row just below the row containing the address and logo, or row 2.

2. Select the cells in this row.

3. Select **Layout**, **Tables**, **Lines** to display the Table Lines dialog box, which enables you to change the line settings of the selected group of cells (see fig. 14.20).

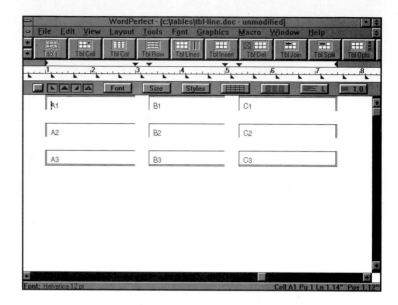

FIG. 14.19

The default lines of cells in an exploded table.

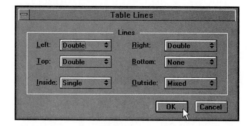

FIG. 14.20

The Table Lines dialog box.

4. To change the top row, click the **T**op button to display the pop-up list of line style options: **N**one, **S**ingle, **D**ouble, **D**ashed, **D**otted, **T**hick, and **E**xtra Thick.

5. Select **T**hick, and then select OK to change the top line in row 2 from a double line to a thick line.

Using this procedure, change the top and right sides of cell A7 to double lines. Notice that this change creates a special effect at the right side of the cell, combining a double line and a single line (see fig. 14.21).

You may find that you want to format text by using the cell margins, but you don't want to see the lines. In your invoice, for example, you want to place your company's logo in cell A1 and use the left side of cell B1 as the left margin for your company's name and address. To turn off the line between the two cells, position the cursor in cell B1 and select **N**one as the left line.

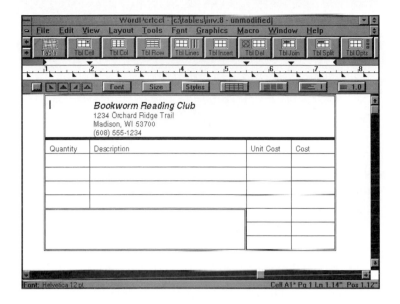

FIG. 14.21

The invoice with modified table lines and the company logo and address added.

As with joining and splitting cells, changing table lines may take some getting used to; however, as you experiment with the different line styles and locations, you will better understand how to use them.

Changing Row Height

WordPerfect automatically determines the amount of vertical space in a row, based on the amount of text in its cells. The cell requiring the most vertical space sets the height for the entire row.

Sometimes, you need to set a specific row height, either to limit the amount of text you can enter in the row's cells or to make sure that a row contains a minimum amount of space whether or not the cells contain data. A good example of this kind of situation is a calendar, in which you may want a fixed row height, such as 1 1/4 inches, regardless of the number of events on any given day (see the sample calendar in "Exploring Other Uses for Tables" in this chapter).

■ **Cue:** You may want to use fixed row heights when creating forms, to ensure that your forms retain their original size and shape.

For this example, you want the top row of your invoice to occupy 2 inches of vertical space, even though the logo and address really need only 1 1/2 inches. To set a specific row height in row 1, follow these steps:

1. Position the cursor in row 1.

2. Select **Layout**, **Tables**, **Row** to display the Format Row dialog box (see fig. 14.22).

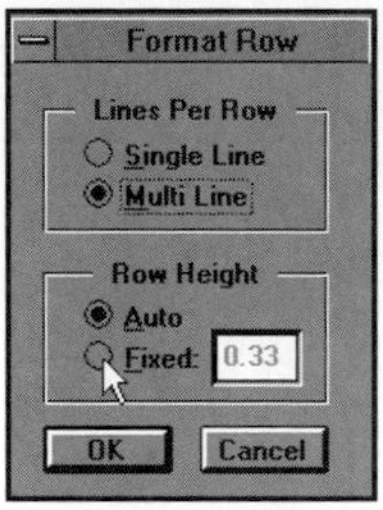

FIG. 14.22

The Format Row
dialog box.

In this dialog box, you can select the following combinations of options:

- **A**uto and **M**ulti Line. This combination, the default, automatically adjusts the row height to accommodate as many lines as are necessary.

- **F**ixed and **M**ulti Line. This combination uses a fixed height and enables you to use multiple lines, but only up to the specified height. You use this combination, for example, when creating a calendar.

- **A**uto and **S**ingle Line. Choosing this combination automatically adjusts the row to accommodate a single line of text, regardless of the text's height (font size). If you choose these options and press Enter from a cell in your table, the cursor automatically moves to the next cell.

- **F**ixed and **S**ingle Line. This combination maintains a fixed height but enables you to enter only one line of text. The font size for that line of text must be small enough to fit into the specified row height.

3. Because you want a fixed height of 2 inches, select **F**ixed and type **2** in the text box. Leave the **M**ulti Line option selected so that you can have as many lines as you need.

4. Select OK to confirm the specified change.

Creating Header Rows

Because tables can consist of up to 32,765 rows, a table may span several pages. If you create a long table, you may want certain information, such as column headings, to repeat at the top of each page. Suppose that in your invoice you want to display the company name and logo and the column headings at the top of each page in case the invoice becomes unusually long and continues on a second page. You put this kind of information in *header rows*.

To create header rows, follow these steps:

1. Position the cursor anywhere inside the table.

2. Select **L**ayout, **T**ables, **O**ptions.

3. In the **A**ttributes section of the Table Options dialog box, type the number of rows you want to designate as header rows in the Header Rows text box.

4. Choose OK to confirm your selection.

You can specify any number of rows as header rows, but WordPerfect always starts counting from row 1. For example, you cannot specify only the second row as a header row.

WordPerfect does not display in the text editing screen the header rows on subsequent pages of the table. When you position the cursor in a header row, the program displays an asterisk (*) on the status bar next to the cell address. To display header rows on subsequent pages, select **F**ile, Print Preview (Shift-F5).

Locking Cells

After you finish setting the attributes for a cell, you can lock the cell to protect it from further changes. To lock a cell, follow these steps:

1. Position the cursor in the cell you want to lock, or select the group of cells you want to lock.

2. Select **L**ayout, **T**ables, **C**ell.

3. In the Cell Attributes section of the Format Cells dialog box, select **L**ock.

4. Select OK to lock the selected cells.

After locking a cell, you cannot enter text into it or modify its contents. To remove cell locks, repeat the preceding steps to deselect the Lock feature.

■ **Cue:** You can lock table cells so that they cannot be modified by anyone.

You can turn off all locks in a table temporarily by selecting **L**ayout, **T**ables, **O**ptions and from the Table Options dialog box, selecting **D**isable Cell Locks. This feature is like a key—it unlocks the cells but leaves the actual locking mechanism in place. After you unlock the cells, you can make any changes you need to the unlocked cells. To deselect this feature and relock the cells, repeat this process.

Positioning Tables

By default, WordPerfect positions tables at the left margin. You can change the position of a table by selecting **L**ayout, **T**ables, **O**ptions. WordPerfect displays the Table Options dialog box, which enables you to position the table at the left margin, at the right margin, in the center, or to extend it fully to both margins. In addition, to position the table a specific distance from the left edge of the paper, you can select **Fro**m Left Edge and enter the distance (again see fig. 14.14).

If your table already extends from margin to margin, selecting **R**ight or Ce**n**ter has no effect. If you select **F**ull and then change your margins or move the table to a location that has different margins, WordPerfect automatically adjusts the table so that it fits within the new margins.

Understanding Table Codes

To complete your knowledge of table structures, you should understand the codes that control the layout of your tables. Using your invoice as an example, position the cursor in cell A1, and press the left-arrow key once. Select **V**iew, **R**eveal Codes (Alt-F3). Figure 14.23 shows the invoice table with the Reveal Codes window open.

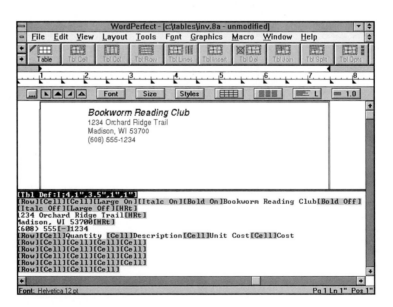

FIG. 14.23

The invoice with codes revealed.

In spite of the many changes you may have made to your table's structure, the Reveal Codes feature displays only three basic table codes:

- [Tbl Def] indicates the table number (each table in your document is numbered sequentially) and the number and width of the table columns.

- [Row] indicates the beginning of a new table row.

- [Cell] indicates the beginning of the contents of a cell.

You cannot delete [Row] and [Cell] codes.

Formatting Table Text

The preceding section focuses primarily on features that help you create the layout, or structure, of a table. You also want to make sure that the text itself contributes to the effectiveness of your presentation. You therefore need to understand text attributes (fonts, boldfacing, italicizing), text alignment, and cell shading.

Understanding Formatting Precedence

Each time you choose a text formatting option, you have to ask yourself whether you are applying it to a column or to a cell (or group of cells). Whether an attribute you assign affects a cell depends on the priority, or precedence. Changes you make to a cell have precedence, or priority, over changes made to columns. For example, if you assign an attribute such as boldface to a cell and then remove that attribute from the column containing that cell, the status of the boldfaced cell is not affected by your adjustment to the column. In the same way, if you right-justify a column and then center one cell in that column, the attribute you apply to the cell (center alignment) overrides the column attribute (right alignment).

Cue: Cell formatting choices take precedence over column attributes.

If you assign attributes globally through the Table Options dialog box, any changes you make to columns or cells do not affect the global attributes; however, global changes do determine the way WordPerfect displays text in all the cells of a table.

Formatting Columns

To modify the text formatting of all cells in a column, position the cursor in any cell in the column and select **L**ayout, **T**ables, Col**u**mn. WordPerfect displays the Format Column dialog box (see fig. 14.24).

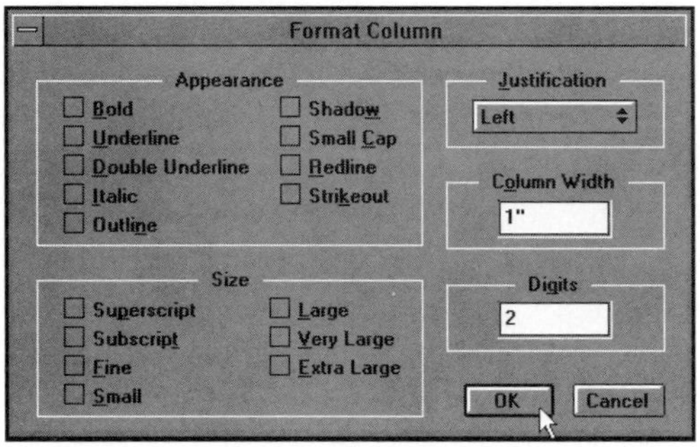

FIG. 14.24

The Format Column dialog box.

T I P To format several columns simultaneously, position the cursor in any cell of the leftmost column of the columns you want to format, and then select that cell and the cells on the same row in each column to the right, that you want to include. Then select **L**ayout, **T**ables, Col**u**mn.

C**o**lumn Width enables you to specify an exact column width, such as for a calendar or a form requiring precise column measurement (for more details, see "Changing Column Widths" in this chapter).

The options in the Appearance section enable you to assign the listed attributes to text entered into any of the cells in the column. These options include Bold, Underline, Double Underline, Italic, Outline, Shadow, Small Cap, Redline, and Strikeout. You can select combinations of attributes; however, whether they print and how they print depends on your printer and printer drivers.

The options in the Size section enable you to specify a variation of the current base font. For example, if your table is formatted in 12-point Helvetica, selecting **L**arge may change the type size to 14 points. For a greater variety of effects, combine Size attributes with Appearance attributes.

Next to column width, justification is perhaps the most commonly needed column format feature. Clicking the Justification button displays a pop-up list of the following justification options:

- Left is the default alignment for most text.

- Right is useful for certain kinds of whole numbers and special treatment of text.

- Center is useful for columns containing data that the reader most likely will scan vertically, such as columns listing "Yes," "No," "N/A," and so on.

- Decimal enables you to align numbers at the decimal point, two digits from the right margin.

- Full should be used sparingly in tables, because text that extends to both margins in relatively narrow columns often has large gaps of white space between words.

Using your invoice as an example, align your columns so that the Quantity column is right-justified and the two Cost columns align at the decimal point. To right-justify the Quantity column, follow these steps:

1. Position the cursor anywhere in column A.

2. Select **L**ayout, **T**ables.

   CUA Press Tables (Ctrl-F9).

3. Select Column to display the Format Column dialog box.

4. Click the Justification button and select Right from the pop-up list.

5. Select OK to right-justify the column.

To align both Cost columns at the decimal point, position the cursor anywhere in column C. Select column C and column D. Then, select **L**ayout, **T**ables, Column to display the Format Column dialog box. Click the Justification button and select Decimal from the pop-up list. Select OK to align the selected columns at the decimal point.

Note that the column headings now assume the new column alignments, as does text or numbers you type into any cell in these columns. Also note that in decimal-aligned columns, WordPerfect displays the message Align char = . on the left side of the status bar to indicate that as you enter text, the program right-justifies it on the left side of the decimal; as soon as you type a period, WordPerfect removes the message and, as you enter text, left-justifies text on the right side of the decimal point.

By default, WordPerfect displays two digits after the decimal point. To change this setting, simply enter a new number in the Digits text box of the Format Column dialog box (again see fig. 14.24). The Digits option affects only columns or cells formatted for decimal alignment.

Formatting Cells

After you format a column of cells, you may find that you need to change the justification or attributes of a single cell or a group of cells within that column. For example, although the two price columns in your invoice now align text at the decimal point, the headings in these columns would look better if they were right-justified, which means that you need to change the formatting of the two cells containing these headings. Remember that cell formatting takes precedence over column formatting.

To change the format of a single cell, position the cursor in the cell and select **L**ayout, **T**ables. Then select **C**ell to display the Format Cell dialog box (see fig. 14.25).

The Format Cell dialog box.

Some of the options in the Format Cell dialog box are similar to the options in the Format Column dialog box, especially the Appearance, Size, and Justification options

To change the format of a group of cells, select the desired cells before you access and select options from the Format Cell dialog box. For example, right-justify the column headings in columns C and D of your invoice by first selecting the cells containing the headings and then selecting **L**ayout, **T**ables. Select **C**ell to display the Format Cell dialog box, and select **R**ight from the Justification pop-up list. Choose OK to change the cell format.

One option in the Format Cell dialog box that you do not find among the column options is Alignment, which enables you to specify the vertical position of the text in a cell: at the top (default), centered, or at the bottom. This option does not enable you to change the way WordPerfect displays text in the document editing window; text always appears at the top of a cell. Alignment does, however, properly align text in Print Preview and in printed tables.

Three other options (in the Cell Attributes area) apply only to cell formatting: Shading, Lock, and Ignore Cell When Calculating.

Shading adds a gray background to a cell. To shade all the column heading cells in your invoice, first select the four cells. Then select **L**ayout, **T**ables, **C**ell to display the Format Cell dialog box, and select **Sh**ading. Before you close the dialog box, also select **B**old to further emphasize the column headers. Then choose OK to apply the format changes, which you can see in figure 14.26.

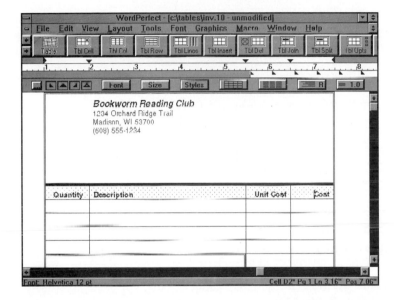

FIG. 14.26

The invoice with new cell attributes.

The Lock option, which protects a cell from being altered, is explained in "Locking Cells" in this chapter. The Ignore Cell When Calculating option enables you to exclude the numbers in selected cells from any math calculations that WordPerfect performs on the table. If you select this option, WordPerfect reads the numbers as text instead of numbers (see "Using Table Math" in this chapter, for more information about using this option).

When you first select the Format Cell dialog box, both the Use Column Justification option and the Use Column Size and Appearance option are checked because the selected cells are using the attributes you applied to the column. If you select an attribute that differs from the column justification format, WordPerfect automatically turns off Use Column Justification; similarly, the program turns off Use Column Size and Appearance if you select an option under Appearance or Size in the Format Cell dialog box. To reassign the column defaults, click Use Column Justification or Use Column Size and Appearance. WordPerfect automatically turns off any cell attributes that conflict with the default column formats.

Setting Global Table Options

You set certain options globally for all cells, regardless of the settings you choose in the Format Column or Format Cell dialog boxes. To display the Table Options dialog box, select **L**ayout, **T**ables, **O**ptions (see fig. 14.27).

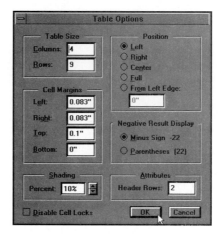

FIG. 14.27

The Table
Options dialog
box.

Three of the options in this dialog box—Table Size, Position, and Attributes (Header Rows)—relate to table structure (see "Editing the Table Structure" in this chapter).

The other options enable you to specify how you want to display information in each cell in your table. For example, each cell is somewhat like a miniature document because each cell has its own margins. If you find that you cannot fit text or a graphic into a cell the way you want it to fit, you can reduce the *cell margins*, which is the space between the cell lines and the text.

If you are using the math feature, you can choose to display negative numbers in parentheses or with a minus sign. If you select shading as a cell attribute, you can specify how dark you want that shading. You cannot, however, specify different shading percentages for shaded cells in the same table.

T I P   Gray shading looks best in a range of 5 percent to 25 percent. If you make your cells any darker, text becomes difficult to read. To black out a cell entirely, select 100 percent shading.

Using Table Math

If you use spreadsheet programs, you probably have noticed the similarity between WordPerfect's tables and a typical spreadsheet layout. In fact, WordPerfect tables "enjoy" a certain amount of mathematical wizardry. Although you cannot create complex formulas, you can use the four basic math operators (addition, subtraction, multiplication, and division) and general balance sheet math functions (Subtotal, Total, and Grand Total) to create formulas.

You add several of these mathematical functions to the sample invoice. When you finish, you will have a table that multiplies quantities times price, adds extended prices, and calculates the sales tax.

Creating Formulas

The first formula you need in your invoice is one that multiplies the quantity in column A and the unit price in column C, and places the product in column D.

Notice that column A cells contain both numbers and letters; Word-Perfect uses only the numbers in a cell for purposes of its calculations. If a cell has more than one line, the program uses the numbers in only the first line. If more than one number is on the first line, WordPerfect combines them, ignoring letters and punctuation. For example, WordPerfect reads 224EXT-5 as 2245. The numbers that WordPerfect uses constitute the value of the cell.

To create the formula, position the cursor in cell D3. Select **L**ayout, **T**ables, Formula. WordPerfect displays the Tables Formula dialog box (see fig. 14.28).

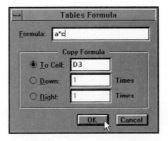

Formulas include cell addresses, such as A3, B3, and so on, and math operators, such as addition (+), subtraction (-), multiplication (*), and division (/). In your invoice, you want to multiply the quantity in cell A3 by the unit price in C3, so you type **A3*C3** in the Formula text box.

CAUTION: Be careful not to include spaces or any other punctuation in the formula; otherwise, WordPerfect displays the message Illegal Character(s). You can, however, use lowercase letters.

WordPerfect follows the usual algebraic order of precedence to calculate formulas. Material within parentheses is calculated first. The calculation moves from left to right. For example, 17–5*2 yields 24, whereas 17–(5*2) gives you 7.

The first time you create a formula, you must copy it from the dialog box to the cell by using the To Cell option (the default). You can change the destination cell by specifying a different cell address in the To Cell text box, although if you have followed the preceding procedures, D3 is already displayed. When your formula and destination cell are correct, select OK to copy the formula to your table.

After you select OK, WordPerfect displays in cell D3 the product of the numbers in A3 and C3 (see fig. 14.29). Also, immediately following the equal sign (=) on the left side of the status bar, the program displays the formula that generates the number in cell D3.

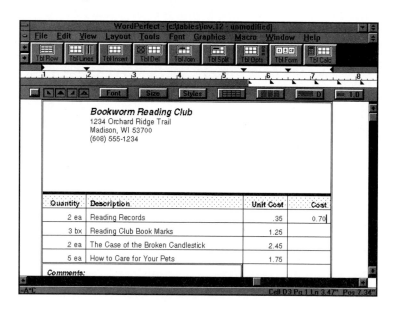

FIG. 14.29

The invoice with a formula in column D.

T I P

You can use only letters to define a formula, and WordPerfect automatically uses the current row number when it calculates the formula. For example, entering the formula **A*C** with the cursor in row 3 is the same as entering **A3*C3**.

Copying Formulas

The formula you need for cells D4, D5, and D6 is the same as the one you just created in cell D3. Rather than creating three new formulas, you can copy the formula from cell D3 to these three cells.

Using your invoice as an example, position the cursor in cell D3, which contains the formula you just created. Select Layout, Tables, Formula. In the Tables Formula dialog box (again see fig. 14.28), WordPerfect shows the formula you assigned to cell D3; leave this formula as is. Select **Down** and type **3** in the text box to specify that you want to copy the formula to the three cells beneath the current one. Select OK to copy the formula to cells D4, D5, and D6.

Move the cursor down one cell to D4 and note the formula displayed on the status bar. When you copy a formula, WordPerfect automatically changes the row or column references to match the new cell location. This process is called *relative cell referencing*. For example, the formula A3*C3 in row 3 automatically becomes A4*C4 when you copy it to row 4.

Cue: WordPerfect provides relative cell referencing to facilitate accurate copying of formulas.

If you were to insert a new row between rows 3 and 4, WordPerfect automatically would change the row references in the formula in the new rows 5, 6, and 7 to reflect their new location.

CAUTION: Just because WordPerfect calculates values, do not assume that the answers are correct. You sometimes may enter an incorrect formula. Always check your results.

Using Totaling Functions

Now that you have a list of extended prices, you need to generate a subtotal of the purchases listed on your invoice before you add the tax and generate a total.

WordPerfect provides three totaling functions: Subtotal, Total, and Grand Total. Each of the following characters, when used alone in a formula, becomes a function and has the following effects:

- The + symbol displays the Subtotal of all values between it and any preceding + symbol in the same column.

- The = symbol displays the Total of all subtotals between it and any preceding = symbol in the same column.

- The * symbol displays the Grand Total of all preceding totals in the same column.

Note that if you have only one set of numbers to total, you must use the + symbol to subtotal them; you cannot generate a total unless you have at least one subtotal. Likewise, you cannot generate a grand total unless you have at least one total.

To enter a totaling function as a formula, follow these steps:

1. Position the cursor in the cell where you want to provide a Subtotal. In your invoice, position the cursor in cell D7.

2. Select **L**ayout, **T**ables.

    Press Layout Tables (Ctrl-F9).

3. Select **F**ormula and type + in the text box.

4. Choose OK to enter the Subtotal function into the cell.

Creating Tax and Total Formulas

To make your invoice completely functional, you need two more formulas: one that calculates a tax and another that adds the tax to the subtotal.

To create a formula to calculate the tax, follow these steps:

1. Position the cursor in cell D8, the cell directly under the Subtotal in your invoice.

2. Select **L**ayout, **T**ables.

    Press Layout Tables (Ctrl-F9).

3. Select **F**ormula, and type **D7*.05** in the Formula text box (for a 5 percent sales tax).

4. Choose OK to enter the tax formula into the cell.

To generate a final total in cell D9 of your invoice, your first thought probably is to use the Total function (=). Because the Total function adds only the subtotals that precede it, however, WordPerfect would exclude the tax from the final total. Instead, create a formula that adds the numbers in the subtotal and tax cells, as follows:

1. Position the cursor in cell D9, cell directly under the tax in your invoice.

2. Select **L**ayout, **T**ables.

   CUA Press Layout Tables (Ctrl-F9).

3. Select **F**ormula, and type **D7+D8** in the Formula text box.

4. Choose OK to enter the formula into the cell (see fig. 14.30).

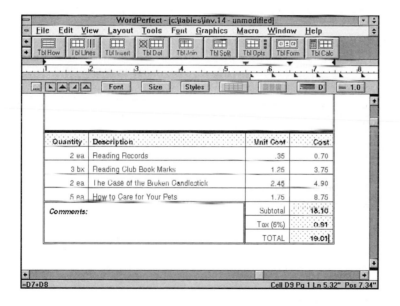

FIG. 14.30

The invoice with all formulas added.

Calculating and Changing Values

When you add a formula, WordPerfect uses the values of the formula's referenced cells to calculate the result. If you change the values of any of the referenced cells, you must recalculate the table to correct the formulas or totals.

For example, you learn from your distributor that the price of a box of bookmarks has gone up from $1.25 to $1.75. In your invoice, edit the unit price cell to reflect the price change. Note that the extended price and totals do not change.

To recalculate a table, select **L**ayout, **T**ables. Then select C**a**lculate to update the table.

If you make many changes to your tables, consider adding the Table Calculate button (Tbl Calc) to your Button Bar.

You may create other cells that contain numbers, but you don't want to include the value of those cells in a subtotal. For example, in your invoice, you want to place an invoice number at the top of column D, but you don't want the program to add the invoice number to the subtotal. You need to select the option that enables you to ignore the cell when calculating (see "Formatting Cells" in this chapter, for details on selecting this option).

If you tell WordPerfect to ignore a cell that is referenced specifically in the formula of another cell, that formula, because it cannot complete its calculation, displays ?? when you recalculate the table. If you tell WordPerfect to ignore a cell that contains a formula, the program does not calculate that formula.

Deleting and Modifying Formulas

If you determine that you no longer need a formula, simply deleting the numbers in the cell does not delete the formula. Instead, you must select the cell and then press Backspace or Del.

If you want to modify the formula, position the cursor in the cell that contains the formula you want to modify and select **L**ayout, **T**ables, **F**ormula. Correct the formula in the Formula text box, and select OK to enter the change in the cell.

Cue: Lock cells that contain formulas in order to prevent changes.

To prevent yourself or someone else from accidentally deleting or overwriting the information in a cell that contains a formula, consider locking the cell (see "Locking Cells" in this chapter). Locking cells with formulas has the added advantage that when you move the cursor to a locked cell, the cursor slips over the locked cell to the next unlocked cell, making data entry quicker and easier.

Creating and Using Tables: The Next Step

Using the procedures you have learned so far, you are ready to create and use nearly any kind of table. In this section you learn some of the special procedures you can use to create tables from existing text and spreadsheets, and you learn how to enhance the look and functionality of your tables with certain advanced features, such as sorting, graphics, merging, and cross-referencing.

This section also provides some examples of what you can do with tables. Even if you don't take the time to learn all the procedures, you should scan the sample figures to see the kinds of table applications that are available with WordPerfect for Windows and that you may use sometime.

Converting Tabular Columns to Tables

You may have existing text you want to place in a table; however, you don't want to retype the text. Fortunately, WordPerfect provides a method for creating a table from text that is formatted in tabular or parallel columns.

Suppose that you have a list of company employees that includes their names, offices, and telephone numbers. The columns of data are separated by single tabs (see fig. 14.31).

Jones, Mary	C361	5-4987
Adams, Bill	B221	5-4999
Hanson, Marge	C377	5-4984

FIG. 14.31

A list formatted in tabular columns.

To convert data in tabular columns to a table, follow these steps:

1. Position the cursor at the beginning of the first line of data. Using the employee list as an example, move the cursor just before the letter *J* in *Jones*.

2. Press F8 and move the cursor to the end of the last line of data (or use the mouse). In this example, select the data to just after the number *4* in *5-4984*. Don't include the final transaction, or you will end up with an extra row in your table.

3. Select **Layout, Tables**.

   CUA Press Layout Tables (Ctrl-F9).

4. Select **Create** to display the Convert Table dialog box (see fig. 14.32).

FIG. 14.32

The Convert
Table dialog
box.

5. Select **T**abular Column (the default), and choose OK.

WordPerfect converts your tabular data to a table (see fig. 14.33).

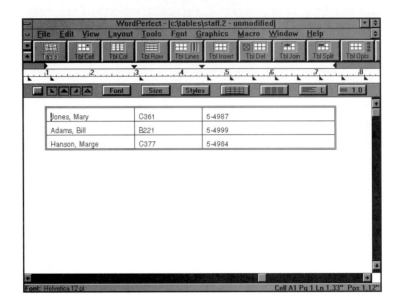

FIG. 14.33

A table con-
verted from
tabular columns.

This procedure seems easy because it is easy; however, the key to converting tabular columns successfully to a table lies in the format of the
original text. Make sure that each column is aligned by a tab setting
that aligns each column correctly. Also make sure that only one tab
separates columns of data. If, for example, you use WordPerfect's default half-inch tab settings and use two tabs to separate the office numbers from the short employee names, but use only one tab to separate
office numbers from the long names, WordPerfect adds extra cells in
the table for the blank tabs, and the result can be quite messy.

Sorting Tables

Although your table looks good, the employee names are not in alphabetical order. WordPerfect enables you easily to sort the data in a table (see Chapter 22, "Sorting and Selecting Data," for more details on this procedure).

To sort a table, simply position the cursor anywhere in the table and select **Tools, S**ort. WordPerfect displays the Sort dialog box, which enables you to select from many alternatives. The default settings alphabetically sort the first word in the first column. Select OK to sort the table.

Unfortunately, WordPerfect sorts the table text and the table lines together. After you complete a sort, therefore, you may have to redefine the lines in one or more cells, even though the names are sorted properly (see "Changing Table Lines" in this chapter for details on redefining lines).

If you want to sort only some of the rows in a table—for example, if you don't want to include your header rows in the sort—select the desired rows before you access the Sort dialog box.

Converting Parallel Columns to Tables

Sometimes your table rows need to be different depths because you have varying amounts of data in the different rows or columns. In early versions of WordPerfect for DOS (5.0 and before), the only way to create columns of data with irregular rows of data was to use the Parallel Columns feature. This feature enables its users to create columns that look like a table you can create with WordPerfect for Windows, but without the table lines (see fig. 14.34).

To convert to a table the data in parallel columns, follow these steps:

1. Position the cursor at the beginning of the first row of the data (for example, just before the letter *S* in *Speaker*).

2. Press F8 and move the cursor to the end of the last row of the data (you also can use the mouse to select the data). (For this example, position the cursor just after the quotation mark following the word *training.*)

3. Select **L**ayout, **T**ables, **C**reate.

4. From the Convert Table dialog box (again see fig. 14.32), select **P**arallel Column, and choose OK.

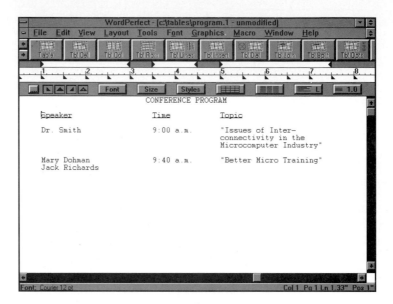

FIG. 14.34

Columns created
with the Parallel
Columns feature.

WordPerfect then converts your tabular data to a table (see fig. 14.35).

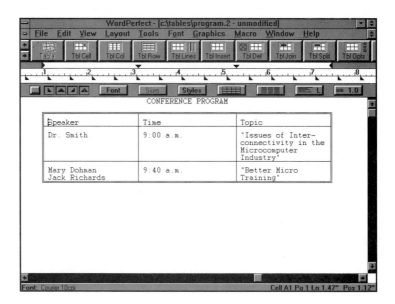

FIG. 14.35

A table con-
verted from
parallel columns.

T I P

To convert a table to parallel columns, select **F**ile, Save **A**s (F3), specify a new document name, and select WordPerfect 5.0 as the file format. WordPerfect saves the table in a Parallel Columns format.

Importing a Spreadsheet to a Table

Spreadsheets have the same kind of layout as tables. Converting a spreadsheet to a table is as simple as opening or retrieving the spreadsheet just as you open or retrieve any other document.

■ **Cue:** You can convert spreadsheets from other programs into WordPerfect tables.

When you convert a spreadsheet to a table, the spreadsheet's blank cells and rows convert to blank cells in your table, as shown in figure 14.36. In addition, after conversion, you may have to change column widths, fonts, and so on, in your table.

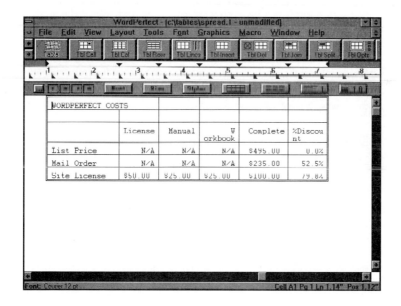

FIG. 14.36

A spreadsheet converted to a table.

The following limitations exist, however, when converting spreadsheets to tables:

- The spreadsheet must be compatible with Lotus 1-2-3 or PlanPerfect. Most other spreadsheet programs have the capability to save spreadsheets as Lotus 1-2-3 compatible files.

- The spreadsheet should fit within your page margins. If the spreadsheet is too wide, WordPerfect displays `Warning: Table extends beyond right margin` on the status bar. Although WordPerfect converts and imports the spreadsheet, unless you reduce the size of the resulting table, the data that extends beyond the right margin does not print.

- Formulas do not convert; you import only the data you see on-screen in your spreadsheet program.

For more information on importing spreadsheets, see Chapter 31, "Importing Data and Working with Other Programs."

Adding Graphics to a Table

Each cell of a table is a self-contained miniature document, and you can place both graphics and text within a cell, just as you do in a document (see Chapter 7, "Introduction to Graphics" for details about creating a graphics box in your document).

Suppose that you want to add a WordPerfect graphic to the upper left corner of your invoice. Follow these steps:

1. Position the cursor in cell A1, which is where you want to place the image.

2. Select **G**raphics, **U**ser, **C**reate, and indicate that you want to use the Figure Editor. (Note that you select **U**ser only because, by default, this graphics box has no border lines.)

3. In the Figure Editor, select **F**ile, **R**etrieve, and then select the graphics file BOOKWORM.WPG.

4. Make any editing changes you want. For this example, select **E**dit, **M**irror to reverse the image horizontally.

5. Select **F**ile, **B**ox Position, and select Full Margins for the Horizontal Position to place the graphic evenly between the two margins of cell A1.

6. Select **F**ile, **C**lose to place the graphic in the table cell (see fig. 14.37).

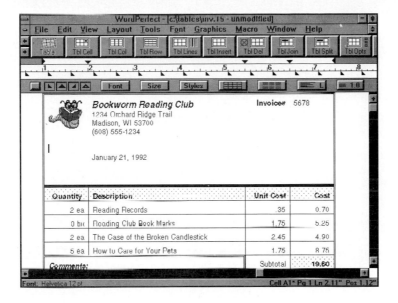

FIG. 14.37

The invoice
with a graphic
image.

To get the results you want, you may have to experiment further,
adjusting the size of the graphic and its position.

 CAUTION: You should save your document before adding graphics, as you should before performing any complex procedure. Then, if you need to, you can go back to your
original table and begin again.

Creating Forms with Irregular Columns

You sometimes may want to use tables to create forms that have somewhat irregular columns throughout the table. You can split and join
cells to accomplish the task, but you must remember that WordPerfect
splits and joins cells along existing column lines. An easier method for
creating a form containing unusually irregular columns is to create two
separate tables, one immediately above the other, resulting in what
looks like one, single table.

For example, to create a form that begins with three columns, then
changes to four, follow these steps:

1. Create the first table, with three columns and as many rows as you want.

2. Position the cursor immediately after the table you just created.

3. Create the second table, with four columns and as many rows as you want.

4. Change the bottom line of the last row in the first table to None. Select **L**ayout, **T**ables, **L**ines, **B**ottom, None.

5. Change the top line of the first row in the second table to Single, which makes the two tables look like they are joined as one (see fig. 14.38).

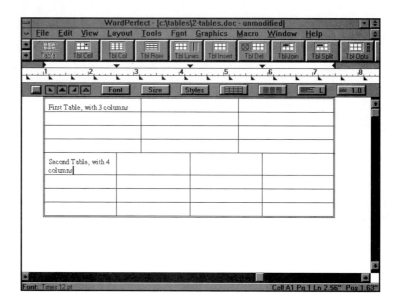

Two tables that look like one.

Note that in figure 14.38, the cursor seems to be in row 5 of the table, but as shown on the status bar, it actually is in cell A1 of the second table.

Placing Tables Side-by-Side

■ **Cue:** To create side-by-side tables, use graphics table boxes and the Text Box Editor.

In the normal body of text of a WordPerfect document, you cannot place two tables side-by-side. Instead, you must create two graphics table boxes and position them side-by-side. You create the actual tables inside the table boxes by using the Text Box Editor.

To create side-by-side tables, follow these steps:

1. Select **G**raphics, **T**able Box, **C**reate, and from the Select Editor dialog box, select **T**ext Editor.

2. Click the Box **P**osition button.

3. Select Margin **L**eft from the **H**orizontal Position pop-up list.

4. In the Size area, set the **W**idth at half the distance between your margins, probably about 3 1/4 inches if you have 1-inch margins on an 8 1/2-inch page.

5. Create the table, using the steps you have learned for creating a table.

   Alternatively, you can close the box for now and come back to the Editor later to create the table.

6. Select Close to place the table box in your document.

7. To create the second table box, repeat the preceding steps, selecting Margin, **R**ight from the **H**orizontal Position pop-up list and setting the desired table **W**idth (again, probably about 3 1/4 inches).

If you don't want the thick top and bottom table box borders that WordPerfect adds by default, position the cursor before the first table box, and select **G**raphics, **T**able Box, **O**ptions. From the Border Styles area of the dialog box, select **N**one from the **T**op pop-up list and **N**one from the **B**ottom pop-up list. Choose OK to make the changes.

Repeat this procedure to finish the second table box.

Placing Tables in Newspaper Columns

WordPerfect does not enable you to create tables in newspaper columns; however, you can create a table box in a newspaper column, such as the table shown in figure 14.39.

To place a table in a newspaper column, follow these steps:

1. Define and create your columns (see Chapter 13, "Working with Text Columns," for this instruction).

2. Position the cursor where you want to create the table.

3. Select **G**raphics, **T**able Box, **C**reate, and in the Select Editor dialog box, indicate that you want to use the Text Editor.

Cue: When measurements are critical, as they are when creating side-by-side tables, set your margins and select your Document Initial Font *before* creating the table boxes.

By default, your table box fills only the right half of the column. If you want to change the position or size of the table box within the column, do so before creating the table; for example, select **B**ox Position and change the Horizontal Position to Margin, **F**ull.

4. Select **L**ayout, **T**ables, **C**reate; then specify the columns and rows you need, and select OK.

5. Edit your table as you edit any table you create.

6. Select Close to place the table box and your table in your columns.

For more information on positioning graphics boxes, see Chapter 17, "Understanding Advanced Graphics."

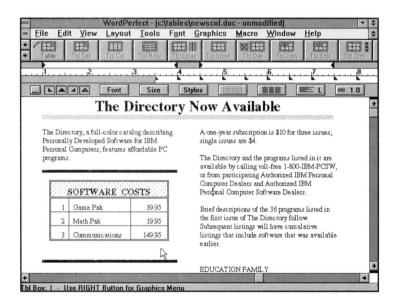

FIG. 14.39

A table box in a
newspaper
column.

Cross-Referencing Tables

If you use WordPerfect's Cross-Reference feature in a document, you must keep in mind that WordPerfect sequentially numbers both tables and table boxes in the same numbering scheme (I, II, III, and so on). For example, a table that follows a table box is numbered II. You cross-reference a table the same way you cross-reference a graphics table box (see Chapter 25, "Assembling Other Document References," for a detailed discussion of the Cross-Reference feature).

Using Merge Codes with Tables

You can place Merge codes in tables, just as you can in normal text. You thus can create forms that, when merged, either prompt the operator for input or merge data from a secondary merge file, or both (see Chapter 21, "Assembling Documents with Merge"). This process sometimes is called "Forms Fill-in" because the predesigned but incomplete form is filled in automatically by WordPerfect or by the operator.

Cue: Use Merge codes in tables to create forms to be filled in.

Using your invoice form as an example, suppose that you want to change the form so that WordPerfect automatically inserts the date, prompts the operator for the invoice number, and calculates the invoice before printing. You add merge codes in the appropriate cells of the table and then save the master form under an easily identifiable name, such as INVOICE.FRM. Refer to Chapter 21, "Assembling Documents with Merge," for complete instructions for using this WordPerfect feature.

In addition, you can create simple macros to automate such merges (see Chapter 20, "Creating Macros"), and you can put these macros on your Button Bar (see Chapter 19, "Using the Button Bar"). For example, if you create an Invoice button that uses a merge macro, when you click the Invoice button, WordPerfect automatically retrieves the invoice form and prompts you for the necessary information.

BUTTON

Exploring Other Uses for Tables

WordPerfect's Tables feature is so rich that describing all the tasks you can accomplish with it would be impossible. The following samples, however, may give you some ideas. Each is accompanied with a brief description of procedures you need to understand. For most procedures, however, you should refer to the previous sections in this chapter.

Calendars

A good use for a table is a personal calendar. Determine first whether you want your calendar in portrait or landscape orientation. Remember that most dot-matrix printers cannot print landscape text. Set your margins, and then divide by seven the available space between the margins to determine how much room you have for each day of the week. If you need more room, reduce your margins or the size of your font.

Create the table with 7 columns and 5 rows (usually). Select all the cells in a column and select **L**ayout, **T**ables, **R**ow. Specify a fixed height, multiple-line row, and enter the vertical measurement you want (for example, **1.50″**). If you want to change the width of any of the columns, select **L**ayout, **T**ables, Col**u**mn, and specify the width you want.

Save the blank form so that you can use it again. Then add the month, dates, and events; save this form under a different name; and print it (see fig. 14.40 for an example of a printed calendar).

JANUARY 1992

SUN	MON	TUE	WED	THU	FRI	SAT
			1 New Year's Day Happy New Year!!	2	3	4
5	6	7	8	9	10	11
12	13	14	15	16	17	18
19	20	21	22	23	24	25
26	27	28	29	30	31	

FIG. 14.40

A sample calendar created with the Tables feature.

Phone Message Forms

A practical example of a form you can prepare with the Tables feature and then distribute on paper is a phone message form. If the standard office-supply forms don't meet your needs, use WordPerfect's Tables feature to create your own (see fig. 14.41 for an example).

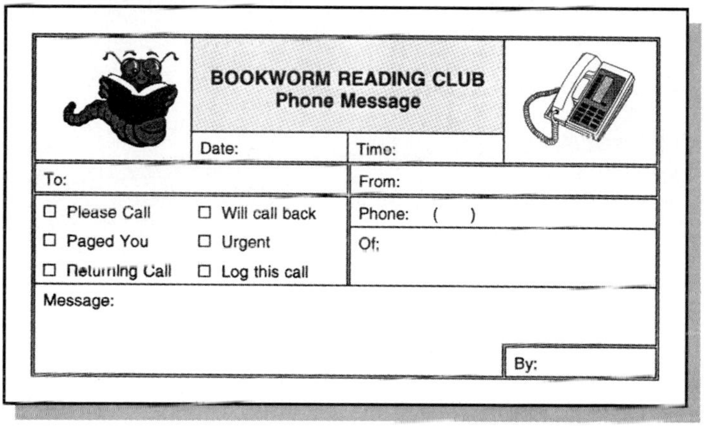

BOOKWORM READING CLUB
Phone Message

Date: Time:
To: From:
☐ Please Call ☐ Will call back Phone: ( )
☐ Paged You ☐ Urgent Of:
☐ Returning Call ☐ Log this call
Message:
By:

FIG. 14.41

A sample phone message form.

Remember that you want your forms (and tables) to be both functional and attractive. The advantage to creating your forms with WordPerfect is that you can test several versions of a form on the people who will use the form, before printing a large quantity of forms.

Other possible uses for tables are order forms (similar to the invoice you created in this chapter) and even crossword puzzles.

Chapter Summary

In this chapter, you have learned about the Tables feature, one of WordPerfect's most powerful and useful features. At some point, nearly everyone needs to create a table, a form, a calendar, or a report that contains a spreadsheet. With the Tables feature, you can perform all these tasks, and more.

You have learned to create tables consisting of any number of rows and columns, to enter text and move within a table, and to delete its cells, rows, and columns. You also have learned in this chapter how to change the structure, or layout, of the table by changing its column widths, by joining and splitting its cells, and by modifying its lines. You now can format text, using attributes, alignment, and shading for effect, and you can use formulas for performing math calculations. Finally, you learned how to use advanced features to create complex forms.

PART

IV

OUTLINE

Producing
Professional
Output

Working with Advanced
   Printing Techniques

Using Lines To Add Effects

Understanding Advanced
   Graphics

Desktop Publishing with
   WordPerfect

Working with Advanced Printing Techniques

C hapter 9, "Basic Printing," discusses basic printer use in WordPerfect—installing and setting up printer drivers, using Print Preview, and general printing. Chapter 10, "Working with Fonts," details how to install and select different fonts in WordPerfect. This chapter focuses on the following advanced WordPerfect printing topics:

- Creating and selecting custom paper definitions
- Printing on envelopes
- Creating and printing labels
- Using the Advance feature
- Using options from the Typesetting dialog box (such as kerning, leading, letterspacing, and printer commands) to improve text appearance

■ **Eric Mark Rintell** is a computer consultant who enjoys advising clients about WordPerfect. He enjoys print-related topics so much that he wrote much of the print-related material in this book.

The chapter is arranged so that you can skip to the topics that interest you.

CAUTION: Most features described in this chapter function only when you have selected a WordPerfect 5.1 printer driver. Before you continue reading this chapter, choose File, Select Printer to access the Select Printer dialog box. Verify that the WordPerfect option is selected and the Print dialog box displays the current printer. If you are using a Windows printer driver, refer to "Using Paper Definitions with Windows Printer Drivers," later in this chapter.

Using the Paper Size Feature

As you become more comfortable with using different fonts and with printing, you may want to print on envelopes, labels, legal-size paper, and so on. You use the Paper Size feature to tell WordPerfect the type of paper and the page orientation you want to use.

This section of the chapter describes the general process for creating and editing a paper definition and includes some specific examples. Print samples in this chapter were printed on an HP LaserJet III laser printer; options and printouts shown may differ for your printer. Some menu options may not be available for a dot-matrix, daisywheel, or inkjet printer.

In the following sections, you learn how to use custom paper definitions and how to print on envelopes and labels.

Creating and Editing Paper Definitions

Each WordPerfect printer driver contains predefined *paper definitions* for the specified printer. If you use a laser printer, for example, the printer driver defines appropriate default print settings for a standard 8 1/2-by-11-inch page (portrait), an 11-by-8 1/2-inch page (landscape), and an envelope (4-by-9 1/2 inches).

If you need to print on a different size envelope or sheet of paper, you must create a new paper definition to define the layout of the paper on which you want to print. The capacity to create a new paper definition is a powerful tool because WordPerfect can support any size or type of paper you can use with your printer.

If you are adding a definition for a paper size you will not use often, read this section but edit the [All Others] paper definition (see "Using the [All Others] Definition," later in this chapter) instead of creating a new definition.

Following are the basic steps for creating a paper definition:

1. Choose **L**ayout, **P**age.

   CUA Press Page (Alt-F9).

2. Choose Paper **S**ize. The Paper Size dialog box opens, as shown in figure 15.1. Notice that your current printer is listed in the upper left corner of the dialog box.

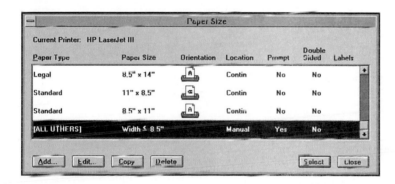

The Paper Size dialog box.

3. Choose **A**dd. The Add Paper Size dialog box opens, as shown in figure 15.2.

The Add Paper Size dialog box.

4. Choose the appropriate options for the paper size you are adding (options are described in the following sections).

5. Choose OK to close the Add Paper Size dialog box.

   Your new paper definition now is listed in the Paper Size dialog box with the options you chose.

6. To begin using the new paper definition, highlight the definition and choose **S**elect; otherwise, choose Close to exit from the Paper Size dialog box.

■ **Cue:** If you have an existing paper definition similar to the definition you want to create, copy the existing definition and edit it.

Editing an existing paper definition is similar to adding a paper definition. To edit a paper definition, follow these steps:

1. Choose **L**ayout, **P**age.

     Press Page (Alt-F9).

2. Choose Paper **S**ize. The Paper Size dialog box opens.

3. Choose **E**dit. The Edit Paper Size dialog box opens; the options in this dialog box are the same as the options in the Add Paper Size dialog box (again see fig. 15.2).

4. Change the options as necessary (options are described in the following sections).

5. Choose OK to close the Edit Paper Size dialog box.

6. Choose Close to close the Paper Size dialog box.

The following sections detail the options in the Add Paper Size and Edit Paper Size dialog boxes and describe how these options affect your paper definitions.

Paper Location

The Paper Location options tell WordPerfect how to feed paper to the printer.

To specify the type of paper feed, choose the Location option and select the appropriate choice from the displayed list. If you place paper in your printer one sheet at a time (for example, envelopes, transparencies, and so on), choose the **M**anual option. Choose the **C**ontinuous option if you have a tractor-feed printer (for example, a dot-matrix or daisywheel printer) or a paper cassette or sheet feeder printer (for example, a laser or inkjet printer). If your printer can take paper from more than one source (for example, more than one paper cassette or sheet-feeder bin), choose **B**in for the Location option; then specify the desired bin in the Bin Number text box.

If you select the **P**rompt to Load Paper option, WordPerfect will remind you to load the correct paper in your printer *before* printing. A dialog box appears, listing the printer port and the type of paper to load. (Fig. 15.3 shows an example of the dialog box.) Place the paper in the printer and choose OK; WordPerfect prints the document. The dialog box may look different, depending on the printer port, paper type, and whether the Windows Print Manager is active.

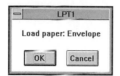

If the Prompt to Load Paper option is deselected, WordPerfect assumes that you have loaded the paper before printing.

Paper Orientation

You can print in portrait or landscape orientation. *Portrait orientation* means that the text is oriented parallel to the short side of the page. *Landscape orientation* means that the text is oriented parallel to the long side of the paper. Refer to figures 15.1 and 15.2 to see the difference between portrait and landscape orientation (shown in the position of the letter A in the printer icons). An upright A represents portrait orientation. A sideways A represents landscape orientation.

To specify portrait printing in the Add Paper Size dialog box, click one of the top Paper Orientation icons; for landscape printing, click one of the bottom Paper Orientation icons. If you don't have a mouse but want to print in landscape format, choose Rotated Font (selected automatically if you click a landscape icon).

The two Paper Orientation icons on the left represent normal printers and the icons on the right represent wide-carriage printers (notice that the "pages" shown in the right-hand icons are wider than those in the left-hand icons). You can choose wide paper by clicking one of the right-hand buttons or by choosing **W**ide Form. *Note:* Don't use this option unless you have a printer that can print on sheets of paper wider than 8 1/2 inches.

CAUTION: Don't select a landscape orientation if your printer isn't capable of landscape printing, because the printer will not print correctly. If you are unsure about your printer's capabilities, check its specifications in the printer manual.

Paper Size

Cue: If you choose a landscape form, WordPerfect automatically selects landscape orientation for you.

With the Paper Size option, you can use one of the predefined paper sizes (**St**andard, **St**and Land, **L**egal, Legal La**n**d, **E**nvelope, **H**alf Sheet, US Government, **A**4, or A4 Land) or specify custom dimensions. The dimensions for the predefined paper sizes (representing how the paper is fed to the printer) are listed to the right of each size in the pop-up list.

If you don't find the paper size you need in the predefined list, choose **O**ther and enter your own paper size. Enter a height and width that are smaller than your top and side margin settings, respectively. (You cannot specify a setting equal to or greater than your current margin settings because the margins will not fit inside the custom paper size. You cannot enter a paper size of 2 inches wide by 10 inches high, for example, because the default margin space takes 2 inches, leaving no room to print text.)

T I P When you enter width and height, keep in mind the direction in which paper is fed into your printer.

Paper Type

Use the Paper **T**ype option to give a descriptive name to your paper definition. (*Note:* This field doesn't affect any printing characteristics.) You can use one of the predefined paper types (**St**andard, **B**ond, Letterhead, **L**abels, **E**nvelope, **T**ransparency, or **C**ardstock) or choose **O**ther and type a descriptive name in the Other text box. If you create a paper definition for a booklet, for example, you may give the definition the name Sales Booklet.

Each time you select the custom paper definition, the specified Paper Type name appears in the upper left corner of the Paper Size dialog box.

Print Options

If you plan to bind a document, you can use the Binding option to shift text away from the bound edges. Choose Binding; then choose **L**eft or **T**op from the pop-up list to specify the binding edge. If your printer can print on both sides of the paper, choose **D**ouble Sided Printing. You can select both of these print options at the same time.

Text Adjustments

If your text doesn't print where your margins indicate that it should print, use the Text Adjustments options to reposition the text on the page. If the text isn't printing at the correct top margin, choose To**p** and specify a distance **U**p or **D**own. If the text isn't printing at the correct side margins, choose Si**d**e and specify a distance **L**eft or **R**ight. If your left margin is set to 1 inch but your text is printing 1 1/4 inches from the left edge, for example, choose Si**d**e and specify a **L**eft distance of **1/4"**.

Changes in text adjustment don't appear in Print Preview; you must print a page from the document to verify that the adjustments are correct. Unlike margin settings, changes in text adjustment affect all future documents that use this paper definition.

Selecting a Paper Definition

After creating a paper definition, you can begin using it immediately in your documents. (You also can use any of the existing paper definitions in the WordPerfect printer driver.) Follow these steps to select a paper definition:

1. Choose **L**ayout, **P**age.

   CUA Press Page (Alt-F9).

2. Choose Paper **S**ize. The Paper Size dialog box opens (again see fig. 15.1). Notice that your current printer is listed in the top left corner of the dialog box.

3. Double-click the desired paper definition with the mouse or highlight the definition and choose **S**elect. WordPerfect inserts the paper definition into your document and closes the Paper Size dialog box.

With a WordPerfect printer driver, you can use more than one page definition in a document. Look at the current page in Reveal Codes after selecting a paper definition. You should see a [Paper Sz/Typ] code that includes the dimensions and form name for the paper. If the [Paper Sz/Typ] code doesn't appear at the top of the page, the paper definition doesn't take effect until the following page.

T I P   If Auto Code Placement isn't on when you select a paper definition, the [Paper Sz/Typ] code appears at the insertion point. Leave Auto Code Placement on to ensure that the [Paper Sz/Typ] code is placed at the top of the page and takes effect with the current page. (For more information on using Auto Code Placement, see Chapter 6, "Formatting Text.")

You can change paper definitions anywhere in a document except within columns or tables. After you have inserted a [Paper Sz/Typ] code in a document, however, WordPerfect doesn't update the code automatically when you edit the paper definition. You must search the document for old [Paper Sz/Typ] codes and replace them with the new paper definition codes.

Paper definitions used in a document are saved with the document. You can use a particular definition as the default definition in all your documents by specifying that definition in Preferences. See Chapter 29, "Customizing WordPerfect with Preferences," for more information.

Using the [ALL OTHERS] Definition

When WordPerfect prints a document, it tries to match [Paper Sz/Typ] codes in the document with paper definitions in the current WordPerfect printer driver. If WordPerfect cannot find an exact match for a [Paper Sz/Typ] code, the program uses the [ALL OTHERS] definition (listed last in the Paper Size dialog box). The [ALL OTHERS] definition is generic in the sense that you can use this definition to print a document on any printer, even one that has different paper definitions from your original printer's definitions.

If you plan to use more than one printer to print a document (for example, a shared document to be printed by different users) on a non-standard sheet (not 8 1/2-by-11-inch), you should use the [ALL OTHERS] definition in your document, because every WordPerfect printer driver has an [ALL OTHERS] definition. You also should use the

[ALL OTHERS] definition (instead of creating a new definition) if you plan to use a paper definition once and then delete it. You cannot create the [ALL OTHERS] definition, but you can select and edit it.

To use the [ALL OTHERS] definition, select it as you would any other paper definition. The Select [ALL OTHERS] dialog box opens (see fig. 15.4). This dialog box contains the same Paper Type and Paper Size options as the Add Paper Size dialog box. (For instructions on using these options, see the section "Creating and Editing Paper Definitions," earlier in this chapter.) After you specify the desired options, the [ALL OTHERS] paper definition contains a generic description of the paper you want to use.

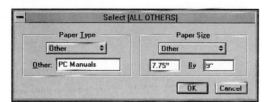

The Select [ALL OTHERS] dialog box.

Editing the [ALL OTHERS] Definition

You can edit the [ALL OTHERS] paper definition as you edit any other paper definition. The Edit Paper Size [ALL OTHERS] dialog box opens instead of the Edit Paper Size dialog box; the Edit Paper Size [ALL OTHERS] dialog box contains fewer options than the Edit Paper Size dialog box (see fig. 15.5). The Location, Prompt to Load Paper, and Text Adjustments options are described in the earlier section "Creating and Editing Paper Definitions." Notice that the Prompt to Load Paper option is selected by default in [ALL OTHERS].

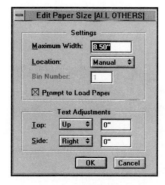

The Edit Paper Size [ALL OTHERS] dialog box.

The Edit Paper Size [ALL OTHERS] dialog box contains a new field, Maximum Width. The default for this field is the maximum paper width your printer can accommodate. If you retrieve a document with a paper size wider than the specified maximum width, WordPerfect adjusts the margins and text on-screen to match the width of the document. WordPerfect also changes the [Paper Sz/Typ] code in the document and marks it with an asterisk (*) to indicate a change in the paper width. If the Maximum Width is 8 1/2 inches, for example, and you retrieve a document with a paper size of 12 inches by 12 inches, which WordPerfect cannot match, the program positions the right margin relative to 8 1/2 inches.

T I P   You can specify a paper size for the [ALL OTHERS] paper definition but no option is available for choosing paper orientation. If your printer is capable of landscape printing, you can print landscape with the [ALL OTHERS] definition by specifying a width that exceeds the Maximum Width.

Copying Paper Definitions

■ Cue: When copying a paper definition, remember to use a unique Paper Type name for each paper definition.

If you need a new paper definition that is similar to an existing definition, you can copy the existing definition and edit it. This method saves time, especially if you need to change only one or two fields. If the new definition uses the same paper size, specify a new form name in the Paper Type text box to avoid confusing the two definitions. To copy a paper definition, follow these steps:

1. Choose **L**ayout, **P**age.

    Press Page (Alt-F9).

2. Choose Paper **S**ize. The Paper Size dialog box opens (again see fig. 15.1).

3. Highlight the printer form you want to copy. For this example, use the standard paper definition.

4. Choose **C**opy. The Add Paper Size dialog box opens (again see fig. 15.2).

5. Make any desired changes in the paper definition (see "Creating and Editing Paper Definitions," earlier in this chapter). For this example, choose Paper **T**ype and specify **O**ther. Then type **Test Copy** in the Ot**h**er text box.

CAUTION: Each paper definition in a printer driver must be unique. If you don't make any changes in the paper definition, choose Cancel to cancel the copy procedure.

6. Choose OK to close the Add Paper Size dialog box.

7. To begin using the edited paper definition, double-click it with the mouse or highlight it and choose Select. Otherwise, choose Close to exit from the Paper Size dialog box.

Deleting Paper Definitions

You can delete any paper definition (including the predefined paper definitions that come with your printer driver) except the [ALL OTHERS] paper definition. Because deleting a paper definition erases it from your printer driver, think carefully before deleting. To delete a paper definition, follow these steps:

1. Choose Layout, Page.

    CUA Press Page (Alt-F9).

2. Choose Paper Size. The Paper Size dialog box opens (again see fig. 15.1).

3. Highlight the paper definition you want to delete. For this example, highlight the Test Copy form you created in the preceding section.

4. Choose Delete.

5. WordPerfect asks you to confirm your deletion; the default is No (don't delete). If you choose Yes, WordPerfect removes the paper definition from the Paper Size dialog box. For this example, choose Yes.

6. Choose Close to exit from the Paper Size dialog box.

Using Paper Definitions with Windows Printer Drivers

If you use a Windows printer driver, you are restricted to one paper definition in a document. (By contrast, you can select more than one paper definition in a document with WordPerfect printer drivers.) Your editing options are limited to the options you can change in your Windows printer driver (most enable you to specify page orientation and paper sizes).

You should change the paper definition at the beginning of your document; if you open the Paper Size dialog box, it should reflect the paper size in your Windows printer driver. The Paper Size dialog box also shows the paper orientation. (In typical Windows style, a narrow sheet represents portrait orientation, and a thick sheet represents landscape orientation.) Note that the letter A isn't rotated for landscape orientation in the dialog box.

CAUTION: Changes you make in your Windows printer driver affect printing in your other Windows applications.

Printing on Envelopes

In this section, you learn how to create a paper definition for printing #10 business envelopes on an HP LaserJet III printer. (If you use a different brand of printer, use the example as a general guideline to creating envelope definitions.) After creating the envelope definition, you use it to print a sample envelope.

Begin by ensuring that you are working in an empty document screen (choose File, New). Then verify that you are using a WordPerfect printer driver. (Choose File, Select Printer to access the Select Printer dialog box; then choose WordPerfect in the Printer Drivers section of the dialog box.)

To create an envelope definition, follow these steps:

1. Choose Layout, Page.

    Press Page (Alt-F9).

2. Choose Paper Size. The Paper Size dialog box opens (again see fig. 15.1).

3. Choose Add. The Add Paper Size dialog box opens.

4. Specify the Add Paper Size dialog box options (see fig. 15.6).

   To distinguish the business envelope from other envelopes, choose Other for Paper Type and type **Business Envelope** in the text box.

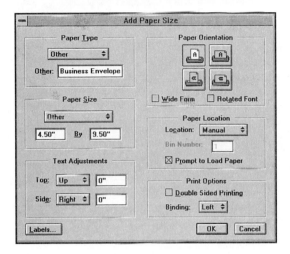

Click the landscape printing icon (the bottom left icon under Paper Orientation) or choose Rotated Fonts to specify landscape printing.

Because envelopes normally aren't kept in the LaserJet's paper tray, choose Manual for Location. Choose Prompt to Load Paper so that WordPerfect will prompt you to place an envelope in the printer at print time.

Choose Other for Paper Size and type **9.5"** (height) by **4.5"** (width). To understand these dimensions, hold the envelope in the position you use to feed it into the laser printer. You insert the short edge first (feeding sideways, or perpendicular to the way you write on an envelope). You choose landscape orientation to ensure that the text prints parallel to the long edge of the envelope.

With a dot-matrix printer, you feed the envelope into the printer as if you were writing on the envelope (long edge first), so you reverse the dimensions (**4.5"** by **9.5"**), with Paper Orientation set for portrait printing.

5. Choose OK to close the Add Paper Size dialog box.

6. Business Envelope now is listed in the Paper Size dialog box. To use the new definition, highlight it and choose **S**elect.

If you press Reveal Codes (Alt-F3), you see the following hidden code at the top of the document:

```
[Paper Sz/Typ:9.5" x 4.5",Business Envelope]
```

With the envelope definition created, you specify appropriate margins and typefaces and then enter the text for the envelope. The following paragraphs describe how to create the sample envelope (see fig. 15.7). If your printer doesn't have the typefaces used in this example, select appropriate alternate typefaces.

T I P

If you use envelopes frequently, create a macro that selects an envelope definition, adjusts the margins, and fills in your return address; then you just type the recipient's address for each envelope.

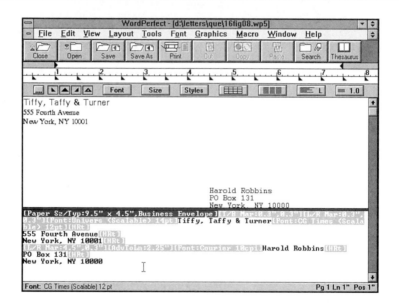

FIG. 15.7

Text and codes (shown in Reveal Codes) for a business envelope.

Cue: On a laser printer, you cannot set the margins to 0 inches because the printer cannot print on the edges of a sheet of paper.

If you use the default 1-inch margins on an envelope, the sender's address looks awkward. To change the margins, press Margins (Ctrl-F8) and change all the margins to .3 inch.

You choose fonts by pressing Font (F9) and selecting appropriate typefaces. For this example, use the Univers (Scalable) font with a 14-point size for the company name. After specifying the font, type the company name: **Tiffy, Taffy & Turner**. *Don't* press Enter after typing the company name; instead, immediately specify the font for the rest of the sender's address. (You are using a large font for the sender's name; if you choose a smaller font *before* pressing the Enter key, WordPerfect adjusts the line spacing.) For this example, specify CG Times (Scalable) with a 12-point size for the remainder of the return address. Press Enter after changing the font.

Next, type the company's street address (**555 Fourth Avenue**), press Enter, type the last line of the address (**New York, NY 10001**), and press Enter again. With Auto Code Placement on (see Chapter 6, "Formatting Text"), you must press Enter after the ZIP code.

At this point, you are ready to enter the recipient's address; however, you want the address to appear in the middle of the envelope. Use the Advance feature (described later in this chapter) to move the insertion point to the specific location where you want the address to appear. Choose **L**ayout, **A**dvance. The Advance dialog box opens (see fig. 15.8). Choose To Line; then choose **A**dvance and type **2.25** in the text box. Choose OK to close the Advance dialog box.

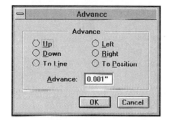

FIG. 15.8

The Advance dialog box.

Next, you adjust the left margin so that the recipient's address is more centered. Press Margins (Ctrl-F8), type **4.5"** for the Left Margin option, and choose OK. Then choose a monospaced font for the recipient's address by pressing Font (F9) and specifying Courier 10 cpi. Type the recipient's name and address as follows:

> ■ **Cue:** Using a monospaced font complies with U.S. Postal Service (X R rules.

> Harold Robbins
> PO Box 131
> New York, NY 10000

To see how the printed envelope will look, press Print Preview (Shift-F5). As figure 15.9 shows, Print Preview provides a good approximation of how the envelope will look when printed. Print the document by pressing Print (Ctrl-P); notice that the LaserJet waits for you to place an envelope in the manual feed area before printing.

Printing on Labels

WordPerfect's Labels feature is a specialized tool for defining and printing on labels. With the Labels feature, you can print mailing lists, file indexes, business stickers, and so on. By using the Labels feature combined with WordPerfect's Merge feature, you can select and print a list of names on labels. This section explains how to define label definitions and how to print on labels. At the end of the section, you create a label definition and use it to print on labels.

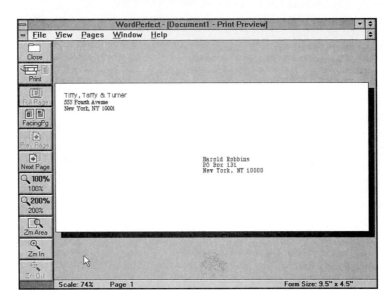

The business envelope shown in Print Preview.

Creating and Editing Label Definitions

Before you can print on a sheet of labels, you must create the label definition (like any other paper definition). You may want to have a ruler and a sample sheet of labels handy when you begin so that you can enter exact measurements. Note that if you edit a label definition, you must search your document for the old definition, delete it, and insert the edited definition.

To create or edit a label definition in a WordPerfect printer driver, follow these steps:

1. Choose **L**ayout, **P**age.

     Press Page (Alt-F9).

2. Choose Paper **S**ize. The Paper Size dialog box opens (again see fig. 15.1).

3. To create a new label definition, choose **A**dd. To edit an existing label definition, highlight the definition and choose **E**dit.

Depending on your choice, the Add Paper Size dialog box or Edit Paper Size dialog box opens (again see fig. 15.2).

4. Look at your sheet of paper to see whether you need to change any options in the dialog box. Pay close attention to the Paper Size, Prompt to Load Paper, and Paper Type options. For Paper Type, choose Labels or Other and type a descriptive name (for example, **Avery 5162**). You should select the Prompt to Load Paper option so that you are reminded to insert the labels when printing.

5. Choose Labels. The Edit Labels dialog box opens, as shown in figure 15.10.

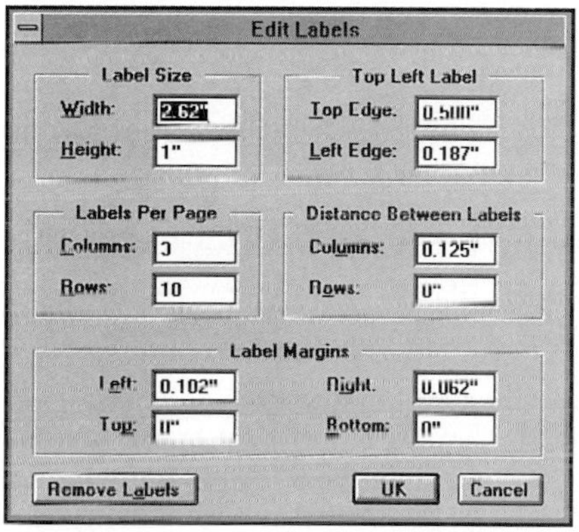

FIG. 15.10

The Edit Labels dialog box.

6. Change the options in the Edit Labels dialog box to match your label sheet (see the next section for details).

7. Choose OK to close the Edit Labels dialog box.

8. Choose OK to close the Add Paper Size or Edit Paper Size dialog box.

9. To begin using your label definition, choose Select in the Paper Size dialog box; otherwise, choose Close to close the dialog box.

T I P

You can use the LABELS.WCM macro included with WordPerfect to create your label definitions. Choose Macro, Play (or press Alt-F10), highlight LABELS.WCM in the Files List window, and choose Play. Answer Yes to the prompt that asks whether WordPerfect should verify that the correct printer is selected for adding label definitions. Select another printer or verify that the correct printer is selected; then make your labels choice from the list (see fig. 15.11).

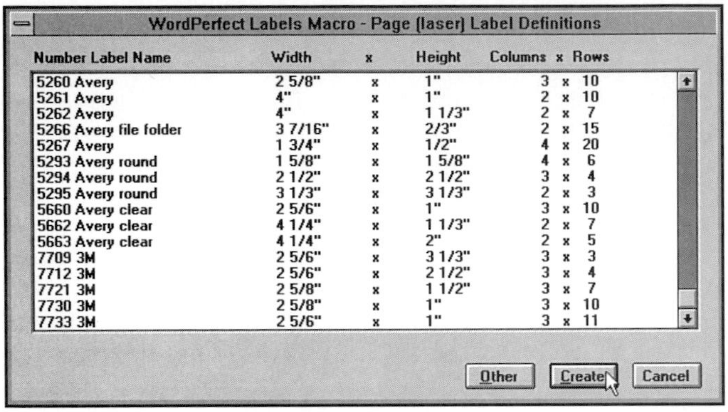

WordPerfect Labels Macro - Page (laser) Label Definitions				
Number Label Name	**Width**	**x**	**Height**	**Columns x Rows**
5260 Avery	2 5/8"	x	1"	3 x 10
5261 Avery	4"	x	1"	2 x 10
5262 Avery	4"	x	1 1/3"	2 x 7
5266 Avery file folder	3 7/16"	x	2/3"	2 x 15
5267 Avery	1 3/4"	x	1/2"	4 x 20
5293 Avery round	1 5/8"	x	1 5/8"	4 x 6
5294 Avery round	2 1/2"	x	2 1/2"	3 x 4
5295 Avery round	3 1/3"	x	3 1/3"	2 x 3
5660 Avery clear	2 5/6"	x	1"	3 x 10
5662 Avery clear	4 1/4"	x	1 1/3"	2 x 7
5663 Avery clear	4 1/4"	x	2"	2 x 5
7709 3M	2 5/6"	x	3 1/3"	3 x 3
7712 3M	2 5/6"	x	2 1/2"	3 x 4
7721 3M	2 5/8"	x	1 1/2"	3 x 7
7730 3M	2 5/8"	x	1"	3 x 10
7733 3M	2 5/6"	x	1"	3 x 11

[Other] [Create] [Cancel]

FIG. 15.11

The WordPerfect Labels Macro-Page Label Definitions dialog box for laser printer definitions.

Understanding the Edit Labels Dialog Box

You can specify up to five settings in the Edit Labels dialog box; you may not need to modify each setting for your labels. The Remove Labels button at the bottom of the dialog box deletes a label definition associated with a paper definition. The following paragraphs explain each setting in the Edit Labels dialog box.

■ **Cue:** If you enter measurements in fractional form, WordPerfect converts them to decimals.

■ *Label Size.* Use the Label Size options to specify the **W**idth and **H**eight of an individual label. Measure the label only and ignore spacing between labels on the sheet. If your label is 5 1/4 inches wide by 3 inches high, enter **5.25"** for **W**idth and **3.0"** for **H**eight.

■ *Top Left Label.* Use these options to tell WordPerfect where the first label is located on a sheet of labels. The **T**op Edge measurement is the distance from the top edge of the page to the top edge of the first label. The **L**eft Edge measurement is the distance from the left edge of the page to the left edge of the first label.

■ *Labels Per Page.* Use the Labels Per Page options to specify the number of labels on a sheet of paper. WordPerfect records the total number of labels in grid format. The **C**olumns count is the number of labels across a sheet of paper (horizontal); **R**ows lists the number of labels from the top of the sheet to the bottom (vertical). If you have a sheet of 12 labels with 3 labels across the top and 4 labels from the top to bottom, type **3** for **C**olumns and **4** for **R**ows.

- *Distance Between Labels.* This measurement specifies the distance separating individual labels on a sheet. You indicate whether white space exists between labels so that WordPerfect can print each label correctly. Columns lists the measurement from the bottom of one label to the top of the next label; **Rows** shows the distance between the right edge of one label and the left edge of the next label.

- *Label Margins.* This option sets the margins for each individual label (not a sheet of labels). You can use this option to tell WordPerfect how much space to leave for the **L**eft, **R**ight, To**p**, and **B**ottom margins. Label margins are a separate measurement from page margins.

Creating a Sample Label Definition

In this section, you learn how to create a paper definition for a sheet of Avery 5164 laser printer labels. After you create the label definition, you design a shipping label and print it on the HP LaserJet III laser printer. This example serves as a guideline for creating and selecting label definitions, entering label text, and printing on labels, regardless of the kind of printer you use.

Begin by ensuring that you are working in an empty document screen (choose File, New). Then verify that you are using a WordPerfect printer driver. (Choose File, Select Printer to access the Select Printer dialog box; then choose WordPerfect in the Printer Drivers section of the dialog box.)

To create the label definition, follow these steps:

1. Choose **L**ayout, **P**age.

    Press Page (Alt-F9).

2. Choose Paper **S**ize. The Paper Size dialog box opens.

3. Choose **A**dd. The Add Paper Size dialog box opens.

4. Choose Paper **T**ype, **O**ther and type **Avery 5164** in the Other text box.

5. Choose Lo**c**ation, **M**anual and select the P**r**ompt to Load Paper option so that WordPerfect will remind you to insert labels when you print the document. (***Note:*** You don't need to change the Paper **S**ize because a sheet of Avery 5164 labels is the same size as a standard sheet of paper.)

6. Choose **L**abels. The Edit Labels dialog box opens.

7. Figure 15.12 shows the Edit Labels dialog box with specifications for a sheet of Avery 5164 labels. Enter the data shown in the figure in your Edit Labels dialog box.

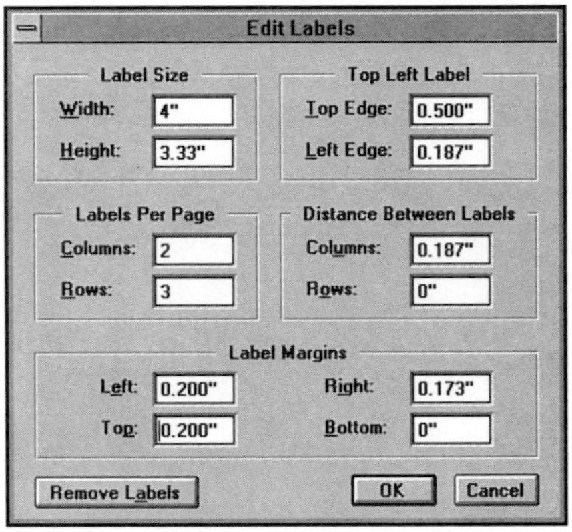

FIG. 15.12

Avery 5164 label specifications in the Edit Labels dialog box.

8. Choose OK to close the Edit Labels dialog box.

9. Choose OK to close the Add Paper Size dialog box.

   Your new paper definition now is listed in the Paper Size dialog box with the options you chose. The Labels column lists the number of labels per sheet (2 columns by 3 rows).

10. To begin using the new paper definition, highlight the definition and choose **S**elect.

When you choose the Avery 5164 definition, WordPerfect places a hidden [Paper Sz/Typ] code at the top of the document. The [Paper Sz/Typ] code for a label includes the label size. For the Avery 5164 label definition, the code appears as follows, indicating the paper size (8 1/2-by-11 inches), paper type (Avery 5164), and label size (4-by-3 1/3 inches):

        [Paper Sz/Typ: 8.5" x 11",Avery 5164,4" x 3.33"]

With the label definition created, insert the text and codes shown in figure 15.13. (The sender and recipient are the same as in the envelope example, earlier in the chapter.) The following paragraphs describe how to create the sample label. The codes have been made as simple as possible for quick entry. If your printer doesn't have the typefaces used in this example, select appropriate alternate typefaces.

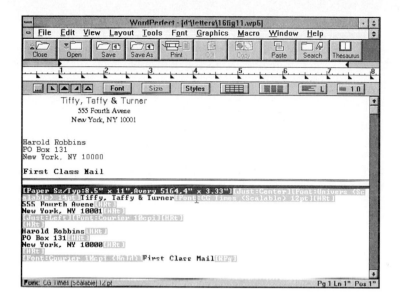

FIG. 15.13

Text and codes (shown in Reveal Codes) for Avery 5164 labels.

Press Font (F9) to specify the fonts. Use the Univers (Scalable) font with a 14-point size for the company name. After specifying the font, type the company name: **Tiffy, Taffy & Turner**. *Don't* press Enter after typing the company name; instead, specify CG Times (Scalable) with a 12-point size for the remainder of the return address. Press Enter after changing the font. Then type the company's street address (**555 Fourth Avenue**), press Enter, type the last line of the address (**New York, NY 10001**), and press Enter again. Center the entire return address.

Use a monospaced font for the recipient's address. Press Font (F9) again and specify Courier 10 cpi for this example. Type the recipient's name and address as follows:

> Harold Robbins
> PO Box 131
> New York, NY 10000

After you finish typing the recipient's name and address, press Enter twice and type **First Class Mail** in boldface. To end the label, use a hard return (Ctrl-Enter).

To copy the label, move the insertion point so that the [Just:Center] code is highlighted. Press Select (F8), End of Document (Ctrl-End), Copy (Ctrl-Insert). Move to the end of the document and paste the copied text and codes by pressing Paste (Shift-Insert). For this example, paste the copied label five times to create a total of six copies.

Cue: To ensure that only one physical sheet of labels is printed, erase the last [HRt] code.

Printing the Sample Labels

To print all the labels, you print the full document. Press Print (Ctrl-P); WordPerfect sends the print job to the Windows Print Manager. Print Manager displays the following prompt:

```
Load Paper: Avery 5164 8.5"x11"
```

Place the Avery 5164 label sheet in the LaserJet with the label side facing up. Choose OK; Print Manager prints the labels. Figure 15.14 shows the printed labels; notice that only six labels have been printed.

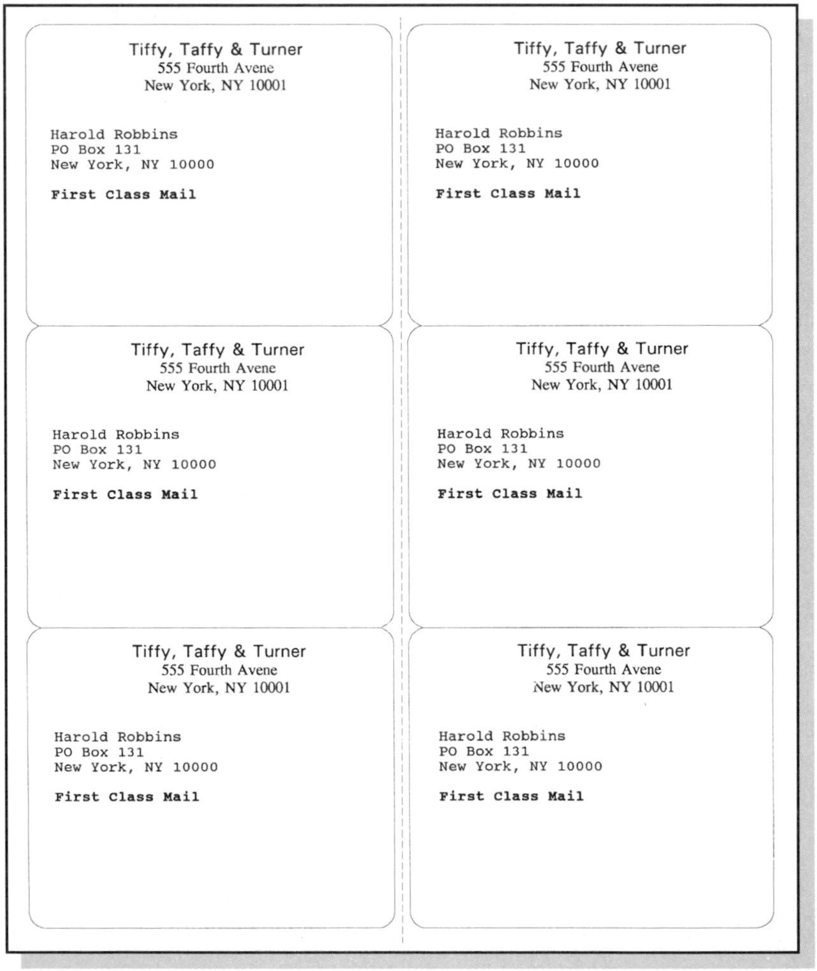

FIG. 15.14

Printed Avery 5164 labels.

Using Label Definitions in a Document

Select label definitions in the same way you select any other paper definition (see "Selecting a Paper Definition," earlier in this chapter). As with other definitions, the best practice is to leave Auto Code Placement turned on so that WordPerfect places the [Paper Sz/Typ] code at the top of the page. (See Chapter 6, "Formatting Text," for information on Auto Code Placement.)

If you edit a label definition, the new definition doesn't affect existing [Paper Sz/Typ] codes. The only way to change the code is to delete the old [Paper Sz/Typ] code and insert the new code.

■ **Cue:** If WordPerfect prevents you from selecting a label form, try setting your page margins to 0 inches.

Printing Logical Pages (Labels)

You may think of a sheet of labels as a page, but WordPerfect treats each label as a *logical page*. A sheet of labels is a *physical page*; if you have a physical page with 12 labels, WordPerfect "sees" 12 logical pages. The measurements you specify in the Label Size section of the Edit Labels dialog box determine the logical page size; these measurements are displayed in the editing window's status bar (and on the Ruler, if you have it turned on).

View your labels in Print Preview before printing to make sure that all your measurements are correct. A mistake in any measurement may cause the labels to print incorrectly. If you need to make changes, edit the label definition, delete the old code, and insert the new code before using Print Preview again.

WordPerfect (deceptively) displays a physical page in Print Preview, regardless of how many logical pages you have chosen to print.

If you access the Print dialog box and print the current page, WordPerfect prints only one label. You can print several labels by choosing the **M**ultiple Pages option. To print your entire labels document, however, choose **F**ull Document. (See Chapter 9, "Basic Printing," for information on printing with the Print dialog box.)

Because label sheets are more expensive than regular paper, print a practice set of labels on a plain sheet of paper. Place the printed page over a sheet of labels and hold the two pages next to a bright light to see whether the labels will print correctly.

T I P

When using a laser printer to print labels, follow these guidelines:

- Use only labels designed for laser printers. Regular labels may jam the printer, or the adhesive may melt from the heat in the printer.

- Don't print on a label sheet that is missing a label. The label sheet can jam the printer.

- Don't run a large label sheet through the printer twice. Glue can weaken and the label can come off.

Entering Text in Logical Pages

■ **Cue:** You can center text vertically on a label by using the **C**enter Page command from the Page (Alt-F9) menu.

Enter label text in the same way as any other document text. Word-Perfect wraps lines automatically, and you can use the Enter key to separate lines. If you type more text than can fit on a label, WordPerfect enters a soft page break. Text appearing after a soft page break prints on the next label. If you cannot fit all the text you want on a label, adjust the top and bottom margins of the label or switch to a smaller font.

After you finish typing the text for the label, press Hard Page (Ctrl-Enter) to advance to the next label. Use the PgUp and PgDn keys to move between labels. Because WordPerfect views each label as a separate page, all headers, footers, page numbering, and so on, that you define at the top of the document apply to each label. If you define a header at the top of the document, for example, the header prints on every label, because every label is a logical page.

T I P   To create blank shipping labels with your return address at the top of each label, use your return address as the header.

If you are working with a mailing list, you may prefer to keep the mailing list in a secondary merge file; your primary merge file can be a document with a label format. With the Merge feature, you can use the same secondary merge file to print individualized letters and mailing labels (see Chapter 21, "Assembling Documents with Merge").

Using Labels in Tractor-Feed Printers

If you are printing on tractor-feed labels (labels on a sheet with holes on each side to guide the paper through the printer, usually a dot-matrix or daisywheel printer), you must change some of the options in the Edit Labels dialog box. For most tractor-feed labels, set the **Top Edge** and **Left** edge measurements to **0"**. The printer should print on the first line of the first label in the upper left corner at the top of the sheet. Set all the Label Margins options to **0"**.

> Print a test label after changing the specifications in the Edit Labels dialog box. Use the results to calculate your margin measurements correctly.
>
> **T I P**

Printing tractor-feed labels may be easier if you treat each row of labels as a physical page. In this method, Lines Per Page is specified with one row and no columns. The paper size (specified in the Add Paper Size dialog box) accounts for the distance between labels. If you have four 1 3/4-inch-wide labels, with 1/2-inch horizontal distance between labels, the paper width is 8 1/2 inches, calculated as follows:

1.75" + .5" + 1.75" + .5" + 1.75" + .5" + 1.75"

If each label is 1 1/2 inches high with 1/4-inch vertical distance between rows of labels, the paper height is 1 3/4 inches (1 1/2 inches plus 1/4 inch).

Treating each row of labels as a physical page doesn't affect the information you enter for Label Size options or the Distance Between Labels Columns measurement. In this example, the Label Size is 1 3/4 inches (**Width**) by 1 1/2 inches (**Height**), and the Distance Between Labels (**Columns**) is 1/2 inch. *Note:* Remember to set the Distance Between Labels Rows measurement to **0"** because you are treating each row as a physical page.

Using Labels with Windows Printer Drivers

Although you can use only one paper definition in a document when you use a Windows printer driver, you can use more than one label definition. The only restriction is that the label size must fit the paper size you have chosen in your Windows printer driver. WordPerfect prints to the margins you specified when you created the label definition.

You create a label definition only once for a Windows printer driver; after you create a label definition, the definition is available to all Windows printer drivers. You select the label definition in the same way you select any other paper definition.

Note: You cannot name label definitions with a Windows printer driver. The only way to distinguish among label definitions with Windows printer drivers is by label size.

To create a label definition for your Windows printer driver, begin by verifying that you are using a Windows printer driver. (Choose File, Select Printer to access the Select Printer dialog box; then choose Windows in the Printer Drivers section of the dialog box.) Then follow these steps:

1. Choose Layout, Page.

      Press Page (Alt-F9).

2. Choose Paper Size. The Paper Size dialog box opens. The Paper Type listed in the Paper Size dialog box is Current Windows Form.

3. Choose Add. A dialog box opens with the message Only label definitions can be added when using Windows printer drivers. Choose OK to continue.

   The Edit Labels dialog box opens (again see fig. 15.10). Most of the options are the same as the options for WordPerfect printer drivers (see "Understanding the Edit Labels Dialog Box," earlier in this chapter). Note that you cannot name the label definition, and the Remove Labels option isn't available.

4. Specify the desired label options; then choose OK to confirm your specifications.

5. To use the labels definition, choose Select; otherwise, choose OK to exit from the Edit Labels dialog box.

Adjusting Textual Appearance

This section explains how to position text on your page and how to exert more control over the spacing between letters, words, lines, and paragraphs. You learn how to control word justification and how to specify whether WordPerfect underlines spaces and tabs. By using the techniques in this section, you can change the appearance of your printed text so that words have less space between them for business correspondence, change the spacing between letters in a flier for a professional look, and tell WordPerfect where you want the next lines of text to appear on a page.

T I P

To use a hidden code in all your documents, place the code in the
Initial Codes screen. (Choose File, Preferences, Initial Codes.) For
more information, see Chapter 29, "Customizing WordPerfect with
Preferences."

Using Advance

Use the Advance feature to place text in a specific location on your
page. Unlike other page codes, Advance isn't affected by Auto Code
Placement. WordPerfect places an advance code in your text at the
insertion point, not at the top of a page or the beginning of a paragraph.
You can use Advance to place text inside a graphic, fill in forms, and
place different fonts and type sizes on a page.

If you choose an up, down, left, or right advance, WordPerfect moves
the insertion point in the specified direction. If the insertion point is
at the 2 1/2-inch position, for example, and you enter a right advance of
1/2 inch, the insertion point moves to the 3-inch position on the same
line.

You also can specify an *absolute advance*, by indicating the exact horizontal or vertical position on a page where you want WordPerfect to
move the insertion point. If you specify a horizontal advance of 3 1/2
inches, for example, the insertion point moves to the position 3 1/2
inches from the left edge of the paper, regardless of the current location of the insertion point. (By contrast, a right advance of 3 1/2 inches
moves the insertion point 3 1/2 inches to the right of the current insertion point location.)

To use the Advance feature, follow these steps:

1. Choose **L**ayout, **A**dvance. The Advance dialog box opens (see
   fig. 15.15).

FIG. 15.15

The Advance
dialog box.

2. Choose an Advance option.

   To specify a directional advance, choose **U**p, **D**own, **L**eft, or **R**ight.

■ **Cue:** To move to a
specific location on the
page, you need two [Adv]
codes to position the
insertion point both vertically
and horizontally.

   To specify an absolute advance, choose To L**i**ne (to specify a vertical position, measured from the top edge of the page) or To P**o**sition (to specify a horizontal position, measured from the left edge of the page). The default for an absolute advance is the current position, displayed in the status bar.

3. Choose **A**dvance and enter the distance that you want to advance the insertion point.

4. Choose OK to close the Advance dialog box. WordPerfect inserts a hidden [Adv] code into your document; you can view the code in Reveal Codes (Alt-F3).

Kerning

Kerning reduces the space between letters to enhance their visual appearance. Not all printers support kerning, but for those that do, WordPerfect offers two options: Automatic Kerning and Manual Kerning. Automatic Kerning automatically reduces the space between certain pairs of letters (for example, AW); Manual Kerning enables you to reduce or increase the space between letters. (To adjust the spacing between all the characters in your document, use WordPerfect's Letterspacing feature; see the section "Using Letterspacing and Word Spacing," later in this chapter.)

Figure 15.16 shows unkerned text and text kerned with WordPerfect's Kerning feature. Notice the different spacing between the letters in each example.

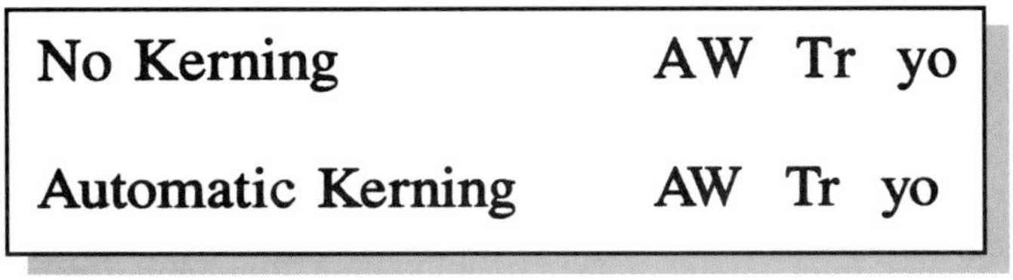

| No Kerning | AW Tr yo |
| Automatic Kerning | AW Tr yo |

FIG. 15.16

Examples of kerning.

Using Automatic Kerning

Automatic Kerning is an on/off code feature; WordPerfect kerns all the letters from the [Kern:On] code until the program reaches the end of the document or a [Kern:Off] code. The recommended practice is to turn on Auto Code Placement so that WordPerfect places the [Kern:On] code at the beginning of a paragraph.

> If you want WordPerfect to kern all your documents automatically, insert a [Kern:On] code in the Initial Codes window of Preferences (see Chapter 29, "Customizing WordPerfect with Preferences").
>
> **T I P**

To turn Automatic Kerning on or off, follow these steps:

1. Place the insertion point where you want kerning to begin in your document.

2. Choose **L**ayout, Typesetting. The Typesetting dialog box opens, as shown in figure 15.17.

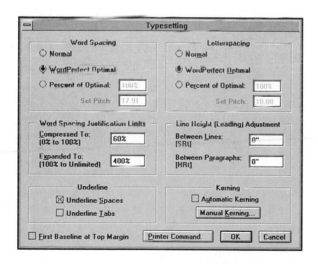

FIG. 15.17

The Typesetting dialog box.

3. Choose Automatic Kerning. An X in the check box indicates that Automatic Kerning is turned on; if you turn off kerning, the X disappears.

4. Choose OK to close the Typesetting dialog box.

You can view the [Kern] code in Reveal Codes (Alt-F3).

Cue: WordPerfect keeps kerning tables in the printer resource (PRS) file.

T I P To see how a font will look when kerned, retrieve the KERN.TST file (usually stored with your printer files) and specify the font. Then print KERN.TST.

Using Manual Kerning

You can use Manual Kerning to increase or decrease the space between letters. Unlike Automatic Kerning, Manual Kerning affects only a specific pair of letters that you choose. You can use Manual Kerning independently of Automatic Kerning. To use Manual Kerning, follow these steps:

1. Move the insertion point between the letter pair whose spacing you want to change.

2. Choose **L**ayout, Typesetting. The Typesetting dialog box opens (again see fig. 15.17).

3. Choose Manual **K**erning. The Manual Kerning dialog box opens, as shown in figure 15.18. The Preview window shows the kerned text.

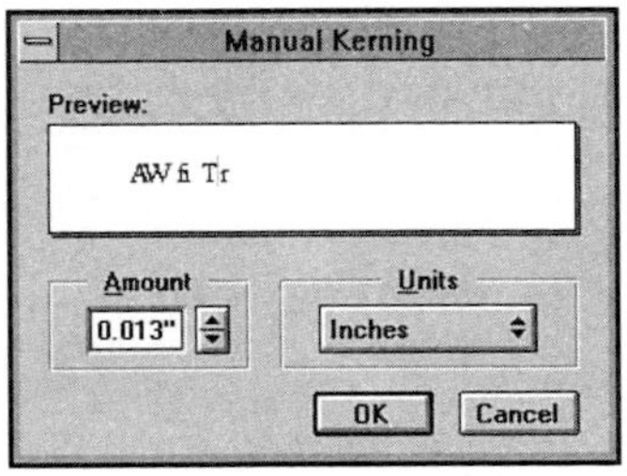

FIG. 15.18

The Manual Kerning dialog box.

4. Choose **U**nits and specify the measurement you want to use (**I**nches, **C**entimeters, **P**oints, or **1**200ths).

5. In the **A**mount text box, click the arrows or enter a specific amount to change the distance between letters. Using a positive number (*expanded* kerning) increases spacing between the letters; using a negative number (*contracted* kerning) decreases spacing. The Preview box in figure 15.18 shows that the letter pairs *AW* and *fi* have been contracted and the letter pair *Tr* has been expanded.

6. When you are satisfied with the visual appearance of the letter spacing in the Preview window, choose OK to close the Manual Kerning dialog box. If you have changed your mind about manual kerning, choose Cancel.

7. Choose OK to close the Typesetting dialog box.

In Reveal Codes (Alt-F3), look at the letter pair you kerned. WordPerfect inserts a code between the letters to adjust the spacing: [AdvRght] for positive spacing (moving the letters farther apart) or [AdvLft] for negative spacing (moving the letters closer together).

Using Letterspacing and Word Spacing

The Letterspacing feature affects the space between *all* letters following a [Wrd/Ltr Spacing] code, and the Word Spacing feature adjusts spacing between words. Not all printers support word spacing and letterspacing. You can set word spacing and letterspacing individually or at once in the Typesetting dialog box (WordPerfect places word spacing and letterspacing in one hidden [Wrd/Ltr Spacing] code).

To set word spacing or letterspacing, follow these steps:

1. Move the insertion point to the text where you want to adjust the letterspacing or word spacing.

2. Choose **Layout**, **Typesetting** to open the Typesetting dialog box (again see fig. 15.17).

3. Choose a Word Spacing option, a Letterspacing option, or both. The options are described in the following paragraphs:

   ■ *Normal.* If you choose this setting, WordPerfect uses the settings specified by the font vendor or printer manufacturer. (*Note:* The Normal word spacing option affects only proportionally spaced fonts.)

   ■ *WordPerfect Optimal.* This option (the default) uses the spacing set by WordPerfect Corporation. With WordPerfect Optimal spacing, in a proportionally spaced font, a space equals half the font point size. In a fixed-space font, the pitch (characters per inch) determines the optimal word spacing. For more information on fonts, see Chapter 10, "Working with Fonts."

   ■ *Percent of Optimal.* Use this setting to modify the WordPerfect Optimal spacing. Enter a number greater than 100 to increase spacing between words and letters. To reduce spacing, enter a number less than 100. The default is 100 percent—the same as choosing WordPerfect Optimal spacing. You need not enter a percent sign (%); WordPerfect enters it for you. With the Set Pitch option, you also can specify the exact number of characters per inch. The percentage and pitch you enter may not work with your printer; if necessary, WordPerfect adjusts the settings.

4. When you finish choosing options, choose OK to close the Typesetting dialog box.

Setting Word Spacing Justification Limits

If you use full justification for your document (see Chapter 6, "Formatting Text," for more information), WordPerfect aligns text between the left and right margins. With Full Justification on, you can use the Word Spacing Justification Limits option in the Typesetting dialog box to adjust the minimum (default 60 percent) and maximum (default 400 percent) spacing between words. If words in your document appear too close together, increase the minimum spacing by changing the **Com**pressed To setting. If the words appear too far apart, decrease the maximum spacing by changing the **Ex**panded To setting.

■ **Cue:** You can set the Expanded To option to an unlimited amount by entering 999.

You can enter measurements in different units by typing a letter after the number: centimeters (**c**), inches ("), points (**P**), or 1200s of an inch (**w**). To enter 12 points when WordPerfect defaults to inches, for example, enter **12p**.

When you use the options under Word Spacing Justification Limits, WordPerfect inserts a hidden [Just Lim:xx,yyy] code into your document, where xx is the minimum justification setting and yyy is the maximum justification setting. If Auto Code Placement is turned on, WordPerfect inserts the code at the beginning of the paragraph where you are working; otherwise, WordPerfect places the [Just Lim] code at the insertion point. If your printer doesn't support the Justification feature, you will not see any difference in your document when you change the justification settings.

Adjusting Line Height (Leading)

Leading (pronounced "ledding") is the amount of space between lines. Leading (called *line height* in WordPerfect) includes the height of the font plus the white space (vertical spacing). You can use the Line Height (Leading) Adjustment option in the Typesetting dialog box to adjust the leading without changing the default line height—in effect, changing the white space between lines. You can change the leading within paragraphs and between paragraphs. Figure 15.19 illustrates different amounts of leading.

This is a paragraph with normal leading. Pay close attention to the spacing between the lines. This figure shows leading between lines, not between paragraphs.

This is a paragraph with expanded leading. Pay close attention

to the spacing between the lines (they are farther apart). This

figure shows leading between lines, not between paragraphs.

This is a paragraph with contracted leading. Pay close
attention to the spacing between the lines (they are closer
together). This figure shows leading between lines, not
between paragraphs.

FIG. 15.19

Examples of adjusted leading.

To adjust the leading in your document, follow these steps:

1. Move the insertion point to the paragraph you want to change.

2. Choose **Layout**, **Typesetting**. The Typesetting dialog box opens (again see fig. 15.17).

3. To change the amount of space between lines, enter a number in the Between Lines text box. To change the amount of space between paragraphs, enter a number in the Between **Paragraphs** text box.

   To expand spacing, enter a positive number; to contract spacing, enter a negative number. The default leading measurement is inches. To use points, type the number followed by **p**; for centimeters, add **c**.

4. Choose OK to close the Typesetting dialog box.

If Auto Code Placement is on, WordPerfect inserts the `[Line Height Adj]` code at the beginning of the paragraph; otherwise, WordPerfect places the code at the insertion point.

The Between **Lines** option adjusts leading by changing the amount of white space created by a soft return `[SRt]`; the Between **Paragraphs** option adjusts the white space created by a hard return `[HRt]`. When you use the Line Height (Leading) Adjustment options, WordPerfect places a hidden `[Line Height Adj:x,y]` code in your document; x is the value you assigned to soft returns (Between Lines); y is the value you assigned to hard returns (Between **Paragraphs**).

Adjusting line spacing may be easier than adjusting leading. If you have an 8-point monospaced font, for example, and you add 4 points of leading, you have the equivalent of 1 1/2 line spacing. If you subsequently select a 12-point fixed-space font, WordPerfect continues to add 4 points to the 12-point font. Instead of 1 1/2 line spacing, you now have the equivalent of 1 1/3 line spacing. To preserve the proportions you set previously, you must change the leading to add 6 points (because 6 points is half of 12 points) instead of 4 points.

The Line Height (Leading) Adjustment feature differs from the Line Height feature. You use the Line Height feature to override WordPerfect's default line height and set a new line height. You use the Line Height (Leading) Adjustment feature to change the amount of space between lines or between paragraphs. For more information on line height, see Chapter 11, "Formatting Pages and Designing Documents."

Using the First Baseline at Top Margin Option

In typography, the *baseline* is the lowest point reached by characters in a line of text, excluding *descenders* (such as the lowest point of the letters *p* and *y*). WordPerfect normally places the top of the first line of text even with the top margin of the page. The position of the baseline for the first line depends on which font you use.

Sometimes you may want the first baseline to remain constant (for example, if your first line includes text in several fonts of different sizes). If you have set a fixed line height (see Chapter 6, "Formatting Text"), you can use the First Baseline at Top Margin option in the Typesetting dialog box to make the first baseline on a page even with the top margin of the page. This option places the first baseline even with the top margin of every page, regardless of which font you use.

When you choose First Baseline at Top Margin, WordPerfect inserts a hidden code. To use this option throughout your document, place the [Bline:On] code at the beginning of the document or in Initial Codes. The code remains in effect until you turn it off with a matching [Bline:Off] code.

Turning on the First Baseline at Top Margin option also affects any WordPerfect feature (such as the Advance feature) that places text in a specific location on a page. An Advance To Line 2" command normally places the baseline of the text slightly below 2 inches from the top of the page (the *top* of the line of text is at 2 inches). With a [Bline:On] code present, however, an Advance To Line 2" command places the baseline of the text you enter on the line 2 inches from the top of the page. Figure 15.20 illustrates the effect of the baseline code on an absolute advance.

> This shows the effect of Baseline margin on an Advance to Line 2" command.
>
> Baseline On with 2" Advance to Line
> No Baseline with 2" Advance to Line

FIG. 15.20

The effect of a baseline code on an absolute advance.

Using the Underline Options

You can use the Underline options in the Typesetting dialog box to control how WordPerfect treats tabs and spaces when you use the Underline feature (Ctrl-U). WordPerfect's default format underlines spaces but not tabs. To change whether WordPerfect underlines spaces, choose Underline **S**paces; to change whether WordPerfect underlines tabs, choose Underline **T**abs. If an option is selected, an X appears in the check box in front of the option.

Changing either Underline setting doesn't affect Auto Code Placement; WordPerfect places a hidden [Underln] code at the insertion point in your text. Any changes in the underline options affect all use of the Underline feature after the hidden [Underln] code. To override WordPerfect's defaults for every new document, place an [Underln:Spaces,Tabs] code in Initial Codes (see Chapter 29, "Customizing WordPerfect with Preferences").

Using the Printer Command Option

Printer commands are specific instructions for your printer. They may be commands that WordPerfect doesn't support or commands unique to a particular situation. The printer codes come from your printer manual.

Suppose that a friend sends you a document (formatted for an HP LaserJet II) that you want to print on your PostScript printer (which has an HP LaserJet II emulation mode). Instead of reformatting the document, you can use the Printer Command feature to place in the document the printer codes to switch your printer into the LJII emulation mode. If you often switch your printer to LJII emulation, you can place the printer commands in a printer command file so that you don't need to reenter the printer codes in each document.

To place a printer command in your file, follow these steps:

1. Place the insertion point at the location in your document where you want to insert the printer code.

2. Choose **L**ayout, Typesetti**n**g. The Typesetting dialog box opens.

3. Choose the **P**rinter Command button. The Printer Command dialog box opens, as shown in figure 15.21.

The Printer Command dialog box.

4. You can choose **C**ommand and type the printer command (up to 40 characters) or choose **F**ilename and type the name of a file containing the printer commands. You cannot choose both options at the same time.

5. Choose OK to close the Printer Command dialog box.

6. Choose OK to close the Typesetting dialog box.

When you use the **C**ommand option to enter printer commands, type any letters or numbers directly. If the printer command contains a character that doesn't print, type the character's ASCII number in angle brackets. If the command uses Esc (ASCII equivalent 27), for example, type **<27>**. (WordPerfect's documentation includes an ASCII conversion chart that shows ASCII equivalents.) If you enter commands with the **C**ommand option, you cannot edit the printer code after you place it in your document; you must delete the old code and enter a new **C**ommand code.

If you need to use the same printer codes in several documents, type a printer command with more than 40 characters, or send different groups of codes to your printer, consider placing the printer commands in a printer command file. Some printer vendors provide a printer command file with the printer. You can create a printer command file in WordPerfect but remember to save it as an ASCII text (DOS) file (use the Save **A**s option from the **F**ile menu). WordPerfect looks for printer command files in the same directory as your downloadable fonts; the directory is specified in Preferences (see Chapter 29, "Customizing WordPerfect with Preferences").

WordPerfect ignores any path names you supply in the Printer Command dialog box. The program doesn't insert the printer command file into your document; instead, it sends the printer command file to your printer when you print the document.

Whether you choose the Command or Filename option, WordPerfect places a hidden [Ptr Cmd] code in your document. You can see the code in Reveal Codes (Alt-F3). [Ptr Cmd] codes aren't affected by Auto Code Placement, so they appear at the insertion point.

WordPerfect doesn't check printer codes for accuracy. If you make a mistake when you enter a printer command (with the Command option or in a file), you will not know until you print the document, when the printer commands appear as text in the printed document. If you make a mistake in the printer commands, you may need to reset your printer to restore it to its normal state. You should reset your printer to ensure that your output prints correctly and to retest your printer codes. (If you know your printer's reset code, you can use it in a command.)

Chapter Summary

In this chapter, you learned how to create paper definitions in WordPerfect and how to create and print envelopes and labels. You also learned how to use the Advance feature to position text on the page, how to change the appearance of your text with kerning and leading, how to control WordPerfect's underlining options, and how to control your printer with printer codes.

Using Lines To Add Effects

When you create a document, you focus first on the content. What you say and how you say it is, after all, the primary objective of written communication. After you have checked your text for correct grammar, proper spelling, appropriate word choice, and convincing logic, however, your work still is not finished. The next task you face is to make your document visually attractive. Two major reasons exist for making your document look appealing:

- You want to attract the attention of your readers before they begin to read. Busy people, in particular, often set aside materials that don't have a professional look. They usually intend to get back to these documents, but rarely do.

- After your readers begin reading, the visual layout and design of the document can help make reading easier, increasing the chance that readers will focus on the content. You don't want them to be distracted by poor document design.

■ **Read Gilgen** is Director of Learning Support Services at the University of Wisconsin, Madison. He started using WordPerfect for academic reasons but admittedly has become addicted to its graphics features.

The next several chapters explore some of the ways you can use Word-Perfect to enhance the visual appeal of your documents. In this chapter, you learn about lines—how to create them, how to edit them, and how to use them in several practical applications.

WordPerfect provides several methods for creating lines. The Tables feature, for example, enables you to create horizontal and vertical lines to highlight and organize blocks of data. Chapter 14, "Working with Tables," discusses this feature. Graphics and text boxes also use several different line types to separate these items from the body of the text, as you learn in Chapter 17, "Understanding Advanced Graphics."

In addition to tables and graphics boxes, you also can create two types of freestanding graphics lines to set off text sections or enhance the look of your documents. The first part of this chapter focuses on horizontal and vertical lines, which you can adjust for length, position, thickness, and shades of gray.

Finally, WordPerfect offers the capability to draw connecting lines and boxes to highlight or set off parts of your text. The last part of this chapter explains this Line Draw feature and shows you how to use it to create an organizational chart.

In this chapter, you learn the following important aspects of using lines to add effects:

- Creating horizontal and vertical lines
- Changing the shape, length, and gray shading of graphics lines
- Positioning and editing lines with the mouse
- Using Line Draw to create connected boxes and lines

One word of caution: the procedures you learn in this chapter are really quite easy and fun. You just may become addicted!

Creating Horizontal Lines

Horizontal lines are used primarily to separate logical sections or segments of text; for example, they can communicate to readers a separation of the preliminary part of a letter (such as the letterhead) and the content, or what the recipient should read.

Creating a Full Horizontal Line

Suppose that you want to create a memo heading. You begin with the date, and the TO, FROM, and RE (or SUBJ) lines, as shown in figure 16.1.

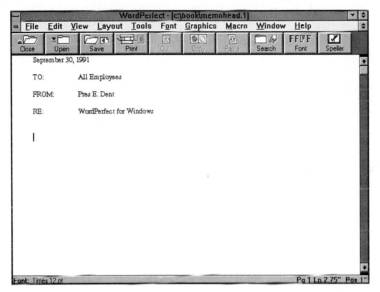

FIG. 16.1

A sample memo heading.

Now you are ready to create a separator line. After positioning the insertion point where you want the line, choose **G**raphics, **L**ine, **H**orizontal. WordPerfect displays the Create Horizontal Line dialog box (see fig. 16.2), enabling you to specify how you want the horizontal line to appear.

Cue: To create a horizontal line that extends from one margin to the other, choose **G**raphics, **L**ine, **H**orizontal and press Enter.

 Press Horizontal Line (Ctrl-F11).

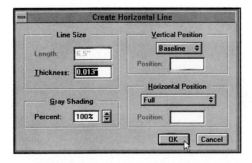

FIG. 16.2

The Create Horizontal Line dialog box.

For now, assume that you are satisfied with the default settings. These settings produce a line with the following characteristics:

- 0.013-inch thickness (1 point or 1/72 inch)
- 100 percent gray shading (black)
- Position at the baseline (at the bottom of the characters) of the current line
- Extending from the left margin to the right margin

Press Enter or choose OK to accept the default settings; the line appears in the text. WordPerfect places in the text a code similar to the following (see fig. 16.3):

```
[HLine:Full,Baseline,6.5,0.013",100%]
```

Your display may differ from that in figure 16.3, depending on your margin settings.

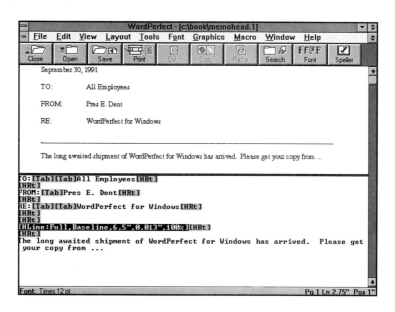

FIG. 16.3

The [HLine] code for the default horizontal line.

Specifying Vertical Position

The horizontal line you just created is anchored to the baseline of the line where the [HLine] code is located. If you move the code, the line moves to the position where you move the code.

You may want the line to be positioned at an exact vertical location on the page, regardless of the position of the surrounding text. In the sample memo, for example, you can create a line that appears exactly three inches from the top of the page.

To set the line at this position, follow these steps at the Create Horizontal Line dialog box:

1. Press Tab to move to the Vertical Position scroll box; then press the down-arrow key to choose **S**pecify. Alternatively, use the mouse to select **S**pecify.

2. Type **3** in the Position text box.

3. Press Enter or choose OK to accept this definition; WordPerfect places the line three inches from the top of the paper.

The [HLine] code now reads 3" rather than Baseline to indicate that—regardless of where the code appears on the page—the horizontal line is always three inches from the top of the page.

CAUTION: If you move the [HLine] code to another page, the horizontal line also moves to that page.

Specifying Horizontal Position and Length

You also can specify the length and horizontal position of the line. To create a three-inch, left-justified signature line, for example, follow these steps at the Create Horizontal Line dialog box:

1. Use the mouse or press Tab to move to the **H**orizontal Position scroll box, and choose Left from the pop-up list.

2. Move to the Line Size section and type the desired length (**3"**) in the Length text box.

3. Press Enter or choose OK to accept this definition. Figure 16.4 shows a left-justified signature line.

When you choose a horizontal position other than Full, the default line length that appears in the Length text box measures from the left or right margin to the insertion point position. If the insertion point is at the left margin and you choose Left for the horizontal position, for example, the Line Size Length text box shows 0", and you must change the measurement. If you choose Right, the length is 6.5" (or whatever distance lies between the left and right margins).

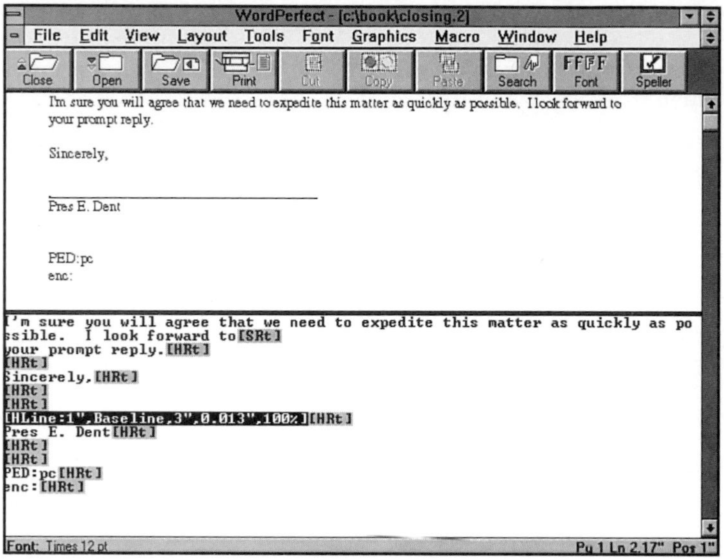

FIG. 16.4

A left-justified
signature line.

T I P   You can begin a line anywhere, even outside the left margin, by specifying the horizontal position. Choose **S**pecify in the **H**orizontal Position scroll box, and then type the desired position in the Position text box. You also can extend past the right margin by setting the length properly.

Specifying Line Characteristics

Single solid lines often are sufficient to create the visual effect you want, but sometimes you may want a thicker line or a line that isn't quite so stark. To create a softer, wider line for the sample memo, follow these steps in the Create Horizontal Line dialog box:

1. In the **T**hickness text box, type **.1** to create a 1/10-inch-thick line.

2. Move to the **G**ray Shading section and type **20** in the Percent text box (or use the arrow keys or mouse to choose the desired percentage from the scroll box).

3. Press Enter or choose OK to accept this definition. Figure 16.5 shows the new line.

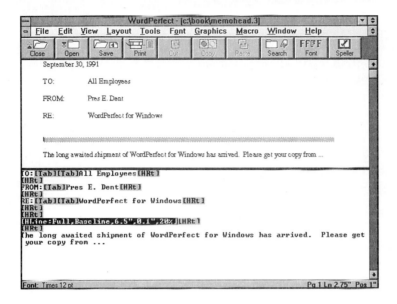

FIG. 16.5

A 20 percent gray, 1/10-inch-thick horizontal line.

> You can choose nearly any percentage of black, depending on the capability of your printer. Any percentage greater than 50 percent prints almost completely black on most printers, however. To print a shade of gray that can be duplicated (photocopied or offset), choose a percentage near 20.

T I P

Editing a Horizontal Line

So far, you have learned how to create various types of lines and position them to precise measurements. But your first attempt may not be exactly what you had in mind. You can delete the [HLine] code and start over, but editing the line's position and characteristics is quite easy.

Position the insertion point just *after* the line you want to edit, because WordPerfect searches first backward and then forward until it finds a line to edit. Then choose Graphics, Line, Edit Horizontal Line to access the Edit Horizontal Line dialog box. This dialog box has the same settings as the Create Horizontal Line dialog box used to create the line (again see fig. 16.2).

Cue: Before editing a line, position your insertion point just *after* the line to be edited.

If you want to edit the line visually with the mouse, you need not use
the dialog box. To modify a line with the mouse, move the mouse
pointer to the line you want to edit. The mouse pointer changes to an
arrow pointing to the line, as shown in figure 16.6. (You may have to
move slowly and carefully to make the arrow appear.) Then press the
left mouse button to select the line for editing.

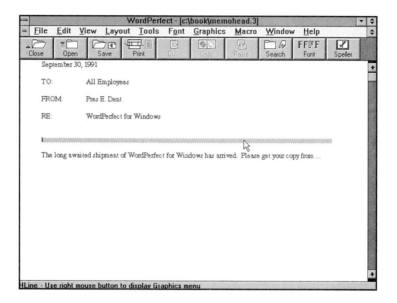

FIG. 16.6

Selecting a line
for editing with
the mouse.

When you select the line—or any graphics element—a dashed box appears around the line, indicating that it is ready for editing. For thin
lines, the box may appear as a single dashed line. The solid black boxes
at the corners are called *sizing handles* (see fig. 16.7).

To change the position of the line, move the mouse pointer into the
middle of the box, until you see the four-direction arrow icon shown in
figure 16.7. Then hold down the left mouse button, drag the line to the
position where you want it, and release the mouse button. Take care
when positioning your line; WordPerfect does not prevent you from
moving a line outside the left or right margin.

CAUTION: Be careful not to drag a sizing handle, or you will
change the shape of your line.

Notice that repositioning the line doesn't affect the text in any way. You
can position the line beneath, above, or even on top of (superimposed
on) text or other graphic elements.

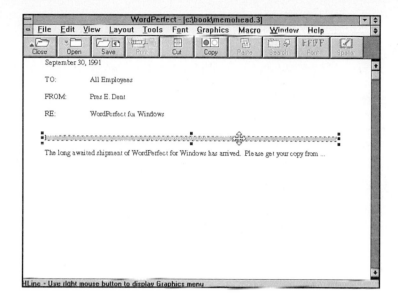

FIG. 16.7

Sizing handles
appearing
around a
selected line.

If you want to change the shape (length or thickness) of the line, position the mouse pointer on one of the sizing handles until you see a two
directional arrow icon. Then hold down the left mouse button, dragging
the handle in any direction to change the thickness, the length, or both
(see fig. 16.8). When the line is the size you want, release the mouse
button.

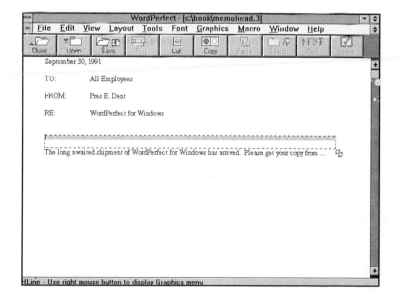

FIG. 16.8

Changing the
thickness of a
horizontal line.

T I P   To delete a line, select the line with the mouse and press Backspace or Del.

To make other changes to the line, you must use the Edit Horizontal Line dialog box. If you aren't using the mouse or you want to manipulate the line settings directly, you can make changes in length, thickness, position, and shading with this dialog box.

Cue: To select a line for editing, position the mouse pointer on the line and click.

You can access the Edit Horizontal Line dialog box by choosing **Graph**ics, **L**ine, Edit **H**orizontal Line (as previously described), but an easier method is to position the mouse pointer on the line so that the arrow icon appears, and click to select the line. You then press the right mouse button and choose **E**dit Horizontal Line from the menu that appears.

T I P   Double-click the mouse while pointing at the line to select it and go directly to the Edit Horizontal Line dialog box.

From the dialog box, you can adjust size, gray shading, and vertical and horizontal positions. (If you change the line's size or position with the mouse, the new measurements appear in the appropriate boxes.) You can type new settings, or choose horizontal and vertical positions from the scroll boxes.

Moving a line also moves the [HLine] code to the nearest line of text. To return a line to its original position, use the mouse to move the line as close as possible to its original position; then edit the line by choosing Baseline from the Vertical Position pop-up list.

Creating Vertical Lines

Like horizontal lines, vertical lines can help to direct the reader's eyes. When used with columns, for example, vertical lines help the reader follow the flow of text from one column to the next. Vertical lines also can provide special effects in newsletters, legal documents, and book-length documents.

The procedures for creating and editing vertical lines are nearly identical to those for horizontal lines, with the exception of the orientation and the default length.

Creating a Full Vertical Line

Suppose that you are a secretary getting ready to leave for your vacation. Your boss, who knows nothing about word processors, asks what he has to do to type his own letters if he wants to. You decide to leave him a "will." To give it a legal appearance, you want to add a page-length line at the left side of your text to set off line numbering in the left margin. After changing the left margin (if necessary), choose **Graphics**, **Line**, **Vertical** to access the Create Vertical Line dialog box, as shown in figure 16.9.

 Press Vertical Line (Ctrl-Shift-F11).

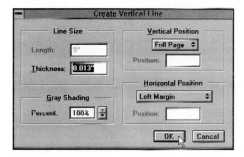

FIG. 16.9

The Create
Vertical Line
dialog box.

For now, assume that you are satisfied with the default settings. These settings produce a line with the following characteristics:

- 0.013 inch thickness (1 point or 1/72 inch)

- 100 percent gray shading (black)

- Position at the left margin (actually, about 1/8 inch to the left of the margin to leave space between the line and the body of text)

- Extending from the top to the bottom margin

Press Enter or choose OK to accept the default settings; the line appears in the text. At the same time, WordPerfect places in the text a code similar to the following:

```
[VLine:Left Margin,Full Page, 9",0.013",100%]
```

After you type the text of the will and turn on line numbering (by choosing **Layout**, **Line**, **Numbering**), you can add horizontal signature and date lines three inches long, at the left and right margins (see fig. 16.10).

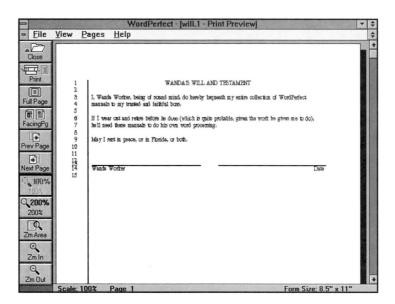

FIG. 16.10

A sample document with vertical and horizontal lines.

The only problem with the example in figure 16.10 is that the line numbering looks crowded at the signature lines. WordPerfect allocates space (line height) as needed to accommodate the largest character on the line; because this line contains no characters, the line height is reduced accordingly. To remedy this problem, you can change the line height for just that line (see Chapter 6, "Formatting Text"). A simpler method is to add a space before either of the [HLine] codes on that line (see fig. 16.11). The printed result now rivals wills prepared in any law office (see fig. 16.12).

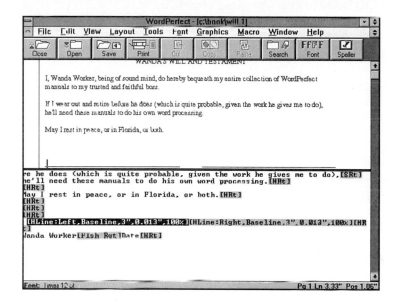

FIG. 16.11

A space next to
the [HLine]
code increases
that line's height.

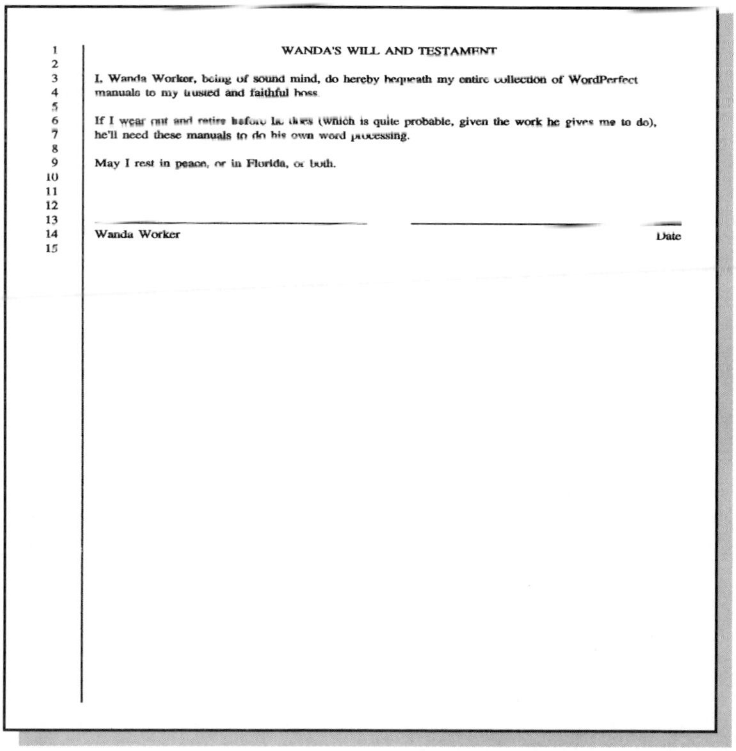

FIG. 16.12

The printed living
will.

Specifying Position, Length, and Characteristics

You use the Create Vertical Line dialog box to change the default position, length, and characteristics of a vertical line (again see fig. 16.9). The options in this dialog box are much like those in the Create Horizontal Line dialog box. The major difference is that you now are concerned with the horizontal (not the vertical) positioning of the line. When you do change the vertical position, you specify the line length, measuring from the current vertical position to the bottom of the page.

The Horizontal Position options include the following:

- *Left Margin*. This option positions the line approximately 1/8 inch to the left of the actual margin so as to provide some white space between the line and the text.

- *Right Margin*. This option positions the line approximately 1/8 inch to the right of the actual margin.

- *Between Columns*. This option enables you to place vertical lines to the right of any column. If you don't have columns, this option is the equivalent of the Right Margin option.

Using Vertical Lines with Columns

A common use of vertical lines is to separate columns of text. With newspaper-style columns, vertical lines can make the flow of the text easier to follow. Vertical lines also can separate parallel columns, although such data may be prepared more easily by using tables and changing the table lines as needed (see Chapter 14, "Working with Tables").

In Chapter 13, you learned how to create columns. If you still have the text you practiced with, use that text for the following exercise. If not, retrieve any unformatted text and add a title followed by two hard returns. Then, at the beginning of the text, define three evenly spaced newspaper-style columns by choosing **L**ayout, **C**olumns (see Chapter 13).

  Press Columns (Alt-Shift-F9).

Suppose that you created a company newsletter similar to the one shown in figure 16.13. On the first page is a two-line title across the top of the page followed by three evenly spaced columns of text.

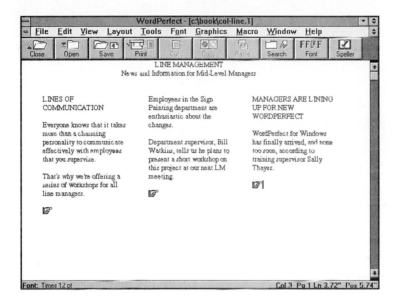

FIG. 16.13

Sample news-
letter with a title
and newspaper-
style columns.

To place vertical lines between the columns, position the insertion point at the beginning of the first column (after the [Col On] code), and follow these steps:

1. Choose **G**raphics, **L**ines, **V**ertical. The Create Vertical Line dialog box appears.

   CUA Press Vertical Line (Ctrl-Shift-F11).

2. Move to the **H**orizontal Position section and choose Between Columns from the scroll box.

3. Press Enter or choose OK to accept the default line length, width, and shading. A nine-inch line appears to the right of the first column.

As figure 16.14 shows, the default line extends from the top of the page to the bottom because the vertical position was set at Full Page. A line that extends only the length of the columns will have a better visual effect, so you must specify a vertical starting point and a line length.

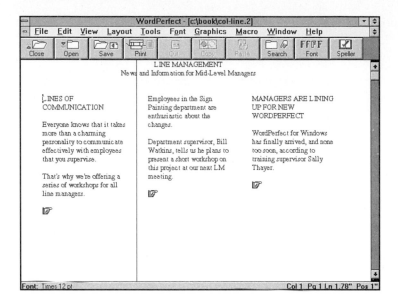

FIG. 16.14

A full-page vertical line between the first and second columns.

After creating the second line, you can go back and edit the first line. With the insertion point at the beginning of the first column of text (after the [Col On] code), follow these steps to create the second line:

1. Choose **G**raphics, **L**ines, **V**ertical. The Create Vertical Line dialog box appears.

   CUA Press Vertical Line (Ctrl-Shift-F11).

2. Move to the **V**ertical Position section and choose Specify from the scroll box.

   This action automatically places in the Position text box the measurement from the top of the page to the current insertion point position, and sets the line length from the current insertion point position to the bottom margin (see fig. 16.15).

3. Move to the **H**orizontal Position section and select Between Columns from the scroll box. Note that the Position box changes to the Right of Column box.

4. Move to the **R**ight of Column box and type **2**.

5. Press Enter or choose OK.

   The line appears between the second and third columns, as shown in figure 16.16.

Changing the settings for a vertical line between columns.

A vertical line beginning at the insertion point position (the top line of text).

You now have two vertical lines, but only the second line is the proper length. The next section explains how to edit the line length.

Editing a Vertical Line

You edit vertical lines by selecting Graphics, Line, Edit Vertical Line to access the Edit Vertical Line dialog box. This dialog box has the same settings as the Create Vertical Line dialog box used to create the line (again see fig. 16.15).

■ **Cue:** Before editing a vertical line, position your insertion point just *after* the [VLine] code.

Position the insertion point just *after* the [VLine] code for the line you want to edit, because WordPerfect searches first backward and then forward until it finds a line to edit.

If you want to edit the line visually with the mouse, you can make several changes without using the dialog box. (Review "Editing a Horizontal Line" in this chapter if you don't remember how to select and edit a line with the mouse, or if you skipped directly to this section.)

The line between the second and third columns is set to the proper length, so you need to look at the dialog box for the correct settings. Follow these steps to see the settings and edit the vertical line:

1. Select the second line with the mouse.

2. Choose **G**raphics, **L**ine, Edit V**e**rtical. (You also can press the right mouse button and choose **E**dit Vertical Line from the resulting menu, or double-click the line to bring up the dialog box.)

   Notice that the length of the line is exactly nine inches minus the measurement in the Position text box of the Vertical Position section.

3. Make a note of the vertical position and choose Cancel or press Esc.

■ **Cue:** You can double-click any graphics line to access its editing dialog box.

4. Double-click the first line to bring up its dialog box.

5. Move to the **V**ertical Position scroll box and select Specify.

6. Move to the **R**ight of Column text box and type the measurement that was used for the second line (the line to the right of the second column).

7. Press Tab.

   WordPerfect calculates and enters the line length measurement in the Line Size Length text box.

8. Press Enter or click OK. The first and second lines now match (see fig. 16.17).

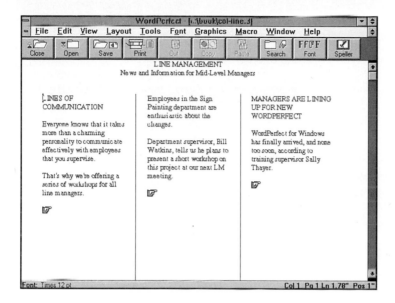

FIG. 16.17

Matching vertical lines that extend from the top of the text.

Combining Vertical and Horizontal Lines

WordPerfect does not limit you to one type of line. You can combine lines to meet your needs. One example of a functional combination of horizontal and vertical lines is the sample shown in figure 16.12, which has signature and date lines as well as a vertical line at the left margin.

You can improve the design of your newsletter, for example, by adding a horizontal line that separates the title from the three columns of text, as shown in figure 16.18.

To create a wide horizontal line with gray shading, follow these steps:

1. Position the insertion point on the line above the columns of text.

2. Choose **G**raphics, **L**ine, **H**orizontal.

   CUA　Press Horizontal Line (Ctrl-F11).

3. Type **.1"** in the **T**hickness text box.

4. Move to the **G**ray Shading section and change the Percent setting to **30%**.

5. Press Enter or choose OK to place the line in the text.

6. Press Enter again to add an extra line between the horizontal line and the columns of text.

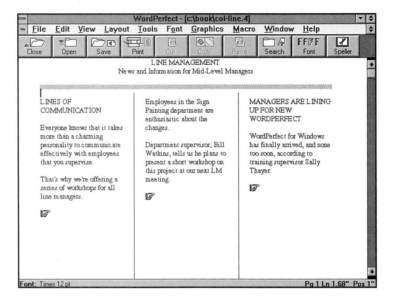

FIG. 16.18

The newsletter with a horizontal line added below the title.

Notice that even though you moved all three columns down one line, the vertical lines remained the same length and in the same position, because you specified the vertical position when you created the lines.

With the additional white space, your newsletter now looks quite attractive.

You can create many other line combinations: lines crossing lines, thick shaded lines beside thin black lines, shaded lines superimposed on text, and more. You also can use lines from empty graphics boxes to surround areas of your document or to create fill-in-the-blank or check boxes. These types of lines are explored in greater detail in the next two chapters.

Using Line Draw

WordPerfect's Line Draw feature enables you to use text-based line and angle characters to create free-form lines and boxes. Although sometimes you can create the same effect with graphics lines, Line Draw often is easier to use.

When you first use Line Draw, you may wonder why you need other types of graphics lines. The answer lies in the printed result. Lines created with Line Draw print correctly only with monospaced fonts such as Courier or Letter Gothic. If you use proportionally spaced fonts, your character-based lines and boxes differ in print and on-screen. By contrast, a graphics line is defined as two points (each end of the line), and the computer program fills in the line between those two points. Therefore, graphics lines and boxes print correctly, regardless of the font you use.

If you plan to use Line Draw to add lines to existing text, create the text with a monospaced font, and use spaces rather than tabs or centering codes to line up the various parts of the text chart. You can use another font for the rest of your document; only the Line Draw section needs the monospaced font.

Cue: When using Line Draw, always use monospaced text and spaces rather than tabs.

One example of a Line Draw application is an organizational chart. The relationship between names and positions can be made clearer by adding boxes and lines (see fig. 16.19).

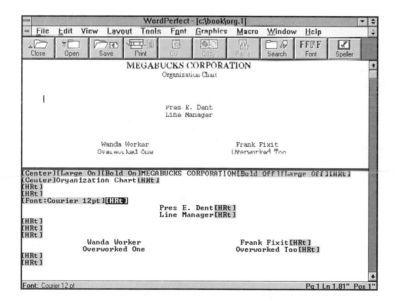

FIG. 16.19

A sample organizational chart before drawing boxes and connecting lines.

To enter Line Draw, press Ctrl-D. Line Draw is not listed on the menu, so you have to remember this command or use Help. When you use Line Draw, WordPerfect is in Draft mode, and the document characters appear thicker and are monospaced. The Line Draw dialog box also appears at the bottom of the screen (see fig. 16.20). At this point, the regular menu items are not active. You can draw lines in the editing area, but you can select options only from the dialog box.

Cue: You access Line Draw by pressing Ctrl-D.

FIG. 16.20

The Line Draw
dialog box.

Moving the Insertion Point in Line Draw

By default, WordPerfect assumes that you want to begin drawing immediately, using a single line. More often, however, you need to move the
insertion point to the corner of a box or the beginning point of a line
before drawing. Choose the **M**ove button by clicking it or by pressing
Alt-M; then use the cursor-movement keys to move the insertion point
to the position where you want to start drawing. For this sample chart,
move to the upper left corner of the manager's name (one row up and
two characters to the left).

> **T I P**   Pressing Home moves the insertion point to the left margin, and End
> moves it to the right margin, even if you have selected the WP51
> keyboard.

As you move the insertion point to areas that previously had no text
and as you draw lines, WordPerfect adds spaces to fill the area from
the left margin to the insertion point.

Drawing Lines

When you are ready to begin drawing, you can choose a line style from
the Characters section of the Line Draw dialog box. Then choose **D**raw
and move the insertion point in the direction you want to draw.
WordPerfect forms the line character-by-character. When you want to
change direction, press the appropriate arrow key (the one that points
in the new direction). The line turns, adding a corner.

For this example, choose the double-line character. Then press the right-arrow key 15 times, the down-arrow key 3 times, the left-arrow key 15 times, and the up-arrow key 3 times to complete the double-line box around the top manager's name. Then choose **M**ove, position the insertion point where the next line should begin, choose the line style, and begin drawing. Fig. 16.21 shows the completed chart. (Because mistakes are easily made, you may need to read the next section before you can finish the example.)

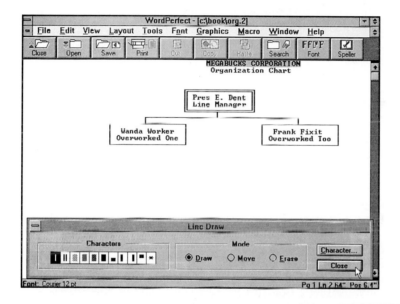

FIG. 16.21

The completed organizational chart.

> To create a box that extends the full width of the screen, start at the left margin and press End, move down, press Home, and move up to complete the box.
>
> T I P

The beginning or ending of a line may show directional arrows. These arrows indicate that the line is not connected to anything. The arrows don't print, but the appropriate line draw characters print in their place.

Erasing Lines

Because you are using a freehand approach to draw lines and even the fastest computers have a bit of delay as you draw, you may make mistakes that you need to correct. To erase all or part of a line, follow these steps:

1. Choose **M**ove and place the insertion point at the beginning of the line you want to erase.

2. Choose **E**rase; then use the arrow keys to move along the path of the line you want to erase.

3. Choose **D**raw to add correct lines or **M**ove to position the insertion point to create another line.

If you move too fast when drawing lines or erasing, you may change existing text. By default, Line Draw operates in Typeover mode so that it doesn't reformat your text. You may have to close the Line Draw dialog box and go back (also in Typeover mode) to correct any text you accidentally erased.

Printing Line Draw Lines

If you use a fixed-pitch (monospaced) font to create your lines, the horizontal lines probably will turn out fine. Some dot-matrix printers, however, don't quite connect the vertical line characters, thus making your vertical lines look like vertical dashes. Most laser printers don't have this problem. Before you print, you can use the Print Preview feature to check the results (and avoid wasting paper).

■ Cue: Check your line drawings in Print Preview. Choose **F**ile, Print Pre**v**iew or press Shift-F5.

If the lines don't join vertically, adjust the Line Height setting. Move the insertion point to the beginning of the Line Draw area and follow these steps:

1. Select **L**ayout, **L**ine, **H**eight to access the Line Height dialog box (see fig. 16.22).

FIG. 16.22

The Line Height dialog box.

2. Use the mouse to click the Fixed button; the default line height appears in the box.

3. Change the line height to an amount less than the amount shown. If you are using a Courier font, for example, which has a line height of 0.167, change the height to **0.15**.

4. Press Enter or choose OK to accept the change.

5. Select Print Preview again to see whether the lines now join. If not, repeat this process using a smaller line height.

After you adjust the line height properly for the Line Draw section, position the insertion point immediately after this section and select automatic line height again (**Layout, Line, Height, Auto**).

By now, you probably have figured out several uses for Line Draw. For example, you can do the folowing:

- Create organizational charts

- Design flow charts

- Illustrate wiring connections

- Diagram floor plans

- Lay out maps

Although Line Draw does have its limitations, particularly in the selection of fonts, still it is another powerful word processing tool.

Chapter Summary

In this chapter, you learned how to create horizontal and vertical graphics lines and how to change the shape, length, and gray shading of graphics lines. You also learned how to position and edit lines with the mouse and how to use Line Draw to create connected boxes and lines.

You now are ready to explore WordPerfect's rich graphics capabilities and learn about integrating text, lines, and graphics to create attractive, professional-looking documents.

Understanding Advanced Graphics

WordPerfect for Windows provides a graphics facility that is easy to learn and easy to use. This chapter builds on the information discussed in Chapter 7, "Introduction to Graphics." In that chapter, the primary WordPerfect graphic object—the figure graphic—is discussed. In this chapter, you review four of WordPerfect's graphics boxes, their options, and their defaults. In addition, you learn about the Figure Editor and how to use the Box Position and Size dialog box. (The fifth type of graphics box, Equations, is discussed in Chapter 27, "Using the Equation Editor.")

In the preceding chapter, graphics rules were introduced. Rules are used to define, separate, and enhance text. Used to enhance the text, graphics create an instant impression or get across an idea quickly.

■ **Joseph E. Rosenman** is the principal consultant of PCC Resources, a NYC consulting concern that specializes in PC installations, word processing, and desktop publishing.

Graphics go one step further than text alone by portraying an idea visually or illustrating a complicated object.

This chapter shows how WordPerfect's Graphics features work and gives you practice in using them. Chapter 18, "Desktop Publishing with WordPerfect," explores the use of graphics and fonts in realistic publication examples.

In this chapter, you learn about the following topics:

- The five graphics types
- The graphics defaults
- The interaction between graphics and text
- The Figure Editor
- The Text Editor
- The Caption Editor
- The Box Position and Size dialog box
- Combinations of graphics
- Sources for clip art and graphics editors

WordPerfect's Five Graphics Boxes

All graphics used in WordPerfect documents are placed in graphics boxes. A graphics box has two aspects, contents and options, and can contain one of three types of information: a graphics file, an equation (a special kind of graphics file), or text. WordPerfect has five kinds of graphics boxes: figure, text, equation, table, and user. The major difference among the five box types is in the type of graphical information each contains and which graphics editor the box uses by default.

The following three editors are available through the Graphics menu:

Editor	Use
Figure Editor	Modifies graphics
Equation Editor	Creates and modifies equations
Text Editor	Creates and modifies text as a graphic

This chapter explains how to use the Figure Editor and Text Editor. The Equation Editor is described in Chapter 27, "Using the Equation Editor."

All five graphics boxes have the same Options parameters, but they differ in their initial settings and in WordPerfect's choice of editor. You review the graphics editors elsewhere in this chapter, and you see how they work with the different types of graphic boxes.

The Figure Options dialog box controls a series of parameters that affect the way the box is displayed on-screen. All the boxes have exactly the same options, but their starting values (the defaults) are different. WordPerfect includes five types of boxes for use under different circumstances. For example, you sometimes may want to use one kind of box for graphics with one format and use another type of box for tables with a different format. You need to set the options only once each for both box types. If WordPerfect had only one type of box, you would have to reset the options again and again as you switched from a picture display to a table display and back again.

■ **Cue:** Options are used to set the border style, the spacing inside and around the box, and the percentage of gray shading used.

Figure Graphics

You choose **Graphics** to gain access to the five graphics boxes, the graphics editors, and graphics rules. (The Equation Editor is discussed in Chapter 27, "Using the Equation Editor," and graphics rules are discussed in Chapter 16, "Using Lines To Add Effects.") Each menu choice brings up a menu containing additional choices. Figure 17.1 shows the primary and secondary menus when you select **Graphics, Figure**.

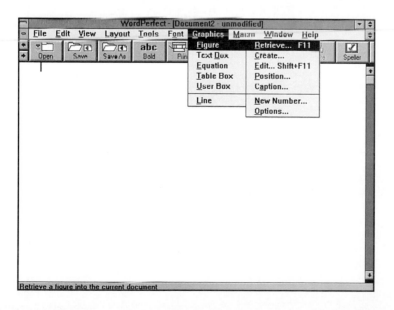

FIG. 17.1

Selecting Retrieve from the Figure menu.

■ **Cue:** **G**raphics, **F**igure **R**etrieve is the most common way to add a graphics figure to a document.

One difference between figure graphics and the other four box types is that the Figure menu includes a Retrieve option. This option is really just a shortcut, because any box that can invoke the Figure Editor can retrieve a graphic. It is assumed that the figure graphic will contain a graphics file.

If you work a great deal with figure graphics, you may want to place the Figure Retrieve command (Graphics, Figure, Retrieve) on the Button Bar.

The options on the Figure menu are described in the rest of this section.

■ *Retrieve.* Retrieving a figure graphic creates a figure graphic box, unless the preceding graphic is being replaced. You automatically jump into the Retrieve Figure dialog box (see fig. 17.2).

Select **G**raphics, **F**igure, **R**etrieve.

Press Figure Retrieve (F11).

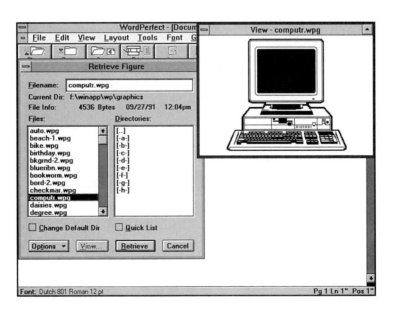

FIG. 17.2

The Retrieve Figure dialog box showing a list of figures.

■ The Retrieve Figure dialog box includes the View command. When used with graphics, this option provides a window that enables you to preview the graphics file before it is retrieved. Using the View feature, you easily can scroll through and preview a directory of graphics files before the files are loaded into the document.

■ *Create.* Choosing **C**reate opens the Figure Editor, where you can retrieve and manipulate a figure.

　　Select **G**raphics, **F**igure, **C**reate.

■ *Edit.* Choosing **E**dit causes the Edit Figure dialog box to appear. This dialog box enables you to select the graphics figure to load into the Figure Editor. If you selected the desired graphics box prior to issuing the Edit command, the graphic is loaded directly into the Figure Editor.

  Press Figure Edit (Shift-F11).

■ *Position.* Choosing **P**osition causes the Box Position and Size dialog box to appear. You use this dialog box to select the graphics figure you want to position. If you selected the desired graphics box prior to issuing the Position command, the Box Position and Size dialog box comes up for the appropriate graphic box.

　　Select **G**raphics, **F**igure, **P**osition.

■ *Caption.* Selecting **C**aption causes the Edit Figure Caption dialog box to appear, which you use to select the graphics figure whose caption you want to create or modify. If you selected the desired graphics box prior to issuing the command, the Caption Editor appears, showing the caption for the appropriate box.

　　Select **G**raphics, **F**igure, **C**aption.

■ *New Number.* Choose **N**ew Number to open the Figure Number dialog box and changes the number of the *next* figure graphic.

　　Select **G**raphics, **F**igure, **N**ew Number.

■ *Options.* Selecting **O**ptions opens the Figure Options dialog box. Any changes to figure options affect only *subsequent* figures.

　　Select **G**raphics, **F**igure, **O**ptions.

> ■ **Cue:** You must select **G**raphics, **F**igure, **C**aption for each figure that uses a caption.

Options for the Graphics Boxes

How the contents of a graphics box are presented can make a big difference in the effect the graphic produces, and in that sense you can view the graphics box itself as the packaging. By using the Options command on the Figure menu, you can select the way the graphics box appears on the page. Figure 17.3 shows the Figure Options dialog box.

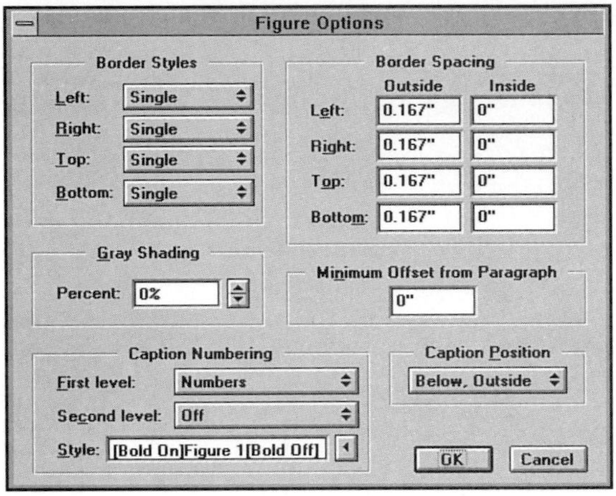

Figure Options

Border Styles
Left: Single
Right: Single
Top: Single
Bottom: Single

Border Spacing
	Outside	Inside
Left:	0.167"	0"
Right:	0.167"	0"
Top:	0.167"	0"
Bottom:	0.167"	0"

Gray Shading
Percent: 0%

Minimum Offset from Paragraph
0"

Caption Numbering
First level: Numbers
Second level: Off
Style: [Bold On]Figure 1[Bold Off]

Caption Position
Below, Outside

OK   Cancel

FIG. 17.3

The Figure
Options dialog
box.

The graphics options include several types of controls that affect the graphics box, which can be summarized as follows:

- Relationship of the graphic to the text
- What kind of box border lines are used
- Gray shading
- Caption information

This information is covered in the rest of this section.

Graphics Box and Text

The graphics box is like a container: the box holds some graphical information and defines a border for the text outside the box. To provide a clean and uniform appearance, you can determine how much space to leave along the border on the inside and outside of the box. The Border Spacing section of the Figure Options dialog box gives you the chance to specify the spacing for all eight sections:

Outside: Left, Right, Top, Bottom

Inside: Left, Right, Top, Bottom

A fundamental aspect of graphics boxes is their relationship to the rest of the text. The Wrap Text parameter, found in the Box Position and Size dialog box, controls whether the text moves aside to leave room for the graphics boxes. The Wrap Text parameter is not the same as word wrap, which is used to keep text within the margins. Wrap Text controls whether text flows around a graphics box or whether the text and graphics are superimposed. When Wrap Text is on, text flows around the graphics box. When Wrap Text is off, text ignores the graphics box and acts as though the graphics box is not present.

Why turn off Wrap Text? In many situations, it is convenient to let the text and graphics overwrite. For example, suppose that you want to place some text in a graphic of a picture frame. You place the picture frame graphic on the page in the desired location, and then you enter and position the appropriate text manually.

The final text-related parameter in the Figure Options dialog box is Minimum Offset from Paragraph. This confusing parameter controls how far from the top of the paragraph WordPerfect can move the graphics box in trying to fit the graphics box on the page. If the graphics box is anchored using the character or paragraph type, the graphic's vertical position changes as text is edited. If the text is placed in such a way that the graphics box is too close to the bottom of the page to fit, WordPerfect can move the box up. In some cases, Word-Perfect cannot adjust the graphics box position. When that happens, the graphics box is moved to the top of the next page.

A value of 0 means that the graphic *must* start at the top of the paragraph. A value of 2 means that the graphic can be pushed "down" as much as 2 inches from the start of the paragraph.

Border Lines for Boxes

Each box has four sides, and each side can have one of six line types—or no lines at all. The line types can be mixed in any fashion, although not every combination is appealing or useful. The following are the Border Styles options in the Figure Options dialog box: Single, Double, Dashed, Dotted,Thick, and Extra Thick.

One of the most significant differences among the different graphics boxes is the choice of borders. The borders dramatically distinguish one type of box from another.

Gray Shading

The interior of the graphics box doesn't have to be white. WordPerfect enables you to specify a gray shade to be used in the box. The amount of shading is represented by a percentage, where 0 percent is white and 100 percent is solid black. The Figure Options dialog box enables you to select from a pop-up list a shading amount in 10 percent incre-ments (10 percent, 20 percent, 30 percent, and so on). If you need a more specific amount, you can enter the exact percentage you want. The printed appearance of the box depends on the capability of the printer: not all printers can render gray shading well. On a high-resolu-tion printer, differences of a few percent may make a difference. On typical office laser printers, however, 10 percent increments provide an adequate difference in shading.

As you approach 100 percent shading, you cannot see black letters placed in a black box. If you select white letters, a 100 percent black background may be appropriate. An example of white-on-black printing is provided toward the end of this chapter.

Creating Captions

You can give a caption to each box. The four parameters available for each caption are First level, Second level, Caption style, and Caption position.

■ Cue: Captions can have a primary number or a primary and a secondary number.

The first and second level captions refer to the type of automatic num-bering used for the box. First level indicates that the box numbers use whole numbers. Second-level captioning adds a decimal portion to the caption number. For example, the text *Figure 3* uses only a first-level numbering, and the text *Figure 4.2* uses first- and second-level numbering.

You have a choice of four numbering systems in captions, which are the following: Off, Numbers, Letters, and Roman Numerals.

You use the Style text box of the Figure Options dialog box to indicate what text to use in the caption and to determine the text's appearance. The words *fig.*, or *Figure* may be appropriate choices for the Style text box. The Style text box gives you four choices for the appearance of the caption, when using automatic numbering. These choices are Bold, Italics, Underline, and Small Caps.

After you have decided how you want the captions to look, you decide where to put them. The caption can be positioned in one of the follow-ing four locations:

Below and Outside the box

Above and Outside the box

Below and Inside the box

Above and Inside the box

Captions do not appear unless the Caption Editor has been invoked for that particular box. The menu commands to start the Caption Editor are **Graphics**, **Figure**, **Caption** (for text boxes, use **Graphics**, Text **Box**, **Caption**, and so on).

T   I   P

Graphics Defaults

The figure box options have been covered in some detail in this chapter. The same considerations apply to the remaining four graphics boxes. The following figures show the default parameters in the dialog box and what the boxes look like using those settings. Please note that all the illustrations are of boxes with an image loaded.

Beginning with the figure box, figures 17.4 through 17.12 show the various boxes and their respective Options dialog box parameters.

Figure 17.4 shows the default box for a figure. The Figure Options dialog box is shown in figure 17.3.

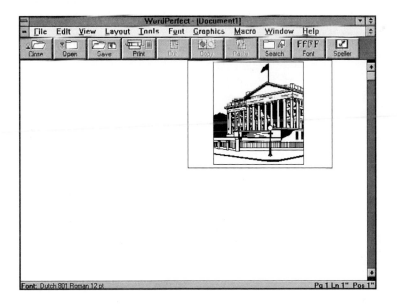

FIG. 17.4

The default box for a figure.

Figure 17.5 shows the default graphics text box. The corresponding dialog box is shown in figure 17.6.

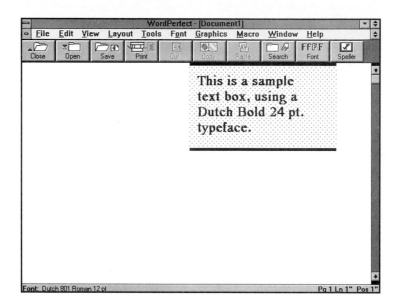

FIG. 17.5

The default text box.

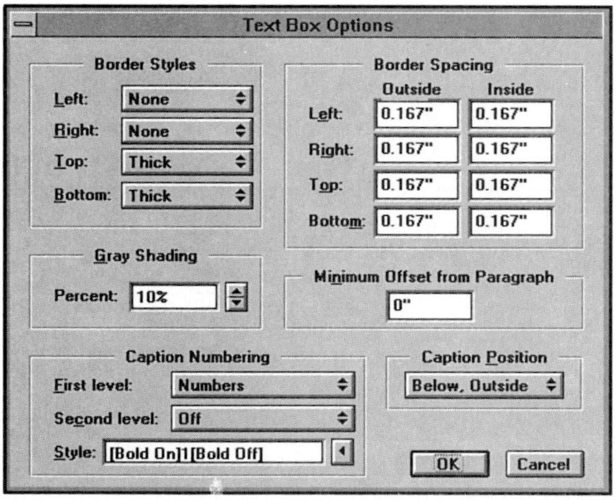

FIG. 17.6

The Text Box Options dialog box.

The default graphics equation box is shown in figure 17.7, and the Equation Options dialog box is shown in figure 17.8. *Note:* A blank Equation Editor box has no default borders.

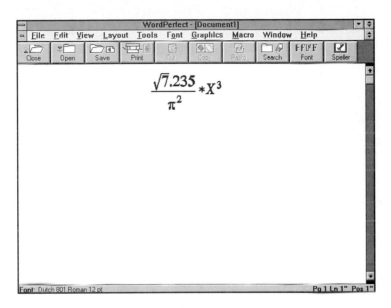

FIG. 17.7

The default box for an equation.

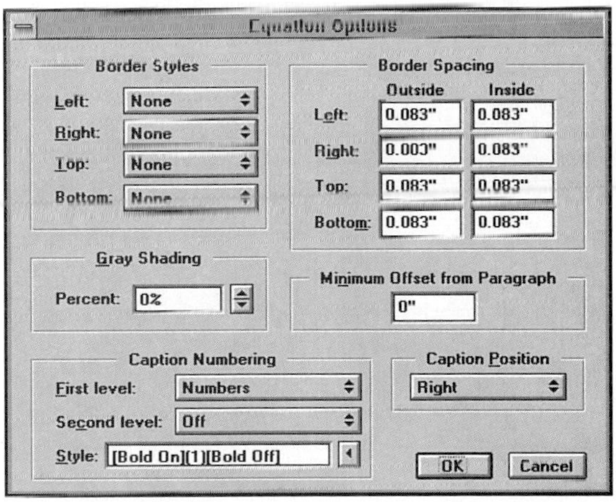

FIG. 17.8

The Equation Options dialog box.

Figures 17.9 and 17.10, respectively, show the graphics box and Options dialog box for a table.

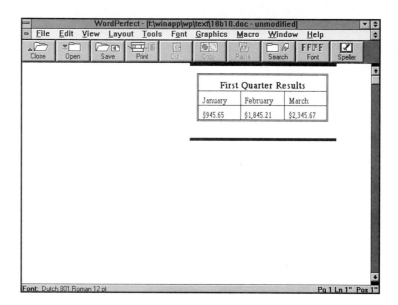

FIG. 17.9

The default box for a table.

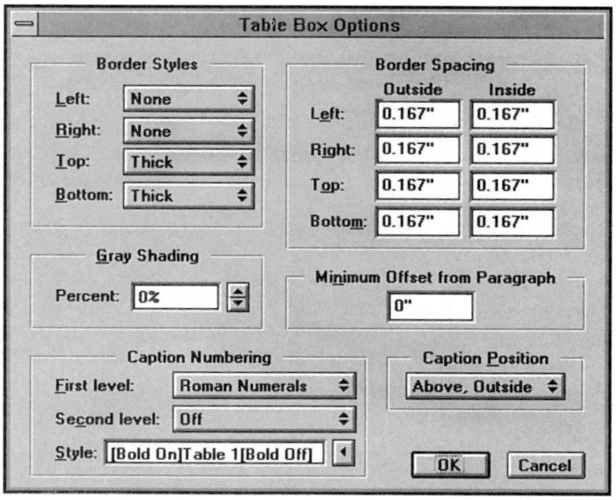

FIG. 17.10

The Table Box Options dialog box.

The user-defined graphics box and its Options dialog box are shown in figures 17.11 and 17.12, respectively. *Note:* A blank user box has no default borders.

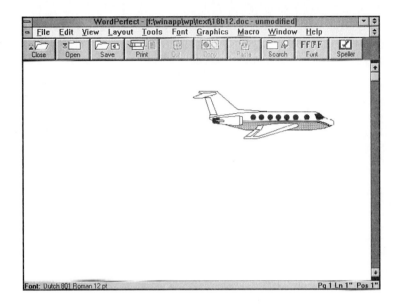

FIG. 17.11

The default user-defined box.

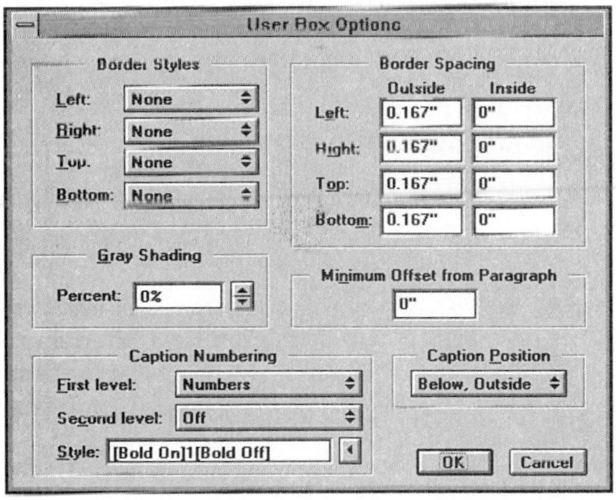

FIG. 17.12

The User Box Options dialog box.

When you select **G**raphics, **T**able Box, **C**reate or **G**raphics, **U**ser Box, **C**reate, WordPerfect asks which editor you want to use. Figure 17.13 illustrates the Select Editor dialog box.

FIG. 17.13

The Select Editor dialog box.

Figure Editor

■ **Cue:** The Figure Editor enables you to alter the appearance of a graphic.

WordPerfect can do much more than load a graphics image into a box. The Figure Editor provides a collection of tools to manipulate the way the image looks. The Figure Editor does *not* alter the image itself, only the way the image is stored in the graphics box.

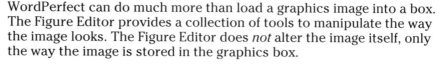

The Figure Editor's Button Bar can be replaced or modified to suit your needs. If you find that you use certain functions frequently, add them to the Button Bar.

The Figure Editor is a full-screen window with its own set of tools and a special Button Bar. You can invoke the Figure Editor in several ways:

■ Select the **G**raphics menu and choose **F**igure, **C**reate

■ Select the **G**raphics menu and choose **F**igure, **E**dit (to select a previously defined figure graphic)

■ If Wrap Text is enabled, double-click the graphics box

■ If Wrap Text is disabled, click with the *right* mouse button to display a pop-up window (see fig. 17.14). This window presents the following options:

Select Box

Edit Figure   Invokes the Figure Editor

Box **P**osition   Invokes the Box Position and Display
                          dialog box

Edit **C**aption   Invokes the Caption Editor

The Figure Editor screen includes an editing window showing the graphics file, an optional Button Bar, a menu line, and a status line (see fig. 17.15).

The Figure Editor has the following five menu options: **F**ile, **E**dit, **V**iew, **W**indow, and **H**elp.

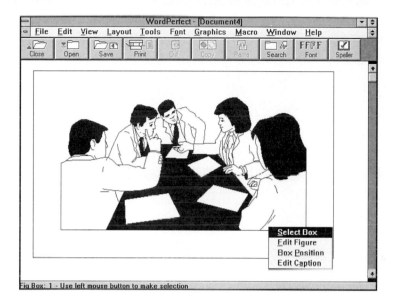

FIG. 17.14

A figure graphic showing the right mouse button window.

FIG. 17.15

The Figure Editor with a graphics file loaded.

Help works the same in the Figure Editor as elsewhere in WordPerfect. The View option controls the way in which the Figure Editor Button Bar is displayed. Button Bars are discussed in Chapter 19, "Using the Button Bar." Although that chapter discusses the main screen Button Bar, all the Button Bar setup and edit features apply to the Figure Editor Button Bar as well. The Window menu choice enables you to switch to other open windows.

The remaining two choices on the Figure Editor menu bar, File and Edit, provide access to all the Figure Editor's functions and features.

Note: Some of the graphics files used as illustrations in this section are not included with WordPerfect for Windows; they are available separately from WordPerfect Corporation. If the graphic is in *vector* format, you probably can alter the appearance of the graphic in the Figure Editor.

Figure Editor File Commands

The Figure Editor's File menu has 6 options (see fig. 17.16). You learn how to use these options in this section.

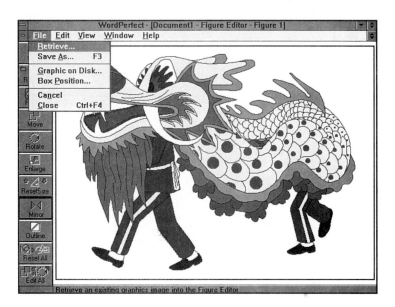

FIG. 17.16

Figure Editor with the File menu open.

You choose **F**ile, **R**etrieve to load a graphics file into the Figure Editor. Examples of supported graphics files include WordPerfect Corporation clip art, PCX files, TIFF files, and HPGL files. When you select **F**ile, **R**etrieve, the Open Figure dialog box appears (see fig. 17.17).

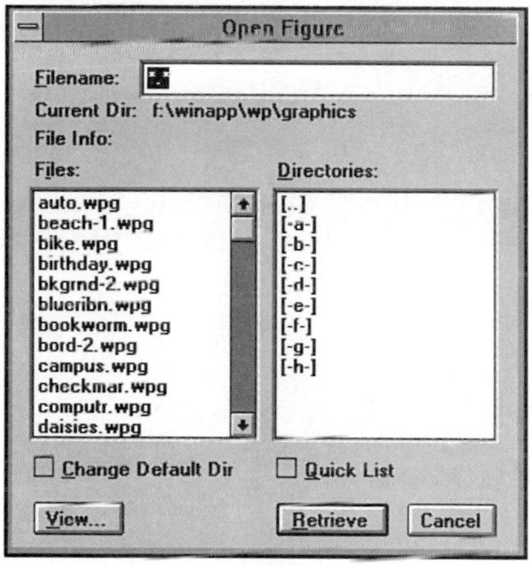

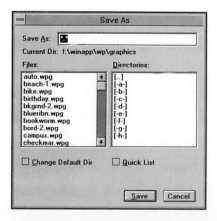

FIG. 17.17

Selecting a figure from the Figure Editor's Open Figure dialog box.

> Some formats, like PCX and TIFF, can be imported with better quality if you first convert them into WPG files with the GRAPHCNV program. Using the GRAPHCNV program is discussed toward the end of this chapter.

T I P

Selecting File, Save As saves the contents of the Figure Editor to disk as a WPG file. This command is useful if a non-WPG format file was imported into the Figure Editor. Note that none of the modifications made to the figure box by the Figure Editor are saved, because those changes affect how the contents of the box are *displayed* and *not* what is within the box. Choosing Save As brings up the Save As dialog box (see fig. 17.18).

 Press Save As (F3).

FIG. 17.18

Using the Figure Editor's Save As dialog box.

Choosing **F**ile, **G**raphics on Disk saves the graphic as a disk file instead of storing it in the document header. Using this option creates a link between the document and any Graphic on Disk files. Saving with this option has the advantage of reducing the size of the document, but also has the disadvantage of requiring that multiple files be kept together for a complete document. If you choose **F**ile, **G**raphics on Disk, the Graphic on Disk dialog box appears (see fig. 17.19).

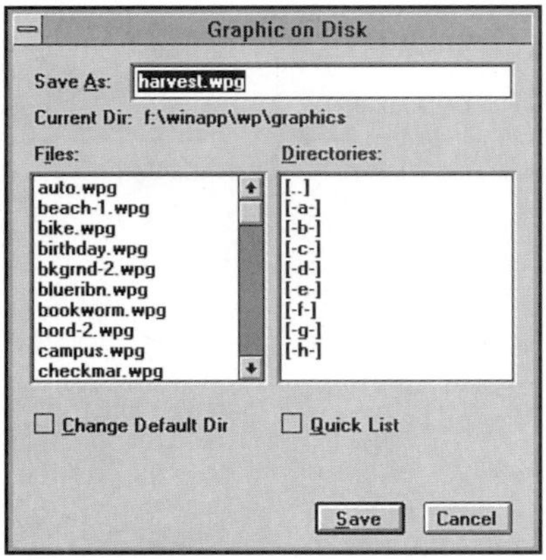

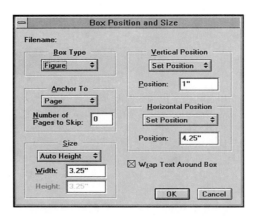

FIG. 17.19

Saving a graphic as a disk file.

Selecting **F**ile, Box **P**osition opens a complex dialog box containing many parameters. Most of these values are set automatically as you use the mouse to move and size the graphics box directly on the editing screen. If you need to specify exact information, or if you want to define the graphics box in a nonstandard way, you must access the Box Position and Size dialog box from the Edit screen or in the Figure Editor by selecting **F**ile, Box **P**osition (see fig. 17.20).

FIG. 17.20

Setting parameters in the Box Position and Size dialog box.

Choosing Cancel discards any changes you may have made and returns you to the editing screen.

Selecting **C**lose ends the Figure Editor session and returns you to the document, which now shows the modified figure box.

 Press Close (Ctrl-F4).

Box Position and Size Dialog Box

Use the **B**ox Type option to change from one type of graphics box to another. The following five choices are available: Figure, Text, Equation, Table, and User.

Use the **A**nchor To option to anchor the graphic box in one of these three ways:

- *Paragraph.* The graphics box moves around with the text and stays with a particular paragraph.

- *Page.* The graphics box is fixed in a particular position on the page.

- *Character.* The graphics box is treated as if it were a text character and is repositioned along with the text.

Note: If you select Page, the Graphics Box code should be at the start of the page. If you select Paragraph, the Graphics Box code should be at the start of the paragraph.

Choosing **N**umber of Pages to Skip causes the graphics box to appear on a subsequent page. This parameter is meaningful only if the graphics box uses the Page anchor type.

You use the **S**ize setting to determine the size of the graphics box. WordPerfect gives you the following four ways to determine the box size:

- *Auto Both.* Use the default box size (for height and width) as determined by the graphic.

- *Set Width.* Specify the width of the box, and WordPerfect determines the height.

- *Set Height.* Specify the height of the box, and WordPerfect determines the width.

- *Set Both.* Specify both the width and the height.

■ **Cue:** Size determines the size of the box, not the graphic in the box. The size of the graphic contained in the box can be changed in the Figure Editor.

■ **Cue:** Vertical Position determines whether the graphic is at the top or bottom of the page.

Select **Vertical** Position to determine how the graphics box is positioned on the page with respect to the top and bottom margins. Table 17.1 shows how this selection changes with the different anchor types.

Table 17.1. Vertical Position Commands according to Anchor Type			
Option	**Paragraph**	**Page**	**Character**
Full Page	n/a	Graphics box fills page from top to bottom	n/a
Top	n/a	Positions box at top margin	Positions top of box with text baseline
Center	n/a	Positions box in center of page	Positions center of box with text baseline
Bottom	n/a	Positions box at bottom margin	Positions bottom of box with text baseline
Baseline	n/a	n/a	Matches baseline of last line of text box with baseline of text
Set Position	n/a	Manually set offset from top of page	n/a
Position	Determines distance from top of paragraph	Distance from top of page (use with Set Position)	n/a

■ **Cue:** Horizontal Position determines whether the graphics box is to the left or right side of the page.

Choosing **Horizontal** Position determines how the graphics box is positioned on the page with respect to the left and right margins. Table 17.2 shows how this parameter changes with the different anchor types.

Turning on **Wrap** Text Around Box causes the text to wrap around the box. The Outside Border Spacing values (from the Figure Options dialog box) determine how close text can come to the box (choose **Graph**ics, **Figure, Options**).

When **Wrap** Text Around Box is turned off, the text ignores the box and acts as if the box doesn't exist. In that case, text and the graphics box overwrite the same space.

Table 17.2. Horizontal Position Commands according to Anchor Types

Option	Paragraph	Page	Character
Margin, Left	Places box at left margin	Places box at left margin	n/a
Margin, Right	Places box at right margin	Places box at right margin	n/a
Margin, Center	Places box in center of margins	Places box in center of margins	n/a
Margin, Full	Expands box to fill space between margins	Expands box to fill space between margins	n/a
Column, Left	n/a	Places box at left column margin	n/a
Column, Right	n/a	Places box at right column margin	n/a
Column, Center	n/a	Places box in center of any two column margins (you can span more than one column)	n/a
Column, Full	n/a	Expands box to fill space between column margins (you can span more than one column)	n/a
Set Position	Manually set offset from left margin	Manually set offset from left margin	n/a
Position	Distance from left margin (use with Set Position)	Distance from left margin (use with Set Position)	n/a

T I P You can open the Position dialog box by using the mouse and following these steps:

1. Position the mouse pointer on the graphics box.

2. Click the right mouse button.

3. Select **P**osition.

   The Box Position and Size dialog box appears.

The Figure Editor status line displays the following information:

Information	Description
File Name	The name of the graphics file that is loaded
Pos X:	The distance left or right from center
Y:	The distance up or down from center
Scale X: Y:	The amount of width and height larger (or smaller) than when the graphic originally was loaded; 100 is "normal"
Rotate:	Rotation in degrees from the center of the graphic
% Change	A value used in keyboard commands; the value can be 1%, 5%, 10%, or 25%; pressing the Ins key changes this number.

Figure Editor Menu Commands

■ **Cue:** The Figure Editor Edit menu contains the commands that change the way the graphic appears.

The Figure Editor enables you to change the way a graphics file appears in the graphics box. These changes do not affect the original graphics file in any way, and the changes are lost if a new graphics file is loaded into the graphics box. You should be aware, however, that not all the Edit menu commands work (or work well) with raster graphics. Figure 17.21 shows the Edit menu. Limitations for bit maps are noted along with descriptions of the Figure Editor options being discussed.

WordPerfect Corporation clip art is used in the examples in this section. Although the sample graphics were chosen for their visual appeal, you can use *any* vector WPG file (such as the clip art included with WordPerfect) as you try the commands.

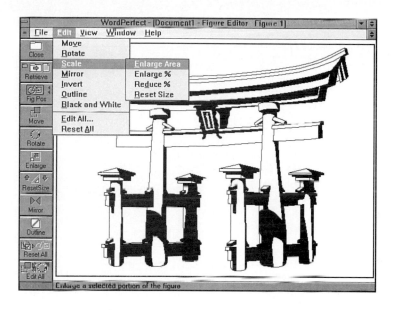

FIG. 17.21

Figure Editor with the Edit menu open.

Selecting Edit, Move moves the graphics figure around within the graphics box. If you use a mouse, you do *not* see the figure's new position until you release the mouse button. The status line is updated as you move the mouse pointer. If you use the arrow keys, the figure moves in discrete jumps. The amount of movement is determined by the % Change value.

Figure 17.22 shows an example of a graphic after being loaded, and figure 17.23 shows the same figure after being moved 25 percent to the right.

Cue: If you move the graphic too far to any side, part of the graphic is clipped off.

FIG. 17.22

An unmodified figure.

FIG. 17.23

The figure moved 25 percent to the right.

Choosing **E**dit, **R**otate causes a rotation pointer to appear on the screen, which helps identify the 0 degree point (see fig. 17.24). You can click and drag with the mouse or click at some point on the screen (the graphic rotates so that it is aligned with the mouse pointer). You also can rotate the graphic in fixed increments by using the Ctrl-left arrow and Ctrl-right arrow keys. Figure 17.24 shows an example of a graphic after being loaded, and figure 17.25 shows the same figure after being rotated 45 degrees.

Note: Raster graphics cannot be rotated.

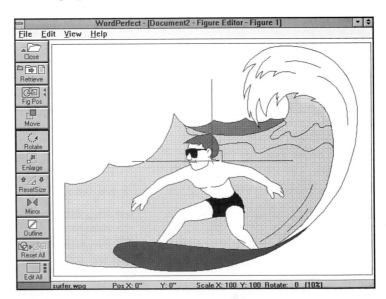

FIG. 17.24

A figure showing the rotation pointer.

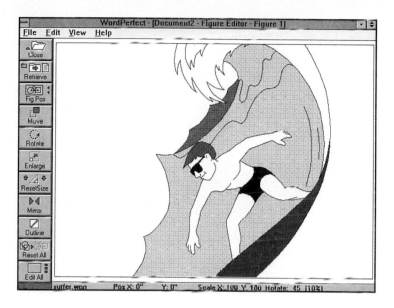

Selecting **Edit, Scale** shrinks or expands the figure within the graphics box. If the figure is expanded larger than 100 percent, parts of the image fall outside the box and are no longer visible. The Scale option also enables you to enlarge a specific portion of the graphic so that it fills the entire box. You have the following four Scale options: **Enlarge Area, Enlarge %, Reduce %,** and **Reset Size.**

To enlarge a specific area of a graphic, follow these steps:

1. Position the enlarge pointer (a crosshair) in the lower left corner of the area to be enlarged.

2. Drag the enlarge box to the desired size.

3. Release the left mouse button.

Figure 17.26 shows a figure ready for enlargement, with the enlarge pointer positioned. Figure 17.27 shows the area of the figure to be enlarged, and figure 17.28 shows the enlarged image.

Cue: The Enlarge Area command enables you to zoom in on a specific portion of a graphic.

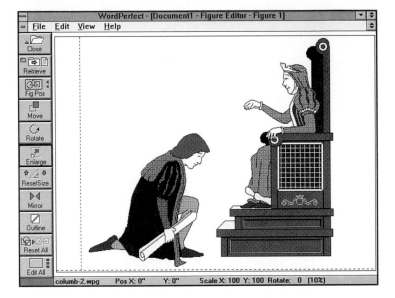

FIG. 17.26

The graphic to be enlarged.

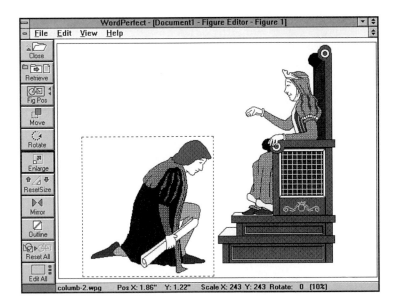

FIG. 17.27

Preparing to enlarge part of a graphic.

FIG. 17.28

The enlarged
graphic section.

The Enlarge % option increases the scale of the figure by the percentage indicated in the Status Line Percentage Change field. The keyboard equivalent of this command is Ctrl-up arrow. Figure 17.29 shows the graphic enlarged 25 percent.

FIG. 17.29

The original
graphic enlarged
25 percent.

The Reduce % option decreases the scale of the figure by the percentage indicated in the status line. The keyboard equivalent of the Reduce % option is Ctrl-down arrow.

The Reset Size option restores the scale to its original values.

Note: Enlarging or reducing raster images results in a substantial loss of quality. These functions are not recommended for use with raster graphics.

Selecting **Mirror** flips the graphic horizontally. If the figure is of a person facing left, choosing **Mirror** turns that person to the right. No keyboard or mouse options apply to this command. Figure 17.30 shows a graphic before using the Mirror option, and figure 17.31 shows the same graphic after using the Mirror option.

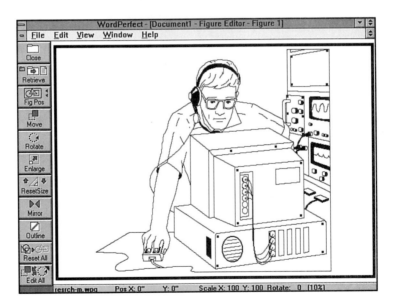

FIG. 17.30

A graphic before mirroring.

Choose **Invert** to switch each dot in the graphic to its complementary color. This command has the effect of turning a color picture into something analogous to a photographic negative. Invert has little or no effect on line art, and only affects vector graphics with solid areas. The effect on raster graphics, however, is dramatic.

Select **Outline** to convert a graphic with solid areas and colors into a line-art graphic. All colors become white (transparent), and all black areas remain black. Figures 17.32 and 17.33 illustrate the effect of the Outline command.

FIG. 17.31

A mirrored graphic.

FIG. 17.32

An original graphic.

Turning the
original graphic
into line art.

The **B**lack and White command on the Edit menu is similar to the Outline command, except that all colors become black (instead of white).
Figure 17.34 shows how this option affects the graphic in figure 17.32.

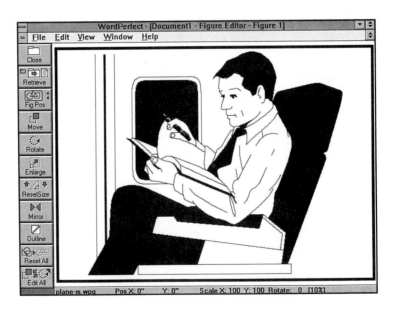

Using the Black
and White option
on a graphic.

Use the Edit All command on the Edit menu to open the Edit All dialog box, which contains all the Figure Editor's Edit options (see fig. 17.35). This dialog box enables you to specify *exactly* what you want if you know the numeric values in advance. Clicking the Apply button causes the graphic to be redrawn using the new settings, without closing the window.

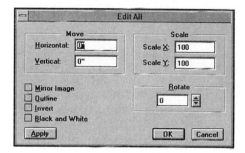

FIG. 17.35

The Figure Editor's Edit All dialog box.

Choosing Reset All from the Edit menu returns all the values to what they were when the figure was first loaded.

Cue: Reset All restores the graphic to its original settings.

Text Boxes and the Text Editor

Text boxes generally contain text being used in a graphical fashion. For example, the text can be emphasized in any one of several ways:

- Placing the text within borders
- Using a gray background
- Using a special or contrasting font
- Rotating to the text
- Straddling columns

The text box provides a simple way to *package* a segment of text and to treat that segment as an independent element. Generally, text boxes are placed in the document in the same way that figure graphics may be placed. The same considerations about the Figure Graphic Options and Box Position and Size dialog boxes apply to the text box.

To access text box features, use the Graphics, Text Box menu selection. All the selections are the same as in Figure Graphics (except that Retrieve is missing). To create a text box, use Graphics, Text Box, Create. To edit a previously defined text box, use Graphics, Text Box, Edit.

Press Alt-F11 (Text Box Create).

 Press Shift-Alt-F11 (Text Box Edit).

Primarily used with text boxes, the Text Editor enables you to enter and rotate text in a graphics box. All the text options found on the Font and Layout menus are available in the Text Editor. Some examples of these effects are the following:

Option	Description
Size	Make larger or smaller
Font	Use different fonts
Attributes	Variations like Bold, Italic, Small Caps, and Outline or Shadow (if available with your printer)
Typesetting	Alter character and word spacing
Tables	Use tables, including linked spreadsheets

 If you frequently use text boxes, you may want to place the Text box create command (**G**raphics, Text **B**ox, **C**reate) on the Button Bar.

The Text Editor gives you access to two special controls, the Box Position dialog box and a Rotate control. Box Position is exactly the same as described in the section "Figure Graphics." Figure 17.36 illustrates the Text Editor window. Note the familiar menu bar at the top of the screen.

Cue: You can rotate text only if your printer supports text rotation.

You can use the Text Editor Rotate control to rotate the text in one of four orientations. Rotation is always in 90-degree increments, so the text can be sideways (left or right) or upside down.

To Rotate text, press Alt-R or click the Rotate button. The Rotate Text dialog box appears, giving you the following four choices: Rotate None, Rotate 90°, Rotate 180°, and Rotate 270°.

Note that the default is None and that rotation always affects the entire text box. No rotation codes are inserted into the text.

Note: Your printer must be able to print rotated text for this feature to work.

You can open the Text Editor to edit a text box directly from the document by double-clicking the text box (as long as word wrap is turned on). Pressing the right mouse button brings up a window which gives you the following options: Edit **C**aption, **E**dit Text Box, and **P**osition.

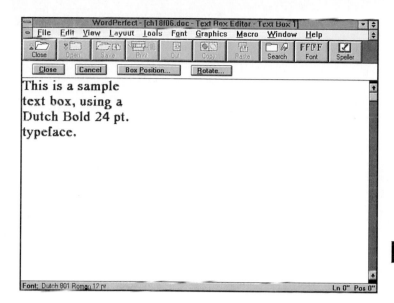

Caption Editor

You can invoke the Caption Editor for any of the five types of boxes. Like the Text Editor, starting the Caption Editor opens a window in which you can enter text. The location of the caption is determined by the Options dialog box. Figure 17.37 shows how the Caption Editor screen (for figure graphics) looks with the default caption.

The only command in the Caption Editor (besides Close and Cancel) is Box Number. Choosing Box Number inserts the box number code at the current insertion point. As with the Text Editor, you can enter text in the Caption Editor. You can use any of the standard font and attribute choices. Captions are generally short, just a few words or a short sentence.

Cue: The Caption Editor works with all five types of boxes.

Some Examples of Graphics

Now that you have become acquainted with advanced graphics commands, you can try them out. This section provides some step-by-step examples of how to create advanced graphics, based on the assumption that you already know how to create and position a figure graphic as explained in Chapter 7, "Introduction to Graphics."

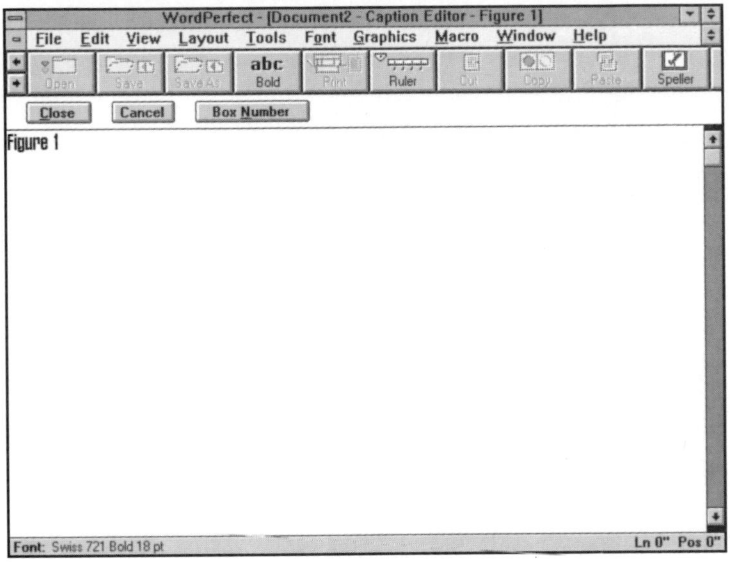

WordPerfect - [Document2 - Caption Editor - Figure 1]

File Edit View Layout Tools Font Graphics Macro Window Help

Open Save Save As Bold Print Ruler Cut Copy Paste Speller

Close   Cancel   Box Number

Figure 1

Font: Swiss 721 Bold 18 pt   Ln 0" Pos 0"

FIG. 17.37

The Caption
Editor screen.

The first example is a combination figure graphic, placed on a blank page. Three graphics boxes are involved, one on each side (mirror images), framing a larger graphic in the center. All the graphics involved in this example are included with WordPerfect.

In the following section, all the steps needed to create the example are described. You can click the menu choices with the mouse instead of using the keyboard. Part of the example involves sizing and moving the graphics. You also can use the mouse, as explained in Chapter 7, "Introduction to Graphics." The example includes precise location information—but you don't really need to be that precise. The mouse enables you to move and size the figure graphics boxes quickly, but they may not match the example exactly.

To create a graphic made up of several individual graphics in combination, follow these steps:

1. Open a new document.

2. Select **G**raphics, **F**igure, **O**ptions.

3. Change all four border styles to None.

4. Close the Options dialog box.

5. Select **G**raphics, **F**igure, **R**etrieve.

    Press Figure Retrieve (F11).

6. Select and retrieve the file BIKE.WPG.

7. Click the graphic with the right mouse button and select Box **P**osition.

8. Set the following parameters:

   Vertical Position: 1.5"

   Horizontal Position: Margin, Right

   Width: 1.6"

9. Click OK to close the Box Position and Size dialog box.

10. Select **G**raphics, **F**igure, **R**etrieve.

     Press Figure Retrieve (F11).

11. Select and retrieve the file BIKE.WPG.

12. Click the graphic with the right mouse button and select Box **P**osition.

13. Set the following parameters:

    Vertical Position: 2.5"

    Horizontal Position: Margin, Left

    Width: 2.25"

14. Double-click on the figure box on the left to open the Figure Editor. Alternatively, you can use the menu command Graphics, Figure, Edit to cause the Edit Figure Box to pop up, prompting you for the figure box number to edit. In this example, you choose number 2.

     Press Figure Edit (Shift-F11).

15. Press Ins until the `% of change` is 1percent.

16. Press the right-arrow key three times to move the figure to the right. When correctly positioned, the status line reads `X:0.168`.

17. Select **E**dit, **M**irror to mirror the graphic.

18. Select **F**ile, **C**lose to exit the Figure Editor.

    Figure 17.38 shows the screen at this stage.

19. Select **G**raphics, **F**igure, **R**etrieve.

     Press Figure Retrieve (F11).

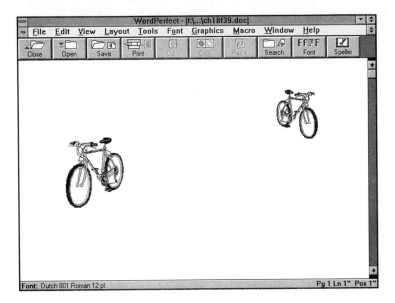

FIG. 17.38

Two bikes, ready to go...

20. Select and retrieve the file AUTO.WPG.

21. Click the auto graphic with the right mouse button and select Box Position.

22. Set the following parameters:

   Vertical Position: 1.25"

   Horizontal Position: Margin, Center

   Width: 4"

23. Click OK to close the Box Position and Size dialog box.

You now have a three-figure graphic (see fig. 17.39). Note that you can size and position the three graphics with the mouse instead of with the Box Position and Size dialog box. Using the mouse is less exact but is faster and creates virtually the same effect.

■ **Cue:** You can use the mouse to adjust the size and position of the graphics.

The next example places one graphic inside another graphic. As in all the examples, the instructions provide explicit size measurements so that the final results will be the same—but you can use the on-screen mouse sizing and moving features to create a similar effect.

Figure 17.40 shows a graphic of a movie screen, in which you place a second graphic of a researcher at work. The second graphic is placed on a 10 percent gray background to help distinguish it from the movie screen graphic. Because the gray background is a box option, use the user box for the second graphic. This procedure enables you to set a gray background for one type of box and to leave the other type of box with a white background.

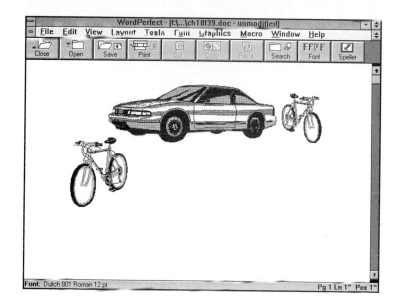

FIG. 17.39

Three graphics boxes.

FIG. 17.40

A movie screen graphic with a blank screen.

1. Open a new document.

2. Select **G**raphics, **F**igure, **O**ptions.

3. Change all four border styles to None.

4. Close the Options dialog box.

5. Select **G**raphics, **U**ser, **O**ptions.

6. Change **G**ray Shading to 10%.

7. Close the Options dialog box.

8. Select **G**raphics, **F**igure, **R**etrieve.

   Press Figure Retrieve (F11).

9. Select and Retrieve PROJECT.WPG.

   This file is not included with WordPerfect for Windows. If you want to practice with other graphics examples, you may do so. Both graphics used in this example are available in WordPerfect's Business Pack.

10. Resize the graphic box so that it fills the page by clicking and dragging with the mouse or by setting the Horizontal Position to Margins, Full in the Box Position and Size dialog box. The latter approach is more precise and places you in the Box Position and Size dialog box for the next step.

11. If you are not there already, enter the Box Position and Size dialog box by doing one of the following:

   ■ Click the figure box with the right mouse button and select Box **P**osition.

   ■ Select **G**raphics, **F**igure, **P**osition and choose Figure Number 1.

12. Deselect the Wrap Text Around Box.

13. Close the Box Position and Size dialog box.

At this point, you have retrieved and sized the first of the two graphics. The next step, placing a smaller graphic into the larger graphic, is a bit tricky. To have both graphics display, the Wrap Text feature must be off. Unfortunately, after you have placed the smaller graphic, you cannot select it with the mouse. This limitation of WordPerfect can be overcome only by advance planning.

If you need to re-select the second graphic, the best way to do that is to move the larger graphic temporarily out of the way. Because the first graphic is positioned at the top of the document and is centered between the margins, you can easily reposition it.

If you try to position the second graphic using the mouse, and the results are unsatisfactory, you can use the Box Position and Size dialog box to enter the appropriate values—as provided in this example. If you don't have access to these graphics examples, you may find that using the samples provided in WordPerfect is unsuitable. You cannot use the same measurements provided in this example for a graphic of a different size.

To place the smaller graphic, follow these steps:

1. Select **G**raphics, **U**ser, **C**reate.

2. When the Select Editor dialog box pops up, chose **F**igure Editor.

3. From the Figure Editor, select **F**ile, **R**etrieve.

4. Select and Retrieve RESRCH-W.WPG.

   This file is available in WordPerfect's Business Pack.

5. Close the Figure Editor.

6. Position the user box so that it fills the movie screen. (Unfortunately, you cannot use the mouse to accomplish this.) Use one of the following:

   ■ Click the user box with the right mouse button and select Box **P**osition.

   ■ Select **G**raphics, **U**ser, **P**osition and choose User Box Number 1.

7. Set the following Parameters:

   Vertical Position: 1.5"

   Horizontal Position: 2.75"

   Size: Set Both

   Width: 4.6"

   Height: 3.5"

8. Close the Box Position and Size dialog box.

Figure 17.41 shows the superimposed graphic.

Any graphic image that has a large blank spot may be suitable for the kind of superimposition used here. The following rules summarize the method needed to produce the superimposed graphics:

1. Place the larger graphic first.

2. Disable Wrap Text on the larger graphic.

3. Approximate the proper size and location of the smaller graphic.

4. Through trial and error, resize and relocate the smaller graphic through the Box Position and Size dialog box until the results are satisfactory.

In addition to placing a graphic in a graphic, another popular technique is to place a text box within the graphic. The next example does exactly that.

FIG. 17.41

A movie screen with "projected" image.

Cue: To make the text larger or smaller, you need to change the font or the font point size.

The third example has fancy text placed inside an ornamental border. This example also uses two graphics boxes, a figure box for the border and a text box for the text. The text is in a fancy typeface (Cloister). You can use any typeface available to you. The font you can select for the text depends on the kind of printer you are using and what typefaces you have available. If you have a large amount of text to place in the box, you should choose a smaller font. (For more information about choosing fonts, see Chapter 10, "Working with Fonts.") Figure 17.42 shows the finished graphic.

To create the graphic, follow these steps:

1. Open a new document.

2. Select **G**raphics, **F**igure, **O**ptions.

3. Change all four border styles to None.

4. Close the Options dialog box.

5. Select **G**raphics, **T**ext, **O**ptions.

6. Change the top and bottom styles to None.

7. Change **G**ray Shading to 0 percent.

8. Close the Options dialog box.

9. Select **G**raphics, **F**igure, **R**etrieve.

 Press Figure Retrieve (F11).

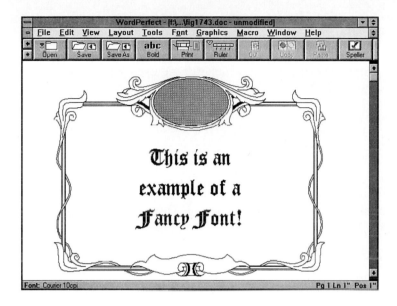

FIG. 17.42

A text box inside
a fancy border.

10. Select and retrieve BORD-2.WPG.

11. Click the graphic with the right mouse button and select Box
    Position.

12. Set the following parameters:

    Horizontal Position: Margin, Full

    Reselect Wrap Text Around Box

13. Click OK to close the Box Position and Size dialog box.

14. Select Graphics Text, Box, Create.

     Press Text Box Create (Alt-F11).

15. Select Layout, Line, Center.

     Press Center (Shift-F7).

16. Select Font, Font.

    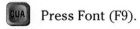 Press Font (F9).

    Note: This example uses 40-point Cloister. You can choose any
    available font and font size for this example (the options available
    depend on the printer you are using). If you choose a font that is
    too large, the text does not fit into the box. If you choose a font

that is too small, most of the box is empty. You often can change the size of the font so that it fits the available space—if your printer supports scalable fonts.

17. Enter the desired text. This example uses **This is an example of a Fancy Font!**

18. Select Box **P**osition.

19. Set the following parameters:

    Size: Set Both

       Width: 4"

       Height: 2.5"

    Vertical Position: 2.5"

    Horizontal Position: Margins, Center

20. Click OK to close the Box Position and Size dialog box.

21. Select **C**lose to exit the Text Editor.

The next example shows what happens when you add a graphic to a page full of text. In this example, you are adding the graphic to a page that *already* has text. If you were to create the graphic box first and *then* add the text, the result would be the same (the text would wrap around the graphic). As you move or resize the graphic, the text flows around the graphics box. Figure 17.43 shows the page without the graphic, and figure 17.44 shows the page after the graphic is added.

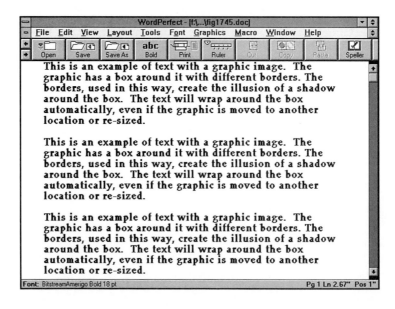

FIG. 17.43

A WordPerfect page with text but no graphic.

To create this kind of graphic, follow these steps:

1. Open a new document.

2. Enter the appropriate text. (Any text is suitable.)

3. Select **G**raphics, **F**igure, **O**ptions.

4. Change the Left and Top borders to Single.

5. Change the Right and Bottom borders to Extra Thick.

6. Close the Options dialog box.

7. Select **G**raphics, **F**igure, **C**reate.

> `CUA` Press Figure Create (F11).

8. Select and retrieve MAP-WORL.WPG.

9. Click the graphic with the right mouse button and select Box **P**osition.

10. Set the following parameters:

    Vertical Position: 2"

    Horizontal Position: Margins Right

11. Click OK to close the Box Position and Size dialog box.

Note the shadow effect produced by using different borders. Any two connecting sides can use thick lines to create this illusion.

Text flows around the figure graphics box, wherever it may be located. Although you precisely positioned the figure box so that the example matches the illustration in fig. 17.44, you easily can move and resize the box using the mouse. Select the figure box with the mouse and try moving and scaling it. If you need more information on how to move and scale a graphics box, refer to Chapter 7, "Introduction to Graphics."

The next example shows how a graphic can be used to enhance text when the two are overlaid. Note that the choice of graphic and text are critical in a document of this kind. Only line art is suitable (unless very light shades or colors are selected), and text that is larger and thicker than normal is required to maintain legibility. Figure 17.45 shows how this combination appears.

To create the overlaid text and graphic, follow these steps:

1. Open a new document.

2. Enter the appropriate text. (Any text is suitable.)

    Note: Choose a point size larger than 15, if available.

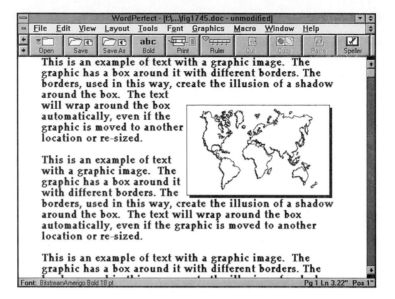

FIG. 17.44

The same page
with a graphic
added.

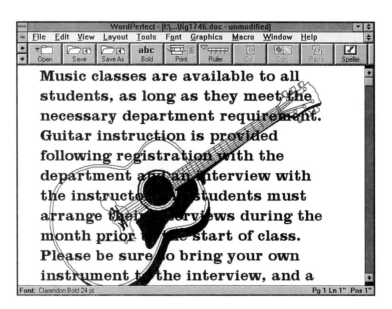

FIG. 17.45

Text on a guitar
background.

3. Select **Graphics**, **Figure**, **Options**.

4. Change all four border styles to None.

5. Close the Options dialog box.

6. Select Graphics, Figure, Retrieve.

CUA   Press Figure Retrieve (F11).

7. Select and retrieve GUITAR-2.WPG.

8. Click the graphic with the right mouse button and select Box Position.

9. Set the following parameters:

> **V**ertical Position: 2"
>
> **H**orizontal Position: Margin, Full
>
> Reselect **Wr**ap Text Around Box

10. Click OK to close the Box Position and Size dialog box.

Even though the graphic chosen is primarily line art, the guitar has two solid areas—and the text *is* obscured in those areas. If you use this technique, be sure that your graphic does not make the text difficult to read.

The next example illustrates a handy technique for reverse printing. Creating a text box with 100 percent gray shading (black) and white letters produces a self-contained white-on-black region. Figure 17.46 illustrates this technique, using a Bitstream Cooper Black typeface.

■ **Cue:** White-on-black printing is not supported by all printers.

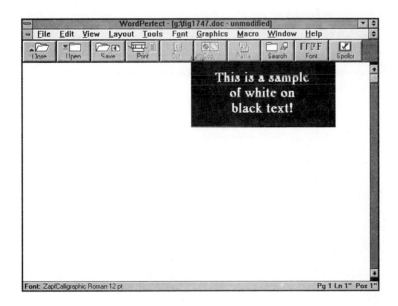

FIG. 17.46

A white-on-black text box.

To create this effect, follow these steps:

1. Open a new document.

2. Select **G**raphics, Text **B**ox, **O**ptions.

3. Change all four border styles to None.

4. Set Grey Shading to 100%.

5. Close the Options dialog box.

6. Select **G**raphics, Text **B**ox, **C**reate.

    Press Text Box Create (Alt-F11).

7. Select **L**ayout, **J**ustification, **C**enter.

    Press Center (Control-J).

8. Select **F**ont, **C**olor, **P**redefined Color, **W**hite.

9. Enter text. Any text can be used in this example.

   On most systems, the text does *not* appear on-screen as you type. If you need to see the text you have entered, select Reveal Codes (Alt-F3) while in the text box. Note also that white-on-black printing is not supported by all printers.

10. **C**lose the Text Editor.

You can make text boxes small enough to contain a single line of text. By selecting the Character Anchor in the Box Position and Size dialog box, you can include small, reverse-print text boxes in lines of text as if they were words with special attributes.

The last example combines some of the techniques discussed in the preceding examples. This example uses clip art that is not included with WordPerfect, so you may not be able to try it out.

The graphics used in this example are included in WordPerfect's Education Pack. If you want to try something similar, select the five graphics included with WordPerfect. Although they are not related, you can practice the techniques of sizing and placement with whatever graphics are available.

This example, shown in figure 17.47, groups five graphics together. The central graphic is the main subject, and the four other graphics are supporting images. Note the use of the captions to help articulate the message. The instructions for this graphic are abbreviated, because you use the same techniques illustrated in the preceding examples.

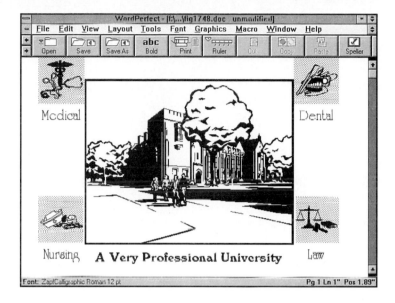

FIG. 17.47

Five graphics combine for one message.

First, initialize the graphics boxes. Follow these steps:

1. Open a new document.

2. Select **Graphics, Figure, Options.**

3. Change all four border styles to None.

4. Close the Options dialog box.

5. Select **Graphics, User, Options.**

6. Set **Gray Shading** to 25%.

7. Close the Options box.

Next, you retrieve, size, and position the main graphic. Although these instructions include exact values, you can approximate the same setting by using the mouse to size and position the graphic. Remember, if you don't have the actual graphics used in this example, try experimenting with any substitute vector art you have available—such as the clip art included in WordPerfect. Follow these steps:

1. Select **Graphics, Figure, Retrieve.**

   CUA Press Figure Retrieve (F11).

2. Select and Retrieve CAMPUS.WPG.

3. Click the graphic with the right mouse button, and select Box **P**osition.

4. Set the following parameters:

> **V**ertical Position: 1.25"
>
> **H**orizontal Position: Margin, Center
>
> **S**ize: Auto Height
> **W**idth: 4.75"
>
> Deselect **W**rap Text

5. Close the Box Position and Size dialog box.

6. Click the graphic with the right mouse button, and select Edit **C**aption.

7. Delete the [Box Num] code.

8. Select Font, Font to chose an appropriate font.

 Press Font (F9).

This example uses Bitstream's Windsor 20 point.

9. Select **L**ayout, **J**ustification, **C**enter.

 Press Center (Control-J).

10. Enter text. In this example, the text used is **A Very Professional University**.

11. Close the Caption Editor.

The next section places the four satellite graphics around the larger main graphic. All the steps needed to place the first satellite graphic are detailed. The remaining three boxes are placed in the same fashion. The table following the steps details the values for the four boxes. You can position and size the four graphics using the mouse. Follow these steps:

1. Select **G**raphics, **U**ser, **C**reate.

2. When the Select Editor dialog pops up, choose the Figure Editor.

3. In the Figure Editor, select **F**ile, **R**etrieve.

4. Select and Retrieve MEDICAL.WPG.

5. Select **F**ile, Box **P**osition.

6. Set the following parameters:

    Vertical Position: 1"

    Horizontal Position: .888"

    Size: Set Both
        Width: 1", Height: 1"

    Deselect **W**rap Text

7. Click OK to close the Box Position and Size dialog box.

8. Close the Figure Editor.

9. Click the graphic with the right mouse button, and select Edit Caption.

10. Delete the [Box Num] code.

11. Select **F**ont, **F**ont to chose an appropriate font.

   Press Font (F9).

This example uses Bitstream's University 24 point.

12. Select **L**ayout, **J**ustification, **C**enter.

   Press Center (Control-J).

13. Enter Text. In this example, the text used is **Medical**.

14. Close the Caption Editor.

These steps complete the placement of the first satellite box. Repeat steps 19 through 32 for each of the three remaining user boxes. The parameters are defined in the following table:

Box	File Name	Vertical Position	Horizontal Position	Size	Caption
User Box #1	MEDICAL.WPG	1"	0.888"	1",1"	Medical
User Box #2	DENTAL.WPG	1"	6.6"	1",1"	Dental
User Box #3	NURSING.WPG	4"	0.888"	1",1"	Nursing
User Box #4	LAW.WPG	4"	6.6"	1",1"	Law

The final effect is that of graphical "bullets" surrounding the central figure. A graphic like this might be suitable in a newsletter or at the top of a flier.

The GRAPHCNV Program

■ **Cue**: The graphics conversion program is needed only if you are unhappy with WordPerfect's automatic translation or if you want to convert files in advance.

WordPerfect converts most graphics formats directly when the graphic is retrieved, but WordPerfect's automatic conversion may not be ideal in all situations. The GRAPHCNV program (included with WordPerfect) gives you additional control over the conversion process. Because WordPerfect doesn't have to perform a conversion on WPG files, previously converted files load more quickly. GRAPHCNV also converts color files into gray-scale format.

GRAPHCNV is a DOS program, not a Windows application, which means that any file conversions you perform must be done from DOS. To run GRAPHCNV, make sure that you have GRAPHCNV in a subdirectory included in the path on your computer, or change to the WPC directory.

To use GRAPHCNV, follow these steps:

1. Type **graphcnv** and press Enter.
2. Enter the name of the original file.
3. Enter the destination file name.

You also can specify the input and output files directly on the command line, as in the following:

    GRAPHCNV NEWFILE.PCX NEWFILE.WPG

NEWFILE.PCX is the file to be converted, and NEWFILE. WPG is the WPG file that is created.

In either example, if the destination file name exists, GRAPHCNV asks whether you want to replace it.

GRAPHCNV has a large number of command line options, summarized in table 17.3. To use a command line option, include the option after you type **graphcnv**, as in the following:

    GRAPHCNV /C=B

This command starts GRAPHCNV and converts all colors to black. File specifications and command line options can be combined, as in the following example:

    GRAPHCNV NEWFILE.PCX NEWFILE.WPG /C=B

Table 17.3 lists the command line options.

Table 17.3. GRAPHCNV Command Line Options

Option	Purpose
/b=#	Sets WPG background color: 1 = black, 2 = blue, 3 = green, 4 = cyan, 5 = red, 6 = magenta, 7 = brown, 8 = white
/c=2	Changes color to black and white
/c=16	Changes color to WordPerfect's 16-color palette
/c=256	Changes color to WordPerfect's 256-color palette
/c=b	Changes color to black (do not use with bit maps)
/c=w	Changes color to white (do not use with bit maps)
/f=#	Changes fill color (after /c or /g conversion): 1 = black, 2 = blue, 3 = green, 4 = cyan, 5 = red, 6 = magenta, 7 = brown, 8 = gray, 9 = dark gray
/g-16	Changes color to WordPerfect's 16 gray scale palette
/g-256	Changes color to WordPerfect's 256 gray-scale palette
/h	Displays a Help screen
/l	On the standard printer, prints a conversion status message for each file processed
/l-filename	Saves to a file a conversion status message for each file processed
/m	Inverts a monochrome bit map
/n=#	Changes line color (after /c or /g conversions); see /f for the color codes
/o	Suppresses the Replace files? prompt
/w	Disables HPGL pen-width conversion. All HPGL pen widths convert to hairline widths.

Graphics Resources

The easiest way to get graphics is to purchase clip-art collections. The best-quality clip art for use with WordPerfect comes from WordPerfect Corporation, but WordPerfect isn't the only source. Often, the only way to get the graphic you need is to create the graphic yourself. You can use many programs to create graphics. Although far from complete, the following section describes some of the more important and better-known possibilities.

DrawPerfect

DrawPerfect is a multifaceted graphics program that works directly with the WPG graphic format. When used with WordPerfect Office and WordPerfect 5.1, DrawPerfect can be started directly from the WordPerfect Graphics Editor. Unfortunately, DrawPerfect isn't available as a Windows application to accompany the release of WordPerfect for Windows.

Some of DrawPerfect's features include the following:

- A graphing facility
- A presentation facility
- A drawing facility
- A Graphics Editor

DrawPerfect's graphing capabilities are an enhanced version of the Chart feature you would expect to find in a spreadsheet. In addition to many graph types, you can incorporate special text and clip art to "dress up" the appearance of the graph. After enhancing the graph, you can put together a "slide show" by using DrawPerfect's presentation feature. You can sequence multiple graphics so that they appear in a predetermined order, using a variety of special effects as new graphics are displayed.

If you need to combine graphics, add lines or effects, prepare unique combinations of graphics, or create original graphics, DrawPerfect is an excellent choice when working with WordPerfect.

Other Graphics Packages

Many graphics products are available that produce excellent output. Depending on what your needs are, the following packages may be useful to you.

Package	Features	Address
CorelDraw!	Windows-based; unsurpassed text special effects; easy-to-use interface; excellent font and clip-art libraries; capability to produce WPG files	Corel Systems Corp. 1600 Carling Ave. Ottawa, Ontario Canada K1Z 8R7 (613) 728-8200

Package	Features	Address
Micrografx Designer	Windows-based; used for precision work; combines best features of CAD with a full-featured drawing program	Micrografx, Inc. 1303 Arapaho Richardson, TX 75081 (214) 234-2694
AutoCAD	Supports the creation of detailed and intricate drawings; best package for creating complex engineering drawings	AutoDESK Inc. 2320 Marinship Way Sausalito, CA 94965 (415) 332-2344
PC PaintBrush	Bit-map drawing program; best choice for creating or editing PCX files; PaintBrush Plus includes scanner support	ZSoft Corporation 450 Franklin Road, Suite 100 Marietta, GA 30067 (404) 428-0008
ColoRIX VGA Paint	Superior editing tools; controls and effects worth extra effort required; available in DOS and Windows versions (DOS version produces WPG files)	RIX Softworks, Inc. 18552 MacArthur Blvd. #200 Irvine, CA 92715 (800) 233-5983
Hijaak	Indispensable for graphics conversions; converts any format that WordPerfect cannot accept into an acceptable format	Inset Systems 71 Commerce Drive Brookfield, CT 06804 (800) 828-8088

Scanners

A useful tool for working with graphics is a scanner. Scanners convert pictures or photographs into a computer graphics format, usually TIFF or PCX files. For certain kinds of graphics work, scanners are essential tools. Several varieties of scanners are available:

Cue: Scanners usually produce TIFF or PCX files.

Scanner Type	Capability
Hand scanners	Can scan copy up to 4 inches wide
Flatbed	Can scan 8 1/2-by-1-inch or 8 1/2-by-14-inch pages; use with books and bulky originals
Gray-scale	Converts color or black and white into shades of gray
Color	Can scan full color originals

Scanning is a time-consuming operation and (especially with color scanning) can produce enormous files. As with all bit-mapped images, you cannot scale scanned images without losing resolution and quality.

Autotracing

Autotracing is a technique that converts bit-mapped files into vector format. Not all graphics convert well, but in many cases an autotraced bit-mapped graphic produces an excellent vector graphic. This situation is true especially for scanned line art, which lends itself to vector format. After being converted to vector format, the graphic can be scaled and modified without loss of resolution.

CorelDraw! and Micrografx Designer include autotrace programs with their software. Several other stand-alone autotrace programs are available for purchase.

Clip-Art Vendors

Many vendors of clip art sell collections in various formats. Most of the collections are available in PCX, EPS, or TIFF format. Some collections are available in CGM format, and a few in WPG format. The following are a few possible sources for clip art:

WordPerfect Corporation
1555 N. Technology Way
Orem, UT 84057
(800) 451-5151

Figure Library
Business-Pak
Holiday-Pak
Leisure-Pak
Education-Pak

Each collection includes more than 200 WPG files.

Metro ImageBase, Inc.
18623 Ventura Boulevard, Suite 210
Tarzana, CA 91356
(800) 525-1552

This clip art is available in EPS and other vector formats.

T/Maker Corporation
1390 Villa St.
Mountain View, CA 94041
(415) 962-0195

This clip art is available in WMF, EPS, and other formats.

Image Club Graphics, Inc.
1902 Eleventh Street
Suite 5
SE Calgary
Alberta, Canada T2G 3G2
(403) 262-8008

Image Club Graphics sells more than 4,000 EPS images.

Presentation Task Force
New Vision Technologies, Inc.
38 Auriga Drive, #13
Nepean, Ontario, Canada K2E 8A5
(613) 727-8184

Presentation Task Force has more than 1,100 CGM images.

3G Graphics, Inc.
11410 N.E. 124th St. #6155-E
Kirkland, WA 98034
(800) 456-0234

3G Graphics sells EPS clip art.

Chapter Summary

This chapter discusses the WordPerfect graphics boxes and editors and shows examples of how they are used. The next chapter, "Desktop Publishing with WordPerfect," shows how you can enhance commonly used documents and publications with graphics and the careful use of typefaces.

Desktop Publishing with WordPerfect

Desktop publishing is using your computer to produce documents of typeset-quality text and graphics. Desktop publishing systems enable you to use both text and graphics on the same page and to print pages on a high-resolution laser printer or typesetter. Although word processing enables you to create and edit your text on-screen, desktop publishing is concerned mainly with page layout: how your text appears, how the layout relates to the document as a whole, and whether the presentation of the text reinforces and enhances the text's meaning.

Several software packages are available that specifically provide desktop publishing capabilities; Ventura Publisher and Aldus PageMaker are the most well-known page-layout programs. Although WordPerfect for Windows is not specifically a desktop publishing package, it has many

■ **Joseph E. Rosenman** is the principal consultant of PCC Resources, a New York City consulting firm that specializes in PC installations, word processing, and desktop publishing.

of the features needed to perform desktop publishing. Because the program provides a what-you-see-is-what-you-get (WYSIWYG) environment, you easily can see and modify your page layouts. Several features in WordPerfect for Windows make using the program as a desktop publisher especially easy:

- On-screen movable tabs and margins
- On-screen graphics movement and rescaling
- Screen fonts that match printing fonts
- Font size and placement that reflect the printed document

Part IV of this book is concerned with ways to enhance text, from using advanced printing features and adding rules to documents, to using graphics. Up to this point, the theme of Part IV has been to go beyond simple words on a page. This chapter brings everything together and shows you how to use WordPerfect's capabilities to create representative documents you might use in daily business.

This chapter discusses the following topics:

- Integration of text and graphics
- Principles of design
- Typeface selection
- Page planning and layout
- Publication enhancements
- Production of a flier, trifold mailer, and newsletter

Integrating Text and Graphics

Generally, you add graphics to text for a specific purpose, and that purpose should dictate how you use the graphics. The publishing industry often uses the phrase "form follows function," referring to the fact that a successful publication is designed according to its purpose. For example, a catalog focuses on presenting the items in the catalog. Design considerations should focus on how to make the list of products most accessible to the reader. Publications may contain elements that are not text, but those elements should enhance the message being communicated.

Graphics can coexist comfortably with text, or they can compete for the reader's interest. If you have an article about house design or landscaping, in which you discuss a diagram of rooms or plots, you are likely to include some illustrations. Should you use a full-scale drawing or a rough illustration? Should you include a single illustration or several in a series? Does a specific section of the text involve the illustration, or is an entire section or chapter involved? All these questions are important in deciding how best to incorporate graphics with text.

An effective presentation must balance all the elements that make up the document. Readers should see the relevant graphic when they are reading about it in the text. Browsing through pages in search of an illustration can be confusing and distracting. A document with many illustrations can break up the text and make following a train of thought difficult. In such cases, grouping several illustrations together periodically, perhaps every three or four pages, would be better.

Often, an illustration or picture can relay information far more effectively and accurately than text. In such cases, adding graphics to a document can be a tremendously useful technique. In other cases, you can add graphics to embellish your text and make it more interesting. Documents that contain graphics provide readers with a break in the monotony of the text, making their reading experience more enjoyable; however, graphics also can be distracting and confusing, especially if they are poorly chosen or inappropriate.

Cue: Graphics should enhance or support the text, not compete with it.

Many publications regularly and effectively use graphics with text. In a book or report, graphics generally are used sparingly. Books and reports provide a thorough presentation of their subjects; graphics serve simply to augment this presentation. On the other hand, newsletters and brochures usually contain many graphics because they must capture and maintain the reader's attention. Newsletters and brochures need to communicate their messages quickly—and graphics help

Designing Successful Publications

You should consider a number of principles while designing a publication. These principles are not exactly rules, but rather are guidelines to help you make your presentation more effective and interesting. If you consider the following "ideals" as you design and produce your publications, the results will be much more effective and elegant:

- *Simplicity.* The more complicated the presentation, the less likely the reader can follow what you are trying to say. Simplicity in presentation invites participation.

■ *Clarity.* Even simple elements can be introduced in a haphazard and confusing fashion. People in western societies usually read from left to right, and top to bottom. Structure the elements—including the text—on the page so that readers can follow this "natural" viewing order as easily as possible.

When you look at the page, what path does your eye follow? Your eye should not jump around too much. If the effect of the page is confusing, redesign the page. A reader should not glance at a page and wonder, "What does this mean? Where should I look for the information? I don't understand."

■ **Cue:** Your choice of typeface and type size can affect your publication dramatically; too many font changes make the page look rough and confusing.

■ *Consistency.* Multiple-page publications should establish and follow a consistent format. Consistency not only unifies the publication, but also helps the reader feel comfortable and familiar with the material. Design elements such as columns, margins, typefaces, type sizes, headlines, subheadings, and so on, should be the same throughout the publication. Change for the sake of change can be deadly in desktop publishing.

■ *Proportion.* Design elements, whether text or graphics, must coexist comfortably on the page. If one element is much larger than the others, the smaller elements become lost, and the reader senses that the publication is out of proportion. Proportion is an aesthetic consideration and, therefore, is difficult to define precisely; nevertheless, proportion is important to a publication's overall look and feel.

■ *White Space.* Also important to your publication's overall effect is your use of *white space*—the portion of the page that is not printed. A lack of white space causes reader fatigue and disinterest.

As you add text, headlines, and graphics to a page, you create points of interest and activity. If you use small, narrow typefaces and the smallest possible spaces between columns (or no columns at all), you can pack a great deal of information on the page, but the page probably will be difficult to read. You need white space on the page to create areas of relaxation and to produce a balanced and effective presentation.

■ **Cue:** To compensate for the presence of busy graphics, leave space around them.

To create white space in your document, you can leave empty places on the page. Leaving ample margins, *alleys* (the space between columns), and *gutters* (the space next to columns at the page margins) is one way to increase the white space on a page. You also can use *open graphics* to create white space on a page. Some graphics are very busy and solid, whereas others are sparse and broad. Do not place your text too tightly against your graphics.

Using *open typefaces* is another way to create white space on a page. Certain typefaces have a closed and tight look, whereas others have an open and broad look. Choosing typefaces with a large *x-height* (the height of the body of its lowercase letters) and with contrasting thin strokes in the letters helps increase the "lightness" of a page. A dense, heavy typeface requires extra white space to compensate for its appearance. Small type also reduces white space. When a page seems tiring, try increasing the point size of the type, making the margins and alleys wider, and increasing the space around graphics. Using additional leading also helps open the page.

A wildly imbalanced page is confusing and difficult to follow; however, you do not have to balance every page perfectly. A good publication has elements of balance and elements of emphasis, creating just the right amount of "visual tension" to keep the reader interested and awake. An example of selective emphasis can be seen in a page with two graphics. Instead of making both graphics equal in size, make the more important graphic ten percent larger. By choosing which elements to emphasize and to what degree to emphasize them, you control and direct the attention of the reader.

In a multiple-page publication, you must take into account the fact that readers view two pages together. You must check to see whether facing pages clash with each other or complement each other. Perhaps you want to mirror the placement of graphics on facing pages, instead of copying them to the same position. For example, you might place a graphic in the left column of the left page and in the right column of the right page. The issues of balance that apply to a single page also apply to facing pages.

> ■ **Cue:** Always consider the appearance of two pages that will open together as a pair of pages, not two individual pages.

The principles discussed in this section can help you organize and lay out the text and graphics used on the page. The other important element on the page, text, is not just letters. The size, shape, and combination of typefaces can have a dramatic impact on the appearance and effectiveness of your document. The next section explores this subject in more detail.

Understanding Typefaces

Understanding typefaces is virtually an art. Sometimes the difference between typefaces is obvious; other times the difference is very subtle. Not everyone has the training or skill needed to distinguish one typeface from another or to select the best typeface for a given project. In fact, a "best" choice does not always exist. Often, one out of a number of typefaces is suitable; your choice will be based on your aesthetic taste.

Even though typography is a complex subject, you can follow basic principles to produce a more effective publication. In order to understand typefaces and make more informed choices, this section compares several different typefaces and explores some ways of looking at and organizing typefaces. Chapter 10, "Working with Fonts," gives the details of working with soft fonts, font cartridges, and so on.

Typeface Essentials

Thousands of different typefaces are available for use, and they are grouped in several ways. In simple terms, typefaces can be divided into four categories:

- *Serif* typefaces have small flourishes or protuberances at the ends of the letters. For example, an uppercase T has three serifs—one on every end. The shape, size, and direction of a serif changes from typeface to typeface.

- *Sans serif* typefaces have no serifs; the ends of the letters are plain. Sans serif typefaces can be constructed of either uniform or variable strokes.

- *Ornamental* typefaces—a miscellaneous category of fonts used primarily in special effects and headlines—include all "fancy" letters. Ornamental typefaces can be script, fancy, irregular, or they can feature any sort of ornamentation or peculiarity.

  Ornamental typefaces almost always are busy and unusual typefaces. They catch your eye, focusing your attention on their letters. Reading a book set in an ornamental typeface would be torturous; used for headlines and to capture attention, however, ornamental typefaces are effective and interesting.

  The term *ornamental* describes the function of the typeface rather than its appearance. Some ornamental typefaces simply are fancy versions of serif and sans serif typefaces; others are original or unique expressions of letters.

  Figure 18.1 shows examples of serif, sans serif, and ornamental typefaces.

- Besides the many alphanumeric typeface sets, a final category of typefaces is available: special symbols. Symbols can include mathematical characters, musical notation, meteorological symbols, and a variety of graphical icons. The best-known set of special symbols is known as *dingbats*.

This is Palatino, a serif typeface; the font is 14-point Palatino. Notice the cross strokes on each letter (in contrast to the following font). Serif typefaces are usually good for smaller point sizes and are used in the body of text in magazines and newspapers.

This is ITC Avant Garde, a sans serif typeface.
The font is 14-point ITC Avant Garde.
Sans serif typefaces look good in larger point sizes.

Park Avenue is a decorative typeface; it is not as easy to read as the other two categories of typefaces. The font is 18-point Park Avenue. Decorative typefaces should be used sparingly for impact.

Examples of serif, sans serif, and ornamental typefaces.

Examples of dingbats.

Dingbats are ornamental characters that you can use to embellish a document. Dingbats include a variety of stars, arrows, boxes, circles, fancy numbers, and an assortment of special symbols (such as a telephone, pointing finger, and pencil). Figure 18.2 shows four rows of dingbats.

As long as the dingbats typeface is available on the printer, you can use them in your documents. Although at this time Word-Perfect does not display dingbats, you can print them (they generally are mapped to character set 12).

Type Styles

Most typefaces are made up of several standard variations, or *type styles*. A type style is the weight or posture of a font. If the weight is thick and dense, the typeface is *heavy* or *boldface*. If the weight is thin, the typeface is *light*. If the typeface slants to the right, it is *italic*. You can combine modifications to create a *boldface-italic* typeface. In fact, most typefaces consist of the following four variations: normal (Roman), boldface, italic, and boldface italic.

For example, you might find four variations of the Swiss font: Swiss Roman, Swiss Bold, Swiss Italic, and Swiss Bold Italic. You also might find several degrees of boldface. Within one font family, you may see Roman, Bold, Extra Bold, and Heavy categories. These categories vary from font to font.

Typography

You can distinguish one typeface from another according to the way its individual elements are put together. The relationship between a typeface's uppercase letters and lowercase letters, the height of the body of its lowercase letters (x-height), the variations of the thickness of its letters, the length of its ascenders and descenders, the type of serifs it has, all combine to create a typeface's individual characteristics (see fig. 18.3).

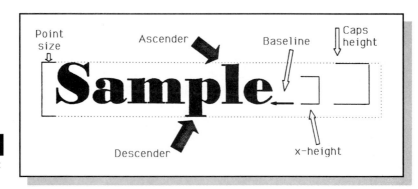

FIG. 18.3

The elements of a typeface.

One element that a typographer might modify when designing a typeface family is its width. Some typefaces are very broad; others are very narrow. Often, an extended typeface family includes several variations of width. Figure 18.4 illustrates the various weights, angles, and widths of Bitstream's Swiss font family.

Although figure 18.4 shows many variations of Swiss, the Swiss font is just one example of a sans serif typeface. Both serif and sans serif typefaces come in many different sizes and styles, some with very subtle differences. Studying a group of typefaces within a particular category can help you understand how fonts differ from one another. The eight samples shown in figure 18.5 are all serif typefaces, but they clearly are not the same.

This is Swiss Roman	ABCabc1234
This is Swiss Italic	*ABCabc1234*
This is Swiss Bold	**ABCabc1234**
This is Swiss Bold Italic	***ABCabc1234***
This is Swiss Light	ABCabc1234
This is Swiss Light Italic	ABCabc1234
This is Swiss Black	**ABCabc1234**
This is Swiss Black Italic	**ABCabc1234**
This is Swiss Condensed	ABCabc1234
This is Swiss Condensed Italic	*ABCabc1234*
This Is Swiss Bold Condensed	**ABCabc1234**
This is Swiss Black Condensed	**ABCabc1234**
This is Swiss Compressed	**ABCabc1234**
This Is Swiss Extra Compressed	**ABCabc1234**

FIG. 18.4

Bitstream's Swiss font family.

This is the Dutch Typeface	ABCabc123
This is the Zapf Calligraphic Typeface	ABCabc123
This is the Bitstream Amerigo Typeface	ABCabc123
This is the Activa Typeface	ABCabc123
This is the Bitstream Charter Typeface	ABCabc123
This is the Bodoni Typeface	ABCabc123
This is the Century Schoolbook Typeface	ABCabc123
This is the ITC Tiffany Typeface	ABCabc123

FIG. 18.5

Examples of serif typefaces.

Each typeface has its own characteristics, as indicated in table 18.1.

Table 18.1. Characteristics of Several Serif Typefaces

Typeface	Characteristics
Dutch (Times Roman)	The "classical" serif font, Dutch is similar to the typeface of news papers, particularly the *London Times*. Dutch is characterized by large uppercase letters, contrasting thin and thick strokes in the letters, and a triangular serif. Lowercase letters have thickened ends instead of clearly defined serifs.
Zapf Calligraphic (Palatino)	Calligraphic is smoother than Dutch. The transitions from thick to thin stroke weights are gradual, and the typeface has a rectangular serif. The ends of letters diminish to thinner strokes than the ending strokes of most serif typefaces, and lowercase letters are also prominently serif— lending a touch of calligraphy to this traditional typeface.
Bitstream Amerigo	This typeface has a chiseled look; the ends of the strokes become very thin as they connect to other parts of the letters. Amerigo is a narrower typeface than Dutch, with thick-ended strokes that are cut at sharp angles. The serifs on Amerigo are small and subtle.
Activa (Trump Mediaeval)	Activa is somewhat wider than Amerigo and has a more typical serif on the ends of the letters. Activa's character calls attention to itself— very good for short text but poorly suited for long documents.
Bitstream Charter	A typeface especially designed to work well with low-resolution laser printers, Charter is a smooth, open, and consistently designed typeface. The large x-height improves readability, and the typeface offers no surprises.

Typeface	Characteristics
Bodoni	Bodoni, the classic "modern" Roman typeface because of its symmetrical construction, is very graceful and smooth. The serifs look like trailing pen strokes, and the large caps height contrasting with the small x-height draws attention to the text without excessive attention being drawn to the individual characters.
Century Schoolbook	Schoolbook is similar to Dutch but is a little more relaxed. In place of the severe straight lines, Schoolbook adds an occasional curve and flourish to its uppercase letters. This typeface is well suited for lengthy documents, especially when you want a friendly tone.
ITC Tiffany	This typeface is more ornate than most serif typefaces. Tiffany's overlapping strokes, bold serifs, and strong variations in stroke weight combine to give the typeface a great deal of character. Tiffany is excellent for titles and captions but not well suited for body text.

Note that the eight samples displayed are all in normal type style. All these typefaces also are available in boldface, italic, and boldface italic variations. Although all eight typefaces may serve similar purposes, each has strengths and weaknesses that make it better suited to a particular job.

Presenting a Page

At the heart of desktop publishing is the act of laying out, or composing, the document. Document composition is usually accomplished at three levels:

- ■ Type selection and spacing
- ■ Page layout and composition
- ■ Document format

The preceding section covers some of the issues related to type. In this section, you learn about some of the guidelines that go into preparing a complete, cohesive, and attractive page.

Creating a Page

■ **Cue:** Every publication is designed to communicate with a specific group of readers: *Know your audience.*

Creating an effective document is not just a matter of putting text on the page. The process of creating a page generally follows these steps:

1. *Determine the information content of the page.* The more you know before you start to create the page, the better. Knowing what you want to accomplish can help you write text that is especially effective and elegant.

2. *Decide on the output media,* such as paper size and type, color, and so on. After you know what you want to accomplish, you need to decide how best to present that page. Color is an expensive and complicated option, but it can be very effective. Colored paper and colored ink can have a dramatic impact on your presentations; however, make sure that the combination doesn't reduce the readability of the page or fatigue or distract the reader.

   A typical document consists of black ink on white paper, although you certainly can choose colored paper. An off-white or cream color might lend a touch of class, whereas a fluorescent green or red might give an altogether unexpected impression. Similarly, colored inks can enhance a document or distract the reader. You can create colored documents in two ways: by printing with more than one color of ink or by using color separations. Color separation is just beginning to be supported by PC-based applications. Although providing some color support, WordPerfect cannot handle the color separation needed to reproduce photographs.

   WordPerfect supports a limited number or colors (4–16), with output quality suitable for "proofing" (examining the printed copy for correctness prior to high-quality printing). If the requirement is for color separations and full-color output, WordPerfect is not up to the task. If your printer supports more than one color, WordPerfect can be used to produce limited color documents.

   Paper doesn't come only in 8 1/2-by-11-inch sheets. Larger sizes, such as 11-by-17-inch paper, which folds neatly into two 8 1/2-by-11-inch pages, might be a good choice. A trifold 8 1/2-by-11-inch page also works well. In addition, other countries use entirely different sizes of paper. You might select standard-weight paper, which is cheaper to mail, or heavyweight paper, which lasts longer and creates a positive impression. Glossy paper is even more expensive but also more attractive.

3. *Generate the text.* After you know what you want to present and the media by which you want to present it, writing the text should be a straightforward process. Create your text in WordPerfect. Later, you can edit your message.

4. *Select graphical elements.* After you write the text, select the graphics you intend to use with it. Are they balanced? Does either your text or your graphics overwhelm the other?

5. *Lay out the page.* You now are ready to position elements on the page. Don't be concerned with the actual text at this stage in the design process; instead, concern yourself with positioning the text blocks. Some text is free-form, which you can place in chunks throughout the page. Other text should remain together, as if it were a graphical element. A paragraph in a book is an example of free-form text, whereas a name and address is an example of text that must stay together.

6. *Select typefaces.* After you have a rough idea of your page layout, you should select the typefaces you want to use. The body of the text probably should be in a standard serif typeface, and the section headlines in a contrasting typeface, possibly a sans serif font. You can set the major heading in a larger version of the contrasting type or in a third typeface—if appropriate, perhaps an ornamental typeface.

   After making an initial selection of typefaces, you might want to reposition the text and graphics. Steps 5 and 6 often are repeated several times as the look of the page is defined. For example, you might find that the headline is too large, bold, or garish, and choose to replace it with something simpler or more appropriate. The page may then look too open, and you might want to decrease the leading. One of the most creative aspects of page layout occurs at this point in the process—positioning graphics and text, selecting the look of the headlines, and choosing the fonts.

7. *Put everything together.* After you select the fonts, you prepare the final layout. At this point, you already have selected and "roughed in" all the graphics, chosen the type, and established the approximate size of the headlines. The final step involves modifying the margins and type sizes to make sure that sufficient white space is left on the page, and verifying that the elements don't clash when you view them as a whole.

For a one-page document, you usually go through the layout process only once. For multiple-page documents, you must repeat all or part of the layout process. You can make the opening page special, but the second and subsequent pages should conform to a common format. If each page is different, readers become confused and distracted.

Fitting Type on the Page

When you type text, the amount of space between the letters of each word (*kerning*) and between lines of type (*leading*) depends on the typeface you have selected. You sometimes might want to vary these settings. The most common modification is an adjustment to the leading. Reducing leading makes the text more difficult to read. Small reductions may be appropriate, such as squeezing two lines of text into a small caption. Opening up (expanding) the leading almost always improves the readability of text and reduces reader fatigue. Minor adjustments in leading can have a significant, although subtle, impact on the appearance and effectiveness of type.

WordPerfect provides adjustments to word and letter spacing, along with traditional kerning. By selecting blocks of text and adjusting the vertical and horizontal spacing, you gain a tremendous amount of control over the appearance of the type. For more information on WordPerfect's vertical and horizontal spacing commands, refer to Chapter 15, "Working with Advanced Printing Techniques."

Enhancing a Page

If your document has few graphics, the endless text can seem uninviting. You can use any of the following devices to enhance the appearance of the document and break up the text:

Cue: Horizontal rules help separate the text and improve readability by adding white space to the page.

Cue: For busy pages, use familiar typefaces in a pull-out; for boring pages, use a contrasting typeface.

- **Rules.** A *rule* is a vertical or horizontal line that you use to separate sections of text. You should use vertical rules sparingly, because they often increase the tension on the page and make the page seem busier. Thick rules generally accompany large and heavy typefaces.

- **Pull-outs.** A *pull-out* (or *pull-out quote*) is an enlarged and emphasized quotation from the text. Possible pull-out techniques include using a fancy or contrasting typeface, text larger than the text from which you take the pull-out, and placing the quotation in a text box that has borders or a gray background, or both (refer to "Creating a Newsletter," in this chapter, for a more detailed discussion of pull-outs).

- **Headlines.** A headline serves not only to introduce important sections of text, but also to create visual excitement on the page and to provide a structure for the reader to follow. Although too many headlines are confusing and overwhelming, an appropriate number creates a feeling of direction.

- *Ornaments.* An *ornament* usually is an artistic fancy, frequently line art, included at the end of an article. Ornaments fill up white space that might otherwise look unbalanced. They rarely have any relevance to the text, so use them sparingly and always at the ends of articles.

- *Headers and footers.* When appropriate, headers and footers can display information that needs to be on every page of a document—information such as the issue date, page number, copyright notice, publication name and identification, chapter title, and so on. Although headers and footers can add visual interest to a page, they always should be appropriate and relevant.

- *Captions.* When you use graphics and tables, don't forget to consider whether a caption might enhance the presentation. Captions provide a further opportunity to introduce a contrasting text element, adding interest to the page.

Even though you might find many places in your document where introducing a different font is appropriate, restraint always is a good idea. For example, unless the fonts used in the text body and headlines are monotonous, you probably should use the same typeface for captions and pull-outs but select different sizes and weights. For a minor headline, you might use the same typeface you use for the major headline but use a smaller type size (assuming the major headline is not an ornamental typeface—ornamental typefaces that are too small look terrible). When you repeat elements in slightly different forms, you create a sense of familiarity and continuity that enhances the effectiveness of the document.

■ **Cue:** Limit most documents to two typeface families: one for the body of the text, and another, usually contrasting, typeface for headlines.

To demonstrate the effectiveness of desktop published documents, the following sections discuss the techniques involved in using WordPerfect for Windows to create a flier, a trifold mailer, and a newsletter.

Creating a Flier

Using desktop publishing to create fliers is common. Fliers can be simple or complex, mostly text or full of graphics. You can use fliers for mailings, handouts, as a part of a larger presentation, or as miniature posters.

The first example is an advertising flier created for a fictitious computer retail chain. The flier has two purposes:

- To advertise a limited-time sale

- To promote the company

The first purpose is obvious; the second, less so. Nearly all advertising seeks to promote the company offering the advertisement. Even if the customer fails to purchase a sale item, a successful advertisement creates a positive impression and promotes name recognition. Balancing the items being sold with the name of the store selling them is therefore important in creating fliers. The completed flier is illustrated in figure 18.6.

Supreme Systems

End-of-Quarter Sale Event
September 23-28   9 AM - 7 PM

Special inventory reduction and close-out of manufacturers discontinued items.

Many items are only available in limited quantities. Full manufacturers warranties apply.

Computers		
8088 with 640K	$299
8088 with 640K +VGA	$699
286 with 1 Meg	$499
286 with 1 Meg +VGA	$999
386 with 1 Meg	$999
386 with 4 Meg	$1199
386 with 4 Meg +VGA	$1599
486 with 4 Meg +VGA	$1999

Modems	
2400 with MNP-5	$119
v.32 / v.42 bis	$299
v.32 bis / v.42 bis	$399

Supreme Systems	Supreme Systems
12345 Transfer Lane	98765 Baseline Drive
Conduit, AH 13243	Modulate, AH 13579
(555) 987-6543	(555) 234-5678

FIG. 18.6

An advertising flier.

Fliers have specific points to communicate. The computer store flier conveys the following information:

- Supreme Systems is having a sale
- Date of the sale
- Store hours
- Selected price list of sale items
- Addresses and phone numbers of participating stores

In a memo, you could present all the necessary information in a short bulleted list—but the goal isn't just to relay some information. By producing a flier, you hope to do the following:

- Catch the customer's attention
- Generate interest and excitement
- Interest the customer in the specific items on sale
- Create name recognition for the advertiser

You have three tools available to accomplish these goals:

- Graphics to add visual interest
- Interesting fonts
- A page layout that invites the customer to read the flier

Using Graphics in the Flier

One of the first characteristics you notice about the Supreme Systems flier is the use of graphics. Four graphics are used in the flier:

- The border
- The banner
- The explosion
- The PC

The border for this flier was created in DrawPerfect, WordPerfect Corporation's graphics program. If you don't want to create your own, you can choose from a number of borders in the various WordPerfect graphics libraries. The full-page border creates instant visual interest and helps define the flier as a single, unified page.

Cue: Use a border around a flier to help define the publication as a single, unified page.

The banner might appear to consist of regular letters at first glance, but is in fact a graphic created by using CorelDRAW! Generally, in fliers the company's name and logo is displayed prominently at the top. The name or logo often is created as a graphic. Creation as a graphic enables modifications to the type that would be impossible using just fonts and a word processor. In this example, note that the two ends of the banner slant upward toward the center of the page. This effect is achieved by altering the appearance of the text through CorelDRAW!'s perspective modifier. The result is a company name that is much more interesting than plain text.

The explosion is a modified graphic from WordPerfect's Business Pack graphics library. Using DrawPerfect, the words *Blowout Prices!* were added to the figure. DrawPerfect made it easy to scale the text to fit the cloud of the explosion and also enabled the text to be rotated to an angle. To place the text in the explosion graphic using WordPerfect would require a considerable amount of time sizing for a correct fit, and even then the graphic couldn't be placed at the angle used in the sample flier.

The PC is one of the standard graphics included with the DrawPerfect Figure Library. As a graphical element, the PC reinforces the *content* of the flier: this sale is primarily about PCs. Note that if many graphics were used, this message would be diluted.

Using Fonts in the Flier

Excluding the banner and the text in the explosion (which are graphics), two typeface families are used in this example. The banner uses ITC Souvenir Demi (the dates and time), as does the name *Supreme Systems* in the address. The body of the flier uses Zapf Humanist Bold and Zapf Humanist Bold Italic.

This combination follows the tried-and-true rule of limiting the number of typefaces to two or three on the page, and of using contrasting typefaces for headlines and text body. Changing the size of the Souvenir font and enlarging the Humanist column headings enhance the variety in the flier.

Cue: Right-justifying short segments of text is acceptable to create symmetry within the document page.

Note the text to the right of the explosion graphic. This text is right-justified. Generally, you should avoid right-justification at all costs (right-justified text is *very* hard to read). In this example, where a small amount of text is framing a roughly circular graphic element, right-justification contributes to a clean, balanced look.

Laying Out the Flier

Within the box created by the border graphic, the text and remaining graphics elements are placed to meet the goals highlighted at the beginning of this section. The page is laid out in four chunks. The first chunk consists of the corporate name, the flier "purpose," the date, and the time. This information is critical and is prominent on the flier.

The next chunk consists of text providing details of the sale and the explosion graphic. The explosion's location near the center of the page is deliberate; the explosion acts as a focal point, producing a visually compelling image that draws the attention of the reader. Note that this area leaves a great deal of white space. The "busyness" of the graphic requires compensatory white space to produce an even and comfortable look. Beginning with the second chunk, the flier has two columns. The shorter lines of text in columns are easier to read than longer lines of text. The explosion graphic is placed in the center—in both columns at once.

The third chunk contains the flier's detailed information. Saving the details for the latter part of the page helps ensure that the prospective customer has read the vital information already. Using the PC graphic helps restore some of the interest that the dry price list might have lost. The final chunk at the bottom of the page contains the names, addresses, and phone numbers of the two stores.

Note the vertical rule separating the two addresses in the fourth chunk. In most cases, the reader will be interested in only one address—not both. The vertical rule helps emphasize that difference. A vertical rule would not be effective in the third chunk (separating the price lists), because the goal there is *not* to separate the prices into two separate lists. The horizontal rules help separate the introductory section from the main body, and again from the name and address section. Note that the horizontal rules are thicker than the vertical rule. This difference serves two purposes: to create a strong sense of separation and to better match the density of the Souvenir typeface used in proximity to both rules.

Settings for the Flier

Table 18.2 summarizes the parameters used in the advertising flier.

Table 18.2. Settings for the Flier

Element	Option	Setting
Justification		Left
Margins (before border is placed)	Top	0.3"
	Bottom	0.3"
	Left	0.3"
	Right	0.3"
Margins (after border is placed)	Left	1"
	Right	1"
Column 1	Left	1"
	Right	4"
Column 2	Left	4.5"
	Right	7.5"
Height Adjustment		0", 0.05"
Fonts	"End of Quarter"	Souvenir Demi 30 pt
	Date and Time	Souvenir Demi 24 pt
	Main Body	Humanist Bold 16 pt
	Column Headlines	Humanist Bold Italic 19.2 pt
	Address Name	Souvenir Demi 20 pt
	Address and Phone #	Humanist Bold 16 pt
Rules	Horizontal	Center, Baseline, 6", 0.04", 100%
	Vertical	Column 1, 8.63", 1.5", 0.013", 100%
	Border Style	All None
Figure Options	Outside Border	All 0"
	Inside Border	All 0"
	Gray Shading	0%
Figure: Border	Box Type	Figure
	Anchor Type	Page
	Vertical Position	Full Page
	Horizontal Position	Margins, Full
	Wrap	No
	Size	Width: 7.89" Height: 10.4"
Figure: Masthead	Box Type	Figure
	Anchor Type	Page
	Vertical Position	0.75"
	Horizontal Position	Margins, Center
	Wrap	Yes
	Size	Width: 6.5" Auto Height: 1.16"

Element	Option	Setting
Figure: Explosion	Box Type	Figure
	Anchor Type	Page
	Vertical Position	0.75" (Figure was moved to the bottom of the box)
	Horizontal Position	Columns 1-2, Center
	Wrap	No
	Size	Width: 2.5" Auto Height: 3.3"
Figure: PC	Box Type	Figure
	Anchor Type	Page
	Vertical Position	6.8"
	Horizontal Position	Column 2, Center
	Wrap	No
	Size	Width: 2.1" Auto Height: 1.52"

Creating a Trifold Mailer

Trifold mailers are double-sided brochures designed to be folded into three parts; put into envelopes, stapled, or taped closed; and mailed. They can contain a variety of information, from a sales pitch or introduction to professional services, to an invitation to a special event.

Trifold publications usually are on 8 1/2-by-11-inch paper in landscape (sideways) orientation, with three even columns on each side. This format provides a total of six 3 1/2-by-8 1/2-inch columns. The outside of a trifold mailer usually includes an address column and an introduction column, which are visible when the trifold is folded (see fig. 18.7). You can use either side column on the outside of the mailer for special information, or you can treat those columns as extensions of the information on the inside.

The inside of a trifold mailer provides three adjacent columns that you can be treat as three separate pages or as a three-part whole (see fig. 18.8). You also can treat the inside as a single 8 1/2-by-11-inch page, but this format generally is less effective than the trifold concept.

DataByte Associates

Professional Services
A full range of computer
support and poltergeist
expulsion services are
provided as part of our
standard benefit.
Reentrant ghoul control
and spectral manifestations
are our specialties.

Expert Consultants
Our entire staff is fully
trained and receives annual
certification in computer
exorcism.

Tireless Researchers
To better serve our clients,
we operate on a 30-hour
day and work 15-hour
shifts. We've discovered
that seeing ghosts is easier
at the end of the extended
shifts.

Informed Sales Staff
Our staff is especially
expert in anything you
need to know!

DataByte Associates
1011 Widebuss Lane
Inverterville, MB 54321

Bulk Rate
U.S. Postage
PAID
Yourtown, State
Permit #

DataByte
Associates

Specialists in the removal
of computer gremlins,
apparitions, phantoms,
and ghosts.

1011 Widebuss Lane
Inverterville, MB 54321
(123) 456-7890

FIG. 18.7

The outside of a
sample trifold
mailer.

Designing the Outside

This trifold mailer is designed so that the left column of the outside is
folded inside. In this example, the left column of the outside contains
the most important information—a description of the service being
sold (again see fig. 18.8). The message in this column is reinforced by
the columns inside the mailer. The name *DataByte Associates* is set in
Bitstream's Bernhard Modern Italic typeface. The section headings are
set in Clarendon Bold, and the body text is in Century Schoolbook.

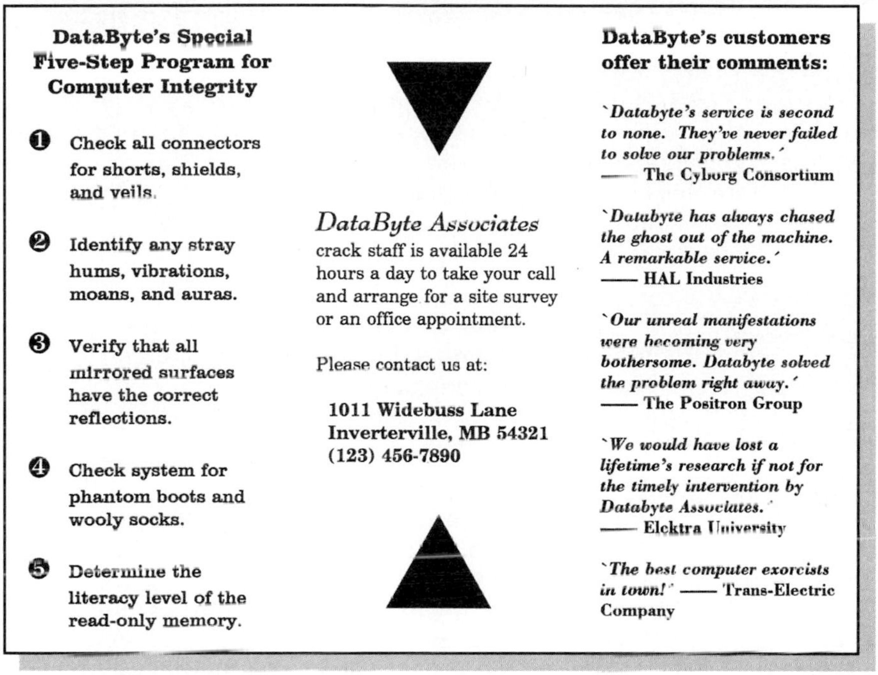

DataByte's Special Five-Step Program for Computer Integrity

❶ Check all connectors for shorts, shields, and veils.

❷ Identify any stray hums, vibrations, moans, and auras.

❸ Verify that all mirrored surfaces have the correct reflections.

❹ Check system for phantom boots and wooly socks.

❺ Determine the literacy level of the read-only memory.

DataByte Associates
crack staff is available 24 hours a day to take your call and arrange for a site survey or an office appointment.

Please contact us at:

**1011 Widebuss Lane
Inverterville, MB 54321
(123) 456-7890**

DataByte's customers offer their comments:

`Databyte's service is second to none. They've never failed to solve our problems.`
—— The Cyborg Consortium

`Databyte has always chased the ghost out of the machine. A remarkable service.`
—— HAL Industries

`Our unreal manifestations were becoming very bothersome. Databyte solved the problem right away.`
—— The Positron Group

`We would have lost a lifetime's research if not for the timely intervention by Databyte Associates.`
—— Elektra University

`The best computer exorcists in town!` —— Trans-Electric Company

FIG. 18.8

The inside of a sample trifold mailer.

The center column of the outside of the mailer is the mailing column, which generally contains a return address, space for the address of the addressee, and postal information. This example includes the standard postal permit box for bulk mailings. Both the postal permit and the return address are in text boxes. The return address is typeset in the same Bernhard Modern and Century Schoolbook used throughout the flier. You can add a logo to the left side of the column, but because the mailer is busy enough already, none is included in this example. Note that this column is in an orientation different from the rest of the trifold.

To create a proper postal format, you must rotate the text in the mailing column either 90 degrees or 270 degrees. Text boxes enable you to rotate text easily, but not all printers can print both orientations on the same page. PostScript printers and the Hewlett-Packard LaserJet III can, but most other printers cannot. Be sure that your hardware meets your desktop publishing needs before undertaking jobs of this sort. If you cannot rotate this column, leave it blank, print the horizontal text on a separate page, and then cut the text and paste it in the proper place before duplicating the flier.

The right column on the outside of the mailer is the main, introductory column. Like a title page in a book, this column introduces the company and the product. In this example, the introductory column contains four elements: the company name, a brief description of the company, the company logo, and the company's address and telephone number.

Note that the company name and address are centered, but the brief description of the company is not. Centered text is difficult to read, but often is expected with a name. An address that is isolated with a graphical element often is centered as well. If the text block were larger and occupied a greater portion of the column, the entire block would be better suited to left justification. The text in this column is set in the same typefaces that are used in the left column, Bernhard Modern and Century Schoolbook.

Designing the Inside

The inside page of the sample trifold mailer has three purposes:

- ■ To elaborate on the product or service
- ■ To provide contact information
- ■ To convince the customer to buy the service

Each column focuses on one of these points. In the left column, using fancy numbers (Zapf Dingbats) to present the five-step program provides a focus for the prospective customer. A numbered list often gives readers a feeling of accomplishment. The type is Clarendon Roman and Clarendon Bold. You might choose Century Schoolbook instead of Clarendon Roman, but the columns benefit from a slightly contrasting typeface. Clarendon is fancier than Century Schoolbook but still is ordinary and readable. Clarendon works well in large point sizes, and you can use it successfully for your text if the text isn't long.

The center column contains the contact information—the address and telephone number, which you cannot post often enough, and an inviting phrase to make the customer feel welcome. In the center column, you could have started listing the quotations that are in the right column, but as a design consideration, you should keep them separate. Instead, the contact information is centered vertically, with two large triangles pointing toward the text. The triangles actually are text characters from Bitstream's Zapf Dingbats typeface. The company name is set in Bernhard Modern, the text in Century Schoolbook, and the address and telephone number in Century Schoolbook Bold.

The right column contains customer testimonials attesting to the company's quality—a form of blatant self-promotion. Testimonials are common, especially when the designer feels the prospective customer might need reassurance. A contrasting typeface, usually italic, often is used to distinguish quotations from the rest of the text. Bitstream's Bodoni Bold and Bold Italic work well in the right column, and they blend with the Clarendon in the column heading and in the other columns on this page.

■ **Cue:** Vertical rules in trifold documents are a bad idea: The slightest error in folding is visible immediately.

Creating Columns

Using columns on a page that is 8 1/2 inches wide, or wider, is all but essential because columns dramatically improve readability. The Columns feature in WordPerfect for Windows is easy to use, but you cannot use all the program's page features in a column. For example, headers and footers span the *entire* width of the page. An alternative to using the Columns feature is to use WordPerfect's Label feature. Because a WordPerfect label is actually a page within a page, this method of creating columns enables you to use the program's page features in your columns. Using WordPerfect's Label feature, you can divide a page into several pages, or columns, such as into four equal quadrants, into halves, or into thirds.

When dividing a page into halves or thirds, using landscape orientation makes sense. You can use standard 8 1/2-by-11-inch paper, 8 1/2-by-14-inch paper, or any other size paper that your printer can accommodate. Refer to Chapter 15, "Working with Advanced Printing Techniques," for a detailed discussion of setting up labels.

The trifold mailer is an interesting project because it involves combining several different components into a single, small publication. As you learn in the following section, producing a newsletter is much more complicated and involves choosing from many possible designs.

Settings for the Trifold Mailer

Table 18.3 summarizes the parameters used in the trifold mailer.

Table 18.3. Settings for the Trifold Mailer

Element	Option	Setting
Paper Size		11" × 8.5
Justification		Left
Line Spacing: pg. 1		1.0"
Line Spacing: pg. 2		1.1"
Line Spacing: pg. 2, column 3		1.0"
Margins	Top	0.5"
	Bottom	0.5"
	Left	0.5"
	Right	0.5"
Column 1	Left	0.5"
	Right	3.5"
Column 2	Left	4"
	Right	7"
Column 3	Left	7.5"
	Right	10.5"
Fonts: Outside left column	"DataByte Associates"	Bernhard Modern Bold Italic 24 pt
	Headings	Clarendon Bold 18 pt
	Body	Century Schoolbook Roman 14 pt
Fonts: Outside right column	"DataByte Associates"	Bernhard Modern Bold Italic 48 pt
	Body	Century Schoolbook Roman 18 pt
Fonts: Inside left column	Title	Clarendon Bold 18 pt
	Body	Century Schoolbook Roman 14 pt
Fonts: Inside center column	Triangles	Zapf Dingbats 100 pt
	"DataByte Associates"	Bernhard Modern Bold Italic 22.5 pt
	Body	Century Schoolbook Roman 16 pt
	Address	Century Schoolbook Bold 16 pt

Element	Option	Setting
Fonts: Inside right column	"DataByte's" Quotation	Clarendon Bold 18 pt Bodoni Bold Italic 16 pt
	Quotation Source	Bodoni Bold 16 pt
Rules	Horizontal, Outside left column	Center, Baseline, 2", 0.013", 100%
	Horizontal, Outside right column	Center, Baseline, 2", 0.013", 100%
Figure Options	Border Style	All None
	Outside Border	All 0.167"
	Inside Border	All 0"
	Gray Shading	0"
Figure: "PC, grave, and ghost" logo	Box Type	Figure
	Anchor Type	Page
	Vertical Position	2.8"
	Horizontal Position	Columns, Right
	Wrap	No
	Size	Width: 2.81" Height: 2.71"
Text Box Options: Postal Box	Border Style	All Single
	Outside Border	All 0.167"
	Inside Border	All 0.167"
Text Box: Postal Box	Justification	Center
	Font	Swiss Bold 10 pt
	Box Type	Text
	Anchor Type	Page
	Vertical Position	Bottom
	Horizontal Position	Column Right, Column 2
	Wrap	Yes
	Size	Width: 1" Height: 1.5"
Text Box Options. Return address	Border Style	All None
	Outside Border	All 0.167"
	Inside Border	All 0.167"
Text Box: Return address	Justification	Left
	Font: "DataByte"	Bernhard Modern Italic 14 pt
	Font: Address	Century Schoolbook Roman 12 pt
	Box Type	Text
	Anchor Type	Page
	Vertical Position	Top
	Horizontal Position	Column Right, Column 2
	Wrap	Yes
	Size	Width: 1.28" Height: 3"

Creating a Newsletter

A newsletter poses some interesting challenges. Because a newsletter is a multiple-page document, you need to consider the publication as a whole. The pages need to be consistent, but at the same time they must be interesting. Unlike a book or report, which usually contains nothing but text, a newsletter is expected to contain nontext elements.

WordPerfect has all the editing and layout tools needed to produce effective newsletters. Several layouts are possible for the body of the newsletter; the example includes two effective layout designs. Techniques to add interest to the newsletter include decorative headers and footers, raised caps and drop caps at the beginning of paragraphs, pull-out quotes, graphics, and ornamental characters. Most of these techniques are explored in the newsletter sample presented in this section.

Designing the First Page

A newsletter generally follows a style or format that is repeated throughout the publication. The first page usually is different from the other pages and probably includes a masthead of some sort. Mastheads usually consist of the publication name, either stylized or plain, and information about the publication, such as the issue number and date.

Cue: You can make newsletter mastheads from a specialized logo or graphic, text using special effects, or any of a number of large or ornamental typefaces.

The masthead can be simple text in a large type size, complex text, or a fancy graphic. Figure 18.9 shows four text samples for the banner of a newsletter called *WordPerfect for Windows*.

The four sample titles are set in Bitstream fonts on an 8 1/2-by-11-inch page and are in the maximum point size that fits the text across the page. The first title is set in 72-point Swiss Bold. The second, third, and fourth titles are set respectively in 86-point Swiss Black Condensed, 76-point Futura Black, and 76-point Zapf Humanist Bold Italic. (To fit in this book, the type in figure 18.9 was reduced in size from the original.)

Each title has a different look, and you certainly could use any of them in a newsletter masthead. The two Swiss fonts communicate a formal and reliable message—no surprises, but little excitement. Futura Black is a fancy, contemporary typeface, making it more interesting visually, but the typeface can be a little distracting. Zapf Humanist Bold Italic, a traditional typeface, is a compromise between Swiss and Futura Black. This italic variation is more interesting than the Roman version.

Many other typefaces are available for masthead titles. The title of the *WordPerfect for Windows* newsletter shown in figure 18.10 is a custom graphic created in CorelDRAW! and saved as a WordPerfect graphic.

WordPerfect For Windows

WordPerfect For Windows

WordPerfect For Windows

WordPerfect For Windows

FIG. 18.9

Newsletter title samples.

The masthead of the newsletter consists of the WordPerfect for Windows graphic and two horizontal rules—each made up of a thick line and thin line—that frame the issue identification and date. The inverted horizontal rules act as a motif throughout the newsletter to integrate its pages. As you see in ensuing figures, each page of the newsletter is framed with these rules, one at the top (except for the first page) and one at the bottom.

The first page is designed with three irregular columns: a narrow column on the left for the credits and two larger columns for text. In this example, the entire first page is dedicated to a single story. The following list contains alternative designs:

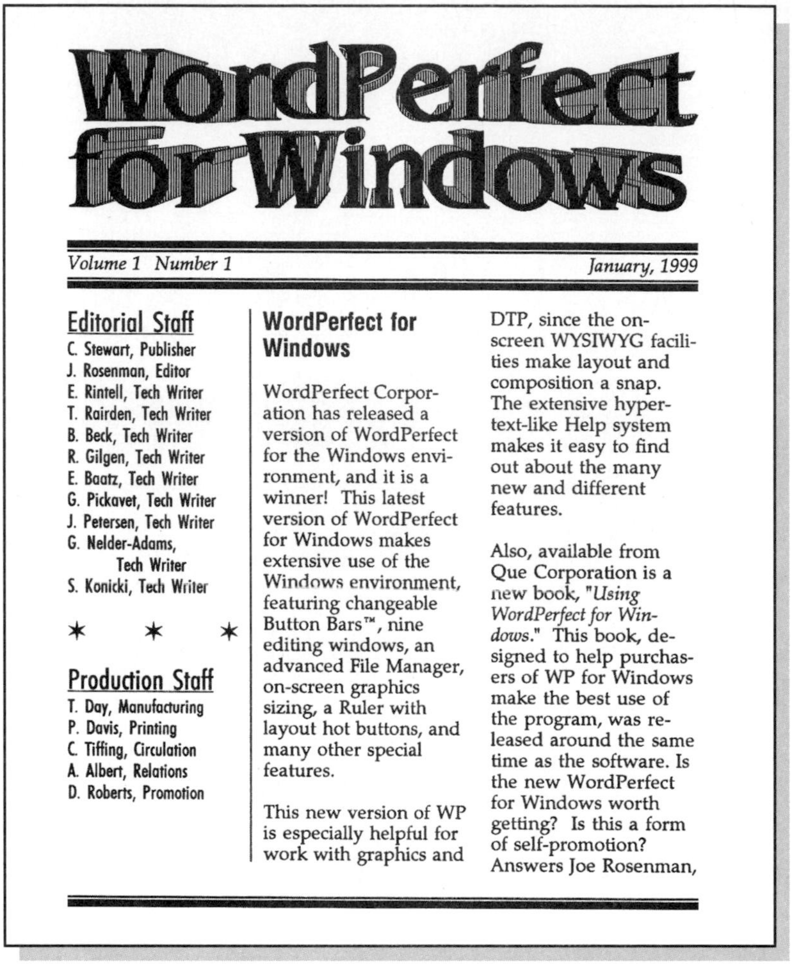

WordPerfect for Windows

Volume 1 Number 1   *January, 1999*

Editorial Staff

C. Stewart, Publisher
J. Rosenman, Editor
E. Rintell, Tech Writer
T. Rairden, Tech Writer
B. Beck, Tech Writer
R. Gilgen, Tech Writer
E. Baatz, Tech Writer
G. Pickavet, Tech Writer
J. Petersen, Tech Writer
G. Nelder-Adams,
        Tech Writer
S. Konicki, Tech Writer

Production Staff

T. Day, Manufacturing
P. Davis, Printing
C. Tiffing, Circulation
A. Albert, Relations
D. Roberts, Promotion

WordPerfect for Windows

WordPerfect Corporation has released a version of WordPerfect for the Windows environment, and it is a winner! This latest version of WordPerfect for Windows makes extensive use of the Windows environment, featuring changeable Button Bars™, nine editing windows, an advanced File Manager, on-screen graphics sizing, a Ruler with layout hot buttons, and many other special features.

This new version of WP is especially helpful for work with graphics and DTP, since the on-screen WYSIWYG facilities make layout and composition a snap. The extensive hyper-text-like Help system makes it easy to find out about the many new and different features.

Also, available from Que Corporation is a new book, "*Using WordPerfect for Windows*." This book, designed to help purchasers of WP for Windows make the best use of the program, was released around the same time as the software. Is the new WordPerfect for Windows worth getting? Is this a form of self-promotion? Answers Joe Rosenman,

FIG. 18.10

Page 1 of the newsletter.

- Place one story in the second column and another in the third column.

- Move the narrow column to the right, and make it a table of contents.

- Move the credits to a narrow column on the second page, and use the first page only for stories.

Of the many ways you can set up the first page, make sure that you keep that page readable and interesting. The first page of a newsletter is the most visible and should invite the reader to pick up the issue and turn to the next page.

The column containing the credits is set in Bitstream's Futura Medium Condensed, which contrasts with the rest of the newsletter's typeface, Zapf Calligraphic. The section headings are in Swiss Bold Condensed. For publication information, using a typeface different from and smaller than the typeface of the newsletter's main text is common practice and helps keep that information from distracting the reader from the body of the newsletter. Combining sans serif headlines with serif Calligraphic text also works well. The Condensed Swiss typeface is especially appropriate for the column headings, because the characters are tall without being wide.

The stars separating the two sections of the credits column are set in the Zapf Dingbats typeface. You can perfectly center the stars by placing the first at the start of the line, centering the second, and aligning the third flush right. Note that by using WordPerfect's positioning codes, the placement of the three stars always is correct, even if you resize the column later.

To adjust the spacing in the second and third columns, the line spacing was changed to 0.98. Although this change is subtle and probably will not be noticed by the reader, minor adjustments of line height can help you fit text onto the pages. In this case, the adjustment of line spacing makes room for two additional lines to fit on the page (one in each column). This change, in turn, makes the text on page 2 fit better in relationship to the graphic of the printer. Any changes greater than 5 to 10 percent will be visible, and you should make them cautiously. Note that the line height change is placed in the second column and, therefore, does not affect the preceding column.

Cue: Reducing the line spacing can make it possible to fit an extra line or two on the page.

A vertical rule separates the credits column from the body text to help differentiate the content of the two sections. You also can use a vertical rule between the second and third columns, but it isn't necessary. If you do use a vertical rule to separate each column on the first page, you should continue this design on the following pages. A vertical rule would hurt readability on the second page and would be impossible on the third page, as you can see in figures 18.11 and 18.12.

Designing the Second Page

The second page consists of two even columns of text, with the header and footer rules that are introduced on the first page. As on the first page, the body typeface is Bitstream's Zapf Calligraphic, and the heading is Swiss Bold Condensed. This page contains three special features: *raised caps*, a pull-out quote, and a graphics figure.

author of the DTP chapter of the Que book, "It could well be."

From all appearances, Word-Perfect Corporation's latest offering continues their tradition of product excellence. We can probably look forward to a series of updates and enhancements, as is the case with all of WPC's programs, but we believe that this program is a winner. §

What is Desktop Publishing?

Just who is a publisher, any-way? If you've ever sat down in front of a typewriter and typed a letter, **you** are. Publishing is a broad category, both functionally

Desktop publishing, in its simplest terms, implies that the publishing is done on someone's desktop.

and practically. Desktop publish-ing, in its simplest terms, implies that the publishing is done on someone's desktop. Gone are the giant presses, gone are the expen-sive typesetting machines, gone are the days of molten lead type and back-breaking labor. Today, the basic ingredients of desktop publishing are very simple: a personal computer, a laser printer, and desktop publishing software.

What is desktop publishing used for? Anything that's printed, including professional announce-ments, resumés, newsletters, pam-phlets, and even books. The desk-top publishing system allows the desktop publisher to combine the skills of the word processor, grap-hics artist, page-layout specialist, typesetter, and printer into one coherent process. Usually, the desktop publishing system pro-duces "camera-ready copy," suitable for offset printing or photo duplicating.

Desktop publishing allows the professional to generate a the doc-ument and determine its appearance—the size of the letters, the style of the characters, the position on the page, etc. Line drawings, which could be pro-duced using a graphics package, can be easily incorporated into the document. Photographs can be scanned into the computer, and

2

FIG. 18.11

Page 2 of the newsletter.

Reprinted by permission of PCC Resources.

Raised Caps

■ **Cue:** Raised caps increase the white space and add visual interest; drop caps add visual interest, but don't increase the white space.

The raised caps feature is especially interesting because it adds visual appeal and interest to the page. Each paragraph begins with a raised capital letter that, in this newsletter, is set in 42-point (three times larger than the text) ITC Tiffany. Each paragraph's initial letter is in a typeface that is larger and different from the text's typeface, making that letter stand out as a graphical element.

Raised caps add interest to the page but require a little extra work. For this newsletter, you can create a paired style that contains some of the necessary steps. The style entry, which you can name Raised Caps, contains the following commands:

incorporated as well. Changes are easily incorporated, and revised copy can be produced in a matter of minutes.

Desktop publishing is faster than traditional printing, and far less expensive. It is inexpensive enough to be purchased by many businesses. In addition, consulting firms like PCC Resources can assist many businesses by providing timely and economical alternatives to traditional publishing.

Are there any negatives to desktop publishing? Yes, several. The quality

Desktop publishing is faster than traditional printing, and far less expensive.

of the camera-ready copy, while excellent, is not as good as traditional typesetting. To the untrained eye,

it would look identical, but to the trained eye (perhaps with a magnifying glass), traditional typesetting would be superior. In addition, because of limitations

PCs CAN BE PUBLISHING PLATFORMS

in current technology, desktop publishing is available only in black and white. High resolution color printing is generally available only through traditional publishing firms. Finally, if you are doing your own desktop publishing, you must invest *time*

in order to learn how to use your software.

Whether you choose to do your publishing in-house, or through a personal computer consulting firm like PCC Resources, desktop publishing offers a quick, economical, and versatile alternative to traditional publishing. Desktop-published documents can provide a more professional presentation than typewritten pages, and can easily incorporate graphics and images to produce an appealing, eye-catching manuscript. §

3

Reprinted by permission of PCC Resources.

FIG. 18.12

Page 3 of the newsletter.

```
Change font to 42-point Tiffany Medium
[Comment]
Change font to 14-point Zapf Calligraphic
Insert an Advance Left code with a distance of 0.02"
```

You can find more information about the Style command in Chapter 12, "Using Styles." Chapter 11, "Formatting Pages and Designing Documents," describes the Advance command.

You must "hard code" the fonts into the style because you cannot interactively determine what font size to use. To *hard code* means to place the value in as already selected. Normally, for example, you could choose a type by selecting Font, but in the style, you determine the choice ahead of time so that the font is no longer a variable. (You could use a macro, of course, but it isn't justified in this situation; a style is much more straightforward and logical.) This style is customized for this particular newsletter.

Follow these steps to create raised caps:

1. Apply the Raised Cap style to the first letter of the first word of the paragraph.

2. Insert a hard return at the end of the line with the raised cap.

3. Add an Advance Up code of **0.11"** at the start of the *next* line.

Note that this method does not work if you are using full justification, because the hard return on the first line leaves that line ragged. If you leave out the hard return, the Advance code might float up to the first line as you modify the text, creating an unexpected and unpleasant effect.

The Advance Left code, [AdvLeft:0.02"], placed after the raised cap helps to kern the two letters so that they look more natural together. Unfortunately, you frequently have to adjust the letter pairs by additional amounts to produce the best result possible. The following adjustments were added to the raised caps, in addition to the 0.02 inch that the style adds automatically:

Raised Cap Letter	Advance Left Value
F	0.01"
J	0.01"
W	0.04"
D	0"

Pull-Out Quotes

You use WordPerfect's Text Box feature to generate the pull-out quote in this newsletter. Although you can change the text box options, the default values work well in this example. The text box default values are a 10 percent gray background, a thick line on the top and bottom, and no line on the left or right.

Use the following parameters for the text box position:

Anchor type:	Character
Vertical Position:	Baseline
Size: Width (Auto Height)	3.06"

Immediately following the text box code, insert an Advance Down code of 0.05 inches so that the text does not print right against the box. Place the text box code and the Advance Left code on the line in which you want the pull-out quote to appear. In this example, the text box is designed to fit within the column margins. The text in the pull-out quote is set in 16-point Zapf Humanist Bold Italic.

Graphics

The last special feature on this page is the graphic in the top right corner. The graphic adds contrast and interest to the page and is related to the text. Set the following options for the figure boxes:

Borders:	None
Inside and Outside Border Space:	0"

The figure box is positioned according to the following parameters:

Anchor type:	Page
Vertical Position:	Top
Horizontal Position:	Margin, Right
Size: Width (Auto Height)	3.06"

Designing the Third Page

The third page of the newsletter is more complex and ambitious than the other pages (again see fig. 18.13). Three columns make the text a little easier to read but a little more difficult to lay out. In addition, the graphic and pull-out quote straddle more than one column. This layout requires additional attention, because the two graphics could clash with each other or compete for space on the page. Note that a newsletter might use two *or* three columns, but not both. The sample newsletter pages switched from two to three columns for illustrative purposes only. With the exception of the first page, the best guideline is to choose one format for your columns and to use it throughout the newsletter.

Like the second page, this page contains raised caps, a pull-out quote, and a graphic. The raised caps are the same as the raised caps on the second page, except for the Advance values. Note that the letter *A* requires an Advance Right value of 0.03 inch, or the code `[AdvRgt:0.03"]`:

Raised Cap Letter	Advance Value
D	0.00"
A	0.03" (Right)
W	0.04" (Left)

On this final page of the newsletter, set line spacing to 0.96 inch to adjust the position of the text so that the pull-out quote and the graphic do not interfere with each other. Placing the two graphics and adjusting the line height (leading) requires considerable tweaking before you can achieve a satisfactory result.

The pull-out quote is a text box, as on the second page, but on this page, the anchor type is Page. As a result, the position on the page is set to an absolute location. If you change the design or move text around, you have to reposition the pull-out quote manually on the page. Although inconvenient, this method is necessary when graphics boxes span more than one column.

The pull-out quote's contents are centered and set in Bitstream's Zapf Humanist Italic. This particular typeface stands out without adding to the clutter on the page. The fact that both the pull-out quote and the graphic span columns adds interest, but also runs the risk of overwhelming the reader. You need to use a friendly and comfortable typeface, and Zapf Humanist Italic fulfills that need.

The figure graphic of a PC also spans two columns. Note that the intrusion into the third column does not take up half the column. WordPerfect adjusts the text to whatever space is left in the column. The figure graphic, like the text box for the pull-out quote, uses the Page anchor type and is set with absolute values. The caption is set in the same typeface as the text, Zapf Calligraphic, but in WordPerfect's Large size, in Small Caps, to distinguish it from the rest of the text.

Cue: Place something in a large blank area at the end of a page to show that nothing is missing—a quotation, observation, ornament, or symbol.

Notice the white space at the end of the third column of the newsletter's last page. You do not have room to begin another article, yet the amount of leftover space is large enough to appear conspicuous. To fill the void, you have several options:

- Insert an interesting quotation or funny saying.
- Present a little-known statistic or fact.
- Include line art.
- Print an artistic symbol.

For this newsletter, select the latter approach, enlarging one of Bitstream's Zapf Dingbats characters as the symbol. Although it adds visual interest to the page, the symbol also shows that nothing is missing from the empty section. Note that the empty section is not completely filled up; you simply provide visual appeal to an otherwise conspicuously blank area. The Dingbat character used (four diamonds) is set at 50 points and is character 12,118. (Character set 12 is user-defined; Chapter 28, "Creating and Displaying Special Characters," explains the use of the character sets.)

Settings for the Newsletter

Table 18.4 gives the settings for the three-page newsletter.

Table 18.4. Settings for the Newsletter

Page 1 Element	Option	Setting
Justification		Left
Margins	Top	0.5"
	Bottom	0.75"
	Left	1"
	Right	1"
Column 1	Left	1"
	Right	2.75"
Column 2	Left	3"
	Right	5.13"
Column 3	Left	5.38"
	Right	7.5"
Line Spacing	Column 1	1"
	Columns 2 and 3	0.98"
Fonts	Issue/Date	Zapf Calligraphic Italic (14 pt)
	Editorial Headline	Futura Medium Condensed (21 pt)
	Editorial Text	Futura Medium Condensed (14 pt)
	Editorial "Stars"	Zapf Dingbats (16.8 pt)
	Section Headlines	Swiss Bold Condensed (18 pt)
	Body Text	Zapf Calligraphic Roman (14 pt)

continues

Table 18.4. *(continued)*

Page 1 Element	Option	Setting
Rules	Thick	Full, Baseline, 6.5", 0.075", 100%
	Thin	Full, Baseline, 6.5", 0.02", 100%
	Vertical	Column 1, 4.08", 5.7", 0.013", 100%
Figure (Masthead)	Border Style	All None
	Outside Border	0" (all sides)
	Inside Border	0.167" (all sides)
	Gray Shading	0%
	Contents	Graphic
	Anchor Type	Page
	Vertical Position	Top
	Horizontal Position	Margins, Full
	Wrap	Yes
	Size	Width: 6.5" Height 2.78"

Page 2 (changes from page 1)

Column 1	Left	1"
	Right	4.06"
Column 2	Left	4.44"
	Right	7.5"
Line Spacing	Column 1	0.99"
	Column 2	1.0"
Fonts	Raised Caps	ITC Tiffany Medium (42 pt)
	Pull-out quotes	Zapf Humanist Bold Italic (16 pt)
Figure (Printer)	Border Style	All None
	Outside Border	0" (all sides)
	Inside Border	0" (all sides)
	Gray Shading	0%
	Contents	Graphics
	Anchor Type	Page
	Vertical Position	Top
	Horizontal Position	Margins, Right
	Wrap	Yes
	Size	Width: 3.06" Height: 2.21"

Page 2 Element	Option	Setting
Text Box (pull-out quote)	Border Style	Top: Thick Bottom: Thick Left: None Right: None
	Outside Border	0.167" (all sides)
	Inside Border	0.167" (all sides)
	Gray Shading	10%
	Contents	Text
	Anchor Type	Character
	Vertical Position	Baseline
	Horizontal Position	n/a
	Wrap	Yes
	Size	Width: 3.06" Height: 1.3"

Page 3 (changes from pages 1 and 2)

Column 1	Left	1"
	Right	3"
Column 2	Left	3.25"
	Right	5.25"
Column 3	Left	5.5"
	Right	7.5"
Line Spacing		0.96"
Fonts	Figure Caption	Zapf Calligraphic Roman, Small Caps (16.8 pt)
	Pull-out quotes	Zapf Humanist Italic (16 pt)
	"Diamond" ornament	Zapf Dingbats (50 pt)
Figure (PC)	Border Style	All None
	Outside Border	0" (all sides)
	Inside Border	0" (all sides)
	Gray Shading	0%
	Contents	Graphics
	Anchor Type	Page
	Vertical Position	2.75"
	Horizontal Position	3.11"
	Wrap	Yes
	Size	Width: 3.08" Height: 2.5"

continues

Table 18.4. *(continued)*

Page 3 Element	Option	Setting
Text Box (pull-out quote)	Border Style	Top: Thick Bottom: Thick Left: None Right: None
	Outside Border	Top: 0" Bottom: 0" Left: 0.167" Right: 0.167"
	Inside Border	0.167" (all sides)
	Gray Shading	10%
	Contents	Text
	Anchor Type	Page
	Vertical Position	7.25
	Horizontal Position	1"
	Wrap	Yes
	Size	Width: 3.0" Height: 1.1"

Finishing the Newsletter

The initial design of a newsletter is usually a great deal of work, but after you finish that design, producing additional pages and issues is much easier. In some cases, using a more elaborate footer and header is appropriate. You can use headers and footers to communicate issue information that needs to be repeated on every page.

You also can incorporate a graphical design onto each page, either in the body of the text or in a header. For example, a company might want its logo repeated on each page. If the logo lends itself to a single line, you can center it in a header. You also can place the graphics or logo in the text of the document as a graphics box using Page (absolute) orientation. Note that if you place a graphics box in a header, text does not fill the space to the side of the graphic unless you place it within the header as well.

Most newsletters are printed on *signatures* of 11-by-17-inch paper. Each signature holds four complete 8 1/2-by-11-inch pages, two on each side. For this reason, newsletters usually consist of multiples of four pages (4, 8, 12, and so on). Generally, you contract with a printer to offset print the camera-ready copy you produce with your laser printer. In some cases, you might provide the printing company with a data file of printing information so that the printers can use their high-resolution equipment to produce the camera-ready copy. PostScript is almost certainly the format of choice when providing the printing company with a data file, because PostScript is widely supported in both the PC and professional printing environments. WordPerfect for Windows completely supports PostScript and enables you to use several PostScript printers and cartridges for HP-compatible laser printers.

You can apply the same techniques used in the newsletter to produce larger publications, such as reports, books, or magazines. If you do not plan to print the final copy on 8 1/2-by-11-inch paper, multiple columns may not be necessary or appropriate in your publication.

Chapter Summary

WordPerfect for Windows provides an excellent platform for desktop publishing. Most of the features that are difficult in WordPerfect 5.1 for DOS, such as moving and sizing graphics and adjusting margins, tabs, and column widths, are simple in WordPerfect 5.1 for Windows. As seen in the examples included in this chapter, WordPerfect is well-suited to many desktop-publishing projects. As you learned in this chapter, WordPerfect for Windows enables you to combine text and graphics, design successful publications, select suitable typefaces, plan and lay out pages, enhance your publications, and create fliers, trifold mailers, and newsletters.

PART

V

Automating Your Work

OUTLINE

Using the Button Bar

Creating Macros

Assembling Documents
with Merge

Sorting and Selecting Data

Using the Button Bar

T he Button Bar is an innovative feature of WordPerfect for Windows, that lets you carry out a command by clicking a mouse button as easily as you can issue a command by pressing a function key. You can put any WordPerfect feature on a Button Bar, and you can customize your Button Bar for your own needs and taste. In this chapter, you learn to do the following:

■ **Gordon Nelder-Adams** is the WordPerfect expert for the Sacramento PC Users Group and a computing assistant at the University of California, Davis.

- ■ Select a different Button Bar
- ■ Add, delete, and move buttons
- ■ Change the position of the Button Bar on-screen
- ■ Change the appearance of the Button Bar
- ■ Create additional specialized Button Bars
- ■ Assign macros to Button Bars

Why Use the Button Bar?

WordPerfect 5.1 for Windows amply refutes the assertion that programs written for the Windows environment make poor use of the keyboard. Like WordPerfect 5.1 for DOS, WordPerfect 5.1 for Windows makes extensive use of function keys to perform most commands. Although using your mouse with the pull-down menu feels natural, after you become familiar with the menu structure, you can travel the structure more quickly with the Alt key than with the mouse. To use the menus to display the Merge dialog box, for instance, you select **Tools**, **Merge**, **Merge**. You can press Alt-T, M, M in less than a second. Performing the same operation with a mouse takes several times longer, even with a speedy computer.

This inherent difference in speed between the keyboard and the mouse forms the basis of some criticism of the Windows environment. Such criticism ignores the fact that Windows does not *prevent* the use of the keyboard and that WordPerfect for Windows *enables* features such as the on-screen display of fonts, icons, and graphics objects that you can manipulate on-screen. WordPerfect, in addressing the subject of accessing features with the mouse, combined several of these capabilities and created the *Button Bar* (see fig. 19.1).

FIG. 19.1

WordPerfect's
Button Bar.

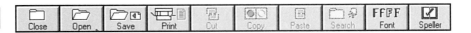

Cue: You cannot use the Button Bar with the keyboard; you must use your mouse.

The Button Bar's name is self-descriptive; it is a bar of on-screen buttons you can click with your mouse. Each button can contain any item from WordPerfect's pull-down menus. Clicking a button performs the action indicated on that button; you don't have to use the keyboard or pull-down menus. The use of buttons is hardly unique—nearly all Windows dialog boxes contain one or more buttons—nor is clicking buttons to access features unique. WordPerfect's Ruler contains several buttons that provide shortcuts to features such as font selection, styles, and others. Programs like Microsoft Word for Windows and Excel also provide buttons.

What is unique about the Button Bar is that you can customize it according to your preferences. You can specify which items you want to display in the Button Bar and the order in which WordPerfect displays them. You can create several different Button Bars for performing various tasks and can switch rapidly between Button Bars. You also can add macros to the Button Bar. You even can control the on-screen location of the Button Bar and determine whether the buttons display text, icons, or both. Finally, if you want more display space on-screen and do not need the Button Bar, you can turn off the Button Bar until you need it again.

After you add a new button to the Button Bar, you activate that button's feature simply by clicking. Clicking a button can be faster than selecting the feature from the menu with either the keyboard or the mouse, especially if the item is in a second-level menu. Furthermore, you don't have to remember a feature's menu location or function key if you can access the feature by clicking its button—a particularly useful aid for beginners or occasional users who have not yet learned the program's full structure.

By adding to the Button Bar the options you use daily, you can perform your tasks more quickly. By creating specialized Button Bars for the options you use less frequently, you can make those tasks easier to perform.

Selecting a Button Bar

You can turn the Button Bar on and off, select from different Button Bars, edit Button Bars, and create new Button Bars through the View menu (see fig. 19.2).

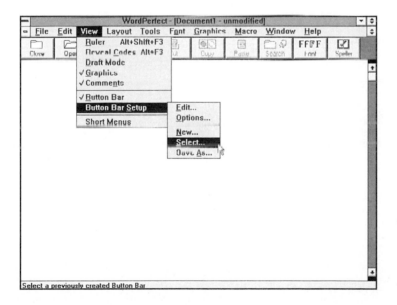

FIG. 19.2

Selecting a Button Bar.

Button Bars are stored as files with the extension WWB. WordPerfect provides two sample Button Bars: WP{WP}.WWB and TABLES.WWB. You should have installed these files when you installed the program, and you can choose from them. WordPerfect remembers which Button

Bar you used most recently and whether it was on-screen when you last exited the program.

If you have not previously selected a different Button Bar, WP{WP}.WWB is selected. If it is not visible on your screen, choose **V**iew, **B**utton Bar. WordPerfect displays Button Bar WP{WP}.WWB or another Button Bar that you or another user previously selected (see fig. 19.3). The space occupied on-screen by the Button Bar is temporarily unavailable to display text.

WP{WP}.WWB

FIG. 19.3

WordPerfect's sample Button Bars.

TABLES.WWB

If the Button Bar displayed is not the one you want, you must select the correct one.

To select a Button Bar, follow these steps:

1. Choose **V**iew, Button Bar **S**etup, **S**elect.

   WordPerfect displays the Select Button Bar dialog box, which is similar to the Open File dialog box. WordPerfect stores Button Bar files in your macro directory, and the Select Button Bar dialog box displays only the file names in that directory with a WWB extension.

2. Select a Button Bar file; then choose Open or press Enter. For this example, select WP{WP}.WWB.

T I P   You can select a Button Bar file by double-clicking its name in the dialog box.

WordPerfect replaces the currently displayed Button Bar, if any, with the Button Bar you select. If your Button Bar was turned off, selecting a Button Bar automatically turns on this feature.

When the Button Bar is on, WordPerfect displays a check mark next to Button Bar in the View menu. To turn off the Button Bar, select View, Button Bar. WordPerfect adjusts your screen to regain text space.

Examining the Button Bar

WordPerfect has designed a unique icon for every feature you can select as a button. Notice that each button contains an icon and the name of its feature (again see fig. 19.3). Later, you learn how to display only names or only icons, but in this section you examine the general aspects of the Button Bar's design.

The first three buttons on WP{WP}.WWB, WordPerfect's default Button Bar, are Close, Open, and Save. All three commands have to do with the manipulation of files; therefore, their icons contain file folders, as do the icons for Retrieve, Save As, and File Manager. Similarly, the Print button contains a printer, and the Cut and Paste buttons show a piece of paper that has been, respectively, cut and rejoined. WordPerfect's use of similar icons makes identifying related features easier.

WordPerfect also uses abstract symbols to group buttons in other ways. For example, the Table button in TABLES.WWB contains a diagonal slash in the upper left corner (again see fig. 19.3). On a color monitor, these slashes are blue. The blue slash is an example of a *category marker*. Buttons that share category markers perform similar functions. For example, each button that contains a blue slash *creates* something.

A small red triangle in the upper right corner denotes a button that *edits* something. (Most "create" buttons have an equivalent "edit" button.) A rounded yellow triangle denotes *viewing* something: Print Preview, the Ruler, Reveal Codes, Button Bar, and so on.

Each category marker has a distinctive shape, and many have distinctive colors. The WordPerfect manual contains a list of all the category markers and their meanings. As you add and use buttons, you will begin to recognize the categories. You will also recognize other repeating patterns, such as the file folder icons representing file access, the cassette tape icons representing macros, and the table icons visible in TABLES.WWB (again see fig. 19.3). Buttons for font attributes, such as Bold, Italic, and Large, contain the letters *abc*, formatted appropriately. Over time, you will learn to associate the button pictures with the features they represent, and you may find that you don't need the descriptions. You can then hide the descriptions so that more space for your text is available on-screen (see "Changing the Button Bar's Position and Style" in this chapter).

In figure 19.3 you can also see that icons and descriptions for the Cut, Copy, and Paste buttons appear gray. Just as WordPerfect dims unavailable menu options, the program dims buttons that are currently unavailable.

Some buttons also serve as visual status indicators. For example, if you include a Ruler button on a Button Bar, you can turn on the Ruler by clicking its button. As long as the Ruler is displayed, the Ruler button looks as if it has been pressed in. WordPerfect creates the appearance of a pressed button by drawing a heavy border around the selected button and shifting the button's contents down slightly on screen (see fig. 19.4). If you click the selected Ruler button, WordPerfect hides the Ruler and the button "pops back up." Buttons for the other View menu options, such as Reveal Codes and Draft Mode, act in a similar fashion.

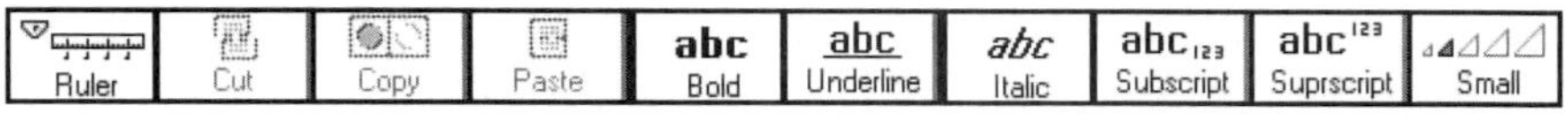

FIG. 19.4

Selected buttons
acting as status
indicators.

The other group of buttons that act as visual indicators are the font attribute buttons, such as Bold, Italic, Superscript, and Large. Although the primary purpose of these buttons is to turn the attributes on and off, whenever your insertion point is between a pair of attribute codes, the button for that attribute appears pressed in. When you edit text that contains many font attributes, the status indicator buttons enable you to know at a glance whether your insertion point is between a pair of attributes codes, without your having to go in and out of Reveal Codes.

Creating Personal Button Bars

WordPerfect's sample Button Bar WP{WP}.WWB includes many of the most commonly used commands: Open, Save, Print, Cut, Paste, Speller, and so on. If you don't use these commands frequently, you should create a personal Button Bar to meet your own needs. You may want to include some, if not most, of these sample buttons. You probably will delete a few buttons, rearrange others, and add still more; but this sample Button Bar is a good starting place. TABLES.WWB, on the other hand, is a special-purpose Button Bar designed for editing tables and shares no buttons with WP{WP}.WWB. When you create a special-purpose Button Bar, starting with an empty bar is probably easier than modifying an existing one.

Which buttons should you put on your Button Bar, and in what order should you display them? The answers to these questions depend on your work style.

When selecting buttons for your Button Bar, however, you may want to avoid the features available through the Ruler. By double-clicking the Ruler's built-in buttons, you can call up the dialog boxes for Tab Set, Margins, Font, Styles, Create Table, Define Columns, and Line Spacing. Therefore, the Font button in WP{WP}.WWB duplicates the Font button on the Ruler. Unless you rarely work with the Ruler on-screen, adding any of these buttons to your Button Bar is probably a waste of space.

 **Cue:** Don't add to your Button Bar buttons that duplicate buttons on the Ruler.

In theory, your main Button Bar should contain the options you use most often; however, after first creating your own Button Bar, you may find yourself bypassing a button in favor of its keyboard or menu equivalent. If so, remove that button from the Button Bar and add a different button. You probably will revise your Button Bar several times before you are comfortable with it, and over time, you may find that your preferences change. Creating and editing Button Bars is so quick and easy that you can experiment with many different combinations of buttons. You may find different Button Bars useful under different situations.

Saving a Button Bar

Before making changes to the sample Button Bar, save it under a new name.

To save the sample Button Bar under a new file name, select **View**, Button Bar **Setup**, Save **As**. WordPerfect displays the Save Button Bar dialog box, which is similar to the Save As dialog box. Type a new Button Bar file name in the Save **As** text box, perhaps your initials if you are creating a personal Button Bar.

WARNING: Make sure that you never use either of WordPerfect's default Button Bar file names—WP{WP}.WWB or TABLES.WWB—for a Button Bar you create. If you do, and later you reinstall or upgrade WordPerfect for Windows, you risk copying the original or upgraded version of the default Button Bar over your own and losing your changes.

You do not have to type the extension WWB because WordPerfect adds it for you. If you use an extension other than WWB, WordPerfect does not recognize the file as a Button Bar. WordPerfect stores Button Bar files in the default macro directory, just as it stores macros and keyboard layouts. You can choose a different directory; however, under normal circumstances you should not because WordPerfect can locate the file only when it's located in the macro directory.

After you type the new file name, select **S**ave or press Enter. The only difference between the Button Bar now displayed on-screen and the original one is the current Button Bar's new file name. Any changes you make are saved in this new Button Bar file.

Editing Button Bars

To edit a Button Bar, follow these steps:

1. From the **V**iew menu, select Button Bar **S**etup, **E**dit. WordPerfect displays the Edit Button Bar dialog box (see fig. 19.5).

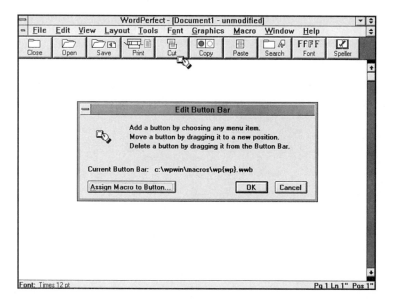

FIG. 19.5

The Edit Button Bar dialog box.

The Edit Button Bar dialog box is somewhat unusual. In addition to the OK and Cancel buttons, the dialog box contains a single button labeled **A**ssign Macro to Button, and editing instructions.

Immediately below these instructions, the dialog box displays the name of the current Button Bar. If the name displayed is not the name you expected, immediately select Cancel and specify the correct Button Bar before you make any changes.

In the dialog box, WordPerfect also displays a small hand holding a button—an image the mouse pointer assumes while you edit the Button Bar.

> Although you normally can use your keyboard or mouse to select menu items, you must use your mouse when editing the Button Bar.
>
> **T I P**

2. To delete the Font button, just drag it off the Button Bar, and release the mouse button.

   When you release the mouse button, WordPerfect deletes the Font button and moves the Speller button to close the gap.

3. Delete the Speller button.

4. To add a Ruler button, use the mouse to choose **View**, **Ruler**.

5. Add the Print Preview button by using the mouse to choose **File**, **Print Preview**.

   WordPerfect displays Print Preview as the last button on the right. If your Button Bar is displayed vertically, the program displays new buttons at the bottom (see the "Changing the Button Bar's Position and Style" for details on vertically displaying the Button Bar).

6. Place the new Print Preview button between Save and Print by dragging the Print Preview button with your mouse.

   WordPerfect places the button between the two buttons it overlaps when you release the mouse button, so you don't have to be too precise. Be careful, though, not to drag the Print Preview button completely off the Button Bar. After you release the mouse button, WordPerfect moves the buttons to the right of the Save button to make room for the Print Preview button's new location.

7. Move the Ruler button to the right of the Print Preview button.

8. Now add the Reveal Codes button (click **View**, Reveal **Codes**) and drag it to the right of the Ruler button.

9. After you finish adding, moving, and deleting buttons, select OK or press Enter. If you change your mind and press Cancel, your Button Bar returns to its original layout.

■ **Cue:** To add a button, you must use your mouse to select from the menu the items you want to add to the Button Bar.

If you add more buttons than can fit on-screen, WordPerfect adds left and right scroll buttons to the left edge of the Button Bar (or to the top if your Button Bar is displayed vertically). You can continue adding

■ **Cue:** Don't add many more buttons than will fit on-screen, or you will waste time scrolling the Button Bar to find the buttons you want.

buttons, but to use a button that you cannot see on-screen, you must scroll the Button Bar left or right until you display the button you want. If you add many buttons, the scrolling process may take longer than accessing the pull-down menus or using the function keys, thus defeating the purpose of the Button Bar. To some extent, however, you can control the number of buttons displayed on-screen by changing the position and style of your Button Bar, as explained in the following section.

Changing the Button Bar's Position and Style

Although by default WordPerfect positions the Button Bar horizontally across the top of the screen, you can change that position. WordPerfect can display the row of buttons horizontally across the bottom of your screen or vertically along either the left or right edge of your screen.

To specify the position of the Button Bar, select **V**iew, Button Bar **S**etup, **O**ptions. WordPerfect displays the Button Bar Options dialog box, which contains four Position options: **L**eft, **R**ight, **T**op, and **B**ottom (see fig. 19.6). Table 19.1 defines the four options.

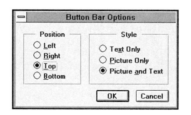

FIG. 19.6

The Button Bar Options dialog box.

Each position has its advantages and disadvantages. If you use a standard VGA screen, positioning the Button Bar at the left or right side of the screen reduces the width of the text display; you may not be able to see a full line of text if you select a small font, narrow margins, or a landscape page orientation. Furthermore, if you position the Button Bar on the right, you occasionally may click the scroll bar instead of the desired button. Depending on your mouse control, however, this risk may be slight.

Table 19.1. Button Bar Position Options

Option	Location On-Screen
Left	Vertically displayed along the left edge of the screen, below the menu. WordPerfect moves your text and the Ruler to the right, and the width of the buttons makes both text and the Ruler narrower.
Right	Vertically displayed along the right edge of the screen, below the menu. The text and Ruler do not move, but they do become narrower because of the width of the buttons.
Top	Horizontally displayed below the menu. WordPerfect displays the Ruler below the Button Bar.
Bottom	Horizontally displayed across the bottom of the screen, below the status line.

The same slight risk applies to positioning the Button Bar across the top of the screen; however, this position is perhaps the most eye-catching and natural location to use. The bottom, by contrast, is a less common position, and buttons located there can be awkward to click. In general, Top and Left are the most useful Button Bar Positions.

Position, however, is only one category in the Button Bar Options dialog box; the other category is Style. The Style options enable you to control what is displayed on the face of each button. These options are even simpler and completely self-descriptive: Text Only, Picture Only, and Picture and Text. The default Style option is Picture and Text.

If you don't need to display both the text and the picture on each button, you can make the buttons smaller. Although the width of the buttons does not change, selecting either Text Only or Picture Only reduces the height of each button. Text Only makes the buttons slightly smaller than Picture Only, but either option makes the buttons approximately half the height of buttons displayed if you select Pictures and Text (see fig 19.7).

Selecting the Position option Top or Bottom and the Style option Text Only or Picture Only makes room for an extra line or two of text. On the other hand, if you select the Position option Left or Right and the Style option Text Only or Picture Only, the Button Bar remains the same width; however, the smaller button size enables you to include more than twice as many buttons on-screen (see fig. 19.8).

Cue: You can display the most buttons by making your Button Bar vertical (left or right) and not selecting the Picture and Text option.

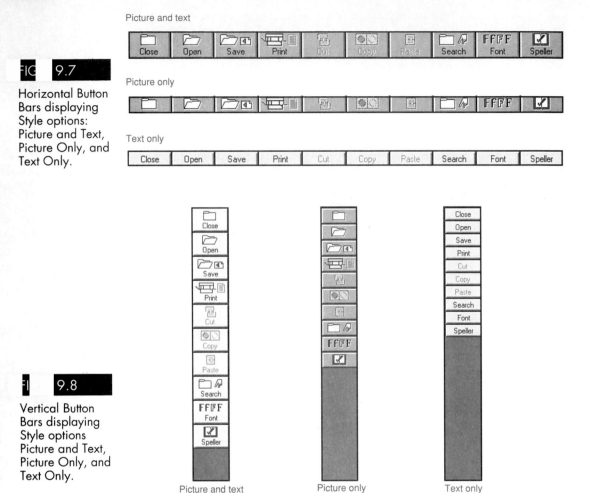

FIG   9.7

Horizontal Button
Bars displaying
Style options:
Picture and Text,
Picture Only, and
Text Only.

Vertical Button
Bars displaying
Style options
Picture and Text,
Picture Only, and
Text Only.

Each Style option also has its advantages and disadvantages. When
Picture and Text is selected, the meaning of each button is completely
clear, but the buttons take up the most room on-screen. With Text
Only, the buttons' meanings are equally clear and take up the least
amount of room on-screen. However, at a quick glance one word or
short phrase looks much like another, and reading your buttons to find
the one you want can slow your use of the Button Bar by a surprising
amount. By contrast, with Picture Only selected, the varied shapes
of the different icons makes distinguishing between them almost
instantaneous—after you learn what each icon means. Although the
meanings of most icons are obvious, some take a little practice to
recognize.

A more severe limitation to the Picture Only option occurs when you assign macros to your Button Bar. Because WordPerfect displays the same icon for every Button Bar macro, you cannot distinguish one macro from another if you select Picture Only. If your Button Bar contains more than one macro, therefore, you should use the Text Only or the Picture and Text option.

The options in the Button Bar Options dialog box are radio buttons; you can select only one Position option and one Style option at a time. After you specify the options you want, select OK or press Enter to accept your changes, or select Cancel (press Esc) to return to your prior selections.

The number of buttons you can display on-screen depends not only on the Position and Style options you specify, but also on your monitor resolution. On a standard VGA monitor with a resolution of 640 by 480 pixels, WordPerfect can display 10 buttons across the width of your screen. If your monitor displays 1024 by 768 pixels on-screen, WordPerfect can display 12 buttons. Equipped with a high-resolution monitor and using a vertical Button Bar, you can display 26 buttons on-screen if you specify Picture Only as your Style option (see fig. 19.9), or a glorious 29 buttons if you specify Text Only.

Button bar ———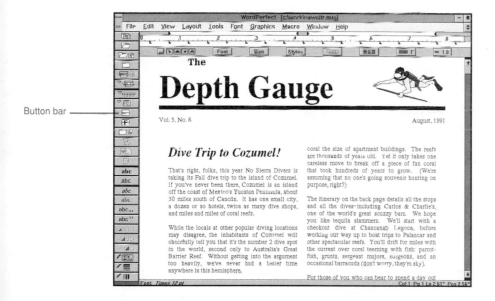

FIG. 19.9

A vertical Button Bar at 1024 by 768 resolution.

Creating Specialized Button Bars

No matter how many buttons you can display on-screen, you can never display enough. If WordPerfect allowed, you could fill your entire screen with the buttons of features you use frequently, let alone features that might come in handy on occasion. But the more buttons you have, the more buttons you have to sort through to find the one you want. At some point, the law of diminishing returns takes effect, and using the Button Bar then takes longer than using the pull-down menus. To resolve this dilemma, you can create several Button Bars.

Few people perform the same tasks on the computer all the time. Unless you have a strictly repetitive job, such as data entry, the longer you spend time at your computer, the larger the variety of features you are likely to use. If you examine the kinds of documents you work with and the features you use in those documents, you should be able to identify several groups of features that you could compile into Button Bars. The following list contains some common commands you may want to include in one or more Button Bars:

- *File commands:* File Manager, Open, Save, Save As, Close

- *Edit commands:* Cut, Copy, Paste

- *Font commands:* Bold, Italic, Underline, Superscript, Subscript, Small, Large, Very Large

- *Document and screen commands:* Print, Print Preview, Ruler, Reveal Codes, Initial Codes, Initial Font, Special Codes

- *Tools and advanced layout commands:* Speller, Thesaurus, Merge Codes, Mark Text, Spreadsheet Link, Table Edit

- *Graphics commands:* Figure Box, Text Box, Equation Box, Table Box, User Box, Line

This list is not exhaustive; you can place every selection in the pull-down menus on a button, including Button Bar itself, which turns off the Button Bar. (For obvious reasons, you cannot click a button to turn on the Button Bar.) Some features, such as Save, Cut, and Paste, you may want to include in more than one Button Bar.

You shouldn't create Button Bars only for the features you use frequently, though. Creating Button Bars for seldom performed tasks can make those tasks more approachable. For instance, one of Word-Perfect's sample Button Bars, TABLES.WWB, is designed specifically for the task of creating and editing tables. The actions involved in editing a table's structure are completely different from the procedures used for editing normal text, and the table edit options are all several levels down in the Layout menu. This Button Bar makes all the hard-to-reach options available by a single click.

You can create specialized Button Bars for any tasks you perform. For instance, to make the task of constructing merge files easier, you can construct a Merges Button Bar, as follows:

1. Access the **View** menu and select Button Bar **Setup, New.**

   Because this Button Bar is not based on an existing Button Bar, selecting New both avoids the possibility of altering another Button Bar by mistake and displays an empty bar so that you don't have to drag off unneeded buttons to make room.

2. Use your mouse to make the following selections in order from the Tools, Merge menu:

   > Field
   > Input
   > Merge Codes
   > Page Off
   > Next Record
   > Merge Convert
   > Merge

3. From the Tools menu, select Date, Code. Drag the Date Code button between Merge Codes and Date Code.

4. Select OK. WordPerfect displays the Save Button Bar dialog box. Type **merges** and select Save.

Your Button Bar for merges should resemble the Button Bar shown in figure 19.10. Because this Button Bar has only eight buttons, you can add several macros without filling the space available on-screen. The buttons you installed let you specify a field name or number to be merged, add an insert code which makes a merge pause and display a dialog box prompt, display a dialog box of merge programming codes, insert a date code, insert two more common merge codes, convert old merge files to the WordPerfect 5.1 merge format, and actually begin a merge to test the file you are creating.

FIG. 19.10

A sample Button Bar for merges.

You can create similar Button Bars for working with WordPerfect's other specialized tools such as Index, List, Table of Contents, Link, and graphics boxes. Other chapters in this book contain suggestions for using the Button Bar with their respective features; they should give you more ideas.

Using Macros with the Button Bar

If your Button Bar is too large to fit on-screen, you must scroll through it to reach buttons hidden at one end or the other, which greatly decreases the Button Bar's efficiency. The problem is compounded further when you create multiple Button Bars, because you must select a different Button Bar before you can use it.

WordPerfect's macros solve this problem. Although macros are not suited to scrolling Button Bars, they are ideal for performing the kind of menu selections required to switch to a different Button Bar or to change its position or style. WordPerfect also enables you to assign macros to your Button Bar so that you can perform such tasks with one click. Carrying this idea one step further, you can create Button Bars that contain nothing but macros. One of the most useful macros you can assign to a Button Bar selects a different Button Bar.

Creating Macros To Control Button Bars

After you create a specialized Button Bar, such as the Merges Button Bar you created in the preceding section, you may want to create a macro that selects this Button Bar for you.

You follow the usual procedure for recording a macro, as explained in Chapter 20. Under **Filename**, type **merges-bb**. (Don't type an extension; WordPerfect automatically supplies one.) Under **Descriptive Name**, type **Select Merge Button Bar**. You may add a more complete description under **Abstract** if you want. Select **Record** or press Enter. Go through the steps to select MERGES.WWB, and then turn off Macro Record.

Of course, after you select a different Button Bar, you are going to want to use a macro to return to your personal Button Bar. Record the macro again, replacing MERGES in the file name with your initials (ABC-BB) and selecting your default Button Bar instead of MERGES.WWB. You should record a version of this macro for each Button Bar you create.

When your personal Button Bar, ABC-BB.WWB, or any other Button Bar is on-screen, you can select MERGES.WWB by playing the macro. Likewise, you can select your own button bar by playing the ABC-BB macro. If you switch Button Bars frequently, you may want to assign these macros to your Macro menu for quicker access (see Chapter 20, "Creating Macros," for details).

If you regularly change the position and style of your Button Bar, you should create macros to automate these tasks. If you want, you can combine the keystrokes of a macro that selects a Button Bar and the keystrokes that change its position and style so that selecting a Button Bar also selects its specified position and style. If you create such a macro, however, you may want to select position and style in all macros that select Button Bars.

Assigning Macros to a Button Bar

After you record a macro, you can play it back several different ways. You can choose Macro, Play, and select the desired macro; you can assign the macro to a Ctrl-key combination; or you can assign the macro to a position on the Macro menu. WordPerfect provides an additional and attractive option: the Button Bar itself. You can assign macros to buttons on the Button Bar.

To assign a macro to your personal Button Bar, follow these steps:

1. Select the Button Bar to which you want to assign a macro.

2. Select View, Button Bar Setup, Edit to display the Edit Button Bar dialog box.

3. Select Assign Macro to Button.

   WordPerfect displays the Assign Macro to Button dialog box. This dialog box, a variant of the Open File dialog box, lists the contents of your macro directory.

   Note the Macro on Disk check box under the Files list. Check this box if you want WordPerfect always to use the most current version of the macro you are assigning to a button. If you do not check this box, WordPerfect saves a copy of the original macro with the Button Bar file. Any later changes you make to this macro will not be reflected in the macro assigned to the button. To update the Button Bar, you will have to add a new button for the edited version of the macro.

4. Double-click the macro name in the Files list box, or highlight the macro name, and select Assign. At the end of your Button Bar,

WordPerfect displays the specified macro with its icon depicting a cassette tape.

5. Select OK to close the Edit Button Bar dialog box and save your changes.

To run this macro, simply click its button. WordPerfect displays the correct Button Bar. You may want to add to this Button Bar the macro that selects your personal Button Bar. To do so, repeat the preceding steps, but select the macro named ABC-BB.WCM (substitute your initials for *ABC*). You now can switch back and forth between the two Button Bars by clicking a button.

Creating a Macros Button Bar

If you use many different Button Bars, you may want to create a *Macros Button Bar*, which contains nothing but macros that select other Button Bars. Then, to each of these other Button Bars, assign a single macro that displays the Macros Button Bar.

To create a Macros Button Bar, follow these steps:

1. Select **V**iew, Button Bar **S**etup, **N**ew.

■ **Cue:** If you put several macros on a Button Bar, you cannot use the Picture Only option with that Button Bar.

2. Using the steps described in the preceding section, assign to this new Button Bar any macros you have created and you want to add.

   Each macro button displays a picture of a cassette tape (see fig. 19.11). If your current Button Bar style is **P**icture Only, you must switch to another Style option to distinguish between the macros.

FIG. 19.11

A Macros Button Bar.

3. Select OK. WordPerfect displays the Save Button Bar dialog box. Type **macros** and select Save.

4. Click the button that selects your personal Button Bar.

5. Using the techniques described in Chapter 20, create a macro to select the Macros Button Bar.

6. Assign this macro to your other Button Bars.

You can assign other macros to your Macros Button Bar as well.

Editing Built-in Button Bars

In addition to the sample Button Bars, WordPerfect for Windows has three built-in, special-purpose Button Bars, which are used with Print Preview, the Figure Editor, and the Equation Editor. When you call up Print Preview, for example, its Button Bar appears down the left of the screen (see fig. 19.12). Its buttons can contain only features that are available in Print Preview's pull-down menus. Likewise, the Figure Editor and Equation Editor Button Bars, can contain only buttons relevant to their respective windows.

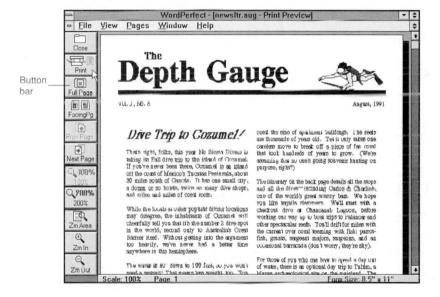

FIG. 19.12

The Print Preview Button Bar.

Just as you work with "normal" Button Bars, you can add, delete, or move buttons on any of the special-purpose Button Bars. You cannot create two or three different Print Preview Button Bars and select among them, however; you can have only one Button Bar for each of these three specialized windows. In fact, their file names have different extensions: WP{WP}.EEB, WP{WP}.FEB, and WP{WP}.PPB.

All the Position and Style options are available for the built-in Button Bars. In Print Preview, however, the height of your screen determines the amount of detail in which WordPerfect can display your document. If you display your Button Bar horizontally, your document appears coarser in Print Preview than if you display the Button Bar vertically. Selecting the Text Only or Picture Only styles may enable you to display all the available buttons on-screen, if you desire.

You can edit the contents, position, and style of the Equation Editor and Figure Editor Button Bars in the same manner. The defaults for each are somewhat different, but you easily can change them if other settings would be more appropriate.

Finally, the File Manager has its own Button Bar facility with essentially the same capabilities as WordPerfect's. Although you cannot assign macros to its buttons, you can create multiple File Manager Button Bars with access to the full range of the File Manager's features. Just as with WordPerfect, the Button Bar makes the File Manager easier to use and more powerful.

Chapter Summary

With WordPerfect's Button Bar feature, you can use your mouse to select options—a process that is quicker than using your keyboard. A button can contain any menu option, no matter how many levels deep, so that you can activate that option with a simple click. In this chapter, you have learned how to add, delete, and move buttons. You can display the Button Bar at the top, bottom, left, or right of your screen. You know how to display buttons with Picture and Text, Picture Only, or Text Only. You have learned to create additional specialized Button Bars. You can create macros to select Button Bars and to change Button Bar options, assign macros to buttons, and create Macro Button Bars. You also learn how to edit built-in Button Bars.

As with any other feature, the more you use the Button Bar, the more comfortable you become with it. Don't be afraid to experiment. Although not all buttons are extremely helpful, many turn difficult tasks into the push of a button.

Creating Macros

WordPerfect provides several tools to help you customize the program according to your uses and needs, and to automate those tasks which you do frequently. Among the most powerful of these tools is the macro.

A macro is a specialized file that performs one or more actions for you. Macros are like tape recordings. When you create a macro, WordPerfect records your actions and saves them in a file. When you "play" that macro file, WordPerfect repeats your actions exactly.

Macros can contain one or more of the following types of information:

- Text
- Menu and dialog box selections
- Insertion point movement and text selection
- Programming commands

You can create macros that repeat words and phrases you frequently use, select a particular format option, move to a different point in a document, select text for some action, or display prompts and menus. Macros can perform a single action or a complex series of actions. The important point is that macros do something useful for you.

■ **Gordon Nelder-Adams** is the WordPerfect expert for the Sacramento PC Users Group and a Computing Assistant at the University of California, Davis. He has created countless simple and advanced macros to automate his own office and a number of law offices in the greater Sacramento area.

Although every document you create is different, you probably create relatively few *types* of documents, and those types of documents are probably formatted similarly. At the same time, you undoubtedly have developed or will develop work habits and always use certain features in the same way, making the same menu choices and dialog box selections over and over again.

By using macros, you can make WordPerfect do some of your work for you. A macro cannot type a letter for you, but it can format a letter any way you like. In fact, you can record as a macro *any* task that you perform repetitively, if you can break that task down into a list of specific steps.

Some users find the concept of macros unnecessarily daunting. Although advanced macros can be full programs in their own right, creating most macros is no more difficult than turning on a tape recorder. Furthermore, macros can make your work easier and more efficient in several ways. The following are some of the advantages of macros:

- *Speed.* Playing a macro is faster than performing the actions yourself for all but the simplest tasks.

- *Accuracy.* After you create a macro to your satisfaction, the macro always plays exactly the same way.

- *Consistency.* You can share macro files with other users so that everyone in an office can perform a given task the same way.

- *Ease of use.* After you record a complex task as a macro, you can play the macro anytime with a single command.

The best way to learn about macros is to create and edit some yourself. This chapter teaches you how to do the following:

- Record macros

- Play macros

- Replace macros

- Assign macros to the menu, keyboard, or Button Bar

- Edit macros

Along the way, you create many useful macros and learn techniques and tips that help you to create your own macros.

If you are familiar with macros created with WordPerfect 5.0 or 5.1 for DOS, you must learn some new techniques when creating macros in WordPerfect for Windows. Because WordPerfect for Windows macros are very different from DOS WordPerfect macros, you must convert or recreate DOS 5.1 or 5.0 macros to use them in WordPerfect for Windows. For more information on converting macros, see the file MACRO.DOC.

Macros for the DOS versions of WordPerfect store and replay actual keystrokes, but WordPerfect for Windows macros record and play the *results* of menu selections. In WordPerfect for Windows, you can select menu items with function keys or from the pull-down menus, using the keyboard or mouse to make your selections. Whichever selection method you use, the macro stores only the result. This difference— particularly significant for editing macros and creating advanced macros—is discussed in "Understanding the Differences from Word- Perfect 5.1 for DOS Macros" later in this chapter.

At the same time, WordPerfect for Windows does not enable you to use the mouse within a macro to select an insertion point or to select text. Whenever you are recording and you move the mouse pointer over the document window, the mouse pointer changes to a circle with a diago- nal line through it, the international "No" symbol. You must use the directional keys to move the insertion point and use function keys or menus to select options.

Recording Macros

The process of creating a basic macro, called *recording*, is much like recording music on a tape recorder. In fact, each WordPerfect icon for macro-related menu items and utility programs includes a picture of a cassette tape. Like a cassette tape, a macro also must have something recorded before you can play it back.

When you record live music, you must make preparations to ensure that the recording will be successful, such as determining the proper placement of microphones and performing tests to balance the sound. Likewise, you should prepare before recording a macro. Follow these general guidelines:

- Save any work in progress so that you don't lose any information if you make a mistake. You don't necessarily have to close your document, but you may have to open one to make sure that the macro works correctly.

- Always record a macro under the same conditions you plan to play it, whether those conditions include an empty document, a few lines of dummy text, or a particular type of formatting. If your macro edits a table, for instance, the insertion point must be in a table for the macro to perform the actions you want to record.

- You first may want to go through the actions without recording them, to make sure that these actions do what you want.

- If the macro is more than a few steps long, you also may want to write down each step as a reference.

After you have saved any open documents, made sure that conditions are the same, and are confident of the actions you are about to perform, you can record the macro. Follow these five basic steps to record any macro:

1. Turn on macro recording.

2. Give the macro a file name. Macros are stored as files on disk like any other document and receive a default WCM extension.

3. Give the macro a descriptive name and (optionally) a short abstract of its purpose. The name and abstract do not affect the function of the macro but are displayed when a macro is assigned to the Macro menu. The abstract can help others (or you) to understand the macro's purpose.

4. Perform the actions you want recorded in the macro.

5. Turn off macro recording.

■ **Cue:** Give macros names that are both short and descriptive so that they take fewer keystrokes to play and are easy to remember.

Before turning off macro recording, you also may have to "clean up" after your macro. If you select some text during the macro, for example, you should make sure that the text is no longer selected before you stop recording.

Now put this theory into practice by creating a simple but useful macro that adds a complimentary close to a letter. The information is typed along the left margin, following the block style of correspondence. If you make any typographical errors in the process of typing its contents, correct them as you usually do and continue.

To record the macro, start from a new document and do the following:

1. Select **Macro**, **R**ecord.

     Press Macro Record (Ctrl-F10).

    The Record Macro dialog box appears, with the insertion point in the **F**ilename text box (see fig. 20.1).

2. Type **vty**, but not the period or an extension. Macro file names should consist of no more than eight letters.

3. Press Tab or Alt-D to move the insertion point to the **D**escriptive Name text box and type **Very truly yours**. If you want, press Tab again or Alt-A to move the insertion point to the **A**bstract text box and type **Complimentary close to a letter**. This step is optional; you can record a macro without a Descriptive Name or an Abstract.

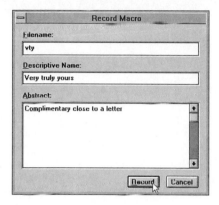

FIG. 20.1

The Record Macro dialog box.

4. Select **R**ecord or press Enter. The message Recording Macro appears on the status line in the bottom left corner of the screen.

5. Type **Very truly yours,** and then press Enter four times.

6. Type **John Q. Perfect** or your own name, and then press Enter. Type **WordPerfect Consultant** or your own job title, press Enter four more times, and then type your initials (see fig. 20.2).

■ **Cue:** When you are recording a macro, the mouse pointer changes to the international "No" sign whenever the pointer is in the document area of the screen.

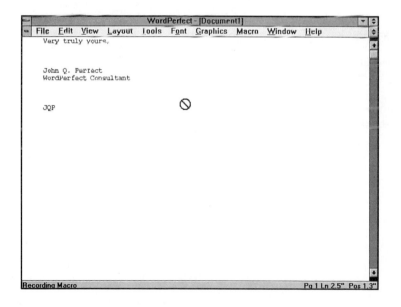

FIG. 20.2

Recording the VTY macro.

7. Select **M**acro, **S**top.

 Press Macro Stop (Ctrl-Shift-F10).

Your hard disk light blinks briefly while WordPerfect saves the macro.

Playing Macros

You can play a macro whenever you want, as often as you want. Each time the macro performs exactly the same actions, as long as the conditions under which you play the macro are similar to those under which it was recorded. If you recorded a macro that edits a table, playing the macro outside a table creates an error message at best or some other, undesired action at worst. In the case of the VTY macro, the worst that can happen if you play it at the wrong time is the insertion of a few short lines of text into a document, text that you can delete easily.

Try testing the VTY macro. From a new document, follow these steps:

1. Select **M**acro, **P**lay.

    Press Macro Play (Alt-F10).

   The Play Macro dialog box appears (see fig. 20.3). A variant of the Open File dialog box, the Play Macro dialog box displays the default macro directory, as specified in **P**references, **L**ocation of Files. The dialog box's left list box contains only files with the default macro extension WCM, as indicated by the contents of the **F**ilename text box, *.wcm.

FIG. 20.3

The Play Macro dialog box.

2. If you know the name of the macro you want to play, type its name and then select **P**lay or press Enter. In this case, type **vty** and

press Enter. You don't need to type the WCM extension, although you can if you want.

Alternatively, if you are unsure of the macro's name, look in the Files list box, scrolling up or down as necessary. For this example, highlight VTY.WCM and then select **P**lay or press Enter.

> You can double-click a macro name to select and play it back in one action.
>
> **T I P**

After a brief pause, the macro plays. In this case, the contents of the complimentary close are inserted into the document.

You always can play a macro by using this method. Later in this chapter, the section "Playing Macros in Other Ways" introduces several alternative methods.

Using Control-Key Macros

WordPerfect provides a number of built-in Ctrl-key shortcuts, such as Ctrl-B for Bold, which enable you to use common commands more quickly and easily. You can use the same principle to play your commonly used macros quickly and easily by using Ctrl-key and Ctrl-Shift-key combinations that are not already used by WordPerfect.

To record a Ctrl-key or Ctrl-Shift-key macro, you begin by selecting **Macro**, **R**ecord (Alt-F9). Instead of typing a name for the macro file, however, you press the keystroke combination you want to use, such as Ctrl-Y or Ctrl-Shift-B. WordPerfect inserts the proper name, in this case CTRLY.WCM or CTRLSFTB.WCM, into the Filename Text box. You can use any letter of the alphabet and the numerals 0 through 9 for your keystroke combinations. Then record the macro as you usually record a macro.

To play the macro, press the key combination. WordPerfect looks for a macro that corresponds to the keys you press. If the program finds a match, the macro plays back; if not, WordPerfect indicates that the macro was not found.

The built-in Ctrl-key shortcuts and other keyboard assignments take precedence over Ctrl-key and Ctrl-Shift-key macros. If, for instance, you name a macro CTRLI.WCM, pressing Ctrl-I turns on italic rather than playing your macro.Unfortunately, WordPerfect already has used most of the "good" Ctrl-key combinations, so you may want to stick to Ctrl-Shift-key combinations for your macros for the sake of consistency.

Stopping Macros

Occasionally, you may want to stop recording or playing a macro for some reason. If you are in the Record Macro or Play Macro dialog box but have not yet selected **R**ecord or **P**lay, you can stop the process by selecting Cancel or pressing Esc.

If you have selected Record and make a mistake, you have several choices. If the mistake is not serious, you can finish recording the macro and then edit the macro to correct the mistake. If the mistake is serious or the macro is fairly simple, however, stopping recording and starting over again may be easier. To stop recording a macro, select **M**acro, **S**top, or press Macro Stop (Ctrl-Shift-F10).

If you have selected a macro and selected **P**lay, you can stop the macro by pressing Esc. If macro pauses in a dialog box, you can stop it by selecting Cancel or pressing Esc.

Replacing Macros

You may want to replace a macro for several reasons. You may have discovered a mistake after recording or stopped in the middle of re-cording. On the other hand, the macro may work exactly as designed, but your needs may have changed. You may decide, for example, to change the VTY macro because your title has changed, or you have decided that your name should appear in uppercase letters.

In either case, you have two basic choices: to edit the macro or to re-place it. Editing a simple macro is not difficult and is discussed later in this chapter. When you edit a macro, however, you must make each entry in the correct form and syntax; any errors prevent the macro from playing. When you record a macro, WordPerfect makes the entries for you, and the syntax is always correct. To change a simple macro, therefore, you may find it easier to record a new version, replacing the original, than to edit the original macro.

To replace a macro, record a new macro with the same name. WordPerfect warns you that a macro by that name already exists and asks whether you want to replace it. If you select **Y**es, WordPerfect deletes the old macro file, and begins recording your new macro in a file with the same name.

Because replacing a macro is essentially identical to creating a new macro, you should make the same preparations: save any existing documents, set the stage for any formatting requirements, and go through a trial run, if necessary.

To replace the VTY macro, start from a new document and do the fol-lowing:

1. Select **M**acro, **R**ecord.

    Press Macro Record (Ctrl-F10).

   The Record Macro dialog box appears.

2. Type **vty**, without a period or an extension.

3. Press Tab or Alt-D to move the insertion point to the **D**escriptive Name text box. Type **Very truly yours,**. If you want, press Tab again or press Alt-A to move the insertion point to the **A**bstract text box and type **Complimentary close to a letter**.

4. Select **R**ecord or press Enter. A dialog box appears, with the prompt `Replace existing macro: c:\wpwin\macros\vty.wcm?` If you have typed the wrong name, you can select **N**o to cancel the operation; to replace the old macro, select **Y**es. Note that the default is No; pressing Enter cancels the new recording.

 **WARNING:** If WordPerfect prompts `Replace existing macro` while you are recording, you already have a macro of that name. If you are not intentionally recording over an older macro, you should select Cancel.

5. Type **Very truly yours,** and press Enter four times.

6. Type **JOHN Q. PERFECT** or your own name all in uppercase, and then press Enter. Type **Perfect Consultant** or some other new title and press Enter four more times; then type your initials.

7. Select **M**acro, **S**top.

    Press Macro Stop (Ctrl-Shift-F10).

   WordPerfect saves the macro.

To test the new VTY macro, select **M**acro, **P**lay, or press Macro Play (Alt-F10); then type **vty** and select **P**lay or press Enter. The new complimentary close is displayed.

Changing Format with Macros

The VTY macro inserts nothing but text. A macro just as easily can change the appearance of your document, however, by inserting formatting codes. Indeed, macros that change formatting are often far more useful than those that only insert text. Although the VTY macro is useful only at the close of a letter, a macro that changes line spacing or font can be used in any document.

A Macro That Changes Tab Settings

By default, WordPerfect's tabs are set at every 1/2 inch. At smaller point sizes, however, this setting can make paragraph indents seem unnaturally large. You therefore may want to set your tabs for every 1/3 inch instead.

To create a tab-setting macro, start from a new document and do the following:

1. Select **M**acro, **R**ecord.

     Press Macro Record (Ctrl-F10).

    The Record Macro dialog box appears.

2. Type **tab3** in the Filename text box without a period or an extension.

3. Press Tab or Alt-D to move the insertion point to the **D**escriptive Name text box. Type **Set tabs every 1/3 inch**. Press Tab again or press Alt-A to move the insertion point to the Abstract text box; then type **Clears existing tabs and sets evenly spaced tabs every 1/3 inch.**

4. Select **R**ecord or press Enter.

5. Select **L**ayout, **L**ine, **T**ab Set. The Tab Set dialog box appears.

6. Select Clear Ta**b**s to delete all existing tabs.

7. Check the E**v**enly Spaced check box. Select **P**osition and type a value of **-1i**. Select Repea**t** Every and type **1/3i**.

8. Select **S**et Tab. Select OK or press Enter.

9. Select **M**acro, **S**top.

     Press Macro Stop (Ctrl-Shift-F10).

If the Ruler is displayed, the tabs now appear every 1/3 inch. Close the document without saving and create a new document to test your macro. Display the Ruler if it is not visible.

To replay the macro, select **M**acro, **P**lay, or press Macro Play (Alt-F10). Type **tab3** and select OK or press Enter. Your tabs change on the Ruler. In Reveal Codes you see a Tab Set code.

If you find this macro useful, you may want to create similar versions. You can create a TAB4 macro, for example, to set tabs every 1/4 inch by following the same steps but changing the name, description, and

Repeat Every value. You also may want to create a macro that sets tabs to every 1/2 inch, which can be particularly useful to restore your original tab setting.

A Macro That Changes Margins

Some of the most useful simple macros are those that change a document's format in common ways. The TAB3 macro is one example. Another task you may perform frequently is changing margins. Although changing margins is not difficult, changing all four margins requires changing four different values in the Margins dialog box. If you find yourself frequently selecting the same values, creating a macro to do the job for you can save a surprising amount of time.

To create a macro that changes left and right margins to 1 1/2 inches, for example, follow these steps:

1. Select **Macro, Record.**

   CUA Press Macro Record (Ctrl-F10).

2. Type **mar15** for the Filename. Press Tab and type **Set 1.5-inch side margins** in the Descriptive Name text box. Select **Record** or press Enter.

3. Select **Layout, Margins.**

   CUA Press Margins (Ctrl-F8).

   The Margins dialog box appears.

4. Type **1.5** for the left margin, press Tab, and then type **1.5** for the right margin. Select OK or press Enter.

5. Select **Macro, Stop.**

   CUA Press Macro Stop (Ctrl-Shift-F10).

When you play the macro, the margins displayed in the Ruler change, and you can see a margin set in Reveal Codes.

You can create many different versions of this macro. You may want to create a companion macro, for instance, to change margins back to 1 inch. You also can change top and bottom margins at the same time; you may want to set margins to 1 1/2 or 2 inches all around to format an extremely short letter, or to a smaller 3/4 or even 1/2 inch to provide room for headers, footers, and page numbers. Because the macro sets specific values, using it is much quicker than changing all four values every time.

You also can include steps 3 and 4, in which the margins are actually changed, in a longer macro, such as the envelope macro described later.

Making Macros Pause

The VTY and TAB3 macros always insert exactly the same information. If you always close a letter the same way, VTY always does the job perfectly. TAB3, however, can set tabs only to every 1/3 inch; if you want to perform a similar action but set tabs to every 1/4 inch, TAB3 cannot do it. Although you can create a second macro, TAB4, to perform that task, WordPerfect provides a method with which you can write a single flexible macro that can do either task.

Whenever you call up a dialog box in the process of recording a macro, a small, unlabeled check box appears in the dialog box's title bar, on the far right end. This check box is the Record Marker. You can select this box with the mouse pointer, or select Toggle Record Marker (Alt-space bar, **T**oggle Record Marker) from the Control menu, which you access by clicking the little box in the upper left corner of the dialog box.

If you check a dialog box's Record Marker, WordPerfect records your selection of the dialog box in your macro but does not record the values you select. As a result, when you play the macro, the macro pauses with the dialog box on-screen. You then can change or set any values as you normally do. When you select OK or press Enter, the macro continues.

T I P   To make a macro pause in a dialog box, select the check box in the right corner of the dialog box's title bar while you are recording the macro.

If you change line spacing frequently, for example, you may want to create a macro to speed the process. (The Ruler enables you to set line spacing to 1, 1 1/2, or 2; but if the Ruler is not displayed, or if you want some other value, you must call up the Line Spacing dialog box.) You can create several individual macros to select different line spacing values, such as DS for double-space, SS for single-space, and so on. The following example, however, creates a macro that calls up the Line Spacing dialog box and enables you to enter any value.

To create the line spacing macro, start with a new document and do the following:

1. Select **M**acro, **R**ecord.

   CUA Press Macro Record (Ctrl-F10).

2. Type **ls** for the **F**ilename, press Tab, and then type **Line spacing** for the **D**escriptive Name. Then you may press Tab to move to **A**bstract and enter a detailed description. Select OK or press Enter.

3. Select **L**ayout, **L**ine.

   CUA Press Layout Line (Shift-F9).

4. Choose **S**pacing. The Line Spacing dialog box appears.

   Note the Record Marker check box in the dialog box's title bar (see fig. 20.4).

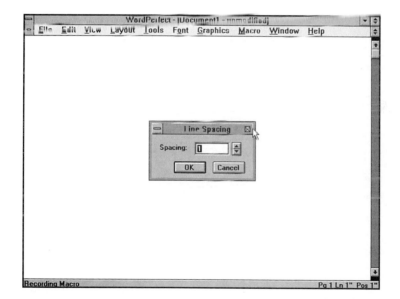

FIG. 20.4

The Record Marker check box.

5. Check the Record Marker box, or select **T**oggle Record Marker from the dialog box's Control menu, which you can access by pressing Alt-space bar, then selecting **T**oggle Record Marker.

6. Do not select a different line spacing value. Select OK or press Enter.

7. Select **M**acro, **S**top.

   CUA Press Macro Stop (Ctrl-Shift-F10).

To test this macro, open a single-spaced document and then select **M**acro, **P**lay (or press Alt-F10); type **ls**, and select **P**lay or press Enter. The Line Spacing dialog box appears. Set the value to 2.0, and then select OK or press Enter. Because the macro contains only one command, the macro changes the line spacing and then quits. Play the macro again, selecting 1.5 spacing instead. You can select any line spacing value between 0.5 and 160, in units of .01 space. (The dialog box's scroll buttons suggest values to the nearest half space.)

If you set the Record Marker in a dialog box, when you play the macro WordPerfect displays the current settings for that dialog box. If you want to suggest different values but still have the opportunity to change them, you must select the dialog box twice while recording the macro. The first time, select your suggested settings and close the box. The second time, set the Record Marker. When you replay the macro, it changes the settings according to the first entry, and then returns to the dialog box and pauses to enable you to revise those settings.

Creating Some Useful Macros

You can create an infinite number of macros: macros that perform a single task, such as applying a text attribute; macros that perform multiple tasks, such as formatting an entire document; macros that always enter the same values; macros that pause to enable you to select different values. The examples that follow—useful macros in their own right—demonstrate different, useful techniques to include in your own macros.

A Macro That Inserts a Special Character

With the WordPerfect Characters dialog box, you can view and select any character from among the WordPerfect character sets. (See Chapter 28, "Creating and Displaying Special Characters," for more details.) If you don't remember the character set or the number of the character you want to insert, however, finding the right character can take some time. If you repeatedly enter a particular character, such as the Greek letter mu (µ), you can create a macro to select the character almost immediately. All you must remember is the macro's name.

To create a macro that inserts a mu, do the following:

1. Select **M**acro, **R**ecord.

    Press Macro Record (Ctrl-F10).

   The Record Macro dialog box appears.

2. Type **mu** for Filename. Press Tab, and then type **Greek letter mu** for the **Descriptive Name**. Select **R**ecord or press Enter.

3. Select **F**ont, **WP** Characters.

 Press WordPerfect Characters (Ctrl-W).

The WordPerfect Characters dialog box appears.

4. Press and hold the mouse button with the mouse pointer under the heading **S**et. A pop-up list of available character sets appears. Select **G**reek. The Greek alphabet appears. Select the lower case mu (μ) character.

Alternatively, select **N**umber and type **8,25**. (This number gives the location of the special character within its character set.)

5. Select **I**nsert and Close.

6. Select **M**acro, **S**top.

 Press Macro Stop (Ctrl-Shift-F10).

To insert a mu, select **M**acro, **P**lay; type **mu**, and then press Enter. You may want to assign such a macro to a particular keystroke combination to make it quicker to play. See "Assigning Macros to the Keyboard" in this chapter.

A Macro That Transposes Two Characters

Even the best typist occasionally makes typographical errors. Transposing two characters is one of the most common errors—for instance, typing *hte* instead of *the*. Rather than delete and retype the characters, you can have WordPerfect correct this situation by recording the following macro:

■ Cue: If you have assigned the MACROS.WWK keyboard, you can press Ctrl-Shift-X to play the TRANSPOS macro for transposing two characters.

1. Type **hte** and then position the insertion point before the *h*.

2. Select **M**acro, **R**ecord.

 Press Macro Record (Ctrl-F10).

The Record Macro dialog box appears.

3. Type **tr** for the **F**ilename. Press Tab, and then type **Transpose two letters** for the **D**escriptive Name. Select **R**ecord or press Enter.

4. Press Shift-right arrow once to select the first character.

 Press Select (F8).

Press the right arrow once.

5. Select **E**dit, **C**ut. WordPerfect cuts the character to the Clipboard. Press the right arrow once to move the insertion point between the *t* and *e*. Select **E**dit, **P**aste. WordPerfect pastes the character from the Clipboard.

6. Select **M**acro, **S**top.

 Press Macro Stop (Ctrl-Shift-F10).

■ **Cue:** You should assign short, simple macros to keystroke combinations, so that you can play them more quickly.

To use the macro, place the insertion point before a transposed letter pair and then select **M**acro, **P**lay, or press Macro Play (Alt-F10). Type **tr** and press Enter. WordPerfect reverses the order of the two characters. You may want to assign this macro to a keystroke as well.

Note that to record this macro, you must type several characters first to have something to cut and scroll between. Without these characters, the macro does not record the desired actions.

A Macro That Prints an Envelope

■ **Cue:** If you assigned the MACROS.WWK keyboard, you can press Ctrl-Shift-E to play the ENVELOPE macro for printing an envelope.

Many people create professional-looking letters in WordPerfect and then type envelopes for those letters. Typing envelopes is completely unnecessary, however, because WordPerfect can print envelopes as easily as a standard document and because a standard business letter already contains the information that should be printed on the envelope.

The following macro copies the name and address of the addressee, creates a new document formatted as an envelope, pastes the name and address, prints the envelope, and closes the envelope document without saving. The macro is written for a WordPerfect printer driver because the procedures for selecting envelopes are significantly different for a Windows printer driver. Your printer must be able to handle envelopes, and you must have an envelope Paper Type available under Layout, Paper Size.

To create the envelope macro, first open a previously saved document or create a dummy letter with a name and address followed by at least two hard returns (created by pressing Enter). Select an insertion point in the first line of the address; then follow these steps to create the macro:

1. Select **M**acro, **R**ecord.

 Press Macro Record (Ctrl-F10).

2. Type **env** for the **F**ilename and **Envelope** for the **D**escriptive Name. If desired, press Tab to move to **A**bstract and type a longer description.

3. Select **R**ecord or press Enter.

4. Press Home to move the insertion point to the beginning of the line.

5. Press Select (F8).

6. Select **E**dit, **S**earch.

 Press Search (F2).

7. Select **C**odes, type **hrt** to highlight the hard return ([HRt]) code, and then select **I**nsert. Select **C**odes and **I**nsert again; then **C**lose the Codes dialog box. The Search **F**or string should read [HRt][HRt]. Select **S**earch. WordPerfect searches from the beginning of the addressee's name for two hard returns, which typically follow an address, and selects everything between for copying.

8. Select **E**dit, **C**opy.

9. Press Select (F8) again to turn off the selection.

10. Select **F**ile, **N**ew.

11. Select **L**ayout, **P**age, Paper **S**ize, and choose an envelope paper type. Press Select or Enter.

12. Select **L**ayout, **M**argins. For a #10 business envelope (adjust margins for other envelope sizes), set the following margins:

Left:	4.0
Right:	0.5
Top:	2.0
Bottom:	0.5

    Select OK or press Enter.

13. Select **E**dit, **P**aste. WordPerfect pastes the name and address on the envelope.

14. Select **F**ile, **P**rint.

 Press Print Document (F5).

Because the envelope is the entire document, you can select **C**urrent Page or leave the setting at **F**ull Document in the Print dialog box. Then select **P**rint.

15. Select **F**ile, **C**lose. A dialog box appears, asking whether you want to save the document. Select No.

16. Select **Macro, S**top.

 Press Macro Stop (Ctrl-Shift-F10).

To use the macro, select an insertion point anywhere on the first line of the name and address block of a letter, select **Macro, P**lay, and type **env**. The macro searches for two consecutive [HRt] codes, so if you want to include an Attention line below the address block, add a nonprinting character such as a space or a tab in any blank line you want included so that the macro searches past that line.

You could embellish this macro by adding, between steps 11 and 12, the formatting and text required to print your return address in the upper left hand corner of the envelope.

Using Macros with Styles and Merges

Macros, merges, and styles are among WordPerfect's most powerful and flexible features. Because their capabilities overlap in many ways, you may find many cases in which you can perform a given task using at least two, if not all, of these features.

If, for example, you regularly want to make a heading appear in a particular way, whether using the boldface and large attributes or selecting a different typeface altogether, you can write a macro that applies the attributes or font changes, or you can create a paired style containing the necessary codes, instead. Likewise, to automate the process of writing a letter, you can write a macro that selects the desired format and types your return address and the date, or you can create a primary merge file that contains the same information (merge files are covered in Chapter 21, "Assembling Documents with Merge").

Powerful as macros are, without complex programming they are not as flexible as merges or styles. If you use a macro to format a series of headings, the macro inserts whatever codes you have specified around each heading; if you later decide to change the appearance of your headings, you must edit each heading by hand (or create another macro to reformat the headings, which can be complicated). If you use a style to format your headings, however, you need only edit the style definition to reformat the headings throughout your document. Likewise, a macro to format the beginning of a letter contains many steps, and if you make a mistake you must recreate the macro from scratch or edit and recompile the macro. You can edit a primary merge file as you do any other document, however, and try half a dozen different versions in the time needed to edit an equivalent macro once.

Although they can create similar if not identical results, macros, merges, and styles are three very different features. *Merge* assembles documents, from a few sentences to form letters to complete manuscripts. *Styles* are "canned" collections of format codes that you can apply as a unit and change globally. *Macros* repeat actions, whether typing text, inserting format codes, or selecting commands. Refer to Chapter 12, "Using Styles," and Chapter 21, "Assembling Documents with Merge," for full treatment of the style and merge features.

Wherever you can perform a task using two or more different codes, functions, or techniques, a good rule of thumb is to use the code, function, or technique that is easiest to change. When you can perform a task using a style or a merge as easily as creating a macro, consider whether the style or merge may be more flexible in the long run. This recommendation doesn't mean that you should never use a macro when another feature will do. Instead, consider which feature is actually more appropriate for the task. If you decide that a macro is not the most appropriate, however, you also should consider using the two features together—that is, create a style or merge to gain the flexibility and ease of use those features provide. Then create a macro to select the style or begin the merge, to take advantage of a macro's speed of execution.

A Macro That Selects a Style

Suppose that you have created several styles to format main headings, subheadings, and so on, and named them Heading1, Heading2, and Heading3. The styles may contain font changes, attributes, spacing changes, a table of contents, or index marks—whatever you need or want. Selecting a style such as Heading1 requires opening the Styles dialog box and then scrolling to find the name and selecting the name with the mouse, or typing the name to highlight.

To create a macro that selects the Heading1 style, follow these steps:

1. Select **M**acro, **R**ecord.

    CUA Press Macro Record (Ctrl-F10).

2. Type **h1** for the Filename, press Tab, and type **Heading1 style** for the **D**escriptive Name. Select **R**ecord.

3. Select **L**ayout, **S**tyles.

    CUA Press Styles (Alt-F8).

    The Styles dialog box appears.

4. Type **Heading1**. (If you do not have a style named Heading1, type the name of one of your paired styles.) The Heading1 style is highlighted.

5. Select **O**n or press Enter.

6. Select **M**acro, **S**top.

 Press Macro Stop (Ctrl-Shift-F10).

To use this macro on existing text, select a heading and play the macro to apply the style. You also can play the macro first and then type the contents of the heading. At the end of the heading, select **L**ayout, **S**tyles (Ctrl-F8); then select O**ff** or press Enter. (When a style is on, Off becomes the default action.) Either method places Heading1 Style On and Style Off codes around your heading. You also can create similar H2 and H3 macros to select Heading2 and Heading3 styles, or create macros to select any styles you use regularly.

If you use several different style libraries, you also may want to create one or more macros that call up the Styles dialog box and then retrieve a different style library.

A Macro That Starts a Merge

Macros can be even more useful in starting merges. Style libraries nearly always are located in a default style directory, but merge files can be located anywhere. Likewise, although you can apply only one style at a time, merges often require a secondary merge file in addition to a primary merge file. If you create many merge files, you can create an advanced macro that presents a menu of your merge files and then plays the merge you select. Unfortunately, such a macro is beyond the scope of this chapter, but you can use the following simpler example to run a specific macro.

Before you create a macro that begins a merge, first create a primary merge file. (If you have not yet created any merge files, for the purposes of this macro you can substitute the name of any other file you have created; during the merge operation WordPerfect retrieves the document, searches for merge codes and, finding none, leaves the insertion point at the end of the document.) Chapter 21, "Assembling Documents with Merge," describes the merge process in detail.

To create a macro that starts a merge, follow these steps:

1. Select **M**acro, **R**ecord.

 Press Macro Record (Ctrl-F10).

2. Type **merge** for the Filename, press Tab, and type **Start a merge** for the Descriptive Name.

3. Select **T**ools, **M**erge.

    Press Merge (Ctrl-F12).

4. Choose **M**erge. The Merge dialog box appears.

5. Type the path and file name of a primary merge file (or some other document, if you have not created any merge files). If you prefer, you can select from a file list by clicking the adjacent Folder icon.

6. If your merge requires a secondary merge file, press Tab to move to the **S**econdary File text box and type the path and file name of your secondary file. (If you are using a "dummy" primary file, skip this step.) Again, you can select from a file list by clicking the Folder icon.

7. Select OK or press Enter. The merge begins.

8. Select **M**acro, **S**top.

    Press Macro Stop (Ctrl-Shift-F10)

You do not have to wait for the merge to stop before pressing Macro Stop. In fact, you should be sure not to answer any merge prompts before you press Macro Stop, or your responses will be recorded in your macro.

A Combination of Macros, Merges, and Styles

Macros, merges, and styles are powerful features when used separately, and the preceding examples show ways in which you can combine macros with the other two features. You also can combine all three. Addressing a standard business letter provides a good example. You can adapt the following basic steps to your formatting preferences or those of your company:

1. Create a Letterhead style for yourself or your office. (See Chapter 12, "Using Styles," for more details.)

2. Starting with a new document, insert the Letterhead style. Add several hard returns.

3. Select **T**ools, **D**ate, **C**ode. WordPerfect inserts a code that always displays the current date whenever the document is retrieved or merged. Add four more hard returns.

4. Select **T**ools, **M**erge, **I**nput. The Insert Merge Code dialog box appears.

5. Type **Enter Name & Address, then press Alt-Enter**. Select OK or press Enter to close the dialog box.

   WordPerfect inserts an input code containing the text you just typed.

6. Insert two hard returns, type **Dear**, and then select **T**ools, **M**erge, **I**nput again.

7. Type **Enter Salutation & press Alt-Enter**. Select OK or press Enter to close the dialog box. Type a colon (**:**) and two more hard returns. See figure 20.5 for an example of this letter.

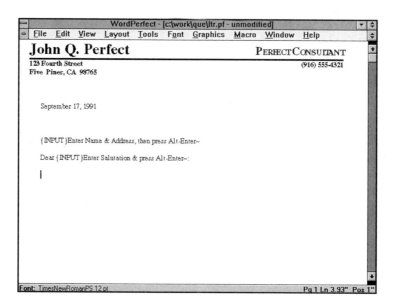

A sample merge letter with a letterhead style.

8. Save the document as LTR.PF in a subdirectory.

9. By following the steps in the preceding section, create a macro named LTR. Type **LTR.PF**, including its path, as the name of the primary file, and do not name a secondary file.

To create a business letter, do the following:

1. Play the LTR macro.

   The macro begins merging LTR.PF, displaying the Letterhead style and the date code. The merge pauses at the first [Input] code and displays the prompt Enter Name & Address, then press Alt-Enter in a Merge Message dialog box.

2. Type the desired information and press Alt-Enter. The merge pauses again after the word *Dear*, with the second prompt displayed.

3. Type **John**, **Dr. Smith**, **Sirs**, or some other appropriate salutation, and press Alt-Enter again. The merge adds the colon and final two hard returns and stops, leaving you to write the body of the letter.

4. When you finish the letter, play the VTY macro to insert the complimentary close and your signature block.

5. Use the ENV macro to print an envelope.

Although creating a business letter "by hand" is not a difficult task, a number of steps are required. This combination of macros, merge operation, and styles reduces the task to a few keystrokes.

Playing Macros in Other Ways

Saving time is one of the most important aspects of using macros. Although the time-saving advantages of long, complex macros are obvious, for shorter macros the advantages are less clear. Recording a macro that selects boldface makes little sense, for example, because you can press Ctrl-B far more quickly than you can select **M**acro, **P**lay (or press Ctrl-F10); type a short macro name; and press Enter. On the other hand, a macro such as ENV can format and print an envelope with greater speed and accuracy than the fastest user. Simple macros such as the line spacing (LS) macro fall somewhere in the middle, where the time needed to play the macro is nearly equal to the time you need to perform the actions yourself. At the same time, the simplest macros are often the most useful because you can use them in many different situations.

When you play a macro normally, you must select the Play Macro dialog box through the cascading menus or function keys, type the name or select the name of the desired macro from the list in the dialog box, and then select **P**lay or press Enter. To make commonly used macros quicker and easier to play, WordPerfect provides several alternative methods. Specifically, you can assign macros to the following items:

- The Macro menu
- Button Bars
- Keyboard layouts

After you assign a macro to one of these three areas, you can play the macro with at most one or two keystrokes or clicks. None of these methods, however, is appropriate for all macros, because the space available in a menu, Button Bar, and keyboard layout is limited, and you cannot find room enough to assign all the macros you can write. In addition, having to sort through a long list of macros takes a significant amount of time.

Instead, assigning macros to one of these areas is ideal for a short list of simple macros that you use most often. Assigning a macro does not prevent you from playing it in the normal fashion, nor does the task prevent you from assigning the macro to another area, or even all three. You may find, however, that some macros are more appropriately assigned to a Button Bar than to the keyboard, and vice versa.

You must record a macro before you can assign it to the menu, Button Bar, or keyboard.

Assigning Macros to the Menu

You can assign up to nine macros to the Macro menu. These macros are listed below the Assign to Menu command, numbered sequentially. Instead of displaying the actual file name of a macro assigned to the menu, WordPerfect displays its descriptive name or an alternative description that you typed while assigning a macro (if you gave it one when you recorded it).

After a macro has been assigned to the menu, you can play the macro by selecting it with the mouse or by pressing Alt-M to bring up the Macro menu and then typing the number next to the macro you want to play.

To assign a macro to the menu, do the following:

1. Select **M**acro, **A**ssign to Menu.

   The Assign Macro to Menu dialog box appears. The dialog box contains a large list box labeled Menu Text, which lists the descriptions of all macros you have assigned previously to the menu (see fig. 20.6). The first entry is highlighted. Below the Menu Text list box the actual path and file name of the highlighted macro are displayed. If you have not assigned a macro yet, the Menu Text list box is empty.

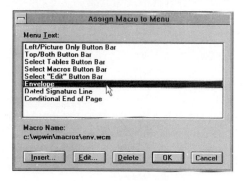

FIG. 20.6

The Assign
Macro to Menu
dialog box.

2. Select Insert. The Insert Macro Menu Item dialog box appears.

3. Select the Folder icon next to the Macro Name text box. The Select File dialog box appears. A variant of the Open File dialog box, the Select File dialog box displays your default macro subdirectory as designated in Preferences, Location of Files.

4. Select the macro you want to assign. WordPerfect returns you to the Insert Macro Menu Item dialog box. The path and file name of the selected macro appear in the Macro Name text box. If you entered a descriptive name when creating the macro, that description appears in the Menu Text list box. If you want to edit the description or did not initially enter one, you may do so now.

5. Select OK. WordPerfect returns to the Assign Macro to Menu dialog box, and the description of the macro is displayed in the Menu Text list box.

6. Select OK again to close the Assign Macro to Menu dialog box.

   The Macro menu now reflects the changes you made (see fig. 20.7).

If you previously have assigned macros to the menu, by default the newly assigned macro appears at the top of the list and becomes macro 1. If you want to add a macro to the middle of the list instead, before performing step 2, highlight the macro above which you want the new macro to appear. Then perform the rest of the steps as listed, and the macro appears in sequence as desired. If you want to assign a macro to the end of the list, scroll down below the last entry before performing step 2.

If you want to remove a macro entry from the Menu Text list, you have two choices. You can delete the entry outright, or you can replace the entry with a new macro.

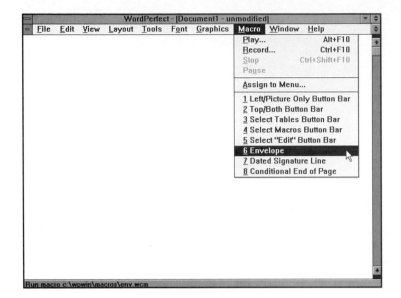

FIG. 20.7

The Macro menu
with some
assigned macros.

To delete an entry from the Macro menu, follow these steps:

1. Select **Macro**, **Assign** to Menu. The Assign Macro to Menu dialog box appears.

2. Highlight the description of the macro you want to remove from the menu.

3. Select **Delete**. WordPerfect removes the description from the list. If you want, highlight and delete other macros at the same time.

4. Select OK to close the Assign Macro to Menu dialog box.

Deleting a macro entry from the Macro menu does not delete the macro file itself, but you no longer can play the macro from the menu. You still can play the macro by selecting **Macro**, **Play**, or by pressing Play Macro (Alt-F10).

You can edit a Macro menu entry merely to revise the description that appears in the Menu Text list. You also can edit the macro name that appears in the entry, which has the effect of removing the current macro from the menu and replacing it with a different macro.

To edit an entry in the Macro menu, follow these steps:

1. Select **Macro**, **Assign** to Menu. The Assign Macro to Menu dialog box appears.

2. Highlight the description of the macro you want to edit.

3. Select Edit. The Insert Macro Menu Item dialog box appears, displaying the macro name and menu text of the selected macro. You can edit either or both entries. To search the list of available macros, select the Folder icon to the right of the Macro Name text box. If you change the name of the selected macro, make sure that the description in the Menu Text box is now accurate.

4. Select OK to return to the Assign Macro to Menu dialog box. If you want, highlight and edit other macros now.

5. Select OK to close the Assign Macro to Menu dialog box.

Again, replacing one macro in the Macro menu with another does not delete the first macro file from disk, but you no longer can access the first macro from the menu.

The principal advantage to assigning macros to the menu is the speed with which you can play them. The principal disadvantage is the limit of nine macros that you can assign to the menu.

Assigning Macros to the Button Bar

Chapter 19, "Using the Button Bar," describes WordPerfect's Button Bar feature in detail. To summarize, you can assign any menu item and any macro to the Button Bar. If you have frequently used macros you want to assign to the Button Bar, do the following:

1. Select View, Button Bar Setup, Edit. The Edit Button Bar dialog box appears.

2. Select Assign Macro to Button.

   The Assign Macro to Button dialog box appears. The box lists the contents of your macro directory.

3. Highlight the macro file name and select Add, or double-click the file name. The macro appears at the end of the Button Bar, with the button showing the macro's name and a cassette tape. Repeat steps 2 and 3 to assign additional macros to buttons, if desired.

4. Select OK to close the Edit Button Bar dialog box and save your changes.

After you assign a macro to a button, you can play the macro by clicking the button. You cannot access Button Bar buttons from the keyboard.

Assigning macros to the Button Bar has several advantages and disadvantages. On the positive side, you can play any macro by clicking a

BUTTON

■ **Cue:** If you display a Button Bar with the Picture Only option selected, you cannot tell one macro from another, because all macro buttons display the same cassette tape icon.

button and you can include many macros by creating additional Button Bars. On the negative side, the number of buttons you can display at once is limited, and scrolling through many buttons defeats the purpose. See Chapter 19 for more information.

Assigning Macros to the Keyboard

By default, WordPerfect for Windows follows common user access (CUA) conventions in assigning actions to function keys, directional keys, and the standard keyboard with the Ctrl, Alt, and Shift keys. You can change your own keyboard layout, however, to move any command or function to some other position you find convenient. The program also comes with a keyboard layout similar to that used by WordPerfect 5.1 for DOS. Although this process is covered in detail in Chapter 29, "Customizing WordPerfect with Preferences," the process also is relevant here because in addition to existing WordPerfect functions, you can assign macros to a keyboard layout.

■ **Cue:** If several users share a computer, each user can create his or her own keyboard layout containing favorite macros without fear of altering each other's macros.

Assigning macros to a keyboard layout can be extremely useful. The most obvious advantage is being able to play such macros with a single keystroke combination. Equally important, you can bundle your most commonly used macros into a single large file, which saves disk space and is easier to transport from computer to computer. You can write macros to select different keyboard layouts.

T I P You do not need to change WordPerfect's key assignments completely to make the keyboard layout feature useful. In fact, changing too many function key defaults can make using the program confusing for you, not to mention others who may share your computer.

If you use the WordPerfect 5.1-compatible keyboard, you already are using an alternate keyboard layout. If you are using the built-in CUA-compliant keyboard, you must create a new keyboard layout file because you cannot change the built-in values directly. A new keyboard layout, however, is identical to the built-in keyboard until you make macro or other assignments

Assigning a macro to a keyboard layout requires two basic processes: retrieving the macro file into the keyboard layout file and selecting a keystroke combination to use to play the macro. See Chapter 29, "Customizing WordPerfect with Preferences," for more information.

To assign a macro to your keyboard layout, do the following:

1. Select **F**ile, **P**references, **K**eyboard. The WordPerfect Keyboard dialog box appears, displaying the name of your currently selected keyboard layout. If necessary, select a different layout or create a new layout before continuing (see Chapter 29).

2. Select **E**dit. The Keyboard Editor dialog box appears. The left side displays a list of assignable items. By default, the list shows commands.

3. With the mouse, click the button next to Item Types, which should be labeled Commands. A pop-up list appears, containing the additional entries Menus, Text, and Macros. Drag down and select Macros.

   Alternatively, with the keyboard, press Alt-I; then press the space bar to drop down the list. Select Macros.

   The contents of the list box change to show any macros that you already have added (see fig. 20.8). If no macros have been added, the box is empty.

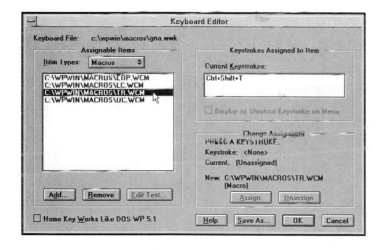

FIG. 20.8

The Keyboard Editor dialog box.

4. Select **Ad**d. The Import Macro to Keyboard dialog box, a variant of the Open Files dialog box, displays the contents of your macro directory.

5. Select a macro to add and then select **I**mport or press Enter. The macro's path and file names appear in the list box.

   If you want to import additional macros to be assigned, repeat steps 4 and 5.

6. Press the keystroke combination you want to use to play a macro, such as Alt-Shift-E. If some other item already is assigned to that keystroke, WordPerfect displays its name and type in the Current line in the Change Assignment section; otherwise, (Unassigned) is displayed.

7. From the Assignable Items list box, select a macro that you now want to assign.

8. Select **A**ssign.

   If you want, repeat steps 6 through 8 to assign additional macros.

9. Select OK to save the new assignments, and then select OK again to close the WordPerfect Keyboard dialog box.

After you assign a macro to a keystroke combination, pressing that combination replays the macro.

T I P   You can assign macros to Ctrl-*letter* and Ctrl-Shift-*letter* key combinations. For *letter* you can use any keyboard character from A through Z and 0 through 9 to name the macro. One of WordPerfect's built-in keyboards, MACROS.WWK, contains 17 Ctrl-Shift-*letter* macros.

T I P   Although keyboard macros are quicker to play deliberately, they are also easier to play accidentally. For this reason, you may want to avoid assigning to keystrokes macros that delete large amounts of text or close documents without saving them.

Managing Macro Files

Whenever you record a macro, WordPerfect saves your actions on disk. When you play the macro, WordPerfect opens the file, interprets the recorded instructions, and performs the specified actions. Recording and playback are the two ways in which you normally use macros. Because each macro is stored as an individual file, however, you can deal with it in other ways as well. You can edit its contents, which is discussed in "Editing Macros" later in this chapter. You also can manipulate the macro file as a whole through such standard file actions as moving, copying, renaming, or deleting.

Using Different Extensions

If you do not include an extension with the file name when you record a macro, WordPerfect appends a WCM extension. Likewise, when you play a macro, by default the Play Macro dialog box displays only files with the WCM extension, and you do not need to type the extension for WordPerfect to play the macro. Not only does this default extension enable you to record and play macros more quickly and easily, it identifies any file ending in WCM as a WordPerfect for Windows macro. Macros created by other WordPerfect Corporation programs have their own unique extensions, as do those of many other programs. You can identify Excel macros, for instance, by their XLM extension.

The WCM extension, however, is not required. When you record a macro you can use some other extension. When you want to play the macro, however, you won't see it displayed in the list of available macros because its name doesn't end in WCM. To play such a macro, you must type its full file name with the different extension for WordPerfect to find it. You also can change the file name pattern in the Play Macro dialog box from *.WCM to *.* to display all files in the macro directory. Despite the different extension, after you tell WordPerfect to play such a file, the program then recognizes the file as a macro and carries out its instructions.

Although you nearly always should use the default extension, you may want to use a different extension for one or more macros for several reasons. First, you may not want WordPerfect to recognize the file as a macro. If you are trying to develop a complex macro, for example, and it doesn't work yet to your satisfaction, using a different extension prevents you or some other user from playing it by accident. Although the macro does not show up in the list of available macros, you can still test it by simply typing its full name.

Second, you may want to identify the macro as a particular kind of macro. You may want to designate all macros assigned to the Macro menu or to a particular Button Bar with a unique extension. If you write advanced macros, you can make one macro call another; therefore, you may want to use an extension signifying that a particular macro or group of macros should be called only from another macro and not played directly by the user.

These techniques, however, are advanced. For normal operation, you should use the default WCM extension, particularly because you never have to type it.

Using Different Directories

Besides changing a macro's file name or extension, you can change its location. Changing locations has some of the same advantages and disadvantages as changing extensions, but also offers some unique advantages, particularly in a network environment.

Every copy of WordPerfect maintains a list that specifies the locations of many important program and user files. You can specify these locations when you install the program, and you can change them at any time in the Location of Files dialog box. You can specify default directories for user files such as documents, graphics, and spreadsheets, as well as program-related files such as printer, Speller, and Thesaurus files. In particular, you can specify a directory that contains macro, keyboard, and Button Bar files.

After you specify a particular directory for any of these items, WordPerfect looks in that directory to read from or write to a related file. If you don't specify a directory for any item, WordPerfect looks for program-related items in the WPWIN directory (or whatever name the main program directory has been given). For documents, graphics, spreadsheets, and macros, WordPerfect looks in the current default directory.

You need not specify a directory for each item. If you have access to dozens or hundreds of directories through a network, for example, specifying a single document directory can become annoying rather than helpful, because WordPerfect always looks at the directory specified in Location of Files rather than the current default directory to open or save new files.

For macros, however, specifying a directory is essential. If the Location of Files dialog box does not specify a macro directory, whenever you create a macro WordPerfect stores the macro file in the current default directory. If you change to a different directory and then try to replay the macro, WordPerfect cannot find the macro. After you specify a macro directory, however, WordPerfect stores new macros in that directory and likewise looks there for macros to play.

To specify a directory for macros, do the following:

1. Select File, Preferences, Location of Files. The Location of Files dialog box appears.

2. Select Files under the heading Macros/Keyboards/Button Bars. If the text box already contains an entry, you can type a new location or leave the entry unchanged. (If you change the current entry, you must copy any existing macro files you want to use to the new location.)

   If the entry is blank, type **c:\wpwin\macros** or another directory path.

3. Select OK or press Enter.

Just as you can play a macro with a different extension, you also can play a macro in a different location. Whenever WordPerfect cannot find the macro you specified, it displays the message File "*filename*" not found. Search for file? If you answer Yes, the Play Macro dialog box appears again, and you can change directories to try to find the file. If you know in advance that your macro is in a different location, you can change directories in the Play Macro dialog box to the correct location before selecting Play.

If you share a computer with others, you can create a separate macro subdirectory for each user and then for each user write a macro that changes the default macro directory in the Location of Files dialog box. You then must copy each macro into every user's macro directory so that anyone can switch to his or her own directory from any other user's directory.

Manipulating and Viewing Macro Files

All macros are not created equal. No matter how carefully you plan your macros before recording, you will find yourself using some macros many times a day and other macros only occasionally; some macros you never use. You may also find some of your macro names hard to remember—you know you created a macro, but you can't remember what you called it. In these cases, you may want to manipulate the macro file.

You don't usually think of macros as being files on disk. You normally record a macro, and once you are satisfied with the way it works, you play it back many times without needing to know where it is located on disk or what the macro file looks like. Because WordPerfect for Windows macros are normal WordPerfect documents, though, you can manipulate macro files as you manipulate any other document. You can copy macro files, rename them, move them to other locations, or delete them. You also can edit macros, as you learn in the following section.

If a macro isn't useful, and you don't want to fix it, you should delete it; a useless macro wastes precious disk space. If you can't remember a macro's name, you should change it. You also may want to copy macros, so you can use them on another machine or share them, or move macros, as you learned in the preceding section. You should periodically examine your macro directory for macros that you don't use or macros that you could improve by renaming or editing them.

WordPerfect enables you to manipulate macro files in several ways. Both the Macro Play dialog box and the Open File dialog box contain an Options button that you can use to delete, copy, move or rename an individual file or to search for specific file names or words within files. The Open File dialog box also contains a View button, which calls up a window that displays the contents of a file. Finally, the WordPerfect File Manager, which you can run independently of WordPerfect for Windows or select through WordPerfect's File menu, is a multipurpose file manipulator that enables you to perform the same actions on multiple files.

When you select **M**acro, **P**lay (Alt-F10), the Macro Play dialog box automatically displays your available macros in the **F**iles list box. This list can be a major help if you can't remember a macro's name, because you can scroll through the list until you find the macro. Once you find the macro, if you want to rename it, do the following:

1. Select the file.

2. Select the Op**t**ions button and drag down to select **M**ove/Rename. Alternately, press Alt-T to select Options, press the space bar to drop down the list of options, and select **M**ove/Rename.

   The Move/Rename File dialog box appears.

3. In the **T**o text box, type a new name for the macro file. You *should* include the WCM extension when renaming a macro, because WordPerfect does not do it for you. You do not need to type a new path, unless you want to move the macro file at the same time you rename it.

4. Select **M**ove. (This button performs either a move or a rename operation.) WordPerfect returns to the Macro Play dialog box.

To move a macro file, follow the same steps but include a different path in the Move/Rename File dialog box.

■ **Cue:** You can move and rename a macro file in the same operation by changing both the path and the file name.

To copy a macro file, again follow the same steps, but select the Copy option instead of Move/Rename. The Copy File dialog box is nearly identical to the Move/Rename File dialog box. You can copy a macro file to a different directory by specifying a different path. You also can copy a macro to the *same* directory by specifying a different name without specifying a path, or you can copy a macro to a different directory and rename the macro at the same time by typing a different path and macro name. Again, remember to include the WCM extension.

Finally, you can delete a macro file by selecting the **D**elete option. WordPerfect asks you to confirm the deletion.

You can perform the same operations using the Options button in the Open File dialog box. Using the Open File dialog box has both advantages and disadvantages. Where the Macro Play dialog box automatically shows the contents of your macro directory, the Open File dialog box shows the contents of your current default document directory. Therefore, you must change to your macro directory before you can manipulate files (your macro directory should appear in your Quick List). Also, in the Open File dialog box, you can only manipulate or open files; you cannot play a macro.

Once you change to your macro directory, the Open File dialog box offers one particular advantage, the View button. When you select View, a window opens that displays the contents of the file which is currently selected in the Files list box. As you scroll the Files list, the View window continually changes to show the current file. Because macros are WordPerfect documents, the View window can display the actual text of your macros, which can be invaluable in locating a particular macro or in discriminating between two similar macros without actually opening the files.

As useful as the options in the Play Macro and Open File dialog boxes are, they can act on only one file at a time. If you want to copy, move, or delete several macros at once, you must use the WordPerfect File Manager.

WordPerfect's File Manager bears no relation to the Windows File Manager and contains many more useful features. To run WordPerfect's File Manager from within WordPerfect, select File, File Manager. The WordPerfect File Manager appears (see fig. 20.9).

The WordPerfect File Manager can display file information in many different ways, including a traditional File List, a View document window, a Quick List, and a window called the Navigator, which graphically displays the subdirectories and path leading to the current directory. Figure 20.9 shows the Navigator, File List and Viewer; you may not see the same windows when you first open the File Manager. See Chapter 30, "Advanced File Management Techniques," for additional information on the File Manager.

In the File Manager you can mark multiple files. If you hold down the Shift key when you press the space bar or click a file name, you can select a range of files; if you hold down the Ctrl key you can select multiple individual files. You can then select Move, Copy, Delete, or other operations from the File menu or from the File Manager's Button Bar.

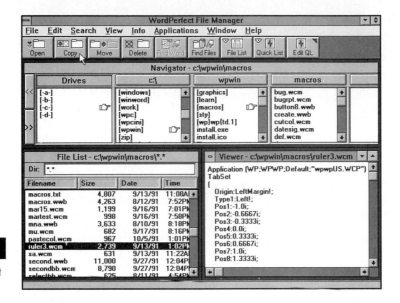

FIG. 20.9

The WordPerfect
File Manager

You also can open or retrieve macro files directly from the File Manager by selecting **O**pen or **R**etrieve from the File Manager's File menu. If you select multiple files to open, each appears in its own window in WordPerfect.

Finally, you can print one or more macros (or other files) from the File Manager. Select one or more files; then select **F**ile, **P**rint. The File Manager opens the macros in WordPerfect and prints them. This method is much quicker than opening and printing each file individually.

Editing Macros

Earlier in this chapter, you learned how to rerecord a macro if you make a mistake while recording the original or if your needs change. If the change you want to make is minor or the macro you want to change is complex, however, you may find editing easier than replacing the original macro.

In WordPerfect for Windows, you can edit a macro file directly. You can change text entries and commands, delete information that is no longer wanted, or add new commands of your own. Before examining the subject in detail, however, you should be aware of a few potential pitfalls.

Understanding the Differences from WordPerfect 5.1 for DOS Macros

If you are familiar with macros created by WordPerfect 5.1 for DOS, you must make some adjustments when working with macros in Word-Perfect for Windows. Macros created by WordPerfect for Windows are different from macros created by WordPerfect 5.1 for DOS in several important ways.

First, the two kinds of macros are stored in entirely different types of files. Macros created by DOS versions of WordPerfect are stored in files that cannot be retrieved directly into the main program. Instead, you can edit WordPerfect for DOS macros only in the program's built-in Macro Editor facility, which is limited in capability, or in the more powerful Editor program, which is a separate program included in the WordPerfect Office program collection (formerly named WordPerfect Library).

WordPerfect for Windows, by contrast, stores its macros as normal documents. A macro file contains a text description of the macro's actions, written in WordPerfect for Windows' specific macro syntax. A compiled version of the macro—the part actually read by the Macro Facility when you play the macro—is stored in the macro file's invisible header, where normal documents contain information about printers, fonts, graphics, and styles.

Second, the syntax that the different versions of WordPerfect use are entirely different. When recording commands and menu selections, macros for DOS versions store and replay actual keystrokes, from the main keyboard as well as function keys. WordPerfect for Windows macros record and play the *results* of menu selections, whether you make those selections by pressing function keys or by selecting menu items with the mouse or keyboard.

For example, a WordPerfect 5.1 macro that selects double-spacing might include the following code:

    {Format}ls2{Enter}{Enter}{Enter}

This line means **Format** (Shift-F8), **L**ine, **S**pacing, 2, plus the keystrokes required to return to the document screen. You can accomplish the same result using different keystrokes, which result in the codes:

    {Format}162{Enter}{Exit}

In a WordPerfect for Windows macro, no matter what keystrokes or mouse movements you use to change line spacing, the result is recorded as follows:

    LineSpacing (Spacing:2.0)

The LineSpacing command is one of more than 600 WordPerfect for Windows *product commands*, which are macro commands that carry out program-specific commands and selections. You can use a product command essentially for any action you can accomplish in WordPerfect for Windows. Macros for future Windows programs released by WordPerfect Corporation will contain their own specific product commands.

WordPerfect for Windows macros also can contain *programming commands*, which are not specific to any one WordPerfect Corporation Windows program. Programming commands include such commands as GO, IF, CALL, ASSIGN, LABEL, MENU, and more. Although most WordPerfect for Windows programming commands have direct equivalents, with similar concepts, in the WordPerfect 5.1 for DOS macro language, their syntax has changed significantly.

When you record a macro in WordPerfect 5.1 for DOS, the program monitors and transcribes your keystrokes to a macro file. When you play the macro, the program reads the macro file, compiles its contents, and plays the recorded keystrokes.

When you record a macro using WordPerfect for Windows, the program's Macro Facility monitors your actions, transcribes those actions into the equivalent product commands, and enters them into the macro file. When you stop recording, the Macro Facility saves the entire file to disk. When you play the macro, the Macro Facility compiles the macro and plays the results.

As a result, editing a WordPerfect for Windows macro has two basic steps:

1. Edit the text description of the macro.

2. Recompile the macro to update the version stored in the header.

In most cases, however, WordPerfect automatically compiles the edited macro the first time you play it.

Understanding Macro Syntax

Because of the more than 600 product commands available, a complete discussion of the syntax and use of each command is beyond the scope of this chapter. Each command follows regular rules of syntax, however, and understanding those rules can help you to avoid creating syntax errors when you edit macros.

Figure 20.10 shows the contents of VTY.WCM. Its first line contains the following statement:

Application (WP; WPWP; Default; "WPWPUS.WCD")

```
Application (WP;WPWP;Default;"WPWPU3.WCD")
Type
(
    Text:"Very trly"
)
DeleteCharPrevious()
DeleteCharPrevious()
Type
(
    Text:"uly yours,"
)
HardReturn()
HardReturn()
HardReturn()
HardReturn()
Type
(
    Text:"John Q. Perfect"
)
HardReturn()
Type
(
    Text:"Perfect Consultant"
)
HardReturn()
HardReturn()
HardReturn()
HardReturn()
Type
(
    Text:"jqp"
)
```

FIG. 20.10

The contents of
VTY.WCM
revealed.

At the beginning of every macro you record, WordPerfect inserts this programming command line, which specifies that any product commands that follow should be interpreted as belonging to WordPerfect for Windows.

With the program-specific product commands and nonspecific programming commands described earlier, WordPerfect has laid the groundwork for macros with the capability of integrating a suite of Windows programs, rather than working only within WordPerfect. WordPerfect's Macro Facility (or a subsequent update) will work with Windows versions of DrawPerfect and WordPerfect Office as well, when those programs are released. Including this command now helps to ensure that WordPerfect for Windows macros will need to be rewritten as little as possible, if at all, to work with those programs.

As a result, you never should edit or delete this command in a recorded macro. If you write advanced macros directly, always include this command as the first line.

After the first line, the rest of the macro is straightforward and repetitive. The macro contains three product commands, each used several times:

```
Type()

DeletePreviousCharacter()

HardReturn()
```

Each WordPerfect product command always is followed by its parameters within parentheses. A command can have no parameters, one parameter, or many parameters. Simple commands such as DeleteCharPrevious, which corresponds to the Backspace key, and HardReturn, which inserts the code [HRt] into a document, do not require parameters, so the parentheses are empty. The Type command has only one parameter. A command that carries out a complex formatting procedure, such as PageSizeSelect, which selects a specific paper size, can have a dozen parameters or more.

The PageMargins command is a good example of a product command with several parameters. The following statement comes from the ENV macro:

```
PageMargins
(
   Left:4.0i;
   Right:0.5i;
   Top:2.0i;
   Bottom:0.5i
)
```

As its name implies, PageMargins sets left, right, top, and bottom margin values—one parameter for each margin. Each parameter contains a parameter name and a value. A colon (:) separates each name from its corresponding value, and a semicolon (;) separates each parameter from the next. WordPerfect places each parameter on a separate line for purposes of clarity, but the command works equally well if you remove all extra spaces and carriage returns between the parentheses.

Making a Simple Text Change

Suppose that you want to change the VTY macro, either because you discovered a mistake, you changed your title, or even changed your name.

For instance, John Perfect wants to change his VTY macro because he has taken on a partner, Robert Expert. He also wants to correct some mistakes he made while originally recording the macro. As you can see in figure 20.10, John left the *u* out of the word *truly*, then backspaced to correct the mistake. As a result, the macro faithfully inserts the error, backspaces twice, then finishes the line. While the macro creates the correct result when played back, it has to perform extra work to do so. By editing, he can combine the two Type commands into one by deleting everything from the *ly* in *trly* through the quotation marks at the beginning of *uly* (see fig. 20.11). The syntax is preserved and the macro is smaller, which makes it slightly quicker to play back. (The difference might not be noticeable in a short macro, but correcting numerous such mistakes in a longer macro would have an effect.)

```
WordPerfect - [c:\wpwin\macros\vty.wcm - unmodified]
File   Edit   View   Layout   Tools   Font   Graphics   Macro   Window   Help
Application (WP;WPWP;Default;"wpwpUS.WCD")
Type
(
    Text:"Very trly"
)
DeleteCharPrevious()
DeleteCharPrevious()
Type
(
    Text:"uly yours,"
)
HardReturn()
HardReturn()
HardReturn()
HardReturn()
Type
(
    Text:"John Q. Perfect"
)
HardReturn()
Type
(
    Text:"Perfect Consultant"
)
HardReturn()
HardReturn()
HardReturn()
Type
(
    Text:"JQP"
)
Select On                                    Pg 1 Ln 2.5" Pos 1.9"
```

FIG. 20.11

Editing
VTY.WCM.

To fix this macro, you can record over the original macro, but if the changes are simple, you may find it easier to edit instead. To edit the macro, you begin by opening the file as you open any other document:

1. Select **File**, **O**pen.

    Press Open File (F4).

   The Open File dialog box appears.

2. Change to your macro directory. If the directory appears in your Quick List, you can double- click the listing to change the directory immediately.

3. Type *vty.wcm* or scroll through the list box and select the macro from the list of available files. Select OK or press Enter.

   The macro appears on-screen.

4. Before making any changes, select Save **As** and give the file a new name such as **vty2.wcm**. If you later make any mistakes you can now safely retrieve the original and start over.

5. If you made and corrected any typographical errors while recording your own VTY macro, delete any DeleteCharPrevious() commands and combine the surrounding commands into one correctly spelled Type command (again see fig. 20.11).

   In this example, edit the phrase *Perfect Consultant* to read *Perfect & Expert, Consultants*. Do not delete any quotation marks or parentheses.

6. Close the document and save your changes.

Test your edited macro by playing back VTY2. If you have made a syntax error, WordPerfect prompts you. You can either retrieve VTY2.WCM and attempt to find your mistake, or start with the original VTY.WCM and try your changes over again. If the macro performs as desired, you can delete the original and rename the new version.

Editing WordPerfect Commands

In one sense, any change you make to a WordPerfect for Windows macro involves editing a command. As in the preceding example, even inserting a line of text or a hard return requires that you use a particular product command.

■ **Cue:** You can build complex macros by copying parts of other simpler macros.

When you edit a macro, you can change a parameter value safely, as long as the new value makes sense in context—you cannot set margins wider than the dimensions of your paper, for example. You also can delete an entire command safely if you no longer want your macro to carry out that function or task. You can delete one or more entire parameters within a command if you do not want to set or change the value for those parameters in effect when you play the macro. Such a command is syntactically correct, but you should verify that it now performs the action you want.

Never edit a command name or a parameter name. Although command names are not case sensitive, WordPerfect looks for a specific spelling. If you change the name, WordPerfect cannot recognize it, and your macro cannot function properly.

In the preceding example, the text string in each Type command represents the value of the parameter named Text. Therefore, changing the contents of the text string quite literally is changing the value of the parameter. By the same token, each DeleteCharPrevious() line is a command all to itself—deleting the line deletes the entire command.

The MAR15 macro created earlier in this chapter contains the following commands:

```
Application (WP; WPWP; Default; "WPWUS.WCD")

PageMargins
(
    Left:1.5i;
    Right:1.5i;
    Top:1.0i;
    Bottom:1.0i
)
```

If you decide instead that you want to set all margins to 1.5 inches, do the following:

1. Open MAR15.WCM.

2. Save the edited macro as MAR152.WCM.

3. Change the value of the Top parameter to read **1.5i**. Make sure to leave the semicolon (;).

4. Change the value of the Bottom parameter to **1.5i** as well. Because Bottom is the last parameter, no semicolon should follow.

5. Close the edited macro and save your changes.

6. Play the edited macro. If you receive a syntax error, open the original macro and repeat the preceding steps. If you receive a message indicating that you must compile the macro, read the following section, "Compiling Macros."

Notice also that when you create the macro, you change only the left and right margins, but the macro also contains the values for top and bottom margins that are in effect at the time. Every time you now play the macro, you set the top and bottom margins to one inch, whether or not some other value was already set and all you wanted to change was the top margin.

To correct this problem, you can do the following:

1. Open MAR15.WCM.

2. Save the edited macro as MARTEST.WCM.

3. Delete the lines containing the Top and Bottom parameters.

4. Delete the semicolon at the end of the Right parameter. The semi-colon tells WordPerfect that another parameter follows, which is no longer true. If you leave the semicolon, you receive an error message stating Parameter expected when you try to play the macro.

5. Close the file, saving your changes.

6. Play the edited macro.

If you receive a syntax error, open the original macro and repeat the preceding steps. If you receive a message saying that you must compile the macro, read the next section.

Compiling Macros

Under most circumstances WordPerfect for Windows compiles your macros automatically. If you edit your own macros, however, from time to time you may receive the following message when you try to play a macro:

"*macroname*" contains no object or its object is out of date. The macro must be compiled before it can be played.

If this message appears, you must use WordPerfect's Macro Facility to compile the macro. Because you receive this message only when trying to play a macro, the Macro Facility may already be playing in the background.

To compile a macro, do the following:

1. Press Alt-Tab repeatedly to cycle through any open windows. If the Macro Facility appears, go on to the next step.

   If the Macro Facility does not appear, continue to press Alt-Tab until you return to WordPerfect. Select **F**ile, **F**ile Manager. In the File Manager, select WordPerfect Macro Facility from the Applications menu. If necessary, press Alt-Tab until the Macro Facility Appears.

2. From the Macro Facility's Macro menu, select **C**ompile Macro. The Compile Macro dialog box, a variant of the Open File dialog box, appears.

3. Select the macro file you want to compile and then select Convert or press Enter. Your macro is compiled.

If your macro contains syntax errors, you receive error messages providing some information on the problem. You can cancel the compilation process to fix the error or continue compiling to see whether additional errors occur.

Using Advanced Macros

The WordPerfect manual does not contain a full list of available product and programming commands. However, the file WPWPUS.WCD contains a list of available WordPerfect product commands and their syntax, and the file MACRO.DOC contains a long list of macro programming commands. (If you are using a foreign edition of WordPerfect the letters *US* are replaced by the two-letter language code for your edition.) The Application programming code's fourth parameter refers to WPWPUS.WCD explicitly, and the Macro Facility uses this file to record and play macros. Therefore, although you can safely view and print WPWPUS.WCD, *do not make changes*, or your macros may not work properly.

The information in WPWPUS.WCD is in a format more useful to WordPerfect than to you, and it does not contain listing for the programming codes. Full documentation is available in a manual titled *WordPerfect Macros*, which you can order from WordPerfect Corporation.

If you are unsure of a product command's syntax, you do not have to resort to a manual. Because WordPerfect creates macros using the correct syntax, you always can record a simple macro that uses the feature. You then can copy the resulting commands into any other macro.

With the exception of the Application command, however, you can insert programming commands only by entering them yourself. If you have created advanced macros in WordPerfect 5.1 for DOS, the concepts behind WordPerfect for Windows' programming commands are familiar to you, but the syntax is significantly different.

Although advanced macros using programming commands are more complex than the basic macros covered in this chapter, they can perform correspondingly more complex actions. With programming commands, you can display prompts and menus in dialog boxes on-screen, accept input from the user, and take various actions depending on the response. WordPerfect's macro language is sophisticated enough to write true programs. Although this practice may be beyond the casual user, WordPerfect's advanced macros make ideal tools to help manage a complex office environment.

Chapter Summary

More than any other feature, WordPerfect's macros enable you to take control and customize WordPerfect according to your needs and preferences. Whenever you perform a task repetitively, you can automate that task by recording a macro. For most tasks, macros provide greater speed, accuracy, consistency, and ease of use than performing the tasks yourself many times.

In this chapter, you learned how to record macros, including planning their steps in advance and setting the stage for their recording. You learned how to play macros, replace short macros if necessary, and edit macros when appropriate. You now know alternative ways to play macros by assigning them to the Macro menu, Button Bars, or keyboard layouts. You know how to combine macros with styles and merges. You also created a number of macros that are useful by themselves. This chapter also provides examples for creating other macros that meet your own needs.

Macros are an extremely powerful feature, but they need not be imposing or difficult. This chapter, however, covers only the basics of creating and using macros. Experiment with other macros of your own. Certainly, you will make mistakes, but you will learn far more about WordPerfect and gain more power over it than you ever can by word processing "the long way."

Assembling Documents with Merge

S uppose that you need to mail the same letter to different people, but you want to personalize the letter for each individual. Word-Perfect's Merge feature can help you complete this task.

A *merge operation* combines into one document, data stored in different files or entered at the keyboard. When you are creating individual letters, for example, you can use merging to combine a standard text passage from one file with a name, address, and other information in another file. When you create a mass-mailing letter, for instance, the Merge feature is particularly helpful.

Merging eases the burden of redundant tasks by combining *fixed data* (standard text and formatting codes) with information that varies from letter to letter (*variable data*). The feature also saves time because you enter the fixed information only once.

■ **Eric Mark Rintell** is an independent computer consultant and has used WordPerfect's Merge feature since the release of WordPerfect 4.1.

Merging isn't limited to letters. You can use Merge to create standard text for catalogs, forms to be filled in on-line, legal contracts, and lists. You also can use the Merge feature for printing envelopes and mailing labels. If any situation calls for combining fixed and variable information more than once, use Merge.

This chapter explains the Merge feature. You learn the components needed in a merge operation, including primary and secondary merge files. You also learn how to perform the following tasks:

■ Compile merge files

■ Use Merge to automate printing of mailing lists on envelopes and labels

■ Use data from other programs in a merge operation

■ Use keyboard input in a merge process

■ Use (and skip) empty fields in merge files

T I P   Some advanced Merge techniques include using programming commands and variables. With programming commands, you can merge complex documents by including or excluding paragraphs, controlling the order of execution, calling macros, and so on. These techniques go beyond the scope of this book. See your WordPerfect for Windows Reference manual for information.

Planning a Merge Operation

WordPerfect performs each merge operation the same way. The process is easy because you do all the setup work in the primary and secondary merge files.

You place all fixed data—such as format codes and unchanging text—in a *primary merge file*, which also contains commands for merge control and the locations of variable information. The primary file for a letter, for example, may contain the sender's name and address and the body of the letter. The primary file also indicates where you want Word-Perfect to place any variable information, such as the name and address of the receiver.

WordPerfect offers several alternatives for using variable information in a merge. Variable information can be stored in a *secondary merge file* or other files or typed from the keyboard as needed. The most popular form is the secondary merge file (used by most examples in this chapter). The organization of the secondary file is important; WordPerfect must "understand" how variable information in the file is combined with the fixed information in the primary file.

Like a database manager, WordPerfect separates the secondary file into records and fields. A *record* is a complete group of variable data that contains all the information needed for one subject or person. Figure 21.2 (shown in the following section of this chapter) contains a list of students' names, their addresses, advisors, and appointment times. Information about each student makes up one record. Records consist of units called *fields*, which further separate the data. In figure 21.2, for example, a student's name is a distinct field in that student's record.

WordPerfect reads the merge commands in the primary merge file, combines variable information from the secondary merge file, other files, or the keyboard, and produces an *output file* that follows the instructions in the primary file.

■ **Cue:** Divide your data into fixed and variable data. In the variable data, try to find any similarities or patterns that can produce a field.

■ **Cue:** The number of records in a secondary file is limited only by disk space.

Setting Up Merge Files

Suppose that you are the registrar for a small community college. Before classes begin, you must send to each full-time student a letter with the following information: when classes begin, who has been assigned as the student's advisor, what time each person is scheduled to meet with the advisor, and how many credits the student must take each semester to keep the full-time designations. Figure 21.1 shows a sample student letter.

The following table lists the data included in the letter shown in figure 21.1, dividing the information into fixed and variable categories.

Fixed Data	Variable Data
School name and address	Student's name
Student's state (NY)	Street address
Arrival date on campus	City
Date classes begin	ZIP code
Advisor meeting date	Appointment time
28 credit hours per semester	Advisor

> The Community College
> 650 Fourth Avenue
> New York, NY 10001
>
> December 20, 1991
>
> Edward Murray
> 76 Main St.
> Apt. 24
> Blue Hill, NY 11330
>
> Dear Edward,
>
> As head of the Registrar's office, let me welcome you to Community College. I am sure that you will enjoy what our college has to offer.
>
> Before you can register for classes, you need to meet with your academic advisor, Mr. Hartley. Your appointment with Mr. Hartley is scheduled for 3:30pm on Friday, January 10.
>
> Classes begin on Monday, January 13. In order to maintain your status as a full time student, you must take at least 28 credit hours a semester. If you have any questions, please don't hesitate to call the Registrar's office at (212) 555-1100.
>
> Sincerely,
>
> Larry J. Fibner

FIG. 21.1

A sample
student letter.

If you list the data, you can decide which information is fixed and which varies, look for patterns in the data, and separate the items into different data fields. The fixed information will be typed in the primary merge file, to appear in every letter. The variable information will be typed in the secondary merge file, and will vary by student. Figure 21.2 shows a list of the variable student data.

Check the list of variable data for any similarities; for example, notice that each student lives in the state of New York (NY). Because the state is the same in each case, you can remove the state data field from the secondary merge file and use the state abbreviation in the primary file as fixed information.

Although all the students live in the same state, not all live in the same city. You therefore must include the city field as a variable in the secondary merge file. Because the list includes two advisors, the advisor name varies by student, and you must include the advisor data field in the secondary merge file.

Name	Street	City	State	ZIP Code	Advisor	Appointment
Edward Murray	76 Main St. Apt. 24	Blue Hill	NY	11330	Mr. Hartley	3:30pm
Charles Rex	34-121 86th St.	New York	NY	10002	Ms. Stewart	3:30pm
Lisa Worley	23 Auerbach Rd	New York	NY	10001	Mr. Hartley	11:15am
Mary Tisch	8 Captains Rd	Garden City	NY	11560	Mr. Hartley	10:15am
Larry Mancey	41 Park Ave	New York	NY	11231	Mr. Hartley	4:15pm
Shari Hurt	781 Central Ave	Garden City	NY	11560	Ms. Stewart	11:00am
Lisa Hartley	63 47th St. Apt. 4A	New York	NY	10001	Ms. Stewart	12:00pm
Larry Riley	23 48th St. Apt. 63	New York	NY	10001	Mr. Hartley	11:30am
Harold Dobner	3 Meadows Rd	Yonkers	NY	11302	Ms. Stewart	1:15pm

FIG. 21.2

A list of student information.

Creating the Secondary Merge File

Now that you know which information is variable, you can create the secondary merge file. First, you must decide how many fields you need for the merge operation. Then, after assigning field names, you construct a secondary merge file.

You need a minimum of four fields for the merge operation: one each for the student's name, address, advisor, and appointment time. If you separate the student's name, street address, and city into separate fields, however, you can do more with the same information in a merge operation. You can use the following sentence in your primary merge file, for example: "Community College encourages a diverse student body and welcomes students from the <city> area." You cannot include such a sentence if you use the minimum four fields, because no <city> field exists, and WordPerfect cannot separate the information in the <address> field into street address, city, state, and ZIP code.

You can break the name field further by placing the first and last names in separate fields. This change enables you to begin a letter with *Dear Edward* instead of *Dear Edward Murray*.

By breaking fields into small logical units, you can integrate the secondary merge file with different primary merge files more easily. You can create a secondary merge file, for example, that you can sort by the student's last name or city. Always think of future needs when you plan the number of fields for your merge files.

■ **Cue:** Break fields containing more than one item of data into smaller fields.

T I P   For more information on sorting secondary merge files, see Chapter 22, "Sorting and Selecting Data."

■ **Cue:** Pick field names that are representative of the data.

The last step in preparing to create the merge files is naming the fields for the secondary merge file. Choose names that indicate the contents of each field. Instead of naming the field containing ZIP codes "Numbers," for example, call it "ZIP" or "ZIP Codes." If you retrieve a secondary merge file after three months and cannot figure out what the fields represent, you didn't name the fields very well.

For the college example, you will use the following field names:

> FirstName
>
> LastName
>
> Street
>
> City
>
> ZipCode
>
> Advisor
>
> ApptTime

■ **Cue:** Make field names descriptive but brief.

You can use spaces and punctuation characters in field names; however, field names are easier to enter if you use just letters. Be descriptive but don't use extra characters that may lead to errors.

Entering Field Names

The first record in the secondary merge file is a special record used for listing the field names. With the field names already chosen, all you must do is insert the names into the secondary merge file.

Follow these steps to insert the field names:

1. Open a blank document by choosing **New** from the **File** menu.

   CUA Press New File (Shift-F4).

2. Choose **Merge** from the **Tools** menu.

   CUA Press Merge (Ctrl-F12).

3. Choose Merge **Codes**. The Insert Merge Codes dialog box appears (see fig. 21.3).

FIG. 21.3

The Insert
Merge Codes
dialog box.

4. Press **F** and then use the direction keys to highlight the {FIELD NAMES}name1~...nameN~~ code.

    If you're using a mouse, scroll until you find the {FIELD NAMES}name1~..nameN~~ code; then click to highlight the code.

5. Choose **Insert**, or press Enter.

    The Merge Field Name(s) dialog box appears. The Field Number area indicates that you are working with the first field.

    > **Cue:** Field names appear in the order in which you enter the fields.

6. Because the first field is the first name of the student, type **FirstName** in the Field Name text box.

7. Choose **Add**; WordPerfect highlights the phrase *FirstName*.

8. Press the Backspace key twice to clear *FirstName* from the input box and to increment the Field Number, whose value has been changed to 2. Notice that *FirstName* is listed in the field names list.

    Your screen should resemble figure 21.4.

9. Type **LastName** for the second field name, and choose **Add**. Press Backspace twice to clear the input box and advance the Field Number to the next field.

    > **Cue:** The order in which fields appear in the secondary merge file is unimportant because you can use the fields in any order in your primary merge file.

    Repeat this step to fill in the remaining field names: **Street** for field name 3, **City** for field name 4, **ZipCode** for field name 5, **Advisor** for field name 6, and **ApptTime** for field name 7.

10. After entering all the field names, choose OK or press Enter to close the Merge Field Name(s) dialog box. A line appears at the top of your secondary merge file that begins with the code {FIELD NAMES}.

11. Choose **Close** or press Esc to close the Insert Merge Codes dialog box.

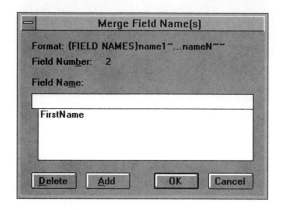

FIG. 21.4

Entering field names in the Merge Field Name(s) dialog box.

T I P

WordPerfect separates field names with a tilde (~). This marker is especially useful for field names that include spaces, such as the following names:

    Student First Name~Student Last Name~

An extra tilde and an {END RECORD} code follow the last field name, ApptTime, to signify the end of the record.

■ **Cue:** To access Reveal Codes, press Alt-F3.

After you finish entering the field names, your document should look like the one in figure 21.5. You can edit a misspelled or incorrect field name just as you edit any other text in a WordPerfect document. If you must add a field name, read "Changing Fields in a Secondary File" in this chapter.

T I P

The {FIELD NAMES} code at the beginning of the record is not text, but a hidden merge code indicating the beginning of the field names record. (In Reveal Codes, you see the hidden [Mrg:FIELD NAMES] code.) If you print this document, only the text you typed and the tildes (~) separating field names appear in print.

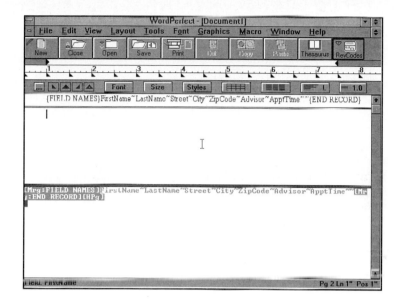

FIG. 21.5

The secondary
merge file with
the {FIELD
NAMES} record
inserted.

Entering Fields and Records

Notice that the left side of the status bar reads Field: FirstName. WordPerfect now expects you to fill in the first field, FirstName. You must enter your data for each record in the order you specified in the {FIELD NAMES} record.

Before you begin entering data, make certain that the insertion point immediately follows the hard page break, which appears in the text on-screen as a horizontal double line (again see fig. 21.5).

If you are entering a large number of fields or records, put {END FIELD} on the Button Bar to save keystrokes and time (see Chapter 19 for instructions).

BUTTON

Most of the data for this example file comes from figure 21.2. To enter the data for the first record, follow these steps:

1. In the first field (the student's first name), type **Edward**. Do *not* press Enter.

2. To enter an {END FIELD} code, choose **Merge** from the **Tools** menu and then choose **End Field**. The {END FIELD} code signifies the end of data for this field (FirstName) and separates fields in a record.

Press Merge End of Field (Alt-Enter).

If you look at the hidden codes in Reveal Codes, the {END FIELD} code appears as shown in figure 21.6.

Notice that the field name on the status bar has changed to LastName. WordPerfect tracks the current field as you enter the data in each field.

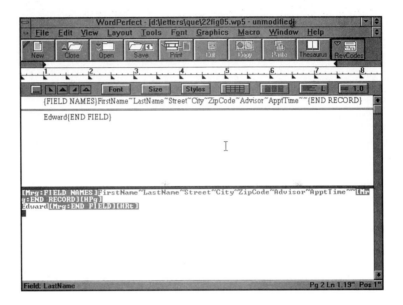

FIG. 21.6

The {END FIELD} code, shown in Reveal Codes as [Mrg:END FIELD][HRt].

3. Type Edward's last name, **Murray**.

4. Enter another {END FIELD} code by choosing **M**erge from the **T**ools menu and then choosing **E**nd Field.

5. Type **76 Main St.** (the first line of Edward Murray's address) and press Enter to move to the next line. Type **Apt. 24** (the second line of the address), and enter another {END FIELD} code.

> **CAUTION:** Don't press Enter to separate fields or records. You can use Enter, however, to place data on different lines within a field. After the Edward Murray record is merged, for example, the street address appears on the line above the apartment number.

6. Type **Blue Hill** for the city, followed by an {END FIELD} code.

7. For the ZipCode field, enter **11330**, followed by an {END FIELD} code.

8. For the advisor, type **Mr. Hartley**, and add an {END FIELD} code.

9. Type **3:30pm** for the time Edward Murray and Mr. Hartley are scheduled to meet. Then enter an {END FIELD} code.

   This entry completes the fields in the record.

10. Choose **Merge** from the **Tools** menu, and then choose **End Record**.

 Press Merge End of Record (Alt-Shift-Enter).

Place End Record on the Button Bar if you need to enter a large number of records.

An {END RECORD} code appears in the file, followed (in Reveal Codes) by a hard page break ([HPg]).The {END RECORD} signifies the end of data and separates records in a secondary merge file. Notice that the status line indicates that WordPerfect is in the FirstName field again, on page 3 of the secondary merge file (see fig. 21.7).

Cue: A hard page break, which appears as an unbroken double line, always follows the last field in a record.

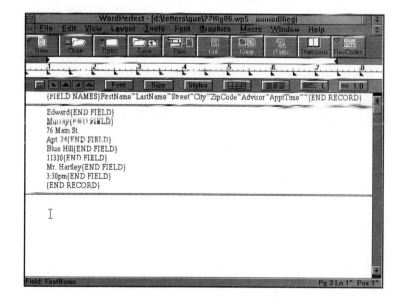

FIG. 21.7

A completed record in a secondary merge file.

11. Save the file by choosing **S**ave from the **F**ile menu.

 Press Save (Shift-F3).

The Save As dialog box appears.

12. Type **STUDENTS.SEC** for the file name.

T I P Use one extension for all secondary merge files. For this example, the SEC extension shows that this file is a secondary merge file.

Enter the remaining student records in the secondary merge file by repeating steps 1 through 10 for each record, substituting the appropriate information for each student. Save the file after entering each record so that you don't lose any work.

The information you type in the fields will appear in the output file. If you make a mistake, edit the text in the fields as you edit any text.

Be sure to maintain consistency regarding the number of fields in each record. In the STUDENTS.SEC file, for example, each record must have seven fields. If a record lacks information in a field, use an empty field (see "Using Empty Fields" in this chapter).

Creating the Primary Merge File

After saving the variable data in the secondary merge file, you can create the primary merge file. This file contains the fixed information, including the body of the letter and the formatting codes.

The college letter looks like any other WordPerfect letter, except for the {FIELD} codes. In a primary merge file, the {FIELD} code, followed by the field name, indicates where you want to place a variable. When you merge the files, the contents of the named fields appear in the output file.

Before you insert any {FIELD} codes, create the letterhead and date for the cover letter. Follow these steps:

1. Open a blank document by choosing **N**ew from the **F**ile menu.

 Press New File (Shift-F4).

2. Choose **J**ustification from the **L**ayout menu, and then choose Center Justification, or press Justify Center (Ctrl-J).

3. Type the following information:

   The Community College
   650 Fourth Avenue
   New York, NY 10001

4. Press Enter three times to leave space between the address and the date.

5. Choose **J**ustification from the **L**ayout menu, and then choose **L**eft Justification, or press Justify Left (Ctrl-L).

■ **Cue:** You can insert a [Date] code to have WordPerfect include the current date—see "Inserting Dates" later in this chapter.

5. Type today's date and press Enter twice. If the mailing will take several days to finish, insert another date or insert a [Date] code.

At this point, if you were typing a letter to one person, you would enter the recipient's name. Because you are sending this letter to several recipients, however, you insert a {FIELD} code into the document to tell WordPerfect to insert in this place the data from the appropriate field in the secondary merge file. Follow these steps to insert the code:

1. Choose **M**erge from the **T**ools menu.

    Press Merge (Ctrl-F12).

2. Choose **F**ield from the cascading menu. The Insert Merge Code dialog box appears, as shown in figure 21.8.

   If you create or edit a great many primary merge files, put **F**ield on the Button Bar to save time.

> **CAUTION:** Don't confuse the Insert Merge Code and the Insert Merge Codes dialog boxes. The Insert Merge Code dialog box puts a specific merge code into a primary merge file; the Insert Merge Codes dialog box is for entering any merge codes into any file.

3. In this dialog box, you type the name of the field whose contents you want to insert when the document is merged. For this example, type **FirstName**. Be careful to spell the field names correctly.

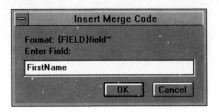

FIG. 21.8

The Insert
Merge Code
dialog box.

CAUTION: You must spell field names exactly the same way in the primary and secondary merge files.

4. Press Enter or click OK to insert the {FIELD} code into the primary merge file and close the Insert Merge Code dialog box.

Your screen should look like figure 21.9.

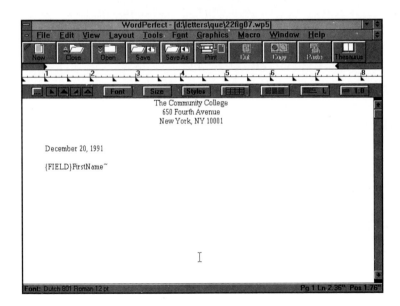

FIG. 21.9

The primary
merge file with
a {FIELD}
code inserted.

5. The information is entered exactly as you would enter it into any letter. Place a space between the FirstName and LastName fields. Press Enter to place the street address on the next line. Press Enter after the Street field; place a comma and a space after the City field. Enter the abbreviation for New York (NY) as text because it is fixed information. Type the rest of the primary merge file (text and {FIELD} codes). The completed file is shown in figure 21.10.

6. After you finish typing the primary merge file, save the document as STUDENT3.LTR by choosing **S**ave from the File menu.

 Press Save (Shift-F3).

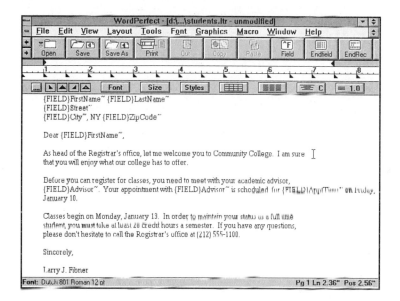

FIG. 21.10

The completed primary merge file.

> **T I P**
>
> You can use a field more than once in a primary merge file. The fields FirstName and Advisor, for example, are used twice in the example letter. You don't need to use all the secondary merge file fields in the primary merge file; WordPerfect ignores fields that don't appear in the primary merge file.

Make sure that you have spelled each field name correctly. You can edit field names in the same way that you edit any other text in a WordPerfect document. WordPerfect does not generate an error message if a field name is misspelled, but leaves a blank space in the output file for the misspelled field.

■ **Cue:** Cascade the secondary merge file (choose **W**indow, **C**ascade) from the primary merge file to view the field names to ensure that you spell them correctly.

T I P You can use graphics in a primary merge file, but you cannot save the graphics in the primary merge file. Use the Graphics on Disk option instead.

Merging Files

■ **Cue:** WordPerfect is not case sensitive in respect to field names. *Firstname*, for example, is the same as *FirstName*.

Now that you have created the primary and secondary merge files, you have everything you need to perform the merge operation. To merge files in WordPerfect, follow these steps:

1. Choose **Merge** from the **T**ools menu.

   CUA Press Merge (Ctrl-F12).

2. Choose **M**erge from the Merge menu to open the Merge Files dialog box (see fig. 21.11).

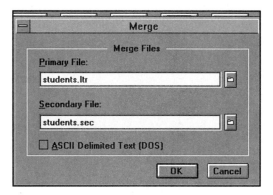

FIG. 21.11

The Merge Files dialog box.

3. Type **students.ltr** in the **P**rimary File text box.

   If the file is not in the current directory, type the full path name in the text box. If you cannot remember the path, click the Folder icon to the right of the text box.

4. Type **students.sec** in the Secondary File text box. If the file is in a different directory, type the full path name or use the Folder icon.

5. Press Enter or click OK.

WordPerfect begins to merge the two files. The left side of the status bar displays Merging during the process. (The display screen, meanwhile, remains blank.)

All merges work in the same simple manner. Once you know how to perform one merge, you can perform any merge.

T I P

If you must interrupt WordPerfect in the middle of a merge, press Esc. WordPerfect aborts the merge; the page number on the right side of the status bar indicates the last record number that was merged before you interrupted the merging process.

After the merge process is complete, WordPerfect displays the last page of the output file.

By scrolling through the output file with the direction keys or the mouse, you can see that the merge process created a separate, personalized letter for each student. You can edit or print the output file the same way you work with any other WordPerfect document with multiple pages. The merged document is a new document consisting of information from the primary and secondary merge files.

■ **Cue:** Use Alt-PgUp and Alt-PgDn to scroll through the merged file a page (record) at a time.

Output files exist only in memory; if the merge process doesn't work as you expected, exit the output file, correct the primary file as necessary, and merge the primary and secondary files again. If you decide to save the merged file on disk, do not save it under the same name as the primary or secondary merge file.

If you plan to reuse an output file, save the file on disk by choosing **S**ave from the **F**ile menu or pressing Save (Shift-F3). With a large output file, however, you may find that running a merge operation each time you need the file is more appropriate than saving the output file—but this process is more time-consuming.

T I P

Merging with Labels and Envelopes

You can use one secondary merge file with different primary merge files. The following sections show how you can use Merge with any paper size or type supported by WordPerfect.

T I P   Remember that a secondary merge file contains variable data; you can use the secondary merge file with several different primary merge files, so you do not have to enter variable data more than once.

The first example is for printers that can print envelopes. The second example discusses label printing and merges. (Both sections assume that you know how to create, edit, and select different forms in WordPerfect. If you need more information on creating forms, see Chapter 11, "Formatting Pages and Designing Documents.")

Merging with Envelopes

After printing your merged letters, all you must do is sign the letters, put them in envelopes, and mail them. You don't even have to address envelopes by hand, because Merge can address them for you.

In this section, you create an envelope merge file that contains your return address and the recipient's name and address. The information in this section assumes that you are using a WordPerfect printer driver with an envelope form. If your driver has no envelope form, you must create one for your printer. For more details on envelope forms, see Chapter 15, "Working with Advanced Printing Techniques."

To create the primary merge file for an envelope, follow these steps:

1. Choose **N**ew from the **F**ile menu to create a blank document.

   CUA Press New File (Shift-F4).

2. Choose **D**ocument from the **L**ayout menu.

   CUA Press Layout Document (Ctrl-Shift-F9).

3. Choose Initial **C**odes. The Document Initial Codes window replaces the document window (see fig. 21.12).

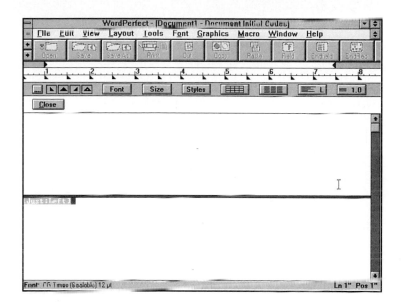

FIG. 21.12

The Document Initial Codes window.

Try to place the formatting codes (such as [Paper Sz/Type], margin **T I P**
codes, and so on) that appear at the beginning of the primary merge
file in Document Initial Codes. This technique reduces clutter in the
merge file by removing repetitive codes from the primary merge file,
and the [Paper Sz/Type] code in Document Initial Codes then
doesn't appear at the top of each envelope when the database is
merged.

4. Choose **Page** from the **L**ayout menu.

     Press Layout Page (Alt-F9).

5. Choose Paper **S**ize from the Page menu. The Paper Size dialog box
   appears.

6. In the dialog box, highlight the envelope paper definition you want
   to print on.

7. Choose **S**elect to close the dialog box.

8. Choose **M**argins from the **L**ayout menu.

     Press Margins (Ctrl-F8).

The Margins dialog box opens.

9. Set all margins to **.3** inch and choose OK.

10. Choose **C**lose to close the Document Initial Codes window.

11. Type the rest of the formatting codes, text, and {FIELD} codes as shown in figure 21.13. The margins have been adjusted to accommodate the sender's name and address and the recipient's name and address. The [AdvToLn] (Advance To Line) code moves the insertion point 2 1/4 inches from the top of the envelope (for more information, see Chapter 15).

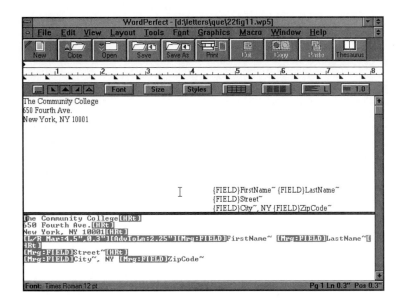

FIG. 21.13

The primary merge file for an envelope.

When you finish creating the envelope form, save your primary file as STUDENTS.ENV. Perform the merge with STUDENTS.ENV as the primary file and STUDENTS.SEC as the secondary file.

CAUTION: If you don't save any changes in the primary and secondary merge files before you begin merging, the changes don't take effect because WordPerfect merges the version of each file found on disk under that file name.

After you perform a merge with some envelopes, find a record that has an address with extra lines and check that the address fits on the envelope. If the address doesn't fit, adjust the margins and the Advance to Line code that appears after the return address. (The Advance To Line code controls the number of inches from the top of the envelope.) If you have no problems, you can print the envelopes.

Merging with Labels

One of the most common uses for the merge process is label printing. Without Merge, printing a mailing list on labels probably is not worthwhile because you must type each label.

Choose a label suitably sized for your needs. If you plan to use the top half of the label for the return address and the bottom half for the recipient's name and address, pick a label that has enough height to accommodate both names and addresses. You may find a 1-by-2-inch label suitable for folders in a filing cabinet, for example, but too small for a name and address.

WordPerfect offers many features that enable you to specify exactly where information prints on a label. Refer to Chapter 15 for details on creating, editing, and printing with labels.

Figure 21.14 shows a primary merge file for the Avery 5164 label definition created in Chapter 15. The following codes are placed in the Document Initial Codes window: [Paper Sz/Type: Avery 5164]. The file uses a proportional font for the name of the school and a monospaced font for the student information to comply with the United States Postal Service OCR codes. Primary merge files for most merges are constructed in the same manner; all you do differently is adjust for the form you want to use for printing.

■ **Cue:** Because WordPerfect views each label as a logical page on a sheet, you must place a hard page break between labels (see Chapter 15).

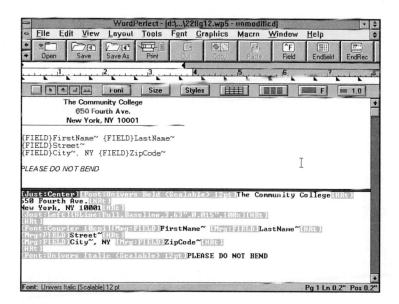

FIG. 21.14

A primary file for a label merge.

Figure 21.15 shows the first page of printed labels. For a more balanced look, a center page code ([Center Pg]) was placed in the Document Initial Codes of the primary merge file. The first label in the upper left corner appears to fit more tightly than other labels because Edward Murray's address contains an additional address line that the other labels don't have.

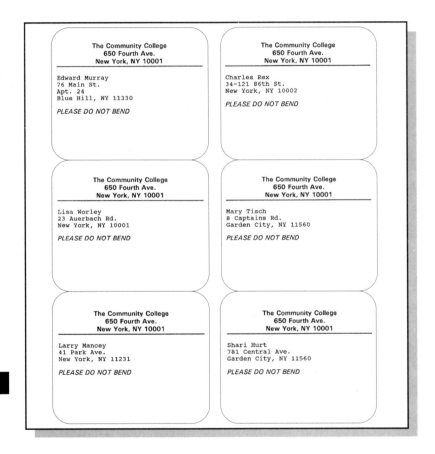

FIG. 21.15

First page of output from a label merge.

Dealing with Special Situations

The examples shown in this chapter provide enough information for most merge situations. This section covers a number of special situations. If you like, you can skip to the area that interests you or is most useful for your merge conditions.

Changing Fields in a Secondary File

After you insert the {FIELD NAMES} record at the beginning of a secondary merge file, you may need to add or delete fields. If you must add a field, type the field name in the {FIELD NAMES} record, followed by a tilde. Consider the following {FIELD NAMES} record:

```
{FIELD NAMES}LastName~FirstName~Telephone~~{END RECORD}
```

If you want to add the field name *Extension* to the end of this record, you must retain the two tildes before the {END RECORD} code, as follows:

```
{FIELD NAMES} LastName~FirstName~Telephone~Extension~~
{END RECORD}
```

To insert a field name, follow these steps:

1. Place insertion point between the two last tildes.

2. Type **Extension~**,

Remember that when you add a field, you must place the data for that field in the same location in every record. If you add a field name in the middle of the {FIELD NAMES} record, for example, you must place the corresponding data in the middle of every record.

> **CAUTION:** If you enter the data in the wrong location in the record, you can ruin the output.

A good rule is to add new field names after the last field name. By placing a new field as the last field, you are less prone to make mistakes because you type the new data just before the {END RECORD} code in each record.

Cue. Add new field names after the last field name in a record.

You need not delete fields in a secondary merge file (unless you need to reduce the disk size of the file). If you don't use a secondary file field in the primary merge file, WordPerfect ignores the field during the merge. When you add new records to the secondary merge file, just include an empty field for any field you no longer use. For more information, see "Using Empty Fields" in this chapter.

> **CAUTION:** Deleting fields, although possible, is not advised. If you delete a field, you must go through the records manually deleting the corresponding data and the {END FIELD} code.

Using Other Secondary Files

You aren't limited to using a WordPerfect secondary merge file with the merge feature. The next sections describe two other approaches, which you can use if your data is not stored in a WordPerfect document.

Using Notebook Files

WordPerfect Corporation's WordPerfect Office includes the Notebook module, which you can use to store names, addresses, telephone numbers, or other information. You can use Notebook files as secondary merge files in WordPerfect for Windows; no special action is required on your part. Simply type the name of the Notebook file as the secondary file in the Merge dialog box.

Using ASCII Delimited Text Files

You can use ASCII delimited text files from other programs in a merge operation without having to re-enter the data in a secondary merge file. Most spreadsheet and database management programs can export files in an ASCII delimited format.

An ASCII delimited file (which you can view with the DOS TYPE command) has a structure similar to a WordPerfect secondary merge file. In a secondary merge file, an {END FIELD} code separates fields; in an ASCII delimited file, predefined characters separate the fields. Make sure that you know what the program uses as delimiters before performing the merge operation

Because you cannot place the {FIELD NAMES} code in the ASCII delimited file, you cannot tell WordPerfect your field names in an ASCII delimited file. You must change the {FIELD} codes in your primary merge file before merging with an ASCII delimited file.

■ **Cue:** If you use the same field and record delimiters often, change the default field and record delimiters (see Chapter 29, "Customizing WordPerfect with Preferences").

You can use the Replace command (**E**dit, **R**eplace) to replace the field names with numbers in your primary merge file. Number the fields in the order in which they appear in the secondary merge file. Don't forget to save the primary file before you perform the merge operation.

To execute a merge with an ASCII delimited file as the secondary merge file, you follow the steps you follow for any merge operation. After you enter the file names in the Merge Files dialog box, select **A**SCII Delimited Text (DOS). In the Text File Delimiters dialog box, specify the special characters used in the ASCII delimited file to denote the end of a field and the end of a record.

WordPerfect should process the merge like any other merge. If a field appears blank, you may have forgotten to change the {FIELD} code in the primary file or counted your fields incorrectly.

Using Keyboard Input

Usually, you will use a disk file (WordPerfect, Notebook, or ASCII) for your secondary merge file. Sometimes, however, you may want to type variable information. You can type the data by placing an {INPUT} merge code instead of a {FIELD} code in the primary file where you want the data to appear. The {INPUT} code is useful for filling in forms or for customizing form letters with individual postscripts.

Cue: A secondary merge file is not required for a merge with keyboard input.

When WordPerfect reaches the {INPUT} code in the primary file, the merge process pauses, a custom message (which you create) appears in a Merge Message dialog box, and the software waits for you to enter the data. To continue merging, you press End Field (Alt-Enter).

Cue: Try to limit your message to no more than 300 characters. Otherwise, when the merge is run, the user will have to scroll to the right in order to read the message.

To use keyboard input in a merge, follow these steps:

1. Place the insertion point in the primary merge file where you want the information to appear.

2. Choose Merge from the Tools menu.

   Press Merge (Ctrl-F12).

3. Choose Input from the Merge menu to access the Insert Merge Code dialog box (see fig. 21.16).

FIG. 21.16

The Insert Merge Code dialog box for inserting a message.

You can put it on the Button Bar to save time if you frequently create primary merge files with keyboard input.

BUTTON

4. Type the message. End your message with a phrase like *(Press Alt-Enter to continue)* so that the user knows how to continue the merge operation.

5. Press Enter or choose OK.

   The dialog box closes and an {INPUT} code appears in your document. Your custom message (followed by a tilde) appears after the {INPUT} code. You can read your entire message in the editing window. If you make a mistake, you can edit the text as you edit any other text; just remember to leave the tilde after the text.

6. Enter additional {INPUT} codes as needed in the primary file. Choose **S**ave from the **F**ile menu or press Save (Shift-F3) to save your primary document.

7. Perform the merge operation.

Each time WordPerfect encounters an {INPUT} code, a Merge Message dialog box appears with your custom message. Type the necessary information and press Alt-Enter to continue merging. The example in figure 21.17 shows a keyboard merge that prompts for the user's name.

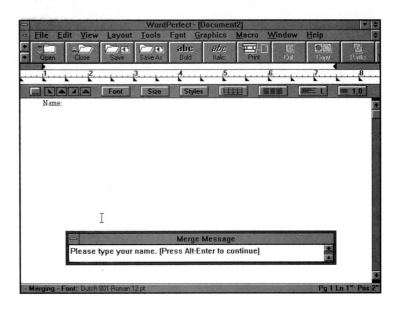

FIG. 21.17

A Merge
Message dialog
box.

Inserting Dates

In the college example, you placed a {DATE} code in the letter. This {DATE} code always displays the current date when a document is retrieved. Although this code is useful for most situations, it may cause confusion for merged documents that are saved on disk. For example, suppose that you execute a merge on November 1, save the merged document, and retrieve the merged document on December 15. The date displayed in the merged document is December 15. Unless you look at the date the file was created, you have no way of knowing when you executed the merge. Luckily, the Merge feature has a solution to this problem: the merge {DATE} code. The merge {DATE} code always displays the date the merge is executed. If you save the merged document with the merge {DATE} code, when you retrieve the merged document on December 15, the date displayed in the merged document is still November 1.

You can insert codes that tell WordPerfect to include the date of the merge in the final document. Follow these steps:

1. Place the insertion point in the primary merge file where you want the date to appear.

2. Choose Tools, **Merge**, Merge **C**odes from the Merge menu to access the Insert Merge Codes dialog box.

3. Highlight the {DATE} code and choose **I**nsert.

4. Choose **C**lose to close the dialog box. A {DATE} code appears in your primary merge file.

The date inserted into the output file is the date of the merge. If you want the output file to display the current date instead of the merge date, insert a {DATE} code by pressing Ctrl-Shift-F5 instead of choosing a merge {DATE} code. The {DATE} code is always updated with the current date, but the merge {DATE} code doesn't change after the merge ends.

Using Empty Fields

When you place variable information in a secondary merge file, each record must have the same number of fields, but sometimes you may lack the data for one or more fields in a particular record. You can use an *empty field* (a field containing only an {END FIELD} code) to resolve this situation in the secondary file, but you may get unexpected results when your primary merge file looks for data that isn't available.

The two examples in this section are based on the following fields for a phone book merge:

```
{FIELD NAMES}LastName~FirstName~BusPhone~Extension~Fax~
Mobile~HomePhone~~{END RECORD}
```

■ **Cue:** Because all records in a secondary merge file must have the same number of fields, use empty fields in a record to skip blank areas.

Each record in the secondary merge file must have these seven fields. You can assume that most people listed in the secondary merge file have all four telephone numbers, but not everyone has an extension.

In the following example, Arnold Norris has a direct business number that doesn't require an extension, and his office doesn't have a facsimile machine. The data for his record follows:

Field	Data
LastName	Norris
FirstName	Arnold
BusPhone	212-555-1212
Extension	none
Fax	none
Mobile	212-111-9876
HomePhone	718-555-2345

Placing Empty Fields in a Secondary File

When you enter a record that lacks data for each field, as in the preceding example, enter {END FIELD} codes in the fields lacking data (choose **M**erge from the **T**ools menu and then choose **E**nd Field, or press Alt-Enter). Don't type a space or enter a hard return.

The entry for Arnold Norris' record in the secondary merge file is as follows:

```
Norris{END FIELD}
Arnold{END FIELD}
212-555-1212{END FIELD}
{END FIELD}
{END FIELD}
212-111-9876{END FIELD}
718-555-2345{END FIELD}
{END RECORD}
```

When you perform the merge, WordPerfect understands that the Extension and Fax fields have no entries.

Skipping Empty Fields in a Primary File

The primary file in the phone book example has the following text and codes:

```
{FIELD}LastName~, {FIELD}FirstName~
Business: {FIELD}BusPhone~ Ext: {FIELD}Extension~
Fax: {FIELD}Fax~
Mobile: {FIELD}Mobile~
Home: {FIELD}HomePhone~
```

After placing the empty fields in the Arnold Norris record, you make sure that the mobile and phone numbers are in the correct fields. When you merge the files, however, the following is the result:

```
Norris, Arnold
Business: 212-555-1212 Ext:
Fax:
Mobile: 212-111-9876
Home: 718-555-2345
```

The information is correct—WordPerfect has not inserted any numbers for an extension or fax number—but the program has inserted unnecessary text for both fields. You can structure the primary file so that Merge ignores the text for blank fields.

Used with the {END IF} code, the command {IF NOT BLANK} fieldname~ takes effect only if the named field contains data. Word Perfect excludes from the output merge file any fixed text between the {IF NOT BLANK} and {END IF} codes if the field is blank in the secondary merge file.

To omit text from a merge, follow these steps:

1. Place the insertion point in the primary merge file where you want to place the text that may be omitted.

2. Choose **Tools**, **Merge**, Merge **Codes** to display the Insert Merge Codes dialog box.

3. Highlight {IF NOT BLANK} and choose Insert.

   The Insert Merge Code dialog box appears and indicates that you are entering the field name for an {IF NOT BLANK} code. The field name you enter in this dialog box appears in the primary merge file, followed by a tilde.

> **T I P**
> Don't confuse the Insert Merge Code and the Insert Merge Codes dialog boxes. The Insert Merge Code dialog box puts a specific merge code into a primary merge file; the Insert Merge Codes dialog box is for entering any merge codes into any file.

4. Type the field name—**EXTENSION**—and press Enter. The Insert Merge Code dialog box closes.

5. Choose **C**lose to close the Insert Merge Codes dialog box.

6. In the primary merge file, enter the text and codes you want to appear in the output file if the field is not blank. Type **Ext: {FIELD} Extension**.

7. Choose **T**ools, **M**erge, Merge **C**odes to access the Insert Merge Codes dialog box.

8. Highlight {END IF} and choose **I**nsert. WordPerfect inserts an {END IF} code into the primary merge file.

9. Choose **C**lose to close the Insert Merge Codes dialog box.

These steps modify the primary file to read as follows:

```
{FIELD}LastName~, {FIELD}FirstName~

Business: {FIELD}BusPhone~ {IF NOT BLANK}Extension~
Ext: {FIELD}Extension~{END IF}

{IF NOT BLANK}Fax~Fax: {FIELD}Fax~

{END IF} {IF NOT BLANK} Mobile~Mobile: {FIELD}Mobile~

{END IF} Home: {FIELD}HomePhone~
```

The first {IF NOT BLANK} code checks to see whether the Extension field is blank. If the field is blank, WordPerfect doesn't insert the text *Ext:* into the output file. If the secondary file contains text in the Extension field, the text *Ext:* and the field contents appear in the output file. The same approach, used for the Fax and Mobile fields, prevents blank lines from appearing in the final document.

After merging the Arnold Norris record with the modified merge file, WordPerfect produces the following output:

```
Norris, Arnold
Business: 212-555-1212
Mobile: 212-111-9876
Home: 718-555-2345
```

Removing Hard Page Breaks

Although by default WordPerfect inserts a hard page break between merge records, you don't always want each record to appear on a separate page.

The phone book scenario from the preceding sections is a good example of a time when you may want more than one name on a page. If you insert a {PAGE OFF} code into your primary merge file, Word-Perfect doesn't insert a hard page break between records.

To prevent page breaks between records, place the insertion point at the beginning of your primary merge file and follow the usual steps for inserting a code. When the Insert Merge Codes dialog box displays, choose {PAGE OFF}.

Merging Directly to the Printer

If you are short on disk space, you can send the output file directly to a printer. After WordPerfect merges a record from the secondary merge file with the primary merge file, the software sends the output immediately to the printer. Because WordPerfect treats each record as a new document, each record is cleared from memory as it prints.

Sending an output file directly to the printer has some drawbacks. Merging to the printer takes longer than merging to the screen. Because each record is a separate document, you cannot edit or save the output file. If a mistake appears in the merged documents, you cannot correct it until the print job is finished.

A {PRINT} code in the primary merge file tells WordPerfect to send the output file directly to the printer. Follow the usual steps to insert the code at the beginning of your primary merge file.

Chapter Summary

The Merge feature is a powerful tool that you can use to combine formatted text with variable information. You need to plan your merge operations before performing them; think about what goes in the primary document (fixed information) and in the secondary document (variable information). This chapter has shown you how to analyze your data's suitability for a merge operation and how to divide your data into fixed and variable information.

You now know how to create and save primary and secondary merge files and how to perform merge operations. You have learned how to perform a merge with envelopes and labels, how to handle special situations in a merge operation, and how to merge directly to the printer.

Sorting and Selecting Data

Y ou probably use databases daily. Each time you find an address or number in a telephone directory or card file, look up the time for a program in a television schedule, or check the definition of a word in a dictionary, you use a database. The shopping list you use at the store and the calendar where you track your appointments also are databases. In each case, the database is a written or printed collection of data that is related in some way. The data is organized—alphabetically, numerically, by date, or by some other method—so that you can find specific information quickly.

■ **Robert M. Beck** is a former judge, now practicing law in Oklahoma City. Also a former newspaper editor and reporter, he is currently a computer consultant for small-to-medium-sized law offices.

Understanding Data Files

A WordPerfect *data file* is an electronic version of the printed database. Figure 22.1 shows a WordPerfect data file with information organized in a line record format.

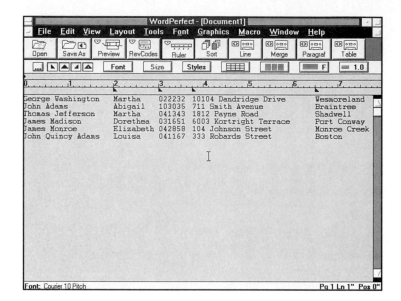

FIG. 22.1

A WordPerfect
line record data
file.

When you store data electronically rather than on paper, you can store large volumes of data in a very small space and find specific data extremely quickly. With your information organized into data files, you can use WordPerfect's powerful Sort feature to sort the files, extract specific information, and use the data with other WordPerfect features (Search, Replace, Merge, Table Math, Macros, and so on) to meet many of your business or personal database needs.

T I P   The Sort functions can handle most needs, but your data may require a specialized database program. WordPerfect Corporation offers two such programs: DataPerfect 2.2 and Notebook 3.01 (included in the WordPerfect Office PC and LAN 3.01 software packages). These programs produce the same data reports as the Sort feature but in much less time than required by WordPerfect.

This chapter shows you how to do the following:

■ Organize your data into data file formats

■ Use a data file to store, sort, and select information

■ Create a directory from the information in a data file

- Sort data file information alphabetically and numerically

- Use a data file to create personalized letters and mailing labels

You can apply the principles used here to any collection of data in a WordPerfect data file. The examples in this chapter are based on the information shown in figure 22.2. If you want to follow the examples but don't have the time to create data files containing all 40 records, create sample data files using any six of the records from figure 22.2.

If you are an experienced user of another program with data-manipulation capabilities, this chapter helps you to expand your skills to include the WordPerfect Sort functions.

You may be a bit overwhelmed at first by the terms in this chapter. As you progress through the chapter, however, you will master the terms and concepts as you learn to take charge of your data with WordPerfect's Sort feature.

> **Cue:** If you have used a DOS version of WordPerfect (such as WordPerfect 5.1), the interface of the Sort feature appears different, but the techniques for using Sort in WordPerfect for Windows are similar to those in the DOS version.

Designing a Data File

Figure 22.2 shows the membership information for an imaginary social organization, the President's Club. In the days before computers made record-keeping easy, the club used the one-page spreadsheet shown in the figure to keep a roster with information about each member arranged in columns and rows.

Recently, the club approved the purchase of a computer system and chose WordPerfect for Windows as the system's primary software program. The club needs one or more data files in which to keep the information required for various activities.

The club has 37 active members and 3 provisional members whose membership status is pending. Most of the members, who live in different cities and states, are married. Except for the annual meeting, the members don't meet regularly but communicate often by letter and telephone. Some members have unlisted telephone numbers, which must be treated as confidential. The club sends cards for birthdays and membership anniversaries. Each person is sponsored for membership by one of several philosophical organizations from which the club accepts membership nominations. When the nominee's membership application is approved, the member is assigned a unique number that the club uses to keep track of all matters related to the member.

Member	Spouse	Member Number	Street Address	City
George Washington	Martha	022232	10104 Dandridge Street	Westmoreland
John Adams	Abigail	103035	711 Smith Avenue	Braintree
Thomas Jefferson	Martha	041343	1812 Payne Road	Shadwell
James Madison	Dorothea	031651	6003 Kortright Terrace	Port Conway
James Monroe	Elizabeth	042858	104 Johnson Street	Monroe Creek
John Quincy Adams	Louisa	041167	333 Robards Street	Boston
Andrew Jackson	Rachel	031567	1006 Hoes Boulevard	Charlotte
Martin Van Buren	Hannah	120582	44 Symmes Expressway	Kinderhook
William Henry Harrison	Anna	020973	386 Christian Canyon Road	Charles City
John Tyler	Letitia Julia	032990	2971 Gardiner Avenue	Greenway
James Knox Polk	Sarah	110295	2925 Childress Street	Mecklenburg
Zachary Taylor	Margaret	112484	2403 Smith Street	Orange
Millard Fillmore	Abigail Caroline	010700	707 Powers Circle	Summerhill
Franklin Pierce	Jane	112304	2340 McIntosh Lane	Hillsboro
James Buchanan		042391	2362 Appleton Street	Mercersburg
Abraham Lincoln	Mary	021209	1284 Todd Court	Hodgenville
Andrew Johnson	Eliza	122908	12220 McCardle Avenue	Raleigh
Hiram Ulysses Simpson Grant	Julia	042722	4231 Dent Street	Point Pleasant
Rutherford Birchard Hayes	Lucy	100422	457 Webb Street	Delaware
James Abram Garfield	Lucretia	111931	1962 Rudolph Street	Orange
Chester Alan Arthur	Ellen	100531	1020 Herndon Drive	Fairfield
Stephen Grover Cleveland	Frances	031837	585 Folsom Street	Caldwell
Benjamin Harrison	Caroline Mary	082033	3861 Scott Parkway	North Bend
Steven Grover Cleveland	Frances	031837	7126 Dimmick Road	Caldwell
William McKinley	Ida	012943	8361 Saxton Street	Niles
Theodore Roosevelt	Alice Edith	102758	21587 Lee Expressway	New York
William Howard Taft	Helen	121557	1617 Carow Avenue	Cincinnati
Thomas Woodrow Wilson	Ellen Edith	122856	1027 Herron Street	Stauton
Warren Gamaliel Harding	Florence	110265	26 Axson Place	Blooming Grove
John Calvin Coolidge	Grace	070472	3071 Galt Road	Plymouth
Herbert Clark Hoover	Lou	081074	711 Kling Street	West Branch
Franklin Delano Roosevelt	Anna Elinor	012082	8531 Goodhue Circle	Hyde Park
Harry S. Truman	Elizabeth	050884	1032 Henry Way	Lamar
Dwight David Eisenhower	Mary	101490	1033 Roosevelt Street	Denison
John Fitzgerald Kennedy	Jacqueline	052917	4301 Daisy Drive	Brookline
Lyndon Baines Johnson	Claudia	pending	8246 Geneva Street	Gillespie
Richard Milhous Nixon	Thelma	010913	8 Taylor Terrace	Yorba Linda
Gerald Rudolph Ford	Elizabeth	071413	1037 Ryan Parkway	Omaha
James Earl Carter	Rosalynn	pending	3810 Wallace Street	Plains
Ronald Wilson Reagan	Nancy	020611	39 Moringlory Drive	Tampico
George Herbert Walker Bush	Barbara	pending	1600 Pennsylvania Avenue	Milton

FIG. 22.2

A spreadsheet listing membership information.

After analyzing these activities and the information in the spreadsheet, you define the following categories for fields in the data file:

- Member's name
- Spouse's name
- Address
- Telephone number
- Listed/unlisted status

State	ZIP Code	Telephone Number	Unlisted	Birthday	Date Admitted	Sponsor
VA	22677-0000	703/321-0222		02/22/32	05/04/86	Fed.
MA	02184-0023	615/444-0077		10/30/35	05/04/86	Fed.
VA	22970-7541	804/273-0481		04/13/43	05/04/86	Dem.-Rep.
VA	24471-1010	703/804-1710		03/16/31	05/28/86	Dem.-Rep.
VA	24574-6357	508/413-5707		04/28/38	04/04/91	Dem.-Rep.
MA	02167-0000	413/411-6704	U	07/11/37	08/23/86	Dem.-Rep.
SC	29408-4019	803/084-9408		03/15/37	06/08/86	Dem.
NY	12106-3702	212/315-5160		12/05/22	07/24/86	Dem.
VA	23030-1065	804/752-0480		02/09/13	04/04/91	Whig
VA	22067-1734	703/103-7360		03/29/17	01/18/91	Whig
NC	27602-5028	704/919-7016		11/02/45	06/15/90	Dem.
VA	22960-3115	413/502-7167		11/24/28	07/09/81	Whig
NY	12781-0707	812/306-5002		01/07/01	03/28/90	Whig
NH	03244-0632	603/107-3106		11/23/14	10/08/89	Dem.
PA	17236-2548	215/412-7178		04/23/11	06/01/88	Dem.
KY	42748-4010	216/419-5136		02/12/08	05/04/86	Rep.
NC	27602-0000	802/484-7256	U	12/29/08	07/31/87	Dem.-Rep.
OH	45163-1531	908/250-4840		04/27/28	07/23/88	Rep.
OH	43015-0077	609/671-6044		10/04/22	01/17/89	Rep.
OH	44453-6203	908/201-6968		11/19/31	09/19/88	Rep.
VT	05456-5824	802/512-8080		10/05/31	11/18/86	Rep.
N.I	07000-1004	201/609-9084		03/18/37	06/24/90	Dem.
OH	44057-5271	609/713-2706		08/20/33	03/13/91	Rep.
NJ	07006-1028	609/806-4117		03/18/37	04/24/91	Dem.
OH	44446-6002	908/409-6600		01/20/43	09/14/91	Rep.
NY	10001-3734	212/412-0397		10/27/28	05/04/86	Rep.
OH	45202-1765	609/555-7121		09/16/57	03/08/90	Rep.
VA	24401-0000	703/812-2175		12/28/56	02/03/91	Dem
OH	43106-6550	908/713-8608	U	11/02/05	08/02/89	Rep.
VT	05056-2837	802/951-4369		07/04/27	01/05/88	Rep.
IA	52358-0217	812/515-7124		08/10/47	10/20/87	Rep.
NY	12638-3410	212/618-7144		01/20/48	05/04/86	Dem.
MO	64769-6537	314/417-8162		05/08/48	12/26/90	Dem.
TX	75020-2871	214/409-5127		10/14/40	03/28/89	Rep.
MA	02147-4356	413/681-0003	U	05/29/17	05/04/86	Dem.
TX	78116-4447	915/399-7772		08/27/08	pending	Dem.
CA	92686-9923	415/833-9333	U	01/09/13	00/00/81	Rep.
NE	68502-1130	308/402-2748		07/14/13	01/21/87	Rep.
GA	31780-5333	404/912-4690	U	10/01/24	pending	Dem.
IL	61283-0000	217/309-3126		02/06/11	01/20/89	Rep.
MA	02187-7720	413/618-7099		06/12/24	pending	Rep.

- Birthday
- Membership anniversary
- Sponsoring organization
- Membership number

Depending on the record structure you choose for this information, you may want to break the address into separate fields (street address, city, state, and ZIP code).

The following sections of this chapter describe the terms, structures, and procedures you need to understand in order to create an appropriate data file for this information. Later in the chapter, you learn how to create the four different types of record format that WordPerfect uses for data files.

If possible, read these sections in order. Each section builds on the preceding sections and the common structural elements in a logical sequence that helps you to understand the concepts presented.

Understanding Basic Terms

A *database* is a collection of related information about any subject, organized in such a way that you can retrieve information, draw conclusions, and make decisions. A WordPerfect database is called a *data file*.

A WordPerfect data file is much like a drawer in a filing cabinet. Each file in the drawer contains sheets of paper with information about a particular subject (a *record*). If the file drawer contains membership files, for example, each file contains specific information about a particular member. In the same way, a record from the WordPerfect data file contains all the data about the subject of that record. Figure 22.3 points out an individual record in the WordPerfect data file shown earlier.

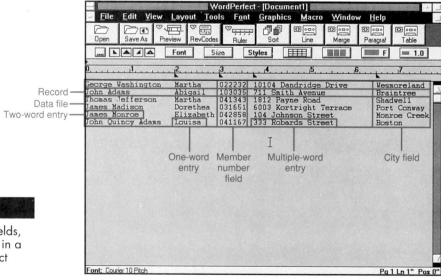

FIG. 22.3

Records, fields, and words in a WordPerfect data file.

Each file in the file drawer contains sheets of paper. For each member, for example, the membership file may contain a form with vital information about the member. This data corresponds to the *fields* in each record of a data file. The fields in a membership data file may include business address, phone number, marital status, and so on.

The smallest unit of information in a data file is a *word*. One character can comprise a word; for example, in the membership data file, the letter *M* in the Marital Status field can indicate that the member is married. Fields can contain more than one word, however; in an inventory data file, for example, a Tools field may include the entry *socket wrench*.

The structure you choose for your data file is called the *record substructure* or *record format*. WordPerfect uses four types of formats for data file records: *line*, *paragraph*, *merge*, and *table-row* format. Every record contains words, but the record's type determines whether that record has field, line, or cell substructures. These formats are explained in detail in the "Choosing a Record Format" section of this chapter.

You create a record format with WordPerfect *formatting codes*. Except for the *merge codes* used in merge records (described in detail in Chapter 21, "Assembling Documents with Merge"), you cannot see most data file formatting codes in the active document window unless you view the document with Reveal Codes. Figure 22.4 shows the formatting codes (in Reveal Codes) for a sample data file in line record format

■ **Cue:** To turn on Reveal Codes, choose **V**iew, Reveal **C**odes or press Reveal Codes (Alt-F3).

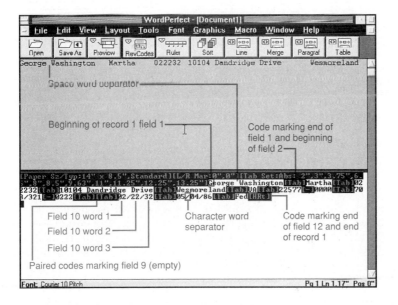

FIG. 22.4

Formatting codes for a data file in line record format.

Defining a record is the process of arranging and entering data on a subject in the proper record structure. When you *manipulate records*, you use WordPerfect's Sort feature to examine, extract, and rearrange information from the data file.

Understanding Formatting Codes

When you type two or more words in a field, you generally press the space bar to separate the words. No code appears for the space on-screen; WordPerfect shows a blank area between the words.

To separate some fields, you press the Tab key. When you enter the last name Smith in one field, press Tab, and enter the first name Alice in the next field, WordPerfect displays the following in Reveal Codes:

    Smith[Tab]Alice

The [Tab] formatting code creates a space that appears in the active document window as a blank between words. When the last word in one field appears close to the first word in the next field, you can determine whether the separation between the two words is created by a space or a hidden [Tab] code only if you use Reveal Codes.

T I P   A common mistake is relying on a word's image in the active document window to determine its location within a record. When WordPerfect sorts or selects data in a data file, the software acts on the record's actual format, not its screen image; use Reveal Codes to find the location of the formatting code or data you want to edit.

Organizing and Formatting Your Data

The physical size of a file drawer limits the number of files you can place in it. Similarly, the amount of storage space available on your computer's disk(s) limits the number of records you can store in a data file. On a system with a large hard disk, you can (theoretically) create one data file with millions of records; as a practical matter, however, your data files should be only as large as necessary to include all required information.

The order of the field sequence you use for your records doesn't matter to WordPerfect. You can place the ZIP code in the first field, for example, and the street address in the second field. Creating and editing records is easier, however, if you use a logical field sequence so that related units follow each other.

WordPerfect performs sorting and selecting operations by analyzing the individual words in each record. Regardless of the record format you use to create a data file, you must enter the data in each record in a manner consistent with other records in the file. If the first field in one record is a last name field, the first field in *every* record in that file must contain a last name, or no entry.

If you must skip a field because no entry is appropriate, press the Tab key (or other field-separator key) twice to leave a blank space in that field and move to the next field. In Reveal Codes, you see the code repeated ([Tab][Tab], for example) for each skipped field.

Formatting Dates

Consistent data entry includes using the same format for information that can be expressed in more than one way. To you, for example, the following expressions convey the same meaning:

> January 14, 1992
> 01/14/92

To WordPerfect, however, the expressions are different. Suppose that you have a data file that includes the following dates in separate records:

> January 21, 1992
> Apr. 24, 1992
> 06/03/92
> 07/26/92
> 08/26/1992

If you define a default sorting operation to place the dates in chronological sequence, WordPerfect arranges the dates in the following order:

> 08/26/1991
> Apr. 24, 1991
> January 21, 1991
> 06/03/91
> 07/26/91

Cue: You cannot use a format such as October 26, 1992, or Oct. 26, 1992, where the month name is spelled out, because the Sort feature cannot arrange the names of months in chronological order.

If you type all the dates in a uniform numeric format (08-26-92, 08/26/92, or 08/26/1992), however, WordPerfect manipulates the dates correctly.

Formatting Text

In the active document window of figure 22.5, the records appear to have a uniform structure. When you examine the records in Reveal Codes, however (shown in the lower half of the figure), you can see that the words aren't arranged in a uniform format. The Pierce and Lincoln records have three words in one field, and the Fillmore, Buchanan, and Johnson records have the same type of information divided into two fields—the first containing two words (the first and last names) and the second containing one word (a six-digit membership number).

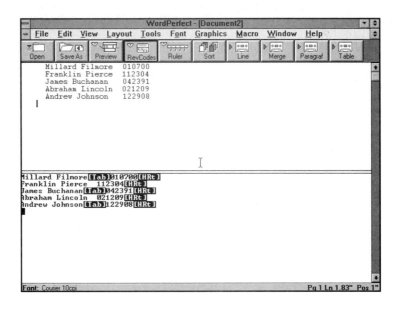

FIG. 22.5

Records with
inconsistent
formatting.

Because the formatting in this example is inconsistent, sorting alphabetically by last name or extracting records by membership number is impossible. Later in this chapter, you learn how to create record structures that help avoid this problem.

Another formatting problem involves separate words that WordPerfect must treat as one word, such as the two-part name Van Buren. The space between Van and Buren causes WordPerfect to treat each word as an individual unit. You can handle this problem in one of two ways.

One solution (usually the easiest) is to enter first and last names in separate fields. When you use this method, WordPerfect has no difficulty sorting and selecting by last name, even with last names that include multiple words. With this method, you can assign middle names to a separate field, or include them as separate words in the first name field.

A second solution takes advantage of formatting codes and characters that visually separate two or more words but that WordPerfect treats as regular characters. These codes and characters include the hard space (Ctrl-space bar), backslash (\ ), and dash character (Ctrl-hyphen).

CAUTION: Avoid confusing the hard space with the space, the backslash (\ ) with the forward slash (/), and the dash character (Ctrl-hyphen) with the hyphen (hyphen). WordPerfect recognizes the space, forward slash, and hyphen as characters that separate words.

For the Van Buren example, the hard space is a good solution. When you press Ctrl-space bar, WordPerfect inserts a [HdSpc] code (visible only in Reveal Codes) between the words. The two words appear to be separated by a blank space in the active document window, but all WordPerfect features except printing treat the two words as a unit.

■ **Cue:** If you use a hard space, the Sort feature cannot operate on the word following the hard space. Use this method only if you don't need WordPerfect to arrange and extract records based on the word following the hard space.

Choosing a Record Format

A data file can contain all four record structures (line, paragraph, merge, and table-row formats). As a practical matter, however, you should keep all records of the same type together in consecutive order because the Sort feature can operate on only one type of record structure at a time. Unless the information in your data file occupies only a few pages, generally you can sort and select records more easily if you limit a data file to one type of record.

To choose the record format, begin by analyzing the data you want to store, and consider how you will use the data after you place it in the data file. Regardless of the record format you choose, you must place the same type of information into the same field, cell, or line location in each record to get the correct results with the Sort feature.

■ **Cue:** Almost any text file contains one or more of the record formats recognized by WordPerfect's Sort feature, even if you didn't intend to use that document as a data file.

The next four sections describe the four WordPerfect record formats for a data file.

Line Records

A line record contains all its fields on one line. The smallest line record contains a one-character word in one field. A field's maximum size is the number of characters that fit on one line between the left and right margins. The available space between margins also determines the maximum number of fields you can define for a line record.

T I P   Many users mistakenly believe that the line record's simple structure is for records containing only a few words in a few fields. In reality, you can use line records to meet most of your data file needs.

A primary advantage of the line record format over the paragraph and merge record structures is that line record fields generally align in columns. Seeing the data on the preceding line may remind you of the type of information that belongs in the current field. In each field of the first record, you also can enter a field heading or description of the type of data in that field.

Paragraph Records

A paragraph record provides a flexible structure for storing information that varies in size from a one-character word to thousands of words. Unlike the line record format, a paragraph record can contain an almost unlimited number of lines spread over many pages. Each line can be subdivided into the same types of fields used in line records, with the words in a field spanning one or more lines.

Simple Paragraph Records

A simple paragraph record spans one or more lines but lacks formatting codes to separate the lines into more than one field. (This paragraph is an example of a paragraph record containing multiple lines, each with only one field.) The flexible formatting of the paragraph record makes it a good choice if your data file includes unstructured information, such as notes or observations about the subjects of the records.

Figure 22.6 shows a simple paragraph record format.

In figure 22.6, the paragraph record contains eight lines. The left margin marks the beginning of each line; the [SRt] code marks the end of each of the first seven lines. The first of the two [HRt] formatting codes marks the end of the eighth line, and the second [HRt] formatting code marks the end of the record.

CAUTION: The combined [HRt][HRt] codes marking the end of a record act as a unit. Removing one code causes inaccurate record manipulation.

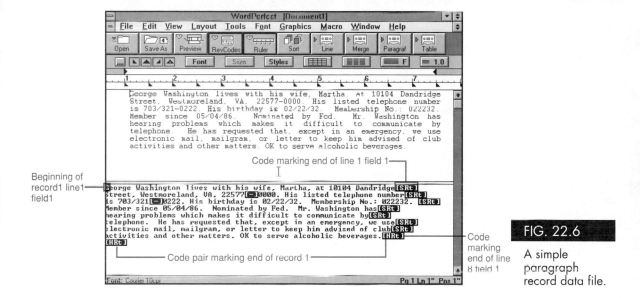

FIG. 22.6

A simple
paragraph
record data file.

The double [HRt] codes impose a major limitation on using the paragraph record format. All lines must contain data or at least one hidden formatting code. A blank, single-field line creates the [HRt][HRt] code combination that the Sort feature interprets as the end of a paragraph record. With a single [HRt] code, the Sort feature treats the paragraph record as two records—at best, separating the record's information and, at worst, causing loss of data.

If you know in advance that some of your records have one or more fields for which no data is available, design the paragraph record so that these fields aren't used as one-field lines. When you type data into a paragraph record and discover that no data is available for a one-field line, don't leave the field empty. Type **none** or some other word into the line.

If you don't want the field to contain any data, you can press Tab and divide the line into two empty fields. This method enables WordPerfect to manipulate the record as a unit, but adding the extra field doesn't alter the appearance of the blank line on-screen. Sorting and selecting operations on this record may be inaccurate, however, if you later insert data into the field without deleting the hidden [Tab] code.

Multiple-Field Paragraph Records

Because of the random nature of the data in a paragraph record, sorting and selecting records is difficult. To solve this problem, you can create a multiple-field paragraph record. The multiple-field paragraph record uses the structure of a line record with one important difference—the paragraph record can contain multiple lines, each of which contains multiple fields. Figure 22.7 shows the format for a paragraph record that includes fixed-field lines.

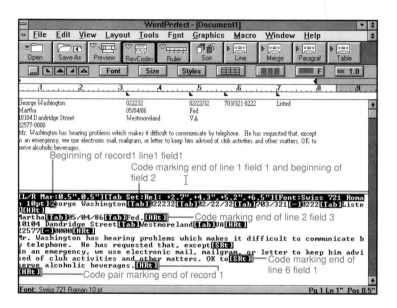

FIG. 22.7

A complex paragraph record.

Except for the last field, WordPerfect locates each field in this example by the [Tab] code following the last character in the last word in the field. ([Tab] is the code most commonly used for this purpose, but you also can use other codes.) The beginning of a line can be at the left margin, or follow the [Indent] or [Indent][Mar Rel] formatting code.

The most complex type of multiple-field paragraph record contains a hanging indent at the beginning of a line. This format is ideal for maintaining a bibliographic data file. Figure 22.8 shows (in Reveal Codes) the structure for this type of paragraph record.

Merge Records

The merge record format is similar to the paragraph record format; this flexible format enables you to store variable information ranging in size from a one-character word to thousands of words.

In a business setting, the merge record format is used most often to manipulate customer, client, or employee data with WordPerfect's Merge feature. The fields in merge records are defined by merge formatting codes.

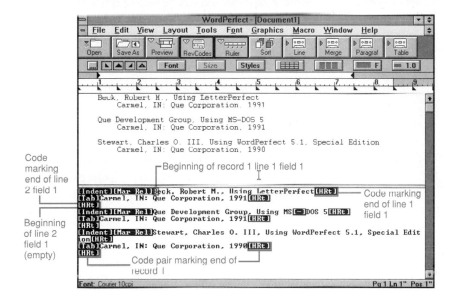

Code marking end of line 2 field 1

Beginning of record 1 line 1 field 1

Code marking end of line 1 field 1

Beginning of line 2 field 1 (empty)

Code pair marking end of record 1

FIG. 22.8

Format for a bibliographic paragraph record.

In addition to different formatting codes, the merge record format uses a special structure. In a merge record, the field is the primary substructure; the line is the secondary substructure of the field. WordPerfect line-wrapping codes mark each line end within a field.

Figure 22.9 shows the structure of a merge record in Reveal Codes.

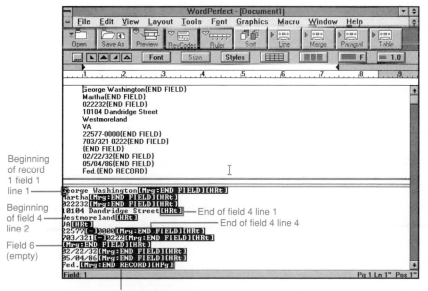

Beginning of record 1 field 1 line 1

Beginning of field 4 line 2

Field 6 (empty)

End of field 4 line 1

End of field 4 line 4

FIG. 22.9

The basic format of a merge record.

Code marking end of field 9 line 1 and end of record 1

■ **Cue:** Because other record formats are fixed, you can create a macro to edit other types of records into merge record format.

Each field can contain a one-character word on one line or thousands of words in lines covering many pages. Regardless of the merge record's internal size, however, its formatting codes prevent you from placing more than one record on a physical page.

For more information on using the Merge feature, see Chapter 21, "Assembling Documents with Merge."

Table-Row Records

The table-row record format combines the best aspects of the other three types of records. At its most basic level, a table-row format data file appears to be a group of connected cells. The smallest table-row record contains a one-character word in one cell.

■ **Cue:** To use the Print Preview feature, choose Print Preview from the File menu or press Print Preview (Shift-F5).

Figure 22.10 shows how a typical table-row record appears in the active window and in Reveal Codes. Figure 22.11 shows the same data file displayed with WordPerfect's Print Preview feature.

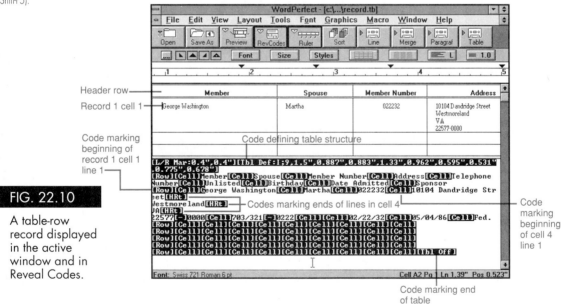

FIG. 22.10

A table-row record displayed in the active window and in Reveal Codes.

The *cell* is the table-row record's primary substructure. You cannot alter or delete a cell by accidentally pressing the space bar, the Del key, or any of the keys that insert tabular formatting codes.

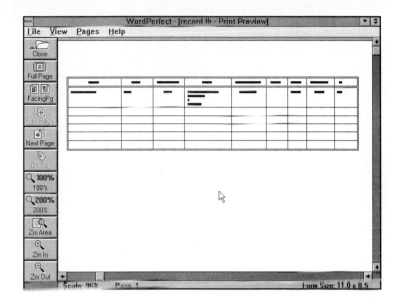

FIG. 22.11

Table-row records dis-played by Print Preview.

Creating a Data File

The only rigid rule for using the Sort feature easily and effectively is that your data files must be organized in a record structure. To get accurate results when sorting and selecting, your files must contain the same type of data in the same substructure in each record.

Each WordPerfect record format—line, paragraph, merge, and table row—has advantages and disadvantages compared to the other record formats. As shown in the figures earlier in this chapter, for example, the line record has the simplest structure, and the table-row record has the most complex structure.

To choose an appropriate format, analyze the data you want to keep in the data file—for example, the data from the President's Club. Also consider how you plan to use the data after you enter it into the data file.

The next four sections describe how to create a simple data file with each of the four record formats.

Creating a Line Record

In the following sections you learn how to create the line record data file shown in figure 22.12. As the figure shows, formatting codes separate each field in the line record. The first field isn't preceded by a

[Tab] code; the field begins at the left margin. The end of the record is indicated by a [HRt] following the last field. All other fields in the record are separated by the [Tab] code. Note that the address field contains three words; spaces separate the words. In the phone number field, a forward slash separates the area code and prefix, and a hyphen separates the prefix and suffix.

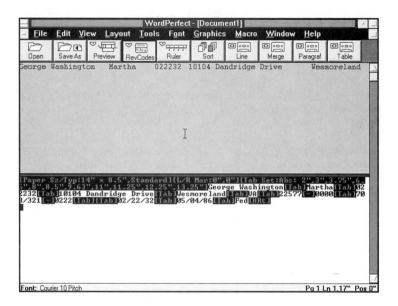

FIG. 22.12

A data file with a line record structure.

The following table shows the formatting codes used in line record formats:

Field-Separating Codes	End-of-Record Codes
[Tab]	[HRt]
[TAB]	[HRt-SPg]
[Cntr Tab]	[HPg]
[Rgt Tab]	[DSRt]
[Dec Tab]	[HyphSrt]
[Flsh Rgt]	[SRt]
[Indent]	

WordPerfect alters the appearance and function of [HRt] to [HRt-SPg] if the code is at the end of the last line on a page or at the beginning of the first line of the following page. The [DSRt], [HyphSRt], and [Cnt] codes appear when words exceed the physical limits of a line. The [SRt] code marks the end of a line record, for example, and the Sort feature treats all words following that code as a separate record. The hyphenation soft return ([HyphSRt]) and deletable soft return ([DSRt]) codes visually separate a word across two or more lines, but the Sort feature ignores the split and treats the word as the last word of the line on which the word begins.

Increasing the Number of Characters in the Line

If you produce documents with a fixed-pitch font (such as Courier 10-point) on 8 1/2-by-11-inch paper, you may think that your line record is limited to 85 characters (with margins at 0 inches). Even with 14-by-8 1/2-inch paper and a landscape format, the line record you can create increases to only 140 characters. You can use a simulated-printer technique, however, to increase the number of characters.

Set your margins at 0; then select a WordPerfect printer definition for any printer with built-in fonts smaller than Courier 10-point. (The IBM 4019 LaserPrinter page definition, for example, includes a built-in Courier 16.66 cpi font. This definition and a landscape form increase the maximum number of characters to 230 per line record.) Use this printer definition to create a 14-by-8 1/2-inch landscape page definition for your line record data file.

For more information, see Chapter 9, "Basic Printing"; Chapter 10, "Working with Fonts"; Chapter 11, "Formatting Pages and Designing Documents"; and Chapter 20, "Creating Macros."

With some dot-matrix printer definitions that have built-in fonts, you can use this technique with a small proportionally spaced font to increase the maximum number of characters to several hundred per record.

If you cannot fit your data on one line even with the adjusted printer definition, a less reliable method is available for line records with large amounts of data. When you enter the data, allow the information in the last field of each record to wrap to more than one line. Then, when you need to manipulate the data, use WordPerfect's Replace feature to add an extra [HRt] code at the end of each record. This action temporarily gives your line records the format of paragraph records (which can include multiple-line fields). Use the Sort feature's paragraph-record settings to manipulate your data file. (Afterward, you can restore the original format of your data file with another macro.)

■ **Cue:** If you use the simulated-printer method and later decide that you need to print the data file, create a macro to rearrange the data into a format your printer can handle.

CAUTION: You can use the [HRt] technique safely only when the data in the last field wraps to other lines.

Creating the Format

Using the standard printer definition, create the following format for the data file:

- 14.0" by 8.5" landscape printer size/type form
- Left and right margins set at 0.0"
- Courier 10 cpi font

Cue: When choosing tab settings, define each tab stop to begin at least 0.1 inch to the right of the last character in the preceding field.

After you define the format for the page, you must establish tab settings for the fields. Select 11 settings instead of 12; [Tab] codes mark the ends of the first 11 fields, but a hard return marks the end of the last field.

For fields containing words with a fixed number of characters—such as the ZIP code or telephone number fields—you know the exact number of characters and the space required. For fields containing variable-length words, however, because you don't know the maximum number of characters, you must make an educated guess.

CAUTION: If you define a field too narrowly and type information in one field that extends into the next field, sorting and selecting operations may not work properly.

In the President's Club data file, the following fields contain words of a set length: member number, state, ZIP code, telephone number, unlisted status, and date admitted. Six fields contain words of variable length, of which three fields—member's name, spouse's name, and street address—have the potential for greatest variation in word size. Assign these fields the most space.

For the sample line record data file shown in figure 22.12, follow these steps to set the tabs:

1. Choose **L**ayout, **L**ine.

   CUA Press Layout Line (Shift-F9).

2. Choose **T**ab Set.

3. Define the tab settings shown in the following table:

Field	Left Edge (Abs)
Member's name	none
Spouse's name	2.0"
Membership number	3.0"
Street address	3.8"
City	6.5"
State	8.0"
ZIP code	8.5"
Telephone number	9.6"
Unlisted	11.0"
Birthday	11.2"
Date admitted	12.2"
Sponsor	13.2"

Adding the Data

When the tab settings are complete, you type the data in the fields. Begin typing at the left margin (the beginning of the first field in the record). To add data to the line record data file, follow these steps:

1. Beginning at the left margin, type the data for the first field. For this example, type **George Washington**.

2. Press Tab.

3. Type the data for the second field. For this example, type **Martha**.

4. Press Tab.

5. Continue typing data as shown in figure 22.12, pressing Tab when you complete each field, until you finish typing the data for the last field. Instead of pressing Tab to end the field, press Enter. WordPerfect inserts the hidden [HRt] code to identify the end of the record.

6. When you finish entering the data in the record, save the data file. For this example, save the file with the name RECORD.LN.

Note: If you want a larger file for sorting and selecting later in this chapter, enter more data from the President's Club example in figure 22.2.

The line-ending formatting codes [HRt], [HRt-SPg], or [HPg] (hard page) mark the end of the last field on a line. If you type past the end of the line or page, WordPerfect inserts [SRt] or [SPg] as line-ending codes. The Sort feature recognizes these codes as markers for the end of a line record. With these codes, related data can be split to a second line.

> **CAUTION:**   If you use the Sort feature to manipulate line records ending with a [SRt] code, the related information split by the code may be fragmented or lost during the sorting and selecting operations.

In some circumstances, WordPerfect inserts deletable soft return ([DSRt]) or hyphenation soft return ([HyphSRt]) formatting codes that appear to split a word into two separate line records. The word spans two lines, but WordPerfect ignores these codes and treats the two lines as one record.

Creating a Paragraph Record

In this section you learn how to create the paragraph record data file shown in figure 22.13.

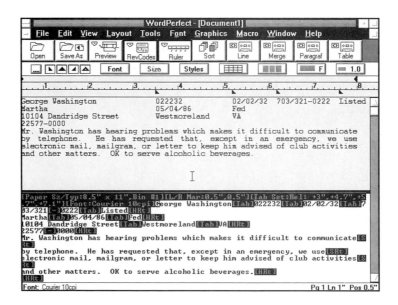

FIG. 22.13

A data file with a paragraph record structure.

The following table shows the formatting codes you can use as field, line, and end-of-record indicators.

Field-Separating Codes	End-of-Line Codes	End-of-Record Codes
[Tab]	[SRt]	[HRt][HRt]
[TAB]	[SPg]	[HRt][HRt-SPg]
[Indent][Mar Rel]	[HyphSRt]	[HRt][Dorm HRt]
[Cntr Tab]	[DSRt]	[HRt-SPg][Dorm HRt]
[Rgt Tab]	[HRt]	[HRt][HPg]
[Dec Tab]	[HRt-SPg]	[HPg][Dorm HRt]
[Indent]	[HPg]	
[Flsh Rgt]		

WordPerfect creates the [SRt], [SPg], [HyphSRt], and [DSRt] codes when the words exceed the physical limits of a line. The [HyphSRt] and [DSRt] codes visually separate a word across two or more lines, but the Sort feature ignores the splitting and treats the word as the last word of the line on which it begins.

WordPerfect alters the appearance and function of dual [HRt] codes to [HRt][HRt-SPg], [HRt][Dorm HRt], [HRt-SPg][Dorm HRt], [HRt-SPg], or [HPg][Dorm HRt] if the code is at the end of the last line on a page or at the beginning of the first line of the following page.

Use the following format to create the paragraph record data file in figure 22.13:

- 8.5" by 11" portrait printer size/type form
- Left and right margins set at 0.5"
- Courier 10 cpi font
- Left Margin (Rel) tabs at 3.0", 4.5", 5.5", and 7.0"

Follow these steps to enter the data in the paragraph record:

1. Beginning at the left margin (the beginning of the first field in the record); type the data for the first field. For this example, type **George Washington**.

2. Press Tab.

3. Type the data for the second field. For this example, type **022232**.

4. Press Tab.

5. Type **02/22/32** and press Tab.

6. Type **703/321–0222** and press Tab.

7. Type **Listed** and press Enter.

8. Using the appropriate formatting codes, continue typing the data as shown in figure 22.13. Be sure to press Enter twice to insert the dual [HRt][HRt] codes that mark the end of the paragraph record.

9. When you finish entering the data in the record, save the data file. For this example, save the file with the name RECORD.PG.

Note: To create a larger file (for sorting and selecting later in this chapter), enter more data from the President's Club example (shown in fig. 22.2).

Creating a Merge Record

In this section you learn how to create the merge record data file shown in figure 22.14.

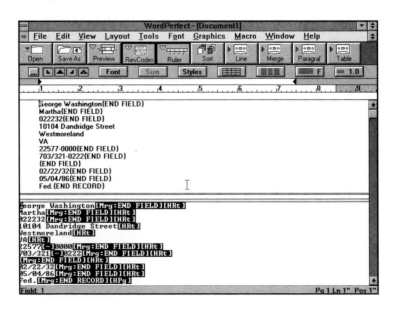

FIG. 22.14

A merge record data file.

In figure 22.14, the first three fields contain single lines defined by the left margin and the {END FIELD} code, which Reveal Codes displays as a [Mrg:END FIELD] code followed by the [HRt] code. The fourth field contains four lines—the [HRt] code marks the end of the first three lines, and the [Mrg:END FIELD] code marks the end of the fourth line and the field. One {END FIELD} code marks the location of field 6, which is empty. The {END RECORD} code—which Reveal Codes displays as the [Mrg:END RECORD] code followed by the [HPg] code—marks the end of the last field and the record.

WordPerfect manipulates records properly even if you accidentally delete the [HRt] code following the {END FIELD} code or the [HPg] following the {END RECORD} code. No safety net exists, however, if you accidentally delete an {END FIELD} or {END RECORD} code. Removing either code causes inaccurate record manipulation. If you delete the {END FIELD} code, for example, WordPerfect treats that field's lines as part of the next field. In the same manner, removing the record's {END RECORD} code causes WordPerfect to treat the record as additional fields in the following record.

The following table shows the formatting codes for a merge record format:

Substructure	Code Shown in Active Window	Code Shown in Reveal Codes
End of field	{END FIELD}	[Mrg:END FIELD][HRt]
End of record	{END RECORD}	[Mrg:END RECORD][HPg]
End of line	none	[SRt]
	none	[SPg]
	none	[HyphSRt]
	none	[DSRt]
	none	[HRt]
	none	[HRt-SPg]
	none	[HPg]

WordPerfect creates the [SRt], [SPg], [HyphSRt], and [DSRt] codes when the words exceed the physical limits of a line. The [HyphSRt] and [DSRt] codes visually separate a word across two or more lines, but the Sort feature ignores the splitting and treats the word as the last word of the line on which it begins.

WordPerfect alters the appearance and function of [HRt] to [HRt-SPg] if the code is at the end of the last line on a page or at the beginning of the first line of the following page.

T   I   P   In WordPerfect for Windows, you can manipulate data files containing merge codes used by older versions of WordPerfect for DOS. These files use the ^R[HRt] code combination to end fields and the ^E[HPg] code combination to end records.

Data files containing merge records don't require special formatting codes to begin creating the file. To create the merge record data file shown in figure 23.14, follow these steps:

1. Beginning at the left margin (the beginning of the first field in the record), type the data for the first field. For this example, type **George Washington**.

2. Choose **Tools**, **Merge**, **End** of Field to insert the [Mrg:END FIELD][HRt] code combination that marks the end of the first field.

    Press Merge End of Field (Alt-Enter).

3. Type the data for the second field. For this example, type **Martha**.

4. Choose **Tools**, **Merge**, **End** of Field to insert the [Mrg:END FIELD][HRt] code combination.

    Press Merge End of Field (Alt-Enter).

5. Continue typing data as shown in figure 22.14.

   If necessary, use the hard space (Ctrl-space bar) to separate two words that you want WordPerfect to treat as one word (such as Van Buren).

   When a field contains more than one line, press Enter after typing each component of the field. For an address field, for example, type each part of the address (street address, city, state, and ZIP code) on a separate line, pressing Enter at the end of each line.

6. When you finish typing the last field in the record, choose **Tools**, **Merge**, **End R**ecord to insert the [Mrg:END RECORD][HPg] codes that mark the end of the merge record.

    Press Merge End of Record (Shift-Alt-Enter).

7. Save the data file with the name RECORD.MG.

Note: Enter more data from the President's Club example (refer to fig. 22.2) if you want a larger data file for the sorting and selecting sections of this chapter.

Creating a Table-Row Record

WordPerfect's Sort feature treats each table row in the table-row record format as one record in much the same way as a line record. The arrangement of data within a cell is identical to the structure of fields and lines in a merge record.

In this section you learn how to create the table-row record data file shown in figure 22.15.

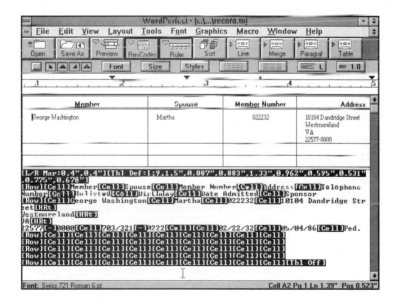

A table-row record data file.

A *cell* is the primary substructure in the table-row record. A *table row* is a horizontal row of cells; each cell can contain many lines. Each vertical row of cells is called a *column*.

A *word* is the smallest unit of information within a cell; a space, forward slash (/), or hyphen separates words in the cell. WordPerfect recognizes two types of words: alphanumeric and numeric. An *alphanumeric word* consists of letters, numbers, and symbols, including the hard space (Ctrl-space bar), backslash (\), and dash character (Ctrl-hyphen). Following are examples of alphanumeric words (separated by semicolons):

George Washington; Martha; February 22, 1932; § 1024

A *numeric word* consists of one or more numerals and certain characters usually associated with numbers, such as the dollar sign ($), comma, and period. You use numeric words primarily for sorting number strings of unequal length. Following are examples of numeric words (separated by semicolons):

$1,000.00; 022232; 15,836

The [Tbl Def:*definition*] code defines the table's cells, rows, and columns. The [Row] code separates the rows of the record. The [Cell] code separates the cells within a row. Except for the last line in a cell, a [HRt] or [SRt] code marks the end of a line within the cell. The [Tbl Off] code marks the end of the last line in the last cell and the end of the table structure. (For more information on creating a table with WordPerfect's Table feature, see Chapter 14, "Working with Tables.")

The following table lists the formatting codes used in table-row record formats:

Structure	Formatting Code
Beginning of table	[Tbl Def:*definition*]
Beginning of row	[Row] [Hrd Row] (Ctrl-Enter)
Beginning or end of cell	[Cell]
Last cell in row	[Row]
Last cell in table	[Tbl Off]
Beginning or end of line	[Cell]
End of line	[SRt] [SPg] [HyphSRt] [DSRt] [HRt] [HRt-SPg]
Last line in cell at end of row	[Row] [Hrd Row]
Last line in last cell in table	[Tbl Off]
End of table	[Tbl Off]

WordPerfect's Table feature creates the [Tbl Def:*definition*], [Row], [Cell], and [Tbl Off] codes when creating the table structure. You cannot edit or delete the individual codes.

WordPerfect creates the [SRt], [SPg], [HyphSRt], and [DSRt] codes when the words exceed the physical limits of a line. The [HyphSRt] and [DSRt] codes visually separate a word across two or more lines, but the Sort feature ignores the splitting and treats the word as the last word of the line on which it begins.

WordPerfect alters the appearance and function of [HRt] if the code is at the end of the last line on a page or at the beginning of the first line of the following page.

A cell's maximum possible width is the distance between the left and right margins of the document. A cell's maximum possible height is the distance between the top and bottom margins. The maximum number of characters on a line and the maximum number of lines in a cell are determined by the active base font.

Theoretically, a table can have a maximum of 32,765 table-row records, each with 32 cells containing many lines. As a practical matter, however, even a small table requires significantly more RAM and disk space than the other types of data files containing the same number of words and records. The programming codes WordPerfect uses to create the table structure impose the additional memory requirements.

To use a data file containing a table with row records, you begin by creating the table structure. To create the table-row data file shown in figure 22.15, follow these steps:

1. Select a printer definition that includes proportionally spaced fonts.

2. Choose the smallest font available for the printer definition.

3. Use the Table feature to create a table with 9 columns and 41 rows. The top row is defined as a header row.

4. Move the insertion point into cell A1 (the first cell in the table) and type the data for the first cell. For this example, type **George Washington**.

5. Move the insertion point into cell B1 (the next cell to the right of cell A1) and type the data for the second cell. For this example, type **Martha**.

6. Continue moving the insertion point to each adjacent cell to the right and enter the remaining data for the first record.

   The address data in cell D1 contains four lines. Press Enter at the ends of the first three lines in this cell. You need not press Enter at the end of the last (fourth) line.

7. Save the data file with the name RECORD.TB.

Note: To use a larger file for sorting and selecting purposes later in this chapter, enter more data from the President's Club example (again see fig. 22.2).

Now you are ready to use WordPerfect's Sort feature to manipulate records. In the next sections, you learn how to arrange and extract records with the Sort feature.

Sorting Data File Records

The Sort feature's two functions—sorting and selecting—give you the power to manipulate data in your documents and to use the data with other WordPerfect functions, such as the Merge feature. You can define conditions that use these functions separately or together to examine, rearrange, and extract data in the active document window.

The *sorting* function organizes records alphabetically or numerically. The *selecting* function filters data to include or exclude records matching parameters that you define. You can sort records without defining selection parameters or select records without sorting them, but many times you may want to use both functions in one data-manipulation operation.

The *output data file* is the document remaining after the Sort feature manipulates the records. The content of the output data file depends on the conditions you define and varies from no records to all records in their original sequence.

■ **Cue:** WordPerfect can sort and select symbols that aren't part of the U.S. English character set (for example, letters in foreign languages) when you use a WordPerfect Language Module that includes those characters.

A *sorting operation* arranges the records in your data file alphabetically or numerically in ascending or descending order. A *selecting operation* (or *extraction operation*) examines each record in the data file and extracts those records matching the defined parameters for the operation. A *sorting-and-selecting operation* analyzes each record in the data file, extracts records matching defined parameters, and arranges the extracted records in a specified order.

A confusing aspect of the Sort feature is the term *select*, which has been used for years in the DOS versions of WordPerfect to describe data extraction operations. Standard Windows terminology uses the same word to describe the act of highlighting text before performing editing operations (*selecting* text). To avoid confusion, this section uses the term "highlight" to describe the process of specifying text in the data file that you want WordPerfect to sort or select.

> To get accurate results, your files must contain the same type of data in the same format in each record.   **T I P**

Understanding Size Limitations

The size of your data file can affect WordPerfect's operating speed. The Sort feature can process a small data file in seconds, but processing a large file may require minutes.

The Sort feature takes significantly longer to manipulate data formatted in table-row records. A sorting operation involving 100 table-row records arranged in 12 single-line cells, for example, can take 5 to 6 times longer than a sorting operation on the identical information arranged in line records. Unless you use a fast computer with large amounts of RAM and disk space, or you are more concerned with accuracy and ease of data entry than with the amount of time required for record manipulation, consider using a record structure other than the table-row format for data files with more than 100 records.

■ **Cue:** Keep your data files as small as possible to ensure the fastest record processing.

This section uses the President's Club example (shown in figure 22.2) to show how to sort data file records. Assume that the President's Club is publishing a private membership directory and needs a list of members arranged in ascending alphabetical order. The next sections describe how to access the Sort dialog box, define the parameters, and execute the sort operation to create a list.

Specifying the Records To Sort

You can sort some of or all the records in the data file. When you want WordPerfect to sort only specified records in the data file, use the Select feature to highlight those records (which must be arranged in consecutive sequence) before accessing the Sort dialog box.

The Sort feature moves hidden formatting codes with the records to which the codes are attached. For this reason, you should always use the Select feature to highlight any records (except table-row records) following hidden document-formatting codes. Begin highlighting immediately to the right of the last hidden document-formatting code. The reason is that when the first record moves from its original position, taking the document formatting, all records above that record's new location use the default document formatting. If you don't highlight the records before using the Sort feature, the data output file may contain improperly formatted records after data manipulation.

> **T I P** You can use a line record at the top of your data file to hold headings describing the data file contents. When you highlight the records to sort, however, don't highlight the line record, or WordPerfect will attempt to sort that information with the rest of the records.

For the President's Club example, retrieve the RECORD.LN file (created earlier in this chapter) in the active document window. If the first record begins with hidden document-formatting codes or is a descriptive line, use WordPerfect's Select feature to highlight all the records, excluding the hidden formatting codes or descriptive line.

Accessing the Sort Dialog Box

Before you can access the Sort dialog box, you must have a data file in the active document window. Unlike the DOS versions, WordPerfect for Windows' Sort feature cannot access the system's hard disk and floppy disk(s) to manipulate data.

WARNING: Always save the data file as a document on disk before manipulating it with the Sort feature. Because the Sort feature cannot access disk drives, the results of data-manipulation operations replace the original data file in the main document window. If you don't save the data file as a document on disk, sorting and selecting operations can cause the loss of some or all data in the data file.

■ **Cue:** Save your data file before accessing the Sort dialog box.

WordPerfect shows all the Sort feature's options in the Sort dialog box. Follow these steps to access the Sort dialog box:

1. Retrieve or create a data file in the main document window.

2. Choose **Tools, Sort**.

 Press Sort (Ctrl-Shift-F12).

WordPerfect displays the Sort dialog box, as shown in figure 22.16.

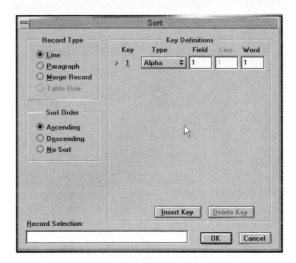

FIG. 22.16

The Sort dialog
box.

Defining the Sort Parameters

The Sort dialog box is divided into four areas—Record Type, Sort Order, Key Definitions, and Record Selection. On first access of the Sort
dialog box in an editing session, the dialog box shows the default line
record parameters shown earlier (see fig. 22.16), unless the insertion
point is in a table-row record. In that case, the default record type is
Table Row; its Key 1 definition lists Cell, Line, and Word with values of
1 in each text box.

When you access the Sort dialog box again, the parameters you defined
for the last record manipulation appear in the dialog box as defaults.

If you use the keyboard instead of a mouse to navigate the Sort dialog
box, press the Tab (forward) and Shift-Tab (backward) keys to move
between the areas of the screen and the individual options.

 **Cue:** If the main docu-
ment window appears blank
but the Sort dialog box
appears, the window
contains at least one hidden
formatting code.

CAUTION: If you switch to WordPerfect for Windows from a DOS
version, you may be accustomed to typing a number
and pressing Enter to move the cursor to the next option. Pressing Enter while defining parameters for the
Sort feature in WordPerfect for Windows immediately
begins record manipulation with the existing parameters.

Choosing OK or pressing Enter starts the data-manipulation operation.
By default, the OK button is active, a status indicated by its darkened

edges; if you press Enter, WordPerfect immediately begins manipulating records with the existing parameters. Press Esc to stop the definition process and display the active document window.

When you define the Record Type, Sort Order, and Key Definitions sections of the screen, the sequence you use doesn't matter. (The fourth section of the dialog box, Record Selection, is explained in the "Defining Selection Parameters" section of this chapter.)

Sort Order Options

The options in the Sort Order section determine whether WordPerfect arranges the records in Ascending or Descending order. If you choose the No Sort option, the Sort feature performs only selecting operations, and the records extracted to the output file retain the sort order of the original data file. Table 22.1 shows the sort order WordPerfect uses for alphanumeric sort operations. Each section of the table (Ascending Order and Descending Order) reads from top to bottom and then left to right.

WordPerfect arranges alphanumeric words according to their ASCII numeric values, except for letters, which are arranged together regardless of case (A followed by a, B by b, and so on).

T   I   P   You can sort numbers alphanumerically if all the numbers have the same number of digits (telephone numbers, Social Security numbers, and so on). If the number of digits varies between records (ages, monetary amounts, and so on), sort numerically to arrange the numbers according to arithmetic value.

For the President's Club example, set the Sort Order to Ascending.

Record Selection

The Record Selection option defines the conditions used by the WordPerfect to extract records from the data file. Record selection is discussed in more detail later in this chapter.

Table 22.1. Alphanumeric Sorting Priorities

Ascending Order

/	#	8
–	&	9
!	@	A
(	\	a
)	0	B
{	1	b
}	2	C
$	3	c
+	4	Z
*	5	z
=	6	[
%	7	]

Descending Order

]	7	%
[	6	–
z	5	*
Z	4	+
c	3	$
C	2	}
b	1	{
B	0	)
a	\	(
A	@	!
9	&	–
8	#	/

Record Type Options

When you access the Sort dialog box, WordPerfect defaults to the Record Type section. These options specify the record format you want to manipulate (**L**ine, **P**aragraph, **M**erge Record, or **T**able Row). The **T**able Row option isn't available unless the insertion point is in a table row when you access the Sort dialog box. When the insertion point is in a table row, Record Type defaults to the **T**able Row option and cannot be changed.

Cue: Be sure to choose the correct record type option; specifying the wrong record type can cause WordPerfect to manipulate the records incorrectly.

WordPerfect doesn't detect the other record structures. You must describe the record structure by choosing the **L**ine, **P**aragraph, or **M**erge Record option. For the President's Club example, set the Record Type section to **L**ine.

CAUTION: When you begin using the Sort feature, you may confuse the term *line record* with the line substructures in the other record types, and use the wrong parameters to define sorting and selecting operations on paragraph and merge records. Remember that a line record contains fields, but paragraph records and merge records contain lines.

Key Definitions

In the Key Definition section of the Sort dialog box, you specify the location within the record for the word or words on which the sorting and selection operation will be based. You also indicate whether each word is numeric or alphanumeric. You can define a maximum of nine keys for each sorting or selecting operation.

Key Numbers

The number of the key (shown below the Key heading in the Key Definitions section) indicates the order in which WordPerfect acts on the key; key1 is the first sort order, key2 the second, and so on. The sorting operation arranges the records as required by the first key, if each record contains a unique word in the location defined by the key.

If you define more than one key, and WordPerfect finds two or more records containing the same key1 word, the software arranges those records as required by the key2 definition. If two or more records contain the same key2 word, WordPerfect arranges those records as required by the key3 definition. This process continues until all key definitions are processed.

Suppose that you must alphabetize records containing customer names. You define the first key as the last name, the second key as the first name, and the third key as the middle name. In this case, WordPerfect first arranges the records alphabetically by last name. Records with the same last name are then arranged alphabetically by first name. Finally, if any records contain the same last and first names, the software arranges them alphabetically by middle name. If two or more records contain the same last, first, and middle names, the records appear in the same sequence as their original locations within the data file.

When you first display the Sort dialog box during an editing session, the dialog box lists only key1, marked with an arrow (>). If you choose Insert Key, WordPerfect adds key definition lines, up to a maximum of nine keys. The default value is 1 in each category for these additional keys.

Each time you choose Insert Key, WordPerfect enters a new key at the cursor location, and all key definitions after the cursor move down in the dialog box. If the cursor is at key3, for example, choosing Insert Key creates a new key definition as the third key; the original key3 definition moves down to become the key4 definition.

Cue: To avoid redefining keys, create all the keys you plan to use before defining any of the keys.

The Delete Key option removes key definitions. To remove a key, move the cursor to that key; then choose Delete Key. You can delete key2 through key9 but not key1. If you delete any key definition other than the last key, all definitions below the deleted key move up one position.

If you use the mouse to point to the key you want to change, the arrow (>) immediately moves to mark the key. When you use Tab or Shift-Tab to move the cursor, however, the arrow doesn't move until after you begin defining the key. For this reason, ignore the arrow when creating keys or deleting keys.

T I P

For the President's Club example, choose Insert Key to create a second key (key2).

Key Types

The Key Definitions section shows three or four categories where you specify the sorting and selecting keys. The number of categories depends on the record type; the categories are aligned from left to right in order of structure within the record. For a merge record, for example, each record contains fields, each field contains lines, and each line contains words; the key definition categories thus are Field, Line, and Word. In each case, the selector box under the Type category shows whether the word defined by the key is numeric or alphanumeric.

If the data to be sorted is in line record format, the categories under Key Definition are Field and Word. A category named Line appears between the Field and Word categories, but its only function is to keep the dialog box structure consistent. You cannot access or define a parameter for the Line category.

The paragraph record categories are Line, Field, and Word; the merge record categories are Field, Line, and Word; and the table-row record categories are Cell, Line, and Word.

You enter the appropriate number in the text box for each category of each key you want to define. Suppose that you want to sort a data file in merge record format. In the first field of each record, you have the person's title (Mr., Ms., Dr., and so on). The second field contains the first name, the third field holds the last name, and the address is in the fourth field. The address field is divided into three lines; the first line is the apartment or suite number, the second line holds the street address, and the third line contains the city, state, and ZIP code. To sort the data file by city name, you define the key as the first word in the third line of the fourth field, entering the definition as follows:

Key	Type	Field	Line	Word
1	Alpha	**4**	**3**	**1**

T I P   For sorting purposes, city names containing two or more words (St. Paul, for example), should be typed with hard spaces (Ctrl-space bar) so that WordPerfect treats the name as one word.

You can indicate the desired items in each category with positive or negative numbers. In a line containing 10 words, for example, you can identify the first word as **1** or **–10**, the second word as **2** or **–9**, and so on. Regardless of the number of words in a line, to sort by the last word, you define the word as **–1**; the second-to-last word is **–2**, and so on.

Suppose that you want to sort the data file based on the ZIP code, which is the last word in the third line of the address field. In this case, you cannot define the word you want to sort with a positive number. The number of words in the line can vary substantially, based on the length of the city name (Reno, NV versus Lakes of the Four Seasons, IN, for example). If you tell WordPerfect to sort on the third word of the third line of the fourth field, the sort is incorrect, because WordPerfect sorts 89511 (the ZIP code for Reno) with the word "the" (the third word in Lakes of the Four Seasons). Instead, you tell WordPerfect to count backward from the end of the line with the following key definition:

Key	Type	Field	Line	Word
1	Alpha	4	3	-1

If the category contains only one structure, you must enter **1** for the value in that category. Suppose that you want to sort the data file by title. Because the title field contains only one line, the Line category definition must be 1.

CAUTION: When you define a key for paragraph records beginning with a hanging indent, the definition for the first field of the first line is –1. The [Indent][Mar Rel] code combination tells WordPerfect that the first word in line 1 of field 1 is shifted one field to the left of field 1. Because no field exists to the left of field 1, however, the Sort feature interprets the codes to mean that the word is in the field at the end of the line. This field always is identified as –1, no matter how many fields are in the line. If the same code combination is used for any other field within a line, subtract one from its actual field number. If the [Indent][Mar Rel] codes are at the beginning of field 3, for example, use 2 as its field number.

For the President's Club example, use the following key definitions:

Key	Type	Field	Line	Word
1	Alpha	1	1	-1
2	Alpha	1	1	1

Field 1 in this example contains the member names. For the primary sort, you want to use the last name, which is always the last word in the field (–1). The secondary sort is based on the first name, which is the first word in the field (1).

Starting the Sort Operation

After you finish defining the parameters for the sorting or selecting operation, you begin record manipulation by choosing OK or pressing

Enter. If you don't want to execute the sort operation, choose Cancel or press Esc to leave the Sort dialog box and return to the main document window.

CAUTION: If you return to the main document window without starting the sort operation, WordPerfect doesn't save any new parameters you have defined in the Sort dialog box.

For the President's Club example, start the sorting operation by clicking OK or pressing Enter. WordPerfect arranges the records in alphabetical order by the member's last name. If two or more records have identical key1 words, those records are placed in alphabetical order using the first name. The sorted data file appears as shown in figure 22.17. Save the output data file with the file name LNFN.ALP.

FIG. 22.17

Line records arranged in alphabetical order by last name and then by first name within last name.

John Adams	Abigail	103035	711 Smith Avenue	Braintree	M
John Quincy Adams	Louisa	041167	333 Robards Street	Boston	M
Chester Alan Arthur	Ellen	100531	1020 Herndon Drive	Fairfield	V1
James Buchanan		042391	2362 Appleton Street	Mercersburg	PA
George Herbert Walker Bush	Barbara	pending	1600 Pennsylvania Avenue	Milton	M
James Earl Carter	Rosalynn	pending	3810 Wallace Street	Plains	G
Stephen Grover Cleveland	Frances	031837	585 Folsom Street	Caldwell	N1
Steven Grover Cleveland	Frances	031837	7126 Dimmick Road	Caldwell	N1
John Calvin Coolidge	Grace	070472	3071 Galt Road	Plymouth	V1
Dwight David Eisenhower	Mary	101490	1033 Roosevelt Street	Denison	T3
Millard Fillmore	Abigail Caroline	010700	707 Powers Circle	Summerhill	N'
Gerald Rudolph Ford	Elizabeth	071413	1037 Ryan Parkway	Omaha	NE
James Abram Garfield	Lucretia	111931	1962 Rudolph Street	Orange	OE
Hiram Ulysses Simpson Grant	Julia	042722	4231 Dent Street	Point Pleasant	OE
Warren Gamaliel Harding	Florence	110265	26 Axson Place	Blooming Grove	OE
Benjamin Harrison	Caroline Mary	082033	3861 Scott Parkway	North Bend	OE
William Henry Harrison	Anna	020973	386 Christian Canyon Road	Charles City	VA
Rutherford Birchard Hayes	Lucy	100422	457 Webb Street	Delaware	OE
Herbert Clark Hoover	Lou	081074	711 Kling Street	West Branch	IA
Andrew Jackson	Rachel	031567	1006 Hoes Boulevard	Charlotte	SC
Thomas Jefferson	Martha	041343	1812 Payne Road	Shadwell	VA
Andrew Johnson	Eliza	122908	12220 McCardle Avenue	Raleigh	NC
Lyndon Baines Johnson	Claudia	pending	8246 Geneva Street	Gillespie	T3
John Fitzgerald Kennedy	Jacqueline	052917	4301 Daisy Drive	Brookline	M
Abraham Lincoln	Mary	021209	1284 Todd Court	Hodgenville	K1
James Madison	Dorothea	031651	6003 Kortright Terrace	Port Conway	VA
William McKinley	Ida	012943	8361 Saxton Street	Niles	OE
James Monroe	Elizabeth	042858	104 Johnson Street	Monroe Creek	VA
Richard Milhous Nixon	Thelma	010913	8 Taylor Terrace	Yorba Linda	CA
Franklin Pierce	Jane	112304	2340 McIntosh Lane	Hillsboro	N

Sorting Paragraph Records

The sorting process is a little more complicated with paragraph records than with other record formats because of the way the lines and fields are structured. This section describes how to sort paragraph records, using the President's Club example saved earlier in this chapter as RECORD.PG.

Assume that the President's Club records must be arranged alphabetically by state (line 3 field 3 word 1), city (line 3 field 2 word 1), and last name (line 1 field 1 word –1). Follow these steps to sort the data file:

1. Retrieve the RECORD.PG file in the active document window.

2. If the first record begins with hidden document formatting codes or is a descriptive line, highlight the paragraph records, excluding the hidden formatting codes or descriptive line.

3. Choose **T**ools, **S**ort.

    Press Sort (Ctrl-Shift-F12).

4. Set the Record Type to **P**aragraph.

5. Set the Sort Order to **A**scending.

6. Choose **I**nsert Key twice to create key2 and key3 definitions.

7. Set key1 to the following parameters:

Type	Line	Field	Word
Alpha	3	3	1

8. Set key2 to the following parameters:

Type	Line	Field	Word
Alpha	3	2	1

9. Set key3 to the following parameters:

Type	Line	Field	Word
Alpha	1	1	–1

10. Start the sorting operation by clicking OK or pressing Enter.

WordPerfect arranges the records in ascending order by state (key1). If two or more records list the same state, those records are arranged in ascending order by city (key2). Finally, if two or more records list identical states and cities, WordPerfect sorts them in ascending order by the member's last name (key3). Figure 22.18 shows the result of the sort.

Save the output data file as STCITYLN.ALP.

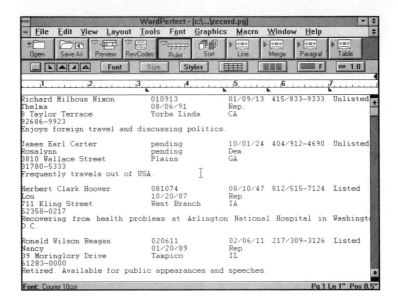

FIG. 22.18

Paragraph
records arranged
in alphabetical
order by state,
city, and last
name.

Extracting Records

The Sort feature's selecting function examines words defined by one or more key parameters in the Sort dialog box and extracts the records matching the parameters. After the Sort feature completes the extraction process, only the matching records remain in the main document window.

CAUTION: When you select records, WordPerfect removes records from the active document window. Sorting and selecting operations take place in RAM and don't alter the original data file stored on disk, but the output data file in the active document window retains the original data file's name. To avoid accidentally replacing the original file on disk, save the revised data file in the active document window with a different name as soon as record manipulation is complete.

Defining Selection Parameters

In a combined sorting and selecting operation, WordPerfect extracts the records matching the selection statement and then arranges the records in the specified order. If you don't want to sort extracted records, choose the **No** Sort option in the Sort Order section of the Sort dialog box.

A *selection statement* defines the word for which the selecting function tries to find a match at the designated location within the record. You type the selection statement in the **R**ecord Selection text box in the Sort dialog box. The selection statement performs the following actions:

■ Assigns one word—called a *string*—to a key

■ Uses symbolic operators to define the extraction operation (including operational sequence) that you want WordPerfect to perform when it finds a match

Understanding Operators

When you move the cursor to the **R**ecord Selection section of the Sort dialog box, WordPerfect displays eight symbolic characters at the lower left edge of the screen, as shown in figure 22.19.

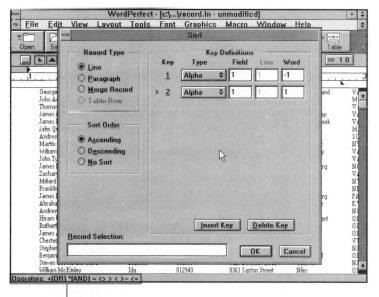

Symbolic character list

The following sections describe the 10 symbolic characters recognized by the selecting function.

The + Operator

The + (plus sign) operator acts as an "or" connection between two different conditions in the selection statement. WordPerfect extracts the record if *either* of the conditions in the statement is true. Consider the following selection statement:

> key1=Adams + key2=VA

With this statement, WordPerfect extracts the record if *Adams* is found at the location specified by key1 OR if *VA* is found at the location specified by key2.

The * Operator

The * (asterisk) operator acts as an "and" connection between two different conditions in the selection statement. WordPerfect extracts the record if *both* conditions in the statement are true. Consider the following selection statement:

> key1=Adams * key2=VA

With this statement, WordPerfect extracts the record if *Adams* is found at the location specified by key1 AND *VA* is found at the location specified by key2.

The = Operator

The = (equal) operator matches conditions. WordPerfect looks in the location specified by the key for the word specified in the statement. If the word appears in the specified location, and no other selecting operators are specified, WordPerfect selects the record. Consider the following selection statements:

> key1=Adams
> key1=150

In the first statement, if the word *Adams* is in the location specified by key1, WordPerfect extracts the record. In the second statement, if the word *150* is in the location specified by key1, WordPerfect extracts the record.

The <> Operator

The <> (not equal) operator searches for nonmatching conditions. WordPerfect looks in the location specified by the key for the word specified in the statement. If the word doesn't appear in the specified location, and no other selecting operators are specified, WordPerfect selects the record. Consider the following selection statements:

    key1<>Adams
    key1<>150

In the first statement, if the word *Adams* is in the location specified by key1, WordPerfect extracts the record. In the second statement, if the word *150* is in the location specified by key1, WordPerfect extracts the record.

The > Operator

The > (greater than) operator extracts records where the contents of the key location exceed the value specified in the statement. Consider the following selection statements:

    key1>Adams
    key1>150

The first statement extracts records with words following *Adams* alphabetically. The second statement extracts records if the number found at the key location is greater than 150.

The < Operator

The < (less than) operator extracts records where the contents of the key location are less than the value specified in the statement. Consider the following selection statements:

    key1<Adams
    key1<150

The first statement extracts records with words that precede *Adams* alphabetically. The second statement extracts records if the number found at the key location is less than 150.

The >= Operator

The >= (greater than or equal to) operator extracts records where the contents of the key location meet or exceed the value specified in the statement. Consider the following selection statements:

    key1>=Adams
    key1>=150

The first statement extracts records containing the word *Adams* or any word following it alphabetically. The second statement extracts records if the number found at the key location is 150 or higher.

The <= Operator

The <= (less than or equal to) operator extracts records where the contents of the key location are less than or equal to the value specified in the statement. Consider the following selection statements:

```
key1<=Adams
key1<=150
```

The first statement extracts records containing the word *Adams* or any word preceding it alphabetically. The second statement extracts records if the number found at the key location is 150 or lower.

The Keyg Operator

A *key* describes in numeric terms the actual location of each word within a record. A *global key* extracts records containing a matching word anywhere within the record.

The *keyg* (global key) operator extracts records where the specified word appears anywhere in the record. Consider the following selection statements:

```
keyg=Adams
keyg=150
```

The first statement extracts records containing the word *Adams* anywhere in the recod. The second statement extracts a record if the number 150 appears anywhere in the record.

The () Operators

Paired ( ) (do-first) operators override the selecting function's default left-to-ght operational sequence. Consider the following selection statement:

```
key2=VA * (key1=Adams + key1=Lincoln)
```

This statement extracts records with *Adams* or *Lincoln* at the location specified by key1 if *VA* is at the location specified by key2. If the parentheses are omitted, the statement extracts all records with *Adams* and *VA* at the locations specified by key1 and key2, respectively. Then the statement extracts all records with *Lincoln* at the location specified by key1.

Specifying the Selection Statement

Before you can use a key definition in a selection statement, you must designate the key parameters in the Key Definition section of the Sort dialog box. If you assign a selection statement to an undefined key and then start the selecting operation, WordPerfect displays an error message and terminates the operation. This limitation doesn't apply if you assign the selection statement to the global key (keyg=*word*), which can be defined only in the **R**ecord Selection section.

■ **Cue:** Although you can define a selection statement that includes 213 characters, keep your statements short to reduce the possibility of errors.

When the parameters are defined, you start record manipulation by clicking OK or pressing Enter. Regardless of the type of record manipulation—sorting, selecting, or a sorting and selecting combination—WordPerfect displays the Sort Status dialog box, which shows the progress of the operation (see fig. 22.20). When the operation is completed, WordPerfect displays the results in the active document window.

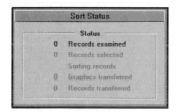

FIG. 22.20

The Sort Status dialog box.

Suppose that the President's Club sends greetings to active (but not pending) members with birthdays in the current month. At the end of each month, the club prepares a chronological list of members with birthdays during the next month. The membership information is in the RECORD.MG data file (created earlier in this chapter), in merge record format. Birth dates are in field 7, stored as three words (month/day/year).

The following steps describe how to define the correct parameters to select the members with October birthdays:

1. Retrieve the RECORD.MG file in the active document window.

2. If the first record begins with hidden document formatting codes or descriptive lines, highlight all the records, excluding the hidden formatting codes or descriptive lines.

3. Choose **T**ools, **S**ort.

    Press Sort (Ctrl-Shift-F12).

4. Set the Record Type to **M**erge Record.

5. Set the Sort Order to Ascending.

6. Choose **Insert** Key three times to create key2, key3, and key4.

7. Set key1 to the following parameters:

Type	Field	Line	Word
Alpha	**7**	**1**	**3**

8. Set key2 to the following parameters:

Type	Field	Line	Word
Alpha	**7**	**1**	**1**

9. Set key3 to the following parameters:

Type	Field	Line	Word
Alpha	**7**	**1**	**2**

10. Set key4 to the following parameters:

Type	Field	Line	Word
Alpha	**3**	**1**	**1**

11. Choose **R**ecord Selection and type the following selection statement:

key2=10 * key4<>pending

12. Start the sorting operation by clicking OK or pressing Enter.

The data file RECORD.MG lists six persons whose birthdays fall in October. Five of these people are members and one has a pending membership status. When WordPerfect performs the extraction, the Sort feature first examines the word defined by key2 (field 7 line 1 word 1). If the word in that location is equal to 10 (the numeric designation for October), the program then examines the word defined by key4 (field 3 line 1 word 1). If the word in that location doesn't equal *pending*, the record is extracted to the output data file. In this example, the selecting function extracts five records.

After extracting the records specified by the selection statement, WordPerfect arranges the extracted records in ascending numeric order by year (key1). If two or more records contain the same year, the matching records are arranged by month (key2).

In this example, because all records contain the same word (the month designation 10) at the key2 location, this step serves no useful purpose. Because key2 must be defined so that WordPerfect can extract the correct records, however, the sorting function must process key2 for those records with the same year at the key1 location.

Finally, if two or more records have identical year and month designations (key1 and key2, respectively), WordPerfect arranges them in ascending order by day (key3). Figure 22.21 shows the result of the sorting and selection process.

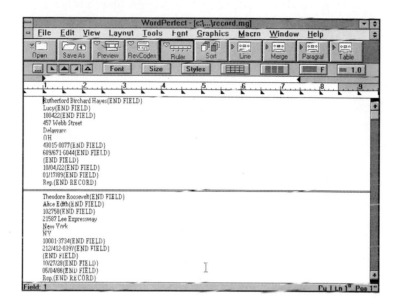

FIG. 22.21

Extracted merge records arranged in chronological order by birth dates.

Save the output data file as BIRTHD10.SF.

Sorting and Selecting Table-Row Records

Table-row records require some special steps to sort and select. This section describes basic sorting and selecting with a table-row record format, using the President's Club data file as an example.

> **T I P**
>
> If you don't want to sort an entire table, you can highlight the rows you want to sort before accessing the Sort dialog box. As an alternative, however, you can define a descriptive header row for your table-row data file. If a row has been defined as a header, WordPerfect excludes it. See Chapter 13, "Working with Text Columns," for information on defining a header row.

The President's Club needs a chart, sorted by ZIP code, listing members who live in New York, Virginia, and Ohio. Records with duplicate ZIP codes must be arranged by last name, and members with the same last name must be arranged by membership number. For this example, use the RECORD.TB data file created earlier in the chapter.

The state abbreviation is the first word in line 3 of the fourth cell in each record; the ZIP code is the first word in line 4 of the same cell. The last name is the last word in the first line of the first cell in each record, and the membership number is the first word in the first line of the third cell.

To use the sorting and selecting functions to create a chart from a table-row data file, follow these steps:

1. Retrieve the RECORD.TB file in the active document window.

2. Move the insertion point to any cell within the table.

3. Choose **Tools, Sort**.

    Press Sort (Ctrl-Shift-F12).

   WordPerfect displays the Sort dialog box, with **Table Row** as the unalterable default setting for the Record Type section.

4. Set the Sort Order section to A**s**cending.

5. Choose **I**nsert Key three times to create key2, key3, and key4.

6. Set key1 to the following parameters:

Type	Cell	Line	Word
Alpha	4	3	1

7. Set key2 to the following parameters:

Type	Cell	Line	Word
Alpha	4	4	1

8. Set key3 to the following parameters:

Type	Cell	Line	Word
Alpha	1	1	−1

9. Set key4 to the following parameters:

Type	Cell	Line	Word
Alpha	4	3	1

10. Choose **R**ecord Selection and type the following selection statement:

> **key1=NY + key1=OH + key1=VA**

11. Click OK or press Enter to start the sorting operation.

WordPerfect extracts the records matching the criteria defined in the selection statement; then the program arranges the records alphabetically by state, numerically by ZIP code within the state, alphabetically by member's last name within the ZIP code, and finally numerically by membership number within the last name. Figure 22.22 shows the result of the selecting and sorting operation.

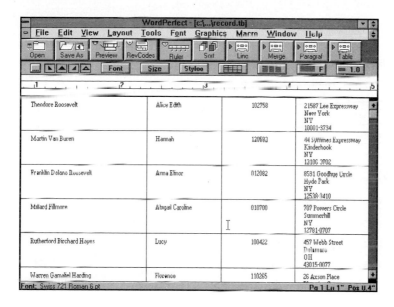

FIG. 22.22

Extracted table-row records arranged according to the defined parameters.

Save the output data file as ZPNYOHVA.TB.

Chapter Summary

This chapter introduces the processes for creating data files with information in line, paragraph, merge, and table-row formats. You learned how to use formatting codes and how to use the Sort dialog box to specify sorting and selecting operations.

You now have the basic skills to use WordPerfect's powerful Sort feature.

PART

VI

Managing Large Projects

OUTLINE

Using Footnotes and Endnotes

Line Numbering, Paragraph Numbering, and Outlining

Assembling Other Document References

Working with Master Documents

Using Footnotes and Endnotes

M ention the word footnotes and most people picture volumes of scholarly works laden with obscure references. Many people also remember, perhaps painfully, the difficult chore of typing footnotes for research papers. But with WordPerfect, footnotes (and endnotes) are easy to create, and they aren't just for academics any more.

Footnotes provide additional information about what is being said in the body of the text without interrupting the flow of that text. Footnotes may contain reference details, such as the name of the author, the title of the work, the page number where the reference is found, and so on. A footnote also may provide parenthetical or interpretive explanations of data or other technical material. Footnotes should not contain essential information, however, because by their very location, the author is telling you that the footnotes are not required reading.

Fortunately, WordPerfect makes creating, editing, moving, and renumbering your footnotes easy. WordPerfect even enables you to use footnotes or endnotes in the same document and to change one kind of note to the other.

■ **Read Gilgin** is Director of Learning Support Services at the University of Wisconsin, Madison. His background is in Latin American literature, and he first began using WordPerfect primarily for its footnotes feature

If you aren't convinced that you need footnotes, skim through this chapter; look at some of the examples and try anything that catches your attention. You just may find yourself joining the ranks of people who are already sold on the ease and usefulness of WordPerfect's footnotes feature.

Choosing between Footnotes and Endnotes

Footnotes typically are located at the bottom of the page on which the note reference, or number, occurs; endnotes are listed together at the end of the document. In WordPerfect, the methods for creating and working with each are nearly identical. Before deciding whether to use endnotes or footnotes, however, you need to determine your audience and the desired effect of your notes.

Endnotes are designed primarily as a convenience to typists. (Can you recall trying to figure out how much space to save at the bottom of each page for your footnotes?) The use of endnotes is now so firmly entrenched in academic publications that publishers often require authors to use endnotes when submitting manuscripts.

Footnotes, on the other hand, are much more convenient for the reader. A quick glance to the bottom of the page provides readers with additional material or references. The reader can then continue without the bothersome interruption of thumbing forward to the list of endnotes. For this reason, this chapter focuses first on footnotes and then explains how endnotes differ.

Using Footnotes

The best time to create a footnote is while you are typing the text to which the note refers because the details of the note are still fresh in your mind and the reference material is readily at hand.

Type the following paragraphs so that you have some text with which you can practice. Remember to indent the quotations by pressing F7 before typing each quotation.

Absurdist writers generally take one of two rather different approaches to their subject. French dramatists tend to illustrate the sense of anguish that besets modern man. Spanish American short story authors, however, tend to laugh at their condition and suggest humorously absurd ways of coping with it. Regarding this latter approach, Montaigne stated:

> Wailing and commiseration imply some valuation of the object bewailed; what we mock at we consider worthless.

The Cuban author Virgilio Piñera, speaking about living under the Batista regime, declared:

> For more than fifty years we have gotten along by joking. If we couldn't literally confront those who were exploiting our country, at least we could ridicule them. This resistance kept our culture from dying completely.

Creating Footnotes

To create the first note for the preceding text, follow these steps:

1. Position the insertion point at the exact location where you want the footnote number. In this example, place the insertion point immediately after the period following the word *worthless* in the first quotation.

2. Select **Layout, Footnote, Create.**

   WordPerfect places the insertion point in a blank footnote editing screen. Using the footnote numbering method you have chosen, the program automatically generates a footnote number—*1* in this example. (See "Changing Footnote Options" for a discussion of how to change the numbering method.) The status line indicates the superscript font that is in effect.

3. Type the text of your footnote, using features you normally use for editing text in WordPerfect. Any feature that appears dimmed in the menus is not available for use in editing footnotes.

   For this example, type the following footnote text:

   > Michele de Montaigne, "On Democritus and Heraclitus" in <u>Essays</u>, tr. J.M. Cohen (Baltimore, Md.: Penguin Books, 1958) pp. 132-133.

Figure 23.1 shows the footnote editing screen displayed after you type the footnote text.

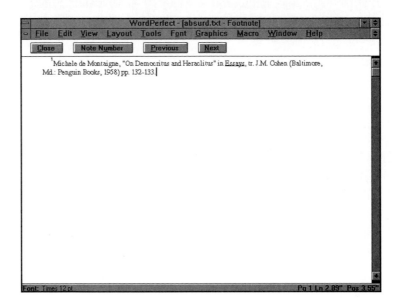

FIG. 23.1

The footnote editing screen with footnote text.

 CAUTION: After you finish typing your footnote, do not add a hard return (do not press Enter); instead, simply stop typing on the last line of the note. By default, WordPerfect separates footnotes with a single blank line. Adding a hard return gives you two blank lines between this note and the next one.

4. Choose **C**lose to include the footnote in your text.

WordPerfect returns the insertion point to the location of the footnote number.

WordPerfect displays the footnote number in the superscript font that is in effect. The footnoted line appears to be double-spaced (see fig. 23.2) because the superscripted number requires extra space; however, when you print the page, the footnoted line is single-spaced (see fig. 23.3).

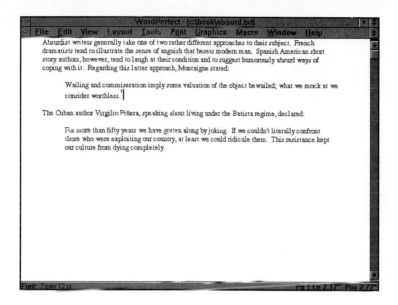

Absurdist writers generally take one of two rather different approaches to their subject. French dramatists tend to illustrate the sense of anguish that besets modern man. Spanish American short story authors, however, tend to laugh at their condition and to suggest humorously absurd ways of coping with it. Regarding this latter approach, Montaigne stated:

> Wailing and commiseration imply some valuation of the object bewailed; what we mock at we consider worthless.

The Cuban author Virgilio Piñera, speaking about living under the Batista regime, declared:

> For more than fifty years we have gotten along by joking. If we couldn't literally confront those who were exploiting our country, at least we could ridicule them. This resistance kept our culture from dying completely.

A footnoted line that appears double-spaced.

Viewing Footnotes

Although the footnote number appears in your text, the footnote itself does not. WordPerfect reserves enough space at the bottom of the current page for the footnote you have just created. To see what the footnote looks like, follow these steps:

1. Select **File**, Print Preview.

2. Select **Pages**, Full Page to view the layout of your footnoted page. Although you cannot read the text, you can view the placement of the footnotes on the page.

3. Select **View**, 100% to see the page at its normal size. This view shows you the top half of the page. Use the scroll bar or the PgDn key to view the bottom half, where footnotes are located.

4. After you finish viewing the footnotes, select **Close** to return to your document.

After working with footnotes for a while, you will find that they always are where they're supposed to be, and you won't need to take these "reassurance steps."

> Absurdist writers generally take one of two rather different approaches to their subject. French dramatists tend to illustrate the sense of anguish that besets modern man. Spanish American short story authors, however, tend to laugh at their condition and to suggest humorously absurd ways of coping with it. Regarding this latter approach, Montaigne stated:
>
> > Wailing and commiseration imply some valuation of the object bewailed; what we mock at we consider worthless.[1]
>
> The Cuban author Virgilio Piñera, speaking about living under the Batista regime, declared:
>
> > For more than fifty years we have gotten along by joking. If we couldn't literally confront those who were exploiting our country, at least we could ridicule them. This resistance kept our culture from dying completely.
>
> ---
>
> [1]Michele de Montaigne, "On Democritus and Heraclitus" in Essays, tr. J.M. Cohen (Baltimore, Md.: Penguin Books, 1958) pp. 132-133.

FIG. 23.3

Sample text and footnote as printed page.

Editing Footnotes

An easier way to view your footnotes quickly and also to make any necessary changes to them is to redisplay the footnote editing screen. Follow these steps:

1. From anywhere in the document, select **L**ayout, **F**ootnote, **E**dit, and then enter the number of the footnote you want to change or view.

2. Make any necessary editing changes. You can use the same tools you use when you create a footnote.

   At this point you have the option of returning to your document or editing other footnotes.

3. If you have created more than one footnote and you want to view or edit other footnotes, you can select **P**revious or **N**ext. These options provide a quick way to browse through your notes.

4. Select **C**lose when you are ready to return to your text.

WordPerfect returns the insertion point to your text at the location of the footnote number you are editing.

If you plan to use footnotes often, you should consider using WordPerfect's Button Bar to automate creating and editing them. A simple example is to add Footnote Create and Footnote Edit to the Button Bar (see Chapter 19).

Numbering Footnotes Automatically

What happens to the footnote numbering sequence if you decide to add, insert, delete, or move a footnote? Fortunately, WordPerfect automatically adjusts the footnote numbers; you don't have to worry about renumbering all the other footnotes.

If you turn on Reveal Codes, you can see that footnotes are actually special codes that use the computer's capability to keep track of numbers (see fig. 23.4). You can delete or move these codes just like any other text, and you can insert new codes wherever you want.

In the following procedures, notice the changes in footnote numbers as you add, insert, delete, and move your footnotes.

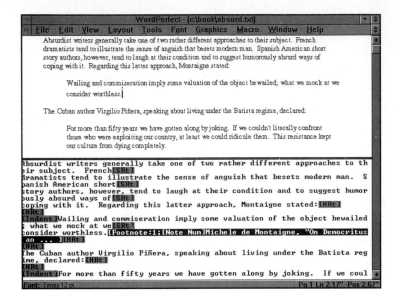

FIG. 23.4

A footnote code
as seen in Reveal
Codes.

Adding Footnotes

Adding footnotes is the same as creating them. You can add footnotes as you create your text, or you can add them later during the editing process.

To add a footnote to your text, follow these steps:

1. Position the insertion point at the exact location where you want the footnote number. Using the example, position the insertion point immediately after the period following the word *completely* in the second quotation.

2. Select **L**ayout, **F**ootnote, **C**reate.

    WordPerfect places the insertion point in a blank footnote editing screen. Note that WordPerfect has automatically incremented the footnote number. All you have to do is type the text of the footnote.

3. For this example, type the following footnote text:

    Virgilio Piñera, <u>Teatro completo</u> (Havana: Ediciones R, 1960), pp. 10-11.

4. If you want to edit another existing footnote, select **N**ext to move toward the end of the document or **P**revious to move toward the beginning of the document. If you have no next or preceding footnote, WordPerfect displays the error message Not Found.

5. After you finish editing your footnote, choose Close to include the footnote in your text.

   WordPerfect returns the insertion point to the location on the editing screen just after the footnote number of the last footnote you edited.

To insert a footnote before another already existing footnote, you follow the same steps you use when creating a new footnote:

1. Move the insertion point to the exact location where you want the footnote number. For this example, position the insertion point immediately after the period following *surrounds him* in the first paragraph.

2. Select Layout, Footnote, Create.

   WordPerfect automatically adjusts the footnote number so that it is one more than the preceding note. In this example, the footnote you add becomes footnote 1.

3. Type the footnote text. For this example, type

   The term "Theatre of the Absurd" was coined by literary critic Martin Esslin,

4. After you finish typing the footnote text, choose Close to include the footnote in your text.

   WordPerfect returns the insertion point to your text at the location of the footnote number for the footnote you just created.

Note that WordPerfect renumbers the other footnotes to account for the new note you just inserted.

Moving Footnotes

As you edit your document, you may have to move sections of text from one place to another. If the text contains footnotes, WordPerfect moves the footnotes with the text and renumbers them according to their new locations.

Sometimes, however, you need to move only the footnote—for example, if you insert a footnote in the wrong location. Cutting and pasting a footnote is the same as cutting and pasting text. The following steps explain how to move a footnote:

1. Position the insertion point immediately to the left of the footnote number you want to move. In this example, position the insertion point immediately to the left of the first footnote number in the first paragraph.

2. Use the mouse or cursor keys to select the footnote number.

 Press Select (F8).

3. Choose **Edit, Cut** to cut the footnote.

 Press Shift-Del.

Remember that this command cuts the footnote number and the entire text of the footnote.

Note that when you cut a footnote, WordPerfect adjusts the other footnote numbers.

4. Position the insertion point where you want to relocate the footnote, and select **Edit, Paste** to insert the footnote.

Press Shift-Ins.

In this example, paste the footnote just after the phrase *French dramatists* in the first paragraph (see fig. 23.5).

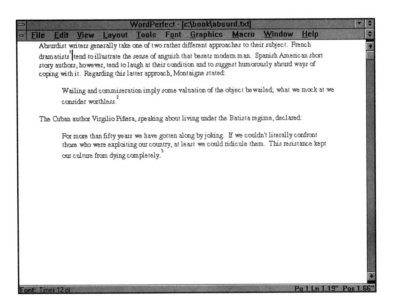

FIG. 23.5

Document after moving a footnote.

Note that the replacement of this footnote adjusts the other footnote numbers again.

Deleting Footnotes

At times, you may want to remove a footnote. For example, you may decide that the footnote information is unnecessary, or you may create a footnote accidentally.

To delete a footnote, position the insertion point immediately following the footnote number in the text, and press Backspace.

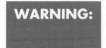 **WARNING:** When you delete a footnote number, you also delete its footnote text. WordPerfect does not warn you of the potential danger when you delete a footnote number.

■ **Cue:** If you accidentally create a footnote (for example, if you meant to select **E**dit but selected **C**reate instead), simply close the footnote editing screen and press Backspace. This procedure removes the note and adjusts all footnotes to their original numbers.

If you accidentally delete a footnote, you can restore it. For this example, follow these steps to delete and restore a footnote:

1. Position the insertion point immediately following the second footnote number.

2. Press Backspace. Note that the other footnote numbers adjust automatically.

3. Select **E**dit, **U**ndelete.

    Press Alt-Shift-Backspace.

4. Press **R**estore to undelete the footnote. Note again that the footnote numbers change.

If you are careful, you can use the Delete key to move a footnote. Delete the footnote, position the insertion point where you want to insert the note, and select **E**dit, **U**ndelete, **R**estore.

T I P

Changing Footnote Options

You have learned how to create, edit, delete, and move footnotes; these procedures are all you need for short documents with standard footnote requirements. If you also need to modify the way your footnotes look, WordPerfect can help.

To access the footnote options, select **L**ayout, **F**ootnote, **O**ptions. WordPerfect displays the Footnote Options dialog box (see fig. 23.6).

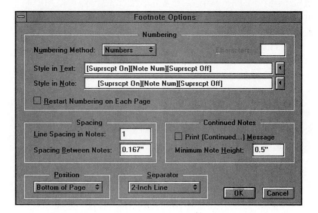

FIG. 23.6

The Footnote Options dialog box.

You don't need to try all these options, because you won't use many of them. Knowing that they are available and understanding how to use them is a good idea, however.

WordPerfect offers three footnote numbering methods:

- Numbers (1, 2, 3)
- Characters (*, **, ***)
- Letters (a, b, c)

Instead of using Numbers—the default numbering method—you may want to use Characters. If you want asterisks, for example, as the character for your notes, you select Characters as your numbering method, and enter an asterisk (*) in the Characters box. If you plan to use a great many references in your document, you probably should avoid using characters. Otherwise you may end up with a long and hard-to-read footnote number (such as ******).

■ **Cue:** You can press Ctrl-W to select special characters from the WordPerfect Character menu (see Chapter 28).

If you have many references but you still want to use characters, WordPerfect provides two ways to reduce the problem of having too many characters. One way is to select **R**estart Numbering on Each Page, which restarts the numbering sequence at the top of each page.

The other way is to use multiple characters by entering as many as five different characters in the Character box. For example, entering *≈≈§# in the Character box produces *, ≈, ≈, §, #, **, ≈≈, and so on.

By default, WordPerfect inserts a superscripted footnote number into the body of the text and, at the bottom of the page, indents a superscripted footnote number five spaces from the left margin. You can edit the Style in Text or Style in Note box by deleting, typing characters, or by adding codes from the pop-up lists at the right side of the style boxes.

■ **Cue:** If you intend to use both footnotes and endnotes in the same document, you may want to use numbers for the footnotes and letters for the endnotes.

WordPerfect assumes that you want single-spaced footnotes, even if the body of your text is spaced differently. If you want the spacing in the footnotes to match your text, enter the appropriate spacing number in the Line Spacing in Notes box. If you want to change the spacing in just one footnote, go to the footnote editing screen for that footnote (**Layout, Footnote, Edit**); insert the line-spacing codes into the footnote itself (**Layout, Line, Spacing**); and then **Close** the footnote editing screen to return to your document.

By default, WordPerfect separates all footnotes with a single blank line. If you want to increase or decrease the size of this space, change the number in the Spacing **B**etween Notes box.

■ **Cue:** You can specify spacing in any increment your printer can handle, and you can use either decimal notation or fractions. 1.5, 1 3/8, and so on.

Normally, WordPerfect reserves enough space at the bottom of the page for all the footnotes on that page. If, however, the number for a long footnote occurs toward the end of the page, WordPerfect may have to begin the footnote on one page and continue it on the next. If you don't have enough room for at least three lines of the footnote, WordPerfect moves the text and its accompanying footnote to the next page.

If you want the program to print the message *Continued...* with footnotes that are split across a page, select the Print (Continued...) **M**essage check box. You can increase the minimum size of your notes (approximately one-half inch, or three lines) by changing the Minimum Note **H**eight box.

If you create footnotes and text in a foreign language, you can place a language code in your document initial codes (**L**ayout, **D**ocument, Initial **C**odes), and WordPerfect displays the *Continued...* message in the language you have selected. (Refer to Chapter 29, "Customizing WordPerfect with Preferences," for more information on language codes.)

T I P

To ask whether you want your footnotes at the bottom of the page may seem silly. After all, isn't that where footnotes are supposed to go? But you do have the option of placing your footnotes immediately below the end of the text rather than flush against the bottom margin. Select the position from the pop-up list in the Position box.

Finally, you can change the kind of line used to separate your footnotes from the body of the text. The Position box lists the choices:

- 2-Inch Line (default)
- No Line
- Margin to Margin (a line across the page)

After you select the options you want, choose OK. WordPerfect closes the dialog box and places a Footnote Options code at the location of the insertion point.

Formatting Footnotes

When you create a footnote, it normally assumes the characteristics in the document initial codes, the document initial font, and other WordPerfect default settings. For example, suppose that your default settings include the Courier type style and one-inch left and right margins. If you place a font code at the beginning of your document and later create a footnote, WordPerfect still displays the footnote in Courier. If you change your margins, the footnote still has one-inch margins.

The most effective way to ensure that your footnotes and the body of your text match is to change the document initial codes and document initial font. Follow these steps:

1. Select **L**ayout, **D**ocument.

    Press Ctrl-Shift-F9.

2. Select Initial **F**ont.
3. Choose the fonts you want to use for both text and footnotes.
4. Select **L**ayout, **D**ocument, Initial **C**odes.
5. Select **L**ayout, **L**ine.

   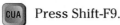 Press Shift-F9.

6. Select **M**argins to set the margins for both text and footnotes.

Another way of changing fonts and margins so that both text and footnotes match is to place the font or margins codes at the beginning of the document, and then place a Footnote Options code *after* these code changes (see fig. 23.7).

FIG. 23.7

A Footnote
Options code
that follows the
font and margin
codes.

The following steps explain how to insert a Footnote Options code after the font and margin codes:

1. Move the insertion point to the beginning of the document.

2. Select the font and the margin settings you want to use for both text and footnotes.

3. Select Layout, Footnote, Options.

4. Specify any changes you want to make.

5. Select OK to place the Footnote Options code in your document.

If you want your footnotes and text to be different, however, you first set the margins and fonts you want for your footnotes in the document initial codes and document initial font. Then at the beginning of the document, set the font and margin codes you want for your text. Be sure to place any Footnote Options codes *before* these code changes (see fig. 23.8).

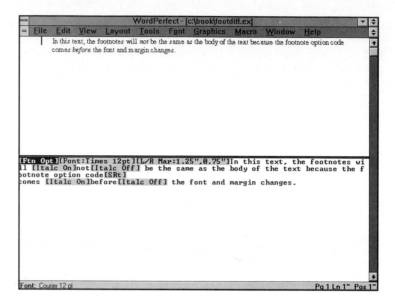

FIG. 23.8

A Footnote
Options code
that precedes the
font and margin
codes.

Continuing Footnotes across Documents

If you create a long document, you probably will save each section or chapter in a separate file. In your final printed version, however, you may want your footnotes to be numbered consecutively from one section or chapter to the next.

One method for creating continuing footnote numbers across multiple documents is manually to change the beginning footnote number in each document. For example, suppose that Chapter 1 has seven footnotes. You would change the beginning footnote number to *8* at the beginning of Chapter 2 (a separate file). Follow these steps to change the beginning footnote number:

1. Select **L**ayout, **F**ootnote, **N**ew Number.

2. Enter the beginning footnote number (**8** in this example), and select OK.

You then continue creating footnotes in that chapter. For this example, WordPerfect automatically numbers the next footnotes *9, 10, 11,* and so on.

Another, perhaps more elegant, method for creating continuing footnote numbers across multiple documents is to use the Master Document feature explained in Chapter 26. This feature enables you to create footnotes without worrying about the beginning and ending numbers of each chapter; WordPerfect automatically calculates the footnote numbers, based on all the footnotes in all the chapters.

The method you choose for creating consecutively numbered footnotes depends on how much you expect the document to be changed over time. If you expect few or no changes, the manual method is sufficient. If the document (several files) is likely to see extensive revisions, however, you are better off learning about and using the Master Document method.

> **T I P**
>
> If you want to use a particularly long footnote more than once, but you don't want to duplicate it, you can use the Cross Reference feature (see Chapter 25, "Assembling Other Document References"). This feature enables you to display a cross-reference, such as *See footnote 3*, in your footnote. WordPerfect automatically changes the reference number if you change the footnote number. Cross-referencing also can encourage the reader to return to where the original discussion was located—for example, to a chart or long quotation.

Using Endnotes

Endnotes serve the same purpose as footnotes: to provide parenthetical or reference information. What makes endnotes different from footnotes is that all endnotes are placed together at the end of the document, unless you specify another location (at the ends of chapters, for instance).

Creating Endnotes

The steps you follow to create endnotes are nearly identical to the steps you use for footnotes:

1. Position the insertion point at the exact location in the text where you want your endnote number.

2. Select Layout, Endnote.

    Except for the additional Placement of Endnotes option, the menu for endnotes is the same as the menu for footnotes.

3. Select Create to create an endnote.

    WordPerfect displays the same kind of editing screen it displays for footnotes. Note, however, that the note number is not super-scripted but is placed at the left margin and is followed by a period.

4. Press Tab or the space bar to separate the note from the period of the note number.

CUA   Press Indent (F7).

5. Type the text of your endnote, using features you normally use for editing text in WordPerfect. Any feature that appears dimmed in the menu is not available for use in editing footnotes.

6. After you finish editing your endnote, select **C**lose.

The style of the endnote differs from the style of the footnote. For example, if you had indented the note, it would look something like the following reference:

```
1. Michele de Montaigne, "On Democritus and Heraclitus" in
   Essays, tr. J.M. Cohen (Baltimore, Md.: Penguin Books,
   1958) pp. 132-133.
```

By default, WordPerfect displays endnotes at the end of the document. If you want your notes displayed on a separate page, go to the end of the document and create a new page (press Ctrl-Enter or choose **L**ayout, **P**age, **P**age Break). You also can add a title and formatting to this page (see fig. 23.9).

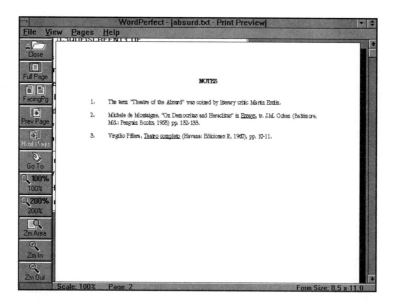

FIG. 23.9

A sample endnote page.

■ Cue: If you want to preview the endnotes, position the insertion point on the endnotes page, and select **F**ile, Print Pre**v**iew.

To edit, add, insert, delete, or move endnotes, see the corresponding footnotes sections in this chapter. The procedures are identical for both footnotes and endnotes. Endnote options are almost the same, except that endnotes have fewer options than footnotes.

Changing Endnotes' Location

Endnotes, by definition, come at the document's end, which is where WordPerfect places them by default. You may, however, want to place some other element, such as an index, a bibliography, or an appendix, at the end of your document, after your endnotes.

To place endnotes somewhere other than at the end of your document, follow these steps:

1. Move your insertion point to the location in your text where you want to place the endnotes. You may want to create a separate page (press Ctrl-Enter or choose **Layout, Page, Page** Break).

2. Select **Layout, Endnote, Placement.**

   WordPerfect then asks whether you want to restart endnote numbering.

3. Choose **Yes** if you want to restart numbering—for example, you want endnotes at the end of each section of a multisection document. If this list is the only endnote list in the document, choose **No**.

   WordPerfect displays in the text a comment box that shows where the endnotes will appear (see fig. 23.10). This comment box does not print.

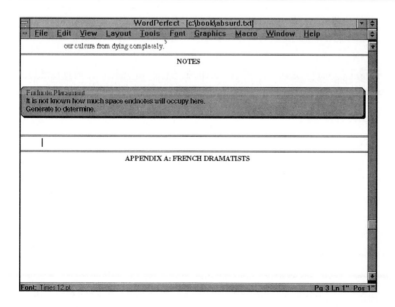

FIG. 23.10

The comment box displayed when changing endnote placement.

The amount of space your endnotes require isn't terribly important unless you are concerned about the overall length of your manuscript. If you want to verify the number of pages the endnotes occupy, you can use the Generate feature. Select **Tools**, **Generate** and answer **Yes** when asked whether you want to proceed.

The comment box changes to display the message Endnote Placement, and the page numbers on subsequent pages increment to reflect the number of pages the endnotes will occupy.

T I P   If you want to display several table references at the bottom of the page but don't want to include them in the footnote numbering sequence of your text references, you can use endnotes for the table references and place the endnotes on the same page as the table.

Changing Footnotes to Endnotes

Footnotes, as you have learned by now, are easy to create and, for readers, are much easier to use than endnotes. At times, however, you may need to use endnotes in a document, even if you used footnotes when you created it. Likewise, you may have used endnotes when creating a document, but now you want to print it with footnotes instead.

■ **Cue:** WordPerfect comes with two macros— FOOTEND.WCM and ENDFOOT.WCM—that you can use to change all footnotes to endnotes or vice versa.

To convert footnotes to endnotes, you find a footnote, cut the footnote text from the edit screen, delete the footnote number, create an endnote, and paste the footnote text into the endnote editing screen. To convert endnotes to footnotes, you simply reverse the process.

To convert footnotes to endnotes, follow these steps:

1. Select **Layout**, **Footnote**, **Edit**.

2. Press Enter to select the footnote number displayed in the dialog box.

3. In the note editing screen, press the right-arrow key until the insertion point is positioned to the immediate right of the note number.

4. Turn on Select and move the insertion point to the end of the note to select all the footnote text.

  Press Select (F8).

5. Select **E**dit, **C**ut (or press Shift-Del).

6. Select **C**lose.

7. Press Backspace to delete the note number for the text you just cut.

8. Select **L**ayout, **E**ndnote, **C**reate.

9. Enter a tab, an indent, or a space (depending on the endnote format you prefer), and then select **E**dit, **P**aste to paste the text.

 Press Shift-Ins.

10. Select **C**lose.

If you want to make changing footnotes to endnotes even easier, you can edit your Button Bar to assign the FOOTEND macro to a button (see Chapter 19).

> You quickly can change all your footnotes to endnotes by defining and turning on newspaper-style columns at the beginning of your document (**L**ayout, **C**olumns, **D**efine, Enter). Then delete the codes [Col Def] and [Col On]. Because you cannot use footnotes in columns, WordPerfect converts all footnotes to endnotes. Be sure to save your document before trying this trick, however, because this action may affect special formatting in your document.

T I P

Chapter Summary

In this chapter, you have learned how to create a footnote or endnote. You have also learned how to view your notes through Print Preview, Footnote (Endnote) Edit, and Reveal Codes and to edit your notes. You can add, insert, move, and delete your notes; you know how to change the font and margin formatting of your notes to match the formatting of your document text. You have seen how to change your note options, and change the placement of your endnotes. The chapter also explains how to convert footnotes to endnotes, and vice versa.

Now all that is left is to begin using footnotes or endnotes to enhance the readability and completeness of your documents. You now know how easily you can create and use footnotes.

WordPerfect does offer, by the way, another approach to creating footnotes; a brute-force method. People who take this approach would rather type—and retype and change—their footnote numbers than learn how to use the more elegant and simpler footnote feature. Smile smugly as you watch them struggle, or perhaps refer them to this chapter.

Line Numbering, Paragraph Numbering, and Outlining

WordPerfect automates the numbering and management of lines, paragraphs, and outlines so that you don't have to remember what the next line number or outline level should be. You also aren't forced to do tedious and error-prone renumbering if you delete an item or add one in the middle. For outlines, these ideas have been extended so that you can easily delete and move groups of related information.

This chapter explores the following automatic numbering features:

- Line Numbering, to number lines automatically
- Paragraph Numbering, to generate paragraph numbers
- Outline, to create outlines and generate paragraph numbers

■ **Eric Baatz** has held a variety of managerial and programming jobs in the New England computer industry over the last 15 years. He is an enthusiastic user of many word processors and desktop publishing systems.

You also learn to do the following:

- Change the defaults for Line Numbering
- Change the number style used for Paragraph Numbering and Outline
- Edit an outline

Line Numbering, the simplest form of automatic numbering, places an incremented number in the left margin next to each line of text. You can begin and end the numbering at any location you choose. You also can have the numbering restart on each page or have the numbers printed at some interval other than every line.

You can create simple lists and complex outlines using *Paragraph Numbering*. Paragraph Numbering formats text, with the amount of indentation and the number style varying with the hierarchical level of each paragraph. For numbers, you can specify Arabic numerals, Roman numerals, bullets, or your choice of characters, all combined with various punctuation marks.

The *Outline* feature extends Paragraph Numbering so that you can create and maintain outlines efficiently. After you turn on Outline, WordPerfect inserts a new number each time you press Enter, and you can move, copy, or delete a level and its sublevels as a unit.

The Line Numbering Feature

Line Numbering places an incremented number in the left margin next to each line of text. (You cannot see the numbers unless you choose **F**ile, **P**rint or File, Print Pre**v**iew.) Use Line Numbering when you want easy, clear references to individual lines. This feature is particularly useful for items that groups of people review, such as legal documents.

Line Numbering includes footnotes and endnotes but not headers, footers, or full-width graphics boxes, including equation boxes.

Understanding Line Numbering Options

You control Line Numbering with the Line Numbering dialog box, which you access by choosing **L**ayout, **L**ine, **N**umbering (see fig. 24.1).

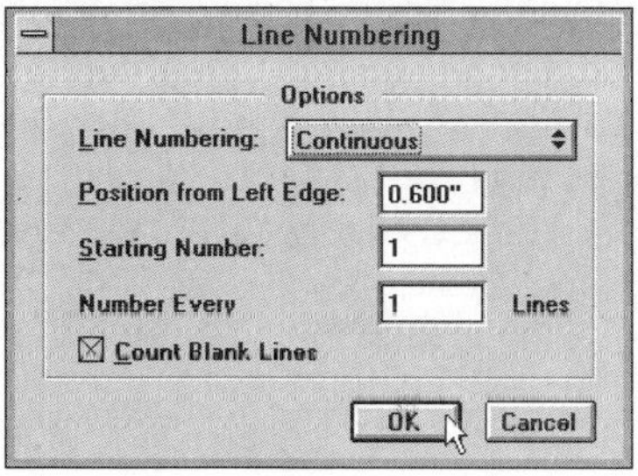

FIG. 24.1

The Line
Numbering
dialog box.

The Line Numbering dialog box offers the following options:

■ The **Line** Numbering scroll box presents a pop-up list when you
hold down the left mouse button while the pointer is on the scroll
box (see fig. 24.2). Make a selection by moving the mouse and
releasing the mouse button when your choice is highlighted. (Alternatively, you can press the space bar from the **Line** Numbering
scroll box to get the list of options.)

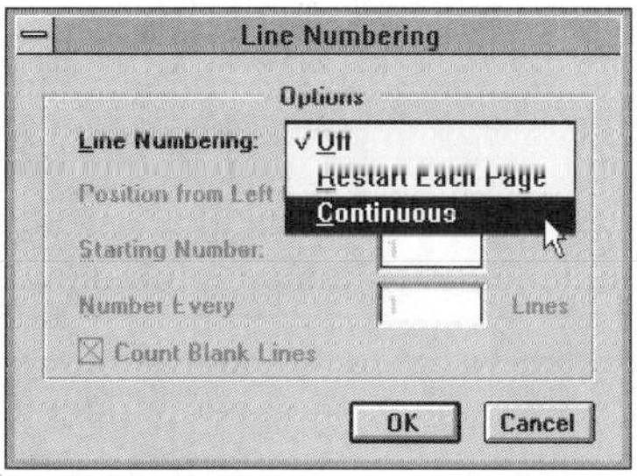

FIG. 24.2

The Line
Numbering
pop-up list of
options.

The choices in the Line Numbering scroll box are described in the
following paragraphs.

The **O**ff option turns off Line Numbering at the beginning of the
current paragraph if the Auto Code Placement feature is on, or at
the beginning of the next line if Auto Code Placement is off.
WordPerfect places a [Ln Num:Off] code in your document. (For
information on Auto Code Placement, see Chapter 6, "Formatting
Text.")

The **C**ontinuous option turns on Line Numbering at the beginning
of the current paragraph if Auto Code Placement is on, or at the
beginning of the next line if Auto Code Placement is off. The line
numbers start with the value in the **S**tarting Number text box and
increase until the end of the document or until you turn off Line
Numbering.

■ **Cue:** If you use Continuous numbering, Print Preview
displays the document as if
you had chosen Restart Each
Page numbering instead;
however, the line numbers
print correctly.

The **R**estart Each Page option turns on Line Numbering at the beginning of the current paragraph if Auto Code Placement is on, or at the beginning of the next line if Auto Code Placement is off. The line numbers start with the value in the **S**tarting Number text box and increase until you start a new page, where the line numbers begin again with the number in the **S**tarting Number text box.

■ The **P**osition from Left Edge text box specifies the distance from the left edge of the paper to the location where the line numbers appear.

Cue: The Position for Left Edge number should be smaller than the number for the left margin; otherwise, the line numbers print on top of your text.

Don't try to type a unit of measure in the **P**osition from Left Edge text box. Deleting the unit and adding a different one also won't change the units used. The Units of Measure dialog box in Preferences controls the units used. (For information on Preferences, see Chapter 29, "Customizing WordPerfect with Preferences.")

Cue: If Auto Code Placement is turned on for your document, you can start Line Numbering only at the beginning of paragraphs.

■ The **S**tarting Number text box specifies the number you want WordPerfect to display on the first numbered line. Ordinarily, you start numbering on the first line of a document or page, using a starting number of 1. If you want the first part of the document to have no line numbers and Line Numbering to start at line 30, however, you must turn on Line Numbering for line 30 and specify a starting number of **30**.

■ In the **N**umber Every *n* Lines text box, you specify how often you want line numbers displayed. Typing **3** in this text box, for example, causes a number to appear on every third line—3 on line 3, 6 on line 6, 9 on line 9, and so on.

■ Use the **C**ount Blank Lines option to specify how you want to treat blank lines—that is, lines consisting of only a hard return code ([HRt]). If this box is checked, WordPerfect counts blank lines. If the box isn't checked, WordPerfect doesn't count blank lines.

Specifying Line Numbering Settings

To use the default Line Numbering settings in the Line Numbering dialog box, follow these steps:

1. Position the insertion point in your document at the location where you want line numbering to begin.

2. Choose **L**ayout, **L**ine, **N**umbering. The Line Numbering dialog box appears (refer to fig. 24.1).

3. Choose **Line Numbering**; then specify **Restart Each Page** or **Continuous**.

4. Choose OK or press Enter.

After you turn on Line Numbering, WordPerfect inserts a [Ln Num:On] code into your document. Placement of the [Ln Num:On] code depends on the setting of Auto Code Placement.

If the default settings for Line Numbering don't meet your needs, change the defaults in the Line Numbering dialog box. If you want to number every fifth line instead of every line, for example, type **5** in the Number Every *n* Lines text box.

Turning Off Line Numbering

If you want to remove all line numbering from the document, delete the [Ln Num:On] code in Reveal Codes.

If you don't know the location of one or more of your Line Numbering codes, choose **Edit**, **Search** to access the Search dialog box. Choose **Codes** and specify the [Ln Num:On] code to search your entire document for that code. (For more information on using the Search feature, see Chapter 4, "Editing a Document.")

T I P

If you want to retain line numbers in part of the document, turn off Line Numbering at the end of the last section you want numbered. ***Note:*** If Auto Code Placement is on, you cannot turn off Line Numbering in the middle of a paragraph, because the [Ln Num:Off] code will appear at the beginning of the paragraph in which you have placed the insertion point.

To turn off line numbering at the end of a section, follow these steps:

1. Move the insertion point to the location where you want the line numbers to stop.

2. Choose **Layout**, **Line**, **Numbering**. The Line Numbering dialog box appears.

3. Choose **Line Numbering** and then choose **Off**.

4. Choose OK or press Enter to return to your document.

Viewing Line Numbers

■ **Cue:** Line numbers are printed in the font that is in effect at the location where the [Ln Num:On] code appears in the text.

Line numbers don't appear on-screen in the editing window. You can use Reveal Codes (Alt-F3) to see the [Ln Num:On] and [Ln Num:Off] codes, but to see the line numbers, you must print the document or use Print Preview.

To view your line numbers in Print Preview, follow these steps:

1. Choose **F**ile, Print Pre**v**iew.

    Press Print Preview (Shift-F5).

2. Click the 100% icon or choose **V**iew, **1**00% to see the numbers more clearly. Figure 24.3 shows a document with line numbers in Print Preview.

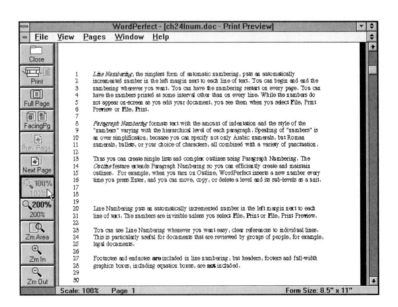

FIG. 24.3

Print Preview showing line numbers in the left margin.

3. Click the Close icon or choose **F**ile, **C**lose. WordPerfect returns to the document editing window.

    Press Close Document (Ctrl-F4).

> **T I P**
>
> If you want printed line numbers to be less conspicuous, change them to a smaller font. Begin by moving the insertion point to the location where you want line numbering to begin. Turn on Line Numbering (choose **L**ayout, **L**ine, **N**umbering). Turn on Reveal Codes (Alt-F3) and move the pointer to highlight the [Ln Num:On] code. Choose **F**ont, **F**ont and change to a smaller font. Then move the pointer just to the right of the [Ln Num:On] code and change back to the larger font. (See Chapter 10, "Working with Fonts," for more information on using fonts.)

Be sure that the font you specify for line numbering is the same size as or smaller than the font used for normal text. Because the font used for the text—not the line numbers—determines line height, using a large font for line numbers may result in those numbers appearing squashed.

The Paragraph Numbering Feature

The Paragraph Numbering feature uses a wide variety of numbering styles to number paragraphs. You specify the part(s) of your document where Paragraph Numbering occurs and the styles of numbers you want to use. As you insert or delete numbered paragraphs, WordPerfect renumbers them for you.

This feature enables you to display information hierarchically, from simple lists to complex outlines, with related paragraphs sharing a number style and identical indentation from the left margin. Unlike Line Numbering, Paragraph Numbering generates numbers you always can see in your document.

The idea at the heart of Paragraph Numbering is that logically similar material should share the same number style and the same amount of indentation from the left margin. Before generating paragraph numbers, therefore, you must decide how much indentation and what types of numbers are appropriate for your material. A simple list, for example, probably has only one level of indentation and uses Arabic numerals or bullets. A complex outline, on the other hand, has many levels and uses various number styles, such as Roman numerals and upper- and lower-case letters.

WordPerfect supports up to eight levels of indentation. Level 1 indentation has numbers at the left margin, level 2 has numbers following one tab, level 3 has numbers following two tabs, and so forth. The example pictured in figure 24.4 shows indentation levels and their WordPerfect codes. Figure 24.4 uses Arabic numerals followed by a period for level 1, lowercase letters followed by a period for level 2, and lowercase Roman numerals followed by a period for level 3.

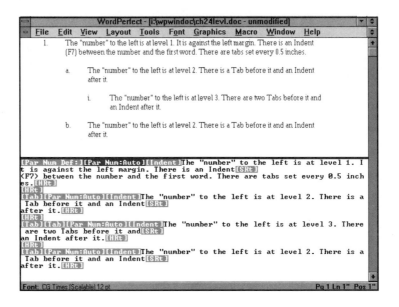

FIG. 24.4

Paragraph Numbering levels and codes.

Your tab settings control the amount of space before and after each number when you start Paragraph Numbering. In figure 24.4, the indent after 1. moves the text to the first tab setting. The tab before a. moves a. to the first tab setting, and the indent after a. moves the text to the second tab setting. Because the default tab settings were used, each tab and indent moves the text one-half inch.

Defining Number Style

You use the Define Paragraph Numbering dialog box (see fig. 24.5) to specify Paragraph Numbering options. To access this dialog box, choose **T**ools, **O**utline, **D**efine.

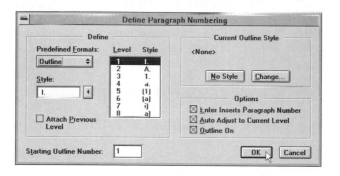

FIG. 24.5

The Define
Paragraph
Numbering
dialog box.

If you plan to number paragraphs often, add a button to your Button
Bar so that you can get to the Define Paragraph Numbering dialog box
with a single click. See Chapter 19, "Using the Button Bar," for more
information.

BUTTON

Note: Many of the Define Paragraph Numbering dialog box options are
specific to the Outline feature (explained later in this chapter). All
choices in the Define section of the dialog box, however—including
user-defined numbering formats—are available for Paragraph
Numbering.

To specify a predefined Paragraph Numbering format, follow these
steps:

1. Move the insertion point to the location where you want paragraph numbering to begin. If you haven't typed the paragraph,
   move the insertion point to the location where you plan to start
   typing. If you have typed the text, move the insertion point to the
   beginning of the text.

   ■ **Cue:** Before typing
   your text, specify tab
   settings by choosing
   Layout, **L**ine, **T**ab Set.

2. Choose **Tools**, **O**utline, **D**efine.

   CUA Press Paragraph Define (Alt-Shift-F5).

3. Choose Predefined **F**ormats and specify the desired format. The
   columns in the Level/Style box change, depending on the specified format. If you choose Outline, for example, the first entry is
   1 I. and the second 2 A., indicating that level 1 style is uppercase Roman numerals followed by a period, and level 2 style is
   uppercase letters followed by a period.

   If you don't like the resulting style, choose a different format.

4. Choose **O**utline On in the Options section of the dialog box to
   remove the X in the check box and disable the Outline feature.

■ **Cue:** If Auto Code Placement is turned on, WordPerfect inserts the [Par Num:Auto] code at the beginning of the paragraph in which the insertion point is located.

5. Choose OK or press Enter to return to your document. This step activates the new definition by generating a [Par Num:Auto] code in your document.

Creating Numbered Paragraphs with Automatic Levels

After you choose the desired numbering style, you can begin typing your text.

> **T I P**
>
> If you want a centered title above your numbered paragraphs, choose **Layout**, **Line**, **Center**; then type the title. Press Enter twice to end the title and place a blank line between the title and the start of the numbered paragraphs.

To create numbered paragraphs with automatic levels, follow these steps:

1. If you are sure that Outline is turned off, go to step 2. If you aren't sure, press Enter. If no paragraph number is generated, Outline is off; go on to step 2. If a paragraph number is generated, turn off the Outline option by choosing **Tools**, **Outline**, Outline Off, or by deleting the [Outline On] code in Reveal Codes.

2. If Auto Code Placement is not on for your document, make sure that the insertion point is at the left margin.

3. Choose **Tools**, **Outline**, **Paragraph** Number.

    Press Paragraph Number (Alt-F5).

   The Paragraph Numbering dialog box appears, as shown in figure 24.6.

■ **Cue:** Your choices in the Define Paragraph Numbering dialog box determine the numbering style that WordPerfect uses.

   Choose **Insert** or press Enter to accept the **Auto** default for Numbering Level. WordPerfect inserts a [Par Num:Auto] code into the text, causing the insertion of the appropriate number and style based on the number of tabs to the left of the insertion point.

4. Press Indent (F7), Tab, or the space bar, and then type the text for the paragraph.

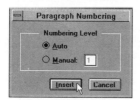

FIG. 24.6

The Paragraph
Numbering
dialog box.

If you use Indent, the paragraph's text is indented to the next tab setting, as in the following example:

    1. This example shows the effect of an Indent after the number, followed by more text that wraps to the next line.

If you use Tab, the first line of the paragraph's text is indented to the next tab setting, and the second and subsequent lines are indented to the number's tab setting, as in the following example:

    1. This example shows the effect of a Tab after the number, followed by more text that wraps to the next line.

5. Press Enter twice to insert a blank line and begin a new paragraph.

6. If you want the new paragraph to have a number, press Tab at least once to move the insertion point to the right so that the desired style of number is generated, and then return to step 3.

    If you don't want the new paragraph to have a number, return to step 4.

If you use a mouse, consider adding the Paragraph Numbering menu item to the Button Bar. You also can define a macro that chooses **Para**graph Number, specifies **A**uto or **M**anual, dismisses the dialog box, and creates an indent; then assign that macro to a button (see Chapters 19 and 20).

BUTTON

Overriding Automatic Levels with Manual Levels

Sometimes you may want a particular number style to be used regardless of how many tabs are to the left of the insertion point. For example, you may want all the numbers to line up at the margin or at a particular tab setting. To create manual levels, choose **M**anual in the Paragraph Numbering dialog box (again see fig. 24.6). Then specify the level of the numbering style that corresponds to the style of number you choose.

Suppose that you choose WordPerfect's predefined Paragraph format, but you want to use lowercase letters. Choose **M**anual and specify a level of **2** in the text box. With this option, WordPerfect inserts a [Par Num:n] code into the document, where *n* is the level number you specified.

Editing Paragraph Numbers

Because paragraph numbers are WordPerfect codes in your document, you can manipulate the numbers using the standard methods of insertion and deletion you already know.

To delete a paragraph number, turn on Reveal Codes (Alt-F3), highlight the [Par Num] code representing the number you want to delete, and press Del.

■ **Cue:** You can decrease a level by choosing **L**ayout, Pa**r**agraph, **M**argin Release, at the cost of cluttering up your document with yet more codes.

To change the level of a paragraph number, highlight the [Par Num] code representing the number whose level you want to change. To decrease the level, press Backspace to delete one or more tabs or indents to the left of the [Par Num] code. To increase the level, press Tab once for each level. If nothing happens when you press Tab, you may not have enough tab settings defined.

To add a paragraph number to an unnumbered paragraph, follow these steps:

1. Place the insertion point at the beginning of the paragraph but after any tabs you have used to adjust the indentation level. (You may want to turn on Reveal Codes for this step.)

2. Choose **T**ools, **O**utline, **P**aragraph Number.

   [CUA] Press Paragraph Number (Alt-F5).

3. The Paragraph Numbering dialog box appears. Choose **A**uto or **M**anual as appropriate.

4. Choose OK or press Enter.

T I P   If you start a series of paragraph numbers, but the first number in the series isn't the number you expected, you may not have defined a new Starting Outline Number when you defined the new style in the Define Paragraph Numbering dialog box. WordPerfect continues to increment the numbers with the Paragraph Numbering style that preceded the new style.

You can use styles, macros, and the Button Bar to simplify the use of Paragraph Numbering. Begin by creating a style that changes the margins so that numbers are indented, creates a tab setting for the left edge of the text following the numbers, and restores the margins and tab settings after the list is finished. Then create a macro that turns on the style and defines the type of numbers to use. Finally, add a button to the Button Bar to which you assign the macro. See Chapter 12, "Using Styles;" Chapter 19, "Using the Button Bar;" and Chapter 20, "Creating Macros."

The Outline Feature

The Outline feature extends the number styles and levels of Paragraph Numbering. Outlines are organized with logically similar material sharing the same style of number and the same amount of indentation from the left margin. How far the indentation extends and the amount of space after each number depends on your tab settings. Level 1 indentation places numbers at the left margin, level 2 numbers follow one tab, level 3 numbers follow two tabs, and so on. WordPerfect supports up to eight levels of indentation.

Note: As in the Paragraph Numbering sections of this chapter, "paragraph number" means any of a wide variety of symbols you use to indicate the beginning of a level. Those symbols include letters, numbers, bullets, characters of your choice, and, with Outline Styles, even WordPerfect codes.

Because Outline is an extension of Paragraph Numbering, the two features share vocabulary, dialog boxes, and WordPerfect codes that define where numbers are placed on a line and how the numbers look. Figure 24.7 shows an outline example with the associated WordPerfect codes. This example uses uppercase Roman numerals followed by a period for level 1, uppercase letters followed by a period for level 2, and Arabic numerals followed by a period for level 3.

In figure 24.7, the indent after I. moves the text to the first tab setting. The tab before A. moves A. to the first tab setting, and the indent after A. moves the text to the second tab setting. Because the default tab settings were used, each tab and indent moves the text one-half inch.

The example in figure 24.7 also shows the other WordPerfect codes that format the text. The style of the numbers is defined by the [Par Num Def] code (see the section "The Define Paragraph Numbering Dialog Box," later in this chapter). Outline is turned on between the [Outline On] and [Outline Off] codes, as described in the next section. Each [Par Num:Auto] code becomes a number of the proper style and value.

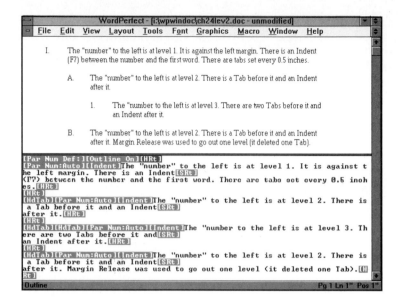

FIG. 24.7

Outline levels
and WordPerfect
codes.

Table 24.1 highlights the differences between Outline and Paragraph
Numbering.

Table 24.1. Contrasting Paragraph Numbering and Outline

Paragraph Numbering	Outline Numbering
Can be done anywhere in the text	Can be done only between the [Outline On] and [Outline Off] codes, but you can put those codes anywhere in your text
Paragraph numbers appear only when specified (good for text with infrequent numbers)	Outline numbers appear each time you press Enter (good for text with frequent numbers); you can delete unwanted numbers
Particular number style can be placed anywhere on a line	Number style determined strictly by indentation
Normal text editing available	Normal text editing and special paragraph editing available (the latter enables easy moving, deletion, and copying of related groups of paragraphs)
All keys keep their normal meanings	Several keys have special meanings; (see table 24.2 for complete list of special keys)

Turning On Outline

You can turn on Outline in one of two ways. For either method, begin by moving the insertion point to the location where you want Outline to take effect. Then choose one of the following methods:

- Choose **T**ools, **O**utline, Outline **O**n. With this method, WordPerfect inserts an [Outline On] code into your document at the insertion point. The style of the numbers generated is determined by the closest preceding Paragraph Numbering definition.

- Choose **T**ools, **O**utline, **D**efine or press Paragraph Define (Alt-Shift-F5). The Define Paragraph Numbering dialog box appears (refer to fig. 24.5). This dialog box enables you to define the style of numbers you want; with the Outline **O**n option selected, this method turns on Outline when you choose OK or press Enter.

When Outline is on, WordPerfect displays the word Outline in the status bar.

Understanding the Outline Keys

With the Outline feature, you can redefine the functions of some keys so that you can add numbers and change the level of a number. You also can move, delete, and copy families of paragraphs (that is, a level of the outline and all its sublevels).

Outline is on when the insertion point is between an [Outline On] code and an [Outline Off] code. If Outline is on, and the closest preceding Paragraph Numbering definition hasn't altered the default settings in the Options section of the Define Paragraph Numbering dialog box, a number of keyboard keys take on special meanings. Table 24.2 describes these special meanings.

The Options section of the Define Paragraph Numbering dialog box controls the effect of pressing Enter.

■ **Cue:** You can create outlines within headers, footers, endnotes, footnotes, and text boxes; these features are completely independent of any outlines within the main body of your document.

Table 24.2. Special Outline Keys

Key	Meaning
Enter	This keystroke inserts a hard return code ([HRt]) into the text at the insertion point, followed by enough tabs to place the next paragraph number at the same level as the preceding paragraph number. These tabs are followed by a new paragraph number (that is, a [Par Num:Auto] code).
Tab	If pressed immediately after you press Enter, this keystroke inserts a hard tab code ([HdTab]) immediately before [Par Num:Auto], moving the number one tab setting to the right and changing the setting to the style of the next level.
Margin Release (Shift-Tab)	If pressed immediately after a tab, this key combination removes the hard tab immediately before the [Par Num:Auto] code. This action moves the number to the left by one tab setting and changes the setting to the style of the preceding level.
Alt-left arrow,* Alt-right arrow*	These keystroke combinations move the insertion point to the preceding (Alt-left arrow) or the next (Alt-right arrow) paragraph number or outline style, regardless of its level.
Alt-up arrow,* Alt-down arrow*	These keystroke combinations move the insertion point to the preceding (Alt-up arrow) or the next (Alt-down arrow) paragraph of the same or lower level.

* Only if you have an extended keyboard

Turning Off Outline

When you complete the outline, return to creating normal paragraphs by turning off Outline. If the insertion point is not at the end of the outline text, move the insertion point there. Then choose **Tools**, **O**utline, Outline Off. WordPerfect inserts an [Outline Off] code into your document. When you turn off Outline, the Enter and Tab keys revert to their normal functions.

If you don't know whether Outline is on or off, look at the status bar. If the word Outline appears, the Outline feature is on.

Creating a Sample Outline

This section shows you how to create the short outline shown in figure 24.8.

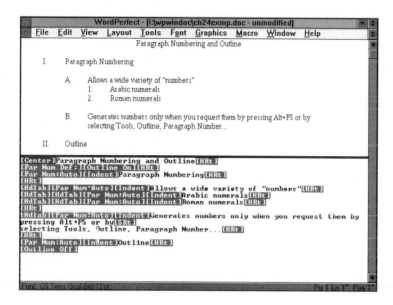

FIG. 24.8

An Outline example shown with codes.

To create the sample outline, begin by moving the insertion point to the location where you want the outline to start. If necessary, specify the tab settings (choose Layout, Line, Tab Set). Because this example has three levels, you need at least three tab settings to the right of the left margin. If the default tab settings are in effect (a tab setting exists every one-half inch), you don't need to change the settings for this example. Then follow these steps:

1. To create the centered title, choose Layout, Line, Center.

    Press Center (Shift-F7).

   Type **Paragraph Numbering and Outline** and press Enter.

2. Choose Tools, Outline, Define.

    Press Paragraph Define (Alt-Shift-F5).

   The Define Paragraph Numbering dialog box appears.

3. Choose Predefined Formats and specify Outline.

■ **Cue:** If Auto Code Placement is turned on for your document, WordPerfect inserts the [Par Num:Auto] code at the beginning of the paragraph in which the insertion point is located.

4. Choose OK or press Enter to return to your document. WordPerfect activates the new definition by inserting a [Par Num Def] code into your document and turning on Outline.

5. Press Enter to create a paragraph number.

6. Press Indent (F7); then type **Paragraph Numbering**.

7. Press twice to create the next paragraph number and leave a blank line between the numbered paragraphs. Note that the number moves with the insertion point.

8. Press Tab to move in one level. The number follows and changes; in this case, from *II* to *A*.

   If you press Tab too many times, press Margin Release (Shift-Tab) to move one tab setting to the left. No code is inserted, but the number moves to the left and changes back one level.

9. Press Indent (F7); then type **Allows a wide variety of "numbers"**.

10. Press Enter; then press Tab to move in one level.

11. Press Indent (F7); then type **Arabic numerals**.

12. Press Enter. Note that the new number lines up with the preceding number.

13. Press Indent (F7); then type **Roman numerals**.

14. Press Enter twice.

15. Press Margin Release (Shift-Tab) to move the indentation one setting left and to change the number from *3* to *B*.

16. Press Indent (F7); then type **Generates numbers only when you request them by pressing Alt+F5 or by selecting Tools, Outline, Paragraph Number...**.

17. Press Enter twice.

18. Press Margin Release (Shift-Tab).

19. Press Indent (F7); then type **Outline**.

20. Choose **T**ools, **O**utline, Outline Off.

Editing an Outline

After you create an outline, you may want to make structural changes such as deleting, adding, or moving numbered paragraphs. The real advantage of using automatic numbering is the ease of editing and renumbering.

You can move quickly from one outline level to another if you have an extended keyboard. Press Alt-left arrow to move the insertion point backward to the preceding paragraph number, regardless of its level. Press Alt-right arrow to move the insertion point forward to the next paragraph number, regardless of its level. Press Alt-up arrow to move the insertion point backward to the preceding paragraph of the same or lower level. Press Alt-down arrow to move the insertion point forward to the next paragraph of the same or lower level.

T I P

Changing and Deleting Outline Paragraph Numbers

To change the level of a single paragraph, you must change its indentation. Place the insertion point on the [Par Num] code for the number you want to change (you may want to turn on Reveal Codes). To move the number to the right (making the number a lower level), press Tab. To move the number to the left (making the number a higher level), press Margin Release (Shift-Tab).

To change the level of a *family* of numbered paragraphs (that is, one paragraph and all the following lower levels), see the section "Moving Outline Numbered Paragraphs," later in this chapter.

To delete a paragraph number, delete the [Par Num] code representing the paragraph number. Because paragraph numbers are just another WordPerfect code, delete the [Par Num] code the same way you delete any other code: turn on Reveal Codes, delete the [Par Num] code, and turn off Reveal Codes.

Adding Outline Paragraph Numbers

If you accidentally delete a paragraph number or if you create an unnumbered paragraph and later decide to add a number, you easily can add a paragraph number. Assuming that Outline is turned on (check the status bar for the word Outline) and that the Outline On option is enabled in the Paragraph Numbering definition, follow these steps:

1. Place the insertion point at the end of the paragraph preceding the paragraph you want to number. (You may want to turn on Reveal Codes.)

2. Press Enter to create a new number.

3. If necessary, press Tab or Margin Release (Shift-Tab) to set the proper indentation and style.

4. Join your text to the new number by deleting any hard returns ([HRt]) between the new number and the following text.

5. If necessary, press Indent (F7), Tab, or the space bar to move the start of your text an appropriate distance to the right.

If you want to add a paragraph number when Outline is off or the Outline On option is disabled, refer to the section "Creating Numbered Paragraphs with Automatic Levels," earlier in this chapter.

Deleting Outline Numbered Paragraphs

Cue: If you highlight the paragraph and press Del, you cannot paste the paragraph elsewhere in the text; you must use Undelete to recover the deleted text.

Because a numbered paragraph is primarily normal text, you can delete the paragraph like any other text. To delete a numbered paragraph, highlight the text you want to delete (including the [Par Num] code) and choose **Edit, Cut** (or press Shift-Del). WordPerfect renumbers the remaining paragraphs to account for the deletion.

If you delete too many or too few WordPerfect codes, you may have to clean up the outline's format after a deletion.

A special mechanism is available for deleting a family of paragraphs that avoids painstaking manipulation of the mouse and the need for cleaning up. Figure 24.9 shows a family of paragraphs, highlighted in the editing window.

The example outline contains other families. The largest family consists of the I, A, 1, 2, and B items.

To delete a numbered paragraph family when Outline is turned on, follow these steps:

Cue: If you decide you don't want to delete the paragraph or family you just deleted, choose **Edit, Undelete.**

1. Place the insertion point on the top level number of the family you want to delete. You may want to turn on Reveal Codes to make sure that the insertion point is on the [Par Num] code.

   For this example, suppose that you want to delete the A, 1, and 2 paragraphs. Highlight the *A*.

2. Choose **Tools, Outline, Delete Family.**

   WordPerfect highlights the text to be deleted and displays a dialog box, as shown in figure 24.10.

3. Choose **Yes** or press Enter.

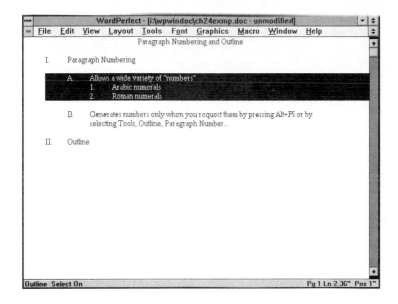

FIG. 24.9

A family of
paragraphs in
the sample
outline.

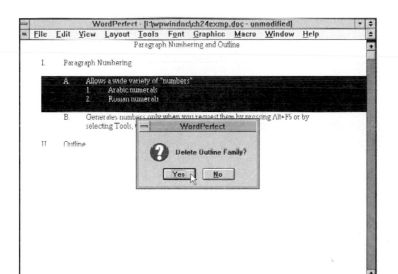

FIG. 24.10

An outline family
selected for
deletion.

Moving Outline Numbered Paragraphs

At times, you may need to move a numbered paragraph within your outline. Begin by highlighting the paragraph you want to move. (Be sure to highlight the [Par Num] code also.) Choose **E**dit, **C**ut. Move the insertion point to the location where you want the paragraph inserted and insert the paragraph by choosing **E**dit, **P**aste.

You can move a paragraph or an entire family of paragraphs vertically or horizontally (changing all levels within the family at the same time) without adding or deleting tabs in front of each numbered paragraph in the family.

You can move a family up, down, left, or right, depending on the contents of the family. The highlighted family in figure 24.9, for example, can be moved up, left, and down, but not right. The following table shows how the movement of the sample family changes the numbering structure.

Direction of Movement	Change in Numbers and Text		
Up	I.	Allows a wide variety of "numbers"	
		A.	Arabic numerals
		B.	Roman numerals
	II.	Paragraph Numbering	
Left	I.	Paragraph Numbering	
	II.	Allows a wide variety of "numbers"	
		A.	Arabic numerals
		B.	Roman numerals
Down	I.	Paragraph Numbering	
		A.	Generates numbers...
		B.	Allows a wide variety of "numbers"
			1. Arabic numerals
			2. Roman numerals

In this example, you cannot move the family to the right because that movement would leave a numbering gap between the family and the paragraph immediately preceding the family.

To change a family of numbered paragraphs (for this example, the family shown in figure 24.9), follow these steps:

1. Move the insertion point to the number at the top level of the family you want to move. You may want to turn on Reveal Codes to make sure that the insertion point is on the [Par Num] code. For this example, move the insertion point to *A*.

2. Choose **Tools**, **Outline**, **M**ove Family. WordPerfect highlights the family, displays the message `Press Arrows to Move Family; Enter when done`, and changes the pointer to a circle with a slash.

3. Press the appropriate arrow to move the family in the desired direction. For this example, press the down arrow twice to move the family to follow *II. Outline*.

4. Press Enter to fix the family in place.

5. If you want to add a blank line before the moved family, press Enter to create a new line and an unwanted paragraph number. Then press Backspace to delete the unwanted number.

   If you want to add a blank line after the moved family, move the insertion point to the end of the family, press Enter, and then press Backspace to delete the unwanted number generated by pressing Enter.

   For this example, press Enter and then Backspace once to delete the unwanted number.

WordPerfect renumbers the outline after you move a paragraph. Figure 24.11 shows the sample outline after the family has been moved.

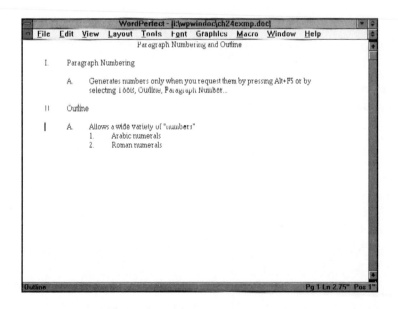

FIG. 24.11

The sample outline after moving the family.

Copying Outline Numbered Paragraphs

Because numbered paragraphs are primarily normal text, copying an individually numbered paragraph is much like moving or deleting that paragraph. Follow these steps to copy a paragraph:

1. Highlight the text and [Par Num] code you want to copy.

2. Choose **E**dit, **C**opy.

    CUA   Press Copy (Ctrl-Ins).

3. Move the insertion point to the location where you want to insert the copy.

4. Choose **E**dit, **P**aste.

    CUA   Press Paste (Shift-Insert).

Copying a family of paragraphs is much like moving the family, except that a copy of the paragraph(s) is created immediately after you choose **T**ools, **O**utline, **C**opy Family. The copy moves, rather than the original family. See "Moving Outline Numbered Paragraphs," earlier in this chapter.

Adding Outline Numbered Paragraphs

To add a numbered paragraph to an existing outline, move the insertion point to the location where you want to insert your text. Press Enter to create a new number. To create a blank line between the preceding text and the new number, press Enter again. If you want to move the text to the right to change the indentation, press Tab; to move text left to the desired indentation, press Margin Release (Shift-Tab).

Adding Outline Unnumbered Paragraphs

To add an unnumbered paragraph to an existing outline, move the insertion point to the location where you want to insert your text and press Enter to create a new number. If you want a blank line between the preceding text and the new number, press Enter again; then press Backspace to delete the unwanted number.

If you want to move the text to the right to change the indentation, press Insert or Tab. To move the text left to the desired indentation, press Margin Release (Shift-Tab).

If you want to add many consecutive paragraphs without numbers when you are in Outline, turn off the Enter Inserts Paragraph Number option in the Define Paragraph Numbering dialog box before adding the paragraphs.

T I P

The Define Paragraph Numbering Dialog Box

The Define Paragraph Numbering dialog box controls the style of paragraph numbers, the starting number, and how several aspects of Outline work. To access the dialog box, move the insertion point to the location where you want the new definition to take effect. Choose **Tools, Outline, Define**. The Define Paragraph Numbering dialog box appears (refer to fig. 24.5). Each section in the dialog box is discussed in the following sections.

If Auto Code Placement is on, the new numbering style takes effect at the beginning of the current paragraph (that is, WordPerfect places a [Par Num Def] code at the beginning of the paragraph). If Auto Code Placement is off, the new numbering style takes effect at the beginning of the next line.

Using the Define Options

The Define section of the Define Paragraph Numbering dialog box offers a number of predefined number formats and some limited customization. The following sections describe the options in this section of the dialog box.

Predefined Formats

With the Predefined Formats option, WordPerfect uses a different number format (style) at each of its eight levels. You can choose one of four predefined combinations or define one of your own. Table 24.3 summarizes the number styles for each level of the predefined formats, using the following symbols:

1 represents an Arabic numeral.
a represents a lowercase alphabetic character.
A represents an uppercase alphabetic character.
i represents a lowercase Roman numeral.
I represents an uppercase Roman numeral.

Table 24.3. Predefined Number Formats

Level	Predefined Formats		
	Paragraph	Outline	Legal [1,1,1]
1	1.	I.	1.
2	a.	A.	1.1
3	i.	1.	1.1.1
4	(1)	a.	1.1.1.1
5	(a)	(1)	1.1.1.1.1
6	(i)	(a)	1.1.1.1.1.1
7	1)	i)	1.1.1.1.1.1.1
8	a)	a)	1.1.1.1.1.1.1.1

Cue: If you want to use different bullets, create a user-defined format and use the WordPerfect Characters dialog box (choose **F**ont, **W**P Characters or press Ctrl-W) to substitute the bullets you want for Word-Perfect's defaults.

To use one of WordPerfect's predefined formats, choose the desired format in the Predefined **F**ormats scroll box. If you prefer to define your own format, you can choose User-Defined in the Predefined **F**ormats scroll box or modify one of the predefined formats. To use the latter method, select the predefined format that most closely resembles what you want and choose that level in the Level/Style box. The style of the number from that level appears in the Style text box (see the next section for a discussion of the Style options).

The WordPerfect characters (expressed as a WordPerfect Character Map number and a character number within that map) used for bullets by levels 1 through 8 are (4,0), (4,1), (0,45), (4,2), (0,42), (0,43), (4,3), and (0,120). Chapter 28, "Creating and Displaying Special Characters," details these and other special characters you may want to use in your documents.

Level Style

Cue: If the Attach **P**revious Level option is enabled for a level, an asterisk (*) precedes that level in the **L**evel Style box.

You don't type anything in the **L**evel Style box; after you select a pre-defined format, the style of the number for each level appears in this box. If you choose one of the levels in the Level Style box, the associ-ated style appears in the Style box.

> **T I P**
>
> Bullets require special care. Your printer may not be capable of printing the WordPerfect characters used as bullets, or WordPerfect may try to use graphics to "draw" the character for your printer. The latter technique may take longer than you find tolerable or may not meet your quality standards. Before using bullets, make an eight-level outline with just the bullets, print the outline, and check the results.

Style

The **S**tyle box holds the number style from the highlighted level in the **L**evel Style box. If you modify the contents of the Style box in any way, the entry in the Predefined Formats box changes to User-Defined.

A *number style* is a single character that represents a class of numbers (a related group of numbers in a similar style; for example, Arabic or Roman) and punctuation characters. The number changes from one numbered paragraph to the next but the punctuation remains the same. The style (I), for example, has two punctuation characters—the opening and closing parentheses—and the I that represents the class of Roman numerals. The first number represented by the style (I) is (I), the second is (II), the third is (III), and so forth.

You place a style in the Style box by choosing a predefined format, by choosing a level in the **L**evel Style box, or by selecting an entry from the list that appears when you click the arrowhead icon to the right of the Style box.

To modify the contents of the Style box, move the pointer to the Style box and delete or type characters. One way you can add characters is by choosing **F**ont, **W**P Characters or pressing Ctrl-W to get the WordPerfect Characters dialog box. You can add any of the more than 1,500 WordPerfect characters as "punctuation" in the number style.

WordPerfect limits the modifications you can make. Basically, you are restricted to something like (I), where you can leave out either or both punctuation characters and change the class of number. The best advice is to experiment and see what is accepted.

Figure 24.12 shows the effect of some nontraditional customization on the sample outline. With a user-defined format, you can use the desired WordPerfect character (in this case, the character found on the WordPerfect character map at location 5,7) as a bullet, and enable Attach **P**revious Level.

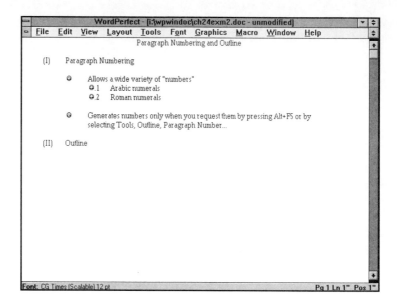

WordPerfect - [i:\wpwindoc\ch24exm2.doc - unmodified]

File   Edit   View   Layout   Tools   Font   Graphics   Macro   Window   Help

Paragraph Numbering and Outline

(I)   Paragraph Numbering

       •   Allows a wide variety of "numbers"
         •.1   Arabic numerals
         •.2   Roman numerals

       •   Generates numbers only when you request them by pressing Alt+F5 or by
         selecting Tools, Outline, Paragraph Number...

(II)   Outline

Font: CG Times (Scalable) 12 pt   Pg 1 Ln 1" Pos 1"

FIG. 24.12

A nontraditional user-defined format on the sample outline.

The Current Outline Style section (discussed later in this chapter) allows for more complex numbers.

Attach Previous Level

Choosing the Attach **P**revious Level option causes the number of the level highlighted in the **L**evel Style box to be stuck together with the number of the preceding level. Each level you change is marked with an asterisk (*) in the **L**evel Style box.

An example is much easier to understand than the definition. The Paragraph predefined format normally produces paragraph numbers like the following:

     1. text and more text
       a.   text and more text
          i.   text and more text

Choosing the Attach **P**revious Level option for levels 2 and 3 produces the following:

     1. text and more text
       1.a. text and more text
          1.a.i.   text and more text

Choosing the Legal predefined format turns on Attach **P**revious Level automatically.

Using the Starting Outline Number Option

You edit the Starting Outline Number text box to specify the starting value of the next paragraph number. With this technique, for example, you can produce the following, which looks like two outlines, one embedded in the other:

■ **Cue:** You always specify the starting outline number using Arabic numerals, no matter what style of numbers is being used.

    I.   first text, first line
    II.   first text, second line
        A. first text, third line
           I.   second text, first line
           II. second text, second line
    III. first text, fourth line
    IV. first text, fifth line

As usual, you set the Starting Outline Number to 1 before first text, first line and also before second text, first line. Set the Starting Outline Number to 3, however, before first text, fourth line.

You can specify that an outline starts with any level you want by specifying the values you want for several levels at one time. The values can be separated by periods, commas, or spaces. To restart the example (the first outline restarts on the line "first text, fourth line") with a first level of III and a second level of B, type **3,2**. The example then looks like the following:

    I.   first text, first line
    II.   first text, second line
        A. first text, third line
           I.   second text, first line
           II. second text, second line
        B. first text, fourth line
    III. first text, fifth line

Using the Current Outline Style Option

The Current Outline Style section of the dialog box indicates which outline style is in effect. The style is <None> unless you choose **Change**. (See "Outline Styles," later in this chapter.) If you want to turn off an outline style, choose **No Style**.

Using the Options Features

The Options section of the Define Paragraph Numbering dialog box offers three check boxes that affect how Outline works. The default setting is *on* for all three features. When you turn off the Enter Inserts Paragraph Number and Auto Adjust to Current Level features (remove the X from each check box), WordPerfect removes most of the difference between Paragraph Numbering and Outline for text entry. The following paragraphs describe the Options features.

■ *Enter Inserts Paragraph Number.* Turn on this feature to ensure that every time you press Enter, a new paragraph number is generated. You can insert a hard return ([HRt]) without inserting a paragraph number by pressing Hard Return (Shift-Enter). This method is the default behavior of Outline that has been referenced throughout this chapter.

  Because turning off this feature means that pressing Enter generates only a hard return ([HRt]), the only way you can insert a number is by choosing **L**ayout, **L**ine, **N**umbering. (You can restore the numbering function of the Enter key by displaying the Define Paragraph Numbering dialog box and turning on the Enter Inserts Paragraph Number feature again.)

■ *Auto Adjust to Current Level.* Turn on this feature to ensure that a number generated by WordPerfect is the same level as the preceding number. If you use the Outline predefined format, for example, you get the following when Auto Adjust to Current Level is on:

  I. text and more text
     A.   pressed Tab to get a second-level number
     B.   did not press Tab and got a second-level number

  Turn off the Auto Adjust to Current Level feature to ensure that a number generated by WordPerfect always is a first-level number. With this option turned off, the preceding example appears as follows:

  I. text and more text
     A.   pressed Tab to get a second-level number
  II. did not press Tab and got a first-level number

■ *Outline On.* Choose Outline On so that Outline is turned on and inserts an [Outline On] code at the insertion point when you choose OK or press Enter.

Outline Styles

With Outline Styles, you can associate a style with each level of para-graph numbering. Where you normally get a number with punctuation (automatically by pressing Enter or on demand by choosing Tools, Outline, Paragraph Number), you can get the benefits of a style.

A wide variety of effects are available. You can use a style to right-justify the paragraph number, for example, so that the number is close to the start of the text without having to make a very small tab setting. You can put an automatic indent after the number. You can make all second-level text indented and italicized (perhaps if the text consists of quotations). Notice that this last style doesn't even use paragraph numbers.

Because outline styles are ordinary styles and because Chapter 12, "Using Styles," presents the concepts and mechanics of styles, the following sections deal only with aspects of styles that are unique to Paragraph Numbering and Outline.

Using Predefined Outline Styles

WordPerfect comes with several outline styles in its LIBRARY.STY file. To use one of the predefined styles, you must tell WordPerfect in Pref-erences where LIBRARY.STY is located. (See Chapter 29, "Customizing WordPerfect with Preferences," for information on using Preferences.)

Figure 24.13 shows three predefined outline styles in the Outline Styles dialog box. You can use the styles "as is" because they adapt to your document by using the paragraph numbering definition in effect when you use the styles. Even if you don't want to use them, the styles are a source of inspiration for what can be done with outline styles.

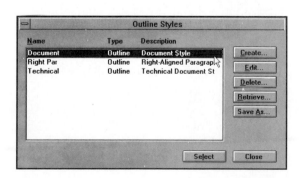

FIG. 24.13

The Outline Styles dialog box with three predefined styles.

The best way to see how an outline style works is to look at its codes (see "Creating and Editing Outline Styles," later in this chapter) and to use the style in a short example.

Using an Outline Style

To use an existing outline style in your document, follow these steps:

1. Move the insertion point to the location where you want the outline style to take effect.

   If Auto Code Placement is on for your document, the change takes effect at the beginning of the paragraph. If Auto Code Placement is off, the change takes effect at the beginning of the next line.

2. Choose **T**ools, **O**utline, **D**efine.

    Press Paragraph Define (Alt-Shift-F5).

   The Define Paragraph Numbering dialog box appears (refer to fig. 24.5).

3. Choose the appropriate options in the sections of the dialog box other than the Current Outline Style section.

4. In the Current Outline Style section, choose **C**hange. The Outline Styles dialog box appears (again see fig. 24.13).

   If a dialog box appears that says File Not Found, Preferences doesn't properly specify the directory or the name of your style library. Correct this problem in Preferences before continuing.

   The Outline Styles dialog box looks almost like the Styles dialog box discussed in Chapter 12, "Using Styles," except that only outline styles are listed. With the exception of the Create button, all the buttons are the same as the Styles dialog box.

5. Choose the style you want in the **N**ame list box. The entire line is highlighted.

6. Choose Se**l**ect. The Outline Styles dialog box closes and the Define Paragraph Numbering dialog box reappears.

7. Choose OK.

Creating and Editing Outline Styles

Creating an outline style is exactly like creating any other style, except that an outline style is effectively eight styles, one for each level of paragraph number, under one name. To create an outline style, follow these steps:

1. Choose **T**ools, **O**utline, **D**efine.

    Press Paragraph Define (Alt-Shift-F5).

   The Define Paragraph Numbering dialog box appears (refer to fig. 24.5).

2. In the Current Outline Style section, choose **C**hange. The Outline Styles dialog box appears (refer to fig. 24.13).

3. Choose **C**reate. The Edit Outline Style dialog box appears, as shown in figure 24.14.

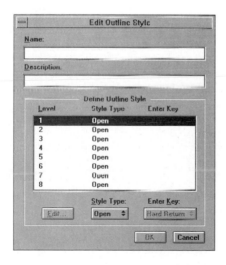

FIG. 24.14

The Edit Outline Style dialog box.

Although the Edit Outline Style dialog box looks considerably different from the Style Properties dialog box discussed in Chapter 12, "Using Styles," only two significant differences exist: the additions of the Define Outline Style section and its Edit button.

4. Type the name of the outline style.

5. Type the description of the outline style. You can type more characters than the Outline Styles dialog box displays.

6. In the Define Outline Style section, choose the **L**evel number for which you want the style to be invoked. The entire line in the list box is highlighted.

7. Choose the appropriate **S**tyle Type option (**O**pen or **P**aired) and Enter **K**ey option (**H**ard Return, Style O**ff**, or Style **O**ff/On). See Chapter 12, "Using Styles," for a complete discussion of these options.

8. Choose **E**dit. The normal Style Edit window appears. The window is divided into two sections; the lower section is a Reveal Codes view of the top section (see fig. 24.15).

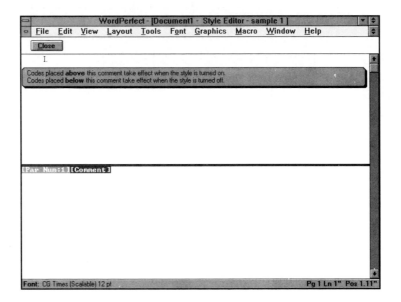

The Style Edit window for level 1 of the Document outline style.

9. Type your text and enter any necessary WordPerfect codes.

10. Choose **C**lose. The Style Edit window closes, and the Edit Outline Style dialog box reappears.

■ **Cue:** If you type many of the same codes for each level, choose **E**dit, **C**opy at the first level and **E**dit, **P**aste at the others.

11. If you want to associate another group of codes with another level, repeat steps 6 through 10 for each level. Note that you can type different codes for each level.

12. After you finish creating outline styles, choose OK. The Edit Outline Style dialog box closes, and the Outline Styles dialog box reappears.

13. If you want to use the new outline style immediately, choose Select; otherwise, choose **C**lose or press Esc. The Outline Styles dialog box closes, and the Define Paragraph Numbering dialog box reappears.

14. If you want to use an outline style immediately, make any other necessary choices in the Define Paragraph Numbering dialog box; then choose OK. Otherwise, choose Cancel or press Esc.

Editing an outline style is just like creating an outline style, except that you must substitute the following for step 3 of the procedure:

> Select the style you want to edit and choose **E**dit. The Edit Outline Style dialog box appears.

Chapter Summary

In this chapter, you have explored three of WordPerfect's numbering systems: Line Numbering, Paragraph Numbering, and Outlining.

The options discussed in this chapter enable you to use Line Numbering to number each line on a page or in your document, change the default settings for Line Numbering to specify when and how Word-Perfect numbers lines, and check line numbering with Print Preview.

You also learned how to use Paragraph Numbering to number paragraphs only when you request a number and how to turn on Outline to number paragraphs automatically. You learned how to delete, add, or move numbered paragraphs; change the paragraph numbering styles; and create an outline style.

Assembling Other Document References

A fter reading other chapters in this book, you can see that WordPerfect is a truly powerful word processor. This power does not stop with composing documents. WordPerfect also provides tools that enable you to perform complex document processing tasks—such as generating several different kinds of references and comparing different versions of a document and marking the changes.

WordPerfect provides a variety of document reference types including lists, tables of contents, tables of authorities, indexes, and cross-referencing. You mark text in a document and have WordPerfect create various reference tables that list items and the page numbers where they appear. The power of these features is most apparent when you revise a document; you can add or delete information anywhere in the document without worrying about the page numbers assigned to your

■ **Gary Pickavet** is the Assistant Superintendent for Business and Data Processing Services for the Santa Barbara County Education Office. He uses WordPerfect regularly for research projects and the preparation of presentation materials.

marked items. After revising the document, you generate the references, and WordPerfect builds a table listing each item with its correct page number.

Before the advent of word processors, good project planning required that you assign a significant chunk of time at the end of the project to design, create, and modify a table of exhibits, table of contents, index, and so on. You spent part of that time laboriously proofreading the references to ensure accuracy. The longer the document, the greater the chance of errors. With automatic generation of references, Word-Perfect makes referencing almost effortless and saves you countless hours.

Lawyers preparing legal briefs, for example, used to spend much time poring over a document, noting all the legal citations. After finding all the legal citations and noting their page numbers, the writer had to create a table of authorities listing each citation and the page numbers. WordPerfect's Table of Authorities feature solves this problem.

Another time-consuming task often performed manually is showing the differences between the old and new versions of a document. WordPerfect includes a Document Compare feature that marks the new version of a document, showing deleted material with the strikeout enhancement and new material with the redline enhancement.

In this chapter you learn how to perform the following tasks:

- Mark text for the various reference types

- Choose a table numbering format (dot leaders, page numbers, and so on)

- Define the document location for reference tables

- Generate document references

- Use automatic cross-referencing

- Compare two documents using redlining (to show added text) and strikeout (to show deleted text)

Creating Lists

■ **Cue:** Use WordPerfect's lists to create tables of maps, exhibits, or figures.

Lists are the most basic reference feature provided by WordPerfect— even with their simplicity, they are extremely powerful. You use lists in a document to create tables of exhibits, maps, or figures. You can create a list of any items you want to mark. WordPerfect generates a list of the marked items with or without page numbers.

You create lists by following these basic steps:

1. Mark the text you want included and specify the list in which you want the text to appear. (You can bypass this step if you want lists generated only from captions of WordPerfect's various graphics boxes. WordPerfect finds these captions for you.)

2. Indicate where you want the list created in the document and how you want the list formatted.

3. Generate the references to assemble the list of marked items and, optionally, the page numbers.

You can define up to 10 lists in a document and choose from 5 numbering formats. When you generate the list, WordPerfect lists the items in the order they appear in the document and creates the list at the location you specified.

Marking Text for Lists

To create a list, you must mark any text you want in the list (except for graphics box captions, described later in this section). WordPerfect uses the text as the item description in the list. If the marked text includes any text enhancement codes (such as boldface or italic), the enhancement also applies to the text in the list. When you mark *Exhibit 1*, for example, and you include the italic enhancement code, the text remains italicized in the list you generate.

Marking text for your list requires several keystrokes. You can make this task much easier by adding a List button to the Button Bar. Refer to Chapter 19, "Using the Button Bar," for instructions.

To mark text you want to appear in a list, follow these steps:

1. Select the text. (For information on how to select text, see Chapter 5, "Selecting and Editing Text.")

   Selected text appears highlighted on-screen.

2. From the **Tools** menu, select **Mark** Text.

    Press Mark Text (F12).

3. Choose **List**.

   Alternatively, if you have the List command on the Button Bar, click the List button.

   The Mark List dialog box appears.

4. Press Alt-down arrow to display the Number pop-up list.

5. Highlight the number of the list on which you want the item placed; click the item or press Enter (see fig. 25.1).

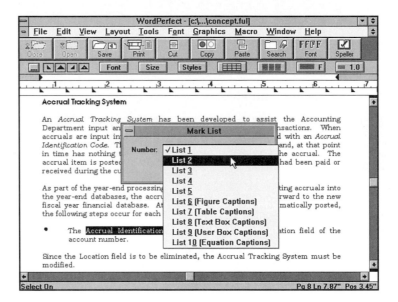

FIG. 25.1

The Mark List
dialog box with
Number pop-up
list.

6. Choose OK or press Enter.

The first five list categories are undefined—that is, you can make them any collection of items you want to have grouped in a table. List categories 6 through 10 are associated with the various WordPerfect graphics boxes. If you use graphics boxes with figure captions in your document, for example, and you choose List 6 from the Number pop-up list, Word-Perfect includes all graphics box figure captions in your list.

If you do not use the graphics boxes or do not use captions for the boxes you do use, you can use the last five list categories for text you select in the document and associate with the list number. Furthermore, you can mix captions that WordPerfect automatically selects, with text you select and associate with the same list number. The better practice, however, is to keep the lists for which *you* mark text separate from WordPerfect's automatically selected lists.

T I P   To help you keep the lists straight as you compose your document, keep a handwritten explanation of each list you use (for example, "Captions" or "Exhibits") and the list number assigned to the category.

When you mark text to be placed in a list, WordPerfect inserts the code [Mark:list,#] at the beginning and the code [End Mark:List,#] at the end of the selected text (# is the actual list number). These codes do not print, but you can see them in the Reveal Codes window.

If you change your mind about what the marked text should say, edit the text between the codes. If you decide you do not want an item included in the list, delete the codes. The next time you generate the document references, WordPerfect modifies or removes the list text as appropriate.

Defining a List and Choosing Numbering Formats

After you mark the text you want included in the list, or if you plan to use a list number reserved for captions (which doesn't require you to mark the text), you define where you want the list to appear in your document and specify the numbering format you want.

You can save keystrokes and time by creating a Def List button to perform the Define List command (see Chapter 19).

WordPerfect offers five numbering formats, including No Numbering, as shown in the pop-up list in figure 25.2. A window in the Define List dialog box shows a sample list using the selected numbering format.

Cue: Begin each new list on a new separately numbered page.

Cue: Remember that the text in your list has the same enhancements it has in the body of your document.

FIG. 25.2

The Numbering Format pop-up list in the Define List dialog box.

The following table shows the result of selecting each numbering format.

Numbering Format	Text Result
No Numbering	Map of the US
Text #	Map of the US 38
Text (#)	Map of the US (38)
Text #	Map of the US 38
Text.....#	Map of the US..................38

To define where you want the list placed and the numbering format, follow these steps:

1. Place the insertion point at the place in the text where you want to start the list.

    If you want to place the list on its own page, insert a hard page break (press Ctrl-Enter). Type a page heading that describes the list; this step is optional but recommended.

2. From the **T**ools menu, select Define.

     Press Define (Shift-F12).

3. Choose Li**s**t, or click the Def List button.

    The Define List dialog box appears (see fig. 25.3).

4. Select **L**ist to display the pop-up list, and choose the list you want to place at the current location.

5. Select Numbering **F**ormat to display and choose styles other than the default presentation.

6. Choose OK.

When you define a list, table of authorities, index, or table of contents, WordPerfect inserts a [Def Mark:] code into your document. You can see the code in the Reveal Codes window. For a list, the code is similar to the following example:

```
[Def Mark:List,1:FlRgtDotLdr]
```

More information about these codes appears in the section "Defining an Index" in this chapter.

After you define where you want the list placed in the document and the numbering format, you generate the list.

Generating Document References

After you mark text, determine on which list to place the text, and define where you want to put the list, you create the list.

WordPerfect generates *all* document references each time you choose the Generate command. Generally, you want to generate references immediately before printing to ensure that all page numbers and cross-references are correct. If you have modified your document since the last time you generated references, WordPerfect reminds you that you may need to generate the references by displaying the dialog box shown in figure 25.4.

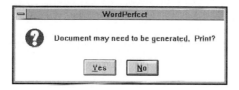

When you choose the Generate command, WordPerfect creates new lists where you indicate. Based on the text currently marked in your document, WordPerfect deletes and rebuilds lists you generated earlier. This process works the same way for the other document tables: tables of contents, tables of authorities, cross-references, and indexes.

If you generate document references often, consider adding a Generate button to the Button Bar.

BUTTON

To generate or update your lists, follow these steps:

1. From the **T**ools menu, select **G**enerate, or click the Generate button.

Press Generate (Alt-F12).

The Generate dialog box appears (see fig. 25.5).

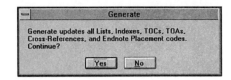

FIG. 25.5

The Generate
dialog box.

2. Choose **Yes** to create or update your lists and any other references in the document.

Creating a Table of Contents

With WordPerfect, you can form a comprehensive table of contents (ToC) for documents you create. Tables of contents can include up to five levels, with each level indented to show the subordinate levels. Like a list (unless you choose otherwise), each marked item appears in the table of contents with the page number where the item appears in the document. The Generate command updates the table of contents entries and their page numbers.

As with lists, you use the following three basic steps to create a table of contents:

1. Mark the text you want to include in the table of contents.

2. Define the location of the table in the document and the numbering format for each level.

3. Generate the table.

Marking Text for a Table of Contents

Selecting items for a table of contents is as easy as highlighting text and any desired enhancement codes and then selecting the desired ToC level.

 You can save keystrokes and time by creating a ToC button to perform the table of contents Mark Text command.

WordPerfect provides five levels of headings and places a blank line before each level 1 ToC entry. Blank lines do not separate subordinate items with levels below 1. Figure 25.6 shows an example of spacing for level 1 headings and subheadings.

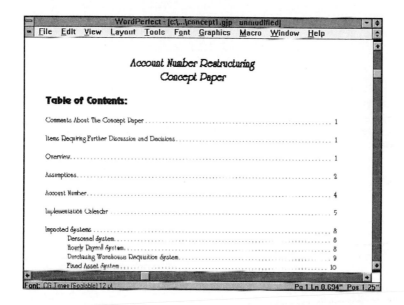

FIG. 25.6

A sample table of contents.

> Use Reveal Codes to exclude text enhancement codes that occur at the beginning of selected text. When you mark a ToC entry including codes, the code applies to the text in the table of contents. If you capture an item with a text enhancement code that you don't want to print in the ToC, you can edit the table of contents after you generate it. Note, however, that any changes you make in the table of contents are replaced the next time you generate the document references.

T I P

To mark text for a ToC entry, follow these steps:

1. Select the text and any enhancement codes you want to apply to the text (for example, boldface or italic).

2. From the **Tools** menu, choose **Mark Text**.

   QUA Press Mark Text (F12).

Cue: Open the Reveal Codes window so that you can easily see whether the selection you mark includes desired enhancement codes.

3. Choose Table of Contents, or click the Mark Text button.

   The Mark Table of Contents dialog box appears (see fig. 25.7).

4. Choose the ToC level number (1 through 5) for this item; then choose OK.

You can see the text and enhancement codes that you want in the table by opening the Reveal Codes window. The mark ToC code [Mark:ToC,#], where # is the level number (1 through 5), precedes the text and codes. At the end of the item is the [End Mark:ToC,#] code. If you want to change the ToC entry, edit the text between codes. WordPerfect inserts the revised text into the table of contents the next time you generate the document references.

If you change your mind after marking text for inclusion and no longer want the item included in the table of contents, delete the [Mark:ToC] or the [End Mark:ToC] code. WordPerfect deletes the matching code and removes the item from the table of contents the next time you generate document references.

Defining a Table of Contents

■ **Cue:** Begin the table of contents on a new page.

When you define a table of contents, you can select the location of the table, the number of levels to include in the table, and formatting for each ToC level.

You can save keystrokes and time by creating a Def ToC button to perform the Define Table of Contents command.

To define the table of contents, follow these steps:

1. Move the insertion point to the desired location for the table of contents.

2. If you want the table of contents to begin on a new page with appropriate headings, as in figure 25.6, and any part of your document falls *before* your selected location for the table of contents, insert a hard page break (Ctrl-Enter).

3. From the Tools menu choose Define.

   CUA   Press Define (Shift-F12).

4. Choose Table of Contents, or click the ToC button.

   The Define Table of Contents dialog box appears (see fig. 25.8).

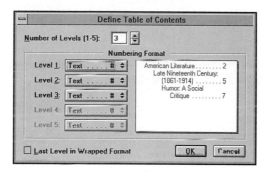

FIG. 25.8

The Define Table of Contents dialog box.

5. Select Number of Levels and enter the number, up to 5, of ToC levels in your document.

6. If you want to change the default numbering format for any of the levels, select the level you want to change and choose one of the five available numbering formats. (For a detailed description of the formats, see the section, "Defining a List and Choosing Numbering Formats," in this chapter.)

   Repeat step 6 for each level that you want to change.

7. Choose Last Level in Wrapped Format to have the ToC entries for the last level (and optionally, their page numbers) follow one another as though they are one paragraph of information. The appended headings wrap at the end of each line, and lines subsequent to the first one are indented.

8. Choose OK, and then press Ctrl-Enter to insert a hard page break at the end of the table of contents page.

9. If the next page is your document text, insert a new page number code to ensure that your document has properly numbered and correct page numbers in the table of contents.

When you define a table of contents, index, list, or table of authorities, WordPerfect inserts into your document a [Def Mark:] code, which you can see in the Reveal Codes window. The code for a table of contents is similar to the following:

```
[Def Mark:ToC,1:FlRgtDotLdr]
```

More information about these codes appears in the section, "Defining an Index," in this chapter.

Generating a Table of Contents

After you define the formatting options and the location for the table of contents, you generate the table.

When you select Generate from the Tools menu, WordPerfect generates all document references—including a table of contents. To generate the table of contents, follow the steps given in "Generating Document References" in this chapter.

Using Multiple Tables of Contents

Cue: Use lists to generate more than one table of contents.

In WordPerfect, you can generate only one table of contents in a document. If your document is complex or has extensive sectioning, however, you may want to have multiple tables of contents. Although you cannot achieve this goal directly with WordPerfect, you can use what you have learned in the section about lists to generate what looks like another table of contents.

To generate a list that masquerades as a table of contents, select a list number you currently are not using. Mark each list item you want to include in the "other" table of contents.

Because WordPerfect does not indent list items to designate subordinate levels as in a table of contents, if you want items in this list indented or designated as hierarchical in some way, you must include formatting codes (underline, boldface, and so forth) in your document text. If you want a blank line after an item, insert a hard return that you include when you mark the list item.

Creating a Table of Authorities

Probably not many professions deal with more paperwork than the legal profession. Court cases require enormous amounts of correspondence, transcripts, and other written materials, such as legal briefs.

A legal brief is a lengthy and complex document that contains many references to prior legal cases and statutes. Creating a legal brief can be a nightmare. Combing through the document to create the table of contents and table of authorities is extremely laborious. Text insertions may change page numbers, requiring another time-consuming scan of the document and revisions to the tables.

A table of authorities is a table used to reference (or index) a legal brief. The table includes legal citations grouped into categories, such as cases, statutes, court rulings, and regulations. Within each group, the appropriate citations are listed with each page number on which each citation appears in the brief.

The WordPerfect Table of Authorities (ToA) feature makes this chore easier. The time savings to a legal office in automating this task is well worth the time required to learn how to use the feature. Figure 25.9 shows a sample table of authorities for a legal brief.

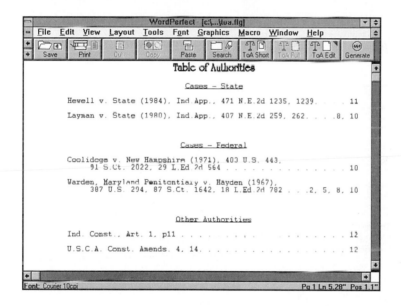

FIG. 25.9

A sample table of authorities.

To use the Table of Authorities feature, you first adjust your Word-Perfect setup files for the options that control the formatting of the ToA. WordPerfect stores these settings, so you do not have to repeat this process every time you use the feature (see Chapter 29 for more information).

Creating a table of authorities is not as difficult as you may think. The several steps involved are straightforward. The general steps follow:

1. Decide what groupings or categories of legal citations you have in the brief.

2. Mark the first occurrence of each legal citation. Specify exactly what the citation reference should say and how it should be formatted when printed in the table of authorities. Assign a short, unique keyword to each kind of legal reference.

3. Mark all citations in the brief with the appropriate keyword.

4. Define where you want to place the table of authorities and the options you want to apply.

5. Generate the document references.

6. Print the legal brief.

WordPerfect sorts the authorities in each section alphabetically. The sections are listed in the order in which you defined them.

Cue: To ensure accurate references, generate the document references immediately before you print.

Adjusting Setup for the Table of Authorities

You can control some of the text-formatting characteristics used by WordPerfect when creating your table of authorities. To set these preferences, choose **F**ile, **P**references. (See Chapter 29, "Customizing WordPerfect with Preferences," for a detailed discussion.)

WordPerfect remembers the preferences you have set and uses them as the defaults each time you define a ToA. When you change your mind, change the option(s), and the new preferences are the default settings when you define a ToA in future documents. You can override these preferences when you define the ToA, described in "Defining a Table of Authorities" in this chapter.

Choosing Sections and Marking Text for a Table of Authorities

Cue: Before you begin marking citations, decide the sections under which you want to group your citations.

Before you begin marking citations for a ToA, you must decide how many sections you plan to have. As you mark each citation the first time, you assign it to a section. You may decide to have three sections, for example: one for federal cases, one for state cases, and one for other authorities (again see fig. 25.9). WordPerfect enables you to designate up to sixteen separate sections.

Before you begin marking text, try to understand how WordPerfect uses the ToA Full Form and ToA Short Form functions. The ToA Full Form, entered only once, contains the text of the complete citation as it appears in the generated table of authorities.

The ToA Short Form is a unique identifier you assign to tie citations together when you generate the table of authorities. You can assign a ToA Short Form as part of the ToA Full Form code.

> As you mark the ToA Full Form and assign the unique identifier, keep track of the citation and the ToA Short Form. Using the same ToA Short Form for more than one ToA Full Form causes an error when you generate the document references. The Full Form citation appears in the table of authorities, but instead of page numbers, an asterisk appears.

T I P

After you create the ToA Full Form for a citation, you mark subsequent occurrences of the same citation with the unique Short Form name you assigned to the citation. This process enables WordPerfect to build the table of authorities with page numbers showing where each citation occurs.

Generally, a citation marked for the first time should be marked as the ToA Full Form. The full form is where you define the actual text to be placed in the table of authorities.

Cue: Mark the full form the first time the citation occurs in the brief.

Many commands are involved in marking, editing, defining, and generating a table of authorities. You can add the various commands to the Button Bar. Consider adding all the commands to a custom Legal Button Bar. For more information on editing, saving, and selecting a Button Bar, see Chapter 19, "Using the Button Bar."

To mark a citation as a ToA Full Form, follow these steps:

1. Select all the citation text that you want included in the ToA.

2. From the **Tools** menu, choose Mark Text.

    Press Mark Text (F12).

3. Choose ToA Full Form.

   The Mark ToA Full Form dialog box appears (see fig. 25.10).

4. Select the Section Number in which you want to include this citation.

   The citation text you highlighted appears in the Short Form text box. You can edit the short form now or as a selection in the Full Form editing screen.

FIG. 25.10

The Mark ToA
Full Form dialog
box.

5. Choose OK.

   The Full Form editing screen appears with the text you selected in
   your document in the text editing area (see fig 25.11).

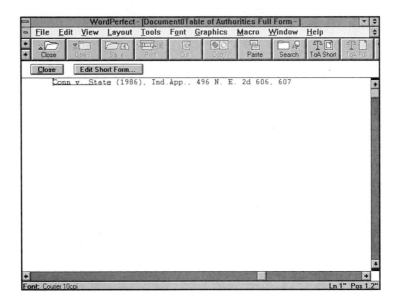

FIG. 25.11

The Full Form
editing screen.

6. Edit the citation as desired. The citation can be up to 30 lines
   long.

   WordPerfect does not always wrap the text lines properly. You
   may need to edit the text of a full form to get a line to break
   properly. If so, position the insertion point about two inches from
   the right margin and press Enter. Experiment with the results of
   this technique until you find a break you like. You may find that
   you like the looks better if you allow a little more or less than two
   inches.

   ■ **Cue:** You can apply text
   enhancements to the full form
   citation.

   You can apply text enhancement (such as boldface or italic) or
   formatting (such as indent) codes to the full form citation.

7. If you want to view or edit the short form or section number, choose Edit Short Form to return to the Mark ToA Full Form dialog box.

8. Choose Close to return to the document.

 CAUTION: If you edit the legal citation in your brief, WordPerfect does not modify the text in the full form. You must edit the full form to change its appearance in your table of authorities.

To edit a full form, follow these steps:

1. Choose View, Reveal Codes to open the Reveal Codes window.

   Press Reveal Codes (Alt-F3).

2. Locate the first occurrence of the citation in the document (normally where you have defined the full form). If the first citation has a short form code, continue to search for subsequent occurrences of the citation until you locate the full form. The short form code does not include the section number and looks like this: [ToA:;Short Form Text]. The full form code has the level number and looks similar to this: [ToA:2;Short Form Text;Full Form].

3. Move the insertion point to the right of the full form code.

 CAUTION: If you do not position the insertion point to the right of the code, the Full Form editing window contains the citation from the preceding full form. If no ToA code exists for the full form before the insertion point, WordPerfect displays the text of the nearest full form following the insertion point.

4. From the Tools menu, choose Mark Text.

   Press Mark Text (F12).

5. Choose ToA Edit Full Form.

   The Full Form editing window appears with the ToA text for editing (again see fig. 25.11).

6. Edit the text as desired.

7. Choose Edit Short Form if you need to change the short form or the section number the citation is assigned to.

8. Choose **C**lose to save the changes.

The edited text does not appear in the table of authorities until you generate the document references.

After you enter the ToA Full Form, you mark subsequent occurrences of the citation using the ToA Short Form name that you associated with the ToA Full Form.

To mark a citation using the ToA Short Form identifier, follow these steps:

1. Place the insertion point immediately before the citation.

2. From the **T**ools menu, choose Mar**k** Text.

    Press Mark Text (F12).

3. Choose ToA **S**hort Form.

   The Mark ToA Short Form dialog box appears (see fig. 25.12). The last short form used appears in the text box.

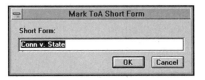

4. Edit the short form, if necessary.

5. Choose OK.

6. Continue steps 1 through 5 until you have marked all citations.

T I P   The short form name must be unique but also should be descriptive to help you associate the short form with the citation. Enter enough text for the short form name to increase the likelihood that it is unique.

When you mark a citation with a short form identifier, WordPerfect inserts into the document a code such as [ToA:;*short form text*;]. If you change your mind and no longer want the citation referenced, delete the code. If you want a different short form identifier for a citation, delete the code and repeat the preceding steps.

If you incorrectly type a ToA Short Form or type it correctly but have no ToA Full Form corresponding to the short form, WordPerfect places the ToA Short Form name, preceded by an asterisk (*), at the beginning of the table of authorities when you generate the table. If this situation occurs, simply locate the incorrect short form, delete the code, and enter the correct short form. If the full form is missing, find the first occurrence of the citation, delete the short form, and create a full form.

Defining and Generating a Table of Authorities

Before WordPerfect can generate the table of authorities, you must define where you want the table placed. You probably also want to title the page and place headings before each section (see fig 25.13).

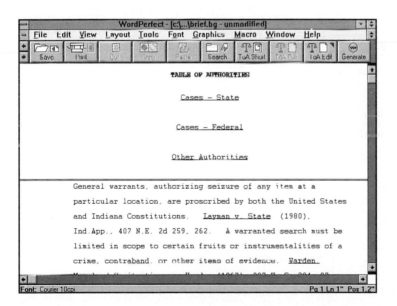

FIG. 25.13

The sections of a table of authorities.

Work through the following steps to define the location for a table of authorities:

1. Because a table of authorities is usually placed at the end of the table of contents, move the insertion point there.

2. Press Ctrl-Enter to place a hard page break at the end of the table of contents and start the table of authorities on a new page. As with all tables, the table of authorities should be a separately numbered part of the document.

Next, follow these steps to create a page heading for a table of authorities:

1. From the **L**ayout menu, select **L**ine, **C**enter.

    Press Center (Shift-F7).

2. From the **F**ont menu, select **B**old.

    Press Bold (Ctrl-B).

3. Type **Table of Authorities**.

   Mark the heading to be generated in the table of contents if you want it included there.

4. Press Bold again to turn off boldface.

Follow these steps to create the first section for a table of authorities:

1. Press Enter two times.

2. From the **L**ayout menu, select **L**ine, **C**enter.

   Press Center (Shift-F7).

3. From The **F**ont menu, select **U**nderline.

   Press Underline (Ctrl-U).

4. Type the heading for the first section (in the example, **Cases - State**).

5. Press Underline again to turn off underlining.

6. Press Enter twice to create blank space between your heading and the table of authorities for the section.

Work through the following steps to define the location and options for a table of authorities section:

1. From the **T**ools menu, choose De**f**ine.

    Press Define (Shift-F12).

2. Choose Table of Authorities.

   The Define Table of Authorities dialog box appears (see fig. 25.14).

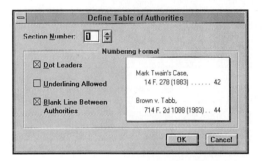

FIG. 25.14

The Define Table of Authorities dialog box.

3. Select Section Number and enter the number that corresponds to the section you are defining at this location. (In the example, the first section is 1.)

4. Choose the options for Numbering Format—Dot Leaders, Underlining Allowed, and Blank Line Between Authorities. These choices default to the WordPerfect Preferences settings; you can override them for this section. (See Chapter 29 for an explanation of the options.)

   WordPerfect updates the window to the right of the Numbering Format options to show you an example of the numbering format you select.

5. Choose OK.

6. If you have more than one type of authority, repeat the steps for creating a section heading; and repeat steps 1 through 5 for defining the location and options for a ToA for the other sections. (In the example, section two is "Cases - Federal" and section three is "Other Authorities.")

7. Press Ctrl-Enter to insert a hard page break at the end of the ToA page.

8. If the next page is your document text, insert a new page number 1 code to ensure that your citations are referenced to the proper page numbers.

For a ToA, the code, visible when Reveal Codes is active, looks similar to the following example:

```
[Def Mark:ToA,1]
```

For more information about these codes, see "Defining an Index" in this chapter.

Now that you have marked your citations and defined your table, you are ready to generate the table of authorities. Follow the steps given in "Generating Document References" in this chapter. Figure 25.15 shows the first page of a printed table of authorities.

```
                        TABLE OF AUTHORITIES

                           Cases - State

    Conn v. State (1986), Ind.App., 496 N. E. 2d
         606, 607 . . . . . . . . . . . . . . . . . 13, 14
    Hewell v. State (1984), Ind.App., 471 N. E. 2d
         1235, 1238 . . . . . . . . . . . . . . . . 13, 14
    Iddings v. State (1981), Ind.App.,  427 N.  E. 2d 10 . . 17
    McReynolds v. State (1986),  Ind., 460 N. E. 2d  960 . . 14
    Pollard v. State (1979),  Ind., 388 N. E. 2d 496 . . . . 20
    State v. McLaughlin (1984),  Ind.App., 471 N. E.
         2d  1125 . . . . . . . . . . . . . . . . . . 17
    Stinchfield v. State  (1977), 174 Ind. App. 623,
         367 N. E. 2d  1150 . . . . . . . . . . . . 17, 18
    Watt v. State (1980), Ind.App., 412 N. E. 2d 90 . . . . . 18


                          Cases - Federal

    Collidge v. New Hampshire (1971), 403 U. S. 443, 91 S.Ct.
         2022, 29 L.Ed.2d 564 . . . . . . . . . . . . 13
    Katz v. United States (1967), 389 U.S. 347, 88 S.Ct.
         507, 19 L.Ed.2d 576  . . . . . . . . . . . . . 18
    United States v. Henry  (1980), 447 U. S. 264, 100 S.Ct.
         2183, 65 L.Ed.2d 115 . . . . . . . . . . . . . 17
    Warden, Maryland Penitentiary v. Hayden (1967), 387 U. S.
         294, 87 S.Ct. 1642,  18 L.Ed.2d 782 . . . . . . . . 13
    Wong Sun v. United States (1963), 371 U. S. 471, 83 S.Ct.
         407,  9 L. Ed. 2d 441 . . . . . . . . . . . . . 19


                         Other Authorities

    Ind. Const., Art. 1, §11 . . . . . . . . . . . . 14, 17
    Ind. Const., Art. 1, §14 . . . . . . . . . . . . . 23
    Rule of Appellate Procedure 4 . . . . . . . . . . . . 29
```

FIG. 25.15

An example of a printed table of authorities.

Creating an Index

Manually generating a good index is time consuming. Sifting through a long document looking for each reference to a word or phrase also can be an error-prone process.

WordPerfect's Index feature creates an alphabetized list of index headings and subheadings for a document. You can mark each occurrence of the words you want to include in the index, use a file with the words you want to use as index words for the document, or use a combination of both methods.

As an alternative to marking each occurrence of a word or phrase in a document for inclusion in the index, WordPerfect offers another way to build your index. A concordance file is a regular WordPerfect file into which you place words that you want included in the index. Word-Perfect reads your list of words in the concordance file, determines on what pages these words appear, and places the entry in the index.

Creating an index follows the same pattern as generating a list or a table of contents. You mark the words you want to include, define the location and numbering format of the index, and then generate the index.

Specifying Text for an Index

You can mark text in two ways: manually mark each occurrence of the index word in the document on-screen or list the words in a concordance file. Each method has advantages and disadvantages, and the methods can be used together.

Marking each occurrence of a word draws your attention to misspelled words. When you generate the index, only exact matches appear with the page numbers for each occurrence. Because misspelled index entries do not match, they appear on separate lines.

Suppose that in your document you mark the text *Instructional Expenses Accounting* as an index, and elsewhere in your document you mark the text *Instructional Expense Accounting*. When you generate the index, because the text is not identical, you will have each entry listed separately (see fig. 25.16).

On the other hand, if you place the text *Instructional Expense Accounting* into a concordance file, *Instructional Expenses Accounting* does not appear at all in the index because it is not an exact match.

Marking Text

Marking each occurrence of an index word provides the greatest flexibility but is the most time-consuming option. This method requires you to find and mark every occurrence of the index word in the document. Items you do not mark are not included in the index.

■ Cue: Any enhancements such as boldface or underlining do not apply to the text in the index.

```
                    WordPerfect - [c:\...\concept.ful]
  File  Edit  View  Layout  Tools  Font  Graphics  Macro  Window  Help
  FFFF     ☑       📄       📄       📄      ⊟✕📄      ⊛        ⇕ 📄       ⇕ 📄      ⇕ 📄
  Font    Speller  Index     List     ToC   Cross-Ref Generate  Def Index  Def List  Def ToC

    Index:

       Account Number . . . . . . . . . . . . . . . . . . . . . . . . . . . . . . . . . . . . . . . . . . . . . . . . . . . . . . . . . 3, 4
       Accrual Identification Code . . . . . . . . . . . . . . . . . . . . . . . . . . . . . . . . . . . . . . . . . . . . . . . . .7
       Accrual Tracking System . . . . . . . . . . . . . . . . . . . . . . . . . . . . . . . . . . . . . . . . . . . . . . 3, 7, 8
       Assumptions . . . . . . . . . . . . . . . . . . . . . . . . . . . . . . . . . . . . . . . . . . . . . . . . . . . . . . . . . . . .2
       Attachment 1 . . . . . . . . . . . . . . . . . . . . . . . . . . . . . . . . . . . . . . . . . . . . . . . . . . . . . . . 6, 15
       Instructional Expense Accounting . . . . . . . . . . . . . . . . . . . . . . . . . . . . . . . . . . 12
       Instructional Expenses Accounting . . . . . . . . . . . . . . . . . . . . . . . . . . . . . . . . . 14

Font: Bookman 12 pt                                              Pg 16 Ln 5.58" Pos 1.5"
```

FIG. 25.16

A sample index
with duplicate
entries.

To mark text as an index word, follow these steps:

1. Select text for the index item.

2. From the **Tools** menu, choose **Mark** Text.

   CUA   Press Mark Text (F12).

3. Choose **Index**.

   BUTTON   Save keystrokes and time by creating an Index button for this
   step. Click the Index button.

   The Mark Index dialog box appears (see fig. 25.17).

   WordPerfect places the highlighted text in the Heading text box.

```
  ▭               Mark Index
  Heading:
  ┌──────────────────────────────────┐
  │ Training                         │
  └──────────────────────────────────┘
  Subheading:
  ┌──────────────────────────────────┐
  │                                  │
  └──────────────────────────────────┘
                    ┌─────────┐  ┌──────────┐
                    │  OK     │  │  Cancel  │
                    └─────────┘  └──────────┘
```

FIG. 25.17

The Mark Index
dialog box.

4. Choose OK to insert into your document an index code containing the selected text.

    If you want to place this reference as a subheading under another heading, type the text of that heading in the **H**eading text box. Press Tab. The insertion point moves to the **S**ubheading text box, and the text you selected in your document appears as the subheading. Choose OK.

When you mark an entry as a heading, WordPerfect inserts the code [Index:*heading text*] to the left of the word or phrase. If you mark an entry as a subheading after typing a heading in the Heading text box, WordPerfect inserts the code [Index:*heading text, subheading text*]. Figure 25.18 shows a Reveal Codes window with an item marked as a subheading.

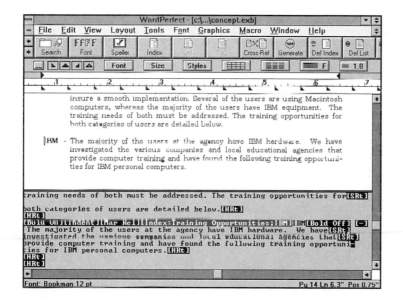

FIG. 25.18

The Reveal Codes window with a subheading code shown.

CAUTION: When you mark text as an index item, WordPerfect inserts the selected text into the index code. If you subsequently modify the text you selected for inclusion as an index item, the text in the index code does not change. You must delete the index code to the left of the revised text in your document and again mark the text for the index.

WordPerfect lists subheadings alphabetically and indents them under a heading. Suppose that you are indexing a document that has a section describing computer training for Macintosh and IBM computers. You may want to mark *Training Opportunities* as the heading and *Macintosh* and *IBM* as subheadings. The resulting index generates as shown in figure 25.19.

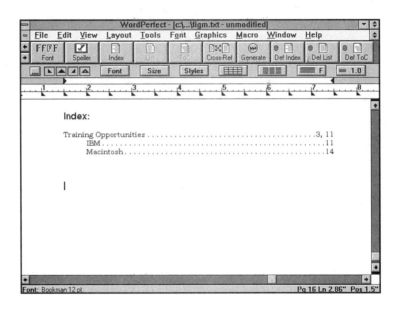

FIG. 25.19

A sample index with heading and subheadings.

T I P   If you want text to appear as a heading above subheading items but without a page number reference, use the text as a heading when defining subheadings in the Mark Index dialog box but do not define the heading text in your document as an index item. Use the text only in the Heading text box when marking index items as subheadings.

If you change your mind after marking text for inclusion in the index and no longer want the item included, delete the [Index:] code. WordPerfect removes the item from the index the next time you generate document references.

Using a Concordance File

You can create an index without marking text by using the Concordance feature.

A *concordance file* contains the words that you want to be your index words. When you define the index for your document (see "Defining an Index" in this chapter), WordPerfect enables you to specify a concordance file for use in generating the index. The words and phrases in the concordance file are your index items, and the referenced page numbers reflect all occurrences of the words in the document.

■ **Cue:** You can save time and ensure that all index references are found by using a concordance file.

WordPerfect includes and shows the page numbers of only items that are an exact match with a concordance entry. An entry of *Print* in the concordance file, for example, does not match *Printing* in your document, and WordPerfect does not create an index reference for *Printing*.

On the other hand, the match is not case sensitive. An entry in the document of *print* matches *Print* in the concordance file and causes that page number to be included in the index.

To create a concordance file, follow these steps:

1. From the File menu, select **New**.

    Press New (Shift-F4).

2. Type the entries that are your index items. Type one entry to a line, pressing Enter at the end of each line.

3. From the File menu, select **Save**.

    Press Save (Shift-F3).

Use WordPerfect's capability to open multiple document windows to keep your concordance file and your document open simultaneously. Each time you find a word in your primary document that is appropriate as an index entry, click the concordance file document window to move to the window. Add the word to the list, click back in your primary document, and continue composing.

T I P

WordPerfect makes each entry in the concordance file a heading. If you want an entry to be listed as a subheading, select **Tools, Mark Text, Index**. Enter the heading under which the subheading is to be listed in the **Heading** text box. Press Tab. The concordance file index word appears in the Subheading text box. Choose OK.

If you want the word in the concordance file to be both a heading and a subheading, for the second time, select **Tools, Mark** Text, **Index**. The word is shown in the Heading text box. Choose OK.

Defining and Generating an Index

You must define where to place the index in the document and the numbering format for the index.

You can save keystrokes and time by creating a Def Index button to perform the Define Index command.

To define an index, follow these steps:

1. Place the insertion point at the location where you want to start the index.

2. You probably want to place the index on a page by itself. To start a new page, insert a hard page break (Ctrl-Enter). You may want to type a page heading (such as **INDEX**).

3. From the **Tools** menu, choose Define.

   CUA Press Define (Shift-F12).

4. Choose **Index**, or click the Def Index button.

   The Define Index dialog box appears (see fig. 25.20).

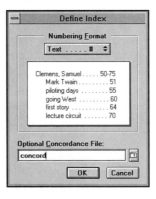

5. Select Numbering **Format** if you want to change the default style shown.

WordPerfect provides five numbering formats. For a detailed description of the formats, see "Defining a List and Choosing Numbering Formats" in this chapter.

6. If you want WordPerfect to generate the index using a concordance file you have defined, select Optional **C**oncordance File and type the file name in the text box.

   Alternatively, click the List Icon to the right of the text box, and a Select File dialog box opens to help you to find the desired file.

7. Choose OK.

The index can be placed anywhere in a document. For marked index entries, however, WordPerfect includes in the index only those entries located before the index definition code in the document. Index entries are listed for all entries in the concordance file, no matter where in the document you locate the index.   **T I P**

The index code, displayed when the Reveal Codes window is open, looks similar to the following example:

    [Def Mark:Index,FlRgtDotldr;c:\wpwin\data\concord]

The elements of this code break down as follows:

- [Def Mark:] is the code used for a list, table of contents, table of authorities, and an index. You insert this code into a Search text box to find the code.

- Index indicates that this [Def Mark:] code is for an index (although you cannot search specifically for an index type [Def Mark:]).

- The next part of the code indicates the numbering format. In this case, FlRgtDotLdr indicates that page numbers are flush right with dot leaders.

- The final part of the code, c:\wpwin\data\concord, shows the concordance file name and full path, if you are using a concordance file.

After you have defined the index, if you want to change its location or numbering format, you must delete the current [Def Mark:Index] code, any previously generated index information, and its matching [End Def] code. Then define the index and desired numbering format in the new location.

T I P Deleting a [Def Mark:] definition code without deleting the matching [End Def] code causes WordPerfect to display the error message [End Def] code does not have matching [Def Mark] during the Generate function. After you acknowledge the error message, WordPerfect cancels the Generate function. You can use the Search function to look for [End Def] codes to find the code causing the problem. When you find the problem code, delete it and generate the document references again.

After you mark what you want included in your index and where you want it placed, you generate the index.

WordPerfect places index entries defined as headings at the left margin and indents subheadings one tab.

When you select **G**enerate from the **T**ools menu, all document references are generated—including indexes. To generate the index, follow the steps given in "Generating Document References" in this chapter.

Preparing Indexes for Multiple Related Documents

If you are using the Master Document feature, you should define the index at the end of the master document. WordPerfect includes in a generated index only manually marked text before an index definition code. If you are using a master document and subdocuments, you must reference *before* the index definition code any subdocuments that have manually marked index text in order to ensure that WordPerfect includes the entries from the subdocument in the generated index. Subdocuments referenced after the index definition code do not have their manually marked index text included in the generated index.

■ **Cue:** Use a concordance file to locate index entries in all linked subdocuments.

If you use a concordance file, WordPerfect includes all references in the master document and any subdocuments in the generated index, regardless of where the subdocument is referenced.

T I P If you have any subdocuments you do not want included in the index and you are not using a concordance file, place the link to the subdocuments after the index definition code.

For more information about the Master Documents feature, see Chapter 26, "Working with Master Documents."

Using Automatic Cross-References

The Automatic Cross-Reference feature makes a complex document much easier for a reader to understand. With automatic cross-references, you can inform the reader where a figure is located or provide a detailed explanation of a concept, as in the following:

Cue: Use automatic cross-references to help your reader find information.

> See fig. 3 on page 22.
>
> Please see the detailed description of the widget, which begins on page 114.

You can cross-reference any item. You control the definition of the referenced items (the targets) and the references to them.

In the past, writers often avoided cross-referencing because the process was time-consuming and subject to errors. Each time the document was revised, the writer had to find all cross-references and review them to see whether they required changing. Writers no longer need to avoid cross-referencing, because this powerful WordPerfect tool makes the task a snap. WordPerfect updates references reliably each time you generate document references.

A *target* is the place in the document you are telling the reader to look. The *target name* is a unique identifier that WordPerfect uses to link targets and their references.

When generating the document references, WordPerfect matches targets and references by using the target name. The target name must be an exact match. During document reference generation, a reference to the name *account* does not match and cross-reference to the target name *accounts*. The matching, however, is not case sensitive; a reference linked to the target name *Accounts* is matched with a target defined as *accounts*.

WordPerfect uses the target name only during document reference generation to link references with their targets. The name does not print when the document prints. To view the target name, activate Reveal Codes.

You can use cross-referencing in different ways. In simple cross-referencing the ratio is one reference to one target—for example, *See the detailed description of helium on page 234.* You can have a reference to multiple occurrences of a unique target name, such as *See the graphics check boxes on pages 2, 12, 20.* You also can reference a single target in different ways, for example, *See fig. 1 on page 4.*

The basic steps for cross-referencing are

1. Mark the referenced item(s)—the targets.

2. Define one or more references to each target.

3. Generate the document references to update the page numbers for all references.

Marking Text for Automatic Cross-Referencing

Cue: Use the Master Document feature to cross-reference between separate files.

You can create cross-references in your document in two ways. You can mark all references and targets separately and then generate the cross-references, or you can mark the reference and target with one operation.

Depending on what works best for you, you can mark a target when you create it and mark its references later. Alternatively, you can mark the references as you write them and mark the target later. Generally, if you are composing a new document and want to handle the references and targets as you write, you should mark the reference before you mark the target.

When you mark the references and targets separately, you must keep a list of the unique target names you have assigned to ensure that references correctly match their targets and to help prevent duplicating names.

Marking a Reference to Text on a Page

To mark a reference separately, follow these steps:

1. Type any desired introductory text, such as **See description on page**.

2. Place the insertion point where you want to insert the reference code.

3. From the **T**ools menu, choose Mar**k** Text.

 Press Mark Text (F12).

4. Choose Cross-Reference.

   To save keystrokes and time for this repetitive step, consider adding a Cross-Ref button to your Button Bar. Click the Cross-Ref button.

   The Mark Cross-Reference dialog box appears (see fig. 25.21).

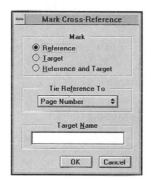

FIG. 25.21

The Mark Cross-Reference dialog box.

5. In the Mark section, choose Reference. (The other options in this section—Target and Reference and Target—are discussed in separate sets of instructions.)

6. Choose Tie Reference To. The pop-up list shown in figure 25.22 appears. Because you want the reference to show the page number of the target, select Page Number.

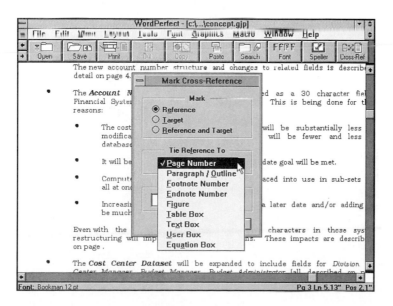

FIG. 25.22

The Tie Reference To pop-up list.

7. Type the target name in the Target **N**ame text box.

8. Make a note of the exact target name because you must enter the exact name when you mark the target elsewhere in your document.

WordPerfect inserts a reference code, such as [Ref(TARGET1):Pg?]. A question mark initially appears in the displayed code text, but the actual page number of the target replaces the question mark when you generate the document references. If more than one target matches the entered target name, the cross-reference lists all those page numbers, separated by commas. If you make a mistake typing the target name, delete the code and mark the reference again.

After marking references to a target, you must mark the target before generating the document references.

To mark a target, follow these steps:

1. Position the insertion point within the first word in the target text.

2. From the **T**ools menu, choose Mar**k** Text.

      Press Mark Text (F12).

3. Choose Cross-**R**eference.

    If you added a Cross-Ref button to the Button Bar, click the Cross-Ref button.

    The Mark Cross-Reference dialog box appears (again see fig. 25.21).

4. In the Mark section, choose **T**arget.

    The Tie Reference To section grays because it is not applicable for targets.

5. The last target name entered displays in the Target **N**ame text box. Choose OK or type the correct target name in the text box, and choose OK.

WordPerfect inserts a target code such as [Target(*target1*)], where *target1* is the target name you assigned to tie this target to its references. If you make a mistake typing the target name, delete the code and mark the target again.

Marking References to Footnotes and Endnotes

Sometimes you want to reference a footnote in the main text of your document. You may want to add, for example, *See discussion in footnote 4 on page 12.* To mark a footnote as a target, you must be in the footnote editing window.

> If you mark a target in the footnote editing window, the target moves to other pages with the footnote if you add or delete text in the document.
>
> **T I P**

To create and mark a footnote as a target, follow these steps:

1. Move the insertion point to the location where you want to define the footnote.

2. From the Layout menu, choose Footnote and then Create.

   The Footnote editing window appears (see fig. 25.23).

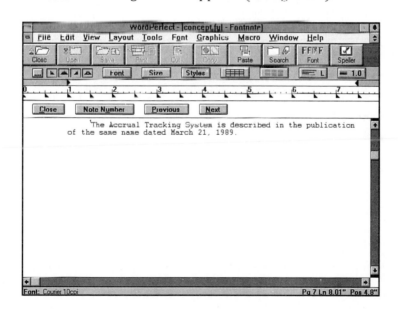

FIG. 25.23

The Footnote editing window.

3. From the Tools menu, choose Mark Text.

    Press Mark Text (F12).

4. Choose Cross-**R**eference. The Mark Cross-Reference dialog box appears.

5. In the Mark section, choose **T**arget.

6. Choose OK if the target name in the Target **N**ame text box is correct. If not, type the correct target name and choose OK.

7. Type the footnote text.

8. Choose **C**lose.

WordPerfect inserts the footnote reference into your document, including the target code.

To mark the reference to the footnote and page number, follow these steps:

1. Type any introductory text (such as **See discussion in footnote**).

2. From the **T**ools menu, select Ma**r**k Text.

  Press Mark Text (F12).

3. Choose Cross-**R**eference.

   If you created a Cross-Ref button on the Button Bar, click the button.

   The Mark Cross-Reference dialog box appears.

4. In the Mark section, choose **R**eference.

5. Choose Tie Re**f**erence To; then select **F**ootnote Number from the pop-up list.

6. Type the target name in the Target **N**ame text box exactly as you assigned it when you marked the target.

7. Choose OK.

   A question mark appears in your document. This question mark is replaced with the footnote number containing the target when you generate references.

8. Complete the introductory text (in the example, **See discussion in footnote ? on page**).

9. Repeat steps 2 through 4.

10. Choose Tie Re**f**erence To; then select **P**age Number.

11. Repeat steps 6 and 7.

Mark endnotes the same way you mark footnotes. Be sure to place the target codes for references to endnotes in the endnotes themselves.

Marking Reference and Target in One Operation

To mark the reference and target in one operation, follow these steps:

1. Place the insertion point where you want to place the reference.

2. Type any desired introductory text.

3. From the **Tools** menu, select **Mark Text**.

   CUA Press Mark Text (F12).

4. Choose Cross-**R**eference.

   If you added a Cross-Ref button to the Button Bar, click the Cross-Ref button.

   The Mark Cross-Reference dialog box appears (again see fig. 25.21).

5. In the Mark section, choose **R**eference and Target.

6. From the Tie Reference To pop-up list, choose a reference type.

7. Type a target name in the Target Name text box and then choose OK.

   The Mark Cross Reference Both dialog box appears (see fig. 25.24).

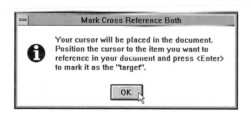

FIG. 25.24

The Mark Cross Reference Both dialog box.

8. Move the insertion point to immediately after the target item, and press Enter. (If you are defining a target for something other than text, place the target in the editing window or caption, as appropriate.)

   WordPerfect inserts the reference and target codes and places the page number at the reference point.

Generating Cross-References

When you choose **G**enerate from the **T**ools menu, WordPerfect generates all document references—including cross-references. To generate cross-references, follow the steps in "Generating Document References" in this chapter.

Using Document Compare

Often you want to revise a document and have someone review the changes to provide you with feedback; however, manually identifying every change is so time-consuming that often the task is not worth the time. In addition, you must provide the original document, to show what text has been removed, and the new document, to show what text is new.

With the Document Compare feature, WordPerfect compares an old version of a document on disk to the document on-screen. WordPerfect notes the differences between the documents.

Phrases containing text that has been removed appear with the strikeout text enhancement. Phrases containing text not in the old version appear with the redline text enhancement. The new text appears in red on your screen if you have a color monitor.

CAUTION: Many people make revisions to a document by retrieving the current document, making the changes, and then replacing the old version of the document with the revised version. After you replace the old version of the document with the version on-screen, you cannot use the Document Compare feature.

■ **Cue:** To delete, copy, move, rename, or find a file quickly, use the Options button on the Open File dialog box.

If you plan to use the Document Compare feature, after you start revising an original document, save the revisions with a new name, rename the original document, or make a copy of the original document. By taking any one of these steps, you maintain the original version for use with the Document Compare feature.

You can now make revisions to your on-screen document. When you have finished making changes, you will be ready to compare the on-screen document with the original document you just saved on disk.

Comparing a New Version to an Old Version

To compare the revised version of the document on-screen to the old version saved on disk, follow these steps:

1. From the Tools menu, select Document Compare, Add Markings.

   The Add Markings dialog box appears with the current path and file name displayed (see fig. 25.25).

FIG. 25.25

The Add Markings dialog box.

2. If necessary, change the file name to match the name of your original document.

   If you want to search for another file, click the List icon to open a Select File dialog box; select another directory or file name.

3. When the File to Compare is correct, choose Compare.

   The message Please Wait... appears on the status line at the bottom of the screen.

WordPerfect modifies the screen version of the document and notes the differences. Text in the old version that is not in the new version is marked with the strikeout enhancement. Text not contained in the old version is displayed with the redline enhancement. Figure 25.26 shows a document that has been marked using the Document Compare feature.

In figure 25.26, strikeout is shown as text with a line through it, and redline is displayed as shaded text. These enhancements are the defaults WordPerfect uses when printing to a laser printer. The actual enhancements that print depend on your printer and the enhancements it supports. Consult your printer manual for more information.

WordPerfect also enables you to change the method of redlining to other than the default. You can change the method of redlining permanently, using the Preferences feature, or just for the current document, using the following steps:

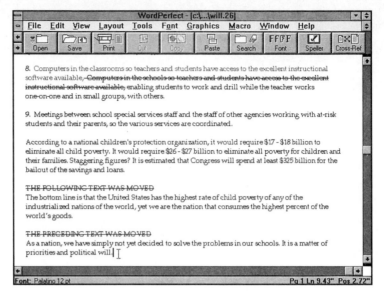

A revised document with changes marked in strikeout and redline.

1. From the **Layout** menu select **D**ocument and then **R**edline Method.

   The Document Redline dialog box appears (see fig. 25.27).

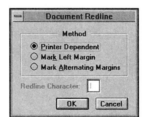

The Document Redline dialog box.

2. If desired, make a choice, as follows:

   ■ Choose **P**rinter Dependent to use the WordPerfect printer driver redlining method.

   ■ Choose Mar**k** Left Margin to place the selected redline character in the left margin of lines.

   ■ Choose Mark **A**lternating Margins to place the selected redline character in the left margin of lines on even-numbered pages and right margin of lines on odd-numbered pages.

3. If you want to change the redline character from the default vertical bar, select **R**edline Character and type the desired character in the box. This option is available only if you choose to use a redline method other than Printer Dependent.

WordPerfect's Document Compare function works with text bounded by punctuation marks, hard return codes, hard page codes, footnote codes, endnote codes, and the end of the document. If you change one word in the middle of a sentence, for example, WordPerfect displays the entire old line with the strikeout enhancement and the entire new sentence with the redline enhancement rather than just the one word.

In figure 25.26, for example, the word *schools* has been changed to *classrooms*. Although only one word changed, the phrase with the word *school* to the left of the comma appears with the strikeout enhancement. Then the phrase with the word *classroom* displays with the redline enhancement.

Purging Marked Changes from a Saved Document

If you save the screen document and replace the latest revision, you can delete the phrases marked with the strikeout and remove the redline text enhancement from added phrases.

> If you saved your revised file immediately before using the Document Compare function, you have no reason to remove the redlining and strikeout from your document. After you print the document with the noted changes, close the document without saving it and open the latest version of the revised document.
>
> **T I P**

To remove Document Compare markings, follow these steps:

1. From the **T**ools menu select Doc**u**ment Compare, **R**emove Markings.

   The Remove Markings dialog box appears (see fig. 25.28).

2. If you want to remove only the phrases marked with the strikeout enhancements and leave the new phrases with the redline enhancement, choose Leave **R**edline Marks.

Cue: Leave added text redlined for emphasis.

FIG. 25.28

The Remove
Markings dialog
box.

3. Choose OK to remove the Document Compare markings.

You also can remove the Document Compare text and redline enhancements by selecting **U**ndo from the **E**dit menu. You must execute this task *immediately* after using the Document Compare function.

Chapter Summary

The automatic generation of document references enables writers to do tasks that were time-consuming and error-prone before the tools now provided with WordPerfect existed. Although most of the document references described in this chapter appeal to most writers, Word-Perfect also offers a table of authorities feature that is specifically designed to help attorneys and law office staff people perform their complex writing tasks.

In this chapter, you have learned how to create lists, tables of contents, tables of authorities, and automatic cross-references. You also learned how to create an index and control the entries included in it by marking text and by using a concordance file.

This chapter also shows you how to compare a current version of a document on-screen with an old version on disk to create a document with the changes from old to new noted in redlining and strikeout enhancements.

Working with Master Documents

S ome people use WordPerfect only for fairly small projects in their daily work. They find WordPerfect invaluable for documents—memos, letters, or reports only a few pages long—with which they must deal daily. Many other people, however, need word processing software that enables them to create and manage extremely large projects and documents. These people, too, find WordPerfect invaluable.

The WordPerfect Master Document feature is designed for the management of very large writing projects. With the Master Document feature, you create a master document, which you can think of as a skeleton or shell of the final large project. At the minimum, a master document contains references to *subdocuments*, other WordPerfect files that are

■ **Gary Pickavet** is the Assistant Superintendent for Business and Data Processing Services for the Santa Barbara County Education Office. He uses WordPerfect regularly for research projects and preparing supporting materials for presentations.

combined into the final document. In the master document, you also define document reference features—the table of contents, indexes, and the table of authorities—that must span the entire finished document. The master document can contain regular text as well.

The basic steps in using the Master Document feature for large writing projects are as follows:

1. Compose and create individual subdocuments.

2. Create a master document that references all the subdocuments to be included in the final project.

3. Define any special features you want to include in the master document (such as a table of contents, index, lists, or table of authorities).

Cue: You can save time with subdocuments. When you make a revision, you open and save a small document instead of a huge one.

These special features are covered in Chapter 25, "Assembling Other Document References." The organization of this chapter assumes that you have read Chapter 25 and are familiar with document references. This chapter covers subdocuments and special considerations required when using reference features with master documents. When you complete this chapter, you will be able to do the following:

- Create a master document and subdocuments

- Expand the master document to combine the subdocuments into the master document

- Generate the document references to create the table of contents, lists, table of authorities, indexes, and cross-references for the expanded document

- Check the spelling of the expanded document

- Print the expanded document

- Condense the master document into the separate subdocuments, optionally saving any changes to the subdocuments

Creating Master and Subdocuments

For purposes of illustration, this chapter uses the example of an Employee Orientation Manual for the business division of an organization.

Because the Employee Orientation Manual contains a great deal of diverse information, it is developed by composing and saving information in separate files. Some of these files come from other departments (such as statistical information from data processing or employee job descriptions from personnel). These separate files are combined to produce an Employee Orientation Manual.

Cue: Use master documents when a project will include files from different authors or departments.

Using the Master Document feature for this project is desirable for several reasons. First, you easily can obtain and combine files from different authors and departments into a finished document. Second, you can revise, print, and distribute individual sections as stand-alone documents, but you can combine the sections into the orientation manual when it is printed. Finally, you can create a comprehensive table of contents and index for the orientation manual and revise them quickly each time you revise a subdocument.

Although not required, you should first create your subdocuments and then create a master document with the links to the subdocuments. Following this sequence makes it easier to create the master document because you know the file names of the subdocuments you want to include.

Cue: Create your subdocuments first to help plan your master document.

Working with Subdocuments

A *subdocument* is a regular WordPerfect document. You create a subdocument the same way you create any WordPerfect document.

CAUTION: Codes contained in a subdocument override those defined in the master document. This factor is not a problem for text enhancement codes (such as boldface, italic, underline, and so on) or font size codes (such as fine, large, and so on) that affect only a section of text; this factor is a problem, though, for codes (such as margins, tabs, and base font codes) that affect an entire document's formatting.

Insert codes that affect the entire document into the master document immediately preceding the subdocuments' respective links; do not insert these codes into the subdocument files. Inserting codes into the master document ensures that all subdocuments are formatted with the same options.

■ **Cue:** Create as many subdocuments as needed to keep the project manageable and logical.

WordPerfect places no limits on the number of subdocuments you can combine into a master document. A subdocument also can be any size: less than one page or as much as hundreds of pages. The only practical limit is the amount of disk storage on your computer. When doing a large project, you want to create as many documents as necessary to keep your project manageable and logical. In fact, subdocuments can contain links to other subdocuments. In this way, a subdocument in one master document may also be a master document itself. This concept is covered in the section "Creating Subdocuments within Subdocuments."

The Employee Orientation Manual includes many separate files. The section containing employee job descriptions is a collection of many separate files, one for each job description. These individual job description files are linked in a master document, JOBDESC, which is a subdocument in the master document ORIENT.MD. JOBDESC is referenced in the master document as a subdocument.

When you insert the links to these subdocuments into a master document, you determine where and in what order the subdocuments are included.

Table 26.1 lists each file to be included in the master document, ORIENT.MD, and the subdocument's description.

As already mentioned, subdocuments are regular WordPerfect documents. You create and edit them just as you create and edit any WordPerfect document. To create each subdocument, follow these steps:

1. Open a new document.

2. Compose your text.

3. Add any formatting unique to that subdocument.

4. Save the document.

When you have created all your subdocuments, you are ready to create the master document.

Building the Master Document

Building a master document requires the following three basic steps:

1. Decide what files you want to link as subdocuments to the master document.

2. Create the master document.

3. Insert the subdocument links into the master document.

Table 26.1. Description of Sample Master Document

File Name	Description
TITLEPG	The title page
WELCOME	A letter welcoming new employees to the organization
DIVISION.MAN	The heart of the manual—a detailed description on items employees need to know
OVERVIEW.BAS	An overview of the services provided by the business office
OVERVIEW.FIN	An overview of the services provided by the accounting and payroll departments
OVERVIEW.CC	An overview of the services provided by data processing
ORG1.CHT	The organizational chart of the managers of the entire organization
ORG2.CHT	The organizational chart of the Business and Data Processing division
OFFCHART	Office diagram charts
STATS	Statistics about the services provided to clients each year
JOBDESC	A master document with separate subdocuments of the job description for every position in the division

After you decide the order of the subdocuments within the master document, you are ready to create the master document. To create the master document, start with a new document (select New from the File menu). A blank document is displayed on your screen.

After you create and display the master document, you can place subdocument links into your master document. These subdocument links tell WordPerfect where to place each subdocument in the master document.

Because you will be adding many subdocuments into the master document, consider adding a button to the Button Bar to perform the Subdocument command.

Cue: To save time, plan the order of your subdocuments before creating the master document.

BUTTON

Cue: It's best to decide the order of your subdocuments before mastering the links to them.

To include a subdocument link in a master document, follow these steps:

1. Move the insertion point to the location where you want to place the subdocument.

2. If you want to start the subdocument on a new page, insert a Page Break code into the master document at the place you intend to insert the subdocument link.

   To insert a Page Break, from the **L**ayout menu, select **P**age and then **P**age Break.

   CUA Press Page Break (Ctrl-Enter).

3. From the **T**ools menu, select **M**aster Document and then **S**ubdocument. If you have a Subdoc button, move the mouse pointer to the button and click. The Include Subdocument dialog box is displayed (see fig. 26.1).

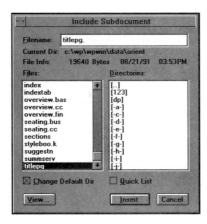

FIG. 26.1

The Include Subdocument dialog box.

4. Use the **F**ilename, F**i**les, or **D**irectories option to select the file name for the first subdocument. In the example, the first subdocument is the title page, so select the file TITLEPG.

T I P   You can double-click the file name of the desired subdocument to insert it into the Master Document at the location of the insertion point. This step also closes the dialog box and returns you to the master document.

WordPerfect inserts a subdocument code into the master document. This code links the subdocument to the master document and tells WordPerfect the name of the file to retrieve to the location of the code.

The subdocument code is represented in your document in the following two ways:

- The subdocument link is represented in the text screen as a comment.

- A hidden code is placed into the document, that you can see only by opening the Reveal Codes window.

To open the Reveal Codes window, select Reveal Codes from the **View** menu (Alt-F3).

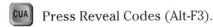 Press Reveal Codes (Alt-F3).

Figure 26.2 shows the two representations of the subdocument link.

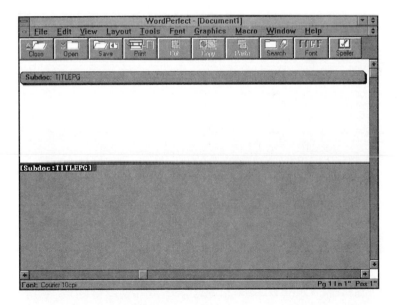

FIG. 26.2

A master document with a subdocument link.

5. If you want the next subdocument link to start on a new page, enter a Page Break before entering the next subdocument link (see step 2).

6. Repeat steps 1 through 5 until you have entered all subdocument links.

7. After entering all subdocument links, name and save the master document. For the example, use ORIENT.MD as the file name for the master document. For more information about saving master documents, see the following section "Saving the Master Document" in this chapter.

Figure 26.3 shows the TITLPG, WELCOME, and DIVISION.MAN files as subdocument links in the master document. The page breaks cause each subdocument to begin on a new page. The bottom half of the screen is the Reveal Codes window, which shows the subdocument link codes.

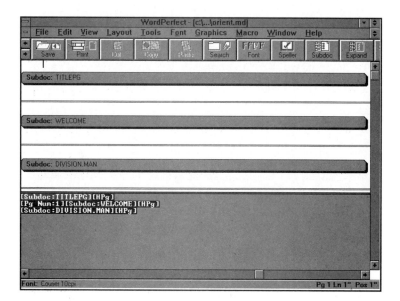

FIG. 26.3

A master document with three subdocument links separated by page breaks.

Adding and Deleting a Subdocument

As you work with your master document, you may find at a later time you want to add new subdocument links or delete existing subdocument links. To add a subdocument link, follow these steps:

1. Select View, Reveal Codes.

 Press Reveal Codes (Alt-F3).

The Reveal Codes window enables you to see precisely where the subdocument link will be added.

2. To insert the new subdocument link, follow steps 1 through 5 for including a subdocument link in a master document in the "Building the Master Document" section of this chapter. When you add a new subdocument link, the subdocument text is included the next time you expand the master document.

At some point, you may decide that you no longer want a particular subdocument included in your master document. Deleting a subdocument link is easy. Follow these steps:

1. Open the Reveal Codes window.

2. Move the insertion point until the [Subdoc:FILENAME] code is highlighted. (The file name is the actual subdocument file name.)

3. Press Delete. The code is removed from your document, and the comment box displayed in the document window disappears.

After you delete a subdocument link, your master document no longer includes that subdocument. After you generate the document references for the master document, entries for the index, table of contents, and so on, are removed for any subdocuments you deleted from the master document.

Expanding the Master Document

After you have created the links to the subdocuments, you can expand the master document to create a document including all the subdocuments. Expanding the document enables you to use WordPerfect functions across all subdocuments and the master document text. You may want to search for text, mark table of contents or index entries, or check the spelling of the expanded document instead of working with individual subdocuments, which is more time-consuming.

To expand the master document, follow these steps:

1. Open the master document so that it is displayed on the screen.

   Save keystrokes and time by adding an Expand button to the Button Bar.

■ **Cue:** Expand the master document so that you can use WordPerfect features across all subdocuments at once.

BUTTON

2. From the **Tools** menu, select Master Document, **Expand** Master. If you have added an Expand button, move the mouse pointer to the button and click.

WordPerfect retrieves the subdocument you named when you entered the subdocument link. If the program cannot find the file, you see the Expand Master Document dialog box with the message Subdocument not Found (see fig. 26.4).

FIG. 26.4

The Expand Master Document dialog box when the subdocument is not located.

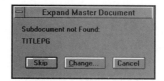

In this dialog box, you can select from three options:

- Choose **S**kip to expand the document without including the referenced subdocument.

- Choose **C**hange to display the Include Subdocument dialog box, and select an alternative directory or file name. The unfound subdocument link is replaced by a subdocument link with the new selected file name.

- Choose Cancel, and the expansion of the master document stops.

CAUTION: If you enter just the file name when you created the subdocument link, without entering the path to the file, you must be in the directory where the subdocuments are located. If you aren't, the Subdocument not found message appears as shown in figure 26.4. In that case, select **C**hange and select the file in the Include Subdocument dialog box.

When WordPerfect expands a master document, each subdocument link code is replaced with two codes: one code marks the beginning of the subdocument's text, and the other code marks the end. The entire subdocument file is placed between the codes. The sample Employee Orientation Manual master document is shown in figure 26.5 with the [Subdoc Start] and [Subdoc End] codes for the TITLEPG subdocument.

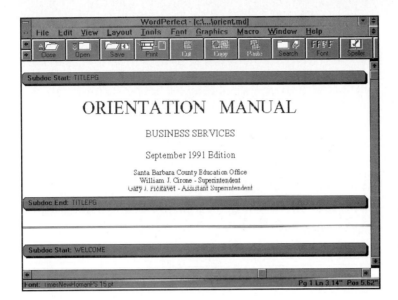

FIG. 26.5

A portion of an expanded master document with Start and End codes.

CAUTION: Never delete the [Subdoc Start:FILENAME] and [Subdoc End:FILENAME] codes in an expanded master document. These codes are used by WordPerfect to keep track of your subdocuments. When you compress a master document, the program removes subdocuments according to these matching codes. If you want to delete a subdocument from your master document, delete the subdocument link from the unexpanded master document (see "Adding and Deleting a Subdocument" in this chapter).

After all subdocuments are retrieved into the master document, return to the top of the expanded master document. Now you can edit any of the text in the expanded document or perform a WordPerfect function, such as a spelling check, on all the documents at once.

Creating a Table of Contents, List, Index, or Table of Authorities

In the last chapter, you learned about the powerful WordPerfect features that can be used to assemble document references. With the Master Document feature, you can create lists, a table of contents, an index,

Cue: With the Master Document feature, you can assemble document references like a table of contents across separate files.

a table of authorities, and cross-references that span subdocuments linked in the master document.

This section describes the steps required to generate a table of contents for a master document. The steps to generate lists, a table of authorities, and an index are similar (see Chapter 25 for detailed information).

You create a table of contents in a master document and its linked subdocuments almost exactly as you create the table of contents in an ordinary document. Follow these three general steps:

1. Mark the text to be included in the table of contents.

2. Define where the table is to be created and the numbering format.

3. Generate the table.

These steps are explained in more detail in the following sections.

This chapter focuses on document references as they are used with the Master Document feature. For detailed information about these features, see Chapter 25, "Assembling Other Document References."

Cue: If you have any subdocuments you do not want included in the index and you are not using a concordance file, place the reference to the subdocuments after the Index definition code.

CAUTION: If you are using the Master Document feature, you should place the Index definition code ([Def Mark:Index]) at the end of the master document. Only text you have manually marked as an index item preceding an Index definition code is included in a generated index.

If you are using a master document and subdocuments, any subdocuments with manually marked index text must be referenced before the Index definition code to include their entries in the generated index in the master document. Subdocuments referenced after the Index definition code do not have their manually marked index text included in the master document's generated index.

If you use a concordance file, all references in the master document and subdocuments are included in the generated index in the master document regardless of where the subdocument is referenced.

Marking Text for the Table of Contents

Normally, the text you want to include in the table of contents is contained in the linked subdocuments. You can, however, mark text in your master document and include it in the table of contents.

The first step in creating a table of contents is marking the text to be included as table of contents entries.

To mark text for a table of contents entry, follow these steps:

■ **Cue:** Open the Reveal Codes window so that you can easily see whether the needed enhancement codes are included in the selection you mark.

1. Open the subdocument in which you want to mark table of contents entries.

2. Select the text and any enhancement codes, such as boldface or italic, to be applied to the text.

    Save keystrokes and time by creating a ToC button to perform the Table of Contents Mark Text command.

3. From the **T**ools menu, select Mar**k** Text.

     Select Mark Text (F12).

4. Select Table of **C**ontents. If you added a ToC button to the Button Bar, move the mouse pointer to the ToC button and click. The Mark Table of Contents dialog box is displayed (see fig. 26.6).

FIG. 26.6

The Mark Table of Contents dialog box.

5. Move the mouse pointer to the up or down triangle icons and click to select the table of contents level number (1 through 5) for this item or type the level number in the Level text box; click OK.

6. Mark all entries in the current subdocument to be included in the table of contents.

7. Save the subdocument.

8. Repeat steps 1 through 7 for each subdocument you link to the master document, as well as any text in the master document you want to include in the table of contents.

T I P   Instead of opening each subdocument and marking text as a table of contents item, expand the master document, and mark the table of contents items. Then compress and save the master document and modified subdocuments.

Defining the Table of Contents

After you have marked the text items for your table of contents, you are ready to define the table of contents and its options.

Defining the table of contents enables you to select the location of the table, the number of levels to include in the table, and the formatting of each table of contents level.

T I P   You should define the table of contents in the master document, not a subdocument. If you define a table of contents in a subdocument, multiple copies of the table of contents appear in the final document.

To define the table of contents, follow these steps:

1. Open the master document. Move the insertion point to the desired location of the table of contents.

    Save keystrokes and time by creating a Def ToC button to perform the Define Table of Contents command.

2. To begin the table of contents on a new page with appropriate headings, insert a page break by choosing Layout, **P**age, **P**age Break.

CUA Press Page Break (Ctrl-Enter).

3. From the Tools menu, select Define.

CUA Select Define (Shift-F12).

4. Select Table of Contents. If you have added a Def ToC button to the Button Bar, move the mouse pointer to the button and click. The Define Table of Contents dialog box is displayed (see fig. 26.7).

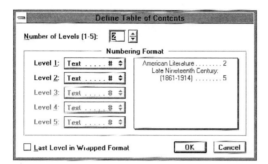

FIG. 26.7

The Define
Table of
Contents dialog
box.

The Define Table of Contents dialog box enables you to select several options. For a detailed description of these options, see Chapter 25, "Assembling Other Document References." The options are as follows:

- The number of levels (1 through 5) you want to include in the table of contents

- The numbering format for each level

- Whether the last level item should be displayed in wrapped format

5. Select Number of Levels and enter the number of table of contents levels in your document.

6. If you want to change the default Numbering Format for any of the levels, select the level (for example, Level 1). Then select one of the five numbering formats available.

WordPerfect can have the table of contents entries for the last level (and optionally, their page numbers) follow one another as if they were one paragraph of information. The appended headings wrap at the end of each line, and lines subsequent to the first one are indented.

7. Select OK.

8. Press Ctrl-Enter to insert a hard page break at the end of the Table of Contents page.

9. Insert a new page number code at the beginning of the first page of your document text (right before the subdocument link of a subdocument begins the body of the document). This code ensures that your master document is numbered properly and the page numbers in the table of contents are correct. For information on inserting a new page number code, see the "Inserting a New Page Number" section in this document.

10. Save the master document with the defined table of contents.

Figure 26.8 shows a table of contents definition in a master document with the Reveal Codes window open.

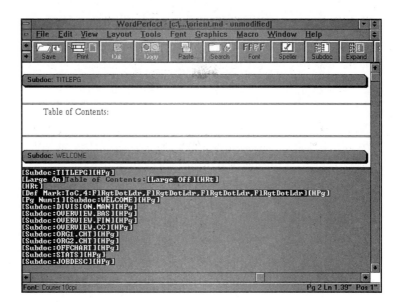

FIG. 26.8

A master document with a table of contents defined.

After you have defined the location of the table of contents and the various formatting options, you are ready to generate the table.

Generating the Table of Contents

After you mark the table of contents items in all the subdocuments and define the location and formatting options for the table of contents in the master document, you can build the table of contents with WordPerfect's Generate command.

Each time you use the Generate command, WordPerfect generates all references in a document. Usually, you generate references immediately before printing to ensure that all page numbers and cross-references are correct. If you modify your document after references are generated and then choose to print your document, WordPerfect reminds you that the references may need to be generated again by displaying a dialog box similar to the one shown in figure 26.9.

■ **Cue:** Generate your document's references right before printing to ensure accuracy.

If the WordPerfect dialog box is displayed, select No (don't print) and follow the steps to Generate the document references. Then select print again.

T I P

After you choose Generate, WordPerfect creates a new table of contents in the location you have indicated. If you previously generated a table of contents, it is deleted and rebuilt based on the text currently marked in your document. The other document references—lists, tables of authorities, cross-references, and indexes—also are deleted and rebuilt when you generate document references.

Because you will probably generate document references often, consider adding a Generate button to the Button Bar.

BUTTON

To generate or update the table of contents for your master document, follow these steps:

1. From the **Tools** menu, select **Generate**. If you added a Generate button to the Button Bar, move the mouse pointer to the button and click. The Generate dialog box is displayed (see fig. 26.10).

    Select Generate (Alt-F12).

FIG. 26.10

The Generate
dialog box.

2. Choose **Yes** to create or update the table of contents and other
references in the document.

Figure 26.11 shows a portion of the generated Table of Contents for the
sample document.

Table of Contents:

Welcome 1

Division Orientation Specifics 2
    Absences: 2
        Illness/Medical Appointments 2
        Vacation 2
        Personal Necessity Leave 3
        Other 3
    Birthdays 3
    Coffee 3
    Correspondence 5
    Counsel Opinions 5
    Desk Procedures 7
    Disaster Preparedness 7
    Fair Labor Standards Act (FLSA) 7
    FAX Machines 9
    Ground Rules 9
    In-Service Events 9
    Lounge 9
    Lunch/Breaks 9
        Financial Accounting/Payroll Staff 9
        Secretarial Staff 10
        Other Staff 10
    Mail 10
    Maintenance and Operations 10
    Meetings 10
        SBAS/DP Managers 11
        School District Business Officials 12
        SBAS and D.P. End-of-Month Coffee 12
        Data Processing Staff 12
        Financial Accounting/Payroll Services Staff 12
        Secretarial Staff 12
    Meeting Room Availability/Scheduling 12

Overview of Services 23
    School Business Advisory Services 23
    Financial Accounting/Payroll 27
    Data Processing 30

Office Diagram Charts 34

Division Statistics 35

ii

FIG. 26.11

A portion of a
master
document's
Table of
Contents.

T I P

If you generate document references for a condensed master document, WordPerfect automatically expands the master document, generates the document references, and then condenses the master document again. When WordPerfect starts to condense the master document, the WordPerfect Generate Condensing Master Document. Update Subdocuments? dialog box shown in figure 26.12 appears. Choose **Yes** to save subdocuments with updated references. WordPerfect saves the subdocuments and returns to the master document, which now has updated references such as the table of contents.

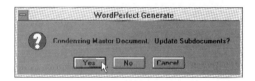

FIG. 26.12

The WordPerfect Generate dialog box.

When you generate document references, they are generated for lists, cross-references, a table of authorities, an index, and a table of contents. This chapter covers the marking of text, table definitions, and references generation for a table of contents example. Other references are done in a similar way. See Chapter 25, "Assembling Other Document References," for more information about using the other reference types.

Printing the Master Document

Expanding your master document produces a complete document of text from the master document and all linked subdocuments. When you generate the document references, you create a complete and accurate document by building and updating the references. Printing this document produces a comprehensive final document.

When you print a master document, it is formatted for the currently selected printer. Subdocuments saved with another printer definition may look different when printed as part of the master document rather than printed by themselves.

You also can print the *condensed* master document, one that has not yet been expanded. Normally, you would not want to print a condensed master document, but because it can contain text of its own as well as the generated table of contents and index, you may want to print it to see those items.

To print only the condensed master document, print the document before expanding it. If the master document is already expanded, condense it and then print. Remember, the subdocument links are displayed as comments and do not print.

Condensing the Master Document

After you are finished working with the expanded master document, you can condense it. When you condense the master document, WordPerfect removes the subdocuments. When the master document is condensed, you are given the option to save changes made to the subdocuments. The revised subdocuments replace the original files on the disk. If you choose not to save the subdocuments, the original files remain as they were when copied into the master document. Changes made to the subdocuments while part of the master document are lost.

BUTTON

If you will be using the Master Document feature often, consider adding the Condense Master command to the Button Bar.

To condense an expanded master document, follow these steps:

1. From the **T**ools menu, select **M**aster Document, **C**ondense Master. The Condense Master Document dialog box with the message Save All Subdocuments? is displayed (see fig. 26.13).

FIG. 26.13

The Condense Master Document dialog box.

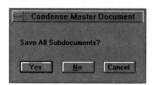

2. Choose **Y**es to save all or individual subdocuments to disk. Choose **N**o to condense the master document without saving any of the subdocuments. If you have made changes to any of the subdocuments, you should select **Y**es. If you choose **N**o, changes made to the subdocuments while part of the master document are lost.

If you select **Y**es to save the subdocuments and WordPerfect finds on disk an existing subdocument with the same file name, the Save Subdocument dialog box with the message Replace Existing File? is displayed (see fig. 26.14). Select **Y**es to replace the file on disk with the subdocument text from your master document.

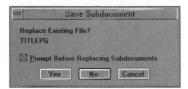

FIG. 26.14

The first Save
Subdocument
dialog box.

If you select **No**, the copy of the file on disk is not replaced. The second Save Subdocument dialog box with the Save As prompt is displayed (see fig. 26.15). This dialog box enables you to specify the directory and file name for saving the subdocument text.

WordPerfect displays the first Save Subdocument dialog box with the Replace Existing File? message for each subdocument (again see fig. 26.14). If you don't want to be prompted for subsequent subdocuments, click to remove the X before the Prompt Before Replacing Subdocuments option. Existing subdocument files on disk are replaced by the appropriate subdocument information without your intervention.

Cue: Remove the X from the Prompt Before Replacing Subdocuments check box to save the files more quickly.

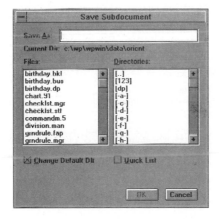

FIG. 26.15

The second
Save Sub-
document
dialog box.

Saving the Master Document

When you are finished working with the master document and want to make the revisions permanent, save it. You can save the master document in either its expanded or condensed form. No real reason exists to save the master document in its expanded form, however, because it can be expanded again at any time. In fact, because saving the expanded document uses more of your hard disk storage space, you should not save an expanded master document unless you have some special reason. If you save the expanded master document in the future, you will not be asked whether you want to condense it.

Cue: Save your documents often. This protects you from data loss because of power failure or computer software problems.

To save a master document, follow these steps:

1. From the **File** menu, select **S**ave.

    Select Save (Shift-F3).

   If the master document has not been condensed, the WordPerfect dialog box with the message Document is expanded, condense it? is displayed (see fig. 26.16).

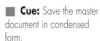

FIG. 26.16

The Word-Perfect dialog box prompt while saving a master document.

■ **Cue:** Save the master document in condensed form.

2. Choose **Yes** to condense the master document. If you don't want to condense the master document, see the "Condensing the Master Document" section of this chapter for information on saving expanded master documents.

Using Other Features in a Master Document

■ **Cue:** Performing an operation across subdocuments in a expanded master document is easier than performing the operation on the subdocuments separately.

Many of WordPerfect's features can be used with the Master Document feature. You can perform functions such as Spelling Check, Search, and Replace more quickly with an expanded master document than on each subdocument. Other features, such as controlling page numbering, are not possible without the Master Document feature unless the individual files are permanently combined into one file.

T I P

When you use Styles in master documents, WordPerfect combines all the styles contained in the master document and subdocuments in the style list of the expanded master document. If you use a style name more than once, WordPerfect uses the first style definition in the expanded document throughout the expanded document.

Inserting a New Page Number

Without the Master Document feature, sequentially numbering a master document is a monumental task. For each file, you need to start the page numbering by inserting the number following the ending page number of the preceding file. If you add text to any file, you need to renumber the pages in all subsequent files.

With the Master Document feature, however, you can insert new page number codes into the master document, and all pages from that point forward are numbered sequentially throughout the following subdocuments. For example, in the Employee Orientation Manual, the first page after the Table of Contents is the Welcome Letter to new employees. By placing a new page number code with a value of 1 in the master document right before the WELCOME subdocument link code, you make the Welcome Letter begin on page 1. All subsequent subdocuments are sequentially numbered from that point.

To turn on page numbering and insert a new page number code with a value of 1, follow these steps:

1. Open the master document.

2. From the **View** menu, select Reveal Codes to open the Reveal Codes window. This window enables you to place the new page number code exactly where you want it.

   CUA Press Reveal Codes (Alt-F3).

3. Move the insertion point to a location immediately before the subdocument link code. The [Subdoc:FILENAME] code in the Reveal Codes window is highlighted. WordPerfect adds the codes immediately to the left of this code.

4. From the **Layout** menu select **P**age, then **N**umbering. The Page Numbering dialog box is displayed (see fig. 26.17).

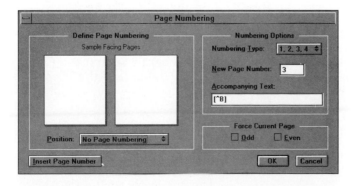

FIG. 26.17

The Page
Numbering
dialog box.

5. Select the appropriate option in the Page Numbering dialog box. For the Orientation Manual, you select **P**osition and choose Bottom Center.

6. Select **N**ew Page Number and type **1**.

7. Select OK to finish. The appropriate codes are inserted into the master document. Figure 26.18 shows the codes immediately to the left of the [Subdoc:WELCOME] code.

8. Save the master document.

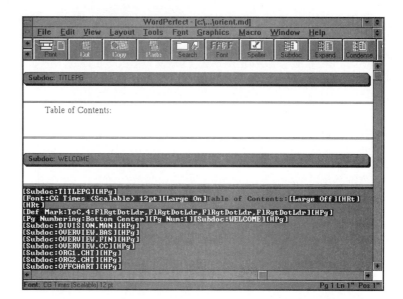

FIG. 26.18

A master document with page numbering codes.

Using Search, Replace, and Speller

You can use the Search, Replace, and Spelling Check features in an expanded master document to perform the operations in the subdocuments. See Chapter 11, "Formatting Pages and Designing Documents," for detailed information on the Search and Replace commands and Chapter 8, "Using the Speller and the Thesaurus," for information about the Speller.

The Orientation Manual has many sections contained in separate subdocuments. Using Search, Replace, or Speller without the Master Document feature requires that you open each subdocument, perform the desired operation, and save the revised file—a tedious and time-consuming task. Also, with so many separate files, you may forget to check some of the files. With the Master Document feature, however, you can expand the master document and perform operations with the confidence that all files will be checked.

To search, replace, or check spelling across all the subdocument files linked to your master document, follow these steps:

1. Open the master document.

2. Expand the master document.

3. Perform the search, replace, or spelling check.

4. Condense the master document.

5. Save the master document. Select Yes to the Save All Subdocuments? prompt.

Adding Footnotes and Endnotes

If you plan to use footnotes or endnotes with the Master Document feature, you should consider several points. Footnote and endnote option codes determine numbering styles, printing format, spacing, and position of the footnotes and endnotes. If you use a footnote or endnote option code, you should have no more than one of each. You should place these codes only in the master document. By placing the codes in the master document, you ensure uniform formatting styles for all footnotes and endnotes in the document. If you put the codes in the individual subdocuments, the options override those in the master document, possibly resulting in the footnotes in each section printing differently.

> **Cue:** To ensure uniform formatting throughout the document, place one footnote and one endnote option code at the beginning of the master document before the occurrence of any footnotes or endnotes.

To enter a footnote or endnote option code, first move the insertion point to the top of the master document. Select **L**ayout, **F**ootnote (or **E**ndnote), **O**ptions. Choose the options you want to change, if any, and select OK.

You add Footnotes and Endnotes to a document by selecting the **L**ayout, **F**ootnote (or **E**ndnote), **C**reate command. In the editing window that opens, enter the desired text and select **C**lose. For detailed information about footnotes and endnotes see Chapter 23, "Using Footnotes and Endnotes."

Numbering Footnotes

With the Master Document feature, you can number footnotes consecutively throughout the document. You also can restart numbering at 1 at the beginning of any subdocument.

To number footnotes consecutively, no special action is required. Simply create the footnotes in each subdocument as you create footnotes for any document. If you print a subdocument by itself, the footnotes are numbered from 1. When you open and then expand a master document that includes that subdocument, the footnotes in all subdocuments are numbered consecutively throughout the master document.

If you want to begin numbering footnotes at 1 for a particular section, place a new footnote number code ([New Ftn Num:1]) to precede the subdocument where you want to begin numbering.

For more information about footnotes, see Chapter 23, "Using Footnotes and Endnotes."

Placing Endnotes

You do not have to follow any special procedures to place endnotes in your subdocuments. You can place endnotes either at the end of each subdocument or at the end of the master document.

If you want the endnotes for each chapter to be placed at the end of the chapter, insert an endnote placement code at the end of the subdocument that contains the end of the chapter. If you want all endnotes to be gathered to one place, insert the endnote placement code at the desired location in the master document. Any endnotes created in the master document or any subdocument prior to the endnote placement code will be listed at the location of the endnote placement code.

To insert an Endnote placement code into a document, move the insertion point to the desired location (usually at the end of the document). Select **L**ayout, **E**ndnote, **P**lacement. An Endnote Placement dialog box appears asking you whether you want to Restart Endnote Numbering? Because the endnote placement is at the end of the document and not the end of the chapter, choose **N**o.

For more information about endnotes, see Chapter 23.

Using Cross-References

With the Master Document feature, you can cross-reference items in different subdocuments. Cross-referencing from one file to another is impossible without the Master Document feature. In the Employee Orientation Manual's subdocument containing disaster preparedness information, you may want to refer the reader to a diagram showing fire escape routes, but the diagram is in the subdocument containing the office diagram charts.

To cross-reference, insert a reference code with a target name into the subdocument containing the disaster preparedness section. Then insert a target code with the same target name into the appropriate chart of the office diagram charts subdocument. When the master document is expanded and the document references generated, the reference page number in the disaster preparedness section refers the reader to the appropriate page number for the fire escape routes.

For more information about cross-references, see Chapter 25, "Assembling Other Document References."

Cue: You can enter reference and target codes in separate files and tie them together using the Master Document feature.

Creating Subdocuments within Subdocuments

You are not limited to a rigid structure of one master document with multiple subdocuments. A subdocument also can be a master document with subdocuments.

The Employee Orientation Manual has a subdocument titled JOBDESC. This subdocument is actually a master document with each job description file defined as a subdocument within JOBDESC. Therefore, if you want to print all employee job descriptions, you can open the file JOBDESC and expand it. The separate job description files are retrieved so that they can be printed.

Cue: A master document can also be a subdocument in another master document.

The file JOBDESC is also defined as a subdocument in the Orientation Manual master document file ORIENT.MD. When the Orientation Manual master document is expanded, the subdocuments within the JOBDESC file also are expanded and placed in the Orientation Manual. Condensing the master document ORIENT.MD condenses the subdocument files in the JOBDESC subdocument and saves them if requested.

Finding Other Uses for Master Documents

■ **Cue:** Use the Master Document feature for any large writing project.

To help you understand Master Documents, this chapter uses a sample Employee Orientation Manual. Now that you are familiar with the Master Document feature, you can see that it is ideally suited for many types of large projects, such as college dissertations, computer program user's manuals, or complex legal contracts in a law firm.

Often individual writers collaborate on a large writing project with the goal of combining their work into one document. Without Word-Perfect's Master Document feature, combining these separate efforts is a time-consuming task that presents many challenges in numbering pages, creating a table of contents, and indexing the final document. Without the Master Document feature, time is taken away from the actual research and writing effort of the authors. Creating a master document saves time because many of these tasks can be handled automatically with WordPerfect's powerful Master Document feature. In fact, any document with parts that are logically maintained or better managed in separate disk files is a good candidate for the Master Document feature.

Chapter Summary

This chapter shows you how to use the Master Document feature to manage a large and complex document. You saw that breaking the document into smaller, easy-to-handle pieces and then combining these pieces when necessary saves time. As part of working with master and subdocuments, you learned how to build a master document to manage a large writing project, place subdocument links into a master document to enable WordPerfect to combine separate files, and generate a table of contents and other document references for an entire project. To save time and ensure accuracy, you learned to perform several WordPerfect features across subdocuments. Finally, you learned how to print the complete expanded master document.

PART

VII

Becoming
an Expert
User

OUTLINE

Using the Equation Editor

Creating and Displaying
  Special Characters

Customizing WordPerfect with
  Preferences

Advanced File Management
  Techniques

Importing Data and Working
  with Other Programs

Using the Equation Editor

Creating mathematical equations within a word processing program can be a specialized and difficult task, requiring the use of multiple type sizes, special characters, varying line spacing, complex alignment of different elements of the equation, and so on. Several programs are available that provide tools for creating complex equations, but which lack many features necessary for more general word processing. Most general-purpose word processors, however, lack the specialized tools for creating complex equations.

WordPerfect's Equation Editor makes the power of a technical word processor available to users of a general-purpose word processor. The Equation Editor's syntax, although specialized, is similar to the language you use to read equations out loud. After you enter a description of an equation, the Equation Editor performs all the formatting for you, placing each element in the correct position, using the appropriate type sizes, and scaling mathematical symbols, such as sums, integrals, roots, and parentheses, to fit. The Equation Editor does not solve equations for you or check the mathematical validity of any equation you create.

■ **Gordon Nelder-Adams** is the WordPerfect expert for the Sacramento PC Users Group and a computing assistant at the University of California, Davis. He does scientific word processing at UC Davis.

You can use the Equation Editor to create complex, multilevel equations that would look at home in a calculus textbook, scientific paper, or engineering diagram. You also can use the Equation Editor for simple fractions, square roots, and other common algebraic functions more likely to be helpful to the average user. Although the Equation Editor's syntax at first may seem confusing, if you can speak the equation out loud, you are half-way to creating it in the Equation Editor. The syntax for creating a fraction, for example, in the Equation Editor is simply "a over b"; to create the same fraction without using the Equation Editor is much more complicated.

Each equation you create is a WordPerfect graphic and can be adjusted in size, shape, and position like any other graphics box. If your printer has a symbol font available, WordPerfect can use its characters to build equations or can create individual graphics characters from the WordPerfect character sets. As a result, you can print your equations on any printer, ranging from a 9-pin impact printer to a PCL laser printer to a PostScript typesetter. Equally important, WordPerfect for Windows displays equations within your document exactly as they will print so that you can see an equation as you create or edit the surrounding text.

In this chapter, you learn to use the Equation Editor to do the following:

- Type entries in the Editing Pane
- View the equation in the Display Pane
- Insert commands, functions, and symbols from the Equation Palette
- Enter characters from the normal keyboard, an equation keyboard, or the WordPerfect Characters dialog box
- Create superscripts and subscripts, fractions, sums and integrals, roots, and matrixes
- Automatically number equations
- Embed equations within text
- Save, retrieve, and print equations

Starting the Equation Editor

The Equation Editor is a specialized graphics editor, and, therefore, the mechanics of creating, saving, and positioning equations are similar to those used for figures and other graphics boxes (see Chapters 7 and 17, "Introduction to Graphics" and "Understanding Advanced Graphics").

To start the Equation Editor and create a new equation, access the **Graphics** menu and select **Equation, Create** (see fig. 27.1).

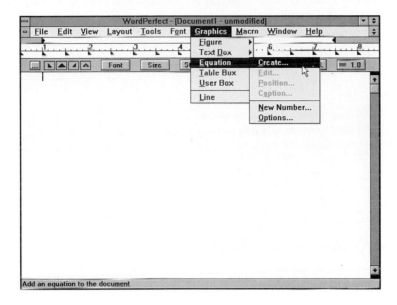

FIG. 27.1

The Equation menu.

To edit an existing equation, select **Equation, Edit** from the **Graphics** menu. The Edit Equation dialog box appears, suggesting the number of the next equation to edit. Accept this number or type a different equation number, and select OK or press Enter.

If you create many equations, add Equation Create to your Button Bar for speedier access.

The quickest way to edit an equation is to double-click the equation with your mouse. The Equation Editor opens and automatically retrieves the equation.

T I P

The Equation Editor now appears on screen, temporarily replacing the normal document editing screen (see fig. 27.2).

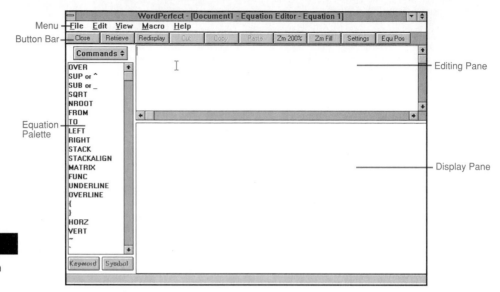

Menu
Button Bar
Equation
Palette

Editing Pane

Display Pane

FIG. 27.2

The Equation
Editor.

Examining the Equation Editor Screen

The Equation Editor consists of five main elements: the Editing Pane, the Display Pane, the Equation Palette, an abbreviated pull-down menu system, and the Equation Editor Button Bar (optional). When you create a new equation, the Editing Pane and Display Pane are empty. You can switch between the Editing Pane, Display Pane, and Equation Palette by using the Next Pane and Previous Pane commands (F6, Shift-F6) or by using your mouse.

The Editing Pane is actually a small text editing window in which you type a description of an equation. Each description can consist of text, variables, symbols, numbers, functions, and commands. These elements are explained in more detail later. You can insert these elements by typing directly from the keyboard, by selecting them in the Equation Palette, or through the WordPerfect Characters dialog box. You also can save the contents of the Editing Pane as a separate file and retrieve other equation descriptions into the Editing Pane to modify or build on. You can perform basic editing functions on the contents of the Editing Pane, including cutting, copying, and pasting. You cannot format text as you can in the normal document editing screen, however, and most function keys have no effect in the Editing Pane. When you want to see the current appearance of your equation, select

View, Redisplay

 Press Redisplay (Ctrl-F3).

to display the equation in the Display Pane. The syntax of your description must be correct, or you will receive an error message, and the equation will not display.

As its name implies, the Display Pane displays an image of your equation as the equation will print. The image usually is magnified for easy viewing; the magnification is adjusted automatically to best display the full equation. If you create a large equation, you can zoom in on a particular segment and scroll the window to display different segments. You cannot, however, make changes to the equation from the Display Pane. If some part of your equation is incorrect, you must return to the Editing Pane to make changes.

WordPerfect does not update the image in the Display Pane automatically, because during the process of building an equation description, incomplete clauses frequently make your syntax incorrect. When you make changes in the Editing Pane, therefore, redisplay the image in the Display Pane after you are done.

When you need to insert a character, symbol, command or function, you can type it from the keyboard or insert it from the Equation Palette (again see fig. 27.2). The Palette displays one of eight menus containing groups of WordPerfect characters most commonly used in the Equation Editor, as well as formatting commands and mathematical functions. The Equation Palette contains menus for commands, functions, Greek letters, arrows, sets, large symbols, and other miscellaneous symbols.

You can scroll among the Palette menus, select a command, function, or symbol, and insert it into the Editing Pane as a keyword or a symbol.

The Equation Editor Button Bar provides immediate mouse access to selected menu items. As with any other Button Bar, you can assign menu commands to individual buttons, change the Button Bar's position on-screen, and display button text, pictures, or both. Unfortunately, although you can create macros in the Equation Editor, you cannot assign them to its Button Bar, nor can you create more than one Equation Editor Button Bar. If you need more room on-screen, you can turn off the Button Bar by selecting View, Button Bar. (For general information on Button Bars, see Chapter 19, "Using the Button Bar.")

BUTTON

Creating an Equation in the Editing Pane

Before examining the Equation Editor's syntax and command structure in detail, create a few simple equations and observe how WordPerfect interprets them. Follow these steps:

1. Access the Equation Editor by selecting **G**raphics, **E**quation, **C**reate.

   The Equation Editor appears. The insertion point is in the Editing Pane, and the Equation Palette displays the Commands menu.

2. Type the following:

   2x + 3y = 24

3. From the **V**iew menu, select **R**edisplay.

    Press Redisplay (Ctrl-F3).

   Alternatively, click the Redisplay button on the Button Bar.

   Your equation is centered in the Display Pane, but the equation doesn't look quite the way you typed it. Instead, it appears as follows:

   $2x+3y=24$

   The Equation Editor does not interpret spaces you type in the Editing Pane as spaces in the printed equation. In many cases, equations require spacing far narrower than a standard space, so the Equation Editor demands that you explicitly enter spacing instructions by using a tilde (~) to create a normal space and an opening single quotation mark (') to create a thin space, which is actually a quarter space.

4. Edit your original equation as follows, and Redisplay.

   2x~+~3y~=~24

   In the Display Pane, your equation now appears as follows:

   $2x + 3y = 24$

5. Now use the space bar to edit the equation, and Redisplay again.

   2x~ +~3y =~ 24

Note that the appearance in the Display Pane doesn't change.

6. Select **C**lose from the **F**ile menu.

Alternatively, click the Close button on the Button Bar.

Your equation appears horizontally centered in your document.

The space characters, ~ and ', can be called *formatting spaces*, because they change the appearance of the equation in the Display Pane and on the printout. Whether normal or thin spaces, however, the Editing Pane treats them like any other letter, number, or character. Spaces created with the space bar, on the other hand, do not affect the appearance of the final equation; but these spaces are essential for working easily in the Editing Pane, for much the same reason that you use them in a normal document. If your equation consists of only letters, numbers, and other special characters, you need not use the space bar at all.

Remember that the Editing Pane is a small text editor in its own right, which wraps text and enables you to use Ctrl-left arrow and Ctrl-right arrow to move left and right a "word" at a time. If your only concern is the printed appearance (as reflected in the Display Pane), you can create an equation clause with dozens of formatting spaces, letters, and numbers without using the space bar once. Step 4 in the preceding steps is a short example.

Such a clause prints properly but is difficult to work with in the Editing Pane. If the last character triggered a line wrap, for instance, the entire clause would wrap to the next line, leaving a large gap. In a large equation, such wasted spaces can make displaying the whole equation in the Editing Pane impossible. Such clauses are also awkward to edit, because pressing Word Right or Word Left (Ctrl-right arrow and Ctrl-left arrow) moves the insertion point completely past the clause. To reach the middle, you must scroll a character at a time or use your mouse to select a new insertion point. Neither procedure is difficult, but both are slower to use for reaching a point within the clause than scrolling by word.

For the reasons listed in the preceding paragraph, you should use the space bar to break up long clauses in the Editing Pane into smaller "words" for easy editing, even though these spaces will not print. Using the space bar to break up a clause is optional; how frequently you do so is up to you.

Creating a Simple Fraction

Regular spaces (spaces created with the space bar) are required in many circumstances. OVER, for example, is the Equation Editor command that creates a fraction. You type **a over b** to create the following equation:

$$\frac{a}{b} \tag{1}$$

Because the printed equation contains no spaces, you don't need to use tildes. You might assume, therefore, that you can omit regular spaces from the typed equation, as well. Typing **aoverb**, however, produces the following equation:

$$aoverb \tag{2}$$

■ **Cue:** Use the space bar in the Editing Pane to separate words and phrases. The spaces don't affect the printed appearance and make your equation text easier to edit.

Without the spaces around OVER, WordPerfect cannot recognize it as a command.

To edit the equation from the preceding section to turn it into a fraction, do the following:

1. From the **G**raphics menu, select **E**quation, **E**dit. The Edit Equation dialog box appears.

2. Type **1**. Select OK or press Enter. The Equation Editor appears; the Editing Pane and Display Pane show their respective views of your first equation.

3. In the Editing Pane, change the equation text to read as follows:

   2x over 3y~ =~ 24

4. Press Redisplay. Your equation now looks like Equation 3.

$$2\frac{x}{3}y \; = 24 \tag{3}$$

Again, this equation is not quite what you want. The Equation Editor recognized the OVER command, but the Editor did not recognize that *2x* and *3y* belong together. The Equation Editor makes very few assumptions about which letters, characters, and symbols should be grouped together and which should not. Just as you must indicate formatting spaces by inserting tildes and opening single quotation marks, you must use braces ({}) to surround groups of characters when you want the Equation Editor to perform some action on the entire group.

5. In the Editing Pane, change the text again to read as follows:

   {2x} over {3y}~=~ 24

6. Press Redisplay. Now the equation appears as desired.

$$\frac{2x}{3y} = 24 \qquad\qquad (4)$$

Creating Superscripts and Subscripts

Many equations contain superscripts and subscripts. WordPerfect's normal text attributes don't work in the Equation Editor, so you need to use commands to create superscripts and subscripts. The "long" form of these commands are SUP and SUB, respectively. In place of SUP, however, you can use a caret (^) to create a superscript and in place of SUB, you can use an underline (_) to create a subscript.

Therefore, to create the following equation:

$$x_1 + y^2 \qquad\qquad (5)$$

type

> x sub 1 ~+~ y sup 2

or

> x_1 ~+~ y^2

As with OVER, you must use regular spaces around SUP and SUB. You don't need to use spaces around the characters ^ and _ because their meanings are always unambiguous, and the Equation Editor reserves their use for these commands. The spaces around the plus sign are optional but help separate the equation text into individual "words" in the Editing Pane.

You can nest multiple levels of super- and subscripts, using braces, if necessary. Examine the following typed equations and their printed appearance:

(a)	(b)	(c)	(d)	
x^e^n	x^e^n−1	x^e^{n−1}	x^e^n_1	**(6)**
x^{e^n}	$x^{e^n}-1$	$x^{e^{n-1}}$	$x^{e^{n_1}}$	

WordPerfect chooses a smaller point size for each successive level. Note the difference that adding braces makes between equations (b) and (c).

Edit your equation in the following way:

1. If necessary, select **G**raphics, **E**quation, **E**dit, and enter the number of the equation to edit.

2. Edit the equation text to match the following:

   {2x_{n–1}^2} over {3y^2}~ =~ 24

3. Redisplay. Your equation should now look like Equation 7.

$$\frac{2x_{n-1}^2}{3y^2} = 24 \tag{7}$$

WordPerfect automatically adjusts the height of the numerator and denominator. Notice that the x in the numerator has a superscript and a subscript and that one appears directly above the other. To use both at the same time in this way, you must enter the subscript first and then the superscript.

Reviewing Key Concepts

Now that you have created a few equations and have some feel for how the Equation Editor works, you are ready to examine some concepts and terminology in more depth. Although learning the syntax of individual commands is important, understanding the concepts on which those commands are based is equally important. At first glance, many commands can appear to be confusing and arbitrary collections of symbols. With a little background knowledge, the same command syntax becomes logical and necessary. In the following sections, you learn some definitions and general rules of syntax. Following that, you examine the parts of the Equation Editor in detail, before returning to more specific examples.

Defining Terms

A *command* is a reserved word or character that tells the Equation Editor to perform a formatting action on the following text. OVER, SUP, and SUB (or ^ and _) are examples of commands. Table 27.1 gives a full list of Equation Editor commands.

A *function* is a word recognized by the Equation Editor as a standard mathematical function such as log or sin. Table 27.2 gives a full list of functions. Table 27.2 is located in the section "Using Functions in the Equations Editor."

A *variable* is any sequence of letters and numbers that the Equation Editor does not recognize as a command, function, or other keyword. Variables can be one or more characters long and must start with a letter of the alphabet but can contain numbers, too. Any word not having a special meaning is treated as a variable. Examples include *x*, *B1*, and *velocity*.

A *symbol* is any character that is not a standard letter or number. Symbols used frequently in the Equation Editor appear in the Equation Palette's Greek, Symbols, Arrows, Large, Sets, and Other menus. The complete set of WordPerfect Characters is available under **W**P Characters in the **E**dit menu or by pressing Ctrl-W.

A *number* is any positive whole number followed by a space, an alphabetic character, a symbol, or a period; thus, although B2 is a variable, 2B is a number followed by a variable. The Equation Editor does not recognize negative numbers and decimals as units but treats minus signs and decimal points as separate parts. You must use braces around numbers such as {−2} or {3.1} to have the Equation Editor treat them as units.

A *keyword* is an alphabetic description of a command, function, or other symbol in the Equation Palette. Commands and functions are keywords by definition. Just as SUP and SUB can be represented by ^ and _, each symbol can be inserted as a keyword or as an individual character. Thus beta is the keyword for the symbol β, and you can use either in the equation text to cause the character to appear in the printed equation.

Table 27.1. Equation Editor Commands

Command Keyword	Description
OVER	Fraction
SUP or ^	Superscript
SUB or _	Subscript
SQRT	Square Root
NROOT	Nth Root
FROM	Limits
TO	Limits
LEFT	Left delimiter
RIGHT	Right delimiter

continues

Table 27.1. *(continued)*

Command Keyword	Description
STACK	Vertical stack
STACKALIGN	Vertical stack with character alignment
MATRIX	Matrix
FUNC	User-defined function
UNDERLINE	Underline
OVERLINE	Overline
{	Start group
}	End group
HORZ	Horizontal move
VERT	Vertical move
~	Normal space
`	Thin space (one-fourth a normal space)
BINOM	Binomial
&	Column separator
#	Row separator
MATFORM	Matrix column format
ALIGNL	Align left
ALIGNR	Align right
ALIGNC	Align center
PHANTOM	Place holder
.	No delimiter
\	Literal
BOLD	Bold attribute
ITAL	Italic attribute
OVERSM	Fraction small
BINOMSM	Binomial small
LINESPACE	Vertical (line) spacing
LONGDIV	Long division
LONGDIVS	Long division (square symbol)
SCALESYM	Scale symbol

Understanding Syntax

An equation text resembles a sentence. Commands act the part of verbs; and numbers, variables, and other symbols take the place of nouns. Just as each language has its own rules of grammar and syntax, the Equation Editor has specific rules that govern how you combine the various elements of an equation. Depending on how poorly you construct a sentence, it can be grammatically correct but mean something other than you intended, or it can be missing an essential part of speech and be meaningless. As long as your equation's syntax is correct, the Equation Editor can show it in the Display Pane, although the displayed equation may not be exactly what you wanted.

Although the Equation Editor performs the mechanics of positioning the various elements of an equation, selecting the proper type sizes, and creating graphic symbols where necessary, your equation text must provide the necessary commands for which actions are to be taken and which groups of characters those commands affect. If your syntax has one or more errors, the Editor displays an Incorrect Format error message and moves the insertion point to a part of your equation text that the Editor recognizes as faulty. (If your equation has more than one error, you may have to edit and attempt to Redisplay several times.)

The following syntax rules apply to all equations. Some commands have additional syntax rules, described later in this chapter.

- *Commands are not case-sensitive.* You can type them all in uppercase, all in lowercase, or in mixed case. OVER, over, and Over are all acceptable.

- *All commands must be separated from variables that come immediately before and after.* You can use the space bar, press Enter, or insert a symbol. Note that you can place a number immediately before a command, but if you place a number immediately after a command, the Equation Editor will interpret the two elements as one variable. The best practice, therefore, is to use spaces around commands at all times.

- *Commands act only on individual elements of an equation, whether those elements are numbers, variables or characters.* If you want a command to act on several elements as a *group*, you must combine them into a single element by surrounding them with braces ({}).

- *You can create groups within groups.*

- *Braces must appear in pairs.* Mismatched braces are the most common cause of syntax errors.

Cue: Mismatched braces are the most common cause of syntax errors.

■ *When formatting your equations for display and printing, the Equation Editor groups elements in the following order of precedence:*

1. Groups formed by braces ({})

2. Diacritical marks (such as overbars, vectors, and tildes)

3. Primes, SUB, SUP, FROM, and TO

4. Roots

5. OVER, BINOM

6. Other elements from left to right

   Groups formed by braces ({}) always take precedence. When the Equation Editor doesn't format a clause as you desired, you can override its defaults by establishing a group.

Using the Equation Editor

As you have seen in examples in this chapter, you can create and edit many equations in the Editing Pane by using only the keyboard without employing the other resources the Equation Editor provides. Making full use of the Equation Editor, however, requires making full use of all its features: the keyboard, specialized equation keyboards, the Equation Palette, the WordPerfect Characters dialog box, and the Equation Editor Button Bar.

Using the Editing Pane

The Editing Pane provides a full text-editing environment with most of the editing features available in a normal document. You can use the normal directional keys to move by character, word, line, or to the top and bottom of an equation, or you can select any insertion point with the mouse. You can select text by using Shift with the directional keys or by using the mouse. You can delete selected text, or you can cut or copy it to the Clipboard and paste it back once or many times. You also can move information between the normal document screen and the Editing Pane by cutting or copying to the Clipboard.

You can enter letters, numbers, and other keyboard characters by typing directly in the Editing Pane. Although many mathematical symbols and characters are available in the Equation Palette, if you need to include the following common characters in an equation, you must enter them from the keyboard:

$$+ - * / = < > ! ? . | @ , ; :$$

You also must enter the following common characters from the keyboard:

~ ' ' " \ # & { } ( ) [ ]

These characters have special meanings to the Equation Editor. You already have seen the tilde (~) and left quotation mark ('). The meanings of the other special characters are described in the section "Using Functions and Commands To Create Equations."

Using an Equation Keyboard

Another WordPerfect feature that you can use in the Equation Editor is an equation keyboard layout. In WordPerfect, you can remap the keyboard, moving commands from one function key to another or assigning macros or special characters to Ctrl- and Alt-key combinations. The 5.1-compatible keyboard layout provided with WordPerfect for Windows is one example of an alternative keyboard layout. WordPerfect also provides a specialized equation keyboard containing many useful symbols such as Greek letters, sums, integrals, and so on. You can use the equation keyboard as is or modify it to suit your needs.

Before you can use the equation keyboard in the Editing Pane, however, you must select it. For instructions, see Chapter 29, "Customizing WordPerfect with Preferences.

The equation keyboard will now be selected when the Editing Pane is active. See the WordPerfect manual for a complete list of shortcut keys. You can add any command or other keyword you use frequently to this keyboard file as a text entry, and assign that text to a keystroke combination. See Chapter 29, "Customizing WordPerfect with Preferences," for more information on editing the equation keyboard.

Using the Equation Palette

The equation keyboard enables you to insert frequently used characters and symbols with a single keystroke combination, but is limited by the number of keys available on a keyboard. Unless you use the equation keyboard frequently, you may have trouble remembering which characters are assigned to which keys. Although not as quick to use, the Equation Palette provides access to many more symbols and mathematical functions and Equation Editor commands. Furthermore, because the Equation Palette displays the contents of each of its groups on-screen, you can browse through them to find the symbol, command, or function you need and then insert it into the Editing Pane.

You can insert commands and functions only as keywords. You can insert items from the other groups as keywords or as the symbols their keywords represent. Greek letters and other symbols always display and print as symbols, regardless of how you enter them in the Editing Pane. Keywords are usually quicker to type than to select through the Equation Palette, but they take up more room in the Editing Pane. Symbols are always individual characters and help make the equation text look more like the printed equation but take longer to select through the Equation Palette (although you can enter some quickly from the equation keyboard).

When inserting commands, functions, and symbols into the Editing Pane, the Palette puts a space before and after the item, whether entered as a keyword or symbol.

The Equation Palette contains the following groups of symbols:

Commands (the default)
Large
Symbols
Greek
Arrows
Sets
Other
Functions

A large button at the top of the Equation Palette displays the currently selected group name. You can select a new group with the mouse or keyboard and insert the desired item into the Editing Pane.

To use the Equation Palette, move the insertion point in the Editing Pane to the desired position, and follow these steps:

1. If necessary, select a different Palette group. Click and hold the group button with your mouse; the Equation Palette pop-up list appears. Drag up or down to select the desired group name and release.

   Alternatively, press Next Pane (F6) from within the Editing Pane to activate the Equation Palette. Press Alt-PgUp or Alt-PgDn to cycle through the Palette groups until you reach the desired item.

2. Select an item with your mouse or with the directional keys. As each item is highlighted, its keyword appears at the bottom of the screen. If the entire group list will not fit in the space available, a vertical scroll bar appears, that you can select with your mouse. You also can continue to scroll using the up- and down-arrow keys or use PgDn and PgUp to move to the bottom or top of the group list.

3. At the bottom of the Palette are two buttons labeled Keyword and Symbol. Click either button to insert the item into the form indicated. (Because commands and functions can be entered only as keywords, the Symbol button is dimmed when either of those menus is displayed.)

    Alternatively, press Enter to insert the item as a keyword, or press Ctrl-Enter to insert the item as a symbol.

If you need more room on-screen, you can turn off the Equation Palette by selecting **V**iew, **P**alette. Select **V**iew, **P**alette again to turn it back on when needed.

■ **Cue:** You can double-click an item to insert it as a keyword or hold down the Ctrl key and double-click to insert the item as a symbol.

Using WordPerfect Characters

Although the Equation Palette provides access to a wide variety of characters commonly used in equations, it doesn't contain every available WordPerfect character. If you need to enter another character into an equation, you have access to the full set of nearly 2,000 characters that WordPerfect recognizes. From the **E**dit menu, select **WP** Characters or press Ctrl-W. The WordPerfect Characters dialog box appears in the lower right corner, partially obscuring the Display Pane. You can choose from the 13 different character sets (0 through 12), select a character, and insert it into the Editing Pane in a manner nearly identical to using the Equation Palette. If you need only one special character, you can close the dialog box after you insert the character, or you can leave the dialog box open and switch between it and the Editing Pane to insert additional characters. You can redisplay equations while the WordPerfect Characters dialog box is open, but they will be partially hidden until you close the box.

■ **Cue:** You can insert any character by using the WordPerfect Characters dialog box (Ctrl-W).

Altering the Equation Display

The Equation Editor attempts to display all equations within the boundaries of the Display Pane at the largest comfortable resolution. This technique presents no problems for small equations, which can be displayed anywhere from two to five times actual size. The status bar at the bottom of the screen displays the current degree of magnification. Actual size is 100 percent, and 500 percent is five times actual size. The default is 200 percent.

When an equation becomes very large, the Equation Editor must reduce it to fit within the Display Pane, and reduction can make the equation difficult to read. You can make an equation easier to read by selecting a specific resolution, zooming in or out, making the equation fill the Display Pane, or selecting a specific area to enlarge. You can select any of these options from the Equation Editor's View menu (see fig. 27.3). Selecting 100% or 200% changes the display to that magnification. Zoom In increases the magnification, and Zoom Out decreases the magnification; either can be used repeatedly to adjust the display in 50 percent increments. When you select Zoom Area, a set of cross hairs appears. Use the mouse to position the cross hairs immediately above and to the left of an area you want to see in greater detail, and then press and drag the rectangular space. When you release the mouse button, WordPerfect enlarges the selected area to fill the Display Pane. Zoom Fill makes the equation smaller or larger as necessary to fill the Display Pane.

When an equation is too large to fit within the Display Pane at the current magnification, one or two scroll bars appear on the right side of the Display Pane, as needed (again see fig. 27.3). You can use the scroll bars to move the equation within the Display Pane without changing its magnification.

Remember that moving or resizing an equation in the Display Pane does not affect the printed appearance of the equation. To change the printed size, see "Positioning and Sizing Equations," in this chapter.

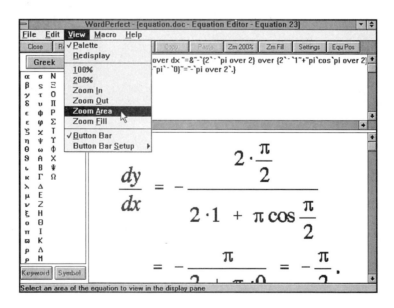

FIG. 27.3

The Equation Editor's View menu.

Using Functions and Commands to Create Equations

Although the Equation Editor automatically performs certain formatting tasks such as printing variables in italic and functions in standard type, you must provide most formatting instructions yourself. You have seen several commands, including OVER, SUP (^), and SUB (_). The following sections explore other useful commands, from basic to complex, which you can use to format equations to your exact needs.

Using Functions in the Equation Editor

The Equation Editor follows accepted mathematical rules in formatting equations. In particular, these rules require setting recognized mathematical functions in regular type and setting variables in italic type. As a result, any word that the Editor doesn't recognize as a function, command, or other keyword, is treated as a variable and automatically set in italic. The words recognized by the Equation Editor as functions are standard terms for trigonometric, logarithmic, and other mathematical functions. Table 27.2 lists the functions and their descriptions.

Table 27.2. Equation Editor Functions

Keyword	Description
cos	Cosine
sin	Sine
tan	Tangent
arccos	Arc cosine
arcsin	Arc sine
arctan	Arc tangent
cosh	Hyperbolic cosine
sinh	Hyperbolic sine
tanh	Hyperbolic tangent
cot	Cotangent
coth	Hyperbolic cotangent

continues

Table 27.2. *(continued)*

Keyword	Description
sec	Secant
cosec	Cosecant
exp	Exponent
log	Logarithm
ln	Natural logarithm
lim	Limit
liminf	Limit inferior
limsup	Limit superior
min	minimum
max	maximum
gcd	Greatest common denominator
arc	Arc function
det	Determinant
mod	Modulo

You can type functions directly or insert them from the Equation Palette. The Palette always inserts functions into the Editing Pane in lowercase letters and puts a space before and after each function. As with commands, functions must have a space, carriage return, or symbol on either side to be recognized by the Equation Editor.

Although you can enter functions in uppercase or lowercase, the lowercase used by the Equation Palette is the normal mathematical practice. The common practice is to use a thin space (`'`) to separate functions from variables. For example, you type the following:

> B'cos'theta ~+~ A

to produce the following equation:

$$B\cos\theta + A \tag{8}$$

The letters A and B are recognized as variables and therefore are italicized; cos is recognized as function and is left alone; the word theta is recognized as a Greek letter. Thin spaces separate cos from the letter B and theta, but full spaces separate the plus sign from the whole first clause and from the letter A that follows.

Using FUNC, BOLD and ITAL to Format Equations

In practice, the Equation Editor displays functions as typed, in normal (nonitalic) font. Unfortunately, the Equation Editor treats everything it does not recognize as a function, command, symbol or other keyword as a variable and italicizes it. Suppose that you want to create the following equation calculating present value:

$$\text{Present Value} = \text{Payment} \left(\frac{1 - (1 + \text{interest rate})^{-\text{number of payments}}}{\text{interest rate}} \right) \qquad (9)$$

You may be tempted to type the following:

Present~ Value ~=~ Payment~ ({1 ~—~ (1 ~+~ interest~ rate)^ {−number~ of~ payments}} over {interest~ rate})

The Equation Editor does not recognize any word except *over* as a keyword, and therefore treats the rest as variables, with the following result:

$$\textit{Present Value} = \textit{Payment} \left(\frac{1 - (1 + \textit{interest rate})^{-\textit{number of payments}}}{\textit{interest rate}} \right) \qquad (10)$$

To format this equation correctly, you must use the command FUNC. FUNC instructs the Equation Editor to treat the item that follows as a function. The item can be a single variable, a grouped word or phrase, or an entire equation. The Editor then formats the indicated text normally instead of italicizing it. To correct the preceding equation text, insert the command FUNC at the beginning and surround the rest of the equation with braces, as follows:

FUNC {Present~ Value ~=~ Payment~ ({1 ~—~ (1 ~+~ interest~ rate)^{−number~ of~ payments}} over {interest~ rate})}

The equation now appears as desired. When you use FUNC, make sure that you properly group the desired text with braces ({}).

Because the Equation Editor formats functions in normal type by default, it also provides the command ITAL to italicize functions. You use ITAL to in the same manner as FUNC, and you can use both simultaneously. You can use FUNC on an entire equation, for example, and use ITAL to italicize a smaller group within the equation (see the preceding equation). You can use a third command, BOLD, to set part (or all) of an equation in boldface type. UNDERLINE and OVERLINE also work in a similar way.

FUNC and BOLD can be particularly effective when used in combination to format simple text, such as to create a headline or a drop capital at the beginning of a paragraph. For instance, the equation text

BOLD { FUNC { Equation~ Editor~ Creates~} ITAL { Headlines! } }

creates the following "equation":

Equation Editor Creates *Headlines!*

Because this headline "equation" is actually a graphic created by using WordPerfect's graphics characters, you can change its point size in the Equation Settings dialog box to anything you desire, whether or not your printer has fonts of that size. From within the Equation editor, select **F**ile, **S**ettings. Under Graphic Font Size, select **P**oint Size, and specify the size you desire. A *point* is 1/72 inch, so 36-point type is roughly one-half inch tall. You can experiment with different point sizes.

You can create drop capitals at the beginnings of paragraphs by using the preceding techniques to create an equation with a single, large letter, and by changing the equation Options and Position so that the equation box is exactly the size of the letter. See "Positioning and Sizing Equations" at the end of this chapter, and Chapter 17, "Understanding Advanced Graphics," for more information on changing the position and size of equation boxes.

Using \ To Format Literals

A problem can occur when you include a common word in your equation text that also happens to be a keyword for a mathematical symbol, such as *and*, *or*, *in*, or *not*. Instead of displaying and printing the word, the Equation Editor uses the symbol.

You can correct this situation by placing a backslash (\) immediately before the misinterpreted word, in the following way:

\and

The backslash is a command that instructs the Equation Editor to treat the following symbol or command as a literal; that is, to display it exactly as typed. If you use braces ({}) in an equation, for instance, the Equation Editor normally assumes that you want to group the text in between and does not print the braces. To cause them to print, place a backslash before each brace, as in the following example:

\{ equation \}

Other common examples include tildes, ampersands, and the backslash itself (\\).

Forming Fractions with the OVER, LEFT, and RIGHT Commands

You have seen the OVER command used to create a fraction in the form

x over y

where x or y can be an individual number or a group. As with multiple levels of superscripts and subscripts, the Equation Editor can create fractions within fractions, as long as each successive level of fractions is grouped properly with braces so that it can be treated as a single item. For instance, the equation text

{{x^2 ~+~ 5} over y} over 2

creates the following result:

$$\frac{\frac{x^2 + 5}{y}}{2}$$ (11)

where $x^2 + 5$ is placed over y, and the entire fraction is then grouped and placed over 2.

You also can use a variant of the OVER command, OVERSM, to set the numerator and denominator in the next smaller size of type. OVERSM works in the same manner as OVER.

Complicated equations frequently include parentheses (( )), brackets ([]), and braces ({}) as delimiters to enclose individual clauses. When surrounding a single line of text, each symbol can be used as is (remember that each brace must be preceded by a backslash to print). Used by themselves, however, these characters cannot enclose multiple-line fractions properly. In the present value equation, for instance, the parentheses are not tall enough to enclose the fraction completely.

You can use the commands LEFT and RIGHT with these and other delimiters to create dynamic delimiters that automatically expand to enclose completely the surrounded portion of an equation. Table 27.3 lists common delimiters.

Table 27.3. Common Dynamic Delimiters

Delimiter	Description
(	Left parenthesis
)	Right parenthesis
[	Left bracket
]	Right bracket
< or LANGLE	Left angle bracket
> or RANGLE	Right angle bracket
\{ or LBRACE	Left brace
\} or RBRACE	Right brace
	or LINE	Single vertical line
DLINE	Double vertical line

You can rewrite the present value equation (in an abbreviated form) as follows:

PV ~=~ PMT~ LEFT [{1 ~—~ (1~+~ i)^n} OVER i RIGHT]

with the following result:

$$PV = PMT \left[\frac{1 - (1 + i)^n}{i} \right] \tag{12}$$

In this example, the parentheses (()) are used normally, the brackets ([]) are used with LEFT and RIGHT to create dynamic delimiters, and the braces ({}) are used to group the numerator. The Equation Editor automatically expands the height of the brackets to match the enclosed text.

You always need to use LEFT and RIGHT together, although you do not need to use the same left and right delimiters. If you want to use a single delimiter, you can substitute a period (.) after the opposite LEFT or RIGHT command to create a "dummy" delimiter.

Creating Sums and Integrals

Although you can create most of the equations you have seen thus far outside the Equation Editor, specialized constructs such as sums and integrals are nearly impossible to create any other way. With the Equation Editor, however, these constructs are no more difficult to produce than a simple fraction.

Use the FROM and TO commands to create a sum or an integral with the following syntax:

operator FROM *x* TO *y*

where *operator* is SUM or INT, and *x* and *y* are the beginning and ending limits. To create Equation 13, you type the following statement:

INT FROM 0 TO INF ~ X^2 ~+~ 2

and to create Equation 14, you type the following statement:

SUM FROM {i=1} TO N F_i ' DELTA t_i

$$\int_0^\infty X^2 + 2 \tag{13}$$

$$\sum_{i=1}^N F_i \Delta t_i \tag{14}$$

FROM and TO always place the limits below and above the symbols, respectively. If you want the limits to appear to the side, use SUP and SUB instead. Note that you must use braces around limits such as {i=1} for them to be treated as a single item.

Also note the use of keywords for symbols. INF is the keyword for infinity and is not case sensitive. Keywords for Greek letters, however, are case sensitive, because the Greek alphabet contains both upper- and lowercase characters. Type **DELTA** or **Delta** to create a capital letter.

To enlarge a sum or integral symbol, use the command SCALESYM following the syntax:

SCALESYM (*% of normal*) *operator*

Thus the equation text

SCALESYM 200 INT

creates an integral sign twice the normal size. You can use this technique, however, only when you print the equation as a graphic (see "Printing Equations" in this chapter). Although SCALESYM is most useful with SUM and INT, you can use it with any character.

Creating Roots

Another specialized mathematical construct is the *root*. The Equation Editor provides two commands for creating roots, SQRT and NROOT. SQRT creates square roots; NROOT creates *n*th roots. Both, however, are dynamic operators and automatically expand to enclose the selected equation. You always need to use braces ({}) to group the desired text, unless you are creating the root of a single number. The statement

SQRT {x^3+1}

for example, creates the following equation:

$$\sqrt{x^3+1}$$ **(15)**

As with other constructs, the information within the braces can be simple or complex and can include additional roots, fractions, or any other command or symbol the Equation Editor can use.

The syntax for NROOT is nearly identical to the syntax for SQRT, with the addition of a parameter for *n*, in the following form:

NROOT *n* {*equation*}

To use a fourth root in an equation, for example, type

NROOT 4 {{9x} over 5}

which creates the following equation:

$$\sqrt[4]{\frac{9x}{5}}$$ **(16)**

Using the Matrix Commands

Use the MATRIX command to arrange groups of numbers or variables into regular columns and rows. When you create a matrix, you must indicate the beginning of each new row with a pound sign (#), and within each row, you must separate each column with an ampersand (&). You can specify further the way each row is formatted by including the MATFORM command together with ALIGNC, ALIGNL or ALIGNR. Table 27.4 describes the matrix commands and their functions.

Table 27.4. Matrix Commands

Command	Function
MATRIX	Creates a matrix structure in the Equation Editor by specifying the row and column location of every subgroup
MATFORM	Specifies the horizontal alignment format to be applied to each subgroup (left, right, or centered within the column) by using the commands ALIGNC, ALIGNL, and ALIGNR
ALIGNC	Aligns its accompanying variable in the center of the current subgroup or matrix column
ALIGNL	Aligns its accompanying variable on the left margin of the current subgroup or matrix column
ALIGNR	Aligns its accompanying variable on the right margin of the current subgroup or matrix column
&	Column separator
#	Row Separator

To create a matrix with three columns and three rows, type

MATRIX {a1 & b1 & c1 # a2 & b2 & c2 # a3 & b3 & c3}

which creates the following equation:

$$\begin{matrix} a1 & b1 & c1 \\ a2 & b2 & c2 \\ a3 & b3 & c3 \end{matrix} \qquad (17)$$

You must have an ampersand (&) separating each column and a pound sign (#) separating each row, and the entire matrix must be surrounded by braces ({}). Each row must have the same number of columns, and you can create a maximum of 48 columns.

Because matrixes typically are bounded by vertical lines, most equation texts for a matrix begin with LEFT LINE and end with RIGHT LINE. You can use other delimiters, however, including brackets ([]) and braces ({}) (remember to precede each brace with a backslash). Thus, the following text:

LEFT LINE~ MATRIX {aaa & bbb & ccc # 11 & 22 & 33 # x & y & z}
~RIGHT LINE

creates the following equation:

$$\left| \begin{array}{ccc} aaa & bbb & ccc \\ 11 & 22 & 33 \\ x & y & z \end{array} \right| \tag{18}$$

Note that if all the elements in a column are not the same width, the Equation Editor by default centers them around a common midpoint. If you prefer to have one or more columns aligned to the left or right, you can include a MATFORM command, which specifies the alignment of each column with the ALIGNL, ALIGNC, and ALIGNR commands. The syntax is as follows:

MATFORM {ALIGN1 & ALIGN2 & ALIGN3 ...}

Place the command after the MATRIX keyword immediately inside the left brace and before the contents of the matrix. Note that you must specify the alignment for every column in the MATFORM command, even if you are changing the alignment for only one column. To realign the first and last columns of the preceding equation, you can change the equation text as follows:

LEFT LINE~ MATRIX {MATFORM {ALIGNL & ALIGNC & ALIGNR} aaa & bbb & ccc # 11 & 22 & 33 # x & y & z} ~RIGHT LINE

which creates the following equation:

$$\left| \begin{array}{ccc} aaa & bbb & ccc \\ 11 & 22 & 33 \\ x & y & z \end{array} \right| \tag{19}$$

As with any other Equation Editor construct, each element in a matrix can be quite complex, as long as the entire expression making up the element is surrounded by braces to create a group.

Creating Multiline Expressions with STACK and STACKALIGN

The Equation Editor assumes that each equation text, no matter how complex, is a single equation centered on a common baseline. Spaces and carriage returns in the Editing Pane can make your equation text easier to read but don't change the printed appearance of the final equation.

Often, however, you want to stack several shorter equations on top of one another within the boundaries of a single large equation text. The Equation Editor provides two commands that perform this task in slightly different ways: STACK and STACKALIGN. The syntax for STACK is as follows:

STACK {line1 # line2 ...}

Again, the pound sign (#) serves as a row separator. To stack two equations in the same box, such as

$2x + 3y = 3200$

$x - 2y = 8$

you type

STACK {2x ~+~ 3y ~=~ 3200 # x ~-~ 2y ~=~ 8}

which produces the following equation:

$$2x + 3y = 3200$$
$$x - 2y = 8$$

(20)

Notice that these two equations are centered around a common midpoint. This alignment is the default alignment, which you can change by using some of the same commands you use to align matrixes, ALIGNL and ALIGNR. For example, to align the two equations along their right edges, edit the equation text as follows:

STACK {2x ~+~ 3y ~=~ 3200 # ALIGNR x ~-~ 2y ~=~ 8}

for the following result:

$$2x + 3y = 3200$$
$$x - 2y = 8$$

(21)

Usually, however, you want to align two or more equations along a specific point such as an equal sign, which you can do with the STACKALIGN command. The syntax for STACKALIGN is nearly identical to the syntax for STACK, except that each line of the equation also must contain an ampersand (&) *following* the character upon which the equations should be aligned. You can edit the preceding equation text again as follows:

STACKALIGN {2x ~+~ 3y ~=&~ 3200 # ALIGNR x ~-~ 2y ~=&~ 8}

to align the equations on their equal signs, as follows:

$$2x + 3y = 3200$$
$$x - 2y = 8$$

(22)

The equations now line up in a pleasing manner. Another example follows.

STACKALIGN {DELTA f ~=& f(a ~+~ DELTA x) ~-~ f(a)

#=&~ SQRT {9 ~+~ 0.3} ~-~ SQRT 9

#=&~ SQRT {9.3} ~-~ SQRT 9}

which creates the following equation:

$$\begin{aligned} \Delta f &= f(a + \Delta x) - f(a) \\ &= \sqrt{9 + 0.3} - \sqrt{9} \\ &= \sqrt{9.3} - \sqrt{9} \end{aligned}$$ (23)

Note that the equation text could have been written in a continuous string without affecting the printed output of the equation(s). Pressing Enter to place each part of the equation on a different line, however, makes the entire equation easier to work with and read. This technique is helpful when you work on large or complex equations.

You also can use the PHANTOM command to help align equations. PHANTOM tells WordPerfect to leave space in an equation for a character or group of characters, but not to print them. Thus

PHANTOM {x+1}

tells WordPerfect to leave a space in the equation the exact width of the clause $x+1$. This command is particularly useful in stacked equations for matching the same clause in the line above or below. PHANTOM also can be used to create placeholders in matrixes.

Using Other Commands and Symbols

Although you probably will use the commands, functions, and Greek menus in the Equation Palette most often, do not overlook several other menus.

The diacritical marks found in the Other menu can be considered commands or symbols, because each prints a characteristic mark but prints that mark above another character. The most common diacriticals are BAR and VEC, which print, respectively, a bar and a vector symbol above another character or group. The Other menu also contains keywords to create several kinds of ellipses, including horizontal, vertical, and diagonal. These commands are used as follows:

x BAR DOTSLOW y VEC

creates the equation

$$\bar{x} ... \vec{y}$$ (24)

The Large menu contains symbols often used in a larger size (and smaller equivalents of each). Some examples are SUM and SMALLSUM for large and small sums, INT and SMALLINT for large and small integrals.

The Arrows menu contains a wealth of single and double arrows pointing in all directions. The left and right harpoons, for example, are useful in chemical equations, such as

$$HCO_3^- \rightleftharpoons H^+ + CO_3^{2-} \tag{25}$$

The Symbols menu contains a host of other common symbols, from primes, mathematical operators such as the partial derivative, multiplication and division symbols, to logical symbols such as *therefore*, and abstract symbols such as *infinity*.

The examples in this chapter provide only a small sample of the many characters and symbols available in the Equation Palette. Virtually any mathematical character or symbol is available, and you can access even more through the WordPerfect Characters dialog box. For more information on other commands and symbols, see the WordPerfect Reference Manual.

Positioning and Sizing Equations

Although created by the Equation Editor, WordPerfect's equations are contained within graphics boxes that are functionally identical to a figure box, a table box, a text box, or a user box. Each type of graphics box has its own default size, border style, caption position, and background shading. Equation boxes do, too. When you first create an equation, it is anchored to the current paragraph and is the full width of the page, even if the equation itself is only an inch or two wide. The height of the equation determines the overall size of the equation box.

As with any other graphics box, you can change an equation box's position, size, anchor type, border style, background shading, and even whether WordPerfect treats the box as an equation, figure, or table box. You can make some of these changes through direct manipulation with your mouse; you can make others through the Box Position and Size, Caption, and Equation Options dialog boxes (see figs. 27.4 and 27.5). Because the procedures for changing these settings in general are described in detail in Chapter 17, "Understanding Advanced Graphics," they need not be repeated here. You may find, however, that several specific combinations of settings are particularly useful for certain equations.

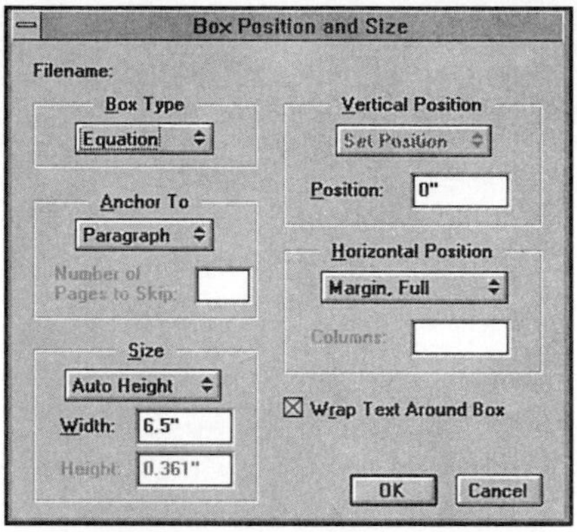

FIG. 27.4

The Box
Position and
Size dialog box
for an equation.

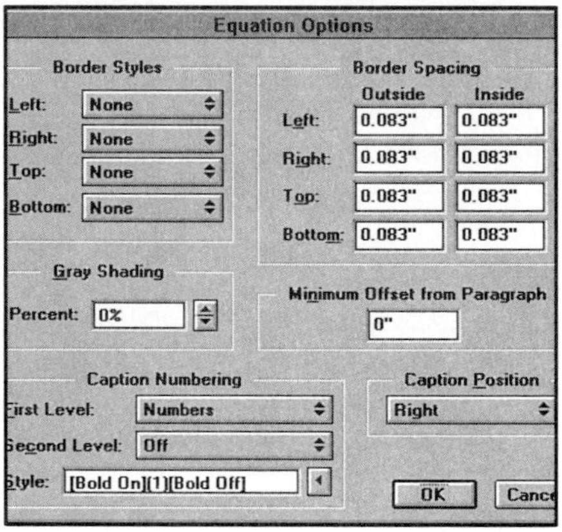

FIG. 27.5

The Equation
Options dialog
box.

Numbering Equations

Although equations do not have captions when created, you can add a
caption after you return to the document screen. Why would you want
to caption an equation? Because the default caption style for equations
is simply a number in parentheses, aligned flush right with the equation. This format is the standard format for numbering equations. Furthermore, equation boxes automatically are numbered in sequence,
just as figure or table boxes are.

You cannot create or edit an equation caption from within the Equation
Editor; you must first close the Editor and return to the normal document window. To add an equation number caption, follow these steps:

1. From the document window, select Graphics, Equation, Caption. The Edit Equation Caption dialog box opens.

2. Enter the number of the box to which you want to add a caption, and select OK or press Enter. The Caption Editor appears on-screen, containing a Flush Right code and an automatic box number (see fig. 27.6).

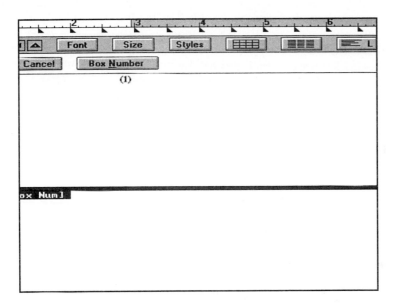

FIG. 27.6

The Caption Editor.

> To edit a caption quickly, click your right mouse button on the equation and select Edit Caption from the small menu that appears.
>
> **T I P**

3. To accept the default caption, select Close. The equation redisplays with an equation number at the right margin.

You can type an actual caption or replace the automatic box number with a fixed number. The default box number, however, changes automatically when you add or delete equations, whereas if you enter a fixed number, you have to make such changes by hand. To change the equation numbering sequence, insert a New Equation Number code (select Graphics, Equation, New Number, and type the desired number).

Embedding Equations in Text

The Equation Editor is undeniably powerful and capable of creating large, complex equations and is also useful for creating small equations that are nevertheless difficult to create using WordPerfect's normal editing capabilities. By default, however, even as simple an equation as

$$\sqrt{8}$$

takes up the full width of the screen and is one-half inch tall. By changing the graphics settings, you can reduce the size of the equation box to the size of the equation itself and include the equation in the flow of text of your document. The best way to reduce the size of the box is to change the equation box to a user box. This technique doesn't change the contents of the box, but only the way it is displayed on the page. By changing the user box options for the entire document, you can control the appearance of all embedded equations as one group of boxes and all displayed equations as another.

To change the equation box to a user box, follow these steps:

1. From the document screen, select **Graphics**, **Equation**, **Position**, and select the desired box number. Change the equation box's settings to the following:

Setting	Value
Box Type	User Box
Anchor to	Character
Vertical Position	Center or Baseline
Horizontal Position	N/A
Size	Auto Both
Wrap text around box	Yes

Compare the settings shown in figure 27.7 to the default settings shown in figure 27.4.

T I P   To change an equation's position quickly from the document, use your right mouse button to click the equation, and select **Position** from the small menu that appears.

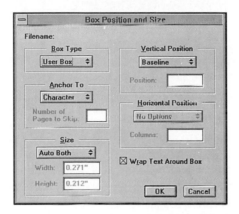

FIG. 27.7

Box Position and Size settings for an in-text equation.

2. If your document will have more than one in-text equation, call up Initial Codes (**L**ayout, **D**ocument, **I**nitial Codes). Otherwise, select an insertion point in front of your equation.

3. Select User Box Options (**G**raphics, **U**ser Box, **O**ptions) to open the User Box Options dialog box. Set Outside Border Space to 0 for left, right, top and bottom.

4. Select OK and, if necessary, close Initial Codes.

Do not follow steps 2 through 4 for additional in-text equations; the user box options need be set only once per document.

When you change the box to a user box, WordPerfect still "knows" that an equation is inside. WordPerfect now treats the whole box differently, however, and applies the user box options for border style, inside and outside border spacing, shading, and numbering. Changing the user box border space to 0 in initial codes tells WordPerfect not to add extra space around all user boxes in the document. Changing the anchor type to Character tells WordPerfect to treat the box as a single large character, and changing the size to Auto Both shrinks the dimensions of the box to the size of the equation itself. (If you do not change user box options, WordPerfect imposes a margin around the equation, which then takes up more space than is desirable within text.) Because WordPerfect automatically numbers different types of boxes in sequence, changing the box type to user box removes the equation from the equation box numbering sequence, which is usually desirable for such small equations.

Saving and Retrieving Equation Files

If you create equations infrequently, or if the equations you create are significantly different from one another, you will have to enter all your equation texts from scratch. If, however, you repeatedly use the same commands or frequently create equations that are slight variations of one another, you can make your task easier by reusing your work. From the Equation Editor, you can save all or part of an equation text to a file on disk. You also can retrieve previously saved equations, or even WordPerfect documents, into the Equation Editor.

To save an equation as a separate file, from within the Equation Editor select **F**ile, Save **A**s. The standard Save As dialog box appears, but without the options for saving in a different file format. The current equation box number is suggested as a file name. Although WordPerfect places no restrictions on naming equation files, you may want to use the extension EQN because the Retrieve Equation dialog box looks for that extension by default. You can save the equation in the current directory or change the directory before saving. You also can save part of an equation by selecting a portion of the equation text before choosing Save As.

You can retrieve a previously saved equation from within the Equation Editor. To insert the retrieved equation text into your current equation, place the insertion point where you want the retrieved text to appear. Select **F**ile, **R**etrieve. The standard Retrieve File dialog box appears, listing all files in the current directory with an EQN extension. If you don't see the equation you want, you can select a different directory or enter ***.*** for the file name to see all files in the directory. When you find the correct file, double-click the file name or highlight it and select **R**etrieve. The contents of the file appear at the insertion point in the Editing Pane.

You can follow the preceding steps to retrieve a standard WordPerfect document into the Editing Pane, as well. The retrieved document is stripped of all codes and formatting, leaving only text, WordPerfect characters, and hard returns [HRt]. Any soft returns are changed to hard returns, and the Equation Editor treats the result according to its usual rules.

If you save many equations as separate files, you may want to create one or more separate directories for those files and add those directories to your Quick List for easy access.

Printing Equations

Not all printers have the special characters and symbols necessary to print equations, so by default WordPerfect prints all equations as graphics. If, however, symbol fonts are available to your printer, whether built-in or through a font-scaling program, you can choose to use your printer's fonts to print your equations. Each method has its advantages and disadvantages.

In general, the appearance of equations printed using printer fonts is of slightly higher quality than the appearance of equations printed as graphics. When you print your equations as graphics, however, you can use the SCALESYM command to size characters arbitrarily, and WordPerfect can be more precise in using smaller type sizes for formatting second- and third-level superscripts and subscripts.

When printing equations as graphics, WordPerfect uses the graphical character information in the WP.DRS file. In addition to emulations of standard characters in Times Roman, Helvetica, and Courier fonts, this file contains outlines for the entire WordPerfect character set. WordPerfect matches your document's base font and size as closely as possible, using Times Roman for all proportionally spaced serif fonts, Helvetica for similar sans serif fonts, and Courier for fixed-width fonts. You can change the size and appearance, however, of a single equation or all equations.

You can choose between printing all equations as graphics or not, by default, through the Equation Preferences settings. You can override that default for any individual equation by changing the Settings options for that equation in the Equation Editor.

To change the settings for all documents, from the document editing screen, select **F**ile, **P**references, E**q**uations. The Equation Preferences dialog box opens (see fig. 27.8). By default, the Print as **G**raphics box is checked, and all equations print as graphics. Logically, if you deselect this option, all equations you create in the future will *not* print as graphics. Changing this setting, however, does not affect any equations you have already created.

Also by default, WordPerfect formats and prints equations in the same point size as a document's initial font. If, however, you prefer your equations to be printed in a larger (or smaller) point size, you can change the default point size in the Equation Preferences dialog box. The **D**efault Font radio button is initially selected. To change the default, select **P**oint Size. The current point size appears in the adjacent box. You can change this value by typing a specific point size, or by using the scroll arrows to change the value.

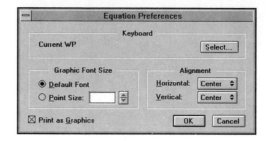

FIG. 27.8

The Equation
Preferences
dialog box.

In the Equation Preferences dialog box, you also can change the default
horizontal or vertical alignment for equations, or select an equation
keyboard layout. When you are done, select OK or press Enter to close
the dialog box and save your preferences.

To override the default settings for Print as Graphics and Graphic Font
Size for an individual equation, select File, Settings from within the
Equation Editor. The Equation Settings dialog box opens. This dialog
box is identical to the Equation Preferences dialog box, except that you
cannot select or change the equation keyboard layout. The default
equation settings reflect the equation preferences in effect when you
created the equation. Select (or deselect) Print as Graphics or change
the Graphic Font Size option to Default Font or to a specific Point Size.
Select OK or press Enter to close the dialog box. You can change the
default *type face* for one or more equations through a somewhat less
direct method. As with several other WordPerfect editing structures,
such as footnotes, you can change the appearance of an equation by
changing the formatting of an options code, in this case an Equation
Options code. Thus, if you want your text to print in Times but your
equations to print in Helvetica, follow these steps:

1. Select Font, Font, and select Helvetica 12 point.

2. Select Graphics, Equation, Options. When the Equation Options
   dialog box opens (refer to fig. 28.5), select OK, with or without
   making any changes (the options selected aren't important here,
   only inserting the Options code into your document).

3. Select Font, Font, and select Times 12 pt.

In Reveal Codes, the result appears as follows:

```
[Font:Helvetica 12pt][Equ Opt][Font:Times 12pt]
```

Because the Equation Options code immediately follows the Helvetica
font code, WordPerfect formats any following equations in Helvetica.
Because a Times font code immediately follows the equation, Word-
Perfect formats any following text in Times. Note that if you print your
equations as graphics and select a font for your equations other than

Times, Helvetica, or Courier, WordPerfect substitutes one of these three fonts for whatever font you select. Also note that you can choose an equation font with a different point size and thus change that value at the same time.

Chapter Summary

The Equation Editor is a specialized tool that makes the task of creating equations, from the simplest to the most complex, quick and easy. In this chapter, you have learned to use the Equation Editor to type entries in the Editing Pane and view the equation in the Display Pane. You learned to insert commands, functions, and symbols from the Equation Palette and enter characters from the normal keyboard, an equation keyboard, or the WordPerfect Characters dialog box. You also learned the commands to create superscripts and subscripts, fractions, sums and integrals, roots, and matrixes. You saw how to number equations automatically and how to embed equations within text. Finally, the chapter showed you how to save, retrieve, and print equations.

Creating and Displaying Special Characters

With WordPerfect, you easily can include any of more than 1,500 WordPerfect characters in a document and print them on almost any printer with graphics capability. Many of these characters are called *special* characters in this book, because they are characters not displayed on a standard PC keyboard and thus require more than a simple keystroke to be entered into your document. Characters that appear on the keyboard are entered by normal typing. You enter the special characters by using the WordPerfect Characters dialog box. Note, however, that non-English keyboards do have keys for some of the special characters.

You also can enter WordPerfect's special characters into dialog box sections, such as the Name and Description sections of the Styles Properties dialog box. Prominent exceptions, however, are dialog box sections that take file names, because these dialog box sections accept only characters supported by the underlying operating system.

■ **Eric Baatz** has held a variety of managerial and programming jobs in the New England computer industry during the last 15 years. He has been an enthusiastic user of many word processors and desktop publishing systems.

WordPerfect makes the entire process of entering and printing characters intuitive. If you have special requirements or want some control over the available tradeoffs, however, this chapter will enable you to produce the document you want.

This chapter shows you how to do the following:

- Enter and print any WordPerfect character

- Create new characters by using the Overstrike feature

- Use WordPerfect's language codes to simplify working with documents that contain passages in different languages

Note: This chapter is written for the U.S. English version of Word-Perfect and a U.S. English keyboard attached to an IBM-compatible computer. If your system is different, the principles of this chapter still hold, although some slight differences may exist in some of the examples.

Using WordPerfect Characters

The characters you enter into your document are called WordPerfect characters, and these characters are divided into 13 groups of related characters, called *character sets*. A character set holds a maximum of 256 characters, numbered from zero to 255.

Each character is identified by a pair of numbers: the character set number and the position of the character within that character set. The letter *A*, for example, is found in character set 0 at character position 65, so *A* is referred to as character number (0,65). The letter Æ, in character set 1 at character position 36, is referred to as character number (1,36). Note that character numbering starts at 0, not 1.

A summary of each character set follows:

- *Character Set 0 (ASCII—American Standard Code for Information Interchange).* This character set has 127 characters. The first 32, such as horizontal tab, are control characters and do not print something visible on-screen or on paper. Most of the characters on your keyboard are ASCII characters.

- *Character Set 1 (Multinational 1).* This set has 234 common multinational characters and diacritics, or accent marks.

- *Character Set 2 (Multinational 2).* This set has 28 less common diacritics.

- *Character Set 3 (Box Drawing).* You can place these 88 characters next to each other to form various types of boxes.

- *Character Set 4 (Typographic Symbols).* These 85 common typographic symbols are not found in character set 0.

- *Character Set 5 (Iconic Symbols).* This set consists of 35 picture symbols (Icons).

- *Character Set 6 (Math/Scientific).* These 235 nonextensible, nonoversized math/scientific characters are not found in character set 0. Nonextensible characters are complete characters, not parts of characters, and nonoversized characters are about the same size as alphabetic characters.

- *Character Set 7 (Math/Scientific Extension).* This set has 229 extensible and oversized math/scientific characters.

  The word *extensible* means that many of these characters are intended to be pieces for you to combine to form larger characters. Combining these characters, however, generally is difficult with WordPerfect's character *metric information* (that is, information about how big characters are and how they are oriented).

- *Character Set 8 (Greek).* This set consists of 207 ancient and modern Greek characters.

- *Character Set 9 (Hebrew).* Character set 9 is made up of 44 Hebrew characters.

- *Character Set 10 (Cyrillic).* This set consists of 148 ancient and modern Cyrillic characters.

- *Character Set 11 (Hiragana and Katakana [Japanese]).* This set has 185 characters for writing both hiragana and katakana.

- *Character Set 12 (User Defined).* You can define up to 256 character positions in this set. Mapping a set of dingbats to this character set is a classic use for character set 12. The section "Changing How WordPerfect Generates Characters" in this chapter deals briefly with one way to use this character set.

■ **Cue:** You may want to try using the Equation Editor to form equations you need and then position them by using graphics boxes.

Although WordPerfect knows each character only by its number, each has an English name. Æ, for example, is called an *AE digraph*. The WordPerfect file CHARACTR.DOC lists every character number and name for all the WordPerfect characters.

You can insert a WordPerfect character anywhere in your document by following these steps:

1. Move the insertion point to where you want the character inserted.

2. Select F**o**nt, **W**P Characters or press WP Characters (Ctrl-W).

    The WordPerfect Characters dialog box appears (see fig. 28.1).

FIG. 28.1

The WordPerfect
Characters
dialog box.

3. Choose the character set you want.

    If the **S**et area of the dialog box does not display the name of the character set you want, move the mouse pointer to the up and down arrows on the right side of the **S**et area. Highlight the name of the character set you want on the pop-up list. Release the left mouse button.

    If you're using the keyboard, press Tab until the Set section is highlighted. Press the space bar to see the list of character set names. Use the up- and down-arrow keys to highlight the name you want and then press the space bar to select your preference, or press the key corresponding to the underlined character in the name you want.

4. Move the mouse pointer to the character you want and click the left mouse button. WordPerfect outlines the character. You may have to use the scroll bar to reveal all the characters. Using standard Windows methods, you also can enlarge the dialog box to make more characters visible at once.

Using the keyboard, press Tab until the flashing outline box around the first character in the Characters list box flashes. Use the arrow keys to move the outline box to the character you want. The list box scrolls to show more characters when the cursor approaches the bottom of the list box.

After you choose the character, the Number text box displays its WordPerfect character number.

■ **Cue:** If you don't see a flashing box right away, try waiting a few seconds after you press Tab to give the outline box a chance to flash.

> You also can specify many common digraphs, symbols, and dia-critics by placing the insertion point in the **Number** area of the WordPerfect Characters dialog box and typing two characters. WordPerfect combines the characters into one and acts as if you had selected that character in the dialog box. For example, enter-ing **AE** produces Æ, and entering **CO** produces ©. Refer to the *WordPerfect Characters* entry in the *WordPerfect for Windows Reference Manual* for a complete list of the recognized character combinations.

T I P

5. Insert the character into the document by clicking **Insert** or press-ing Enter. The dialog box remains open so that you can insert another character.

   Otherwise, click the Insert and Close button or press A to insert the chosen character and close the dialog box.

   You also can click the **Close** button or press Esc to close the dialog box without inserting a character.

How the character looks after insertion depends on which WordPerfect mode you are in when you insert the character. See the section "Dis-playing Special Characters" later in this chapter for details.

You also can insert WordPerfect characters into almost any dialog box area, such as the Name and Description areas of the Styles Properties dialog box. Because you generally cannot access menus with a mouse when a dialog box is on-screen, you must get to the WordPerfect Char-acters dialog box by pressing Ctrl-W. Ctrl-W is disabled when you enter file names into dialog box sections, however, because file names must consist of characters that the underlying operating system supports.

Non-ASCII WordPerfect characters take up more disk space than ASCII characters. As a result, you cannot fit as many non-ASCII characters into dialog box text areas, for example, as you can ASCII characters.

Creating Shortcuts for Special Characters

Although selecting Font, WP Characters (or pressing Ctrl-W) to use the WordPerfect Characters dialog box is flexible and easy, you may find the process inconvenient if you frequently enter special characters. Fortunately, WordPerfect offers many customization techniques to fit your needs.

BUTTON

You can create a macro to generate a special character and then assign the macro to a button. See Chapter 19, "Using the Button Bar"; Chapter 20, "Creating Macros"; and Chapter 29, "Customizing WordPerfect with Preferences," for information about each technique.

Displaying Special Characters

The default WordPerfect display is WYSIWYG. With Windows graphics, on-screen you see a representation of every WordPerfect character that you insert into your document. Because the screen has fewer pixels per inch than a printer, however, what you see on-screen differs some from what prints. Still, on-screen you can distinguish one character from another and one style of character from another (for example, italic from roman characters). Of course, line breaks are always the same on-screen as they are on paper.

If you enable Reveal Codes (by selecting View, Reveal Codes or by pressing Alt-F3), the top half of the screen continues to be drawn in graphics mode, but the lower half uses a character mode to show text and WordPerfect codes. If the character on the top of the screen corresponds to one of the character boxes Reveal Codes can display, the character is displayed on the lower part of the screen. If the character does not correspond to a Reveal Codes character box, then a small solid box (■) that looks like WordPerfect character number (4,2) is displayed to act as a visual placeholder. Although Reveal Codes cannot display the character for you, the character is really in your document. If you move the Reveal Codes cursor to the small solid box, the box expands to show the special character number that the box represents (see fig. 28.2).

If you enable Draft mode (by selecting View, Draft Mode), WordPerfect uses the same predefined, fixed-size characters as Reveal Codes to represent the characters in your document. If you enable Draft mode, the screen is updated more quickly, which results in a more responsive interface. The drawback is that the screen looks much less like the eventual document than in WYSIWYG mode. See figure 28.3 for an example of Draft mode.

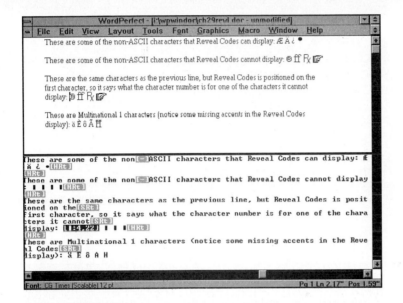

FIG. 28.2

The Reveal
Codes display
showing a
WordPerfect
character
number.

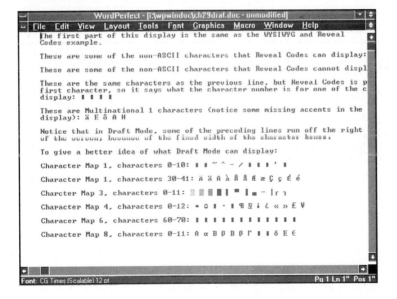

FIG. 28.3

Displaying a
document in
Draft mode.

Printing Special Characters

Printing a document containing special characters generally requires no special effort or preparation. To print the current document, including the special characters, follow these steps:

1. Select **File**, **P**rint.

    Press Print (F5).

   The Print dialog box appears.

2. Choose your options. (See Chapter 9, "Basic Printing," for details about how to use this dialog box.)

3. Click **P**rint or press Enter.

Your printer may not be capable of printing all the characters you have included in your document, even though WordPerfect goes through much effort to get all the characters out of your printer. For example, like WordPerfect, the Hewlett-Packard (HP) LaserJet IIIP laser printer divides its characters into character sets, although HP calls them *symbol sets*. The WordPerfect driver for that printer knows which characters are in which symbol set and switches from one to another so that you have the maximum number of characters available. Even then, the HP LaserJet IIIP prints only 212 of the 234 Multinational 1 characters.

To find out which special characters your printer supports, follow these steps:

1. Select **File**, **O**pen.

    Press Open File (F4).

   The Open File dialog box opens.

2. Select the CHARMAP.TST file.

3. Select **File**, **P**rint.

    Press Print (F5).

   The Print dialog box appears.

4. Make your usual selections (for example, **T**ext Quality), but make sure that you set **G**raphics Quality to Do **N**ot Print.

> Experiment with the Print dialog box's **T**ext Quality settings. A setting of **H**igh generally produces the highest quality text but the slowest printing times. A setting of **D**raft generally produces lower quality but faster printing. Those generalities, however, are not true of laser printers. Laser printers use one level of text quality (very high) no matter which **T**ext Quality setting you choose.
>
> **TIP**

5. Click **P**rint or press Enter.

Your printer takes time to print all these pages (some printers can take a very long time). Compare the results to the character sets shown in Appendix P of the *WordPerfect 5.1 for Windows Reference Manual*. A blank is substituted on your pages for every character your printer cannot print (see fig. 28.4).

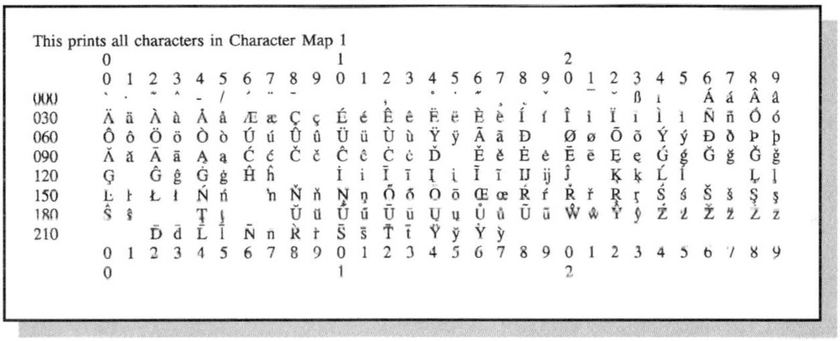

This prints all characters in Character Map 1

	0										1										2									
	0	1	2	3	4	5	6	7	8	9	0	1	2	3	4	5	6	7	8	9	0	1	2	3	4	5	6	7	8	9
000	`	˙	˜	^	¯	/	´	¨	¯				¸		˚	˙	˝	˛	˛	ˇ		¯	˘	ß	ı		Á	á	Â	â
030	Ä	ä	À	à	Å	å	Æ	æ	Ç	ç	É	é	Ê	ê	Ë	ë	È	è	Í	í	Î	î	Ï	ï	Ì	ì	Ñ	ñ	Ó	ó
060	Ô	ô	Ö	ö	Ò	ò	Ú	ú	Û	û	Ü	ü	Ù	ù	Ÿ	ÿ	Ã	ã	Đ		Ø	ø	Õ	õ	Ý	ý	Ð	ð	Þ	þ
090	Ă	ă	Ā	ā	Ą	ą	Ć	ć	Č	č	Ĉ	ĉ	Ċ	ċ	Ď		Ě	ě	Ė	ė	Ē	ē	Ę	ę	Ǵ	ǵ	Ğ	ğ	Ǧ	ǧ
120	Ģ		Ĝ	ĝ	Ġ	ġ	Ĥ	ĥ			İ	i	Ī	ī	Į	į	Ĩ	ĩ	Ĳ	ĳ	Ĵ		Ķ	ķ	Ĺ	ĺ			Ļ	ļ
150	Ŀ	ŀ	Ł	ł	Ń	ń		ŉ	Ň	ň	Ņ	ņ	Ő	ő	Ō	ō	Œ	œ	Ŕ	ŕ	Ř	ř	Ŗ	ŗ	Ś	ś	Š	š	Ş	ş
180	Ŝ	ŝ			Ţ	ţ			Ŭ	ŭ	Ű	ű	Ū	ū	Ų	ų	Ů	ů	Ũ	ũ	Ŵ	ŵ	Ŷ	ŷ	Ź	ź	Ž	ž	Ż	ż
210			D̄	d̄	L̄	l̄	N̄	n	R̀	r̀	S̄	s̄	T̄	t̄	Ÿ	y̆	Ẏ	ỳ												
	0	1	2	3	4	5	6	7	8	9	0	1	2	3	4	5	6	7	8	9	0	1	2	3	4	5	6	7	8	9
	0										1										2									

FIG. 28.4

Determining which characters an HP LaserJet IIIP printer can print.

If your printer cannot produce every character you want, you probably have two choices: have WordPerfect draw the missing characters for you, using your printer's graphics capabilities, or buy font cartridges or soft fonts that contain the characters. The characters a printer can print on its own, however, generally print the fastest and have the highest quality.

When WordPerfect cannot print a character by using a printer's built-in fonts or soft fonts, the program tries to draw the character as a graphic, which is placed on the page in the desired character's position. For WordPerfect to draw a character, your setup must meet these guidelines:

- You need the WP.DRS file that comes with WordPerfect.
- Your printer must have graphics capability.
- You must set the **G**raphics Quality and **T**ext Quality areas in the Print dialog box according to table 28.1.

Table 28.1. Text and Graphics Quality Settings and WP.DRS Characters

Graphics Quality	Text Quality	Drawn Characters
Any setting	Do **N**ot Print	Do not print
Do **N**ot Print	Any setting	Do not print
High, **M**edium, or **D**raft	High	Print at high quality
High	**M**edium or **D**raft	Print at high quality
Medium	**M**edium or **D**raft	Print at medium quality
Draft	**M**edium or **D**raft	Print at draft quality

Figure 28.5 shows the HP LaserJet IIIP printing the same text as in figure 28.4, but this time with the **G**raphics and **T**ext Quality settings on **H**igh. These settings cause WordPerfect to use the WP.DRS file to draw characters the printer cannot print with available fonts.

This prints all characters in Character Map 1

	0										1										2									
	0	1	2	3	4	5	6	7	8	9	0	1	2	3	4	5	6	7	8	9	0	1	2	3	4	5	6	7	8	9
000	`	.	˜	^	-	/	´	¨	¯	'	'	'	¸	'	˚	·	˝	˛	˙	ˇ	´	¯	˘	ß	ı	ȷ	Á	á	Â	â
030	Ä	ä	À	à	Å	å	Æ	æ	Ç	ç	É	é	Ê	ê	Ë	ë	È	è	Í	í	Î	î	Ï	ï	Ì	ì	Ñ	ñ	Ó	ó
060	Ô	ô	Ö	ö	Ò	ò	Ú	ú	Û	û	Ü	ü	Ù	ù	Ÿ	ÿ	Ã	ã	Đ	đ	Ø	ø	Õ	õ	Ý	ý	Ð	ð	Þ	þ
090	Ă	ă	Ā	ā	Ą	ą	Ć	ć	Č	č	Ĉ	ĉ	Ċ	ċ	Ď	ď	Ě	ě	Ė	ė	Ē	ē	Ę	ę	Ǵ	ģ	Ğ	ğ	Ǧ	ǧ
120	Ģ	ģ	Ĝ	ĝ	Ġ	ġ	Ĥ	ĥ	Ħ	ħ	İ	i	Ī	ī	Į	į	Ĩ	ĩ	Ĳ	ĳ	Ĵ	ĵ	Ķ	ķ	Ĺ	ĺ	Ľ	ľ	Ļ	ļ
150	Ŀ	ŀ	Ł	ł	Ń	ń	Ņ	ŉ	Ň	ň	Ŋ	ŋ	Ő	ő	Ō	ō	Œ	œ	Ŕ	ŕ	Ř	ř	Ŗ	ŗ	Ś	ś	Š	š	Ş	ş
180	Ŝ	ŝ	Ť	ť	Ţ	ţ	Ŧ	ŧ	Ŭ	ŭ	Ű	ű	Ū	ū	Ų	ų	Ů	ů	Ũ	ũ	Ŵ	ŵ	Ŷ	ŷ	Ź	ź	Ž	ž	Ż	ż
210	Ŋ	ŋ	D̄	d̄	L̄	l̄	N̄	n̄	R̀	r̀	S̄	s̄	T̄	t̄	Y̆	y̆	Ỳ	ỳ	D’	d’	Ơ	ơ	Ư	ư						
	0	1	2	3	4	5	6	7	8	9	0	1	2	3	4	5	6	7	8	9	0	1	2	3	4	5	6	7	8	9
	0										1										2									

FIG. 28.5

Part of CHARMAP.TST, showing characters drawn using WP.DRS.

WordPerfect-drawn characters look different from surrounding characters because they consist of single thin lines. Drawn characters also take much longer to print than characters built into your printer. Experiment to find out how long your printer takes to print your documents with drawn characters. The HP LaserJet IIIP, for example, takes about 3 minutes to print CHARMAP.TST when **T**ext Quality is set to Do **N**ot Print, and about 18 minutes to print CHARMAP.TST when using WP.DRS.

Another potential drawback to having WordPerfect draw characters is that your printer may not have enough memory to draw the number of WP.DRS characters in your document. As a result, your document may start printing but not finish or may stop after printing part of a page. You may be able to reduce the amount of memory your printer needs by reducing the quality level at which the characters are drawn (refer to table 28.1). Again, only experimentation tells you whether this problem exists for you.

You can improve the quality of the characters that WordPerfect draws by buying the International-Expanded WP.DRS from WordPerfect Corporation's international information office. This inexpensive file is about 75 percent larger than the standard WP.DRS file and draws characters in one of three "full-bodied" fonts, whichever one (WP Courier, WP Helvetica, or WP Roman) is the best match for the font your document is using when a character must be drawn. Character Set 11, however, still is drawn with single-line characters.

Compare figure 28.5 to figure 28.6 to see the difference that International-Expanded WP.DRS makes.

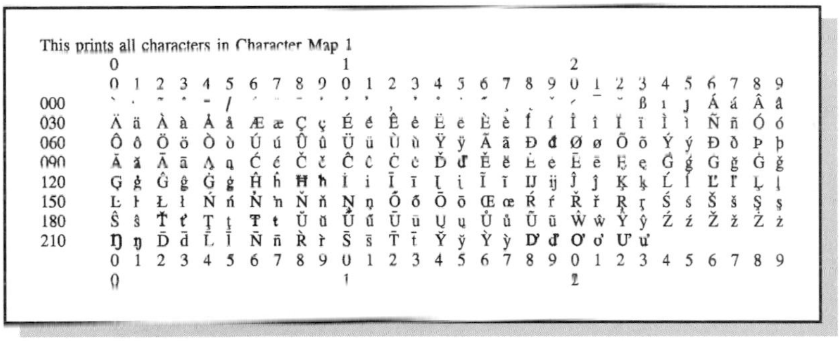

This prints all characters in Character Map 1

	0										1										2									
	0	1	2	3	4	5	6	7	8	9	0	1	2	3	4	5	6	7	8	9	0	1	2	3	4	5	6	7	8	9
000	`	·	˜	ˆ	¯	/	´	¨	¯	˙	˝	'	¸	'	˚	·	˛	¸	̦	ˇ	´	¯	˘	ß	ı	ȷ	Á	á	Â	â
030	Ä	ä	À	à	Å	å	Æ	æ	Ç	ç	É	é	Ê	ê	Ë	ë	È	è	Í	í	Î	î	Ï	ï	Ì	ì	Ñ	ñ	Ó	ó
060	Ô	ô	Ö	ö	Ò	ò	Ú	ú	Û	û	Ü	ü	Ù	ù	Ÿ	ÿ	Ã	ã	Đ	đ	Ø	ø	Õ	õ	Ý	ý	Ð	ð	Þ	þ
090	Ă	ă	Ā	ā	Ą	ą	Ć	ć	Č	č	Ĉ	ĉ	Ċ	ċ	Ď	ď	Ě	ě	Ė	ė	Ē	ē	Ę	ę	Ǵ	ǵ	Ğ	ğ	Ġ	ğ
120	Ģ	ģ	Ĝ	ĝ	Ġ	ġ	Ĥ	ĥ	Ħ	ħ	İ	i	Ī	ī	Į	į	Ĩ	ĩ	Ĳ	ĳ	Ĵ	ĵ	Ķ	ķ	Ĺ	ĺ	Ľ	ľ	Ļ	ļ
150	Ŀ	ŀ	Ł	ł	Ń	ń	Ṅ	ŉ	Ň	ň	Ņ	ņ	Ő	ő	Ō	ō	Œ	œ	Ŕ	ŕ	Ř	ř	Ŗ	ŗ	Ś	ś	Š	š	Ş	ş
180	Ŝ	ŝ	Ť	ť	Ţ	ţ	Ŧ	ŧ	Ŭ	ŭ	Ű	ű	Ū	ū	Ų	ų	Ů	ů	Ũ	ũ	Ŵ	ŵ	Ŷ	ŷ	Ź	ź	Ž	ž	Ż	ż
210	Ŋ	ŋ	D̄	d̄	L̄	l̄	N̄	n̄	R̀	r̀	S̄	s̄	T̄	t̄	Y̆	y̆	Ỳ	ỳ	Ď	ď	Ơ	ơ	Ư	ư						
	0	1	2	3	4	5	6	7	8	9	0	1	2	3	4	5	6	7	8	9	0	1	2	3	4	5	6	7	8	9
	0										1										2									

FIG. 28.6

Part of CHARMAP.TST, showing characters drawn with the International-Expanded WP.DRS

Although the HP LaserJet IIIP needs the same time to print CHARMAP.TST using the International-Expanded WP.DRS as it does using the standard WP.DRS, the general rule is that using the International-Expanded WP.DRS takes longer.

TIP

If you use WP.DRS frequently, consider buying third-party soft fonts or printer cartridges that contain the characters you need, or consider buying a WordPerfect language module. The latter includes the International-Expanded WP.DRS and language-specific printer fonts and keyboard drivers. Call WordPerfect Corporation's international information office for more information.

T   I   P   If you have an expert understanding of your printer, you can use PTR.EXE to determine exactly how your printer generates each special character, and you can change how that is done. For an overview of PTR.EXE, see the "Printer Program" section of the *WordPerfect for Windows Reference Manual.* For the complete story on PTR.EXE, consult *WordPerfect Printer Definition Program for IBM Personal Computers and PC Networks (Technical Reference for Version 5.1).*

Creating and Editing Overstrike Characters

■ **Cue:** Whenever possible, use a WordPerfect character rather than create a similar character by overstriking. WordPerfect characters are more portable between printer drivers and do not interfere with checking the spelling of a document.

Overstriking is a technique for creating special characters. You can combine many different characters and any combination of font attributes into one indivisible character. For example, distinguishing a zero from the letter *O* in the font you are using may be difficult, so you may want to put a slash through the zero.

To create an overstrike character, follow these steps:

1. Move the insertion point to where you want the character inserted.

2. Select **F**ont, **O**verstrike, **C**reate.

    The Create/Edit Overstrike dialog box appears. See figure 28.7 for a filled-in example.

3. Enter the characters you want to overlay. The order in which you enter characters is not important. If you enter more characters than fit into the text box, the characters scroll to the right.

T   I   P   The text box can hold 29 bytes. Because WordPerfect codes and WordPerfect characters are more than 1 byte long, you can enter fewer than 29 characters if you include font characteristics or WordPerfect characters in the text box.

FIG. 28.7

Creating a bold italic slashed zero as an overstrike character.

You can type the characters on the keyboard or use Ctrl-W to access the WordPerfect Characters dialog box. Optionally, you can change the font of each character by moving the mouse pointer to the arrowhead at the right end of the dialog box and holding down the left mouse button. Highlight the characteristic you want from the pop-up list and release the left mouse button. Enter the character that you want to have that characteristic.

4. Click OK or press Enter to insert the overstrike code that represents the character.

The code appears as [Ovrstk:*codes*], where *codes* represents the characters and font attributes that make up the overstrike character. The code for the overstrike character in figure 28.7, for example, is the following:

```
[Ovrstk:[Bold On][Italc On]/0[Bold Off][Italc Off]]
```

An overstrike character is a single character that you can delete by pressing Backspace once. If you have enabled Reveal Codes (select **View**, Reveal Codes, or press Alt-F3), however, placing the Reveal Codes cursor on the overstrike character shows the character's parts.

If you have enabled WordPerfect's normal WYSIWYG mode, an overstrike character is shown on-screen much as it appears in print.

If you have enabled Draft mode (select **View**, **D**raft Mode), an overstrike character is represented on-screen by the last character entered in the Create/Edit Overstrike dialog box.

If you want to change an overstrike character, you need not delete the character and start over. Instead, you can edit the overstrike character.

To edit an overstrike character, follow these steps:

1. Move the insertion point to immediately after the overstrike character you want to edit.

2. Select Font, **O**verstrike, **E**dit.

   The Create/Edit Overstrike dialog box appears, with the pieces of the overstrike character in the text box.

3. Add or delete characters in the text box.

4. Click OK or press Enter to replace the old overstrike character with the edited one.

Working with Multiple Languages

Working with multiple languages is more than being able to enter, display, and print non-English characters. You also need to be able to do things such as correct spelling and manage your documents (for example, by specifying that a particular section of a document is in a different language).

WordPerfect supports multiple languages in several ways:

- You can buy WordPerfect for a particular language. The menus, prompts, and other messages are in that language, as are the dictionaries that come with WordPerfect. These dictionaries are used by WordPerfect's thesaurus, spelling checker, and hyphenation functions.

- You can mark a section of your document as being in any of the more than 20 languages supported by WordPerfect. Within that section, WordPerfect inserts dates in the customary style of that language and performs sorts based on that alphabet. If you have the dictionaries for that language (you can buy them separately), WordPerfect's thesaurus, spelling checker, and hyphenation functions use them in the marked sections.

- You can edit WordPerfect's WP.LRS file to change what is printed for the footnote *continued* message, for the labels in a document summary, and for the spelling of the days of the week and months of the year used in WordPerfect-generated dates.

Entering WordPerfect Language Codes

When you buy WordPerfect, you receive a version for a specific language and country. You can buy an English version of WordPerfect for the United States, for example, or an English version for Australia. WordPerfect refers to the combination of language and country as your *package language* and abbreviates the language with a two-letter package *language code*. The package language for the United States example is English-United States, and the package language code is US. For the Australian example, it's English-Australian and OZ.

The package language code is used with the Language Resource File (see the section "Using the Language Resource File" in this chapter) and becomes your default language code.

Anytime you want and as often as you want, you can change the current language code for your document to any of the more than 20 languages that WordPerfect supports. The language code determines which dictionary, thesaurus, and hyphenation files WordPerfect uses; how the date is formatted; how the words in the date are spelled; and what order WordPerfect uses for sorting, but does not change the language used for WordPerfect menus or messages. You change the language code for your document by following these steps:

1. Move the insertion point to where you want the change to take place, or select the text you want to affect.

2. Select **Tools, Language**.

   The Language dialog box appears, listing all languages that WordPerfect supports (see fig. 28.8). Your current language code is highlighted.

The Language dialog box.

3. Select a language.

4. Click OK or press Enter.

A [Lang:xx] code is inserted, where *xx* is the two-letter code on the right end of the line you selected in the Language dialog box, such as [Lang:SV]. The new language stays in effect until Word-Perfect encounters a different language code.

If you have selected a range of text, WordPerfect places the language code for the new language before the text, and inserts the language code for the original language after the selected text.

A language code inserted into your document's Initial Codes controls how the footnote *continued* message and the document summary labels are printed, as well as the language with which your document starts.

If you buy dictionaries for a language not displayed in the dialog box, add a section to the Language Resource File; or if you want to prevent WordPerfect from checking spelling in a section of your document, select Other from the list box in the Language dialog box and enter the appropriate two letters into the text box below the list box.

If you check spelling after inserting a language code for which you do not have the dictionaries, or if WordPerfect cannot find the dictionaries, you see an error message (see fig. 28.9).

FIG. 28.9

The message shown if the dictionaries for language code ZZ cannot be found.

When you see the error message, you have the following choices:

■ Click the Select **D**ictionary button to enter the directory and name of the dictionary to use.

■ Select **S**kip Language so that WordPerfect skips the spelling check until it encounters another language code.

■ Click the **E**xit button to stop the spelling check.

Using Dictionary, Thesaurus, and Hyphenation Files

You can get spelling checker, thesaurus, and hyphenation files for languages other than your package language by contacting WordPerfect Information Services and buying a language module. Use the usual WordPerfect installation procedure to install the files (see Appendix A). Choose option 7 (Language) from the initial menu and follow the directions.

Cue: You may want to override the installation procedure's default directory for the location of the language module files to save space on the disk where the default directory is located.

You can store the language module files for several languages in one directory; their file names are unique because the names include their language code. The English-United States dictionary and thesaurus files, for example, are named WP{WP}US.LEX and WP{WP}US.THS, and the equivalent Swedish files are WP{WP}SV.LEX and WP{WP}SV.THS.

WordPerfect handles hyphenation differently for different languages, so a given language module may not contain a hyphenation file.

Using the Language Resource File

Whenever WordPerfect prints a *continued* message in footnotes or a document summary, it uses the language code in your Initial Codes (select **F**ile, **P**references, **I**nitial Codes) or, by default, your package language to find your language's section of the WP.LRS file. That section of the file contains the phrases to be used for the *continued* message and for the labels for the document summary. The implication is that all those messages are printed in the same language, regardless of any language code you insert into your document.

When WordPerfect generates a date (select **T**ools, **D**ate, **T**ext, or press Ctrl-F5), WordPerfect uses the current language code to find that language's section of the WP.LRS file to get the spellings for any words used in the date.

■ **Cue:** Changes you make to WP.LRS take effect only when you next start WordPerfect.

Because WP.LRS is a WordPerfect secondary merge file, you can edit it as a normal WordPerfect file. To make changes, however, you must know the format of secondary merge files and know which areas WordPerfect for Windows ignores (because these areas are used by other versions of WordPerfect). See the *WordPerfect for Windows Reference Manual* for details.

Chapter Summary

In this chapter, you learned how to enter special characters into your document and how to take into account tradeoffs in printing special characters. You also learned how to create new characters with the overstrike method and how to work with multilingual documents.

With WordPerfect, you easily can use any of more than 1,500 characters in your document. In its default display mode, WordPerfect can present all those characters on-screen and can print them by supplementing your printer's internal character sets, if your printer supports graphics, with drawn representations of the remaining characters.

Support of multilingual documents goes beyond character sets. With supplemental dictionaries, WordPerfect supports spelling, thesaurus, and hyphenation functions for multiple languages in one document.

Customizing WordPerfect with Preferences

When you install WordPerfect for Windows, it is ready to go to work for you. Assumptions are built into the basic setup of the software that reflect the most common or frequent ways we work. These assumptions or settings are called *defaults*.

Default settings can be changed temporarily in the numerous ways you have learned in the preceding chapters. These temporary changes are in effect only for the current document and can be changed again in separate sections of your document. Because these changes apply only to the current document, you can have several documents open at the same time with each document set up differently. Every time you start a new document, WordPerfect begins with the default settings.

■ **Judith Petersen** is a WordPerfect instructor/ resource staffperson for the Leon County (Florida) School Board Vocational Program. In her own business, Judy is a lawyer and computer software consultant/trainer for businesses and individuals in the Tallahassee area.

Default settings also can be changed permanently. When you change a default setting permanently, the new setting becomes the default. From the time you change the setting, every time you start a new document WordPerfect begins with your *customized* default settings.

You can customize WordPerfect to meet your most frequent use patterns. You can change document settings, such as paper size and margins, as well as hardware settings, such as keyboard layouts, mouse sensitivity, and on-screen document display. You can change the colors used by WordPerfect and the location of special files, such as backup documents or macros. You customize these options and more by using the File Preferences menu.

You use a variety of other menu selections to make temporary setting changes, as well as some default changes, such as the default button bar. Changes you make using menus other than Preferences are discussed elsewhere in this book.

In this chapter, you learn to do the following with the Preferences menu:

- Customize the location of your files
- Create both timed backups and original document backups
- Customize the environment
- Understand WYSIWYG and Draft modes
- Customize the display
- Customize your print jobs
- Customize keyboards
- Use Initial Codes
- Customize document summaries
- Date your documents
- Customize Merge preferences and display Merge codes
- Customize a table of authorities
- Customize the Equation Editor

Introducing the Preferences Menu

A quick review of the Preferences menu gives you an idea of how much of the program you can tailor to your circumstances (see fig. 29.1).

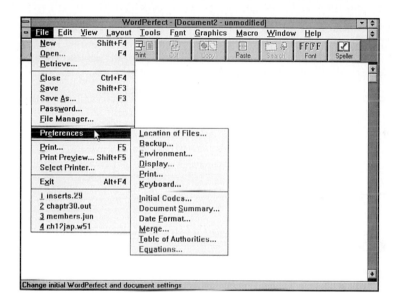

FIG. 29.1

Preferences menu options.

WordPerfect includes a variety of features, many of which use or generate files that can be managed more easily if they are stored in separate directories. The *Location of Files* feature enables you to change or create these directories at any time.

Use *Backup* to turn the timed backup feature on and off, to establish the interval for timed backups, and to choose to make original document backups.

Environment enables you to decide when WordPerfect will beep, which hyphenation dictionary to use and when you are prompted for hyphenation decisions, and how the menus are displayed. You can rearrange the Ruler display and make it appear automatically. You also can implement several WordPerfect features, such as Undo, Auto Code Placement, and Fast Save.

In the *Display* dialog box, you can set Reveal Code and Draft mode colors, specify the units of measure used by WordPerfect and displayed in the status bar, use horizontal and vertical scroll bars, and choose a character to represent a hard return. You can specify whether WordPerfect uses sculptured dialog boxes, side-by-side columns, merge codes on-screen, and graphics in black and white or color.

■ **Cue:** If you want to use the default Preference settings for one work session, type **wp /x** to start WordPerfect. When you exit the WordPerfect session, your personally customized settings are restored.

You can customize *Print* settings, including the way redlined text appears, graphics and text quality, binding offset, and the number of copies. The ratio of font size selections can also be changed.

WordPerfect comes with several keyboard layouts, and you can create and edit your own layout. Use *Keyboard* to choose a different layout or create other key combinations.

Using *Initial Codes*, you can embed in your future documents many of the formatting changes available in other sections of the menu, such as margins, tab settings, line spacing, hyphenation zone, and page numbering.

The *Document Summary* options can change the phrase used to find the subject of a document, set the default descriptive type, and automatically prompt for a document summary when you save or exit a document.

You use *Date Format* to specify how Date Code and Date Text appear in your document.

You can specify the field and records delimiters that WordPerfect recognizes in a DOS text file using *Merge*.

Table of Authorities enables you to specify the use of dot leaders and underlining and to determine whether a blank line is inserted between authorities when you generate a table of authorities in your document.

In the *Equations* dialog box you create and select equation keyboards, set graphics font type and size, align the equation in its box, and control whether graphics or font sets are used to print the equation elements.

■ **Cue:** Back up the WP{WP}.SET file, as well as your INI, GRP, PIF, and customized ICO files, every week.

WordPerfect saves settings you established with Preferences in a file named WP{WP}.SET. If this file accidentally is deleted or corrupted, delete the file and begin again at the WordPerfect factory settings.

Customizing Location of Files

As computer users install more programs on their computers, hard disk management becomes very important. WordPerfect provides help with hard disk management by enabling you to have separate directories for documents, backup files, printer files, and others. This feature also enables you to share directories. With shared directories you can, for example, use the WordPerfect 5.1 directory as the location for printer drivers, and the spreadsheet directory can be the documents subdirectory for your favorite spreadsheet program.

When you installed WordPerfect, a number of subdirectories were created for the WordPerfect files, macros, and keyboards, and for shared program files such as the speller, thesaurus and File Manager. You can customize this directory structure further using the Preferences, Location of Files dialog box (see fig. 29.2).

■ **Cue:** The *default* directory is the directory that you specify in the Location of Files dialog box. You can change the specified directory any time, resulting in a new default directory.

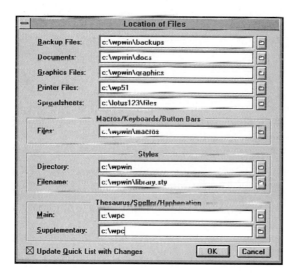

FIG. 29.2

The Location of Files dialog box.

To change a default directory, follow these steps:

1. Choose File, Preferences.

    Press Preferences (Ctrl-Shift-F1).

2. Choose Location of Files.

   The Location of Files dialog box appears.

3. To choose an item, click the item, use the Tab key to move from item to item, or press Alt plus the underlined letter.

4. Type the name of the new directory in the text box, click the file folder button at the right of each text box, or press Alt and the up or down arrow to open the Select Directory dialog box as shown in figure 29.3.

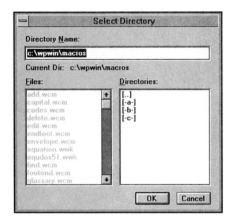

FIG. 29.3

The Select Directory dialog box.

5. Type a new name into the Directory Name text box or click the drive letter to access directories in the Directories list box. *Note:* If you click a drive letter in which there are no directories, no directory name appears in the text box.

6. Choose OK to return to the Location of Files dialog box.

7. Repeats steps 3 through 6 until you have made all the changes you want, then choose OK to return to your document.

■ **Cue:** When you specify a directory that does not exist, Word-Perfect asks whether you want the directory created for you.

Because this process is so easy, you can create several separate macro, graphics, and document directories to use, for example, in desktop publishing or manuscript creation only. Specify a different default directory if you intend to spend an afternoon using specialized macros to create a newsletter, and then another default directory when you are ready to move to a different task.

Backing Up Your Work

If you are just beginning to venture into the world of computers, you must accept that backing up your work is as necessary as saving your work. Think for a moment how often you find the digital display flashing on your clock. When the power failure that turns off and resets your clock occurs, your computer also turns off and reboots. You lose the document you are working on, or at least the editing changes you made since you last saved.

WordPerfect helps prevent this kind of data loss by creating timed backups, every 20 minutes, of the documents that are open. You can change the time interval or turn off this feature if you choose.

Another backup situation arises when you edit a document and save it using the same file name. The new version of the document file replaces the previous version when you save the editing changes. As an additional document protection, you can choose to have the previous file renamed when you save the edited file. This feature is called *original document backup*.

Creating Timed Backups

WordPerfect for Windows can create timed backups at any interval. To authorize timed backups and establish a backup interval, follow these steps:

1. Choose **File**, Preferences.

   CUA Press Preferences (Ctrl-Shift-F1).

2. Choose **B**ackup.

   The Backup dialog box shown in figure 29.4 appears.

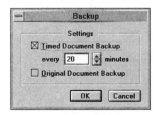

FIG. 29.4

The Backup dialog box.

3. Choose **T**imed Document Backup. (If you use the Tab key, remember to press the space bar to toggle the feature on.) An X appears in the check box.

4. Type a number of minutes in the text box, or click the up and down arrows to add or subtract one minute per click of the mouse button.

5. Choose OK to save your changes and return to the document.

WordPerfect names the timed backup file WP{WP}.BK1 (for document window 1). If you exit WordPerfect for Windows using the **File**, **Exit** (Alt-F4) command, the program deletes the backup file and a directory called WP{WP}td.1 that contains several other files. If a power outage occurs or you exit by turning off the computer, however, these files remain on your disk.

When you restart WordPerfect, the Timed Backup dialog box appears (see fig. 29.5) to prompt you that backup files are present. The dialog box lists, one at a time, a backup file for each document that was open at the time power was interrupted. To save a timed backup file, choose **R**ename and rename the file; to read the file, choose **O**pen; to delete the file, choose **D**elete.

FIG. 29.5

The Timed Backup dialog box.

T I P

Even experienced users fail to follow the warning to save a file before sorting. If you fail to heed this advice, and you scramble a file with an improper sort after extensive editing, exit WordPerfect immediately by rebooting. When the Backup File Exists message appears, choose **O**pen. Most or all of the editing changes you made should be in the renamed file.

Creating Original Document Backups

A second backup option is available. You can save the preceding version of a file with a BK! extension every time you save your work. WordPerfect saves two versions of the file on the disk: the current version and the version immediately preceding the current version. To create original document backups, follow these steps:

1. Choose **F**ile, **Pr**eferences.

    Press Preferences (Ctrl-Shift-F1).

2. Choose **B**ackup.

   The Backup dialog box shown in figure 29.4 appears.

3. Choose **O**riginal Document Backup. (If you use the Tab key, remember to press the space bar to toggle the feature on.) An X appears in the check box.

4. Choose OK to save your changes and return to the document.

WordPerfect for Windows offers three solutions to the problem of using too much hard disk space for original document backup files: use Location of Files to set up a backup directory on a floppy disk you insert when you start WordPerfect; use the File Manager to move BK! files to floppy disks frequently; delete BK! files that are more than a month old.

T I P

Customizing the Environment

You can customize a whole array of "environmental" settings in WordPerfect in one dialog box from the Preferences menu. The following sections explain each Environment Settings choice that WordPerfect offers you, including Settings, Beep On, Menu, Ruler, Prompt for Hyphenation, and Hyphenation.

To access the environmental settings follow these steps:

1. Choose **F**ile, **P**references.

   Press Preferences (Ctrl-Shift-F1).

2. Choose **E**nvironment.

   The Environment Settings dialog box appears (see fig. 29.6).

Take a moment to study figure 29.6. In four of the six areas in the Environment Settings dialog box you make your choices by turning the toggle for each setting off or on. When a setting is *on* you see an X in the check box next to the setting name. Conversely, when you turn off a setting, the X does not appear in the check box. In each area of the dialog box that shows check boxes you can turn on any, all, or none of the settings.

In the two hyphenation areas of the Environment Settings dialog box, you make your choices by activating a radio button. Unlike the check box areas, you cannot choose more than one setting in each case— when one radio button is on (filled with a dark circle), the other related buttons are off (empty).

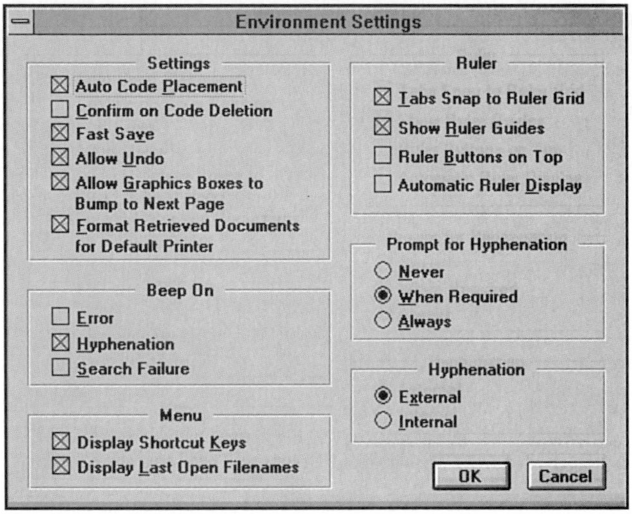

FIG. 29.6

The Environ-
ment Settings
dialog box with
the default
settings.

You can choose your Environment Settings by the following three
methods:

- Using the mouse, click the check box or radio button for each
  option.

- Using the keyboard, press the underlined letter in each option.

- Using the Tab key, press Tab to move the pointer to the option
  you want, and then press the space bar for check boxes or Alt
  plus the up- or down-arrow keys for radio buttons.

After you choose your Environment Settings, to return to your document, choose OK or press Enter.

Auto Code Placement

A number of WordPerfect codes behave as expected only if they are
placed at the beginning of a paragraph or the top of a page or document. The Auto Code Placement feature places these codes at the top
of the current page or at the beginning of the paragraph in which the
insertion point is located. The code takes effect at that point and continues throughout the remainder of the text until you change it later in
the document.

Table 29.1 lists the features subject to Auto Code Placement and the location of the code when Auto Code Placement is on.

Table 29.1. Effect of Auto Code Placement Feature

Code	Placement
Center Top to Bottom	Page
Columns	Paragraph
Headers and Footers	Page
Hyphenation	Paragraph
Letterspacing	Paragraph
Justification	Paragraph
Line Numbering	Paragraph
Line Height	Paragraph
Line Spacing	Paragraph
Margins, Left/Right	Paragraph
Margins, Top/Bottom	Page
Page Numbering	Page
Paper Size/Type	Page
Paragraph Numbering	Paragraph
Suppress	Page
Tab Set	Paragraph
Word Spacing	Paragraph
Word Spacing Justification Limits	Paragraph

If Auto Code Placement is not active, WordPerfect inserts codes into your document at the location of the insertion point. If the code formats a page of text and is not placed at the beginning of the page, the code takes effect on the following page. If the code formats a line of text, a hard return is added at the insertion point location, and the code starts the next line of text. Using the Auto Code Placement feature automates the preferred placement of codes in your document.

T I P Remember that subsequent editing of your text can result in codes being moved to accommodate the changes. Before printing, check to be sure that page codes are still located where you want them in your document.

In some circumstances, Auto Code Placement enables WordPerfect for Windows to make sense of an otherwise impossible command. When working in a table, for example, selecting another Paper Size/Type results in an error message announcing that margins overlap. If Auto Code Placement is on, WordPerfect places the Paper Size/Type code at the top of the page.

Auto Code Placement identifies a paragraph by the location of hard returns. Paragraphs of text that include hard returns, as in a table, are not uncommon. Auto Code Placement regards each line of tabular material as a separate paragraph. If you change margins in the middle of a table with the Auto Code Placement feature, WordPerfect places the margin code at the beginning of the line in which the insertion point is located.

Some of the codes listed in table 29.1 can be placed around text that you already selected. If Auto Code Placement is on, WordPerfect places the code at the beginning of the first paragraph that contains highlighted text and continues to the end of the last paragraph containing highlighted text. To place codes only at the beginning and end of the highlighted text, you must first turn off Auto Code Placement.

Confirm on Code Deletion

When you have the Reveal Codes window open, you can navigate with little difficulty through deleting, moving, and otherwise rearranging codes. With the Reveal Codes window closed, you cannot delete codes unless the codes are within a block of text that you delete in the document window.

To delete text and remain in the full-sized document screen, you can activate the Confirm on Code Deletion feature. With the Confirm on Code Deletion feature, when the Reveal Codes window is closed, a message box prompt for confirmation appears every time you attempt to delete a code. The default setting for this feature is off. To turn on the Confirm in Code Deletion feature, choose the option in the Environment settings dialog box.

Fast Save

If you choose the Fast Save option, WordPerfect formats your documents completely except for printing features. Using Fast Save makes the process of saving much quicker; however, printing the document takes longer. Fast Save is on by default when you install WordPerfect. To turn off Fast Save, in the Environment Settings dialog box, choose the Fast Save option.

When WordPerfect prints a document saved with Fast Save, the program not only formats the print job, but also saves the document on the disk in a temporary file. If disk space is a problem, you can turn off Fast Save.

Allow Undo

The Undo feature enables you to undo the last change made to your document. You can remove text, restore deletions, "unsort" an ill-conceived sort, or return to the last formatting with Allow Undo. Remember, however, that Undo voids only the last change made. If you type text, backspace to erase a letter, then type more text, Undo removes only the text typed since you backspaced. If you insert several codes, Undo removes only the last code. You should experiment with Undo to get a feel for how it works.

Allowing Undo is the default setting in Preferences. To remove the Undo feature, in the Settings section of the Environment Settings dialog box, choose Allow Undo.

Don't confuse Undo with Undelete. Undo restores deleted text to its original location. Undelete enables you to restore the deleted text to the present location of the insertion point.

Allow Graphics Boxes To Bump to Next Page

When you create a graphics box and anchor it to a page position, as with other page codes the final location of the graphic can be influenced by later text editing changes. WordPerfect, however, manages the placement of graphics boxes in a different way. Refer to Chapters 7 and 17 for detailed information on positioning graphics boxes.

When you anchor the box to a position relative to the *page* (rather than a paragraph or character position), WordPerfect uses a default setting that enables editing or formatting changes to "bump" the graphics box to the next page. The graphics box code remains in its original position relative to the accompanying text.

When you choose to disable bumping to the next page, the graphics box code does not relocate with later additions or deletions of text. Instead, formatting or text changes cause the text to wrap around the graphics box and then move to the next or preceding page, leaving the original position of the box on the page intact.

To customize WordPerfect to allow the relocation of graphics boxes, in the Settings area of the Environment Settings dialog box, choose Allow **G**raphics Boxes to Bump to Next Page.

Format Retrieved Documents for Default Printer

A delightful feature of WordPerfect is the capability of having any number of printer drivers installed, even though some of those printers may never be attached to your computer. Having several printer drivers enables you to move files between your office, your home, and the offices of your customers.

If you installed fonts or set up cartridge fonts in each printer driver, you can create documents at home that are ready to print when you return to the office. Remember, however, that the capability to print fonts depends on the appropriate printers being on-line. The capability to display the fonts depends on the printer driver installation. Refer to Chapter 9, "Basic Printing," and Chapter 10, "Working with Fonts," for the information needed to configure printers and install the fonts.

Cue: The default printer is simply the printer selected at the moment. Change the default printer at any time by selecting another printer using **F**ile, Se**l**ect Printer.

If you have several printer drivers, you usually want to retrieve your documents formatted for the printer you intend to use. Otherwise, a complex document created with proportional fonts, for example, may suddenly be scrambled into something unrecognizable because your default printer does not support that spacing.

With the default setting to Format Retrieved Documents for the Default Printer feature, WordPerfect reformats all documents to suit the printer that is active at the time of retrieval. If you turn off this feature, WordPerfect searches for the printer driver that was active when the document was saved last. If you installed the necessary printer drivers, WordPerfect selects the matching driver and designates it as the current default printer, adding it to the list of selectable printers, if necessary. If WordPerfect does not find this driver, WordPerfect displays a message stating that the document is not formatted for the default printer and reformats the document for the default printer.

The default setting for this feature is on. To turn off the feature, in the Settings area of the Environment Settings dialog box, choose Format Retrieved Documents for Default Printer.

Customize the Beep

The computer beep may be the real inspiration for the now famous cartoon featuring a sledge hammer prepared to "Strike any key when ready." Although WordPerfect for Windows has the good manners to *blip* rather than *beep*, you can choose to eliminate all sound effects.

In the Beep On area of the dialog box, you can set WordPerfect for Windows to beep in one of or all the following situations:

- *Error.* When WordPerfect displays an error message
- *Hyphenation.* When WordPerfect prompts you to hyphenate
- *Search Failure.* When a search fails to find a match

Customize Menu Display

You can customize WordPerfect's pull-down menus. The Short Menu option removes a number of advanced features from each menu, making it easier for newcomers to WordPerfect to find the basic commands. You select the Short Menu option through the View menu.

Further customizing of the menu display is possible using the Preferences option. You can remove the display of shortcut keystrokes from the menu. You also control whether WordPerfect lists the names of the last four open files.

A final means of customizing the menus is to add shortcut keystrokes to any menu item that does not yet have one. You do this by creating a new keyboard and adding the shortcuts you create to the matching menu item. Instructions for making this change are in the "Customizing Keyboards" section in this chapter.

Display Shortcut Keys

You can access many of the menu commands from the keyboard by pressing combinations of the Ctrl, Alt, Shift, and function keys. The default menu system displays these shortcut keys on the menus next to each command. You can change the default, however, to remove the shortcut keys. Figure 29.7 shows a menu with shortcut keys; figure 29.8 shows a menu without the shortcut keys.

To customize WordPerfect not to display the shortcut keys on the menus, in the Menu area of the Environment Settings dialog box, choose Display Shortcut **K**eys.

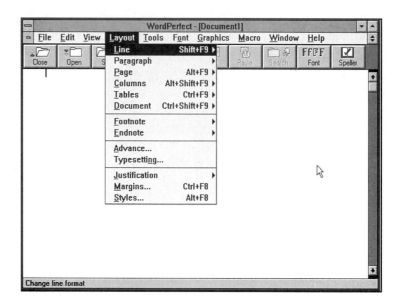

FIG. 29.7

The Layout pull-down menu with shortcut keys.

Display Last Open Filenames

An interesting WordPerfect for Windows feature is the display at the bottom of the File menu listing the last four files you opened or created, then saved. You can reopen any of these files by selecting it on the File menu. This feature is on by default when you install WordPerfect.

To instruct WordPerfect not to display the names of the last four files you opened, in the Menu area of the Environment Settings dialog box, choose Display **L**ast Open Filenames.

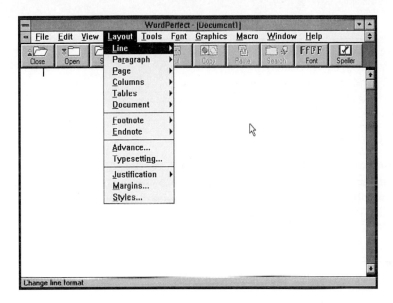

FIG. 29.8

The Layout pull-down menu without shortcut keys.

If you cannot find a file you just saved, you may have a typo in the file name or you may have saved it to a different directory. Check in the File pull-down menu for a display of the file name you used.

T I P

Customize the Ruler

You can customize the Ruler layout only through the Preferences menu. The following sections briefly cover Ruler changes you can make. For a complete discussion of tab features and using the Ruler, refer to Chapter 6, "Formatting Text."

Tabs Snap to Ruler Grid

Displaying the Ruler activates invisible gridlines at 1/16 inch, 1/5 centimeter, or the interval appropriate for the unit of measure you choose. When you move or place a tab, the tab *snaps to* the gridline nearest your placement.

To activate the grid, in the Ruler area of the Environment Settings dialog box, choose Tabs Snap to Ruler Grid.

> **T I P** When setting up tabs with the Ruler grid active, you can override the grid setting to place an individual tab. Simply hold down the Shift key while you place the tab.

Show Ruler Guides

When you use the Ruler to position tabs, by default a dotted vertical line extends from the bottom of the tab to the bottom of the screen as you use the mouse to move the tab along the Ruler. To turn off this feature, in the Ruler area of the Environment Settings dialog box, choose Show **R**uler Guides.

Ruler Buttons on Top

When you first display the Ruler, by default the Button Bar appears on the bottom of the Ruler. The Button Bar is a handy tool that enables you to perform the commands for selecting styles, creating tables, setting justification and line spacing options in one simple step, creating columns, and selecting fonts. For more information on the Button Bar, refer to Chapter 19, "Using the Button Bar."

To move the Button Bar to the top of the Ruler, in the Ruler area of the Environment Settings dialog box, choose Place Ruler **B**utton on Top.

Automatic Ruler Display

■ **Cue:** When Automatic Ruler Display is off, you can display the Ruler at any time while you work on a document by choosing Ruler in the View menu.

After using the Ruler feature for a while, you may find that you want it available to you all the time. By default, WordPerfect does not display the Ruler. Furthermore, when you select the Ruler from the View menu, the Ruler appears only in that document window. To display the Ruler all the time in all open documents, in the Ruler area of the Environment Settings dialog box, choose Automatic Ruler **D**isplay.

Customize Hyphenation

You can customize the circumstances under which WordPerfect asks you for hyphenation decisions. You also can choose the dictionary WordPerfect uses when hyphenating. Before you customize the hyphenation option in Preferences, refer to Chapter 6, "Formatting Text," for more information about how the following hyphenation features work.

Choose Hyphenation Prompt

WordPerfect uses a dictionary of hyphenation rules to decide how to hyphenate a word. The options available in Preferences establish how much input you can have in hyphenation decisions:

- *Never.* If the word cannot be found in the dictionary or the dictionary indicates that no hyphenation for the word exists, the word wraps to the next line.

- *When Required.* The word is hyphenated according to the instructions in the dictionary. If the word cannot be found, WordPerfect prompts you for a hyphenation decision. When Required is the default option.

- *Always.* WordPerfect prompts you to decide where to place the hyphen in every word that can be hyphenated.

Specify Hyphenation Dictionary Location

WordPerfect has an external spelling and hyphenation dictionary contained in a file called WP{WP}US.LEX. The external hyphenation dictionary is the default setting. The dictionary contains approximately 115,000 words with all possible hyphenation positions for each word.

WordPerfect also includes a small internal hyphenation dictionary. The internal dictionary not only contains fewer words, but many of the words have fewer hyphenation options. You can choose which dictionary to use; however, making a decision based on disk space is not realistic. Refer to Appendix A, "Installing and Setting Up WordPerfect for Windows," for a discussion on file size and disk space considerations.

Depending on the hyphenation zone settings, WordPerfect hyphenates everything without regard to how many consecutive lines end with hyphens or how many letters remain on the line, sometimes leaving only two letters on a line. You can use the internal dictionary to limit the number of ways WordPerfect hyphenates because the internal dictionary has fewer words and fewer hyphen options.

> **T I P**   You can exercise some control over WordPerfect's hyphenation by judicious setting of the hyphenation zone. (See Chapter 6 for a full presentation of this feature.)

Customizing the Display

The most obvious effect of WordPerfect's Graphical User Interface (GUI) is the WYSIWYG (what you see is what you get) appearance of text in the document editing area. WordPerfect displays text boldfaced, underlined, or italicized and immediately redisplays the text as you edit, thereby maintaining justification, margins, and other formatting effects on-screen. You can customize this display a number of ways with Preferences Display Settings dialog box.

To access the display settings, follow these steps:

1. Choose **File**, **Preferences**.

   CUA   Press Preferences (Ctrl-Shift-F1).

2. Choose **Display**.

   The Display Settings dialog box appears (see fig. 29.9).

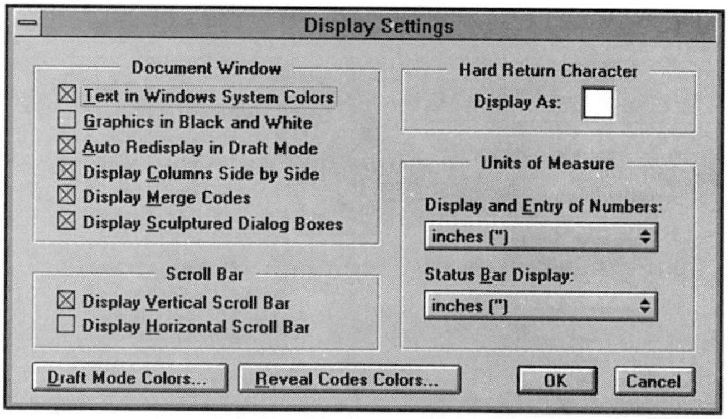

FIG. 29.9

The Display Settings dialog box with default settings.

In the Display Settings dialog box you make your choices in the following ways:

- Where you see a square check box you turn the toggle on or off for each setting. When a setting is *on*, you see an X in the check box next to the setting name. Conversely, when you turn off a setting, the X does not appear in the check box.

- Where you see text boxes, you can make your choice by typing numbers and characters in each box.

- Where you see a pop-up list after you choose an option, make your choice by highlighting the appropriate list item.

You can choose your display settings by the following methods:

- Using the mouse, click the appropriate check box, text box, or up and down arrows for each option.

- Using the keyboard, press the underlined letter in each option.

- Using the Tab key, press Tab to move the pointer to the option you want and then press the space bar for check boxes or Alt plus the up- or down-arrow key for radio buttons.

After you choose your display settings, to return to your document, choose OK or press Enter.

Customizing the Display in Draft Mode

Draft mode is one way you can change your view of the document window. To change to Draft mode, simply choose View, **Draft** Mode. After you choose Draft Mode, a check mark appears beside this option in the View menu.

You can type and edit faster in Draft mode, still having easy access to GUI features, such as the Ruler, Button Bar, and scroll bars, that remain on-screen. Because your text enhancements are not visible in Draft mode, you can customize the screen colors so that font attributes such as boldface, underline, and italic show up in different colors. The one other setting you can customize in Draft mode is the automatic redisplay of text as you edit.

You can consider working in WordPerfect's Draft mode when a monospaced screen font is acceptable; your document contains graphics, columns, or font changes; and you don't have a fast 386 or 486 computer. If you work predominantly with standard monospaced typewriter-style fonts, the WYSIWYG screen may not be the efficient way to do your work.

The following two sections cover the two options in the Display Settings dialog box you can use to customize the Draft mode display.

Auto Redisplay in Draft Mode

WordPerfect for Windows automatically redisplays text on-screen when you edit. You press keys, such as Tab, Enter, and the arrow keys, and WordPerfect immediately reformats the text. Having text "jump around" in this manner is distracting for some people. In Draft mode, you can turn off this feature. In the Display Settings dialog box, choose **A**uto Redisplay in Draft Mode.

When Automatic Redisplay is turned off, WordPerfect does not reformat the text until you use the directional keys or mouse pointer to scroll through the document.

■ **Cue:** The shortcut keystroke that reformats text when Automatic Redisplay is turned off is Redisplay (Ctrl-F3).

Draft Mode Colors

Enhancements that change the size or appearance of your text do not display graphically while you work in Draft mode. Using Preferences, however, you can custom-color your text to indicate enhanced text.

To customize the color selections, follow these steps:

1. In the Display Settings dialog box, choose **D**raft Mode Colors. The Draft Mode Colors dialog box appears.

2. The Draft Mode Colors dialog box includes six predefined color configurations. Choose Color Display Settings at the top of the box; the following options are available:

   ■ *Color.* Including monochrome, CGA, EGA, and VGA monitors

   ■ *Monochrome.* For true two-color monitors

   ■ *Blue on White.* White with blue letters, easy on the eyes

   ■ *LCD Display.* Frequently used for laptop computers

   ■ *LCD Display - No Intensity.* No shading contrasts

   ■ *Plasma Display.* Shades of red used primarily on laptop and portable computers

   ■ *Custom.* Your own creation

3. If you choose Custom, in the Foreground Palette, choose your foreground color; in the Background Palette, choose your background color.

4. In the Appearance, Sizes, and Other sections of the dialog box, choose an appearance, size, or other group item.

5. Choose OK to return to your document.

   If you are dissatisfied with the appearance of your screen, or if you want to return to the original palette before you exit the document, reopen the Draft Mode Colors dialog box and choose **Reset** to return to the factory settings and try again.

T I P

With the colors offered, a good contrast can be obtained by using white as the background color, black for the text, red for your most frequent enhancement, blue for next frequent enhancement, and then dark green. Good combinations for Highlighted Text, Bold/Underline, or Combination are dark blue background with cyan text, dark cyan background with yellow text, or black background with intense white text. These combinations are easy on the eyes after hours of work.

If you have a laptop, portable, or other monochrome color graphics setup, experiment with the preset configurations, including LCD options, for some excellent ideas on getting the most from your display.

Customizing the Display in WYSIWYG Mode

You can change the display in the document editing window to display columns side-by-side, show graphics in black and white, and display the text in Windows system colors. The following sections cover the customizing options WordPerfect offers you for the default on-screen display.

Text in Windows System Colors

Because all your text enhancements are displayed graphically in WYSIWYG mode, configuring text colors is not necessary. WordPerfect uses the Colors option in the Windows Control Panel to set the colors of document text and background, as well as the active and inactive windows title bars and borders. The default settings in the Windows Control Panel are for black text displayed on a white background.

When you change the text color selected in the Windows Control Panel, the change extends to the numbers and markings on the Ruler, as well as text displayed in list and text boxes in WordPerfect dialog boxes.

If, however, you have a color printer and want text that will print in color to be displayed in the same color on the screen, turn off the **Text** in Windows System Colors option in the Document Window section of the Display Settings dialog box.

T I P Notice that Windows also controls the color of the WordPerfect title bar at the top of your screen and the active and inactive document and dialog box bar colors. You can change any of these colors in the Windows Control Panel menu by selecting the Colors icon. Select Color Palette to open the window to a full color display. Use the Screen Element pop-up list to choose the area of the screen you want to color differently; choose the color. Although changing colors does not effect much of your WordPerfect display, it does dress up the display a little.

Graphics in Black and White

Because of today's graphics, GUIs, 256 colors, and high-resolution monitors, displaying graphic images in black and white seems like returning to the dark ages of computer technology. The WordPerfect for Windows configuration displays graphics in color. Unless you have a color printer, however, the black and white graphics display is *true* WYSIWYG.

WordPerfect Corporation's WPG graphics files use checkered patterns of varying densities to represent shades of gray. The entire DrawPerfect figure library, for example, uses the same checkered patterns. Seeing the graphic as it appears on the printed page (true WYSIWYG) may help you determine whether you want to use that graphic or another one.

To change to black-and-white display, in the Display Settings dialog box, choose **G**raphics in Black and White.

Display Columns Side by Side

When you work with newspaper or parallel columns rather than tabbed columns, the default display setting shows the columns side-by-side on-screen. Displaying columns side-by-side slows the reformatting speed of the program. You also will find side-by-side columns make moving from column to column a more cumbersome process.

If you want to speed up the display, turn off the side-by-side display in the Display Settings dialog box by choosing Display **C**olumns Side by Side. Reverse this process to return to side-by-side display.

Display Merge Codes

The WordPerfect default setting is to display merge codes in primary and secondary files. A primary file displays the field number followed by the tilde symbol (for example, 4~) to mark the locations where data is to be merged. If you turn off this feature, these codes appear only in the Reveal Codes window.

To remove the display of merge codes, in the Display Settings dialog box, choose Display **M**erge Codes.

Refer to Chapter 21, "Assembling Documents with Merge," for more information about displaying merge codes.

Display Sculptured Dialog Boxes

By default, the dialog boxes in WordPerfect for Windows are shaded like other screen features, and chiseled lines surround separate sections of the dialog box. If you change the dialog boxes to display in flat white without chiseled lines, the sculptured buttons and colored title bar on top remain.

Again, this graphical feature diminishes program display speed slightly. To speed display, turn off the sculptured boxes in the Display Settings dialog box; then choose Display **S**culptured Dialog Boxes.

■ **Cue:** Sculptured dialog boxes are not available for EGA and monochrome monitors.

Display the Scroll Bars

Scroll bars are strips on the side and bottom of the screen, that enable you to scroll through your document six lines at a time by clicking the up- and down-arrow buttons, clicking in the gray area of the bar for screen up and screen down, or dragging the slide button.

When you install WordPerfect, the vertical scroll bar appears on the right side of the screen. The horizontal scroll bar at the bottom of the screen does not appear.

T I P   If you're going to be working with landscape forms or with font sizes too small to display actual size properly on your screen (typically 10 point or smaller at VGA 640 by 480 resolution, 8 point or smaller at SVGA 800 by 600 resolution) or 12 cpi monospaced fonts, you should activate the horizontal scroll bar.

To display the horizontal scroll bar or remove the vertical scroll bar, in the Display Settings dialog box, choose Display Vertical Scroll Bar or Display **H**orizontal Scroll Bar.

Hard Return Character

Much of visible formatting of your document depends on the placement of hard returns. Although you can locate a misplaced hard return by hunting in the Reveal Codes window, you are likely to notice immediately a symbol used to display hard returns in the document screen. Many computer users first learned word processing with programs that displayed hard returns and find the visible hard return a reliable way to work.

You may choose a hard return display character from the WordPerfect Character Set, which is accessed by pressing Ctrl-W. Commonly used symbols include ¶ (4,5) and ↵ (5,9).

To choose a display character, open the Display Settings dialog box and follow these steps:

1. In the Hard Return Character area, choose **D**isplay As.

2. With the insertion point in the text box, press Ctrl-W to open the WordPerfect characters dialog box.

3. Choose the Set bar to open the Character Set pop-up menu.

4. Choose a character set, then choose a **C**haracter from the set.

   WordPerfect displays a dotted outline around the character.

5. Choose the Insert and Close button.

   The character appears in the Display As box.

6. Choose OK to return to your document.

Refer to Chapter 28, "Creating and Displaying Special Characters," for more information on using character sets and available characters.

Units of Measure

When you install WordPerfect, the program display is in inches. The units of measure are reflected in the Ln and Pos information in the status bar and in other areas such as the Ruler and the Margins dialog box. To change the units of measure, follow these steps:

1. In the Display Settings dialog box, choose the Display and Entry of Numbers button or the Status Bar Display button.

2. From the pop-up list, choose one of the following units of measurement:

   inches (") (8 1/2")

   inches (i) (8 1/2i)

   centimeters (1/100th of a meter)

   points (p) (in WordPerfect, this setting is 1/72", not 1/72.27")

   1200ths of an inch (w) (300w is 1/4")

3. If you want to make additional Display Settings selections with the keyboard, press the space bar to close the box; if you have finished customizing your display settings, choose OK to save your changes and return to your document.

WordPerfect calculates measurements to six decimal places although only three decimal places appear in any numeric text box. Because WordPerfect for Windows also converts fractions, you do not need to convert ruler inches (such as 1/16) to decimal inches.

WordPerfect is capable of converting any measurements to the format being used. For WordPerfect to convert one unit of measure to another, the highlighted letter in parentheses must immediately follow the measurement. If you are working in inches, for example, and enter an amount in centimeters followed by a *c*, WordPerfect converts the centimeters to inches.

> **T I P** Working with 1200ths of an inch can be useful when you are designing complex graphics layouts because you can specify very small increments. The amounts are easy to calculate (600 = 1/2 inch, 120 = 1/10 inch). You do not need to change to this format in order to use it. Even though you are measuring in inches, you can enter a measurement as 360w (3/10").

Reveal Codes Colors

You can customize the colors in the Reveal Codes window for three features: the text, the codes, and the mouse pointer. To customize the Reveal Codes colors, follow these steps:

1. In the Display Settings dialog box, choose Reveal **C**odes Colors.

2. In the Reveal Codes Colors dialog box, choose **T**ext, **C**odes, or **C**ursor.

3. Choose colors of the foreground and background for the Text, Codes, or Cursor.

4. Choose the next feature you want to customize, and then repeat step 3 for each item you want to change.

5. Choose OK to return to your document.

> **T I P** An effective color scheme that is easy to read and sets out the hidden codes well contains a white background, red text, blue codes, black insertion point, and intense white text.

Customizing Your Print Jobs

All the selections grouped here as printing preferences are available in the Preferences Print Settings dialog box and the Print dialog box from the File pull-down menu. WordPerfect shows the permanent changes you make in Preferences as the defaults in the document Print dialog box. Changes you make for an individual print job in the Print dialog box temporarily override the defaults set in Preferences. Setting each of these options for an individual print job is discussed in Chapter 9, "Basic Printing." In Preferences, you customize WordPerfect for all print jobs.

If you usually print two-sided print jobs or print a standard number of multiple copies, setting up printing preferences in the Preferences menu is the way to customize your system (see fig. 29.10).

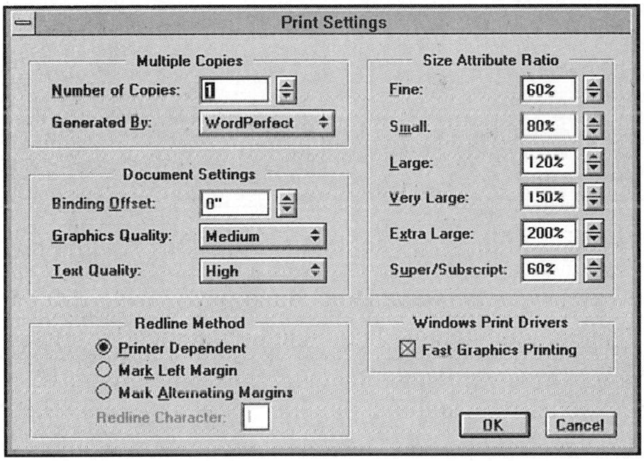

Print Settings

Multiple Copies		Size Attribute Ratio	
Number of Copies:	1	Fine:	60%
Generated By:	WordPerfect	Small:	80%
		Large:	120%
Document Settings		Very Large:	150%
Binding Offset:	0"	Extra Large:	200%
Graphics Quality:	Medium	Super/Subscript:	60%
Text Quality:	High		

Redline Method
- ⦿ Printer Dependent
- ○ Mark Left Margin
- ○ Mark Alternating Margins
- Redline Character:

Windows Print Drivers
- ☒ Fast Graphics Printing

[OK] [Cancel]

FIG. 29.10

The Print Settings dialog box with the default settings.

> **T I P**
>
> Remember that when you change settings through Preferences in the Print Settings dialog box you customize *all* future print jobs, including the printing of documents created before you changed the settings.

The following sections explain each Print Settings choice that WordPerfect offers you, including Multiple Copies, Document Settings, Redline Method, Size Attribute Ratio, and Windows Print Drivers.

To access the Preferences print settings follow these steps:

1. Choose **F**ile, **P**references.

   CUA Press Preferences (Ctrl-Shift-F1).

2. Choose **P**rint.

   The Print Settings dialog box appears (refer to fig. 29.10).

In the five areas of the Print Settings dialog box you make your choices in the following ways:

- Where you see a square check box, you turn the toggle for each setting off or on. When a setting is *on* you see an X in the check box next to the setting name. Conversely, after you turn off a setting, the X does not appear in the check box.

- Where you see round radio buttons, you make your choice by activating a radio button. When one radio button is on (filled with a dark circle), the other related buttons are off (empty).

- Where you see text boxes, you can make your choice by typing numbers and characters in each box.

- Where you see a pop-up list after you choose an option, make your choice by highlighting the appropriate list item.

You can choose your Print Settings by the following methods:

- Using the mouse, click the appropriate check box, radio button, text box, or up and down arrows for each option.

- Using the keyboard, press the underlined letter in each option.

- Using the Tab key, press Tab to move the pointer to the option you want and then press the space bar.

Multiple Copies

In the Multiple Copies area of the Print Settings dialog box you can make two choices as follows:

- Choose the standard number of copies you print of most of your documents.

- Choose whether you want WordPerfect or your printer to generate the copies. If you choose *WordPerfect*, the program creates the specified number of copies and then sends them to the printer so that they print in collated order. If you choose *Printer*, Word-Perfect sends only one copy of the document to your printer with directions to make the specified number of copies; the printer does not collate the copies.

To make the Multiple Copies choices, do the following:

1. In the Print Settings dialog box, Choose **N**umber of Copies.

2. Type the number of copies you want, or choose the correct number from the pop-up list.

3. By default, WordPerfect generates your multiple copies. If you want your printer to generate the multiple copies, choose Generated **B**y.

4. Choose **P**rinter or **W**ordPerfect from the pop-up list.

5. If you are not choosing other print settings, choose OK to save your changes and return to your document.

Binding Offset

When you print a *duplex*, or two-sided, print job, you can specify an inside margin binding offset to ensure that the text on each page is moved a measured amount toward the outside edge of the page. This offset leaves room for stapling or spiral binding while maintaining the margins appropriate for your text. To change the binding offset for all print jobs, follow these steps:

1. In the Print Settings dialog box, choose Binding **O**ffset in the Document Settings area.

2. Type a measurement for the amount you want WordPerfect to add to the inside margins, or choose the correct measurement from the pop-up list.

   Because the program converts a fraction (5/64 or 3/32, for example) to its decimal equivalent, feel free to use the demarcations on a standard ruler.

3. If you are not choosing other print settings, choose OK to save the changes and return to your document.

Graphics Quality

The print quality you specify for the graphics and text in your document can slow printing dramatically, or even make it impossible. The higher the quality of graphics printing you select, the longer your laser printer takes to assemble your document, or the longer your dot-matrix printer takes to print each line of your job.

Graphics can also tax, or even surpass, your printer memory. The graphics images are assembled in your printer as part of your document. The number of graphics, the size of each one, and the graphics print quality all make escalating printer memory demands. One large graphic or several small ones, printed at final quality, can result in one page that exceeds a megabyte in size. The standard memory included with laser printers is 512K, or half that amount.

The options available for graphics and text print quality are as follows:

- *Draft.* Fastest option but extremely low quality; useful if Print Preview does not adequately show what you need to preview

- *Medium.* Zigzagged curves on graphics; text quality usually the same as High

- *High.* Final quality graphics and text printing

- *Do Not Print.* Prints only text or only graphics, depending on which is selected *not* to print

If you are using a Windows printer driver, you can choose only Draft, Set in Printer, or Do Not Print. To select final quality printing, choose Set in Printer; then choose Final, using Setup in the Windows Select Printer dialog box. Whichever option you choose is selected for both text and graphics.

To select print quality, follow these steps:

1. In the Print Settings dialog box, choose **G**raphics Quality.

2. Choose **H**igh, **M**edium, **D**raft, or Do **N**ot Print from the pop-up list.

3. If you are not choosing other print settings, choose OK to save your changes and return to your document.

T I P   If your document prints with only a portion of your graphic or text, your printer ran out of memory while assembling the print job. Use Do **N**ot Print text to print only the graphics. Then choose to print only the text and hand-feed the page of graphics into the printer.

If this choice does not do the job, try using fewer font sizes and type changes. You also can move a large graphic to a separate page, leaving its box empty in your document. Print the graphic; then print the remainder of the graphics; then print the text—hand-feeding the same page for each print job.

Text Quality

If most of your print jobs are draft quality or you print only the graphics part of a document, permanently change the text print quality settings by following these steps:

1. In the Print Settings dialog box, choose **Text Quality**.

2. Choose **H**igh, **M**edium, **D**raft, or Do **N**ot Print from the pop-up list.

3. If you are not choosing other print settings, choose OK to save your changes and return to your document.

Redline Method

Redlining involves changing the appearance of text so that editing additions and strikeouts stand out from original text when you review the edited document. Then you can use Document Compare to incorporate these suggestions into the document. Chapter 10, "Working with Fonts," discusses redlining in more detail, and Chapter 11, "Formatting Pages and Designing Documents" covers changing the redline method for a single document in the Layout menu.

To change the default redline method, that is, change the appearance of redlined text, follow these steps:

1. In the Print Settings dialog box, choose one of the following from the Redline Method area:

   ■ *Printer Dependent.* This redline method can be a colon, vertical line, forward slash, or other character for dot-matrix printers and is usually a shaded background for laser printers.

   ■ *Mark Left Margin.* This option marks the left margin with a redline character.

   ■ *Mark Alternating Margins.* This option marks alternating margins with a redline character.

2. The Redline Character text box is active only if you choose not to use the printer-dependent method. The default redline character displayed is the vertical bar (|) found above the backslash on your keyboard. If this character does not mark text to your satisfaction, choose a different character.

With the pointer in the text editing box, you can type any character from the keyboard, or you can choose any character from the WordPerfect character sets by pressing Ctrl-W. (Chapter 28, "Creating and Displaying Special Characters," describes using WordPerfect characters.)

3. If you are not choosing other print settings, choose OK to save your changes and return to your document.

Size Attribute Ratio

As you work in your document, you can change the current font by using the Font dialog box available in Font menu. You can either select a specific named font and point size from the list boxes or choose a proportionately smaller or larger font from the Size section of the dialog box. The size selections available are Superscript, Subscript, Fine, Small, Large, Very Large, and Extra Large.

The ratio of smaller and larger font sizes is a percentage of the current font you set in the Preferences, Print menu. To change the percentage ratios, follow these steps:

1. In the Size Attribute Ratio area of the Print Settings dialog box, choose from **F**ine, **Sm**all, **L**arge, **V**ery Large, **E**xtra Large, and **Su**per/Subscript. Type the percent you want to use in each box, or click the up- and down-arrow buttons to change in one-percent increments.

2. If you are not choosing other print settings, choose OK to save your changes and return to your document.

If you have a large selection of fonts installed for occasional use but actually use only a handful of fonts regularly, you can change the percentages to select the font size you desire.

Windows Print Drivers Fast Graphics Printing

If you are using a Windows printer driver, printing can be very slow, especially when the document includes graphics. The Fast Graphics Printing feature is on, by default, when you install WordPerfect.

If you have problems printing with your Windows printer driver, try printing without this option. To turn off the Fast Graphics Printing feature, in the Print Settings dialog box, choose Fast Graphics Printing (or press Ctrl-S) to toggle the feature off and remove the X from the check box.

Chapter 9, "Basic Printing" includes a discussion of the installation and use of Windows printers and the Fast Graphics Printing feature.

Customizing Keyboards

WordPerfect for Windows has five keyboard layouts. The CUA compliant keyboard is the default keyboard and is designed to take advantage of working in the Windows environment.

The second keyboard layout is similar to the keyboard layout in WordPerfect 5.1. This keyboard features old favorites like F3 for Help, F1 for Undelete, and the Home and arrow-key combinations to move around the screen and document. You can use these keystrokes, however, only in the document editing window. In dialog boxes, you must use Windows-style keystrokes.

WordPerfect for Windows adds to the keyboard many command keystrokes unknown to WordPerfect 5.1. Two major additions are keystrokes that extend the text selection (previously done with Block On and the directional keys) and the Ctrl-letter key combinations that are shortcut keystrokes for popular commands.

You can find information to help you familiarize yourself with the new layouts and command structures in the following places in this book:

■ A table inside the front cover sets out the Windows keyboard structure you encounter when you use the CUA keyboard or work in dialog boxes.

■ Appendix B includes a chart showing the terminology changes between WordPerfect and WordPerfect for Windows. An additional chart lists the keystrokes used on the CUA keyboard, and another chart the DOS 5.1 compatible keyboard. Note particularly the keystrokes that are unassigned and, therefore, available for your use. A summary version of this chart appears inside the back cover.

■ The tear-out card inside the back cover includes templates for both keyboards.

The third layout is a macro keyboard, which includes a variety of macros that create memos, letters, and envelopes as well as performs other WordPerfect jobs.

The last two keyboard layouts are the equation keyboards, discussed in later sections of this chapter. One equation keyboard is based on the WordPerfect for Windows CUA keyboard. The other option is an equation keyboard based on WordPerfect 5.1 keystrokes.

The equation keyboard is unique because it is the only WordPerfect feature for which you can select two keyboards: one keyboard that is active in the document window and an equation keyboard that activates only when you are working in the Equation Editor.

Selecting a Keyboard

Appendix A covers the process for selecting the initial default keyboard during installation of WordPerfect for Windows.

You can change keyboards at any time by following these steps:

1. Choose **File**, **Preferences**.

    CUA Press Preferences (Ctrl-Shift-F1).

2. Choose **Keyboard**.

    The Keyboard dialog box displays the currently active keyboard (see fig. 29.11).

FIG. 29.11

The Keyboard dialog box.

3. Choose **Select**.

    The Select Keyboard File dialog box appears (see fig. 29.12).

4. Choose the name of the keyboard file you want to use from the Files list, or type the file name in the **File**name text box.

5. Choose Select to return to the Keyboard dialog box; then choose OK to return to your document.

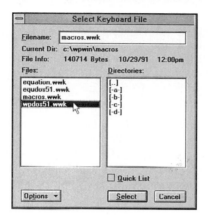

FIG. 29.12

The Select
Keyboard File
dialog box.

Creating a Keyboard

After you try using other keyboard layouts, you may begin to feel the
temptation to create a few shortcuts of your own. The process for creating your own shortcuts is very simple because the Keyboard Editor
does much of the work for you in editing or creating a keyboard (see
fig. 29.13).

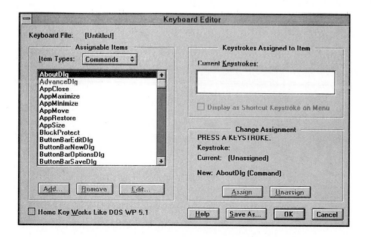

FIG. 29.13

The Keyboard
Editor dialog
box.

The Editor includes an Item Types pop-up list from which you choose **C**ommands, **M**enus, **T**ext, or **M**acros, as described in the following list:

- *Commands*. This option contains a comprehensive list of assignable commands. This lengthy list includes almost every task that you can accomplish with a series of keystrokes. These commands open dialog boxes.

- *Menus*. This option provides a listing of all the menus available. These commands open pull-down menus and highlight your choices of menu options.

- *Text*. This option provides a list of text items you have created.

- *Macros*. This option provides a list of all macros you have added to the list.

Because WordPerfect adds the Commands and Menus list items to the Editor, assigning Commands or Menus is a one-step process. If you choose Text or Macros, WordPerfect activates the Add button below the list box, enabling you to add macros or text items to the Keyboard Editor. Assigning Text or Macros is a two-step process: add the item; assign the item to a key.

To create a new keyboard, follow these steps:

1. In the Keyboard dialog box, choose **C**reate to display the Keyboard Editor dialog box, which shows that the Keyboard File is [Untitled].

2. Use either of the following methods to assign items to the keyboard:

    - Press the keystroke combination you want to use. With the mouse, choose **I**tem Types and then select from the pop-up list either Commands, Menus, Text, or Macros. (Refer to the two following sections for special instructions in adding Text or Macros.) Scroll through the list to choose the item you want.

    - Choose **I**tem Types to open the pop-up menu; then type the underlined letter for **C**ommands, **M**enus, **T**ext, or **M**acros. Press Tab to move to the list box; then scroll through the list to choose the item you want. Press the keystroke combination you want to use.

    In the Change Assignment area (lower right) of the dialog box, Keystroke indicates the strokes you pressed, New has the name of the item you chose, and the Assign button is now active.

3. Choose **A**ssign. The name of the item you chose now appears after Current, and the keystroke combination appears in the Current Keystroke text box in the upper right corner of the dialog box. The Unassign button is active (see fig. 29.14).

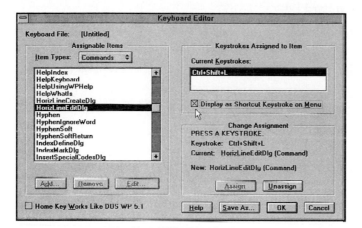

FIG. 29.14

The Change Assignment area in the Keyboard Editor dialog box.

4. Repeat steps 2 and 3 for every keystroke combination you want to add to the selected keyboard.

5. Choose **S**ave As, name your keyboard in the Save Keyboard File dialog box, and then choose OK to save.

6. Press OK twice to return to your document.

CAUTION: You must choose a keystroke combination in order to assign anything to the keyboard. When you choose the item you want to assign, press the correct keystrokes. If you use the keyboard to maneuver within the Keyboard Editor and list box, those movement keystrokes will appear in the keystroke assignment area.

After pressing the keystrokes, carefully read the information in the lower right corner of the Editor to make sure that every item is filled in correctly before you proceed. If you find an error, repeat the keystrokes until they display correctly.

Assigning Text to Your Keyboard

To assign text to a keystroke, do the following:

1. In the Keyboard dialog box, choose Create to display the Keyboard Editor.

2. Press the keystroke combination you want to use and choose **Text** from the **I**tem Types pop-up list.

3. Choose A**d**d to display the Add Text dialog box (see fig. 29.15).

The Add Text dialog box with a closing paragraph.

4. In the Name text box, type a short name for your text.

5. Type the complete text in the Text text box.

6. Choose OK to return to the Keyboard Editor. The short name you typed appears in the list box.

7. Choose the short name you want to assign to the keyboard.

   Notice that Keystroke in the lower right corner of the Keyboard Editor dialog box indicates the strokes you pressed, New has the name of the text item you chose, and the Assign button is active.

8. Choose **A**ssign.

   The name of the text item appears after Current, and the keystroke combination appears in the Current Keystroke text box. The **U**nassign button is active.

9. Repeat steps 4 through 8 for every keystroke combination you want to add to the selected keyboard.

10. When you finish adding to the keyboard, save and rename the customized keyboard.

11. Choose OK twice to return to your document.

The text you enter should be unformatted. WordPerfect removes any formatting you include when it saves the text. You also can paste text into the Text box by pressing Shift-Ins. A text item can contain up to 4,000 characters, including spaces and hard returns.

You also can include characters from the WordPerfect Character Set as text. To add symbols, press Ctrl-W when you are in the text area of the Add Text or Edit Text box. Refer to Chapter 28 for more information about special characters and customizing a keyboard with selections from the WordPerfect Character Set.

Cue: Use the Keyboard Editor to add scientific symbols or foreign letters to the keyboard.

Assigning Macros to Your Keyboard

You can create your own macro. Refer to Chapter 20, "Creating Macros," for more information. To assign a macro to the keyboard, follow these instructions:

1. In the Keyboard dialog box, choose Create to display the Keyboard Editor dialog box.

2. Choose Macro from the Item Types pop-up list.

3. Choose Add to display the Import Macro to Keyboard dialog box (see fig. 29.16).

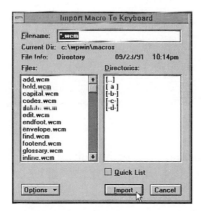

FIG. 29.16

The Import Macro to Keyboard dialog box.

4. Choose a macro to import from the Files list box, or type a macro file name in the Filename box. Choose Import to return to the Keyboard Editor. The macro name appears in the Items list box.

   Notice that in the lower right corner of the Keyboard Editor dialog box, Keystroke indicates the strokes you pressed, New has the name of the macro you added, and the Assign button is active.

5. Choose **A**ssign. The name of the macro now appears after Current, and the keystroke combination appears in the Current Keystroke text box. The **U**nassign button is active.

6. Repeat steps 2 through 5 for every keystroke combination you add to the keyboard.

7. When you finish assigning macros to the keyboard, save and name your keyboard.

8. Choose OK twice to return to your document.

Refer to the discussion in Chapter 20 for more information about assigning macros to the keyboard.

 CAUTION: Only compiled macros can be assigned to the keyboard. The first time you play a macro you have recorded, WordPerfect compiles it. To assign a macro to your keyboard, first record your macro; then play the macro and assign it to your keyboard.

Adding Your Keystrokes to the WordPerfect Menus

You can add shortcut keystrokes to any menu option that doesn't currently have a shortcut. To add a shortcut to the menu, follow these steps:

1. In the Keyboard dialog box, choose **C**reate to display the Keyboard Editor, which shows that the Keyboard File is [Untitled].

2. Choose **I**tem Types to activate the appropriate list; then choose the item you want to assign to the keyboard, press the keystrokes you want to use, and choose Assign.

   For more information on assigning items to the keyboard, refer to "Creating a Keyboard" earlier in this chapter.

3. After you assign the keystrokes, choose the Current **K**eystroke box in the Keystrokes Assigned to Item area of the dialog box. Your keystroke selection appears in the Current Keystroke list box.

4. Choose the keystrokes you want displayed on the WordPerfect menus.

   The Display as Shortcut Key on **M**enu check box activates.

5. Choose the Display as Shortcut Key on **M**enu check box so that an X appears.

6. Repeat steps 4 through 7 for every keystroke combination you want to add to the menus.

7. Choose **S**ave As and name your keyboard in the Save Keyboard File dialog box. Then choose OK to save.

8. Choose OK twice to return to your document.

Retaining Home Key Options

An old friend on the DOS WordPerfect 5.1 keyboard, the Home key functioning with the arrow keys to move around the screen and document, is missing on the new keyboard layout. You can add this feature to your customized keyboard, however. In the Keyboard Editor dialog box, choose **H**ome Key Works Like DOS WP 5.1 so that an X appears in the check box.

Editing a Keyboard

You can continue to fine-tune your home-brewed keyboard using the Keyboard Editor. If you try to edit the original CUA keyboard, you see that the Edit button is not available when the CUA keyboard is active. By your choosing to create a keyboard first, the CUA keyboard becomes the basis of your creation. Once you save the new keyboard, you can then edit the new keyboard further.

To assign additional keystroke commands to a keyboard you have created, follow these steps:

1. In the Keyboard dialog box, choose **E**dit to display the Keyboard Editor.

2. Choose **I**tem Types and activate the appropriate list; then choose the item you want to assign to the keyboard.

   For more information on assigning items to the keyboard, refer to "Creating a Keyboard" earlier in this chapter.

3. Repeat step 2 for every keystroke combination you want to add to the selected keyboard.

4. If you want to add a keystroke shortcut to the WordPerfect menus, choose Current **K**eystroke and choose the shortcut keys from the box.

5. Choose the Display as Shortcut Key on Menu; an X appears in the check box.

6. Choose OK three times to save your changes and return to your document.

Editing Text Assigned to a Keyboard

After you assign text to the keyboard, you easily can edit the text. If a new production manager is hired, you don't need to create a new closing for your business letter. Simply edit the new production manager's name into the letter closing that already exists.

To edit text assigned to the keyboard, follow these steps:

1. In the Keyboard dialog box, choose Edit to display the Keyboard Editor.

2. In Item Types, choose Text to display the names of text items in the list box.

3. Choose the name of the text you want to edit.

4. Choose the Edit Text button.

   The Edit Text dialog box appears.

5. Edit the name or the text as necessary.

6. Choose OK to return to the Keyboard Editor.

7. After you finish editing the keyboard, choose OK three times to save your changes and return to your document.

Removing Text or Macros Added to a Keyboard

You can remove text or a macro you added to a keyboard by following these steps:

1. In the Keyboard dialog box, choose Edit to display the Keyboard Editor.

2. In Item Type, choose Text or Macro to display the items in the list box.

3. Choose the text item or macro you want to remove.

4. Choose **R**emove.

5. When you finish changing the keyboard, choose OK three times to save your changes and return to your document.

   The keystroke assignment you removed no longer works.

You also can change a keyboard assignment by assigning something else to the keystroke.

T   I   P

Using Initial Codes

WordPerfect has a wide array of default settings, such as 1-inch margins on all four sides, 8 1/2-by-11-inch paper size, tabs every 1/2 inch, a period used for decimal tabs, 6 lines per inch, single-spacing, and more. You can change these settings permanently, that is, for all subsequent documents until you change the settings again, using Preferences Initial Codes.

If you print primarily on letterhead, for example, Initial Codes enables you to set a top margin for a letterhead. If you use legal size paper for most print jobs, include an 8 1/2-by-14-inch Paper Size/Type code. If you always want the Widow/Orphan protection on, include this code.

A Document Initial Codes screen, which enables you to customize a single document, is available in the Layout menu. When you customize one document in the Document Initial Codes screen, you override the settings in Preferences Initial Codes for that specific document.

WordPerfect keeps you abreast of the codes you include in Preferences Initial Codes by including the new settings in the Document-Default Initial Codes screen (see fig. 29.17). If you tailor the codes for any individual document, this screen appears as a reminder of the initial codes you set earlier. For more information about Document Initial Codes, refer to Chapter 11, "Formatting Pages and Designing Documents."

The codes you insert in either Initial Codes screen are not displayed in the Reveal Codes window and, therefore, cannot be accidentally deleted. Using Initial Codes settings also ensures that the codes you specify are placed at the beginning of your document.

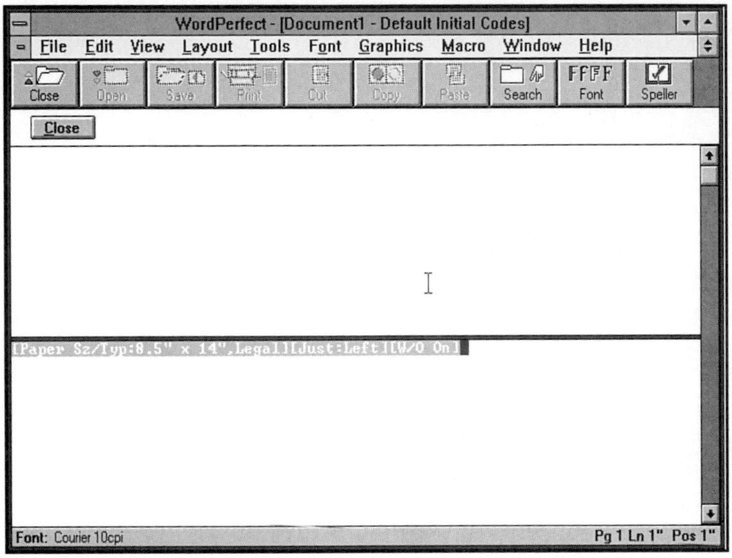

FIG. 29.17

The Document-Default Initial Codes screen (through Preferences).

You cannot insert every code in Preferences Initial Codes. When the Initial Codes screen is active, the pull-down menu dims any option that cannot be selected. If you attempt to add text or other codes, such as hard returns, tabs, or inserts, WordPerfect removes these unavailable items when you close Initial Codes. The codes you can use in Preferences Initial Codes are the following:

Base Font	Line Height
Column Definition	Line Numbering
Column On	Line Spacing
Decimal/Align Character	Margins Left/Right
Endnote Number	Margins Top/Bottom
Endnote Options	New Page Number
Footnote Number	Page Number Style
Graphics Box Number	Paper Size/Type
Graphics Box Options	Print Color
Hyphenation On/Off	Suppress
Hyphenation Zone	Tab Set
Justification	Underline Spaces and Tabs
Kerning	Widow/Orphan On/Off
Language	Word Spacing
Letterspacing	

To change permanently any of the default settings to one from this list, follow these steps:

1. Choose File, Preferences.

    Press Preferences (Ctrl-Shift-F1).

2. Choose Initial Codes.

   The Initial Codes screen is now active.

3. Choose the codes you want to insert in the same manner you insert any WordPerfect codes.

4. Choose Close to return to your document.

   All new documents begin with the default Initial Codes you set up.

Customizing the Document Summary

Creating a document summary enables you to maintain a database about your documents from which you can obtain information without retrieving individual documents. Document summaries act like 3-by-5 cards containing a substantial amount of information about each of your documents. In addition to the document creation date and revision date which WordPerfect automatically fills in, you can include eight separate pieces of information about your document. Refer to Chapter 30, "Advanced File Management Techniques," for information on searching document summaries for information, and to Chapter 11, "Formatting Pages and Designing Documents," for detailed information about Document Summary features.

Using Subject Search Text

One category of information in a document summary is the subject of the document. If you want that information filled in for you automatically, WordPerfect searches your document for the text RE: and extracts the 150 characters that follow RE: into the Subject box of the Document Summary Preferences dialog box (see fig. 29.18). If you use *Reference:*, *Subject:*, or other text to identify the subject of your documents you can change the default subject in Preferences by following these steps:

1. Choose **F**ile, **P**references.

   CUA Press Preferences (Ctrl-Shift-F1).

2. Choose Document **S**ummary.

3. Type your preferred search text in the **S**ubject Search Text box to replace the RE:.

4. Choose OK to return to your document.

FIG. 29.18

The Document
Summary
Preferences
dialog box.

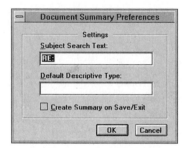

Using Default Descriptive Type

WordPerfect provides a default descriptive type such as *letter* or *proposal*. If one type of document predominates in your work, you can specify your own descriptive type as the default, following these steps:

1. Choose **F**ile, **P**references.

   CUA Press Preferences (Ctrl-Shift-F1).

2. Choose Document **S**ummary.

3. Choose **D**efault Descriptive Type.

4. Type the descriptive type you want to appear each time you create a document summary.

5. Choose OK to save the changes and return to your document.

You can override this default entry by typing a different descriptive type in the Descriptive Type text box of the Document Summary dialog box.

Creating a Summary on Save/Exit

You can instruct WordPerfect to prompt you to fill in the document summary each time you save or exit your document. The summary box prompt appears each time you save or exit the document until you fill in the document summary.

To create a prompt to complete the summary when you save or exit, follow these steps:

1. Choose **F**ile, **P**references.

   CUA Press Preferences (Ctrl-Shift-F1).

2. Choose Document **S**ummary.

3. Choose **C**reate Summary on Save/Exit.

   An X appears in the check box.

4. Choose OK to return to your document.

If you decide you no longer want the document summary prompt, follow the same steps to turn off the feature, removing the X from the check box.

Dating Your Documents

With WordPerfect for Windows, you can insert the current date and time into your document from the clock in your computer. The date can display in a variety of formats, including the day of the week, the time, 24-hour format, or any one of these alone.

If you choose to use Date Text, the current information is obtained from your computer clock, and the text is placed in your document at the insertion point location. You can select Date Code to place a code at the insertion point location. The information displayed by Date Code is updated to the current date and time every time you retrieve your document.

■ **Cue:** Use the Windows Control Panel or the DOS TIME and DATE commands to reset the clock in your computer when necessary.

Inserting the Date or Time into Your Document

Use the Date Text command to insert the current date (or time, if you use that format) into your document in text form. Use the Date Code command to insert a code into your document that retrieves the current date or time whenever you open the document (see fig. 29.19).

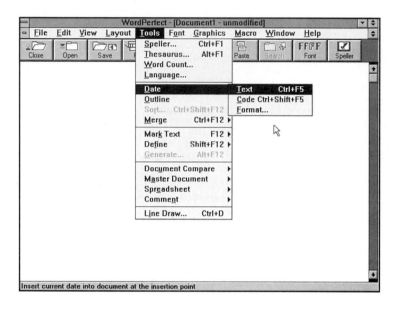

FIG. 29.19

The Date cascading menu.

To insert the date, follow these steps:

1. Choose **Tools**, **D**ate.

2. Choose **T**ext to insert Date Text; choose **C**ode to insert a Date Code.

    Press Date Text (Ctrl-F5).

    Press Date Code (Ctrl-Shift-F5).

The Date Code command is very useful when a document is edited repeatedly over a period of time. When you choose Date Code rather than Date Text, you do not have to correct the date each time you retrieve and print. You may, however, need the date on a document to verify when a document was mailed. With Date Code, retrieving the document later displays only the date the document is retrieved! If recording mailing dates is important in your work, on the day you prepare the document for mailing, replace all occurrences of Date Code with the current date. You can use the Replace feature to perform this task.

Changing the Date Format

WordPerfect displays the current day in Month ##, 199# default format. You can change this format in your document to one of a variety of formats that WordPerfect provides, or you can design your own format. To change the format, follow these steps:

1. Choose **Tools, Date**.

2. Choose **Format** to activate the dialog box shown in figure 29.20.

<table>
<tr><td colspan="3" align="center">Document Date/Time Format</td></tr>
<tr><td>Predefined Dates ▼</td><td>Date Codes ▼</td><td>Time Codes ▼</td></tr>
<tr><td colspan="3">Edit Date Format:
[Month] [Day #], [Year ####]</td></tr>
<tr><td colspan="3">Date Preview: November 1, 1991</td></tr>
<tr><td colspan="3" align="right">OK   Cancel</td></tr>
</table>

FIG. 29.20

The Document Date/Time Format dialog box.

3. Choose **Predefined Dates** and select a format from the pop-up list or choose **Date Codes** or **Time Codes** to create your own format. Refer to tables 29.2, 29.3, and 29.4 for the available date and time formats in the Format menu.

   After you choose Date or Time Code changes, the new format appears in the **E**dit Date Format text box in code form and in Date Preview in text form.

If you design your own date or time display, you may need to add commas or spaces as necessary to set up the correct display. For example, if you choose to add [Weekday] before the default date format, you are offered the following display:

```
[Weekday][Month] [Day #], [Year ####]
```

4. In the Edit Date Format text box, move the pointer between [Weekday] and [Month]; then type a comma and press the space bar. You can add additional text, such as **Today is**.

5. Choose OK or press Enter to return to your document.

When you create a new date format, the changes you make appear as the default format in the Document Date/Time Format dialog box. This is the format that WordPerfect uses when you insert a date in the remainder of your WordPerfect session or until you design a different format. When you start WordPerfect again, the program returns to the default format.

T I P   When you insert a Date Code, the code spells out specifically the format in effect at the time the code was chosen. If you are using a different date format when you next retrieve the document, the format included within the code is the way the date is displayed. To change the display, delete the code and insert a new Date Code reflecting the desired format.

Table 29.2. WordPerfect Predefined Dates

Dates
March 5, 1991
Mar 5, 1991
5 March 1991
Wednesday, March 5, 1991
Wednesday, 5 March 1991
3/5/91

Table 29.3. WordPerfect Date Codes

Codes	Variables
[Day #]	Day of Month
[Day 0#]	Day of Month (zero added)
[Day _#]	Day of Month (space added)
[Month #]	Month Number
[Month 0#]	Month Number (zero added)
[Month _#]	Month Number (space added)
[Month]	Month Name
[Year ##]	2-Digit Year
[Year ####]	4-Digit Year
[Weekday]	Day of the Week
[Abbr.Weekday]	Abbreviated Day of Week

Table 29.4. WordPerfect Time Codes

Codes	Variables
[Hour(12)#]	12-Hour Clock Hour #
[Hour(12)0#]	12-Hour Clock Hour # (zero added)
[Hour(12) _#]	12-Hour Clock Hour # (space added)
[Hour(24)#]	24-Hour Clock Hour #
[Hour(24)0#]	24-Hour Clock Hour # (zero added)
[Hour (24)_#]	24-Hour Clock Hour # (space added)
[Minute#]	Minute Number
[Minute0#]	Minute Number (zero added)
[Minute_#]	Minute Number (space added)
[AM/PM]	AM/PM Mark

Changing the Date Format in Preferences

If you decide to use a different date format almost exclusively, change the format in the Preferences menu. You can override this format in any document by choosing a format from the Tools, Date menu as described in the preceding section.

To change the date or time format for all future documents, follow these steps:

1. Choose **F**ile, **P**references.

     Press Preferences (Ctrl-Shift-F1).

2. Choose Date **F**ormat to access the Date/Time Preferences dialog box, shown in figure 29.21.

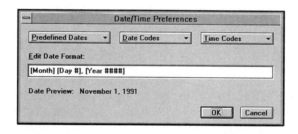

3. Choose a **P**redefined Dates format, or choose **D**ate Codes or **T**ime Codes to alter the predefined choices or design your own format. Refer to tables 29.2, 29.3, and 29.4 for the available date and time formats.

4. If necessary, add commas or spaces to set up the correct display after the new format is displayed.

5. Choose OK to return to your document.

Customizing Merge Preferences

In the Preferences Merge Settings dialog box, you can specify which delimiter to use to begin and end fields and records. You specify a delimiter, for example, if you want to use a database file exported as a DOS text file, or for secondary merge files created with pre-4.0 versions of WordPerfect. Chapter 21, "Assembling Documents with Merge," discusses how WordPerfect handles merging with DOS text secondary documents. Chapter 21 also covers the use of field and record delimiters.

The default field delimiter is a comma, and the default record delimiter is [CR]. To change the delimiters, follow these steps:

1. Choose File, Preferences.

   CUA Press Preferences (Ctrl-Shift-F1).

2. Choose Merge.

   The Merge Preferences dialog box appears (see fig. 29.22).

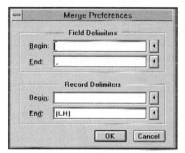

FIG. 29.22

The Merge
Preferences
dialog box.

3. Choose Field Begin or End, or Record Begin or End. An X appears in the check box when the feature is on.

4. In the text box next to the choice you made in step 3, type the delimiter you want to use, or click the arrow button at the right of the text box and choose Tab, Line Feed, Form Feed, or Carriage Return from the pop-up list.

5. Follow steps 3 and 4 for the other three delimiters, and then choose OK to return to your document.

Because so many addresses include commas within a field (for example, 123 North Main St., Suite 130), use quotation marks around the comma (",") for a field delimiter. This style has become a standard with many programs, so you should have no difficulty saving your database files as DOS text files using this delimiter.

T I P

Customizing the Table of Authorities

A table of authorities is usually subject to strict rules governing its set up. Choose Tools, Define, Table of Authorities to view the Define Table of Authorities dialog box. See Chapter 25, "Assembling Other Document References," for a detailed discussion of tables of authorities.

You can change the default ToA settings by following these steps:

1. Choose File, Preferences.

   [CUA] Press Preferences (Ctrl-Shift-F1).

2. Choose Table of Authorities.

3. In the TOA Preferences dialog box (see fig. 29.23) choose the option you want by toggling on or off the X in the check box, based on the following descriptions:

   ■ *Dot Leaders.* By default, the page numbers print flush to the right margin with dot leaders (a series of periods and spaces) between the last character of the citation and the page numbers. If you prefer blank spaces instead of dot leaders, remove the X from this option.

   ■ *Underlining Allowed.* In the text of a brief, court case references normally are underlined. WordPerfect gives you the option to display the underlining in the ToA. The default for this option *does not* display underlining in the ToA. If you want the underlining retained for the table, choose this option.

   ■ *Blank Line Between Authorities.* WordPerfect places a blank line between each authority unless you don't want blank lines. To prevent the insertion of a blank line, remove the X from this option.

4. Choose OK to return to your document.

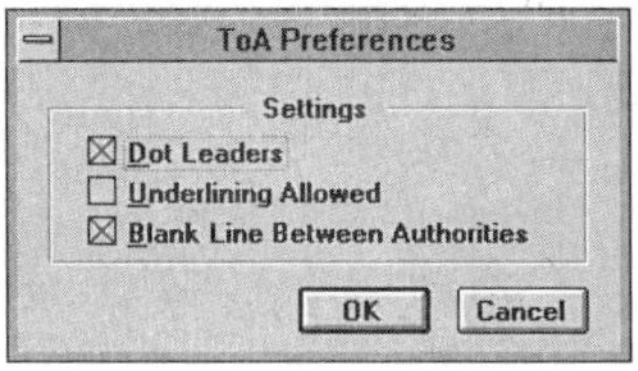

FIG. 29.23

The ToA Preferences dialog box.

Customizing the Equation Editor

When you activate the Equation Editor, in the Equations Setting dialog box you can change the font size and the alignment of an equation within the equation box, as well as decide whether the equation prints as graphics. The Equations Settings dialog box also displays the keyboard being used.

The default setting for all these features can be changed in the Preferences menu. For a detailed discussion of these features and how they are used, see Chapter 27, "Using the Equation Editor." Pay particular attention to the sections on the equation keyboard and printing equations.

Standardizing Equation Settings

When you install WordPerfect, you access the Equation Settings dialog box with the Settings or File pull-down menu. The Equation Preferences dialog box is identical to the Equation Settings dialog box in all respects except that the Keyboard area has an active Select button, enabling you to choose a keyboard to use while you're in the Equation Editor (see fig. 29.24).

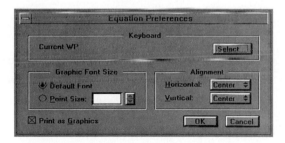

FIG. 29.24

The Equation Preferences dialog box.

You must be in the document window, not in the Equation Editor, to change these settings using Preferences as follows:

1. Choose File, Preferences.

    Press Preferences (Ctrl-Shift-F1).

2. Choose Equations.

The Equation Preferences dialog box appears.

Specifying a Graphic Font Size

The size of the font you used just before the equation, or the document's initial font size, usually determines the font size of your equation. You can permanently change the font size so that all equations are consistent. While in the document window, follow these steps:

1. In the Equation Preferences dialog box, choose Point Size.

2. In the text box, type the point size you want, or click the arrows to change the point size.

3. Choose OK to return to your document.

To return to the default font, follow the preceding steps and choose Default Font.

Changing Alignment

By default, WordPerfect centers an equation vertically and horizontally inside the equation's box. To space the equations differently, open the Preferences menu while you are in the document window, and follow these steps:

1. In the Equation Preferences dialog box, choose Horizontal or Vertical to access the pop-up Alignment list.

2. Choose Left, Center, or Right alignment; release the mouse button or press the space bar to close the box.

3. Choose OK to return to your document.

Choosing To Print as Graphics

Choosing to print equations as graphics enables WordPerfect to use the WordPerfect Character Set and to scale the elements of an equation as you choose. The equations print in WP Helvetica, WP Roman, or WP Courier, whichever is closest in appearance to the font in use just before the equation.

If you have a printer that has scalable fonts with adequate symbol fonts, you can turn off this feature and take advantage of your printer capabilities. To turn off Print as Graphics, follow these steps:

1. In the Equation Preferences dialog box, choose Print as **G**raphics.

2. Choose OK to return to your document.

Using an Equation Keyboard

Two equation keyboards, detailed in Chapter 27, come with WordPerfect. One is based on the CUA default keyboard but contains over 30 commands from the Equation Editor assigned to keystrokes. The other is based on the WordPerfect 5.1 keyboard and has no equation text assigned to it.

To use an equation keyboard while in the Equation Editor, you must first assign a keyboard to the Equation Editor by selecting it from the Preferences Equation Settings dialog box. The keyboard is not active until you open the Equation Editor. You can use any other keyboard while in the document window and at the same time have an equation keyboard selected to use whenever you open the Equation Editor.

You can also create an equation keyboard to suit your purposes and edit it any time after you create it. You can include commands that open dialog boxes, menu commands, text, symbols, and macros on the keyboard. All these features are identical to those available in the Preferences Keyboard Editor.

You begin the keyboard select/create/edit process as follows:

1. In the Equations Preferences dialog box shown in figure 29.24, choose **S**elect.

2. In the Keyboard dialog box (see fig. 29.25) choose the **C**urrent WP, **S**elect another equation keyboard, C**r**eate, or **E**dit an equation keyboard.

FIG. 29.25

The Keyboard dialog box.

When you choose Select, WordPerfect opens the Select Keyboard File dialog box. The CUA-based keyboard is named EQUATION.WWK and the 5.1-based keyboard is EQUDOS51.WWK. If you choose to create a keyboard, you begin with the CUA-based keyboard format in the Keyboard Editor. If you want to create a keyboard based on the WordPerfect 5.1 commands, you have to select the EQUDOS51.WWK equation keyboard and edit it to meet your specifications.

Once you have created or selected a keyboard, you can edit it freely. The steps for editing a keyboard are set out in the sections included under "Customizing Keyboards."

If you choose to edit the EQUATION.WWK keyboard, you can scroll through the text included in the Text list box and note the keyboard assignments for each as displayed in the Current Keystroke list box. You can delete or add text to this list.

Refer again to Chapter 27 for more information and strategies on creating and using equation keyboards.

Chapter Summary

By using the commands and options on the Preferences menu, you can change default settings and customize commands and features to suit your needs as a computer user. In this chapter, you learned to customize units of measure, a table of authorities, and the Equation Editor for specialized tasks. In addition to these features, you also learned to customize features and options to make your screen more understandable and to make your time at the computer more productive.

This chapter provides information to enable you to customize the location of your files, as well as to create both timed backups and original backups to protect your work. You learned how to use the Auto Code Placement and the Confirming on Code Placement features in your work. In addition, you learned how to customize the print job to meet your printing needs and how to use fast graphics printing to save time.

You learned to tailor the menu display and understand the advantages and disadvantages of working in WYSIWYG and Draft modes. You gained some control of what items to display on-screen—when to display scroll bars and hard return characters, for example. You also learned to customize hyphenation and merge preferences for a document. Finally, you learned to customize your keyboard, use Initial Codes, and manipulate the default date on documents.

By taking advantages of the options available to you through the Preferences menu, you can make your time on the computer more productive and enjoyable.

Advanced File Management Techniques

I n Chapter 3, you learned about basic, everyday file management procedures, such as copying, deleting, renaming, and so on. You learned primarily how to interact with the Open File dialog box and its file management procedures; you also learned to use the File Manager to browse through your directories and to create new ones.

WordPerfect's File Manager program is powerful and flexible. Just how does the File Manager help you become an expert user? Perhaps an analogy can answer that question. Suppose that you go to a library which has no card catalog. Furthermore, the books are placed randomly on the shelves. Every person who asks for help depends on a librarian's being able to find what is needed, but in order to do that the librarian has to have read *and* remembered everything in the collection, as well as memorized the location of each work.

■ **Read Gilgen** is Director of Learning Support Services at the University of Wisconsin, Madison. He has taught workshops on and written a series of articles about DOS and file management.

Fortunately, librarians have shelving systems, catalogs, and references in order to find and retrieve needed information efficiently. Likewise, your hard disk and collection of floppy disks become, over time, a massive library of information. Your computer effectiveness depends to a large extent on your ability to find and retrieve that information speedily. The File Manager, when used properly, can find materials quickly and easily, surpassing the retrieval capabilities of most libraries. To avoid learning about the File Manager is akin to counting on being able to find the exact library book you want simply by browsing through the stacks.

In this chapter, you learn how to use the File Manager to perform more quickly and efficiently many of the tasks you learned in Chapter 3. You also learn certain file management procedures that cannot be accomplished without using the File Manager.

You learn how to use the File Manager to perform the following tasks:

- Change directories
- Open, copy, and delete files
- Move, rename, and print files
- Find files on your hard disk
- Change the File Manager layouts
- Change file attributes
- Launch applications

The first portion of this chapter focuses on using the File Manager for commands you already know, such as Copy, Delete, and Move, and you learn how much more you can do with these commands in the File Manager. The last part of the chapter describes ways you can customize the File Manager and explains how you can make it automate the running of programs and editing of files.

T I P The WordPerfect File Manager is a program that can run by itself under Windows or as part of WordPerfect for Windows. To start the File Manager on its own, select the WP File Manager icon from the Windows Program Manager menu or window.

Understanding and Using File Manager Windows

For now, you should use the File Manager with WordPerfect. Start WordPerfect for Windows as you normally do; then start the File Manager: select **File**, **File Manager**. you should see two windows, as shown in figure 30.1. (Your display will vary depending on your current directory and its contents.)

■ **Cue:** To switch quickly between WordPerfect for Windows and the File Manager, press Alt-Tab to leave both programs active and enable you to move more quickly between them.

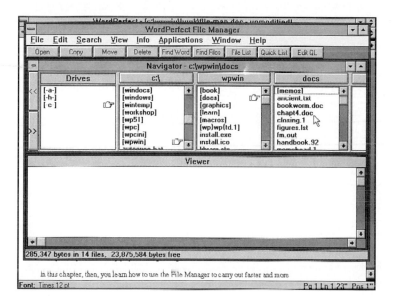

FIG. 30.1

WordPerfect's File Manager with the Navigator and Viewer windows.

The upper window is the Navigator, which helps you see the tree structure of the disk drive you select. This window is the active window. The lower window is the Viewer, which enables you to look at the contents of any file you select in the Navigator window.

Actually, four different windows can appear, depending on your preferences and changes made to the layout. The four File Manager window types, described in the following sections, include:

- The Navigator
- The Viewer
- The File List
- The Quick List

Using the Navigator

In Chapter 3, you learned how to browse your directories using the Navigator. The leftmost column of the Navigator displays all the currently available drives, including any network drives (see "Getting System Information" in this chapter). The second column of the Navigator displays a list of the directories and files in the root directory of drive C. To see additional subdirectories, you select a directory and press Enter (or double-click with the mouse). The File Manager enables you to open a virtually unlimited number of Navigator windows. Select View, Navigator, or simply press Ctrl-N. You then can browse through your directories using this second Navigator Window (see fig. 30.2).

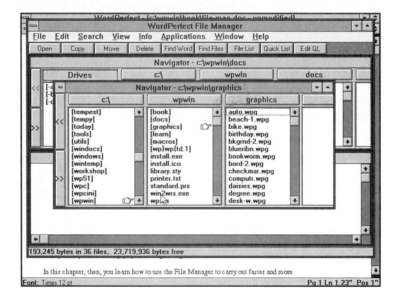

FIG. 30.2

Opening multiple Navigator Windows.

Using the Viewer

The Viewer displays the contents of any file you select while in the Navigator.

Cue: The Viewer window cannot display text and graphics at the same time; text is shown when both are included in a file.

The Viewer window correctly displays ASCII text, text created in WordPerfect (Versions 4.2 and later), WordPerfect graphics, and Windows 3.0 bit-mapped graphics (see fig. 30.3). Other documents may partially display, appear with "garbage" characters, or not display at all.

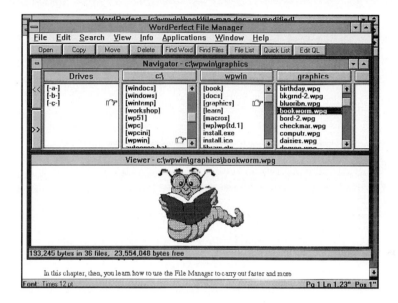

FIG. 30.3

The Viewer
window
displaying a
graphics file.

If for some reason the Viewer window is not displayed, you can open the Viewer by selecting **View**, **Viewer**, or simply by pressing Ctrl-V. You cannot display multiple Viewer windows.

If you continue to browse directories, the Viewer window retains the contents of the last file you selected until you select another file or exit the File Manager.

Using the File List

At times, while browsing with the Navigator, you find a list of files that you need to know more about. In the Navigator, only the file names are listed. The File List shows you size, date, and time information about files. Select **View**, **File List**, or press Ctrl-F. The File Manager displays a list of the files in the last (right-hand) column of the Navigator window, similar to the list in figure 30.4.

A more precise method of displaying files from the directory you want is to locate the name of the desired directory in the buttons above the Navigator columns. Clicking a column heading button automatically opens a File List for the directory you select (see fig. 30.5).

At the top of the window, you see the current path name. Directly beneath that name is a Dir text box displaying *.*, which means that all the files in the current path are displayed.

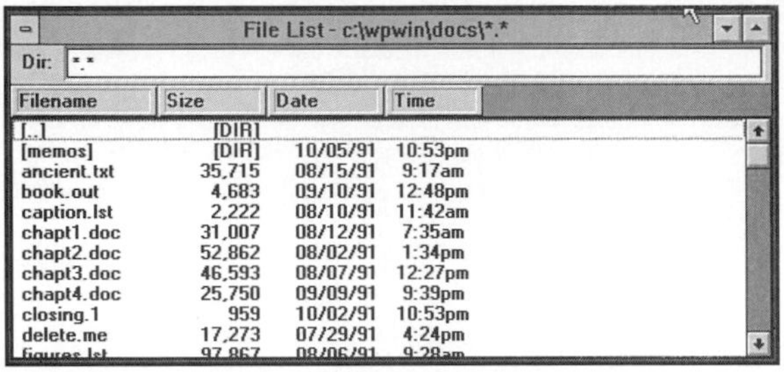

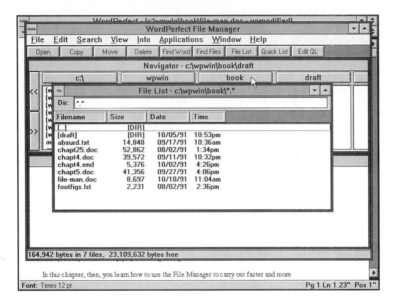

FIG. 30.4

The File
Manager's File
List.

FIG. 30.5

A File List
selected by
clicking a
Navigator
column button.

At the top of the list itself is [..] followed by [DIR]. These codes refer
to the parent directory (as in a genealogical chart). Other entries followed by [DIR] are subdirectories (or, to continue the analogy, "chil-
dren" of the current directory).

The file names are alphabetized by file name. Unlike the list of files you
get in WordPerfect's dialog boxes, the File List window also includes
information on the size in bytes and the date and time the files or directories were created or last modified. To select a file, move the cursor to
the file name and press Enter, or position the mouse pointer on the file
name and click. This file becomes the current (active or default) file,
and the commands you issue apply to this file. (You learn how to select
multiple files in "Copying Multiple Files" in this chapter.)

As with the Navigator, you can open virtually unlimited numbers of File
Lists.

Using the Quick List

In Chapter 3, you learned how to create and use Quick Lists. In the File Manager, you can open a Quick List window to help you change quickly and easily to your most frequently used directories. Select **View**, **Q**uick List, or simply press Ctrl-Q. You cannot display multiple Quick List windows.

Creating and editing a Quick List in the File Manager is the same as doing so from WordPerfect dialog boxes. See Chapter 3 for more information on creating and editing a Quick List.

Determining and Changing Active Windows

When you first start the File Manager, the Navigator window is active. The title bar in an active window is colored (on a color monitor) and contains both Minimize and Maximize buttons at the right side (see the Navigator window in fig. 30.1). Inactive windows, on the other hand, may be gray or dimmed and won't display the Minimize or Maximize buttons.

To change active windows, click with the mouse pointer anywhere inside the window you want to make active. You also can use the keyboard to switch from one File Manager window to the next by pressing Next Document (Ctrl-F6). If you have several windows open at once, using the mouse is probably better because pressing Ctrl-F6 cycles through all the open windows, one at a time.

 CAUTION: Knowing which window is active is extremely important. For example, you may have one file selected in one window but a different file selected in another window. If you use the delete command, you will delete the file in the active window only.

Closing File Manager Windows

You close File Manager windows just as you close WordPerfect documents. First, make sure that the window you want to close is active. Then press Ctrl-F4, or click the minus button to the left of the title bar of the active window and select **C**lose. Double-clicking the minus button also closes the window. (Refer to the Navigator window in figure 30.1 for the location of the minus button.)

If you experimented with several of the window types, your screen may be cluttered with windows. Later in this chapter, you learn to arrange your windows to use several at a time.

If you simply want to clear up your screen and start over again (a good idea at this point), close the File Manager program (Alt-F4). You are returned to WordPerfect. Then start the File Manager program again by selecting **F**ile, **F**ile Manager. The default Navigator and Viewer windows appear (again see fig. 30.1).

Using File Manager Commands

In Chapter 3, you learned how to use basic file management commands, all of which also are available in the File Manager. For example, you learned how to use the File Manager's **F**ile, **C**reate (or Ctrl-T) to create new directories. (Please see Chapter 3 to review these procedures or for more details.) Several optional command procedures, however, are available only in the File Manager.

Changing Directories

You can change directories in the Navigator, File List, or Quick List by using the procedures previously described. The File Manager also enables you to change a directory by selecting **F**ile, Chan**g**e, or by pressing Ctrl-G. The File Manager displays the Change Directory dialog box shown in figure 30.6.

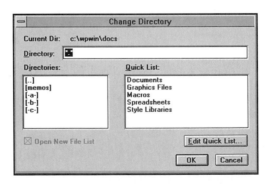

FIG. 30.6

The Change Directory dialog box in the File Manager.

The Change Directory dialog box displays the current directory at the top of the box. If you know what directory you want, simply type the full path name. If you are not sure of the directory name, you can

browse using the directory list in the left window, or select one of the
directories from your Quick List in the right window. When you find the
directory you want, select OK or press Enter. Pressing Esc or selecting
Cancel returns you to the File Manager without changing directories.

Unless you already have a File List displayed, after you select OK and
change directories, the File Manager automatically opens a File List
window to display the files in the directory you choose. If a File List is
already open, the Open New File List check box enables you to display
your new selected list in the already open File List (the default) or to
create a new File List for the new lists. You can open a virtually unlimited number of File Lists, using the Change Directory dialog box to select different directories for display.

■ **Cue:** You can use the
Change Directory dialog
box to edit your Quick List
(select the **E**dit Quick List
button and follow the
procedures you learned in
Chapter 3).

In WordPerfect, changing a directory, by default, also changes the
active or current directory for all dialog boxes that open files (Open,
Retrieve, Select, or Play). Changing a directory in the File Manager,
however, applies only to the active window in the File Manager. Likewise, changing a directory in the File Manager does not affect the
current or default directory in WordPerfect.

Opening a File

To open or retrieve a file, first select the file you want in the Navigator
or the File List window. Then select File, Open (or press Ctrl-O) and
select Open. An even easier method is simply to double-click the file
name, or select the file name and press Enter.

You cannot open a file from the Viewer or Quick List window. If either
of these windows is active when you press Ctrl-O, a dialog box appears
asking you to supply the name of the file you want to open.

You can select several files (but no more than nine) to open at
one time. See "Copying Multiple Files" for information on how to
select more than one file simultaneously.

T I P

Copying a File

To copy a single file, first select in the Navigator or the File List window
the file you want to copy. Then select File, Copy, or press Ctrl-C. The
File Manager displays the Copy File(s) dialog box, shown in figure 30.7.

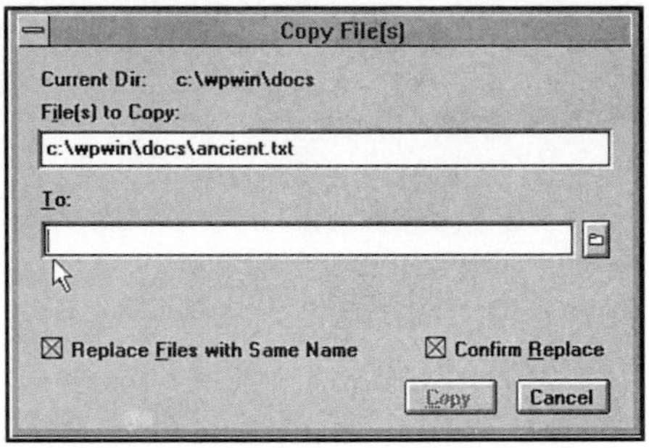

FIG. 30.7

The Copy File(s)
dialog box.

Copying files in the File Manager is nearly the same as copying files in
the Open dialog box in WordPerfect. The File Manager, however, has
four additional options:

- In the File(s) to Copy text box you can use wild-card characters
  (* or ?) to copy multiple files. For example, you can enter ***.RPT** to
  copy all the files whose names end in RPT.

- If you forget where you want to copy the files to, you can select
  the Folder icon at the right of the To text box, or press Alt and the
  up- or down-arrow key to open a Select Directory dialog box. Use
  this dialog box to find the target drive or directory you want. Selecting a drive or directory and choosing OK or pressing Enter
  copies the name of the drive or the path name of the directory
  into the To text box.

- The Replace Files with Same Name check box enables you to replace in the target drive or directory files that have the same
  names as files you are copying. Deselecting this option means that
  the File Manager won't even try to replace files with the same
  names.

- The Confirm Replace check box is displayed only if the Replace
  Files option has been selected. Deselecting this option means that
  the File Manager will replace files in the target drive or directory
  without prompting you first.

CAUTION: When you copy a file onto another by the same name,
the target file is erased and replaced by the new file. If
you're not sure about the name, stop the process and
use the File Manager's Viewer to view the target file
before you copy.

Copying Files by "Dragging and Dropping"

The power and advantages of the File Manager over WordPerfect's simple Open File options are even more evident in the File Manager's capability to use the mouse to copy files ("dragging and dropping" files) and to copy multiple files at one time.

If you have more than one file list on-screen (File List or Navigator or both), you can "drag and drop" files from one list to the other. Select the file you want by holding down the Ctrl key and the mouse button and moving the mouse horizontally until a Copy icon appears. Then move the Copy icon to the second file list and release the mouse button. If you move the icon to a location that cannot receive the copy (for example, to the Viewer), you see the international "no" symbol (a circle with a diagonal line through it— ⊘).

After you release the mouse button, the Copy File(s) dialog box appears with the information in the File(s) to Copy and To text boxes already filled in (again see fig. 30.7). Select OK or press Enter to copy the file. See "Copying Files," for other options.

Copying Multiple Files

Copying many files is tedious at best when you use WordPerfect's Open File Copy option. In the File Manager, however, selecting multiple files to copy simultaneously is easy. You can use the selection procedure described in this section anytime you want to copy, move, delete, open, or print more than one file at once.

Suppose that you have saved in your C:\WPWIN\DOCS directory Chapters 1 through 4 of the book you are working on, and that you now want to copy these chapters to the C:\BOOK directory. Because all four file names are listed consecutively, position the mouse pointer on the first and hold down the left mouse button while you drag the pointer to the last file in the group and then release the mouse button. You also can hold down the Shift key while you move the cursor up or down. All selected files appear in reverse video (see fig. 30.8).

You also want to include the outline, BOOK.OUT, with the chapters, but you don't want to include the CAPTIONS.LST file. To select noncontiguous files, hold down the Ctrl key and use the mouse to select the files you want. After you have selected all the files you want, release the Ctrl key.

■ **Cue:** To select multiple noncontiguous file names from a file list, hold down the Ctrl key and click each file name you want to select.

File List - c:\wpwin\docs*.*			
Dir:	*.*		
Filename	**Size**	**Date**	**Time**
[..]	[DIR]		
[memos]	[DIR]	10/05/91	10:53pm
ancient.txt	35,715	08/15/91	9:17am
book.out	4,683	09/10/91	12:48pm
captions.lst	2,222	08/10/91	11:42am
chapt1.doc	31,007	08/12/91	7:35am
chapt2.doc	52,862	08/02/91	1:34pm
chapt3.doc	46,593	08/07/91	12:27pm
chapt4.doc	25,750	09/09/91	9:39pm
closing.1	959	10/02/91	10:53pm
delete.me	17,273	07/29/91	4:24pm
figures.lst	97,867	08/06/91	9:28am

FIG. 30.8

Selecting multiple files in the File Manager.

After you select a group of files, you can select File, Copy (or press Ctrl-C). This time, however, the Copy File(s) dialog box looks different because you are about to copy several files (see fig. 30.9).

Copy File(s)

Current Dir: c:\wpwin\docs

Files to Copy:

c:\wpwin\docs\book.out
c:\wpwin\docs\chapt1.doc
c:\wpwin\docs\chapt2.doc
c:\wpwin\docs\chapt3.doc
c:\wpwin\docs\chapt4.doc

To Directory:

0 of 5 files copied
0 of 160,895 bytes copied

0%

☒ Replace Files with Same Name   ☒ Confirm Replace

[Copy]   [Skip]   [Copy All]   [Cancel]

FIG. 30.9

The Copy File(s) dialog box for copying multiple files.

The Copy File(s) dialog box lists the full path names of all files to be copied. You still must indicate the directory or drive to which they will be copied. Type the path name of the target drive or directory, or use the Folder icon at the right to select from among your drives or directories.

The text box at the bottom of the Copy File(s) dialog box shows by percentage how many files have been copied and how many remain. The two check boxes for replacing files with the same name are the same as the check boxes for copying single files.

You have the following options for copying selected files:

- Copy **A**ll tries to copy all files you have marked.

- **C**opy and **S**kip enable you to copy files selectively, that is, to copy some and skip others from the list.

If you copy to a floppy drive and the disk gets full before all the selected files have been copied, the File Manager stops and prompts you to remove the full disk and to insert another disk before continuing.

Deleting Files

By now it should be clear that the File Manager is considerably more powerful than WordPerfect's Open File options for copying. The following sections describe similar advantages for deleting and moving or renaming files.

To delete a single file, first select the file you want to delete in the Navigator or the File List window. Then select Fi**l**e, **D**elete or press Ctrl-D. The File Manager displays the Delete File(s) dialog box (see fig. 30.10).

FIG. 30.10

The Delete File(s) dialog box.

Deleting files in the File Manager is nearly the same as deleting files in the Open dialog box in WordPerfect. However, in the **F**ile(s) to Delete text box, you can use wild-card characters (* or ?) to delete multiple files. For example, you can enter ***.91** to delete all the files whose names end in 91.

CAUTION: The Delete File(s) dialog box is the only warning you get that you are about to delete a file, so be careful. After the file is gone, you cannot retrieve it, unless you have MS-DOS 5.0 or a utility that enables you to recover deleted files.

If you accidentally delete a critical file, immediately get help or use a file-recovery program, such as Norton Utilities. The longer you wait, the less likely you can recover deleted files.

Before you delete a large number of files, make sure that you have backup copies of your critical files. Accidentally deleting the wrong files is just too easy when you work with many different files at once.

Deleting Multiple Files

Deleting multiple files is similar to copying multiple files. Use the same methods to select the files you want to delete; then select **F**ile, **D**elete or press Ctrl-D. The Delete File(s) dialog box (see fig. 30.11) then gives you the following options:

■ Delete **A**ll deletes all the listed files without further warning.

■ **D**elete and **S**kip enable you to delete files selectively from the list.

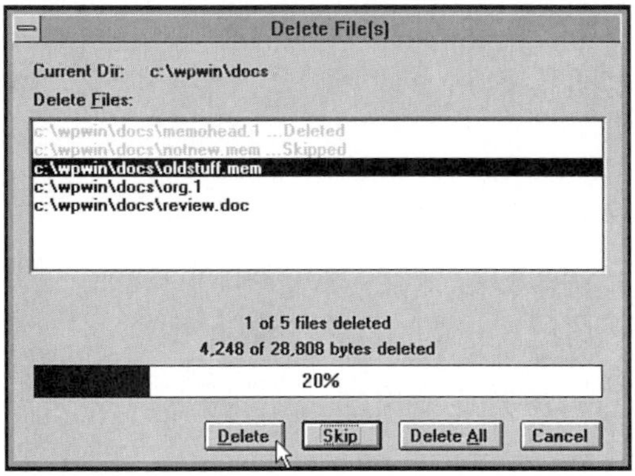

FIG. 30.11

Deleting multiple files with the Delete File(s) dialog box.

The text box at the bottom tells you how many files you are about to delete, how much disk space is taken up by those files, and the percentage of deletion that has been completed (after you begin deleting the files).

Deleting (Removing) a Directory

You also can delete an entire directory by selecting a directory entry from the Navigator or File List and then pressing Ctrl-D (or selecting **F**ile, **D**elete). If you want to delete the C:\WPWIN\BOOK directory, for example, the normal Delete File(s) dialog box first appears. If the name you specify in the Delete **F**iles text box is a directory name and you choose **D**elete, a Delete Directory/File(s) dialog box appears, as shown in figure 30.12.

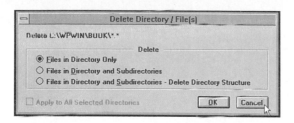

FIG. 30.12

The Delete
Directory/File(s)
dialog box.

You then have the following options for deleting a directory:

- Delete all the files contained in the selected directory, but leave the directory structure and other subdirectories as they are (the default)

- Delete all the files contained in the selected directory as well as in any subdirectories of the selected directory

- Delete all the files contained in the selected directory and its subdirectories, and remove the directory structure (the directory names)

After making your selection, choose OK. Select Cancel or press Esc to abort the process.

 **WARNING:** The capability to delete entire directories requires extra caution because of its destructive nature. Be sure that you know what you are deleting before you proceed.

Renaming and Moving Files

Many procedures described in this chapter build on the simple procedures you learned in Chapter 3. The purpose of these file management commands is to help you better organize and maintain your collection of files. Being able to move or rename files is just one part of good file management practice.

Renaming a file with its path is essentially the same as moving a file, in that by renaming the file you move it to a new location, either to a new name or to a new directory.

To move (or rename) a single file, first, in the Navigator or the File List window, select the file you want to move. Then select File, Move/Rename or press Ctrl-R. The File Manager displays the Move/Rename File(s) dialog box, shown in figure 30.13.

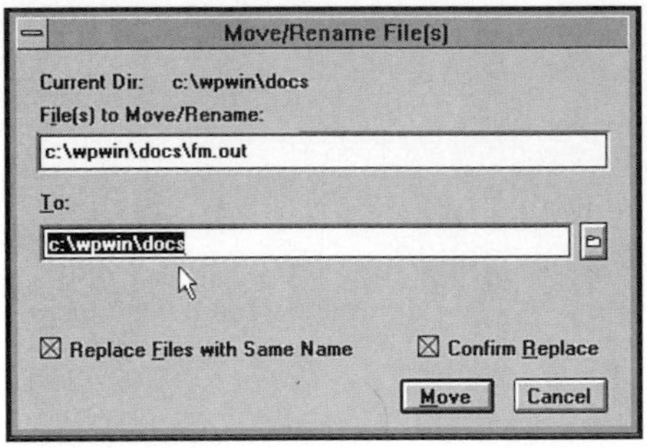

FIG. 30.13

The Move/
Rename File(s)
dialog box.

Moving files in the File Manager is nearly the same as deleting files in the Open dialog box in WordPerfect. The dialog box is identical to the File Manager's Copy File(s) dialog box in that you can use wild cards, select a To directory from the Folder icon, or replace with or without confirmation files with the same name (see "Copying Files").

The only difference between the Copy File(s) and Move/Rename File(s) dialog boxes is that in the latter the directory already is listed in the To text box. All you must do is add the new file name to rename the file. If you want to move the file, enter a new directory name but don't add the file name (unless you also want to change the name). When you are ready to rename or move the file, select **M**ove or press Enter.

■ **Cue:** When you move files, you copy and delete in one operation.

Moving or renaming a file accomplishes the following tasks simultaneously:

- ■ Copies the file to the new location (or to a new name)

- ■ Deletes the original copy (or name)

Whenever you select multiple files, the File Manager assumes that you want to move them, so the dialog box looks just like the Copy File(s) dialog box (refer to fig. 30.9). Again, select the destination directory and then select the appropriate replacement options (see "Copying Multiple Files" for information on selecting multiple files). You have the following options for moving your files:

- ■ Move **A**ll moves all the listed files, if possible, to the destination directory.

- ■ **M**ove and **S**kip enable you to move files selectively, that is, to move some and skip others from the list.

The text box at the bottom again shows the number of files involved and the percentage of the process that has been completed.

If you have more than one File List displayed (File List or Navigator) you can "drag and drop" files from one list to the other. Select the file or group of files you want to move by holding down the mouse button and moving the mouse horizontally until a Move icon appears. Then move the Move icon to the second file list and release the mouse button. If you try to move the icon to a location that cannot receive the copy, you see the international "no" symbol (a circle with a diagonal line through it).

Move selected files with the mouse by holding down the left mouse button and moving horizontally until the Move icon appears. Copy selected files by first holding down the Ctrl key and then holding down the left mouse button and moving horizontally until the Copy icon appears.

T I P

Printing Files from the File Manager

More often than not, you create, save, and then print a document while working in WordPerfect. Sometimes, however, you want a quick printed copy of something you already have created. You can avoid having to retrieve a file before printing by having the File Manager print the document.

To print a single file from the File Manager, you first select the file you want printed. If you have the Viewer window active, you can verify the file before printing, although the Viewer doesn't show special formatting or graphics. To print the file, select File, Print (or press Ctrl-P) and choose Print. After the file prints, press Alt-Tab to switch from the editing screen to the File Manager.

If you cannot print the file as is, WordPerfect tells you that the file must be formatted for the current printer or that the format is incompatible with the WordPerfect or Windows printer driver.

Finding Files

With today's larger hard disks, you can store literally thousands of files on one disk. Finding a file, therefore, can be a daunting task. You have learned about the File Manager's tools for browsing directories to find specific file names. Using this approach has two major disadvantages:

■ Directories may contain so many files that scanning the file names to find the one you want is impractical.

■ A given file name may seem entirely adequate for describing the contents of a file when you first create it. Only days later, however, the file name may no longer be meaningful.

In Chapter 3, you learned how to use the Find option in the Open File dialog box for finding files by their names or by words found in the files themselves. See Chapter 3 if you need to refresh your memory concerning file name and word searches.

These features work exactly the same in the File Manager, but as you expect, the File Manager offers several more options for helping you find just the file or files you want. For example, with the File Manager's Advanced Find option, you can search for files by the date they were last saved.

Searching the File List and Viewer Windows

The File Manager can search active File List or Viewer windows for specific strings of characters. This feature works much like WordPerfect's Search feature, except that you cannot search for codes. To search for words in an active window, select Search, Search Active Window or press F2. A dialog box similar to the one shown in figure 30.14 appears. If the Viewer is active, `Viewer Search` appears on the title bar. If the File List is active, `File List Search` appears.

FIG. 30.14

The File List Search dialog box.

■ **Cue:** If the Search commands appear dimmed on the menu, your active window is a Navigator or Quick List window, not a Viewer or File List Window.

Suppose that you are looking for the file you created for Chapter 4 of a book you are writing. Searching in the File List, you can search for text strings such as *chap* or *4*. You find the file name you are looking for, but what appears in the Viewer doesn't seem right. You can then switch to the Viewer window and search for the word *Manager*, which you know is in the Chapter 4 file.

When doing a search, if the first occurrence is not the one you want, you can repeat the search by selecting **S**earch, Search **N**ext (or by pressing Shift-F2) until you find the text you want. If you begin at a location other than the beginning of the list or viewed document, select **S**earch, Search **P**revious (or press Alt-F2) to repeat the search backwards.

■ **Cue:** You can search File Lists and Viewer documents by using the WordPerfect commands **S**earch (F2), Search **N**ext (Shift-F2), and Search **P**revious (Alt-F2)

Using Search Patterns in Find File and Find Word Searches

Active window searches, as already explained, look only for exact matches to one string of characters and search only in the active window. Find File and Find Word searches, however, enable you to search directories, subdirectories, and even entire disk drives and to use wild cards or logical operators. (See Chapter 3 for more information on searching directories for file names or searching the contents of files for specific words.)

The following are examples of valid search patterns that use wild cards:

Pattern	Files Selected May Contain
report	*report*
ma?y	*Mary, Macy, many,* and so on
"find file"	Only the exact phrase: *find file*
"find file*"	Finds an exact pattern as part of something longer: *find file, find files, find filename*

The following are examples of valid searches that use logical operators:

Pattern	Files Selected Contain
Mary Johnson or Mary;Johnson	*Mary* and *Johnson*
Mary,Johnson	*Mary* or *Johnson*
Fred,Mary;Johnson	*Fred* or *Mary* and also *Johnson*
Johnson "sales rep"	*Johnson* and the exact phrase *sales rep*
-Smith	Does not contain *Smith*
hard-headed	Contains *hard* but not *headed*

TIP Remember that you can include WordPerfect special characters in the search pattern by pressing Ctrl-W (or selecting F**o**nt, **W**ordPerfect Characters) and selecting the character you want. (See Chapter 28 for information about special characters.)

Using Advanced Find

If the preceding methods still aren't enough to help you find the file or files you need, you can use the Advanced Find feature to search an active window by selecting **S**earch, **A**dvanced Find, or by pressing Ctrl-F2. The File Manager displays the Advanced Find dialog box (see fig. 30.15).

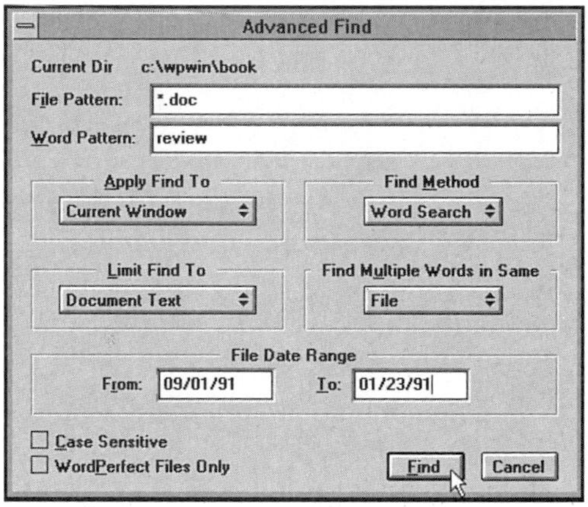

FIG. 30.15

The Advanced Find dialog box with search criteria entered.

This dialog box combines several of the search features found in other Search menus and adds some new features. Among the things you can do are the following procedures:

- You can specify a file pattern in the F**i**le Pattern text box.
- You can specify a word pattern in the **W**ord Pattern text box. You can combine both File and Word searches; for example, you can search for *review* in all files that fit the pattern **.DOC.*
- You can apply the search to the current window, only to selected items, to an entire directory, to subdirectories, or to an entire drive. You access the pop-up menu for this option by pointing to the scroll button with the mouse and pressing the left mouse

button, or by selecting the scroll button and pressing the space bar. The next three options work the same way.

- If you specify a word pattern, you can select the Find **M**ethod that is used to find that pattern. Word Search uses the methods described in "Using Search Patterns in Find File and Find Word Searches," and String Search looks for an exact match to the string of characters. If you did not specify a word pattern, this option is dimmed.

- If you specify a word pattern, you can limit the search to specific parts of documents, including only the text of a document; the first page of a document; or text from fields of the document summary, such as author, typist, keywords, and so on.

- If you specify multiple words in your word pattern, you can limit the search for these words to an entire file or to a page, section, paragraph, or sentence.

- You can limit your search to files that were last modified between dates you specify. You type the dates in the format MM/DD/YY (for example, 01/23/92).

- If you specify a word pattern, you can make the search find only words that match both characters and case. For example, selecting a **C**ase Sensitive search for *WordPerfect* finds *WordPerfect* but not *Wordperfect*.

- You can limit your search to WordPerfect files only, or search all files that meet the other search criteria.

The possible combinations for search criteria are truly amazing. With this added power, however, comes the increased likelihood that you will make mistakes as you set up your searches. If a search doesn't yield the results you expect, select **S**earch, **A**dvanced Find again. The criteria you just used for your search appear. Examine your choices and make changes as necessary to perform the search you want.

Narrowing a Search

When you choose Find, the File Manager searches for files or words that match the patterns you have specified. It then lists the results, that is the file names, in a Search Results window, which is identical to a File List window.

Suppose that the File Manager finds several files which match your criteria but too many for you easily to find the file you want. You can further narrow your search by changing the criteria and applying the search to just the active window (that is, the Search Results window).

You can repeat this process until the list is small enough for you to find the file you want.

Using the File Manager Button Bar

BUTTON

By default, WordPerfect displays a text-only Button Bar at the top of the File Manager window; this Button Bar contains some of the more commonly used file management commands (again see fig. 30.1). Selecting items from the menus can be tedious and time-consuming. Although using equivalent command keys is somewhat faster, the Button Bar is a much easier and faster way for you to select your commands. Chapter 19 discusses how to use and modify the Button Bar.

You select and deselect the File Manager Button Bar just as you do in WordPerfect. For example, to turn off the Button Bar, you select **View**, **B**utton Bar. Do this again to turn the Button Bar back on (a toggle feature).

Changing File Manager Layouts

The default File Manager layout consists of the Navigator in the top half of the File Manager window and the Viewer in the bottom half. Additional windows you choose, such as File Lists, the Quick List, or Search Results windows, appear on top of these two windows.

Although the Navigator is a useful and powerful tool, you may find that a different combination—of File Lists and the Quick List, for example— better serve your needs.

Selecting a Defined Layout

You can select from among six defined layouts, by choosing **View**, **Lay**outs. Then choose from the following:

1 Wide Navigator, Viewer (default)

2 Wide File List, Viewer

3 Narrow File List, Viewer

4 File List, Viewer

5 Quick List, File List, Viewer

6 Navigator, File List, Viewer

You can, of course, make any changes you want to the WordPerfect File Manager layout. This section gives some changes you can make and explains how to save your changes in your own layout.

Sizing the Windows

By default, the windows you see when you start the File Manager share equal space on-screen. This arrangement is referred to as *tiled* windows. You can change the size or position of either or both of the windows. You may, for example, want a narrow Navigator listing in order to have a larger viewing area.

You can use the mouse to drag the sides or the corners of your WordPerfect File Manager windows until they are positioned exactly where you want them. Figure 30.16 shows a layout with a large Viewer and two relatively small File Lists. (See your Windows manual for details on moving and sizing windows.)

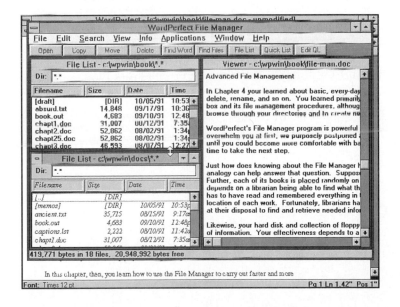

FIG. 30.16

A customized WordPerfect File Manager layout.

To return your windows layout to an evenly shared arrangement, you *tile* them by selecting **W**indow, **T**ile from the WordPerfect File Manager menu or by pressing Shift-F4.

If you have many windows, tiling may make them too small to be of practical use. In this case, you can *cascade* the windows by selecting **W**indow, **C**ascade from the WordPerfect File Manager menu (or by pressing Shift-F5). A portion of each window is then always visible, and you click the visible part of a window to bring it to the front and make it active. You also can select a window from the menu by selecting **W**indow and choosing from the windows listed.

If you experiment with your layout to the point that it becomes hopelessly messed up, you can quickly restore some degree of order by tiling or cascading the File Manager windows.

Customizing the File List Column Headings

By default, the column headings for the File List are Filename, Size, Date, and Time. You can add Full Path, Attributes, Desc. (Descriptive) Name, and Desc. Type. (The latter two are based on information you provide in the Document Summary for documents you create).

To remove a column heading, position the mouse pointer on the column heading button and drag it off the column heading bar.

To add a column heading, position the mouse pointer on the column heading bar and hold the left mouse button down. A list of column heading options appears (see fig. 30.17). Selecting the heading you want places it on the column heading bar.

You can rearrange the buttons by dragging them left or right. You also can resize them by positioning the mouse pointer on the left or right edge of the button until a double arrow appears and then dragging the edge left or right.

Changing Fonts

By default, the displays in the WordPerfect File Manager windows are in boldfaced Helvetica type. You can change this font as follows:

1. Select the window you want to change.

2. Select **V**iew, **F**ont (or press F9).

3. Select the font, point size, boldface and/or italic from the Font dialog box.

4. Choose OK.

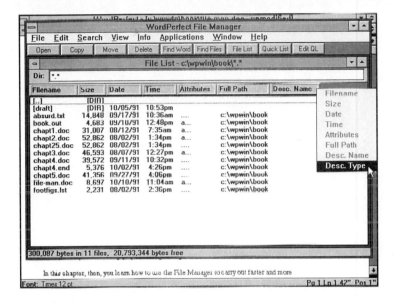

FIG. 30.17

Adding a
column heading
to a customized
File List.

The font changes the display of the current window only (for example,
see the second File List in fig. 30.16). Changing the active window font
does not affect the files themselves or how they print.

You can display more text in the Viewer window by reducing the
font size.

T I P

Saving Layouts

After you set up a custom layout, you need to save it before exiting the
File Manager. To save your layout, select View, Layouts, Setup from
the WordPerfect File Manager menu. The Window Layouts dialog box
appears (see fig. 30.18).

In the Layout Name text box, type the descriptive name you want to
use for your layout; then select Save. The current layout is saved under
the new name.

Making sure that the Save Current Layout On Exit option under File,
Preferences is not selected is a good idea (see Chapter 29, "Customizing WordPerfect with Preferences"). When this option is not selected,
inadvertent changes you may make to your layout are not saved.

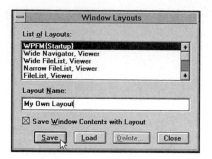

FIG. 30.18

The Window
Layouts dialog
box.

Changing the Start-Up Layout

The WPFM{Startup} definition is listed among the layout names in the List of Layouts (again see fig. 30.18). This layout is used when you start the WordPerfect File Manager, but you can select a different layout as the default or start-up layout.

If, for example, you want to make your new layout the start-up layout, you select WPFM{Startup} from the list (so that it appears in the Layout Name box); then select Save to save your customized layout as the new start-up layout.

Now when you start the File Manager, your own special layout is used.

Getting System Information

The WordPerfect File Manager enables you to check your system resources and print information about them. For most people, this capability generally is a mere curiosity. For those who provide support for end users, however, this feature can be valuable in determining and solving problems.

To view this information, select Info from the WordPerfect File Manager menu. You can access the following types of information:

■ *System information.* Indicates the DOS version, the number of reported drives, the processor type, whether a math co-processor is installed, and the number of parallel and serial ports reported (see fig. 30.19)

Note that several items are reported to the File Manager by other parts of your computer system. If other software, hardware, or the Windows system itself is not set up properly, the report you get may differ from the actual setup.

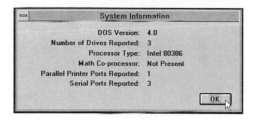

FIG. 30.19

File Manager's System Information report.

- *Windows information.* Indicates the Windows version, operating mode (386 Enhanced, for example), the type of system (MS-DOS), network, keyboard, shell being used, type of mouse, screen display, language, loaded and run programs, and amount of free memory

- *Printer information.* Shows Windows-installed printers only, not those driven by WordPerfect printer drivers

- *Disk information.* Indicates type of drives; volume name; and total, free, and used disk space

You can print any of this information by selecting **Info**, Print Info **Re**port. You have the option of printing to the printer or saving the information to a file.

Changing File Attributes

Every file stored on your disk carries not only the data you create but also bits of file information that tell the disk operating system (DOS) how to deal with that file. These system-level attributes take precedence over commands issued by applications or DOS.

The four system-level attributes are described in the following paragraphs.

- *Read-Only.* This attribute prevents a file from being modified or deleted. The file can be opened, modified in WordPerfect, and then saved under a different name. The file also can be copied. This attribute ensures that the original copy is protected from inadvertent changes.

- *Hidden.* This attribute keeps a file from appearing in the DOS directory or WordPerfect file listing. You still can view the file in the File Manager File List window by selecting **View**, **Options** and then selecting the Hidden/System Files option in the Display in List box. This option is sufficiently buried in the menus that hiding files will more than likely keep them hidden.

■ *Archive*. This attribute tells DOS whether the file has been backed up since the last time it was modified. Selecting this attribute forces DOS BACKUP or any other backup program to include the file in a backup even if it hasn't been modified. Deselecting this attribute excludes the file from a backup even if it has been modified.

■ *System*. Files with this attribute are special files required by your computer's operating system. You can display these files, but you should never delete or modify system files. This attribute is only for your information and serves to warn you not to change or modify the file or its file attributes. Doing so may render the file unusable for its intended application.

> **WARNING:** Never delete, modify, or change the attribute for system files.

To change the attributes of a file, follow these steps:

1. Select the file (or files) you want to change from a File List window.

2. Select **F**ile, Change **A**ttributes (or press Ctrl-A). The Change File Attributes dialog box appears (see fig. 30.20).

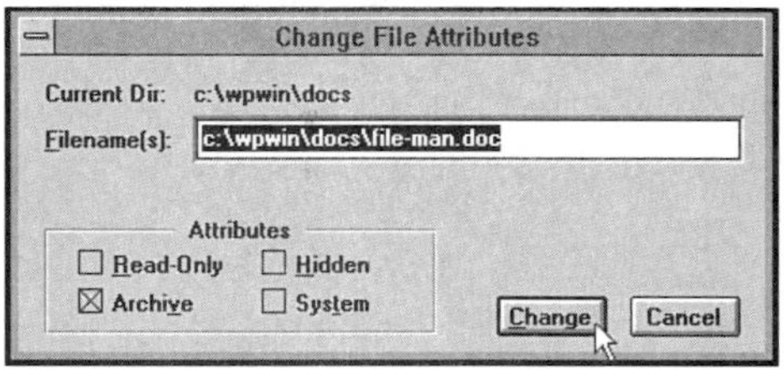

FIG. 30.20

The Change File Attributes dialog box.

3. Select the check box(es) for the attributes you want to change.

4. Select **C**hange or press Enter.

Note that you can set all four attributes at once.

You can change the attributes of entire directories by selecting the directory and then selecting **F**ile, Change **A**ttributes from the WordPerfect File Manager menu. After you select your options and select **C**hange, you get another dialog box asking whether you want to change only the files in the directory or all files in the subdirectories as well as all files in the directory.

If you change a file's attribute to Hidden, you cannot see the file or change its attributes again because it is hidden even from the File Manager. To remove the Hidden attribute from the file, you must first select **V**iew, **O**ptions from the WordPerfect File Manager menu and choose to display hidden files. Then you can deselect the Hidden attribute.

Printing and Saving Information from the File Lists

At times you want to keep the information displayed in one or more of your File Manager lists. For example, you may set up a database application and need a printed list of the program files in order to document what you have done.

The File Manager enables you to copy your lists, by means of the Clipboard, to a WordPerfect file or to a printer.

Using the Clipboard

You can use the Clipboard to create or compile names of files from selected items in your active windows. If, for example, you want to obtain a complete list of all files in your C:\BOOK directory, you select the directory so that it is displayed in your File List and then follow these steps:

1. Select **E**dit, **S**elect All (or press Ctrl-S).

   All the files in the list are selected. If Select All is not available on the menu (if it is gray), select **E**dit, **U**nselect All (or press Ctrl-U) first. Note that you cannot select a file listing from the Viewer window.

2. Select **E**dit, **C**opy to Clipboard (or press Ctrl-Ins).

The list of files is copied to the Clipboard. If you have another list of files in another window, or you select a new list for your active window, you repeat the first step to select that list, but then press Alt-Ins to append the second list to the end of the first list.

When you are finished, you can switch back to WordPerfect and paste the contents of the Clipboard into a document.

If you want to copy just the file names to the Clipboard, select files from the Navigator window, or while in the File List window, use the mouse to drag off the column headings for everything except the file names. Then select the files and copy to the Clipboard.

For more information on using the Clipboard, see Chapter 31, "Importing Data and Working with Other Programs."

Printing File Lists

The method described in the preceding section enables you to create files of your lists that then can be modified or formatted in WordPerfect before printing.

If you simply want a straight printout of the list of files in an active File List, select File, Print Window from the WordPerfect File Manager menu. A dialog box offers you the option of printing the entire list or just the files you have selected.

If you want more or less information in your printout, again in an active File List, add or remove the column header buttons before printing (see "Changing File Manager Layouts" in this chapter). Otherwise, the columns you have selected print with a header that includes the date and time of the printout.

Launching Applications

When you start a program in the Windows environment, you actually make a request to "launch" that program. For example, when you start WordPerfect, you probably select the WordPerfect icon from the Windows Program Manager. The Program Manager, in turn, checks its resources to determine where the WordPerfect files are located and, without any other intervention on your part, starts the WordPerfect program.

The WordPerfect File Manager also can launch programs. You can set up the File Manager so that it starts programs as you request them, or you can ask the File Manager to open a file and by association the File Manager automatically starts the proper program before opening the requested file.

Adding Applications to the File Manager

You probably will not do all your computer work in WordPerfect. You may also use an electronic mail, spreadsheet, or database program. With the WordPerfect File Manager Applications feature, you can set up these programs so that you can easily access them from the File Manager.

To add a program to the File Manager's Applications menu, follow these steps while using File Manager:

1. Choose **A**pplications, **A**ssign. The Applications dialog box appears (see fig. 30.21).

```
┌─────────────────────────────────────────┐
│ ═              Applications              │
│ List of Applications:                    │
│ ┌──────────────────────────────────────┐│
│ │WordPerfect                           ││
│ │WordPerfect Macro Facility            ││
│ │Speller                               ││
│ │                                      ││
│ └──────────────────────────────────────┘│
│ Descriptive Name:                        │
│ ┌──────────────────────────────────────┐│
│ │All Alone But Having Fun              ││
│ └──────────────────────────────────────┘│
│ Command Line:                            │
│ ┌────────────────────────────────────┬─┐│
│ │c:\windows\sol.exe                  │□││
│ └────────────────────────────────────┴─┘│
│ ☐ Send Selected Files to this Application│
│ [ Add ] [Change] [Delete] [ OK ] [Cancel]│
└─────────────────────────────────────────┘
```

FIG. 30.21

The Applications dialog box.

The List of Applications area in the dialog box lists the applications you already have set up. If you want to change an application in this list, select the application and then select Change.

2. Type a description in the Descriptive **N**ame box. For example, you might describe the Windows Solitaire game as **All Alone But Having Fun**.

3. In the Command **L**ine box, enter the DOS command that Windows must use to start the program (C:\WINDOWS\SOL.EXE, for example). You also can choose the appropriate executable file by using the Folder icon at the right of the text box and browsing to find the file you want.

4. Select **A**dd and then choose OK to add this program to your list of applications.

To run the application, you no longer need to exit or minimize the File Manager. Simply choose **A**pplications and select the program you want to run (All Alone But Having Fun, for example).

The Applications list is limited to 15 applications.

Associating Applications with Files

Many files on your disk have certain characteristics that identify them as having been created by a specific application. For example, WordPerfect files have unique file headers, some spreadsheets have formats understood only by spreadsheet programs, and so on.

You can tell the WordPerfect File Manager to associate certain types of files you are using with the applications that were used to create them. Then the File Manager can automatically start the proper application when you select a file.

You may, for example, have several files you created with WordStar before you began using WordPerfect. Because WordPerfect can detect WordStar files and can convert them to a WordPerfect format, you want the WordPerfect File Manager to know that any WordStar file you select should automatically start the WordPerfect program and then open the WordStar file.

Other files may not have a unique structure but may have unique file name extensions. You also can have the WordPerfect File Manager start an application when you select a file with a specific file extension. Files with the PLN extension, for example, can automatically start in the PlanPerfect application.

Automatic start-up of associated applications works only when the WordPerfect File Manager is started first from the Windows Program Manager. If you start WordPerfect first and then start the WordPerfect File Manager, the latter is "linked" to WordPerfect, and everything you try to open is sent to WordPerfect.

To set up (or verify) associated applications, select **F**ile, **P**references, **A**ssociate. The Associate dialog box appears (see fig. 30.22).

Suppose that you need to edit standard DOS text files (such as INI, or initialization files) and want to use a text editor rather than Word-Perfect. You can *associate* the text editor with these files in two ways:

■ Text files are considered a *type* of file. That is, the WordPerfect File Manager can tell whether they are text files or some other format. Therefore, you can associate the DOS text file type with your text editor.

■ If you want to associate just initialization (INI) or batch (BAT) files, for example, you can associate these file extensions with your text editor.

The associated file types information is stored in the WPFM.INI file, usually located in your \WPC directory. The associated file extensions information is stored in your WIN.INI file, usually in your \WINDOWS directory. You can edit or add to either of these files directly from your text editor.

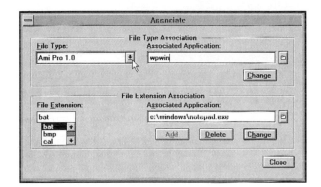

FIG. 30.22

The Associate
dialog box.

Using the WordPerfect File Manager as a Program Manager

Using the combined power of the Applications and Associate features, you can set up the File Manager as your primary program manager.

Consider, for example, that the majority of work you do is related to documents of one type or another. If you start the File Manager first, you can open any of your documents, and the proper application automatically starts.

For new documents, you can select the application from the application menu (WordPerfect, for example). But you also can select executable files (applications) from the File List by selecting File, Run from the WordPerfect File Manager menu or by double-clicking the application's file name (NOTEPAD.EXE, for example).

The WordPerfect File Manager is set up to recognize that file names with EXE, COM, or PIF extensions are applications and should automatically be run when selected.

Most automatic launch (or run) features work only if you start the WordPerfect File Manager separately from the Windows Program Manager. They do not work if you link the WordPerfect File Manager to WordPerfect by starting the File Manager from within WordPerfect.

Chapter Summary

The WordPerfect File Manager is a powerful yet easy-to-use program. It is simple enough for beginners, yet it offers tremendous flexibility and powerful features to meet the needs of almost any user. As you master the features discussed in this chapter and in Chapter 3, you will have the tools you need to manage your work more effectively.

In this chapter, you have learned to use the Navigator, Viewer, File List, and Quick List windows for working with your files. You can search for files based on file names and file contents. You have learned to customize and save WordPerfect File Manager layouts. You also can get (and print) information about your computer system, change file attributes, and print and save file lists. Finally, you can set up and use applications programs from the WordPerfect File Manager.

Importing Data and Working with Other Programs

I n most offices, so many tasks need to be done that people use several programs every day; they use word processors, spreadsheets, graphics programs, and databases, for example. When so many different programs are used, exchanging data from one program to another becomes a necessity.

One reason for the success of Windows is that it establishes standards for the sharing of information. For example, Windows requires programs to use certain data formats in the Clipboard, a utility that stores

■ **Steve Konicki** Is a computer consultant who specializes in Microsoft Windows and Windows applications.

data and oversees its exchange between programs. Because of these standards, the Clipboard can perform document conversions of simple text, complex formatting, detailed graphics, or spreadsheets, that other methods cannot. Windows also offers *Dynamic Data Exchange* (DDE), a sophisticated method of sharing data. DDE creates a link between the Windows program that created a data file and other Windows programs, such as WordPerfect. When data is changed in the originating program, the DDE link updates the data in WordPerfect.

WordPerfect for Windows takes the simplicity of the Windows graphical user interface to a new level of power with the capability of exchanging data between programs. As well as supporting the Windows Clipboard and DDE, WordPerfect provides its own tools for exchanging data between programs. WordPerfect can convert into its own format documents written in 42 other formats and translate its own documents into the same 42 formats. In addition, WordPerfect directly imports data from many of the most powerful spreadsheets.

Even with the powerful data exchange methods provided by WordPerfect and Windows, the conversion process is not always flawless. In today's offices, documents commonly have many elements that can complicate the conversion process. These elements include special tab placements, indents, font changes, mixed text justification, headers, footers, page numbering, styles, bullets, graphics, graphics text boxes, tables, and equations.

The newsletter shown in figure 31.1 illustrates many elements common to complex documents. The newsletter contains a graphics banner, some small graphics in the body of the text, newspaper-style columns, headlines and subheads, indents, font changes, and a schedule created as a WordPerfect graphics text box. Although you may never want to convert a document as complex as this newsletter, it is a good example because from time to time you may need to convert documents that include some of the elements used in the newsletter.

Cue: Learn the strengths of a number of conversion methods so that you will know which to use for a particular task.

No single conversion method will always be completely successful at translating documents like this newsletter from one word processor to another. Therefore, you need to learn the strengths of a number of conversion methods so that you will know which to use for a particular task. This chapter covers the following topics:

- Standard strategies for exchanging files between WordPerfect for Windows and other programs

- Alternative methods you can try if normal conversion methods do not produce acceptable results

- Some advanced conversion strategies

CASA TIMES

SEPTEMBER/OCTOBER, 1991

CASA COMMUNITY CLEAN-UP DAY WAS A ROUSING SUCCESS AND A GOOD TIME FOR ALL. THANK YOU FROM CASA TO ALL WHO CAME AND GAVE OF THEMSELVES.

MANAGER'S CORNER

The Camden Association for Senior Activity (CASA) Community Center is open from 7:00 am to 10:00 pm every weekday. Mel is in charge from 7 a.m. to 2 p.m.. We are staffing the remaining hours with volunteers for 2-hour shifts. Please sign up. Schedule your shift around a favorite activity! See Mel to sign up.

The appearance of the center has improved dramatically. To help keep it that way, maintenance/repair jobs need to be tackled quickly. If you are handy with a hammer, will recycle cans, run errands (Mel needs to stay on the premises!), whatever, let Mel know. We need volunteers.

In fact, we want to build a list of skills, talents, abilities that we can call upon occasionally. We know many of you can only offer your services from time to time. Please let us know the things we can call on you for. Fill in your name, phone # and skills on the back of the newsletter.

DANCING, CASA STYLE

CASA will be growing in 1992. The board has scheduled a fund-raising dance on Saturday, Nov. 28 at 9:30 pm. Admission is $3.00 at the door OR pre-pay your 1992 CASA dues and dance for free. Remember when it comes to dancing, age is not a number but a state of mind.

NOTES FROM THE BOARD

With all the new ideas and directions for the center, the Board has been kept hopping. Great progress has been made on completing the list of "manager jobs" mentioned in the last newsletter. Snack machines were approved, since health code will make a kitchen impossible.

We have increased membership dramatically, from 159 as of the membership meeting in July, to 280 fully-current members. Fourty-eight folks joined in August alone, and several paid for a year. We are grateful to see this happening now since the bookstore, snack machines and other improvements required startup funds.

SOCIAL COMMITTEE IS STARTING UP

Are you interested in assuring that CASA has enough social activities? Are you willing to do something about it? We are forming the social planning committee for the next year. Dances, picnics and holiday celebrations are just a few of the events we will need help with.

Our first planning committee meeting will be Saturday, Sept. 21, at 12:15 p.m. Please join use to help make CASA the kind of place where everyone in the community wants to spend time. Come and share your ideas even if you cannot serve on the committee.

THE CASA BOOKSTORE

Our new bookstore, which will feature new and used books of all kinds, is coming along very nicely. We are building our new book titles somewhat slowly, so that we can be sure to stock the books you really want. More are coming in all the time. But there is a large stock of used books. If there is a book you want or need, order it from us at the CASA Bookstore and help it become a real asset to the community. We also carry gift items, so drop by and see how we can serve you.

DONATIONS STILL NEEDED

We still need a display case with glass front, a typewriter or printer, a garden hose, an electric stapler. Also, coffee cups and a coffee urn, are desperately needed. It's deductable! Please drop off your recent newsmagazines. We serve cake, cookies and coffee every day between 2 p.m. and, drop by and help or just come by and have coffee and goodies.

YOU CAN BE INVOLVED

A very personal plea–CASA needs someone to write the newsletter. Bennie can't be Chairman of the Board AND editor AND writer of the newsletter. Writing skills not necessary. Just interest and enthusiasm.

BIRTHDAYS

Remember! Birthdays at CASA are celebrated the first Saturday, with a potluck dinner at 6:30. Bring a covered dish. Celebrate with us on October 5!

SUNDAY	MONDAY/FRIDAY	SATURDAY	CASA SCHEDULE
11:00 Box Lunch	7:00 Center Opens	11:00 Box Lunch	
6:15 Supper Together	11:30 Lunch Together	6:15 LifeStyles (Box Supper)	
8:00 CASA Tonight	6:15 Happy Hour Supper	1st Sat. Birthdays Potluck at 6:30	
8:00 BINGO (Room A)	8:00 CASA Tonight	8:00 CASA Tonight	
TUESDAY-Movies	Friday-CASA Bake Sale	THURSDAY-7:30 CASA Board Meeting - All are welcome!	

FIG. 31.1

A document like this newsletter can tax any conversion strategy.

These conversion strategies work with documents created in a wide range of programs, including word processors, spreadsheets, graphics programs, and databases.

Because most WordPerfect users will not use all the data exchange methods covered in this chapter, general information about conversion strategies is provided. These strategies are grouped by program type. When you need information on using another program's files in WordPerfect, you can refer to the section that deals with that type of program.

T I P You can skip this chapter if you intend to use only WordPerfect or you do not intend to share information between WordPerfect and other programs. Reading this chapter, however, may teach you techniques that help you use WordPerfect more effectively.

Understanding Conversion Strategies

Because in the past, sharing data files between computer programs was often a tedious and difficult task, you may not have given much thought to sharing data files. The ideal way to share information is for programs to use the same data formats. In reality, however, most computer programs create files in their own formats, and conversions of one kind or another are necessary. Today, however, WordPerfect makes exchanging files between programs much easier.

The following examples are just a few of the numerous scenarios in which conversion of data from another program into a WordPerfect document is beneficial:

- A letter written in another word processor has several pages you need immediately for a document you are writing in WordPerfect.

- A spreadsheet detailing your office's budget and expenditures for the last three months contains data you need for a report being prepared in WordPerfect.

- A graph showing your corporation's profit in the last fiscal year was prepared in a format not supported by WordPerfect, but you need it right away for a brochure you are preparing in WordPerfect.

- For an annual report being written in WordPerfect, you want to include information contained in a database file listing your firm's clients and the amounts they purchased from your firm last year.

- Your sales staff has prepared a slide show in one of the popular presentation graphics programs, and you want part of the show for an information package being prepared for the local media.

Often the goal of sharing data between WordPerfect and other programs is to retain not only the original file's content, but also its appearance. Each file-sharing problem listed can be solved by

WordPerfect, but converting a complex document is far from a perfect procedure. The conversion strategy depends on the job and project goal. A method that works well with one document may not work well with another. Use your imagination when converting a complex document and be patient enough to try several methods or, if necessary, a combination of methods.

CAUTION: Before you convert a file, make a backup in case the conversion does not work well. If one conversion technique doesn't work, you need a copy of the original file to try other methods.

The following list summarizes several conversion strategies:

- Use WordPerfect's Convert function to translate the file to WordPerfect format.

  WordPerfect's Convert function generally produces satisfactory results for files with uncomplicated formatting. Files with complicated formatting, such as graphics text boxes, tables, and graphics, do not convert properly. Therefore, use Convert only on document text, and then import any tables or graphics and rebuild the document.

- If the other word processor being used can translate files to WordPerfect format, use that program to convert the document.

  Using another word processor's conversion function to translate files to WordPerfect format usually produces a result similar to WordPerfect's Convert function. Experiment with WordPerfect and other programs you use often to see which program's conversion does a better job.

- Use the Windows Clipboard to copy all or part of the file, and paste the copied sections into WordPerfect.

  If a file contains graphics or complex formatting, using the Clipboard to copy the file into WordPerfect produces better results than a conversion. Like the Convert function, however, the Clipboard is not flawless. With some documents, a two-step conversion process is better: first copy the text into WordPerfect, and then copy the graphics. You may find that using WordPerfect's Convert on the document text and using the Clipboard to copy the graphic and rebuild the document is better.

- Use Windows Dynamic Data Exchange to import information into WordPerfect.

Using Windows Dynamic Data Exchange to import data from another Windows program into WordPerfect for Windows produces a satisfactory result when current, complete information is more important than appearance. DDE does not preserve the document's original formatting.

■ Save the original document in Rich Text Format (RTF) if the originating program supports RTF, and import the converted document into WordPerfect.

If WordPerfect cannot convert a document, but the word processor that created the document supports RTF (Rich Text Format), use RTF to save the file. RTF is a special type of formatting used by many Windows programs. RTF enables programs to exchange information about typefaces, font sizes, margins, tabs, and type attributes like boldface, italic, or underline. Exporting a document to WordPerfect in RTF yields an excellent result with formatted text. But RTF has no graphics conversion capabilities, so import graphics and text separately.

■ Use an intermediate format if the original program and WordPerfect support a common format.

With a document that WordPerfect is incapable of converting, convert the document into a third format supported by both the original word processor and WordPerfect. With this method, formatting may be saved, although how much depends on many factors, including how well the first program handles the conversion to the intermediate format.

■ Convert the file into generic DOS ASCII text and import that into WordPerfect.

If WordPerfect and the program that created a document do not share an intermediate format, you can use the original word processor to save the file in generic ASCII text and import the ASCII file into WordPerfect. Converting the file into ASCII yields the least desirable result because all formatting is lost; consequently, you must completely reformat the document. Convert a file to ASCII when you need unformatted text or when ASCII conversion is the only way to accomplish the task.

Converting Word Processing Files

This section discusses several different strategies for converting word processor files. The section begins with using WordPerfect's Convert to import documents from other word processors. You are likely to use this strategy most often. This section also covers the following:

- Using WordPerfect to convert its own files into the format used by other word processors

- Using other word processors to convert WordPerfect documents into the formats used by the other word processors

- Using Windows Clipboard and Dynamic Data Exchange to import documents, or parts of them, into WordPerfect

- Using a third word processor format as an intermediate format when WordPerfect and the program that originated a document do not share a common document format

Using WordPerfect's Convert

WordPerfect for Windows converts files from 42 word processor formats into WordPerfect format and converts its own files into the formats of these 42 word processors. The Convert function is internal to WordPerfect for Windows, not an external program as in Word-Perfect 5.1 for DOS. Therefore, conversions are faster and easier to do. The formats used by WordPerfect's Convert are listed in table 31.1.

Cue: Because the Convert function is internal to WordPerfect for Windows, conversions are faster and easier to do than in DOS.

Convert loads when you select a document for editing and WordPerfect detects that the file is not in WordPerfect format. For example, to open an Ami Pro document titled NOV30SUM.SAM, follow these steps:

1. Select WordPerfect's File menu and choose Open to display the Open File dialog box.

    Press Open File (F4),

   Alternatively, click Open on the Button Bar.

2. Exit your default WordPerfect document directory (assuming that is the directory you are in) by double-clicking the bracketed double periods [. .], which indicate that you are in a subdirectory.

   Alternatively, Tab to the directories list, press the space bar to highlight the bracketed periods, and press Enter.

   Continue double-clicking the bracketed periods or pressing Enter until the current directory listing in the Open File dialog box shows that you are in the root directory (probably C:\ or D:\).

   The dialog box displays a list of directories.

3. Enter the directory where you store Ami Pro documents by double-clicking the directory name.

   Alternatively, scroll through the list with the directional keys until the directory name is highlighted, and press Enter.

4. Scroll through the list of files until the highlight is on the file name NOV30SUM.SAM.

5. Double-click the file name NOV30SUM.SAM or press Enter.

   The Convert File Format dialog box displays the document format that has been detected by Convert (see fig. 31.2).

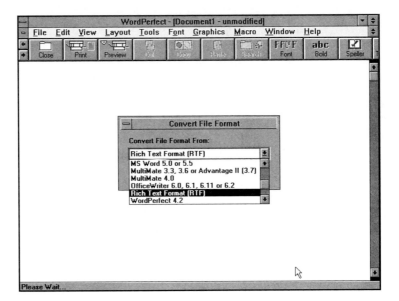

FIG. 31.2

The Word-
Perfect Convert
File Format
dialog box.

6. If Convert has correctly identified the document as an Ami Pro file, choose OK. When the Convert process is complete, the document appears on-screen.

Table 31.1. Formats Used by WordPerfect's Convert

Ami Pro 1.2	MultiMate Advantage II (3.7)
Ami Pro 1.2a	MultiMate 4.0
Ami Pro 1.2b	Navy DIF Standard
ANSI Text (Windows)	OfficeWriter 6.0
ANSI Delimited Text (Windows)	OfficeWriter 6.1
ANSI Generic Word Processor (Windows)	OfficeWriter 6.11
ASCII Text (DOS)	OfficeWriter 6.2
ASCII Delimited Text (DOS)	Rich Text Format (RTF)
ASCII Generic Word Processor (DOS)	Spreadsheet DIF
DisplayWrite 4.0	WordStar 3.3
DisplayWrite 4.2	WordStar 3.31
DisplayWrite 5.0	WordStar 3.34
IBM DCA/FFT	WordStar 4.0
IBM DCA/RFT	WordStar 5.0
Kermit (7-bit transfer)	WordStar 5.5
MS Word for Windows 1.0	WordStar 6.0
MS Word for Windows 1.1	WordPerfect (for DOS) 4.2
MS Word for Windows 1.1a	WordPerfect (for DOS) 5.0
MS Word (for DOS) 5.0	WP for Windows 1.0/WP (DOS) 5.1
MS Word (for DOS) 5.5	XyWrite 3.55
MultiMate 3.3	XyWrite 3.56
MultiMate 3.6	

Before you use Convert on a document, you must know the word processor format used to create the file, in case WordPerfect incorrectly detects the file's format. If you created the original document, you probably remember its format. If the document is in the directory of another word processor, the file probably was created in that word processor's format. If you get a file from another person, ask in what format the file was created. If you cannot be sure of the original format, convert a backup copy. WordPerfect doesn't often mistake a document format, but the error can happen, and the conversion will be unsatisfactory. If WordPerfect does identify incorrectly the file you want to convert, scroll through the Convert File Format dialog box until you find the correct format and then choose OK.

■ **Cue:** Be sure that you know a file's format before you try to convert it to WordPerfect format.

■ **Cue:** WordPerfect's Convert does a good job with documents from Word for Windows 1.0, 1.1, and 1.1a.

Before you make any editing changes in a converted document, examine the new document carefully to determine whether the conversion result is acceptable. If important formatting or other details have been lost or improperly converted, you may want to try one of the other conversion strategies before proceeding.

WordPerfect's Convert feature works best on documents with fairly simple formatting and a minimum of graphics. Convert does not do a good job translating graphics text boxes, tables, and other WordPerfect graphics. The following sections evaluate how well WordPerfect's Convert runs with documents prepared in a few popular word processors.

Word for Windows

WordPerfect's Convert does a good job with documents from Word for Windows 1.0, 1.1, and 1.1a, especially considering that conversion of nearly any document often results in the loss of some formatting and graphics elements. Figure 31.3 shows ARTICLE.DOC loaded in Word for Windows. Figure 31.4 shows the document after conversion by WordPerfect for Windows.

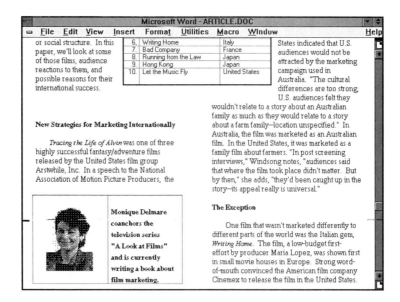

FIG. 31.3

A Word for Windows document.

WordPerfect's Convert successfully translated the photo in the graphics text box, which is unusual for a word processor's convert function. Convert also was successful (except for some minor font problems), with a graphics text box listing movie titles. Note that the newspaper-style columns of the body text were not successfully translated, and minor adjustments to the typeface used in the document's body type are necessary.

This conversion is an example of how even a good translation can create additional work, because you have to adjust various elements of the converted file before it looks exactly like the original document. WordPerfect's conversion of Word for Windows documents, however, is usually excellent. In many Word for Windows documents, Convert preserves two-column formatting, indents, tables, and centered headlines, as well as translating many graphics elements.

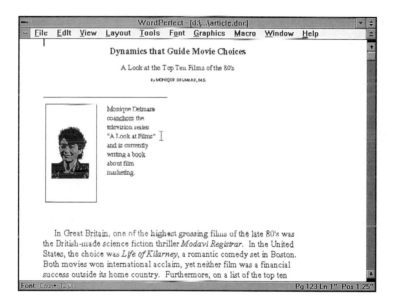

FIG. 31.4

The same Word for Windows document after being converted to WordPerfect for Windows.

Ami Pro

WordPerfect does a good job converting documents created in Ami Pro. Most formatting is retained, although details like fonts and type attributes like boldface and italic need touch-ups, and graphical elements can be lost. Although the Convert function is designed to support Ami Pro Versions 1.2, 1.2a, and 1.2b, many documents created in earlier versions of Ami Pro also can be converted.

As of this writing, WordPerfect's Convert cannot translate Ami Pro 2.0 documents. That limitation is likely to change in later versions of WordPerfect. To check your version of WordPerfect to see whether it supports Version 2.0 of Ami Pro or higher, scroll through the Convert File Format dialog box, which lists the word processor formats supported by WordPerfect (see "Using WordPerfect's Convert").

Ami Pro 2.0 converts its own documents into WordPerfect format, and Ami Pro 2.0 can convert WordPerfect into Ami Pro format. In figure 31.5, you see the excellent job Ami Pro does converting the newsletter shown at the beginning of this chapter. Ami Pro preserved the two-column formatting of the body type and most other formatting elements, such as indents and type justification, and Ami Pro preserved the small graphics in the body of the newsletter. You need to adjust the fonts used in the document. With this document, saving the banner and the graphics text box as separate graphics and pasting them into the document after the conversion produces a better result.

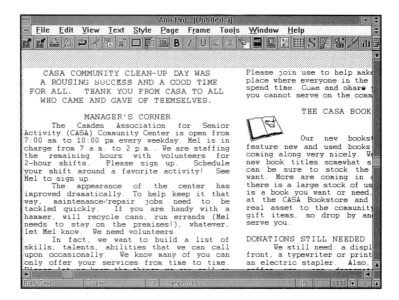

FIG. 31.5

The newsletter converted from WordPerfect to Ami Pro 2.0.

Microsoft Word 5.0 and 5.5

WordPerfect does an excellent job of converting documents created in Microsoft Word 5.0 and 5.5 when formatting is kept simple (see figs. 31.6 and 31.7). Most formatting is retained, although details like fonts and type attributes like boldface and italic need touch-ups. WordPerfect also converts its own documents into Word 5.0 and 5.5 formats.

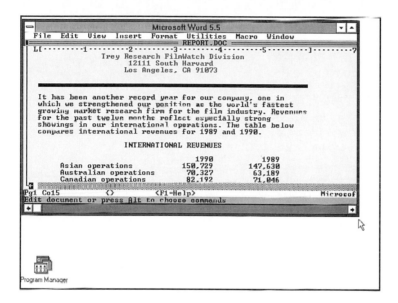

FIG. 31.6

A Word 5.5 document.

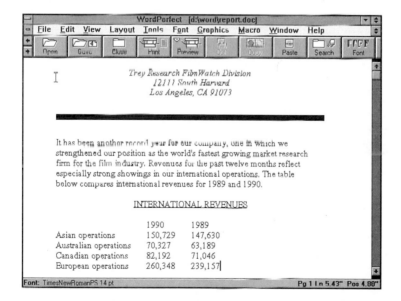

FIG. 31.7

The Word 5.5 document after conversion into WordPerfect.

WordPerfect cannot translate graphics used in Word documents. If you want to use a graphic from a Word 5.0 or 5.5 document, convert the text to WordPerfect format, and then paste the graphic into the document.

Using the Windows Clipboard

■ **Cue:** The Clipboard often produces a much better translation than a program's convert function.

The Windows Clipboard can be one of the most important options you have for converting documents. The Clipboard often produces a much better translation than a program's convert function, because in many cases the Clipboard preserves formatting details like margins, indents, columns, typeface, and font size, as well as boldface, italic, underlining, and other complex elements. The Clipboard also can transfer tables and graphics from one document to another.

The Clipboard is an area of memory set aside by Windows for the exchange of data between Windows programs. Windows programs are required to use certain standardized data formats when copying information to the Clipboard. This requirement means that although Windows programs like WordPerfect and Word for Windows do not use the same format for saving their documents to disk, they do share common formats for copying documents, or parts of documents, to the Clipboard.

This formatting requirement makes the Clipboard an important document conversion tool. Because programs translate their own data into these standardized formats and because each Windows program is designed to interpret these data formats in exactly the same way, the Clipboard often can accurately convert documents other methods cannot convert. You can get accurate results regardless of whether a document is simple text or a complex incorporation of formatting methods, font changes, tables, graphics, and spreadsheet information.

With many documents, the Clipboard can exchange text and graphics simultaneously from one Windows word processor to another. Even when the Clipboard cannot translate all elements of a complex document at the same time, the Clipboard still is a powerful tool for converting documents. You can use the Clipboard to translate parts of a complex document and paste data from the original document into a second word processor, where you can assemble a near-duplicate of the original document.

For example, figures 31.8, 31.9, and 31.10 show the two-step process used to convert a flier from Ami Pro to WordPerfect. Figure 31.8 shows the original document. In step 1, the flier's text is translated into WordPerfect format using Ami Pro's conversion feature (see fig. 31.9). In step 2, the graphics banner is pasted from the Ami Pro document into WordPerfect by way of the Clipboard (see fig. 31.10). Although the small type in the banner may need retouching in Windows Paintbrush, the entire operation took less than 10 minutes. People who frequently translate complex documents between Windows word processors, especially documents with graphics, will find themselves using the Clipboard often.

> **T I P**
>
> The Clipboard is useful for translating documents between Windows and DOS programs, and even between two DOS programs. Because of this capability, the Clipboard can be an important tool for solving the problem of a word processor whose documents cannot be read by WordPerfect, especially when WordPerfect and the first word processor do not share a common intermediate format.

FIG. 31.8

A flier prepared in Ami Pro.

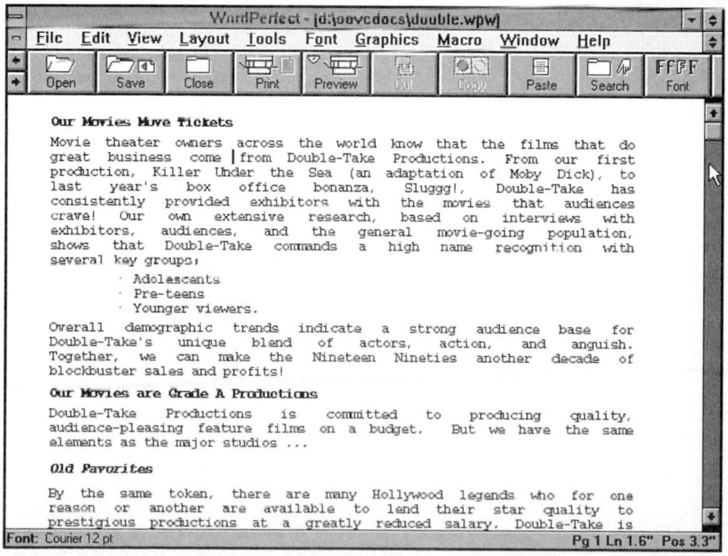

FIG. 31.9

The Ami Pro text converted to WordPerfect.

FIG. 31.10

The graphic banner pasted into Word-Perfect via the Clipboard.

■ **Cue:** You can use the Clipboard to transfer data between Windows and DOS programs and even between two DOS programs.

The Clipboard has different capabilities depending on whether you are transferring data between two Windows programs or from a DOS program to another program. As mentioned, the Clipboard can transfer both formatted text and graphics between Windows programs. When copying a document from a DOS program, the Clipboard can transfer only unformatted text. (Most of the time, trying to copy graphics between Windows and DOS programs using the Clipboard does not yield a good result.)

The following paragraphs explain ways to copy with the Clipboard. The first set of steps describe copying data from Windows and DOS programs to the Clipboard. Then you learn how to paste data from the Clipboard into a second program. Please note that you must follow different procedures for copying data to the Clipboard from Windows programs, DOS programs when Windows is running in 386 Enhanced mode, and DOS programs when Windows is running in Standard mode. You must use the right procedures, or the Clipboard will not work properly.

To copy data to the Clipboard from a Windows program or a DOS program with Windows running in 386 Enhanced mode, follow these steps:

1. Start the program from which you want to copy data.

2. Load the file containing the data you want to copy.

3. If you are running a Windows program, maximize it to full screen.

   If you are running a DOS program in 386 Enhanced mode, the program should be running in a window; if the program has started full screen, press Alt-Enter to reduce the program to a window.

4. Place the mouse pointer in the upper left corner of the data you want to copy.

5. Drag the pointer toward the lower right corner until you have selected the data you want to copy. When you have correctly selected the data you want to copy, release the mouse button.

6. Copy the selected data into the Clipboard.

   If you are copying data from a Windows program, choose **E**dit, **C**opy.

   If you are copying data from a DOS program, open its Control menu by clicking the Control menu box, the hyphen-shaped icon on the DOS program's title bar (or press Alt-space bar on the keyboard). Choose **E**dit, **C**opy.

   The data is copied to the Clipboard.

When Windows is running in Standard mode, DOS programs can run only full screen or shrunk to an icon, so the preceding procedure for copying data to the Clipboard from a DOS program does not work. But Windows still enables you to paste text from a DOS program into the Clipboard as long as your DOS program runs in Character mode rather than Graphics mode. (Check your program documentation if the following procedure doesn't work.) Instead of choosing text with the mouse when Windows is in Standard mode, you can copy only the DOS program's full screen. You can easily edit the text after it is pasted into another program. Here is the procedure for copying data to the Clipboard from a DOS program when Windows is in Standard mode:

1. Start the program from which you want to copy data.

2. Load the file containing the data you want to copy.

3. Make sure that the data you want to copy is on-screen.

4. Press the Print Screen key on your keyboard.

   The data is copied to the Clipboard.

After data has been copied to the Clipboard, the next step is to paste the data into the destination program. As with copying data to the Clipboard, you follow different procedures for pasting data from the

Clipboard into Windows programs, into DOS programs when Windows is running in 386 Enhanced mode, and into DOS programs when Windows is running in Standard mode. If you do not use the right procedures, the Clipboard does not work properly.

To paste data into a Windows program or a DOS program when Windows is running in 386 Enhanced mode, follow these directions:

1. Start the program into which you want to paste the data from the Clipboard. If you are copying into a DOS program, ensure that the DOS program is running in a window.

2. Open or create the document into which you want to paste the data.

3. Place the insertion point in the document where the data is to be inserted.

4. Paste the data into the program.

   If you are pasting into a Windows program, open the program's **E**dit menu and choose **P**aste.

   If you are pasting into a DOS program, click the Control menu and choose **E**dit, **P**aste, or on the keyboard press Alt-space bar, E, P.

   The data is pasted into the destination document.

To paste data from the Clipboard into a DOS program when Windows is running in Standard mode, follow these steps:

1. Start the program into which you want to paste the data from the Clipboard.

2. Open or create the document into which you want to paste the data.

3. Position the insertion point within the program's data file at the point where you want to paste the data.

4. Press Alt-Esc to switch back to Windows without quitting the program you want to paste the data into. The target program is reduced to an icon at the bottom of the Windows Desktop.

5. Click the target program's icon once to open the program's Control menu. Using the keyboard, press Alt-Esc until the description line beneath the program's icon is highlighted; then press Alt-space bar to open the Control menu.

6. Click **P**aste or scroll down the list until Paste is highlighted and press Enter.

   The data is pasted into the destination document.

In order to use the Clipboard to paste data from one DOS program into another DOS program, follow the preceding directions for copying data from a DOS program, and the directions for copying data into a DOS program. Be sure that you follow the directions appropriate for the Windows operating mode you use.

Using Dynamic Data Exchange (DDE)

Windows Dynamic Data Exchange (DDE) is most useful for importing information into WordPerfect if the important consideration is current, complete information rather than appearance. DDE creates a link between data imported into WordPerfect from another Windows program and the originating program and data file. This link can automatically update the WordPerfect document with any changes made in the source file. Numerous Windows applications, including Word for Windows and Ami Pro, use DDE to link their data files with WordPerfect.

Creating a DDE link between a WordPerfect document and another program's data file is easiest when both WordPerfect and the second program are running, and the data file to be linked is loaded in the second application. To create a DDE link, follow these steps:

1. Start the program whose file you want to link and load the source file.

2. Start WordPerfect and load the document into which you want to import the data.

3. Place the insertion point in the WordPerfect document where you want to create the link.

4. Select WordPerfect's **Edit** menu and choose **Link**; then choose **Create**. The Create DDE Link dialog box appears (see fig. 31.11).

■ **Cue:** Use Windows Dynamic Data Exchange (DDE) for importing information into WordPerfect if the important consideration is current, complete information rather than appearance.

FIG. 31.11

The Create DDE Link dialog box.

5. Select the appropriate source application and file name from the list in the **S**ource File and Item section of the Create DDE Link dialog box.

6. In the **L**ink Name text box, type a name for the link or accept the name chosen by WordPerfect.

7. Select **A**utomatic or **M**anual Update Mode.

   In Manual Update mode, the link is updated only when you choose. More information on automatic updating follows.

8. Select **T**ext if you want WordPerfect to import the data as text, or choose **G**raphics if you want WordPerfect to import the data as a graphics box.

9. Choose OK.

The DDE link has been established. After a few moments, the data you have linked appears at the place you chose in your WordPerfect document.

WordPerfect is a *DDE client*. This term means that WordPerfect receives DDE messages from other programs (the messages that update a document, for example), but WordPerfect does not send updates to the program that created the document. Any changes you make to linked data within WordPerfect are not sent to the data's originating program. Therefore, you have to update the data in the originating program if you make changes in WordPerfect.

Following the preceding directions links an entire data file to your WordPerfect document. If you want to link only a portion of the document, a Paste Link enables you to choose only the data you want to import. In order to create a Paste Link, follow these steps:

1. Start the program whose file you want to link to a WordPerfect document, and load the file to be linked.

   In this file, you select the data you want to link to the WordPerfect document.

2. Place the mouse pointer in the upper left corner of the data you want to link.

3. Drag the mouse toward the lower right corner until you have selected the data you want to link.

4. Copy the selected data into the Clipboard by choosing **E**dit, **C**opy.

5. Start WordPerfect, and load the file in which you want to create the Paste Link.

6. Choose **E**dit, **L**ink, **P**aste Link.

   A copy of the source data is pasted into your WordPerfect document, and this data is linked to the source.

A DDE link is updated automatically when the source file and the destination file are open at the same time. Both files need to be loaded in their originating programs. Automatic updating works only when the source file is opened first. If both files are open and the source has been changed, however, you can update the second file at any time by opening the **E**dit menu, choosing **L**ink, and then choosing **U**pdate. The Update DDE Link dialog box appears. If the document contains more than one link, you can scroll through the box to choose the link to update or choose **A**ll to update all links in the document at once. Choose OK to update the selected links and return to your document.

■ **Cue:** A DDE link is updated automatically when the source file and the destination file are open at the same time.

Using an Intermediate Format

If a word processor cannot convert its own documents to WordPerfect format and WordPerfect cannot convert the word processor's documents, your next step may be to use an intermediate format. Find out whether both WordPerfect and the other word processor can convert documents to a common third format. For example, if the second word processor supports DisplayWrite 4.0, convert the file to DisplayWrite format. Then use WordPerfect to convert the file from DisplayWrite 4.0 format to WordPerfect format.

■ **Cue:** If a word processor cannot convert its own documents to WordPerfect format and WordPerfect cannot convert the word processor's documents, you may be able to use an intermediate format.

When using an intermediate format, the ideal is to find a format that both the original word processor and WordPerfect handle well. The more formatting information that is preserved in the conversion process, the less extra work you have to do following the conversion.

Rich Text Format (RTF)

Rich Text Format (RTF) was designed as an answer to the problems created by the need to convert documents from one word processor's format to another. RTF is a standardized document format used by Windows word processors and other programs. The basic idea behind RTF is for word processors to use the same codes to represent document formatting details like margins, indents, columns, justification, typeface, font size, boldface, italic, underline, and other formatting elements. Theoretically, word processors using this common format can convert nearly all elements of one another's documents.

Although RTF is not perfect, it actually is quite successful at translating documents between word processors. RTF is one of the formats used by Windows programs to copy data into the Clipboard, where other programs can use the data. The section on the Clipboard covers how the Clipboard often can transfer documents between word processors without losing important formatting details. One reason for the Clipboard's success is its use of RTF. Many Windows programs—including WordPerfect, Word for Windows, Ami Pro, and Aldus PageMaker—offer RTF translation.

Because RTF is so good at translating formatting detail between word processors, you might use it as your first choice for translating documents. RTF does not translate graphics, graphics text boxes, or tables, however.

T I P If you plan to translate a document with RTF as the intermediate format, be sure to save graphics elements separately so that you can import them later into WordPerfect and rebuild the document.

ASCII Text

Like RTF, ASCII text is read by almost all word processors. Unlike RTF, however, ASCII conversions lose formatting information, such as indents, margins, fonts, and attributes (italic, boldface, and underline). Only carriage return information is preserved. In some conversions, word wrap is represented by a carriage return at the end of each line. You may have to remove the carriage returns manually after a conversion using ASCII text.

An ASCII translation results in the loss of special effects, such as graphics text boxes and tables. If the original document includes special effects, convert them separately so that you can import them into WordPerfect later and rebuild the document.

Using Spreadsheet Information

Spreadsheet data is so much a part of the modern business environment that important spreadsheet cells are integrated into both simple day-to-day business memos and important and detailed reports. Word-Perfect for Windows brings a great deal of simplicity and power to using spreadsheet information in your documents. WordPerfect has its own Spreadsheet Link function and the capability to read data directly from many of the most powerful spreadsheets. WordPerfect reads directly the following spreadsheets:

- Lotus 1-2-3 Versions 1.0 through 3.1

- Microsoft Excel 3.0

- Quattro and Quattro Pro

- PlanPerfect Versions 3.0 through 5.1

Figure 31.12 shows an Excel spreadsheet pasted into a WordPerfect document using WordPerfect's Import Spreadsheet function.

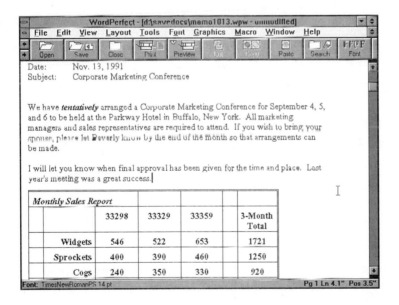

FIG. 31.12

An Excel spreadsheet pasted into WordPerfect.

Strategies for importing spreadsheet information into WordPerfect include the following:

- Use WordPerfect's Spreadsheet Import function.

- Create a WordPerfect Spreadsheet Link. You can configure the link so that it automatically updates the spreadsheet information in your document every time the document is opened or only when you choose to update the document.

- Establish a Windows DDE link that you can configure to update the information in your WordPerfect document whenever the source spreadsheet and the WordPerfect document are open at the same time or only when you choose to update the data.

- Use the Windows Clipboard to copy information from the spreadsheet into your WordPerfect document.

- Use a third Windows program, such as Windows Write, as an intermediate format to save information for import into WordPerfect.

Using the Import Spreadsheet Function

■ **Cue:** The Import Spreadsheet function does not create a permanent link between the original spreadsheet and the document in which it is used.

WordPerfect's Import Spreadsheet function imports a spreadsheet into a document. This function, however, is best used for a quick memo or other document you use once, because any changes in the spreadsheet must be updated manually in the document. Unlike WordPerfect's Spreadsheet Link feature or the Windows DDE, the Import Spreadsheet function does not create a permanent link between the original spreadsheet and the document in which it is used.

For this reason, read about the other options WordPerfect gives you for importing spreadsheet data before you use the Import Spreadsheet function. Pay particular attention to the WordPerfect Spreadsheet Link and the Windows DDE link. Both features automatically update WordPerfect documents with changes made to the spreadsheet.

To use the Import Spreadsheet function, follow these steps:

1. Place the insertion point where the spreadsheet file is to be located.

2. Select the **T**ools menu and choose Spr**e**adsheet; then choose **I**mport to open the Import Spreadsheet dialog box.

3. Type the path and file name of the spreadsheet you want to import, or choose the List button to open the Select File dialog box. Browse directories for the correct spreadsheet.

4. In the **R**ange text box, type the range of cells you are importing from the spreadsheet file. See the explanation of spreadsheet size limitation in the section "Handling Wide Spreadsheets."

5. Select **T**able to import the spreadsheet file as a table; select Te**x**t to import the spreadsheet file as text.

6. Choose OK to complete the task.

Creating a WordPerfect Spreadsheet Link

Creating a WordPerfect Spreadsheet Link is an excellent way to import spreadsheet data into a WordPerfect document. A Spreadsheet Link can automatically update a WordPerfect document with any changes in the linked spreadsheet each time you open the WordPerfect file. You also can configure the link to update the spreadsheet information only when you choose to update the link. If you use a Spreadsheet Link, important spreadsheet information in your WordPerfect documents need never be outdated, and you don't have to update the information line-by-line in the WordPerfect document.

To create a WordPerfect Spreadsheet Link, follow these steps:

1. Place the insertion point at the location in your WordPerfect document where the spreadsheet is to be imported and linked.

2. Select the **T**ools menu, and choose Spreadsheet; then choose **C**reate Link.

   You see the Create Spreadsheet Link dialog box.

3. In the **F**ilename text box, type the path and file name of the spreadsheet you want to link, or click the List button to open the Select File dialog box so that you can browse directories for the spreadsheet.

   > ■ **Cue:** You must use the mouse to select the list button in the Create Spreadsheet Link dialog box.

4. In the **R**ange text box, type the range of cells you want to link.

5. Select **T**able to link the spreadsheet as a WordPerfect table; select Te**x**t to link the spreadsheet as text.

6. Choose OK to insert the linked data at the insertion point in the WordPerfect document.

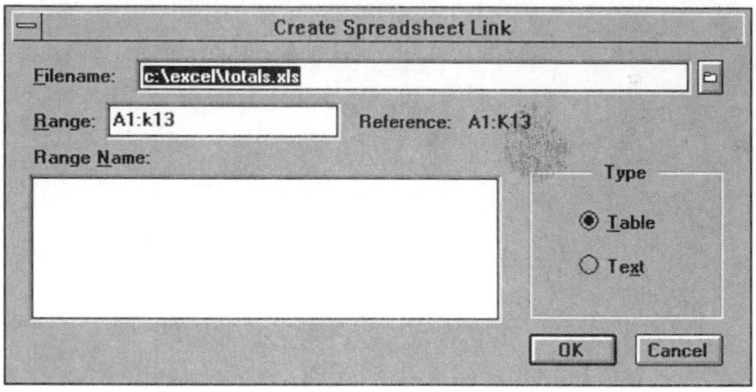

FIG. 31.13

The Create
Spreadsheet
Link dialog box.

To change an existing Spreadsheet Link, follow these instructions:

1. Move WordPerfect's insertion point inside the Spreadsheet Link you want to edit.

2. Select the **T**ools menu, choose Spr**e**adsheet, and then choose **E**dit Link.

   The Edit Spreadsheet Link dialog box appears.

3. In the **R**ange text box, enter the new range of cells you want to link.

   If you want to link a different spreadsheet to the document, change the file name of the spreadsheet in the **F**ilename text box, or click the List button to open the Select File box and browse for a new spreadsheet.

4. Choose **T**able to link the spreadsheet as a WordPerfect table; choose Te**x**t to link the spreadsheet as text.

5. Choose OK to insert the new spreadsheet at the insertion point.

Creating a DDE Spreadsheet Link

Another way you can link spreadsheet data to a WordPerfect document is by using Windows Dynamic Data Exchange. As noted earlier in this chapter, DDE enables a Windows program to import data from another Windows program and link the data to the originating program. Thereafter, when the data is changed in the originating program, the data can be automatically updated in the program into which the data was imported. If you wish, you can configure the link to be updated only when you choose to update manually.

DDE is not as powerful as a WordPerfect Spreadsheet Link, because before the link can be updated automatically, both the WordPerfect file into which you have imported spreadsheet data and the source file must be open, and the source file must be opened first. With a WordPerfect Spreadsheet Link, the imported data can be updated automatically each time the WordPerfect file is opened, regardless of whether the source spreadsheet file is open.

Creating a DDE link between a WordPerfect document and a spreadsheet is easiest when the spreadsheet program is loaded with the file to be linked to your WordPerfect document. To create the link, follow the instructions given in "Using Dynamic Data Exchange (DDE)."

Using the Clipboard

When your goal is to copy spreadsheet data quickly into a WordPerfect document, using the Windows Clipboard is often the fastest. The section of this chapter titled "Using the Windows Clipboard" gives directions on using the Clipboard to copy data between applications.

Figure 31.14 shows the result of using the Clipboard to copy part of a spreadsheet from Lotus 1-2-3 Release 2.3 into WordPerfect. The Clipboard can copy large amounts of data; however, when dealing with spreadsheets, you should copy blocks that you are certain fit on the WordPerfect page. If you copy more data than fits on the page, a warning indicates that the data extends beyond the printable boundaries of the WordPerfect page and that the page cannot be printed without reformatting.

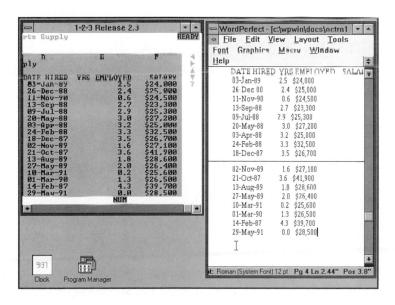

FIG. 31.14

Data copied from Lotus 1-2-3 to WordPerfect document.

Handling Wide Spreadsheets

■ **Cue:** If your spreadsheet is too wide for your WordPerfect document, you have several ways to accommodate the spreadsheet.

WordPerfect requires that spreadsheet data fit between the margins of your document. If you import a spreadsheet that is wider than your document, WordPerfect truncates each line or wraps it to the next line, depending on the format you choose when importing the spreadsheet.

If a spreadsheet is imported as a table, WordPerfect limits the spreadsheet to 32 columns that must fit between the margins of your document. If the spreadsheet's 32 columns are wider than the margins in an 8 1/2-by-11-inch sheet of paper, try the following methods for fitting the spreadsheet into your document:

■ Reduce the column widths in the spreadsheet before importing the spreadsheet into WordPerfect.

■ Before you import the spreadsheet, position WordPerfect's insertion point just above the location where the spreadsheet data is to be placed and change to a smaller font. Reducing the size of the font decreases the width of each column.

■ Reduce the width of your left and right margins in WordPerfect to create more room for the spreadsheet.

■ Choose **L**ayout, **T**ables, **O**ptions to have WordPerfect size the table so that it does not exceed the space between the margins.

■ Choose **L**ayout, **P**age, Paper **S**ize, and reset your document to print in landscape mode if your printer supports this mode.

When importing a spreadsheet as text, WordPerfect accepts up to 20 columns that must fit between the margins. If your spreadsheet's 20 columns are wider than the margins of your paper, WordPerfect inserts a soft return and wraps each row to the next line of the document. You may want to make more room for each row by printing your document in landscape mode.

Dealing with Problem Spreadsheets

To use spreadsheets other than Lotus, Excel, PlanPerfect, Quattro, or Quattro Pro, you must convert your spreadsheet. Most spreadsheet programs enable you to convert a spreadsheet into Lotus format or one of the other formats used by WordPerfect. For more information on converting a spreadsheet, see the documentation for your spreadsheet program.

Using an intermediate program can be an important alternative if WordPerfect cannot convert data from your spreadsheet and the Clipboard fails to copy a spreadsheet into WordPerfect satisfactorily. Use the Clipboard to make a copy of a spreadsheet file, and paste the copied file into Windows Write or Notepad. Correct the formatting to look like the original spreadsheet. Then import or paste the new file into WordPerfect.

Using WordPerfect with Graphics Programs

In the short time since the introduction of Windows, it has attracted the best graphing, drawing, and painting programs. Thanks to the intuitive nature of the Windows graphical user interface, Windows graphics programs are easy to learn, and acceptable results are possible for even the novice.

Windows is the ideal environment for WordPerfect. Perhaps more than any other word processor, WordPerfect for Windows makes using graphics in documents fun because you can so easily import graphics and move them about the document page. In addition, WordPerfect's WYSIWYG capabilities make appealing documents simple to produce.

WordPerfect works easily with more than 75 of the most popular Windows and non-Windows graphics programs because WordPerfect can import graphics using a wide range of graphics formats. Table 31.2 lists some of the graphics formats WordPerfect for Windows can import.

■ **Cue:** WordPerfect works easily with more than 75 of the most popular Windows and non-Windows graphics programs.

Table 31.2. Some Graphics Formats Imported by WordPerfect
BMP: Windows Bit Map (16 or 256 color)
CGM: Computer Graphics Metafile
DHP: Dr. Halo PIC format
DXF: AutoCAD format
EPS: PostScript and Encapsulated PostScript
GEM: GEM Draw format
HPGL: Hewlett-Packard Graphics Language Plotter File
IMG: GEM Paint format
MSP: Microsoft Windows 2.x Paint format
PCX: PC Paintbrush format
PIC: Lotus 1-2-3 PIC format
PNTG: Macintosh Paint format
PPIC: PC Paint Plus format
TIFF: Tagged Image File format
WMF: Windows Metafile format
WPG: WordPerfect Graphics format

The sections that follow highlight a few of the more popular business graphics programs that work well with WordPerfect.

CorelDRAW!

CorelDRAW! is one of the most advanced business and technical illustration programs available. It is also one of the simplest programs to learn. CorelDRAW! enables you to create detailed color drawings of complex objects and to manipulate drawings to include 3-D, shaping and molding, stretching or mirroring, and realistic perspective.

CorelDRAW! includes more than 150 fonts to use in your graphics or to convert for use with Windows font management software. CorelDRAW! also includes almost 4,000 business symbols and clip-art figures, and Corel Trace, a utility that makes graphic images produced in a digital scanner clearer, sharper, and easier to resize before being imported into WordPerfect.

CorelDRAW! saves its drawings in WordPerfect Graphics format (WPG), as well as several other formats supported by WordPerfect; consequently, importing a CorelDRAW graphic is as simple as selecting WordPerfect's Graphics menu, choosing Figure and then Retrieve.

Arts & Letters

Arts & Letters is rapidly becoming a top Windows graphics program because of its simplicity and power. Arts & Letters produces high-quality technical drawings, as well as banners, pie and bar graphs, maps, and newspaper ads. Arts & Letters also can produce screens for printing T-shirts, towels, and ceramics, as well as newsletters, fliers, and bulletins. Arts & Letters includes 5,000 clip-art images, offers 10,000 more, and enables you to edit any clip-art image.

Although Arts & Letters does not directly support the WordPerfect Graphics format (WPG), Arts & Letters does save graphics in several formats, including Encapsulated PostScript (EPS), Computer Graphics Metafile (CGM), and Tagged Image File Format (TIFF), supported by WordPerfect.

To import an Arts & Letters graphic, select WordPerfect's Graphics menu; choose Figure and then Retrieve.

Using Database Conversions

Businesses that need to keep track of their customers and the volume of business being done with the company, often keep records in database programs like dBASE. Because no widely popular Windows database programs currently exist, converting a WordPerfect document into a format that can be used by a database remains a difficult, but possible, task.

To make a conversion, follow these steps:

1. Save the document in DIF spreadsheet format.

2. Use the spreadsheet's conversion function to import the DIF file into a spreadsheet.

3. Adjust the formatting to ensure that the data is displayed properly.

4. Use the spreadsheet's conversion function to convert the spreadsheet into a DBF database file, and import the data into the database program.

Database information can be imported to WordPerfect in the following ways:

- Use the Windows Clipboard to copy the information from the database into WordPerfect.

- Print an ASCII text database report to a file on disk, and import the file into WordPerfect.

- Prepare a delimited file (a data exchange format) that can be used directly in WordPerfect by a merge or can be converted into secondary merge format. Your database program can do this conversion quickly and easily.

  Chapter 21, "Assembling Documents with Merge," explains how to use delimited text in a merge or secondary merge.

T   I   P   To use the Clipboard to paste a database file into WordPerfect, Windows must be running in 386 Enhanced mode, and the database program should be running in a window. Use the Clipboard to copy data from a DOS program into a Windows program (see "Using the Windows Clipboard").

Different database programs have different methods of preparing to export a file as delimited ASCII text. For information on doing this procedure in your database program, consult the program documentation. The steps used to prepare a delimited dBASE file that can be used in a merge are as follows:

1. Start dBASE.

2. Load the file you want to convert to delimited ASCII format. (For a file named CUSTOMER, type **USE CUSTOMER** at the dot prompt.)

3. Enter the words **copy to CUSTOMER delimited** to create the delimited ASCII text file CUSTOMER.TXT.

   If you want only certain fields to be contained in the delimited file, list the field names after the word *copy*. For example, type **copy NAME STREET CITY STATE to CUSTOMER delimited**, and only the customer's name, street, city, and state fields are included in the delimited file.

4. Quit dBASE by typing **QUIT** at the dot prompt.

Chapter Summary

In this final chapter of *Using WordPerfect for Windows*, Special Edition, you have learned some of the advanced techniques for using Word-Perfect with data files prepared in other programs. Important topics covered included general conversion strategies and strategies for using spreadsheet data in WordPerfect. You also learned to import or export data files from other word processors. Other topics covered include making files readable with conversion functions, converting documents into an intermediate word processing format, and using the Windows Clipboard to copy documents and graphics into WordPerfect from other programs. Finally, you learned how graphics programs and database files can be used with WordPerfect.

Appendixes

OUTLINE

Installing and Setting Up
   WordPerfect for Windows

WordPerfect: Windows vs.
   DOS

Installing and Setting Up WordPerfect for Windows

W hether you are a novice computer user working on a system that came with Windows 3 installed, a power user who has worked with microcomputers for 10 years and intensely dislikes INSTALL programs, or someone in between, WordPerfect's INSTALL routines accommodate you pretty well. This appendix helps you with initial and update installations of WordPerfect for Windows and with setting up WordPerfect in the way that best suits your style of computer and word processing program use.

WordPerfect's files are shipped compressed, using a WordPerfect Corporation proprietary compression utility, on seven 5 1/4-inch high-density (1.2M) or 3 1/2-inch high-density (1.44M) disks.

■ **Tony Rairdon** is a strategic marketing consultant with extensive experience using WordPerfect Corporation products.

CAUTION: You must use this INSTALL program to install WordPerfect on your system. You cannot decompress and install the individual files without the program, and you need what INSTALL does with several Windows files to access WordPerfect easily.

The WordPerfect INSTALL program does the following:

- Checks your system for compatibility with WordPerfect (optional with custom installation)
- Decompresses and installs the program files into the appropriate subdirectories
- Installs and activates your printer driver(s) in WordPerfect
- Installs the WordPerfect Corporation Group file (from which you can start WordPerfect) in the Windows 3 subdirectory and modifies Windows to recognize the new group

You should have *at least* 10M available on the hard disk to which you're installing WordPerfect. A full installation requires more than 9M; a less-than-full installation is possible, but you don't save much space and may sacrifice some of the program's capabilities. Leaving out the Learning/Workbook and Graphic Images files, for example, saves only about 370K; leaving out the thesaurus capability saves only about 390K.

WordPerfect for Windows does not require any alterations or additions to the PATH statement in your AUTOEXEC.BAT file in order to find and load its various DLLs and other files. Instead, WPWIN.EXE gathers the necessary information before loading the main program file, WPWINFIL.EXE, to which the program passes the locations of the various DLLs and auxiliary programs.

T I P To get the best performance from WordPerfect for Windows, and Windows in general, your CONFIG.SYS file should contain the directive Files=60, and you should have SmartDrive or an alternative disk cache active. You should also defragment your hard drive periodically (weekly works well for many people) with a utility such as Norton's SpeedDisk or Central Point's Optimize.

Installing WordPerfect for Windows

WordPerfect 5.1 for Windows is a Windows application, and it requires that Microsoft Windows 3.0, be installed on your system before you can install WordPerfect. Its installation, however, generally runs more smoothly from DOS, outside of Windows.

After you make sure that your system has the necessary hardware (see Appendix B), software, and disk space for WordPerfect, insert the Install/Program 1 disk into a drive. At a DOS prompt, switch to that drive and type **install**.

The installation program opening screen appears, and asks whether you want to continue. Press Y (for Yes, the default) or press Enter. You then see the INSTALL main menu, shown in figure A.1.

You perform your initial installation from this menu; you also may perform interim and maintenance updates on the entire program or on just specific portions, to either stand-alone systems or to network servers. (This appendix deals with stand-alone installations. See "Appendix M: Networking WordPerfect" in the WordPerfect for Windows Reference Manual, if you are installing to a network.)

```
WordPerfect Installation Options                    Installation Problems?
                                                        (800) 228-6076

▶ 1 - Basic        Install standard files to default locations, such as c:\wpwin\,
                   c:\wpwin\graphics\, and c:\wpwin\macros\.

  2 - Custom       Install standard files to locations you specify.

  3 - Network      Install standard files to a network drive.  Only a network
                   supervisor should use this option.

  4 - Printer      Install additional or updated WordPerfect printer files.

  5 - Interim      Install Interim Release program files.  Use this option only
                   if you are replacing existing WordPerfect for Windows files.

  6 - Copy         Install every file on a diskette to a location you specify
                   (useful for installing all the Printer .ALL files).

  7 - Language     Install additional WordPerfect Language Modules.

  8 - README       View WordPerfect for Windows README files.


Selection: 1                                    (F1 for Help; Esc to exit)
```

FIG. A.1

The INSTALL main menu.

The following list explains the available installation options:

- *Basic.* Basic installation briefly checks your system, then installs the main program files in C:\WPWIN; the Shared Resource program files (printers, the spelling checker and thesaurus, File Manager, and others) in C:\WPC; the macros, keyboard and button bar files in C:\WPWIN\MACROS; and the graphics and workbook tutorial files in their own respective subdirectories.

- *Custom.* Custom installation generally gives you more control than the Basic version over where files are placed and which other installation activities (such as system check and printer installation) take place. If you actively manage your hard disk and prefer a hierarchical directory structure to a flat one, use Custom rather than Basic installation.

- *Network.* This option enables network administrators to customize installation onto a network server and create or modify a network environment file, specifying the type of network and location of user SET files. This appendix, however, deals with stand-alone installations.

- *Printer.* With this option, you can install additional WordPerfect printer drivers or update the drivers you already have installed if you receive new printer disks from WordPerfect Corporation.

- *Interim.* Use this installation option if you have received a new interim release of WordPerfect for Windows. Interim looks for your current WordPerfect directory structure and replaces the WordPerfect program files and printer drivers (as you enable the program to) with the newer versions from your new disks.

- *Copy.* Copy decompresses and copies all the files on a disk to a subdirectory you designate on your hard disk or a floppy disk. This option can be helpful in recovering specific files that may have been changed or corrupted on your hard drive and in installing all the printer files.

- *Language.* With the Language option, you can install additional language modules, each containing a spelling checker, thesaurus, and hyphenation for the particular language. When you choose a language from the Language dialog box under the Tools menu, you invoke the appropriate date formats and sort orders. If you have installed the language module for that language, you also can spell check, automatically hyphenate, look up alternative words in that language, and use the character set and a keyboard specific to that language. Appendix H of the manual that comes with your software covers the language module feature in more detail, and includes a list of available language modules.

■ *README.* This option enables you to view the README files from each disk.

Initial Installations

For your initial installation of WordPerfect for Windows, use either the Basic or the Custom option. The following sections cover these two options as well as the initial installation choices for keyboards and printer drivers. The sections on README files and recovering disk space also are part of the initial installation process.

Choosing Basic Installation

If you choose the Basic option, INSTALL checks your hard drive to determine whether enough space is available before the installation actually starts. If enough space is *not* available, a warning box appears to tell you how much space is available and how much space WordPerfect requires (see fig. A.2).

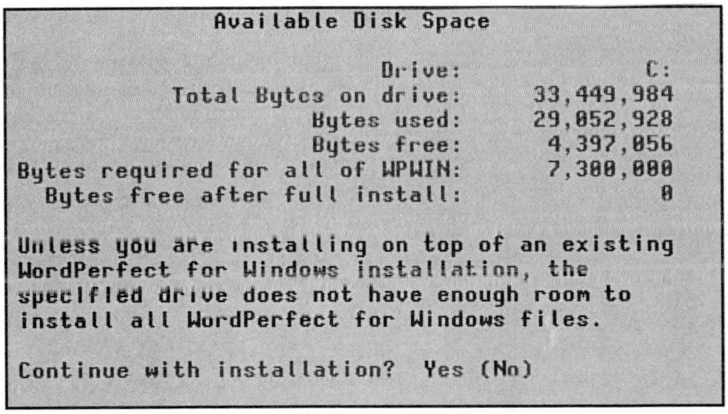

```
              Available Disk Space

                         Drive:              C:
            Total Bytes on drive:    33,449,984
                     Bytes used:    29,052,928
                     Bytes free:     4,397,056
     Bytes required for all of WPWIN:    7,300,000
      Bytes free after full install:            0

     Unless you are installing on top of an existing
     WordPerfect for Windows installation, the
     specified drive does not have enough room to
     install all WordPerfect for Windows files.

     Continue with installation?  Yes (No)
```

FIG. A.2

The Available Disk Space warning/ information box.

A similar box appears if enough room *is* available to tell you how much disk space you have left after the installation. In both instances, you have the option of proceeding. If you try to proceed with too little space for the program's essential files, the installation eventually aborts. You are left with a disk that needs cleaning up and without functional WordPerfect.

After you respond **Yes** to the warning/information box, the Basic INSTALL proceeds automatically, prompting you only when you need to swap disks, up to the keyboard selection discussed later in this appendix.

Choosing Custom Installation

If you choose the Custom installation, INSTALL asks where to place the various file groups, as shown in figure A.3. To choose a directory other than C:\WPWIN for the program files, press Enter, type the drive and directory where you want to put the program, and press Enter again. INSTALL then changes the other entries to correspond with the program location you specified. You may also change (or supply, in the case of the Documents subdirectory) any of or all the other file group locations before returning to the Custom Installation menu.

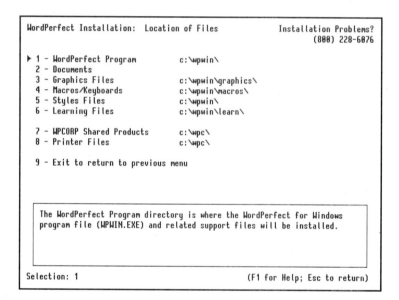

FIG. A.3

The Custom
Installation
Location of Files
screen.

If you designate directories that do not exist, INSTALL creates them for you on the fly. (The exceptions to this practice are the Documents and Printer subdirectories; INSTALL queries you before creating these subdirectories if they do not already exist.)

After completely specifying the directory structure in which you want WordPerfect installed (see fig. A.4 for an example), press **9** or **E**xit to return to the Custom Installation menu, then press **3** or **P**erform Installation or press Enter.

INSTALL checks the space available on the drive(s) you have designated for the selection before the program actually starts the installation. If there is *not* sufficient space, a warning box displays the amounts of available space and WordPerfect's required space (again see fig. A.2).

```
WordPerfect Installation:  Location of Files        Installation Problems?
                                                       (800) 228-6076

   1 - WordPerfect Program        f:\wpwin\
   2 - Documents                  f:\wpwin\docs\
   3 - Graphics Files             f:\wpwin\graphics\
   4 - Macros/Keyboards           f:\wpwin\macros\
   5 - Styles Files               f:\wpwin\styles\
   6 - Learning Files             f:\wpwin\learn\

   7 - WPCORP Shared Products     f:\wpc\
   8 - Printer Files              f:\wpc\ptr\

 ▶ 9 - Exit to return to previous menu




 ┌─────────────────────────────────────────────────────────────┐
 │                                                               │
 │                                                               │
 │                                                               │
 │                                                               │
 └─────────────────────────────────────────────────────────────┘
 Selection: 9                          (F1 for Help; Esc to return)
```

FIG. A.4

The Custom Installation Location of Files screen completed for a typical custom installation.

A similar box appears if enough room *is* available, telling you how much disk space you will have left after the installation. In both instances, you have the option of proceeding. If you try to proceed with too little space for the program's essential files, the installation eventually aborts, and you are left with a disk that needs cleaning up and without functional WordPerfect.

After you respond **Yes** to the warning/information box, the Custom INSTALL proceeds with a series of file group installations. For each group, INSTALL asks whether or not you want to install the files and tells whether they are necessary or optional. Unless disk space is a serious concern, you should probably answer **Yes** to all the questions, enabling INSTALL to put the full program on your system. INSTALL prompts you to swap disks, as necessary, to implement your file group installation responses.

Choosing Keyboards

After most files have been transferred, INSTALL offers you the choice of WordPerfect's CUA keyboard, which uses the same keystrokes that Windows and most Windows applications use, or a keyboard similar to the WordPerfect 5.1 keyboard. If you press Enter or **1**, WordPerfect uses the default CUA (Common User Access) keyboard. If you press **2**, WordPerfect is set up initially for the 5.1 keyboard.

Either way you answer this question, INSTALL transfers the WordPerfect 5.1-style keyboard file to your \WPWIN\MACROS subdirectory so that you easily can choose that file later (choose File, Preferences, Keyboard) if you want to try the CUA keyboard first.

T I P Many keys on the WordPerfect for Windows 5.1-style keyboard have different functions from WordPerfect 5.1 because of Windows-standard key allocations. WordPerfect for Windows also adds Alt-Shift and Ctrl-Shift function keys to 5.1's normal Shift, Alt, and Ctrl function keys. Furthermore, the Windows CUA keystrokes always apply in the Help screens and dialog boxes, even if you have selected the 5.1 keyboard, because the functions are Windows rather than WordPerfect applications.

Choosing Printer Drivers

After keyboards, INSTALL moves on to printer selection, which enables you to install WordPerfect Corporation's highly regarded printer drivers as an alternative to the standard Windows printer drivers. If you don't install one or more WordPerfect printer drivers, you have only the Windows printer drivers—adequate but not impressive—to work with.

The Windows drivers tend to be slow and inflexible. The drivers, for example, enable you to have only one page size or orientation in a document. Each different paper size or orientation must be printed as a separate job. You also cannot edit the Windows printer drivers to add additional paper sizes and types to the sizes and types that come preinstalled, or to intervene in font management. Finally, according to the Microsoft Windows User's Guide, Windows supports most commonly used printers with specific drivers; WordPerfect, on the other hand, has more than 900 printer-specific drivers. If your printer isn't directly supported by a Windows driver, you must run your printer in a mode emulating one of the supported printers (if your printer has that capability) or use the Generic/Text driver, which has no graphics or fonts capabilities and generally is extremely limited.

The comparatively fast WordPerfect printer drivers enable you to create additional paper sizes and types as you need them without leaving WordPerfect; to have multiple page sizes and orientations (such as letterhead, second sheet, and envelope) in the same document; and, with WordPerfect's PTR.EXE, to fine-tune and modify the drivers to best suit your needs.

If you install the WordPerfect printer drivers, you can toggle between WordPerfect and Windows drivers anytime you choose so that you lose nothing (except some disk space) and gain the capabilities outlined in this section by answering **Yes** to the question, Do you wish to install WordPerfect printer drivers? A list of available printer drivers appears on-screen. Use the Pg Dn, Pg Up, and directional keys to position the pointer at each printer driver you want to install (you can choose more than one) and press Enter or the space bar to select each one. INSTALL highlights each printer driver and marks it to the left with a diamond. After making your selection(s), press F7 to INSTALL the selected drivers.

Cue: Press **N** and then type the first two or three letters of your printer's brand name to speed your way with Name Search through WordPerfect's list of more than 900 printer selections.

> **T I P**
>
> If you're upgrading from WordPerfect 5.1 and have added many forms (paper sizes and types) or fonts to your 5.1 printer drivers or have fine-tuned the Automatic Font Changes and Substitute Fonts, you probably should skip installing the 5.1 drivers during INSTALL.
>
> Instead, after you finish the installation and bring up WordPerfect for Windows, choose File, Preferences, Location of Files, and in the Printer Files text box type the path for your 5.1 printer files. Alternatively, you can have INSTALL place the files in your WordPerfect for Windows directory structure, and then use File Manager or another file management utility to copy the *.ALL and *.PRS files from your 5.1 printer directory over the files in your WordPerfect printer directory.

Many printers are supported by more than one driver. If a driver marked with an asterisk (*) is the only driver supporting your printer, you must order an Additional Drivers disk from WordPerfect Corporation or download the driver from the WordPerfect Corporation Bulletin Board. (You can find the number for the bulletin board in the list of WordPerfect Corporation's telephone numbers in the Introduction to this book.) Detailed instructions appear on-screen when you choose one of the asterisk-marked drivers.

In the unlikely event you don't find your printer on the list, you may need to order a driver for it from WordPerfect Corporation or you may need to use it in a mode that emulates one of the more than 900 supported printers. With the printer selection list on the screen, press Printer Selection Help (F1) for more information on both possibilities.

The initial printer driver installation installs the printer driver library file(s) (*.ALL) in the designated directory on your system but does not actually generate the printer-specific driver file(s) (*.PRS, for Printer

Resource). The first time you load WordPerfect after the installation, you briefly see an information box that displays an Updating Printer Information message while the program generates the PRS files for the printers you selected. (See Chapters 9 and 15 for more information on printer selection.)

Viewing the README Files

At the end of your installation sequence, you are given the opportunity to view the README files. Don't skip this step. These files usually contain useful and valuable information pertaining to features and capabilities that were included in the program too late to be covered in the printed documentation. INSTALL has put the README files onto your hard drive already; this menu option gives you the opportunity to view them during your installation so that you will be familiar with their contents.

T I P   You easily can access the README files whenever you want to, simply by opening them from within WordPerfect. (When the Convert File Format dialog box offers you the ASCII Text (DOS) Format From, press Enter or choose OK. You may need to reset your margins or font size if the lines are breaking inappropriately.) You also may want to print the README files to keep in the back of your WordPerfect Reference Manual.

Recovering Disk Space after Installation

If you are short of hard disk space, you can recover a fair amount of it *after* your installation by using the File Manager (see Chapter 3, "Managing Files") or another file management utility to delete files you don't need.

For example, if you have a VGA, Super VGA, or 8514A video interface, INSTALL cannot tell whether it is color or monochrome; the program installs all four "VGA and up" drivers, covering both modes for both WordPerfect and File Manager (see table A.1). You can recover more than 300K of hard disk space when you eliminate the two drivers you do not need on your system.

Appendix N of the WordPerfect documentation identifies most of the more than 160 files that INSTALL places on your hard disk. In carefully reviewing that appendix, you may identify a number of files you don't need to have on your system. If, for instance, you know you will never use WordPerfect's Equation Editor, you can recover almost 100K by deleting the two Equation Editor keyboards (EQUATION.WWK and EQUDOS51.WWK) and the Equation Editor display resource file WP.QRS. If you install the File Manager but then decide you prefer to use another file management utility, you can recover more than 600K by eliminating all the files associated with File Manager.

Table A.1. Video DLLs for WordPerfect and File Manager

Video Standard	WordPerfect in \WPWIN	File Manager in \WPC
VGA	WPWPVGA.DLL	WPFMVGA.DLL
Monochrome VGA	WPWPMVGA.DLL	WPFMMVGA.DLL

Interim Releases

WordPerfect Corporation, like most software companies, is constantly working on new versions of its products. Major additions to the capabilities of the program are indicated by new "major version" numbers, which precede the decimal point in the version number. Lesser, but still significant, enhancements are indicated by minor version numbers, which follow the decimal point. This version of WordPerfect for Windows is 5.1; it parallels the capabilities and features of WordPerfect 5.1 for DOS.

In addition to major and minor version releases, WordPerfect Corporation regularly adds enhancements to and fixes minor problems with all its software products. Occasionally the company incorporates a series of those changes and fixes into what is referred to as an *interim*, or *maintenance*, release. The version number does not change with interim releases, but the dates of the files, the dates shown in the Help, About WordPerfect screen are revised, and all subsequent shipments from WordPerfect Corporation are of the new interim release.

WordPerfect Corporation constantly adds new printer drivers to support new printers in the marketplace and revises those printer drivers it has previously released in order to improve functionality. The new and updated drivers are available from WordPerfect Corporation as soon as they are completed to meet users' needs. Periodically, there is also a new printer driver released, incorporating all the latest changes and additions into a new set of disks with all file dates revised to the date of the release.

If you have a specific problem with either the program or a printer driver that an interim release resolves, WordPerfect Corporation provides the update to you free of charge. The Problems Resolution group, with which you talk on the Technical Support phone lines, handles these updates. If you simply want to have the "latest and greatest" version and do not have a specific problem that the update fixes, you may order it for a nominal charge from WordPerfect Corporation Orders. (See the Introduction for a list of pertinent toll-free phone numbers.)

To install an interim release (maintenance update) of WordPerfect, use the Interim option from INSTALL's main menu (again see fig. A.1). This option bypasses the Basic and Custom options and the directory organization choices (with Custom). Interim searches out the information on your existing installation and uses it to install the interim release. After you choose Update, the Interim Release Update Installation menu appears (see fig. A.5).

```
WordPerfect Interim Release Installation           Installation Problems?
                                                     (800) 228-6076

  ▶ 1 - WordPerfect Program

    2 - Shared Program                 Select an option to update the
                                       corresponding set of files.
    3 - Shared Utilities

    4 - Graphics/Learning

    5 - Language Module

    6 - Printer

    7 - Exit Install


  ┌──────────────────────────────────────────────────────────────────┐
  │ The WordPerfect Program option installs the updated WordPerfect for│
  │ Windows program files.                                             │
  │                                                                    │
  │                                                                    │
  └──────────────────────────────────────────────────────────────────┘
  Selection: 1                          (F1 for Help; Esc to return)
```

FIG. A.5

The Update Installation menu.

Choose each of the file groups you want to update, and follow the prompts for each group. The update installation proceeds in much the same manner as your initial installation, prompting you to swap disks when required.

Printer Additions and Updates

If you need only to change printers or add a printer, or you want to update your printer driver from a new Printer disk and you are using WordPerfect printer drivers, the Printer option on the INSTALL main menu is even more direct than Update. Before choosing Printer from the main menu, place either Printer Disk 1 or a printer disk numbered 5 or higher in your floppy disk drive. Choose **Printer** to bypass all other menus and go directly to the screen from which you select the printer drivers.

Just as you did on the initial installation, choose each printer driver you want to update by using the PgDn, PgUp, and directional keys or Name Search to position the pointer at each printer driver; press Enter or the space bar to select each one. INSTALL highlights each printer driver you select and marks it to the left with a diamond. After making your selection(s), press F7.

Adding Printers

If you are adding a new printer, INSTALL adds the ALL printer library file to the directory where your other printer files are stored but does not generate the PRS with which you actually print. As a result, you won't see the new printer listed in the Printer Select dialog box until you do the following:

1. Choose **File**, Select Printer to bring up the Select Printer dialog box, which lists the printer(s) you have been using. (If you have also been using the Windows printer drivers, be sure that the WordPerfect radio button is selected in the Printer Drivers section of the dialog box.)

2. Choose **Add** to bring up the Add Printers dialog box, which displays a list of all the printers available in the ALL files in the designated printers subdirectory. (If you see only printers you have already used, choose the Additional Printers (*.ALL) radio button in the Printers section of the dialog box to open the full list.)

3. Select your new printer; then choose **Add** or press Enter. The Copy Printer dialog box opens with your new printer listed in the text window. Choose OK or press Enter again. The PRS is generated, and you return to the Select Printer dialog box with the new printer listed and highlighted.

4. Choose **Select** or press Enter to select and begin using the new printer.

Updating Existing Printers

If you are updating a printer that is already installed on your system, INSTALL detects the old file and displays the warning box shown in figure A.6.

```
                        Warning
f:\wpc\ptr\wpps1.all already exists.

WPCorp .ALL files can have soft fonts added to
them by other software products.  If your .ALL
files have these additional fonts, you may not
wish to overwrite them.

Overwrite this file?  Yes (No)
```

FIG A.6

The Printer
Overwrite
Warning box.

T I P   Anytime you want to modify something that currently works, as in updating a printer file or even the main program files, it's a good idea to save a copy of the working files to another directory. Then you can proceed with the update or other modification. If you have any problems with the update or modification, you easily can recopy the old working files back over the altered or updated files

If you are using only the printer fonts that came installed on the printer, type **Y**es or press Enter, and INSTALL proceeds with the update.

WARNING: If you have added any fonts to your printer with a cartridge or soft font installation program, you probably don't want to update your driver by simply accepting the overwrite. That process wipes out the fonts you added when the Update routine overwrites the *.ALL file. If you subsequently choose Update for that printer from the Printer Select dialog box, you wipe the added fonts out of your actual printer driver, the *.PRS file, and then do not have access to the fonts from your Fonts menu. Note that any forms (paper size/type) you create, Automatic Font Changes, or Substitute Fonts modifications you make with PTR.EXE survive an update.

T I P

INSTALL copies the updated new printer library file (ALL) to your drive, but the driver file with which you actually print (the PRS) has not been updated. To get the new driver into service, you must go into WordPerfect. Choose File, Select Printer; select the printer you want to update by clicking it *once* (if it's not already highlighted), and choose Update.

Preserving Installed Fonts

If you know that a new printer driver has significant improvements or solves a problem you have experienced, but you have installed fonts you want to preserve, follow these steps:

1. Before doing anything else in your update, use File Manager, DOS, or another file management utility to copy your current ALL and PRS files to another directory.

2. Now run INSTALL, **Printer** or INSTALL, **Update** (including the **Printer** option) to overwrite your old files with the new ALL printer library files in your printer subdirectory. (Press Enter or type **Yes** in response to the warning box this time.)

3. Exit from INSTALL. Change to your printer subdirectory and, at the DOS prompt, type **PTR** and press Enter. WordPerfect's PTR.EXE printer utility appears.

4. To retrieve your old ALL file into PTR, press Shift-F10; then type the full path and file name (for the directory into which you copied it before updating) and press Enter.

5. PTR displays a list of all the printers contained in the ALL file. Use the directional keys (PTR.EXE doesn't support a mouse) to highlight your printer in the list; then press Enter to look at or edit it.

6. From the choices presented, choose Fonts by highlighting it; then press Enter to see the available Font Libraries.

7. Highlight in turn each of the libraries you want in the new driver, press **4** for Copy, type the full path (your WordPerfect printer directory) and file name for the new ALL, and press Enter. The fonts are copied to the new file. (If you're not sure which families you need or want, just press Enter rather than **4**, and you are shown a list of what's in the library you had highlighted; then press F7 to return to the list of families and proceed as described.)

8. Exit from your old printer file back to an empty Printers screen in PTR.EXE by pressing F7 and following the prompts.

9. Press Shift-F10, type the path and file name of your new ALL, and press Enter to retrieve the new ALL file, which now also contains the font libraries you copied to it from the old ALL file, into PTR.

10. Highlight your printer and press Enter.

11. With Fonts highlighted, press Enter again. Highlight each of the font libraries you have just copied into the printer and type an asterisk (*) in front of each one to select it and make its fonts available. (One or more other families already should be marked with an asterisk. Leave them alone.)

12. Exit from the printer using F7; answer **Yes** to save the printer modifications in the ALL file, and exit PTR by pressing F7.

13. Start WordPerfect; choose **F**ile, Se**l**ect Printer, and select the printer with which you're concerned; choose **U**pdate. You now have the latest driver with your old fonts and your old AFCs and Substitute Fonts intact in it.

 **Cue:** When you update a printer, don't forget to reselect the printer to make the updates effective during your current WordPerfect session.

Reinstallations

If you want to reinstall WordPerfect and do not want to use the INSTALL **U**pdate option (for example, you want WordPerfect on a different drive, or you want a Custom installation rather than Basic, and you don't want to create it manually), use either the Basic or Custom installation routines.

WARNING: When you choose either Basic or Custom from the INSTALL main menu and you have a prior installation in place, INSTALL may gather invalid information from some of the files (both WordPerfect and Windows) previously created. This condition may cause problems, and definitely *will* cause problems if you are reinstalling to a different drive from your original installation. Avoid these problems by taking care of the critical files before you start INSTALL (see the following list of steps).

To prevent problems that may be caused when you reinstall using Basic or Custom from the INSTALL main menu, before starting INSTALL, follow these steps:

1. Copy or move all document, macro, and Button Bar files you have created; printer files (*.ALL and *.PRS) you have modified with PTR.EXE; and graphics you have saved to another directory structure. You also should copy or move your default WordPerfect settings file, WP{WP}.SET, unless WordPerfect is not functioning correctly when you decide to reinstall.

> **T I P**
>
> If WordPerfect acts a bit unpredictably, a corrupted WP{WP}.SET file may be at fault. Before going to the extreme of deleting and reinstalling the whole program, delete just the SET file and then restart WordPerfect. The program comes up with all default functions and creates a new SET file, incorporating any changes you make whenever you make a change in Preferences or exit the program.

2. Delete all files in the \WPC and \WPWIN directories and their subdirectories.

3. Delete all WP*.INI files and WPCORP.GRP from your main Windows directory.

4. Run INSTALL with the Basic or Custom option.

5. Copy or move all files from step 1 back to the appropriate directories for your new installation.

Follow this procedure to ensure that the reinstallation runs as smoothly as your initial installation.

Setting Up and Starting WordPerfect

Now that you have installed WordPerfect for Windows, put the program to work. Open Windows, double-click the WordPerfect group icon, and double-click the WordPerfect icon.

WordPerfect appears on-screen with all defaults at the factory settings. The only way in which WordPerfect reflects your input now is in the location of its various files, and that input reflects your preferences only if you used the Custom option of INSTALL.

WordPerfect can be extensively fine-tuned to suit your individual needs. Chapter 29, "Customizing WordPerfect with Preferences," discusses customizing in-depth. In this appendix, however, the concentration is on what you need to begin working effectively.

Having loaded Windows and WordPerfect, you may want to refer to Chapter 1, "Preparing To Use WordPerfect for Windows," before you proceed in this appendix.

Defining a Documents Subdirectory

Soon after you begin creating a document, you have to deal with the process of saving your work. Whether you did a Basic or Custom installation, your default directory for saving files is the same subdirectory where your principal WordPerfect program files are stored (if you didn't specify one in the Custom Location of Files screen). Because managing and retrieving your documents is far easier when you store the documents in their own subdirectory, set up WordPerfect to add a \DOCS subdirectory below your \WPWIN directory.

You can set up the \DOCS subdirectory from DOS, with DOS commands and a third-party file and hard disk management program, or with WordPerfect's File Manager (covered fundamentally in Chapter 3 and in depth in Chapter 30). The easiest way to set up the subdirectory, however, is to go from WordPerfect's main edit screen into **F**ile, **P**references, **L**ocation of Files. Choose **D**ocuments, type the drive and full path name of the directory you want to use for your documents, and press Enter. If the directory does not yet exist, WordPerfect displays a dialog box stating that the directory does not exist and asks whether you want to create it (see fig. A.7). Choose OK to create the directory and return to the edit screen.

FIG. A.7

The Create Directory dialog box in Preferences, Location of Files.

> **T I P** Be sure that the Update Quick List with Changes feature is turned on so that the new documents subdirectory appears in Quick List.

Activating the Ruler

WordPerfect traditionally has had a very clean screen, and in its default mode this version for Windows is no exception. One of the principal advantages, however, of the graphical user interface is that you easily can work with *graphical* presentation and manipulation ("click and drag") of many aspects of the document's formatting. The Ruler in WordPerfect (as in many Windows applications) is an excellent example.

To see the Ruler on-screen and evaluate its usefulness to you, choose **View**, **R**uler, or press View Ruler (Alt-Shift-F3). If you want to have the Ruler come up whenever you load WordPerfect, see Chapter 29, "Customizing WordPerfect with Preferences." Chapter 6, "Formatting Text," introduces the Ruler and demonstrates how to format text with this versatile tool.

Using WordPerfect Start-Up Switches

WordPerfect has a number of start up options you can use by adding the appropriate switch to the command line you type to load the program (see table A.2). More than one switch may be used at one time—just make sure to put spaces between them. To use one or more of the switches when loading WordPerfect via its icon into a group in the Windows Program Manager, do the following:

1. Access the Windows Program Manager.

2. Click *once* to select the WordPerfect icon. (Clicking twice launches WordPerfect.)

3. Choose **F**ile, **P**roperties.

4. At the end of the command line, add the switch and its parameters (**/m-START**, for example), and then choose OK or press Enter.

If you use a single command to load Windows and run WordPerfect from the DOS command line, or you run WordPerfect from the Windows Program Manager's File Run dialog box, simply add the start-up switch(es) to the end of your command line string. This procedure is the best way to invoke the switches for one-time use.

Table A.2. Start-Up Options for WordPerfect 5.1 for Windows

Option	Description
filename	Starts WordPerfect with a specific file already open. Include the full path if the file is not in your document default directory.
/m-*macroname*	Executes a specific macro when WordPerfect starts.
/d-*drive\directory*	Specifies the drive\directory where you want WordPerfect to store the temporary buffers and overflow files it creates.
/x	Overrides Preferences settings with WordPerfect default settings for the current session only. The settings stored in your WPWP.INI files and your other WP*.INI files remain in effect.
/nb	Turns off Original Backup (to save disk space).
/sa	Turns on Stand-alone mode; disregards network setup. This option may provide greater speed of operation when the network facilities are not required.
/nt-*network* #	Accesses network-oriented features for a stand-alone system.
/ps-*path*	Accesses a path to personal setup files (WP*xxx*.SET), so that an individual user can override the network-wide settings established in the master setup file WP{WP}.SET; use with the /u switch.
/u-*username*	Identifies specific network user and machine.

WordPerfect: Windows vs. DOS

I f you are a current user of the MS-DOS version of WordPerfect 5.1, you probably have followed with interest the development of Word-Perfect 5.1 for Windows. But you probably also have been confused by all the new terminology, along with all the claims and counter-claims about the benefits of this new software interface.

The information in this appendix will help you

- Evaluate the advantages and costs in changing from WordPerfect 5.1 for DOS to WordPerfect 5.1 for Windows

- Make a smooth transition from WordPerfect 5.1 for DOS to Word-Perfect 5.1 for Windows

What follows, then, is an overview and a "translation" guide rather than a comprehensive comparison of WordPerfect 5.1 for DOS and

■ **Read Gilgen** is Director of Learning Support Services at the University of Wisconsin, Madison. He has used WordPerfect since 1983.

WordPerfect 5.1 for Windows (hereafter WordPerfect for DOS and WordPerfect for Windows). When you see something about which you would like to know more, please refer to the appropriate chapters in this book.

Why Use WordPerfect 5.1 for Windows?

You have spent a great deal of energy learning to use the MS-DOS version of WordPerfect 5.1. Is changing to WordPerfect for Windows worth the effort? What costs are involved? Can you really switch without losing valuable time? This section describes some of the advantages and costs involved in switching from WordPerfect for DOS to WordPerfect for Windows.

Advantages

Perhaps the biggest advantage to adopting WordPerfect for Windows is its graphical user interface (GUI), which means that everything you create on-screen is represented graphically and therefore more accurately. WordPerfect for Windows now displays proportionally spaced fonts in their actual type style, graphics images, and special characters. WYSIWYG (what you see is what you get) takes on a whole new meaning in this environment.

In addition to the text in a GUI environment, other visual, graphics elements exist to make your work easier. For example, scroll bars help you see where in your document you are working relative to your entire document and enable you to move quickly and easily from one location to another. Drop-down menus provide you with a quick list of features and also are (nearly) consistent with the menus of other GUI applications or programs.

WordPerfect for Windows employs dialog boxes, which make "telling" the program what to do easy. A dialog box often presents options in the form of buttons that you "press" (click with the mouse). The program's icons—pictorial representations of procedures—enhance your ability to locate and select features quickly. Because WordPerfect for Windows displays both words and icons, debates about whether the program is for left-brain or right-brain people are no longer important.

Because of the graphical interface, the mouse becomes much more important in WordPerfect for Windows. Now you can "point and shoot" rather than using command or function keys—that is, you can move the mouse to the feature you want and click to access it. Likewise, the mouse enables you to select blocks of text and to position and size graphics images more effectively.

WordPerfect for Windows, however, is not just another Windows application like all other Windows word processors. The program also provides you with the rich array of features you have come to expect from WordPerfect, plus many features you simply cannot find in similar products (compare, for example, WordPerfect for Windows' File Manager with the one that comes with Windows).

Finally, unlike most software upgrades, you need not worry about compatibility. WordPerfect 5.1 for Windows files are completely interchangeable with WordPerfect 5.1 for DOS files. In fact, WordPerfect for Windows makes converting to and from other word processing programs easier than ever.

Costs

Any major change or upgrade of software brings with it both costs and benefits. Often the reason for software upgrades or new software programs is to take advantage of advances in hardware technology. WordPerfect 5.0, for example, was designed to work better with rapidly developing laser printing technologies, but it also required hard disks and additional memory to run efficiently.

Today's computers not only are faster, they also offer dramatic improvements in graphics (in color and resolution), memory, and storage capacity. WordPerfect Corporation has developed WordPerfect 5.1 for Windows to take advantage of those capabilities. With old technologies, however, WordPerfect for Windows cannot perform up to its maximum potential.

WordPerfect 5.1 for Windows works best with the following hardware:

- For satisfactory performance, WordPerfect for Windows requires an IBM PC or IBM PC-compatible computer with an 80386 processor or better. The minimum requirement is an 80286 processor, and an 80386SX processor also works. Satisfactory performance, however, depends on the speed and power offered by the more powerful processors. (Note that WordPerfect for Windows does not work on PC/XT-type computers; these computers cannot operate Windows in the Standard or Enhanced mode. WordPerfect for Windows does not operate in Windows' Real mode.)

- The program requires at least 4M (megabytes) of RAM. The stated minimum is 2M, but performance deteriorates drastically with this smaller amount.

■ You need at least 8M hard disk space free to install WordPerfect for Windows.

■ You should have a graphics monitor with the quality of at least a VGA monitor. Color is also a plus. You can use WordPerfect for Windows with an EGA monitor, but because resolution (crispness of the characters) is more important with a GUI interface, working with a monitor that is lower in quality than a VGA monitor is difficult and tiring.

■ WordPerfect for Windows works best when you use a mouse. Although you can use WordPerfect for Windows without a mouse, don't even try.

You will find other costs related to software, such as the Windows program itself and other programs you may need to purchase to take full advantage of Windows' data interchange capabilities. Purchases you may have to make include the following:

■ MS-DOS 3.1 or later

■ Windows 3.0 or later

■ Other applications such as spreadsheet, communications, and database programs. Although you can run many MS-DOS applications in a Windows DOS mode (that is, as a standard DOS program), with these programs, you lose the flexibility that Windows provides you to switch quickly from one program to another or to copy data between programs.

Finally, you will encounter the human costs of time and energy associated with learning any new program. Fortunately, if you already know WordPerfect 5.1 for DOS, you will be surprised at how much you already know about WordPerfect 5.1 for Windows. If you are new to WordPerfect, WordPerfect for Windows makes learning about and using the program easier than ever. Not everyone, however, finds the graphical interface easy to use. Inveterate keyboard users may fight with the menu system until they discover that WordPerfect for Windows can be keyboard driven. In addition, WordPerfect for DOS devotees may find that certain Windows conventions, based on the Common User Access (CUA) standard, are foreign to them.

In short, if you already have the hardware or are thinking about upgrading anyway, if word processing is your primary application, and if you're not afraid to try something new, you probably are ready for WordPerfect for Windows.

New Features

If you're currently using WordPerfect 5.1, you want to know what's new in WordPerfect 5.1 for Windows. Although everything that is new cannot be listed, this section discusses the major new or significantly enhanced features (in alphabetical order), providing brief descriptions and references to the chapters in this book where you can find more detailed information. The major procedural differences (both optional and required) are discussed in "Comparing Procedures," in this chapter.

Button Bar

The Button Bar is one of the more exciting new features because you can use it to customize WordPerfect for Windows to the way *you* work. Many WordPerfect for DOS users have to resort to macros to help streamline commonly used, but cumbersome, procedures.

In WordPerfect for Windows, you can place any procedure as a button on a Button Bar, which you can access simply by clicking it with the mouse. For example, if you frequently work with graphics, you can place a button on the Button Bar to set figure box options with a single mouse click instead of by selecting Graphics, Figure, Options. You can create special macros and assign them as buttons. You even can create many different Button Bars and assign them as menu-like buttons on a master Button Bar. Refer to Chapter 19, "Using the Button Bar," for more information on customizing your Button Bars.

Convert

WordPerfect for DOS long has had a separate conversion program for translating files from a limited number of other word processing or database files to WordPerfect. Using this conversion program was cumbersome, however, because you had to exit WordPerfect before converting the files.

In WordPerfect for Windows, this conversion capability now takes place automatically when you open files or is accomplished as an option when you save files. Convert currently includes 42 different formats. These formats are as follows:

Formats	Versions
Ami Pro	1.2, 1.2a, 1.2b
ANSI (Windows)	Text, Delimited Text, Generic Word Processor
ASCII (DOS)	Text, Delimited Text, Generic Word Processor
DisplayWrite	4.0, 4.2, 5.0
IBM	DCA/FFT, DCA/RFT
Kermit	7-bit transfer
Microsoft Word (Windows)	1.0, 1.1, 1.1a
Microsoft Word (DOS)	5.0, 5.5
Multimate	3.3, 3.6, 3.7 (Advantage II), 4.0
Navy DIF Standard	—
OfficeWriter	6.0, 6.1, 6.11, 6.2
Rich Text Format	RTF
Spreadsheet DIF	—
WordPerfect	4.2, 5.0, 5.1 (DOS/Windows)
WordStar	3.3, 3.31, 3.4, 4.0, 5.0, 5.5, 6.0
XyWrite III Plus	3.55, 3.56

Note that Kermit, Navy DIF, and Spreadsheet DIF convert from those formats to WordPerfect for Windows and not vice versa. In addition, the file format is identical in the DOS and Windows versions of WordPerfect 5.1. See Chapter 31, "Importing Data and Working with Other Programs," for more information about converting files.

DDE Links

With WordPerfect for Windows, you can use Dynamic Data Exchange (DDE) links not only to transfer data from one file to another, but to update the data automatically whenever the source file is changed. For example, you can link a fiscal year report to data in a spreadsheet, and as the spreadsheet changes, so does the data in the report. This feature, however, works only with Windows applications that support DDE. WordPerfect for DOS can create links only with Lotus 1-2-3 compatible spreadsheets, and such links are not updated automatically. For a detailed discussion of DDE, refer to Chapter 31, "Importing Data and Working with Other Programs."

Macro Features

Although WordPerfect for Windows offers some dramatic changes in macros (the macro language, in particular), the program also provides new capabilities that make creating and using macros easier than ever. For example, you now can pause while recording your macro, do whatever you need to do, and then resume recording the macro. You also can assign macros to your Macro menu, to Ctrl-*letter* and Ctrl-Shift-*letter* key combinations, and to buttons on your Button Bar. You can retrieve, edit, and save your WordPerfect for Windows macros just as you work with any other document. Although WordPerfect for DOS macros do not work with WordPerfect for Windows, the Macro facility enables you to convert many WordPerfect for DOS macro commands and codes into WordPerfect for Windows formats. For more information about macros, see Chapter 19, "Creating Macros."

Multiple Documents

In WordPerfect 5.1 for DOS, you can have two documents open at once, but often two aren't enough. With WordPerfect for Windows, no longer are you limited to two documents: you can have up to *nine* open documents, depending on memory and disk space. See Chapter 1, "Preparing To Use WordPerfect for Windows," for more information.

Quick List

The List Files feature of WordPerfect 5.1 for DOS is powerful and easy to use, but you still need to understand DOS commands to find files and change locations on your hard disk. WordPerfect for Windows offers the Quick List feature, which makes choosing a file easier than ever. With Quick List, you can create a list of descriptive names that refer to drives and directories you use. When you need to access a directory, you simply select from among the descriptive names, such as *Drafts for Chapter Six*. See Chapter 3, "Managing Files," for a detailed discussion of the Quick List feature.

Ruler

Another advantage of WordPerfect for Windows' graphical interface is that it gives you the capability to use the Ruler to make adjustments on-screen to margins, tab settings, columns, fonts, spacing, justification, tables, and more. In WordPerfect for DOS, you often have to wade through several levels of menus to find and use many formatting features. WordPerfect for Windows menus are no less complex, but the Ruler puts many commonly used formatting procedures where you can see and have immediate access to them. For example, the Ruler enables you to use the mouse to drag a tab setting to a different location, to change it, or to remove it altogether. See Chapter 6, "Formatting Text," for further discussion of the Ruler.

Undo

WordPerfect for DOS users long have wanted the capability to "undo" an action, not just to undelete a deletion. WordPerfect for Windows enables you to do both. See Chapter 4, "Editing a Document."

WordPerfect Characters

In WordPerfect for DOS, you can use over 1,500 special foreign, typographic, and scientific characters. Unfortunately, using them is hampered by a difficult Compose feature, the need to look up the characters in a reference manual, and the inability to see most of the characters on-screen.

Now, because of its graphical interface, WordPerfect for Windows can display on-screen any of the over 1,500 characters in its 11 character sets; therefore, you now can select the characters from an on-screen list. Chapter 28, "Creating and Displaying Special Characters," discusses these character sets in detail.

WPG Images

When WordPerfect Corporation first offered graphics capabilities in WordPerfect for DOS, the company provided a basic sampling of 30 graphic images in the WordPerfect Graphics (WPG) format. WordPerfect for DOS, Version 5.1, comes with 30 different WPG images. Continuing the tradition, WordPerfect 5.1 for Windows includes 36 new

WPG graphics, most of which come from the WordPerfect/DrawPerfect Figure Library collections. See Chapters 7, "Introduction to Graphics," and 17, "Understanding Advanced Graphics," for more information.

Comparing Terminology

Because of the Windows environment, and to comply more closely with CUA (Common User Access) terminology, several terms in WordPerfect 5.1 for Windows are different from terms in WordPerfect 5.1 for DOS. The following brief glossary (see table B.1) lists most of these changes.

Table B.1. New Terminology

WordPerfect for DOS Term	WordPerfect for Windows Term	Comments
Block	Select	To select, you can use the mouse, the Select key, or the Shift key and directional keys.
Block Copy	Copy	
Block Move	Cut	
Block Retrieve	Paste	
Exit	Close	
Format	Layout	
Left/Right Indent	Double Indent	
List Files	File Manager	
Macro	Macro Play	You can assign macros to the Macro menu or to a Button Bar, or you can create Ctrl-*letter* and Ctrl-Shift-*letter* macros.
Macro Define	Macro Record	You can pause the recording of a macro.
Menu	Dialog box	WordPerfect for DOS uses numbered or mnemonic menus; WordPerfect for Windows uses dialog boxes that employ buttons, text boxes, and pop-up lists, with mnemonic choices.
Pull-down menus	Menu	The main access menu

Table B.1. (continued)

WordPerfect for DOS Term	WordPerfect for Windows Term	Comments
Retrieve	Open	You can have as many as nine documents open at once.
Retrieve into Current Document	Retrieve	
Setup	Preferences	
Switch	Next Document, Previous Document	You can move forward or backward through as many as nine documents.
Tab Align	Decimal Tab	

Comparing Procedures

As you work with WordPerfect for Windows, you eventually will find that you still can do just about everything you could do in WordPerfect for DOS. Many of the steps you used to accomplish those tasks, however, have changed to comply with the Common User Access (CUA) standard or Windows procedures (or both) or to simplify previously complicated procedures. In spite of the changes, most WordPerfect 5.1 for Windows procedures are functionally the same as they are in WordPerfect 5.1 for DOS.

This section discusses the important procedural changes in WordPerfect for Windows, including brief descriptions of each change and references to the chapters in this book where you can find detailed information. If WordPerfect for Windows enables you to perform a procedure the same way you do in WordPerfect for DOS, that option is indicated in the description of the procedure.

Auto Code Placement

Under normal circumstances, you want certain format codes to take effect at the beginning of a page or a paragraph. For example, if you change a tab setting or the left and right margins, you usually don't want that change to take place in the middle of a paragraph.

WordPerfect for Windows automatically places such codes at the beginning of the current paragraph or, if page-related, at the beginning of the current page.

WordPerfect for DOS always places format codes in the text at the point of the cursor, which sometimes causes problems, especially for codes that should be placed at the top of the page. If you need to "fine-tune" your code placement, as in WordPerfect for DOS, you can turn off the Auto Code Placement feature. See Chapter 29, "Customizing WordPerfect with Preferences," for a discussion of the Auto Code Placement feature.

Clipboard

WordPerfect for Windows' Clipboard is somewhat like the memory storage area WordPerfect for DOS uses to hold text you are moving or copying. In WordPerfect for Windows, however, you can make multiple cuts or copies to the Clipboard before pasting from the Clipboard to your document, by using Append rather than Cut or Copy from the Edit menu. In addition to moving text, you can copy graphics images from other Windows programs and paste them into WordPerfect for Windows documents. For more information about the Clipboard, see Chapter 5, "Selecting and Editing Text."

File Manager

File Manager now is a separate program you can use outside or within WordPerfect 5.1 for Windows. File Manager includes all the features found in WordPerfect 5.1 for DOS' List Files, plus many more. For example, a navigator enables you to explore your subdirectories, a file viewer enables you to look at graphics and your documents, a sophisticated finder helps you locate files anywhere on your disk, either by file name or by keywords in the files, and a utility reports information about your system, your printers, and your disk drives. Refer to Chapter 3, "Managing Files," and Chapter 30, "Advanced File Management Techniques," for discussions of File Manager.

Graphics

You can create graphics lines and boxes in WordPerfect for Windows exactly as you do in WordPerfect for DOS—by manually specifying size and location; however, WordPerfect for Windows displays both text and graphics on-screen. In addition, you can use the mouse to position your graphics and size the graphics boxes, so you easily can view the effect these changes have on your document. Chapter 17, "Understanding Advanced Graphics," discusses WordPerfect for Windows' graphics in greater detail.

Macros

You no longer need a separate, special editor for your macros. You can retrieve, edit, and save WordPerfect for Windows macros just as you do a document. The macro programming language has changed drastically to account for WordPerfect for Windows' new user interface. Also, the first time you use a macro, WordPerfect for Windows compiles it to make it work faster. A macro conversion utility is available to assist you in converting macros, but be prepared to learn a whole new language and methodology. See Chapter 20, "Creating Macros," for more information.

Menu versus Command Key Access

Looking at your WordPerfect for Windows screen, you may find that the primary, and seemingly the only, way to perform WordPerfect for Windows procedures is to use the mouse to access menus and dialog boxes. Indeed, WordPerfect for Windows was designed with the mouse and this visual approach in mind. Nevertheless, at least three other approaches are available. You can combine any of the following methods to perform procedures in WordPerfect for Windows. Chapter 1, "Preparing to Use WordPerfect for Windows," discusses these methods.

- *Keystroke equivalents.* Every menu option contains an underlined letter you can type to access that option's feature rather than use the mouse to point and click. You use the Alt key to access the menu bar itself. For example, to use keystroke equivalents to create a table, press Alt, **L**ayout, **T**able, **C**reate (the boldface characters represent the keys you press). From the dialog box, you press and hold down Alt and type the letter of the item you want, or Tab to the command button you want and press Enter.

- *Function key equivalents.* You can access many WordPerfect for Windows features by using function keys, although the function key assignments for the CUA keyboard layout are different from those of the WordPerfect for DOS layout. These function keys often take you part way into a menu sequence and enable you to finish from menus or dialog boxes.

■ *Ctrl-key equivalents*. Many menu items also have Ctrl-key equivalents you can use as shortcuts to access a feature. For example, to turn on italic, you can press Ctrl-I, which is equivalent to Font, Italic; Ctrl-P prints the current document, and so on.

Reveal Codes

With the Reveal Codes option turned on, you can move the insertion point by pointing to codes in the Reveal Codes area and clicking the mouse. In WordPerfect for DOS, you can click the mouse only in the text (not Reveal Codes) area.

Save and Save As

When you save a WordPerfect for Windows file, you can choose Save to save the file with its same name, or you can choose Save As to save the file with a new name, location, or file format. If you do not change the name, location, or file format, WordPerfect for Windows does not ask whether you want to overwrite the current file, as does WordPerfect for DOS. Because WordPerfect for Windows uses Open and Save As for its document conversion functions, the Text In/Out feature no longer is necessary and, therefore, is not available. See Chapter 2, "Creating, Printing, and Saving a Document," for more information about Save and Save As.

Search

After typing the search string in the WordPerfect for Windows Search dialog box, you now press Enter or click the Search button to begin the search. Codes are inserted into the search string from a window that lists all searchable codes. Chapter 4, "Editing a Document," explains the Search feature in more detail.

Special Codes

If you ever struggled in WordPerfect for DOS to remember the keystrokes you must type to insert a hard space or a tab with dot leaders, you will appreciate the WordPerfect for Windows dialog box that contains only special codes. You simply choose the code you want and insert it in your text. See Chapter 4, "Editing a Document," for more information about special codes.

Speller and Thesaurus

Not only can you use both the Speller program and the Thesaurus program from within WordPerfect for Windows, you also can run either as separate programs directly from the Windows Program Manager without having to run WordPerfect for Windows first. Although you cannot check spelling or change documents in other word processors or text editors, you can use the Speller or Thesaurus to look up words while working in other Windows applications. Chapter 8, "Using the Speller and the Thesaurus," discusses these programs in more detail.

WordPerfect Characters

You now can display on-screen all the more than 1,500 characters in the 11 WordPerfect Character sets. In place of the Compose feature in WordPerfect for DOS, WordPerfect for Windows enables you to select characters from a dialog box that displays the characters you can choose. You no longer have to turn to the reference manual to find the characters you need. An International-Expanded WP.DRS file is available (at extra cost) to enable you to print more characters in a full-bodied font, as opposed to the standard stick-figure look you get with many characters. See Chapter 28, "Creating and Displaying Special Characters," for a detailed discussion of the WordPerfect Character sets.

WYSIWYG versus Draft Mode

By default, WordPerfect for Windows displays text and graphics on-screen almost exactly as they actually appear when printed (some call this WYSIAWYG, or "what you see is almost what you get"). Thus, proportional fonts appear proportional on-screen—in the same point size you selected—and graphics, including lines, boxes, and equations, appear on-screen as they do when printed.

For people who prefer the thicker, monospaced characters of WordPerfect for DOS, a Draft mode is available in WordPerfect for Windows. You can use the View menu to switch quickly from one mode to another, and using the Preferences menu, you can match your WordPerfect for DOS display even more closely by specifying the colors used for Draft mode. Refer to Chapter 29, "Customizing WordPerfect with Preferences," for more information.

Windows-Specific Considerations

WordPerfect for Windows is a software application that runs under the Windows environment. Windows, in turn, runs under the Microsoft Disk Operating System (MS-DOS). By comparison, WordPerfect for DOS is a software application that runs directly under MS-DOS.

WordPerfect for Windows dictates many of the procedures and keystrokes you must use, whereas dialog box procedures and keystrokes and printing and file saving procedures are controlled by Windows or MS-DOS. When you encounter a problem, it could be a result of any of these three programs. When WordPerfect for Windows runs smoothly, it does so because of an amazingly complex cooperation among them all.

To set up or change memory allocation, swap files, screen colors, or mouse definitions, or to optimize Windows for better WordPerfect for Windows performance, consult your Windows documentation.

For more information on the Windows environment, see table B.2, "Common User Access Keystrokes," and B.3, "Keyboard Comparison," in this chapter, and Appendix A, "Installing and Setting Up WordPerfect for Windows."

Comparing Keyboard Layouts

When you first use WordPerfect for Windows, you may wonder why certain keys function as they do. In some cases, the keystrokes used to access certain features are determined by the Windows environment. In other cases, required keystrokes are determined by the keyboard layout you have selected. This section describes the Common User Access (CUA) interface, the CUA and WordPerfect for DOS keyboard layouts. Table B.3 provides a comprehensive listing of keystrokes for WordPerfect for DOS, the WordPerfect for Windows DOS equivalent keyboard layout, and the WordPerfect for Windows CUA equivalent keyboard layout.

Common User Access (CUA) Keystrokes

The Windows environment and applications that run under Windows generally adhere to what is known as the *Common User Access* (*CUA*) interface, which means that basic menu items, their arrangement, and certain basic keystrokes are similar among all Windows programs. This common interface makes using different programs easier because you don't have to learn a new set of keystrokes for each program. Table B.2 lists the most commonly used CUA keystrokes.

Table B.2. Common User Access Keystrokes

Key	Effect
Alt	Activates the menu bar
Alt-*letter*	Select menu or dialog box item
Tab	Cycle forward through dialog box options
Shift-Tab	Cycle backward through dialog box options
Alt-F4	Close a dialog box or exit an application
Esc	Cancel or back out of a procedure
Alt-Esc	Cycle through open applications (windows, icons, or both)
Alt-Tab	Switch between the two most recent active Windows applications
Home	Move insertion point to beginning of line
Ctrl-Home	Move insertion point to beginning of document
End	Move insertion point to end of line
Ctrl-End	Move insertion point to end of document
Ctrl-Esc	Display Task List (active applications)
Shift and directional keys	Select text
F1	Help

WordPerfect for Windows CUA Keyboard Layout

The default WordPerfect for Windows keyboard is compliant with the CUA keyboard but contains other WordPerfect-specific commands. Because WordPerfect Corporation needed to make several basic changes to the keyboard, the company decided to rework the entire keyboard—especially the function keys—so that new users of WordPerfect will find the keyboard easy and logical to use. Thus, certain related tasks are grouped together on the same keys (for example, on F2, Shift-F2, Ctrl-F2, Alt-F2, and so on), working around the required CUA keystrokes. Compatibility with earlier MS-DOS versions of WordPerfect was a secondary consideration.

The WordPerfect for Windows keyboard interface takes advantage of the new Enhanced keyboards, especially the F11 and F12 function keys. It also enables you to use more combinations of keys, such as Alt-Shift-F11, which opens the Text Box Edit screen.

WordPerfect for Windows ships with a CUA-compliant function key template that includes several Ctrl-*letter* equivalents to menu choices, such as Cut, Copy, Paste, Undo, and Print Document.

WordPerfect for Windows DOS-Compatible Keyboard Layout

Although the default WordPerfect for Windows keyboard is CUA compliant, WordPerfect for Windows also provides a WordPerfect for DOS-compatible keyboard for people migrating from WordPerfect for DOS or for people who need to work in both environments. Although this keyboard layout isn't exactly the same as the WordPerfect 5.1 for DOS keyboard, the layout is close enough to make people who are making the transition to WordPerfect for Windows feel quite familiar with the program.

Note that the Windows environment and CUA keystrokes are required after you leave the WordPerfect for Windows menus and enter Windows-like dialog boxes. Suppose that you select the WordPerfect 5.1 keyboard and press Shift-F10 (Open). After typing the name of the file you want to open, you decide to edit the file name. Pressing Home and the right-arrow key places the insertion point on the second character of the file name, because the CUA keystrokes are in effect in the dialog box (Home moves the insertion point to the beginning of the line).

This dual interface takes some getting used to. In fact, although initially you may find that the WordPerfect for Windows DOS keyboard layout is useful for making the switch from WordPerfect for DOS, in the long run it may be worth the effort to use and learn the default WordPerfect for Windows CUA keyboard layout, because keystrokes then are consistent in all areas of the program. Likewise, nothing happens if you press F7 to exit the dialog box. You have to press Alt-F4 (the CUA Close key) or click Cancel.

Keyboard Layout Comparisons

Table B.3 presents a side-by-side keystroke comparison of three keyboards. The first column lists the keystrokes. The second column is the WordPerfect for DOS keyboard. The third and fourth columns are WordPerfect for Windows columns, the third being the DOS-compatible version, and the fourth being the CUA-compatible version. This table may help those who already are used to WordPerfect for DOS to make a smoother transition to WordPerfect for Windows.

If you are interested in modifying or creating a keyboard layout, some keys cannot be changed, but others normally should not be changed. You should not change the following

1. Keystrokes that cannot be mapped: Esc, Enter, Tab, Backspace, Hyphen, Alt-Hyphen, Alt-=, and Alt with the numbers 0 through 9.

2. Keystrokes that depend on a base key normally should not be changed because if the base key is changed, the keystroke does not function as stated.

Where a keystroke functions differently because of the situation in which it is used (for example, you are in a dialog box), the situation is enclosed in angles (for example, <dialog>). Keystrokes have been left blank if they have no function or if they duplicate functions that have been assigned to an easier key combination.

Table B.3. Keyboard Comparison

Key	WordPerfect 5.1 for DOS	WordPerfect DOS Compatible	WordPerfect CUA Compatible
FUNCTION KEYS			
F1	Cancel Back up one step Undelete	Help	Help
Shift-F1	Setup	Preferences	Help: What Is?
Alt-F1	Thesaurus	Thesaurus	Thesaurus
Ctrl-F1	Shell	Next Pane	Speller
Ctrl-Shift-F1	—	Previous Pane	Preferences
F2	Search	Search	Search
Shift-F2	Backward Search	Search Next	Search Next
Alt-F2	Replace	Replace	Search Previous
Alt-Shift-F2	—	Search Previous	—
Ctrl-F2	Spell	Speller	Replace
F3	Help	Undelete	Save As
Shift-F3	Switch	Next Document	Save
Alt-F3	Reveal Codes	Reveal Codes	Reveal Codes
Alt-Shift-F3	—	Previous Document	View Ruler
Ctrl-F3	Screen	Redisplay Screen	Redisplay Screen
Ctrl-Shift-F3	—	Draft Mode	Draft Mode
F4	Indent	Indent <Pop-up List> Open/Close	Open File <Pop-up List> Open/Close
Shift-F4	Left/Right Indent	Double Indent	New File

continues

Table B.3. (continued)

Key	WordPerfect 5.1 for DOS	WordPerfect DOS Compatible	WordPerfect CUA Compatible
Alt-F4	Block	Select Block <Dialog> Close/Cancel	Close Application (Exit) <Dialog> Close/Cancel
Alt-Shift-F4	—	Cell Select (Tables)	—
Ctrl-F4	Move	Sentence Select	Close Document
Ctrl-Shift-F4	—	Paragraph Select	Clear Document
F5	List	File Manager	Print Document
Shift-F5	Date/Outline	Tools Menu (Date/Outline)	Print Preview
Alt-F5	Mark Text	Tools Menu (Mark Text)	Paragraph Number
Alt-Shift-F5	—	Generate	Paragraph Define
Ctrl-F5	Text In/Out	—	Date Text
Ctrl-Shift-F5	—	—	Date Code
F6	Bold	Bold	Next Pane
Shift-F6	Center (twice for dot leaders)	Center (twice for dot leaders)	Previous Pane
Alt-F6	Flush Right (twice for dot leaders)	Flush Right (twice for dot leaders)	Next Window
Alt-Shift-F6	—	Previous Window	Previous Window
Ctrl-F6	Tab Align	Decimal Tab	Next Document
Ctrl-Shift-F6	—	Next Window	Previous Document
F7	Exit	Close	Indent
Shift-F7	Print	Print	Center (twice for dot leaders)

continues

Key	WordPerfect 5.1 for DOS	WordPerfect DOS Compatible	WordPerfect CUA Compatible
Alt-F7	Columns/Table	Layout Menu (Cols/Tables)	Flush Right (twice for dot leaders)
Alt-Shift-F7	—	Print Preview	Hard Decimal Tab
Ctrl-F7	Footnote	Layout Menu (Footnote)	Hanging Indent
Ctrl-Shift-F7	—	Clear	Double Indent
F8	Underline	Underline	Select Block
Shift-F8	Format	Layout Menu	Select Cell
Alt-F8	Style	Styles	Styles
Alt-Shift-F8	—	Special Codes	Special Codes
Ctrl-F8	Font	Font	Margins
F9	End Field	End Field	Font
Shift-F9	Merge Codes	Merge Codes	Layout Line
Alt-F9	Graphics	Graphics	Layout Page
Alt-Shift-F9	—	—	Layout Columns
Ctrl-F9	Merge/Sort	Tools Menu (Merge/Sort)	Layout Tables
Ctrl-Shift-F9	—	—	Layout Document
F10	Save	Save As	Menu
Shift-F10	Retrieve	Open	—
Alt-F10	Macro	Macro Play	Macro Play
Ctrl-F10	Macro Define	Macro Record	Macro Record
Ctrl-Shift-F10	—	Macro Stop	Macro Stop
F11	Reveal Codes	Reveal Codes	Figure Retrieve
Shift-F11	—	View Ruler	Figure Edit
Alt-F11	—	Draft Mode	Text Box Create

Table B.3. (continued)

Key	WordPerfect 5.1 for DOS	WordPerfect DOS Compatible	WordPerfect CUA Compatible
Alt-Shift-F11	—	—	Text Box Edit
Ctrl-F11	—	—	Horizontal Line Create
Ctrl-Shift-F11	—	—	Vertical Line Create
F12	Block	Select Block	Mark Text
Shift-F12	—	Cell Select	Define Menu
Alt-F12	—	—	Generate
Ctrl-F12	—	—	Merge
Ctrl-Shift-F12	—	—	Sort

ESCAPE, PRINT SCREEN, and BREAK KEYS

Key	WordPerfect 5.1 for DOS	WordPerfect DOS Compatible	WordPerfect CUA Compatible
Esc	Repeat	Cancel, Back up one level	Cancel, Back up one level
Shift-Esc	—	(Cancel)	(Cancel)
Alt-Esc	—	Next Application	Next Application
Alt-Shift-Esc	—	Previous Application	Previous Application
Ctrl-Esc	—	Task Dialog	Task Dialog
Ctrl-Shift-Esc	—	Task Dialog	Task Dialog
Print Screen	—	Copy screen to Clipboard	Copy screen to Clipboard
Shift-Print Screen	Copy screen to printer	—	—
Ctrl-Print Screen	Print	—	—
Alt- Print Screen	—	Copy active window to Clipboard	Copy active window to Clipboard
Ctrl-Break	—	Cancel	Cancel

continues

ALPHANUMERIC KEYS

Key	WordPerfect 5.1 for DOS	WordPerfect DOS Compatible	WordPerfect CUA Compatible
Alt-0–9	Assignable as Variables	—	—
Ctrl-2	Compose	—	—
Ctrl-6	Deselect/Reselect Keyboard	—	—
-	Hyphen	Hyphen	Hyphen
Home, -	Hard Hyphen	Hard Hyphen	—
Alt-Hyphen	Hyphen	Document System Menu	Document System Menu
Ctrl-Hyphen	Soft Hyphen	Soft Hyphen	Hard Hyphen
Ctrl-Shift-Hyphen	Soft Hyphen	Soft Hyphen	Soft Hyphen
Alt-=	Pull-Down Menus	—	—
Home, /	Cancel Hyphenation Code	Cancel Hyphenation Code	Cancel Hyphenation Code
Ctrl-/	—	Cancel Hyphenation Code	Cancel Hyphenation Code
Ctrl-B*	Page Number Code	Font Bold	Font Bold
Ctrl-C	—	Copy	Copy
Ctrl-D	—	Line Draw	Line Draw
Ctrl-F	—	Justify Full	Justify Full
Ctrl-G	—	Go To Dialog	Go To Dialog
Ctrl-I	Tab	Font Italic	Font Italic
Ctrl-J	Hard Return	Justify Center	Justify Center

Table B.3. (continued)

Key	WordPerfect 5.1 for DOS	WordPerfect DOS Compatible	WordPerfect CUA Compatible
Ctrl-K	Delete to End of Line	—	—
Ctrl-L	Delete to End of Page	Justify Left	Justify Left
Ctrl-M	Space	—	—
Ctrl-N	—	Font Normal	Font Normal
Ctrl-P	—	Print Current Document	Print Current Document
Ctrl-R	—	Justify Right	Justify Right
Ctrl-S	—	Font Size Menu	Font Size Menu
Ctrl-U	—	Font Underline	Font Underline
Ctrl-V	Compose	Paste	Paste
Ctrl-W	Cursor Up	WordPerfect Characters	WordPerfect Characters
Ctrl-X	Cursor Right	Cut	Cut
Ctrl-Y	Cursor Left	—	—
Ctrl-Z	Cursor Down	Undo	Undo
Backspace	Delete Left	Delete Left	Delete Left
	Delete Block	Delete Selected Text or Graphics <Dialog> Clear Text Box	Delete Selected Text or Graphics <Dialog> Clear Text Box
Home, Backspace	Delete from cursor to beginning of word	Delete from insertion point to beginning of word	—
Alt-Backspace	—	Undo	Undo
Alt-Shift-Backspace	—	Undelete	Undelete

continues

Key	WordPerfect 5.1 for DOS	WordPerfect DOS Compatible	WordPerfect CUA Compatible
Ctrl-Backspace	Delete Word	Delete Word	Delete Word
Delete	Delete Right Delete Block	Delete Right Delete Selected Text or Graphics <Dialog> Clear Text Box	Delete Right Delete Selected Text or Graphics <Dialog> Clear Text Box
Home, Delete	Delete from cursor to end of word	Delete from insertion point to end of word	—
Shift-Delete	—	Cut	Cut
Alt-Delete	—	Delete Row (Table)	Delete Row (Table)
Ctrl-Delete	Delete Row (Table)	Delete Word	Delete to end of line
Insert	Insert/Typeover	Insert/Typeover	Insert/Typeover
Shift-Insert	—	Paste	Paste
Alt-Insert	—	Insert Row (Table)	Insert Row (Table)
Alt-Shift-Insert	—	Append Row (Table)	Append Row (Table)
Ctrl-Insert	Insert Row (Table)	Copy	Copy
Tab	Tab Next Cell	Tab Next Level, Next Cell	Tab Next Level, Next Cell
Home, Tab	Hard Left Tab	Hard Left Tab	—
Home, Home, Tab	Hard Left Tab with dot leader	Hard Left Tab with dot leader	—
Shift-Tab	Margin Release Previous Level, Previous Cell	Margin Release Previous Level, Previous Cell	Margin Release Previous Level, Previous Cell
Alt-Tab	—	Next Application	Next Application
Alt-Shift-Tab	—	Previous Application	Previous Application

Table B.3. (continued)

Key	WordPerfect 5.1 for DOS	WordPerfect DOS Compatible	WordPerfect CUA Compatible
Ctrl-Tab	—	Tab (even in a table)	Tab (even in a table)
Ctrl-Shift-Tab	—	Margin Release (even in a table)	Margin Release (even in a table)
Enter	Hard Return Default Menu Selection	Hard Return <Dialog> Default Action	Hard Return <Dialog> Default Action
Home, Enter	Invisible Soft Return	Invisible Soft Return	—
Shift-Enter	—	Hard Return (even in outline)	Hard Return (even in outline)
Alt-Enter	—	Merge End of Field	Merge End of Field
Alt-Shift-Enter	—	Merge End of Record	Merge End of Record
Ctrl-Enter	Hard Page Hard Row (Tables) Start Next Column (Columns)	Hard Page Start Next Column (Columns) Hard Row (Tables)	Hard Page Hard Row (Tables) Start Next Column (Columns)

*The following Ctrl-Characters are not assigned: A, E, H, O, Q, T

DIRECTIONAL KEYS

Note: In WordPerfect for Windows, you can hold down the Shift key while moving the insertion point in any of the following ways to Select (Block) text from the current insertion point to the ending insertion point. Moving the insertion point farther while holding down the Shift key extends Select (Block). Additional insertion point movement without the Shift key turns off Select. Also, the Home key in the DOS and DOS Compatible keyboards modifies subsequent insertion point movements (for example, Home-Down moves down one screen, and so on.)

Home	(Modifier)	(Modifier)	Position to beginning of line after codes

Key	WordPerfect 5.1 for DOS	WordPerfect DOS Compatible	WordPerfect CUA Compatible
Home, Home	(Modifier)	(Modifier)	Position to beginning of line before codes
Alt-Home	—	—	Position to top of current page/column/cell
Ctrl-Home	Go To	Go To	Position to top of document after codes (twice positions before codes)
End	Position to end of line	Position to end of line	Position to end of line
End, End	—	Position to last cell in row	Position to last cell in row
Alt-End	—	—	Position to bottom of current page/column/cell
Ctrl-End	Delete to End of Line	Delete to End of Line	Position to bottom of document
PgUp	Position up one page	Position up one page	Position up one screen
Alt-PgUp	—	Position up one screen	Position up one page
Ctrl-PgUp	Assign Variable	Screen Left	Screen Left
PgDn	Position down one page	Position down one page	Position down one screen
Alt-PgDn	—	Position down one screen	Position down one page
Left arrow	Position to preceding character	Position to preceding character	Position to preceding character
Home, left arrow	Position to left side of screen	Position to left side of screen	—
Home, Home, left arrow	Position to beginning of line after codes	Position to beginning of line after codes	—
Home, Home, Home, left arrow	Position to beginning of line before codes	Position to beginning of line before codes	—

continues

Table B.3. (continued)

Key	WordPerfect 5.1 for DOS	WordPerfect DOS Compatible	WordPerfect CUA Compatible
Alt-left arrow	—	Position to preceding column/cell/paragraph number	Position to preceding column/cell/paragraph number
Ctrl-left arrow	Position to beginning of preceding word	Position to beginning of preceding word	Position to beginning of preceding word
Right arrow	Position to next character	Position to next character	Position to next character
Home, right arrow	Position to right side of screen	Position to right side of screen	—
Home, Home, right arrow	Position to end of line	Position to end of line	—
Home, Home, Home, right arrow	Position to end of line, last column in table	Position to end of line, last column in table	—
Alt-right arrow	—	Position to next column/cell/paragraph number	Position to next column/cell/paragraph number
Ctrl-right arrow	Position to beginning of next word	Position to beginning of next word	Position to beginning of next word
Up arrow	Position up one line	Position up one line <Character> Decrement	Position Up One Line <Incrementor> Decrement
Home, up arrow	Position to top of screen	Position to top of screen	—
Home, Home, up arrow	Position to top of document after codes	Position to top of document after codes	—
Home, Home, Home, up arrow	Position to top of document before codes	Position to top of document before codes	—

Key	WordPerfect 5.1 for DOS	WordPerfect DOS Compatible	WordPerfect CUA Compatible
Alt-up arrow	—	Position up one row, beginning of cell (tables)	Position up one row beginning of cell (tables)
Ctrl-up arrow	Position up one paragraph	Position up one paragraph	Position up one paragraph
Down arrow	Position to next line	Position to next line <Incrementor> Increment	Position to next line <Incrementor> Increment
Home, down arrow	Position down one screen	Position down one screen	—
Home, Home, down arrow	Position to end of document	Position to end of document	—
Alt-down arrow	—	Position down one row, beginning of cell (tables)	Position down one row beginning of cell (tables)
Ctrl-down arrow	Position down one paragraph	Position down one paragraph	Position down one paragraph
- (Numeric)	Position to top of screen	Position to top of screen	—
+ (Numeric)	Position to bottom of screen	Position to bottom of screen	—

Chapter Summary

Changing versions of software is difficult, even under the best circumstances. Fortunately, you really don't have to relearn WordPerfect. The major changes between WordPerfect 5.1 for DOS and WordPerfect 5.1 for Windows aren't related to features but to the environment or interface required to use those features. This appendix should help make the transition a bit easier. The rest is up to you.

INDEX

A

absolute advance, 485
absolute tabs, 177
Add Markings dialog box, 871
Add Paper Size dialog box, 462
  Paper Location options, 463
  Paper Orientation options,
    463-464
  Paper Size options, 464
  Paper Type options, 464
  Print options, 465
Add Printer dialog box, 250
  Info button, 257
Adobe Type Manager (ATM) for
  Windows, 287
Advance dialog box, 473
Advance feature, adjusting
  textual appearance, 485-486
Advanced Find, 18, 1042-1043
advanced macros, 687
[AdvLft] code, 489
[AdvRght] code, 489
[AdvToLn] code, 708
alignment, 1020
[ALL OTHERS] code, 466-468
alphanumeric words, 747
Alt-F4 shortcut key
  combination, 42
Ami Pro documents, converting
  to WordPerfect, 1067

anchoring boxes relative to
  page, 976
appearance attributes, 302
  changing for fonts, 304-306
Applications dialog box, 1053
Applications menu, 18
archive file attribute, 1050
Arrows menu (Equation
  Editor), 935
Arts & Letters, 1087
ascenders, 281
ASCII
  delimited text files in merge
    operations, 712-713
  text, 1078
Associate dialog box, 1054
attributes
  appearance, 302
  fonts, changing, 302-306
    applying to existing text, 307
  size, 302
    changing for fonts, 302-304
Auto Code Placement feature,
  165, 311-312, 1123
auto codes
  hard returns, 974
  placement, 972-974
AutoCAD, 575
Automatic Cross-Reference
  feature, 863
  basic steps, 864

generating, 870
marking text for, 864-866, 869
marking footnotes/
endnotes, 867-869
targets, 863
Automatic Kerning feature, 487
autotracing, 576

B

backslash (\) (Equation Editor),
926-928
backups, 968-971
original document, 969-971
timed, 965, 969-970
base fonts, 297-298
baseline, 492
Basic installation (WordPerfect
for Windows), 1097
beep, customizing, 977
binding offset, 993
Bit Map (BMP) graphics
format, 198
bit-mapped fonts, 282
black-and-white graphics, 986
blank lines, inserting into
documents, 52-53
[Bline:Off] code, 492
Block Protect feature, 316-317
boilerplate text, 60
BOLD command (Equation
Editor), 926
[Bold Off] code, 127
[Bold On] code, 127
boldface text, 126-127
removing boldface, 127
Box Position and Size dialog
box, 528
boxes
anchoring, relative to
page, 976
free-form, 516-518
moving insertion point, 518
graphics, see graphics boxes
brainstorming, 70-71

Button Bar, 11, 14, 37-39, 49,
624-625, 1044, 1117
assigning macros to,
638-640, 669
controlling Button Bars,
638-639
built-in, editing, 641-642
category marker, 627
columns, automating
tasks, 403
commands commonly
included in, 636
contents, 627-628
creating, 629
editing, 630-632
Macros Button Bar,
creating, 640
position, changing, 632-635
saving, 629-630
selecting, 626-627
specialized, creating, 636-638
style, changing, 632-635
Button Bar Options dialog box,
632-635
buttons
radio, 971
ruler, 980

C

calendars, creating, 453
cancelling print jobs, 267
Caption Editor, 555
cartridges, 283
erasable, 285
fixed, 284
fonts, 976
modular, 284
cascading windows, 27, 1046
category marker, 627
cell margins, 436
[Cell] code, 431
cells, 406, 736, 747
formatting, 434-435
joining in tables, 423

locking, 429
selecting/deleting from
  tables, 413-415
splitting, 424
center justification, 183
[Center Pg] code, 710
Center tabs, 173
centering pages, 319-320
Change Directory dialog
  box, 1030
Change File Attributes dialog
  box, 1050
characters
  hard return, 988-989
  overstrike, 956-958
  posture, 281
  special, 17
  transposing with macros,
    657-658
  weight, 281
  width, 281
  WordPerfect, 1120, 1126
clicking, 30
clip art, 200
  resizing box, 202-204
  vendors, 576-577
Clipboard, 149, 1123
  converting documents,
    1070-1075
  creating/compiling names of
    files, 1051-1052
  linking spreadsheet
    data, 1083
closing documents, 67-68
[Cndl EOP] code, 318
codes
  auto placement, 972-974
  controlling page division, 315
    avoiding orphans and
      widows, 318
    Block Protect feature,
      316-317
    Conditional End of Page
      feature, 317-318

hard page breaks, 315
soft page breaks, 315
deleting
  confirming, 974
  formatting codes, 312
formatting, 727-728
  table-row, 748-749
hard return, 988-989
Initial Codes, 966
initial, setting, 340-341
margins, setting, 313-314
merge, 727
  displaying, 987
  in tables, 453
placing formatting codes,
  311-312
styles
  deleting 369-370
  editing, 364
table codes, 431
[Col Def] code, 384, 795
[Col On] code, 384, 795
ColoRIX VGA, 575
colors, 986
  contrast, 985
  Draft mode, 984-985
  Reveal Codes, 990
  text, 985
columns, 747
  Button Bar usage, 403
  changing with Ruler, 398-400
  deleting from tables, 421-422
  formatting, 432-433
  headings, File Manager, 1046
  inserting into tables, 420-421
  irregular, 449-450
  limitations, 402
  macro usage, 403
  newspaper, 381-382
    defining with Define
      Columns dialog box,
      385-388
    defining with Ruler,
      383-385

editing, 391-392
previewing, 392-394
parallel, 381
converting to tables,
445-447
defining, 395-397
editing, 400-401
inserting, 401-402
moving, 402
typing text in, 397-398
restoring columns deleted
from tables, 422
side-by-side, 987
tabular, converting to tables,
443-444
trifold mailers, 603
using vertical lines with,
510-513
widths, changing in table
structure, 417-419
working with text within, 388
displaying one column at a
time, 390
moving insertion point,
389-390
commands, 33, 914
choosing menu options, 34-35
commonly included in Button
Bars, 636
dialog boxes, 36
Button Bar, 37-39
File Manager, 1030-1035
MATRIX, 930-932
option, 1000
options for selecting, 1124
printer, 16
product, 680
programming, 680
SCALESYM, 941
STACK, 933-934
STACKALIGN, 933-934
WordPerfect, editing, 684-686
comments
adding to documents, 134-136
converting to text, 137

Common User Access, *see* CUA
compiling macros, 686-687
Computer Graphics Metafile
(CGM) graphics format, 197
concordance files, 859-860
Condense Master Document
dialog box, 894
condensed
master documents, 893-895
typeface, 281
Conditional End of Page feature,
317-318
Confirm on Code Deletion
feature, 974
context-sensitive help, 15, 40
How Do I option, 41
What Is option, 41
continuing footnote numbers,
creating, 790-791
contracted kerning, 488
formats used by, 1065
converting formats, 1060-1061
Ami Pro documents, 1067
Clipboard, 1070-1075
Convert function
(WordPerfect), 1062-1066
Dynamic Data Exchange
(DDE), 1075-1077
importing
databases, 1087-1088
graphics, 1085-1087
intermediate formats, 1077
ASCII text conversions, 1078
Rich Text Format
(RTF), 1078
linking spreadsheet data, 1085
creating DDE Spreadsheet
Link, 1082-1083
creating WordPerfect
Spreadsheet Link,
1081-1082
manipulating wide
spreadsheets, 1084
using Clipboard, 1083

with Import Spreadsheet
function, 1080-1081
with Spreadsheet Link
function, 1079-1080
Microsoft Word documents,
1068
strategies, 1061-1062
Word for Windows
documents, 1066-1067
Copy File(s) dialog box, 94,
676, 1034
Copy Printer dialog box,
250, 256
copying
files, 93-95, 1031-1034
numbered paragraphs, 820
paper definitions, 468-469
table math formulas, 439
text, 149
WordPerfect printer
drivers, 256
CorelDRAW!, 574, 1086
Create DDE Link dialog
box, 1075
Create Horizontal Line dialog
box, 499
Create Spreadsheet Link dialog
box, 1081-1082
Create Vertical Line dialog
box, 507
Create/Edit Overstrike dialog
box, 956
cross hairs, 274
Ctrl-Backspace key
combination, 114
Ctrl-Del key, 114
CUA commands, 1128
Alt-Enter (Merge End of
Field), 698, 746
Alt-F1 (Thesaurus), 236
Alt-F2 (Search Previous), 129
Alt-F3 (Reveal Codes),
117-118, 163, 402, 430, 849
Alt-F4 (Exit), 68, 85

Alt-F5 (Paragraph Number),
806-808
Alt-F7 (Flush Right), 173, 181
Alt-F8 (Styles), 352
Alt-F9 (Layout Page), 315, 355,
461-462, 465, 707
Alt-F10 (Macro Play), 648
Alt-F11 (Text Box Create), 554
Alt-F12 (Generate), 891
Alt-Shift-Backspace
(Undelete), 151
Alt-Shift-Enter (Merge End of
Record), 699
Alt-Shift-F3 (View Ruler), 164,
383, 399, 409
Alt-Shift-F5 (Paragraph
Define), 805, 813, 828-829
Alt-Shift-F9 (Columns), 510
Alt-Shift-F11 (Text Box
Edit), 554
Center (Shift-F7), 173, 180,
365, 813, 852
Close (Ctrl-F4), 67, 802
Columns (Alt-Shift-F9), 510
Ctrl-A, 1050
Ctrl-B, 126
Ctrl-Enter (Page Break), 880
Ctrl-F1 (Speller), 219
Ctrl-F2 (Replace), 131-133, 188
Ctrl-F3 (Redisplay), 909
Ctrl-F4 (Close), 67, 802
Ctrl-F5 (Date), 57
Ctrl-F6 (Next Document), 70
Ctrl-F7 (Hanging Indent), 172
Ctrl-F8 (Margins), 169, 313,
354, 707
Ctrl-F9 (Tables), 408, 433, 440
Ctrl-F10 (Macro Record),
646, 651
Ctrl-F11 (Horizontal Line), 499
Ctrl-F11 (Horizontal Line), 515
Ctrl-F12 (Merge), 701, 704, 713
Ctrl-G (Go To), 59-60
Ctrl-J (Justify Center), 700
Ctrl-L (Justify Left), 701

Ctrl-S, 302, 1051
Ctrl-Shift-F1 (Preferences), 258, 390
Ctrl-Shift-F6 (Previous Document), 70
Ctrl-Shift-F7 (Double Indent), 171
Ctrl-Shift-F9 (Document), 299, 706, 788
Ctrl-Shift-F10 (Macro Stop), 647, 650-651
Ctrl-Shift-F11 (Vertical Line), 507, 512
Ctrl-Shift-F12 (Sort), 752, 761, 767
Ctrl-T, 85
Ctrl-U (Font Underline), 126
Ctrl-W (WP Characters), 948
Cut (Shift-Delete), 149
Date (Ctrl-F5), 57
Define (Shift-F12), 843, 860
Document (Ctrl-Shift-F9), 299, 706
Double Indent (Ctrl-Shift-F7), 171
Exit (Alt-F4), 68, 85
F2 (Search), 128-129
F3 (Save As), 66, 152
F4 (Open File), 109, 683, 952, 1063
F4 (Open), 87, 102-104
F5 (Print), 62, 152, 289, 952
F7 (Indent), 170
F8 (Select), 784
F9 (Font), 155
F11 (Retrieve Figure), 201
F12 (Mark Text), 835, 841, 847, 856, 867
Flush Right (Alt-F7), 173, 181
Font (F9), 155
Font Size Menu (Ctrl-S), 302
Generate (Alt-F12), 891
Go To (Ctrl-G), 59-60
Hanging Indent (Ctrl-F7), 172

Horizontal Line (Ctrl-F11), 499, 515
Indent (F7), 170
Justify Center (Ctrl-J), 700
Justify Left (Ctrl-L), 701
Line (Shift-F9), 167-168, 175, 354, 740
Macro Play (Alt-F10), 648
Macro Record (Ctrl-F10), 646, 651
Macro Stop (Ctrl-Shift-F10), 647, 650-651
Margins (Ctrl-F8), 169, 313, 354, 707
Mark Text (F12), 835, 841, 847, 856-867
Merge (Ctrl-F12), 701, 704, 713
Merge End of Field (Alt-Enter), 698, 746
Merge End of Record (Alt-Shift-Enter), 699, 746
New (Shift-F4), 694, 700, 706, 859
Next Document (Ctrl-F6), 70
Open (F4), 87, 102-104, 109, 683, 952, 1063
Page (Alt-F9), 315, 355, 461-462, 465, 707
Page Break (Ctrl-Enter), 880
Paragraph Define (Alt-Shift-F5), 805, 813, 828-829
Paragraph Number (Alt-F5), 806-808
Paste (Shift-Insert), 149
Preferences (Ctrl-Shift-F1), 258, 390
Previous Document (Ctrl-Shift-F6), 70
Print (F5), 62, 152, 289, 952
Print Preview (Shift-F5), 272, 802
Redisplay (Ctrl-F3), 909
Release (Shift-Tab), 172
Replace (Ctrl-F2), 131-133, 188

Retrieve Figure (F11), 201
Reveal Codes (Alt-F3),
   117-118, 163, 402, 430, 849
Ruler (Alt-Shift-F3), 164, 383,
   399, 409
Save (Shift-F3), 64, 152, 896
Save As (F3), 66, 152
Search (F2), 128-129
Search Next (Shift-F2), 129
Search Previous (Alt-F2), 129
Select (F8), 784
Shift-Alt-Enter (Merge End of
   Record), 746
Shift-Delete (Cut), 149
Shift-F2 (Search Next), 129
Shift-F3 (Save), 64, 152, 896
Shift-F4 (New), 694, 700,
   706, 859
Shift-F5 (Print Preview),
   272, 802
Shift-F7 (Center), 173, 180,
   365, 813, 852
Shift-F9 (Line), 167-168, 175,
   354, 740
Shift-F12 (Define), 843, 860
Shift-Ins, 784
Shift-Insert (Paste), 149
Shift-Tab (Release), 172
Sort (Ctrl-Shift-F12), 752,
   761, 767
Speller (Ctrl-F1), 219
Styles (Alt-F8), 352
Tables (Ctrl-F9), 408, 433, 440
Text Box Create (Alt-F11), 554
Text Box Edit
   (Alt-Shift–F11), 554
Thesaurus (Alt-F1), 236
Undelete (Alt-Shift-
   Backspace), 116, 151
Vertical Line (Ctrl-Shift-F11),
   507, 512
WP Characters (Ctrl-W), 948
CUA (Common User Access)
   compliant keyboard, 997
   keystrokes, 1128

current directory, 81
   changing, 91-92
   listing files in, 88-89
Current Print Job dialog box, 261
Custom installation
   (WordPerfect for Windows),
   1098-1103
customizing
   beep, 977
   default settings, 964
   display, 982-990
      in Draft Mode, 983-984
      WYSIWYG mode, 985
   document summary, 1009
   environment, 971-981
   Equation Editor, 1019-1022
   file location, 967-968
   hyphenation, 980-982
   keyboards, 966, 997-1007
   merge preferences, 1016-1017
   print jobs, 990-997
   rulers, 979-980
   sound, 977
   table of authorities, 1018
   WordPerfect, 964

D

/d-drive\directory start-up
   option, 1112
dangling headings, 318
data files, 721
   choosing record formats,
      731-736
   creating, 737
      line record data files,
         738-742
      merge record data files,
         745-747
      paragraph record data
         files, 743-744
      table-row record data files,
         747-750
   designing, 723-726
   formatting codes, 728

organizing data, 728
  formatting dates, 729
  formatting text, 730-731
  records, sorting, 750-751
    paragraph records, 761
    size limitations, 751
    Sort dialog box,
      accessing, 752
      options, 754-759
    sort parameters, defining,
      753-759
    specifying records, 751
    starting, 760
databases, 726
  importing, 1087-1088
dates
  format, 1013-1016
  formatting, 729, 966,
    1013-1016
  in documents, 1011-1013
  inserting into merge
    operations, 715
DDE, 1076
Decimal Align character, 179
Decimal Align tabs, 173
decorative typefaces, 280
[Def Mark:] code, 861
defaults, 81
  descriptive type, 1010
  directory, 81, 86
  settings, 963
    customized, 964
    changing, 967
    format settings, 162
  style libraries, 372-373
Define Columns dialog box,
  385-388
Define Paragraph Numbering
  dialog box, 826
  Current Outline Style
    option, 825
  Define options, 821
    Attach Previous Level
      option, 824
    Level Style box, 823

Redefined Formats option,
  821-822
Style box, 823-824
Starting Outline Number
  option, 825
Define Table of Contents dialog
  box, 889
defining
  documents subdirectory, 1110
  indexes, 860-862
  lists, 837-839
  records, 728
  table of authorities, 851-854
  table of contents, 842-844
    in master document,
      888-890
Del key, 114
deletable soft returns, 184
Delete Column dialog box, 414
Delete File dialog box, 95
Delete Row dialog box, 413
Delete Table dialog box, 414
deleting
  codes, confirmation, 974
  directories, 1036-1037
  files, 95-96, 1035-1036
    multiple, 1036
  footnotes, 785
  formatting codes, 312
  formulas, 442
  lines, 114
  numbered paragraphs,
    816-817
  paper definitions, 469
  selections, 151
  style codes, 369-370
  subdocuments, 882-883
  tables, 415
  text, 113-115
  WordPerfect printer
    drivers, 256
  words, 114
    from dictionary (Speller),
      234-235
descenders, 281, 492

dialog boxes
    Add Markings, 871
    Add Paper Size, 462-465
    Add Printer, 250, 257
    Advance, 473
    Applications, 1053
    Associate, 1054
    Box Position and Size, 528
    Button Bar Options, 632-635
    Change Directory, 1030
    Change File Attributes, 1050
    Condense Master
      Document, 894
    Copy File(s), 94, 676, 1034
    Copy Printer, 250, 256
    Create DDE Link, 1075
    Create Horizontal Line, 499
    Create Spreadsheet Link,
      1081-1082
    Create Vertical Line, 507
    Create/Edit Overstrike, 956
    Current Print Job, 261
    Define Columns, 385-388
    Define Paragraph Numbering,
      821-826
    Define Table of Contents, 889
    Delete Column, 414
    Delete File, 95
    Delete Row, 413
    Delete Table, 414
    Display, 966
    Display Settings, 982
    Document on Disk, 263-266
    Document Redline, 872
    Document Summary, 343-345
    Edit Equation Caption, 937
    Edit Horizontal Line, 506
    Edit Label, 476-477
    Edit Labels, 475
    Edit Outline Style, 829
    Edit Paper Size, 462-467
    Edit Spreadsheet Link, 1082
    Equation Preferences,
      942, 1019
    Equation Settings, 942

Expand Master Document, 884
Figure Options, 525-529
Find, 99
Format Column, 432-433
Generate, 892
Go To, 60, 389
Import Spreadsheet, 1080
Insert Merge Codes, 694,
  701, 715
Insert Special Codes, 179
Labels Macro-Page Label
  Definitions, 476
Language, 959
Line Draw, 518
Line Numbering, 798-801
Location of Files, 101, 246
Macro Play, 676 677
making choices in, 36-39
Mark Cross-Reference, 868
Mark Table of Contents, 887
Move/Rename File(s), 96-97,
  676, 1038
Open File, 87-89, 90-92, 95-96,
  99-100, 102-104, 676-677, 1063
Outline Styles, 827-828
Page Numbering, 329
Paper Size, 461
Paragraph Numbering, 805-807
Password, 89
pausing macros in, 654
Position, 544
Position Hyphen, 187
Preferences Location of
  Files, 967
Print, 62, 262, 952-954
Print Settings, 268
Printer Command, 494
Printer Setup, 252-253
Remove Markings, 873
Retrieve Figure, 201
Retrieve File, 87
Save As, 12, 64
Save Subdocument, 895
sculptured, displaying, 987
Search, 128

Select [ALL OTHERS], 467
Select Printer, 61, 249,
    257, 259
Select Sheet Feeder, 253, 257
Sort, 445, 752-759
Split Column/Row, 424
Style Properties, 352, 366-367
Styles, 352
Tab Set, 175-177
Table Options, 436
Typesetting, 489
WordPerfect, 891
dictionaries, 965
    hyphenation, 981
    supplementary, 230-232
        viewing/modifying, 232
    Speller
        compressing, 235-236
        expanding, 235-236
        main, 217
        specifying, 220-221
        supplementary, 217
        words, 234-235
dingbats, 584
direction keys, scrolling
  documents, 55
directories, 80
    accessing, 1029
    changing, 91-92, 967, 1030
        with Quick List, 100
    creating with File Manager,
        84-85
    current, 81
        changing, 91-92
        listing files in, 88-89
    default, 81, 86
        changing, 967
    deleting, 1036-1037
    parent, 80
    root, 80
    structure, customizing, 967
disk
    printing documents from,
        263-264
    saving documents to, 64-67

space, recovering after
    installation, 1102-1103
display, 966
    customizing, 982-990
        in Draft Mode, 983-984
        menu, 977
        WYSIWYG mode, 985
Display dialog box, 966
Display Pane (Equation
  Editor), 908
    displaying large equa-
        tions, 922
display pitch, 342
Display Settings dialog box, 982
displaying
    files, 978
    merge codes, 987
    ruler, 980
    scroll bars, 987-988
    sculptured dialog boxes, 987
    shortcut keys, 978
    WordPerfect characters, 950
Document Compare feature, 870
    comparing new/old
        documents, 871-873
    removing Document Compare
        markings, 873-874
document initial fonts, 299-300
Document on Disk dialog
  box, 263
    Document Summary
        option, 266
    Odd/Even Pages option, 266
    Range option, 264-265
Document Redline dialog
  box, 872
document summaries
    choosing options, 346-348
        Delete option, 347
        Extract option, 346
        Print option, 347
        Save As option, 347
    creating, 343-345
        when saving or exiting
            documents, 346

customizing, 1009
Save/Edit, 1011
Document Summary dialog box,
343-345
options, 966
documents
adjusting textual appear-
ance, 485
Advance feature, 485-486
baseline, adjusting, 492
kerning, 486-489
leading, 491-492
Letterspacing feature,
489-490
Printer Command feature,
494-495
Underline options, 493
Word Spacing feature,
489-490
Word Spacing Justification
Limits option, 490
applying paired styles to
existing text in, 363
closing, 67-68
comments, 134-135
converting to text, 137
editing, 135-136
hiding, 136
comparing, 871-873
removing Document
Compare markings,
873-874
converting, 15
Ami Pro documents, 1067
ASCII text, 1078
Clipboard, 1070-1075
Dynamic Data Exchange
(DDE), 1075-1077
intermediate formats, 1077
Microsoft documents, 1068
Rich Text Format (RTF),
1078
Word for Windows
documents, 1066-1067

date and time, inserting,
1011-1013
defining subdirectory, 1110
deleting style codes from, 369
editing with Search and
Replace, 133
entering text, 50-52
formatting
built-in settings, 50-51
for default printer, 976
importing
databases, 1087-1088
graphics, 1085-1086
inserting
blank lines, 52-53
dates during merge
operations, 715
text, 60, 113
WordPerfect characters,
948-949
label definitions in, 481-484
laying out, 589
creating pages, 590-591
enhancing appearance,
592-593
fitting type on pages, 592
linking spreadsheet
data, 1085
creating DDE Spreadsheet
Link, 1082-1083
creating WordPerfect
Spreadsheet Link,
1081-1082
manipulating wide
spreadsheets, 1084
using Clipboard, 1083
with Import Spreadsheet
function, 1080-1081
with Spreadsheet Link
function, 1079-1080
looking up words with
Thesaurus, 237
master
condensed, 893-895
creating, 876-878

expanding, 883-885
including subdocument
links, 880-882
printing, 893-894
sample, 879
saving, 896
table of contents in,
886-893
multiple
fonts within, 300-301
open, 1119
navigating, 27-33
opening, 86-87
planning, 72-73
outlining, 75-76
prewriting, 73-75
printing, 61, 64, 260
canceling print jobs, 267
Current Print Job dialog
box, 261
from disk, 263-264
from screen, 262-263
multiple pages, 266
print settings, modifying,
267-269
saving
styles in, 367
to disk, 64-67
scrolling, 53-54
with direction keys, 55
with mouse, 54
searching, 128-129
and replacing text, 131-133
for codes, 130-131
repeating searches, 129
specifying search
criteria, 129
spell checking, 223-226
correcting irregular
capitalization, 227-229
editing words, 226-227
eliminating duplicate
words, 228
in multiple languages, 230
looking up words, 229-230

using styles in, 361-362
checking styles in Reveal
Codes screen, 362
windows, 25-26
[DORM HRt] code, 315
dot leaders, 1018
double-clicking, 30, 144
downloading fonts, 283
specifying path for, 294
Draft mode, 16, 983-984
colors, 984-985
versus WYSIWYG, 1126
dragging, 30, 143
DrawPerfect graphics
program, 574
drives, 80
available, 1026
duplex printing, 993
Dynamic Data Exchange (DDE),
17, 1058, 1119
converting documents,
1075-1077

E

Edit Equation Caption dialog
box, 937
Edit Horizontal Line dialog
box, 506
Edit Labels dialog box, 475-477
Edit menu, 34
Edit Outline Style dialog box, 829
Edit Paper Size [ALL OTHERS]
dialog box, 462, 467
Paper Location options, 463
Paper Orientation options,
463-464
Paper Size options, 464
Paper Type options, 464
Print options, 465
Edit Spreadsheet Link dialog
box, 1082
editing, 15
[ALL OTHERS] definition,
467-468

built-in Button Bars, 641-642
Button Bars, 630-632
comments in documents,
  135-136
contents of text boxes,
  366-367
documents with Search/
  Replace, 133
footers, 323-324, 328
footnotes, 780
headers, 323-324, 328
horizontal lines, 504-506
keyboards, 1005-1006
label definitions, 474-477,
  481-484
    sample, 477-480
macros, 678, 683-684
newspaper columns, 391-392
outlines, 814-815
    adding numbered
      paragraphs, 820
    adding outline paragraph
      numbers, 815-816
    adding unnumbered
      paragraphs, 820-821
    copying numbered
      paragraphs, 820
    deleting numbered
      paragraphs, 816-817
    modifying outline
      paragraph numbers, 815
    moving numbered
      paragraphs within
      outline, 818-819
    styles, 829-831
overstrike characters, 957-958
paper definitions, 460-465
paragraph numbers, 808-809
parallel columns, 400-401
Quick List entries, 104
style codes, 364
style names, 365
table structure, 416-417
    changing column widths,
      417-419

deleting rows/columns,
  421-422
header rows, creating, 429
inserting rows/columns,
  420-421
joining cells, 423
locking cells, 429
positioning tables, 430
restoring deleted rows/
  columns, 422
row height, changing,
  427-428
size, changing, 419
splitting cells, 424
table codes, 431
table lines, changing,
  424, 427
text assigned to key-
  boards, 1006
vertical lines, 514
WordPerfect commands,
  684-686
words when spell checking
  documents, 226-227
Editing Pane (Equation Editor),
908, 918-919
    creating equations in, 910-911
    simple fractions, 912-913
    subscripts, 913-914
    superscripts, 913-914
editing screen, 21
empty fields, 715-718
Encapsulated graphics
  format, 198
End Centering/Alignment code
  [End C/A], 181
[End Def] code, 861
endnotes, 791
    changing footnotes to, 794-795
    creating, 791-792
    location, changing, 793-794
    versus footnotes, 776
Enter key, 52

envelopes, 377
  printing on, 470-473
    with envelope merge files,
      706-708
    with macros, 658-660
environment, 965
  customizing, 971-981
equation keyboards, 1021-1022
Equation Editor, 524, 905-906
  Arrows menu, 935
  backslash (\), 926-928
  commands, 914
    BOLD, 926
    FUNC, 925-926
    MATRIX, 930-932
    STACK, 933-934
    STACKALIGN, 933-934
  creating sums/integrals, 929
  customizing, 1019-1022
  displaying large
    equations, 922
  Editing Pane, 918-919
    creating equations in,
      910-911
    simple fractions, 912-913
    subscripts, 913-914
    superscripts, 913-914
  embedding equations in text,
    938-939
  equation keyboard
    layout, 919
  Equation Palette, 919-921
  functions, 914, 923-924
  keywords, 915-916
  Large menu, 935
  numbering equations, 936-937
  numbers, 915
  Other menu, 934
  positioning equations, 935
  printing equations, 941-943
  retrieving equation files, 940
  roots, creating, 930
  saving equation files, 940
  screen, 908-909
  sizing equations, 935
  starting, 907-908
  symbols, 915
  Symbols menu, 935
  syntax, 917-918
  using WordPerfect characters
    with, 921
  variables, 915
equation keyboard layout
  (Equation Editor), 919
Equation Palette (Equation
  Editor), 908, 919-921
Equation Preferences dialog
  box, 942, 1019
Equation Settings dialog box, 942
equations, 966
  alignment, 1020
  graphics, printing, 1020
  keyboard, 998
erasable cartridges, 285
exiting
  documents, creating
    document summaries, 346
  WordPerfect for Windows, 42
Expand Master Document dialog
  box, 884
expanded
  kerning, 488
  typeface, 281
extensible characters, 947
extensions (file names), 64
extracting records, 762
  defining selection
    parameters, 763-766
  specifying selection
    statements, 767-769
extraction operations, 750

F

FaceLift for Windows
  (Bitstream), 286-287
Fast Save option, 975
fields, 690-691, 726
  empty, 715-718

entering in secondary merge
files, 694-700
typing data into, 741-742
Figure Editor, 213, 524-526,
536-538
  File menu, 539-541
  menu options, 526-527, 544,
  547, 553
figure graphics
  creating, 201-202
  retrieving, 205
Figure Options dialog box,
525-529
file extension, PRS, 256
File List window, 1025-1028
File Manager, 13, 83, 1023, 1123
  accessing system
    information, 1048-1049
  Button Bar, 1044
  column headings, 1046
  commands, 1030-1035
  creating directories, 84-85
  features, 18-20
  file lists, 1051-1052
  files, opening, 1031
  finding existing directories, 84
  launching programs, 1052
    adding programs to
      Manager's Applications
      menu, 1053-1054
    associating programs with
      files, 1054-1055
  layouts, changing, 1044-1048
  printing, 1039
  screen, 84
  setting up as primary
    program manager,
    1055-1056
  switching to WordPerfect, 84
  windows, 1025-1030
    closing, 1029-1030
    File List, 1025-1028
    Navigator, 1025-1026
    Quick List, 1025, 1029

sizing, 1045
Viewer, 1025-1026
File menu, 34
files, 80
  attributes, 1049-1051
    changing, 1050
  backing up, 968-971
  concordance, 859-860
  contents, displaying, 1026
  copying, 93-95, 1031-1034
  creating/compiling names of
    with Clipboard, 1051-1052
  data files
    choosing record formats,
      731-736
    creating, 737-750
    designing, 723-726
    formatting codes, 728
    organizing data, 728-731
    records, sorting, 750-759
  deleting, 95-96, 1035-1036
    multiple, 1036
  displaying, 978
  equation, 940
  file names, 80
  finding, 99-100
    lost files, 110
  idea files, 70
  LIBRARY.STY style library
    file, 375-377, 380
  lists, searching, 1040-1041
  listing, 1027-1028
    in current directory, 88-89
  locating, 1039-1043
  location, 965
    customizing, 967-968
  locking, 89
  managing with macros
    changing directories in,
      674-675
    file extensions, 673-674
    manipulating macro files,
      675-678
    viewing macro files,
      675-678

merge, 690-691, 704-706
creating, 693-694, 700-704
entering field names,
694-696
entering fields, 697-700
entering records, 697-700
fields, changing, 711
placing empty fields in, 716
setting up, 691-692
skipping empty fields in,
717-718
substituting with ASCII
delimited text files,
712-713
substituting with keboard
input, 713-714
substituting with Notebook
files, 712
moving, 1037-1038
opening, 87, 108-109, 1031
organizing, 81-83
output, 691
data files, 750
placing printer commands in,
494-495
README, 1102
renaming, 96-97, 1037-1038
retrieving, 108, 111
saving, 1125
before sorting, 970
Files list, 88-89
Find command, 18
Find dialog box, 99
Find File search, 1041
Find Word search, 1041
finding
files, 99-100
words, 97-99
fixed
cartridges, 284
data, 689
pitch, 162
fixed-space fonts, 281

fliers, creating, 593-595
fonts in fliers, 596
graphics in fliers, 595-596
laying out, 597
settings, 597-599
Font menu, 35
fonts, 281, 1046-1047
attributes, changing, 302,
304-306
applying to existing
text, 307
size attributes, 302-304
base, 297-298
bit-mapped, 282
built-in, 282
cartridges, 283, 976
erasable, 285
fixed, 284
modular, 284
document initial, 299-300
downloading, 283
specifying path for, 294
fixed-space, 281
in fliers, 596
initial, 297-298
setting, 339
installing, 976
in Windows printer driver,
295-296
in WordPerfect printer
driver, 288-294
internal, 282
monospaced, 162, 281
outline, 282
proportionally spaced, 162, 281
Redline, 341-342
scalable, 282
selecting, 296
specifying document initial
fonts, 299-300
specifying initial fonts,
297-298
using multiple fonts in
documents, 300-301

size, 996, 1020
soft, 282-283
    adding to WordPerfect
        printer driver, 291-294
    selecting, 291-293
Strikeout, 341-342
swappable, 293
typeface packages, 285
    Adobe Type Manager
        (ATM) for Windows, 287
    FaceLift for Windows
        (Bitstream), 286-287
    Intellifont for Windows
        (Hewlett-Packard), 286
    Morefonts (Micrologic
        Software), 285
footers, 321-322
    discontinuing, 325-326
    editing, 323-324, 328
    incorporating graphics
        into, 327
    margins, setting, 170
    page numbers in, 324
    searching and replacing, 328
    spell checking, 327
    suppressing, 325
footnotes, 776
    adding, 782-783
    changing to endnotes,
        794-795
    creating, 777-778
        continuing footnote
            numbers, 790-791
    deleting, 785
    editing, 780
    formatting, 788-789
    moving, 783-784
    numbering automatically, 781
    options, changing, 786-788
    versus endnotes, 776
    viewing, 779
foreground document, 26
Format Column dialog box,
    432-433

formats
    changing with macros, 651
        margins, changing, 653-654
        setting tabs, 652-653
    choosing numbering formats
        for lists, 837-839
    converting, 1060-1061
        importing databases,
            1087-1088
        importing graphics,
            1085-1087
        linking spreadsheet data,
            1079-1085
        strategies, 1061-1062
        with ASCII text, 1078
        with Clipboard, 1070-1075
        with Dynamic Data
            Exchange (DDE),
            1075-1077
        with intermediate
            formats, 1077
        with Rich Text Format
            (RTF), 1078
        with WordPerfect Convert
            function, 1062-1067, 1068
    creating for line record data
        files, 740
    dates, 1013-1016
    for WordPerfect Convert
        function, 1065
    intermediate, converting
        documents, 1077
        with ASCII text, 1078
        with Rich Text Format
            (RTF), 1078
    record, 727
        choosing, 731-736
formatting, 161
    Auto Code Placement
        feature, 165
    codes, 727-728
        table-row, 748-749
    dates, 729
    default settings, 162

documents
 built-in settings, 50-51
 for default printer, 976
footer margins, setting, 170
footnotes, 788-789
header margins, setting, 170
indents, setting, 170-172
line spacing/height, 166-168
margins, setting, 169-170
pages, 310
 centering pages, 319
 controlling page division,
  315-318
 deleting formatting
  codes, 312
 headers/footers, 321-328
 initial codes, setting,
  340-341
 initial font, setting, 339
 numbering, 328-333
 on-screen display pitch,
  changing, 342
 placing codes, 311-312
 positioning with Advance
  command, 319-320
 Redline font method,
  341-342
 selecting paper size/type,
  333-339
 setting margins, 313-314
 Strikeout font method,
  341-342
positioning text on lines,
 181-182
spaces, 911
table text, 431
 cells, 434-435
 columns, 432-433
 global table options,
  setting, 436
tabs, 172-173
text, 730-731
versus styles, 350-351
with Ruler, 163-164

formulas
 deleting, 442
 modifying, 442
 for table math, 437-439
  copying formulas, 439
free-form
 boxes, 516-518
  moving insertion point, 518
 lines, 516-518
  drawing, 518-519
  erasing lines, 520
  moving insertion point, 518
  printing, 520-521
freewriting, 72
full justification, 182
FUNC command (Equation
 Editor), 925-926
functions, 148, 914
 Equation Editor, 923-924

G

Generate dialog box, 892
global
 keys, 766
 table options, setting, 436
Go To command (Edit menu),
 58-60
Go To dialog box, 60, 389
GRAPHCNV program, 572
 command line options, 573
Graphic Edit mode, 202-203
Graphical Interchange Format
 graphics format, 198
graphical user interface
 (GUI), 193
graphics, 1124
 adding to tables, 448-449
 black-and-white, 986
 boxes, 199-200, 524-525
  adjusting size of, 541
  anchoring, 541
  border lines, 529
  captions for, 531

changing from one to
    another, 541
defaults, 536
Equation Editor, 524
Figure Editor, 524-527,
    536-541
gray shading in, 530
moving to next page,
    975-976
positioning on page,
    542-544
relationship to text, 528-529
Text Editor, 524
clip art, 200
    resizing box, 202-204
combining with text, 210
creating
    adding to text, 565
    figure graphics, 201-202
    grouping graphics
        together, 569-571
    made of several individual
        graphics, 556-558
    overlaying text and
        graphics, 565-567
    placing one graphic inside
        another, 558-561
    placing text inside
        ornamental borders,
        562-564
    reverse printing, 568
enlarging specific areas, 547
Figure Editor, 213
font size, 1020
formats
    Bit Map (BMP), 198
    Computer Graphics
        Metafile (CGM), 197
    Encapsulated, 198
    Graphical Interchange
        Format, 198
    Hewlett-Packard Graphics
        Language (HPGL), 197
    PC Graphics (PCX), 197

    PostScript (EPS), 198
    Tagged-Image, 198
    WP Graphics (WPG), 197
GRAPHCNV program, 572
    command line options, 573
handling, 14
Importing, 1085-1086
    Arts & Letters, 1087
    CorelDRAW!, 1086
in fliers, 595-596
in newsletters, 613
incorporating into headers/
    footers, 327
integrating with text, 580-581
multiple, 207-210
obtaining, 573-575
    clip-art vendors, 576 577
    with autotracing, 576
    with scanners, 575
placing in styles, 359
quality, 993-994
raster, 194-195
retrieving figure graphics, 205
    moving check mark box, 206
vector, 194
Graphics menu, 35
grid rulers, tabs snap to, 979-980
guide rulers, showing, 980

H

hard hyphens, 184
hard page breaks, 315
    removing from merge
        records, 719
hard return, 52
    characters, 988-989
hard tabs, setting, 178
headers, 321-322
    discontinuing, 325-326
    editing, 323-324, 328
    incorporating graphics
        into, 327
    margins, setting, 170
    page numbers in, 324

rows, 428
searching and replacing, 328
spell checking, 327
suppressing, 325
headings, dangling, 318
headword, 238
help
context-sensitive, 15, 40
How Do I option, 41
What Is option, 41
standard help features, 42
Help menu, 35
Hewlett-Packard Graphics
Language (HPGL) graphics
format, 197
hidden codes, 39, 117-123
[AdvLft], 489
[AdvRght], 489
[AdvToLn], 708
[ALL OTHERS], 466-467
[Bline:Off], 492
[Bold], 127
[Cell], 431
[Center Pg], 710
changing size of Reveal Codes
window, 124
[Cndl EOP], 318
[Col Def], 384, 795
[Col On], 384, 795
colors, 990
[Def Mark:], 861
[DORM HRt], 315
[End Def], 861
[HPg], 315
[HRt-SPg], 315
[Insert Pg Num], 332
[Just Lim], 490
[L/R Mar], 312
[Lang], 960
[Line Height Adj], 491
[Ln Num:On], 801
[Mrg:FIELD NAMES], 696
option, 1125
[Outline On], 806
[Ovrstk], 957

[Paper Sz/Typ], 337, 466, 709
[Par Num], 806, 808, 815
[Pg Num:1], 329-330
screen, checking document
styles, 362
[SPg], 315
[Style], 351, 363
[Subdoc End], 884
[Subdoc Start], 884
[Suppress:HA], 325
[Suppress:PgNum], 333
[T/B Mar], 312
[Tbl Def], 431
[ToA:;Short Form Text], 849
[ToA:2;Short Form Text;Full
Form], 849
[Und Off], 127
[Und On], 127
[Underln], 493
window, 124
working with Reveal Codes
on, 124
[Wrd/Ltr Spacing], 489
see also, Reveal Codes,
hidden codes
hidden file attribute, 1049
highlighting text, 142
canceling highlighting, 147
with keyboard, 145-146
with mouse, 142-144
with Select mode, 147
Hijaak, 575
[HLine] code, 500
Home key options, retaining, 1005
horizontal lines
combining with vertical lines,
515-516
creating, 498-500
horizontal position/length,
specifying, 501-502
line characteristics,
specifying, 502-503
specifying vertical
position, 501
editing, 504-506

How Do I context-sensitive help
  option, 41
[HPg] code, 315
[HRt-SPg] code, 315
hyphenation, 184
  adding words, 190
  automating, 185
  choosing hyphenation points,
    187-188
  codes, 184
  customizing, 980-982
  dictionary, location, 981
  hard hyphens, 184
  preventing, 185
  removing hyphens, 188-190
  setting Hyphenation Zone, 186
hyphenation soft returns, 184

I

I-beam pointer, 30, 142
icon-based interface, 13
icons, 49
idea files, 70
Import Spreadsheet dialog box,
  1080
Import Spreadsheet function,
  linking spreadsheet data,
  1080-1081
importing
  databases, 1087-1088
  graphics, 1085-1086
    Arts & Letters, 1087
    CorelDRAW!, 1086
  spreadsheets, 1080-1081
    into tables, 447-448
indents, setting, 170-172
indexes
  creating, 854-855
  defining, 860-862
  generating, 860-862
  marking text for, 855-858
    with Concordance feature,
      859-860
  preparing for multiple related
    documents, 862

Info menu, 18
initial
  codes, 966, 1007-1009
    setting, 340-341
  fonts, 297-298
    setting, 339
Ins key, 60, 113
Insert Merge Codes dialog box,
  694, 701, 715
Insert mode, 60
[Insert Pg Num] code, 332
Insert Special Codes dialog
  box, 179
inserting
  parallel columns, 401-402
  special characters with
    macros, 656-657
  text, 60, 113
insertion point, 30, 389-390
  moving, 53-57
    for Line Draw feature, 518
    with direction keys, 55
    with Go To command (Edit
      menu), 58-60
    with keyboard, 56
    with mouse, 54
INSTALL program, 1094
  main menu, 1095
    preserving installed fonts,
      1107-1108
    printer options, 1105-1107
installing
  fonts
    in Windows printer driver,
      295-296
    in WordPerfect printer
      driver, 288-294
  WordPerfect for
    Windows, 1095
    Basic installation, 1097
    Custom installation,
      1098-1103
    installation options, 1096
    interim releases, 1103-1108
  WordPerfect printer drivers,
    246-248

Intellifont for Windows (Hewlett-Packard), 286
interim releases (WordPerfect for Windows), 1103-1104
  preserving installed fonts, 1107-1108
  printer updates, 1105-1107
internal fonts, 282
irregular columns, 449-450
italic
  type, 281
  typeface, 585

J–K

[Just Lim] code, 490
justification, 182-183

[Kern] code, 488
kerning, 486-489, 592
keyboards
  assigning
    macros to, 670-672
    text, 1002-1003
  choosing
    during installation, 1100
    menu options, 36
  creating, 999-1001
  CUA Compliant, 997
  customizing, 966, 997-1007
  editing, 1005-1006
    text assigned, 1006
  equation, 998, 1021-1022
  highlighting text, 145-146
  layout comparisons, 1130
  macros, 997
    assigning, 1003-1004
    removing, 1006
  moving insertion point with, 56
  navigating WordPerfect documents, 31-33
  substituting secondary merge files with keyboard input, 713-714
  text, removing, 1006

Windows CUA keyboard layout, 1129
keyg operator, 766
keys, 766
  Ctrl-Backspace key combination, 114
  Ctrl-Del key combination, 114
  Del, 114
  direction, scrolling documents, 55
  Enter, 52
  Ins, 60, 113
  Outline, 811-812
  shortcut display, 978
keystrokes, adding to menus, 1004-1005
keywords, 915-916

L

[L/R Mar] code, 312
labels
  definitions, creating/editing, 474-477
    sample, 477-480
    using in documents, 481-484
  printing, 474
    with merge operation, 709
  using in tractor-feed printers, 483
  using with Windows printer drivers, 483-484
Labels Macro-Page Label Definitions dialog box, 476
[Lang] code, 960
language codes, 959-961
Language dialog box, 959
Large menu (Equation Editor), 935
launching programs with File Manager, 1052
  adding programs to Manager's Applications menu, 1053-1054

associating programs with files, 1054-1055
Layout menu, 35
layouts
    defined, 1044
    File Manager, 1044-1048
    modifying appearance, 156-157
    saving, 1047
    start-up, 1048
leading, 491-492, 592
left aligned tabs, 173
left justification, 182
letterheads, 377
Letterspacing feature, 489-490
LIBRARY.STY style library file, 375-377, 380
light typeface, 585
Line Draw dialog box, 518
Line Draw feature, 516-518
    drawing lines, 518-519
    erasing lines, 520
    positioning insertion point, 518
    printing lines, 520-521
[Line Height Adj] code, 491
Line Numbering, 798
    options, 798-800
    settings, specifying, 800-801
    turning off, 801
    viewing line numbers, 802-803
Line Numbering dialog box, 798-800
    specifying settings, 800-801
line records, 756
    data files, creating, 738-742
    formats, 731
        formatting codes used in, 738-739
line spacing macros, creating, 654-656
line substructures, 756
lines, 727
    Conditional End of Page feature, 317-318
    formatting spacing/height, 166-168
    free-form, 516-518
        drawing, 518-519
        erasing lines, 520
        moving insertion point, 518
        printing, 520-521
    horizontal
        combining with vertical lines, 515-516
        creating, 498-500-503
        editing, 504-506
    positioning text on, 181-182
    spacing, creating line spacing macros, 654-656
    table lines, changing, 424, 427
    vertical
        combining with horizontal lines, 515-516
        creating, 506-510
        editing, 514
        using with columns, 510-513
linking spreadsheet data, 1085
    creating
        DDE Spreadsheet Link, 1082-1083
        WordPerfect Spreadsheet Link, 1081-1082
    manipulating wide spreadsheets, 1084
    with Clipboard, 1083
lists
    choosing numbering formats, 837-839
    creating, 835
    defining, 837-839
    generating, 839
    marking text for, 835-837
[Ln Num:On] code, 801
locating lost files, 110
Location of Files dialog box, 101, 246
Location of Files feature, 217
locking files, 89

logical pages, 481
  entering text into, 482
looping, 72

M

/m-macroname start-up
  option, 1112
Macro menu, 35
Macro Play dialog box, 676-677
macros, 17, 661, 1124
  advanced, 687
  assigning to Button Bars,
    638-640
    controlling Button Bars,
      638-639
  changing format with, 651
    margins, changing, 653-654
    setting tabs, 652-653
  columns, automating
    tasks, 403
  combining with merges and
    styles, 663-665
  compiling, 686-687
  creating Macros Button
    Bar, 640
  editing, 678, 683-684
    WordPerfect commands,
      684-686
  features new to WordPerfect
    for Windows, 1119
  files, managing, 673
  keyboards, 997
    assigning to, 1003-1004
  line spacing, creating, 654-656
  managing files
    changing directories
      located in, 674-675
    file extensions, 673-674
    manipulating macro files,
      675-678
    viewing macro files,
      675-678
  pausing in dialog boxes, 654

  playing, 648-649
    alternative methods,
      665-666
    assigning to Button
      Bar, 669
    assigning to keyboard,
      670-672
    assigning to menu, 666-669
  printing envelopes, 658-660
  recording, 645-648
  removing from key-
    boards, 1006
  replacing, 650-651
  selecting styles, 661-662
  starting merges, 662-663
  stopping, 650
  syntax, 680-682
  to insert special characters,
    656-657
  transposing characters,
    657-658
  WordPerfect 5.1 for DOS
    versus WordPerfect for
    Windows, 679-680
Macros option, 1000
maintenance releases, *see*
  interim releases
managing macro files, 673
manipulating records, 728
Manual Kerning, 488
margins
  changing with macros,
    653-654
  setting, 169-170, 313-314
Mark Cross-Reference dialog
  box, 868
Mark Table of Contents dialog
  box, 887
Master Document feature,
  875, 896
  Cross-Reference feature,
    using with, 901
  endnotes, adding, 899-900
  footnotes, adding, 899-900

inserting new page
numbers, 897-898
Replace feature, using
with, 899
Search feature, using
with, 899
Spelling Check feature, using
with, 899
master documents
condensed, 893-895
creating, 876-878
expanding, 883-885
including subdocument links,
880-882
printing, 893-894
sample, 879
saving, 896
table of contents in, 886
defining table of contents,
888-890
generating table of
contents, 890-893
marking text for, 887-888
uses, 902
MATRIX commands, 930-932
measurement units, 989-990
menu bar, 22
menu-based interface, 13
menus
adding keystrokes, 1004-1005
Applications, 18
assigning macros to, 666-669
choosing, 34-35
creating tables, 408-409
display, customizing, 977
Edit, 34
Equation Editor
Large menu , 935
Arrows menu, 935
File, 34
Font, 35
Graphics, 35
Help, 35
Info, 18

Layout, 35
Macro, 35
option, 1000
Preferences, 965-966
Tools, 35
View, 34
Window, 35
merging, 661, 689, 727
combining with styles and
macros, 663-665
directly to printer, 719
inserting dates into
documents, 715
merge codes, 727, 966
displaying, 987
in tables, 453
merge record format, 734
merge record data files,
creating, 745-747
planning, 690-691
preferences, customizing,
1016-1017
printing
envelopes, 706-708
labels, 709
files, setting up, 691-692
removing hard page breaks
from merged files, 719
starting with macros, 662-663
with ASCII delimited text files,
712-713
with empty fields, 715-718
with keyboard input, 713-714
with Notebook files, 712
merging files, 704-705
Micrograf Designer, 575
Microsoft Word documents,
converting to WordPerfect,
1068
mnemonic menu options, 36
modes
Draft, 16, 983-984
colors, 984-985
Graphic Edit, 202-203
Insert, 60

Select, highlighting text, 147
Typeover, 60, 113
WYSIWYG, 985
modular cartridges, 284
monospaced fonts, 162, 281
MoreFonts (Micrologic
Software), 285
mouse
choosing menu options, 35
double-clicking, 144
dragging, 143
highlighting text, 142-144
navigating WordPerfect
documents, 29-31
quadruple-clicking, 144
scrolling documents, 54
Shift-clicking, 144
triple-clicking, 144
Move/Rename File(s) dialog
box, 96, 676, 1038
moving
around WordPerfect
documents, 27-33
files, 96-97, 1037-1038
footnotes, 783-784
graphics boxes to next page,
975-976
insertion point, 53-57
in Line Draw feature, 518
with direction keys, 55
with Go To command (Edit
menu), 58-60
with keyboard, 56
with mouse, 54
numbered paragraphs within
outline, 818-819
parallel columns, 402
tables, 415
text, 149
within tables, 411
[Mrg:FIELD NAMES] code, 696
multiple
style libraries, 371
fonts in documents, 300-301
graphics, 207-210

languages, 958
language codes, 959-961
language resource file, 962
spelling checker/
thesaurus/hyphenation
files, 961
pages, printing, 266
table of contents, 844

N

Navigator, 18, 1025
finding existing directories, 84
window, 1025-1026
/nb start-up option, 1112
newsletters
creating, 606
designing first page, 606-609
designing second page,
609-613
designing third page,
613-615
finishing, 618-619
settings for, 615-618
newspaper columns, 381-382
defining
using Define Columns
dialog box, 385-388
using Ruler, 383-385
editing, 391-392
placing tables in, 451-452
previewing, 392-394
Notebook files in merge
operations, 712
/nt-network start-up option, 1112
number style, 823
numbered paragraphs
adding, 820
copying, 820
deleting, 816-817
moving within outlines,
818-819
numbering pages, 328-333
numbers, 915
numeric words, 748

O

Open File dialog box, 87, 95-96,
102-104, 676-677, 1063
  changing current directory,
  91-92
  Files list, 88-89
  finding files, 99-100
  Options button, 92
    copying files, 93-95
  View window, 90
open styles, 351
  creating, 352-355
opening
  documents, 86-87
  files, 87, 108-109
operators, sorting/selecting,
763-766
  (), 766
  keyg, 766
options
  commands, 1000
  Fast Save, 975
  Home key, retaining, 1005
  Macros, 1000
  menus, 1000
  text, 1000
organizing files, 81-83
original document backups,
969-971
ornamental typefaces, 584
ornaments, 593
orphans, 318
Other menu (Equation
Editor), 934
Outline feature, 798, 809
  accessing, 811
  editing outlines, 814-815
    adding numbered
    paragraphs, 820
    adding outline paragraph
    numbers, 815-816
    adding unnumbered
    paragraphs, 820-821

  copying numbered
    paragraphs, 820
  deleting numbered
    paragraphs, 816-817
  modifying outline
    paragraph numbers, 815
  moving numbered
    paragraphs within
    outline, 818-819
  outline keys, 811-812
  sample, 813-814
  styles, 352
  transitional, 76
  turning off, 812
  versus Paragraph Num-
    bering, 810
outline font, 282
[Outline On] code, 806
Outline styles, 827-828
  creating, 829-831
  editing, 829-831
Outline Styles dialog box,
  827-828
output files, 691, 750
overstriking, 956-958
[Ovrstk] code, 957

P

Page Numbering dialog box, 329
pages
  controlling page division, 315
    avoiding orphans and
      widows, 318
    Block Protect feature,
      316-317
    Conditional End of Page
      feature, 317-318
    hard page breaks, 315
    soft page breaks, 315
  creating, 590-591
    fitting type on page, 592
  enhancing appearance,
  592-593

formatting, 310
centering pages, 319
controlling page division,
315-318
deleting formatting
codes, 312
headers/footers, 321-328
initial codes, setting,
340-341
initial font, setting, 339
numbering, 328-333
on-screen display pitch,
changing, 342
placing codes, 311-312
positioning with Advance
command, 319-320
Redline font method,
341-342
selecting paper size/type,
333-339
setting margins, 313-314
Strikeout font method,
341-342
logical, 481
entering text into, 482
physical, 481
paired styles, 352
applying to existing text in
documents, 363
creating, 356-359
paper definitions, 333-339,
460-461
copying, 468-469
creating/editing, 462-465
deleting, 469
selecting, 465-466
using Windows printer
drivers, 470
Paper Size dialog box, 461
Paper Size feature, 460
paper definitions
creating/editing, 460-465
selecting, 465-466
[Paper Sz/Typ] code, 337,
466, 709

[Par Num] code, 806, 808, 815
Paragraph Numbering, 798,
803-805
defining numbering style,
805-806
editing paragraph numbers,
808-809
numbered paragraphs with
automatic levels, 806-807
overriding automatic
levels with manual
levels, 807
versus Outline feature, 810
Paragraph Numbering dialog
box, 805-807
paragraph records
data files, creating, 743-744
format, 732-734
sorting, 761
paragraph styles, 379
paragraphs, 727
parallel columns, 381
converting to tables, 445-447
defining, 395-397
editing, 400-401
inserting, 401-402
moving, 402
typing text in, 397-398
parent directory, 80
Password command (File
menu), 89
Password dialog box, 89
passwords, 89
path name, 81
PC Graphics (PCX) graphics
format, 197
PC PaintBrush, 575
[Pg Num] code, 330
[Pg Numbering:location]
code, 329
phone message forms,
creating, 455
physical page, 481
pitch, 281

playing macros, 648-649
    alternative methods, 665-666
        assigning to Button Bar, 669
        assigning to keyboard,
            670-672
        assigning to menus, 666-669
point size, 281
points, 926
Pos indicator, 52
Position dialog box, 544
Position Hyphen dialog box, 187
PostScript (EPS) graphics
    format, 198
posture, 281
Preferences Location of Files
    dialog box, 967
Preferences menu, 965-966
previewing newspaper columns,
    392-394
prewriting, 73-75
primary file name, 64
primary merge files, 690-691
    creating, 700-704
    skipping empty fields in,
        717-718
Print dialog box, 62, 262
    Graphics Quality area, 953-954
    Text Quality area, 953-954
Print Manager, 270-271
Print Preview, 16, 271-273
    limitations, 276
    Pages menu options, 275-276
    View menu options, 273-274
print queue, 270
Print Settings dialog box, 268
print wheels, 294
Printer Command dialog box, 494
Printer Command feature,
    494-495
printer commands, 16
printer drivers, 242, 976
    choosing during installation,
        1100-1102

installing fonts
    in Windows printer
        drivers, 295-296
    in WordPerfect, 288-294
    Windows, 244-245, 257
        configuring, 260
        selecting, 258-259
        updating, 260
        using labels with, 483-484
        using paper definitions
            with, 470
    WordPerfect, 243-244
        adding to list of available
            printers, 249-251
        copying, 256
        deleting, 256
        installing, 246-248
        updating, 257
Printer Setup dialog box,
    252-253
printers
    default, formatting
        documents, 976
    drivers, 976
        Windows, 996
    feeding paper to, 462
    merging directly to, 719
    selecting, 61, 251
    tractor-feed, using labels
        in, 483
    WordPerfect, setting up,
        252-256
printing
    [ALL OTHERS] definition,
        466-467
        editing, 467-468
    binding offset, 993
    canceling print jobs, 267
    customizing, 990-997
    documents, 61, 64, 260
        Current Print Job dialog
            box, 261
        from disk, 263-264
        from screen, 262-263

duplex jobs, 993
envelopes
  with envelope merge files,
    706-708
  with macros, 658-660
equations, 941-943
  as graphics, 1020
file lists, 1052
from Files Manager, 1039
graphics
  fast, 996
  quality, 993-994
labels with merge
  operation, 709
Line Draw lines, 520-521
master documents, 893-894
multiple
  copies, 992-993
  pages, 266
on envelopes, 470-473
on labels, 474
  label definitions, creating/
    editing, 474-477
  label definitions, in
    documents, 481-484
  label definitions, sample,
    477-480
Paper Size feature, 460
  paper definitions, creating/
    editing, 460-465
  paper definitions,
    selecting, 465-466
print settings, modifying,
  267-269
selections, 152
settings, customizing, 966
size attribute ratio, 996
tables, 415
text quality, 995
WordPerfect characters,
  952-955
product commands, 680
program manager, setting up
  File Manager as, 1055-1056
programming commands, 680

proportionally spaced fonts,
  162, 281
PRS file extension, 256
/ps-path start-up option, 1112
publications
  composition, 589
    creating pages, 590-591
    enhancing appearance,
      592-593
    fitting type on pages, 592
  designing, 581-583
pull-down menu commands
  Append, 150
  Applications menu, Assign
    command, 1053
  Control menu, Toggle Record
    marker command, 654
  Edit menu
    Copy command, 1073
    Convert Case
      command, 157
    Cut command, 784
    Go To command, 58-60
    Link, Create
      command, 1075
    Link, Paste Link
      command, 1077
    Move/Rename, 96
    Paste command, 784, 1074
    Replace command, 131
    Search command, 128
    Select command, 158
    Select All command, 1051
    Undelete command,
      115-117, 412
    Undelete, Restore
      command, 785
    Undo command, 15, 413
  File Manager (File menu)
    Create Directory
      command, 84-85
  File menu
    Change Attributes
      command, 1050
    Close command, 67

Exit command, 68, 85
File Manager
  command, 686
New command, 694,
  706, 859
Open command, 87, 102-
  104, 109, 683, 952, 1063
Password command, 89
Preferences, Associate
  command, 1054
Preferences, Display
  command, 417
Preferences, Keyboard
  command, 671
Preferences, Location of
  Files command, 86-87, 675
Print command, 62, 952
Print Preview command,
  779, 802
Print Window
  command, 1052
Retrieve command, 111-112
Save As command, 66-67
Save command, 64-66, 896
Select Printer command, 61
Font menu
  Bold command, 126
  Overstrike, Create
    command, 956
  Underline command, 126
  WP Characters, 948
Graphics menu
  Equation, Caption
    command, 937
  Equation, Create
    command, 907, 910
  Equation, Edit
    command, 907
  Equation, Position
    command, 938
  Line, Edit Horizontal
    command, 503
  Line, Edit Vertical
    command, 514

Line, Horizontal command,
  499, 515
Lines, Vertical command,
  507, 512
Table Box, Create
  command, 451
User, Create
  command, 448
Layout menu
  Advance command,
    319-320, 485
  Columns command, 510
  Columns, Define
    command, 395
  Document command,
    706, 788
  Document, Redline Method
    command, 872
  Endnote command, 791
  Endnote, Placement
    command, 793
  Footnote command, 867
  Footnote, Create
    command, 777-778,
    782-783
  Footnote, Edit command,
    780, 794
  Footnote, New Number
    command, 790
  Footnote, Options
    command, 786
  Justification commands, 156
  Line, Center command,
    813, 852
  Line commands, 156,
    354, 740
  Line, Numbering
    command, 798-800
  Line, Tab Set command, 813
  Margins command, 313,
    354, 707
  Page commands, 157, 355,
    461-462, 465, 707
  Page, Page Break
    command, 58

Page, Paper Size
command, 1084
Styles command, 159, 352
Tables, Cell command,
429, 435
Tables, Column command,
418, 432, 453
Tables command, 408,
416, 440
Tables, Create command,
445, 452
Tables, Delete
command, 421
Tables, Formula command,
437-439, 442
Tables, Join command, 423
Tables, Lines, Bottom
command, 450
Tables, Lines command, 425
Tables, Options command,
419, 429-430, 436, 1084
Tables, Row command,
427, 453
Tables, Split
command, 424
Typesetting command, 487
Macro Facility Macro menu,
Compile Macro
command, 686
Macro menu
Assign to Menu
command, 666
Play command, 648
Record command, 646, 651
Stop command, 647, 651
Open File Options menu
Copy command, 93-94
Delete command, 95-96
Find command, 97-99
Tables menu, Insert
command, 420
Tools menu
Comment, Create
command, 135
Date, Text command, 57

Define command, 843, 860
Document Compare, Add
Markings command, 871
Document Compare,
Remove Markings
command, 873
Generate command, 839, 891
Language command, 959
Mark Text command, 835,
841, 847, 856, 867
Master Document
command, 880
Master Document,
Condense Master
command, 894
Master Document, Expand
Master command, 884
Merge command, 701,
704, 713
Merge, End of Field
command, 746
Merge, Merge Codes
command, 715
Outline, Define command,
805, 813, 828-829
Outline, Outline Off
command, 806
Outline, Paragraph
Number command, 806
Sort command, 445, 752,
761, 767
Spreadsheet, Create Link
command, 1081
Spreadsheet, Edit Link
command, 1082
Spreadsheet, Import
command, 1080
Typesetting menu, 157
View menu
Button Bar Setup, Edit
command, 630, 669
Button Bar Setup, New
command, 637
Button Bar Setup, Options
command, 632

Button Bar Setup, Select
command, 626
Redisplay command, 909
Reveal Codes
command, 849
Ruler command, 409, 416
Window menu, Tile
command, 71, 75
pull-outs, 592, 612

Q

quadruple-clicking, 144
Quick List feature, 100, 1119
creating, 101-103
editing entries, 104
window, 1025, 1029
Quote paired style, 380

R

radio buttons, 971
ragged left and right, 183
raised caps, 609-612
raster graphics, 194-195
read-only file attribute, 1049
README files, 1102
record formats, 727
choosing, 731
line record format, 731
merge record format, 734
paragraph record format,
732-734
table-row record format, 736
record substructures, 727
recording macros, 645-648
records, 690-691, 726
defining, 728
entering in secondary merge
files, 697-700
extracting, 762
defining selection
parameters, 763-766

specifying selection
statements, 767-769
manipulating, 728
Redline fonts, 341-342
redlining, 995-996
references, 238
reinstalling WordPerfect,
1108-1109
relative
cell referencing, 439
tabs, 177
Remove Markings dialog
box, 873
renaming files, 96-97
replacing
macros, 650-651
styles, 367-369
resizing clip art box, 202-204
restoring deleted text, 115-117
Retrieve command (File
menu), 111
Retrieve Figure dialog box, 201
Retrieve File dialog box, 87
retrieving
files, 108, 111
style libraries, 374-375
Reveal Codes, 39, 117-123, 966
changing size of Reveal Codes
window, 124
hidden codes
[AdvLft], 489
[AdvRght], 489
[AdvToLn], 708
[ALL OTHERS], 466-467
[Bline:Off], 492
[Bold], 127
[Cell], 431
[Center Pg], 710
[Cndl EOP], 318
[Col Def], 384, 795
[Col On], 384, 795
colors, 990
[Def Mark:], 861
[DORM HRt], 315

[End Def], 861
[HPg], 315
[HRt-SPg], 315
[Insert Pg Num], 332
[Just Lim], 490
[L/R Mar], 312
[Lang], 960
[Line Height Adj], 491
[Ln Num:On], 801
[Mrg:FIELD NAMES], 696
[Outline On], 806
[Ovrstk], 957
[Paper Sz/Typ], 337,
    466, 709
[Par Num], 806, 808, 815
[Pg Num], 329-330
[SPg], 315
[Style], 351, 363
[Subdoc End], 884
[Subdoc Start], 884
[Suppress:HA], 325
[Suppress:PgNum], 333
[T/B Mar], 312
[Tbl Def], 431
[ToA:;Short Form Text], 849
[ToA:2;Short Form
    Text;Full Form], 849
[Und Off], 127
[Und On], 127
[Underln], 493
[Wrd/Ltr Spacing], 489
option, 1125
screen, checking document
    styles, 362
window, 124
working with Reveal Codes
    on, 124
Rich Text Format (RTF), 1078
right-aligned tabs, 173
right justification, 183
Roman type, 281
root directory, 80
roots, 930
[Row] code, 431

rows
    deleting from tables, 421-422
    header, 428-429
    height, changing, 427-428
    inserting into tables, 420-421
    restoring rows deleted from
        tables, 422
Ruler, 14, 163-164, 1120
    activating, 1111
    buttons on top, 980
    changing columns, 398-400
        widths, 417-419
    creating tables, 409-410
    customizing, 979-980
    defining newspaper columns,
        383-385
    displaying automatically, 980
    grid, tab snap to, 979-980
    guides, showing, 980
    setting tabs on, 174-175
rules, 592

S

/sa start-up option, 1112
sample style library, 375-377, 380
sans serif typefaces, 280, 584
Save As dialog box, 12, 64
Save Subdocument dialog
    box, 895
saving
    Button Bars, 629-630
    documents
        creating document
            summaries, 346
        to disk, 64-67
    Fast Save, 975
    files, 1125
    layouts, 1047
    master documents, 896
    selections, 152
    styles
        in documents, 367
        in style libraries, 373-374
    tables, 415

scalable fonts, 282
SCALESYM command, 941
scanners, 575
screens
    Equation Editor, 908-909
    making screens print, 61, 64
    printing documents from,
        262-263
scroll bars, 22
    displaying, 987-988
scrolling, 987-988
    documents, 53-54
        with direction keys, 55
        with mouse, 54
sculptured dialog boxes,
    displaying, 987
Search dialog box, 128
searching, 1125
    documents, 128-129
        and replacing text, 131-133
        for codes, 130-131
        repeating searches, 129
        specifying search
            criteria, 129
    file list, 1040-1041
    Find File search patterns, 1041
    Find Word search
        patterns, 1041
    headers/footers, 328
    narrowing, 1043
    Viewer window, 1040-1041
secondary merge files,
    690-691, 706
    creating, 693-694
        field names, entering,
            694-696
        fields, entering, 697-700
        records, entering, 697-700
    fields, changing, 711
    placing empty fields in, 716
    substituting
        with ASCII delimited text
            files, 712-713

    with keyboard input,
        713-714
    with Notebook files, 712
Select [ALL OTHERS] dialog
    box, 467
Select
    feature, 60
    mode, highlighting text, 147
Select Printer command (File
    menu), 61
Select Printer dialog box, 61,
    249, 259
    Info button, 257
Select Sheet Feeder dialog box,
    253, 257
selecting
    fonts, 296
        specifying document initial
            fonts, 299-300
        specifying initial fonts,
            297-298
        using multiple fonts in
            documents, 300-301
    operations, 750
    text, 141
selections-selected text
    applying styles to, 159
    deleting, 151
    modifying appearance, 153
        changing case, 157
        fonts/font size, 154
        layout, 156-157
        text, 154
    performing functions on, 148
    printing, 152
    rectangular, 158-159
    saving, 152
    statements, 763
        specifying, 767-769
    undeleting, 151
serif typefaces, 280, 584
Setup program, 13
sheet feeders, 253
Shift-clicking, 144

shortcut keys, 16
  Alt-F4 (exiting WordPerfect
    for Windows), 42
  display, 978
signatures, 618
size attributes, 302
  changing for fonts, 302-304
  ratio, 996
sizing handles, 504
soft fonts, 282-283
  selecting, 291-293
soft hyphens, 184
soft page breaks, 315
soft returns, 52
Sort dialog box, 445, 752-754
  Key Definition section,
    756-759
  Record Selection option, 754
  Record Type section, 756
  Sort Order section, 754-755
sorting-and-selecting
  operations, 750
sorting data file records, 750-751
  operators, 763-766
  paragraph records, 761
  size limitations, 751
  Sort dialog box, 752-759
  sort parameters, defining,
    753-759
  specifying records, 751
  starting, 760
  table-row records, 769-771
  tables, 445
sound, customizing, 977
special
  characters, 17
    inserting with macros,
      656-657
  codes, 1125
specialized Button Bars,
  creating, 636-638
spell checking headers and
  footers, 327
Speller, 216-217, 1126
  main dictionary file, 217

options, 219
  setting, 221-222
  specifying dictionaries,
    220-221
  specifying spelling to
    check, 222-223
setting up, 217-218
spell checking documents,
  223-226
  correcting irregular
    capitalization, 227-229
  editing words, 226-227
  eliminating duplicate
    words, 228
  in multiple languages, 230
starting, 218-219
supplementary dictionaries,
  230-232
  supplementary dictionary
    file, 217
Utility
  adding dictionary words,
    234-235
  compressing dictionaries,
    235-236
  deleting dictionary words,
    234-235
  expanding dictionaries,
    235-236
  running, 233
wild-card character word
  searches, 229-230
Word text box, 229-230
[SPg] code, 315
Split Column/Row dialog
  box, 424
Spreadsheet Link function,
  1079-1080
STACK command, 933-934
STACKALIGN command, 933-934
standard help features, 42
starting
  Equation Editor, 907-908
  Speller, 218-219
  Thesaurus, 236

Windows, 20
WordPerfect for Windows,
   20, 1109
   activating Ruler, 1111
   defining documents
      subdirectory, 1110
   problems, 24-25
   selecting start-up switches,
      1111-1112
status line, 22
   Long Prompts, 23
   Pos indicator, 52
   quick help, 23
stopping macros, 650
Strikeout fonts, 341-342
strings, 763
[Style Off:Headings] code, 363
[Style On:Headings] code, 363
Style Properties dialog box, 352,
   366-367
[Style] code, 351
styles, 349-351, 661
   codes, deleting, 369-370
   combining with merges and
      macros, 663-665
   creating
      from existing text, 359-360
      open styles, 351-355
      outline styles, 352
      paired styles, 352, 356-359
   editing style codes, 364
   envelopes, 377
   letterheads, 377
   libraries, 371
      default, 372-373
      multiple, 371
      retrieving, 374-375
      sample, 375-377, 380
      saving styles in, 373-374
   lists, deleting style codes
      from, 369-370
   names, editing, 365
   of typeface, 585
   open, 351
      creating, 352-355

outline, 352
paired, 352
   applying to existing text in
      documents, 363
   creating, 356-359
paragraphs, 379
placing graphics in, 359
quotation, 380
replacing with another style,
   367-369
saving styles in doc-
   uments, 367
selecting with macros,
   661-662
using in documents, 361-362
versus formatting, 350-351
Styles dialog box, 352
subdirectories, 80
[Subdoc End] code, 884
[Subdoc Start] code, 884
subdocuments, 875-878
   adding, 882-883
   creating, 876-878
      within subdocuments, 901
   deleting, 882-883
subject-search text, 1009-1010
suffix (file names), 64
[Suppress:HA] code, 325
[Suppress:PgNum] code, 333
swappable fonts, 293
symbol sets, 952
symbols, 915
Symbols menu (Equation
   Editor), 935
syntax
   Equation Editor, 917-918
   of macros, 680-682
system
   file attribute, 1050
   information, accessing,
      1048-1049

T

[T/B Mar] code, 312
Tab Set dialog box, 175-177
Table of Authorities, 966
    adjusting setup for, 846
    Blank Line Between
      Authorities, 1018
    choosing sections for,
      846-851
    creating, 844-846
    customizing, 1018
    defining, 851-854
    dot leaders, 1018
    generating, 851-854
    marking text for, 846-851
    underlining, 1018
Table of Contents
    creating, 840
    master document, creating
      in, 886
        defining table of contents,
          888-890
        generating table of
          contents, 890-893
        marking text for, 887-888
    defining, 842-844
    generating, 844
    marking text for, 840-842
    multiple, 844
Table Options dialog box, 436
table-row-record data files, 747
    formats, 727
        data files, creating, 747-750
        record format, 736
        selecting, 769-771
        sorting, 769-771
tables, 405-406
    adding graphics, 448-449
    converting
        parallel columns to,
          445-447
        tabular columns to,
          443-444
    creating, 408-410
        calendars, 453
        forms with irregular
          columns, 449-450
    cross-referencing, 452
    cutting, pasting, deleting text
      in, 412-413
    deleting, 415
    entering text into, 411
    importing spreadsheets into,
      447-448
    mathematics, 437
        copying formulas, 439
        creating formulas for,
          437-439
        formulas, deleting/
          modifying, 442
        tax formulas, creating,
          440-441
        total formulas, creating,
          440-441
        totaling functions, 440
        values, calculating/
          changing, 441-442
    Merge codes in, 453
    moving, 415
        within, 411
    phone message forms,
      creating, 455
    placing
        in newspaper columns,
          451-452
        side by side, 451
    planning, 407
    printing, 415
    saving, 415
    selecting/deleting cells,
      413-415
    sorting, 445
    structure
        changing column widths,
          417-419
        deleting rows/columns,
          421-422
        editing, 416-417

header rows, creating, 429
inserting rows/columns, 420-421
joining cells, 423
locking cells, 429
positioning tables, 430
restoring deleted rows/ columns, 422
row height, changing, 427-428
size, changing, 419
splitting cells, 424
table codes, 431
table lines, changing, 424, 427
text, formatting, 431
cells, 434-435
columns, 432-433
global table options, setting, 436
tabs, 172-173
absolute, 177
relative, 177
setting
absolute tabs, 177
adjusting Decimal Align Character, 180
from Tab Set dialog box, 175-177
hard tabs, 178
on Ruler, 174-175
relative tabs, 177
with macros, 652-653
snap to ruler grid, 979-980
tabular columns, converting to tables, 443-444
Tagged-Image graphics format, 198
targets (Automatic Cross-Reference), 863
tax formulas, 440-441
[Tbl Def] code, 431
terminology in WordPerfect for Windows, 1121-1122

text
adding graphics to, 565
adjusting appearance, 485
Advance feature, 485-486
baseline, adjusting, 492
kerning, 486-489
leading, 491-492
Letterspacing feature, 489-490
Printer Command feature, 494-495
Underline options, 493
Word Spacing feature, 489-490
Word Spacing Justification Limits option, 490
applying
font attribute changes to, 307
paired styles to existing text, 363
Block Protect feature, 316-317
boilerplate, 60
boldface, 126-127
colors, 985
combining with graphics, 210
converting to comments, 137
creating styles from existing text, 359-360
cutting, pasting, deleting in tables, 412-413
deleting, 113-115
embedding equations in, 938-939
enhancing, 154
overlaying text and graphics, 565-567
entering
into documents, 50-52
into tables, 411
formatting, 730-731
greeking, 273
highlighting, 142
canceling highlighting, 147
rectangular sections of, 158-159

with keyboard, 145-146
with mouse, 142-144
with Select mode, 147
in columns, 388
    displaying one column at a
        time, 390
    moving insertion point,
        389-390
inserting, 60, 113
integrating with graphics,
    580-581
keyboards, assigning to,
    1002-1003
lowercase, 157
marking
    for automatic cross-
        referencing, 864-869
    for indexes, 855-860
    for lists, 835-837
    for table of authorities,
        846-851
    for table of contents,
        840-842
    in master document,
        887-888
modifying fonts/font size, 154
overwriting, 113
positioning on line, 181-182
quality, 995
relationship to graphics
    boxes, 528-529
removing from key-
    boards, 1006
restoring deleted text, 115-117
selecting, 141
subject-search, 1009-1010
transferring, 149
    appending selections, 150
    moving or copying
        selections, 149
    to other Windows
        applications, 150
typing in parallel columns,
    397-398

underlining, 126-127, 493
uppercase, 157
text boxes, 553-554
    editing contents of, 366-367
Text Editor, 524, 554
text option, 1000
The Elements of Software Design:
    The New Edition, 48
Thesaurus, 236, 1126
    headwords, 238
    looking up words, 237-239
    references, 238
    replacing words, 239
    starting, 236
tiling windows, 27, 1045
timed backups, 969-970
title bar, 21
[ToA:;Short Form Text] code,
    849
[ToA:2;Short Form Text;Full
    Form] code, 849
Tools menu, 35
total formulas, creating, 440-441
totaling functions, 440
tractor-feed printers, using
    labels in, 483
transferring text, 149-150
transitional outlines, 75-76
trees, 80, 1025
trifold mailers, creating, 599-605
triple-clicking, 144
type, 280-281
typefaces, 280, 583
    categories, 584-585
    condensed, 281
    decorative, 280
    expanded, 281
    individual characteristics,
        586, 589
    packages, 285
        Adobe Type Manager
            (ATM) for Windows, 287
        FaceLift for Windows
            (Bitstream), 286-287

Intellifont for Windows
    (Hewlett-Packard), 286
Morefonts (Micrologic
    Software), 285
sans serif, 280
serif, 280
styles, 585
Typeover mode, 60, 113
Typesetting dialog box, 489

U

/u-username start-up option, 1112
[Und Off] code, 127
[Und On] code, 127
underlining, 1018
    text, 126-127, 493
[Underln] code, 493
Undo feature, 15, 975, 1120
undoing changes, 975
unnumbered paragraphs,
    adding, 820-821
Update Installation menu, 1104
Using Microsoft Windows 3,
    Second Edition, 257, 271

V

variable data, 689
variables, 915
vector graphics, 194
vertical lines
    combining with horizontal
        lines, 515-516
    creating, 506-510
    editing, 514
    using with columns, 510-513
View
    menu, 34
    window, 90
Viewer, 18
    window, 1025-1026
        searching, 1040-1041

viewing
    footnotes, 779
    line numbers, 802-803

W

WCM file extension, 673-674
What Is context-sensitive help
    option, 41
When a Writer Can't Write:
    Studies in Writer's Block and
    Other Composing Process
    Problems, 69
widows, 318
wild-card characters, 81, 229-230
Windows
    menu, 35
    Print Manager, 270-271
    printer drivers, 244-245, 257
        configuring, 260
        selecting, 258-259
        updating, 260
    starting, 20
windows
    active, changing, 1029
    cascading, 27, 1046
    File Manager, 1025-1030
    printer drivers, 996
    tiled, 27, 1045
Word for Windows documents,
    converting to WordPerfect,
    1066-1067
Word Processing in a Community
    of Writers, 69
Word Spacing feature, 489-490
Word Spacing Justification
    Limits option, 490
WordPerfect
    built-in settings, 51
    characters, 946-949, 1120, 1126
        displaying special
            characters, 950
        inserting into documents,
            948-949

printing special
    characters, 952-955
    shortcuts for creating, 950
characters, using with
  Equation Editor, 921
DOS-compatible keyboard
  layout, 1129-1130
exiting WordPerfect for
  Windows, 42
features new to Windows,
    13-17, 1117
    Button Bar, 1117
    Dynamic Data Exchange
      (DDE), 1119
    format conversion
      capabilities, 1117-1118
    macro features, 1119
    new WPG formats, 1121
    opening multiple
      documents, 1119
    Quick List feature, 1119
    Ruler feature, 1120
    Undo feature, 1120
    WordPerfect
      characters, 1120
File Manager, switching
  between to Windows, 84
INSTALL program, 1094
macros for DOS version
  versus Windows version,
  679-680
multiple languages, 958
    language codes, 959-961
    language resource file, 962
    spelling checker/thesaurus/
      hyphenation files, 961
printer drivers, 243-244
    adding to list of available
      printers, 249-251
    copying, 256
    deleting, 256
    installing, 246-248
    updating, 257

printers
    selecting, 251
    setting up, 252-256
  reinstalling, 1108-1109
  starting/setting up, 20, 1109
    activating Ruler, 1111
    defining documents
      subdirectory, 1110
    problems, 24-25
    selecting start-up switches,
      1111-1112
  switching from DOS to
    Windows, 1114
    advantages, 1114-1115
    comparing procedures,
      1122-1126
    disadvantages, 1115-1116
  terminology in Windows,
    1121-1122
  writing with, tips, 69-72
    planning documents, 72-76
WordPerfect dialog box, 891
word wrapping, 52
WP Graphics (WPG) graphics
  format, 197
WPG formats, 1121
[Wrd/Ltr Spacing] code, 489
writer's block, 69-70
    brainstorming, 70-71
    freewriting, 72
writing with word processors,
  tips, 68-72
    planning documents, 72-73
      outlining, 75-76
      prewriting, 73-75
WYSIWYG (what you see is what
  you get), 10, 13, 982
    mode, 985
    versus Draft mode, 1126

X-Z

/x start-up option, 1112
XLM file extension, 673-674

Free Catalog!

Mail us this registration form today, and we'll send you a free catalog featuring Que's complete line of best-selling books.

Name of Book _____

Name _____

Title _____

Phone (___) _____

Company _____

Address _____

City _____

State _____ ZIP _____

Please check the appropriate answers:

1. Where did you buy your Que book?
   - ☐ Bookstore (name: _____)
   - ☐ Computer store (name: _____)
   - ☐ Catalog (name: _____)
   - ☐ Direct from Que
   - ☐ Other: _____

2. How many computer books do you buy a year?
   - ☐ 1 or less
   - ☐ 2-5
   - ☐ 6-10
   - ☐ More than 10

3. How many Que books do you own?
   - ☐ 1
   - ☐ 2-5
   - ☐ 6-10
   - ☐ More than 10

4. How long have you been using this software?
   - ☐ Less than 6 months
   - ☐ 6 months to 1 year
   - ☐ 1-3 years
   - ☐ More than 3 years

5. What influenced your purchase of this Que book?
   - ☐ Personal recommendation
   - ☐ Advertisement
   - ☐ In-store display
   - ☐ Price
   - ☐ Que catalog
   - ☐ Que mailing
   - ☐ Que's reputation
   - ☐ Other: _____

6. How would you rate the overall content of the book?
   - ☐ Very good
   - ☐ Good
   - ☐ Satisfactory
   - ☐ Poor

7. What do you like *best* about this Que book?
   _____
   _____

8. What do you like *least* about this Que book?
   _____
   _____

9. Did you buy this book with your personal funds?
   - ☐ Yes   ☐ No

10. Please feel free to list any other comments you may have about this Que book.
    _____
    _____
    _____

que

Order Your Que Books Today!

Name _____

Title _____

Company _____

City _____

State _____ ZIP _____

Phone No. (___) _____

Method of Payment:

Check ☐   (Please enclose in envelope.)

Charge My: VISA ☐   MasterCard ☐

American Express ☐

Charge # _____

Expiration Date _____

Order No.	Title	Qty.	Price	Total

You can **FAX** your order to **1-317-573-2583**. Or call **1-800-428-5331, ext. ORDR** to order direct.
Please add $2.50 per title for shipping and handling.

Subtotal	
Shipping & Handling	
Total	

que

BUSINESS REPLY MAIL
First Class Permit No. 9918   Indianapolis, IN

Postage will be paid by addressee

11711 N. College
Carmel, IN 46032

BUSINESS REPLY MAIL
First Class Permit No. 9918   Indianapolis, IN

Postage will be paid by addressee

11711 N. College
Carmel, IN 46032